1989 CRB Commodity Year Book

PREPARED AND PUBLISHED BY

Commodity Research Bureau
a Knight-Ridder Business Information Service
100 CHURCH ST., SUITE 1850
New York, N.Y. 10007

We are pleased to say that this is the 50th anniversary issue of the year book, which has been published since 1939. The 1989 issue covers activity in commodities, currencies, and financial markets during 1988. The commodity markets continued their recovery from 1986's price slump, and the CRB Futures Price Index ended 1988 about 8 percent above a year earlier. Prices of many raw materials not traded in the futures markets, particularly industrial metals, rose.

Overall trading volume in the U.S. futures markets was a record 245.9 million contracts, up 7 percent from the previous year. Interest rate futures, accounting for 42 percent of total volume, continued to be the major markets. Agricultural commodities were the second most heavily traded group, accounting for 25 percent of overall volume. They were followed by energy products with 11 percent, currencies with 9 percent, precious metals with 7 percent, and stock indices with 6 percent.

Trading in the agricultural markets surged, as the U.S. drought affected prices of grains, oilseeds, and livestock, while other factors boosted volume in the imported commodities--cocoa, coffee, and sugar. Altogether, volume in the agricultural markets in 1988 swelled by 39 percent over the previous year's level.

The other big gainer was the energy group, where trading volume expanded by 29 percent, led by crude oil and unleaded gasoline. Growth in this group has been impressive, with trading volume having risen almost six-fold from 1984 to 1988.

Other groups showing higher trading volume in 1988 were currency futures, up 6 percent, and interest rate futures, up 5 percent. However, stock index futures lost considerable ground, as trading volume plunged by 43 percent, following the 1987 market crash. This was in contrast to strong growth in stock indices in the mid-1980s. Moreover, trading in precious metals slowed in 1988, and was down 8 percent from the previous year.

Among the individual futures markets, the leaders in volume terms in 1988 were Treasury bonds, Eurodollars, crude oil, soybeans, the S&P 500 Index, corn, and gold.

The U.S. economy's performance in 1988 exceeded the expectations of those who had projected slow growth or a contraction, following the stock market crash. The economy expanded at a real rate of 2.7 percent, led by growth in manufacturing. Industrial production increased by 5 percent during the year and was bolstered by strength in exports. Durable goods orders were very strong, rising a whopping 15.7 percent during the year. Consumer spending was better than expected, with retail sales up by 4.2 percent on a real basis, and personal consumption expenditures up 3.5 percent. With steady growth in jobs, the economy was considered to be at full employment. By year's end, the unemployment rate had dropped to 5.3 percent.

Despite worries about accelerating prices in early 1988, inflation at the consumer level was the same as in 1987. The Consumer Price Index rose by 4.4 percent in both 1988 and 1987. Meanwhile, the Producer Price Index jumped by 4 percent in 1988 from 2.2 percent in 1987, registering the biggest gain since 1981.

The Federal Reserve raised the discount rate by half a point to 6.5 percent in August to dampen inflation fears. It allowed the fed funds rate to drift higher during the year. The dollar strengthened in 1988, after having fallen the three previous years. The U.S. trade deficit declined during 1988 for the first time since 1980.

The year book contains one feature article, entitled "Food and Energy Prices as Inflation Indicators." The author is Walter Emery, who was the Director of Research at CRB for many years before his retirement in 1986. The article discusses the usefulness of the CRB Futures Price Index and the group futures indices in examining the inflationary pressures from rising raw materials prices in the economy. The study focuses on the food and energy sectors, and looks at supply/demand factors that have been important in shaping prices in these sectors in recent years. Also discussed are government and private reports that provide statistics and information important to the food and energy markets. The CRB Futures Price Index has received widespread attention from analysts, traders, and the press, and the article should be valuable to those wishing to familiarize themselves with the index.

We wish to express our appreciation for the assistance provided by government agencies, particularly the U.S. Department of Agriculture and Bureau of Mines, and by the commodity exchanges and various trade associations. We have attempted to list these organizations on page 4T.

The Editorial Board
February 1989

TABLE OF CONTENTS

ACKNOWLEDGMENTS

The editors wish to thank the following for source material:

Aluminum Association
American Bureau of Metal Statistics
American Gas Association
American Iron and Steel Institute
American Metal Market
American Paper and Pulp Association
American Petroleum Institute
Atomic Industrial Forum Inc.
Chicago Board of Trade
Chicago Mercantile Exchange
Citrus Associates of N.Y. Cotton Exchange
Coffee, Sugar & Cocoa Exchange
Commodity Exchange, N.Y.
Commodity Futures Trading Commission
Consolidated Gold Fields, PLC
Edison Electric Institute
F.W. Dodge Corp.
Federal Power Commission
Federal Reserve Board
Florida Department of Citrus
Futures Industry Association
Johnson Matthey Ltd.
The Journal of Commerce
General Services
Gill & Duffus Ltd.
Handy & Harman
International Cotton Advisory Committee
International Monetary Market (Chicago)
International Tea Committee
Kansas City Board of Trade
MidAmerica Commodity Exchange
Minneapolis Grain Exchange

National Coffee Association of U.S.A., Inc.
New York Cotton Exchange
New York Futures Exchange
New York Mercantile Exchange
Newsprint Service Bureau
Nuclear Exchange Corp.
Nuclear Regulatory Commission
Oil World
Portland Cement Association
Random Lengths
Rubber Manufacturers Association
Rubber Study Group
The Silver Institute
Society of the Plastics Industry Inc.
Leather Industries of America Inc.
Tea Council Inc.
Textile Economics Bureau Inc.
Textile Organon
U.N. Conference On Trade and Development
U.N. Food and Agriculture Organization
U.S. Bureau of Mines
U.S. Department of Agriculture
U.S. Department of Commerce
U.S. Department of Energy
U.S. Department of the Interior
U.S. Department of Labor
U.S. Department of the Treasury
The Wall Street Journal
Winnipeg Commodity Exchange
Wool Services Co.
Zinc Institute

The editors wish to thank the following for their contribution to the 1989 edition:

Barbara Lahey, production manager

Liam Boyle, publishing production
Debra Cruz, production assistant
Carolann Dirig, administrative assistant
Albert Marin, chart production
Luis Vazquez, chart production

THE COMMODITY PRICE TREND

The CRB Futures Price Index, containing prices in 21 commodity markets, rose by 8 percent in 1988, after an 11 percent gain in 1987. In comparison, the Consumer Price Index increased by 4.4 percent in both 1988 and 1987. In 1988, a rise in food prices because of the drought was countered by a decline in energy prices.

The fact that 1988's consumer inflation rate didn't exceed 1987's was considered welcome news, given strong fears of inflation in the first half of the year. However, some analysts were worried about the rise in the Producer Price Index. A 4 percent increase in the PPI in 1988 was sharply above 1987's gain of 2.2 percent and the largest rise since 7.1 percent in 1981. The jump in the index would have been even larger, if energy prices hadn't been relatively soft. Prices of crude materials rose by 6 percent in 1988, and prices of intermediate goods, less food and energy, rose by 7.2 percent.

Moreover, prices of many items used in manufacturing--industrial metals, plastics, and chemicals--increased by up to 20 percent in 1988. Capacity utilization rates for industries producing these materials were around 90 percent at year-end, while the overall capacity utilization rate was a high 84.2 percent. The numbers suggested that inflation was heating up at the producer level.

CRB Futures Index Rises in 1988

During 1988, the CRB Futures Price Index continued its upward climb, and reached a four-year high of 270.5 in June. Agricultural commodities leapt with the drought, and other markets jumped on board. The index retreated during the fall with harvest pressures, but the drop was stemmed by price strength in copper and the soft commodities.

Oilseeds and Grains - Soy complex and grain prices rose in the spring, with dry weather throughout much of the U.S. In June, nearby soybean futures soared to $10.99/bu., a 15-year high, as the Midwest was in the midst of a severe drought. Soymeal futures also reached a 15-year high, while soyoil rose to the best level in three years. Corn futures climbed to $3.59/bu., a level last seen in 1984; and oats, having more than doubled in price, reached an all-time high of $3.93/bu. Chicago wheat (SRW) shot up to $4.08 mid-summer, and Kansas City wheat (HRW) reached $4.11, both 6-year highs. Minneapolis spring wheat reached $4.61, the best level in seven years.

Soybean and corn prices slumped with the harvest in the fall, but gained ground in a post-harvest advance at year-end. Wheat futures were firm in the fall and added to summer's gains, on relatively tight supplies, and expectations for good Export Enhancement Program business.

Suffering most from the 1988 drought were: spring wheat production, down 58 percent from the previous season, oats-down 42 percent, corn-down 30 percent, soybeans-down 20 percent, and hard red winter wheat-down 14 percent.

Livestock - The livestock index ended 1988 above a year earlier, as cattle and hog prices were higher, while bellies were lower. Cattle had a strong rally in 1988's first half, but plunged as summer's drought encouraged slaughters. However, the July 1 cattle inventory was the lowest since numbers were first collected in 1983, and it seemed likely that modest declines in all cattle inventories would continue through 1989. Cattle futures climbed in second-half 1988.

Strong packer demand and small hog runs bolstered hog prices in the spring. Higher slaughters induced by the drought and huge levels of pork in storage weighed on hogs and bellies from July-September. Pork belly futures made an 8-year low in mid-1988. However, hog prices picked up late in the year.

Imported - During the year, sharp gains were seen in the imported group (softs) index, which nonetheless ended the year about unchanged from late 1987. The imported index reached a 2-year high in July, on sugar's sharp speculative run-up, later retraced on the downside. Sugar also had a late year advance on indications world sugar production and consumption would be closely in line in 1988/89.

Coffee futures plunged in August on heavy liquidation, fueled by reports Colombia was leaving the ICO. Weather problems in Brazil later helped the market, although it received an October setback on bearish interpretations of the new International Coffee Agreement. In December, coffee prices skyrocketed on dry-weather damage to crops in Brazil and Central America and tight supplies. Cocoa, a severe bear market in 1988 because of large Ivory Coast supplies, reached a 13-year low of $1,103/tonne. The market later recovered somewhat with a plan for a French trade house to store and/or sell 400,000 tonnes of Ivorians.

Industrials - The industrials group was unable to add to 1987's sharp gains and ended 1988 unchanged. In the fall, crude oil prices retreated to $12.15/bbl., a 2-year low, on indications OPEC was producing about 21 million bpd, well above its quota. Prices rebounded on late-year optimism about the cartel's new agreement, which took effect in 1989. Cotton futures lost ground with declining mill use and export sales, but improved at year's end on brightening export prospects. Offsetting losses in the industrials was copper's advance in second-half 1988 to $1.65/lb., an all-time high. A Peruvian miners' strike, production declines in Chile, Zaire, and Zambia, and low producer and consumer inventories underscored the advance.

Precious Metals - The precious metals index had another up and down year, similar to 1987, but at lower levels. A summer rally in metals was mostly coat-tailing on strength in other commodities. Later, gold and silver fell sharply with ample supplies of both and expectations for further production increases in gold, due to inexpensive leaching methods.

Platinum rallied late in 1988 on some traders' views world supplies would be tight in the year ahead. However, Ford Motor Co.'s December announcement that it had developed a substitute for platinum in catalytic converters sent the market plunging. Strength in the dollar at year's end weighed on precious metals.

The Fundamental Outlook

The CRB Futures Index ended 1988 at 251.8, up 8 percent from the year-earlier level. The index slipped in early 1989, with a drop in the imported group and slight declines in the metals, soybean complex, grains, and livestock.

However, some moderate gains in the CRB Futures Price Index were possible in 1989, with expected price strength in several of the components, including wheat, cattle, coffee, and, to a lesser extent, petroleum. However, gains in these markets would have to outweigh anticipated weakness in other components, particularly gold, silver, corn, cocoa, and pork bellies, which were all burdened with excess supplies.

Meanwhile, prices of some materials outside the CRB Futures Index--a number of industrial metals, chemicals, and plastics--were expected to remain firm in the first half of 1989. Energy prices were likely to be slightly higher in 1989, based on expectations that OPEC would be more disciplined in abiding by its production ceiling than in 1988. With a high capacity utilization rate and full employment, inflation pressures were strong in early 1989, but were expected to be contained by the Federal Reserve's actions.

CRB FUTURES PRICE INDEX (1967=100)
Weekly high low & close

Monthly CRB Futures Price Index   (High, Low & Close 1967 = 100)

Year		Jan.	Feb.	Mar.	Apr.	May	June	July	Aug.	Sept.	Oct.	Nov.	Dec.	Range
1983	High	242.7	245.1	242.1	247.3	252.7	249.5	261.7	281.6	283.8	275.4	275.6	277.6	283.8
	Low	234.8	232.1	232.8	244.7	247.2	244.2	245.2	263.5	272.5	264.6	265.9	270.4	232.1
	Close	242.7	232.1	242.1	246.7	249.7	246.2	259.9	278.7	273.5	264.6	273.9	277.6	—
1984	High	278.3	276.1	283.0	283.2	284.2	280.3	268.3	259.8	256.3	254.8	258.7	253.2	284.2
	Low	273.2	266.1	274.7	275.1	275.3	268.4	249.4	253.3	250.3	252.0	252.7	244.0	244.0
	Close	273.6	272.5	283.0	275.1	280.1	271.0	249.4	257.1	251.4	254.8	253.8	244.2	—
1985	High	247.9	248.1	245.2	247.1	239.7	233.8	228.0	221.7	224.5	225.6	227.7	231.1	248.1
	Low	241.7	236.6	238.2	239.3	230.9	226.6	219.3	217.7	217.2	221.9	223.8	227.6	217.2
	Close	247.1	238.2	244.4	239.3	232.3	226.6	220.7	219.7	222.9	225.6	227.7	229.2	—
1986	High	231.1	216.6	216.5	213.5	216.1	205.7	203.7	207.1	212.3	213.4	213.3	212.0	231.1
	Low	219.9	209.9	209.4	203.0	205.5	201.6	196.9	201.0	208.2	209.7	208.4	207.5	196.9
	Close	219.9	209.9	209.6	213.5	205.5	201.6	200.1	207.1	210.9	211.3	210.7	209.1	—
1987	High	213.9	213.7	210.1	221.7	235.6	234.6	227.8	226.8	227.3	232.7	237.1	234.7	237.1
	Low	208.3	204.2	205.7	209.4	222.6	223.1	220.7	222.4	223.5	222.7	221.1	227.5	204.2
	Close	212.6	205.4	208.7	221.7	224.9	225.9	225.9	223.0	223.8	223.4	234.6	232.5	—
1988	High	239.3	232.9	233.5	236.0	248.4	270.5	265.8	251.0	248.6	246.5	247.0	252.8	270.5
	Low	230.4	224.3	224.5	232.7	232.5	249.8	242.0	243.7	237.1	237.6	236.0	244.1	224.3
	Close	230.4	225.7	233.0	234.4	248.4	265.1	246.2	246.2	238.8	243.9	244.9	251.8	—
1989	High	251.6												
	Low	241.1												
	Close	242.4												

Source: Commodity Research Bureau

T.006A

COMMODITY RESEARCH BUREAU FUTURES PRICE INDEX
(1967=100)

MONTHLY HIGH, LOW & CLOSE

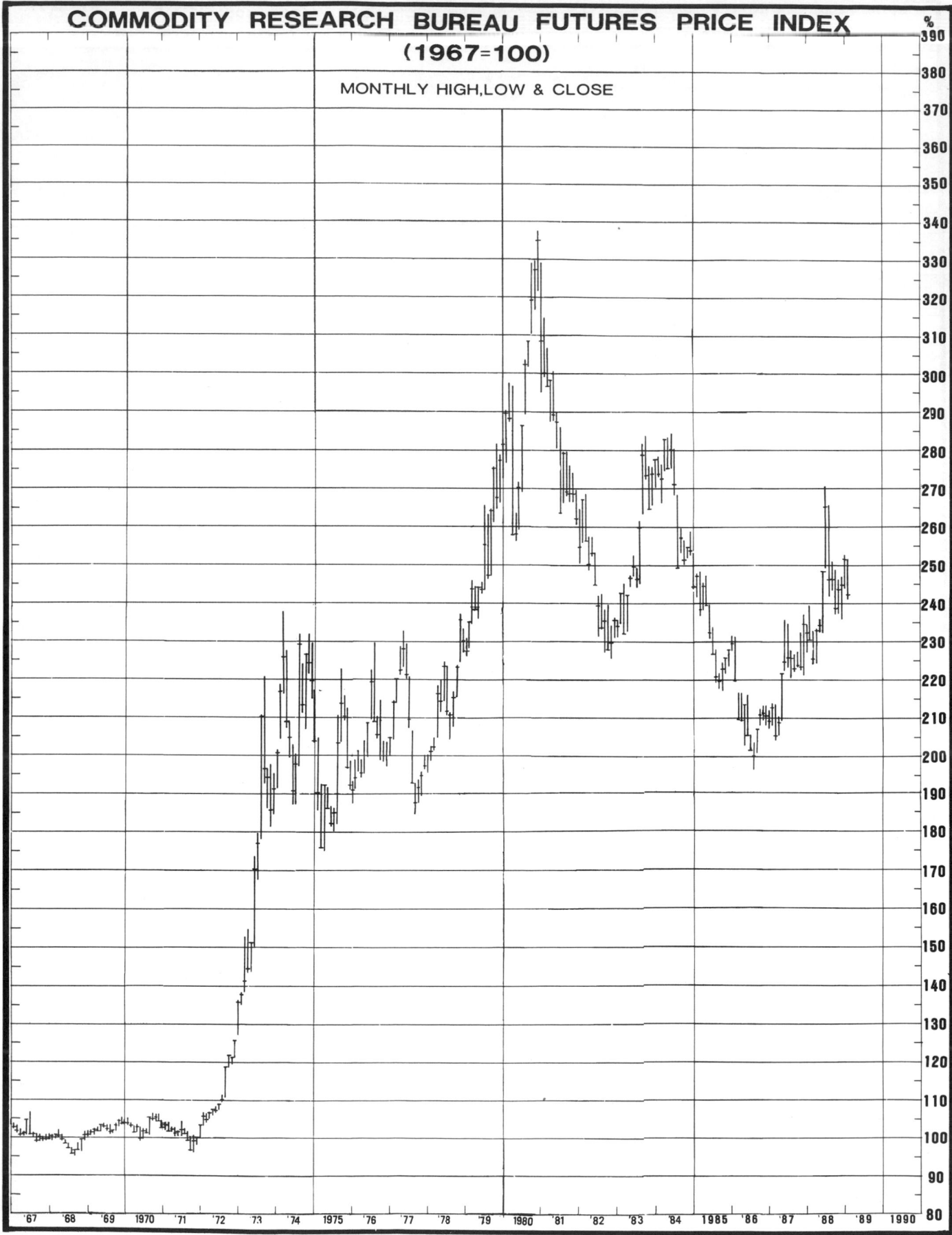

8T

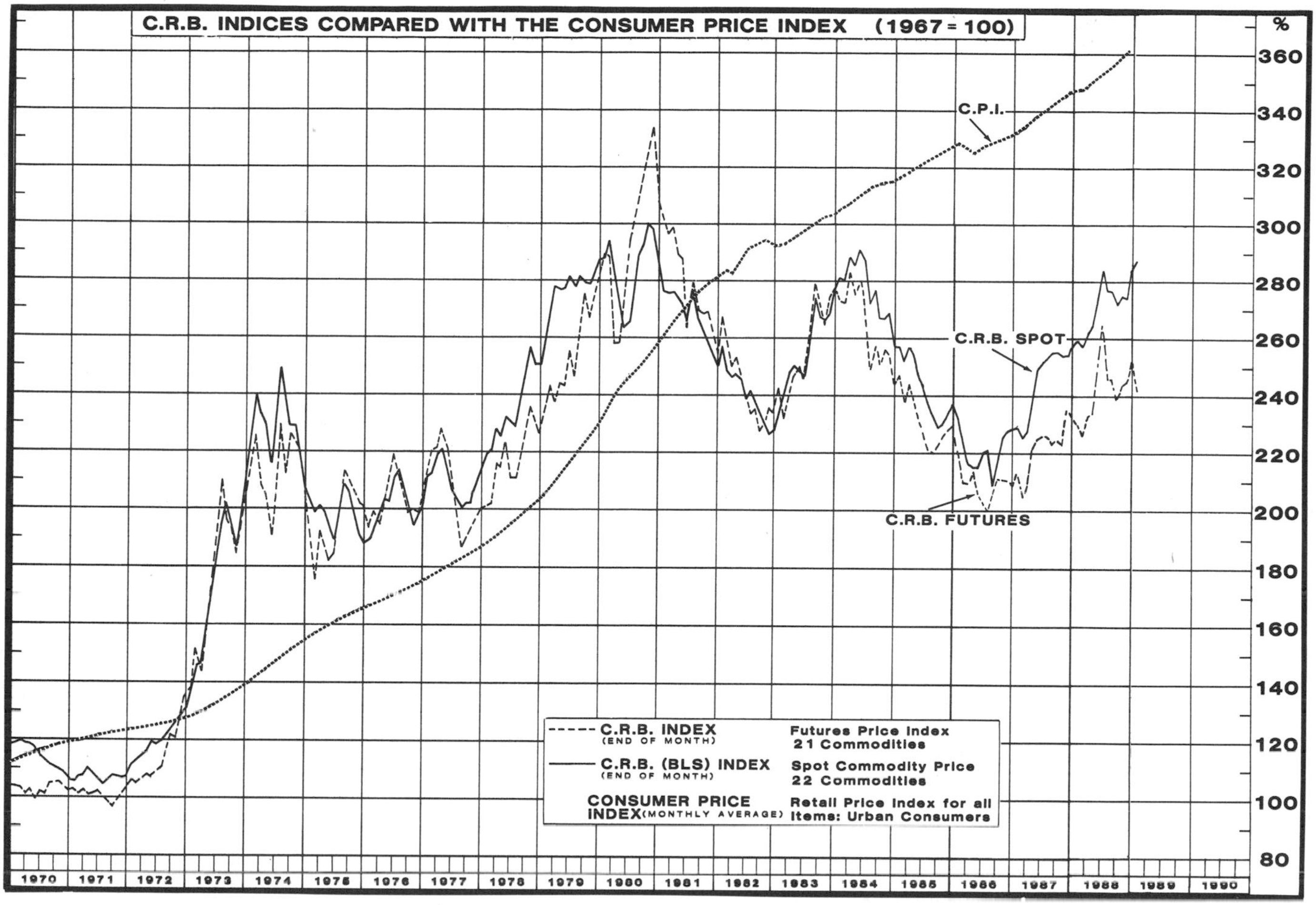

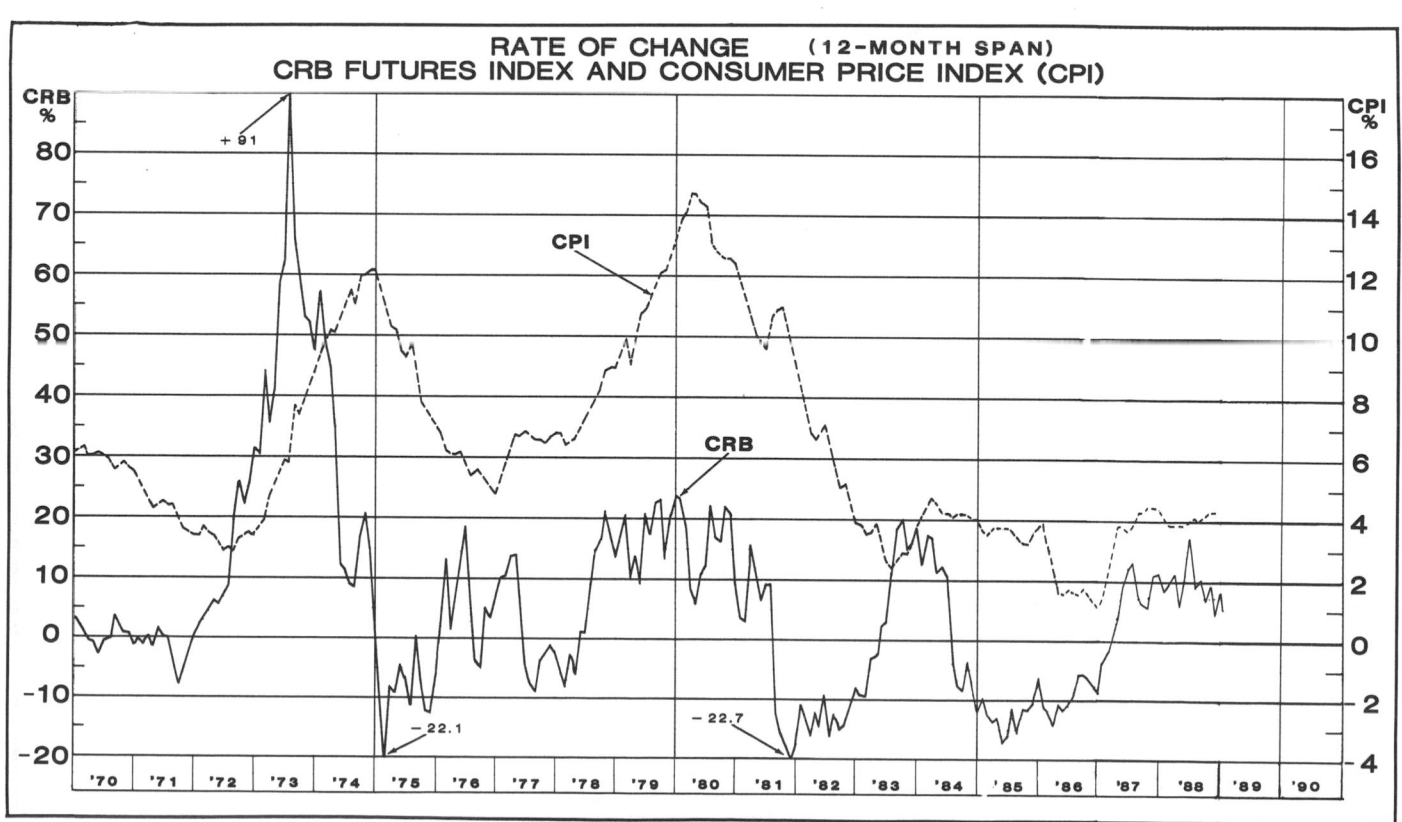

C.R.B. INDICES COMPARED WITH THE CONSUMER PRICE INDEX (1967 = 100)
%
360
340
320
300
280
260
240
220
200
180
160
140
120
100
80
C.P.I.
C.R.B. SPOT
C.R.B. FUTURES
C.R.B. INDEX (END OF MONTH)
Futures Price Index 21 Commodities
C.R.B. (BLS) INDEX (END OF MONTH)
Spot Commodity Price 22 Commodities
CONSUMER PRICE INDEX (MONTHLY AVERAGE)
Retail Price Index for all Items: Urban Consumers
1970
1971
1972
1973
1974
1975
1976
1977
1978
1979
1980
1981
1982
1983
1984
1985
1986
1987
1988
1989
1990

RATE OF CHANGE (12-MONTH SPAN)
CRB FUTURES INDEX AND CONSUMER PRICE INDEX (CPI)
CRB %
80
70
60
50
40
30
20
10
0
-10
-20
CPI %
16
14
12
10
8
6
4
2
0
2
4
+ 91
CPI
CRB
− 22.1
− 22.7
'70
'71
'72
'73
'74
'75
'76
'77
'78
'79
'80
'81
'82
'83
'84
'85
'86
'87
'88
'89
'90

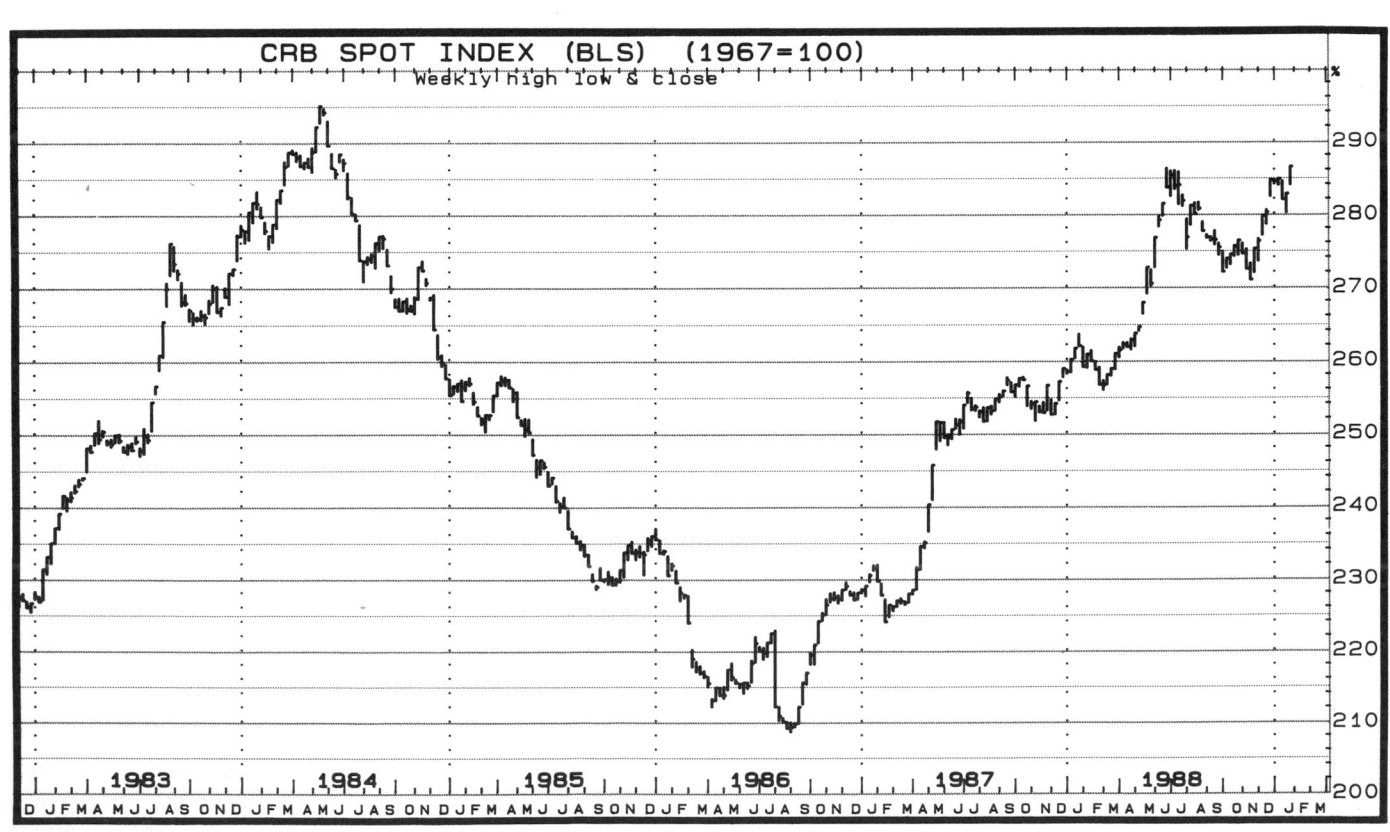

CRB SPOT (BLS) INDEX-ALL COMMODITIES (1967=100)

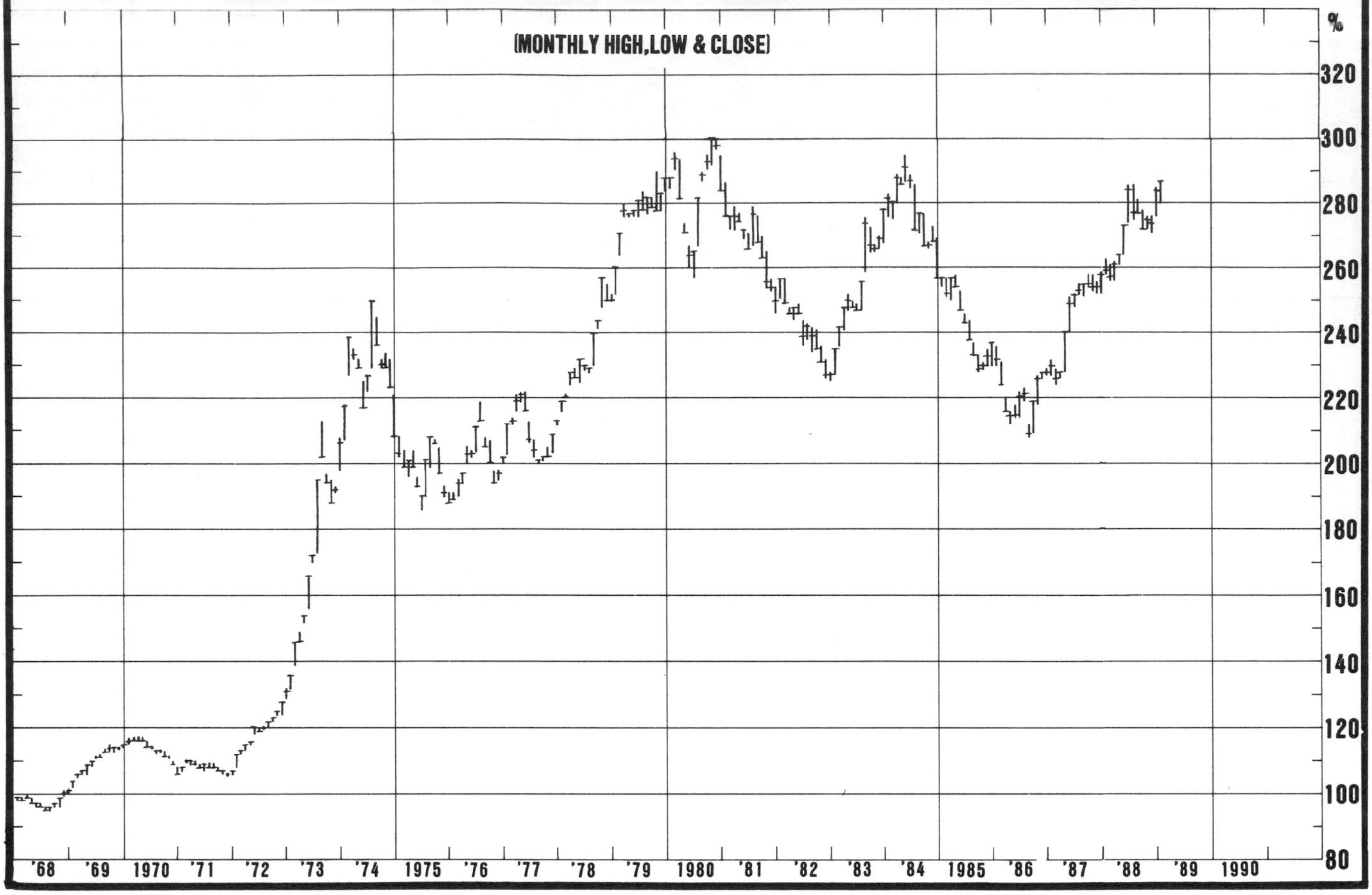

(MONTHLY HIGH,LOW & CLOSE)

%

320
300
280
260
240
220
200
180
160
140
120
100
80

'68 '69 1970 '71 '72 '73 '74 1975 '76 '77 '78 '79 1980 '81 '82 '83 '84 1985 '86 '87 '88 '89 1990

CRB SPOT INDEX (BLS) (1967=100)

Weekly high low & close

290
280
270
260
250
240
230
220
210
200

1983 1984 1985 1986 1987 1988

D J F M A M J J A S O N D J F M A M J J A S O N D J F M A M J J A S O N D J F M A M J J A S O N D J F M A M J J A S O N D J F M A M J J A S O N D J F M

10T

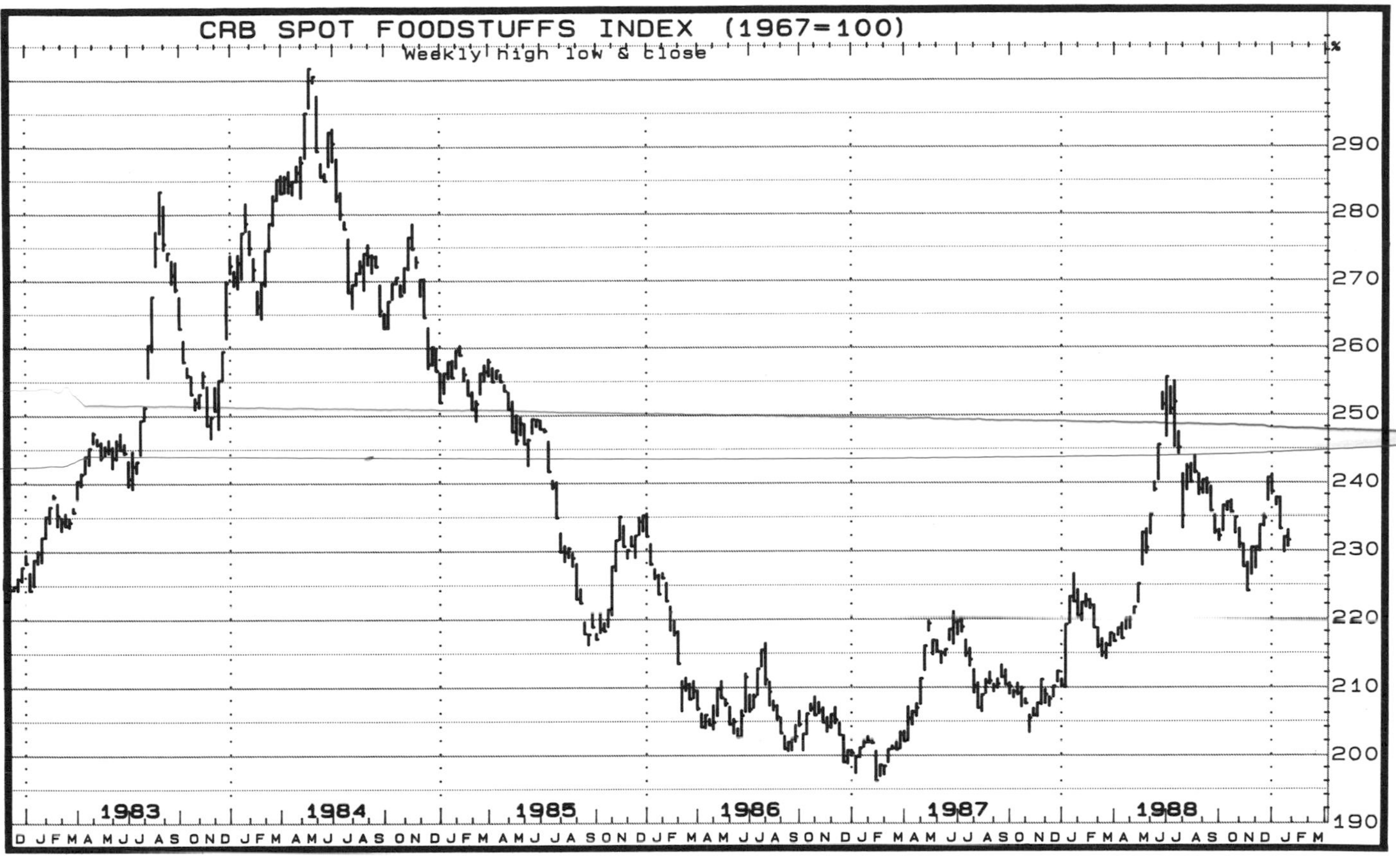
CRB SPOT FOODSTUFFS INDEX (1967=100)
Weekly high low & close
%
290
280
270
260
250
240
230
220
210
200
190
1983
1984
1985
1986
1987
1988
D J F M A M J J A S O N D J F M A M J J A S O N D J F M A M J J A S O N D J F M A M J J A S O N D J F M A M J J A S O N D J F M A M J J A S O N D J F M

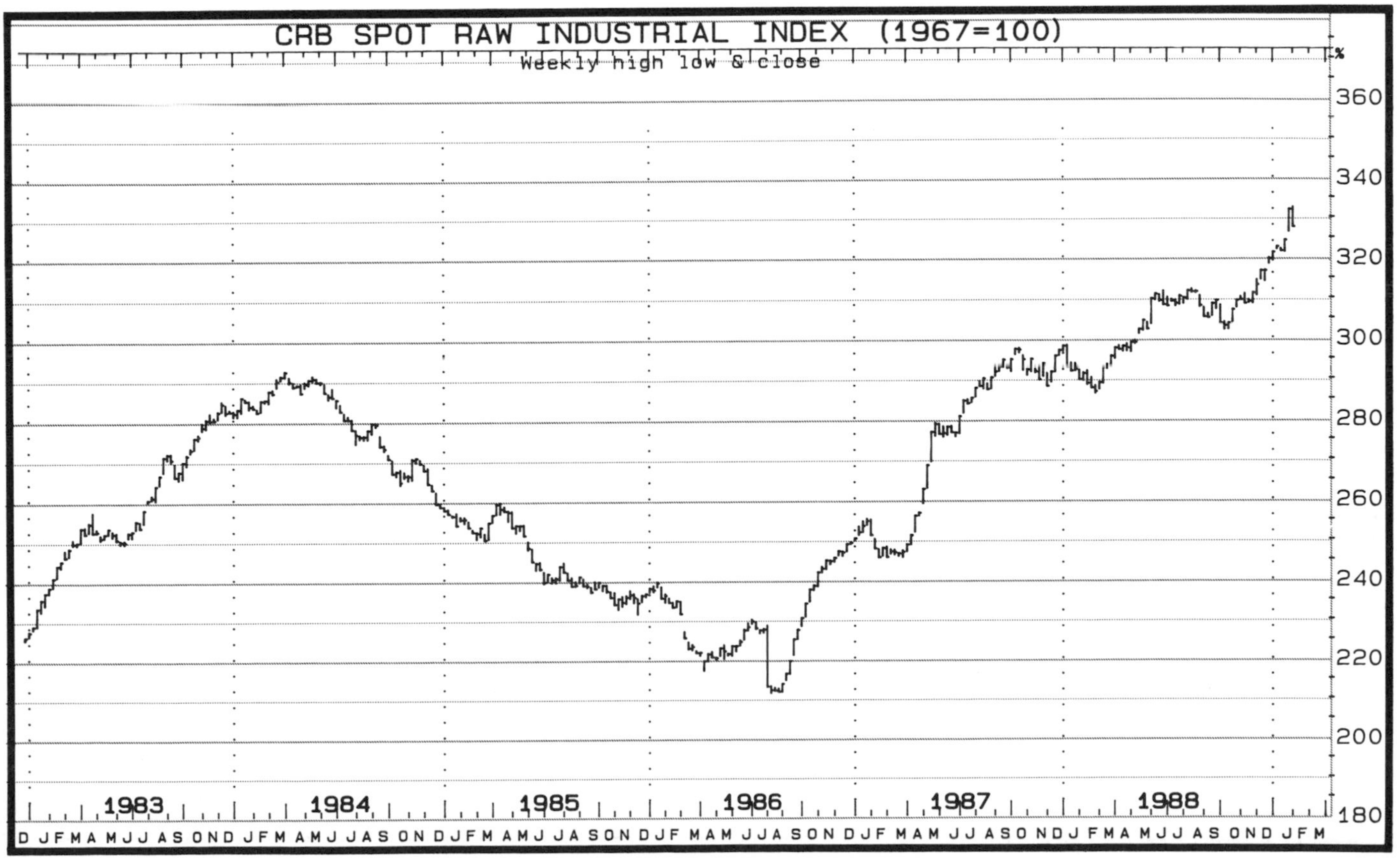
CRB SPOT RAW INDUSTRIAL INDEX (1967=100)
Weekly high low & close
%
360
340
320
300
280
260
240
220
200
180
1983
1984
1985
1986
1987
1988
D J F M A M J J A S O N D J F M A M J J A S O N D J F M A M J J A S O N D J F M A M J J A S O N D J F M A M J J A S O N D J F M A M J J A S O N D J F M

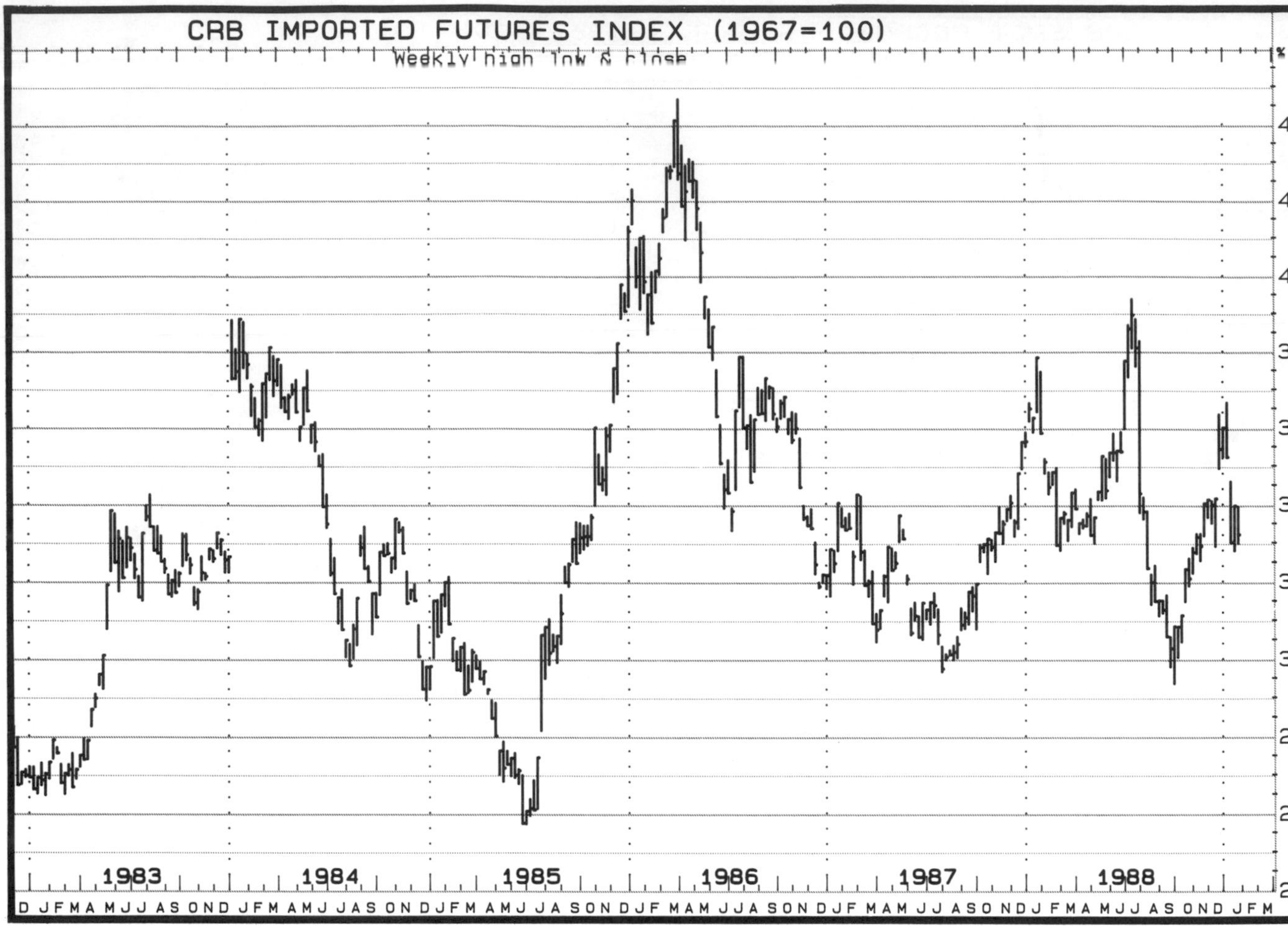

CRB IMPORTED FUTURES INDEX (1967=100)
Weekly high low & close

CRB INDUSTRIALS FUTURES INDEX (1967=100)
Weekly high low & close

12T

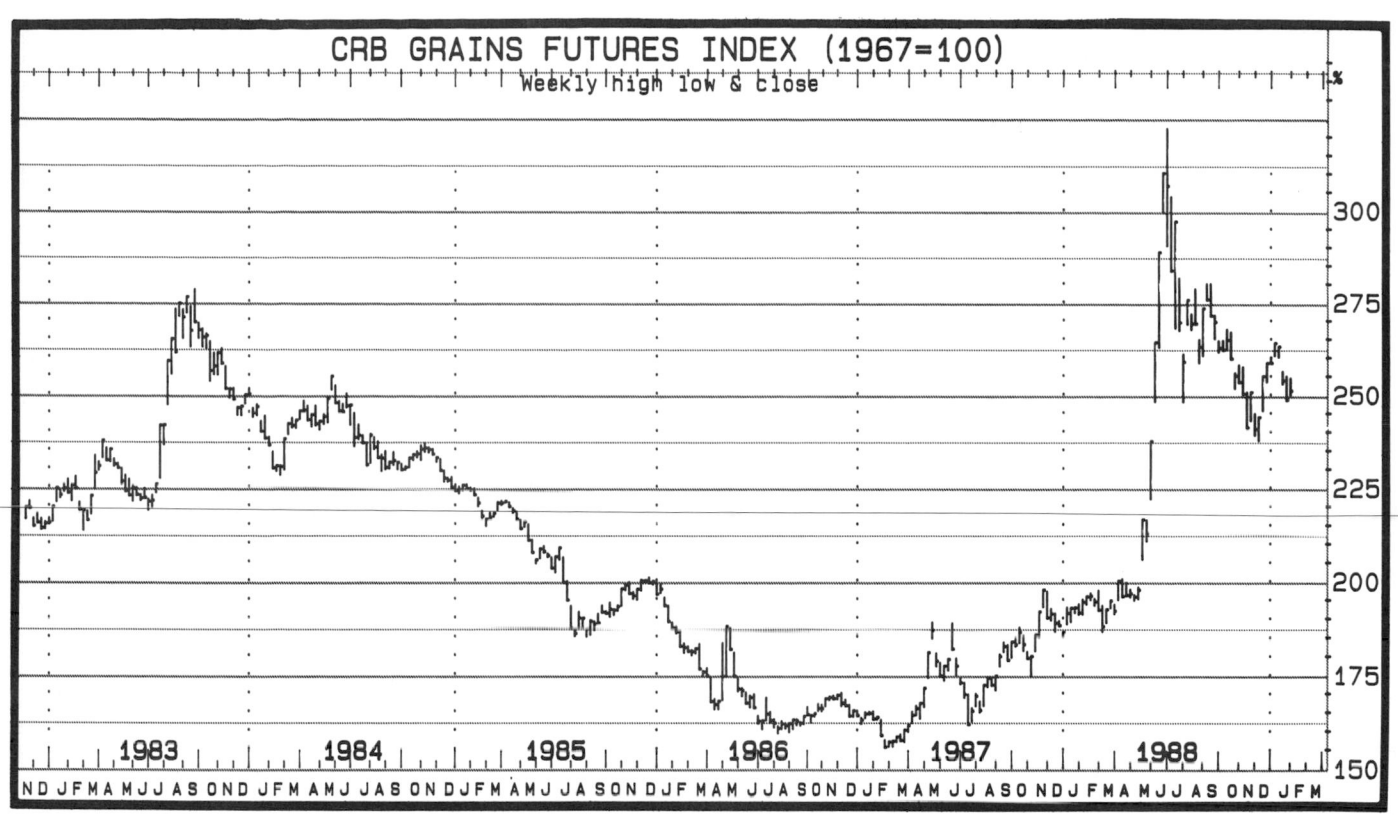

CRB GRAINS FUTURES INDEX (1967=100)
Weekly high low & close
%
300
275
250
225
200
175
150
1983
1984
1985
1986
1987
1988
N D J F M A M J J A S O N D J F M A M J J A S O N D J F M A M J J A S O N D J F M A M J J A S O N D J F M A M J J A S O N D J F M A M J J A S O N D J F M

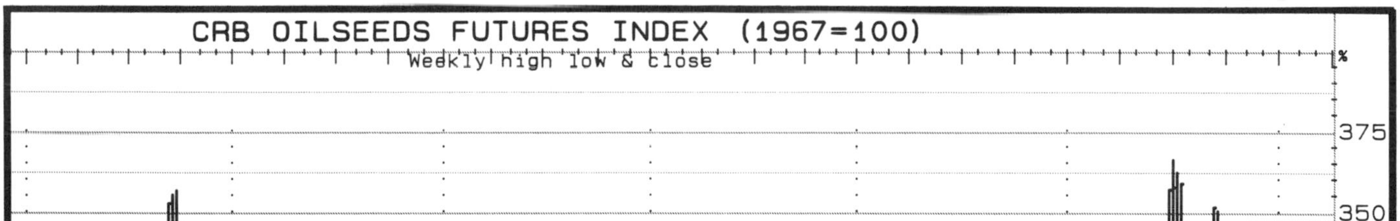

CRB OILSEEDS FUTURES INDEX (1967=100)
Weekly high low & close
%
375
350
325
300
275
250
225
200
175
150
1983
1984
1985
1986
1987
1988
D J F M A M J J A S O N D J F M A M J J A S O N D J F M A M J J A S O N D J F M A M J J A S O N D J F M A M J J A S O N D J F M A M J J A S O N D J F M

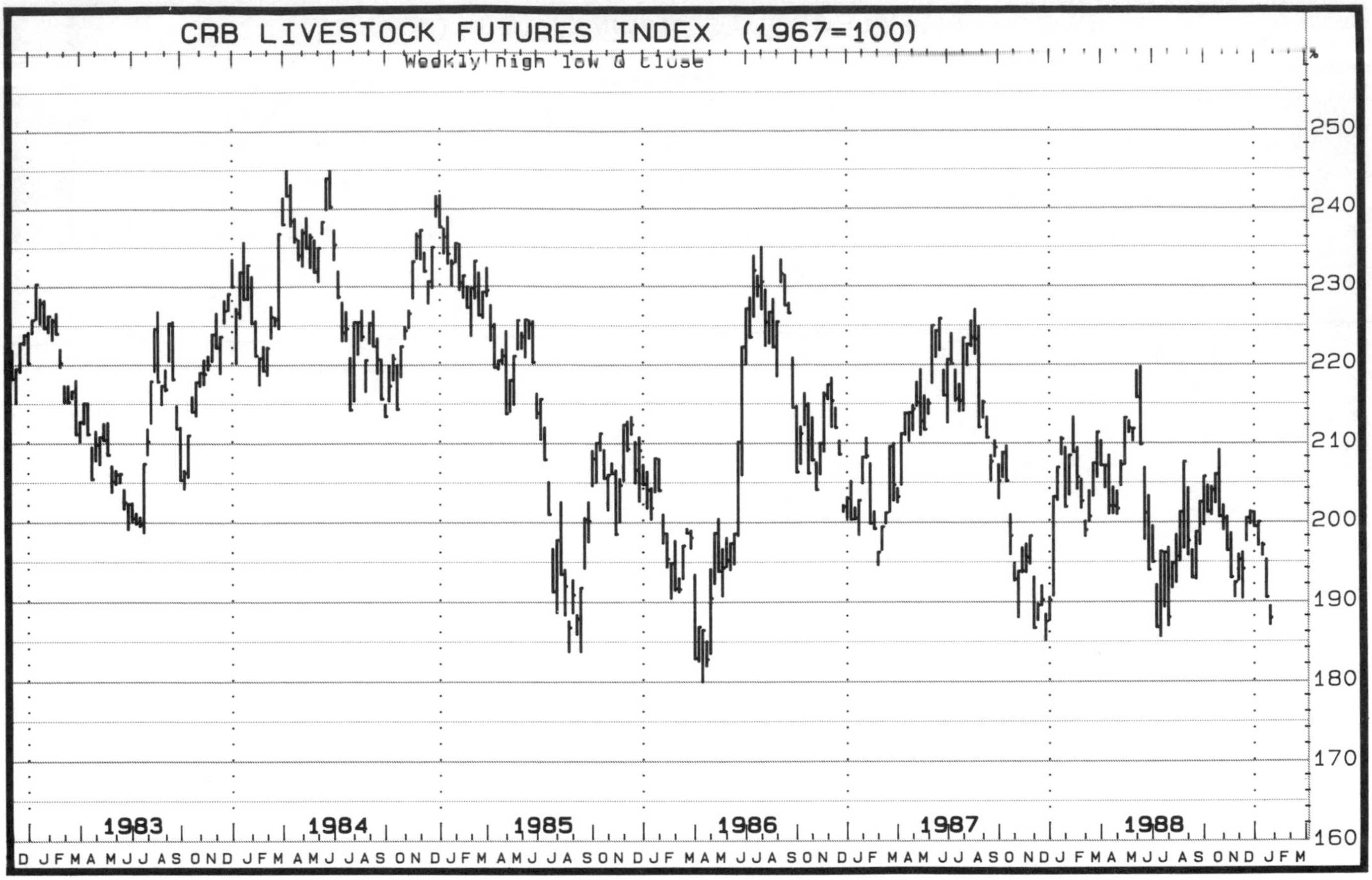

CRB LIVESTOCK FUTURES INDEX (1967=100)

Weekly high low & close

250
240
230
220
210
200
190
180
170
160

1983 1984 1985 1986 1987 1988

D J F M A M J J A S O N D J F M A M J J A S O N D J F M A M J J A S O N D J F M A M J J A S O N D J F M A M J J A S O N D J F M A M J J A S O N D J F M

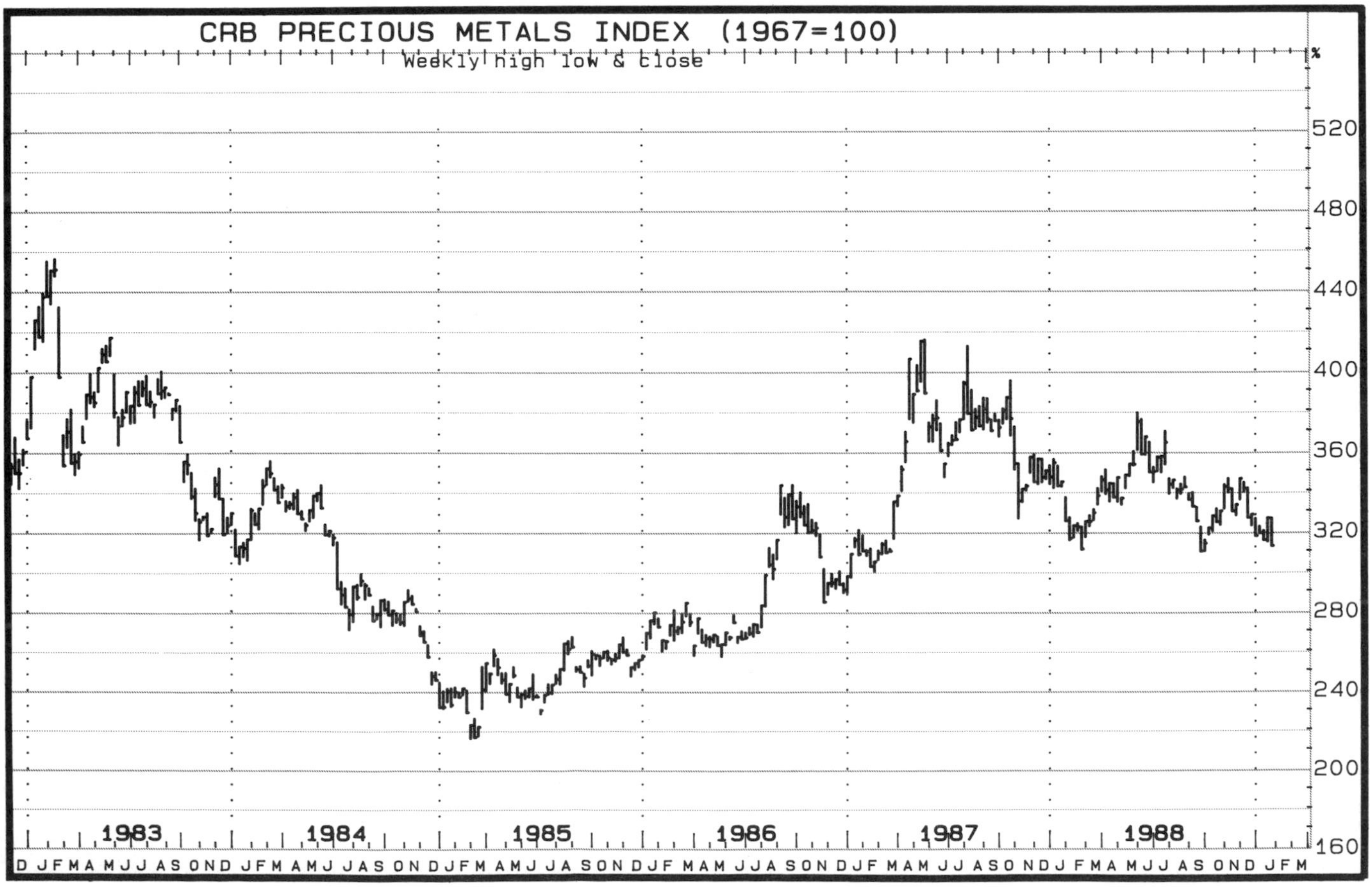

CRB PRECIOUS METALS INDEX (1967=100)

Weekly high low & close

520
480
440
400
360
320
280
240
200
160

1983 1984 1985 1986 1987 1988

D J F M A M J J A S O N D J F M A M J J A S O N D J F M A M J J A S O N D J F M A M J J A S O N D J F M A M J J A S O N D J F M A M J J A S O N D J F M

14T

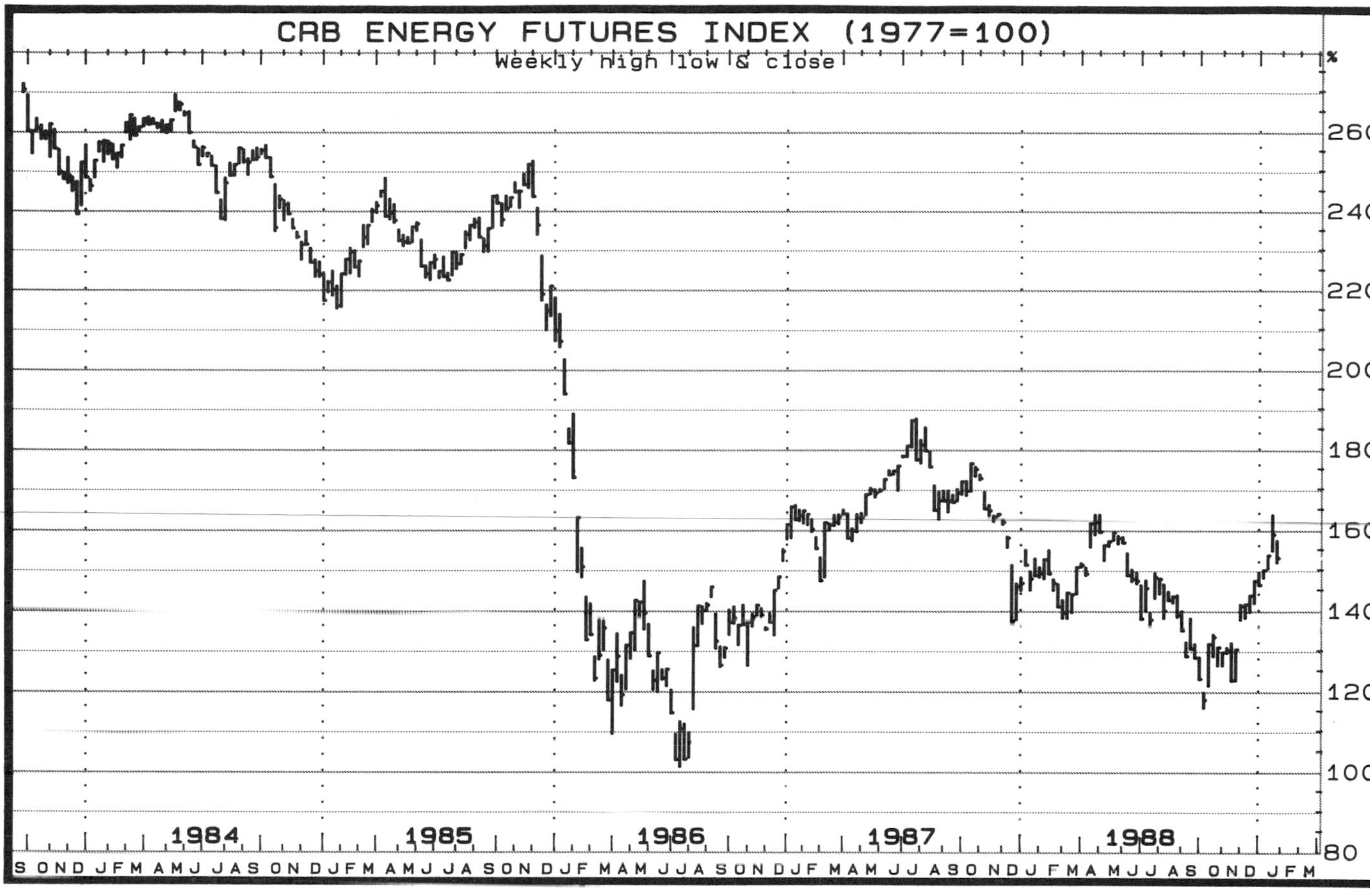

CRB ENERGY FUTURES INDEX (1977=100)
Weekly high low & close

```
          1984        1985        1986        1987        1988
S OND JFM AMJ JAS ON DJFM AMJ JA SON DJF MAM JJA SON DJF MAM JJ ASO NDJ FMA MJJ AS OND JFM
```

CRB COMMODITY PRICE INDEX (1967=100)

COMMODITY PRICE INDEX
23 SPOT PRICES

BURLAP	RUBBER
BUTTER	SOYBEAN OIL
COCOA	STEEL SCRAP
COPPER SCRAP	STEERS
CORN	SUGAR
COTTON	TALLOW
HIDES	TIN
HOGS	WHEAT(MPLS.)
LARD	WHEAT(K.C.)
LEAD	WOOL TOPS
PRINT CLOTH	ZINC
ROSIN	

CRB SPOT INDEX

CRB FUTURES INDEX

COMMODITY PRICE INDEX
21 FUTURES PRICES

CATTLE (LIVE)	LUMBER
COCOA	ORANGE JUICE
COFFEE	PLATINUM
COPPER	PORK BELLIES
CORN	SILVER (N.Y.)
COTTON	SOYBEANS
CRUDE OIL	SOYBEAN MEAL
GOLD (N.Y.)	SOYBEAN OIL
HEATING OIL (NO.2)	SUGAR"11" (WORLD)
HOGS	WHEAT (CHI.)
OATS (CHI.)	

```
     1987                                              1988                                         1989
  2  16  30  13  27  11  25   8  22   5  19   4  18   1  15  29  13  27  10  24   8  22   5  19   2  16  30  14  28  11  25   9  23   6  20   3
  |  OCT  |  NOV  |  DEC  |  JAN  |  FEB  |  MAR  |  APR  |  MAY  |  JUN  |  JUL  |  AUG  |  SEP  |  OCT  |  NOV  |  DEC  |  JAN  |
```

15T

FOOD AND ENERGY PRICES AS INFLATION INDICATORS

BY WALTER L. EMERY

The significance attached to commodity price movements as indications of inflationary forces far exceeds their representation in national economic indices. For example, the farm sector represents only about 10 percent of the Gross National Product, while food accounts for only 16 percent of the Consumer Price Index, and farm commodities represent about one-third of that.

However, the importance of commodity price movements was highlighted by recent efforts by officials of the Group of Seven nations to establish an index of commodity prices to use, in conjunction with other indicators, as a measure of inflationary pressures.

One advantage of the Commodity Research Bureau Futures Price Index as an inflation indicator is that it not only reflects spot price quotations, but also measures price expectations as far as nine months ahead. For example, cash cattle (and nearby futures) in late August 1988 were depressed by increased drought-induced marketings, while deferred cattle futures prices advanced on expectations of reduced marketings in the first half of 1989.

The CRB Futures Price Index is accorded wide acceptance by most government and business economists as a valuable inflation indicator. It tracks well over a period of time with both the Consumer Price Index (CPI) and the Producer Price Index (PPI). Studies have also shown that it tends to lead the CPI by 6 or 7 months.[1]*

Two commodity categories of the CPI which are given particularly close attention by business and government economists, as well as by those concerned directly with interest rate movements, are the Food and Energy sectors. These categories can be monitored on a daily basis, using relevant CRB group futures indices. The group indices are a valuable aid in forecasting rates of change for these two closely watched sectors of the CPI, which is published only monthly.

The CPI energy sector can be monitored via the CRB Energy Group Index, which consists of crude oil, heating oil, and unleaded gasoline.

The food sector of the CPI can be monitored daily via the CRB Grains Group Index, which consists of CBOT wheat, corn, oats and soymeal; the Oilseeds Group Index, which consists of soybeans, flaxseed, and rapeseed; the Livestock and Meats Group Index, which consists of live cattle, hogs, and pork bellies (the makings of bacon); and the Imported Group Index, which consists of cocoa, coffee, and world sugar.

Grains and oilseeds together account for 29 percent of the CRB Futures Price Index; livestock and meats-14 percent; imported-14 percent; and energy-10 percent. The index also includes industrial commodities and precious metals.

For some perspective on movements in the CRB group indices as indicators of changes in inflation rates, it is essential to look beyond the daily index figures to those factors which may influence prices in the food and energy sectors of both the CRB Futures Index and the CPI. The aim of this article is to acquaint the reader with some of the more important influences on these areas of commodity prices and to show how they may effect changes in the rate of inflation.

Factors Influencing the Energy Markets

The major sources of energy are the fossil fuels, which are being depleted, as demand outstrips new discoveries. The most important fossil fuels are petroleum, natural gas, and coal. By far the most important known fossil fuel reserves consist of coal.

The bulk of energy used in the U.S. is consumed directly as fuel, with the remainder used to generate electricity. In 1987, about 57 percent of the nation's electricity was generated by burning coal, 11 percent by natural gas, and less than 5 percent by oil. Nuclear power accounted for about 18 percent and hydroelectric power about 10 percent of electricity generation.[2]

Given this background and that most of our transportation system requires gasoline or fuel oil, concern about the contribution of energy costs to inflationary pressures focuses on crude oil and petroleum products.

Media attention tends to focus on the ongoing efforts of the Organization of Petroleum Exporting Countries (OPEC) to control production quotas and crude oil prices for its thirteen members. In 1987, OPEC accounted for about 33 percent of the estimated 56.2 million barrels of crude oil produced per day (bpd) worldwide, but had an estimated 75 percent of the world's known crude reserves.[3] Yet, the ability of OPEC to dictate world petroleum prices has been dissipated to some extent by growth of non-OPEC oil production, by energy conserving measures, and by alternative sources of energy.

OPEC

Spot crude oil and petroleum futures prices respond to news of upcoming OPEC meetings and trade expectations of possible official action on production quotas and/or export prices. Upward market response has usually been of a temporary nature for several reasons. Foremost is the fact that when a majority of OPEC members have agreed upon a concrete plan of action to limit production or bolster prices, some members have failed to observe quota restrictions and/or have undercut official export prices by one means or another.

Despite the cease-fire in the 8-year Iran-Iraq war, these two OPEC members have strong incentives to step up crude oil production and exports, even at reduced prices, to finance the rebuilding of their war-torn economies. Moreover, political differences, as between the active Shiite and predominant Sunni Moslem countries, could continue to make any working agreement on OPEC production quotas and prices difficult-- over the short term or long run.

U.S. dependency upon crude oil supplied by Arab

FOOTNOTES WILL FOLLOW ARTICLE

members of OPEC has been reduced sharply. (Most U.S. crude imports come from Saudi Arabia, Canada, Venezuela, and Mexico.)[4] Yet, overall U.S. imports of oil have increased. The heaviest dependence on imports was about 46 percent in 1977, whereas imports were as low as 31 percent of consumption in 1982 and 1983.

According to former Saudi oil minister Sheik Ahmed Zaki Yamani, it will be only a matter of time (as early as the mid-1990s) before the world will again be dependent upon Persian Gulf oil.[5] Thus the potential exists for higher prices for crude oil and its products, if OPEC can "get its act together."

There are a number of factors that can have at least a short-term influence on energy market sentiment, aside from those having to do with OPEC considerations. Some of them are related to weekly oil statistics released by the American Petroleum Institute (API) concerning production, imports, and stocks. Any significant changes in production, imports, or primary inventories from recent averages in any of these categories could evoke a market response, which might develop into an energy sector price-trend change. It should be noted that an import hike in a given week could reflect no more than a bunching of tanker arrivals, and that any stock change could be influenced not only by shifts in demand for products, but also by changes in refinery runs in response to shifting "crack" or processing margins.

In addition, *seasonal factors* play a part not only in demand and stock levels, but also in prices. Crude oil demand in the important oil-consuming nations of the Northern Hemisphere tends to be slowest in the spring and summer months and strongest in the fall and winter heating oil demand period. Gasoline demand tends to lead price movements in the petroleum complex in the spring and summer when driving peaks. Heating oil or distillate demand tends to be strongest following the start of the heating season (October 1 in the U.S.); usually stocks have been built up somewhat ahead of this period. Market response to these seasonal considerations can be influenced considerably by the level and location of inventories.

Weather developments can also affect demand for petroleum products. Long-range forecasts of a severe winter cold spell can prompt a build-up in heating oil inventories, but liquidation of those stocks can occur if the cold spell fails to materialize. Severe weather can adversely affect offshore drilling operations, at least temporarily, as can hurricanes in the Gulf of Mexico, which can also disrupt nearby refinery operations.

Demand for Energy

Over the relatively near term, there appears to be little prospect of reducing demand for gasoline, which is by far the most important segment of the energy complex in the U.S. Despite more efficient use of fuel in motor vehicles, studies show that the number of automobiles in the country continues to increase and that the average number of miles driven also increases --tending to offset the greater mileage per gallon.

Most energy-conserving measures appear to have already been instituted. These include: better-insulated homes which tend to reduce heating oil needs; computer-controlled lighting, heating, and air conditioning to use minimum energy in large office buildings; and more fuel-efficient jumbo jet airplanes. However, these developments may be partially offset by increased use of air conditioners in homes, if the greenhouse effect of carbon dioxide pollution and a trend to a warmer climate really gets under way.

Yet, over the foreseeable future, the best possibility for reducing the oil imbalance in the U.S. would seem to be the curbing of demand. This could happen if a recession occurred in the U.S. and the reduced level of economic activity meant less energy use. Prices of crude oil and many oil products then would tend to decline. Thus, economic indicators in this country and projections of the economic outlook in other industrialized nations are likely to influence market sentiment, although the old rule of thumb that a given increase in economic growth is matched by a like change in energy use apparently no longer holds. However, shifts in the economic outlook are likely to be reflected in the discount or premium for deferred petroleum complex futures relative to nearby contracts.

Although the prospects for further, significant gains in fuel conservation do not appear encouraging, government actions may inhibit consumption of gasoline. For example, a higher federal gasoline tax has been proposed. Its purpose (aside from significantly increasing tax revenues) would be to inhibit the use of motor fuel.[6] It would increase prices to the consumer and thus contribute to inflationary pressures, particularly if the economy were strong and use of motor fuel was reduced only slightly by such a tax.

In addition, an import tax to be initiated when the price of crude oil declines below a stated level has been proposed, in the hope of stimulating domestic oil production and leading to self-sufficiency for national security reasons. A significant increase in the import tax would tend to have at least an initial upward influence on much of the U.S. oil economy and on inflationary sentiment.

Other proposals include the easing or lifting of environmental regulations to allow oil exploration off the coast of California and in Alaska's National Wildlife Refuge. Both areas are believed to contain significant oil deposits. Thus from the U.S. oil supply side, some alleviation of increasing dependency upon foreign oil could occur over a period of time. Restoration of depletion allowances to U.S. producers and additional deregulation of natural gas are other measures that have been proposed. All of the foregoing considerations may at one time or another surface, exerting an influence on oil prices and inflation.

U.S. oil production in 1987 dropped to the lowest level in several years (by 4.5 percent to 8.29 million bpd and 14 percent below the 1970 peak), while demand rose by 1.8 percent. As a result, net petroleum imports rose to an average of about 5.8 million bpd (of which crude accounted for 4.5 million bpd and petroleum products 1.3 million). This was the highest import level in seven years, significantly exceeding pre-1973-74 Arab oil import levels, but below the all-time peak of 8.6 million bpd in 1977, which represented 46 percent of consumption.[7]

According to an Energy Department forecast, U.S. oil imports (of crude and refined products) by the mid-1990s will have reached 8-10 million bpd. Oil has become nearly as important a share of the U.S. trade deficit as imported manufactured goods (second only to imported motor vehicles).[8] These considerations point up the importance of crude oil to the U.S. economy and the dependency on imports.

There appears to be little near-term prospect for significant *substitution* of petroleum with its obvious competitors--natural gas and coal. Coal has the greatest reserves worldwide and in the U.S., and natural gas reserves in the U.S. far exceed those of oil. However, petroleum demand and prices can be influenced by developments in these competing fossil fuels.

Industrial consumers are the most important users of natural gas, followed by residential and electric utility use. Large users of natural gas include steel mills, paper mills, and auto manufacturing plants, some of which can switch to fuel oil (no. 6) when it becomes cheaper than natural gas--a factor which tends to limit any significant price gains for natural gas.[9]

Coal, a major source of air pollution as it produces far more carbon dioxide per kilowatt-hour generated than oil or gas, must be converted to gaseous or liquid form, if it is to provide a growing share of U.S. energy needs. It could do so, if technological and environmental problems are worked out. Yet, a significant increase in the use of coal as a substitute for petroleum in the U.S. appears to be a long-term market factor.

Other substitutes for fossil fuels include alcohol fuel using methanol (mostly from natural gas but also from coal) or gasohol, using ethanol produced from corn processing. Ethanol in blended fuels increases octane, but may cause reduced mileage per gallon. Moreover, costs are a consideration. It is estimated that crude oil prices would have to rise to $22-$24 per barrel for ethanol to become competitive with the current federal subsidy, assuming $2 per bushel corn.

Nuclear and hydroelectric power also are likely to receive increasing attention to meet growing demand for electricity, especially in view of concern about the "greenhouse" effect of burning fossil fuels. However, their use as substitutes for petroleum appears unlikely to make much of a dent in the foreseeable future, partly because of costs and the long lead time involved in the construction of facilities.

Petrochemicals

The petrochemical industry is often overlooked as a component of the petroleum complex, but is of basic importance to the economy and to the longer term outlook for inflationary pressures. Demand has soared for such chemicals as ethylene, propylene, styrene, and vinyl chloride used in making plastics--the largest consumer of petrochemicals.[10] Thus, demand for petrochemical feedstocks derived from petroleum refining operations is a factor to watch.

A myriad of plastic products touches virtually every facet of everyday living, and demand for such products increases as living standards increase. Worldwide demand for olefins--the basic building blocks made by the petrochemical process--is expected to continue strong into the mid-1990s.[11] However, recession in any of the major industrialized nations of the world could interrupt the trend to increased usage. Meanwhile, low crude oil prices worldwide have contributed to keeping petrochemical feedstock prices in check and, in turn, have contributed to reduced or stable consumer prices for a multitude of petroleum-based products.

In summary, the factors influencing fuel prices are complex, and long-term price effects of some developments could differ from short-term price impacts. On the supply side, much depends on the bench mark crude price OPEC considers low enough to discourage the development of alternative means of energy supply, further energy conservation efforts, and non-OPEC production, yet high enough to discourage above-quota production.

Factors Influencing Food Prices

The CPI is the most widely used measure of retail price inflation. Major factors influencing retail food prices are farm prices, the costs of processing and distributing food, and consumer demand. The latter is primarily affected by changes in disposable personal income.

According to the USDA, processing and marketing costs account for about 66 percent of the consumer's food dollar. Labor represents about 50 percent of these costs; packaging, 15 percent; transportation, 11 percent; and energy, 9 percent. Plastics account for 15 percent of packaging costs, and the increased use of plastics makes the food industry more vulnerable to any sharp rise in petroleum prices.[12]

Raw farm commodities generally account for less than one-third of a food's retail price. Foods from animal products tend to have a higher farm value share than those from crops, because farm production costs are relatively greater for animal products than crops. The more highly processed crop products have the lowest ratio of farm value to retail price. This means that a given change in the farm price has a smaller impact on the retail price. The USDA notes that pork, poultry, and certain fruits and vegetables have a strong influence on the CPI for all food.

Of the 12.3 percent of U.S. disposable personal income allotted to food in 1986, USDA studies show that the portion of income spent on food averages 42 percent in the 20 percent of households with the lowest before-tax incomes. [13]

Per capita consumption of food (retail weight equivalent) has fluctuated around 1,400 pounds annually in the past 25 years or more. However, over that period, the mix of food consumed and the extent of processing has changed considerably. For example, we consume less red meat, but more poultry, fish, grains, and cereal products than formerly. Fresh fruit and vegetable consumption has also risen, as has the demand for a variety of convenience foods.[14]

The aging of the U.S. population is expected to affect food expenditures. According to the USDA, foods that may be most affected by the projected changing age distribution of the population are pork, fresh fruits and vegetables, and margarine. From a 1980 base year to 2020, per capita expenditures for fruits could increase 7 percent; vegetables by 7 percent; meat, poultry, fish, and eggs by 6 percent; and fats and oils by 6 percent. Least affected would be total food, up 2 percent; dairy products, up 3 percent; and miscellaneous foods, up 1 percent. Older people, in general, eat out less frequently, so food consumed away from home is projected to decline about 4 percent over 1980-2020.[15]

As indicated earlier, the price influence of food market factors on the food sector of the CPI tends to diminish as the distance from the raw material stage increases. For example, the U.S. farmer in 1987 received 26 percent of the retail price of flour, but only 7 percent of the retail price of white bread.[16] At the consumer price level, the price of a loaf of bread may be little affected by a wheat price-depressing factor, because of transportation, storage, processing, and other marketing costs. Price response at the retail level also depends upon the size and location of inventories at the crude, intermediate, and finished goods levels.

Looking well ahead, there are a number of potential food price factors to be aware of. *Biotechnology* or gene transfer for plants or animals holds the promise of a sharp expansion in U.S. agricultural products, including meats, and suggests eventually cheaper food, partly depending on how fast this technology is made available to producers. *Alternative or sustainable agriculture*, using fewer external inputs like chemical pesticides, herbicides and fertilizer, and entailing sustainable soil and water quality, could mean more diversification of crop and livestock production, and at least initially reduced crop yields, with a resultant reduction in agricultural output and firmer prices. While increased concern about the environment may encourage greater interest in alternative agriculture, farmer acceptance of such measures is expected to be a very gradual process.

Two other potential developments may influence food prices in the not-too-distant future. They are concern over the greenhouse effect of air pollution on crop production and the ongoing Uruguay round (1987-92) of the General Agreement on Tariffs and Trade (GATT) talks.

Back-to-back droughts influenced by the greenhouse effect could have a drastic effect on crop and livestock production and on prices in the U.S. In the Uruguay round of GATT negotiations, the U.S. proposed eliminating all trade-distorting government support to agriculture over a 10-year period. In the event of such a development, most commodity prices would tend to rise as land planted to affected crops, particularly in higher-cost producing areas, would be curtailed.

Food price stimulus shifts or trend changes can come about from either the supply side or the demand side. Shifts in demand tend to be of a longer term and less obvious nature than such dramatic developments in production as those caused by widespread drought. Domestic demand for major field crops and also for livestock and poultry products does not usually vary greatly and tends to be predictable.

However, changes in export demand for crops such as wheat, soybeans, and corn, or products such as soybean meal or broiler meat, where export demand is a significant share of total demand, are much less predictable than shifts in domestic demand. Accordingly, they tend to exert a greater, though perhaps more short-lived, effect on food prices.

Regarding export potential, with the world population reaching the 5-billion mark in 1987, and estimated to be growing at a 1.7 percent annual rate, there are about 88 million additional mouths to feed every year.[17] However, the most rapid growth is expected in the developing countries, where food deficits are already sizable and imports are restricted because of large national debts, unfavorable trade balances, sagging economies, and subsistence incomes. This indicates the need for long-term assistance, if food import requirements are to be translated into food purchases.

In weighing those factors which influence food and feed price direction, the availability of supplies in other competing export countries (such as Canada, Australia, and the EC for wheat) is an important consideration. Significant weather developments in countries like China and India, with their huge populations, and the Soviet Union with its climate restrictions on production must also be monitored. Significant changes in the domestic crop outlook in these countries are important to U.S. export prospects. USDA's world supply/demand estimates, released monthly, are an excellent means of monitoring this area of concern.

Supply side (production) changes for field crops tend to come about gradually over one or two crop years, in response to a period of either high prices, which prompt increased plantings, or low prices, which discourage plantings. (Crop seasons are reversed in the Southern Hemisphere.) Production response tends to occur within the parameters imposed by government price support and other program benefits to participating farmers.

Supply shifts in livestock production evolve over a longer period, due to biological considerations--with the lag in poultry production response to price or profit developments much less than that for hogs and cattle. Moreover, the near-term price impact for livestock can be opposite to longer term influences. For example, the prospect of higher feed prices may prompt a price-depressing pick-up in marketings of potential breeding stock near term, which reduces the animals available for marketing later on. Conversely, the expectation or advent of lower feed prices tends to prompt the retention of animals for breeding, with resultant near-term price firmness, while the longer term outlook is for increased marketings.

Market responses to weekly and other USDA and trade reports covering major field crops such as wheat, corn, and soybeans are reflected immediately in the CRB Grains and Oilseeds Group Futures Indices. Reports of substantial export sales, especially for nearby shipment, can exert a strong influence on grain or oilseed prices. Reports of congestion at export points or of a labor strike that disrupts the movement of commodities can often temporarily depress prices at the farm level. Also, weekly government or trade reports on export sales and commitments can be market factors, if they depart significantly from expectations.

Monthly USDA supply/demand estimates for grains and oilseeds for the U.S. and the world can influence prices over the intermediate term, as well as the short term. Seasonal reports on planting intentions and later reports on planted acreage can set the stage for longer term price movement. The importance of these reports depends in part upon yield prospects--which may be monitored by USDA crop production estimates during the growing season and usually by trade estimates which precede official crop reports. At times, an official production estimate, although below the previous report or year-earlier production, may exert an initial downward influence on prices, if it is larger than estimated by the trade.

The foregoing, broad-brush observations should provide a framework within which to evaluate the following factors that influence major grain, oilseed, and livestock prices, and relationships between the CRB Futures Price Index (and the group indices) and both the CPI and the PPI.

Grains and Oilseeds

Grain supply in the U.S. tends to be influenced considerably by government farm policy, as implemented through Farm Acts which cover five crop years, and by farmer response to price incentive, acreage reduction, and other provisions each season. These programs are usually designed to deal with excessive supplies, and they require participating farmers to curtail planted acreage for eligibility for price support and other program benefits. A program calling for significant acreage reductions can lead to sharply higher prices, given a combination of reduced planted acreage and extremely poor crop yields.

On the other hand, a period of high prices associated with reduced supplies tends to encourage calls for lower acreage set-asides. Increased plantings combined with favorable yields may produce another surplus, with the cycle repeating itself and farm programs usually a step behind supply/demand conditions. In any case, acreage reduction programs tend to be only about two-thirds effective, as farmers take less productive land out of cultivation and increase inputs on remaining, more fertile acres.

The 1985 Farm Act was designed to reduce excess supplies by increasing acreage set-asides for program participation and also to move more of the basic commodities in surplus into domestic and export channels by way of reduced price support levels. In the past, high U.S. support prices provided an umbrella for foreign producers who, by shaving prices below U.S. support levels, usurped U.S. export business. Some export markets were subsequently regained, aided by export subsidy programs, but at the expense of sharply lower farm prices.

At this writing, Congressional work was about to begin on the 1990 Farm Bill, which will set government price supports, acreage set-asides, and export assistance through the mid-1990s.

Farm price support decisions are complicated by GATT negotiations. International cooperation on reducing farm subsidies, if successful, could spell lower production and potentially higher grain and oilseed prices.

Bringing government farm policy into closer focus, grain and soybean prices can be influenced by farmer responses to program provisions covering the coming season. A gauge of farmer response can be obtained from the USDA Prospective Plantings report (often released in late March); by later reports of producer sign-ups for acreage set-aside provisions of the program; and by the USDA Planted Acreage report (usually released in late July).

Other factors which influence planting decisions include reports on subsoil moisture conditions for both fall and spring-seeded crops, as influenced by fall rains, winter snow pack, and windy winter conditions when snowfall is light. The Weekly Crop and Weather bulletin issued by the USDA covers crop conditions and stages of development, topsoil and subsoil moisture, and weather developments.

Later, USDA's monthly crop estimates during a growing season attract market attention, particularly if they vary significantly from expectations, as indicated by earlier-released trade estimates of production. Reports of too little or too much rain, temperature extremes, and plant disease find reflection in prices. Generally, the closer to harvest, the more accurate production prospects tend to be. Markets frequently develop into "weather markets" with sharp but unsustained price moves occurring when adverse weather conditions are forecast or materialize, particularly during the planting, fruiting, or harvesting stages of a crop. Weather markets have tended to peak around the time of harvest in the Northern Hemisphere.

For most major field crops, a calendar year spans at least a portion of two crop years. For example, the 1987 U.S. corn crop year (1987/88 season) extended from September 1, 1987, the earliest stages of harvest, through August 31, 1988 (which covered distribution of the 1987 corn crop into domestic use, exports, and carryover). The 1988/89 crop year extends from September 1, 1988, through August 31, 1989. Thus for much of 1988, the market had to contend with movement of 1987-crop corn into domestic and export channels, and at the same time contend with factors which influenced the size and disposition of the drought-affected 1988 corn crop.

After harvest, when total supply for the season is generally well-established, "effective supply" still enters into the pricing structure, even though market attention tends to shift to the demand side of the equation, as the season progresses. Effective supply may be defined roughly as that which appears to be readily available to the commercial market at the then-current price level. It is influenced not only by storage and crop-quality considerations, but also by producer holding in anticipation of higher prices. If such a holding pattern occurs at a time when exporters have previously made significant export sales commitments for early shipment from the "new" crop, prices can move higher until these commitments are covered by purchases in the cash market.

Some provisions of the "market-oriented" 1985 Food Security Act have weakened market prices. Grain held in the farmer-owned reserve or owned by the CCC can be acquired at less than loan prices through the use of generic certificates. These certificates can also be used to redeem loans at prices below loan levels. Outstanding certificates represent a pool of potential free stocks or supplies. The loan level no longer supports prices under the current farm program.

Throughout the crop year, the market is concerned with the demand side of the equation and the rate of distribution into domestic and export channels, as revealed by various government and trade reports.

The domestic demand side tends to be more predictable than exports, and for food grains is basically determined by population growth rates and changes in disposable personal income. Overall feed grain domestic demand is influenced primarily by changes in livestock and poultry numbers and the profitability of feeding. Soybeans are influenced by both considerations-- soybean oil by population growth rates and soybean meal by animal numbers and composition.

The rate of domestic use of grains can be monitored by periodic USDA reports of grain stocks in all positions (including free stocks) and also by monthly USDA supply/demand reports for the U.S. These reports can influence specific grain prices considerably, if they significantly differ from expectations.

Seasonal considerations also enter into domestic use and price patterns. For example, feed demand for corn, the nation's largest crop, tends to be heaviest in winter when pasture usually is not available. However, prices usually tend to rise seasonally from harvest levels into the following summer, although prices tend to peak early in drought years.

Export demand for U.S. grain is influenced by a number of factors including: prices relative to those of competing foreign producers, freight differences, quality considerations, crop conditions and availability in major exporting countries and in some important grain-importing countries; changes in the exchange rate of the U.S. dollar, versus the currencies of major importers of U.S. grains and oilseeds; and the availability of credit and foreign export subsidies. Seasonally, exports of

U.S. grains and oilseeds tend to be slowest in the July-September quarter.

The U.S. operates a number of programs to assist agricultural exports. These include the Export Enhancement Program, CCC Export Guarantee programs, the Targeted Export Assistance Program, and food aid programs under PL 480 and Section 416 authority. Substantial exports have been made under these programs. Any changes in the programs could influence exports and prices of the commodities involved. Export programs, by reducing domestic supply, can increase prices, potentially to levels which permit release of CCC-owned stocks--which then can be a price-depressing influence.

Wheat and rice are the world's most important food grains. International trade in wheat, however, far exceeds that in rice. A natural disaster, such as widespread drought or a weak or late monsoon in Southeast Asia, that adversely affects production in major wheat/rice producing and/or consuming countries can exert a strong impact on export demand and prices for U.S. wheat. Monthly USDA world supply/demand reports can indicate actual and potential dislocations of supply and demand.

According to the USDA, assuming income growth as projected, countries that are expected to show increased import growth (for grains and oilseeds) to the year 2000 are Mexico, Egypt, Taiwan, Iran, Nigeria, Saudi Arabia, Venezuela, Algeria, Iraq, Romania, Morocco, Malaysia, and possibly India.[18]

Probably the best guide to the longer term influence of grain and oilseed supply/demand factors on price and inflation potential is the stocks-to-use ratio worldwide and in major producing and/or consuming nations. Large stocks predicted for the end of a season relative to forecast use in that season can lessen or even offset the price-constructive influence of a crop shortfall in a major grain-consuming country. On the other hand, a low or declining stocks-to-use ratio can pave the way for higher and potentially inflationary prices.

There are rules of thumb for supply/demand ratios for grains that have in the past been associated with periods of increasing or high prices. The Canadian Wheat Board has noted that the ratio of ending stocks to world wheat consumption tends to be cyclical, with 40 percent being the highest ratio of stocks to use in the last 25 years (in the late 1960s when prices were low) and the lowest ratio about 20 percent (in the early 1970s peak price years for wheat). The indicated ratio at the end of the 1987/88 season was about 33 percent, and the forecast for 1988/89 was 23 percent--the lowest since 1972/73. According to the USDA, the world coarse grain stocks-to-use ratio was forecast at the lowest ratio since 1983/84. USDA also has noted that cereals constitute 75 percent of the diet in Asia and 50 percent-70 percent in Africa, while 12 percent of the world's population lives in these areas and only 25 percent of the world's cereals are grown there. It is estimated that the ratio of world cereal stocks to use at the end of 1988/89 will be the lowest since 1974/75. (The monthly USDA supply/demand reports provide estimates of stocks-to-use ratios.)

When evaluating the potential inflationary impact of a development which affects grain and oilseed prices, one must also consider the size and location of commercial stocks of grains and oilseeds and finished products. Large stocks of consumer food products on grocers' shelves can mute or at least delay any inflationary impact of reduced grain or vegetable crops on the CPI food sector. Yet, retail food prices can be expected to reflect reduced supplies, as retail food stocks are drawn down.

In summary, the foregoing considerations may provide some insight into the multitude of short and long-term influences on grain and oilseed prices, which may find reflection in rates of change in the food sector of the CPI. One must attempt to distinguish between: 1.) factors which may prompt no more than a one-time response in the CPI food sector, and 2.) those longer term developments, which may or may not support the prospect of the food sector of the CPI continuing to lead the underlying uptrend in the CPI for all items.

Livestock and Meat Sector

Some observations are helpful when considering the role of livestock and poultry prices in shaping the trend of the CPI food sector. Meat consumption continues to shift toward poultry and away from beef. Meat and food prices advanced sharply relative to the CPI for all items in the 1973-79 period. However, since 1980, as meat supplies expanded, the meat and food indices increased at a much lower rate than the CPI index for all items through 1986--with the meat index moderating increases in the food index. Any sustained change in these relationships will be influenced considerably by changes in livestock numbers, as determined basically by the size of breeding stock and the stage of cattle and hog production cycles, and by changes in poultry numbers, as determined primarily by hatchery supply flock size.

The cattle cycle is a long one and for the past several years has not conformed to earlier patterns, which indicated a period of about ten years (peak to peak in numbers) involving an expansion phase of 6-7 years and a liquidation phase of only 2-4 years. The current cycle, which reached a peak in 1982, involved an expansion phase of only three years, while the liquidation phase was in its seventh year in mid-1988. The interval between a cattleman's decision to initiate the breeding process in response to price incentive and its impact on retail beef is around 2 1/2 years.[19]

The hog cycle used to average around four years from one peak to the next. However, the production cycle became erratic, as hog production shifted to expensive confinement systems, which entailed sizable capital costs and encouraged large producers to continue turning out hogs as long as returns exceeded cash costs (a situation favoring less production response than formerly to adverse market conditions). In any case, it takes 9-10 months to bring a hog to slaughter weight.[20]

The broiler production cycle is the shortest of all, and thus production can respond quickest to changes in market conditions. The breeding to slaughter period for broilers is about 2 1/2 months, and for turkeys is about 5 1/2 months.[21]

Before the drought in the summer of 1988, we were generally considered to be approaching stabilization of the liquidating phase of the cattle cycle after cattle and calf numbers had reached 99 million head, the lowest level since 1961, on January 1, 1988. The expansion phase is expected to be delayed somewhat, as some heifers and cows intended for breeding were sent to market instead. The initial stages of herd rebuilding entail reduced marketings, as heifers and cows are retained for breeding. Thus the stage may be set for lower marketings in 1989 and beyond than anticipated earlier, with resultant higher beef prices.

Hog number expansion began in mid-1986 and continued well into 1988. Drought-induced higher feed costs could hasten culling of the breeding herd and set the stage for initiation of the downward phase of the hog production cycle, perhaps sometime in 1989.

As broiler numbers respond most quickly to profit and/or demand incentive, their production cycle tends to have less bearing on broiler prices (and on the CPI food sector) than broiler prices relative to other meat prices--pork, in particular. However, higher feed costs could slow expected production gains.

Longer term, livestock and poultry meat prices can also be influenced by shifts in dietary considerations which affect demand for various meat products. Also, the trend to further processing of meats and the increased demand for convenience foods can result in higher meat costs for the consumer, even in the event of a modest increase in meat supplies.

Many factors affect the near-term and long-term supply and price of livestock and poultry and meat products. The market's evaluation of all these factors can be monitored on a daily basis by observation of the CRB Livestock and Meat Group Futures Index. Changes in the trend of this index can provide a clue as to the rate of change in the CPI food index over a period of time.

The basic USDA livestock reports that set the stage for subsequent cattle and hog slaughter (meat production) are: 1.) the semi-annual inventory of cattle numbers and composition by class and weight of animal, as of year-end and mid-year (reports are released in January and July); and 2.) the semi-annual Hogs and Pigs report, which is usually released in late June and December. Later, quarterly reports of (a) the number and weight groups of cattle on feed, and (b) hog numbers, weights, and farrowing intentions provide a clue as to slaughter rates for coming months. These reports can exert a strong but, at times, no more than temporary influence on prices, particularly if they fail to support data in the semi-annual USDA reports. Monthly USDA reports of cattle on feed fine-tune the earlier quarterly expectations. Weekly and daily USDA estimates of cattle and hog receipts at major markets and slaughter estimates influence short-term price movement.

Some developments prompt shifts in the near-term availability of livestock for slaughter, and generally result in short-term price movement unlikely to have any lasting effect on the CPI food sector. These developments include: weather-delayed movement of animals to market and extreme heat, which can mean weight loss, if not increased death loss, for both livestock and poultry.

Other Foods

Some other items included in the CPI food sector can also be monitored by observation of the futures price movement of cocoa, coffee, domestic sugar, frozen concentrated orange juice (FCOJ), and soybean oil.

Both cocoa and coffee are produced in developing countries and are subject to international agreements designed to balance supply and demand by either absorbing excess supplies in a stockpile or reducing export quotas when prices are low, and releasing such supplies withheld from the market when prices exceed specified targets. Changes in terms of these agreements can influence prices.

Significant price moves in cocoa and coffee occur primarily as a result of important changes in production from one season to the next. Coffee has at times moved sharply higher because of freeze damage during June-August in Brazil, the world's largest producer. Such a development primarily affects the following season's crop, but it also influences the price of the crop just harvested. Much of the world's cocoa is produced in West Africa, with too little or too much rain in the critical late-summer growth period an important market factor prior to the main crop harvest which begins in October. Disease is also a matter of concern.

U.S. domestic sugar prices are influenced primarily by: changes in U.S. sugar beet and sugar cane production, competition from sugar substitutes, and provisions of the U.S. sugar program, as implemented by price support and import quota changes.

FCOJ prices are influenced not only by orange crop developments in Florida, the major producing state, but also by production and export developments in Brazil, the other major FCOJ producer. Freeze damage to Florida oranges or orange trees is always a matter of concern from late November through January.

Soybean oil is the world's leading edible oil, and the U.S. is the largest producer. Soybean oil price movements affect other fats and oils. In turn, its price is influenced by competition from other edible oils, such as palm oil, sunflower oil, and rapeseed oil. The rate of U.S. soybean crushing activity--as indicated by monthly USDA reports and periodic Fats and Oils Situation reports--and weekly export reports also provide clues to soybean oil's price direction.

The USDA issues seasonal forecasts for world cocoa and coffee production. USDA also issues production estimates for U.S. sugar and oranges, while monthly supply/demand estimates are issued for soybean oil.

U.S per capita consumption is significant for some groups of commodities included in one or another segment of the CPI food sector, but whose price movement is generally less visible than for those commodities which are traded on futures exchanges. These include dairy products, and fresh and processed fruits and vegetables. Fresh vegetables for the commercial market are generally irrigated (much comes from California). However, drought can have a significant impact on some non-irrigated crops for canning, such as dry edible beans, tart cherries, green peas, sweet corn and snap beans in the North Central States, where such production is concentrated. Price changes (as expressed in index numbers) for many of these commodities can be monitored by the monthly PPI for finished goods (or by supermarket prices comparisons).

The most authoritative information on crop production and other factors which influence prices and in turn the food sector of the CPI are USDA's seasonal estimates of planted acreage and production, and monthly reports of developments which affect supply/demand and prices. USDA's monthly *Agricultural Outlook* magazine is a very useful source of information on commodities not traded on futures exchanges, as well as grains, oilseeds, livestock and poultry. These reports, along with the monthly USDA cold storage holdings reports, can provide useful clues to the food price outlook.

The CRB Index, CPI, and PPI

Mention has been made previously of the help that the CRB group futures indices provide in monitoring food and energy price changes, and how they offer clues to subsequent shifts in the rate of change in the volatile food and energy sectors of the monthly reported CPI.

Movement in the overall CRB Futures Price Index (which also includes industrial commodities and precious metals prices) can be a valuable aid in forecasting shifts in the rate of change in the CPI.

The timing and extent of retail price responses to raw commodity price stimuli depend partly on market psychology, the level of inventories at the various stages of processing and marketing, and on whether long-term supply contracts exist. Where the costs of labor and other processing inputs are much more significant in the final cost to the consumer than the cost of the raw commodity, a sizable decline in the raw commodity price may not have a significant impact on the rate of change in the CPI group index including the product.

Raw commodity futures price indices bear a relationship to both the PPI and the CPI. As various studies have indicated, there is a correlation between the CRB Futures Price Index and the rate of change in the PPI for crude and finished goods (whose prices tend to be reflected in later, similar changes in the CPI). However, only the CPI includes prices of imports and services, which can have an important influence on the CPI. Interim peaks in the CRB Futures Index have occurred around the same time or somewhat earlier than peaks in the rate of change in the PPI for finished goods. Troughs in the CRB Futures Index have occurred slightly before troughs in the PPI.[22] And studies have shown that the CRB Futures Index has tracked well with the CPI and has tended to lead the CPI by about six months.[23]

In Summary

Obviously, the food and energy sectors must be viewed together with underlying factors that influence the rate of inflation, such as shifts in the foreign exchange value of the U.S. dollar and in interest rates, as well as developments in such major components of the CPI as housing and transportation.

Nevertheless, one who is concerned with the potential inflationary impact of food and energy market influences on the CPI would do well to monitor the CRB Energy, Grains, Oilseeds, Livestock and Meats, and Imported group futures indices, as well as the overall CRB Futures Price Index. Attention should be focused on the trends of these indices. Supply and demand developments which affect food and energy prices and influence CRB group index trend changes may be monitored by a wealth of USDA and other government reports, many of which were referred to earlier in this article.

Footnotes

1 *The CRB Futures Price Index*, New York, Commodity Research Bureau, 1988.
2 Dept. of Energy, *Monthly Energy Review*, June 1988.
3 Ibid.
4 *New York Times*, January 15, 1988.
5 *New York Times*, March 3, 1988.
6 *New York Times*, June 28, 1988.
7 Dept. of Energy, *Monthly Energy Review*, June 1988.
8 *New York Times*, November 19, 1987.
9 *New York Times*, January 5, 1988.
10 *New York Times*, March 15, 1988.
11 Ibid.
12 USDA, *National Food Review*, April-June 1988.
13 Ibid.
14 USDA, *Agricultural Outlook*, August 1986.
15 USDA, *National Food Review*, April-June 1988.
16 Ibid.
17 USDA, *Farmline*, July 1988.
18 USDA, *Agricultural Outlook*, September 1987.
19 USDA, *National Food Review*, April-June 1988.
20 Ibid.
21 Ibid.
22 American Institute for Economic Research, Research Reports, October 23, 1978.
23 *The CRB Futures Price Index,* New York, Commodity Research Bureau, 1988.

FUTURES VOLUME HIGHLIGHTS 1988 in Comparison with 1987

Rank	Contracts With Volume Over 100,000	1988 Contracts	%	1987 Contracts	%	RANK
1.	T-Bonds, CBOT	70,307,872	28.60%	66,841,474	29.20%	(1)
2.	Eurodollar, CME	21,705,223	8.83%	20,416,216	8.92%	(2)
3.	Crude Oil, NYMEX	18,858,948	7.67%	14,581,614	6.37%	(4)
4.	Soybeans, CBOT	12,497,096	5.08%	7,378,760	3.22%	(6)
5.	S&P 500 Index, CME	11,353,898	4.62%	19,044,673	8.32%	(3)
6.	Corn, CBOT	11,105,516	4.52%	7,253,212	3.17%	(7)
7.	Gold (100 oz.), COMEX	9,496,402	3.86%	10,239,805	4.47%	(5)
8.	Japanese Yen, CME	6,433,132	2.62%	5,358,556	2.34%	(9)
9.	Sugar #11, CSC	5,819,121	2.37%	3,853,499	1.68%	(16)
10.	Deutschemark, CME	5,662,109	2.30%	6,037,048	2.64%	(8)
11.	Live Cattle, CME	5,477,205	2.23%	5,229,294	2.28%	(12)
12.	Soybean Meal, CBOT	5,313,081	2.16%	3,797,970	1.66%	(17)
13.	Swiss Franc, CME	5,283,406	2.15%	5,268,276	2.30%	(10)
14.	T-Notes (6 1/2-10 Year), CBOT	5,200,949	2.12%	5,253,791	2.30%	(11)
15.	No. 2 Heating Oil, NY, NYMEX	4,935,015	2.01%	4,293,395	1.88%	(14)
16.	Soybean Oil, CBOT	4,896,194	1.99%	3,912,417	1.71%	(15)
17.	Silver (5,000 oz.), COMEX	4,664,655	1.90%	5,055,652	2.21%	(13)
18.	Wheat, CBOT	3,377,738	1.37%	1,929,306	0.84%	(24)
19.	Unleaded Reg. Gas, NYMEX	3,292,055	1.34%	2,056,238	0.90%	(22)
20.	British Pound, CME	2,616,068	1.06%	2,592,177	1.13%	(20)
21.	Copper, COMEX	2,112,459	0.86%	2,569,178	1.12%	(21)
22.	Live Hogs, CME	2,008,750	0.82%	2,040,478	0.89%	(23)
23.	NYSE Composite Index, NYFE	1,668,732	0.68%	2,915,915	1.27%	(18)
24.	Platinum, NYMEX	1,460,455	0.59%	1,361,546	0.59%	(28)
25.	T-Bonds, MIDAM	1,414,390	0.58%	1,015,454	0.44%	(30)
26.	Canadian Dollar, CME	1,408,783	0.57%	914,563	0.40%	(33)
27.	T-Bills (90-Day), CME	1,373,553	0.56%	1,927,006	0.84%	(25)
28.	Cotton #2, NYCE	1,370,249	0.56%	1,395,980	0.61%	(27)
29.	Wheat, KCBOT	1,338,711	0.54%	971,095	0.42%	(31)
30.	Municipal Bond Index, CBOT	1,274,316	0.52%	1,613,107	0.70%	(26)
31.	Cocoa (10 M Tons), CSC	1,268,050	0.52%	895,465	0.39%	(34)
32.	Pork Bellies, CME	1,186,599	0.48%	1,097,010	0.48%	(29)
33.	MMI Maxi, CBOT	1,175,531	0.48%	2,630,887	1.15%	(19)
34.	Coffee "C", CSC	1,149,710	0.47%	964,586	0.42%	(32)
35.	Soybeans, MIDAM	863,934	0.35%	417,620	0.18%	(39)
36.	5 Year T-Note, NYCE	789,630	0.32%	383,613	0.17%	(41)
37.	Feeder Cattle, CME	702,438	0.29%	645,877	0.28%	(35)
38.	T-Notes (5 Year), CBOT	506,595	0.21%			
39.	Silver (1,000 oz.), CBOT	481,566	0.20%	509,965	0.22%	(36)
40.	US Dollar Index, NYCE	446,525	0.18%	403,783	0.18%	(40)
41.	Corn, MIDAM	429,219	0.17%	311,722	0.14%	(42)
42.	Wheat, MGE	423,542	0.17%	310,599	0.14%	(43)
43.	Lumber, CME	371,489	0.15%	437,089	0.19%	(38)
44.	Orange Juice, (Frozen Conc.), NYCE	358,039	0.15%	266,641	0.12%	(45)
45.	Oats, CBOT	354,578	0.14%	291,108	0.13%	(44)
46.	Wheat, MIDAM	294,236	0.12%	189,610	0.08%	(47)
47.	Cmdty Rsrch Bureau Index, NYFE	205,951	0.08%	136,832	0.06%	(50)
48.	Palladium, NYMEX	139,883	0.06%	160,284	0.07%	(48)
49.	Gold (Kilo), CBOT	103,335	0.04%	159,627	0.07%	(49)
	Contracts with Volume Over 100,000 Contracts 1/			767,190	0.34%	
	Contracts with Volume Under 100,000 Contracts	894,359	0.36%	779,481	0.34%	
TOTAL		245,871,290	100.00%	228,876,684	100.00%	

1/ Contracts over 100,000 traded in 1987 but not over 100,000 in 1988.

COMMODITY FUTURES CONTRACTS TRADED 1984 - 1988

	CONTRACT UNIT	1988	1987	1986	1985	1984
Wheat	5,000 bu	3,377,738	1,929,306	2,090,316	2,127,962	2,974,886
Corn	5,000 bu	11,105,516	7,253,212	6,160,298	6,392,812	9,108,526
Oats	5,000 bu	354,578	291,108	140,952	99,024	155,110
Soybeans	5,000 bu	12,497,096	7,378,760	6,133,668	7,392,128	11,362,691
Soybean Oil	60,000 lb	4,896,194	3,912,417	3,182,963	3,647,408	4,009,548
Soybean Meal	100 tons	5,313,081	3,797,970	3,049,005	3,339,268	3,822,179
Plywood	76,032 sq.ft.					4,466
Silver	5,000 oz	4,165	12,092			
Silver	1,000 oz	481,566	509,965	511,239	1,034,830	1,887,257
Gold	100 oz	84,965	24,893			
Gold	Kilo	103,335	159,627	124,546	168,527	302,717
GNMA Mrtges, CDR	$100,000		7,583	24,078	84,396	862,450
GNMA II	$100,000					37,615
Cash Settle GNMA	$100,000			7,351		
T-Bonds	$100,000	70,307,872	66,841,474	52,598,811	40,448,357	29,963,280
T-Notes (6 1/2-10 yr)	$100,000	5,200,949	5,253,791	4,426,476	2,860,432	1,661,862
T-Notes (5-year)	$100,000	506,595				
30-Day Interest Rate	$5,000,000	19,476				
Corporate Bond Index	$1,000 x Index	49	10,591			
Crude Oil	1,000 bbl					628
CBOE 250 Index	$500 x Index	55,840				
Institutional Index	$500 x Index		175			
Municipal Bond Index	$1,000 x Index	1,274,316	1,613,107	906,980	334,691	
Major Market Index	$100 x Index			36,292	2,062,083	1,514,737
MMI Maxi	$250 x Index	1,175,531	2,630,887	1,738,916	422,091	
NASDAQ-100	$250 x Index			3,743	139,888	
CHICAGO BOARD OF TRADE		116,758,862	101,626,958	81,135,634	70,553,897	67,667,952
Live Hogs	30,000#	2,008,750	2,040,478	1,936,864	1,719,861	2,169,030
Pork Bellies, Fzn.	38,000 lb	1,186,599	1,097,010	1,100,339	1,457,386	1,908,045
Live Cattle	40,000#	5,477,205	5,229,294	4,690,538	4,437,327	3,553,270
Feeder Cattle	42,000 lb	702,438	645,877	411,441	455,881	316,985
Lumber	130,000 bd.ft.	371,489	437,089	502,530	581,548	753,568
Gold	100 oz	137	261,639		7	8,841
Leaded Regular Gas	1,000 barrels					4,045
No. 2 Fuel Oil	1,000 barrels					4,601
T-Bills (90-day)	$1,000,000	1,373,553	1,927,006	1,815,162	2,413,338	3,292,817
Domestic CD (90-day)	$1,000,000		98	3,062	84,106	928,662
Eurodollar (3-month)	$1,000,000	21,705,223	20,416,216	10,824,914	8,900,528	4,192,952
European Currency Unit	125,000		300	43,826		
British Pound	25,000	2,616,068	2,592,177	2,701,330	2,799,024	1,444,492
Canadian Dollar	100,000	1,408,783	914,563	734,071	468,996	345,875
Deutschemark	125,000	5,662,109	6,037,048	6,582,145	6,449,384	5,508,308
Japanese Yen	12,500,000	6,433,132	5,358,556	3,969,777	2,415,094	2,334,764
Mexican Peso	1,000,000				12,737	15,364
Swiss Franc	125,000	5,283,406	5,268,276	4,998,430	4,758,159	4,129,881
Australian Dollar	100,000	75,960	53,335			
French Franc	250,000	3,932	10,437	2,685	9,335	8,388
S&P 500 Index	$500 x Index	11,353,898	19,044,673	19,505,273	15,055,955	12,363,592
S&P 100 Index	$200 x Index			3,514	1,662	166,202
S&P OTC 250	$500 x Index			5,270	94,919	
CHICAGO MERCANTILE EX.		65,663,682	71,334,072	59,831,171	52,115,247	43,449,682

	CONTRACT UNIT	1988	1987	1986	1985	1984
Rice, Rough Old	200,000 lb				9	2,978
Rice, Rough New	200,000 lb	47,627	31,114	3,095		
Cotton Short Staple	50,000 lb			3	1,751	
CHIC. RICE & COTTON EX.		47,627	31,114	3,098	1,760	2,978
Coffee "C"	37,500 lb	1,149,710	964,586	1,073,142	650,768	499,133
Sugar #11	112,000 lb	5,819,121	3,853,499	3,583,814	3,012,929	2,449,549
Sugar #12	112,000 lb			19,058	99,851	109,448
Sugar #14	112,000 lb	84,999	69,928	72,526	17,433	
White Sugar	50 M tons	726	903			
Cocoa	10 M tons	1,268,050	895,465	777,765	800,573	1,127,752
CPI-W	$1,000 x Index		2	8,776	1,324	
COFFEE SUGAR & COCOA		8,322,606	5,784,383	5,535,081	4,582,878	4,185,882
Copper	25,000 lb	2,112,459	2,569,178	1,872,209	2,444,552	2,506,365
High Grade Copper	25,000 lb	924				
Silver	5,000 oz	4,664,655	5,055,652	3,849,687	4,821,206	6,742,508
Gold	100 oz	9,496,402	10,239,805	8,400,175	7,773,834	9,115,504
Aluminum	40,000 lb	2,610	8,500	52,627	77,063	82,661
Moody's Index	$500 x Index		11,482			
COMMODITY EXCHANGE		16,277,050	17,884,617	14,174,698	15,116,655	18,447,038
Wheat (5,000 bu)	5,000 bu	1,338,711	971,095	744,023	735,447	956,668
Value Line Index	$500 x Index	79,872	505,551	953,985	1,204,659	910,956
Mini Value Line	$100 x Index	14,171	28,457	18,678	19,032	30,179
KANSAS CITY BD. OF TRD.		1,432,754	1,505,103	1,716,686	1,959,138	1,897,803
Wheat	1,000 bu	294,236	189,610	344,749	347,355	404,508
Corn	1,000 bu	429,219	311,722	406,694	456,661	604,992
Oats	1,000 bu	12,917	6,958	2,169	1,746	7,067
Soybeans	1,000 bu	863,934	417,620	680,156	843,231	1,301,916
Soybean Meal Old	20 tons		17	3,231	10,981	
Soybean Meal New	20 tons	8,558	3,191	2,256		
Live Cattle	20,000#	48,349	44,112	58,752	64,510	81,112
Live Hogs	15,000#	34,230	44,364	80,818	74,388	112,877
Refined Sugar	40,000 lb					24
Silver	1,000 oz			649	4,510	19,497
New York Silver	1,000 oz	12,063	9,578	9,342	57,886	12,611
Gold	33.2 oz			0	76	41,690
New York Gold	33.2 oz	14,652	17,957	21,111	31,467	19,285
Platinum	25 oz	2,874	4,342	5,944	1,368	213
Copper	12,500 lbs		2	892	4,043	492
Copper New	55,000 lbs		29	1,753		
T-Bonds	$50,000	1,414,390	1,015,454	467,639	297,033	251,300
T-Bills	$500,000	22,203	25,592	34,690	36,904	30,486
T-Notes	$100,000	4,159				
British Pound	12,500	28,240	10,979	17,270	21,239	8,901
Swiss Franc	62,500	77,176	97,571	102,019	110,047	99,385
Deutschemark	62,500	49,993	85,009	74,662	85,439	67,507
Japanese Yen	6,250,000	44,257	58,836	47,601	32,912	34,677
Canadian Dollar	$50,000	9,282	7,749	6,150	3,370	3,315
MIDAMERICA COMMODITY EX.		3,370,732	2,350,692	2,368,547	2,485,166	3,101,855

	CONTRACT UNIT	1988	1987	1986	1985	1984
Wheat	5,000 bu	423,542	310,599	283,900	297,509	338,487
White Wheat	5,000 bu	380	1,415	686	3,402	2,245
High Fructose Corn Syrup	48,000 lb	49	5,963			
Oats	5,000 bu	1,807				
MINNEAPOLIS GRAIN EX.		**425,778**	**317,977**	**284,586**	**300,911**	**340,732**
Cotton #2	50,000 lb	1,370,249	1,395,980	1,015,392	636,492	1,137,141
Orange Jce, Fzn. Conc.	15,000 lb	358,039	266,641	211,543	190,758	317,364
Propane	100,000 gal		5,799	11,966	13,724	22,005
European Currency Unit	100,000	23,936	42,198	72,195		
Five Year Treasury Note	100,000	789,630	383,613			
U.S. Dollar Index	$500 x Index	446,525	403,783	166,494	74,573	
NY COTTON EXCHANGE		**2,988,379**	**2,498,014**	**1,477,590**	**915,547**	**1,476,510**
NYSE Composite Index	$500 x Index	1,668,732	2,915,915	3,123,668	2,833,614	3,456,798
Russell 2000	$500 x Index	32	5,644			
Russell 3000	$500 x Index		10,734			
Cmdty Rsrch Bureau Index	$500 x Index	205,951	136,832	59,324		
NEW YORK FUTURES EX.		**1,874,715**	**3,069,125**	**3,182,992**	**2,833,614**	**3,456,798**
Palladium	100 oz	139,883	160,284	145,562	133,223	159,019
Platinum	50 oz	1,460,455	1,361,546	1,624,635	693,256	571,127
Potatoes(Cash Settlement)	100,000 lb		6,240	16,558	16,903	26,595
No. 2 Heating Oil, NY	1,000 bbl	4,935,015	4,293,395	3,275,044	2,207,733	2,091,546
Leaded Reg. Gasoline, NY	1,000 bbl			829,733	667,172	653,630
Unleaded Gasoline, NY	1,000 bbl	3,292,055	2,056,238	439,352	132,611	2,736
Propane	42,000 gal	23,749	15,312			
Crude Oil	1,000 bbl	18,858,948	14,581,614	8,313,529	3,980,867	1,840,342
NEW YORK MERCANTILE EX.		**28,710,105**	**22,474,629**	**14,644,413**	**7,831,765**	**5,344,995**
TOTAL FUTURES		**245,871,290**	**228,876,684**	**184,354,496**	**158,696,578**	**149,372,225**
PERCENT CHANGE		7.43%	24.15%	16.17%	6.24%	6.82%

OPTIONS VOLUME HIGHLIGHTS

1988 IN COMPARISON WITH 1987

RANK	EXCHANGE	1988 CONTRACTS	%	1987 CONTRACTS	%	RANK
1.	Chicago Board of Trade	26,279,633	53.48%	25,466,032	55.14%	1)
2.	Chicago Mercantile Exchange	12,348,986	25.13%	13,033,142	28.22%	(2)
3.	New York Mercantile Exchange	5,606,093	11.41%	3,260,642	7.06%	(4)
4.	Commodity Exchange	2,973,594	6.05%	3,610,981	7.82%	(3)
5.	Coffee Sugar & Cocoa Exchange	1,697,058	3.45%	472,476	1.02%	(5)
6.	New York Cotton Exchange	154,137	0.31%	88,703	0.19%	(7)
7.	Kansas City Board of Trade	30,178	0.06%	33,228	0.07%	(8)
8.	New York Futures Exchange	24,311	0.05%	206,631	0.45%	(6)
9.	MidAmerica Commodity Exchange	21,653	0.04%	12,921	0.03%	(9)
10.	Minneapolis Grain Exchange	1,847	.00%	1,229	.00%	(10)
	TOTAL	49,137,490	100.00%	46,185,985	100.00%	

OPTIONS CONTRACTS TRADED 1984 - 1988

OPTION	CONTRACT UNIT	1988	1987	1986	1985	1984
Corn	5,000 bu	1,591,223	661,519	575,634	363,549	
Soybeans	5,000 bu	3,245,134	1,242,072	775,139	840,786	72,969
Wheat	5,000 bu	445,575	124,598	9,314		
Silver	1,000 oz	8,303	10,009	3,081	10,820	
T-Bonds	$100,000	19,509,425	21,720,402	17,314,349	11,901,116	6,636,209
T-Notes	$100,000	1,011,626	1,421,852	1,000,682	177,292	
Muni Bonds	$1,000 x Index	171,788	118,632			
Soybean Oil	60,000 lbs	124,131	85,735			
Soybean Meal	100 tons	172,428	81,213			
CHICAGO BOARD OF TRADE		**26,279,633**	**25,466,032**	**19,678,199**	**13,293,563**	**6,709,178**
Live Hogs	30,000#	130,206	147,859	105,516	57,042	
Live Cattle	40,000 #	1,067,593	1,222,397	718,099	326,724	20,722
Pork Bellies	38,000 lbs	12,143	15,112	1,981		
Feeder Cattle	42,000 lbs	163,433	134,830			
Lumber	130,000 bd.ft.	22,171	6,483			
Eurodollar	$1,000,000	2,599,839	2,569,957	1,757,426	743,080	
British Pound	25,000	543,380	569,062	496,591	329,071	
Deutschemark	125,000	2,734,079	3,125,687	2,205,579	1,562,438	727,634
Swiss Franc	125,000	1,069,798	1,053,323	817,897	324,806	
Japanese Yen	12,500,000	2,944,889	2,250,813	864,586		
Canadian Dollar	100,000	313,901	48,690	26,465		
Australian Dollar	100,000	6,811				
T-Bill	$1,000,000	5,916	11,634	63,768		
S&P 500	$500 x Index	734,827	1,877,295	1,886,445	1,090,068	672,884
CHICAGO MERCANTILE EXCH		**12,348,986**	**13,033,142**	**8,944,353**	**4,433,229**	**1,421,240**
Sugar	112,000 lbs	1,536,345	432,927	254,491	91,400	11,960
Coffee	37,500 lbs	65,204	25,639	5,319		
Cocoa	10 M tons	95,509	13,910	999		
COFFEE SUGAR & COCOA EXCH		**1,697,058**	**472,476**	**260,809**	**91,400**	**11,960**
Gold	100 oz	1,698,696	2,080,067	1,646,791	1,395,896	1,432,514
Silver	5,000 oz	872,106	918,064	579,425	531,315	99,843
High Grade Copper	25,000 lbs	2				
Copper	25,000 lbs	402,790	612,850	127,501		
COMMODITY EXCHANGE		**2,973,594**	**3,610,981**	**2,353,717**	**1,927,211**	**1,532,357**
Wheat	5,000 bu	30,178	33,228	18,302	16,856	878
Value Line Index	$500 x Index					
KANSAS CITY BOARD OF TRADE		**30,178**	**33,228**	**18,302**	**16,856**	**878**
Soybeans	1,000 bu	21,043	12,317	6,635	8,790	
Soft Red Winter Wheat	5,000 bu	533	530	7,492	6,076	2,149
Gold	33.2 oz	77	74	91	678	318
MIDAMERICA COMMODITY EXCH		**21,653**	**12,921**	**14,218**	**15,544**	**2,467**
Spring Wheat	5,000 bu	1,847	1,229	3,259	5,414	624
MINNEAPOLIS GRAIN EXCHANGE		**1,847**	**1,229**	**3,259**	**5,414**	**624**
Cotton	50,000 lbs	124,260	73,480	60,507	29,218	3,078
Orange Juice, Fzn. Conc.	15,000 lbs	5,873	685	3,354	435	
Five Year U.S. T-Note	$100,000	13,479				
U.S. Dollar Index	$500 x Index	10,525	14,538	198		
NEW YORK COTTON EXCHANGE		**154,137**	**88,703**	**64,059**	**29,653**	**3,078**
NYSE Composite Index	$500 x Index	23,304	206,631	296,303	195,634	246,359
CRB Index	$500 x Index	1,007				
NEW YORK FUTURES EXCHANGE		**24,311**	**206,631**	**296,303**	**195,634**	**246,359**
Heating Oil	42,000 gal	125,812	143,605			
Crude Oil	1,000 bbl	5,480,281	3,117,037	135,266		
NEW YORK MERCANTILE EXCHANGE		**5,606,093**	**3,260,642**	**135,266**	**0**	**0**
TOTAL OPTIONS		**49,137,490**	**46,185,985**	**31,770,613**	**20,044,744**	**9,928,141**
PERCENT CHANGE		**6.39%**	**45.37%**	**58.50%**	**101.90%**	**275.09%**

SOURCE: FUTURES INDUSTRY ASSOCIATION

Alcohol

Salient Statistics of Alcohol in the United States In Millions of Gallons[3]

Year	Ethyl Alcohol & Spirits Production[5]	Ethyl Alcohol & Spirits Stocks Dec. 31	Denatured Alcohol[2] Production	Denatured Alcohol[2] Consumption Total	Denatured Alcohol[2] Consumption For Fuel Use	Denatured Alcohol[2] Stocks Dec. 31	Production of Methanol (Synthetic)
1976	498.8	85.3	225.3	225.6	—	3.2	940.1
1977	498.3	71.4	223.8	224.6	—	2.6	971.8
1978	506.7	71.2	227.7	228.8	—	2.7	970.4
1979	570.3	53.6	260.7	260.9	—	4.1	1,109.5
1980	643.2	72.0	301.2	281.5	14.5	10.1	1,077.3
1981	571.2	83.3	230.7	227.1	5.7	5.4	1,291.7
1982	601.1	95.0	284.9	277.9	41.9	6.6	1,137.7
1983	698.5	78.6	354.4	356.7	65.8	6.6	1,202.1
1984	631.3	150.6	416.9	410.5	116.7	24.5	1,232.8
1985	681.0	46.9	512.2	513.8	222.9	26.5	753.5
1986	645.4	47.5	408.0	444.6	226.7	23.8	1,085.1
1987[1]	730.3	43.4	442.3	460.5	208.3	9.7	1,098.2
1988[4]	760	41	475	482	216	8	940

[1] Preliminary. [2] At denaturing plants. [3] Ethyl alcohol in proof gallons; denatured alcohol in wine gallons. [4] Estimate. [5] Represents alcohol and spirits of 190° of proof and over. *Source: Alcohol and Tobacco Division*   T.1

U.S. Production of Ethyl Alcohol[1] & Spirits In Millions of Tax Gallons[2]

Year	Jan.	Feb.	Mar.	Apr.	May	June	July	Aug.	Sept.	Oct.	Nov.	Dec.	Total
1975	52.0	40.4	44.5	41.4	39.8	39.1	41.3	40.1	39.6	53.8	46.4	48.0	526.4
1976	41.6	36.2	44.0	39.3	36.0	37.0	45.5	46.0	43.3	39.3	42.8	47.7	498.8
1977	36.5	37.7	42.8	39.2	43.5	43.2	40.3	40.9	41.0	44.7	48.9	39.7	498.3
1978	35.8	41.1	50.4	42.2	31.3	48.7	42.5	45.4	50.5	40.3	38.0	40.7	506.7
1979	42.8	41.3	49.3	47.3	42.9	48.2	43.8	46.0	53.7	49.4	51.0	54.6	570.3
1980	57.4	52.7	55.3	55.2	54.2	45.7	52.8	46.4	57.3	64.6	47.9	53.7	643.2
1981	49.2	44.3	49.3	51.0	44.0	42.2	45.1	55.8	53.1	44.0	47.8	45.4	571.2
1982	42.9	39.8	48.2	37.6	41.9	52.6	51.9	44.3	53.3	61.9	61.7	65.0	601.1
1983	60.9	58.6	59.4	46.1	56.6	60.2	63.8	56.9	59.2	55.6	53.9	47.2	698.5
1984	49.3	45.9	54.1	58.2	50.9	49.7	48.4	48.4	51.8	60.5	50.4	63.7	631.3
1985	63.3	44.8	60.6	55.6	56.3	63.7	58.5	55.5	59.4	64.1	51.8	47.1	681.0
1986	45.6	51.5	56.5	52.5	55.6	50.1	48.9	50.2	56.7	62.2	54.2	60.8	645.4
1987[3]	62.2	54.9	55.8	60.2	62.0	56.6	60.1	63.4	63.8	63.0	60.6	66.9	730.3
1988[3]	62.6	61.2	64.2	60.7	69.8	61.2	65.9						

[1] At industrial alcohol plants. [2] A "tax gallon" is the alcoholic equivalent of a U.S. gallon at 60 degrees Fahrenheit, containing 50% of ethyl alcohol by volume. [3] Preliminary. *Source: Internal Revenue Service*   T.3

Average Wholesale Price Index of Ethyl Alcohol, in N.Y. 1982 = 100

Year	Jan.	Feb.	Mar.	Apr.	May	June	July	Aug.	Sept.	Oct.	Nov.	Dec.	Average
1975	201.6	206.3	219.2	219.2	217.8	218.0	216.8	214.6	215.8	217.1	218.2	216.6	215.1
1976	217.2	230.2	233.0	233.6	233.0	233.0	233.0	232.5	233.0	233.0	232.3	233.0	231.4
1977	231.6	233.0	232.3	232.3	232.3	233.0	238.8	244.9	243.6	243.1	242.5	243.9	237.6
1978	243.9	231.0	230.3	226.4	226.4	225.8	226.4	226.6	226.4	218.8	226.4	226.5	227.9
1979	234.8	239.2	239.2	243.6	248.1	249.4	260.1	265.4	277.6	284.3	291.5	292.2	260.5
1980	311.7	319.6	325.0	338.4	361.4	369.4	370.3	369.2	369.2	369.3	369.2	369.2	353.9
1981	369.2	369.2	370.3	370.3	368.5	368.5	387.3	387.3	387.3	396.8	392.0	383.3	379.2
1982	382.2	353.5	349.6	346.4	N.A.	338.7	341.1	345.2	336.6	335.5	335.9	N.A.	346.5
1983	336.4	335.2	334.4	333.3	333.2	333.2	337.2	337.1	337.0	337.0	340.4	340.4	336.2
1984	341.1	340.5	340.5	339.7	339.9	340.0	346.9	344.0	341.7	341.0	342.4	342.4	341.7
1985	339.3	334.2	326.2	326.0	326.0	326.0	325.7	328.1	327.3	324.6	325.3	324.9	327.8
1986	323.8	261.5	317.3	316.6	316.3	315.7	315.3	313.5	313.7	312.0	311.9	311.6	310.8
1987[1]	90.3	89.8	90.1	89.2	89.2	89.7	N.A.	91.7	90.4	91.5	91.8	91.0	90.4
1988	91.4	83.8	83.3	85.7	88.0	87.7	90.3	88.1	86.5	90.0			

[1] Data prior to 1987 are on Dec. 1973 = 100 base. *Source: Bureau of Labor Statistics* (0614-0341)   T.2

1

Aluminum

In 1988, the aluminum industry saw results from its moves in late 1986 to early 1987 to scale back its operations in an effort to cut excess inventories and raise prices.

Spot aluminum prices gained sharply during the year, starting off in January at 89.7 cents/lb. and moving to more than $1.24 in August. They subsequently eased slightly.

The thirteen primary aluminum producers in the U.S. have a total production capacity of 3.89 million tonnes. However, only four refiners with 15 plants in operation accounted for 63 percent of total capacity.

In 1987, U.S. primary production totaled 3.34 million tonnes, for an 85 percent capacity utilization rate.

During the first seven months of 1988, primary aluminum production in the U.S. totaled 2.27 million tonnes, for an implied annual rate of 3.91 million tonnes, more than 100 percent of current rated aluminum production capacity.

Reports in the U.S. metals market press indicated U.S. primary aluminum pourings from January-July of 1988 were running at just over 4.0 million tonnes annualized, 102 percent of rated capacity.

Domestic consumption of aluminum in 1987 was 2.20 million tonnes and recovery was 1.98 million tonnes; both numbers were higher than earlier estimates. For the first seven months of 1988, consumption was 1.24 million tonnes, for an implied annual total of 2.12 million. Recovery for the same period amounted to 1.12 million tonnes, for an implied annual total of 1.92 million.

Total U.S. imports of aluminum for consumption in 1987 were 1.66 million tonnes. Imports during the first nine months of 1988 were 1.12 million tonnes.

Worldwide production in 1988 was estimated at 154 million tonnes. The U.S. was the largest producer with an estimated 26 percent of global output. It was followed by the Soviet Union with 14 percent and by Canada with 9 percent.

Production increases have been confined to areas of the world that have cheap and plentiful water power which can be used in the mining process. Canada, Venezuela, Australia and Brazil are prominent among those countries with growing aluminum industries.

In 1988, aluminum fell under the gaze of the Environmental Protection Agency, and in a new listing of hazardous wastes in September, the agency indicated that spent potliners from aluminum reduction plants were one of six wastes covered by the new reporting and disposal rules.

Futures Markets

Aluminum futures are traded on the New York Commodity Exchange (COMEX) and the London Metal Exchange (LME).

World Production of Primary Aluminum In Thousands of Metric[3] Tons

Year	Australia	Austria	Canada	China	France	West Germany	Hungary	Italy	Japan	Norway	Spain	Switzerland	Brazil	United Kingdom	United States	USSR	World Total
1983	478	94	1,091	400	361	743	74	196	256	713	358	76	401	253	3,353	2,000	13,904
1984	758	96	1,227	400	342	777	74	230	287	765	381	79	455	288	4,099	2,100	15,714
1985	851	94	1,282	410	293	745	74	221	227	712	370	73	549	275	3,500	2,200	15,367
1986[1]	882	93	1,364	410	322	765	74	243	140	712	350	80	758	276	3,037	2,300	15,341
1987[2]	1,004	93	1,530	410	300	730	74	240	41	725	350	80	840	297	3,343	2,400	16,016

[1] Preliminary. [2] Estimate. [3] Data prior to 1980 are in thousands of short tons. *Source: Bureau of Mines*   T.4

U.S. Production of Primary Aluminum (Domestic & Foreign Ores) In Thousands of Metric Tons

Year	Jan.	Feb.	Mar.	Apr.	May	June	July	Aug.	Sept.	Oct.	Nov.	Dec.	Total[1]
1983	253	223	248	245	265	261	284	297	299	320	318	340	3,353
1984[2]	342	324	350	348	365	351	349	344	329	338	325	334	4,099
1985[2]	329	289	312	295	304	288	292	289	280	285	265	271	3,499
1986[2]	273	251	281	275	284	241	231	230	231	243	239	252	3,036
1987[2]	262	238	266	263	271	272	282	286					

[1] Final annual totals. [2] Preliminary. *Source: Bureau of Mines*   T.9

U.S. Production of Primary Aluminum (Domestic & Foreign Ores) In Thousands of Metric Tons

Year	Jan.	Feb.	Mar.	Apr.	May	June	July	Aug.	Sept.	Oct.	Nov.	Dec.	Total[1]
1983	253	223	248	245	265	261	284	297	299	320	318	340	3,353
1984	342	324	350	348	365	351	349	344	329	338	325	334	4,099
1985	329	289	312	295	304	288	292	289	280	285	265	271	3,499
1986	273	251	281	275	284	241	231	235	231	243	239	252	3,036
1987[2]	262	238	266	263	271	272	282	286	286	301	301	316	3,343
1988[2]	320	304	330	324	336	323	334	333	327				

[1] Final annual totals. [2] Preliminary. *Source: Bureau of Mines*   T.9

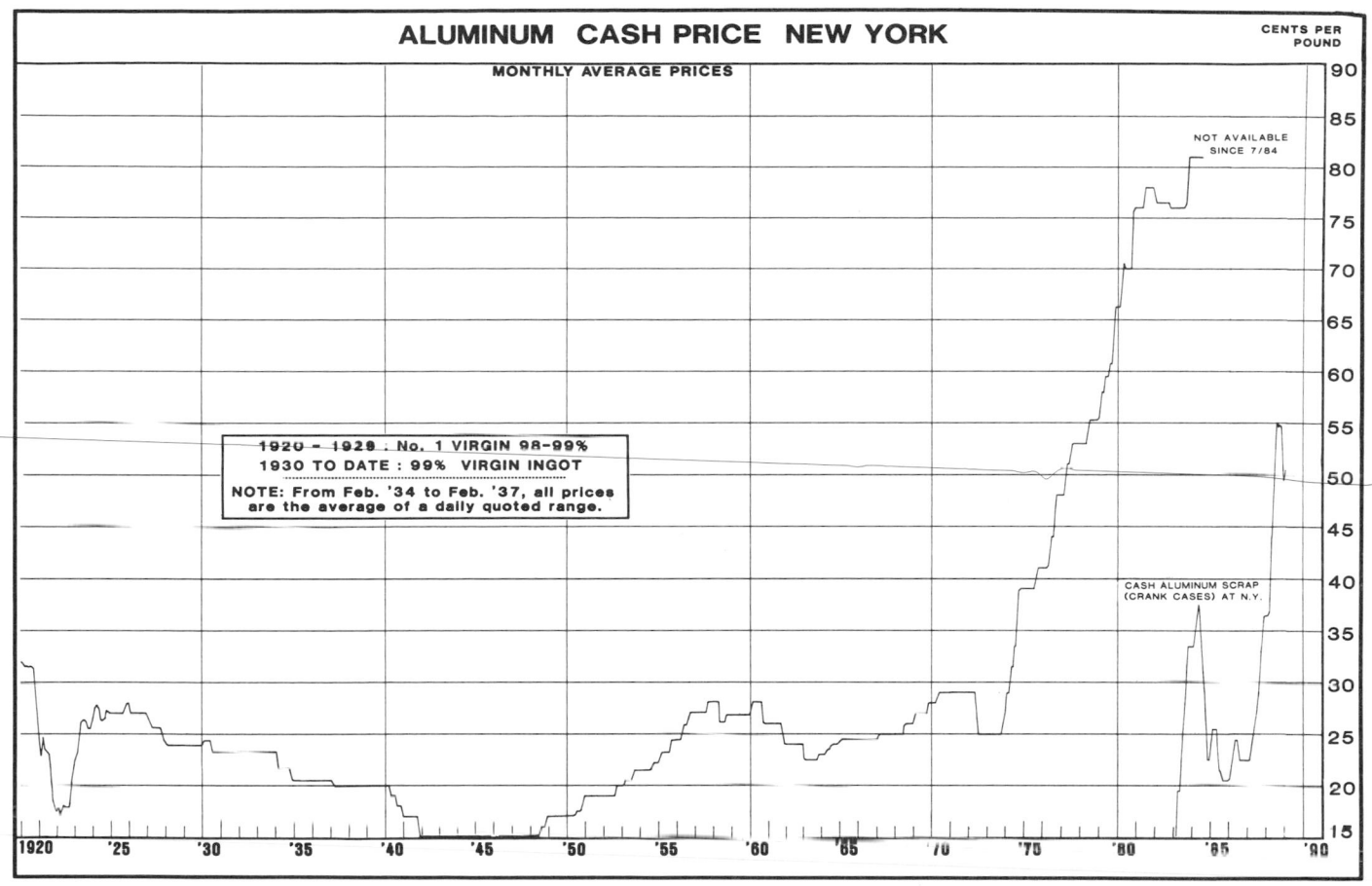

ALUMINUM CASH PRICE NEW YORK

CENTS PER POUND

MONTHLY AVERAGE PRICES

NOT AVAILABLE SINCE 7/84

1920 - 1929 : No. 1 VIRGIN 98-99%
1930 TO DATE : 99% VIRGIN INGOT
NOTE: From Feb. '34 to Feb. '37, all prices are the average of a daily quoted range.

CASH ALUMINUM SCRAP (CRANK CASES) AT N.Y.

Salient Statistics of Aluminum in the U.S. In Thousands of Metric Tons

Year	Net Import Reliance as a % of Apparent Consumption	Production Primary	Production Secondary	Primary Shipments[1]	Recovery from Scrap Old	Recovery from Scrap New	Apparent Consumption	Plate, Sheet, Foil	Rolled Structural Shapes[2]	Extruded Shapes[3]	Net Shipments[5] by Producers All	Castings Permanent Mold	Castings Die	Castings Sand	Castings All	Total All Net Shipments
1980	7[7]	4,654	1,260	5,515	617	960	4,595	3,346	606	1,165	5,242	193	443	121	769	6,011
1981	7[7]	4,489	1,394	5,644	758	1,031	4,614	3,097	472	1,079	4,689	132	524	108	826	5,515
1982	7	3,274	1,466	5,090	782	884	4,370	2,749	391	871	4,094	108	480	81	728	4,823
1983	17	3,353	1,564	5,857	820	953	5,035	3,249	423	1,038	4,798	137	592	76	861	5,659
1984	7	4,099	1,760	6,552	825	935	5,279	3,259	451	1,182	5,003	161	679	90	990	5,994
1985	16	3,500	1,762	6,382	850	912	5,174	3,291	357	1,267	5,031	168	698	93	1,011	6,042
1986[4]	26	3,037	1,773	6,545	784	989	5,143	3,397	337	1,335	5,179	155	749	77	1,032	6,211
1987[6]	24	3,343	1,986	6,813	852	1,134	5,469	3,740	346	1,351	5,549				949	6,498

[1] To Domestic Industry. [2] Also rod, bar & wire. [3] Also rod, bar, tube, blooms & tubing. [4] Preliminary. [5] Consists of total shipments less shipments to other mills for further fabrication. [6] Estimate. [7] Net exports. *Source: U.S. Bureau of Mines*   T.8

U.S. Supply and Distribution of Aluminum In Thousands of Metric Tons

Year	Apparent Consumption	Production Primary	Production From Old Scrap	Imports	Exports	Inventories (Dec. 31) Private	Inventories (Dec. 31) Government	Year	Apparent Consumption	Production Primary	Production From Old Scrap	Imports	Exports	Inventories (Dec. 31) Private	Inventories (Dec. 31) Government
1981	4,615	4,489	758	848	787	2,996	2	1985	5,174	3,500	850	1,420	908	2,343	2
1982	4,370	3,274	782	878	748	2,812	2	1986	5,143	3,037	784	1,967	753	2,235	2
1983	5,035	3,353	820	1,091	776	2,265	2	1987[1]	5,469	3,343	852	1,849	916	1,894	2
1984	5,279	4,099	825	1,477	734	2,653	2	1988[2]	5,300	4,030	1,000	1,620	1,200	2,000	2

[1] Preliminary [2] Estimate *Source: U.S. Bureau of Mines*   T.8A

ALUMINUM

High, Low & Closing Prices of December Aluminum Futures in New York   In Cents Per Pound

Year of Delivery		Yr. Prior to Delivery Nov.	Dec.	Jan.	Feb.	Mar.	Apr.	May	June	July	Aug.	Sept.	Oct.	Nov.	Dec.	Life of Delivery Range
1987	High	51.90	52.00	54.20	58.00	58.20	62.00	67.00	70.90	77.10	80.00	84.00	86.00	81.00	89.00	89.00
	Low	50.45	50.45	52.00	53.95	55.60	57.15	61.80	65.00	68.50	74.00	72.50	75.50	76.00	77.50	50.45
	Close	50.75	52.00	53.80	57.25	57.15	62.00	66.20	68.45	77.10	75.50	82.50	79.75	77.00	88.00	—
1988	High	74.25	80.00	81.25	81.00	90.50	91.00	94.00	111.00	115.00	117.25	113.75	107.00	105.50	105.00	117.25
	Low	68.10	71.50	73.75	74.00	78.00	79.50	79.50	95.00	105.00	109.00	98.00	96.00	99.00	98.50	54.60
	Close	70.15	79.00	73.75	80.50	90.50	79.50	94.00	107.50	114.50	114.25	100.00	104.50	101.00	105.00	—
1989	High	—	98.50													
	Low	—	89.00													
	Close	—	97.00													

Source: Commodity Exchange, Inc. (Comex)—N.Y.   T.11A

Month-End Open Interest of Aluminum Futures at New York   In Contracts

Year	Jan.	Feb.	Mar.	Apr.	May	June	July	Aug.	Sept.	Oct.	Nov.	Dec.
1986	2,386	2,179	2,476	1,717	1,444	1,098	1,215	869	854	948	781	977
1987	828	722	985	883	754	661	542	521	554	441	394	270
1988	293	267	327	320	229	278	204	218	182	166	159	152

Source: Commodity Exchange, Inc. (Comex)—N.Y.   T.11B

Volume of Trading of Aluminum Futures at New York   In Contracts

Year	Jan.	Feb.	Mar.	Apr.	May	June	July	Aug.	Sept.	Oct.	Nov.	Dec.	Total
1986	8,409	9,600	7,982	8,572	3,250	4,475	2,218	2,855	1,600	1,104	1,699	863	52,627
1987	1,688	1,688	1,431	640	895	745	408	390	527	319	268	222	8,500
1988	277	390	476	239	360	402	136	43	93	91	48	55	2,610

Source: Commodity Exchange, Inc. (Comex)—N.Y.   T.11C

Average Price of Cast Aluminum Scrap (Crank Cases) in Chcago Area[1] In Cents per Pound

Year	Jan.	Feb.	Mar.	Apr.	May	June	July	Aug.	Sept.	Oct.	Nov.	Dec.	Average
1982	20.50	20.50	19.85	19.50	19.25	16.32	16.00	16.00	16.00	16.00	14.95	14.50	17.45
1983	15.12	17.50	19.50	19.50	23.50	25.50	27.65	31.80	33.50	33.50	33.50	33.50	26.17
1984	34.83	35.50	36.59	37.50	35.64	32.98	30.50	29.11	25.55	23.07	22.50	23.67	30.62
1985	25.50	25.50	25.50	25.50	23.23	21.50	21.40	20.50	20.50	20.50	20.50	22.55	22.55
1986	21.23	22.50	23.60	24.50	24.50	23.36	22.50	22.50	22.50	22.50	22.50	22.50	22.89
1987	22.50	22.50	24.18	25.50	26.75	27.50	29.14	33.07	33.50	36.36	36.50	36.50	29.50
1988	36.50	37.90	44.15	48.83	53.93[1]	55.00	54.65	54.85	54.69	50.64	49.50	50.50	49.26

[1] Dealer buying prices—prior to May 1988 prices are for the N.Y. area. *Source: American Metal Market* T.12

Aluminum Products (Ingot & Mill Products) Shipments[1] in the U.S. In Million Pounds

Year	Jan.	Feb.	Mar.	Apr.	May	June	July	Aug.	Sept.	Oct.	Nov.	Dec.	Total
1982	862	946	1,074	1,014	972	1,127	881	1,114	1,016	980	959	1,099	12,039
1983	971	972	1,185	1,054	1,224	1,205	1,077	1,212	1,202	1,103	1,141	1,275	13,622
1984	1,107	1,268	1,388	1,133	1,301	1,293	1,115	1,244	1,139	1,304	1,153	1,210	14,655
1985	1,166	1,137	1,291	1,228	1,304	1,208	1,199	1,228	1,264	1,278	1,123	1,032	14,456
1986	1,187	1,176	1,401	1,340	1,390	1,202	1,114	1,131	1,116	1,219	1,042	1,062	14,386
1987[2]	1,182	1,253	1,347	1,398	1,301	1,433	1,346	1,261	1,334	1,307	1,219	1,353	15,584
1988[2]	1,165	1,163	1,398	1,246	1,313	1,425	1,271	1,354	1,372				

[1] Mill products & pig & ingot (net shipments). [2] Preliminary. *Source: Bureau of the Census* T.10

U.S. Aluminum Inventories, Total (Ingot, Mill Prod. & Scrap) In Million Pounds

Year	Jan. 1	Feb. 1	Mar. 1	Apr. 1	May 1	June 1	July 1	Aug. 1	Sept. 1	Oct. 1	Nov. 1	Dec. 1
1982	6,607	6,644	6,722	6,639	6,665	6,664	6,557	6,607	6,490	6,415	6,412	6,373
1983	6,180	6,140	6,075	5,870	5,723	5,558	5,418	5,451	5,353	5,236	5,273	5,191
1984	4,994	5,200	5,225	5,295	5,435	5,579	5,618	5,775	5,794	5,881	5,889	5,922
1985	5,850	5,900	5,824	5,796	5,749	5,712	5,595	5,579	5,512	5,439	5,324	5,241
1986	5,165	5,165	5,158	5,153	5,197	5,044	5,044	5,083	5,057	4,977	4,927	4,902
1987[1]	4,928	4,868	4,784	4,702	4,584	4,515	4,474	4,393	4,303	4,152	4,211	4,245
1988[1]	4,175	4,344	4,401	4,388	4,423	4,388	4,258	4,272	4,213	4,198		

[1] Preliminary. *Source: Bureau of Mines* T.5

Aluminum Exports (Metal & Alloys, Crude) from the U.S. In Thousands of Metric Tons

Year	Jan.	Feb.	Mar.	Apr.	May	June	July	Aug.	Sept.	Oct.	Nov.	Dec.	Total
1982	22.1	18.8	46.0	26.6	19.9	48.5	24.2	42.6	23.6	59.5	42.1	27.3	401.2
1983	50.9	12.2	14.0	46.4	8.2	14.9	37.1	33.2	44.5	27.4	50.8	24.1	360.7
1984	24.5	20.1	19.9	7.6	23.4	24.0	22.1	37.5	23.9	17.9	32.9	32.3	286.2
1985	43.9	34.6	24.9	31.0	32.8	58.8	41.8	28.5	29.6	21.4	20.5	13.1	383.0
1986	24.1	28.1	20.0	14.1	18.7	12.6	12.1	17.2	18.0	21.2	19.1	23.5	228.6
1987	17.0	26.3	23.5	26.0	16.8	16.1	29.0	30.6	30.7	22.7	32.1	39.1	309.9
1988	20.3	15.1	21.8	23.0	38.0	47.8	45.9	48.8	43.0				

Source: Bureau of the Census T.7

Aluminum General Imports (Metal & Alloys, Crude) into the U.S. In Thousands of Metric Tons[1]

Year	Jan.	Feb.	Mar.	Apr.	May	June	July	Aug.	Sept.	Oct.	Nov.	Dec.	Total
1982	38.5	65.9	61.7	61.0	51.0	66.5	42.2	78.2	52.8	52.7	60.1	47.8	679.4
1983	48.2	42.6	33.2	66.9	84.6	82.9	72.1	65.7	56.6	58.2	63.6	40.3	714.9
1984	70.9	94.9	114.3	68.8	108.8	73.9	66.8	68.0	89.9	93.0	68.6	57.4	975.3
1985	75.6	62.7	88.9	73.2	80.4	84.8	75.9	80.4	103.4	95.0	76.7	64.0	960.9
1986	90.5	110.9	140.9	144.4	167.3	137.0	131.2	136.1	106.1	118.3	100.4	85.2	1,468.4
1987	126.0	124.6	111.1	106.3	114.9	133.6	120.6	106.1	105.3	124.2	103.6	101.6	1,378.0
1988	111.6	101.4	115.6	98.1	101.5	88.8	87.7	88.2	101.8				

[1] Data prior to 1983 are in thousands of short tons. *Source: Bureau of the Census* T.6

Antimony

Antimony compounds are used as stabilizers to retard light and heat degradation in plastics. They are also used to flameproof plastics, textiles and other combustibles; and as decolorizing and refining agents in optical glass and other special glass products. Antimony-lead alloys are used in lead-acid storage batteries and where increased strength and corrosion resistance are desired.

There were nine plants producing primary antimony metal and oxide in the U.S. at the start of 1988, but two were closed during the year in response to low prices. Reported primary antimony consumption was estimated to have increased to 11,500 short tons in 1988 from 11,086 in 1987, while apparent consumption was estimated to have jumped to 46,000 tons from 40,965. Imports were estimated at 32,000 tons, up almost 20 percent from 1987.

The use of antimony oxide as a flame retardant continued to be the dominant market for primary antimony in 1988, accounting for about 65 percent of consumption. Antimony use in lead-acid batteries increased to 11 percent from 10 percent in 1987 and was believed to have reversed its long-term decline and leveled off. The chemical industry accounted for 9 percent of consumption, glass 5 percent, and other uses 10 percent.

The U.S. government's stockpile target of 36,000 tons was reached through sales in 1987, and there was no change in 1988. Year-end industry stocks were estimated at 7,000 tons, little changed from 6,835 for 1987.

World antimony production was estimated at 64,400 tons in 1988, up slightly from 63,200 a year earlier.

World Mine Production of Antimony (Content of Ore)   In Short Tons

Year	Australia	Bolivia	Austria	China[1]	Czecho-slovakia	Italy	Mexico[2]	Morocco	Peru[5]	Turkey	South Africa	United States	USSR	Yugo-slavia[4]	World Total[1]
1983	593	10,969	726	16,500	990	—	2,777	500	786	926	6,947	838	10,000	1,047	55,881
1984	1,267	10,231	577	16,500	1,100	269	3,377	1,071	741	1,121	8,201	557	10,300	1,050	60,309
1985	1,650	9,838	526	16,500	1,100	546	4,702	830	655	1,210	8,150	N.A.	10,400	1,400	61,833
1986[3]	1,650	11,350	550	16,500	1,000	330	4,400	830	740	1,200	8,200	N.A.	10,500	1,300	66,020
1987[1]		10,000					4,000				8,000			1,200	63,200

[1] Estimate.   [2] Includes antimony content of miscellaneous smelter products.   [3] Preliminary.   [4] Metal.   [5] Recoverable.
Source: Bureau of Mines   T.13

Salient Statistics of Antimony in the United States   In Short Tons

Year	Net Import Reliance as a % of Apparent Consumption	Ship-ments of Mine	Production Primary[2] Mine	Production Primary[2] Smelter	Sec-ondary (Alloys)[2]	Imports[5] Ore Gross Weight	Imports[5] Ore Sb Content	Imports[5] Metal Gross Weight	Ex-ports[3]	Ores & Concen-trates	Industry Stocks, Dec. 31[2] Metallic	Industry Stocks, Dec. 31[2] Oxide	Industry Stocks, Dec. 31[2] Sulfide	Industry Stocks, Dec. 31[2] Resi-dues & Slag	Total[6]	Prod. of Anti-monial Lead[2]
1985	N.A.	N.A.	N.A.	16,449	15,030	14,381	6,638	5,129	362	1,164	807	3,954	16	99	6,040	N.A.
1986[1]	N.A.	N.A.	N.A.	17,978	15,029	10,833	5,855	7,940	595	1,030	956	4,019	19	106	6,130	N.A.
1987[4]	N.A.			19,000	16,000		5,800	8,300	1,500	1,400	1,600	4,100	30	100	6,000	

[1] Preliminary   [2] Antimony content.   [3] Antimony ore, metal & compounds.   [4] Estimate.   [5] Imports for consumption.   [6] Including primary antimony residues & slag.   *Source: Bureau of Mines*   T.15

Industrial Consumption of Primary Antimony in the United States   In Short Tons (Antimony Content)

Year	Ammu-nition	Anti-monial Lead	Sheet & Pipe	Bearing Metal & Bearings	Cable Cover-ing	Solder	Type Metal	Total All Metal Products	Flame Retar-dant	Ammun. primers	Ceramics & Glass	Rubber Pdt's.	Pig-ments	Plas-tics	Total	Grand Total
1985	410	568	N.A.	177	N.A.	336	31	1,638	7,530	27	1,187	25	147	998	2,529	11,697
1986[1]	N.A.	605	40	156	68	279	9	1,589	6,885	23	1,027	41	250	975	2,482	10,956
1987[2]		700		80		270		1,800	5,700	50	1,050		200	800	2,250	11,500

[1] Preliminary.   [2] Estimated coverage based on 77% of the industry.   *Source: Bureau of Mines*   T.16

Antimony Imported (for Consumption) into the U.S. and Price Ranges

Year	Antimony Ore Value Ths. $	Needle or Liquated Antimony Gross Weight Sh. Tons	Needle or Liquated Antimony Value $ Ths.	Antimony Metal Short Tons	Antimony Metal Value $ Ths.	Antimony Oxide Short Tons	Antimony Oxide Value $ Ths.	Foreign Metal (Duty Paid Delivery New York) ¢ Lb.	Antimony Trioxide ¢ Lb.	Metal[2] ¢ Lb.	Domestic (Based on Antimony in Alloy)
1985	12,381	112	256	5,129	10,983	8,815	20,765	120–147	145–165	131.1	200
1986[1]	5,892	385	596	7,940	15,242	11,221	21,529	105–141	125–150	121.9	200
1987[3]		200		8,300		10,000				110.0	200

[1] Preliminary.   [2] N.Y. Dealer Price, 99.5% to 99.6%, C.I.F. U.S. ports.   [3] Estimate.   *Source: Bureau of Mines*   T.17

Apples

World Production of Apples, Fresh (Dessert & Cooking) In Thousands of Metric Tons

Crop Year	Argen-tina	Aus-tralia	Canada	France	Hun-gary	Italy	Japan	Mex-ico	Nether-lands	South Africa	Spain	Tur-key	United States[2]	West Germany	Yugo-slavia	World Total
1975	608	368	460	2,125		2,127	989	230	430	341	1,091		3,415	2,035	370	16,910
1976	576	275	409	1,598		2,143	879	329	380	381	1,008		2,936	1,487	483	15,501
1977	820	301	411	1,186		1,828	959	297	315	289	672		3,057	1,176	381	13,934
1978	810	258	452	1,768		1,874	844	313	510	367	1,015		3,446	1,783	381	16,589
1979	972	345	435	1,769		2,023	853	338	450	372	1,097		3,694	1,951	428	16,605
1980	908	345	553	1,802		1,966	960	282	450	450	859		4,005	1,880	483	17,179
1981	804	294	422	1,502		1,773	846	280	260	486	1,008		3,517	773	508	14,099
1982	817	301	478	1,978		2,642	924	394	440	423	891		3,684	2,637	746	18,418
1983	872	267	485	1,575	1,141	2,057	1,048	302	364	513	1,012	1,750	3,800	1,313	557	19,048
1984	922	352	434	2,005	1,088	2,241	812	486	388	557	970	1,900	3,780	1,799	584	20,495
1985	594	290	479	1,793	967	2,120	910	440	270	516	988	1,900	3,594	1,410	368	18,744
1986	1,000	341	405	1,862	1,050	1,990	944	629	374	525	871	1,950	3,598	1,885	605	20,347
1987[3]													4,782			
1988[3]													3,690			

[1] Preliminary. [2] Commercial crop. [3] Estimate. Source: Foreign Agricultural Service, U.S.D.A. T.18

Salient Statistics of Apples[1] in the United States

Year	Production Total	Production Util-ized	Growers Prices Fresh ¢ Lb.	Growers Prices Proc-essing $ Ton	Fresh	Canned	Dried	Frozen	Juice & Cider	Other[3]	Avg. Farm Price ¢ Per Lb.	Farm Value Million $	Fresh	Dried[5]	Imports Fresh & Dried[5]	Fresh Per Capita Con-sump-tion Lbs.
			Millions of Pounds			Utilization of Quantities Sold / Processed[5] — Millions of Pounds							Foreign Trade[4] Domestic Exports — Metric Tons —			
1975	7,530	7,103	8.80	56.80	4,357	1,027	230	207	1,192	91	6.50	460.9	102.3	3.7	57.8	19.0
1976	6,472	6,467	11.50	108.00	3,916	920	229	220	1,109	73	9.10	586.5	123.7	4.6	55.7	17.1
1977	6,740	6,710	13.80	122.00	3,860	1,076	226	161	1,267	121	10.60	708.6	142.4	8.2	63.6	16.9
1978	7,597	7,544	13.90	117.00	4,210	1,224	221	207	1,495	186	10.40	781.4	154.8	7.3	78.5	17.5
1979	8,126	8,101	15.40	114.00	4,289	1,337	256	137	1,954	130	10.90	881.2	237.3	5.5	71.2	17.5
1980	8,818	8,800	12.10	84.00	4,934	1,202	195	168	2,137	165	8.70	761.3	311.3	7.6	76.8	19.1
1981	7,740	7,693	15.40	102.00	4,442	1,002	190	173	1,798	87	11.10	851.1	269.2	8.3	128.3	16.8
1982	8,122	8,110	13.20	118.00	4,537	1,249	210	191	1,808	116	10.00	809.0	261.8	16.1	98.7	17.9
1983	8,379	8,358	14.80	103.00	4,621	1,204	283	170	1,985	95	10.50	879.3	228.7	12.0	126.0	18.3
1984	8,333	8,318	15.50	111.00	4,666	1,177	289	198	1,886	102	11.20	927.6	205.2	9.3	132.6	18.4
1985	7,924	7,836	17.30	103.00	4,228	1,255	242	194	1,842	74	11.70	915.6	147.1	5.5	160.9	17.3
1986[2]	7,933	7,907	19.10	116.00	4,532	1,179	199	257	1,649	91	13.40	1,060	—168.3—		165	18.0
1987[2]	10,543	10,242	12.20	80.30	5,622	1,285	269	254	2,740	73	8.50	870.6	—293.2—		170	20.5
1988[6]	8,134															

[1] Commercial crop. [2] Preliminary. [3] Mostly crushed for vinegar, jam, etc. [4] Year beginning July. [5] Fresh weight basis. [6] Estimate.
Source: Statistical Reporting Service, U.S.D.A. T.19

U.S. Price[1] of Apples Received by Growers (for Fresh Use) In Cents per Pound

Year	Jan.	Feb.	Mar.	Apr.	May	June	July	Aug.	Sept.	Oct.	Nov.	Dec.	Average
1979	13.5	13.9	14.1	13.9	13.9	13.0	16.2	14.9	14.9	13.3	14.2	14.3	14.2
1980	14.1	14.9	16.6	17.0	17.9	21.0	24.6	17.5	15.7	12.5	11.5	10.7	16.2
1981	10.7	12.4	12.1	11.3	10.7	10.5	12.7	14.6	16.0	16.0	16.1	15.7	13.2
1982	14.1	15.7	16.0	14.5	16.2	17.7	15.2	16.4	16.4	14.6	13.9	13.1	15.3
1983	11.8	12.3	12.8	11.3	11.4	10.5	11.2	14.4	18.0	16.5	15.3	14.6	13.3
1984	14.4	15.2	15.3	15.0	15.1	14.7	18.6	18.3	20.7	18.4	17.3	17.8	16.7
1985	14.7	14.5	15.0	14.9	13.6	12.3	17.5	18.2	17.7	17.3	17.5	17.7	15.9
1986[1]	16.7	17.2	17.2	17.2	20.7	21.1	28.0	30.0	22.3	20.1	18.5	17.9	20.6
1987[1]	18.2	18.9	18.0	19.1	22.4	24.6	25.3	16.0	15.7	12.7	11.6	10.7	17.8
1988[1]	11.4	13.3	12.8	11.3	11.1	10.9	19.7	26.1	25.1	20.8	18.9		

[1] Preliminary. Source: Bureau of Labor Statistics (0111-0215.99) Economic Res. Service, U.S.D.A T.20

Arsenic

The sole U.S. refiner of arsenic closed in 1985, but world refined arsenic trioxide output has been more than adequate to supply U.S. needs. Imports were estimated at 30,000 tonnes in 1988. Nearly all the arsenic consumed by industry is in compounds. Major U.S. consumers include four producers of agricultural chemicals and three producers of wood preservatives. Metallic arsenic is used primarily in nonferrous alloys, and about 15 tonnes of high-purity arsenic were used in both 1987 and 1988 to make gallium arsenide integrated circuits, which were expected to replace silicon chips in high-speed computers and other applications. While gallium arsenide offers superior performance to other semiconductors, its development was presenting technological problems in 1988.

Arsenic use in semiconductors in 1988 was trivial in comparison with total U.S. consumption, which was estimated at more than $30 million. But since it was highly purified, it accounted for about 5 percent of the value of arsenic consumed. The wood preservatives industry accounted for about 69 percent of 1988's U.S. apparent arsenic consumption of 23,700 tonnes. Another 23 percent went into agricultural herbicides and desiccants, 4 percent into glass, 2 percent to nonferrous alloys, and the rest went to other uses.

Because arsenic complicates the smelting and refining of the metals with which it is found in nature, the cost of keeping this poisonous metal from contaminating the environment has risen, further reducing the incentive to recover it. The EPA has strict controls on arsenic emissions from copper smelters and glass factories.

World refinery production of arsenic was estimated at 55,000 tonnes in 1988, unchanged from 1987 output. U.S. imports primarily come from Canada, Mexico, and France. Canada's gold resources contain substantial amounts of arsenic, and world copper and lead reserves contain some 11 million tonnes of arsenic.

There were no available alternatives to arsenicals as growth regulators for grapefruit and for control of some grape diseases. But creosote and pentachlorophenol can substitute for chromated copper arsenate as wood treatments, where odor and paintability are not problems.

World Production of White Arsenic (Arsenic Trioxide) In Metric[4] Tons

Year	Portugal	Bolivia	Belgium	Canada[5]	Chile	France	West Germany	USSR	Japan	Mexico	Peru	Rep. of Korea	Sweden	Namibia[3]	World Total
1977	245				—	6,661	400	8,300	131	6,332	1,507	713	6,613	2,882	33,784
1978	279				—	6,500	400	8,400	100	6,884	1,457	604	6,700	2,647	33,971
1979[4]	345				—	5,550	—	7,700	182	6,537	1,415	590	5,080	2,221	29,620
1980	200	81			—	5,300	360	7,700	284	6,932	2,475	N.A.	6,500	1,288	31,199
1981	196	127	3,000	2,000	—	5,200	360	7,750	95	6,517	2,164	170	6,900	1,370	43,731
1982	200	261	3,000	2,000	—	6,000	360	7,800	100	4,740	1,910	306	9,000	1,895	45,572
1983	180	107	3,000	2,000	—	4,727	360	7,900	300	4,557	1,009	560	9,000	1,126	42,126
1984	180	144	3,000	3,000	3,500	3,828	360	8,000	500	5,496	1,090	N.A.	10,000	2,504	48,402
1985	170	361	3,000	3,000	4,000	8,000	360	8,100	500	6,312	1,257	N.A.	10,000	2,471	54,731
1986[1]	150	200	3,000	3,000	6,000	10,000	360	8,100	500	6,000	1,210	N.A.	10,000	1,936	55,456
1987[2]			3,000	3,000	6,000	10,000		8,000		6,000	1,000		10,000	2,000	55,000

[1] Preliminary. [2] Estimate. [3] Output of Tsumeb Corp. Ltd. only. [4] Data prior to 1979 are in short tons. [5] Includes low-grade dusts that were exported to the U.S. for further refining. *Source: Bureau of Mines*
T.21

Salient Statistics of White Arsenic in the U.S. In Metric[5] Tons

Year	Trioxide (As₂O₃)	Metallic Arsenic	Arsenic Acid	Sulfide	Arsenic Compounds	Trioxide Mexican 99.13% As₂O₃ ¢ lb.[3]	Value of Imports Thous. $	Trioxide Domestic[4] 95% As₂O₃ ¢ lb.	Metal Domestic 99% As 12/31	Peru	Canada	France	Mexico	South Africa	Sweden	Bel.-Lux.	Exports (compounds) Gross Weight
1977	5,981	357	382	—	1,109	18	1,962	13.1	190	—	22	1,352	3,089	—	1,323		
1978	10,306	369	565	—	473	27	5,918	23¼	190	—	136	5,077	2,603	—	2,281	189	
1979	12,325	405	176	39	1	30	7,728	24¼	190	477	277	3,242	3,125	—	5,014	184	969
1980	12,528	266	271	11	1	46	9,190	31¾	300	—	486	2,780	3,720		4,770	388	1,518
1981[5]	17,199	294	1,511	—	4	78	17,742	40	275	50	5,581	749	3,566	17	4,902	1,251	523
1982	14,599	136	699	18	362	59	18,205	40	245	—	3,352	1,992	2,276	—	4,192	1,030	2,658
1983	10,186	243	2,385	1,127	26	45	13,920	33	225	—	2,525	667	2,531	17	3,430	946	85
1984	13,985	304	2,506	20	35	42	14,581	33	210	—	4,767	1,261	3,115	—	3,914	843	76
1985	16,472	407	1,993	2	23	42	17,999	33	210	—	3,669	3,608	3,399	113	2,996	1,498	158
1986[1]	25,728	395	1,381	16	10	44	20,851	33	185	—	1,924	6,274	4,408	1,210	7,069	1,255	217
1987[1]	27,000	530	——2,300——			44			140								80

[1] Estimate. [2] Preliminary. [3] F.O.B. Laredo, TX. [4] F.O.B. Tacoma, Wash. [5] Data prior to 1981 are in short tons. *Source: Bureau of Mines*
T.22

Barley

World barley production in 1988/89 was projected at 167.8 million tonnes, 7 percent less than a year earlier. Output in the European Community was put at 51.4 million tonnes, up 10 percent from 1987/88. The EC share of world output was 31 percent. The USSR had a crop of 47.5 million tonnes, down 19 percent from the previous season, but still 28 percent of the world's output. Eastern European countries produced 16.1 million tonnes. The Canadian crop, severely impacted by drought, declined by 29 percent to 10 million tonnes.

World exports of barley in 1988/89 were placed at 18 million tonnes, up 13 percent from the previous season. The EC was the dominant exporter with 10 million tonnes. Canada was expected to export 3.5 million tonnes, slightly above a year earlier. Australia's sales were expected to be nearly 2 million tonnes, up somewhat from the previous season. U.S. shipments were forecast to decline significantly in 1988/89. The world's major barley importer, Saudi Arabia, was forecast to take 5 million tonnes, 11 percent more than the previous season. The USSR was forecast to import 3 million tonnes, up 30 percent. Japan and Eastern European countries were also important buyers.

World use of barley was forecast to be 174.1 million tonnes, 5 percent less than the previous year. Western Europe accounted for 27 percent of use, while Eastern Europe consumed 10 percent. The USSR was the largest consumer with 51.5 million tonnes.

Global ending stocks of barley were expected to decline by 22 percent to 22.9 million tonnes. The U.S. share of world stocks was 15 percent.

U.S. barley production in 1988/89 was 283 million bushels, 46 percent less than a year earlier. A severe drought concentrated in the upper Great Plains took a large toll on the crop. The national average yield was just over 38 bushels per acre, 27 percent less than the previous season. Harvested acreage fell to 7.4 million.

U.S. stocks of barley at the beginning of the season were put at 321 million bushels, down 4 percent from a year earlier. With the smaller crop, total supplies were forecast at 624 million bushels, 29 percent less than in 1987/88. Usage of barley was projected to decline by 16 percent to 465 million bushels. Use of barley for feeding was forecast to fall by 7 percent to 240 million bushels. Food, seed, and industrial usage was put at 175 million bushels, the same as a year earlier. Exports were forecast to drop by 60 percent to 50 million bushels.

The largest markets for U.S. barley in 1987/88 were Saudi Arabia, Algeria, Israel, Iraq and Bulgaria. For the 1988/89 season, the major markets were Saudi Arabia and Algeria, while East Germany and Poland increased purchases. Barley has been included under USDA's Export Enhancement Program.

U.S. ending stocks were projected to be 159 million bushels, 50 percent less than in 1987/88. That level was closer to inventories during 1975 to 1983.

The price support loan rate in 1989 is $1.34/bu., versus $1.44 a year earlier. The acreage reduction requirement is 10 percent, down from 20 percent in 1988.

Futures Market

Feed barley futures are traded on the Winnipeg Commodity Exchange.

World Barley Supply and Demand   In Millions of Metric Tons

Crop Year	Exports Aus-tralia	Can-ada	EC-12	Total Non-U.S.	U.S.	Total Exports	Imports U.S.S.R.	Total Imports	Pro-duction	Utilization West Europe	Non-U.S.	U.S.	Total Util-ization	Stocks[2] Non-U.S.	U.S.	Total Stocks
1981–82	1.7	5.5	3.5	12.0	2.0	14.1	3.6	14.1	157.0	48.3	149.1	8.1	157.2	13.7	3.2	17.0
1982–83	.6	6.1	3.9	12.5	1.0	13.4	2.2	13.4	166.9	49.5	152.6	8.9	161.5	15.6	4.7	20.3
1983–84	3.6	4.2	3.8	14.5	2.1	16.6	.5	16.6	164.7	49.1	160.7	9.8	170.5	10.5	4.1	14.6
1984–85	4.7	2.4	7.6	16.8	1.2	18.0	4.7	18.0	175.5	50.7	157.8	10.3	168.1	19.1	5.4	24.4
1985–86	3.7	4.8	7.3	17.6	.8	18.4	2.9	18.4	178.0	48.2	161.8	10.9	172.7	22.6	7.1	29.7
1986–87	2.2	6.0	6.2	15.6	3.0	18.5	3.0	18.5	182.7	47.0	169.8	10.3	180.1	25.0	7.3	32.3
1987–88[1]	1.7	3.4	7.0	13.0	2.9	15.9	2.4	15.9	181.2	46.6	175.3	9.4	184.7	21.8	7.0	28.8
1988–89[3]	1.8	3.0	10.5	16.5	1.0	17.5	2.5	17.5	166.0	45.9	162.1	9.0	171.2	20.1	3.5	23.6

[1] Preliminary.   [2] End of crop year season.   [3] Estimate.   *Source: Foreign Agricultural Service, U.S.D.A.*   T.29A

World Production of Barley   In Thousands of Metric Tons

Crop Years	China	United States	Aus-tralia	Canada	Rep. of Korea	Den-mark	Moroc-co	France	India	Japan	USSR	West Ger-many	Spain	Turkey	United King-dom	World Total
1981–2	7,500	10,436	3,450	13,724	749	6,044	1,039	10,231	2,293	383	37,500	8,687	4,757	5,900	10,230	157,000
1982–3	7,000	11,233	1,939	13,966	749	6,357	2,334	10,036	1,993	390	41,000	9,460	5,269	6,400	10,954	166,900
1983–4	6,800	11,081	4,890	10,209	815	4,423	1,228	8,759	1,867	380	50,000	8,944	6,662	5,425	9,980	164,700
1984–5	7,300	13,046	5,554	10,279	804	6,072	1,405	11,699	1,834	396	41,800	10,284	10,000	6,000	11,055	175,500
1985–6	6,200	12,876	4,868	12,387	571	5,251	2,225	11,470	1,556	378	46,500	9,690	9,980	5,800	9,740	178,000
1986–7[1]	6,100	13,293	3,548	14,634	453	5,134	2,966	9,950	1,952	344	53,900	9,377	7,331	6,300	10,015	182,700
1987–8[2]	6,300	11,529	3,468	13,957		4,355		10,385			58,400	8,571	9,282	6,000	9,130	181,200
1988–9[2]	6,300	6,153	3,400	10,125		5,300		10,500			45,500	8,600	11,600	6,200	10,000	166,000

[1] Preliminary.   [2] Estimate.   *Source: Foreign Agricultural Service, U.S.D.A.*   T.23

BARLEY

U.S. Barley Acreage and Prices

Year Beginning June 1	National Program	Set-aside	Planted	Harvested for Grain	Yield per Harvested Acre In Bushels	Received by Farmers[1]	Feed (No. 2)	Malting (No. 3)	Portland No. 2 Western	National Avg. Loan Rate	Target Price	Placed Under Loan (Mil. Bu.)	Total Payments to Participants[6] (Mil. $)
	Acreage (Million Acres)						Minneapolis[2] or Better			Govt. Price Support Operations			
							Dollars per Bushel						
1979–0	7.8	.7	8.1	7.5	50.9	2.29	2.16	2.87	2.69	1.71	2.40	30.0	22[8]
1980–1	8.7	—	8.3	7.3	49.7	2.84	2.60	3.64	3.34	1.83	2.55	31.2	31[7]
1981–2	10.2	—	9.6	9.0	52.4	2.44	2.21	3.06	2.87	1.95	2.60	60.5	63[8]
1982–3	—	.4	9.5	9.0	57.2	2.18	1.76	2.53	2.52	2.08	2.60	92.6	60[10]
1983–4	—	1.1	10.4	9.7	52.3	2.47	2.48	2.84	2.91	2.16	2.60	32.4	72[3]
1984–5	—	.5	12.0	11.2	53.4	2.29	2.09	2.55	2.59	2.08	2.60	56.9	50[10]
1985–6	—	.7	13.2	11.6	51.0	1.98	1.53	2.24	2.23	2.08	2.60	158.4	160[10]
1986–7[4]	—	2.0	13.1	12.0	50.8	1.61	1.44	1.89	1.96	1.56	2.60	16.5	346[3]
1987–8[5]	—	2.9	11.0	10.1	52.7	1.81	1.78	2.04	2.09	1.49	2.60		333[3]
1988–9[5]	—	2.9	9.7	7.4	38.2	2.70				1.44	2.51		

[1] Excludes support payments. [2] Duluth beginning March 1987. [3] Deficiency & diversion payments. [4] Preliminary. [5] Estimate. [6] Available for total feed grains only. [7] Disaster payments. [8] Deficiency & disaster payments. [9] Deficiency, disaster & diversion payments. [10] Deficiency payments. *Source: Economic Research Service, U.S.D.A.*

T.24

Production of Barley in the United States, by States In Millions of Bushels

Year	Arizona	California	Colorado	Idaho	Kansas	Minnesota	Maryland	Oklahoma	Montana	North Dakota	Oregon	Pennsylvania	Utah	South Dakota	Washington	Wyoming
1979	3.2	47.4	18.7	54.9	2.3	40.8	3.8	2.5	40.6	75.9	8.3	4.0	10.4	20.8	17.0	8.7
1980	4.5	44.1	15.9	59.0	2.1	34.6	3.4	1.7	44.1	48.0	10.1	3.8	10.8	15.2	32.3	8.6
1981	4.1	40.3	18.6	63.1	1.7	57.7	5.0	1.6	56.8	105.6	11.7	4.1	11.1	20.1	44.1	9.0
1982	3.8	38.4	15.9	75.9	2.5	51.0	5.4	1.1	76.4	103.4	15.5	3.4	12.9	23.4	49.4	9.4
1983	2.8	29.4	16.5	67.0	4.6	43.5	5.0	1.5	77.7	114.7	16.5	3.6	11.4	23.1	54.4	10.0
1984	5.4	29.0	20.2	88.4	6.7	61.8	5.5	2.1	59.1	153.7	17.4	3.6	11.6	30.3	63.7	10.4
1985	6.0	24.8	21.8	71.9	9.7	71.0	5.5	1.9	30.0	184.3	19.3	4.3	11.8	32.4	56.6	10.6
1986	2.9	23.6	21.0	72.2	10.4	55.0	4.9	1.3	85.0	176.0	20.8	3.9	11.6	35.9	45.0	10.9
1987	2.2	17.8	14.5	61.5	4.8	49.6	6.0	.8	94.5	139.2	15.4	3.4	11.8	34.0	35.5	10.4
1988[1]	1.4	17.1	11.2	51.0	3.0	22.7	4.8	1.0	28.8	42.0	14.8	3.6	9.4	8.1	33.6	8.4

[1] Preliminary. *Source: Crop Reporting Board, U.S.D.A.*

T.25

High, Low & Closing Prices of May Barley Futures at Winnipeg In Canadian Dollars per Tonne

Year of Delivery		June	July	Aug.	Sept.	Oct.	Nov.	Dec.	Jan.	Feb.	Mar.	Apr.	May	Life of Delivery Range
		Year Prior to Delivery							Delivery Year					
1983	High	127.90	127.50	116.80	108.70	105.00	110.50	107.10	111.30	109.50	107.50	109.20	108.20	127.90
	Low	127.90	114.80	106.30	102.50	100.70	101.50	105.50	104.90	101.90	100.00	104.80	100.30	100.00
	Close	127.90	115.70	107.80	104.80	101.50	105.80	106.20	108.50	103.60	106.80	107.30	101.20	—
1984	High	109.00	110.50	131.00	142.10	141.00	138.00	137.00	137.00	133.00	132.00	134.60	149.00	149.00
	Low	107.30	107.50	116.20	128.50	128.80	132.30	131.70	131.80	124.80	128.30	127.60	132.10	107.30
	Close	107.50	110.50	128.60	137.20	134.00	133.90	136.20	132.60	128.90	132.00	133.00	142.00	—
1985	High	136.00	138.50	137.00	134.30	135.20	138.80	139.10	138.10	137.80	138.20	142.00	149.00	149.00
	Low	130.10	124.30	129.80	129.70	132.20	133.80	136.50	136.20	130.40	134.00	138.20	128.50	124.30
	Close	131.50	137.50	130.10	134.20	134.20	138.10	137.10	137.80	134.80	138.00	142.00	129.60	—
1986	High	—	131.10	120.40	117.00	116.90	116.20	115.60	114.40	105.40	102.60	102.30	116.00	131.10
	Low	—	121.90	113.70	111.10	113.00	114.50	112.60	104.50	100.40	98.70	84.60	87.80	84.60
	Close	—	122.00	114.10	113.70	115.70	115.45	113.60	104.90	100.90	102.20	92.80	115.10	—
1987	High	—	86.50	85.50	89.90	88.20	87.40	85.40	85.50	83.40	80.30	79.50	86.50	89.90
	Low	—	85.30	83.50	83.20	83.20	82.70	84.00	83.00	77.20	76.50	74.00	76.00	74.00
	Close	—	85.30	83.60	88.90	84.00	85.10	84.40	83.50	78.30	78.30	76.30	78.10	—
1988	High	87.30	82.00	74.70	74.30	72.60	76.00	74.90	78.50	76.80	73.70	78.00	101.40	101.40
	Low	77.10	73.20	72.50	72.30	70.50	69.00	71.20	72.80	73.10	69.50	74.50	76.10	69.00
	Close	83.00	75.20	72.50	72.40	70.60	74.60	74.30	73.40	74.20	73.70	78.00	98.50	—
1989	High	135.10	140.00	138.20	145.50	142.40	139.50	139.10						
	Low	111.00	120.00	129.80	138.00	135.00	129.70	131.40						
	Close	130.00	130.30	138.20	139.20	138.70	132.00	138.10						

Source: Winnipeg Commodity Exchange

T.26

Average Cash Price of No. 2 (or better) Feed Barley, in Duluth[2]   In Cents Per Bushel

Year	June	July	Aug.	Sept.	Oct.	Nov.	Dec.	Jan.	Feb.	Mar.	Apr.	May	Average
1981–2	209	226	235	221	226	231	206	220	227	216	216	224	221
1982–3	212	185	172	169	154	158	159	163	172	173	201	195	176
1983–4	196	195	242	261	260	253	239	255	256	265	274	277	248
1984–5	259	218	213	205	210	206	188	198	199	197	205	205	209
1985–6	190	166	146	140	141	149	160	157	—	—	—	131	153
1986–7	123	116	113	127	150	163	123	—	—	164[2]	176	186	144
1987–8	173	159	160	176	178	182	174	172	177	188	194	198	178
1988–9[1]	241	231	208	224									

[1] Preliminary.   [2] Prior to March 1987 prices are at Minneapolis.   *Source: Economic Research Service, U.S.D.A.*   T.27

Month-End Open Interest of Barley Futures at Winnipeg   In Contracts (20 Tonne)

Year	Jan.	Feb.	Mar.	Apr.	May	June	July	Aug.	Sept.	Oct.	Nov.	Dec.
1981	14,560	13,335	13,836	16,380	14,252	12,968	15,101	16,620	16,086	10,971	10,591	8,832
1982	8,485	7,838	7,096	6,684	6,774	6,298	7,019	7,427	8,148	8,697	8,697	7,826
1983	9,952	10,972	9,535	10,458	11,064	12,592	12,688	18,486	19,110	17,099	15,083	10,673
1984	10,279	10,698	9,693	12,649	10,439	13,752	12,451	14,125	15,380	9,836	11,345	9,334
1985	10,984	11,828	9,622	8,152	9,187	9,187	8,808	9,529	9,948	10,166	9,948	7,624
1986	7,702	9,550	8,679	9,275	8,109	8,286	8,223	8,729	9,709	8,605	8,771	8,121
1987	8,107	8,695	8,981	9,759	11,167	11,389	9,004	9,086	11,273	13,089	13,030	12,003
1988	18,516	22,409	22,371	28,798	25,665	33,487	34,075	34,081	34,065	29,142	23,490	22,076

Source: Winnipeg Commodity Exchange   T.28

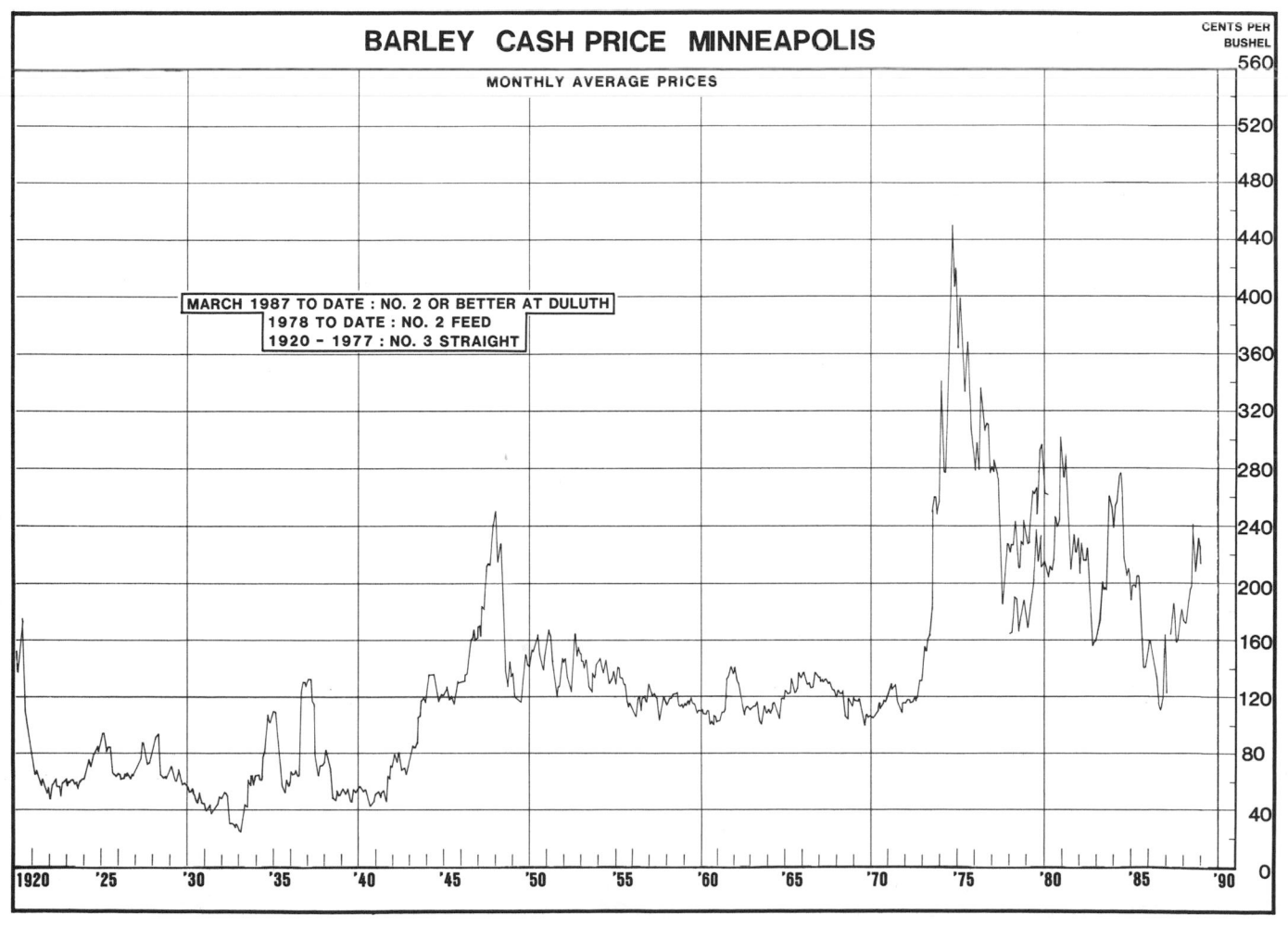

BARLEY CASH PRICE MINNEAPOLIS

MONTHLY AVERAGE PRICES

MARCH 1987 TO DATE : NO. 2 OR BETTER AT DULUTH
1978 TO DATE : NO. 2 FEED
1920 – 1977 : NO. 3 STRAIGHT

BARLEY

Salient Statistics of Barley in the United States   In Millions of Bushels

| Year Begin. June 1 | Supply | | | | Disappearance | | | | | | | Ending Stocks | | |
| | Begin-ning Stocks | Produc-tion | Im-ports | Total Supply | Domestic Use | | | | | Ex-ports | Total Disapp. | Gov't. Owned[1] | Privately Owned[2] | Total Stocks |
					Food	Alc. Bever-ages	Seed	Feed & Residual	Total					
1978–9	173.1	454.8	10.5	638.4	6.0	147.5	13.6	217.6	384.7	25.7	410.4	2.5	225.5	228.0
1979–0	228.0	383.2	11.8	623.0	7.0	150.9	14.0	204.2	376.1	54.8	430.9	3.2	188.9	192.1
1980–1	192.1	361.1	10.2	563.4	7.0	155.3	13.2	173.9	349.4	76.7	426.1	3.4	133.9	137.3
1981–2	137.3	473.5	9.6	620.4	6.9	150.9	16.3	198.4	372.5	100.1	472.6	3.3	144.5	147.8
1982–3	147.8	515.9	10.7	674.4	7.2	145.5	17.4	240.4	410.5	47.2	457.7	6.0	210.7	216.7
1983–4	216.7	508.9	7.1	732.7	7.0	142.5	19.5	282.8	451.8	91.4	543.3	11.9	177.5	189.4
1984–5	189.4	599.2	10.1	798.7	—— 149.0 ——		21.6	303.9	474.5	76.8	551.3	14.6	232.8	247.4
1985–6	247.4	591.4	9.0	847.8	—— 147.2 ——		21.4	332.6	501.2	21.8	523.0	57.4	267.4	324.8
1986–7	324.8	610.5	8.7	944.0	—— 156.1 ——		17.9	297.7	471.7	136.7	608.4	75.5	260.9	335.6
1987–8[3]	335.6	529.5	13.7	878.8	—— 156.1 ——		17.9	257.5	431.5	126.1	557.6	50.1	270.9	321.2
1988–9[4]	321.2	282.6	20.0	623.8	—— 175.0 ——			239.8	414.8	50.0	464.8			159.0
1989–0[4]	159.0													

[1] Uncommitted inventory.   [2] Includes quantity under loan & farmer-owned reserve.   [3] Preliminary.   [4] Estimate.
Source: Economic Research Service, U.S.D.A.

T.29

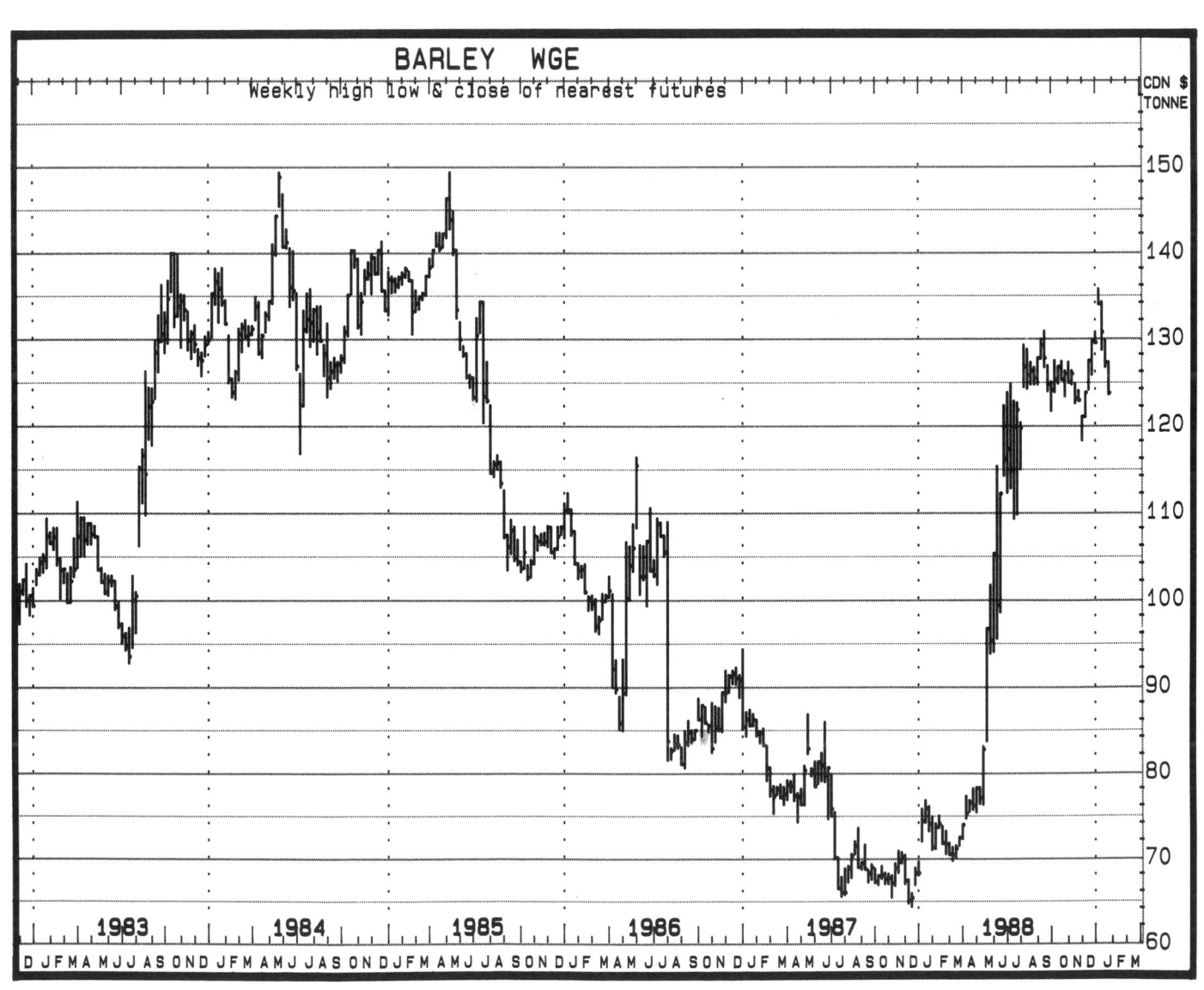

Bauxite

In 1988, bauxite producers did not participate as fully as aluminum refiners in the recent boom for lightweight metal. Bauxite is the raw product from which alumina is refined. Alumina is further reduced to make aluminum. In the conversion process, 2.3 pounds of bauxite make one pound of alumina.

The U.S. has limited production capacity, notably in some lower grade ores, and several surface mines operate in Alabama, Arkansas, and Georgia. Four other nations are responsible for the bulk of the world's production. They are Australia, which is the largest producer, followed by Guinea, Brazil and Jamaica. Australia is also the world's leading producer of alumina.

While there is some production of bauxite in the U.S., most of the country's bauxite is imported from China, which supplies the bulk of the calcinated bauxite consumed, and from Guinea and Jamaica, which supply much of the crude bauxite imported.

For the first six months of 1988, domestic bauxite production was estimated at 310,000 tonnes of abrasive, metallurgical, and refractory grades. Small production increases were not believed to be indicative

of any upward trend. U.S. production was reported by three companies, operating four surface mines.

In 1988, the amount of calcinated bauxite imports appeared to decline, following the full-year 1987 total of 270,000 tonnes of refractory grade and 43,000 tonnes of other grade. From January-May 1988, the import total was 91,000 tonnes of refractory grade and 40 tonnes of other grades.

In 1987, total imports of crude bauxite were 9.15 million tonnes, while the total for the first five months of 1988 was estimated at 4.40 million tonnes. In January-May 1988, Guinea was the leading crude bauxite exporter to the U.S. with 1.97 million tonnes, followed by Jamaica with 1.26 million tonnes, and Australia with 718,000 tonnes.

Australia continued to be the major U.S. supplier of alumina in the first five months of 1988, with a total of 1.38 million tonnes, versus a five-month 1987 total of 1.81 million tonnes. For 1987, total alumina imports were 4.06 million tonnes.

The U.S. government maintains a stockpile of metal grade, refractory grade, and abrasive grade bauxite.

World Production of Bauxite   In Thousands of Metric Tons

Year	Aus-tralia	Brazil	China	France	Greece	Guinea	Guy-ana[2]	Hun-gary	Indo-nesia	Ja-maica[3]	Malay-sia	Suri-nam	USSR[3]	U.S.[3]	Yugo-slavia	World Total
1977	26,086	1,120	1,500	2,059	2,885	10,841	2,731	2,949	1,301	11,390	616	4,805	4,600	2,013	2,044	81,931
1978	24,293	1,160	1,500	1,978	2,663	11,527	2,425	2,899	1,008	11,739	615	5,188	4,600	1,669	2,565	80,975
1979	27,583	2,388	1,500	1,969	2,812	11,326	2,312	2,976	1,052	11,618	387	5,010	4,600	1,821	3,012	85,522
1980	27,179	5,538	1,500	1,921	3,286	11,862	1,844	2,950	1,249	12,054	920	4,646	4,600	1,559	3,138	89,220
1981	25,441	5,770	1,500	1,827	3,216	11,112	1,681	2,914	1,203	11,682	701	4,006	4,600	1,510	3,249	85,347
1982	23,625	6,289	1,500	1,662	2,853	11,827	1,783	2,627	700	8,378	589	4,205	4,600	732	3,668	79,335
1983	24,372	7,199	1,600	1,663	2,455	12,421	1,087	2,917	778	7,683	502	3,400	4,600	679	3,500	78,634
1984	31,537	6,433	1,600	1,607	2,296	13,160	1,333	2,994	1,003	8,937	680	3,454	4,600	856	3,347	87,771
1985	31,839	6,251	1,650	1,530	2,453	13,100	1,675	2,815	830	5,975	492	3,000	4,600	674	3,250	84,310
1986[1]	32,431	6,224	1,650	1,379	2,500	12,130	1,466	3,022	750	6,964	566	3,847	4,600	510	3,300	85,938
1987[2]	32,800	6,500			2,500	12,300	1,800			7,200		2,400	4,600	560	3,300	86,360

[1] Preliminary.   [2] Estimate.   [3] Dry Bauxite equivalent of ore processed.   *Source: Bureau of Mines*   T.30

U.S. Salient Statistics of Bauxite   In Thousands of Metric Tons

Year	Net Import Reliance as a % of Apparent Consumption	Av. Price F.O.B. Mine $ per Ton	Mine Production Crude	Mine Production Dried Equivalent	Value ($1,000)	Recovery[1] of Processed Bauxite Crude Ore Treated	Recovered[1] Total	Recovered[1] Dried Equiv.	Dry Equivalent Imports[2] (for Consumption)	Exports[2]	Consumption	Stocks, Dec. 31 Producers & Processors	Consumers	Govt.	Total
1977	91	5–15	2,436	2,013	27,555	419	169	294	12,989	26	14,528	685	7,264	15,087	23,036
1978	93	5–15	2,066	1,669	23,185	379	154	236	13,847	13	14,738	556	7,806	14,661	23,023
1979	93	5–15	2,186	1,821	24,875	466	235	336	13,780	15	15,697	620	7,958	14,661	23,239
1980	94	6–16	1,869	1,559	22,353	355	179	277	14,087	21	15,962	662	7,681	14,661	23,004
1981	94	8–20	1,847	1,510	26,489	419	187	328	12,802	20	13,525	897	7,395	14,661	22,953
1982	96	8–20	896	732	12,334	234	120	184	10,122	49	9,217	614	6,548	16,326	23,488
1983	96	13–20	826	679	11,309	293	140	225	7,601	74	9,100	552	5,061	16,326	21,939
1984	96	13–20	1,054	856	15,643	361	168	294	9,435	82	10,519	499	4,382	17,338	22,219
1985	96	13–20	787	674	12,855	330	166	284	7,158	56	8,206	220	3,423	18,357	22,000
1986[3]	96	13–17	617	510	10,366	250	128	196	6,456	69	6,901	152	3,147	18,472	21,771
1987[4]	97	13–17	560						9,156	65	7,300		3,000		
1988[4]			600						8,500						

[1] Calcined, or sintered.   [2] Including concentrates.   [3] Preliminary.   [4] Estimate.   *Source: Bureau of Mines*   T.31

Bismuth

Long a part of the pharmaceuticals industry, bismuth has undergone a further revolution thanks to the steel industry, where sharply increased demand fueled a two year bull market in bismuth. Bismuth prices moved from $2.60/lb. at the beginning of 1987 to $6.05 in mid-1988.

In 1988, demand from the chemical side of the market, which includes manufacturers of stomach remedies and cosmetics, as well as industrial and laboratory chemical manufacturers, appeared to be at a record pace, which was expected to keep prices spiraling higher.

While all of 1987's chemical usage of bismuth was 1.65 million pounds, the total for the first six months of 1988 was 928,266 pounds, or an implied 1.86 million pounds for the full year, a potential 13 percent gain. Metallurgical additive use totaled 1.8 million pounds in 1987; that figure for 1988's first six months was 504,812 pounds. Total 1987 bismuth use was pegged at 3.52 million pounds, compared to a six-month tally in 1988 of 1.81 million pounds.

There were some shifts is supply during 1988, notably between Peru and China. In 1987, Peru accounted for 971,003 pounds of U.S. bismuth imports, and was the largest supplier of bismuth to U.S. industry. In the first five months of 1988, however, imports of Peruvian bismuth totaled only 120,325 pounds.

At the same time, China, which accounted for only 16,529 pounds of U.S. bismuth imports in 1987, supplied 117,939 pounds through the first five months of 1988, a considerable gain.

Mexico was the main supplier for 1988's first five months, followed by Belgium, which is no longer combined with Luxembourg, as it was through 1987. In 1987, a combined Belgium/Luxembourg led all exporters to the U.S. with 959,030 pounds, or just over a third of the 3.48 million pounds imported in 1987.

The leading world producers over the last five years have been Australia, followed by Peru, Mexico, and Canada.

Consumers of bismuth cluster in the industrial areas of the Northeastern U.S. According to the U.S. Bureau of Mines, 48 companies east of the Mississippi River account for 90 percent of consumption. U.S. bismuth production in 1987 was accounted for by one firm in Nebraska, and figures for domestic production were unavailable as they constitute proprietary information.

World Mine Production of Bismuth   In Thousands of Pounds

Year	Romania (Ore)	Australia (concentrates)	Bolivia (concentrates)	Canada	China (Ore)	France (Metal)	South Korea (Metal)	Yugoslavia (Metal)	Japan (Metal)	Mexico (Metal)	Peru (Metal)	West Germany (Ore)	USSR (Metal)	World Total
1977	180	2,054	1,435	363	500	115	293	163	1,538	1,607	1,420	24	140	9,872
1978	180	2,324	677	320	530	N.A.	269	29	1,375	2,156	1,347	20	150	9,412
1979	180	2,200	22	306	570	N.A.	192	51	1,010	1,662	1,162	22	160	7,548
1980	180	2,650	24	377	570	N.A.	271	183	745	1,698	1,096	0	160	7,954
1981	180	2,600	24	370	570	N.A.	220	225	1,054	1,446	1,409	0	170	8,268
1982	180	3,310	11	417	570	N.A.	209	108	1,071	1,336	1,676	0	170	9,058
1983	180	3,110	13	445	570	N.A.	220	99	1,263	1,202	1,495	—	180	8,777
1984	180	2,980	7	366	570	N.A.	278	66	1,241	955	1,433	—	180	8,256
1985	180	3,090	351	489	570	N.A.	298	150	1,415	2,039	1,731	—	185	10,498
1986[1]	180	2,200	180	440	570	N.A.	220	110	1,400	1,980	1,500	—	185	8,965
1987[2]		2,400	200	200			200		1,400	2,000	2,000			9,400

[1] Preliminary.   [2] Estimate.   *Source: Bureau of Mines*   T.35

U.S. Salient Statistics of Bismuth   In Thousands of Pounds

Year	Experimental	Metallurgical Additives	Other Alloys	Fusible Alloys	Chemicals[4]	Other Uses	Total Consumption	Consumer Stocks Dec. 31	Exports of Metal & Alloys	Peru	Mexico	Japan	Total	Price[1] $ Per Pound
1977	.6	461.6	18.6	611.2	1,274.5	13.1	2,379.6	436.1	95.3	632.4	182.2		2,013.3	6.01
1978	.6	485.3	21.8	836.0	1,149.7	18.6	2,511.9	781.9	96.3	334.7	535.3		2,657.8	3.38
1979	3.2	703.8	22.0	721.0	1,248.7	28.5	2,727.2	629.7	427.8	648.7	604.8	185.5	2,167.3	3.01
1980	1.2	467.9	26.5	650.9	1,115.6	26.7	2,288.8	674.0	128.7	619.1	860.4	138.4	2,217.4	2.64
1981	.2	307.0	26.0	657.0	1,387.6	15.0	2,392.7	509.0	78.7	859.3	724.1	124.1	2,436.2	2.32
1982	.5	124.6	21.4	571.6	1,144.8	13.6	1,876.4	541.6	52.8	864.1	699.5	41.4	2,026.2	1.61
1983	1.7	522.8	20.0	622.8	1,103.7	13.0	2,285.3	577.5	306.1	653.7	706.6	68.3	1,972.0	1.72
1984	—	424.5	20.0	608.8	1,573.0	22.0	2,648.4	480.0	311.5	391.8	430.5	209.2	1,948.4	4.27
1985	—	668.2	21.0	610.1	1,325.0	20	2,643.5	507.1	268.7	173.3	678.2	99.4	1,998.9	5.18
1986[2]	—	772	28	639.0	1,462	18	2,919	763	92.6	235.8	800.0	219.6	2,489.6	3.25
1987[3]	—	1,088	24	735.9	1,650	24	3,521	648	83.7	971.0	862.6	35.8	3,484.7	3.65
1988[3]	—	1,100	24	750	1,800	12	3,700	600	100	600	1,000	30	3,300	5.80

[1] N.Y., average ton lots; effective Oct. 1981, domestic producers' list price was suspended. Major foreign producer price is recorded.   [2] Preliminary.
[3] Estimate.   [4] Includes pharmaceuticals.   *Source: Bureau of Mines*   T.36

Broilers

Due to higher net returns over the summer, U.S. 1988 broiler production increased more than 4 percent from the previous year. The 12-city broiler price averaged 56 cents for 1988, compared to 47.4 cents in 1987. Prices moved higher in the second quarter, as fast food restaurants began to feature chicken products, while production was being cut because of lower returns in the early part of the year.

U.S. per capita consumption of broilers in 1988 was projected at 62.4 pounds, up from 60.3 a year earlier. Broiler exports in 1988 were expected to be slightly below 1987's record 752 million pounds. The slowdown was attributed to reductions in broiler sales to Iraq and Egypt, both major Export Enhancement Program (EEP) markets in 1987. The two countries were attempting to increase domestic chicken production in 1988. Japan continued as the largest importer of U.S. broilers.

Although high feed costs in the early part of 1989 should limit production increases, broiler production remains profitable, and growth in 1989 is expected to be near the long-run trend of 4 percent annually. Prices during 1989 were forecast to average 51-57 cents. Per capita consumption, meanwhile, was expected to rise to more than 65 pounds during 1989. Exports, however, were expected to drop from the previous year's level.

Broiler Supply and Prices in the United States

Year & Quarters	Number (Mil.)	Avg. Wt. (Lbo.)	Federally Inspected Slaughter — Liveweight Pounds (Mil. Lbs.)	Certified RTC Wt. (Mil. Lbs.)	Total Production RTC[2] (Mil. Lbs.)	Per Capita Consumption (Lbs.)	Prices — Farm	City[4] (Cents/Lb.)
1984	4,272	4.17	17,801	12,999	13,017	53.0	33.7	55.6
1985	4,439	4.20	18,623	13,569	13,762	55.5	30.2	50.7
1986	4,643	4.24	19,676	14,266	14,316	56.7	34.5	57.0
1987[1]	4,971	4.29	21,333	15,498	15,594	60.2	28.3	47.4
1987 I[1]	1,188	4.33	5,149	3,735	3,762	14.7	30.0	50.0
II	1,252	4.29	5,365	3,907	3,933	15.2	28.9	48.1
III	1,302	4.20	5,470	3,965	3,984	15.2	29.0	48.8
IV	1,230	4.35	5,355	3,895	3,916	15.1	25.3	42.5
1988 I[3]	1,267	4.35	5,511	3,996	4,021	15.5	26.8	45.5
II	1,303	4.30	5,611	4,079	4,105	15.7	32.7	55.7
III	1,316	4.20	5,529	4,633			41.1	66.1
IV								

[1] Preliminary. [2] Total production equals fed, inspec. slaughter plus other slaughter minus cut-up & further processing condemnation. [3] Forecast. [4] 12-city weighted average. *Source: Economic Research Service, U.S.D.A.*   T.38

Salient Broiler Statistics in the United States

Year	Commercial[2] Production — Number (Millions)	Live weight (Mil. Lbs.)	Average — Live weight Per Bird (Lb.)	Farm Price (¢ Lb.)	Gross Income (Mil. $)	Total Chickens[2] Supply & Distribution — Commercial Broilers	Other Chickens	Total (In Millions of Pounds)	Storage Stocks Jan. 1	Export & Shipments	Consumption–Civilian — Military	Total	Per Capita (in Lbs.)
1982	4,149	16,760	4.04	26.9	4,502	12,167	744	12,911	136	675	36	12,251	53.1
1983	4,184	17,038	4.09	28.6	4,873	12,400	717	13,117	149	591	36	12,548	53.8
1984	4,282	17,863	4.17	33.7	6,018	13,017	672	13,689	135	580	36	13,083	55.7
1985	4,479	18,851	4.20	30.1	5,680	13,762	636	14,397	139	582	36	13,784	58.0
1986	4,646	19,651	4.24	34.5	6,780	14,316	629	14,945	171	734	37	14,104	59.1
1987[1]	5,003	21,520	4.29	28.7	6,175	15,594	650	16,244	187	920	35	15,298	62.8
1988[3]						16,279	636	16,915	213	882	35	16,046	65.1

[1] Preliminary. [2] Ready-to-cook basis. [3] Estimate. *Source: Economic Research Service, U.S.D.A.*   T.39

Average Wholesale Broiler[1] Prices RTC   In Cents Per Pound

Year	Jan.	Feb.	Mar.	Apr.	May	June	July	Aug.	Sept.	Oct.	Nov.	Dec.	Avg.	4-Region Ave. Retail	Hens-N.Y.[2] 8–16 Lbs.
1982	45.2	44.5	44.8	42.6	45.8	47.0	46.1	43.4	43.6	42.3	40.3	42.0	44.0	71.6	60.8
1983	43.1	45.2	41.9	40.9	46.9	49.1	52.8	54.2	54.5	50.4	56.3	57.1	49.4	72.8	60.5
1984	62.1	61.2	62.0	56.0	57.6	55.5	57.3	51.5	53.6	48.8	52.1	49.0	55.6	81.4	74.4
1985	52.8	51.9	49.7	47.8	50.9	53.4	50.2	50.1	52.2	48.3	53.7	48.7	50.8	76.3	75.5
1986	51.7	49.0	50.3	50.0	54.6	58.3	69.1	69.7	61.0	61.6	57.5	50.0	56.9	83.5	72.2
1987	51.8	49.8	48.5	48.6	50.5	45.5	47.0	52.6	46.4	43.2	44.6	39.8	47.4	78.5	57.8
1988	43.9	44.9	48.4	48.7	56.3	61.5	66.5	68.9	62.8	57.7					

[1] Ice packed, ready-to-cook. [2] In retail stores (urban areas), whole or cut-up ready to cook. *Source: Bureau of Labor Statistics*   T.37

Butter

The U.S. Dairy Termination Program, which gave dairymen monetary incentives to dispose of their herds through slaughter or export, has now ended. But the impact on the dairy industry is expected to continue. Between April 1986 and August 1987, the program removed the capacity for producing over 12 billion pounds of milk. While the program was intended to slow milk production by reducing the cow herd, this was likely to prove short-lived. During the Oct.-Dec. 1987 period, milk production was 3 percent above a year earlier. While cow numbers were lower, output per cow rose. During third quarter 1988, the number of cows on farms fell by 1 percent from a year earlier, while milk output per cow posted a 2 percent increase. With higher grain prices due to the drought, milk production was expected to decline somewhat in 1989.

Milk marketings in June-Aug. 1988 were 1 percent above a year earlier, and butter and cheese production absorbed most of the increase in available supplies. During the June-Aug. period, butter production rose 8 percent. Over the Jan.-Aug. period, butter production was 819.5 million pounds, some 11 percent more than in the same period of 1987.

Commercial use of butter in June-Aug. 1988 was up almost 2 percent from a year earlier. Commercial use of dairy products by domestic consumers was expected to increase modestly at the end of 1988. While rises in consumer incomes remained favorable, higher prices had the potential to limit increases in sales, according to USDA. In 1989, domestic commercial use was expected to grow further. Export demand, at least during the winter, was likely to be good.

The milk equivalent of September 1 commercial stocks of dairy products was 5.22 billion pounds, 2 percent less than in 1987. These stocks were considered somewhat low. Cheese stocks were very low, while butter stocks were more plentiful. On September 1, 1988, butter stocks were 64.8 million pounds, 33 percent more than in 1987 and 50 percent above 1986.

Total Commodity Credit Corporation (CCC) removals of butter during the Jan.-Sept. 1988 period were 268.4 million pounds, up from 135 million in 1987. Purchases in 1989 were expected to be lower, primarily due to growth in commercial use. On October 1, 1988, the CCC's uncommitted inventories of butter were 161.3 million pounds, 96 percent above the level of October 1, 1987. Stocks were higher than a year earlier, but below the level of 1986.

While prices of cheese and non-fat dry milk rose sharply in 1988, butter prices were up only marginally. In September 1988, the price of grade A butter in Chicago averaged 134.27 cents/lb., down from August and up less than 2 percent from January. This was still 4 percent below the 1987 average price of 140.20 cents. By comparison, the price of cheese in September was 14 percent above January and 9 percent above the 1987 average price. The apparent reason for the price difference was that cheese stocks were very tight, while butter stocks were much higher than a year earlier.

World butter production was forecast at 6.5 million tonnes, 2 percent less than in 1987. Production in 1989 was forecast to be near 1988 levels. The Soviet Union was the world's largest butter producer, with 1988 output forecast at 1.76 million tonnes, up 1 percent from 1987. Reportedly, the Soviets had increased milk production substantially, but were using more for fresh use and other products. In 1989, the Soviets were expected to raise butter output by another 2 percent.

The European Community (EC) is the second largest producer of butter. Due to reduced supplies of milk, EC butter output in 1988 was expected to be 1.62 million tonnes, down 13 percent from 1987. In 1989, EC butter production was forecast to fall another 2 percent. New Zealand's 1988 butter output was 279,000 tonnes, 12 percent above 1987. That country's production in 1989 was expected to fall back to 265,000 tonnes.

Supply and Distribution of Butter in the United States In Millions of Pounds

Year	Supply Prod-uction	Supply Cold Storage Stocks[1] Jan. 1[2]	Supply Im-ports	Supply Total Supply	Domestic Disappearance Total	Domestic Disappearance Don-ated	Domestic Disappearance Per Capita —Lbs.—	Exports	Distribution Ship-ments[4]	Distribution Dept. of Agr. Jan. 1 Stocks[5]	Distribution Dept. of Agr. Dec. 31 Stocks[5]	Distribution Dept. of Agr. Removed by U.S.D.A. Programs	Total Use	93 Score Wholesale Prices Calif. AA $ Lb.	93 Score Wholesale Prices Chi. AA $ Lb.
1978	994	185	2	1,181	969	75	4.4	1	4	151	192	112	974	1.2666	1.1058
1979	985	207	2	1,194	1,011	90	4.5	1	4	192	153	82	1,016	1.4327	1.2374
1980	1,145	178	2	1,325	1,017	123	4.5	1	2	153	268	257	1,020	1.6135	1.4079
1981	1,228	305	3	1,536	974	108	4.3	130	2	268	382	352	1,107	1.6855	1.4897
1982	1,257	429	3	1,689	1,011	115	4.3	210	2	382	439	382	1,222	1.7187	1.4839
1983	1,299	467	3	1,769	1,150	258	4.9	119	1	439	464	413	1,270	1.7229	1.4832
1984	1,103	499	3	1,605	1,162	248	4.9	131	2	464	273	202	1,295	1.7459	1.4947
1985	1,248	310	4	1,562	1,164	243	4.9	180	1	273	181	334	1,345	1.6894	1.4197
1986	1,202	217	4	1,423	1,114	201	4.6	55	2	181	220	288	1,171	1.7140	1.4522
1987[3]	1,104	252	5	1,361	1,128	225	4.6	85	1	220	96	187	1,214		
1988[6]	1,300	147			1,100					96					

[1] Includes butter-equivalent of butteroil. [2] Includes stocks held by U.S.D.A. [3] Preliminary. [4] Includes U.S.D.A. shipments to Territories. [5] Includes butteroil.
[6] Estimate. *Source: Department of Agriculture*

T.43

World (Total) Butter[1] Production   In Thousands of Metric Tons

Year	Australia	Brazil	Canada	E. Germany	Czechoslovakia	Argentina	Denmark	France	Ireland	W. Germany	Netherlands	N. Zealand	India	Poland	Sweden	USSR	South Africa	United Kingdom	United States
1981	79	60	125	281	127	32	108	599	125	545	183	247	620	260	64	1,318	15	170	557
1982	76	70	134	266	138	37	121	624	140	556	216	248	650	265	70	1,403	17	216	570
1983	88	70	118	291	149	34	131	637	164	627	271	252	670	300	73	1,562	19	240	589
1984	111	70	119	309	152	29	104	621	171	572	241	287	690	322	77	1,588	18	205	500
1985	114	70	108	316	150	32	110	595	163	515	229	293	700	308	74	1,596	17	202	566
1986	105	65	109	320	150	32	112	633	160	567	264	299	720	289	66	1,700	15	222	545
1987[2]	104	65	95	322	150	34	96	569	145	464	199	248	750	290	64	1,742	11	174	501
1988[3]	94	75	108	310	150	33	90	510	130	400	165	279	800	290	63	1,760	12	131	545

[1] Factory (including creameries and dairies) & farm.   [2] Preliminary.   [3] Forecast.   *Source: Foreign Agricultural Service, U.S.D.A.*   T.44

Production of Creamery Butter in Factories in the United States   In Millions of Pounds

Year	Jan.	Feb.	Mar.	Apr.	May	June	July	Aug.	Sept.	Oct.	Nov.	Dec.	Total
1981	123.1	108.4	115.5	117.3	115.5	95.9	82.7	82.3	85.2	99.5	93.4	109.5	1,228
1982	127.3	115.9	123.4	——————	334.0	——————	——————	256.4	——————	——————	300.0	——————	1,257
1983	139.1	119.2	123.6	124.0	120.7	103.7	91.4	84.6	84.7	100.5	98.1	109.6	1,299
1984	127.3	108.9	107.6	103.0	105.1	81.8	72.7	70.2	67.5	84.4	79.8	95.1	1,103
1985	116.8	104.6	105.9	111.4	112.9	95.6	92.4	92.1	92.1	109.3	99.4	115.4	1,248
1986	136.7	119.3	119.2	122.7	114.7	93.0	79.7	69.9	80.2	85.3	80.3	101.3	1,202
1987[1]	109.2	97.8	107.6	104.2	101.7	83.1	76.2	66.4	77.9	91.2	87.9	108.5	1,104
1988[1]	124.7	117.1	116.4	111.7	107.9	91.7	75.9	74.2	83.0				

[1] Preliminary.   [2] Estimate.   *Source: Crop Reporting Board, U.S.D.A.*   T.45

Commercial Disappearance of Creamery Butter in the U.S.   In Millions of Pounds

Year	1st Quarter	2nd Quarter	3rd Quarter	4th Quarter	Total	Year	1st Quarter	2nd Quarter	3rd Quarter	4th Quarter	Total
1981	188.9	214.2	222.9	243.2	869.2	1985	200.0	203.9	241.5	272.9	918.2
1982	211.4	217.6	217.3	251.0	897.3	1986	198.6	220.1	234.4	269.8	922.9
1983	209.5	198.6	217.0	256.6	881.7	1987[1]	222.7	222.1	218.4	239.3	902.5
1984	194.0	241.3	215.6	251.9	902.7	1988[1]	191.3	218.2			

[1] Preliminary.   *Source: Economic Research Service, U.S.D.A.*   T.46

Cold Storage Holdings of Creamery Butter in the U.S., on First of Month   In Millions of Pounds

Year	Jan.	Feb.	Mar.	Apr.	May	June	July	Aug.	Sept.	Oct.	Nov.	Dec.
1981	304.6	332.1	372.3	407.4	450.4	473.6	507.5	515.5	515.6	489.5	470.0	451.1
1982	429.2	430.3	440.4	447.8	—	—	541.6	—	—	510.0	—	—
1983	466.8	485.4	522.0	529.0	555.7	576.1	589.6	588.4	581.8	552.3	523.9	506.7
1984	499.4	510.6	532.5	529.3	532.4	538.5	516.7	489.6	462.7	426.3	374.3	335.9
1985	206.6	377.3	289.4	291.7	272.7	283.2	286.8	280.7	264.6	247.0	231.6	206.9
1986	205.5	206.3	242.4	283.3	305.0	330.8	342.8	337.6	304.4	279.6	253.3	218.5
1987	193.0	206.6	231.6	254.0	247.9	251.1	237.9	211.2	187.3	176.2	165.6	158.5
1988[1]	143.2	157.3	198.8	221.1	239.8	282.5	294.7	295.7	290.0	247.6	240.1	

[1] Preliminary.   *Source: Crop Reporting Board, U.S.D.A.*   T.47

Wholesale Price of 92 Score Creamery (Grade A) Butter at Chicago   In Cents Per Pound

Year	Jan.	Feb.	Mar.	Apr.	May	June	July	Aug.	Sept.	Oct.	Nov.	Dec.	Average
1981	147.3	147.3	147.3	147.3	147.3	147.5	147.9	148.0	148.5	150.6	148.9	148.1	148.0
1982	147.5	147.5	147.8	147.4	147.3	147.3	147.6	148.1	148.4	147.4	148.2	147.9	147.7
1983	147.3	147.3	147.3	147.3	147.3	147.3	147.8	151.0	147.6	147.3	143.1	143.1	147.3
1984	140.4	141.3	142.1	142.9	142.9	150.0	155.6	150.6	158.1	158.1	158.1	145.6	148.8
1985	141.5	141.3	141.3	141.9	141.9	141.9	141.5	140.7	141.2	141.6	139.5	139.1	141.1
1986	138.8	138.8	137.5	138.8	138.8	139.1	143.7	153.9	154.2	153.5	151.9	145.5	144.5
1987	137.3	136.8	137.8	138.8	138.4	144.6	149.0	148.1	145.3	136.8	135.6	134.0	140.2
1988	131.9	131.0	131.0	131.0	131.0	133.5	135.9	135.6	134.3				

Source: Economic Research Service, U.S.D.A.   T.48

Cadmium

Cadmium was one of 1988's biggest bull markets, and strategic metals traders most likely profited by the price boom. However, prices declined mid-year.

In the first quarter of 1988, the domestic producer price of cadmium metal was between $3.00 and $3.50 a pound, which was more than double its level in the first quarter of 1987. The U.S. Bureau of Mines reported, "The market was so tight that all major cadmium producers did not have material to sell and would not make any commitments for near-term sales at a specific price."

Producer prices soared to close the first quarter of 1988 at $8.50 to $10.60 a pound, about a 300 percent price hike, while dealer prices closed in a range of $8.50 to $9.10 a pound. However, these high prices brought more supplies on stream, and prices began to sag by early summer 1988.

Stocks held by metal and compound producers at the end of the second quarter were down to between $8.00 and $8.25 a pound, with AMAX's producer price back down to between $8.00 and $8.50. However, this was considerably above price levels of $1.30-$1.50 per pound that prevailed in the mid-1980s.

U.S. refinery output of cadmium comes from four companies, each of which operates one plant.

At the end of 1987, metal producers held 126 tonnes of cadmium stocks, with compound producers holding 98 tonnes. At the end of the second quarter of 1988, producers were holding 259 tonnes of high priced cadmium, and compound producers were holding 123 tonnes.

U.S. cadmium consumption is expected to grow through increased demand for nickel-cadmium batteries and cadmium telluride usage in photovoltaic solar cells.

World resources of cadmium are estimated at nine million tonnes, or about .03 percent of global zinc resources, of which cadmium is a by-product. Cadmium is recovered mostly through the smelting of zinc ores. It is also recovered through recycling of nickel-cadmium batteries and some alloys.

World Refinery Production of Cadmium   In Metric Tons

Year	Australia	Belgium	Canada	China	Finland	France	W. Germany	Italy	Japan	Mexico	Norway	Poland	Un. King.	USSR	United States[3]	Zaire	World Total
1976	649	1,200	1,314		428	532	1,275	436	2,500	710	80	750	190	2,700	2,047	266	16,998
1977	670	1,440	1,185		527	790	1,336	448	2,844	908	97	754	295	2,750	1,999	246	18,288
1978	747	1,164	1,265		611	694	1,182	378	2,531	897	120	761	291	2,800	1,653	186	17,310
1979	804	1,440	1,455		590	689	1,266	527	2,597	830	115	773	424	2,850	1,823	212	18,679
1980	1,012	1,524	1,303	250	581	789	1,194	568	2,173	778	130	698	375	2,850	1,578	168	18,238
1981	1,031	1,176	1,298	270	621	663	1,192	489	1,977	590	117	580	278	2,900	1,603	230	17,381
1982	1,010	996	854	300	566	793	1,030	475	2,034	607	104	570	354	2,900	1,007	280	16,387
1983	1,106	1,260	1,456	300	616	513	1,094	385	2,214	642	117	570	340	3,000	1,052	308	17,444
1984	1,082	1,472	1,605	300	614	568	1,111	452	2,423	671	150	570	390	3,000	1,686	318	19,114
1985	1,000	1,252	1,717	300	610	337	1,095	526	2,535	734	159	600	370	3,000	1,603	296	18,634
1986[1]	1,000	1,300	1,421	300	620	400	1,185	411	2,400	700	155	600	350	3,000	1,486	300	18,257
1987[2]	1,000	1,400	1,500						2,400	700					1,500		18,400

[1] Preliminary.   [2] Estimate.   [3] Primary & secondary metal.   *Source: Bureau of Mines*   T.49

Salient Statistics of Cadmium in the United States   In Metric Tons of Contained Cadmium

Year	Net Import Reliance as a % of Apparent Consumption	Production Primary Producers Metallic	Ship-ments	Value Mil. $	Cadmium Sulfide[3]	Imports (for Consumption) Metallic	Flue Dust[3]	Total	Price[5] $ per lb.	Exports Cadmium Metal, Alloys, Dross, Flue Dust	Value Ths. $	Con-sump-tion[4]	Stocks, Dec. 31 Industry Metallic	Com-pounds	Distrib-utors
1975	41	1,990	742	4.2	895	2,375	314	2,689	3.36	180	589	3,055	1,881	121	
1976	64	2,047	2,707	10.5	729	3,094	223	3,317	2.66	229	713	5,381	1,242	148	
1977	51	1,999	1,837	7.1	639	2,332	13	2,345	2.96	107	316	3,818	1,452	72	255
1978	63	1,653	1,957	5.9	698	2,881	—	2,881	2.45	326	864	4,510	1,152	45	296
1979	64	1,823	2,468	9.5	813	813	—	2,572	2.76	211	550	5,099	517	52	327
1980	55	1,578	1,271	5.2	801	2,617	—	2,617	2.84	236	464	3,534	841	42	439
1981	63	1,603	1,382	3.8	527	3,090	—	3,090	1.93	239	332	4,378	1,077	68	215
1982	73	1,007	1,832	2.6	374	2,305	—	2,305	1.11	11	126	3,728	635	167	150
1983	72	1,052	1,495	1.8	670	2,196	—	2,196	1.13	170	351	3,763	209	49	91
1984	51	1,686	1,811	2.6	771	1,889	—	1,889	1.69	106	208	3,300	208	59	52
1985	57	1,603	1,791	2.4	477	1,988	—	1,988	1.21	86	342	3,720	136	111	59
1986[2]	66	1,486	2,030	1.9	645	3,174	—	3,174	1.25	38	188	4,385	303	73	65
1987[1]	66	1,515	1,916		540	2,701	—	2,701	1.90	241			126	98	38
1988[1]		2,000	2,200		420	2,200	—	2,200		500			220	120	20

[1] Estimate.   [2] Preliminary.   [3] Cd content.   [4] Apparent Primary cadmium in all forms.   [5] Sticks & Balls in 1 to 5 short ton lots.
Source: Bureau of Mines   T.50

Castor Beans

World castor seed production in 1988/89 was estimated by *Oil World* at 908,000 tonnes, up from the previous season's drought-reduced crop of 784,000. Output in China, the leading producer, was forecast at 275,000 tonnes, 6 percent above the year before. India's crop was placed at 275,000 tonnes, up 24 percent, while Brazil's was pegged at 169,000 tonnes, up 48 percent. China, by far the largest castor seed exporter, was expected to ship 120,000 tonnes in 1988/89, down 9 percent from 1987/88. Pakistan and the Philippines both export small quantities. Brazil, Japan, and the European Community are the leading importers.

Castor oil production worldwide was forecast at 348,500 tonnes in 1988/89, up 2 percent. While output in Brazil, the largest producer, was expected to be down 2 percent at 99,500 tonnes, production levels in India and China were slated to rise by 17 percent and 7 percent, respectively. World exports of castor oil were expected to fall slightly, as a decline in Brazilian shipments more than offset a rise in Chinese and Indian exports. France, the leading importer, was expected to boost its purchases by 5 percent to 43,000 tonnes.

World castor oil prices ex-Rotterdam in the first five months of 1988 averaged $1,084/tonne. Due to tight supplies, prices had been rising since late 1985, when they averaged $590/tonne.

World Production of Castorseed Beans   In Thousands of Metric Tons

Crop Year	China	Brazil	Ecuador	Ethiopia	India	Romania	Paraguay	Israel	Mexico	Pakistan	Thailand	USSR	Philippines	Sudan	World Total
1983–4	179	172	6	1	405	6	17		4	24	25	65	18	2	949
1984–5	164	225	6	1	469	8	16		4	17	23	58	24	1	1,040
1985–6	280	416	6	1	305	6	38		4	20	32	62	12	1	1,207
1986–7[1]	235	263	5	1	237	8	22		4	20	35	63	7	1	926
1987–8[2]	260	114	6	1	210	8	28			20	33	66	8	2	784
1988–9[2]	275	169	6		260		31				34	65			908

[1] Preliminary.   [2] Estimate.   *Source: Foreign Agricultural Service, U.S.D.A.; "The Oil World."*   T.51

Castor Oil Consumption[1] in the United States   In Thousands of Pounds

Crop Year	Oct.	Nov.	Dec.	Jan.	Feb.	Mar.	Apr.	May	June	July	Aug.	Sept.	Total
1983–4	5,488	4,749	4,965	4,764	4,990	5,296	5,599	6,723	5,663	7,958	7,859	6,812	70,866
1984–5	6,937	5,581	4,178	4,519	5,178	5,930	5,169	7,480	7,158	5,320	5,816	3,839	67,105
1985–6[2]	4,807	3,614	3,840	2,833	5,016	4,935	4,528	5,282	5,602	7,054	6,084	6,111	59,706
1986–7[2]	6,982	5,569	4,743	5,754	5,867	6,251	5,939	6,749	6,984	4,964	3,357	7,078	70,237
1987–8[2]	7,254	7,115	6,943	5,240	6,529	6,984	5,353	6,307	5,457	4,823	7,054	5,466	
1988–9[2]	5,723												

[1] In inedible products (Resins, Plastics, etc.).   [2] Preliminary.   *Source: Bureau of the Census.*   T.52a

Castor Oil Stocks in the United States   In Thousands of Pounds

Crop Year	Oct. 1	Nov. 1	Dec. 1	Jan. 1	Feb. 1	Mar. 1	Apr. 1	May 1	June 1	July 1	Aug. 1	Sept.1
1983–4	5,501	5,688	6,086	4,860	5,006	2,101	N.A.	N.A.	N.A.	N.A.	N.A.	N.A.
1984–5	6,998	7,432	5,669	11,734	10,403	11,129	18,518	24,952	19,072	21,623	16,652	16,001
1985–6[1]	14,632	17,087	28,477	21,031	24,754	25,586	26,263	19,739	30,125	24,740	29,809	26,919
1986–7[1]	22,212	26,907	31,876	29,376	35,042	30,039	39,369	30,616	40,460	40,821	43,204	41,246
1987–8[1]	33,738	36,060	31,757	48,027	43,191	37,297	47,945	41,480	37,969	32,051	26,885	16,472
1988–9[1]	9,662	13,827										

[1] Preliminary.   *Source: Bureau of the Census.*   T.52b

Monthly Average Wholesale Prices of Castor Oil No. 1, Brazilian Tanks at New York   In ¢ per Lb.

Year	Jan.	Feb.	Mar.	Apr.	May	June	July	Aug.	Sept.	Oct.	Nov.	Dec.	Average
1983	45.50	45.50	45.50	46.80	49.50	49.50	53.40	61.80	78.50	78.50	78.50	78.50	59.29
1984	78.50	78.50	78.50	78.50	78.50	73.70	69.00	77.30	65.00	65.00	65.00	65.00	72.71
1985	65.00	65.00	65.00	65.00	65.00	36.00	36.00	36.00	36.00	36.00	36.00	34.00	47.92
1986	34.50	34.50	34.50	34.50	33.38	32.25	32.38	32.56	31.70	31.63	32.00	33.00	33.08
1987	32.80	32.25	34.27	36.00	36.00	36.00	42.50	42.50	43.10	44.00	44.00	46.50	39.16
1988	46.50	46.50	52.50	51.38	49.88	49.50	48.75	48.00	48.00				

Source: Foreign Agricultural Service, U.S.D.A.   T.53

Cattle and Calves

The July 1, 1988, cattle and calf inventory totaled 108 million head, down 1 percent from a year earlier and the lowest midyear inventory since numbers were first collected in 1973. Both beef and dairy cow inventories fell 1 percent from 1987, while beef replacement heifers were unchanged and dairy replacement heifers were down 4 percent. The decline in cow numbers almost assures that modest declines in the all-cattle inventory will continue through 1989 and possibly in 1990.

While first-half 1988 heifer slaughter remained relatively large, cow slaughter fell nearly 7 percent. Beef cow slaughter, at 1.6 million head, was down 9 percent. Dairy cow slaughter for January-June totaled 1.4 million head, a 3 percent decline. There was some uncertainty about the impact of 1988's drought on heifer retention and cow and heifer slaughter over the second half of 1988. However, net returns to cow/calf producers reached $50 per head in 1988 and were expected to be near that level in 1989, creating an incentive to minimize drought-related culling.

There may also have been some positive impacts from the drought. Lack of summer forage and early movement of cattle off grass were expected to minimize the bunching of feeder cattle marketed in the fall. In addition, it was possible that Corn Belt grain producers were in the market for stocker cattle in order to salvage drought-damaged corn by chopping and feeding it. The drought was expected to induce some producers to abandon or modify plans for expanding beef and dairy herds. However, the reduced cattle inventory for 1988, coupled with USDA's decision to permit haying and grazing on idled acreage in drought-impacted counties and with other Government assistance, was likely to contain the amount of drought-forced liquidation from that seen in drought periods of the 1930s, 1940s, and 1970s.

Costs and returns for beef cow-calf operations showed marked improvements in 1986, 1987, and probably in 1988, except in areas impacted by drought. The late 1988 uncertainty was when producers would begin retaining sufficient replacement heifers to expand the breeding herd. Expanding U.S. cattle inventories were not expected before 1990 or 1991. The first sign of the rebuilding process is a reduction in cow slaughter. This had already occurred for the beef cow herd. However, a reduction in heifer slaughter, which allows for increasing the calf crop in upcoming years, had yet to occur. Expanding calf crops typically are not seen until one or more years after reduced cow and heifer slaughter occurs.

The mix of cattle slaughtered has changed considerably over the years. A much smaller proportion of animals slaughtered are calves. In 1950, for example, commercial cattle slaughter was under 18 million head, and commercial calf slaughter was nearly 10 million. By contrast, commercial cattle slaughter in 1987 had increased two-fold to 35.6 million head, and commercial calf slaughter was about one-fourth as large as in 1950 at 2.8 million head. The trend toward a smaller proportion of the calf crop slaughtered as calves will likely begin to stabilize at some point. In recent years, the slaughter of mature cattle has been predominantly fed cattle from feedlots. The average carcass weight for mature cattle has increased sharply over the years. The average federally inspected cattle carcass weight for 1987 was 662 pounds per head, compared with 541 pounds in 1950. Thus the decline in annual beef production was far less than the decline in cattle inventories.

Given some of the structural changes within the cattle sector during the 1980s, the cattle cycle in the 1990s was not expected to show as rapid an annual expansion rate as the average of the previous six cycles. Depending on the number of years of expansion in the 1990s, the herd peak may only reach 105 to 110 million head, versus the previous cyclic peak of 115 in the early 1980s.

Fed beef production was expected to decline about 6 percent in 1989, as feedlot marketings drop to the lowest level since 1980-81. Cow slaughter could decline another 2-3 percent, but an aging herd was considered likely to keep slaughter near 13-15 percent of the January 1 inventory. Nonfed steer and heifer slaughter was expected to remain near to slightly below 1988's 1.2-1.3 million head. The sharpest year-to-year declines were expected in the spring and summer, when total beef production was likely to drop 6-8 percent.

U.S. beef imports in 1988 totaled about 2,350 million pounds, carcass weight, 4 percent above the year before. U.S. imports were forecast to decline 6 percent in 1989. Australian producers were expected to hold back some cattle from slaughter to rebuild herds, and Australian shipments to Japan were likely to increase. U.S. beef exports were forecast to reach 670 million pounds in 1989. Beef exports were high in 1986 and 1987, with larger shipments to Japan and shipments of meat mandated by the Food Security Act of 1985, which went mainly to Brazil. U.S. beef exports to Japan were to continue growing, with the additional increases in the quota during the transition period leading toward liberalization of the Japanese market.

U.S. imports of live cattle come mainly from Mexico and Canada. Imports from Mexico, affected by various economic policies, can change dramatically year to year. If Mexico's domestic meat situation did not stabilize, its exports to the U.S. were projected to be as low as 500,000 head in 1989.

Tight fed beef supplies led to record high cattle prices in May 1988. By mid-June, larger supplies had forced cattle prices sharply lower, but Choice retail beef prices continued to move higher, hitting a record $2.60/lb. in June. The previous record was $2.54 in June 1982. For consumers, the higher retail prices were partially offset by a trend toward higher valued cuts that contain less bone and fat in the package. Retail prices for Choice beef were forecast to rise only 1-3 percent in 1989, following 1988's increase of 3-4 percent.

Futures Markets

Live cattle futures and options on futures are traded on the Chicago Mercantile Exchange (CME) and the Mid America Exchange. Feeder cattle futures and options are traded on the CME.

Cattle Supply and Distribution in the United States   In Thousands of Head

Year	Cattle & Calves on Farms Jan. 1	Imports	Calves Born	Total Supply	Livestock Slaughter—Cattle and Calves Commercial Federally Inspected	Other[2]	All Commercial	Farm	Total Slaughter	Deaths on Farms	Exports	Total Disappearance
1983	115,001	921	43,925	159,847	37,614	2,112	39,726	410	40,136	5,494	56	45,693
1984	113,700	753	42,500	156,953	38,910	1,969	40,879	390	41,259	5,464	71	46,805
1985	109,749	836	41,045	151,630	37,933	1,745	39,678	370	40,048	5,051	125	45,224
1986	105,468	1,407	41,141	148,016	39,108	1,588	40,696	350	41,046	5,038	108	46,192
1987[1]	102,000	1,200	40,026	143,226	37.147	1,315	38,462	358	38,820	4,800	131	43,751
1988[3]	98,994											

[1] Preliminary.   [2] Wholesale and retail.   [3] Forecast.   *Source: Economic Research Service, U.S.D.A.*   T.56

United States Beef Supply and Utilization

Year	Commercial production	Farm production	Beginning stocks	Imports	Total supply	Exports	Shipments	Military purchases	Ending stocks	Total disappearance	Per capita disappearance	Retail weight per capita	Population
	Million Pounds										*Pounds*		*Million*
1984 I	5,708	61	325	470.5	6,564.5	90.0	10.8	24	326	6,113.6	26.16	19.36	233.70
II	5,819	26	326	371.0	6,542.0	70.5	13.2	36	303	6,119.3	26.13	19.34	234.20
III	5,949	26	303	513.7	6,791.7	86.6	14.2	27	320	6,343.9	27.03	20.00	234.70
IV	5,933	61	320	467.9	6,781.9	81.6	9.1	25	358	6,308.2	26.74	19.78	236.00
Year	23,418	171	325	1,823	25,746	328.8	47.3	112	358	24,900	106.05	78.48	234.80
1985 I	5,692	60	358	420	6,530	82	12	28	334	6,073	25.7	19.0	236.20
II	5,923	26	334	537	6,820	77	12	31	296	6,405	27.0	20.0	236.80
III	6,167	25	296	633	7,121	91	12	30	308	6,680	28.1	20.8	237.40
IV	5,775	60	308	481	6,624	78	15	26	317	6,188	26.0	19.2	237.90
Year	23,557	171	358	2,071	26,157	328	51	115	317	25,347	106.9	79.1	237.00
1986 I	5,769	55	420	502	6,745	102	13	24	395	6,236	25.9	18.9	240.7
II	6,246	24	395	482	7,147	83	12	33	427	6,626	27.5	20.1	241.2
III	6,273	24	427	640	7,364	144	14	30	385	6,820	28.2	20.6	241.8
IV	5,925	55	385	505	6,871	193	13	23	412	6,253	25.8	18.8	242.4
Year	24,213	158	420	2,129	26,920	521	52	110	412	25,935	107.4	78.4	241.6
1987[1] I	5,754	56	412	543	6,764	127	14	32	411	6,213	25.6	18.1	242.9
II	5,737	25	411	627	6,800	136	13	23	337	6,315	25.9	18.4	243.4
III	6,084	24	337	681	7,106	159	14		381	6,552	26.8	19.0	243.9
IV	5,850	56	381	418	6,705	183	12		386	6,125	25.5	17.8	244.5
Year[1]	23,405	161	412	2,269	26,247	604	52	104	386	25,205	103.3	73.4	243.8
1988[2] I	5,696	56	386	703	6,841	134	15		419	6,272	25.6	18.1	245.2
II	5,784	25	419	668	6,896	156	15		330	6,395	25.9	18.4	
III													
IV													
Year[2]	23,291	161	386	2,375	26,213	636	61		375	25,141	102.2	72.5	246.0

[1] Preliminary. [2] Forecast.   *Source: Economic Research Service, U.S.D.A.*   T.56b

U.S. Cattle on Feed in 13 States, Quarterly   In Thousands of Head

Year	Number on Feed[1]	Placed on Feed	Marketings	Other Disappearance	Year	Number on Feed[1]	Placed on Feed	Marketings	Other Disappearance
1985	10,653	23,366	22,887	1,378	1987	9,245	24,874	22,971	1,379
I	10,653	5,315	5,907	373	I	9,245	5,680	5,747	371
II	9,688	5,206	5,787	437	II	8,807	5,906	5,619	428
III	8,670	5,480	5,969	244	III	8,666	6,590	6,022	242
IV	7,937	7,365	5,224	324	IV	8,992	6,698	5,583	338
1986	9,754	23,583	22,856	1,236	1988[2]	9,769			
I	9,754	5,270	5,763	316	I	9,769	5,796	5,810	390
II	8,945	5,221	5,821	375	II	9,365	5,898	5,854	418
III	7,970	6,336	5,876	233	III	8,991	5,959	6,151	223
IV	8,197	6,756	5,396	312	IV	8,576		5,560	

[1] Beginning of period.   [2] Preliminary.   *Source: Economic Research Service, U.S.D.A.*

CATTLE AND CALVES

World Cattle and Buffalo Numbers as of January 1   In Millions of Head

Year	Argen-tina	Aus-tralia	Brazil	Canada	China	Colom-bia	France	W. Ger-many	India	Poland	Turkey	Mexico	South Africa	USSR	Un. King-dom	United States	World Total
1982	57.9	24.6	93.0	12.1	N.A.	24.2	23.5	15.0	260.0	11.5	17.0	34.7	13.1	115.9	13.0	115.4	959
1983	58.0	22.5	93.0	11.7	76.1	24.0	23.7	15.1	263.7	11.0	16.5	33.9	12.5	117.2	13.2	115.0	1,033
1984	54.4	22.2	93.3	11.6	78.1	21.7	23.5	15.6	267.5	11.1	16.0	33.9	12.1	119.6	13.1	113.7	1,033
1985	54.7	22.8	94.7	11.3	82.6	21.2	23.1	15.7	271.4	10.9	15.5	33.9	12.0	121.1	13.0	109.7	1,041
1986	53.5	23.4	95.2	11.0	86.8	19.9	22.8	15.6	275.3	10.8	15.0	32.2	11.8	120.9	12.7	105.5	1,039
1987	51.7	23.5	97.0	10.8	91.7	18.8	22.2	15.3	273.6	10.5	14.5	33.6	12.0	122.1	12.5	102.0	1,037
1988[2]	50.8	23.5	98.3	10.8	94.7	18.0	21.1	14.9	264.9	10.2	14.0	35.4	12.2	120.6	11.8	99.0	1,024
1989[1]	50.5	24.0	98.8	11.0	98.0	17.8	20.8	14.8	267.9	10.3	13.5	36.9	12.3	119.5	11.6	97.8	1,030

[1] Forecast.   [2] Preliminary.   *Source: Foreign Agricultural Service, U.S.D.A.*   T.54

U.S. Cattle on Feed in 7 States   In Thousands of Head

Year	Jan. 1	Feb. 1	Mar. 1	Apr. 1	May 1	June 1	July 1	Aug. 1	Sept. 1	Oct. 1	Nov. 1	Dec. 1
1983	8,316	8,052	7,604	7,268	7,221	7,331	7,278	6,861	6,704	6,951	7,683	7,814
1984	8,006	7,917	7,515	7,568	7,376	7,318	7,125	6,811	6,747	7,442	8,221	8,544
1985	8,635	8,169	7,877	7,814	7,495	7,444	7,057	6,404	6,155	6,461	7,582	7,892
1986	7,920	7,664	7,322	7,293	7,107	7,096	6,543	6,331	6,404	6,811	7,546	7,826
1987	7,643	7,304	7,163	7,232	7,233	7,560	7,193	6,693	6,818	7,535	8,364	8,412
1988[1]	8,066	7,856	7,572	7,726	7,504	7,814	7,421	6,840	6,674	7,129		

[1] Preliminary.   *Source: Economic Research Service, U.S.D.A.*   T.54a

U.S. Cattle Placed on Feedlots in 7 States   In Thousands of Head

Year	Jan.	Feb.	Mar.	Apr.	May	June	July	Aug.	Sept.	Oct.	Nov.	Dec.	Total
1983	1,509	1,179	1,394	1,566	1,843	1,595	1,174	1,582	2,003	2,358	1,711	1,736	19,744
1984	1,566	1,301	1,764	1,515	1,798	1,445	1,323	1,680	2,265	2,546	1,945	1,624	20,772
1985	1,449	1,342	1,594	1,417	1,666	1,267	1,078	1,510	1,988	2,779	1,776	1,540	19,346
1986	1,581	1,220	1,650	1,565	1,756	1,162	1,544	1,802	2,103	2,403	1,814	1,435	20,035
1987	1,591	1,442	1,719	1,681	1,984	1,422	1,274	1,915	2,429	2,604	1,609	1,305	21,020
1988[1]	1,660	1,369	1,833	1,531	2,170	1,367	1,246	1,618	2,184				

[1] Preliminary.   *Source: Economic Research Service, U.S.D.A.*   T.54b

U.S. Cattle Marketings in 7 States   In Thousands of Head

Year	Jan.	Feb.	Mar.	Apr.	May	June	July	Aug.	Sept.	Oct.	Nov.	Dec.	Total
1982	1,522	1,413	1,547	1,414	1,413	1,510	1,482	1,689	1,575	1,527	1,485	1,430	18,007
1983	1,643	1,506	1,593	1,470	1,583	1,570	1,497	1,651	1,682	1,626	1,459	1,425	18,701
1984	1,569	1,621	1,594	1,523	1,637	1,544	1,553	1,683	1,489	1,657	1,501	1,414	18,785
1985	1,782	1,540	1,559	1,603	1,589	1,572	1,670	1,670	1,603	1,573	1,380	1,401	18,989
1986	1,750	1,470	1,593	1,631	1,635	1,648	1,692	1,659	1,637	1,587	1,447	1,514	19,263
1987	1,803	1,478	1,561	1,541	1,514	1,702	1,703	1,722	1,641	1,690	1,458	1,577	19,390
1988[1]	1,759	1,527	1,573	1,614	1,719	1,692	1,765	1,720	1,662				

[1] Preliminary.   *Source: Economic Research Service, U.S.D.A.*   T.54c

Condition[1] of Pasture and Range Feed in the United States, on First of Month   In Percent of Normal

Year	Apr. 1	May 1	June 1	July 1	Aug. 1	Sept. 1	Oct. 1	Nov. 1	Dec. 1
1983	84	80	85	88	76	63	66	73	N.A.
1984	74	75	79	80	75	70	66	74	N.A.
1985	79	83	81	77	70	75	76	79	N.A.
1986	N.A.	76	80	83	76	79	83	85	N.A.
1987	N.A.	81	84	82	78	76	79	71	N.A.
1988	N.A.	73	68	46	51	54	60	59	N.A.

[1] Indicates current supply of feed for grazing on non-irrigated pastures & ranges relative to that expected from existing stands under very favorable weather conditions. [80 & over, good to excellent; 65–79, poor to fair; 50–64, very poor; 35–49, severe drought; under 35, extreme drought.]
Source: Statistical Reporting Service, U.S.D.A.   T.57A

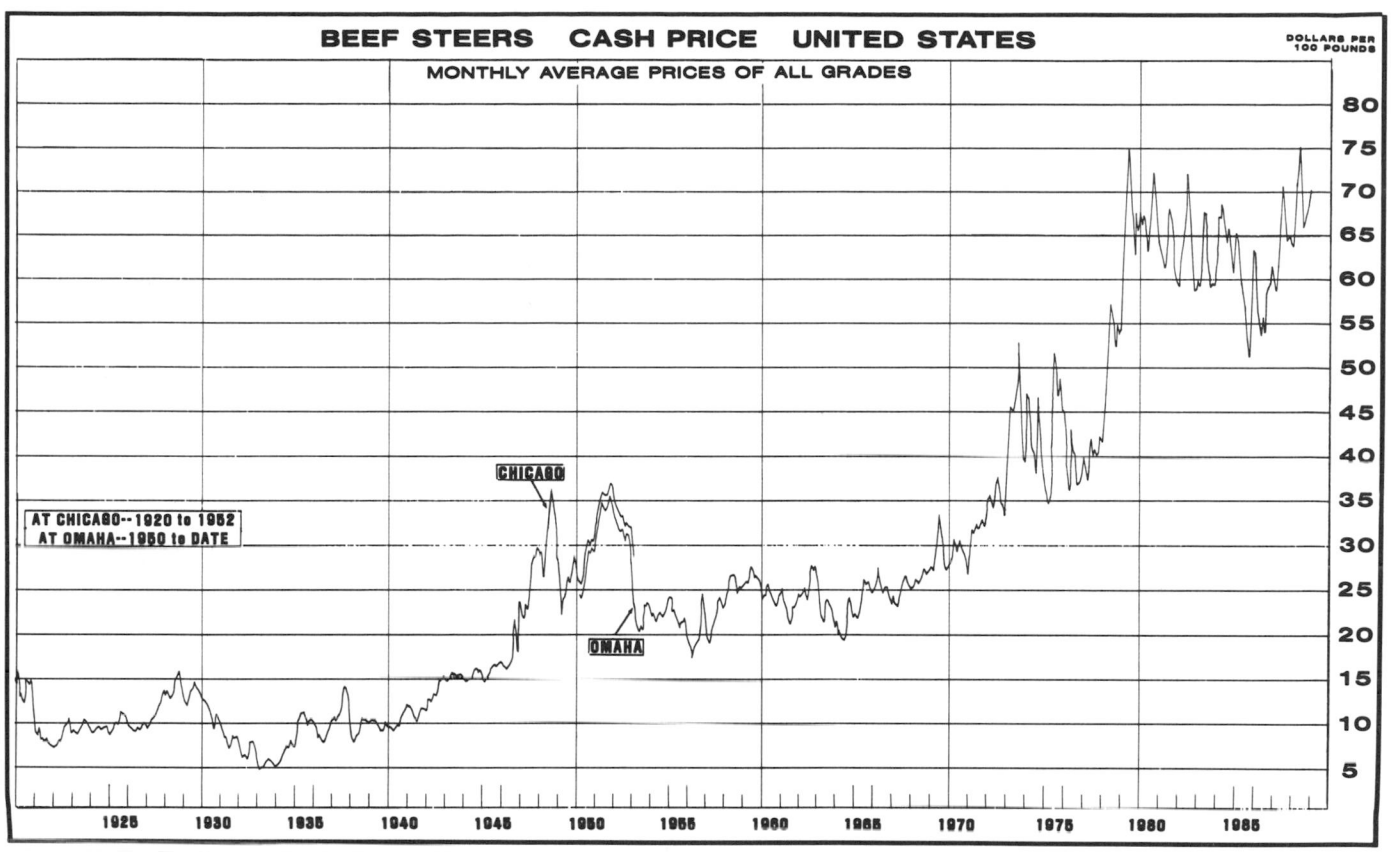

BEEF STEERS   CASH PRICE   UNITED STATES

DOLLARS PER 100 POUNDS

MONTHLY AVERAGE PRICES OF ALL GRADES

AT CHICAGO--1920 to 1952
AT OMAHA--1950 to DATE

CHICAGO

OMAHA

Average Wholesale Prices of Beef Steers at Omaha, Choice (900–1100 Lbs.)   In Dollars Per 100 Pounds

Year	Jan.	Feb.	Mar.	Apr.	May	June	July	Aug.	Sept.	Oct.	Nov.	Dec.	Average
1984	67.08	67.07	68.60	67.86	65.89	64.28	65.79	64.36	62.68	60.85	64.24	65.32	65.33
1985	64.35	62.80	59.58	58.72	57.58	56.69	53.26	51.94	51.29	58.02	63.30	62.94	58.37
1986	59.69	56.42	55.55	53.69	55.79	54.08	58.27	59.04	59.43	59.73	61.54	59.82	57.74
1987	58.79	61.02	61.58	66.30	70.66	68.83	65.80	64.50	64.81	64.81	64.20	63.93	64.60
1988	65.00	68.31	71.53	72.71	75.15	70.58	65.96	67.08	67.71	69.13	70.07		

Source: Economic Research Service, U.S.D.A.   T.65

Average Prices of Steers (Stocker & Feeder) Kansas City   In Dollars Per 100 Pounds

Year	Jan.	Feb.	Mar.	Apr.	May	June	July	Aug.	Sept.	Oct.	Nov.	Dec.	Average
1984	64.39	65.97	66.30	64.15	60.82	59.28	62.17	61.34	62.01	62.74	63.96	64.26	63.11
1985	66.00	67.02	66.66	66.06	64.25	59.11	57.43	57.81	56.27	59.12	60.05	62.04	62.08
1986	61.34	61.68	59.99	56.68	62.21	53.69	57.98	62.20	61.51	61.94	62.77	62.83	60.38
1987	65.75	69.01	68.47	70.56	70.53	70.21	71.22	75.31	77.10	73.21	74.92	73.69	71.32
1988	80.26	81.64	83.12	82.61	78.99	70.77	74.14	79.45	79.89	82.99			

Source: Economic Research Service, U.S.D.A.   T.61

Federally Inspected Slaughter of Cattle in the United States   In Thousands of Head

Year	Jan.	Feb.	Mar.	Apr.	May	June	July	Aug.	Sept.	Oct.	Nov.	Dec.	Total
1984	2,951	2,836	2,954	2,728	3,169	3,062	2,996	3,260	2,903	3,313	2,923	2,784	35,880
1985	3,134	2,661	2,761	2,848	3,052	2,774	3,023	3,089	2,877	3,097	2,669	2,778	34,765
1986	3,204	2,613	2,726	3,096	3,123	3,017	3,213	3,101	3,019	3,164	2,693	2,944	35,913
1987[1]	3,084	2,564	2,805	2,875	2,780	2,945	3,009	2,972	2,977	3,024	2,640	2,793	34,468
1988[1]	2,832	2,679	2,812	2,707	2,830	2,983	2,897	3,120	2,927	2,871			

[1] Preliminary.   *Source: Crop Reporting Board, U.S.D.A.*   T.66

CATTLE AND CALVES

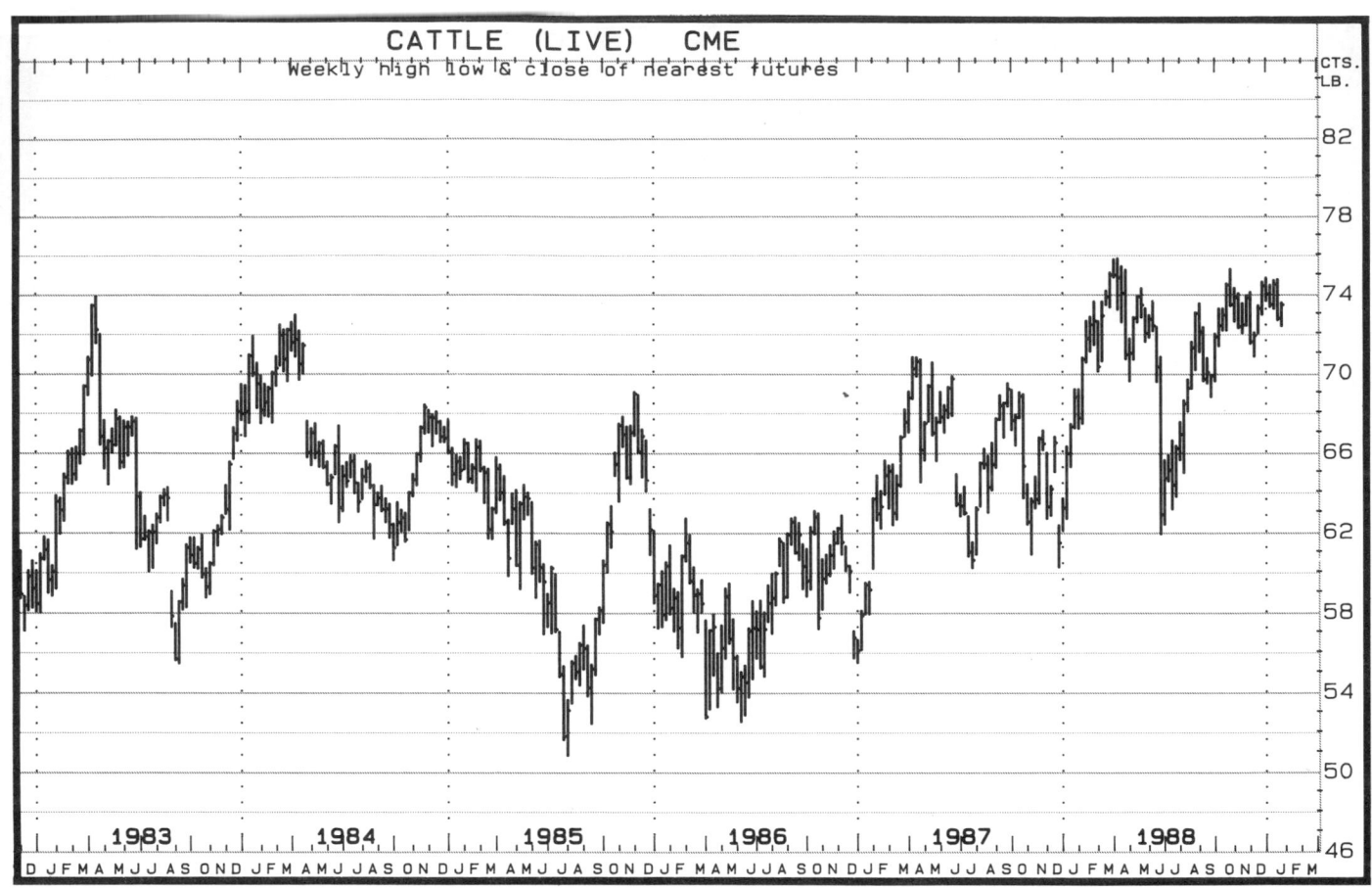

CATTLE (LIVE) CME
Weekly high low & close of nearest futures

High, Low & Closing Prices of June Live Beef Cattle Futures at Chicago In Cents per Pound

Year of Delivery		Apr.	May	June	July	Aug.	Sept.	Oct.	Nov.	Dec.	Jan.	Feb.	Mar.	Apr.	May	June	Life of Delivery Range
					Year Prior to Delivery								**Delivery Year**				
1982	High	72.30	71.90	70.40	67.95	66.97	67.35	66.72	66.05	63.55	61.60	64.75	66.87	70.10	73.65	74.00	74.00
	Low	70.40	68.05	66.85	64.82	64.02	64.42	64.60	61.80	54.75	56.00	60.65	62.72	66.20	69.30	69.57	54.75
	Close	70.40	69.80	67.00	67.02	65.37	65.27	65.20	63.30	55.77	61.40	62.92	66.42	69.57	73.37	70.00	—
1983	High	—	65.50	63.30	64.55	63.72	63.25	62.50	61.80	62.00	63.90	66.47	69.77	71.15	68.05	67.70	71.15
	Low	—	63.90	60.00	60.50	61.77	58.40	58.02	58.52	58.55	60.75	62.90	64.80	65.10	64.30	65.75	58.02
	Close	—	64.10	62.75	62.85	62.30	59.27	59.62	60.80	61.10	62.72	65.27	69.62	66.12	66.05	66.85	—
1984	High	—	—	62.25	64.65	66.55	65.70	65.55	66.30	67.65	68.35	69.35	69.85	69.70	67.35	67.25	69.85
	Low	—	—	61.35	61.10	62.95	63.00	63.20	63.60	65.05	65.45	65.10	67.00	65.62	64.60	63.32	61.10
	Close	—	—	61.80	64.15	63.25	64.90	63.75	65.45	67.05	66.05	69.10	68.70	66.17	64.62	66.05	—
1985	High	—	—	66.55	67.35	67.40	67.70	67.10	68.15	68.10	69.00	69.50	67.75	66.92	64.27	61.47	69.50
	Low	—	—	66.00	65.00	65.00	65.70	65.20	66.30	66.50	66.35	66.55	64.60	62.32	59.05	56.80	56.80
	Close	—	—	66.55	65.00	67.37	66.40	66.75	67.70	67.85	68.35	67.37	67.20	62.65	60.10	56.80	—
1986	High	—	66.60	66.05	64.55	62.75	62.25	63.40	62.45	63.05	63.15	62.50	60.52	57.55	59.35	57.10	66.60
	Low	—	65.60	63.00	58.10	59.10	56.25	60.00	59.90	60.15	58.65	57.40	58.20	53.17	53.40	52.42	52.42
	Close	—	65.90	63.35	60.20	59.60	62.22	61.47	62.42	61.40	61.97	61.37	58.25	57.20	54.07	56.97	—
1987	High	57.50	57.00	57.95	60.00	58.75	59.25	57.45	58.07	57.50	61.17	62.50	64.35	67.25	70.45	69.75	70.45
	Low	53.35	53.70	53.30	55.85	57.00	56.30	55.25	56.50	54.90	55.67	59.45	59.80	62.75	65.47	66.90	53.30
	Close	56.35	54.20	55.60	58.30	58.75	56.82	57.05	57.20	55.55	61.02	62.40	63.42	67.20	67.67	69.62	—
1988	High	63.20	65.00	64.90	64.90	68.40	69.65	68.20	65.32	65.92	68.90	71.25	72.50	72.37	74.22	73.57	74.22
	Low	61.20	62.10	62.30	62.60	63.67	67.22	60.60	60.80	62.00	65.30	66.70	67.37	68.60	70.60	69.47	60.60
	Close	63.20	62.40	64.40	64.45	68.15	67.32	62.52	63.77	65.50	66.85	68.40	70.87	70.90	72.15	70.60	—
1989	High	69.20	70.90	75.05	75.20	74.80	74.60	74.90	74.00	74.92							
	Low	68.60	69.00	69.50	71.85	71.55	72.30	73.25	71.80	71.32							
	Close	69.20	69.80	73.75	73.05	74.10	73.77	73.87	72.20	74.17							

Source: Chicago Mercantile Exchange

T.62

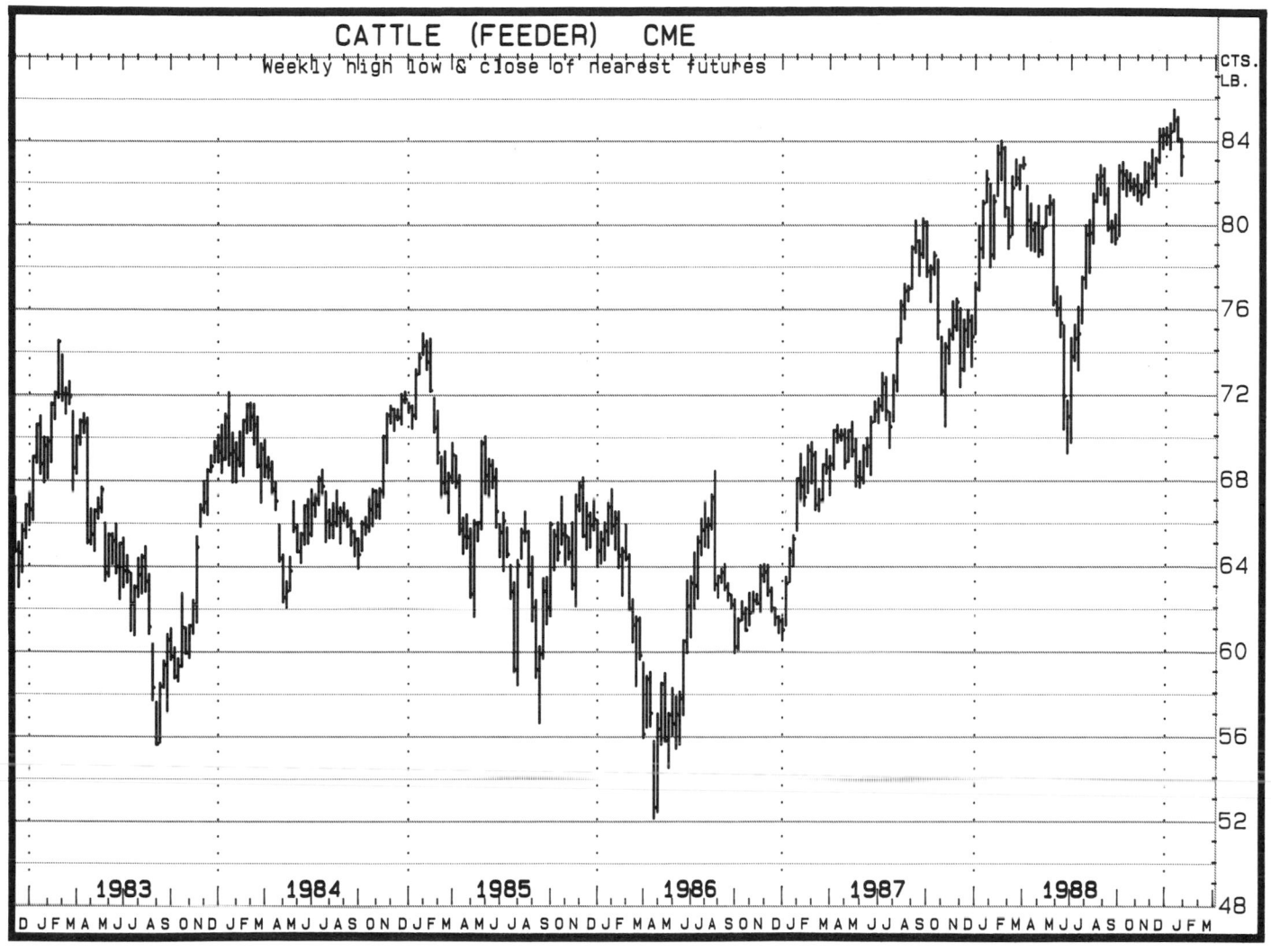

CATTLE (FEEDER) CME
Weekly high low & close of nearest futures

Month-End Open Interest of Live Beef Cattle Futures at Chicago   In Contracts

Year	Jan.	Feb.	Mar.	Apr.	May	June	July	Aug.	Sept.	Oct.	Nov.	Dec.
1983	49,014	56,500	59,992	59,771	58,548	47,307	42,292	49,524	52,174	48,215	49,014	51,629
1984	54,669	57,351	59,793	50,190	44,142	41,790	38,689	37,004	38,416	45,984	64,085	57,242
1985	58,769	57,744	63,236	57,324	56,216	49,594	45,674	48,583	50,888	65,037	68,592	59,361
1986	53,559	55,203	52,551	52,245	55,736	58,420	66,835	64,662	60,580	57,668	64,658	56,421
1987	74,535	91,671	89,788	90,237	94,846	81,881	75,265	85,244	87,859	74,625	75,523	71,804
1988	82,663	101,448	106,864	88,267	90,617	83,150	76,716	84,759	72,772	81,758	79,862	75,383

Source: Chicago Mercantile Exchange

T.64

Volume of Trading of Live Beef Cattle Futures at Chicago   In Thousands of Contracts

Year	Jan.	Feb.	Mar.	Apr.	May	June	July	Aug.	Sept.	Oct.	Nov.	Dec.	Total
1983	370.4	332.7	455.8	489.0	389.1	328.9	302.2	324.9	344.1	335.4	297.9	277.9	4,248.2
1984	457.4	397.6	404.2	323.2	256.4	215.5	265.3	202.6	181.0	245.9	345.7	258.5	3,553.3
1985	340.7	290.3	327.9	304.3	412.0	317.2	440.5	370.2	400.2	445.3	405.0	383.8	4,437.3
1986	492.6	381.0	408.2	462.1	424.2	374.5	448.7	373.0	387.1	376.9	289.4	273.0	4,690.5
1987	376.6	426.7	474.2	456.6	523.7	357.8	394.8	412.7	485.8	580.4	363.1	377.0	5,229.3
1988	425.1	455.6	543.9	468.0	467.8	571.3	463.4	511.8	415.0	417.5	383.9	353.9	5,477.2

Source: Chicago Mercantile Exchange

T.63

CATTLE AND CALVES

Beef Steer-Corn Price Ratio at Omaha[1]

Year	Jan.	Feb.	Mar.	Apr.	May	June	July	Aug.	Sept.	Oct.	Nov.	Dec.	Average
1983	24.5	23.4	22.7	21.9	21.8	21.2	19.6	18.1	17.8	18.4	18.3	19.8	20.6
1984	21.6	22.1	21.1	20.4	19.7	19.1	20.4	20.7	21.3	22.4	24.6	25.6	21.6
1985	24.8	24.1	22.2	21.5	21.5	21.0	20.4	21.7	21.8	25.7	27.8	26.7	23.3
1986	25.6	24.4	24.0	22.9	23.0	22.3	28.9	36.7	42.1	42.7	39.7	38.8	31.0
1987	40.8	43.9	41.9	42.2	40.2	38.9	41.4	43.9	42.1	41.4	38.4	36.7	41.0
1988[1]	36.4	37.4	38.4	39.3	38.6	27.9	24.5	26.2	26.4	26.4			

[1] Bushels of No. 2 yellow corn equal in value to 100 pounds liveweight of choice slaughter steers, 900–1100 lbs.
Source: Economic Research Service, U.S.D.A.

T.56c

U.S. Farm Value, Income & Wholesale Prices of Cattle & Calves

Year	Farm Value of All Cattle—Jan. 1 Per Head $	Total Million $	Gross Income From C. & C.[2] Million $	Prime	Steers[3] Choice	At Omaha Good	Helfers Good	Choice	Feeder Steers All Weights at K.C.	Cows, Utility Omaha	Vealers, Choice So. St. Paul	Cows, Com-mercial Omaha	Beef, Dressed (CarLots) Steer, Choice	Heifer, Choice	Cow[5] Can-ners[6]
									Dollars Per 100 Pounds						
1982	415	47,967	30,390	N.A.	64.22	59.47	59.82	62.79	62.79	39.96	77.70	40.35	101.68	98.54	78.96
1983	406	46,769	29,240	N.A.	62.52	56.99	58.53	61.42	61.39	39.35	72.97	39.40	97.87	94.45	78.48
1984	396	44,976	31,219		65.34	59.14	61.18	64.59	63.11	39.81	63.98	40.75	100.17	96.62	74.70
1985	402	44,139	29,536		58.37	53.28	55.52	58.24	62.08	38.32	58.28	37.91	90.68	88.48	74.13
1986[1]	391	41,280	29,363		57.74	52.04	54.76	57.56	60.38	37.22	59.92	36.96	89.00	87.72	71.31
1987[1]	407	41,492			64.60	58.53	60.11	64.34	71.32	44.83	78.92	44.84	97.20	96.21	83.70

[1] Preliminary. [2] Excludes interfarm sales & Gov't. payments. Cash receipts from farm marketings + value of farm home consumption.
[3] Weighted average prices of beef steers, sold out of first hands for slaughter. [5] All weights. [6] & cutter.
Source: Statistical Reporting Service, U.S.D.A.

T.60

Average Price Received by Farmers for Beef Cattle   In Dollars Per 100 Pounds

Year	Jan.	Feb.	Mar.	Apr.	May	June	July	Aug.	Sept.	Oct.	Nov.	Dec.	Average[1]
1983	54.30	57.10	59.70	61.00	59.90	58.30	55.80	54.20	52.30	51.70	51.20	54.50	55.50
1984	57.20	59.70	61.70	60.10	58.60	57.60	57.60	56.60	55.70	54.10	54.80	57.00	57.30
1985	57.40	58.50	57.30	56.20	55.30	53.60	50.20	49.40	49.10	52.10	54.70	53.70	53.70
1986	53.20	53.00	52.40	50.30	51.00	50.10	52.90	54.40	54.60	54.40	54.60	53.20	52.60
1987	56.40	58.80	59.30	62.60	63.00	62.50	61.10	61.90	63.70	62.90	62.00	62.20	61.10
1988[2]	65.40	67.40	68.30	69.00	69.30	65.00	63.20	65.90	67.20	67.10	67.10		

[1] Weighted average by quantities sold. [2] Preliminary. *Source: Crop Reporting Board, U.S.D.A.*

T.68

Average Price Received by Farmers for Calves   In Dollars Per 100 Pounds

Year	Jan.	Feb.	Mar.	Apr.	May	June	July	Aug.	Sept.	Oct.	Nov.	Dec.	Average[1]
1982	57.00	58.90	61.90	62.10	64.20	61.70	60.40	61.80	59.00	58.30	58.10	58.80	59.80
1983	62.40	66.50	68.40	66.70	66.20	64.30	60.30	57.40	56.10	57.20	59.40	60.60	61.70
1984	61.10	63.90	63.70	62.30	60.80	59.20	59.10	59.10	56.60	58.20	59.40	59.40	59.90
1985	64.10	65.40	65.90	65.40	65.60	62.60	60.00	61.40	58.30	60.20	61.40	58.80	62.10
1986	60.10	62.70	61.90	58.90	58.00	58.10	59.40	61.10	63.40	62.70	62.20	62.20	61.10
1987	66.40	70.60	72.50	75.10	77.40	78.80	80.30	82.30	85.90	81.40	82.90	83.00	78.50
1988[2]	88.20	92.60	93.50	93.20	93.40	84.90	87.70	90.90	89.00	87.80	88.10		

[1] Weighted average by quantities sold. [2] Preliminary. *Source: Crop Reporting Board, U.S.D.A.*

T.69

Federally Inspected Slaughter of Calves & Vealers in the U.S.   In Thousands of Head

Year	Jan.	Feb.	Mar.	Apr.	May	June	July	Aug.	Sept.	Oct.	Nov.	Dec.	Total
1983	221	204	246	202	194	211	214	262	258	259	266	262	2,798
1984	253	236	264	226	233	218	258	294	245	282	275	247	3,030
1985	270	236	261	252	246	221	274	272	271	298	268	298	3,168
1986	289	256	276	284	257	240	281	262	263	276	238	272	3,195
1987[1]	248	225	251	215	189	214	220	202	229	233	211	242	2,679
1988[1]	205	203	216	169	171	204	207	227	207	197			

[1] Preliminary. *Source: Crop Reporting Board, U.S.D.A.*

T.67

Cement

U.S. cement consumption and production slipped in 1988 to 92 million and 78.1 million short tons, respectively, down from 93.9 million and 78.2 million tonnes in 1987. That ended an upturn that began after the recession of 1982. Imports also declined to 17 million tons from a record 17.5 million in 1987, with import reliance as a percent of consumption remaining at an all-time high of 19 percent. In 1982, imports of 3 million tons accounted for only 4 percent of U.S. usage.

The increase in imports was attributed to surplus capacity in the bulk cargo markets that reduced shipment charges, and to the internationalization of the U.S. cement industry. About 60 percent of U.S. clinker capacity was foreign-owned in 1988, and with many plants up for sale, that ratio was expected to increase. Cement capacity in the U.S. declined in the 1980s. In 1987, after two new plants opened, clinker capacity was 87 million tons and finished capacity was 101 million. No new capacity was planned in 1988, and capacity utilization in the East and in southern California was close to 100 percent.

For 1989, the Commerce Department expected cement consumption to drop by 1.8 percent. Domestic shipments were forecast to decline by 2.7 percent. Imports were expected to be about unchanged. However, the need to repair the nation's infrastructure was expected to create record demand in the 1990s.

World Production of Hydraulic Cement by Selected Countries   In Millions of Short Tons

Year	Rep. of Korea	Brazil	Canada	China	France	West Germany	India	Italy	Japan	Poland	Spain	South Africa	Turkey	United Kingdom	United States	USSR	World Total
1983	23.5	23.0	8.7	119.3	27.0	33.6	28.0	43.2	89.2	17.9	33.8	8.7	15.0	14.8	71.3	141.3	1,010.4
1984	22.5	21.8	9.5	133.5	25.0	31.9	32.0	41.6	86.9	18.4	28.0	9.0	17.3	14.9	78.7	143.5	1,037.0
1985	22.5	22.7	11.2	157.1	26.0	28.4	36.4	40.4	80.3	16.5	26.7	7.8	19.4	14.7	78.9	144.1	1,055.7
1986[1]	25.8	27.9	11.1	178.0	25.9	29.2	35.3	39.0	78.5	17.4	26.5	6.9	22.0	14.8	79.9	149.0	1,099.9
1987[2]				180	26	29.5	36	39	79		27				79.0	150	1,110.5

[1] Preliminary.   [2] Estimate.   *Source: Bureau of Mines*   T.70

Salient Statistics of Cement in the United States

Year	Net Import Reliance as a % of Apparent Consumption	Production — Portland (Million Tons)	Production — Others[2] (Million Tons)	Production — Total (Million Tons)	Capacity Used[3] %	Shipments From Mills — Total Mil. Tons	Shipments From Mills — Value[4] $ Mil.	Average Value (F.O.B. Mill) $ per Ton	Stocks at Mills Dec. 31	Imports[5] (Million Tons)	Exports[5] (Million Tons)	Apparent Consumption	Raw Materials — Cement Rock	Raw Materials — Limestone[6]	Raw Materials — Clay & Shale	Raw Materials — Gypsum & Anhy. (Mil. Short Tons)	Total (All)
1983	6	67.5	2.9	70.4	64.6	70.9	3,534	49.95	6.7	4.2	.1	73.4	21.6	73.1	8.7	3.5	113.5
1984	10	74.4	3.3	77.7	71.8	80.2	4,152	51.80	6.9	8.7	.1	84.3	27.0	78.5	9.1	4.0	124.8
1985	16	74.6	3.3	77.9	73.0	83.0	4,286	51.61	7.2	14.1	.1	87.5	24.3	77.6	8.8	4.0	121.4
1986	18	75.2	3.6	78.8	73.7	87.6	4,408	50.32	6.7	16.1	.1	91.5	23.5	79.0	9.0	4.1	122.2
1987[1]	20			78.3		88.0		51.00	6.2	18.0	.1	93.0					

[1] Preliminary.   [2] Masonry, natural & pozzolan (slag-line).   [3] At Portland-cement mills.   [4] Value received f.o.b. mill, excluding cost of containers.   [5] Hydraulic & clinker cement.   [6] Including oyster shells.   *Source: Bureau of Mines*   T.71

Average Price of Bulk Cement In 20 Cities   In Dollars per Short Ton[1]

Year	Jan.	Feb.	Mar.	Apr.	May	June	July	Aug.	Sept.	Oct.	Nov.	Dec.	Average
1985	356.9	359.7	361.1	359.6	365.4	363.8	360.5	360.9	358.5	357.1	355.2	356.8	359.6
1986	360.5	360.7	360.4	360.4	355.0	353.4	351.0	350.1	351.5	351.6	348.8	341.8	353.8
1987[1]	63.28	63.25	63.66	63.50	63.50	64.35	64.25	64.25	63.73	63.73	63.73	63.73	63.75
1988	64.08	64.07	64.44	65.01	65.02	66.39	65.45	65.48	64.42				

[1] Data prior to 1987 are for the price index of Portland cement (1967 = 100).   *Source: Bureau of Labor Statistics (1322-0131.99)*   T.74

Shipments of Finished Portland Cement from Mills in the United States   In Millions of Barrels[3]

Year	Jan.	Feb.	Mar.	Apr.	May	June	July	Aug.	Sept.	Oct.	Nov.	Dec.	Total[1]
1984	20.4	25.6	29.2	34.3	41.5	43.1	42.1	46.9	39.9	43.3	36.5	25.7	435.8
1985	21.8	21.7	31.7	39.4	44.2	42.6	45.9	46.9	43.3	46.0	33.2	26.7	445.1
1986	28.9	23.7	32.3	41.5	43.2	44.8	46.9	46.6	45.9	49.1	35.1	30.7	470.5
1987[2]	25.5	24.9	34.1	41.5	43.2	47.8	49.3	45.6	47.6	50.0	38.3	30.8	480.4
1988[2]	21.0	26.3	36.4	39.9	45.4	50.1	43.8	49.6	47.6	47.3			

[1] Does not necessarily agree with monthly figures. These are compiled from producers' annual reports and are final.   [2] Preliminary   [3] A barrel is approx. 376 pounds.   *Source: Bureau of Mines*   T.73

Cheese

While the Dairy Termination Program is now over, the effect of a reduction in herds will still be felt in seasons to come. According to USDA, during the first three quarters of 1988, milk cow numbers remained 1 percent below 1987 levels. However, the elimination of low-yielding cows and herds meant higher average yields. During the July-September 1988 period, milk output per cow rose 2 percent above a year earlier. Despite the drought and summer's extreme heat, cows did acclimatize and dairymen made needed adjustments. With higher grain prices expected to carry into 1989, milk output per cow was likely to decline.

June-Aug. milk marketings were 1 percent above a year earlier, and the milk equivalent of major manufactured products was up 2.8 percent from a year earlier. Cheese and butter production absorbed most of the increase in supplies. Over the Jan.-Aug. 1988 period, cheese output was 4.32 billion pounds, 2 percent above the same period in 1987. American cheese production was 1.9 billion pounds, almost 2 percent above 1987.

Production of other cheeses was 1.78 billion pounds, 5 percent over 1987. Production of cottage cheese was 639 million pounds, or 2 percent below 1987.

Commercial disappearance of all milk and dairy products fell almost 1 percent in the first 8 months of 1988 on a milk-equivalent milk fat basis. During June-August 1988, commercial disappearance of American cheese was up 7.5 percent, while use of other varieties was off slightly. Commercial use of dairy products by domestic consumers appears to have grown modestly over the rest of 1988. The USDA noted that use of dairy products could nearly match 1987 levels, unless cheese sales increased, due to the end of direct government donations.

Commercial stocks of American cheese on September 1, 1988, were only 286.4 million pounds, 17 percent below the 1987 level and the lowest level on that date since 1958. Low stocks were of concern, since an increase in cheese sales could easily trigger higher prices for cheese and milk. Stocks of other varieties of cheese on September 1 were 109.5 million pounds, 13 percent above the 1987 level. September 1 government stocks of all dairy products were 5.7 billion pounds, almost 9 percent above a year earlier. Stocks of American cheese fell 46 percent to 102.2 million pounds.

During Jan.-Sept. 1988, Commodity Credit Corporation (CCC) removals of American cheese were nearly 230 million pounds, 12 percent above 1987. Small amounts of cheese were expected to be purchased in late 1988. Uncommitted CCC inventories on October 1, 1988 were nearly 44 million pounds, down 55 percent from a year earlier and 92 percent less than October 1, 1986.

With the reduction in stocks, prices of cheese began to rise during August and September. In the July-Sept. period, prices of cheddar cheese at Wisconsin assembly points averaged 126.8 cents per pound, which compares with 125.1 cents in the same period of 1987.

World cheese output in 1988 was projected at 10.3 million tonnes, 2 percent above 1987. The largest cheese producer is the European Community, and its 1988 output was put at 4.3 million tonnes, up 2 percent.

World Cheese (Total[1]) Production   In Millions of Metric Tons

Year	Argentina	Australia	Brazil	Canada	Mexico	Czechoslovakia	Denmark	France	West Germany	Italy	Netherlands	New Zealand	USSR	Sweden	Switzerland	United Kingdom	United States
1981	226	130	217	177	175	113	243	1,168	448	610	465	84	656	103	128	241	1,940
1982	229	153	220	170	230	120	245	1,200	446	645	481	112	699	108	129	244	2,060
1983	245	158	200	183	230	123	249	1,245	446	656	485	114	744	115	135	244	2,186
1984	239	161	200	192	188	130	293	1,287	465	661	515	110	780	116	130	245	2,120
1985	210	160	205	213	187	131	253	1,300	495	684	522	118	809	109	126	260	2,305
1986	256	170	185	226	262	132	252	1,320	530	694	534	127	844	106	131	256	2,363
1987[2]	277	177	195	246	298	132	271	1,342	553	704	552	113	861	107	128	263	2,424
1988[3]	265	176	190	260	335	132	262	1,375	570	700	553	129	865	112	131	308	2,495

[1] Farm & factory production.   [2] Preliminary.   [3] Estimate.   *Source: Foreign Agricultural Service, U.S.D.A.*   T.75

Supply and Distribution of All Cheese in the United States   In Millions of Pounds

Year	Production Whole Milk[2]	Production All Cheese[3]	Supply Jan. 1 Commercial Stocks	Imports[4]	Total Supply	Cheese 40-Lb. Blocks Wisc. Assembly Points ¢ per lb.	Exports & Shipments[5]	Gov't. Jan. 1 Stocks	Gov't. Dec. 31 Stocks	Amer. Cheese Removed by U.S.D.A. Programs	Total Disap.	Military	Civilian	Civilian Per Capita
1981	2,642	4,278	691	248	5,169	139.44	60	169	515	563	4,240	12	4,168	18.15
1982	2,752	4,542	976	269	5,677	138.27	100	515	647	643	4,722	15	4,607	19.88
1983	2,928	4,820	1,064	286	6,171	138.28	87	647	793	833	4,905	18	4,798	20.52
1984	2,648	4,674	1,266	306	6,246	137.96	108	793	621	447.3	5,184	18	5,058	21.42
1985	2,855	5,081	1,062	303	6,441	127.72	125	621	544	629.0	5,501	18	5,358	22.47
1986	2,798	5,209	944	295	6,450	127.30	99	543.7	420	468.4	5,660	18	5,544	23.02
1987[1]	2,717	5,344	789	265	6,398	123.19	89	420.1	81.2	282.0	5,945	—5,856—		24.01
1988[6]	2,810	5,500	453			122.0		81.2	40.0	300.0				

[1] Preliminary.   [2] Whole milk American cheddar.   [3] All types of cheese except cottage, pot and baker's cheese.   [4] Imports for consumption.   [5] Commercial.   [6] Estimate.   *Source: Department of Agriculture*   T.76

Cheese Production in the United States   In Millions of Pounds

Year	American Whole Milk	American Part Skim	American Total	Swiss, Including Block	Mun-ster	Baick	Lim-burger	Neuf-cha-tel	Cream Cheese	Italian Varie-ties	Blue mold	All Other Varie-ties	Total of All Cheese[2]	Cottage Cheese Low-Fat	Cottage Cheese Curd[4]	Cottage Cheese Cream-ed[5]
1979	2,190	4.4	2,194	213.3	63.6	14.4	1.6	5.2	207.1	929.1	34.6	54.1	3,717	150.4	668.5	840
1980	2,376	5.4	2,381	218.9	70.0	15.4	1.6	4.3	224.3	982.7	33.0	52.9	3,984	179.8	667.4	825
1981	2,642	5.9	2,664	214.4	67.4	13.9	1.2	— 241.3 —		994.4	30.2	66.6	4,278	208.3	647.5	773
1982	2,752	6.9	2,759	221.1	71.7	14.3	1.5	— 262.8 —		1,087.8	31.0	92.4	4,542	217.6	628.9	749
1983	2,928	4.1	2,932	209.5	69.6	14.2	1.1	— 270.0 —		1,200.2	31.5	90.6	4,820	215.9	618.2	743
1984	2,649	2.7	2,652	208.0	76.0	16.0	1.2	— 276.5 —		1,318.8	34.1	92.2	4,674	229.3	606.2	736
1985	2,855	2.4	2,857	222.9	82.1	20.1	1.0	— 293.8 —		1,491.3	33.3	77.7	5,081	244.4	598.8	716
1986[1]	2,798	2.1	2,800	227.3	88.5	20.4	1.1	— 321.5 —		1,632.8	34.2	83.2	5,209	265.5	600.1	705
1987[3]	2,717	2	2,719	— 2,625 —									5,344			700
1988[3]	2,748	2	2,750	— 2,800 —									5,550			

[1] Preliminary.   [2] Excludes full-skim cheddar and cottage cheese.   [3] Estimated.   [4] Includes cottage, pot, and baker's cheese with a butterfat content of less than 4%.   [5] Includes cheese with a butterfat content of 4 to 19%.   *Source: Economic Research Service, U.S.D.A.*   T.77

Wholesale Price of Cheese, 40-lb Blocks, Wisconsin Assembly Points   In Cents Per Pound

Year	Jan.	Feb.	Mar.	Apr.	May	June	July	Aug.	Sept.	Oct.	Nov.	Dec.	Average
1979	141.0	135.0	135.6	137.4	137.6	138.9	140.9	145.8	148.8	146.6	144.7	144.4	141.4
1980	146.7	147.2	150.8	153.5	154.2	154.8	155.5	157.0	161.5	165.3	164.1	164.1	156.2
1981	164.0	164.0	166.9	167.0	167.8	167.9	167.8	167.8	167.8	168.5	169.2	168.4	167.2
1982	168.4	168.4	168.4	168.4	168.4	168.4	168.4	168.4	168.3	168.6	168.6	168.6	168.4
1983[1]	139.3	138.4	138.0	137.6	137.4	137.4	137.0	137.1	139.2	140.7	140.7	136.7	138.3
1984	135.8	135.5	135.9	135.9	135.9	136.0	136.7	138.6	144.3	143.8	139.7	137.5	138.0
1985	136.5	134.3	132.1	129.9	128.0	126.8	124.7	124.3	124.3	124.3	123.8	123.9	127.7
1986	123.8	124.5	123.2	125.0	126.0	125.4	126.7	129.5	129.7	130.2	133.4	130.4	127.3
1987	127.8	122.5	122.3	122.4	122.0	122.0	123.2	125.5	126.6	121.9	121.3	120.8	123.2
1988	118.4	110.1	115.0	115.1	115.0	116.2	118.3	127.6	134.6				

[1] Prices prior to Jan. 1983 are for American Cheese, fresh single daises at Chicago.   *Source: Statistical Reporting Service, U.S.D.A.*   T.79

United States Total Cheese Production[1]   In Millions of Pounds

Year	Jan.	Feb.	Mar.	Apr.	May	June	July	Aug.	Sept.	Oct.	Nov.	Dec.	Total
1979	292.5	272.2	323.0	318.8	340.4	343.8	318.8	309.0	290.7	308.0	289.4	308.7	3,717
1980	312.3	303.1	339.7	336.6	360.5	359.9	332.7	317.6	317.0	332.1	317.2	354.4	3,984
1981	342.8	317.8	374.1	379.5	394.2	390.9	353.0	340.6	334.4	343.4	334.1	372.7	4,278
1982	351.3	331.0	391.7	— 1,203 —			— 1,121 —			— 1,143 —			4,542
1983	384.8	359.3	425.3	413.1	439.4	444.7	402.1	381.3	373.0	391.9	389.3	415.4	4,820
1984	382.1	366.0	412.3	409.9	432.9	415.4	379.9	371.3	357.9	381.2	368.9	396.3	4,674
1985	395.0	361.5	416.0	435.3	461.1	447.2	443.8	427.3	403.6	432.9	415.4	441.8	5,081
1986	433.9	400.0	457.1	459.5	482.5	457.4	436.6	421.7	410.1	410.2	401.0	439.4	5,209
1987[2]	413.6	400.9	457.4	462.1	477.8	465.6	453.8	426.0	430.7	448.6	431.8	469.7	5,344
1988[2]	432.8	428.8	483.9	473.1	490.2	474.4	454.2	441.7	448.5				

[1] Excludes cottage and full skim American.   [2] Preliminary.   *Source: Statistical Reporting Service, U.S.D.A.*   T.78

Cold Storage Holdings of All Varieties of Cheese in the U.S., on First of Month   In Millions of Pounds[2]

Year	Jan.	Feb.	Mar.	Apr.	May	June	July	Aug.	Sept.	Oct.	Nov.	Dec.
1979	436.4	436.6	446.2	448.6	462.2	495.3	519.9	555.3	548.5	540.6	526.9	528.2
1980	512.1	515.8	508.9	495.1	510.5	544.4	582.7	620.0	613.8	610.6	590.9	565.4
1981	578.8	601.7	596.3	593.6	632.4	649.8	685.7	714.2	719.4	694.3	682.4	677.5
1982	709.6	711.7	696.4	722.4	—	—	803.9	—	—	864.3	—	—
1983	963.5	1,032	1,088	1,118	1,132	1,138	1,162	1,194	1,231	1,248	1,235	1,215
1984	1,205	1,201	1,220	1,217	1,182	1,208	1,193	1,186	1,148	1,115	1,078	1,044
1985	986.2	968.9	944.4	907.7	898.6	911.0	954.2	963.5	962.9	941.0	891.8	877.5
1986	852.9	835.8	813.2	815.7	838.4	873.3	892.8	915.6	916.2	859.0	805.0	757.0
1987[1]	693.6	680.8	652.4	646.5	645.1	666.8	659.0	642.5	606.6	580.8	538.0	495.9
1988[1]	457.1	452.8	445.9	443.1	453.3	460.1	481.8	492.1	458.0	411.0	392.8	

[1] Preliminary.   [2] Quantities are given in "net weight."   *Source: Crop Reporting Board, U.S.D.A.*   T.80

Chromite

Riding the stainless steel stampede, chromite, in the form of chromium ferroalloys, was one of 1988's hottest metals markets. The almost total U.S. dependence on imported supplies of chromite and ferrocarbon steels and the primacy of South Africa in refining and metals production made chromium a focus of legislative interest to spur domestic production.

In the U.S., Chrome Corp. developed chromium resources in Montana's Stillwater complex using a new kiln roast pre-reduction refining process developed by West Germany's Krupp Industrie. Construction was planned for a ferrochromite plant at Columbus, Montana, with an annual rated capacity of 60,000 tonnes a year. Completion was expected by 1991, and an additional 60,000 tonnes of capacity was planned after completion of the first section.

For the first six months of 1988, chromite consumption in the U.S. increased by 8 percent over the same 1987 period. According to the U.S. Bureau of Mines, total 1987 chromite consumption was 504,272 tonnes. For the first six months of 1988, chromite consumption was estimated at 253,089 tonnes.

U.S. consumption of ferrochromium in the first six months of 1988 totaled 184,164 tonnes, for an implied annual rate of 368,328 tonnes, a potential 3 percent decline from 1987's 380,396 tonnes.

In the first six months of 1988, imports of fer-rochromium for consumption were 214,179 tonnes; this was greater than the 184,167 tonnes consumed in that period and indicates that stock building was taking place. The U.S. receives about 45 percent of its high carbon ferrochromium imports from South Africa. In the first six months of 1988, that country supplied 95,129 tonnes of ferrochromium, valued at $48.9 million dollars. Zimbabwe was second with 31,991 tonnes of ferrochromium, valued at $26.6 million.

The 1989 outlook for high carbon ferrochromium was very promising. Good demand for stainless steel, as well as for carbon steels, prevented ferrochromium producers from catching up with backlogged orders. At least 600,000 tonnes of added capacity were on the drawing boards for completion by 1990's end. This would boost 1988's worldwide production of ferrochromium, amounting to 3 million tonnes, by 20 percent. The new production capacity was expected to lead to the closure of smaller, less efficient production facilities. The long-term outlook for demand appeared to be very strong.

Worldwide resources of chromium ore amount to about 36 billion short tons of shipping grade chromite, with about 99 percent located in southern Africa. The rest of the world's resources are measured in millions of tons.

World Mine Production of Chromite In Thousands of Short Tons (Gross Weight)

Year	Albania	Brazil	Cuba	Finland	Greece	India	Japan	Pakistan	Philippines	Zimbabwe	Turkey	South Africa	Iran	USSR	Madagascar	World Total[1]
1979	827	375	31	480	50	342	13	3	613	597	410	3,634	150	2,535	141	10,277
1980	840	345	31	399	46	352	15	3	547	610	411	3,763	90	3,200	198	10,915
1981	783	261	23	454	27	369	12	2	484	591	442	3,164	35	3,200	110	10,018
1982	744	304	30	380	32	401	12	4	355	476	499	2,680	45	3,240	49	9,348
1983	755	171	37	271	30	397	9	7	294	463	381	2,762	55	3,240	50	9,063
1984	794	282	41	492	68	466	8	3	288	525	537	3,756	55	3,240	66	10,756
1985[2]	909	303	40	500	65	617	13	6	300	591	660	4,077	55	3,240	140	11,630
1986[1]	940	315	51	500	68	680	12	5	202	600	660	3,840	55	3,250	110	11,394
1987[1]		300		500		700			300			3,700				

[1] Estimate. [2] Preliminary. *Source: Bureau of Mines*   T.81

U.S. Salient Statistics of Chromite In Thousands of Short Tons

Year	% Net Import Reliance of Apparent Consumption	Shipments from Gov't Stockpiles	Exports	Imports (For Consumption)	Re-exports	Consumption by Primary Consumer Groups (Gross Weight) Total	Metallurgical	Refractory	Chemical	Consumer Stocks, Dec. 31 Metallurgical	Refractory	Chemical	Total Stocks	$ Per Metric Ton South Africa[2]	Turkish[4]
1979	90	—	27	1,024	28	1,214	774	198	242	416	161	330	907	56	110
1980	91	—	6	982	44	977	577	160	240	219	135	322	675	55	110
1981	90	—	71	898	67	889	503	148	238	230	128	370	728	55	110
1982	85	—	8	507	57	558	283	80	195	120	113	313	546	52	110
1983	76		11	190	5	320	64	72	184	140	76	239	456	52	110
1984	80		55	305	4	512	226	97	189	24	70	233	327	52	110
1985	75		101	414	4	560	273	65	222	44	49	207	300	42	125
1986[1]	79		92	488	1	427	377	50	[5]	275	39	[5]	314	42	125
1987[3]	75		10	400	1	400					21		334	46	100

[1] Preliminary. [2] Cr_2O_3, 44% (Transvaal). [3] Estimate. [4] 48% Cr_2O_3. [5] Included in metalurgical. *Source: Bureau of Mines*   T.82

Coal

U.S. coal production was estimated at a record 940.9 million short tons for 1988 and was expected to reach 945.6 million in 1989, according to the Department of Energy. The 1988 drought, which reduced hydroelectric power supplies during the summer's severe heat wave, contributed to a 4.5 percent increase in coal use at electric utilities to a record 750 million tons. But a return to more normal weather and a recovery in hydroelectric production was expected to put 1989's increase in utilities' coal usage at 1.3 percent.

DOE placed 1988 U.S. coal exports at 86 million tons, falling to 82 million in 1989. The National Coal Association projected 1988 exports at 89 million tons, thanks to a strong world steel industry. Metallurgical coal, used to make coke for steel production, accounted for about two-thirds of U.S. exports. U.S. export sales were also helped by labor problems in Australia and Poland. U.S. coal consumption at coke plants was estimated at 39 million tons.

U.S. coal stocks in consumers' hands totaled 185.5 million tons on December 31, 1987, reflecting inventory building ahead of mineworkers' contract talks. But the UMW signed a five-year contract without a strike, and stockpiles were projected to drop to 149.8 million tons by the end of 1989. That would be the lowest level since 1978. Total 1988 U.S. coal consumption was estimated at 871.6 million tons, up 4 percent from 1987. A one percent increase was expected for 1989.

World Production of All Coal[3]   In Millions of Metric Tons

Year	Australia	East Germany	Canada	Czecho-slovakia	Tur-key	West Germany	Greece	India	Spain	China	Poland	South Africa	United Kingdom	United States	U.S.S.R.	Yugo-slavia
1984	277	296	115	259	30	191	32	152	40	736	242	163	51	808	668	65
1985	171	312	122	253	39	201	36	157	40	813	249	173	89	802	680	68
1986[2]	339	311	114	253	46	209	38	174	39	828	259	175	108	806	705	69
1987[1]		309	122	253	44	212	42	185	35	935	266	175	104	830	878	60

[1] Estimate. [2] Preliminary. [3] Includes anthracite, subanthracite, bituminous, subbituminous, lignite & brown coal.   *Source: United Nations.*   T.83

Bituminous Coal Production[1] in the United States   In Millions of Short Tons

Year	Jan.	Feb.	Mar.	Apr.	May	June	July	Aug.	Sept.	Oct.	Nov.	Dec.	Total
1984	67.6	73.4	81.2	72.5	80.7	76.1	74.4	90.4	78.5	69.4	64.0	63.5	891.8
1985	67.9	66.9	77.3	76.2	78.0	72.7	68.8	79.2	73.6	79.7	68.9	69.6	878.9
1986	78.3	72.7	77.6	74.9	73.1	72.7	67.8	76.5	75.0	76.8	68.7	70.3	886.0
1987[2]	74.3	71.3	75.4	70.5	70.3	76.6	69.2	80.1	81.9	85.6	78.9	79.2	915.2
1988[2]	75.3	76.8	83.9	75.3	74.0	76.4	69.2	88.2	83.2	84.0	86.1	83.1	955.4

[1] Includes small amount of lignite.   [2] Preliminary.   *Source: Bureau of Mines*   T.88

U.S. Stocks of Bituminous Coal for All Industrial & Retail Dealers, at End of Month   In Million Short Tons

Year	Jan.	Feb.	Mar.	Apr.	May	June	July	Aug.	Sept.	Oct.	Nov.	Dec.
1984	156.4	163.0	167.7	175.3	184.7	187.4	186.0	193.5	201.3	200.4	195.3	190.4
1985	176.8	170.3	172.6	178.0	180.6	180.9	172.1	168.9	168.9	172.8	170.4	163.0
1986	158.1	156.5	159.2	166.3	170.2	168.8	155.6	155.0	157.7	163.1	167.0	168.1
1987[1]	162.7	163.3	166.0	169.5	170.8	168.9	156.1	152.3	158.5	167.8	175.6	178.5
1988[1]	169.5	165.5	166.8	170.6	171.3	166.5						

[1] Preliminary.   *Source: Bureau of Mines*   T.87

Average U.S. Price of Coal   In Dollars per Short Ton

Year	Electric Utilities	End-Use Sector Coke Plants	Other Industrial[2]	Ex[3] ports	Im[3] ports	Year	Electric Utilities	End-Use Sector Coke Plants	Other Industrial[2]	Ex[3] ports	Im[3] ports
1981	32.32	62.86	39.46	52.57	28.47	1985	34.53	54.30	37.21	48.18	36.04
1982	34.91	64.97	41.01	56.37	30.40	1986	33.30	50.83	35.84	45.95	36.02
1983	34.99	59.30	39.32	52.16	33.59	1987	31.83	46.55	33.71	42.77	32.04
1984	35.12	56.58	39.29	50.72	35.37	1988					

[1] Based on the cost including insurance & freight (C.I.F. cost).   [2] Manufacturing plants only.   [3] Based on the free alongside ship (F.A.S.) value.
Source: Energy Information Administration   T.90

COAL

Salient Statistics of the Bituminous Coal Industry in the United States

Year	Production — Under-ground (Millions Net Tons)	Production — Sur-face	Production — Total Pro-duction	Value — Total Million $	Value — Avg. Per Ton $	Num-ber of Mines	Thous. of Men Em-ployed	Avg. Tons Per Miner Per Hour — Under-ground	Avg. Tons Per Miner Per Hour — Sur-face	Avg. Tons Per Miner Per Hour — Total	Im-ports	Exports to: Grand Total (Thousands of Short Tons)	Canada	Europe	Asia
1982	338.6	495.0	833.5	22,621	27.14	5,363	214.4	1.37	3.48	2.14	742	105,244	18,205	51,211	29,957
1983	299.9	478.1	778.0	20,111	25.85	4,265	173.5	1.62	3.87	2.52	1,271	76,870	16,809	32,979	21,895
1984	351.5	540.3	891.8	22,750	25.51	4,902	175.7	1.72	4.10	2.65	1,286	80,793	20,140	32,766	21,306
1985	350.1	528.9	878.9	22,060	25.10	4,547	167.0	1.79	4.32	2.76	1,952	91,361	16,112	44,677	21,803
1986[1]	359.8	526.2	886.0	20,998	23.70	4,203	152.7	2.00	4.69	3.04	2,212	84,017	14,031	42,488	18,765
1987[2]	372.2	543.0	915.2								1,747	77,645	16,000	40,000	22,000

[1] Preliminary. [2] Estimate. *Source: Energy Information Administration*   T.84

United States Production of Coal by Principal States In Millions of Short Tons

Year	Anthra-cite Pennsyl-vania	Bituminous — Alabama	Colo-rado	Illinois	Indiana	Ken-tucky	Mon-tana	Ohio	Pennsyl-vania	Vir-ginia	West Vir-ginia	Texas	Wyo-ming	Total Bitu-minous	Total U.S.
1982	4.6	26.6	18.3	60.3	31.8	150.2	27.9	36.5	74.8	39.8	128.5	34.8	108.4	833.5	838.1
1983	4.1	23.8	16.7	56.8	31.8	131.2	28.9	33.8	65.7	35.0	115.0	38.9	112.2	778.0	782.1
1984	4.2	27.1	18.0	63.8	37.6	159.5	33.0	39.3	73.3	40.4	131.0	41.1	130.9	891.8	895.9
1985	4.7	27.8	17.2	59.2	33.3	152.3	33.3	35.6	66.7	40.9	127.8	45.5	140.7	878.9	883.6
1986	4.3	25.8	15.2	61.9	32.9	153.9	34.0	36.4	67.4	41.2	129.9	48.6	136.8	886.0	890.3
1987[2]	3.6	25.5	14.4	59.2	34.2	165.2	34.4	35.8	66.9	44.5	136.7	50.5	146.9	915.2	918.8
1988[1]	3.5	26.2	15.0	59.6	31.9	162.1	38.4	32.5	73.9	48.3	143.7	53.8	161.8	955.4	958.9

[1] Estimate. [2] Preliminary. *Source: Bureau of Mines*   T.85

U.S. Consumption & Stocks of Bituminous Coal & Lignite In Millions of Short Tons

Year	Stocks—Dec. 31 — Electric Power Utilities	Oven Coke Plants	Steel & Rolling Mills / Other Indus-trials	Producers & Distrib.	Total	Consumption — Electric Power Utilities	Coke Plants — Beehive / Ovens	Steel & Rolling Mills / Other Indus-trials	Retail De-liveries[2]	Total
1982	175.1	4.6	—— 9.4 ——	36.1	225.2	592.6	—— 40.9 ——	—— 63.5 ——	6.6	703.6
1983	149.1	4.3	—— 8.6 ——	33.4	195.4	624.2	—— 37.0 ——	—— 65.6 ——	7.1	733.9
1984	173.0	6.2	—— 11.2 ——	33.5	223.9	663.3	—— 44.0 ——	—— 73.2 ——	7.7	788.2
1985	149.2	3.4	—— 10.4 ——	32.7	195.7	692.8	—— 41.0 ——	—— 74.8 ——	6.5	815.1
1986	154.7	3.0	—— 13.4 ——	31.6	199.7	684.2	—— 36.0 ——	—— 111.1 ——	6.4	801.8
1987[3]	163.9	3.9	—— 14.6 ——	27.8	206.3	716.9	—— 36.9 ——	—— 111.7 ——	5.7	834.3

[1] Preliminary. [2] To other consumers. (Residential & Commercial) [3] Estimate. *Source: Energy Information Administration*   T.86

Statistical Trends in the Pennsylvania Anthracite Industry

Year	Production (Millions of Net Tons) — Total	Sur-face	Under-ground	Value of Produc-tion Million $	Avg. Value Per Net Ton	Stocks (Dec. 31) — Electric Utilities	Prod. & Distrib.	Exports to: — Total (1,000 Short Tons)	Canada	France	Nether-lands	South Korea	Apparent Con-sump-tion	Avg. No. of Men Working Daily (1,000)	Num-ber of Mines	Avg. Tons Per Miner Per Hr.
1981	5.4	4.8	.6	239.1	44.28	5,537	370	2,249	361	77	22		4,084	3.1	232	.92
1982	4.6	4.0	.6	229.3	49.85	6,080	672	980	316	57	—	550	3,349	2.7	220	.59
1983	4.1	3.6	.5	214.4	52.29	6,507	498	776	296	58	30	357	2,823	2.1	224	1.01
1984	4.2	3.6	.6	202.5	48.22	6,710	565	680	301	—	52	292	3,088	2.1	149	1.02
1985	4.7	4.0	.7	215.3	45.80	7,189	416	1,286	277	19	32	535	2,917	2.3	217	1.05
1986[1]	4.3	3.7	.6	189.7	44.12	7,099	512	1,460	437	—	8	868	2,533	2.0	221	1.03
1987[2]	3.6	2.9	.6			6,940	537	1,181	470			400	2,604			

[1] Preliminary. [2] Estimate. *Source: Energy Information Administration*   T.91

Pennsylvania Anthracite Coal Production[1] In Thousands of Short Tons

Year	Jan.	Feb.	Mar.	Apr.	May	June	July	Aug.	Sept.	Oct.	Nov.	Dec.	Total
1984	299	262	292	240	397	308	405	458	445	367	349	340	4,162
1985	340	336	397	300	403	506	407	409	381	447	386	396	4,708
1986	261	243	260	300	294	297	298	330	333	431	373	340	4,292
1987[2]	256	264	305	339	333	359	426	358	359	362	323	303	3,560
1988[2]	215	268	279	265	296	282	246	360	315	384	307	258	3,475

[1] Represents production in Pennsylvania only. Production outside which is small, is included in Bituminous Production series.
[2] Preliminary. *Source: Bureau of Mines*   T.92

Cobalt

Cobalt is a strategic material, and the U.S. relies completely on imported supplies. This is not an entirely comfortable position, given the fact that fully 40 percent of global production is from sources considered politically unreliable. Consequently, a small flurry of government-supported cobalt processing research papers was released by the U.S. Bureau of Mines over 1988, and there was some movement to reopen domestic cobalt mines.

Most of the world's cobalt is recovered as a by-product of either copper or nickel mining (only Morocco mines cobalt as a primary ore). However, the rejuvenated U.S. recovery program is also considering lead ores as a commercial source of cobalt. The last U.S. cobalt mine was closed in 1971, and the last refinery was shut down in 1985. According to the U.S. Bureau of Mines, new mine and refinery production is expected to come on stream within two years.

While new leaching processes have made cobalt mining economically possible, political uncertainties surrounding areas where cobalt is most plentiful have contributed to a steady tone in prices. In recent years, cobalt production has been a casualty of Angola's civil war, as well as other regional fighting. The main transport for cobalt and copper exports by Zaire and Zambia had been the Benguela Railroad. The Benguela (a vestige of a European colony, the Belgian Congo) is 90 percent owned by one of 1988's more newsworthy takeover candidates, Societe Generale de Belgique. The railroad remained closed throughout the year, because of the Angolan civil war.

According to reports in 1988, the countries of southern Africa affirmed plans to redevelop the railway through the implementation of a ten-year plan. The three-phase plan hopes to open the railway to limited international traffic by late 1989.

In 1988, the price of cobalt ranged from a low of $6.75/lb. to a high of $7.25; the lows were reached in March-April, and prices rose slightly thereafter.

In 1987, total U.S. cobalt consumption was 15.09 million pounds, with metal accounting for 9.21 million, scrap for 2.4 million, and chemical compounds exclusive of oxides for 2.16 million. For the first three months of 1988, cobalt consumption was 4.39 million pounds, and metal accounted for a little more than half, or 2.3 million.

World cobalt resources are pegged at about 12 million tons. The vast majority of these resources are located in nickel-bearing laterite deposits, and most of the rest are in nickel-copper sulfide deposits, and in sedimentary copper deposits in Zaire and Zambia.

Other than nickel, there are few adequate substitutes for cobalt.

World Mine Production of Cobalt   In Short Tons of Recovered Cobalt Content

Year	Australia	Zaire	USSR	France	Canada	Cuba	Philippines	Finland	W. Germany	Japan[3]	Norway[3]	Morocco	Zambia	New Caledonia	World Total
1980	2,177	17,000	2,300	745	1,767	1,778	1,467	1,141	330	3,160	1,405	924	4,850	395	34,538
1981	1,616	17,000	2,400	493	2,293	1,890	1,099	1,140	160	2,669	1,592	870	4,410	407	33,895
1982	1,631	12,450	2,550	626	1,548	1,653	514	1,141	165	2,141	1,092	873	3,584	299	27,081
1983	1,270	12,450	2,650	144	1,746	1,787	182	1,141	0	1,511	969	—	3,526	440	26,149
1984	1,190	19,850	2,850	128	2,563	1,540	71	1,047	0	998	1,313	—	5,093	550	35,880
1985	915	22,050	3,000	120	2,278	1,565	1,004	1,050	0	1,407	1,804	—	6,393	745	40,115
1986[2]	970	22,050	3,100	110	2,745	1,550	100	1,050	—	1,475	1,740	—	6,350	770	39,850
1987[1]	500	20,000	3,000		3,000	1,500		1,000					4,000	750	34,900

[1] Estimate.   [2] Preliminary.   *Source: Bureau of Mines*   T.93

U.S. Salient Statistics of Cobalt   In Thousands of Pounds of Contained Cobalt

Year	Net Import Reliance as a % of Apparent Consumption	Cobalt Pdt's Production	Consumer Stocks Dec. 31	Imports for Consumption	Consumption By End Uses											Price $ Per Pound[3]
					Steel Full Alloy	Stainless & Heat Resisting	Catalysts[4]	Super Alloys	Tool Steel	Magnetic Alloys	Nonferrous Alloys	Drier in Paints, etc.[5]	Cutting & Wear-Resistant Mater.	Welding & Hard Facing Rods	Total	
1980	93	3,274	2,540	16,302	116	47	1,656	6,285	321	2,267	150	1,331	1,344	620	15,321	25
1981	92	3,302	1,411	15,594	141	35	1,279	4,195	170	1,687	131	1,378	1,076	488	11,680	14.58
1982	92	2,863	1,327	12,870	114	51	789	3,319	161	1,544	175	1,114	638	446	9,468	8.56
1983	95	3,232	1,441	17,221	82	54	1,064	4,034	248	1,711	169	1,503	666	472	11,319	5.76
1984	95	3,499	1,368	25,310	31	74	1,296	4,766	353	2,209	176	1,258	831	399	12,994	10.40
1985	94	2,876	1,131	17,708	N.A.	61	1,253	6,380	203	1,455	N.A.	1,139	1,017	N.A.	13,541	11.43
1986[1]	85	2,420	1,479	12,288	N.A.	76	1,445	6,446	256	1,791	N.A.	1,593	726	N.A.	14,442	7.49
1987[2]	86		1,028	16,000				6,000		1,500		1,700	750		16,000	6.50
1988[2]			1,000	17,000				5,800		1,800		1,850	800		17,000	

[1] Preliminary.   [2] Estimate.   [3] Annual spot for cathodes.   *Source: Bureau of Mines*   T.94

Cocoa

All the world loves chocolate, but not enough, it seems, to eat through the large crops that are being produced by the developing countries that rely heavily on strong cocoa prices to contribute to their foreign exchange earnings.

World production for the 1987/88 (Oct.-Sept.) cocoa crop year was forecast by the USDA at a record 2.12 million tonnes, 7 percent greater than 1986/87's out-turn of 1.97 million tonnes.

In an effort to staunch the flow of cocoa at cheap prices, the Ivory Coast, the world's largest producer with estimated output of between 650,000 and 700,000 tonnes, made a decision in January 1988 to try and prop the market. The country's Caisse de Stabilisation, which regulates the sale of primary products such as coffee and cocoa, refused to authorize cocoa sales at below the equivalent of FF 1,250 per 100 kilos, CIF, a level which was way above the terminal market at the time it was initiated.

As a result, the entire Ivory Coast cocoa system from the farmer to the cocoa processor became involved in an intricate cat and mouse game. With the default of a large international dealer on some tonnages of Ivorian cocoa that had been sold short into the market, there was a frenzy in the cash market, which saw Ivorian differentials go to large premiums over the London terminal.

By late in 1988, it had become apparent that a bold move was going to have to be made to resolve the supply impasse. A major French shipper, Sucres et Denrees S.A., widely believed to have the unofficial backing of the French government, stepped to center stage, and entered into an arrangement with the Ivory Coast to purchase and provide out-of-country storage for a large quantity of new-crop cocoa. The total amount, estimated at 400,000 tonnes, is a significant quantity of cocoa; and therefore the French merchant house was seen as a de facto buffer stock manager.

The cocoa futures market at first responded to rumors of the deal by rallying sharply, as manufacturers bought in differential contracts to lock in low prices, and speculators came in to cover shorts. However, as the cocoa deal was confirmed, and more details released, the market's second and more sober judgement was that the arrangement carried downside price risk, and futures sold off in late 1988.

Brazil is the world's second largest producer, and its 1987/88 crop was forecast at 402,000 tonnes of cocoa, a 13 percent gain over 1986/87's 355,000 tonnes. Malaysia was fast becoming a force to be reckoned with in the world cocoa market. A strong effort to improve the quality of Malaysian cocoa, as well as a government commitment to increase cocoa plantings, has catapulted Malaysia into the front ranks of cocoa producers. Malaysia's 1987/88 crop was estimated at 220,000 tonnes, a 31 percent gain over 1986/87's 167,000 tonnes.

World cocoa bean grindings in 1987/88 were estimated by the USDA to be an all-time high of 1.97 million tonnes. While this was the fourth straight year in which production exceeded consumption, consumption increases have been a regular feature of the world cocoa market.

Cocoa production for 1988/89 was forecast at 2.269 million tonnes, another record. According to one crop forecaster, were it not for some deterioration in growing conditions in much of West Africa and Brazil's Bahia area, the estimate would have been significantly larger.

In recent years, origin grindings have played an important and expanding role in the global cocoa economy. First concieved of as a way of capturing some of the value added on semi-finished cocoa products, they have also served to increase domestic consumption of finished cocoa products and have accounted for part of the recent growth in world demand.

Switzerland continued to have the world's highest per capita rate of cocoa consumption, according to the USDA. On a bean-equivalent basis, the Swiss averaged 4.1 kilograms per capita during the first six years of this decade, followed by Austria and West Germany. The U.S. averaged only about 1.8 kilograms and the Soviets only about 0.7 kilograms. Although the U.S. is not the leading consumer on a per capita basis, it is the largest net importer, accounting for more than 25 percent of world cocoa imports.

Futures Markets

Cocoa futures are actively traded on the Coffee, Sugar, and Cocoa Exchange in New York and on the London Terminal Market.

World Cocoa Supply and Demand   In Thousands of Metric Tons

Crop Year[1]	Stocks Oct. 1	Net World Crop[2]	Total Availability	Seasonal Grindings	Closing Stocks	Stock Change	Crop Year[1]	Stocks Oct. 1	Net World Crop[2]	Total Availability	Seasonal Grindings	Closing Stocks	Stock Change
1978–9	388	1,477	1,865	1,457	408	+ 20	1984–5	342	1,926	2,267	1,836	431	+ 90
1979–0	408	1,610	2,018	1,489	529	+121	1985–6	431	1,944	2,376	1,851	525	+ 93
1980–1	529	1,643	2,172	1,598	574	+ 45	1986–7	525	1,957	2,482	1,902	580	+ 55
1981–2	574	1,717	2,291	1,593	698	+124	1987–8[3]	580	2,142	2,722	1,995	727	+147
1982–3	698	1,508	2,206	1,627	579	− 119	1988–9[4]	727	2,261	2,988	2,080	908	+181
1983–4	579	1,498	2,077	1,735	342	− 237							

[1] Crop year season is Oct.–Sept.   [2] The Net World Crop is obtained by adjusting the Gross World Crop for one percent loss in weight.   [3] Preliminary.   [4] Forecast.   *Source: Gill and Duffus, Ltd.*

T.95

World Production of Cocoa Beans in Principal Producing Countries In Thousands of Metric Tons

Crop Year (Oct.–Sept.)	Brazil	Camer-oon	Co-lombia	Domin-ican Rep.	Ecua-dor	Equator-ial Guinea[1]	Ghana	Indon-esia	Ivory Coast	Mal-aysia	Mex-ico	Papua New Guinea	Nigeria	Sierra Leone	Togo	Vene-zuela	World Total
1980–1	351	120	36	33	85	8	258	13	417	49	30	27	160	10	16	14	1,694
1981–2	315	120	39	43	88	8	225	17	465	61	41	29	183	9	11	15	1,737
1982–3	339	106	40	43	55	9	179	20	360	68	34	29	160	10	10	15	1,545
1983–4	309	109	41	42	55	9	159	23	411	90	35	28	125	9	21	12	1,545
1984–5	415	120	42	39	128	9	175	32	565	100	42	31	170	11	7	11	1,967
1985–6	380	119	46	39	112	9	219	34	555	130	39	33	130	9	14	11	1,947
1986–7	365	123	52	45	77	8	228	39	611	167	38	34	100	8	12	14	1,993
1987–8[3]	400	129	54	49	71	8	180	45	690	220	50	35	145	9	12	14	2,143
1988–89[2]	400	125	55	50	80	8	225	50	700	245	50	35	160	9	12	16	2,292
1989–90																	

[1] Includes Fernando Po & Rio Muni. [2] Forecast. [3] Preliminary. *Sources: Foreign Agricultural Service; U.S.D.A.* T.96

World Absorption (Consumption) of Cocoa[2] In Thousands of Metric Tons

Year	Japan	Aus-tralia	Bel-gium	Brazil	Canada	China	Colom-bia	France	W. Ger-many	Neth-erlands	Spain	Italy	Switz-erland	USSR	United King.	United States	World Total
1980	25	11	23	200	12	15	31	48	158	133	35	34	17	130	65	142	1,510
1981	29	12	29	195	17	15	35	52	167	141	37	35	18	120	85	190	1,599
1982	32	9	29	170	16	15	38	52	175	148	37	39	18	130	88	199	1,608
1983	34	8	33	198	16	10	39	53	180	157	38	36	18	145	77	194	1,652
1984	34	6	36	214	22	12	33	52	194	161	35	40	19	150	90	209	1,750
1985	34	2	36	247	21	8	39	42	207	167	39	47	20	155	91	205	1,850
1986	36	1	35	236	20	25	41	39	201	183	39	40	20	163	87	200	1,873
1987[1]	36	1	35	227	19	14	45	38	209	196	40	44	19	153	95	236	1,905
1988[3]	37	1	37	231	20	20	53	38	228	219	45	44	22	131	100	246	1,997
1989																	

[1] Preliminary. [2] Figures represent the "absorption," "disappearance" or "grindings" of cocoa beans in each country—in other words, net imports of cocoa beans adjusted for changes in stock. [3] Estimate. *Source: Gill & Duffus, Ltd.* T.98

Raw Cocoa Grindings in Selected Countries In Thousands of Metric Tons

Year	Total	1st Quarter	2nd Quarter	3rd Quarter	4th Quarter	Total	1st Quarter	2nd Quarter	3rd Quarter	4th Quarter	Total	1st Quarter	2nd Quarter	3rd Quarter	4th Quarter
			France					Germany (West)					Holland		
1980	43.1	12.5	10.9	9.1	10.7	151.2	40.2	35.4	32.9	42.6	132.6	35.1	31.4	29.5	36.7
1981	47.0	12.6	12.0	9.6	12.9	159.4	41.7	37.6	35.4	44.7	141.0	36.0	34.3	32.7	38.0
1982	45.5	13.1	12.3	9.7	10.4	167.0	45.1	39.9	35.8	46.3	148.4	38.4	34.9	33.7	41.3
1983	47.8	12.2	12.9	10.9	11.7	170.5	45.7	41.0	43.0	49.8	156.9	40.5	37.9	35.2	43.4
1984	47.2	14.0	12.5	11.1	9.7	193.5	49.9	48.6	42.4	52.6	161.4	44.4	40.0	35.0	42.1
1985	42.5	12.4	10.6	8.3	11.2	206.8	57.0	51.7	44.0	54.0	167.4	44.6	41.7	37.0	44.1
1986	39.4	10.9	10.6	8.2	9.7	201.0	53.6	50.6	42.6	54.2	182.6	46.2	45.1	40.3	51.0
1987	37.8	9.9	9.0	9.2	9.7	208.7	55.2	49.2	46.4	57.8	195.6	49.1	47.3	42.8	56.3
1988[1]		10.0	8.6				60.0	54.0	53.0			56.1	51.7	50.5	
1989															
			Italy					United Kingdom					United States		
1980	33.8	8.0	8.4	8.1	9.3	65.3	15.5	16.1	15.5	18.2	142.2	33.5	31.5	34.9	42.4
1981	35.1	8.6	8.1	5.8	12.6	85.3	21.7	21.3	19.2	23.1	190.2	48.4	46.0	48.8	47.1
1982	39.2	9.6	10.1	6.0	13.6	88.1	25.3	21.1	19.6	22.1	199.1	47.7	50.6	50.1	50.7
1983	36.4	8.4	7.9	8.1	12.0	76.7	19.8	18.1	17.4	21.3	193.6	45.9	46.7	47.8	53.2
1984	39.8	8.0	5.6	9.8	16.5	89.6	22.3	21.9	21.1	24.2	164.4	42.4	41.6	40.9	39.5
1985	47.4	11.1	10.5	8.8	17.0	91.3	26.5	24.5	20.0	20.3	153.8	39.0	37.5	40.5	36.8
1986	39.8	10.9	9.1	7.8	12.0	87.2	21.1	22.0	20.1	24.0	153.6	33.8	37.0	42.3	40.6
1987	44.2	11.3	9.9	9.9	13.2	95.1	24.5	22.9	22.4	25.3	181.3	39.7	46.5	49.9	45.4
1988[1]							26.3	25.0	22.4			45.0	47.7	49.0	

[1] Preliminary. *Source: Gill and Duffus, Ltd.* T.97

COCOA

Imports of Cocoa Butter—Selected Countries In Metric Tons

Year	South Africa	Australia	Austria	Belgium	Canada	Finland	France	West Germany	Italy	Japan	Netherlands	Norway	Sweden	Switzerland	UK	USA	USSR	Yugoslavia
1980	1,007	4,532	2,485	12,388	3,717	2,057	14,285	22,790	1,211	6,264	16,445	1,855	4,155	9,117	29,597	34,658	—	1,054
1981	1,444	4,410	3,461	11,960	4,505	2,228	14,170	29,358	1,667	10,352	11,021	1,875	4,234	10,208	19,549	43,196	—	1,965
1982	1,464	5,419	3,382	12,281	4,860	2,333	14,008	30,564	1,631	10,615	16,225	2,083	4,451	9,982	25,820	37,325	—	1,009
1983	1,270	6,067	3,535	12,128	5,313	2,428	16,690	30,581	2,151	9,947	20,224	1,892	4,704	10,224	31,581	47,981		653
1984	1,699	6,445	3,763	13,451	5,437	2,156	17,325	35,241	2,337	8,436	25,072	2,139	5,103	9,798	30,203	51,711	4,200	248
1985	1,792	8,538	3,682	15,416	5,535	2,039	19,908	33,378	3,056	8,632	24,595	1,957	4,929	11,175	31,372	70,146	7,150	1,130
1986	N.A.	8,204	4,387	13,793	5,377	1,966	19,397	25,513	3,246	8,474	14,925	2,295	4,866	11,369	32,669	70,264	3,450	N.A.
1987[1]		8,370	3,897	14,312	5,833	1,971	23,704	27,436	3,509	9,330	16,152	2,734	5,272	11,932	29,689	79,773	1,000	
1988[2]		8,800	3,750	14,400	6,100	1,950	24,000	28,000	3,500	9,700	16,400	2,800	5,500	12,200	30,000	80,500		

[1] Preliminary. [2] Estimate. *Source: Gill & Duffus Group PLC*   T.97a

Imports of Cocoa Liquor and Cocoa Powder (Selected Countries) In Metric Tons

	Cocoa Liquor							Cocoa Powder								
Year	France	West Germany	Netherlands	Japan	UK	USA	USSR	Belgium	France	West Germany	Italy	Japan	Netherlands	Sweden	UK	USA
1979	15,872	795	4,136	2,129	4,784	47,828	5,000	3,642	4,368	10,846	5,266	2,215	2,970	2,656	1,747	64,080
1980	15,688	1,922	7,634	2,927	1,928	43,796	5,200	3,335	5,905	10,693	6,142	2,656	3,018	3,457	1,885	65,606
1981	15,457	2,151	9,262	3,499	1,914	33,109	16,000	3,503	7,963	12,935	6,478	2,616	3,255	3,551	2,393	77,879
1982	13,871	2,196	13,519	3,684	2,283	31,419	8,700	3,770	7,609	13,524	6,673	2,832	2,974	3,872	3,284	60,563
1983	15,164	2,288	14,216	4,303	3,829	45,477	15,425	3,895	8,527	13,886	7,964	3,157	3,009	3,806	3,014	78,968
1984	20,268	3,075	13,622	2,928	2,184	45,547	32,000	4,204	9,652	13,554	7,462	3,260	3,574	3,996	3,654	89,978
1985	24,031	3,570	14,822	2,792	3,400	53,042	37,510	4,586	8,269	16,624	8,313	3,841	4,669	3,928	2,591	81,775
1986	28,426	2,006	10,915	3,346	4,091	50,705	30,110	4,844	8,984	15,654	9,059	4,844	4,669	3,980	3,258	89,454
1987[1]	31,171	391	8,805	3,402	1,870	38,105	21,680	5,229	8,967	16,989	9,330	5,517	3,624	3,982	3,987	103,455
1988[2]	31,500		8,650	3,600	2,000	38,000		5,000	9,000	17,000		5,800	3,500	4,000	3,900	100,000

[1] Preliminary. [2] Estimate. *Source: Gill & Duffus Group PLC*   T.97b

United States Imports of Cocoa (Includes Shells) In Thousands of Long Tons

Year	Jan.	Feb.	Mar.	Apr.	May	June	July	Aug.	Sept.	Oct.	Nov.	Dec.	Total
1979	27.3	26.7	14.6	12.8	8.8	13.7	11.8	15.7	5.7	10.1	10.0	8.0	165.2
1980	11.1	9.2	8.0	19.5	15.4	12.0	16.9	9.6	8.2	9.6	9.4	19.9	148.5
1981	13.5	27.8	19.2	30.4	27.1	24.1	19.3	22.0	20.3	24.1	5.8	11.5	245.0
1982	10.0	29.0	17.6	15.3	16.8	11.9	13.0	20.3	14.3	14.4	14.4	17.4	194.2
1983	46.0	42.7	19.0	36.4	14.4	11.1	9.6	7.2	6.1	5.3	7.7	8.2	213.7
1984	15.5	21.3	28.7	16.9	24.7	15.3	13.3	10.8	10.4	5.0	10.8	18.2	190.9
1985	42.2	43.7	39.1	9.9	30.5	15.6	13.9	12.5	10.9	10.2	12.6	25.0	266.1
1986	29.4	17.1	15.1	9.3	19.0	16.1	21.2	22.5	11.8	7.8	14.9	17.2	201.5
1987[1]	26.1	28.0	22.8	30.5	20.6	10.2	10.6	14.0	5.6	22.1	23.9	43.9	258.5
1988[1]	27.0	30.0	26.7	18.3	14.7	21.0	14.4						

[1] Preliminary. *Source: Department of Commerce*   T.102

Bahia (Brazil) Crops In Thousands of Bags of 60 Kilos

Year	Total Crop Brazilian Crop Year	Temporao Brazilian Crop Year	To Early Nov. (Arrivals)	Main Crop (Oct.–Apr.)	Temporao International Crop Year	Total Crop International Crop Year
1979–80	5,387	3,129		2,257	2,383	4,640
1980–81	5,041	2,383		2,658	2,892	5,550
1981–82	4,609	2,892		1,718	3,170	4,888
1982–83	5,284	3,170		2,114	3,084	5,198
1983–84	5,876	3,084		2,792	1,786	4,578
1984–85	5,030	1,786	604	3,244	3,126	6,370
1985–86	6,027	3,126	583	2,901	2,774	5,674
1986–7	6,623	2,774	792	3,849	1,546	5,395
1987–8[1]	4,993	1,546	866	3,448	2,485	5,933
1988–9[1]			378			

[1] Preliminary. *Source: Gill & Duffus Group PLC*   T.102a

New York Cocoa Bean Futures[1] Prices In Cents Per Pound

Year	Jan.	Feb.	Mar.	Apr.	May	June	July	Aug.	Sept.	Oct.	Nov.	Dec.	Average
1979	193.0	177.0	176.0	157.5	165.0	172.0	158.0	157.0	166.0	159.0	154.5	155.0	160.4
1980	163.8	173.5	157.0	147.0	135.0	125.3	134.5	120.0	122.0	119.0	120.0	108.0	135.4
1981[2]	92.1	88.8	92.5	91.6	82.6	69.6	88.0	96.5	100.6	94.8	88.3	91.7	89.8
1982	95.6	89.6	83.8	75.2	73.3	66.2	66.1	66.0	71.6	70.8	64.8	69.6	74.4
1983	77.6	83.9	80.1	81.4	89.8	99.8	99.6	99.7	93.0	91.3	97.1	112.0	92.1
1984	115.2	110.8	113.0	112.8	118.8	108.2	97.1	98.6	104.3	99.8	100.6	95.5	106.2
1985	98.3	100.0	98.9	101.6	96.1	91.5	95.7	98.2	101.3	102.5	97.9	102.0	98.7
1986	100.6	95.5	91.0	84.9	81.4	81.4	87.6	89.1	95.6	90.6	87.4	85.6	89.2
1987	86.1	84.8	87.2	89.9	89.8	87.0	92.9	88.7	87.1	83.9	84.2	82.1	87.0
1988	86.3	77.9	72.6	71.2	74.3	70.9	71.2	63.1	54.0				

[1] Avg. of the daily closing price of the nearest 3 active futures trading month converted to ¢ per lb.   [2] Prices prior to 1981 are for spot cocoa bean (ACCRA) in N.Y.   *Source: Bureau of Labor Statistics (0191-0221); N.Y. Cocoa Exchange.*   T.105

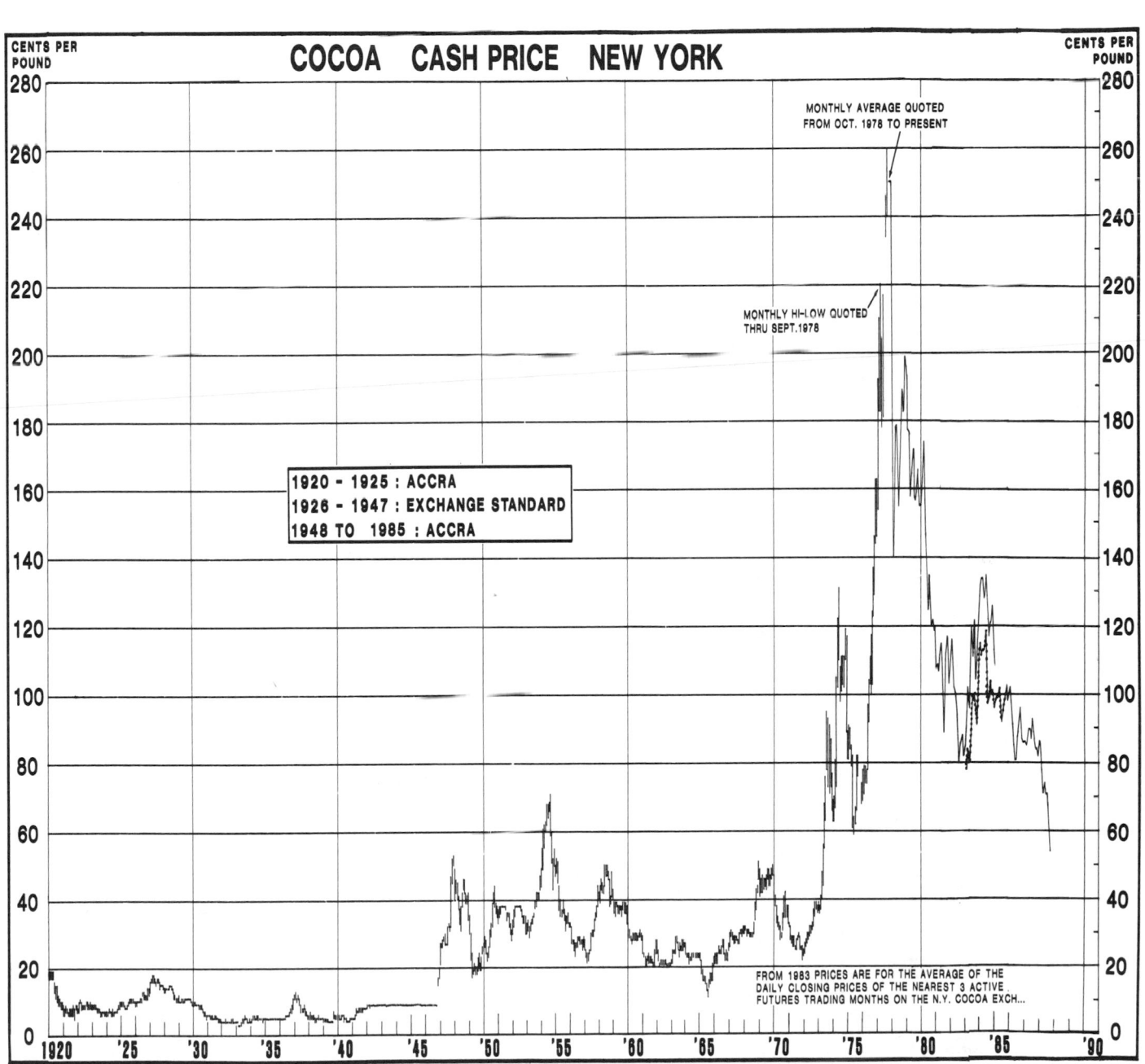

COCOA   CASH PRICE   NEW YORK

MONTHLY AVERAGE QUOTED
FROM OCT. 1978 TO PRESENT

MONTHLY HI-LOW QUOTED
THRU SEPT. 1978

1920 - 1925 : ACCRA
1926 - 1947 : EXCHANGE STANDARD
1948 TO 1985 : ACCRA

FROM 1983 PRICES ARE FOR THE AVERAGE OF THE
DAILY CLOSING PRICES OF THE NEAREST 3 ACTIVE
FUTURES TRADING MONTHS ON THE N.Y. COCOA EXCH...

COCOA

Visible Stock of Cocoa in Philadelphia (Delaware River) Warehouses, at End of Month   In Ths. of Bags

Year	Jan.	Feb.	Mar.	Apr.	May	June	July	Aug.	Sept.	Oct.	Nov.	Dec.
1982	190.1	163.4	174.1	163.2	154.0	125.7	104.6	64.2	51.8	64.3	69.3	98.5
1983	123.6	192.4	281.5	356.5	344.7	338.9	297.7	258.5	204.5	119.8	69.2	43.0
1984	59.5	69.9	105.4	98.8	148.3	168.0	158.3	187.6	165.3	99.7	83.6	217.1
1985	221.3	282.0	333.6	420.9	416.4	389.1	315.9	323.9	320.7	316.3	289.1	280.6
1986	281.3	276.4	258.8	255.8	237.9	201.3	208.7	182.0	209.5	137.1	136.7	188.5
1987	209.8	210.8	228.9	224.1	243.6	276.2	291.4	259.7	236.6	177.9	189.6	206.3
1988	164.6	149.2	154.9	211.1	227.3	232.0	238.1	193.3	185.5	157.6	123.4	112.0

Source: Coffee, Sugar & Cocoa Exchange, Inc.   T.107

Visible Stock of Cocoa in New York Warehouses[1], at End of Month   In Thousands of Bags

Year	Jan.	Feb.	Mar.	Apr.	May	June	July	Aug.	Sept.	Oct.	Nov.	Dec.
1982	33.4	61.3	66.7	57.3	99.0	98.6	115.8	137.7	108.8	97.1	96.1	68.9
1983	64.7	80.1	80.0	88.9	136.4	184.8	178.7	173.5	138.6	109.5	103.0	93.9
1984	59.3	53.2	52.3	52.5	70.7	57.2	93.8	99.9	109.2	62.8	36.3	32.4
1985	34.7	22.0	13.2	36.4	167.8	170.9	161.3	155.7	164.6	150.6	131.8	107.1
1986	99.2	96.9	95.6	89.7	87.4	90.3	88.9	103.6	102.1	87.5	70.6	59.9
1987	51.9	43.5	40.0	39.4	55.2	46.1	58.7	43.5	49.4	44.8	107.7	149.1
1988	138.7	115.4	100.1	96.8	102.8	135.4	140.8	146.8	114.3	105.8	73.7	59.8

[1] In licensed & unlicensed warehouses of storage companies licensed by the Coffee, Sugar & Cocoa Exch.   *Source: Coffee, Sugar & Cocoa Exch., Inc.*   T.106

U.S. Spot Cocoa Prices for Selected Origins of Cocoa Beans and Products   (Dollars per metric ton)

Crop Year (Oct.–Sep.)	Cocoa Beans				Chocolate Liquor		Cocoa Butter		Cocoa Cake 10–12% Fat
	Ivory Coast	Brazil	Dominican Republic	Ecuador	Ecuador	Brazil	African	Other	
1982/83	2,031	1,999	1,815	1,886	2,310	2,440	4,294	4,191	872
1983/84	2,569	2,611	2,361	2,477	3,025	3,119	5,281	5,178	1,610
1984/85	2,433	2,407	2,197	2,239	2,784	2,919	5,331	5,276	951
1985/86	2,281	2,207	2,020	2,048	2,552	2,720	4,940	4,897	825
1986/87	2,155	2,087	1,942	1,975	2,554	2,634	4,643	4,608	965
1987/88	1,952	1,807	1,664	1,700	2,216	2,280	4,001	3,919	916
July '88	1,928	1,778	1,606	1,646	2,150	2,244	3,886	3,789	883
Aug. '88	1,869	1,639	1,434	1,483	1,914	1,998	3,482	3,391	825
Sept. '88	1,861	1,497	1,237	1,309	1,669	1,745	3,066	2,965	752

Source: The Cocoa Merchants Association. All prices are nominal net ex-dock or ex-warehouse, U.S. Eastern seaboard North of Hatteras, for merchandise physically available in interstate commerce, in truckload quantities, regular commercial quality. *Foreign Agricultural Service, U.S.D.A.*   T.99a

Month–End Open Interest of Cocoa Futures at New York   In Contracts

Year	Jan.	Feb.	Mar.	Apr.	May	June	July	Aug.	Sept.	Oct.	Nov.	Dec.
1982	14,554	14,421	15,129	14,036	15,563	14,083	15,954	14,678	16,439	18,615	17,600	19,988
1983	25,989	22,401	22,155	24,796	29,457	29,403	28,447	29,275	28,282	27,890	29,266	29,153
1984	29,712	26,116	26,511	22,277	26,795	23,817	23,691	23,397	22,106	22,505	21,253	20,936
1985	25,616	23,817	27,701	23,588	21,103	21,515	20,487	19,106	20,720	20,224	17,981	16,044
1986	19,259	19,521	21,341	19,654	24,246	23,100	26,017	25,781	25,636	25,189	22,577	26,109
1987	24,868	23,444	23,199	23,313	25,155	25,156	33,285	30,588	32,109	32,042	27,643	26,978
1988	28,603	29,088	33,806	33,799	35,027	38,464	38,593	38,283	38,057	38,336	37,039	36,762

Source: Coffee, Sugar & Cocoa Exchange, Inc.   T.103

Volume of Trading of Cocoa Futures at New York   In Contracts

Year	Jan.	Feb.	Mar.	Apr.	May	June	July	Aug.	Sept.	Oct.	Nov.	Dec.	Total
1982	42,498	44,744	52,468	52,591	38,332	50,693	45,504	45,457	61,137	67,652	48,243	56,744	607,964
1983	88,429	96,636	82,115	91,851	83,275	135,536	102,212	112,031	103,023	70,032	97,781	98,619	1,162,540
1984	151,282	113,788	102,622	103,415	113,757	107,219	75,180	101,732	75,294	69,322	74,357	33,927	1,127,752
1985	86,748	83,988	94,863	72,564	64,716	62,989	74,583	57,842	52,912	58,358	53,056	37,954	800,573
1986	52,774	61,836	70,859	74,249	57,525	77,335	79,029	65,963	75,673	64,729	54,090	43,703	777,765
1987	67,268	61,641	73,341	67,954	68,521	93,849	111,728	66,990	71,591	70,164	81,605	60,813	895,465
1988	84,590	83,826	92,644	85,144	111,277	121,184	128,859	106,031	87,684	137,635	142,016	87,160	1,268,050

Source: Coffee, Sugar & Cocoa Exchange, Inc.   T.104

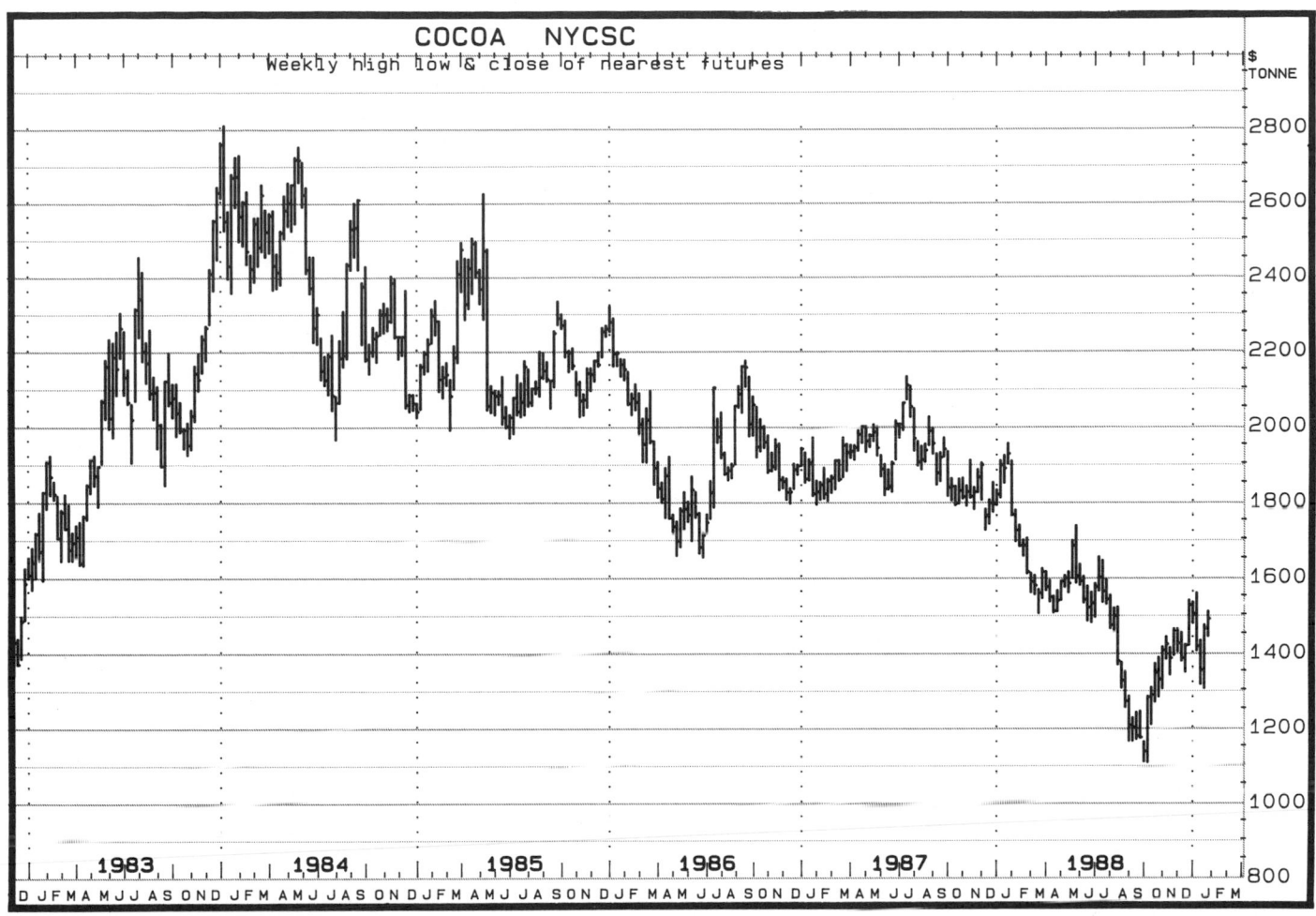

COCOA NYCSC
Weekly high low & close of nearest futures

High, Low & Closing Prices of March Cocoa Futures at New York   In Dollars per Tonne

Year of Delivery		Year Prior to Delivery										Delivery Year			Life of Delivery Range
	Feb.	Mar.	Apr.	May	June	July	Aug.	Sept.	Oct.	Nov.	Dec.	Jan.	Feb.	Mar.	
1983 High	2145	2105	1875	1835	1663	1640	1604	1696	1669	1495	1650	1840	1919	1816	2295
Low	2071	1840	1738	1657	1508	1485	1451	1534	1435	1383	1447	1565	1640	1688	1383
Close	2071	1854	1802	1660	1605	1518	1527	1604	1467	1465	1603	1826	1704	1691	—
1984 High	2015	1958	1990	2325	2390	2460	2440	2195	2124	2272	2759	2805	2626	2645	2805
Low	1785	1790	1780	1895	2070	2055	2080	1907	1953	1967	2175	2353	2355	2425	1653
Close	1838	1835	1990	2168	2224	2369	2113	2089	1989	2224	2755	2521	2462	2617	—
1985 High	2455	2510	2500	2560	2430	2234	2305	2350	2248	2291	2133	2309	2332	2210	2602
Low	2240	2350	2343	2401	2230	1998	1990	2150	2118	2056	2034	2018	2071	1985	1985
Close	2363	2489	2435	2401	2280	2000	2275	2199	2224	2117	2052	2271	2140	2139	—
1986 High	2135	2190	2170	2105	2048	2207	2295	2392	2365	2239	2305	2315	2140	2059	2392
Low	2000	1955	2025	1980	1967	1991	2125	2170	2173	2117	2180	2118	1975	1899	1899
Close	2028	2150	2027	2041	2013	2153	2262	2336	2191	2214	2298	2146	2000	2011	—
1987 High	2283	2200	2106	1960	2007	2098	2176	2248	2076	2003	1937	1965	1884	1915	2412
Low	2148	2015	1931	1884	1825	1895	1970	2011	1920	1876	1837	1787	1797	1827	1787
Close	2165	2039	1952	1906	1904	2034	2176	2034	1927	1886	1935	1820	1857	1906	—
1988 High	2030	2043	2115	2118	2055	2180	2031	1994	1895	1930	1908	1950	1773	1600	2180
Low	1957	1980	2025	1971	1913	1986	1922	1825	1816	1794	1727	1758	1580	1500	1500
Close	2000	2033	2066	1985	2034	2021	2005	1844	1850	1866	1814	1760	1584	1502	—
1989 High	1902	1774	1712	1799	1699	1638	1520	1268	1340	1517	1536				
Low	1750	1670	1625	1653	1540	1495	1251	1125	1125	1307	1371				
Close	1750	1682	1705	1695	1601	1495	1254	1146	1297	1476	1500				

Source: N.Y. Coffee, Sugar & Cocoa Exchange, Inc.   T.108

Coconut Oil and Copra

Copra, dried coconut meat, is processed or crushed into coconut oil and copra meal. The USDA projected world 1988/89 copra output at 4.73 million tonnes, nearly 8 percent more than in 1987/88. The Philippines, the largest producer, was expected to harvest about 2 million tonnes, up over 14 percent from the previous season. A drought that began in late 1986 and ran into 1988 reduced the previous crop. Typhoons in late 1988 may have cut final output in 1988/89. Indonesia, on the other hand, has been a steady producer, with an estimated 1988/89 crop of 1.27 million tonnes, almost 2 percent more than in 1987/88. The Philippines and Indonesia accounted for some 70 percent of total world copra output and were the leading processors. Other important producers were India, with 330,000 tonnes in 1988/89, and Sri Lanka, where output also was recovering from drought.

World 1988/89 copra exports were projected at 340,000 tonnes, up 17 percent from the previous season. The Philippines was expected to ship 130,000 tonnes, well above 1987/88's drought-reduced total of 100,000 tonnes. Papua New Guinea and the New Hebrides and Solomon Islands in the South Pacific were large exporters, primarily for processing in the European Community, Japan, and South Korea.

Due to the larger Philippine crop, the world 1988/89 copra crush was estimated at 4.54 million tonnes, about 4 percent more than in 1987/88. Global ending copra stocks were projected to increase to 11,000 tonnes from 5,000 in 1987/88.

World 1988/89 coconut oil production was forecast at 2.81 million tonnes, up more than 4 percent from a year earlier. The Philippines was expected to produce almost 1.15 million tonnes, up 7 percent from the previous season. Indonesian output was estimated at 720,000 tonnes. World coconut oil exports were forecast at 1.27 million tonnes, about 2 percent more than a year earlier. The Philippines remained the leading exporter, with expected shipments of 850,000 tonnes, above 840,000 the previous season.

World 1988/89 coconut oil consumption was estimated at 2.91 million tonnes, up 5 percent from 1987/88. The major users were Indonesia, the European Community, and the U.S. Coconut oil consumption had been fairly steady over the previous five years, while use of competing oils like palm and rapeseed had risen significantly. Price increases for coconut oil have been lower than those for substitutes. In the U.S., where most coconut oil is used in inedible products like soap, imports were increasing after a period of decline. World ending stocks of coconut oil were estimated at 33,000 tonnes, down from 36,000 a year earlier.

World copra meal production was put at 1.62 million tonnes, up 5 percent from 1987/88. The larger Philippine crop was expected to result in nearly 640,000 tonnes of meal, up 7 percent from 1987/88. World exports were forecast at 1.08 million tonnes, up 7 percent. The Philippines and Indonesia had more than 90 percent of the market. Ending stocks were forecast at 47,000 tonnes, up substantially from 20,000 a year earlier.

World Copra Production by Principal Countries   In Thousands of Metric Tons

Crop Year	Naupu	Fiji	India	Indonesia	Jamaica	Malaysia	Mexico	Mozambique	Papua-New Guinea	Philippines	Solomon Isl.	Sri Lanka	Tanzania	Thailand	Ivory Coast	New Hebrides	Vietnam	World Total
1979–0	46	25	329	1,158	29	210	120	68	145	1,960	32	93	29	50	21	34	39	4,553
1980–1	42	25	329	1,284	25	208	130	55	158	2,256	32	128	29	30	24	47	39	4,986
1981–2	42	25	335	1,205	28	206	100	50	132	2,077	33	174	29	35	26	44	40	4,790
1982–3	42	25	268	1,091	29	208	110	50	120	2,015	31	131	29	30	27	45	40	4,600
1983–4	42	25	300	1,225	30	214	100	55	158	1,237	43	62	29	35	36	47	60	3,781
1984–5	42		360	1,260		199	100	55	176	1,813	45	240		93	60	39	65	4,714
1985–6[1]			380	1,250		190	100	55	160	2,500	31	242		65	53	41	70	5,348
1986–7[2]			320	1,270		175	115	65	149	2,100	28	125		74	48	36	70	4,796
1987–8[2]			300	1,250		166	110	65	150	1,750	35	100		74	46	40	70	4,389
1988–9[2]			330	1,270		155	110	65	150	2,000	35	140		74	45	40	80	4,728

[1] Preliminary.   [2] Forecast.   *Source: Foreign Agricultural Service, U.S.D.A.*   T.109

World Coconut Oil Supply and Distribution   In Thousands of Metric Tons

Crop Year	Production					Exports	Imports	Consumption						Ending Stocks		
	Malaysia	India	Indonesia	Philippines	Total	Exports	Imports	EC-12	India	Indonesia	Philippines	United States	Total	Philippines	United States	Total
1983/4	125	189	672	786	2,273	1,053	908	374	199	577	223	415	2,424	104	50	253
1984/5	125	226	708	919	2,628	1,103	1,179	410	226	574	253	386	2,578	115	59	227
1985/6	104	236	720	1,587	3,324	1,512	1,608	571	236	710	286	461	3,056	178	140	399
1986/7	99	198	731	1,320	2,988	1,354	1,477	558	198	610	265	488	2,879	179	123	385
1987/8[1]	99	186	720	1,071	2,690	1,318	1,292	513	186	570	290	475	2,783	120	130	318
1988/9[2]	95	205	720	1,147	2,807	1,354	1,273	522	205	600	300	475	2,909	117	105	297

[1] Preliminary.   [2] Forecast.   *Source: Foreign Agricultural Service, U.S.D.A.*   T.110

Supply & Distribution of Coconut Oil in the United States   In Millions of Pounds

Year Begin. Oct. 1	Copra Tonne Rotterdam U.S. $	Coconut Oil CIF Rotterdam U.S. $	Imports[2]	Stocks Oct. 1[3]	Total Supply	Exports & Shipments	Disappearance Total Domestic	Disappearance Edible Pdt's.	Disappearance Inedible Pdt's.	Production of Coconut Oil (Refined) Total	Production of Coconut Oil (Refined) Jan.– March	Production of Coconut Oil (Refined) April– June	Production of Coconut Oil (Refined) July– Sept.	Production of Coconut Oil (Refined) Oct.– Dec.
1981–2	333	500	960	204	1,164	29	976	337.9	411.5	700.3	193.3	175.3	171.9	159.8
1982–3	414	608	882	160	1,042	21	876	340.0	493.9	665.7	162.1	162.4	168.7	172.5
1983–4	707	1,123	916	145	1,061	50	901	299.0	602.0	692.6	163.1	186.0	167.1	176.4
1984–5	476	746	891	110	1,001	20	904	275.0	376.0	616.2	161.3	175.7	145.1	134.1
1985–6	200	304	1,217	130	1,347	22	1,016	332.8	683.0	564.0	130.7	133.9	147.6	151.8
1986–7[1]	285	413	1,087	309	1,396	49	1,039	319.4	720.4	715.4	197.9	180.4	155.4	181.7
1987–8[1]	385	547	992	308	1,300	55	1,008	245.0	763.0	803.7	194.2	214.9	195.3	199.3
1988–9[1]	398	567	992	237	1,229	55	970				165.1	182.0	166.3	

[1] Preliminary. [2] Imports for consumption. [3] Includes G.S.A. stockpile & in U.S. bond. *Sources: Bureau of the Census; Agricultural Marketing Service*
T.112

U.S. Consumption of Coconut Oil in End Products (Edible & Inedible Pdts.)   In Millions of Pounds

Year	Jan.	Feb.	Mar.	Apr	May	June	July	Aug.	Sept.	Oct.	Nov.	Dec.	Total
1979	72.7	66.3	83.3	69.1	69.9	62.0	50.4	58.5	58.0	54.4	55.3	48.5	748.5
1980	55.9	49.9	59.5	55.8	58.1	56.3	56.2	51.0	62.5	66.9	63.1	58.3	693.5
1981	67.6	65.0	71.1	68.2	64.0	70.4	58.0	70.4	66.7	73.2	59.8	52.2	786.6
1982	63.3	59.6	61.7	58.5	64.7	64.2	62.2	63.9	66.1	60.2	70.5	60.6	755.5
1983	62.0	64.8	61.1	64.8	80.2	74.9	70.5	61.2	64.3	68.4	66.2	61.0	799.4
1984	71.5	68.5	66.0	67.0	72.6	70.9	61.8	70.7	48.1	63.4	56.6	45.3	762.4
1985	53.4	57.1	46.1	52.5	51.7	52.8	53.2	57.2	61.2	53.0	57.7	50.0	645.9
1986	67.7	43.8	44.7	52.5	45.7	50.0	49.5	67.2	52.8	78.7	65.9	52.2	670.7
1987	63.7	58.0	76.2	74.1	72.8	81.4	73.8	79.1	82.5	89.6	70.0	72.8	895.0
1988[1]	76.1	71.2	59.1	59.6	66.8	65.8	55.1	53.8	48.7	66.0			

[1] Preliminary. *Source: Bureau of the Census*
T.114

Stocks of Coconut Oil (Crude & Refined) in the United States[2]   In Millions of Pounds

Year	Jan. 1	Feb. 1	Mar. 1	Apr. 1	May 1	June 1	July 1	Aug. 1	Sept. 1	Oct. 1	Nov. 1	Dec. 1
1979	154.6	211.3	216.0	89.1	47.5	156.4	119.5	132.2	138.7	167.1	235.0	218.8
1980	309.7	357.7	248.4	246.5	211.2	211.9	220.6	191.6	210.1	182.6	225.6	264.6
1981	300.1	309.2	359.6	322.5	309.5	289.5	285.1	265.8	260.3	227.7	170.0	168.7
1982	173.1	153.6	186.0	160.7	153.0	170.8	194.8	184.3	166.9	159.7	144.5	144.5
1983	127.2	143.8	144.7	144.0	162.9	168.9	123.6	127.7	131.8	145.3	162.5	175.6
1984	175.2	215.5	193.8	165.0	150.2	121.8	78.7	90.9	100.2	111.0	119.8	107.3
1985	121.4	128.0	91.9	81.3	75.9	86.0	116.0	121.7	140.5	130.0	177.4	162.8
1986	206.5	259.0	262.1	285.1	247.4	289.3	275.0	273.4	273.8	308.0	295.5	320.5
1987	323.3	323.6	355.7	318.1	336.9	271.2	203.6	243.9	240.8	270.2	288.5	370.9
1988[1]	367.7	358.8	370.7	371.7	356.0	353.6	336.6	287.5	335.0	333.3	328.2	

[1] Preliminary. [2] Includes coconut oil held in U.S. customs bond. *Source: Bureau of Census*
T.115

Average Price of Coconut Oil (Crude) Tank Cars at New York[1]   In Cents Per Pound

Year	Jan.	Feb.	Mar.	Apr.	May	June	July	Aug.	Sept.	Oct.	Nov.	Dec.	Average
1979	46.3	47.2	47.0	49.9	53.2	57.3	57.3	53.7	44.8	42.5	42.4	40.2	48.5
1980	40.8	40.6	37.5	34.1	29.3	29.5	30.4	29.9	29.1	27.9	29.4	27.8	32.1
1981	26.3	25.0	23.9	24.3	26.0	27.4	28.1	26.4	24.3	26.6	26.6	25.4	25.9
1982	24.8	24.8	22.9	23.0	23.3	23.1	21.1	19.3	19.8	20.0	N.A.	N.A.	22.2
1983	N.A.	20.3	21.0	25.6	28.4	35.8	33.7	N.A.	N.A.	N.A.	N.A.	44.9	27.5
1984[1]	49.2	54.3	53.0	50.8	63.0	69.9	73.3	70.0	64.6	65.6	56.2	52.6	60.2
1985	42.2	40.2	41.0	41.0	N.A.	N.A.	31.7	27.5	25.0	24.0	22.8	17.4	31.3
1986	20.6	18.0	15.6	15.5	13.8	13.9	13.8	13.0	13.3	16.8	19.8	20.7	16.2
1987	21.40	20.88	19.30	20.38	21.44	24.25	25.75	25.13	24.40	24.69	24.50	27.15	23.27
1988	28.81	26.06	25.45	25.25	26.50	30.45	31.88	28.30	27.38				

[1] Prior to 1984, prices are at the U.S. Pacific Coast. *Source: Bureau of Labor Statistics*
T.116

Coffee

In late 1988, the coffee market threw the world's producers and consumers a curve ball in the guise of a strong rally, and prices leapt up by forty cents a pound, due to the confluence of poor crop reports from Central and South American production areas.

The 1988/89 Brazilian crop of 25 million bags was fated to be a small one, due to both the natural growing cycle and residual damage to the tree population brought on by the country's 1985/86 drought.

The Brazilian crop in 1989/90 was initially expected to be very large, as drought-damaged trees surged back into full productive capacity. However, a cold 1988 winter growing season put some of the larger estimates to rest. But the real shocker was a return of drought weather similar to 1985/86's, causing severe damage to the 1989/90 crop. Estimates of the coffee crop were in the low 20 million bag area, and the market was taking notice once again.

Added to the significant problems in Brazil in 1988 were late and smaller Central American coffee crops, notably in El Salvador and war-torn Nicaragua, and a very rainy harvest period in Colombia, which caused losses in both the quantity and quality of the output of the world's largest milds producer.

Central American coffee crops in 1988/89 were estimated originally at around 17 million bags, while trade estimates were focusing on a total of around 13.5 to 14 million bags.

Colombia's crop was originally forecast at 12 million bags, but due to the heavy rains, the crop was downgraded to 10 million bags, with a larger percentage of poorer grade coffee than usual.

Coffee has been the subject of one of the most successful commodity agreements in the history of trade. While not holding as firm a grasp on the price pipeline as the de Beers Central Selling Organization, coffee producers have been able to get prices which are much higher than the cost of production for their crop. The International Coffee Agreement, which is made up of quota supply and demand triggers, was expected to face many problems when it came up for renewal in September 1989.

Before the bull market, the talk at 1988's ICO meetings had centered on the two-tier market, which had developed between member and non-ICO consumer nations. By virtue of the fact that they did not require quota stamps on their coffee imports, non-member nations allowed producers to dispose of their excess production at way below member-nation prices.

The appearance of inequity between the member and non-member nations caused many to question the efficacy of their ICO memberships, a serious issue for the producers, who depend heavily on coffee revenues for their foreign exchange earnings. Consequently, the next round of talks in September 1989 was a potential turning point for the developing country coffee producers.

Coffee production, which has been subsidized by the higher ICO prices, has been growing steadily over the past decade, and it is reasonable to assume that a worldwide crop of about 100 million bags will become the norm. The 1988/89 estimate is below that mark at 93.2 million bags, and is down 10 percent from the revised 1987/88 record of 101.2 million bags. However, better technology in coffee husbandry and improved strains of coffee trees, that take three years rather than the five to seven years it once took for a full Arabica strain of tree to come to fruit, should allow output to expand.

Coffee consumption is more difficult to assess, due to coffee movement across borders, as well as unreported offtake from stocks on hand, which represent almost 50 percent of available production, at an estimated 46 million 60-kilo bags. However, it appears that offtake, which is measured in terms of disappearance (net imports, less changes in stock levels in ICO member nations, and guesstimates about the same in non-member nations) and consumption in producing nations, should total about 93 million bags.

Futures Markets

Washed Arabica futures are traded on the Coffee, Sugar, and Cocoa Exchange (CSCE) in New York. Robusta coffee futures are traded in London and Paris.

World Coffee Supply and Distribution   In Thousands of 60 Kilo Bags

Country by Time Period	Beginning Stocks	Production	Imports	Total Supply Distribution	Domestic Use	Exports Beans	Exports RSTD/GRND	Exports Soluble	Exports Total	Ending Stocks
1977/78	25,667	70,677	627	96,971	18,828	47,657	183	897	48,737	29,406
1978/79	29,406	78,978	729	109,080	19,466	61,906	222	2,433	64,561	25,059
1979/80	25,053	81,789	690	107,532	19,973	59,244	217	2,573	62,034	25,525
1980/81	25,525	86,261	653	112,439	20,595	56,835	166	2,821	59,822	32,022
1981/82	32,022	98,189	769	130,980	21,232	60,584	223	4,059	64,866	44,882
1982/83	44,597	82,170	773	127,540	20,806	62,539	202	2,490	65,231	41,503
1983/84	41,412	88,603	606	130,621	21,089	65,036	349	2,772	68,157	41,375
1984/85	41,375	90,266	456	132,097	23,015	68,348	308	3,344	72,000	37,082
1985/86	37,082	95,232	387	132,701	21,349	66,709	248	2,611	69,568	41,784
1986–87	41,784	79,337	265	121,386	22,219	67,602	299	2,399	66,300	32,867
1987–88[1]	32,867	103,527	346	136,740	23,756	64,114	295	2,822	67,231	45,753
1988–89[2]	45,753	93,160	315	139,228	24,799	64,815	430	2,860	68,105	46,324

Note: Total may not add because of rounding.   [1] Preliminary.   [2] Estimate.   *Source: Foreign Agricultural Service, U.S.D.A.*   T.117a

World Green Coffee (Total) Production   In Thousands of 60 Kilo Bags (132.276 Lbs. Per Bag)

Crop Year	Papua-N. Guinea	Brazil	Cameroon	Colombia	Costa Rica	Ethiopia	Guatemala	India	Indonesia	Ivory Coast	Mexico	Salvador	Uganda	Zaire (Congo, K)	World Total
1980–1	870	21,500	1,959	13,500	2,140	3,264	2,702	1,977	5,365	6,090	3,862	2,940	2,133	1,526	86,344
1981–2	910	33,000	1,850	14,342	1,782	3,212	2,653	2,540	5,785	4,160	3,900	2,886	2,885	1,425	98,189
1982–3	640	17,750	1,830	13,300	2,300	3,670	2,530	2,170	4,750	4,510	4,530	3,100	3,000	1,354	82,778
1983–4	925	30,000	1,000	13,000	2,070	3,300	2,340	1,667	5,515	1,420	4,530	2,400	2,700	1,350	88,595
1984–5	775	27,000	2,316	11,000	2,516	2,587	2,703	3,250	5,600	4,609	4,250	2,680	2,800	1,540	90,266
1985–6	860	33,000	2,067	12,000	1,514	2,833	2,650	2,033	5,800	4,420	4,826	2,300	2,700	1,610	95,232
1986–7	756	13,900	2,267	11,000	2,460	2,700	2,843	3,200	5,900	4,405	5,297	2,275	2,700	1,875	79,337
1987–8[1]	1,042	38,000	1,600	13,000	2,450	2,900	2,650	2,000	5,800	4,550	4,650	2,200	3,100	1,970	103,300
1988–9[2]	1,050	25,000	2,300	12,700	2,700	3,000	2,800	3,500	5,800	4,400	5,100	2,100	3,000	1,900	93,300
1989–90															

[1] Preliminary.   [2] Estimate.   *Source: Foreign Agricultural Service, U.S.D.A.*   T.117

World Green Coffee (Exportable)[3] Production   In Thousands of 60 Kilo Bags

Crop[2] Year	Papua-N. Guinea	Brazil	Cameroon	Colombia	Costa Rica	Ethiopia	Guatemala	Indonesia	Ivory Coast	Kenya	Mexico	Salvador	Uganda	Zaire (Congo, K)	World Total
1980–1	837	13,500	1,926	11,675	1,932	1,664	2,381	4,137	6,026	1,648	2,362	2,740	2,090	1,346	66,064
1981–2	901	24,500	1,815	12,492	1,539	1,596	2,328	4,630	4,095	1,434	2,450	2,686	2,840	1,240	77,311
1982–3	631	9,750	1,785	11,445	2,077	2,108	2,195	3,636	4,445	1,501	2,830	2,900	2,954	1,159	62,366
1983–4	923	21,500	945	11,140	1,837	1,728	2,000	4,375	1,306	1,038	3,030	2,200	2,653	1,150	67,676
1984–5	762	16,500	2,261	9,135	2,281	1,087	2,373	4,590	4,582	1,488	2,635	2,480	2,752	1,340	67,449
1985–6	842	24,000	1,987	10,130	1,276	1,293	2,350	4,800	4,391	1,951	2,625	2,120	2,650	1,410	73,426
1986–7	738	4,900	2,134	9,000	2,225	1,000	2,543	4,950	4,375	1,732	3,797	2,095	2,649	1,670	57,520
1987–8[1]	1,021	27,500	1,467	11,280	2,215	1,250	2,350	4,750	4,518	1,950	3,070	2,020	3,047	1,760	80,009
1988–9[4]	1,028	14,000	2,160	10,400	2,310	1,200	2,300	4,720	4,168	1,730	3,450	1,920	3,446	1,675	68,597

[1] Preliminary.   [2] Coffee marketing year begins in July in some countries & in others about Oct.   [3] Exportable production represents total harvested production minus estimated domestic consumption.   [4] Estimate.   *Source: Foreign Agricultural Service, U.S.D.A.*   T.118

Coffee United States Trade—Quantity and Value

		Imports				Exports				Reexports			
		Green	Roasted[1]	Soluble[1]	Total	Green	Roasted[1]	Soluble[1]	Total	Green	Roasted[1]	Soluble[1]	Total
1983	Ths. Bags	16,449	197	1,019	17,665	14	147	199	360	599	30	22	651
	Mil. $	2,592	32	141	2,765	3	44	51	98	104	10	3	117
1984	Ths. Bags	17,734	284	1,075	19,093	29	141	188	358	888	7	5	900
	Mil. $	3,061	50	153	3,264	5	44	46	95	163	2	1	167
1985	Ths. Bags	18,698	258	994	19,950	22	167	140	328	695	7	12	714
	Mil. $	3,128	49	139	3,315	4	52	35	90	122	2	3	127
1986	Ths. Bags	19,843	274	933	21,050	45	169	122	336	1,085	17	5	1,107
	Mil. $	4,359	65	183	4,607	11	50	33	94	255	5	1	261
1987	Ths. Bags	19,906	288	925	21,119	57	138	180	375				
	Mil. $	2,706	47	145	2,898	10	39	40	89				

[1] 60 kilogram bags of 132.276 pounds each.   [2] Converted to bags of green bean equivalent (GBE) at 1.19 pounds green to 1 pound roasted and 2.6 pounds green to 1 pound soluble.   *Source: Compiled from U.S. Department of Commerce, Bureau of Census data.*

COFFEE

Origin of Green Coffee Imports (for Consumption) into the U.S. In Thousands of 60 Kilo Bags

Year	Angola	Brazil	Colombia	Costa Rica	Domin. Repub.	Ecuador	Ethiopia	Guatemala	Indonesia	Ivory Coast	Mexico	Peru	Philippines	Salvador	Venezuela	Grand Total
1980	120	3,505	3,404	298	343	539	406	1,374	1,315	438	1,337	573	179	1,374	35	18,153
1981	21	3,243	1,727	226	359	701	547	645	1,516	602	1,393	439	270	779	27	16,555
1982	63	3,372	1,710	248	500	773	578	844	1,118	998	1,377	513	308	919	16	17,416
1983	27	3,417	1,755	226	430	857	519	887	1,079	674	1,495	439	276	1,214	26	16,449
1984	5	3,866	2,170	258	447	961	423	1,118	1,030	1,144	1,553	557	296	1,052	88	17,734
1985	27	4,148	2,554	360	439	974	195	1,054	1,041	951	1,812	543	407	1,366	107	18,698
1986	6	2,200	2,629	413	488	1,371	243	1,658	1,346	694	2,125	675	440	1,108	224	19,483
1987[1]	3	3,928	2,549	551	446	1,285	421	1,439	911	476	2,764	573	105	1,117	163	19,906

[1] Preliminary. *Source: U.S. Department of Commerce* T.122

Total Coffee Imports (for Consumption) into the U.S. In Thousands of 60 Kilo Bags

Year	Jan.	Feb.	Mar.	Apr.	May	June	July	Aug.	Sept.	Oct.	Nov.	Dec.	Total
1980	2,020	1,366	1,421	1,642	1,566	1,663	1,533	1,386	1,062	1,292	1,386	1,715	18,153
1981	1,858	1,738	1,395	1,299	1,356	1,026	922	1,213	1,150	1,487	1,565	1,547	16,555
1982	1,287	1,195	1,490	1,147	1,476	1,335	1,282	1,602	1,640	2,005	1,356	1,602	17,416
1983	1,556	1,332	1,373	1,253	1,502	1,034	1,319	1,230	1,532	1,685	1,380	1,253	16,449
1984	1,598	1,299	1,440	1,905	1,615	1,059	1,722	1,735	1,432	1,614	1,127	1,187	17,734
1985	1,622	1,681	1,702	1,430	1,324	1,751	1,217	1,757	1,773	1,385	1,272	1,785	18,698
1986	2,360	1,836	1,645	1,667	1,810	1,286	1,549	1,513	1,641	1,535	1,449	1,192	19,483
1987	1,092	1,218	1,841	1,789	1,883	2,181	1,717	1,481	1,770	2,631	1,246	1,056	19,906
1988	1,175	1,683	1,426	1,179	1,141	832	1,543	1,621	1,238	1,272			

Source: U.S. Dept. of Commerce T.121

Average Spot Price of Coffee (Brazilian[1]) at N.Y. In Cents Per Pound

Year	Jan.	Feb.	Mar.	Apr.	May	June	July	Aug.	Sept.	Oct.	Nov.	Dec.	Average
1980	189.0	213.0	205.0	208.0	218.0	211.0	195.0	206.0	206.0	210.0	210.0	208.0	206.6
1981	218.0	218.0	218.0	218.0	129.0	115.5	115.5	127.0	127.0	129.5	147.0	150.0	159.4
1982	151.0	136.0	136.0	145.0	145.0	145.0	145.0	145.0	145.0	145.0	133.0	133.0	142.0
1983	133.0	133.0	133.0	141.5	141.5	141.5	141.5	143.0	143.0	143.0	143.0	143.0	140.0
1984[1]	150.0	151.0	151.0	148.0	148.0	147.0	145.0	145.0	146.0	140.0	138.0	138.0	145.6
1985	140.0	145.0	141.0	138.0	138.0	140.0	134.0	133.0	133.0	137.0	155.0	175.0	142.4
1986	241.0	226.0	235.0	228.0	218.0	193.0	188.0	185.0	193.0	187.0	167.0	146.0	200.6
1987	126.5	119.8	103.4	102.1	109.2	108.0	99.8	95.9	96.6	105.4	118.6	119.4	108.7
1988	119.0	127.4	127.3	122.8	121.7	122.5	121.0	111.5	115.1	113.2	116.8	131.1	120.8
1989	146.6												

[1] Prices prior to 1984 are for Santos No. 4 at N.Y. *Sources: Bureau of Labor Statistics (0191-0101.01); Wall St. Journal; CRB.* T.120

U.S. Average Monthly Wholesale Prices of Coffee In Cents per Pound

Year	Jan.	Feb.	Mar.	Apr.	May	June	July	Aug.	Sept.	Oct.	Nov.	Dec.	Average
Ground Roast—All Packs													
1985	276.7	277.3	277.8	277.7	279.0	273.0	273.5	273.6	273.9	273.7	275.0	284.0	276.3
1986	334.5	357.5	361.7	367.6	368.9	373.9	366.5	358.0	352.6	350.9	347.7	347.6	357.3
1987	329.6	329.4	319.4	310.1	302.5	300.2	296.4	296.0	279.0	281.4	284.3	283.4	301.0
1988	286.1	287.2	292.8	295.6	295.2	295.7	287.4	288.5	289.4	292.4			
1989													
Ground Roast in One Lb Cans													
1985	259.7	259.9	261.3	260.8	267.3	258.3	254.6	254.9	254.6	254.6	256.6	268.6	259.3
1986	334.2	345.4	346.7	345.7	350.7	349.4	348.4	350.3	341.7	343.8	334.5	334.5	343.8
1987	311.4	314.3	298.1	296.6	297.3	296.9	291.7	292.5	281.0	282.0	285.6	284.6	294.3
1988	284.0	283.2	294.9	294.2	294.2	298.0	279.5	284.1	283.4	286.7			
1989													
Soluble Per 16 Ounces													
1985	795.1	789.5	791.5	793.3	790.1	791.1	799.2	801.8	804.1	804.8	817.8	837.8	801.3
1986	932.4	995.4	1012.8	1020.3	1016.1	1014.0	1003.4	956.4	970.8	952.2	977.7	977.7	985.8
1987	943.2	885.2	861.9	861.9	866.5	866.5	846.3	846.3	825.6	830.6	830.6	830.6	857.9
1988	805.8	805.8	815.3	812.6	812.6	812.6	922.0	922.0	922.0	922.0			

Source: Bureau of Labor Statistics; Foreign Agricultural Service, U.S.D.A.

COFFEE "C" NYCSC
Weekly high low & close of nearest futures

High, Low & Closing Prices of May Coffee Futures in New York In Cents per Pound

Year of Delivery		Mar.	Apr.	May	June	July	Aug.	Sept.	Oct.	Nov.	Dec.	Jan.	Feb.	Mar.	Apr.	May	Life of Delivery Range
1982	High	126.25	124.00	123.87	111.00	126.75	120.25	123.50	130.25	138.00	133.80	137.88	147.30	149.00	143.75	144.95	149.00
	Low	120.10	117.50	111.50	80.50	81.25	98.28	96.10	123.00	124.25	122.23	128.75	137.25	124.50	129.20	135.10	80.50
	Close	122.60	122.25	112.50	87.50	121.45	98.28	123.00	129.00	126.23	133.63	137.88	141.26	128.56	141.72	138.25	—
1983	High	116.50	118.50	117.50	121.25	117.50	114.00	131.00	131.15	135.40	132.30	127.90	123.95	126.90	126.85	135.17	135.40
	Low	114.00	107.50	109.25	113.50	103.51	107.50	111.00	124.00	126.25	121.60	120.25	118.90	120.35	120.10	124.55	103.51
	Close	114.76	113.00	118.51	118.28	108.25	113.10	129.45	130.49	131.78	125.00	120.60	120.12	123.23	124.80	134.17	—
1984	High	117.00	117.75	126.00	124.50	124.00	127.25	130.05	137.30	139.90	144.10	139.65	145.00	152.30	154.23	158.50	158.50
	Low	109.50	113.00	116.00	121.50	121.60	122.25	125.25	129.30	134.50	134.30	134.25	132.75	141.90	147.00	147.80	108.50
	Close	115.13	116.75	123.38	122.51	122.26	125.80	129.25	135.50	138.78	135.94	137.05	144.84	151.37	152.20	154.00	—
1985	High	131.50	138.50	152.00	146.28	140.15	146.00	143.15	135.35	139.15	140.25	147.90	150.70	146.20	147.30	147.50	152.00
	Low	125.28	130.00	137.50	137.75	132.90	133.25	132.75	131.31	134.50	135.60	138.65	139.85	139.25	138.85	143.00	122.01
	Close	131.38	138.50	142.25	137.76	133.48	144.15	133.80	135.05	135.72	140.25	147.24	139.96	144.43	145.80	143.50	—
1986	High	142.50	145.00	144.50	148.75	143.50	142.13	144.45	161.18	171.45	214.09	272.62	261.00	257.00	243.70	234.25	272.62
	Low	136.59	137.00	141.55	142.28	136.20	137.75	137.15	136.20	155.25	174.90	217.80	207.78	231.15	215.25	202.00	130.25
	Close	141.75	143.00	144.00	144.88	138.65	140.75	140.60	161.18	171.45	241.09	218.51	246.96	246.44	229.07	204.05	—
1987	High	265.00	261.00	250.00	210.50	198.50	205.00	219.50	189.00	173.00	150.50	137.50	130.50	126.80	121.30	128.00	291.83
	Low	247.00	239.10	210.25	177.00	169.95	165.50	173.00	165.38	149.26	132.50	122.20	115.50	99.90	98.10	114.50	98.10
	Close	265.00	247.38	210.25	180.25	184.50	199.50	192.78	169.38	151.25	138.00	126.99	129.31	100.04	119.30	122.08	—
1988	High	131.00	128.00	129.75	124.00	114.90	123.90	123.75	131.00	134.85	133.25	134.50	144.40	137.50	136.00	139.75	150.00
	Low	111.75	110.50	119.20	110.00	107.00	109.50	116.50	118.55	128.75	128.15	128.00	134.40	131.70	130.60	130.10	107.00
	Close	111.75	123.01	124.00	111.31	109.45	122.90	118.88	129.06	131.58	128.38	134.29	135.31	134.51	130.60	131.10	—
1989	High	144.40	144.00	140.60	143.75	135.00	126.75	132.00	129.70	128.13	158.00						
	Low	140.00	135.75	133.35	130.25	118.75	112.13	120.55	123.70	122.00	121.40						
	Close	142.50	136.90	136.00	131.25	124.13	122.50	132.00	124.88	122.80	152.86						

Source: N.Y. Coffee, Sugar & Cocoa Exchange, Inc.

T.125

COFFEE

Month-End Open Interest of Coffee Futures at New York   In Contracts

Year	Jan.	Feb.	Mar.	Apr.	May	June	July	Aug.	Sept.	Oct.	Nov.	Dec.
1983	10,752	10,336	11,739	11,752	11,317	7,885	8,042	9,351	9,439	9,420	8,600	7,706
1984	8,086	10,963	13,012	11,649	9,841	9,437	10,303	10,405	10,300	10,400	10,143	12,431
1985	14,435	12,454	12,973	13,230	12,606	10,561	11,783	10,148	10,066	11,873	11,776	13,167
1986	13,062	15,758	15,611	16,285	16,765	15,492	17,011	15,908	19,171	18,769	15,081	14,928
1987	15,679	16,881	18,811	21,389	22,110	21,326	22,936	25,480	25,910	24,179	21,491	21,921
1988	22,724	26,352	23,017	20,830	23,901	20,655	22,636	23,080	23,008	21,693	18,287	23,156

Source: N.Y. Coffee, Sugar & Cocoa Exchange, Inc.   T.124

Volume of Trading of Coffee "C" Futures at New York   In Contracts

Year	Jan.	Feb.	Mar.	Apr.	May	June	July	Aug.	Sept.	Oct.	Nov.	Dec.	Total
1983	30,567	32,884	44,211	37,399	44,917	45,575	26,065	32,818	22,579	38,999	34,428	36,999	427,441
1984	33,327	44,890	46,793	46,833	51,174	42,891	34,956	48,979	43,159	29,703	37,457	36,094	499,133
1985	48,733	54,809	52,365	58,531	38,755	54,725	42,222	39,425	23,615	58,870	83,845	94,671	650,768
1986	113,305	95,509	76,787	82,308	75,176	87,323	78,670	106,366	93,465	112,685	89,713	61,835	1,073,142
1987	69,564	81,427	78,671	104,350	71,189	86,564	77,621	106,182	77,207	85,315	72,846	53,650	964,586
1988	67,955	119,075	85,154	80,772	73,379	125,684	91,569	118,956	88,460	83,713	85,366	129,627	1,149,710

Source: N.Y. Coffee, Sugar & Cocoa Exchange, Inc.   T.123

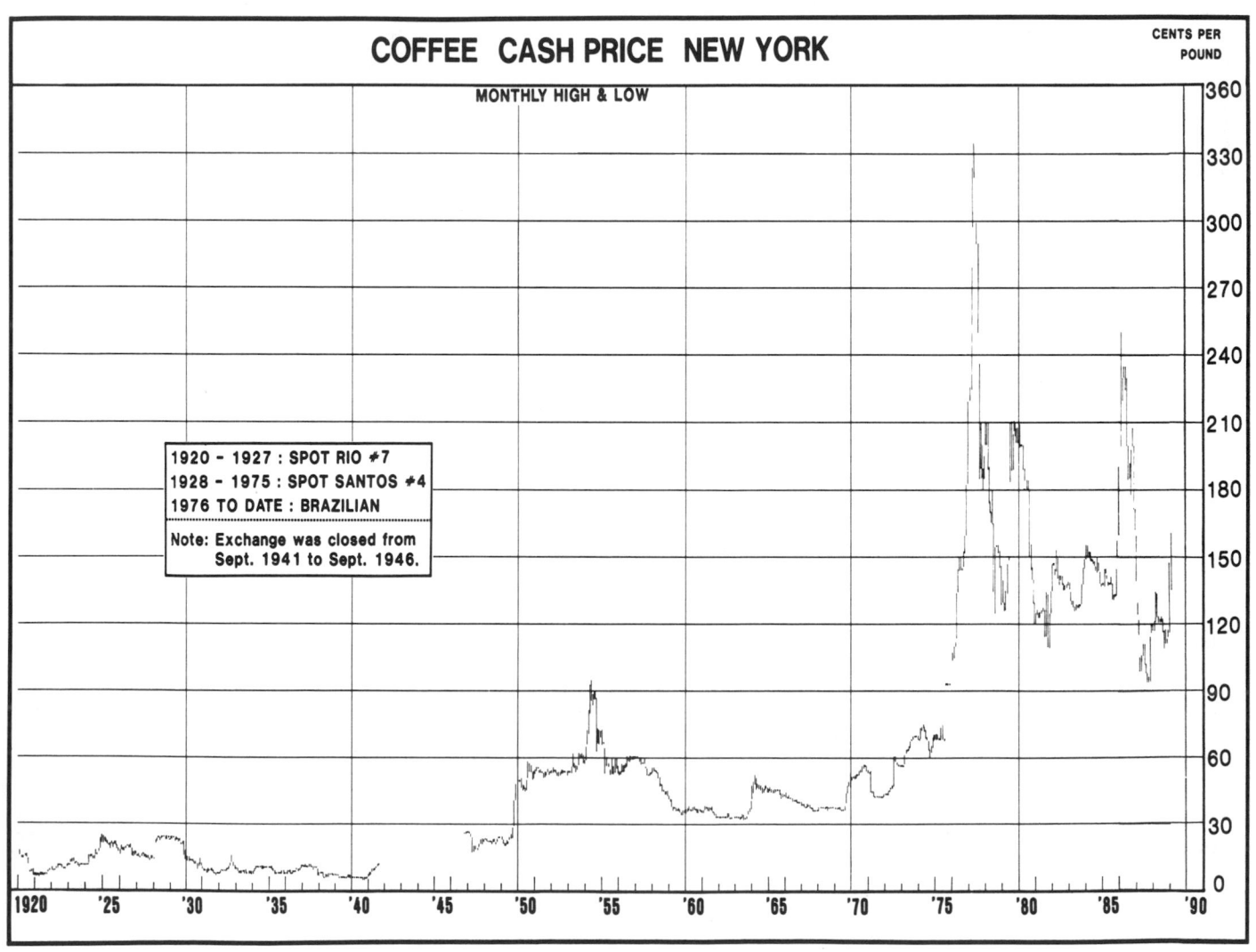

COFFEE CASH PRICE NEW YORK

CENTS PER POUND

MONTHLY HIGH & LOW

1920 – 1927 : SPOT RIO #7
1928 – 1975 : SPOT SANTOS #4
1976 TO DATE : BRAZILIAN

Note: Exchange was closed from Sept. 1941 to Sept. 1946.

Coke

U.S. Salient Statistics of Coke   In Thousands of Short Tons

Year	Product-ion[2]	Domestic Consump-tion	Producers' Stocks—Jan. 1 Total	Oven Coke at Plants Mer-chant	Fur-nace	Petrol-eum Coke	Ex-ports	Im-ports	Exports to Can-ada	Mex-ico	Bel./ Lux.	Neth-erlands	Korea Rep.	Tur-key	Vene-zuela	Avg. Price of Coke Exports $ SH. Ton
1977	53,509	54,144	6,487	314	6,173	2,127	1,241	1,829	634.9	49.4						
1978	49,009	56,948	6,444	136	6,308	2,050	693	5,722	299	37.4						
1979	52,943	53,826	3,534	184	3,350	2,214	1,440	3,974	598	61.0						
1980	46,132	41,278	5,185	595	4,590	1,042	2,071	659	812	75.0						
1981	42,786	44,046	8,627	1,106	7,521	846	1,170	527								
1982	28,115	25,776	6,724	403	6,324	900	993	120	449.7	72.0	99.3	132.7	4.5	—	40.1	61.81
1983	25,808	29,850	8,190	331	7,858	1,344	665	35	471.2	55.8	24.7	24.0	—	—	7.0	68.53
1984	30,561	29,899	3,518	286	3,233	1,096	1,045	582	477.0	72.8	106.4	150.2	64.8	80.1	65.8	66.48
1985	28,651	29,270	3,716	353	3,363	968	1,122	578	407.3	97.3	108.8	68.0	.1	57.6	42.6	68.40
1986	25,540	25,351	2,553	404	2,148	1,232	1,004	329	476.9	78.3	59.0	60.7	—	17.4	20.4	65.23
1987[1]	28,037	29,387	2,066	288	1,778	1,206	574	922	248.2	106.4	21.5	15.3	.2	32.0	89.6	83.58
1988[3]	31,000	32,000	1,064	218	846	1,350	800	2,000								79.00

[1] Preliminary.   [2] Beehive and oven, coke & breeze.   [3] Estimate.   *Source: Bureau of Mines*   T.127

Petroleum Coke Production in the United States   In Thousands of Short Tons

Year	Jan.	Feb.	Mar.	Apr.	May	June	July	Aug.	Sept.	Oct.	Nov.	Dec.	Total
1985	2,469	2,215	2,502	2,608	2,748	2,892	2,962	2,978	2,684	2,942	2,899	3,305	33,204
1986[1]	3,161	2,825	3,027	2,865	3,191	3,176	3,059	3,230	3,171	3,066	2,925	3,206	36,903
1987[1]	3,208	2,919	3,044	2,974	3,087	3,121	3,190	3,138	3,047	3,060	3,158	3,384	37,380
1988[1]	3,464	3,164	3,414	3,159	3,357	3,274	3,326	3,343	3,179				

[1] Preliminary.   *Source: Bureau of Mines*   T.128

United States Coke Production & Stock   In Thousands of Short Tons

Year	Production Beehive & Oven (Byproduct) Jan.–Mar.	Apr.–June	July–Sept.	Oct.–Dec.	Total	Stocks Oven-coke Plants Jan. 1	Apr. 1	July 1	Oct. 1	Petroleum Coke Jan. 1	Apr. 1	July 1	Oct. 1
1980	13,042	12,320	10,052	10,718	46,132	5,185	5,832	7,426	9,018	1,042			
1981	11,178	9,853	11,175	10,580	42,786	8,627	7,586	4,990	5,198	846	948	758	765
1982	8,828	7,507	6,270	5,509	28,115	6,724	7,455	7,871	7,969	900	939	1,091	1,244
1983	5,579	6,451	6,753	7,025	25,808	8,190	5,781	4,569	3,875	1,344	1,317	1,231	964
1984	7,696	8,227	7,522	7,115	30,561	3,518	3,153	2,966	3,441	1,096	1,116	912	991
1985	7,211	7,601	7,150	6,689	28,651	3,716	3,471	3,279	3,217	968	1,086	1,100	950
1986	7,252	7,156	5,513	5,618	25,540	2,553	2,319	2,174	2,141	1,232	1,457	1,366	1,296
1987[1]	5,937	7,073	7,438	7,589	28,037	2,066	1,853	1,546	1,436	1,206	1,437	1,309	1,086
1988[1]	7,347	8,311				1,064	902	1,140		1,350	1,441	1,636	1,427

[1] Preliminary.   *Source: Energy Information Administration*   T.131

Average Price[2] of U.S. Coke Exports

Year	Jan.	Feb.	Mar.	Apr.	May	June	July	Aug.	Sept.	Oct.	Nov.	Dec.	Average
1984								—— 64.64 ——			—— 58.31 ——		66.48
1985	—— 83.30 ——			—— 56.97 ——				—— 68.64 ——			—— 74.09 ——		68.40
1986	—— 95.31 ——			—— 72.58 ——				—— 55.03 ——			—— 55.93 ——		65.23
1987[1]	—— 88.36 ——			—— 85.34 ——				—— 80.57 ——			—— 80.73 ——		83.58
1988	—— 79.31 ——												

[1] Preliminary.   [2] Based on the free alongside (F.A.S.) value.   *Source: Bureau of Labor Statistics (0522-0101)*   T.130

Copper

U.S. mine production of copper increased nearly 14 percent in 1988 to 1.430 million tonnes, according to a preliminary estimate from the Bureau of Mines (BOM). However, global mine production rose only marginally to 8.500 million tonnes, from 8.475 million in 1987. Despite expanded mining operations, Chile's output rose by only 1 percent to 1.432 million tonnes. Falling average ore grades and some production problems with new refining processes affected the level of output. Meanwhile, labor unrest reduced Peru's output to about 300,000 tonnes, from 392,300 in 1987.

U.S. apparent copper consumption rose 4.9 percent in 1988 to 2.220 million tonnes from a year earlier, with growth in manufacturing during the year. But net import reliance as a percent of consumption dropped by half to 13 percent.

U.S. primary refined copper production increased 23 percent to 1.410 million tonnes, and U.S. producers posted substantial profits. Prices repeatedly set all-time highs, and cost-reduction programs kept break-even prices under 60 cents/lb., a level competitive with the most efficient foreign producers.

The producer price for copper cathodes at 1988's end was 6.75 cents above 1987's ending cash price of $1.50/lb. The physical shortage that suddenly turned a 6-year-old buyers' market into a runaway bull market in mid-1987 continued throughout 1988. But prices collapsed early in 1988, as consumers tried to live off of their overpriced inventories. Prices bottomed at 93.5 cents on February 26.

However, expectations that production would soon overtake consumption continually proved to be wrong, and by the fall of 1988, consumers were again scrambling to obtain copper. Futures remained inverted in both the U.S. and London, and cash cathodes were quoted as high as $1.68/lb. in December. For the year, the BOM estimated the average producer price at $1.205, up 46 percent from 82.5 cents in 1987. After bottoming at 5,204 tons on December 9, COMEX copper stocks ended the year at 13,397 short tons, down from 18,635 at the end of 1987.

Copper producers were working on several major expansion projects, as 1988 ended. In 1989, the Ok Tedi mine in Papua New Guinea was expected to reach a production capacity of 500,000 tonnes of concentrate, containing 150,000 tonnes of copper and 350,000 ounces of gold.

In Chile, the $1.1 billion Escondida project, expected to be the world's third largest copper mine when fully operational in 1991, got under way. The open-pit mine in Chile's Atacama Desert was expected to produce 320,000 tonnes of refined copper a year. With 662 million tonnes of ore reserves, graded at 2.1 percent copper, mine life was estimated at 52 years, and cost of production was estimated at 40 cents/lb.

A World Bank forecast predicted copper prices would fall below 70 cents early in 1989 and remain depressed through the 1990s, because of lower industrial growth and increased production. However, price strength continued into 1989, and the market remained inverted, as increased production was used to replenish depleted pipelines.

Futures Markets

Copper futures are traded on the COMEX in New York. Cash copper and futures are traded on the London Metal Exchange. Options are traded on both exchanges.

World Mine Production of Copper (Content of Ore)   In Thousands of Metric Tons

Year	Australia	Canada[3]	Chile	China	Finland	Japan	Mexico	Peru	Zambia	Poland	Zaire	South Africa	Philippines	United States[3]	USSR[3]	World Total[1]
1981	231.3	691.3	1,081	170.0	38.5	51.5	232.9	342.1	588.0	294.6	555.1	199.4	302.3	1,538	570.0	7,777
1982	245.3	612.4	1,242	175.0	37.8	50.7	229.2	353.8	574.5	376.0	519.0	188.7	292.1	1,147	560.0	7,622
1983	261.5	653.0	1,255	175.0	39.3	46.0	196.0	318.8	541.0	402.3	536.5	205.0	271.4	1,038	570.0	7,659
1984	235.7	721.8	1,308	180.0	31.3	43.3	303.5	353.9	532.7	431.0	562.0	198.2	233.4	1,103	590.0	7,999
1985	259.8	738.6	1,360	185.0	28.0	43.2	276.1	391.3	458.6	431.3	557.9	195.4	222.2	1,106	600.0	8,080
1986[2]	245.4	698.5	1,399	185.0	25.9	34.9	285.0	397.4	461.9	434.0	563.0	184.2	222.6	1,147	620.0	8,125
1987[1]	223.0	767.3	1,418	300.0	20.4	22.0	300.0	392.3	470.0	437.0	564.0	213.0	215.0	1,270	630.0	8,475

[1] Estimate.   [2] Preliminary.   [3] Recoverable.   Source: Bureau of Mines   T.132

Commodity Exchange Inc. (COMEX) Warehouse Stocks of Copper   In Thousands of Short Tons

Year	Jan. 1	Feb. 1	Mar. 1	Apr. 1	May 1	June 1	July 1	Aug. 1	Sept. 1	Oct. 1	Nov. 1	Dec. 1
1981	179.6	179.3	179.8	173.3	182.4	175.5	170.6	168.8	167.5	171.6	173.1	171.4
1982	187.6	189.3	193.6	195.7	198.5	201.5	202.2	207.4	211.8	207.1	210.3	246.3
1983	274.4	278.5	293.6	306.1	325.9	336.5	347.4	360.1	374.5	389.3	396.1	404.2
1984	409.2	417.7	409.9	403.2	392.3	372.5	361.6	335.6	320.6	310.8	300.7	288.1
1985	276.3	258.2	238.8	224.8	214.3	201.0	186.4	167.7	155.0	149.0	136.4	124.6
1986	120.3	120.1	118.5	116.4	114.5	108.5	103.4	95.7	90.6	86.6	81.0	84.0
1987	93.3	102.8	108.9	97.5	88.4	71.4	65.3	69.0	73.5	89.2	66.2	33.7
1988	18.5	16.9	16.8	11.8	10.2	19.0	16.9	24.6	22.3	13.6	9.5	5.9
1989	13.4	14.9										

Source: Commodity Exchange, Inc. N.Y. (COMEX)   T.144

U.S. Salient Statistics of Copper   In Thousands of Metric Tons

Year	New Copper Produced — From Domestic Ores — Mines	Smelters	Refineries	From Foreign Ores[2]	Total New	Secondary Recovered[7]	Imports[3] Unmanufactured	Refined	Exports Ore, Concentrate[4]	Refined[5]	Stocks—Dec 31 N.Y. Commodity Exch.	Primary Producers (Refined)	Blister & Materials in Solution	Appar. Consumption[6] Refined Copper (Reported)	Primary & Old Copper[8]
1978	1,358	1,270	1,327	122	1,449	502	532	403	187	92	163	153	263	1,819	2,321
1979	1,447	1,313	1,413	104	1,517	604	282	204	231	74	90	64	275	1,735	2,432
1980	1,181	994	1,126	89	1,215	613	555	427	107	14	163	49	272	1,862	2,179
1981	1,538	1,295	1,419	125	1,544	592	447	331	151	24	170	151	277	2,025	2,292
1982	1,147	941	1,050	176	1,227	518	525	258	195	31	248	268	233	1,658	1,762
1983	1,038	888	1,028	154	1,182	449	675	460	50	81	371	154	174	1,804	2,013
1984	1,103	990	1,090	75	1,165	461	552	445	69	91	251	125	245	2,123	2,107
1985	1,106	939	1,004	54	1,057	503	444	378	116	38	109	66	146	1,976	2,144
1986	1,147	908	1,074	N.A.	1,074	477	598	502	174	12	84	36	135	2,103	2,136
1987[1]	1,256	972	1,146		1,146	499	568	469	125	9	17	29	150	2,152	2,217
1988[9]	1,350	1,000	1,400		1,400			350		75			140	2,300	

[1] Preliminary.   [2] Also from matte, etc., refinery reports.   [3] For consumption.   [4] Blister (copper content)."   [5] Ingots, bars, etc.   [6] Withdrawals from total supply on domestic account.   [7] From old scrap only.   [8] Old scrap only.   [9] Estimate.   *Source: Bureau of Mines*   T.133

Consumption of Refined Copper[2] in the United States   In Thousands of Metric Tons

Year	Cathodes	By-Products Wire Bars	Ingot & Ingot Bars	Cakes & Slabs	Billets	Other	By Class of Consumer Wire Mills	Brass Mills	Chemical Plants	Ingot Makers	Foundries	Miscellaneous	Total Consumption
1978	1,026.1	794.7	111.9	117.1	114.6	24.9	1,517.4	619.2	.4	7.5	12.4	32.3	2,189.3
1979	1,099.0	701.9	92.1	105.6	129.5	30.4	1,499.6	610.2	.4	6.3	11.9	30.1	2,158.4
1980	960.2	583.0	67.6	84.3	117.4	49.7	1,308.9	511.6	.3	5.0	10.9	25.3	1,862.1
1981	1,198.9	489.2	66.7	121.8	101.9	46.7	1,449.6	536.2	.4	5.4	11.3	22.2	2,025.2
1982	1,211.0	195.1	45.1	92.4	82.2	32.4	1,232.8	393.2	.4	4.4	7.6	19.7	1,658.1
1983	1,448.1	77.4	53.2	115.3	101.8	8.2	1,269.9	500.3	.6	3.2	11.3	18.8	1,803.9
1984	1,635.4	72.1	74.4	127.7	118.5	8.2	1,401.7	514.0	.7	5.3	19.8	34.6	1,976.0
1985	1,563.4	70.3	64.2	115.8	139.6	22.8	1,401.7	564.9	.9	1.4	20.6	22.9	2,101.5
1986	1,717.7	52.5	105.9	81.6	127.9	16.9	1,491.9	564.9	.9	1.4	20.6	22.9	2,102.6
1987[1]	1,849.2	14.4	113.3	68.4	86.5	20.0	1,595.6	514.5	1.2	1.4	16.6	22.5	2,151.8
1988[3]							1,425	540					2,300

[1] Preliminary.   [2] Primary & secondary.   [3] Estimate.   Source: Bureau of Mines   T.134

U.S. Mine Production of Recoverable Copper, by Selected States   In Thousands of Metric Tons

Year	Arizona	California	Colorado	Idaho	Michigan	Missouri	Montana	Nevada	New Mexico	Pennsylvania	Tennessee	Utah	Maine	Other States[2]	Total
1978	891.4	N.A.	1.2	3.9	N.A.	10.8	67.3	20.5	127.8	—	11.3	186.3	—	37.1	1,357.6
1979	949.0	N.A.	.4	3.6	N.A.	13.0	69.9	N.A.	164.3	—	N.A.	193.1	—	53.3	1,446.6
1980	770.1	N.A.	.5	3.1	N.A.	13.6	37.7	N.A.	149.4	—	N.A.	157.8	—	48.9	1,181.1
1981	1,040.8	N.A.	N.A.	4.2	N.A.	8.4	62.5	N.A.	154.1	—	N.A.	211.3	—	56.8	1,538.2
1982	769.5	N.A.	.6	3.1	N.A.	7.9	65.0	N.A.	N.A.	—	N.A.	189.1	—	111.8	1,147.0
1983	678.2	N.A.	N.A.	3.6	—	7.7	33.3	N.A.	N.A.	—	N.A.	169.8	—	145.5	1,038.1
1984	746.5	N.A.	N.A.	3.7	—	5.8	N.A.	N.A.	N.A.	—	N.A.	N.A.	—	317.6	1,091.3
1985	796.6	N.A.	N.A.	3.6	N.A.	13.4	15.1		— Not Available —					277.1	1,105.8
1986	789.2						— Not Available —							358.1	1,147.3
1987[1]	764.1						— Not Available —							491.8	1,255.9
1988[3]	740						— Not Available —							610	1,350

[1] Preliminary.   [2] Also includes N.A. States.   [3] Estimate.   *Source: Bureau of Mines*   T.135

U.S. Scrap Copper Intake by Refiners   in Thousands of Short Tons

Year	Jan.	Feb.	Mar.	Apr.	May	June	July	Aug.	Sept.	Oct.	Nov.	Dec.	Total
1983	23.2	22.1	25.5	25.5	22.0	22.5	20.1	21.0	20.1	25.4	20.6	18.2	266.2
1984	17.6	19.2	19.9	21.3	22.0	18.7	18.4	19.8	17.3	22.3	21.2	15.0	232.9
1985	28.1	29.4	32.0	23.9	40.7	27.5	25.6	24.2	28.5	36.1	31.8	35.1	363.0
1986[1]	34.2	31.3	30.4	34.3	33.2	32.7	29.0	26.1	34.8	37.1	28.1	33.0	406.2
1987[1]	28.7	31.6	40.1	42.3	34.0	35.1	29.5	33.2	34.5	35.8	30.8	37.1	414.7
1988[1]	34.5	35.6	43.2	36.9	37.2	36.9	29.7	37.1	39.5				

[1] Preliminary   *Source: American Bureau of Metal Statistics, Inc.; Bureau of Mines*

COPPER

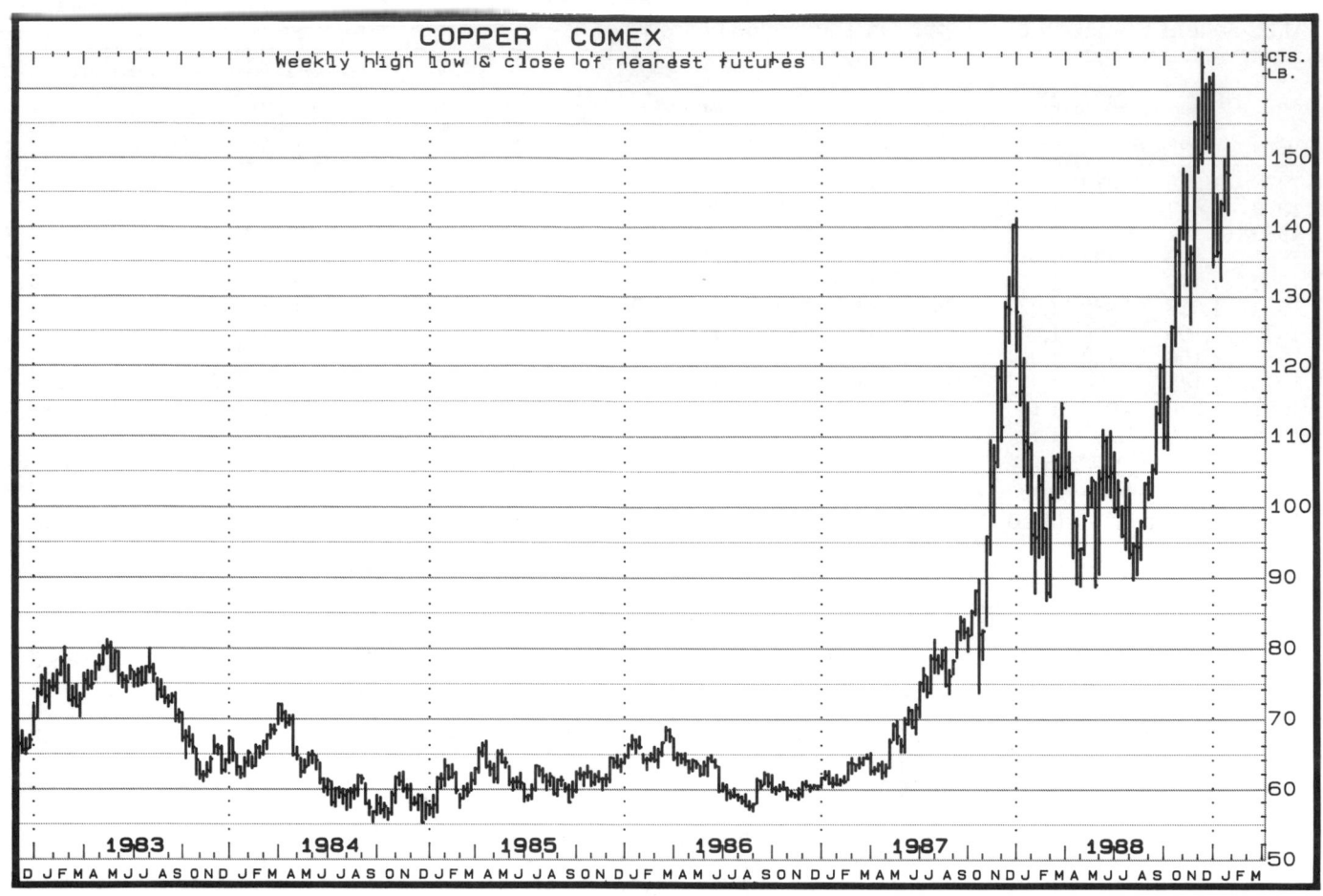

COPPER COMEX
Weekly high low & close of nearest futures

High, Low & Closing Prices of May Copper Futures on the Commodity Exch., Inc., N.Y. (COMEX) ¢ Lb.

Year of Delivery		Year Prior to Delivery									Delivery Year					Life of Delivery Range
		Mar.	Apr.	May	June	July	Aug.	Sept.	Oct.	Nov.	Dec.	Jan.	Feb.	Mar.	Apr.	May	
1983	High	82.25	81.20	82.70	71.30	75.60	72.00	71.90	71.50	70.85	72.65	77.95	81.45	78.40	78.70	80.90	108.30
	Low	77.00	76.80	73.00	60.80	65.35	63.25	62.40	62.00	64.30	67.00	71.00	75.00	70.80	73.80	76.70	62.00
	Close	78.00	80.70	72.60	67.60	68.65	67.20	62.95	67.95	68.90	70.70	76.60	75.20	75.15	77.40	78.05	—
1984	High	85.40	86.00	87.60	83.80	85.05	83.00	78.95	71.70	70.65	69.40	68.10	67.30	71.80	71.75	65.65	88.60
	Low	78.05	81.70	83.70	80.25	80.60	77.30	69.80	64.90	64.00	64.60	62.50	63.90	65.60	63.90	61.40	61.40
	Close	82.60	84.30	84.80	81.25	82.45	77.60	70.25	66.10	69.15	68.30	65.70	66.10	71.75	64.45	64.55	—
1985	High	71.80	79.10	73.35	71.75	67.10	66.60	65.15	62.75	62.70	60.90	64.40	64.20	63.15	66.55	65.30	92.00
	Low	65.60	72.00	69.10	65.35	61.80	62.00	58.90	58.45	59.05	56.40	56.20	57.95	59.10	60.80	60.60	56.20
	Close	71.75	72.40	70.95	67.35	61.90	66.05	60.55	62.75	59.85	57.85	63.15	59.60	62.60	60.95	62.20	—
1986	High	65.65	68.50	68.00	64.35	66.15	64.70	62.90	63.85	63.45	65.35	68.00	67.50	69.15	66.30	63.95	69.15
	Low	62.80	63.55	63.00	61.65	61.50	61.60	60.00	61.15	60.80	61.60	64.50	64.55	63.60	62.15	61.60	60.00
	Close	65.65	63.55	63.95	62.00	63.45	63.05	60.55	61.50	62.10	64.45	67.15	66.05	66.15	62.25	62.85	—
1987	High	70.10	67.75	65.55	65.50	62.10	60.95	63.45	61.55	61.85	62.00	62.85	64.15	65.20	63.70	69.45	70.10
	Low	66.35	63.80	63.65	61.30	59.90	58.60	57.75	59.25	59.65	60.40	60.60	60.85	62.40	61.30	62.40	57.75
	Close	68.30	63.80	64.35	61.60	60.10	59.40	61.80	59.80	61.55	61.75	60.95	63.40	62.45	62.30	65.70	—
1988	High	65.65	64.50	68.35	69.50	74.25	75.65	80.30	86.50	104.40	108.20	109.00	100.80	107.30	107.50	103.90	109.00
	Low	63.25	62.80	63.50	66.05	69.90	70.50	71.90	71.80	78.50	89.10	83.00	79.10	87.40	88.50	93.00	57.75
	Close	63.25	63.30	65.35	69.20	73.70	72.70	77.90	77.20	95.60	108.20	85.85	86.30	105.30	93.80	98.80	—
1989	High	85.40	83.30	83.40	85.00	89.00	93.60	97.00	114.25	125.50	133.00						
	Low	79.10	77.30	77.45	78.70	81.60	83.70	89.80	95.30	103.40	120.30						
	Close	82.00	81.85	80.25	83.00	85.50	93.60	95.20	112.00	124.00	125.00						

Source: Commodity Exchange, Inc. of N.Y. (COMEX)

T.141

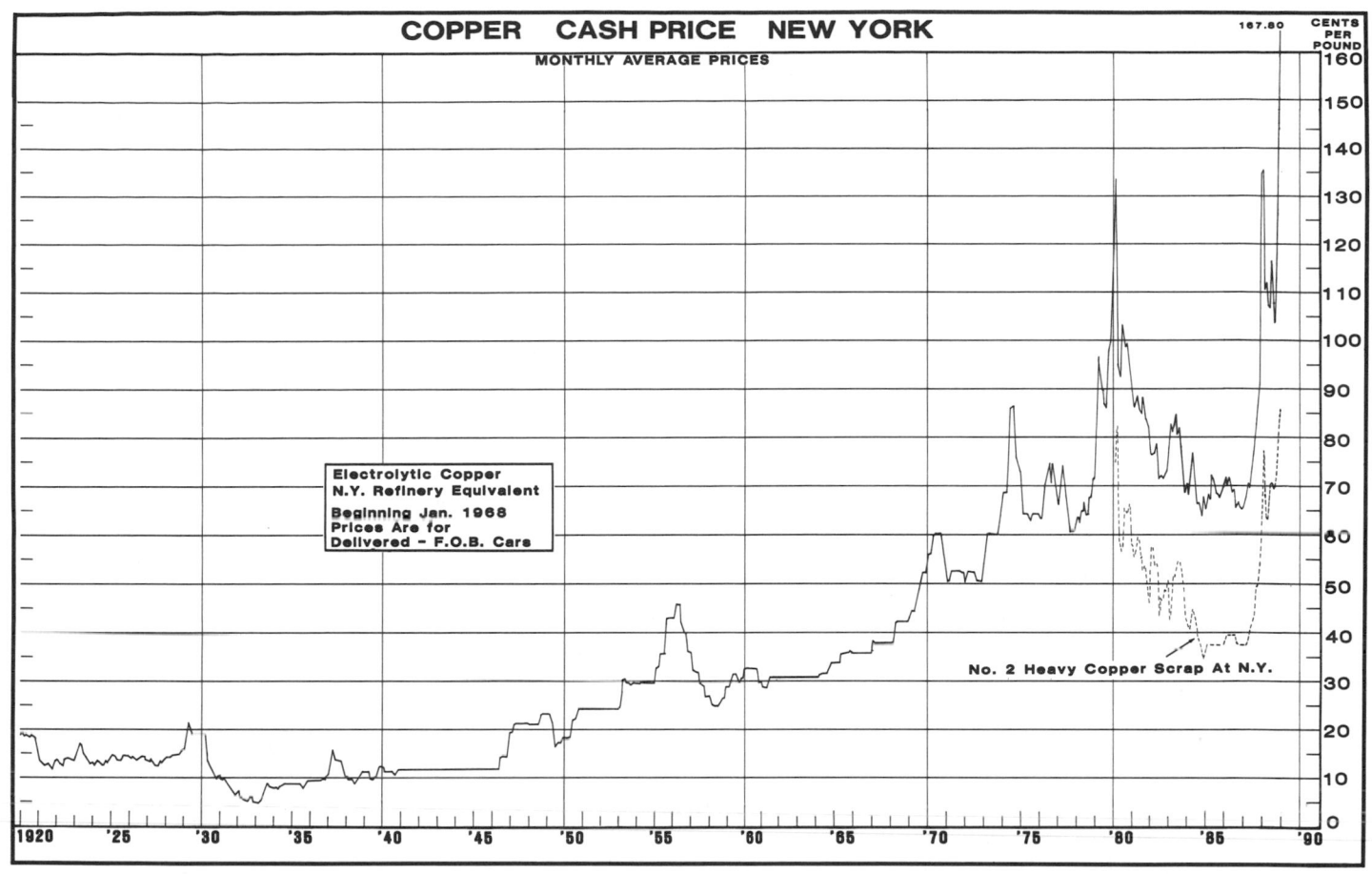

COPPER CASH PRICE NEW YORK

MONTHLY AVERAGE PRICES

Electrolytic Copper
N.Y. Refinery Equivalent
Beginning Jan. 1968
Prices Are for
Delivered – F.O.B. Cars

No. 2 Heavy Copper Scrap At N.Y.

Producers' Prices of Electrolytic (Wirebar) Copper, Delivered U.S. Destinations   In Cents Per Pound

Year	Jan.	Feb.	Mar.	Apr.	May	June	July	Aug.	Sept.	Oct.	Nov.	Dec.	Average
1979	76.15	89.41	94.65	98.66	91.04	87.66	86.02	89.94	95.07	98.84	98.44	106.08	92.75
1980	118.05	133.83	106.23	94.61	93.16	92.39	103.10	100.60	98.73	99.41	96.98	89.20	102.19
1981	88.64	86.07	87.32	88.44	86.33	85.68	84.71	87.98	85.63	83.28	82.09	80.94	85.59
1982	79.42	79.35	76.45	76.99	78.78	71.43	71.78	71.83	71.37	71.92	72.28	73.17	74.56
1983	79.03	82.72	81.09	82.44	84.80	80.90	81.81	79.80	76.75	71.58	68.64	70.43	78.33
1984	69.08	69.51	74.18	76.58	71.56	69.19	66.34	66.44	65.39	63.92	67.71	65.28	68.77
1985	66.23	68.32	67.19	72.17	71.89	68.86	68.53	68.32	67.66	68.60	68.37	70.10	68.85
1986	71.57	70.21	71.78	70.55	68.69	69.15	65.47	64.12	66.82	65.61	65.06	65.91	67.91
1987	67.29	67.87	70.50	69.83	73.54	76.71	83.10	84.94	88.04	91.52	109.59	134.71	84.80
1988	135.63	110.58	111.99	107.51	106.91	116.46	107.90	103.62	118.04	126.38	159.08	167.80	114.50

Source: American Metal Market   T.136

Month-End Open Interest of Copper Futures at COMEX   In Contracts

Year	Jan.	Feb.	Mar.	Apr.	May	June	July	Aug.	Sept.	Oct.	Nov.	Dec.
1980	63,132	60,834	41,546	31,618	31,923	32,454	37,303	38,497	46,737	54,201	52,666	44,225
1981	47,300	47,641	48,699	49,784	52,527	52,325	54,011	54,781	57,153	58,054	52,654	52,226
1982	56,469	60,458	62,817	67,700	74,353	65,938	66,049	64,615	69,845	79,365	85,824	92,146
1983	113,044	121,875	116,706	105,451	99,198	101,350	109,829	106,882	108,357	104,204	104,087	106,898
1984	115,648	100,663	107,730	96,293	92,254	82,836	82,946	84,991	83,606	88,418	83,433	86,502
1985	94,398	82,182	82,195	85,676	82,369	84,913	78,227	75,187	77,106	75,868	76,106	77,790
1986	89,213	79,497	91,606	73,828	71,286	65,698	62,060	60,118	65,370	70,396	74,353	77,988
1987	75,844	77,526	76,775	67,052	72,441	89,640	87,353	64,979	62,572	49,383	44,425	41,206
1988	44,423	34,590	40,060	30,434	28,841	37,556	27,437	33,608	36,473	38,036	36,013	31,083

Source: Commodity Exchange, Inc. of N.Y. (COMEX)   T.142

COPPER

U.S. Imports (for Consumption) of Copper (Unmanufactured), by Sources and Types   In Ths. Tonnes

Year	Ore & Concentrates	Blister	Matte	Refined	Scrap	Australia	Canada	Mexico	W. Germany	Chile	Peru	Philippines	Yugoslavia	Zaire	Zambia	South Africa	Total U.S. Imports
1980	52.4	44.5	.4	426.9	22.8	5.4	152.4	8.3	.5	126.6	52.5	8.9	4.5	5.0	64.9	2.2	547.0
1981	39.1	30.1	2.7	330.6	27.0	1.5	108.5	23.8	—	137.8	52.0	20.4	2.4	24.7	44.1	—	429.6
1982	118.1	97.4	4.1	258.4	28.1	3.7	111.0	64.4	—	233.0	26.8	27.1	—	19.6	10.5	—	506.0
1983	90.6	46.4	3.3	459.6	23.1	—	153.8	44.7	—	292.4	38.9	11.4	—	29.1	24.7	14.0	622.9
1984	11.1	38.9	2.1	444.7	23.0	3.8	177.6	9.5	—	149.4	63.0	6.7	—	28.0	59.5	.5	519.8
1985	2.9	13.0	4.0	377.7	23.0												420.6
1986	4.2	34.5	.7	502.0	27.2	1.1	223.5	24.1	.3	182.5	46.9	1.0	—	36.0	28.7	10.1	568.7
1987[1]	2.3	24.1	6.9	469.2	33.1	—	236.8	18.7	24.0	206.8	37.2	—	4.2	24.0	19.8	9.8	535.6
1988[3]	1.5		6.0	350.0	35.0												500.0

Note: Includes refined; black, blister, & converter; scrap; & copper content of ore, matte, and regulus. [1] Preliminary. [2] Estimate. *Source: Department of Commerce; Bureau of Mines*
T.137

United States Exports of Refined Copper[1] to Selected Countries   In Thousands of Metric Tons

Year	Total U.S. Exports	United Kingdom	China Mainland	Belgium	Brazil	Canada	France	W. Germany	Korea Rep.	Italy	Netherlands	Taiwan	Sweden	Mexico	Japan
1979	73.7	6.5	3.1	2.5	6.2	4.5	12.5	3.5		11.4	6.6	1.2	2.8	.5	2.0
1980	14.5	2.0	—	.6	1.5	2.9	1.9	.8		1.4	.6	.3	.1	.9	.8
1981	24.4	1.3	—	—	.8	6.4	1.1	1.1		.7	—	—	—	7.2	3.9
1982	30.6	1.3	16.1		.4	2.8	1.1	1.9		.1	3.3	—	—	—	.8
1983	81.4	.4	2.2	.7	—	1.7	.6	2.2		—	60.6	1.0	.1	5.3	5.7
1984	91.4	.7	.1	—	—	2.9	.8	1.2		—	6.4	3.2	—	2.8	71.2
1985	37.9	.7	—	.5	—	3.5	.3	1.3		17.3	1.5		4.2	5.0
1986	12.5	2.2	—	—	.1	3.7	.4	1.4	1.3	.1	–	2.2	.1	.2	—
1987[2]	9.2	.9	—			1.7	.4	.4	1.8	.2	—	.2		.5	2.5
1988[3]	75.0	4.0	6.0			3.5	3.0	2.0	8.0	6.0	10.0	2.0		8.5	14.0

[1] Bars, ingots or other forms.   [2] Preliminary.   [3] Estimate.   *Source: Department of Commerce*
T.138

Dealers' Buying Price of No. 2 Heavy Copper Scrap in the Chicago Area[2]   In Cents Per Pound

Year	Jan.	Feb.	Mar.	Apr.	May	June	July	Aug.	Sept.	Oct.	Nov.	Dec.	Average
1979	47.07	58.82	65.46	68.93	63.14	59.05	57.79	58.85	62.03	62.89	62.25	65.00	60.94
1980	74.91	82.35	70.30	60.18	57.60	56.50	65.36	64.88	64.21	65.37	66.08	58.36	65.51
1981	57.60	55.50	57.14	59.50	58.20	55.32	52.68	53.50	53.00	50.16	48.08	46.00	53.89
1982	57.43	57.20	53.76	53.99	53.38	43.24	47.12	46.49	47.83	48.79	48.61	50.75	50.73
1983	42.55	46.71	51.50	51.50	53.74	54.50	54.50	53.54	51.74	48.12	43.30	42.50	49.52
1984	41.17	40.60	43.59	44.50	43.30	42.21	39.36	38.50	38.08	36.20	34.50	35.67	39.81
1985	37.50	37.50	37.50	37.50	37.50	37.50	37.50	37.50	37.50	37.50	37.50	37.50	37.50
1986	38.23	39.50	39.50	39.50	39.50	39.50	39.50	37.79	37.50	37.50	37.50	37.50	38.59
1987	37.50	37.50	37.86	39.50	41.15	42.50	44.68	49.07	49.50	53.32	55.39	64.73	46.06
1988	77.10	68.00	63.50	63.12	70.07	70.59	69.80	69.54	72.36	78.93	83.66	85.50	72.68
1989	89.83												

[1] Prior to May 1988, prices are for the N.Y. area.   *Source: American Metal Market*
T.140

Volume of Trading of Copper Futures at COMEX   In Contracts

Year	Jan.	Feb.	Mar.	Apr.	May	June	July	Aug.	Sept.	Oct.	Nov.	Dec.	Total
1979	154,378	228,837	234,044	234,554	212,934	186,097	139,912	210,387	208,869	200,123	163,074	145,732	2,301,033
1980	243,069	205,232	185,692	121,708	102,054	130,678	148,698	125,062	169,370	132,850	127,110	156,556	7,848,080
1981	116,295	131,960	143,662	140,605	104,376	158,396	125,109	190,763	148,456	114,960	144,453	128,345	1,647,380
1982	112,118	166,562	135,434	179,854	174,157	249,276	197,828	245,973	169,909	231,771	273,546	226,257	2,362,625
1983	306,001	381,645	320,574	278,655	226,482	309,540	213,832	295,470	188,201	230,063	289,111	147,340	3,186,914
1984	199,461	259,881	217,635	269,765	196,382	223,551	152,424	215,226	149,465	170,568	279,151	172,856	2,514,311
1985	254,052	261,784	167,686	310,487	215,079	209,506	146,396	195,882	138,803	178,728	200,142	166,007	2,444,552
1986	190,983	206,513	197,818	240,770	106,750	200,547	89,818	145,468	123,779	121,361	162,963	85,439	1,872,209
1987	124,845	178,598	165,216	170,827	208,696	306,029	272,794	214,181	193,035	276,491	278,985	179,481	2,569,178
1988	210,209	222,625	194,722	151,177	130,289	179,991	120,088	142,945	141,899	186,220	258,725	173,569	2,112,459
1989	216,282												

Source: Commodity Exchange, Inc. of N.Y. (COMEX)
T.143

U.S. Foreign Trade of Refined Copper In Thousands of Metric Tons

Year		Jan.	Feb.	Mar.	Apr.	May	June	July	Aug.	Sept.	Oct.	Nov.	Dec.	Total
1984	Imports	56.1	31.8	51.0	60.3	43.5	49.6	63.0	33.6	29.1	51.9	26.9	24.6	521.3
	Exports	17.5	14.4	8.9	6.8	14.7	1.6	14.0	2.3	2.2	1.9	2.8	6.9	93.9
1985	Imports	46.7	21.8	31.8	22.3	26.8	41.5	27.2	25.7	34.6	22.0	40.4	49.9	390.7
	Exports	5.3	5.8	10.8	3.7	1.3	3.9	5.7	6.8	1.5	1.3	.9	1.1	48.1
1986	Imports	51.9	43.9	49.5	38.2	54.9	36.8	36.0	36.0	37.3	31.7	55.6	31.2	503.1
	Exports	1.3	1.5	1.2	1.0	2.4	.9	.8	1.8	1.7	.6	.9	.8	14.9
1987[1]	Imports	34.4	38.7	55.8	38.9	60.2	69.3	37.0	45.0	28.6	35.9	40.8	31.1	515.6
	Exports	.8	1.9	2.4	2.8	.8	1.1	.6	.5	.8	.7	2.3	3.2	17.9
1988[1]	Imports	49.4	38.0	39.0	33.7	25.9	25.1	22.3	27.7	25.7				
	Exports	4.9	2.0	3.8	5.7	7.7	9.5	3.5	4.4	14.3				

[1] Preliminary. *Source: U.S. Dept. of Commerce.*

Refined Copper Stocks in the U.S.A.   In Thousands of Short Tons (Recoverable Copper Content)

Year	Jan. 1	Feb. 1	Mar. 1	Apr. 1	May 1	June 1	July 1	Aug. 1	Sept. 1	Oct. 1	Nov. 1	Dec. 1
1975	194.9	242.7	259.2	297.8	320.6	334.6	338.2	349.5	341.8	312.3	314.9	324.6
1976	360.7	363.4	370.9	347.8	343.0	325.2	317.1	350.4	355.8	356.1	372.8	416.5
1977	473.8	469.3	487.0	472.3	442.1	447.6	435.0	408.9	370.6	409.4	418.0	456.9
1978	471.1	488.7	491.6	470.2	480.5	465.5	464.0	430.9	418.0	405.9	416.4	408.9
1979	367.0	318.4	287.5	262.1	237.4	197.8	176.0	174.6	158.0	154.6	148.6	167.3
1980	186.3	203.5	228.2	237.1	269.1	277.3	295.7	310.6	301.0	274.6	265.0	246.0
1981	253.0	261.6	249.4	236.8	245.5	243.4	264.7	276.9	276.0	275.5	281.6	301.2
1982	338.6	351.9	375.9	387.3	409.8	422.5	448.1	463.7	449.9	436.2	438.2	470.8
1983	484.5	489.6	501.6	508.9	524.1	519.4	498.7	509.0	522.7	509.1	514.2	505.2
1984	475.3	497.8	499.6	483.3	478.3	463.4	483.2	493.4	490.7	467.1	475.2	457.3
1985	469.7	452.9	380.9	368.2	358.4	363.2	344.1	331.4	310.9	275.7	257.3	264.1
1986	270.7	271.0	261.6	242.0	231.1	201.4	188.0	209.6	214.4	188.1	189.0	211.3
1987	238.4	211.5	206.8	170.1	175.7	161.6	136.4	141.0	140.4	151.3	121.1	86.7
1988[1]	81.4	79.8	81.6	89.0	83.1	75.7	42.0	48.8	52.5	42.9	40.6	39.8

[1] Preliminary. *Source: American Bureau of Metal Statistics, Inc.*   T.145

Refined Copper Stocks Outside the U.S.A.   In Thousands of Short Tons (Recoverable Copper Content)

Year	Jan. 1	Feb. 1	Mar. 1	Apr. 1	May 1	June 1	July 1	Aug. 1	Sept. 1	Oct. 1	Nov. 1	Dec. 1
1975	591.2	628.8	624.5	655.8	723.1	766.0	784.7	861.5	933.4	1,007	1,072	1,108
1976	1,135	1,150	1,149	1,086	1,048	1,045	1,040	1,080	1,112	1,102	1,102	1,141
1977	1,117	1,158	1,200	1,166	1,183	1,185	1,195	1,210	1,229	1,247	1,240	1,225
1978	1,201	1,231	1,139	1,139	1,104	1,099	1,052	1,059	1,001	960.2	962.0	963.1
1979	942.2	878.2	862.4	765.1	758.8	756.7	727.2	687.1	696.6	648.2	635.4	641.3
1980	619.5	598.3	560.9	534.6	516.5	525.9	531.2	530.9	553.2	527.9	489.1	472.6
1981	476.2	485.2	471.0	463.0	458.8	449.8	446.0	454.9	454.7	433.4	419.4	403.0
1982	432.5	446.3	448.4	459.6	452.0	458.7	479.3	492.0	503.6	522.7	575.1	642.9
1983	699.9	760.8	766.4	759.1	795.5	780.0	722.2	683.0	757.4	767.2	765.2	810.4
1984	832.8	817.5	730.0	653.0	618.5	519.3	551.9	526.5	516.0	493.9	483.9	430.0
1985	425.0	420.7	385.7	361.9	364.6	380.4	368.8	464.0	546.7	558.4	533.6	486.6
1986	502.8	501.5	451.8	435.7	422.6	418.7	396.8	430.4	455.1	455.4	458.5	464.8
1987	473.7	467.5	410.5	397.5	387.4	348.5	337.8	336.8	341.1	303.5	245.8	258.8
1988[1]	263.4	286.2	283.4	275.9	260.3	299.8	321.4	360.6	332.8	315.6	297.9	

[1] Preliminary. *Source: American Bureau of Metal Statistics, Inc.*   T.150

Refined Copper Production Outside the U.S.A.   In Thousands of Short Tons (Recoverable Copper Content)

Year	Jan.	Feb.	Mar.	Apr.	May	June	Refined July	Aug.	Sept.	Oct.	Nov.	Dec.	Total	Crude Primary	Secondary
1979	359.8	347.9	360.1	336.9	345.1	364.9	358.1	377.2	366.5	400.9	388.0	382.6	4,388	—4,791—	
1980	384.2	382.8	408.4	398.3	418.7	396.8	392.2	402.9	386.1	394.4	371.8	389.9	4,727	—4,968—	
1981	359.7	347.9	393.6	390.0	388.0	391.4	377.0	377.7	378.8	379.9	366.9	393.8	4,545	—4,891—	
1982	398.2	381.0	442.6	391.8	365.2	403.9	368.4	365.8	386.1	405.8	411.8	372.6	4,693	—5,065—	
1983	386.8	366.3	411.8	400.0	401.2	418.0	381.9	404.3	395.9	404.5	393.1	409.5	4,773	—5,201—	
1984	380.3	376.9	412.4	375.1	374.1	382.5	357.4	381.5	373.8	405.2	380.8	358.7	4,559	—5,114—	
1985	371.6	338.8	388.5	376.1	377.4	351.4	384.2	385.6	380.4	387.6	385.5	394.9	4,522	—5,217—	
1986	366.5	351.5	401.7	409.7	373.1	361.2	361.7	374.8	400.3	407.4	396.4	403.6	4,608	—5,132—	
1987	385.8	375.4	410.6	412.2	399.8	403.6	393.3	370.6	389.1	405.5	400.7	388.3	4,735	—5,203—	
1988[1]	400.6	392.6	433.0	376.1	396.1	401.9	368.4	386.1	391.8						

[1] Preliminary. *Source: American Bureau of Metal Statistics, Inc.* T.148

Refined Copper Production in the U.S.A.   In Thousands of Short Tons (Recoverable Copper Content)

Year	Jan.	Feb.	Mar.	Apr.	May	June	Refined July	Aug.	Sept.	Oct.	Nov.	Dec.	Total	Crude Primary	Secondary
1979	135.6	135.8	152.2	149.8	154.6	149.4	132.3	144.9	137.5	148.7	170.0	155.5	1,766	—1,542—	
1980	161.0	149.5	162.3	170.4	158.7	167.2	52.4	28.7	27.3	61.0	85.8	136.9	1,361	—1,205—	
1981	133.5	116.3	152.2	155.8	135.0	158.3	131.7	124.0	140.5	127.3	124.9	147.9	1,647	—1,429—	
1982	117.5	123.4	121.5	116.4	107.5	108.6	81.8	77.6	80.6	80.1	92.1	90.8	1,198	—1,026—	
1983	97.3	100.6	131.9	125.5	112.2	114.5	73.1	90.6	91.2	110.4	89.1	100.2	1,237	—1,077—	
1984	98.8	100.7	117.1	120.5	127.9	125.6	123.0	126.1	101.8	119.5	95.4	101.4	1,358	—1,270—	
1985	113.5	101.2	118.8	122.4	124.1	100.8	99.9	96.8	93.0	112.9	119.7	106.7	1,310	—1,387—	
1986	109.5	98.3	103.5	115.0	122.4	112.1	109.3	108.9	106.7	114.4	116.6	138.1	1,355	—1,323—	
1987	118.0	110.5	105.4	127.7	118.5	95.5	107.7	106.4	121.8	131.3	123.3	127.7	1,394	—1,308—	
1988[1]	124.5	127.2	145.6	122.5	133.7	116.7	112.7	146.0	133.8	121.1					

[1] Preliminary. *Source: American Bureau of Metal Statistics, Inc.* T.149

Refined Copper Deliveries to Fabricators in the U.S.A.

In Ths. of Short Tons (Recoverable Copper Content)

Year	Jan.	Feb.	Mar.	Apr.	May	June	July	Aug.	Sept.	Oct.	Nov.	Dec.	Total
1979	191.1	174.8	193.5	182.4	204.7	192.4	166.4	179.3	157.4	190.4	161.4	156.7	2,151
1980	173.5	153.7	193.5	167.8	176.3	175.0	98.7	85.0	83.7	106.6	128.7	154.5	1,697
1981	153.0	154.2	196.5	165.1	169.1	158.8	150.6	152.7	157.5	159.5	131.6	131.2	1,880
1982	134.6	112.2	131.5	114.2	121.0	111.4	106.2	110.6	131.8	113.3	78.4	119.2	1,384
1983	126.2	141.1	185.3	156.0	165.9	164.4	91.0	105.2	141.2	137.1	110.2	145.3	1,669
1984	118.3	146.1	185.7	184.4	190.7	163.8	150.7	159.3	166.0	167.1	149.5	124.2	1,906
1985	170.2	188.7	159.8	153.0	144.3	135.2	122.3	130.0	153.3	151.5	137.9	120.7	1,767
1986	123.8	120.1	150.5	155.3	164.5	131.5	113.1	127.1	160.7	141.1	114.7	128.4	1,631
1987	160.2	138.7	166.9	152.3	165.6	152.3	131.6	127.2	141.1	189.7	193.8	166.1	1,886
1988[1]	151.7	152.5	168.1	154.8	159.0	168.3	123.7	172.1	172.8	155.4			

[1] Preliminary. *Source: American Bureau of Metal Statistics, Inc.* T.147

Refined Copper Deliveries to Fabricators Outside the U.S.A.

In Ths. of Short Tons (Recoverable Copper Content)

Year	Jan.	Feb.	Mar.	Apr.	May	June	July	Aug.	Sept.	Oct.	Nov.	Dec.	Total
1979	424.2	395.9	460.4	342.0	349.1	383.3	376.8	357.7	408.5	390.2	377.6	386.4	4,658
1980	386.2	403.2	400.0	407.6	396.9	376.6	357.3	346.7	389.5	406.5	374.4	375.8	4,653
1981	336.8	353.7	383.2	385.4	380.8	382.7	346.0	355.9	393.4	369.5	373.9	364.5	4,426
1982	373.4	380.1	423.6	387.4	348.3	365.4	341.4	342.8	354.9	343.5	331.3	301.6	4,294
1983	303.2	322.9	371.1	325.7	392.2	454.4	407.4	308.3	360.7	389.4	350.2	397.4	4,383
1984	375.0	448.8	477.8	377.1	453.1	358.8	372.5	371.5	382.7	394.6	420.7	360.6	4,793
1985	356.6	372.1	408.2	369.8	379.8	395.9	300.4	319.9	384.6	422.0	419.6	375.9	4,505
1986	364.5	396.9	403.4	403.2	375.6	387.9	331.0	334.1	376.2	384.9	380.9	380.8	4,519
1987	386.0	413.0	413.9	406.8	426.7	401.8	384.1	359.4	425.8	468.1	387.8	374.8	4,848
1988[1]	371.2	390.8	438.5	388.2	365.6	396.9	341.1	399.5	396.1				

[1] Preliminary. *Source: American Bureau of Metal Statistics, Inc.* T.146

Corn

World corn production in 1988/89 was projected by USDA at 390 million tonnes, 13 percent less than a year earlier. A drought-induced decline in U.S. production was responsible for the lower world total. The U.S. accounted for 32 percent of world output. China was the second largest producer, with a crop estimated at 75 million tonnes, 6 percent less than a year earlier. Production declines occurred in Eastern Europe and Brazil, while the USSR boosted its output by 11 percent. Global corn use was estimated at 462 million tonnes, the same as the year before. The major corn consumers were the U.S., China, and the USSR.

World trade in corn was estimated at 71 million tonnes, or 11 percent more than the previous year. Despite the smaller crop, U.S. exports were projected to increase. Thailand was expected to expand its exports to 1.9 million tonnes from 800,000 tonnes the previous year. South African exports were put at 2 million tonnes, up from 780,000 tonnes. However, Argentine exports were slated to fall sharply to 2 million tonnes. Japan remained the largest importer and was expected to purchase 16.7 million tonnes.

Due to climatic conditions, Soviet coarse grain production is quite variable. Despite a larger corn crop in 1988, the Soviets were expected to import 17.8 million tonnes of corn in 1988/89, up substantially from 7.3 million in 1987/88. The Soviets were using imported corn to produce more meat and dairy products in order to upgrade diets. Another country importing more corn was South Korea, where purchases were expected to reach close to 6 million tonnes.

With the decline in world production and a small rise in usage, global ending stocks in 1988/89 were projected at 76.6 million tonnes, 47 percent less than the previous season. The U.S. share of world stocks was expected to fall to 57 percent from 74 percent in 1987/88.

The U.S. crop in 1988 was 4.92 billion bushels, down 30 percent. Harvested acreage was 58.2 million acres, 4 percent less than the previous year and down from 69.2 million in 1986. A drought gripped the Corn Belt during the spring and most of the summer of 1988, reducing the national average yield to 84.6 bu./acre from 1987's record 119.4 bushels.

The drought had its beginnings with less than normal precipitation in the Midwest in the winter of 1988. Some areas, particularly the upper Great Plains, had extremely dry conditions along with warmer than normal temperatures. By the time of spring planting, the extreme dryness was expanding rapidly into Iowa, Illinois, and Ohio. Rains typically received in the spring did not arrive, and June was particularly dry. In terms of heat and dryness, the drought of 1988 was one of the worst of the century.

U.S. 1988/89 carry-in stocks of 4.26 million bushels, while less than in 1987/88, were substantial. The total supply of U.S. corn was placed at 9.19 billion bushels, 23 percent less than in 1987/88. Tighter supplies and higher prices indicated that use of corn would decline. Total use, including exports, was put at 7.53 billion bushels, 2 percent less than the previous year. The USDA estimated that corn used for feed would total 4.3 billion bushels, 9 percent less than the previous season. Livestock producers indicated the drought would not substantially alter their plans to expand output.

Corn used for food, seed, and industrial purposes was expected to decline marginally to 1.23 billion bushels. The use of corn in products such as ethanol and corn sweeteners had expanded earlier, but appeared to be approaching the saturation level.

U.S. corn exports were projected at 2 billion bushels, 15 percent more than a year earlier. In 1987/88, the major importers of U.S. corn were Japan, the USSR, South Korea, Taiwan, and Mexico. In 1988/89, the USSR was the major buyer. The U.S. and USSR signed a new trade agreement under which the Soviets were to buy a minimum of 4 million tonnes of corn per year. Sales to other Asian countries were off in 1988/89, due partly to large export availabilities in Thailand.

While total U.S. corn use fell slightly from the previous season, the sharp drop in production meant that ending stocks would decline substantially. The 1988/89 carryover was projected by the USDA at 1.66 billion bushels, or 61 percent less than the previous season. This represented the tightest inventory level since the 1983 season, when ending stocks were just over a billion bushels. Free stocks of corn, or those not enrolled under one of the government programs, were projected to be 660 million bushels, well below 2.3 billion bushels in 1987/88. Commodity Credit Corporation stocks were expected to be drawn down substantially.

U.S. Government Program

For 1989, the crop support loan rate is $1.65/bu., compared to $1.77 a year earlier. The target price was reduced to $2.48/bu. from $2.93. The acreage reduction requirement is 10 percent, down from 20 percent in 1988.

Futures Markets

Corn futures and options are traded on the Chicago Board of Trade.

World Production of Corn or Maize In Millions of Metric Tons

Crop Year	United States	Argentina	Brazil	Mexico	South Africa	France	China	India	Italy	Bulgaria	Hungary	Yugoslavia	Romania	Indonesia	USSR	World Total
1985–6	225.5	12.4	21.0	10.5	8.1	12.4	63.8	6.9	6.4	3.0	6.5	9.9	14.0	4.6	14.4	479.7
1986–7	209.6	9.3	26.5	10.0	7.2	11.5	70.9	7.5	6.4	1.4	6.6	12.0	15.5	5.0	12.5	477.2
1987–8[1]	179.4	9.0	24.0	9.9	7.0	12.3	79.8	5.5	5.6	2.8	5.6			4.8	14.8	445.2
1988–9[2]	118.7	8.5	22.0	10.3	8.0	12.0	75.0	7.5	6.0					5.0	16.5	386.1

[1] Preliminary. [2] Estimated. *Source: Foreign Agricultural Service, U.S.D.A.*   T.151

CORN

World Coarse Grains Supply & Demand   In Millions of Metric Tons/Hectares

Crop Year	Area Harvested	Yield	Production	World Trade[1]	Utilization Total[2]	Ending Stks[3]	Stocks as % of Util
1982/83	339.2	2.31	784.3	90.0	753.3	181.9	24.1
1983/84	335.1	2.05	687.6	93.4	758.8	110.7	14.6
1984/85	334.7	2.44	815.3	100.4	782.2	143.9	18.4
1985/86	341.2	2.47	842.8	83.2	778.3	208.4	26.8
1986/87[4]	337.1	2.48	834.8	83.9	810.6	232.6	28.7
1987/88[4]	323.1	2.45	790.5	83.1	813.7	209.5	25.7
1988/89[5]	323.3	2.20	712.7	89.8	806.2	115.9	14.4

Note: "Stocks as percent of utilization" represent the ratio of marketing year ending stocks to total utilization.   [1] Trade data as expressed in this table exclude intra-EC trade. The trade year is October/September.   [2] For countries for which stocks data are not available (excluding the USSR) utilization estimates represent "apparent" utilization, i.e., include annual stock level adjustments.   [3] Stocks data are based on an aggregate of differing local marketing years and should not be construed as representing world stock levels at a fixed point in time. Stocks data are not available for all countries and exclude those such as the People's Republic of China and parts of Eastern Europe. World Stock Levels have been adjusted for estimated year-to-year changes in USSR grain stocks, but do not purport to include the absolute level of USSR grain stocks.   [4] Preliminary.   [5] Projection.   *Sources: Prepared or estimated on the basis of official statistics of foreign governments, other foreign source materials, reports of U.S. Agricultural Attaches and Foreign Service Officers, results of Office Research and Related Information.*   150a

Acreage and Supply of Corn in the United States   In Millions of Bushels

Year Beginning Sept.[5]	Planted All Purposes	Harvested For Grain	Harvested For Silage	Harvested For Forage	Yield, Per Harv. Acre-Bus.	Carry-over, Sept. 1 On Farms[5]	Carry-over Off Farms[5]	Carry-over Others[5]	Carry-over Total	Grain Production	Imports[2]	Total (All Supply Grain)
		In Millions of Acres										
1982–3	81.9	72.7	8.3	.3	113.2	1,243.3	— 930.7—		2,537	8,235	.7	10,772
1983–4	60.2	51.5	7.8	.3	81.1	1,510.4	—1,609.5—		3,523	4,175	2.7	7,701
1984–5	80.5	71.9	7.5	N.A.	106.7	347.9	— 375.4—		1,006	7,674	3.5	8,684
1985–6	83.3	75.1	7.2		118.0	678.9	— 701.8—		1,648	8,877	10.6	10,536
1986–7	76.7	69.2	6.3		119.3	2,049.4	—1,990.1—		4,040	8,250	2.1	12,292
1987–8[1]	65.7	59.2	5.9		119.4	2,284.5	—2,597.2—		4,882	7,064	4.0	11,950
1988–9[4]	67.5	56.7			82.3	2,002.8	—2,256.8—		4,260	4,671	5.0	8,936

[1] Preliminary.   [2] Includes grain equivalent of cornmeal & flour.   [3] Interior mills & elevators and terminal mkts.   [4] Estimate.   [5] Data prior to 1986–7 are as of Oct 1.   *Source: Economic Research Service, U.S.D.A.*   T.152

U.S. Corn Supply and Disappearance   In Millions of Bushels

Year & Periods Begin. Sept. 1	Beginning Stocks	Production	Imports	Total Supply	Food, Alcohol & Industrial	Seed	Feed & Residual	Total	Exports	Total Disappearance	Gov't. Owned[1]	Privately Owned[2]	Total
1984–5	1,006	7,674	3.5	8,684	1,070	21.2	4,079	5,170	1,865	7,036	224.9	1,423	1,648
Sep.–Nov.	1,006	7,674	.9	8,681	249.7	—	1,294	1,544	506.2	2,050	206.7	6,424	6,631
Dec.–Feb.	6,631	—	.4	6,632	241.5	—	1,183	1,424	583.9	2,008	209.7	4,414	4,623
Mar.–May	4,623	—	1.1	4,624	283.8	17.0	1,009	1,310	478.9	1,789	221.7	2,614	2,836
June–Aug.	2,836	—	1.1	2,837	295.0	4.2	592.8	892.0	296.4	1,188	224.9	1,423	1,648
1985–6	1,648	8,877	10.6	10,536	1,140	19.5	4,095	5,255	1,241	6,496	545.7	3,494	4,040
Sep.–Nov.	1,648	8,877	1.0	10,526	278.0	—	1,216	1,494	417.7	1,911	388.6	8,226	8,615
Dec.–Feb.	8,615	—	1.3	8,616	264.0	—	1,300	1,564	465.3	2,029	509.4	6,078	6,587
Mar.–May	6,587	—	2.3	6,589	293.0	16.1	1,086	1,395	204.4	1,599	550.9	4,439	4,990
June–Aug.	4,990	—	6.0	4,996	305.0	3.4	494.3	802.7	153.8	956.5	545.7	3,494	4,040
1986–7[3]	4,040	8,250	2.1	12,292	1,175	16.7	4,714	5,905	1,504	7,410	1,443	3,439	4,882
Sep–Nov.	4,040	8,250	.8	12,290	280.0	—	1,384	1,664	321.1	1,985	968.2	9,337	10,306
Dec.–Feb.	10,306	—	.3	10,306	270.0	—	1,472	1,742	315.4	2,058	1,362	6,886	8,248
Mar.–May	8,248	—	.5	8,249	310.0	16.4	1,090	1,416	500.2	1,917	1,492	4,841	6,332
June–Aug.	6,332	—	.5	6,333	315.0	.3	768.0	1,083	367.7	1,451	1,443	3,439	4,882
1987–8[4]	4,882	7,064	4.0	11,950	1,212	17.2	4,727	5,956	1,735	7,690	835.0	3,425	4,260
Sep.–Nov.	4,882	7,064	.6	11,946	292.0	—	1,488	1,780	398.0	2,178	1,683	8,085	9,769
Dec.–Feb.	9,769	—	.9	9,769	282.0	—	1,444	1,726	408.3	2,134	1,768	5,868	7,635
Mar.–May	7,635	—	1.6	7,637	315.0	16.7	955.8	1,288	513.8	1,801	1,305	4,531	5,836
June–Aug.	5,836	—	.9	5,836	323.0	.5	838.9	1,162	414.4	1,577	835.0	3,425	4,260
1988–9[4]	4,260	4,671	5.0	8,936	— 1,215 —		4,500	5,715	1,775	7,490	25.0	1,196	1,446
Sep.–Nov.	4,260	4,671											

[1] Uncommitted inventory.   [2] Includes quantity under loan & farmer-owned reserve.   [3] Preliminary.   [4] Estimate.
Source: Economic Research Service, U.S.D.A.   T.154

Corn Production Estimates and Cash Prices in the U.S.

Crop Year	Corn for Grain Production Estimates						St. Louis No. 2 Yellow	Gulf Ports No. 2 Yel. (Export)	Los Angeles No. 2 Yel.	Season Farm Avg. Price[1]	K.C. White No. 2	Value of Production (Million Dollars)
	Aug. 1	Sept. 1	Oct. 1	Nov. 1	Dec. 1	Final						
	In Thousands of Bushels						$ per bushel					
1979–0	7,108,938	7,268,175	7,390,365	7,585,535	7,763,771	7,928,139	2.68	2.98	3.74	2.52	4.70	19,877
1980–1	6,645,842	6,534,370	6,466,622	6,461,244	6,647,534	6,639,396	3.40	3.59	4.48	3.11	4.96	20,554
1981–2	7,734,941	7,940,421	8,081,444	8,097,231	8,200,951	8,118,650	2.63	2.87	3.92	2.50	2.60	20,200
1982–3	8,315,088	8,318,678	8,314,938	8,329,808	8,397,334	8,235,101	2.87	3.06	3.93	2.55	3.35	22,039
1983–4	5,236,558	4,390,443	4,259,408	4,120,983	4,203,777	4,174,678	3.49	3.67	4.22	3.21	4.70	13,535
1984–5	7,667,721	7,551,991	7,497,831	7,527,206	7,649,995	7,674,020	2.81	3.00	3.78	2.63	3.27	20,085
1985–6	8,265,554	8,468,504	8,602,994	8,716,534	8,865,006	8,876,706	2.37	2.52	3.43	2.23	2.49	21,029
1986–7	8,316,156	8,268,141	8,220,201	8,222,576	8,252,834	8,249,864	1.68	1.83		1.50		12,387
1987–8[2]	7,230,950	7,140,505	7,139,255	7,166,020	—	7,064,143	2.05	2.25		1.94		12,541
1988–9[2]	4,479,385	4,462,475	4,552,735	4,671,235						2.60		12,631

[1] Includes an allowance for unredeemed loan & purchase agreement deliveries valued at the average loan rate. [2] Preliminary.
Source: Economics Research Service; Crop Reporting Board, U.S.D.A. T.153

Production of Corn (For Grain) in the United States, by States   In Millions of Bushels

Year	Illinois	Indiana	Iowa	Kansas	Kentucky	Michigan	Minn.	Missouri	Nebraska	No. Car.	Ohio	Pa.	So. Dak.	Wisconsin	Texas
1980	1,066	602.9	1,463	110.9	103.6	247.0	610.1	109.7	603.5	103.8	440.7	96.0	121.9	348.4	117.0
1981	1,454	654.0	1,759	148.1	149.0	273.6	744.7	213.4	791.2	140.9	360.0	134.4	180.6	378.0	127.5
1982	1,499	790.0	1,578	139.1	154.5	293.2	734.5	199.0	748.0	155.4	456.0	126.1	193.7	361.8	119.7
1983	624.1	340.9	743.9	85.6	46.1	165.6	367.1	72.9	470.5	76.8	224.0	72.5	104.4	223.1	104.8
1984	1,247	705.9	1,445	119.4	146.0	220.1	689.1	154.4	806.2	145.8	460.2	148.5	186.3	344.5	144.2
1985	1,535	756.5	1,707	152.1	159.1	286.7	724.5	272.8	953.6	128.4	511.8	151.8	252.0	358.5	156.5
1986	1,404	695.4	1,627	181.6	139.8	257.3	707.6	280.7	896.0	93.8	476.2	127.7	233.7	365.8	149.0
1987	1,201	631.8	1,307	141.6	118.6	185.3	635.0	243.0	812.2	69.0	362.4	95.4	228.3	330.4	133.8
1988[1]	684.0	374.4	863.2	138.0	72.5	104.0	309.6	144.4	792.0	76.3	220.4	61.4	112.5	136.5	136.5

[1] Preliminary. *Source: Crop Reporting Board, U.S.D.A.* T.157

Distribution of Corn in the United States   In Millions of Bushels

Year Beg. Sept.	Wet-Milled Products					Dry-Milled Products		Alkaline Cooked Pdt's.	Total Ship-ments	Seed	Live-stock Feed[3]	Exports (Incl. Grain Equiv. of Pdt's.)	Total Utiliza-tion	Domestic Disappear-ance
	HFCS	Glucose & Dextrose	Starch	Alcohol		Alcohol								
				Fuel	Beverage[2]	Fuel	Bev-erage							
1979–0	127	170	130	10	20	0	20	158	640	20.0	4,549	2,415	7,604	5,189
1980–1	165	183	120	20	20	15	20	160	718	20.2	4,157	2,408	7,283	4,875
1981–2	185	183	130	55	30	25	10	162	797	19.4	4,169	2,010	6,975	4,966
1982–3	215	188	127	100	30	40	10	170	895	14.5	4,521	1,834	7,249	5,416
1983–4	256	189	147	120	30	40	10	164	975	19.1	3,818	1,902	6,694	4,793
1984–5	310	187	143	140	30	90	10	160	1,091	21.2	4,079	1,865	7,036	5,170
1985–6	328	188	152	155	30	115	10	101	1,100	19.5	4,005	1,241	6,496	5,255
1986–7	339	185	155	— 200 —		125	10	161	1,191	16.7	4,714	1,504	7,410	5,905
1987–8[1]	359	187	167	— 200 —		— 136 —		163	1,229	17.2	4,727	1,735	7,690	5,956
1988–9[4]	370	190	171	— 190 —		— 110 —		165	1,215	19.0	4,500	1,775	7,490	5,715

[1] Preliminary. [2] Also includes nonfuel industrial alcohol. [3] Feed & waste (residual, mostly feed). [4] Forecast.
Source: Economics Research Service, U.S.D.A. T.155

U.S. Exports[2] of Corn (Including Seed), By Country of Destination   In Thousands of Metric Tons

Yr. Begin. Sept.[1]	USSR	China	Canada	Egypt	West Germany	Greece	Israel	Bra-zil	Japan	Mexico	Nether-lands	Rep. of Korea	Spain	Tai-wan	Total Exports
1982–3	3,082	2,161	250	1,516	332	221	420		13,179	3,987	421	3,904	2,132		47,105
1983–4	6,122	0	260	1,240	(EC-6,160)			131	14,165	2,908		3,018	2,096	3,013	48,249
1984–5	14,680	0	427	1,348	(EC-3,939)			209	11,632	1,668		1,467	1,899	2,968	47,486
1985–6	6,376	0	319	1,539	(EC-1,840)			1,062	8,922	1,567		1,239	1,729	2,748	31,468
1986–7	3,844	1,027	347	2,147	(EC-1,618)			1,162	12,058	2,957		3,703	426	2,997	38,224
1987–8	5,184	279	134	822	(EC-1,055)			0	15,830	2,772		4,664	1,627	4,004	43,846

[1] Data prior to 1983–4 are for crop year beginning Oct. 1. [2] Exports of grain only. Does not include corn exported under the food for relief or charity program. *Source: U.S. Bureau of Census.* T.165

CORN   CASH   PRICE   CHICAGO

CENTS PER BUSHEL

Monthly Average Prices

1920 – 1975 No. 3 Yellow
1975 To Date No. 2 Yellow

Average Cash Price of Corn, No. 2 Yellow (5 Days) at Chicago   In Cents Per Bushel

Crop Yr	Sept.	Oct.	Nov.	Dec.	Jan.	Feb.	Mar.	Apr.	May	June	July	Aug.	Average[1]
1980–1	344	343	343	354	356	349	348	353	347	341	341	309	344
1981–2	272	261	260	252	263	263	267	269	273	272	261	236	263
1982–3	217	207	238	244	254	274	298	312	311	328	333	360	298
1983–4	352	347	351	338	330	329	352	361	361	362	345	323	346
1984–5	295	281	279	272	279	279	284	290	285	283	276	250	279
1985–6	231	230	246	249	251	248	244	246	257	255	206	172	208
1986–7	151	150	167	167	158	149	160	167	189	188	170	156	152
1987–8[2]	162	171	185	189	195	201	203	202	209	273	291	278	223
1988–9[2]	277	279	263										

[1] Weighted average by carlot sales.   [2] Preliminary.   *Source: Economic Research Service, U.S.D.A.*

T.161

Average Cash Price of Corn, No. 2 Yellow at Omaha   In Dollars Per Bushel

Crop Yr	Sept.	Oct.	Nov.	Dec.	Jan.	Feb.	Mar.	Apr.	May	June	July	Aug.	Average
1980–81	3.01	3.16	3.34	3.30	3.29	3.18	3.17	3.24	3.24	3.19	3.15	2.79	3.17
1981–82	2.51	2.44	2.39	2.37	2.47	2.45	2.48	2.61	2.65	2.65	2.54	2.23	2.48
1982–83	2.23	2.12	2.35	2.37	2.42	2.62	2.82	3.09	3.10	3.11	3.18	3.39	2.73
1983–84	3.32	3.23	3.24	3.17	3.11	3.03	3.25	3.33	3.35	3.37	3.22	3.11	3.23
1984–85	2.94	2.71	2.61	2.55	2.60	2.61	2.68	2.73	2.68	2.70	2.61	2.39	2.65
1985–86	2.35	2.26	2.28	2.36	2.33	2.31	2.31	2.34	2.43	2.42	2.01	1.61	2.25
1986–87	1.41	1.40	1.55	1.54	1.44	1.39	1.47	1.57	1.76	1.77	1.59	1.47	1.53
1987–88	1.51	1.57	1.68	1.75	1.79	1.84	1.86	1.87	1.96	2.64	2.72	2.55	1.98
1988–89	2.57	2.61	2.47										

Source: Economic Research Service, U.S.D.A.

T.161a

Weekly Outstanding Export Sales & Cumulative Exports—U.S. Corn In Thousand Metric Tons

Marketing Year 1988/89 Week Ending	1988/89 Outst. Sales	1988/89 Cumul. Exports	Marketing Year 1987/88 Week Ending	1987/88 Outst. Sales	1987/88 Cumul. Exports	Marketing Year 1986/87 Week Ending	1986/87 Outst. Sales	1986/87 Cumul. Exports
Sept. 1,'88	10,092	59	Sept. 3,'87	6,462	212	Sept. 4,'86	6,309	72
8	11,310	568	10	6,874	818	11	6,547	381
15	11,637	1,534	17	6,633	1,682	18	6,728	926
22	11,531	2,400	24	6,620	2,434	25	6,912	1,497
29	12,089	3,374	Oct. 1	6,456	3,264	Oct. 2	6,850	2,255
Oct. 6	11,265	4,387	8	6,074	4,104	9	6,712	2,924
13	11,046	5,346	15	5,635	5,106	16	6,504	3,699
20	10,882	6,553	22	7,118	5,994	23	6,336	4,491
27	10,503	7,710	29	7,966	6,529	30	5,880	5,307
Nov. 3	9,921	8,709	Nov. 5	8,030	7,358	Nov. 6	6,005	5,842
10	9,747	9,595	12	8,032	8,170	13	5,997	6,536
17	10,919	10,663	19	7,785	8,785	20	5,968	7,274
24	10,101	11,734	26	8,146	9,585	27	5,751	7,936
Dec. 1	9,598	12,822	Dec. 3	7,554	10,702	Dec. 4	5,536	8,790
8	8,919	13,830	10	7,065	11,630	11	5,454	9,466
15	8,581	14,728	17	7,344	12,443	18	5,868	9,901
22	10,062	15,669	24	7,195	13,215	25	5,807	10,661
29	11,806	16,323	31	6,876	13,879	Jan. 1,'87	5,978	11,119
Jan. 5,'89			Jan. 7,'88	6,644	14,757	8	5,645	11,807
12			14	6,512	15,482	15	5,307	12,302
19			21	7,220	16,471	22	5,330	12,898
26			28	8,756	17,134	29	5,289	13,463
Feb.			Feb. 4	9,109	17,684	Feb. 5	5,292	14,139
			11	9,171	18,400	12	5,443	14,797
			18	8,963	18,997	19	5,637	15,510
			25	9,913	20,031	26	7,581	16,061
			Mar. 3	9,759	20,940	Mar. 5	7,880	16,666
			10	10,213	21,846	12	7,766	17,469
			17	10,629	22,650	19	9,806	18,166
			24	10,740	23,657	26	9,605	19,294
			31	10,908	24,387	Apr. 2	9,506	20,296
			Apr. 7	10,517	25,257	9	9,637	21,135
			14	9,856	26,555	16	10,164	21,993
			21	9,132	27,655	23	9,253	23,338
			28	8,776	28,779	30	8,504	24,676
			May 5	8,505	29,570	May 7	7,758	25,876
			12	7,856	30,990	14	8,216	27,090
			19	7,439	31,818	21	7,453	28,408
			26	7,160	32,694	28	7,240	28,828
			June 2	6,694	33,486	June 4	6,532	29,737
			9	6,517	34,487	11	6,174	30,520
			16	6,402	35,132	18	5,531	31,340
			23	6,589	36,209	25	5,240	32,018
			30	5,710	36,793	July 2	5,488	32,600
			July 7	5,977	37,309	9	5,368	33,145
			14	5,949	38,093	16	4,829	33,925
			21	5,326	39,030	23	4,250	34,841
			28	4,765	39,923	30	3,748	35,859
			Aug. 4	4,361	40,604	Aug. 6	3,193	36,550
			11	3,461	41,453	13	2,647	36,964
			18	2,794	42,276	20	2,081	37,650
			25	2,146	43,072	27	1,200	38,586

Source: U.S.D.A. Export Sales Report (U.S.D.A.)

T.161b

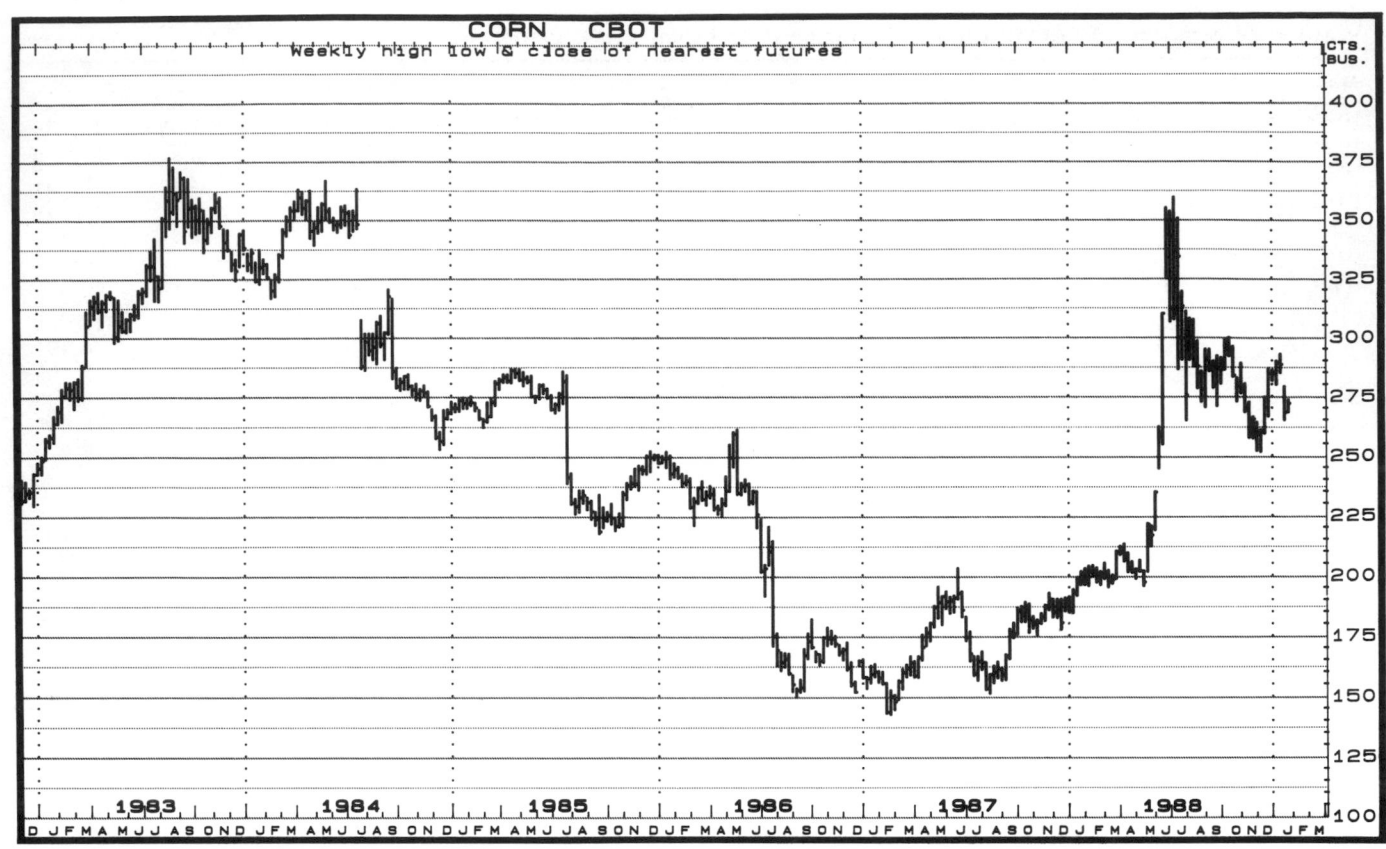

CORN CBOT
Weekly high low & close of nearest futures

High, Low & Closing Prices of May Corn Futures at Chicago   In Cents per Bushel

Year of Delivery		Mar.	Apr.	May	June	July	Aug.	Sept.	Oct.	Nov.	Dec.	Jan.	Feb.	Mar.	Apr.	May	Life of Delivery Range
						Year Prior to Delivery							Delivery Year				
1985	High	312¾	322	321	330	328¼	302¾	301¼	295¾	292¼	285¼	280¼	281	282	286	284¾	330
	Low	300	310	304¾	309¾	289¾	291¼	286½	285½	283¼	272¾	274	269¾	270	280¼	279	269¾
	Close	309¼	314	316½	326¾	297¼	295½	286½	287½	284½	276	278½	271¼	281¼	283¼	283	—
1986	High	282¾	284	279½	274½	264¾	242	243½	247¾	250¾	256½	255¼	245¾	235¾	241	260½	291¼
	Low	274¾	275½	264½	262½	238½	231	231½	238¼	241	242½	243	226¾	222½	224¾	233	222½
	Close	282¾	279	267½	263¾	240½	235	240¾	246½	243½	252¼	244¾	227	234¾	238¼	257	—
1987	High	225½	223¼	226½	212½	198¼	192½	193½	192½	192	184½	168¼	165¼	166	179	195	226½
	Low	214	207	207½	195¾	185½	182¾	180	180¼	183¾	167	160¼	149¼	152¾	157¼	178¼	149¼
	Close	219	223¼	208¼	196	186¾	183	191½	187¼	184	167½	163	153¾	162½	179	181½	—
1988	High	187	199	221	225½	202¼	188½	195¾	203	204¼	202	208	210¼	212	213	219	225½
	Low	175½	182½	195¼	198½	184¼	177½	180	189	185¼	189½	190¼	201	202	198½	195½	174
	Close	184¾	197½	203	202¾	188¾	181¾	193¼	190	202	191¼	202½	209¼	209¾	202¼	216	—
1989	High	235	240½	259	366	369	319¾	312½	303¼	294¾	291¾						
	Low	223½	235¼	234¾	253	281	285	290	279¼	267½	268½						
	Close	232¼	238½	258½	345¼	291¼	302¼	293¼	288½	274½	289¾						

Source: Chicago Board of Trade   T.162

Corn (Shelled & Ear) Stocks in the United States   In Millions of Bushels

Year	On Farms				Off Farms				Total Stocks			
	Mar. 1	June 1	Sept. 1	Dec. 1	Mar. 1	June 1	Sept. 1	Dec. 1	Mar. 1	June 1	Sept. 1	Dec. 1
1985	N.A.	2,008	N.A.	N.A.	N.A.	828	N.A.	N.A.	N.A.	2,836	1,648	8,615
1986	N.A.	3,143	2,049	6,796	N.A.	1,847	1,990	3,510	6,587	4,990	4,040	10,305
1987	5,024	3,492	2,285	6,100	3,224	2,840	2,597	3,668	8,248	6,332	4,882	9,768
1988[1]	4,421	3,241	2,003		3,214	2,595	2,257		7,635	5,836	4,260	

[1] Preliminary.   *Source: Crop Reporting Board, U.S.D.A.*   T.156

Volume of Trading of Corn Futures at Chicago   In Millions of Bushels

Year	Jan.	Feb.	Mar.	Apr.	May	June	July	Aug.	Sept.	Oct.	Nov.	Dec.	Total
1980	3,287	3,227	3,493	3,690	3,265	3,362	6,722	7,310	6,287	6,609	6,455	6,027	59,735
1981	4,848	4,495	5,036	5,222	3,867	4,785	5,459	5,019	3,626	3,127	3,913	3,978	53,375
1982	2,802	3,390	3,634	3,355	2,754	3,538	3,122	3,552	3,127	3,239	4,634	2,594	39,741
1983	3,638	3,114	5,355	4,440	3,943	4,511	5,627	7,431	5,882	5,180	5,734	3,518	59,623
1984	3,518	3,866	4,248	4,407	4,259	4,111	4,868	3,975	3,289	2,883	3,619	2,439	45,543
1985	2,406	2,369	2,746	2,608	2,346	2,494	3,231	2,743	2,629	2,597	3,545	2,248	31,964
1986	2,629	2,153	2,203	2,840	3,029	2,390	2,605	2,217	2,486	3,103	2,591	2,555	30,801
1987	2,343	2,901	3,088	3,646	3,579	3,984	2,978	2,498	2,620	3,380	2,923	2,327	36,266
1988[1]	3,040	3,333	3,212	3,478	4,235	2,039	6,818	5,352	4,353	4,661	5,597	4,733	56,711

[1] Preliminary.   Source: Chicago Board of Trade   T.164

Month–End Open Interest of Corn Futures at Chicago   In Millions of Bushels

Year	Jan.	Feb.	Mar.	Apr.	May	June	July	Aug.	Sept.	Oct.	Nov.	Dec.
1980	838.9	799.0	789.8	787.7	766.7	721.6	1,048.8	1,382.4	1,398.0	1,587.9	1,575.5	1,315.0
1981	1,216.5	1,107.5	1,002.4	846.5	737.5	572.6	568.8	637.8	637.7	724.7	674.6	630.7
1982	708.0	625.6	650.0	610.0	594.5	552.6	581.8	596.6	594.7	663.5	712.1	657.8
1983	776.9	778.5	872.5	832.4	760.0	727.2	792.5	1,127.1	1,134.4	1,163.4	1,138.0	1,062.1
1984	1,022.3	964.0	1,034.3	901.5	776.8	717.8	704.0	712.2	730.6	738.4	657.8	649.4
1985	659.2	588.2	629.0	587.6	507.9	499.2	603.1	661.4	605.7	698.0	714.4	622.1
1986	587.2	545.1	559.5	574.2	574.0	564.3	558.7	594.0	671.7	792.1	677.4	605.5
1987	673.9	705.5	719.0	690.1	628.6	593.7	586.2	568.8	629.4	679.7	672.9	638.3
1988	734.6	777.5	823.9	777.5	911.8	1,177.8	1,187.9	1,121.6	1,178.5	1,262.5	1,085.4	1,123.4

Source: Chicago Board of Trade   T.163

Corn Price Support Data in the United States

Year Begin. Oct.1	National Avg. Loan Rate	Grain Reserve Loan Rate ¢ Bush.	Target Price	Placed Under Loan	% of Production	Acquired by CCC	Total Deliveries[2]	CCC Inventory	Under CCC Loan	Farmer Owned Reserve	Owned by CCC 9/30	Total Stocks	CCC Owned	Under CCC Loan
1980–1	225	240	235	840	12.6	1	42	237.8	100.8	185.4[4]	242	1,392	254	966
1981–2	240	255	240	1,978	24.1	172	45	302.4			280	2,537	248	1,234
1982–3	255	290	270	1,579	18.9	349	0	1,150			1,143	3,523	429	2,400
1983–4	265		286	162	3.9	9		201			201	1,006	1,230	1,450
1984–5	255		303	1,097	14.3	65		240			240	1,648	296	1,056
1985–6	255		303	3,130	35.3	419		546			546	4,040	477	2,811
1986–7[1]	192		303	4,900	59.4	1,575		1,700			1,700	4,882	1,265	4,905
1987–8[1]	182		303					835				4,260		
1988–9[1]	177		293									1,446		

[1] Preliminary.   [2] Includes "delivered to CCC" from original program and deliveries from reseal program and over-deliveries as determined by weight of farm-stored grain when delivered to CCC.   [3] Less than 500,000 bushels.   [4] Called Reserve Corn under extended loan.
Source: Agricultural Stabilization and Conservation Service, U.S.D.A.   T.159

Corn Under Price Support through the End of the Month
(Cumulative Total from Current Season's Crop)   In Millions of Bushels

Crop Year	Aug.	Sept.	Oct.	Nov.	Dec.	Jan.	Feb.	Mar.	Apr.	May	June	July	Aug.	Sept.
1980–1		2.3	44.6	145.0	386.0	746.7	795.2	816.0	830.6	836.0	838.1			
1981–2		13.5	81.9	418.7	1,049	1,642	1,826	1,903	1,940	1,951	1,962			
1982–3		15.5	76.2	334.5	870.2	1,369	1,505	1,551	1,561	1,567	1,572			
1983–4		.4	14.6	58.1	98.3	138.0	149.1	158.3	160.2	161.1	161.3			
1984–5		2.3	47.2	278.5	631.5	969.6	1,028	1,055	1,063	1,068	1,070			
1985–6	11.1	56.9	369.8	1,069	2,016	2,055	2,828	2,916	2,996	3,278	3,040			
1986–7	8.1	59.2	535.6	1,583	2,810	3,922	4,455	4,612	4,765	4,814	4,839	4,850		
1987–8	3.8	290.3	967.9	2,385	3,051	3,899	4,092	4,140	4,168	4,181	4,187	4,187		
1988–9	1.3	16.0	95.3											

Source: U.S. Department of Agriculture   T.158

CORN OIL

Supply & Distribution of Corn Oil   In Millions of Pounds

Year Beginning Oct.	Supply				Food Uses					Disappearance		Non-Food Uses			Total Domestic Disappearance	Total Exports & Shipments
	Production	Imports	Stocks Oct. 1	Total Supply	Short-ening	Margar-ine	Salad & Cooking Oil	Other	Total Food Uses	Foots & Loss	Other	Total Non-Food Uses			
1978–9	737	—	73	810	223	314							619	121
1979–0	791	—	70	861	222	335							654	141
1980–1	864	—	66	930	217	383			625				673	181
1981–2	873	—	76	949	217	357			593				692	202
1982–3	981	—	55	1,036	217	395			637				723	223
1983–4	1,054	—	90	1,144	196	458			693				762	311
1984–5	1,195	—	70	1,265	206	511			774				930	260
1985–6	1,253	—	75	1,328	200	524			834				863	344
1986–7	1,400	—	120	1,520	248	491							1,143	268
1987–8[1]	1,415	—	109	1,524	220	560							1,050	375
1988–9[2]	1,460	—	99	1,559									1,080	385

[1] Preliminary. [2] Forecast.   *Source: Economic Research Service, U.S.D.A.*   T.166

Crude Corn Oil Production in the United States   In Millions of Pounds

Crop Year	Oct.	Nov.	Dec.	Jan.	Feb.	Mar.	Apr.	May	June	July	Aug.	Sept.	Total
1978–9	65.4	59.8	55.8	47.6	54.9	69.4	67.4	69.7	60.6	61.5	63.9	60.3	736.3
1979–0	61.8	63.3	63.0	62.3	60.0	70.7	64.3	68.3	65.1	66.2	69.9	76.2	791.1
1980–1	80.6	68.0	59.0	65.8	63.6	76.2	69.6	74.3	76.1	76.2	76.4	77.8	863.6
1981–2	81.4	69.2	66.5	56.7	64.9	76.4	71.6	77.1	73.9	76.5	79.3	78.0	871.5
1982–3	79.2	72.6	78.4	78.9	73.1	88.2	79.8	85.9	83.6	82.7	92.0	88.2	982.6
1983–4	87.0	85.7	83.2	92.1	87.5	91.1	88.5	94.5	84.4	90.6	86.4	82.0	1,053
1984–5	88.8	75.5	89.6	87.7	84.2	107.3	107.0	110.1	107.7	130.1	101.9	104.0	1,194
1985–6	114.2	101.5	97.1	72.8	97.9	102.2	109.8	118.4	106.3	108.6	119.9	104.1	1,253
1986–7	134.6	120.2	114.0	100.1	102.2	119.3	111.2	123.8	117.5	123.0	114.7	119.5	1,400
1987–8[1]	121.5	115.9	110.6	107.1	110.2	113.4	117.3	125.6	125.4	131.7	132.1	124.5	1,435
1988–9[1]	123.7												

[1] Preliminary.   *Source: Economic Research Service, U.S.D.A.*   T.167

U.S. Corn Oil Consumption in Refining   In Millions of Pounds

Crop Year	Oct.	Nov.	Dec.	Jan.	Feb.	Mar.	Apr.	May	June	July	Aug.	Sept.	Total
1983–4	82.4	82.4	81.6	72.6	64.2	91.8	75.1	85.9	74.6	85.1	93.0	86.5	1,053
1984–5	82.1	86.7	91.0	84.0	71.3	89.4	75.5	106.0	97.4	109.1	96.2	90.8	1,080
1985–6	106.0	95.8	87.1	94.1	87.8	100.9	95.1	103.4	91.2	105.2	97.4	98.1	1,162
1986–7	101.2	98.9	98.3	95.7	98.4	104.0	88.7	83.1	90.9	82.6	77.1	92.3	1,111
1987–8[1]	99.2	90.5	78.3	77.7	93.4	90.0	91.7	103.6	104.1	100.6	119.0	110.6	1,159
1988–9[1]	101.3												

[1] Preliminary.   *Source: Bureau of the Census*   T.167A

Corn Oil Spot Price, Crude, Wet Mill at Chicago   In Cents Per Pound

Year	Oct.	Nov.	Dec.	Jan.	Feb.	Mar.	Apr.	May	June	July	Aug.	Sept.	Average
1978–9	34.0	35.0	31.0	35.0	34.0	33.3	32.1	33.0	30.0	31.0	32.3	32.5	32.8
1979–0	32.8	29.9	33.3	27.5	29.0	26.0	20.0	23.0	22.0	27.3	29.8	28.0	27.4
1980–1	28.0	27.5	28.0	26.3	25.0	23.8	25.5	24.4	24.5	25.8	22.3	21.5	25.2
1981–2	20.0	21.0	25.0	24.0	29.0	25.0	25.0	24.0	23.5	23.0	20.5	21.0	23.4
1982–3	23.0	23.8	24.0	22.5	24.5	21.5	21.0	22.5	22.0	20.0	25.0	36.0	23.8
1983–4	27.5	28.0	25.8	27.0	25.3	26.5	30.0	38.8	35.7	26.0	23.8	29.0	26.6
1984–5	30.5	34.2	30.7	28.7	30.0	31.0	32.5	31.5	30.8	N.A.	N.A.	N.A.	31.1
1985–6	20.9[2]	20.2	20.1	20.8	18.7	17.1	17.9	18.0	17.3	17.0	16.7	16.7	17.0
1986–7	19.6	20.5	21.5	22.5	24.6	22.7	20.9	21.4	22.9	21.5	20.0	19.1	21.4
1987–8[1]	20.68	20.69	21.49	23.09	22.46	21.26	20.44	21.61	26.43	29.56	26.58	24.94	23.27

[1] Preliminary.   [2] Prior to Oct. 1985 prices are for F.O.B. Decatur (tank cars).   *Source: Economic Research Service, U.S.D.A.*   T.168

Cotton

The USDA estimated that 1988/89 world cotton production would rise by 5 percent to 84.3 million bales. A larger U.S. crop partly accounted for the gain, and producers like Mexico, Spain, Turkey and the USSR were expected to have bigger crops. Output in China, the leading producer, was forecast at 19.5 million bales, the same as in 1987/88. The USSR was projected to harvest 12.7 million bales, up 12 percent from 1987/88, when a series of storms disrupted the harvest.

World mill consumption of cotton was placed at 82.7 million bales, down 1 percent from 1987/88. U.S. mill use fell, as textile sales slowed. In other countries, demand for the natural fiber remained quite strong. Many countries were consuming more of their production in an effort to develop textile industries which could export value-added products. China remained the largest consumer, with mill use projected at 20 million bales, the same as 1987/88. Soviet mills were expected to consume 9.3 million bales, equal to a year earlier. Pakistan was developing a textile export sector, and mill use was projected at 3.6 million bales, up 7 percent.

Global exports were put at 23.87 million bales, near 1987/88's. A sharp decline in U.S. exports was expected. Foreign exports were estimated at 18.87 million bales, 11 percent more than last season. However, China's exports were pegged at 1.5 million bales, down from 2.3 million a year earlier. Soviet exports were expected to rise to 3.6 million bales. Pakistan's shipments were projected to be 3.6 million bales, up 50 percent from a year earlier.

World carry-in stocks of cotton were smaller in 1988/89. But with the larger crop, global supplies were estimated at 116.5 million bales, 1 percent above 1987/88. World ending stocks were projected to be 33.6 million bales, up 4 percent. U.S. ending stocks were expected to climb 60 percent to 9.2 million bales, or 27 percent of the world total. China was forecast to carry out 6.6 million bales, 18 percent less than a year earlier. Soviet stocks were expected to increase somewhat.

The 1988/89 U.S. cotton crop was 15.2 million bales, 3 percent more than the previous season. Harvested acreage was 11.6 million, up 16 percent. The national average yield was 627 pounds per acre. Severe drought in the Midwest spared the cotton states. Early in the season, there had been concern that dryness in Louisiana and Mississippi would reduce yields. Much needed rains were received in time, and the crop developed well. States which harvested larger crops included Mississippi, Arkansas, Texas and Arizona.

With carry-in stocks of 5.8 million bales, the total U.S. supply cotton in 1988/89 was forecast at 21 million bales, up 6 percent from a year earlier. Mill use of cotton was projected to fall by 9 percent to 6.9 million bales, due to sluggish sales of major textile products like denim and yarns. Denim, having accounted for much of the recent growth in mill consumption, appeared to be losing favor with consumers. However, household goods and sportswear remained in good demand, and mills specializing in their production were reported to be operating at near capacity.

U.S. cotton exports were projected to fall to 5 million bales, 24 percent below 1987/88. Reasons for the drop included U.S. prices, which were not competitive with foreign growths, and larger foreign export surpluses. The major markets for U.S. cotton continued to be Japan, South Korea, and Taiwan. China purchased some U.S. cotton for the first time since 1984.

Projected U.S. ending stocks were 9.2 million bales.

U.S. Government Program

The 1989 price support loan rate is 50 cents/lb., compared to 51.8 cents in 1988. The target price is 73.4 cents, versus 77 cents the previous year. To qualify for program benefits, producers must reduce base acreage by 25 percent, compared to 12.5 percent in 1988. No paid diversion had been announced as of this writing.

The marketing loan plan B was to be used in 1989, as it was in 1988 and 1987. Under the plan, cotton pledged as collateral for a price support loan may be repaid at the lower of the adjusted world price or the loan level. The USDA calculates the world cotton price each week, and it remains in effect until the next week.

Futures Market

Cotton futures are traded on the New York Cotton Exchange (NYCE).

Supply and Distribution of All Cotton in the United States   In Thousands of (480-Lb. Net Weight) Bales

Crop Year Beginning Aug. 1	Carryover, Aug. 1 — Privately Owned — At Mills	In Public Storage	Else-where	Total Stocks	CCC Held	"Free" Stocks	Current Crop[2] Less Ginnings	New Crop[3]	Total[4]	Imports	City Crop	Total	Mill Consumption	Exports	Total
1980–1	955	1,822	250	3,000	542	2,458	10,627	44	10,671	27	1	13,897	5,891	5,926	11,817
1981–2	883	1,688	25	2,668	652	2,595	15,106	40	15,146	26	0	17,767	5,264	6,567	11,831
1982–3	830	5,269	300	6,632	3,759	2,016	11,486	2	11,488	20	0	17,907	5,512	5,207	10,719
1983–4	792	6,978	167	7,937	4,766	3,171	7,502	163	7,665	12	0	15,235	5,928	6,786	12,714
1984–5	830	1,839	106	2,775	590	2,185	12,382	70	12,452	24	0	15,379	5,540	6,215	11,755
1985–6	768	3,070	264	4,102	1,809	2,293	12,918	145	13,066	33	0	17,181	6,399	1,960	8,359
1986–7	812	8,502	34	9,348	6,829	2,519	9,293	1	9,294	3	0	18,465	7,452	6,684	14,136
1987–8[1]	713	4,000	313	5,026	3,100	1,926	14,358	136	14,494	2	0	18,217	7,617	6,582	14,199
1988–9[5]	737	4,683	171	5,771	3,362	2,409	14,817			2			6,900	5,000	11,900

[1] Preliminary.   [2] Less ginnings prior to Aug. 1.   [3] Ginnings prior to Aug. 1 end of season.   [4] Includes inseason ginnings.   [5] Estimate.
Source: Economic Research Service, U.S.D.A.   T.170

COTTON

Cotton World Supply and Demand   In Thousands of 480-lb. Bales

Yr. Begin. Aug. 1	Beginning Stocks				Production				Consumption				Exports			
	US	USSR	PR China	World Total	US	USSR	PR China	World Total	US	USSR	PR China	World Total	US	USSR	PR China	World Total
1978–9	5,347	2,465	2,500	26,158	10,856	11,907	9,950	59,639	6,352	9,075	13,100	63,286	6,180	3,756	15	19,790
1979–0	3,958	1,895	1,460	21,735	14,629	12,833	10,100	65,736	6,506	9,100	14,100	66,155	9,229	3,770	12	23,244
1980–1	3,000	2,154	1,548	21,177	11,122	13,498	12,400	64,996	5,891	9,150	15,100	65,969	5,926	4,070	6	19,713
1981–2	2,668	2,585	2,392	20,455	15,646	13,277	13,600	71,195	5,264	9,150	16,200	66,131	6,567	4,295	0	20,239
1982–3	6,632	2,527	1,892	25,181	11,963	11,939	16,500	68,080	5,513	9,200	16,400	68,249	5,207	3,890	75	19,452
1983–4	7,937	1,900	3,101	25,198	7,771	9,976	21,300	65,557	5,928	8,750	16,000	68,307	6,786	3,202	760	19,166
1984–5	2,775	707	8,305	23,952	12,982	11,928	28,701	88,215	5,540	9,000	16,000	69,871	6,215	2,994	944	20,198
1985–6	4,102	1,460	20,146	42,436	13,432	12,777	19,000	79,561	6,399	9,400	18,400	75,810	1,960	3,170	2,822	20,260
1986–7¹	9,348	2,260	17,925	47,174	9,731	12,157	16,300	70,441	7,452	9,350	20,200	82,496	6,684	3,365	3,169	25,952
1987–8¹	5,026	2,070	10,875	34,457	14,760	11,345	19,500	80,513	7,617	9,300	18,800	82,328	6,582	3,300	2,200	24,000
1988–9²	5,771	1,315	9,400	32,654	14,714	12,000	21,000	85,343	6,900	9,400	19,300	82,608	5,300	3,300	2,200	23,882

¹ Preliminary.   ² Estimate.   *Source: Foreign Agricultural Service, U.S.D.A.*   T.168a

World Production of Cotton   In Thousands of Bales (480-Lb. Bales)

Year Begin. Aug. 1	Argentina	Brazil	PR. China	Egypt	India	Iran	Mexico	Pakistan	Israel	Sudan	Colombia	Turkey	United States	USSR	World Total
1977–8	1,011	2,237	9,411	1,832	5,548	817	1,620	2,643	294	911	639	2,639	14,389	12,154	63,515
1978–9	797	2,623	9,958	2,014	6,191	612	1,563	2,176	363	637	371	2,191	10,856	11,694	59,446
1979–0	667	2,650	10,137	2,221	6,260	455	1,509	3,344	346	523	574	2,191	14,629	12,070	64,642
1980–1	384	2,862	12,429	2,428	6,256	262	1,620	3,281	359	446	527	2,297	11,122	12,224	63,741
1981–2	696	2,941	13,632	2,293	6,559	356	1,440	3,435	423	712	404	2,242	15,641	11,267	69,125
1982–3	511	2,976	16,526	2,115	6,481	431	840	3,783	400	959	151	2,246	11,963	10,380	66,436
1983–4	827	2,615	21,298	1,879	5,870	420	1,038	2,271	427	1,034	352	2,398	7,771	9,976	65,684
1984–5	787	4,431	28,720	1,833	7,927	512	1,110	4,631	402	933	575	2,664	12,982	11,928	88,199
1985–6	551	3,644	19,046	1,999	8,979	482	970	5,587	455	652	520	2,379	13,432	12,778	80,114
1986–7	482	2,909	16,261	1,850	7,418	510	638	6,061	308	757	490	2,379	9,731	12,217	70,822
1987–8¹	1,148	3,491	19,500	1,615	6,793	441	1,025	6,738	271	684	607	2,465	14,760	11,345	80,471
1988–9²	827	3,963	20,652	1,797	8,719	505	1,161	6,615	326	615	605	2,984	14,934	12,600	86,408

¹ Preliminary.   ² Estimate.   *Source: International Cotton Advisory Committee*   T.169

World Consumption³ of All Cottons in Specified Countries   In Thousands of Bales (480 Pounds Net²)

Yr. Beg. Aug. 1	Argentina	Brazil	PR. China	Egypt	Poland	France	W. Germany	India	Italy	Japan	Mexico	Pakistan	Un. Kingdom	United States	USSR	World Total
1977–8	478	2,241	12,050	1,295	697	846	807	5,288	837	2,988	737	1,872	413	6,509	8,550	60,435
1978–9	503	2,440	13,228	1,319	727	822	777	5,715	975	3,371	757	1,975	447	6,352	8,530	63,210
1979–0	468	2,589	13,972	1,295	782	846	789	5,944	1,047	3,408	757	1,898	400	6,506	8,510	65,116
1980–1	382	2,601	15,024	1,477	735	747	792	6,258	958	3,286	759	2,119	220	5,891	8,250	65,281
1981–2	359	2,631	16,230	1,341	700	743	795	5,837	1,028	3,383	708	2,334	207	5,264	7,855	65,090
1982–3	477	2,603	16,509	1,186	650	765	928	6,259	1,052	3,291	630	2,426	207	5,513	7,600	66,535
1983–4	515	2,553	16,195	1,194	700	745	989	6,651	1,140	3,277	528	2,311	207	5,926	7,900	68,174
1984–5	484	2,753	16,003	1,340	750	728	1,000	7,147	1,212	3,181	556	2,503	201	5,540	8,630	69,983
1985–6	580	3,180	18,478	1,424	698	704	980	7,099	1,185	3,098	634	2,449	217	6,399	9,290	76,255
1986–7¹	588	3,485	20,508	1,387	730	722	1,117	7,870	1,419	3,431	550	3,212	229	7,452	9,525	83,690
1987–8¹	533	3,500	19,061	1,351	725	712	1,072	7,750	1,511	3,550	683	3,436	240	7,700	9,300	83,214
1988–9⁴	551	3,600	19,980	1,400	716	689	1,040	7,850	1,390	3,215	717	3,592	235	7,000	9,400	83,433

¹ Preliminary.   ² Except for the U.S. which are in running bales.   ³ Includes estimates for hand spinning in some countries. Excludes cotton burned or otherwise destroyed.   ⁴ Estimate.   *Source: International Cotton Advisory Committee*   T.173

COTTON   CASH PRICE   UNITED STATES

CENTS PER POUND

MONTHLY AVERAGE PRICES

MIDDLING UPLAND AT N.Y.
1920 - JULY 1940 - 7/8"
AUG. 1940 - JULY 1956 - 15/16"
AUG. 1956 - 1964 - 1"

STRICT LOW MIDDLING – 1"
1965 - TO DATE - 1"

Average Spot Cotton Prices,[2] C.I.F. Northern Europe   In Cents Per Pound (Equivalent U.S. ¢/Lb.)

Crop Year (Aug.-July)	M 1" U.S. Orleans/ Texas	Pakistan N.T. Sind SG	Central Amer.[3] M 13/32"	U.S. Memphis M 13/32"	Greece M 13/32"	Egypt Giza /69/75/81 FG	SM 11/16–3/32" Mexico M 13/32"	Peru Tang- uis #3	Argen- tine "C" 11/6"	USSR[4] Vtoroi	Tanza- nia A.R. MWANZA[5]	Turkey Izmir (12 MIR)	SM 11/8" U.S. Calif.	Aus- tralian M-13/32
1978–79	67.22		75.23	76.25	83.09		75.99	97.79		77.92		73.46	82.96	
1979–80	75.36	75.41	83.63	87.49	84.00	136.37	85.86	101.14		85.89	92.33	90.25	90.69	
1980–81	89.14	84.94	93.47	101.23	100.53	137.66	94.91	104.15	83.18	92.80	103.25	96.65	101.85	
1981–82	66.76	65.65	72.87	76.30	81.00	115.73	75.28	83.42	63.75	73.02	88.08	77.55	79.79	
1982–83	68.11	65.59	76.14	77.94	85.74	110.07	76.39	82.58	41.58	70.68	87.50	83.44	84.94	
1983–84	78.41	75.20	86.81	87.09	94.37	134.07	87.42	102.50	83.27	91.15	95.14	92.74	94.90	90.83
1984–85	65.95	56.22	66.96	73.69	74.36	134.01	70.14	82.64	60.96	—	78.36	74.58	76.20	67.79
1985–86	52.26	37.35	51.38	58.28	50.98	111.40	52.94	74.26	48.34	47.63	55.81	54.13	59.43	50.15
1986–87[1]	56.38	55.48	63.09	62.17	63.53	112.59	64.86	85.50	68.82	62.85	67.41	64.87	74.27	67.05
1987–88[1]	72.14	66.47	72.93	76.29	83.85	145.11	75.18	117.60	61.93	76.18	87.96	86.21	81.17	75.99
Aug. '88	57.74	50.31	56.94	60.75	59.75	154.25	58.94	89.75	53.56	58.06	68.00	73.75	68.81	59.19
Sept. '88														
Oct. '88														

[1] Preliminary.   [2] Generally for prompt shipment.   [3] Cent. Amer. 1986–7 to date. Prior data for Guatemala SM 11/16".   [4] Prior to 11/81 PERVY-SM 1/16".   [5] No. 1/2 until 2/86; No. 3 since.   *Source: International Cotton Advisory Committee*

T.172

COTTON

Average Price of Strict Low Middling, 1¹⁄₁₆ ″, Cotton at Designated U.S. Markets   ¢/Lb. (Net Weight)

Year	Aug.	Sept.	Oct.	Nov.	Dec.	Jan.	Feb.	Mar.	Apr.	May	June	July	Average
1978–9	59.78	60.04	64.08	65.65	64.39	61.48	60.59	58.70	58.05	60.90	63.38	61.87	61.58
1979–0	62.08	62.15	62.88	63.40	66.20	72.40	80.66	79.24	79.05	78.27	72.41	79.01	71.48
1980–1	85.60	87.51	85.78	87.05	87.23	85.11	83.30	81.52	81.15	78.46	78.12	75.08	82.99
1981–2	66.44	60.81	60.63	57.47	55.11	57.82	57.26	59.73	62.03	62.44	61.10	64.96	60.48
1982–3	60.38	58.98	58.58	58.20	59.65	60.16	61.72	66.05	65.33	66.88	70.74	70.27	63.08
1983–4	72.93	71.68	72.01	73.41	73.04	70.55	71.38	74.89	75.64	79.44	75.00	67.35	55.00
1984–5	63.01	61.17	61.15	60.43	60.45	59.97	58.65	60.18	61.71	60.11	59.76	59.55	60.51
1985–6	57.87	56.38	56.14	56.03	56.25	58.39	59.81	61.75	62.62	63.95	65.24	65.73	60.01
1986–7	26.81	33.56	43.95	45.74	54.18	57.17	54.75	54.60	57.72	65.94	70.42	73.07	53.16
1987–8	75.89	71.41	64.30	64.66	62.26	59.69	57.83	59.64	60.07	61.55	62.86	57.40	63.13
1988–9	55.20	51.25	52.20	53.40	54.80								

Note: Grade 41.   *Source: Department of Agriculture*   T.190

Average Spot Cotton, 1³⁄₃₂″, Price (SLM) at Designated U.S. Markets   In Cents Per Pound (Net Weight)

Year	Aug.	Sept.	Oct.	Nov.	Dec.	Jan.	Feb.	Mar.	Apr.	May	June	July	Average	1¹⁄₃₂″	1″
1978–9	60.01	60.27	64.31	65.94	64.68	61.77	60.88	59.03	58.44	61.30	63.79	62.26	61.89	59.92	55.24
1979–0	62.47	62.54	63.28	63.81	66.58	72.78	81.05	79.63	79.44	78.66	72.80	79.40	71.87	69.53	63.39
1980–1	86.00	87.91	86.18	87.45	87.63	85.57	83.70	81.92	81.55	78.86	78.52	75.48	83.39	80.95	75.70
1981–2	66.84	61.22	61.08	57.91	55.52	58.24	57.70	60.12	62.41	62.82	61.48	N.A.	60.89	58.28	54.13
1982–3	60.76	59.36	58.97	58.57	60.02	60.53	62.09	66.43	65.72	67.31	71.20	70.73	63.47	61.17	56.41
1983–4	70.52	69.29	69.49	70.82	70.44	68.03	68.98	72.56	73.37	77.18	72.74	65.11	73.55	70.71	66.32
1984–5	63.45	61.60	60.71	59.99	60.01	59.52	58.21	59.74	61.27	59.67	59.32	59.99	60.29	58.30	55.98
1985–6	57.40	55.89	55.66	55.55	55.77	57.92	59.34	61.28	62.15	63.48	64.77	66.20	59.62	57.87	55.81
1986–7	27.39	35.56	44.53	46.27	54.71	57.70	55.26	55.12	58.24	66.46	70.94	73.59	53.81	50.78	47.77
1987–8	76.42	71.99	64.84	65.17	62.76	60.14	58.28	60.12	60.55	62.03	63.34	57.88	63.03	60.81	59.33
1988–9	55.69	51.80	52.66												

Source: Agricultural Marketing Service, U.S.D.A.   T.191

Average Spot Prices of U.S. Cotton,[1] Base Quality—(SLM) at Designated Markets   In Cents Per Pound

Yr. Begin. Aug. 1	Atlanta	Augusta	Charleston	Dallas	Fresno	Galveston	Greenville	Greenwood	Houston	Little Rock	Lubbock	Memphis	Montgomery	Phoenix	Average
1978–9	—	62.50	—	58.33	67.66	—	62.09	61.84	59.45	—	58.27	61.68	61.92	61.98	61.58
1979–0	—	73.92	—	66.91	73.76	—	73.24	72.73	—	—	66.43	72.55	72.57	71.98	71.48
1980–1	—	85.21	—	80.65	82.80	—	84.54	84.30	—	—	79.66	83.81	84.28	81.70	82.99
1981–2	—	61.87	—	58.32	61.02	—	61.57	61.34	—	—	57.96	61.00	61.34	59.93	60.48
1982–3	—	—	—	61.62	64.49	—	63.50	63.35	—	—	60.84	63.33	63.50	63.17	63.08
1983–4	—	—	—	70.79	77.02	—	73.28	73.14	—	—	70.35	73.25	72.93	74.13	73.11
1984–5	—	—	—	58.94	61.29	—	61.08	60.98	—	—	58.93	60.73	60.56	61.57	60.51
1985–6	—	—	—	58.96	60.35	—	60.52	60.69	—	—	59.17	60.40	60.17	59.84	60.01
1986–7	—	—	—	51.03	60.97	—	51.66	51.99	—	—	51.20	51.70	51.34	55.38	53.16
1987–8	—	—	—	61.14	66.02	—	63.37	62.41	—	—	61.09	62.54	62.79	65.69	63.13

[1] Mixed Lots, Net Weight, uncompressed in warehouse.   *Source: Agricultural Marketing Service, U.S.D.A.*   T.177

Avg. Price[1] Received by Farmers for Upland Cotton in the U.S.   In Cents Per Pound

Year	Aug.	Sept.	Oct.	Nov.	Dec.	Jan.	Feb.	Mar.	Apr.	May	June	July	Average[1]
1978–9	57.4	56.2	59.6	61.1	59.0	57.0	55.6	53.5	54.7	56.0	58.8	61.9	58.1
1979–0	59.2	57.3	61.2	61.0	59.8	60.9	64.9	62.9	61.0	63.6	62.2	71.5	62.3
1980–1	73.7	73.9	75.3	77.6	80.9	76.6	70.8	71.9	72.7	72.5	71.2	70.4	74.4
1981–2	65.0	58.1	63.2	61.1	51.5	50.3	49.1	50.4	54.3	55.8	58.1	59.9	54.0
1982–3	52.7	56.0	60.9	61.0	57.7	57.0	57.7	62.2	60.4	63.6	62.6	67.1	59.1
1983–4	64.6	62.8	63.1	67.0	66.2	62.7	65.0	70.1	67.2	72.7	68.0	65.9	66.0
1984–5	67.3	65.6	64.4	62.0	56.1	52.2	49.5	56.1	57.0	57.5	60.3	60.5	57.8
1985–6	56.6	55.9	57.3	56.5	53.7	54.0	56.9	58.1	59.2	58.5	58.5	61.5	56.8
1986–7	46.8	48.6	50.0	52.6	52.7	52.1	46.4	47.5	50.4	60.0	66.2	68.3	51.5
1987–8[2]	65.3	64.9	65.1	65.6	64.6	60.6	56.8	57.7	59.4	58.9	61.2	58.6	63.7
1988–9[2]	52.6	51.8	53.9	56.7	56.1								

[1] Weighted average by sales.   [2] Preliminary.   *Source: Crop Reporting Board, U.S.D.A.*   T.187

Purchases Reported by Exchanges in Designated U.S. Spot Markets   In Running Bales

Yr. Begin August 1	Aug.	Sept.	Oct.	Nov.	Dec.	Jan.	Feb.	Mar.	Apr.	May	June	July	Total
1983	236,607	270,662	688,534	1,022,458	1,639,279	1,697,601	750,963	424,475	162,863	171,484	59,012	126,720	7,250,658
1984	258,511	154,557	271,195	558,999	1,153,086	1,015,087	570,259	287,483	303,501	159.540	123,089	131,035	4,986,342
1985	166,725	152,795	258,891	395,097	570,460	671,758	389,436	416,654	487,813	626,319	968,185	690,947	5,795,080
1986	585,628	638,356	392,451	422,542	1,353,241	1,055,081	633,852	354,643	501,265	354,008	163,307	160,474	6,614,848
1987	152,935	252,669	650,349	718,829	1,065,457	622,727	571,851	463,739	266,545	572,702	336,191	117,645	5,791,639
1988	288,187	166,692	230,724	163,642	323,025								

[1] Purchases are for 10 markets; commencing February 1980 purchases are for nine markets; and commencing March 28, 1983 purchases are for eight markets.   *Source: Agricultural Marketing Service: U.S.D.A.*   T.190a

Month–End Open Interest of Cotton Futures at New York   In Contracts

Year	Jan.	Feb.	Mar.	Apr.	May	June	July	Aug.	Sept.	Oct.	Nov.	Dec.
1983	29,544	34,165	36,109	33,990	35,026	33,851	31,402	33,981	31,531	29,272	30,868	30,758
1984	32,246	28,060	34,212	29,596	30,569	22,239	21,734	21,576	20,419	22,547	19,211	16,614
1985	19,790	17,660	18,678	14,101	16,481	15,381	19,386	20,861	21,011	22,889	23,196	21,748
1986	23,326	20,824	20,112	20,121	23,702	22,505	25,321	27,642	23,406	24,432	20,534	23,035
1987	26,077	23,482	23,190	25,753	27,990	28,140	35,719	39,148	39,840	39,750	34,600	33,204
1988	38,121	32,220	30,164	26,656	32,811	27,979	30,250	37,102	37,607	35,795	27,662	30,573

Source: N.Y. Cotton Exchange   T.182

Volume of Trading of Cotton Futures at New York   In Contracts

Year	Jan.	Feb.	Mar.	Apr.	May	June	July	Aug.	Sept.	Oct.	Nov.	Dec.	Total
1982	100,242	104,444	103,697	106,892	95,597	151,068	116,211	99,674	101,119	94,265	98,597	83,988	1,255,202
1983	97,947	123,620	139,032	132,447	139,953	153,932	143,116	156,680	121,972	113,759	137,472	90,187	1,550,117
1984	124,735	133,891	127,448	126,780	139,988	111,050	71,522	51,941	39,519	83,631	86,729	39,907	1,137,141
1985	61,860	57,034	61,921	65,709	47,606	47,604	41,069	40,524	42,747	55,046	63,829	51,543	636,492
1986	73,576	77,152	57,433	74,520	57,479	64,742	75,545	94,025	130,989	111,359	113,812	84,618	1,015,392
1987	110,165	106,520	88,621	106,620	110,303	132,180	98,339	127,048	131,214	124,319	126,582	107,124	1,395,980
1988	114,672	119,832	97,533	118,614	127,880	149,303	89,907	100,447	108,285	135,221	124,221	84,334	1,370,249

Source: N.Y. Cotton Exchange   T.183

High, Low & Closing Prices of May Cotton Futures at New York   In Cents per Pound

Year of Delivery		Year Prior to Delivery										Delivery Year					Life of Delivery Range
		Mar.	Apr.	May	June	July	Aug.	Sept.	Oct.	Nov.	Dec.	Jan.	Feb.	Mar.	Apr.	May	
1982	High	84.90	85.35	83.66	82.50	81.27	79.40	73.80	71.90	70.45	67.40	67.95	67.65	66.75	68.95	68.50	87.50
	Low	82.75	83.20	81.80	78.70	79.10	71.45	68.55	68.30	64.40	63.11	65.55	64.65	64.01	65.40	67.50	63.11
	Close	84.20	83.26	82.90	79.00	79.30	69.15	69.15	69.45	65.29	65.70	67.82	64.94	65.92	68.30	68.43	—
1983	High	74.65	76.75	76.50	77.50	77.50	74.90	72.15	69.25	68.15	68.90	68.40	71.25	76.42	75.30	71.60	77.50
	Low	73.50	74.20	73.74	69.45	74.50	69.50	66.75	65.80	65.81	66.20	66.35	66.26	70.30	70.25	69.77	65.80
	Close	74.53	76.40	73.30	76.60	74.66	69.90	67.25	67.42	66.62	67.41	67.33	71.20	75.32	71.08	71.03	—
1984	High	74.60	75.50	80.00	83.40	82.70	83.80	89.40	82.15	83.80	82.05	78.25	78.79	81.85	82.54	84.40	84.40
	Low	70.60	73.25	73.20	79.25	78.20	80.30	78.15	78.70	80.31	78.35	74.75	74.05	77.70	77.90	81.50	66.75
	Close	73.80	73.80	80.00	80.00	81.00	82.80	79.30	81.65	80.98	78.42	77.13	78.09	81.74	82.39	82.39	—
1985	High	81.85	78.00	79.25	79.15	75.25	71.80	69.00	72.05	71.30	67.66	68.20	66.85	68.25	70.45	68.98	79.25
	Low	77.70	75.80	77.45	75.00	69.60	68.74	67.60	67.36	66.45	66.20	65.70	63.28	63.26	64.75	66.10	63.26
	Close	81.74	78.00	78.60	75.00	69.75	69.15	68.00	69.85	66.95	66.95	65.76	64.18	67.60	66.40	66.33	—
1986	High	67.55	67.88	66.65	64.25	62.90	61.10	60.90	62.39	63.45	62.10	63.60	64.48	65.85	67.25	68.05	70.55
	Low	66.35	66.52	61.86	62.00	59.95	59.30	59.25	60.45	60.50	59.60	58.80	59.50	61.90	60.70	66.00	58.80
	Close	67.55	66.52	63.13	63.00	60.25	60.05	60.48	67.34	60.75	62.06	60.32	63.45	65.69	66.80	67.20	—
1987	High	46.70	41.85	40.55	37.30	35.25	38.40	48.90	50.90	52.96	59.50	60.15	57.00	58.70	64.85	66.10	66.10
	Low	40.50	38.30	36.70	33.60	31.56	32.40	35.44	45.51	46.35	52.60	53.30	52.10	54.00	55.55	62.85	31.56
	Close	41.00	40.70	36.73	33.93	34.40	38.40	47.50	47.00	52.96	59.25	54.30	54.60	57.05	64.45	65.61	—
1988	High	56.80	65.23	74.60	74.25	78.35	81.70	78.85	74.60	73.00	71.20	68.90	64.50	64.90	66.05	67.00	81.70
	Low	52.62	55.90	64.00	68.50	71.75	76.20	72.65	65.00	67.81	63.90	61.60	59.20	60.71	60.25	66.00	50.50
	Close	56.22	65.23	71.30	72.50	78.05	78.50	74.05	68.75	70.05	67.65	62.41	61.28	62.88	66.05	66.73	—
1989	High	59.90	58.75	63.60	68.70	62.90	56.80	56.18	57.80	57.20	59.79						
	Low	57.55	55.35	57.00	60.70	55.70	49.03	50.10	51.75	53.22	55.70						
	Close	58.80	56.90	61.75	60.88	56.15	51.72	51.42	56.00	56.70	58.45						

Source: N.Y. Cotton Exchange   T.184

COTTON "2" NYCE
Weekly high low & close of nearest futures

United States Government Crop Forecasts and Actual Cotton Crops

	Forecasts of Production (1,000 Bales of 480 Lbs.[1])					Actual Crop	Forecasts of Yields (In Lbs. Per Harv. Acre)					Actual Yield
Year	Aug. 1	Sept. 1	Oct. 1	Nov. 1	Dec. 1		Aug. 1	Sept. 1	Oct. 1	Nov. 1	Dec. 1	
1976	10,734	10,375	10,251	9,891	10,264	10,581	466	451	445	435	451	465
1977	13,535	13,302	13,317	13,832	14,496	14,389	506	495	500	503	525	520
1978	11,820	11,155	10,873	10,981	10,841	10,856	462	425	429	418	421	420
1979	13,710	14,245	14,356	14,544	14,527	14,629	497	525	528	535	534	547
1980	12,812	11,689	11,589	11,224	11,125	11,122	461	421	419	408	411	404
1981	14,789	15,507	15,476	15,560	15,733	15,646	515	540	540	543	546	542
1982	11,143	11,029	11,365	11,947	12,102	11,963	563	569	587	605	613	590
1983	7,810	7,776	7,550	7,497	7,725	7,771	503	501	487	504	506	508
1984	12,569	13,276	13,272	13,271	13,292	12,982	583	615	620	613	610	600
1985	13,780	13,655	13,638	13,875	13,810	13,432	638	632	633	644	644	630
1986	10,676	10,506	10,006	9,875	9,792	9,731	573	565	539	546	539	552
1987	12,907	12,846	13,336	13,936	14,281	14,760	615	616	640	671	695	706
1988	14,934	14,709	14,714	14,837	15,197		616	605	605	612	627	

[1] Net Weight bales.   Source: Crop Reporting Board, U.S.D.A.

T.175

U.S. Production of Cotton (Upland) & American-Pima In Thous. of 480-Lb. Net Weight Bales

Crop Year								Upland							New Mexico	Total Amer. Pima
Crop Year	Ala-bama	Ari-zona	Arkan-sas	Cali-fornia	Geor-gia	Loui-siana	Missis-sippi	Mis-souri	No. Car.	Okla-homa	So. Car.	Ten-nessee	Texas	New Mexico	Total Amer. Pima
1978	291	1,068	660	1,940	111	478	1,378	188	45	355	115	235	3,792	101	93.4
1979	324	1,280	606	3,408	152	690	1,437	157	43	522	116	171	5,515	104	98.6
1980	275	1,354	444	3,109	86	460	1,143	177	52	205	77	200	3,320	107	104.2
1981	422	1,556	604	3,535	159	742	1,565	168	95	440	164	315	5,663	141	79.6
1982	460	1,095	534	3,073	235	870	1,760	204	102	238	155	339	2,700	78	98.7
1983	183	725	323	1,971	112	532	900	73	43	145	53	151	2,380	70	94.7
1984	447	1,097	612	2,913	281	1,056	1,650	187	120	183	170	337	3,680	87	130.4
1985	545	928	703	3,114	370	742	1,655	204	117	285	180	419	3,910	71	155.1
1986	330	675	602	2,245	185	673	1,190	196	109	210	87	396	2,535	62	205.9
1987	397	849	901	2,989	338	977	1,745	330	98	346	106	634	4,635	89	284.6
1988[1]	380	890	1,050	2,900	350	950	1,850	300	135	280	145	580	4,900	100	347.2

[1] Preliminary. Source: Crop Reporting Board, U.S.D.A.   T.176

Gross Entries of Cotton into U.S. Government Loan Program   In Thousands of Running Bales (480-Lb.)

Crop Yr.	Aug.	Sept.	Oct.	Nov.	Dec.	Jan.	Feb.	Mar.	April	May[1]	June[1]	July[1]	Total
1978–9	0	5	26	89	215	584	352	189	68	16	14	[2]	1,560
1979–0	0	[2]	23	294	319	600	316	110	51	35	8	[2]	1,759
1980–1	0	[2]	8	253	528	912	343	204	36	28	16	[2]	2,328
1981–2	0	9	132	293	1,081	2,796	1,120	473	117	39	21	2	6,083
1982–3	0	46	143	674	1,857	1,590	4,503	4,160	43	23	13	3	5,062
1983–4	0	0	165	227	253	513	188	264	127	9	32	5	1,765
1984–5	0	1	11	98	563	776	1,057	324	62	44	32	5	2,977
1985–6	31	202	771	1,497	1,406	2,375	781	159	61	12	40	60	7,365
1986–7	22	136	775	1,146	1,124	1,664	662	504	97	40	30	6	6,204
1987–8	[2]	25	400	839	745	1,503	1,305	321	170	44	18	9	5,381
1988–9	10	192	1,131	2,015	2,649								

NOTE: Seasonal totals are net, due to allowances for rejections. [1] Entries after April 30 represent late reporting. [2] Less than one thousand bales. Sources: N.Y. Cotton Exchange; Commodity Credit Corporation   T.178

U.S. Daily Rate of Upland Cotton Mill Consumption[2] on Cotton-System Spinning Spindles
In Thousands of 480 Lb. Running Bales[3]

Crop Yr.	Aug.	Sept.	Oct.	Nov.	Dec.	Jan.	Feb.	Mar.	Apr.	May	June	July	Average
1978–9	22,941	22,780	24,090	23,809	21,735	24,114	23,567	25,306	23,358	24,193	24,454	20,127	23,373
1979–0	23,617	24,177	25,188	24,099	21,813	24,160	25,353	25,654	24,899	24,781	23,883	18,473	23,836
1980–1[3]	22.1	22.8	23.9	22.9	19.0	21.8	22.3	21.5	21.7	22.1	21.3	19.3	21.7
1981–2	21.4	20.7	22.4	20.1	16.0	18.9	19.9	19.7	20.5	19.6	18.4	16.0	19.5
1982–3	19.3	19.0	20.8	19.5	17.0	20.2	21.5	22.0	21.5	22.0	21.7	18.4	20.2
1983–4	22.6	22.4	22.9	22.3	18.7	23.5	22.4	21.9	21.5	22.1	20.1	17.7	21.6
1984–5	21.4	20.4	21.4	19.5	16.9	20.0	20.9	20.8	21.0	21.9	21.0	18.5	20.3
1985–6	22.9	22.5	24.6	23.9	19.5	23.8	24.9	24.6	24.8	25.2	24.4	20.9	23.4
1986–7	26.7	26.2	27.3	26.5	23.1	27.3	28.1	29.4	28.7	29.3	28.3	27.0	27.3
1987–8[1]	30.3	30.1	31.0	30.3	24.4	28.4	29.5	29.5	27.8	27.6	26.5	21.7	28.1
1988–9[1]	28.2	27.0	26.9	25.4									

[1] Preliminary. [2] Not seasonally adjusted. [3] Data prior to 1980 are in running bales. Source: Bureau of the Census; U.S.D.C.   T.180

COTTON

Consumption of American and Foreign Cotton in the United States   In Thousands of Running Bales

Year	Aug.	Sept.	Oct.	Nov.	Dec.	Jan.	Feb.	Mar.	Apr.	May	June	July	Total
1980–1	443	456	597	458	475	435	446	539	435	441	531	385	5,641
1981–2	429	517	448	403	400	378	398	493	410	392	460	317	5,038
1982–3	386	474	416	391	425	404	430	549	431	441	543	369	5,259
1983–4	453	560	459	446	468	469	448	548	430	442	503	354	5,628
1984–5	428	509	428	390	423	399	418	519	419	439	525	369	5,268
1985–6	458	562	493	477	486	595	499	492	620	503	489	522	6,198
1986–7	534	523	683	529	576	546	562	734	573	586	708	540	7,096
1987–8[1]	606	753	621	606	610	568	590	738	556	551	662	433	7,294
1988–9[1]	563	676	538	509									

[1] Preliminary.   *Source: Bureau of the Census*   T.188

Exports of American Cotton from the United States   In Thousands of Running Bales

Year	Aug.	Sept.	Oct.	Nov.	Dec.	Jan.	Feb.	Mar.	Apr.	May	June	July	Total
1980–1	402	393	237	436	541	669	2,352	733	498	458	320	264	7,303
1981–2	990	261	262	478	737	653	754	873	676	484	498	396	7,062
1982–3	342	351	293	382	377	438	368	487	612	464	831	409	5,354
1983–4	383	322	261	441	632	663	719	896	723	607	422	365	6,434
1984–5	452	264	292	484	629	793	766	625	544	426	353	252	5,880
1985–6	193	187	207	223	187	396	180	176	163	76	55	21	2,064
1986–7[1]	261	346	314	529	3,149	429	499	595	529	512	422	400	7,985
1987–8[1]	395	295	346	580	681	626	698	735	541	488	523	303	6,211
1988–9[1]	249	249											

[1] Preliminary.   *Source: Foreign Agricultural Service, U.S.D.A.*   T.185

U.S. Exports of American Cotton to Countries of Destination   In Thousands of 480-Pound Bales

Yr. Beg. Aug. 1	Bangla-desh	Can-ada	Hong Kong	France	W. Ger-many	Egypt	Italy	Japan	Indo-nesia	Spain	Swe-den	United King-dom	Rep. of Korea	P.R. China	Tai-wan	USSR	World Total
1980–1	33	267	205	42	112		54	1,139		60	10	38	1,303	1,375	351		5,926
1981–2	50	167	243	58	119		106	1,626		57	17	43	1,412	848	777	0	6,567
1982–3	88	238	158	45	163		105	1,286		72	23	50	1,322	20	378	192	5,207
1983–4	135	227	283	154	195	0	252	1,709	320	114	28	67	1,269	12	495	351	6,785
1984–5	60	195	125	132	195	126	301	1,464	258	118	22	72	1,257	6	513	329	6,211
1985–6	14	98	1	8	85	120	91	520	105	29	15	35	513	0	46	0	1,958
1986–7[1]	89	70	324	114	263	68	263	1,330	1,723	60	15	56	46	0	52	0	6,684
1987–8[1]	42	153	88	67	376	93	406	1,569	287	83	19	69	1,450	0	424	98	6,582

[1] Preliminary.   *Source: Bureau of the Census*   T.189

U.S. Fiber Prices   In Cents per Pound

Year	Cotton[1] Actual	Cotton[1] Raw[5] Equivalent	Rayon[2] Actual	Rayon[2] Raw[5] Equivalent	Polyester[3] Actual	Polyester[3] Raw[5] Equivalent	Price Ratios[4] in Percent Cotton/Rayon	Price Ratios[4] in Percent Cotton/Polyester
1982	68	76	84	88	77	80	.86	.95
1983	78	86	80	84	73	76	1.02	1.13
1984	76	84	84	88	79	82	.95	1.02
1985	66	73	79	82	66	69	.89	1.06
1986	61	68	76	79	62	65	.86	1.05
1987	73	81	81	84	66	69	.96	1.17
1988 Jan.	69	77	83	86	69	72	.90	1.07
Feb.	66	73	83	86	69	72	.85	1.01
Mar.	67	74	87	91	72	75	.81	.99
Apr.	68	76	87	91	72	77	.84	1.01
May	69	77	89	93	74	77	.85	1.00
June	71	79	89	95	76	79	.85	1.03
July	66	73	91	95	76	79	.77	.92

[1] SLM-1¹⁄₁₆″ at group B Mill points, net weight.   [2] 1.5 and 3.0 denier, regular rayon staple.   [3] Reported average market price for 1.5 denier polyester staple for cotton blending.   [4] Raw fiber equivalent.   [5] Actual prices converted to estimated raw fiber equivalent as follows: cotton, divided by 0.90, rayon and polyester, divided by 0.96.   *Source: USDA, Agricultural Marketing Service and trade reports.*

U.S. Imports of Cotton Cloth (Raw Cotton Equivalent) In Thousands of Bales (Net Weight—480 Lbs.)

Year	Jan.	Feb.	Mar.	Apr.	May	June	July	Aug.	Sept.	Oct.	Nov.	Dec.	Total
1984	99.2	96.5	102.1	97.9	79.1	98.9	101.7	91.3	80.1	80.6	66.0	59.8	1,053.2
1985	60.5	85.4	86.0	77.3	94.0	81.5	81.2	72.6	91.8	95.5	98.9	100.2	1,024.9
1986	116.4	109.1	128.9	116.6	106.5	104.8	127.1	109.6	100.2	98.8	96.3	107.9	1,322.2
1987[1]	119.9	142.1	136.4	119.6	119.3	140.4	143.3	140.4	130.1	146.6	143.8	135.3	1,617.2
1988[1]	98.7	102.6	107.6	98.6	90.4	87.3	86.0	91.6	87.2				

[1] Preliminary. *Source: Bureau of the Census*

U.S. Exports of Cotton Cloth (Raw Cotton Equivalent) In Thousands of Bales (Net Weight—480 Lbs.)

Year	Jan.	Feb.	Mar.	Apr.	May	June	July	Aug.	Sept.	Oct.	Nov.	Dec.	Total
1980	50.6	54.2	52.4	45.2	42.4	47.2	34.6	44.3	48.0	42.0	38.4	40.9	540.2
1981	34.8	28.2	35.8	35.7	30.9	30.8	21.7	25.9	25.8	27.5	26.6	21.9	345.6
1982	18.2	18.6	20.4	20.6	24.3	24.8	22.7	15.7	18.4	20.7	18.4	16.4	239.2
1983	20.1	15.1	18.2	17.2	14.2	15.9	12.7	14.0	15.4	16.0	15.3	14.8	188.8
1984	14.2	12.3	13.6	13.4	14.2	16.9	13.5	12.8	15.7	16.7	14.1	13.5	170.9
1985	18.7	15.2	19.8	21.2	17.3	18.6	15.7	21.6	24.7	17.4	15.6	14.7	220.5
1986	17.5	20.1	23.6	23.5	27.4	23.6	17.3	30.1	26.2	26.1	28.2	30.0	293.6
1987[1]	20.2	27.5	25.4	21.7	20.3	22.1	19.0	23.0	19.9	20.6	20.5	19.9	260.6
1988[1]	18.5	18.1	23.9	20.4	19.3	20.4	16.8	19.3	25.0				

[1] Preliminary. *Source: Bureau of the Census* T.193

United States Cotton Ginnings To: In Thousands of Running Bales

Crop Year	Aug. 1	Aug. 16	Sept. 1	Sept. 16	Oct. 1	Oct. 15	Nov. 1	Nov. 15	Dec. 1	Dec. 15	Jan. 1	Jan. 15	Feb. 1	Total Crop
1981–2	44	N.A.	427	645	1,725	3,299	5,541	7,688	10,156	12,023	13,460	14,276	14,778	15,150
1982–3	40	N.A.	453	578	1,529	2,660	5,288	7,202	8,823	9,627	10,574	10,974	11,300	11,526
1983–4	2	N.A.	315	397	763	1,748	3,348	4,638	6,003	6,880	7,209	7,389	7,476	7,504
1984–5	163	N.A.	634	780	1,175	2,277	4,321	7,025	8,972	10,478	11,079	11,682	12,319	12,545
1985–6	70	N.A.	681	1,073	2,431	4,342	6,246	8,216	10,052	11,372	12,365	12,776	12,948	12,988
1986–7	145	N.A.	624	1,022	2,407	3,618	5,292	6,369	7,491	8,263	8,588	9,093	9,270	9,438
1987–8	1	N.A.	429	1,242	3,196	5,359	7,531	9,135	11,076	12,581	13,274	13,733	14,177	14,359
1988[1]	136	N.A.	804	1,152	2,277	4,109	6,088	9,449	11,698	13,258	14,276			

[1] Preliminary. *Source: Bureau of Census* T.171

Cotton Government Loan Program in the United States

Crop Yr. Beginning Aug.	Acreage Prospective Planting Intentions (Thousand Acres)	Acreage Harvested (Thousand Acres)	Loan Rate Avg. at Spot[2] Mkts. (¢ Per Lb.)	Loan Rate Target Price (¢ Per Lb.)	Gov't. Owned	Stocks—Aug. 1 Loan	Stocks—Aug. 1 Total Stock	Loan Entries	Total Supply	Loan Cotton Repossessed	Total Distribution
1983–4	9,281	7,348	55.00	76.00	334	4,432	4,766	1,782	6,416	5,958	5,958
1984–5	10,759	10,380	55.00	81.00	121	469	590	2,974	3,564	1,755	1,755
1985–6	10,957	10,229	57.30	81.00	152	1,657	1,809	7,396	9,205	2,376	2,376
1986–7[1]	9,711	8,468	55.00	81.00	766	6,063	6,829	6,204	13,033	9,933	9,933
1987–8[3]	10,354	10,353	52.25	79.40	189	2,911	3,100	5,379	8,479	5,117	5,117
1988–9[3]	11,578	11,891	51.80	75.90	161	3,201	3,362	6,100	9,462	3,050	5,117

[1] Preliminary. [2] Strict low middling, 1 1/16″ at 10 markets. [3] Estimate. *Source: Department of Agriculture* T.174

COTTON

Average Producer Price of Gray Cotton Broadwovens   Index 1982 = 100[1]

Year	Jan.	Feb.	Mar.	Apr.	May	June	July	Aug.	Sept.	Oct.	Nov.	Dec.	Average
1982	244.0	243.6	242.8	242.2	242.7	240.3	240.4	240.1	239.0	237.4	237.1	236.4	240.0
1983	234.8	234.1	234.2	236.1	236.1	236.7	237.5	239.7	241.5	242.6	243.6	244.3	238.4
1984	244.9	246.2	246.7	248.2	248.1	247.8	248.0	244.9	242.9	242.0	240.9	239.7	245.0
1985	239.5	237.3	237.1	235.5	235.7	235.3	235.1	232.3	231.7	231.8	231.7	231.6	234.6
1986	228.0	228.4	228.6	229.7	230.1	230.0	230.0	228.1	226.9	226.2	227.2	229.4	228.6
1987[1]	101.8	101.8	101.9	102.5	103.0	103.3	106.0	103.9	107.1	109.5	110.6	111.5	105.2
1988[2]	112.7	114.3	114.5	115.9	116.2	116.1	115.9	115.5	115.7	112.2	111.8		

[1] Data prior to 1987 are for cotton yarn—1967 = 100.   [2] Preliminary.   *Source: Bureau of Labor Statistics (0337-01)*   T.181

Cotton Cloth[1] Production in the United States   In Millions of Linear Yards

Year	First Quarter	Second Quarter	Third Quarter	Fourth Quarter	Total Year	Year	First Quarter	Second Quarter	Third Quarter	Fourth Quarter	Total Year
1981	966	961	942	987	3,856	1985	1,030	1,002	933	955	3,921
1982	979	961	868	987	3,794	1986	1,129	942	936	963	4,364
1983	1,068	1,052	1,032	1,040	4,192	1987[2]	1,163	1,217	1,199	1,195	4,772
1984	1,069	1,031	947	955	4,002	1988					

[1] Cotton broadwoven goods over 12 inches in width.   [2] Preliminary.   *Source: Bureau of the Census*   T.192

U.S. American Upland Cotton—Ginnings, by Staple Length   In Thousands Running of Bales

Year beginning August	(13/16") 26 & under	(7/8") 28	(28/32") 29	(15/16") 30	(31/32") 31	(1") 32	(1 1/32") 33	(1 1/16") 34	(1 3/32") 35	(1 1/8") 36	37 & Over	All staple lengths
1981	2	25	155	805	1,924	1,700	1,124	2,725	4,419		2,194	15,073
1982	2	16	78	412	935	676	454	985	3,509		4,362	11,430
1983	3	22	65	251	482	471	513	1,012	2,531		2,063	7,413
1984	7	45	122	414	761	719	715	1,149	2,858		5,630	12,419
1985	—	5	38	234	825	889	883	1,679	4,182	2,380	1,721	12,837
1986	—	2	13	58	226	491	1,058	1,859	3,184	2,159	186	9,237
1987[1]	1	4	18	71	277	698	1,505	2,643	5,119	——3,748——		14,083

[1] Preliminary.   *Source: Agricultural Marketing Service, U.S.D.A.*   T.179

Raw Cotton Equivalent of U.S. Textile Imports   In Thousands of Pounds

Year and month	Yarn, Thread, and Woven Fabric				Pile fabrics and mfrs.	Bed clothes and towels	Gloves hosiery, and hdkf.	Primarily Manufactured Products						Grand total imports
	Yarn	Woven Fabric 100 percent cotton	Blends	Total All				Other wearing apparel	Lace fabric and articles	Household and clothing articles	Misc. products	Floor covering	Total All	
1983	40,881	274,467	64,108	380,706	7,721	70,067	25,383	597,423	5,957	11,855	28,426	7,526	754,796	1,135,502
1984	52,897	360,791	90,126	505,533	12,572	106,468	26,609	733,111	9,651	18,652	37,741	14,649	959,942	1,465,575
1985	53,818	341,896	93,569	491,874	17,916	127,494	30,052	865,476	10,372	19,681	46,197	17,984	1,137,294	1,629,166
1986	103,249	431,289	97,468	634,678	19,576	133,637	27,054	988,906	6,787	30,095	46,410	18,389	1,275,799	1,910,477
1987	131,969	559,245	82,529	776,258	20,153	152,745	31,591	1,234,040	7,113	30,758	53,153	20,657	1,559,438	2,335,692

Source: Bureau of the Census

Raw Cotton Equivalent of U.S. Textile Exports   In Thousands of Pounds

Year and month	Semi-Manufactured					Manufactured Products								Grand total exports
	Yarn	Sewing thread crochet, darning and embroidery cotton	Fabric standard constructions	Other fabric	Total all	Blankets, spreads, pillow cases, and sheets	Towels	Wearing Apparel Knit	Wearing Apparel Other than knit	Other household and clothing articles	Floor covering	Industrial products	Total all	
1983	18,854	11,577	51,667	7,747	90,636	8,725	5,705	27,957	44,113	13,736	13,986	11,601	128,977	219,614
1984	11,186	8,369	55,848	5,997	82,047	9,008	4,470	25,904	42,360	13,894	9,813	15,014	124,032	206,081
1985	16,843	8,466	74,919	5,134	105,892	9,802	3,582	25,326	30,158	11,037	8,155	16,541	107,332	213,224
1986	9,892	6,049	118,154	6,202	140,925	8,192	4,515	27,413	46,437	13,860	9,793	20,992	133,904	274,828
1987	13,491	5,207	99,536	5,643	124,803	8,516	6,224	47,823	60,584	13,189	12,142	21,673	173,200	298,004

Source: Bureau of the Census

Cottonseed and Products

The level of cottonseed output depends on the amount of cotton ginned. World cottonseed output for 1988/89 was estimated by USDA at 32.09 million tonnes, up 4 percent from 1987/88. China continued to be the world's largest producer, but drought in parts of the country was expected to cut yields. China's cottonseed output was estimated at 6.92 million tonnes in 1988/89, below 7.22 million in 1987/88, but up from 1986/87.

In the U.S., the second largest producer, the 1988/89 cottonseed supply was estimated at 6.1 million tonnes. Although planted acreage was up 17 percent, a production increase of 5 percent to 5.49 million tonnes was expected. Cottonseed yields returned to trend levels of 0.46 tonnes/acre from 1987/88's record 0.57 tonnes.

Around the world, smaller output was expected in Egypt, Pakistan, and Turkey. A slight improvement was anticipated in India, Syria, Australia, Greece and Spain.

About 99 percent of all cottonseed is utilized in the producing countries, which either process it into oil and meal or feed it as whole seed to cattle. World trade in seed is less than 300,000 tonnes. The largest importer is Japan, which was expected to take 138,000 tonnes in 1988/89.

Global cottonseed oil production in 1988/89 was pegged at 3.60 million tonnes, compared with the previous year's output of 3.45 million. Global cotton oil inventories as of October 1, 1988, were put at 150,000 tonnes. The 1988/89 carryover was expected to fall to 150,000 tonnes, if cotton oil remained competitive with other vegetable oils.

Global exports of cottonseed oil were forecast at 390,000 in 1988/89, down 10,000 tonnes from 1987/88.

World Production of Cottonseed   In Thousands of Metric Tons

Crop Year	Sudan	Argentina	Brazil	China	Egypt	India	Mexico	Pakistan	Peru	Turkey	South Africa	USSR	United States	World Total
1982–3	421	290	1,198	6,117	769	3,047	313	1,648	60	782	53	5,094	4,304	26,665
1983–4	438	326	995	7,883	680	2,647	377	1,021	100	835	68	4,815	2,791	25,680
1984–5	435	293	1,758	10,639	664	3,447	459	2,014	145	928	89	4,760	4,671	33,910
1985–6		200	1,405	7,050	695	3,652	355	2,468	167	810	94	5,100	4,789	30,631
1986–7[1]		203	1,085	6,018	645	3,218	240	2,640	142	829	135	4,870	3,448	27,110
1987–8[2]			1,375	7,220	564	3,054		2,946		837		4,485	5,224	30,860
1988–9[2]			1,427	7,200	550	3,550		2,850		1,006		5,020	5,399	32,360

[1] Preliminary.   [2] Estimated.   Source: Foreign Agricultural Service, U.S.D.A.   T.194

Salient Statistics of Cottonseed in the United States

Yr. Begin. Aug. 1	Stocks	Production	Total Supply	Crush	Exports	Other	Total Disappearance	Farm Price $/Ton	Value of Production Mil. $	Oil Mil. Lbs.	Meal Ths. Sh. Tons	Linters Ths. Running Bales
			In Thousand Short Tons								*Products Produced*	
1982–3	781	4,744	5,525	3,800	12	1,342	5,154	77.0	366.2	1,134	1,588	1,029
1983–4	371	3,076	3,447	2,583	50	698	3,331	166.0	511.5	777	1,134	699
1984–5	116	5,149	5,265	3,514	60	1,285	4,859	100.0	512.0	1,174	1,732	955
1985–6	406	5,279	5,685	3,417	9	1,912	5,338	66.0	348.4	1,070	1,526	936
1986–7	347	3,801	4,148	2,520	17	1,422	3,959	78.0	296.5	781	1,112	
1987–8[1]	180	5,760	5,958	3,396	50	2,153	5,599	83.0	478.8	1,040	1,558	
1988–9[2]	359	5,951	6,110	3,600	50	2,085	5,735	120.0	714.1	1,055	1,655	

[1] Preliminary   [2] Forecast   Source: Economic Research Service, U.S.D.A.

Supply & Distribution of Cottonseed Oil in the United States   In Millions of Pounds

Crop Year[3] Beginning Oct.	Production	Imports for Consumption	Stocks Oct. 1	Total Supply	Exports	Total	Domestic	Per Capita Consump. of Salad & Ck. Oils – in Lbs. –	Shortening	Margarine	Salad & Cooking Oils	Other	Total	Foots & Loss	Other	Total
					Disappearance				*Food Uses*			*Utilization*		*Nonfood Uses*		
1982	1,134	2	104	1,240	546	1,150	604	21.9	142	31	444	16	634			
1983	777	18	90	885	303	835	532	24.0	143	35	366	17	562			
1984	1,174	—	50	1,224	433	1,117	684	19.8	156	N.A.	399	N.A.	607			
1985–6	1,070	—	107	1,177	442	1,092	650	23.5	202	N.A.	373	N.A.	627			
1986–7	781	11	85	877	214	787	573	24.2	135	36	408	14	593			
1987–8[1]	1,040	0	90	1,130	350	1,035	685	24.7	160		600		760			
1988–9[2]	1,055	0	95	1,150	375	1,060	685									

[1] Preliminary.   [2] Estimate.   Source: Economic Research Service, U.S.D.A.   T.201

COTTONSEED AND PRODUCTS

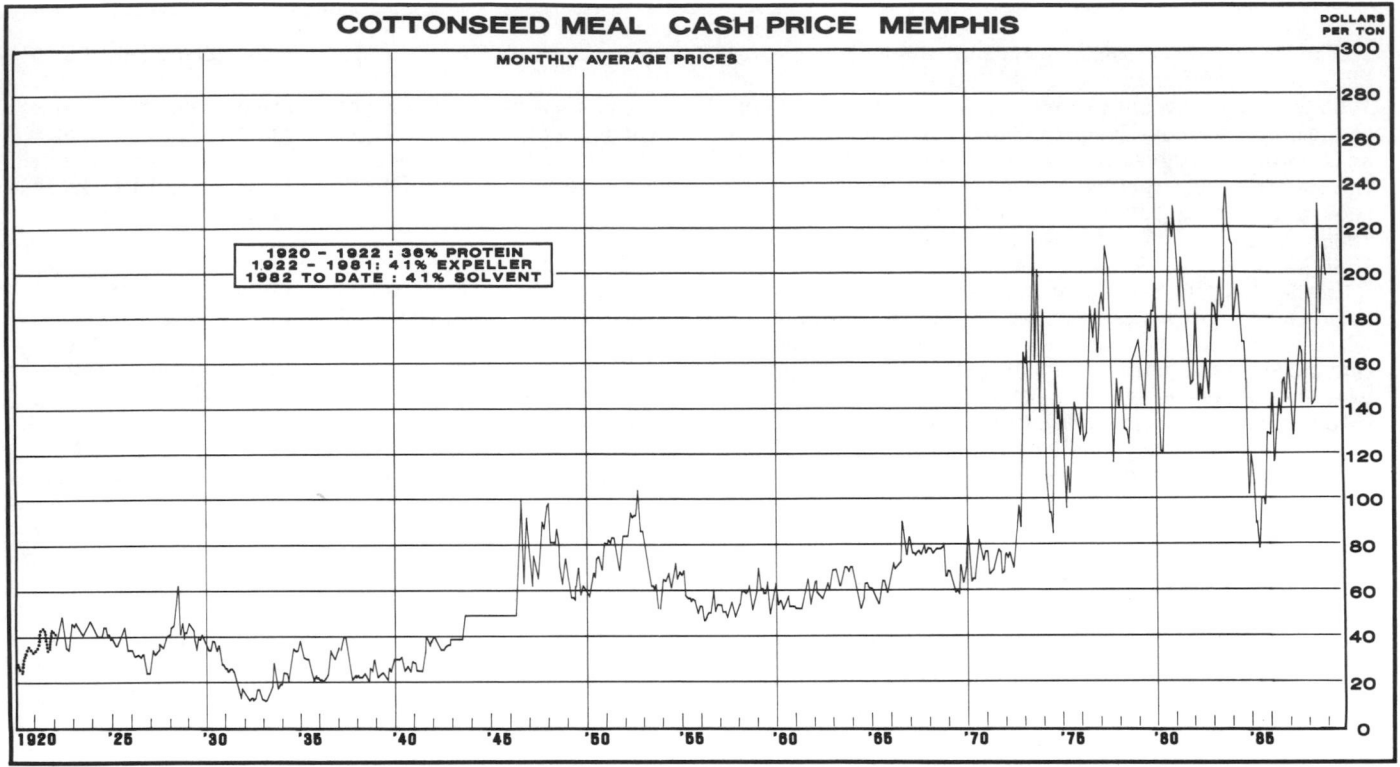

COTTONSEED MEAL CASH PRICE MEMPHIS

DOLLARS PER TON

MONTHLY AVERAGE PRICES

1920 – 1922 : 36% PROTEIN
1922 – 1981 : 41% EXPELLER
1982 TO DATE : 41% SOLVENT

U.S. Consumption of Cottonseed Oil in End Products[1] In Millions of Pounds

Year	Oct.	Nov.	Dec.	Jan.	Feb.	Mar.	Apr.	May	June	July	Aug.	Sept.	Total
1983–4	39.7	46.8	46.9	47.5	55.5	52.1	48.8	57.3	50.1	45.6	54.3	42.4	587.0
1984–5	42.8	55.1	63.5	54.2	58.4	59.2	52.3	64.0	50.2	45.2	43.1	35.5	623.4
1985–6	58.8	50.5	49.1	47.8	53.0	53.3	60.9	53.2	50.8	63.6	40.4	44.8	639.4
1986–7	57.3	52.7	53.0	52.0	45.6	49.6	50.9	47.8	45.1	50.0	50.5	47.9	608.7
1987–8[2]	52.7	62.1	57.1	53.6	60.9	77.1	65.2	76.0	80.3	76.8	50.9	53.8	766.5
1988–9[2]	79.4										68.7	74.8	

[1] Includes small amount exported but does not include imported oil. [2] Preliminary *Source: Bureau of the Census*   T.206

U.S. Exports of Cottonseed Oil (Crude & Refined) In Millions of Pounds

Year	Jan.	Feb.	Mar.	Apr.	May	June	July	Aug.	Sept.	Oct.	Nov.	Dec.	Total
1983	41.8	58.8	97.0	25.8	53.0	23.8	42.5	15.5	20.6	10.5	18.4	21.8	429.5
1984	36.4	39.9	31.8	32.9	46.5	12.8	29.9	8.8	13.1	11.0	37.1	77.3	377.5
1985	47.1	72.7	37.7	38.9	22.9	20.6	17.5	13.1	36.2	19.1	30.1	65.6	421.5
1986	21.9	39.6	32.6	52.6	59.6	27.3	25.1	46.7	13.2	9.3	20.9	25.2	374.0
1987	7.1	14.1	27.5	10.5	25.0	27.0	9.6	12.2	25.8	17.1	32.9	32.8	241.6
1988[1]	24.4	36.7	37.1	50.4	29.9	88.5	18.5	18.7					

[1] Preliminary. *Source: Dept. of Commerce*   T.205

Average Wholesale Price of Cottonseed Meal (41% Solvent) at Memphis In Dollars Per Short Ton

Year	Jan.	Feb.	Mar.	Apr.	May	June	July	Aug.	Sept.	Oct.	Nov.	Dec.	Average
1983	169.40	165.60	153.00	173.40	167.50	164.90	186.90	227.00	237.50	245.00	219.20	214.00	232.34
1984	212.60	178.10	187.30	194.10	190.00	177.50	169.30	168.90	151.60	114.90	101.60	119.40	163.78
1985	109.75	105.60	89.10	82.75	78.10	94.40	99.75	100.00	96.90	116.50	128.75	127.82	102.45
1986	146.25	128.75	115.60	129.25	133.75	132.50	137.00	150.60	152.50	141.90	157.50	160.50	140.51
1987	146.25	138.10	128.00	133.75	149.60	154.50	166.90	163.80	141.50	150.60	177.50	195.00	157.13
1988	187.50	160.00	144.00	143.10	147.50	230.00	223.75	181.00	205.00	212.50	203.00		

Source: Economic Research Service, U.S.D.A.   T.196

Cottonseed Crushed (Consumption) in the United States   In Thousands of Short Tons

Year	Aug.	Sept.	Oct.	Nov.	Dec.	Jan.	Feb.	Mar.	Apr.	May	June	July	Total
1982–3	290.3	285.8	391.5	481.7	432.6	435.6	368.7	321.7	240.5	214.6	164.2	172.3	3,800
1983–4	166.6	120.7	187.9	301.8	296.6	347.8	289.7	294.7	205.6	173.2	124.3	74.1	2,579
1984–5	70.2	72.6	274.3	423.1	424.2	453.4	394.5	395.3	316.2	279.5	219.6	191.3	3,514
1985–6	194.6	197.0	338.0	411.4	368.8	431.5	361.0	349.8	281.3	213.8	154.5	115.3	3,417
1986–7	141.4	167.7	208.5	262.2	283.2	323.5	278.4	255.8	214.7	171.3	134.2	78.8	2,520
1987–8[1]	71.4	137.7	251.8	344.2	363.2	373.4	352.2	340.1	310.7	312.5	275.5	263.6	3,396
1988–9[1]	216.8	179.5	299.3										

[1] Preliminary.   *Source: Bureau of Census*   T.197

Production of Cottonseed Cake and Meal in the United States   In Thousands of Short Tons

Year	Aug.	Sept.	Oct.	Nov.	Dec.	Jan.	Feb.	Mar.	Apr.	May	June	July	Total
1982–3	129.8	129.3	173.5	219.4	197.3	195.1	167.0	146.7	107.8	97.1	71.4	78.9	1,713
1983–4	78.8	55.3	86.7	144.5	140.9	162.4	134.7	136.2	95.1	76.7	55.9	35.8	1,203
1984–5	32.2	32.6	127.3	198.4	198.7	207.7	180.4	181.6	145.0	128.8	99.1	86.2	1,619
1985–6	87.9	90.7	153.1	187.6	169.4	199.1	166.4	159.1	128.6	97.5	71.5	51.9	1,563
1986–7	64.4	77.7	95.0	121.2	130.3	151.1	128.7	116.1	100.0	80.0	61.3	37.3	1,163
1987–8[1]	32.2	58.3	121.7	156.9	169.3	169.4	160.2	155.7	144.0	144.0	124.7	120.6	1,557
1988–9[1]	100.7	80.1	135.4										

[1] Preliminary.   *Source: Bureau of Census*   T.198

U.S. Production of Crude Cottonseed Oil   In Millions of Pounds

Year	Aug.	Sept.	Oct.	Nov.	Dec.	Jan.	Feb.	Mar.	Apr.	May	June	July	Total
1982–3	92.0	88.8	129.8	157.3	143.3	137.6	117.7	102.6	75.8	69.0	53.1	55.7	1,223
1983–4	54.6	37.1	58.6	94.6	93.6	109.5	91.3	96.6	69.3	55.4	40.1	24.4	825
1984–5	21.7	21.6	84.3	132.5	132.5	141.5	124.3	123.3	96.3	87.0	67.7	62.9	1,096
1985–6	60.9	60.7	105.6	129.8	117.1	136.4	115.5	112.0	93.5	69.6	50.1	37.8	1,089
1986–7	48.0	54.5	64.5	83.5	91.4	103.7	90.3	83.3	70.6	55.6	43.5	25.4	814
1987–8[1]	22.6	46.9	84.0	118.2	124.8	125.7	115.8	113.2	104.4	105.8	91.2	91.0	1,144
1988–9[1]	72.7	56.9	98.6										

[1] Preliminary.   *Source: Bureau of Census*   T.199

United States Production of Refined Cottonseed Oil   In Millions of Pounds

Year	Aug.	Sept.	Oct.	Nov.	Dec.	Jan.	Feb.	Mar.	Apr.	May	June	July	Total
1982–3	91.3	76.7	91.5	127.3	124.5	119.2	113.4	103.1	82.6	78.0	60.1	56.5	1,124
1983–4	55.2	39.2	54.6	91.1	97.7	99.7	98.4	100.6	89.1	71.5	43.4	30.5	871
1984–5	25.7	27.8	64.5	121.4	117.6	135.8	122.2	101.9	93.3	95.4	74.6	68.2	1,043
1985–6	55.9	57.0	87.5	117.1	112.0	119.3	109.3	112.9	95.0	63.7	54.9	42.4	1,027
1986–7	60.3	51.2	73.5	90.9	97.6	103.7	96.8	90.3	74.9	59.8	51.0	45.5	896
1987–8[1]	45.8	56.9	71.5	110.3	120.9	122.1	117.8	132.6	116.5	119.2	103.3	109.6	1,227
1988–9[1]	83.2	61.7	93.9										

[1] Preliminary.   *Source: Bureau of Census*   T.202

U.S. Stocks of Cottonseed Oil (Crude & Refined) at End of Month   In Millions of Pounds

Year	Aug.	Sept.	Oct.	Nov.	Dec.	Jan.	Feb.	Mar.	Apr.	May	June	July
1982–3	115.2	103.6	121.1	148.9	172.2	175.3	175.1	158.1	164.6	130.4	113.6	108.9
1983–4	96.7	89.6	82.5	108.6	144.6	152.5	152.1	172.6	167.4	131.7	111.5	86.1
1984–5	61.2	49.8	57.6	74.6	79.4	89.6	98.6	114.2	114.7	107.7	105.8	124.4
1985–6	131.2	106.9	106.2	127.9	130.2	162.0	184.1	197.7	179.7	168.0	154.5	110.4
1986–7	90.4	84.9	77.0	101.1	130.6	165.4	188.1	207.5	204.2	236.2	190.8	165.9
1987–8[1]	127.3	90.2	107.2	136.1	169.8	210.0	197.6	184.7	177.2	197.8	175.6	176.0
1988–9[1]	172.9	160.4	163.7									

[1] Preliminary.   *Source: Bureau of Census*   T.203

COTTONSEED AND PRODUCTS

COTTONSEED OIL   CASH PRICE   NEW YORK

CENTS PER POUND

1920 – 1968: Refined Cottonseed Oil in Tanks
1969 – 1974: Prime Summer Yellow
1975 – to Date: Crude, F.O.B. Southeastern Mills (Tanks Cars)

Average Price of Crude Cottonseed Oil, F.O.B. Southeastern Mills (Tank Cars)   In Cents Per Pound

Year	Jan.	Feb.	Mar.	Apr.	May	June	July	Aug.	Sept.	Oct.	Nov.	Dec.	Average
1981	25.3	24.2	25.3	27.3	26.7	26.6	27.9	24.6	20.7	20.5	20.4	19.8	24.1
1982	19.9	19.5	19.1	20.4	21.0	21.1	20.9	20.3	18.0	16.9	16.8	16.3	19.2
1983	16.3	17.8	18.3	21.4	23.4	21.6	23.6	33.3	36.2	31.7	29.0	28.7	25.1
1984	29.8	29.1	30.1	31.4	41.1	42.6	36.3	32.7	31.0	30.6	31.0	29.3	32.9
1985	27.4	30.1	30.2	32.3	33.3	32.6	29.1	23.8	20.7	18.3	18.9	20.6	26.4
1986	19.9	17.6	15.8	17.5	17.7	17.9	17.6	15.1	14.3	15.4	17.4	17.7	17.0
1987	18.38	18.56	17.85	17.88	18.94	19.25	19.00	16.70	15.44	16.75	17.00	18.35	17.84
1988	21.31	20.19	19.60	21.00	22.88	26.65	30.25	15.00	23.00				

Source: Economic Research Service, U.S.D.A.

T.204

U.S. Exports of Cottonseed Oil to Important Countries   In Thousands of Metric Tons

Yr. Beg. Oct. 1	Canada	Costa Rica	Dom. Rep.	Egypt	W. Ger-many	Guat-emala	India	Salv-ador	Japan	Rep. of Korea	Nether-lands	South Africa	Mex-ico	United Kingdom	Venez-uela	Total
1981–2	4.3	3.1	27.3	156.2	2.3	9.9	0	14.4	41.2	3.0	10.2			3.5	91.2	384.4
1982–3	4.3	.5	6.6	66.3	3.3	15.3	0	14.1	34.6	2.5	5.1	1.2		1.5	73.8	247.5
1983–4	3.5	0	4.5	31.2	7.9	1.1	—	5.3	16.7	2.9	2.1	1.8	.2	3.0	55.4	137.4
1984–5	3.3	1.0	3.9	55.9	—	9.8	—	15.6	22.8	1.8	5.8	2.0	.1	1.5	70.0	196.2
1985–6	2.7	—	5.9	37.8	4.9	11.1	—	29.7	26.3	4.5	8.0	1.6	9.5	.5	48.6	200.7
1986–7	2.9	—	1.9	0	.1	2.2	—	10.9	17.9	5.8	5.0	.5	3.1	0	44.6	97.7
1987–8[1]	4.6	—	6.3	31.5	.1	1.2	—	31.0	21.6	11.5	1.6	1.5	7.3	—	51.3	185.3

[1] Preliminary.   *Source: U.S. Bureau of the Census*

T.202A

Currencies

Despite continued fears about the U.S. trade deficit and federal budget deficit in the foreign exchange markets, the value of the dollar rose in 1988. As measured by the FINEX U.S. Dollar Index, it climbed 8.3 percent in 1988 to 92.50 from its December 31, 1987, close of 85.42 (on a base of 1973=100). The FINEX Index, based on the Federal Reserve Board's trade-weighted dollar index, is updated continuously seven days a week and uses both bids and offers in determining its value. The Fed's index, based on bids only, is released at the end of each business day.

The Fed estimated the average nominal value of its dollar index at 93.0 in the fourth quarter of 1988, little changed from 92.3 in the fourth quarter of 1987. However, when adjusted for changes in consumer prices in the U.S. and the 10 countries in the dollar index, the real value of the dollar index averaged 88.7 (1973=100) in the fourth quarter, up 2.2 percent from the same period in 1987.

The currencies and their percentages in the FRB and FINEX indices are: Deutshemark, 20.8; yen, 13.6; French franc, 13.1; pound sterling, 11.9; Canadian dollar, 9.1; lira, 9.0; Dutch guilder, 8.3; Belgian franc, 6.4; Swedish krona, 4.2; and Swiss franc, 3.6.

The dollar began 1988 under the most severe pressure since the collapse of the Bretton Woods agreement and the introduction of floating exchange rates in 1973. On January 4, the dollar set record postwar lows of 120.25 yen and 1.5630 Deutschemarks (.0083 cent and 63.98 cents, respectively in U.S. terms). However, heavy intervention by the Group of 7 (G-7) central banks boosted the dollar and forced heavy short-covering in the cash market. Soon the market found fundamental reasons to remain long dollars. The U.S. economy avoided the recession many feared would develop after the October 1987 stock market crash, and U.S. exports increased more rapidly than imports, allowing a reduction in the U.S. trade deficit.

Also, the Federal Reserve Board showed its commitment to fight inflation by raising short-term interest rates and keeping a tight lid on the expansion of the money supply. As a result, the U.S. offered a very attractive real rate of return for short-term funds, even after the cost of any hedging in the foreign exchange market.

In 1988, the dollar was strongest from May through August. The European central banks and the Fed intervened frequently during those months to slow the dollar's gains, especially against the Deutschemark. On March 7, the pound sterling topped 3 marks for the first time, despite attempts by the Bank of England to prevent it. The Thatcher government was attempting to restrain inflation with high interest rates, and was using its budget surplus to retire long-term government debt. West Germany was suffering from high unemployment, and low interest rates there were driving funds overseas. The German economy surprised its skeptics by expanding strongly in the third and fourth quarters of 1988 (largely on exports to the rest of Western Europe). But when the Federal Reserve Board raised the discount rate to 6.5 percent on August 9, the greenback climbed to 1.9245 marks, a gain of almost 23 percent from the January low. The yen had lost 12 percent against the dollar, which was trading at 135.20.

However, the dollar's strength apparently drove it above the trading ceiling agreed upon by the G-7 in 1987 and affirmed at the Toronto economic summit in June. On August 25, central banks outside the U.S. raised interest rates, and the dollar lost almost 1 percent against the mark. However, the yen was also softening, and the dollar reached its 1988 high of 137.25 yen on September 2.

In March 1988, the Canadian dollar climbed above 80 U.S. cents for the first time since 1984. Canada's yield curve was inverted in 1988, and while the underlying rate of inflation was in line with the U.S. CPI, Canadian T-bill yields were more than 200 basis points higher. Expectations that the Canadian Senate would ratify the U.S.-Canada free trade pact negotiated in 1987 helped the Canadian dollar, after Prime Minister Mulroney's Progressive Conservatives won the Canadian general election on November 21.

Futures Markets

The Chicago Mercantile Exchange's International Monetary Market (IMM) has futures contracts and options on futures on the British pound, Swiss franc, Deutschemark, Japanese yen, and the Australian and Canadian dollars. The FINEX division of the New York Cotton Exchange trades futures and options on the U.S. Dollar Index. Cash currency options are traded on the Philadelphia Stock Exchange.

Monthly Close of the CRB Currency Futures Index 1977 = 100

Year	Jan.	Feb.	Mar.	Apr.	May	June	July	Aug.	Sept.	Oct.	Nov.	Dec.
1979	Not calculated prior to Sept 1979.								125.1	120.2	121.3	122.9
1980	122.9	120.5	115.1	120.2	122.7	123.6	121.7	124.5	125.0	123.8	121.9	122.5
1981	118.7	115.2	116.3	112.9	109.3	107.2	103.1	104.2	106.4	109.8	112.7	111.6
1982	109.4	105.6	104.7	106.6	104.0	99.7	100.2	93.9	97.7	96.2	98.8	102.4
1983	99.4	98.8	98.8	99.8	99.0	98.5	96.8	95.7	97.4	97.1	96.3	96.2
1984	93.9	97.1	97.7	95.1	94.1	92.2	88.8	89.8	86.2	86.5	84.3	83.1
1985	81.6	78.0	84.2	83.4	84.8	85.5	91.4	90.3	93.9	95.9	98.7	98.8
1986	99.5	103.9	103.3	108.5	104.3	109.6	112.4	113.2	112.3	109.2	112.0	114.4
1987	118.5	119.5	123.3	125.7	123.4	122.9	120.6	123.8	122.6	128.7	134.8	141.3
1988	134.0	133.6	138.3	137.0	134.5	129.2	127.1	125.1	126.7	131.3	136.3	133.7

Source: Commodity Research Bureau.

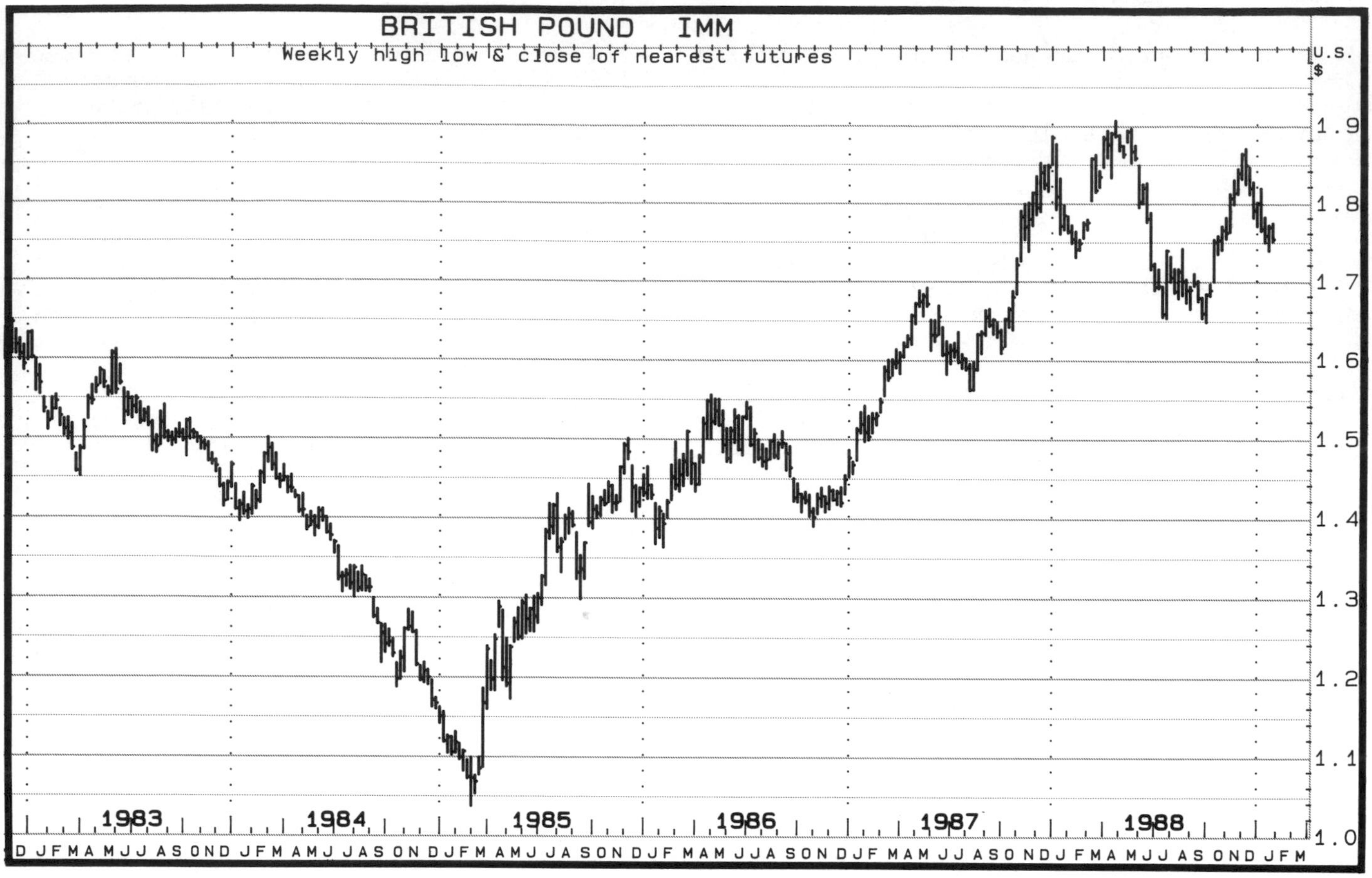

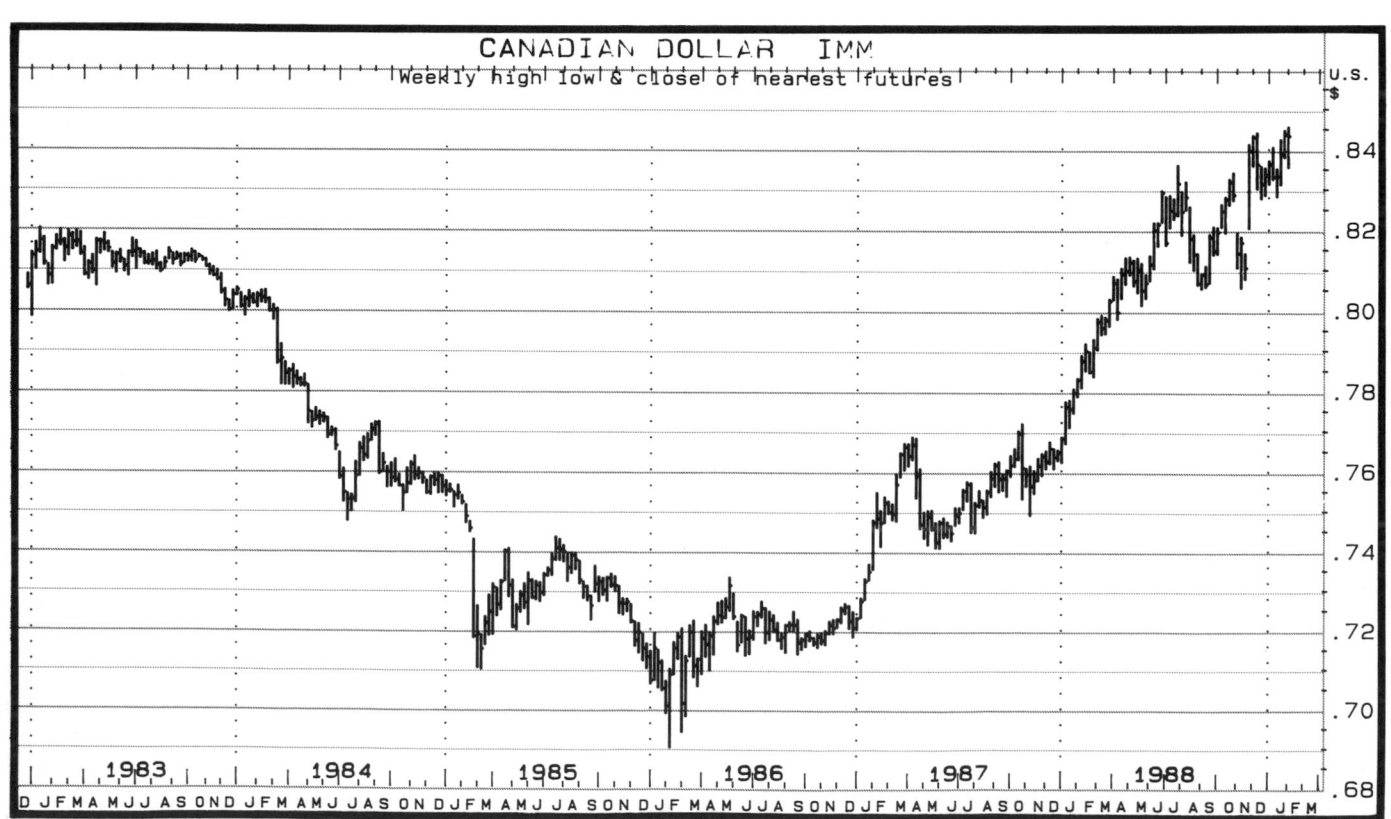

BRITISH POUND IMM
Weekly high low & close of nearest futures
U.S. $
1.9
1.8
1.7
1.6
1.5
1.4
1.3
1.2
1.1
1.0
1983
1984
1985
1986
1987
1988
D J F M A M J J A S O N D J F M A M J J A S O N D J F M A M J J A S O N D J F M A M J J A S O N D J F M A M J J A S O N D J F M A M J J A S O N D J F M

CANADIAN DOLLAR IMM
Weekly high low & close of nearest futures
U.S. $
.84
.82
.80
.78
.76
.74
.72
.70
.68
1983
1984
1985
1986
1987
1988
D J F M A M J J A S O N D J F M A M J J A S O N D J F M A M J J A S O N D J F M A M J J A S O N D J F M A M J J A S O N D J F M A M J J A S O N D J F M

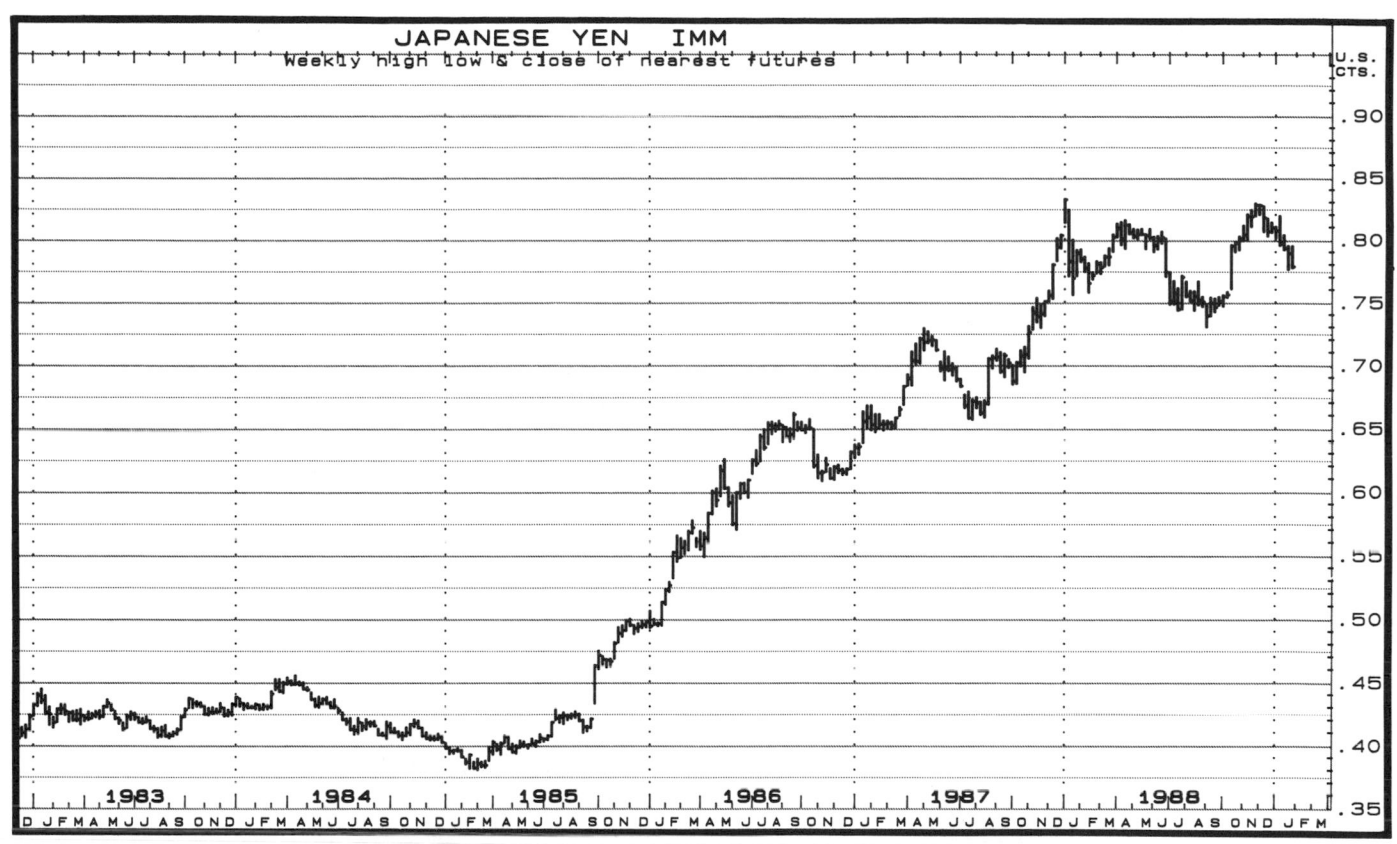

JAPANESE YEN IMM
Weekly high low & close of nearest futures
U.S. CTS.
.90
.85
.80
.75
.70
.65
.60
.55
.50
.45
.40
.35
1983
1984
1985
1986
1987
1988
D J F M A M J J A S O N D J F M A M J J A S O N D J F M A M J J A S O N D J F M A M J J A S O N D J F M A M J J A S O N D J F M A M J J A S O N D J F M

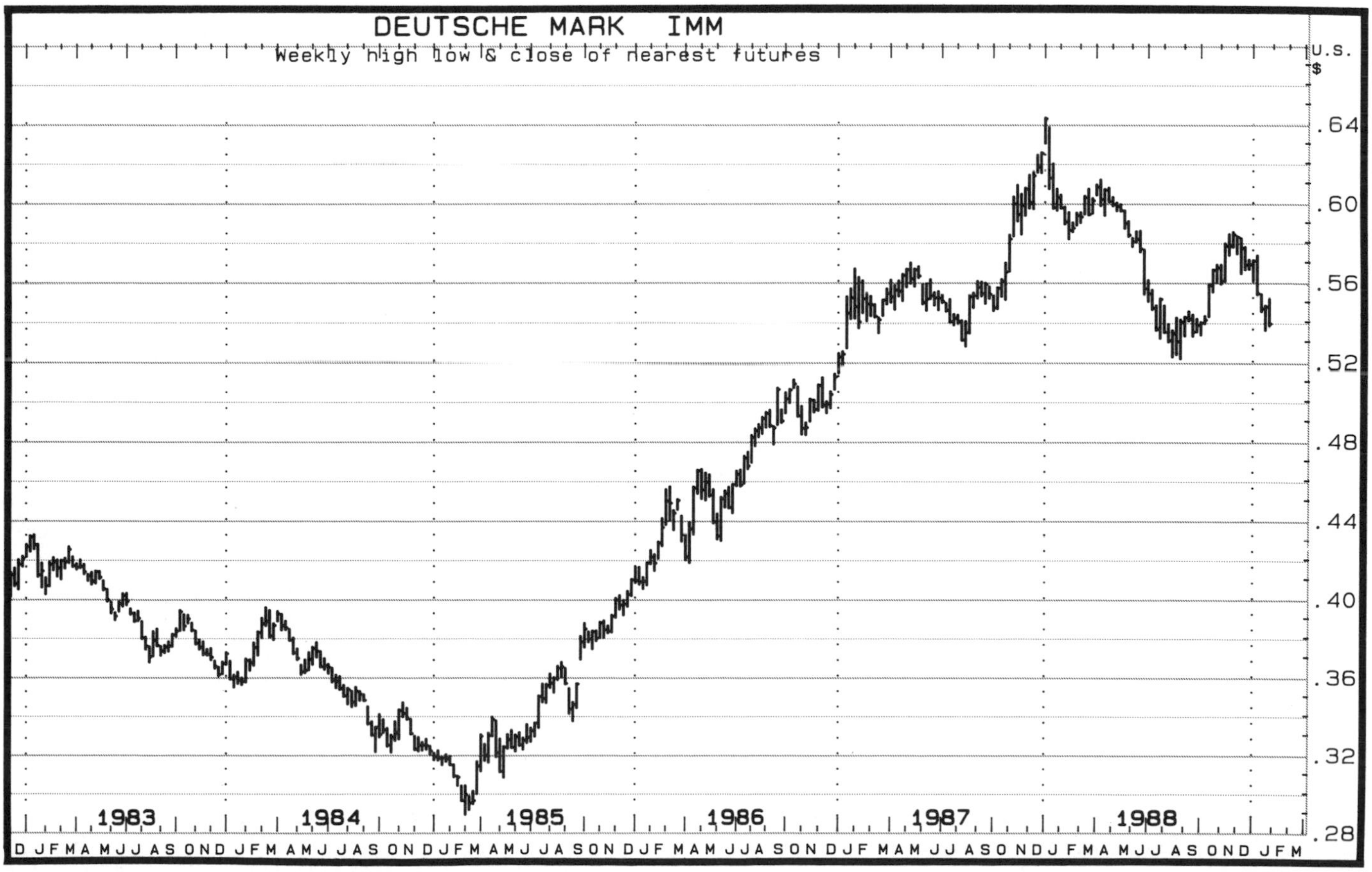

DEUTSCHE MARK IMM
Weekly high low & close of nearest futures
U.S. $
.64
.60
.56
.52
.48
.44
.40
.36
.32
.28
1983
1984
1985
1986
1987
1988
D J F M A M J J A S O N D J F M A M J J A S O N D J F M A M J J A S O N D J F M A M J J A S O N D J F M A M J J A S O N D J F M A M J J A S O N D J F M

CURRENCIES

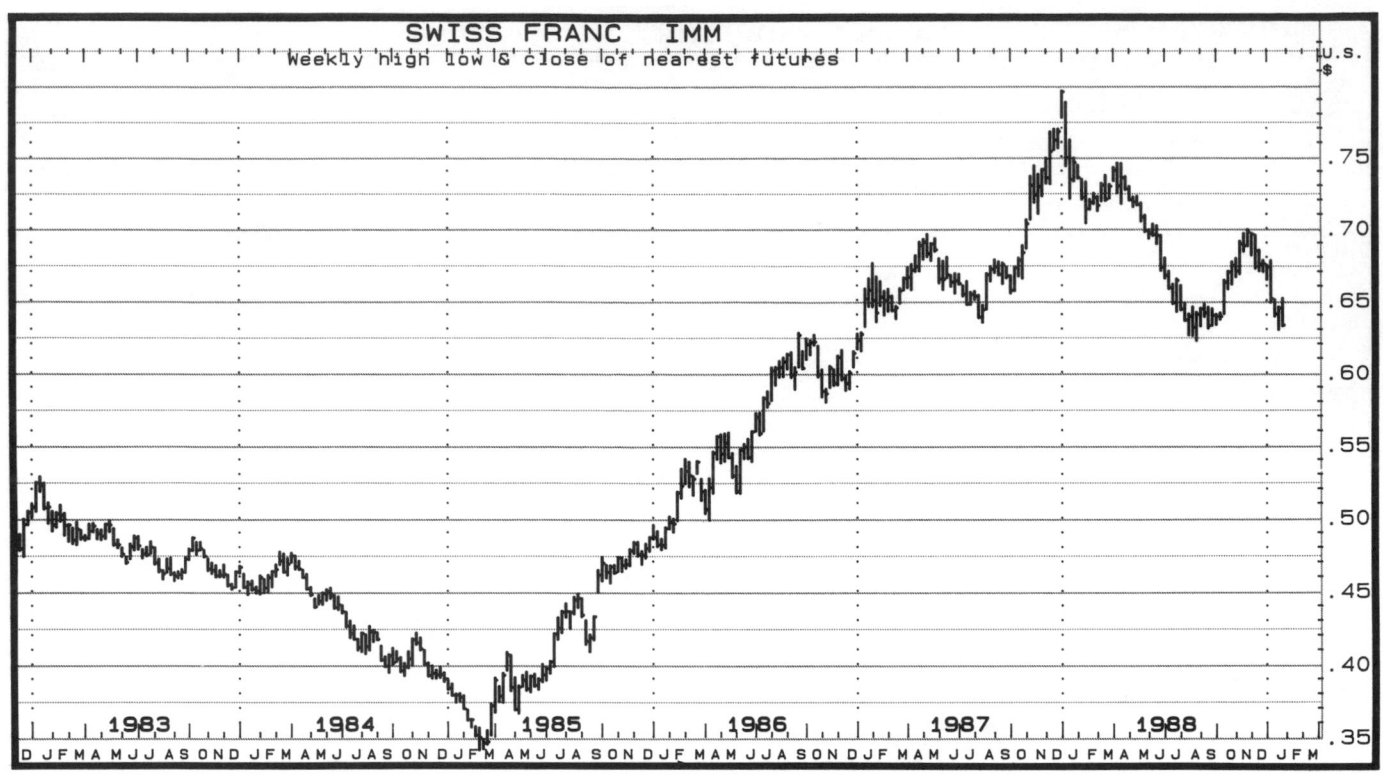

SWISS FRANC IMM
Weekly high low & close of nearest futures

Canadian Dollars per U.S. Dollar

Year	Jan.	Feb.	Mar.	Apr.	May	June	July	Aug.	Sept.	Oct.	Nov.	Dec.	Average
1983	1.228	1.227	1.226	1.232	1.228	1.232	1.233	1.233	1.232	1.232	1.237	1.247	1.232
1984	1.248	1.248	1.269	1.279	1.294	1.304	1.323	1.303	1.314	1.318	1.316	1.320	1.295
1985	1.324	1.354	1.383	1.364	1.375	1.367	1.352	1.357	1.369	1.366	1.376	1.395	1.365
1986	1.407	1.404	1.400	1.387	1.375	1.389	1.380	1.388	1.387	1.388	1.387	1.379	1.389
1987	1.360	1.334	1.319	1.319	1.341	1.338	1.326	1.325	1.315	1.309	1.316	1.307	1.325
1988	1.284	1.268	1.249	1.235	1.237	1.217	1.208	1.224	1.226				

Source: Economic Research Service, U.S.D.A.

T.0581

German Marks per U.S. Dollar

Year	Jan.	Feb.	Mar.	Apr.	May	June	July	Aug.	Sept.	Oct.	Nov.	Dec.	Average
1983	2.389	2.428	2.408	2.439	2.465	2.548	2.590	2.673	2.670	2.601	2.682	2.749	2.553
1984	2.810	2.698	2.596	2.647	2.746	2.738	2.848	2.882	3.028	3.066	2.997	3.102	2.846
1985	3.169	3.300	3.296	3.087	3.103	3.062	2.906	2.792	2.836	2.643	2.594	2.511	2.942
1986	2.437	2.330	2.276	2.268	2.226	2.232	2.148	2.060	2.040	2.005	2.023	1.988	2.169
1987	1.858	1.823	1.834	1.810	1.787	1.819	1.848	1.855	1.812	1.798	1.682	1.634	1.796
1988	1.654	1.697	1.676	1.671	1.693	1.757	1.846	1.886	1.852				

Source: Economic Research Service, U.S.D.A.

T.0582

Japanese Yen per U.S. Dollar

Year	Jan.	Feb.	Mar.	Apr.	May	June	July	Aug.	Sept.	Oct.	Nov.	Dec.	Average
1983	232.5	236.1	238.0	237.6	234.7	240.0	240.4	244.4	242.9	232.3	234.9	234.3	237.5
1984	233.7	233.5	225.2	225.2	230.4	233.4	243.0	242.0	245.3	246.7	243.5	247.8	237.5
1985	254.1	260.2	257.8	251.5	251.6	248.8	241.1	237.3	236.2	214.6	203.8	202.7	238.3
1986	199.8	184.8	178.6	174.7	166.9	167.4	158.1	154.1	154.6	156.4	162.8	162.2	168.4
1987	154.7	153.3	151.3	142.8	140.4	144.5	150.3	147.3	143.2	143.1	135.4	128.3	144.5
1988	127.6	129.1	127.0	124.9	124.7	127.4	133.0	133.6	139.0				

Source: Economic Research Service, U.S.D.A.

T.0583

British Pound Per U.S. Dollar

Year	Jan.	Feb.	Mar.	Apr.	May	June	July	Aug.	Sept.	Oct.	Nov.	Dec.	Average
1983	.6341	.6525	.6706	.6505	.6358	.6456	.6539	.6654	.6669	.6675	.6766	.6971	.6592
1984	.7102	.6931	.6864	.7036	.7190	.7257	.7572	.7608	.7954	.8197	.8066	.8428	.7517
1985	.8861	.9141	.8903	.8066	.8001	.7817	.7241	.7226	.7329	.7031	.6946	.6919	.7790
1986	.7014	.6999	.6809	.6671	.6564	.6625	.6631	.6726	.6809	.7006	.7017	.6945	.6818
1987	.6641	.6541	.6278	.6128	.6000	.6139	.6213	.6249	.6077	.6007	.5634	.5471	.6114
1988	.5553	.5689	.5453	.5325	.5346	.5628	.5862	.5889	.5933				

Source: Economic Research Service, U.S.D.A.   T.0580

Month–End Open Interest of British Pound Futures in Chicago   In Contracts

Year	Jan.	Feb.	Mar.	Apr.	May	June	July	Aug.	Sept.	Oct.	Nov.	Dec.
1983	20,803	24,311	19,495	24,032	32,900	21,098	22,643	23,505	19,183	18,641	23,105	16,968
1984	20,972	27,563	17,939	20,035	17,876	13,072	15,710	15,105	15,473	18,921	21,701	15,624
1985	22,230	23,911	29,487	31,486	50,437	38,496	46,123	41,685	24,982	28,699	35,562	25,082
1986	38,235	40,880	28,187	39,520	30,584	24,702	26,211	27,788	37,506	36,992	34,127	23,145
1987	27,615	41,391	37,799	40,247	42,731	33,006	39,754	43,281	26,290	41,563	46,132	28,593
1988	36,094	43,301	45,691	42,376	45,172	16,530	16,199	19,574	12,790	19,073	28,514	16,277

Source: International Monetary Market (Chicago)   T.0584

Month–End Open Interest of Canadian Dollar Futures in Chicago   In Contracts

Year	Jan.	Feb.	Mar.	Apr	May	June	July	Aug.	Sept.	Oct.	Nov.	Dec.
1983	21,733	15,270	13,594	13,015	11,695	13,608	12,453	10,466	5,764	6,544	6,979	5,131
1984	5,624	5,607	9,572	12,306	10,484	7,684	8,244	8,197	6,397	7,737	10,641	7,775
1985	9,248	12,208	11,132	10,503	12,479	8,145	8,817	9,461	4,771	4,801	8,516	13,929
1986	18,922	15,075	9,748	13,670	14,977	9,400	13,739	17,501	9,358	12,377	14,648	14,937
1987	23,106	24,837	27,963	24,537	25,406	19,674	19,033	23,449	21,422	19,138	19,321	14,908
1988	25,446	23,411	24,339	25,940	29,846	33,848	30,069	28,513	17,849	23,452	28,227	21,974

Source: International Monetary Market (Chicago)   T.0585

Month–End Open Interest of Deutschemark Futures in Chicago   In Contracts

Year	Jan.	Feb.	Mar.	Apr.	May	June	July	Aug.	Sept.	Oct.	Nov.	Dec.
1983	16,806	16,653	18,195	22,944	25,382	23,269	27,585	23,531	30,077	24,460	23,385	22,804
1984	24,830	38,569	37,871	33,228	34,665	25,166	29,713	34,871	37,068	42,785	44,888	33,746
1985	49,483	45,759	48,190	47,318	52,909	50,400	56,977	54,966	42,696	50,796	57,347	53,525
1986	56,622	70,411	53,054	58,819	58,486	38,698	50,631	57,849	45,708	47,807	58,346	44,292
1987	60,164	57,902	41,702	46,932	52,082	32,140	42,132	48,534	31,167	43,385	59,808	32,536
1988	36,616	47,177	35,369	40,603	66,274	47,134	52,040	63,215	36,267	52,715	56,077	35,504

Source: International Monetary Market (Chicago)   T.0586

Month–End Open Interest of Japanese Yen Futures in Chicago   In Contracts

Year	Jan.	Feb.	Mar.	Apr.	May	June	July	Aug.	Sept.	Oct.	Nov.	Dec.
1983	26,913	31,388	23,095	31,378	39,661	28,279	32,731	27,510	37,616	36,891	34,976	32,998
1984	28,988	34,456	42,730	30,390	28,035	16,121	18,197	20,172	15,431	21,592	19,828	13,542
1985	13,755	16,206	21,333	17,893	18,251	22,258	37,861	35,896	32,581	37,658	39,605	28,058
1986	31,732	33,792	31,305	38,348	38,363	37,443	47,528	49,571	30,463	43,062	41,052	23,172
1987	32,164	31,988	43,282	47,410	51,681	27,969	38,334	52,905	37,058	46,297	60,299	42,656
1988	54,303	61,820	53,572	43,499	49,763	42,550	49,262	63,746	31,690	48,882	55,538	32,647

Source: International Monetary Market (Chicago)   T.0587

Month–End Open Interest of Swiss Franc Futures in Chicago   In Contracts

Year	Jan.	Feb.	Mar.	Apr.	May	June	July	Aug.	Sept.	Oct.	Nov.	Dec.
1983	28,628	29,288	22,848	30,877	33,679	26,930	29,997	25,367	31,106	23,808	26,793	21,450
1984	23,067	30,948	25,407	25,118	25,548	18,402	19,093	21,229	18,812	21,485	23,562	17,861
1985	24,406	28,898	22,446	27,144	32,175	27,891	34,160	35,850	25,988	28,190	35,047	27,351
1986	29,412	39,151	28,521	34,855	30,766	32,254	35,466	44,717	26,619	32,621	34,495	23,138
1987	33,581	36,210	29,102	31,854	33,551	24,351	29,387	31,898	23,328	29,809	40,772	24,298
1988	28,279	32,494	24,835	27,511	41,433	25,519	29,120	35,550	20,240	34,238	37,544	21,478

Source: International Monetary Market (Chicago)   T.0588

CURRENCIES

Index of Real Trade-Weighted Dollar Exchange Rates for Soybeans—1980 = 100

Year	Jan.	Feb.	Mar.	Apr.	May	June	July	Aug.	Sept.	Oct.	Nov.	Dec.
1985 U.S. Markets	151.9	155.8	156.2	149.5	150.9	149.9	145.8	144.3	145.5	137.5	135.1	133.6
U.S. Competitors	203.4	204.4	210.1	216.4	226.3	236.0	233.3	221.4	218.8	219.4	215.1	207.6
1986 U.S. Markets	131.5	125.8	122.4	121.5	119.1	120.2	117.0	114.2	114.1	113.6	115.8	114.9
U.S. Competitors	201.5	195.0	198.1	194.2	192.8	192.4	187.7	182.1	186.2	184.2	182.2	188.8
1987 U.S. Markets	110.7	109.8	109.5	106.6	105.1	106.7	108.4	108.0	105.4	104.9	100.1	97.2
U.S. Competitors	183.9	185.0	191.1	184.9	185.5	185.2	190.5	188.0	188.6	194.1	195.8	191.0
1988[1] U.S. Markets	97.5	98.8	97.4	96.5	97.0	99.4	103.2	104.5	104.2	105.4		
U.S. Competitors	187.0	185.5	187.1	190.1	196.3	204.9	213.0	227.2	234.8	274.0		

[1] Preliminary. [2] Real indexes adjust nominal exchange rates for differences in rates of inflation, to avoid the distortion caused by high-inflation countries. A higher value means the dollar has appreciated. Federal Reserve Board Index of trade-weighted value of the U.S. dollar against 10 major currencies. Weights are based on relative importance in world financial markets. *Source: Economic Research Service, U.S.D.A.* T.0590

Index of Real Trade-Weighted Dollar Exchange Rates for Wheat—1980 = 100

Year	Jan.	Feb.	Mar.	Apr.	May	June	July	Aug.	Sept.	Oct.	Nov.	Dec.
1985 U.S. Markets	128.9	131.0	132.0	131.3	132.7	132.0	130.8	129.4	130.1	127.3	125.8	124.9
U.S. Competitors	144.6	150.2	153.7	151.5	152.7	154.0	149.7	147.3	148.9	145.0	145.2	144.3
1986 U.S. Markets	123.4	120.2	119.9	118.8	117.3	118.1	117.1	116.0	117.2	125.1	124.3	125.6
U.S. Competitors	142.3	139.3	136.1	135.0	133.5	135.8	135.3	134.2	134.7	132.5	131.7	130.7
1987 U.S. Markets	123.9	123.8	124.1	121.5	120.8	121.4	122.6	122.4	121.0	120.4	117.8	116.0
U.S. Competitors	128.4	126.4	126.1	124.5	124.5	124.7	124.8	125.1	124.2	125.7	125.8	122.9
1988[1] U.S. Markets	115.6	115.8	114.6	112.9	113.0	113.1	115.0	115.4	115.4	115.6		
U.S. Competitors	122.2	122.2	121.0	120.8	121.0	122.0	124.6	128.0	129.3	135.2		

[1] Preliminary. [2] Real indexes adjust nominal exchange rates for differences in rates of inflation, to avoid the distortion caused by high-inflation countries. A higher value means the dollar has appreciated. Federal Reserve Board Index of trade-weighted value of the U.S. dollar against 10 major currencies. Weights are based on relative importance in world financial markets. *Source: Economic Research Service, U.S.D.A.* T.0590A

Index of Real Trade-Weighted Dollar Exchange Rates for Corn—1980 = 100

Year	Jan.	Feb.	Mar.	Apr.	May	June	July	Aug.	Sept.	Oct.	Nov.	Dec.
1985 U.S. Markets	133.9	135.8	135.9	132.5	133.5	132.6	130.3	131.4	132.2	125.9	123.7	123.1
U.S. Competitors	208.1	212.8	213.5	205.9	211.2	217.1	212.2	206.5	206.9	198.5	195.1	192.1
1986 U.S. Markets	120.6	115.1	112.7	111.3	109.2	110.4	107.7	106.0	105.4	105.3	107.5	108.8
U.S. Competitors	187.8	182.2	175.7	175.8	174.1	174.7	169.2	163.6	166.4	163.7	163.9	164.2
1987 U.S. Markets	105.5	104.9	104.2	100.5	98.9	99.8	101.6	100.6	98.4	98.0	94.4	91.7
U.S. Competitors	160.2	159.0	162.0	160.2	158.3	158.9	160.7	160.4	160.8	166.1	164.7	160.3
1988[1] U.S. Markets	91.3	91.8	90.7	89.4	89.5	90.5	93.0	93.4	93.2	93.7		
U.S. Competitors	161.1	162.8	163.7	166.7	171.1	180.6	190.5	201.8	205.5	233.4		

[1] Preliminary. [2] Real indexes adjust nominal exchange rates for differences in rates of inflation, to avoid the distortion caused by high-inflation countries. A higher value means the dollar has appreciated. Federal Reserve Board Index of trade-weighted value of the U.S. dollar against 10 major currencies. Weights are based on relative importance in world financial markets. *Source: Economic Research Service, U.S.D.A.* T.0591

Index of Real Trade-Weighted Dollar Exchange Rates for Cotton—1980 = 100

Year	Jan.	Feb.	Mar.	Apr.	May	June	July	Aug.	Sept.	Oct.	Nov.	Dec.
1985 U.S. Markets	134.1	136.6	137.8	135.0	136.0	135.5	133.1	132.3	133.1	127.8	126.0	125.6
U.S. Competitors	112.1	113.6	123.0	123.0	122.4	120.3	120.5	119.6	119.6	117.9	117.8	116.6
1986 U.S. Markets	124.5	119.9	117.5	116.4	114.1	115.2	112.4	110.9	111.9	113.1	114.8	114.3
U.S. Competitors	113.2	111.9	111.5	109.9	109.2	111.0	110.8	110.2	108.0	105.2	104.0	106.5
1987 U.S. Markets	111.7	111.1	110.6	107.7	106.0	106.9	108.3	107.7	105.8	105.8	102.6	99.8
U.S. Competitors	105.8	105.9	104.7	102.6	101.2	99.6	100.6	99.9	99.1	104.1	102.7	110.7
1988[1] U.S. Markets	99.7	100.0	98.5	97.7	97.7	98.7	101.1	101.7	101.9	102.5		
U.S. Competitors	109.8	108.9	109.0	103.1	103.4	101.3	100.3	99.2	97.6	96.3		

[1] Preliminary. [2] Real indexes adjust nominal exchange rates for differences in rates of inflation, to avoid the distortion caused by high-inflation countries. A higher value means the dollar has appreciated. Federal Reserve Board Index of trade-weighted value of the U.S. dollar against 10 major currencies. Weights are based on relative importance in world financial markets. *Source: Economic Research Service, U.S.D.A.* T.0591A

CRB CURRENCY FUTURES INDEX (1977=100)
Weekly high low & close

United States Merchandise Trade Balance In Millions of Dollars

Year	Jan.	Feb.	Mar.	Apr.	May	June	July	Aug.	Sept.	Oct.	Nov.	Dec.	Total
1985	−11,408	− 8,095	− 8,960	−10,588	−10,387	−12,068	−10,447	− 9,846	−14,559	−10,561	−12,267	−13,311	−126,461
1986	−12,166	− 9,027	− 9,961	−11,618	−10,706	−10,212	−13,056	−12,157	−13,144	−12,470	−13,140	−10,623	−138,279
1987[1]	−13,453	−10,956	−10,628	−11,613	−12,410	−13,721	−14,431	−13,747	−12,484	−15,298	−11,932	−11,445	−152,119
1988[1]	−10,005	−11,430	− 7,924	− 8,692	− 8,004	−11,751	−10,485	−11,203	− 9,013				

[1] Preliminary. *Source: Bureau of the Census*

Index of Real Trade-Weighted Dollar Exchange Rates for Total Agriculture[2] 1980 = 100

Year		Jan.	Feb.	Mar.	Apr.	May	June	July	Aug.	Sept.	Oct.	Nov.	Dec.
1985	U.S. Markets	137.2	139.8	140.7	136.9	137.9	136.8	134.3	133.9	134.9	129.7	128.0	127.3
	U.S. Competitors	149.8	153.5	156.0	154.4	155.9	156.1	152.0	148.6	149.8	146.6	145.9	144.5
1986	U.S. Markets	125.7	121.7	119.7	118.6	116.7	118.1	115.9	114.3	114.5	115.4	116.6	117.6
	U.S. Competitors	142.8	140.0	139.8	139.2	138.3	141.0	140.2	139.0	140.2	138.2	137.8	136.7
1987	U.S. Markets	114.5	113.9	113.5	110.8	109.7	110.7	111.9	111.6	109.8	109.6	106.0	103.8
	U.S. Competitors	133.3	132.5	132.7	130.4	130.0	130.8	132.1	132.4	130.5	131.2	129.7	127.4
1988	U.S. Markets	103.6	104.2	103.0	101.6	101.8	102.9	105.2	105.9	105.6	106.0		
	U.S. Competitors	126.3	126.7	126.4	125.1	125.5	126.4	129.1	131.7	132.7	136.2		

[1] Preliminary. [2] Real indexes adjust nominal exchange rates for differences in rates of inflation, to avoid the distortion caused by high-inflation countries. A higher value means the dollar has appreciated. Federal Reserve Board Index of trade-weighted value of the U.S. dollar against 10 major currencies. Weights are based on relative importance in world financial markets. *Source: Economic Research Service, U.S.D.A.* T.0589

Eggs

World egg production was forecast to rise by about 1 percent in 1988. The USSR was expected to have the largest gain in production, as hen numbers and yields continued to increase. Japan was also expected to show an increase in production, in response to rising domestic demand. The major producers of eggs in 1988 were the USSR, with approximately 21 percent of world output, the European Community, with an estimated 20 percent, and the U.S., with an estimated 17 percent.

U.S egg production dropped by about 1 percent in 1988, as producers downsized the laying flock early in the year, due to long periods of negative net returns. Chicks placed were well below year-earlier levels through the first part of 1988, an indication of lower future flock numbers. Per capita consumption of eggs in the U.S. in 1988 was forecast to decline by as much as 3 percent from 1987, in part because of health concerns. Consumption also was expected to fall in 1989. Net returns to producers approached break-even in late 1988, as wholesale prices showed late seasonal strength.

Output of egg products was up significantly in the first part of 1988, led by an increase of nearly 12 percent in liquid egg production for immediate consumption in January-August. In the same period, close to 6 percent more shell eggs were used in producing liquid, frozen, and dried egg products. Egg breakings under federal inspection were 5 percent higher in the first nine months of 1988 than in the year-earlier period.

A substantial sale of table eggs to Mexico late in 1988 boosted overall export sales, and exports were expected to be significantly higher than in 1987. Jamaica was expected to continue importing hatching eggs in an effort to rebuild its poultry industry after the destruction left by Hurricane Gilbert in September. Japan continued as the largest U.S. egg export market and imported a much greater quantity of U.S. eggs in 1988. Overall, about 2.4 percent of U.S. production was exported in 1988, compared with 1.9 percent in 1987. Exports were expected to weaken in 1989 because of higher prices.

Total U.S. egg imports were expected to be significantly lower in 1988. For the January-August period, total egg imports were down 32 percent from the year-earlier period. Egg product imports were down 10 percent for the same period, while shell egg imports were 56 percent lower than the year-earlier level. Imports of table eggs picked up somewhat late in the summer, as domestic prices increased relative to foreign prices. W. Germany was expected to be the largest foreign supplier.

Wholesale prices for grade A large eggs in New York City averaged 62.1 cents per dozen in 1988, after price fluctuations late in the year. In 1989, negative net returns to producers were expected in the first part of the year, but returns were likely to turn positive in the second half, with low feed costs and stronger prices.

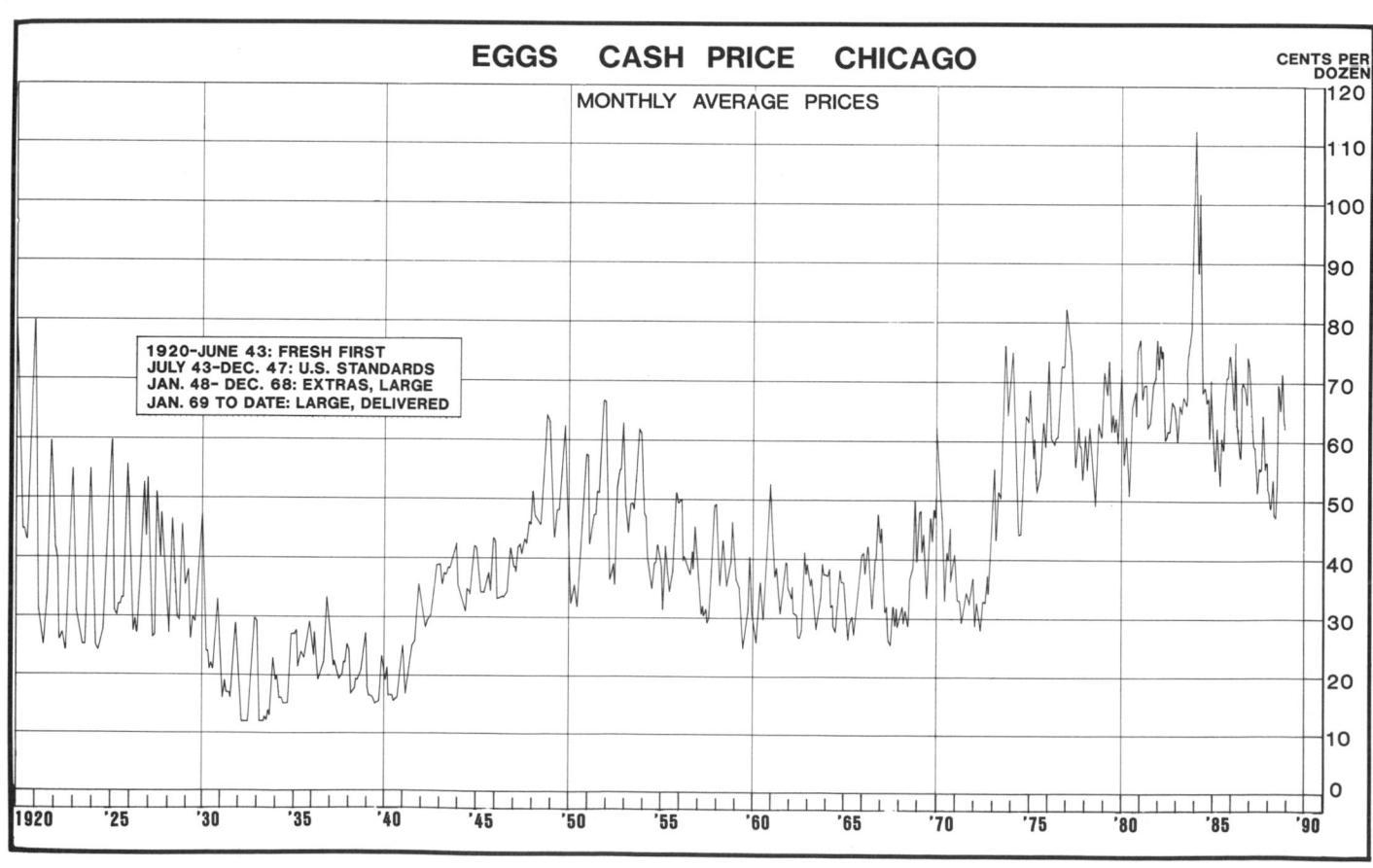

EGGS CASH PRICE CHICAGO

MONTHLY AVERAGE PRICES

CENTS PER DOZEN

1920-JUNE 43: FRESH FIRST
JULY 43-DEC. 47: U.S. STANDARDS
JAN. 48- DEC. 68: EXTRAS, LARGE
JAN. 69 TO DATE: LARGE, DELIVERED

World Production[2] of Eggs   In Billions of Eggs

Year	Argentina	Aus-tralia	Bel. & Lux.	Brazil	Canada	Israel	France	West Germany	Italy	Japan	Nether-lands	Poland	Spain	South Africa	USSR	United Kingdom[3]	United States
1981	3.3	3.6	3.3	10.2	5.9	1.4	15.2	13.2	11.4	33.3	9.8	8.8	11.8	2.6	70.9	13.7	69.9
1982	3.2	3.4	3.3	10.2	5.9	1.8	15.9	13.1	11.2	34.3	10.7	7.6	12.4	3.1	72.4	13.5	69.6
1983	3.3	3.5	3.2	10.0	6.1	1.8	15.0	13.0	10.9	34.8	10.7	7.6	12.2	3.3	75.1	13.2	67.9
1984	3.2	3.5	3.1	9.5	5.9	2.1	14.9	13.2	10.8	35.5	11.1	8.2	10.1	3.3	76.5	13.0	68.5
1985	3.2	3.3	3.0	11.8	5.9	2.1	14.9	12.8	10.9	35.7	11.1	8.6	10.2	3.2	77.3	13.1	68.3
1986	3.2	3.2	2.9	13.0	5.9	1.8	15.0	12.3	10.3	37.1	10.9	8.3	10.9	3.2	79.9	13.2	68.5
1987[1]	3.3	3.2	2.9	15.4	5.7	1.7	14.5	12.3	10.7	39.6	10.9	7.9	10.5	3.4	81.9	13.3	69.6
1988[4]	3.4	3.2	2.8	15.8	5.7	1.7	15.2	12.1	11.0	40.3	10.8	8.3	10.9	3.7	85.0	13.4	68.7

[1] Preliminary.   [2] Relates to farm production in Canada and the United States. Information for many countries is not explicit on this point.   [3] Farm production, years ending May.   [4] Estimate.   *Source: Foreign Agricultural Service, U.S.D.A.*
T.210

Salient Egg Statistics in the United States

Year	Hens & Pullets — On Farms Dec. 1[2] — Millions	Hens & Pullets — Avg.[9] Number During Year — Millions	Rate of Lay Per Layer During Year[3] Number	Eggs — Total Pro-duced Billions	Eggs — Price (in ¢) Per Dozen	Eggs — Consumed[4] on Farms Billions	Eggs — Sold Billions	Gross Income[5] Billion $	Total Egg Pro-duction[6]	Imports[7]	Exports[8] and Shipments Million Dozen	Used for Hatching Million Dozen	Civilian Consumption Total	Civilian Consumption Per Capita Eggs (Number)
1981	293.8	287.8	243	69.8	63.1	.44	69.38	3.67	5,825	5	257	507	5,043	265.5
1982	289.6	286.4	243	69.7	59.5	.43	69.27	3.46	5,802	2	185	506	5,089	265.3
1983	278.5	276.3	247	68.2	61.1	.42	67.75	3.47	5,659	23	112	500	5,056	261.2
1984	285.8	278.0	245	68.2	72.3	.39	67.80	4.11	5,708	32	86	530	5,105	260.9
1985	279.8	276.7	247	68.4	57.1	N.A.		3.25	5,688	13	101	548	5,031	254.7
1986	280.1	276.9	248	68.5	61.6			3.52	5,705	14	130	567	5,023	249.5
1987[10]		280.0	248	69.6	62.5				5,797	6	136	596	5,066	249.4
1988[10]		279.0	250	68.4	65.0				5,700	4	160	605	5,000	244.0

[1] Preliminary.   [2] Of laying age.   [3] Number of eggs produced during the year divided by the average number of hens & pullets of laying age on hand during the year.   [4] Consumed in households of farm producers.   [5] Value of sales plus value of eggs consumed in households of producers.   [6] Farm production, plus nonfarm output estimated at 1 percentage point less each year.   [7] Shell-egg equivalent of eggs and egg products.   [8] Shell eggs & shell equivalent of frozen & dried egg products.   [9] Average number of layers on farms during the year.   [10] Estimate.   *Source: Agricultural Marketing Service, U.S.D.A.*
T.211

Average Wholesale Prices of Shell Eggs (Large) Delivered, Chicago   In Cents Per Dozen

Year	Jan.	Feb.	Mar.	Apr.	May	June	July	Aug.	Sept.	Oct.	Nov.	Dec.	Average
1981	71.4	67.2	66.6	69.7	62.2	62.9	67.5	68.7	70.7	71.3	77.3	72.1	69.0
1982	76.2	74.2	75.2	68.3	60.4	60.8	61.7	61.6	65.9	66.8	66.2	64.1	66.8
1983	60.2	62.7	66.2	64.9	68.4	68.0	66.2	74.4	76.2	77.9	88.4	98.6	72.7
1984	112.3	102.6	88.3	101.8	74.3	68.1	69.0	66.5	67.2	60.7	70.4	62.2	78.6
1985	58.4	55.1	62.3	57.3	52.9	60.8	58.6	66.4	70.5	70.7	74.6	73.2	63.4
1986	70.6	65.7	76.9	62.6	62.0	57.3	69.4	70.0	69.4	66.3	74.1	72.8	68.1
1987[1]	64.4	62.0	59.2	59.0	51.8	55.6	55.4	58.7	64.8	55.5	56.3	52.1	57.9
1988[1]	51.2	48.9	53.6	47.9	47.1	52.8	69.8	65.4	71.4	63.1			

[1] Preliminary.   *Source: Economic Research Service, U.S.D.A.*
T.212

Total Egg Production in the United States   In Millions of Eggs

Year	Jan.	Feb.	Mar.	Apr.	May	June	July	Aug.	Sept.	Oct.	Nov.	Dec.	Total[2]
1981	6,020	5,421	6,009	5,761	5,855	5,608	5,799	5,835	5,685	5,919	5,859	6,079	69,825
1982	5,958	5,333		17,557			17,231			17,419		6,030	69,718
1983	5,931	5,354	5,928	5,622	5,711	5,526	5,666	5,639	5,493	5,699	5,570	5,772	68,169
1984	5,685	5,326	5,796	5,643	5,742	5,525	5,750	5,766	5,622	5,856	5,747	6,040	68,230
1985	5,950	5,293	5,923	5,670	5,721	5,499	5,661	5,686	5,545	5,761	5,658	5,889	68,256
1986	5,856	5,292	5,899	5,641	5,779	5,593	5,689	5,701	5,536	5,793	5,730	5,950	68,459
1987[1]	5,915	5,350	6,020	5,792	5,853	5,616	5,790	5,786	5,686	5,931	5,803	6,016	69.558
1988[1]	5,982	5,607	5,976	5,691	5,770	5,518	5,677	5,701	5,546				

[1] Preliminary.   [2] Dec. 1 previous year thru Nov. 30.   *Source: Crop Reporting Board, U.S.D.A.*
T.219

EGGS

Total Eggs—U.S. Supply and Distribution   In Millions of Dozen

| Year & Quarters | Supply | | | | Utilization | | | | | |
| | Production | Imports[1] | Beginning Stocks[1] | Total Supply | Ending Stocks[1] | Exports & Shipments[1] | Eggs Used for Hatching | Domestic Disappearance | | |
								Military	Civilian[1] Total	Per Capita (Number)
1983 I	1,434	5.0	20.3	1,442	18.1	30.2	128.4	6.3	1,277	66.2
II	1,405	2.9	18.1	1,409	17.4	29.2	129.2	6.9	1,243	64.3
III	1,400	7.4	17.4	1,411	13.2	26.7	120.1	6.5	1,258	64.9
IV	1,420	8.2	13.2	1,432	9.3	26.4	122.4	5.4	1,278	65.8
1984 I	1,401	13.9	9.3	1,414	10.2	17.5	133.0	4.2	1,259	64.6
II	1,409	7.6	10.2	1,413	13.7	15.3	138.0	5.3	1,255	64.2
III	1,428	7.2	13.7	1,436	13.4	26.7	128.4	3.7	1,277	65.2
IV	1,470	3.4	13.4	1,476	11.1	26.5	130.2	4.4	1,315	66.9
1985 I	1,431	2.2	11.1	1,444	11.0	24.6	136.1	5.1	1,272	64.0
II	1,408	3.3	11.0	1,422	12.2	24.5	139.7	5.6	1,245	62.6
III	1,408	2.3	12.2	1,422	13.1	25.1	133.7	4.5	1,250	62.7
IV	1,442	4.9	13.1	1,460	10.7	27.0	138.6	5.0	1,284	64.2
1986 I	1,421	3.6	10.7	1,435	8.7	33.5	139.2	4.6	1,254	62.5
II	1,418	4.0	8.7	1,431	11.9	28.2	145.1	4.2	1,245	62.0
III	1,411	2.2	11.9	1,425	11.5	36.5	141.4	4.5	1,235	61.3
IV	1,456	3.9	11.5	1,471	10.4	31.4	141.2	4.2	1,288	63.8
1987[2] I	1,440	2.6	10.4	1,453	11.9	30.9	147.6	4.5	1,263	62.4
II	1,438	1.2	11.9	1,452	13.8	28.5	154.2	4.1	1,255	61.9
III	1,439	1.0	13.8	1,453	13.5	27.6	147.8	4.6	1,264	62.2
IV	1,479	.8	13.5	1,493	14.4	49.3	146.4		1,283	63.0
1988[2] I	1,464	.9	14.4	1,479	12.7	39.7	150.2		1,276	62.4
II	1,415	.7	12.7	1,428	20.1	40.5	153.5		1,214	59.3
III	1,410		20.1		17.7		150.5			
IV										

[1] Shell eggs & the approx. shell-egg equivalent of egg product.   [2] Preliminary.   *Source: Economic Research Service, U.S.D.A.*   T.213

Shell Eggs: Civilian Per Capita Disappearance in the United States   Number of Eggs

Year	Jan.	Feb.	Mar.	Apr.	May	June	July	Aug.	Sept.	Oct.	Nov.	Dec.	Total[1]	Processed[2]	Total
1979	21.3	18.5	21.0	20.0	20.1	19.2	20.1	19.9	19.8	20.2	20.2	21.8	242	36	278
1980	21.1	19.0	20.9	19.4	19.8	18.7	19.0	19.6	19.4	19.8	20.0	20.7	237.3	35	272
1981	——58.5——			——56.7——			——57.3——			——60.7——			233.1	33	265
1982	——58.6——			——57.0——			——56.5——			——59.1——			231.2	34	265
1983	——57.8——			——55.5——			——55.0——			——57.6——			225.9	35	261
1984	——55.7——			——54.8——			——55.2——			——57.7——			223.4	38	261
1985	——55.3——			——52.2——			——52.5——			——54.7——			214.6	38	253
1986	——54.0——			——51.5——			——51.2——			——53.8——			210.5	39	250
1987[3]	——52.1——			——51.0——			——50.8——			——52.3——			206.2	43	249
1988[3]	——51.8——			——48.0——											

[1] Monthly totals do not necessarily add to yearly figures due to rounding.   [2] Liquid, frozen, & dried egg (egg solids) converted to shell egg equivalent.   [3] Preliminary.   *Source: Economic Research Service, U.S.D.A.*   T.214

Egg-Feed Ratio[1] in the United States

Year	Jan.	Feb.	Mar.	Apr.	May	June	July	Aug.	Sept.	Oct.	Nov.	Dec.	Average
1979	7.8	7.7	8.0	7.4	6.9	6.7	6.1	6.1	6.4	6.1	6.8	7.3	6.9
1980	6.6	6.0	6.4	6.0	5.4	5.6	5.7	6.0	6.2	5.7	6.0	6.6	6.0
1981	5.9	5.7	5.6	5.9	5.2	5.2	5.5	5.8	6.4	6.5	7.2	6.7	6.0
1982	6.6	6.8	7.1	6.6	5.6	5.3	5.7	5.4	6.0	6.3	6.3	6.0	6.2
1983	5.7	5.8	6.1	5.8	6.0	5.8	5.7	6.1	6.0	6.2	6.9	7.7	6.0
1984	8.8	8.5	7.4	8.6	6.5	5.8	5.8	5.8	5.9	5.7	6.5	6.3	6.8
1985	5.4	5.6	6.3	5.7	5.5	5.9	5.8	6.5	7.1	7.3	7.5	7.4	6.3
1986[2]	7.2	6.9	7.6	6.4	6.4	5.7	6.9	7.3	7.3	7.0	8.0	7.9	7.0
1987[2]	7.2	7.1	6.6	6.6	5.9	6.0	5.7	5.6	6.5	6.0	6.4	5.8	7.6
1988[2]	9.6	9.3	5.8	5.2	4.9	5.2	4.9	4.9	5.4	5.3	5.4		

[1] Pounds of laying feed equivalent in value to one dozen eggs.   [2] Preliminary.   *Source: Economic Research Service, U.S.D.A.*   T.215

Hens and Pullets of Laying Age in the U.S., First of Month   In Millions

Year	Jan. 1	Feb. 1	Mar. 1	Apr. 1	May 1	June 1	July 1	Aug. 1	Sept. 1	Oct. 1	Nov. 1	Dec. 1
1981	295.2	292.4	291.3	286.3	284.5	282.5	280.9	284.5	283.8	287.2	290.5	293.8
1982	291.7	290.1	288.4	—	—	282.7	—	—	281.9	—	—	289.6
1983	285.8	283.3	280.5	276.9	273.0	271.8	270.1	269.7	271.5	272.2	276.4	278.5
1984	277.2	276.5	277.0	278.9	276.1	276.2	276.5	274.3	277.8	280.5	282.2	285.8
1985	286.9	281.7	279.0	276.2	272.6	269.1	269.7	271.2	273.8	276.0	280.9	279.8
1986	280.2	279.5	279.2	277.3	275.0	272.9	270.7	272.3	272.6	275.8	279.3	279.9
1987[1]	282.6	283.6	282.5	282.2	278.7	277.2	275.3	276.8	278.6	282.4	282.9	285.5
1988[1]	282.7	282.5	280.3	275.2	272.6	270.1	267.2	268.7	270.1	274.3	276.1	275.4

[1] Preliminary.   *Source: Crop Reporting Board, U.S.D.A.*   T.216

Eggs Laid Per Hundred Layers in the United States   In Number of Eggs

Year	Jan.	Feb.	Mar.	Apr.	May	June	July	Aug.	Sept.	Oct.	Nov.	Dec.	Average
1981	2,049	1,857	2,081	2,018	2,065	1,991	2,051	2,053	1,991	2,049	2,005	2,083	2,426
1982	2,048	1,850	6,159			6,112			6,105			2,097	2,435
1983	2,084	1,899	2,127	2,045	2,096	2,039	2,099	2,084	2,021	2,078	2,008	2,078	2,468
1984	2,054	1,925	2,085	2,032	2,079	1,999	2,086	2,088	2,013	2,080	2,023	2,109	2,046
1985	2,093	1,887	2,134	2,066	2,112	2,041	2,093	2,086	2,017	2,069	2,018	2,103	2,060
1986	2,092	1,894	2,120	2,043	2,110	2,058	2,095	2,092	2,019	2,087	2,051	2,115	2,065
1987[1]	2,089	1,890	2,132	2,069	2,106	2,033	2,097	2,083	2,024	2,098	2,042	2,115	2,065
1988[1]	2,109	1,991	2,147	2,065	2,123	2,054	2,118	2,116	2,037	2,118	2,064		

[1] Preliminary.   *Source: Crop Reporting Board, U.S.D.A.*   T.221

Egg-Type Chicks Hatched by Commercial Hatcheries in the United States   In Millions

Year	Jan.	Feb.	Mar.	Apr.	May	June	July	Aug.	Sept.	Oct.	Nov.	Dec.	Total
1981	37.8	36.1	44.5	48.3	46.1	40.5	32.3	33.8	32.3	35.9	33.7	33.1	454.2
1982	36.7	36.4	44.2	46.6	47.3	39.4	35.4	33.5	31.2	32.3	30.2	31.1	444.4
1983	32.6	33.0	39.3	36.7	38.3	37.5	30.5	30.9	31.8	32.3	29.6	34.4	406.9
1984	36.9	37.5	45.7	47.9	49.0	46.5	38.4	34.8	33.1	31.4	30.1	27.1	458.5
1985	28.3	28.4	36.9	40.9	39.0	33.8	32.1	32.5	33.6	33.6	33.6	34.2	406.8
1986	34.5	34.8	39.5	42.4	42.5	37.3	33.6	33.4	32.6	32.4	27.5	33.3	423.7
1987	34.2	35.8	41.7	42.4	40.9	37.3	33.4	34.7	31.8	34.0	30.6	31.2	427.8
1988[1]	29.5	28.5	34.8	35.1	35.8	33.0	24.8	27.3	30.6	30.6	29.2		

[1] Preliminary.   *Source: Crop Reporting Board, U.S.D.A.*   T.220

U.S. Cold Storage Holdings of Shell Eggs, 1st of Month   In Thousands of Cases (One Case = 30 Dozen)

Year	Jan.	Feb.	Mar.	Apr.	May	June	July	Aug.	Sept.	Oct.	Nov.	Dec.
1981	31	28	18	31	31	25	41	39	20	19	21	38
1982	35	28	19	39	—	—	32	—	—	29	—	—
1983	34	35	25	18	23	32	44	24	25	25	45	18
1984	13	28	17	36	35	41	42	20	31	23	37	35
1985	31	30	29	23	26	30	21	30	20	22	23	28
1986	24	28	21	20	32	44	38	25	33	29	20	29
1987	22	20	25	32	28	38	32	34	32	33	51	40
1988[1]	43	67	53	67	14	21	30	28	25	23	24	26

[1] Preliminary.   *Source: Crop Reporting, Board U.S.D.A.*   T.217

U.S. Cold Storage Holdings of Frozen Eggs, 1st of Month   In Millions of Pounds[1]

Year	Jan.	Feb.	Mar.	Apr.	May	June	July	Aug.	Sept.	Oct.	Nov.	Dec.
1981	24.3	24.3	24.2	22.3	21.9	22.7	24.2	26.9	27.2	25.5	25.6	23.7
1982	21.6	21.2	19.4	17.4	—	—	22.7	—	—	28.3	—	—
1983	25.4	25.5	25.7	23.1	22.5	21.2	21.1	20.4	19.0	16.4	14.2	13.4
1984	11.8	11.0	11.4	12.0	12.1	12.7	12.8	16.4	17.5	16.6	16.7	17.9	16.2
1985	13.4	14.9	13.9	13.5	13.2	14.4	15.3	18.0	18.4	16.4	15.1	13.8
1986	13.2	12.7	12.8	10.7	12.5	11.6	14.2	15.1	15.0	14.0	14.0	13.0
1987	12.8	14.3	13.5	14.5	14.9	17.4	16.9	17.3	17.5	16.5	17.9	17.4
1988[2]	17.3	18.3	18.3	14.3	17.3	20.3	25.3	22.9	24.6	22.2	20.0	18.0

[1] Converted on basis 39.5 pounds frozen eggs equals 1 case.   [2] Preliminary.   *Source: Crop Reporting Board, U.S.D.A.*   T.218

Electric Power

U.S. electricity sales rose an estimated 4 percent in 1988 to 2.556 trillion kilowatt-hours (kwh), reflecting the effects of a colder-than-normal winter and a very hot summer on both consumer and industrial demand. According to the Department of Energy, the weather added nearly 1 percentage point to the weather-normalized underlying growth rate of 3 percent for electricity sales.

Total U.S. electricity generation was projected to grow by 4 percent in 1988 to 2.684 trillion kwh; 1989 generation was forecast at 2.739 trillion, a 2 percent gain. Net electricity imports were estimated to have slipped to 40.5 billion kwh from 46.3 billion in 1987, because the 1988 drought curtailed Canadian hydroelectric production. The drought also cut U.S. hydropower output by an estimated 8.5 percent to 228.5 billion kwh, the lowest output since 1977. Assuming a return to near-normal water levels, U.S. hydropower production was expected to rebound to 276.6 billion kwh in 1989.

The hydropower shortage forced utilities to use more expensive petroleum-fired standby generators to meet summer demand. In August, utilities generated 267 billion kwh, 8 percent above their August 1987 output. Petroleum-fired production increased 42 percent from August 1987 to 16 billion kwh, and petroleum consumption increased 43 percent from a year earlier to 27 million barrels. This contributed to a $449 million increase in August 1988 electric bills, according to the National Oceanic and Atmospheric Administration, which put the total U.S. bill for August at $4.3 billion. The average residential electric bill was estimated at $104, about $11 more than the average for August.

The U.S.-Canada trade treaty was expected to increase Canadian electricity sales to the U.S. Quebec has long-term sales contracts with New York and New England utilities; and BC Hydro, Canada's third largest electric utility, announced plans to form an export subsidiary to increase sales to the U.S. from an annual level of $155 million. BC Hydro said it was considering two new transmission connections to Washington state utilities and two coal-fired plants strictly for exportable power, which would be sold as guaranteed supplies.

Although BC Hydro sees its market stretching south to the Mexican border, most sales would be to the Pacific Northwest, which had a 1988 production surplus of 1,000 megawatts in Washington, Oregon, Idaho, and Montana. However, continued strong economic growth --including a rebirth of the region's electricity-hungry aluminum industry--raised concerns that the surplus might not be adequate to meet demand through the end of the century.

In the Northeast, power grids were strained to capacity by the heat wave, forcing many brownouts. This contributed to the defeat of a Massachusetts referendum to shut two nuclear power plants in that state. Meanwhile, in New York, the governor's plan to buy the Shoreham reactor (in order to scrap it) failed to receive legislative approval, and the plant's fate was in limbo as 1988 ended.

World Electricity Production   In Billions of KWH

Year	Aus-tralia	Brazil	Canada	Czech-oslov.	France	West Germany	Italy	Japan	Norway	Poland	Sweden	Spain	South Africa	United Kingdom	United States	USSR
1979	92.1	126.5	363.2	68.1	241.1	374.2	180.5	589.6	89.1	117.5	92.4		90.3	299.9	2,319	1,238
1980	96.3	139.5	377.5	72.6	243.3	368.8	185.7	577.5	84.1	121.9	93.4		95.0	284.9	2,354	1,295
1981	102.5	142.2	390.9	74.1	263.4	367.1	178.9	583.2	92.8	115.0	102.8	110.0	97.4	276.7	2,359	1,325
1982	104.9	152.0	387.5	74.7	265.4	365.2	181.8	581.1	92.6	117.6	99.5	113.5	119.9	271.3	2,302	1,367
1983	106.3	162.0	408.4	76.0	281.3	372.0	180.1	555.5	105.5	125.9	108.9	114.7	108.3	275.6	2,368	1,396
1984	112.9	178.5	438.0	78.3	307.2	392.9	179.5	580.4	106.2	135.3	123.3	118.1	121.6	280.4	2,479	1,493
1985	121.7	192.7	459.0	80.6	325.7	406.7	182.3	598.1	102.7	137.7	136.5	125.6	121.5	293.7	2,565	1,544
1986[1]	127.7	201.6	468.6	84.8	343.0	406.4	189.0	557.1	96.4	140.3	138.0	127.7	145.4	298.2	2,583	1,599
1987[3]	133.8		482.1	83.4	353.0	418.5	201.0	660.0	140.3	145.8	129.6	129.4	156.0	301.9	2,670	1,692

[1] Preliminary. [2] Estimate. *Source: United Nations*   T.222

Installed Capacity, Capability & Peak Load of the U.S. Electric Utility Industry   In Millions of Kilowatts

Year	Total Electric Utility Industry	Hydro	Gas Turbine & Steam	Nuclear Power	Internal Combustion	Investor Owned	Cooperatives	Sub-Total Gov't.	Municipal Utilities	Federal	Power Districts, State Projects	Capability at Winter Peak Load	Non-Coincident Winter Peak Load	Margin of Reserve (%)	Total Generation	Peak Load Factor (%)
1979	598.4	75.4	463.0	54.6	5.5	464.1	13.8	120.5	34.5	58.3	27.6	554.3	368.9	36.9[2]	2,247	64.4
1980	613.7	76.4	475.3	56.5	5.6	477.1	15.4	121.2	34.6	59.1	27.5	572.2	384.6	23.5	2,293	61.1
1981	635.0	77.2	491.3	60.8	5.6	490.8	18.4	125.7	35.1	61.0	29.5	581.1	391.1	25.2	2,311	61.6
1982	650.1	78.1	503.8	63.0	5.1	499.1	21.5	129.5	35.8	62.5	31.2	596.9	373.3	29.2	2,241	62.1
1983	658.2	79.0	507.1	67.1	5.0	505.5	22.2	130.5	36.6	63.0	30.9	611.6	410.8	25.0	2,310	59.5
1984	672.5	80.6	516.5	70.5	4.8	514.9	24.7	132.9	36.7	63.3	32.8	622.1	436.4	25.3	2,416	59.7
1985	688.7	83.0	520.3	80.4	5.0	530.4	24.6	133.8	37.0	63.7	33.0	636.5	423.7	25.9	2,470	62.0
1986	707.7	85.2	524.1	92.4	5.9	544.2	26.4	137.1	38.6	63.9	34.6	646.7	422.9	24.8	2,487	60.7
1987[1]	718.1	85.9	524.3	101.6	6.2	552.8	26.4	138.9	39.4	64.7	34.9	663.0	448.3	23.4		60.8

[1] Preliminary. [2] New series starting 1980. *Source: Federal Power Commission*   T.223

Available Electricity & Energy Sales in the United States   In Billions of Kilowatt Hours

Year	Generation — Electric Utility Industry — Hydro	Steam	Nuclear	Total[5]	Other Sources[2]	Total	Sales to Ultimate Customers — Total Million $	Total[4]	Residential	Inter-Departmental	Commercial	Industrial	Street & Highway	Other Public Authorities	Railways & Railroads
1975	300.0	1,439	172.5	1,918	85	2,003	46,855	1,733	586.1	5.4	418.1	661.6	13.9	43.6	4.3
1976	283.7	1,558	191.1	2,038	87	2,125	53,463	1,850	613.1	6.4	440.6	725.2	14.4	45.6	4.3
1977	220.5	1,648	250.9	2,124	88	2,212	62,610	1,951	652.3	7.2	469.2	757.2	14.4	46.2	4.2
1978	280.4	1,645	276.4	2,206	79	2,300	69,853	2,018	679.2	7.1	480.7	782.1	14.8	49.5	4.3
1979	279.8	1,708	255.2	2,247	71	2,318	79,640	2,084	696.0	7.4	494.7	817.6	14.8	49.6	4.3
1980	276.0	1,756	251.1	2,283	68	2,351	95,462	2,126	734.4	6.4	524.1	793.8	14.8	48.3	4.3
1981	260.7	1,759	272.7	2,295	70	2,365	111,016	2,151	730.5	6.2	521.7	819.6	14.7	53.7	4.2
1982	309.2	1,647	282.8	2,238			121,584	2,100	732.7	5.4	517.0	770.4	14.2	55.7	4.3
1983	332.1	1,682	293.7	2,308			129,507	2,158	750.9	5.4	546.3	780.0	14.1	56.7	4.3
1984	321.2	1,766	327.6	2,415			142,281	2,286	780.7	5.8	583.8	836.1	14.1	61.0	4.5
1985[1]	281.1	1,803	383.7	2,470			149,162	2,306	792.9	5.3	605.9	820.3	14.6	62.2	4.7
1986[3]	290.8	1,781	414.0	2,487			152,814	2,355	820.8	5.2	630.3	817.4	14.9	62.0	4.7
1987[3]	249.7	1,865	455.3	2,572			155,712	2,440	849.3	4.4	658.2	846.9	14.7	62.2	4.8
1988[3]	230		550	2,740			156,000	2,460	860	3.7	665	860	11.4	64.0	5.0

[1] Preliminary.   [2] Includes generation of industrial and railway electric plants.   [3] Estimate.   [4] Also includes interdepartmental (averages about 600 million kwh).   [5] Includes internal combustion.   *Sources: Federal Power Commission; Edison Electric Institute*   T.224

Electric Power Production by Electric Utilities in the U.S.   In Billions of Kilowatt Hours

Year	Jan.	Feb.	Mar.	Apr.	May	June	July	Aug.	Sept.	Oct.	Nov.	Dec.	Total
1975	164.3	147.1	155.5	146.2	153.2	162.4	176.8	179.7	155.2	154.9	152.8	169.4	1,918
1976	178.3	156.7	164.2	153.2	157.4	173.4	186.4	186.4	165.0	163.7	169.1	183.9	2,038
1977	196.4	162.7	169.1	156.9	169.3	180.8	198.9	196.1	176.2	166.4	167.1	184.2	2,124
1978	197.3	173.7	173.2	159.7	175.2	187.4	202.6	205.6	185.6	175.6	176.3	191.7	2,206
1979	209.7	186.3	182.8	170.0	178.1	186.7	202.3	204.9	180.8	179.7	177.5	188.7	2,247
1980	200.0	188.7	187.5	168.7	175.7	189.4	216.8	215.4	191.5	178.6	178.6	195.6	2,286
1981	206.5	179.6	185.6	172.5	177.8	202.7	220.4	210.4	186.8	181.4	175.6	195.6	2,295
1982	209.4	180.3	187.7	172.6	177.1	186.1	210.6	205.7	180.7	173.0	173.4	184.7	2,241
1983	195.6	172.5	182.5	170.4	174.4	191.0	220.2	230.0	195.6	182.9	182.9	212.3	2,310
1984	216.6	189.6	200.1	181.1	192.2	209.6	221.2	229.3	195.2	190.9	190.4	200.0	2,416
1985	227.9	198.2	195.0	184.9	196.8	205.4	226.7	226.1	202.5	194.8	192.4	219.3	2,470
1986	217.5	192.3	196.8	186.1	197.3	215.0	242.7	225.2	206.7	197.8	196.4	213.6	2,487
1987[1]	222.7	194.0	201.8	189.5	206.1	225.6	247.9	247.6	213.0	203.0	200.3	220.5	2,572
1988[1]	237.6	216.8	213.9	195.8	208.1	232.2	257.0	267.1					

[1] Preliminary.   *Source: Federal Power Commission*   T.225

Use of Fuels for Electric Generation in the United States

Year	Consumption of Fuel — Coal (Thousand Short Tons)	Fuel Oil (Thousand Barrels)[2]	Gas (Million Cubic Feet)	Total Fuel in Coal Equivalent (Thousand Short Tons)	Net Generation by Fuels[3] (Million Kw. Hr.)	Lbs. of Coal Per Kw. Hr. (Pounds)	% of Total Net Fuel Generation	Average Cost of Fuel Per Kw. Hr. (¢)	Heat Rate BTU Per Kw. Hr.	Cost Per Million BTU Consumed (¢)
1975	406,032	506,081	3,157,669	686,236	1,441,611	.952		1.12	10,383	108.3
1976	448,431	555,583	3,080,627	740,112	1,558,951	.950		1.20	10,369	115.3
1977	477,215	623,656	3,190,571	798,425	1,648,775	.969		1.38	10,449	131.8
1978	481,624	635,839	3,188,370	811,814	1,646,163	.986		1.53	10,495	145.3
1979	527,051	523,297	3,490,523	837,371	1,708,029	.981		1.62	10,470	155.4
1980	569,274	420,214	3,681,595	916,952	1,753,749	.980		2.07	10,489	197.0
1981	596,797	351,111	3,640,154	922,133	1,755,401	.992		2.42	10,506	230.2
1982	593,666	249,771	3,225,518	858,869	1,644,062	.996		2.46	10,517	234.0
1983	625,211	245,497	2,910,767	861,621	1,678,021	.993		2.40	10,539	227.1
1984	664,399	204,479	3,111,342	909,156	1,758,882	.990		2.41	10,385	232.0
1985	693,841	173,414	3,044,083	926,793	1,794,276	.990		2.27	10,429	217.7
1986[1]	685,056	230,482	2,602,370	907,720	1,770,925	.989		1.92	10,423	184.5
1987[4]	717,894	199,378	2,844,051	944,420	1,854,895	.981		1.84	10,354	177.7

[1] Preliminary.   [2] 42-gallon barrels.   [3] Excludes wood & waste fuels.   [4] Estimate.   *Source: Federal Power Commission*   T.226

Fertilizer

Fertilizer chemicals used in the U.S. are based on nitrogen, phosphorous and potassium. Nitrogen fertilizer is derived from ammonia, made from natural gas and nitrogen; phosphorous is from phosphoric acid, made from phosphate rock and sulfuric acid; and potassium fertilizer is from potassium chloride, more commonly called potash. According to the U.S. Department of Commerce, fertilizer chemicals based on nitrogen account for 53 percent of total fertilizer consumption. Those based on phosphorous account for 26 percent, and those based on potassium for 21 percent.

Although planted acreage was low by historical levels in 1988, fertilizer prices were higher, as export demand rose. The weaker dollar made U.S. fertilizer more competitive abroad. Domestic fertilizer nutrient consumption in 1988 was estimated at 19.4-19.6 million tons, up slightly from 19.2 million in 1987.

The USSR is the leading producer of ammonia, followed by China and the U.S. Around 80 percent of ammonia production in the U.S. is used for fertilizers. Although domestic ammonia production was threatened by the acreage slump, the industry recovered somewhat in 1988 due to higher overall prices for fertilizer. In 1988, U.S. consumption of nitrogenous fertilizers increased by an estimated 3-4 percent. Prices rose an estimated 15 percent from a year earlier. Ammonia plants reached full capacity towards the end of 1988, and this was expected to continue in 1989, leading to significantly higher prices.

The U.S. leads the world in production and consumption of phosphate fertilizers. U.S. production of phosphoric acid was 11.4 million tons in 1988, up from 10.5 million in 1987. Marketable phosphate rock production was 41.08 million tonnes through November of 1988, 11 percent higher than 1987. Consumption was running ahead of year-earlier levels at 34.66 million tonnes through October. U.S. exports of phosphate rock through November were slightly below the 1987 level. Consumption of phosphatic fertilizers is expected to increase by about 5 percent in 1989, due to larger planted acreage.

Close to 95 percent of U.S. potash sales are used directly in the fertilizer industry. Only about 15 percent of potash used in the U.S. is produced domestically. Even at full capacity, domestic producers can supply only 20-25 percent of U.S. potash needs. Canada, the primary supplier of potash to the U.S., reached an antidumping agreement with the U.S. that provides a floor for prices. As a result of the agreement, potash prices reached record levels in the spring of 1988, as the price of potassium chloride rose to $157/ton in April. Excess supplies in Canada were expected to temper further price increases for potash.

Fertilizer prices were higher in 1988, as supplies were drawn down, due largely to higher exports. The number of U.S. fertilizer companies has fallen sharply, and it is estimated that the by 1990-91, the number will have fallen by more than 50 percent from 1988. However, higher exports and increased planted area in 1989 should move prices higher, perhaps by as much as 9 percent.

World Production of Ammonia   In Thousands of Short Tons of Contained Nitrogen

Year	Bulgaria	Canada	China	France	East Germany	West Germany	India	Italy	Japan	Mexico	Netherlands	Poland	Romania	United Kingdom	United States	USSR	Total
1979	.9	2.2	9.7	2.4	1.2	2.4	2.5	1.6	2.6	1.5	2.1	1.7	2.6	1.8	15.4	13.4	78.4
1980	.9	2.3	11.0	2.3	1.3	2.3	2.4	1.5	2.3	1.7	2.1	1.6	2.5	1.8	16.2	13.9	81.2
1981	1.1	2.4	13.4	2.5	1.3	2.2	3.5	1.3	2.0	2.0	2.0	1.5	2.6	2.0	15.7	14.2	84.8
1982	1.1	2.3	14.0	2.2	1.3	1.7	3.8	1.2	1.8	2.2	1.8	1.5	2.9	1.9	13.0	15.4	83.7
1983	1.2	3.2	15.2	2.2	1.3	1.9	3.9	1.2	1.7	2.1	1.9	1.6	3.0	1.9	11.3	18.6	88.7
1984	1.3	3.9	15.4	2.6	1.3	2.2	4.4	1.3	1.8	2.0	2.5	1.6	3.2	2.0	13.4	19.5	96.9
1985	1.3	4.0	16.5	2.2	1.3	2.1	4.8	1.6	1.8	2.0	2.6	1.4	3.2	1.9	13.2	20.1	98.9
1986[1]	1.3	3.9	17.0	2.2	1.3	1.7	6.0	1.7	1.6	1.8	2.4	1.4	3.2	1.5	11.5	21.6	99.3
1987[2]	1.3	3.0	16.0	2.2	1.4	2.1	5.8	1.6	1.7	2.0	3.1	2.0	3.1	1.6	13.3	22.1	102.7

[1]Preliminary.   [2] Estimate.   *Source: Bureau of Mines*   T.227

U.S. Salient Statistics of Nitrogen[1] (Ammonia)   In Thousands of Short Tons

Year	Net Import Reliance as a % of Appar. Con.	Production (Fixed)	Imports Fixed	Exports (Ammonia)	Apparent Consumption Fixed (Ammonia) Elemental	Apparent Consumption Fixed	Producer Stocks (Year End)	Urea F.O.B. Gulf[2] Coast	Urea Deliv. Corn Belt	Ammonium Nitrate: Deliv. Corn Belt	Ammonia F.O.B. Gulf Coast
1979	7	15,420	1,603	647	14,386	16,565	1,752	145–150	165–170	118–120	128–132
1980	9	16,244	1,921	681		17,754	1,483	170–175	155–170	110–115	120–125
1981	5	15,732	1,719	506		16,467	1,960	130–135	170–180	138–150	132
1982	8	13,029	1,737	610		14,145	1,970	122–125	135–145	125–145	120
1983	18	11,297	2,169	298		13,719	1,422	135–140	160–167	135–145	175
1984	13	13,368	2,699	438		15,346	1,705	147–149	168–200	135–150	147
1985	8	13,238	2,306	1,010		14,439	1,800	82–95	110–137	112–133	108
1986	14	11,499	2,048	531		13,305	1,511	75–78	90–110	100–120	75
1987[3]	7	13,284	2,357	1,000		15,251	1,600	144–117	125–135	100–120	90

[1] Elemental, Fixed, & Natural Nitrates.   [2] Prilled.   [3] Preliminary.   *Source: Bureau of Mines*   T.228

World Production of Phosphate Rock, Basic Slag & Guano   In Ths. of Metric Tons (Gross Weight)

Year	Algeria	Brazil	China	Christmas Island	Israel	Jordan	Morocco	Nauru Island	Senegal	South Africa	Syria	Togo	Tunisia	United States	USSR	World Total
1979	1,084	1,628	8,517	1,367	2,086	2,825	20,032	1,828	1,835	3,221	1,272	2,920	4,154	51,611	24,400	131,825
1980	1,025	2,612	10,726	1,713	2,307	3,911	18,824	2,087	1,632	3,185	1,319	2,933	4,582	54,415	30,300	144,193
1981	916	3,238	11,500	1,423	1,919	4,244	18,562	1,480	1,699	2,718	1,321	2,215	4,596	53,624	30,700	143,001
1982	947	2,732	11,720	1,328	2,148	4,390	17,754	1,359	1,182	3,161	1,455	2,800	4,196	37,414	31,300	127,382
1983	893	3,208	12,500	1,094	2,969	4,749	20,106	1,684	1,521	2,887	1,229	2,081	5,924	42,573	33,100	140,889
1984	1,000	3,855	11,800	1,259	3,312	6,263	21,245	1,358	1,912	2,585	1,514	2,696	5,346	49,197	33,300	151,568
1985	1,207	4,214	6,970	1,187	4,076	6,067	20,737	1,508	1,814	2,433	1,270	2,452	4,530	50,835	33,750	148,606
1986[1]	1,203	4,509	6,700	880	3,673	6,249	21,178	1,494	1,850	2,920	1,606	2,314	5,951	38,710	33,900	138,740
1987[2]	1,073	4,777	9,000	842	3,798	6,801	20,955	1,376	1,880	2,623	1,986	2,644	6,390	40,954	34,100	145,148

[1] Preliminary.   [2] Estimate.   *Source: Bureau of Mines*   T.229

U.S. Salient Statistics of Phosphate Rock   In Thousands of Metric Tons

Year	Mine Production	Marketable Production	Value Mil. $	Imports for Consumption	Exports	Apparent Consumption	Stocks, Dec. 31 (Producer)	Price—$ Avg. Per Metric Ton (f.o.b. Mine)	Avg. Price of Fla. & No. Car. $ Tonne—F.O.B. Mine (−60% to +74) Domestic	Export	Average
1979	185,757	51,611	1,046	886	14,358	39,591	14,500	20.26	18.91	24.60	20.57
1980	209,883	54,415	1,257	486	14,276	40,791	13,709	23.10	21.01	30.03	23.51
1981	183,733	53,624	1,438	13	10,395	35,144	19,619	26.82	25.17	33.74	27.68
1982	104,135	37,414	950	31	9,842	28,760	18,287	25.40	28.78	28.92	25.93
1983	125,691	42,573	1,021	9	12,010	34,838	14,500	23.97	22.64	25.70	23.48
1984	163,012	49,197	1,182	9	11,528	41,758	11,897	23.99	22.67	26.28	23.48
1985	175,227	50,835	1,236	34	9,136	37,532	15,534	24.31	23.08	26.72	23.81
1986	135,683	40,320	897	528	7,848	34,456	13,277	22.67	21.64	25.02	22.31
1987[1]	148,426	40,954	793	464	8,454	35,683	10,884	20.00	18.93	22.87	19.77

[1] Preliminary.   [2] Estimate.   *Source: Bureau of Mines*   T.230

U.S. Salient Statistics of Potash   In Thousands of Metric Tons (K_2O Equivalent)

Year	Net Import as % of Consumption	Production	Sales by Producers	Value Mil. $	Imports for Consumption	Exports	Apparent Consumption	Producer Stocks Dec. 31	Avg. Value Per Ton of Product—$	Avg. Value of K_2O Equiv.	Average Price[2] $ Per Tonne
1979	66	2,225	2,388	279.2	5,165	635	6,918	251	61.38	116.92	95
1980	65	2,239	2,217	353.9	4,972	840	6,349	273	82.98	159.63	133
1981	65	2,156	1,908	328.9	4,796	491	6,213	520	89.62	172.40	137
1982	65	1,784	1,784	265.6	3,858	519	5,123	520	78.42	148.87	109
1983	75	1,429	1,513	220.8	4,440	300	5,653	391	74.85	145.97	100
1984	74	1,564	1,639	241.8	4,829	446	6,022	312	75.95	147.55	109
1985	76	1,296	1,266	178.4	4,593	513	5,346	336	71.22	140.89	96
1986	75	1,202	1,147	144.9	4,212	547	4,843	378	63.24	126.28	82
1987[1]	72	1,262	1,485	195.7	4,073	470	5,088	155	67.38	131.73	75

[1] Preliminary.   [2] Unit of K_2O, standard 60% muriate f.o.b. mine.   *Source: Bureau of Mines*   T.232

World Production of Marketable Potash   In Thousands of Metric Tons (K_2O Equivalent)

Year	Canada (sales)	Chile	China	Brazil	France	Germany East	Germany West	Israel	Italy	Jordan	Spain	USSR	United States	United Kingdom	World Total
1979	7,074	22	16	—	1,921	3,395	2,616	737	182	—	668	6,635	2,225	277	25,768
1980	7,532	25	12	—	1,894	3,422	2,737	797	156	—	658	8,064	2,239	321	27,857
1981	6,549	21	20	—	1,831	3,460	2,591	839	142	—	732	8,449	2,156	285	27,075
1982	5,309	22	26	—	1,704	3,434	2,056	1,004	146	9	692	8,079	1,784	245	24,510
1983	6,938	21	29	—	1,536	3,431	2,419	1,000	184	172	657	9,294	1,429	308	27,418
1984	7,527	18	40	—	1,739	3,465	2,645	1,100	163	295	677	9,776	1,564	325	29,334
1985	6,661	21	40	—	1,750	3,465	2,583	1,100	205	561	659	10,367	1,296	343	29,151
1986[1]	6,752	20	40	10	1,617	3,485	2,161	1,255	158	660	795	10,200	1,202	403	28,758
1987[2]	7,465	20	40	30	1,650	3,500	2,140	1,300	160	720	750	10,400	1,262	435	29,812

[1] Preliminary.   [2] Estimate.   *Source: U.S. Bureau of Mines*   T.231

Flaxseed and Linseed Oil

World 1988/89 flaxseed production was estimated at 1.84 million tonnes, down 19 percent from 1987/88. Canada, previously the largest producer, saw its crop drop to 420,000 tonnes. Yields fell 37 percent because of the 1988 drought; acreage was down 7 percent. Argentina took the lead with a crop of 480,000 tonnes, which was off 13 percent due to lower acreage. India's crop was unchanged at 400,000 tonnes. The USSR was among the few countries that expanded production, and its crop was put at 260,000 tonnes, compared with 230,000 in 1987/88. Both acreage and yields rose in the USSR. In the U.S., acreage fell substantially, and yields were slightly lower, resulting in a crop of 90,000 tonnes, 53 percent less than a year earlier.

Flaxseed demand continued to fall, as substitute fibers replaced flax, and latex paints eliminated the need for linseed oil. The decline was expected to continue.

The world flaxseed crush was estimated at 1.72 million tonnes, off 11 percent from a year earlier. Argentina, with extensive capacity built for soybeans and sunflowerseeds, was the largest flaxseed processor. India, the U.S., and West Germany were also major processors. Canada exports most of its crop. Some is crushed in the U.S. and exported back to Canada as linseed oil. World flaxseed exports were estimated at 570,000 tonnes, down 19 percent from 1987/88. Canada was the largest exporter, while the leading importer was West Germany. World ending stocks were projected at 270,000 tonnes, down 48 percent from a year earlier.

Global linseed oil output was estimated at 590,000 tonnes, down about 12 percent from 1987/88. World consumption was projected at 550,000 tonnes, off about 5 percent. Linseed oil is used mainly as a drying agent in paints and varnishes, but small amounts are purified for food use. Global linseed oil exports were estimated at 260,000 tonnes, down 13 percent. Argentina was the largest exporter, followed by West Germany. The major importers were the USSR, Poland, and China.

World 1988/89 linseed meal output was expected to drop 10 percent to 1.11 million tonnes. World meal exports were forecast at 530,000 tonnes, down 12 percent. Argentina and West Germany, with a combined market share near 74 percent, dominated exports. The major importers were Belgium, the Netherlands and other European Community countries. Consumption was put at 1.26 million tonnes, down 6 percent. Ending stocks worldwide were expected to be unchanged at 30,000 tonnes.

Futures Markets

Flaxseed futures are traded on the Winnipeg Commodity Exchange (WCE).

World Production of Flaxseed   In Thousands of Metric Tons

Crop Year	Argentina	Australia	Czechoslovakia	Canada	Bangladesh	Egypt	France	Hungary	India	Mexico	Poland	Romania	Turkey	Uruguay	United States	USSR	World Total
1980–1	610	7	15	442		27	35	10	423	8	29	44	3	21	196	196	2,096
1981–2	600	7	12	468		18	18	11	483	12	24	38	2	14	185	165	2,086
1982–3	765	3	15	752	8	38	31	11	375	1	20	43	2	6	261	150	2,502
1983–4	660	4	15	444	8	16	22	11	444	4	19	23	2	9	175	259	2,139
1984–5	626	6	15	694	8	20	29	9	389	3	18	35	2	7	178	248	2,316
1985–6	460	10	15	902	8	22	34	7	380	3	18	36	2	6	211	201	2,356
1986–7[1]	622	8	15	1,026	8	23	26	6	340	3	20	32	2	6	293	233	2,690
1987–8[2]	555			729		25	27		400			35		6	190	230	2,280
1988–9[2]	450			410					400						90	260	1,800

[1] Preliminary. [2] Estimate. *Source: Foreign Agricultural Service, U.S.D.A.*   T.233

U.S. Supply and Distribution of Flaxseed   In Thousands of Bushels

Year Beginning June	Stocks, June 1 Farm	Stocks, June 1 Terminal	Stocks, June 1 All Other	Total Stocks	Imports	Production	Total Supply	Seed	Crushing	Exports	Other[2]	Total Distribution
1977–8	1,070	—1,934—		2,961	859	14,280	18,100	557	11,615	1,001	−388	11,784
1978–9	2,890	—2,606—		5,315	1,557	8,614	15,486	724	13,009	91	−922	12,811
1979–0	977	—1,607—		2,584	1,916	12,014	16,514	650	12,425	174	−1,753	11,322
1980–1	2,681	—2,337—		5,018	2,510	7,728	15,256	547	11,927	76	−27	12,447
1981–2	1,136	—1,597—		2,733	3,502	7,289	13,524	691	11,231	11	−359	11,574
1982–3	1,175	— 775—		1,950	1,921	10,278	14,149	486	8,722	638	1,091	10,937
1983–4	1,956	—1,258—		3,212	4,756	6,903	14,871	438	12,733	52	−68	13,155
1984–5				1,716	3,796	7,022	12,534	511	9,935	238	201	10,885
1985–6				1,649	2,927	8,293	12,869	517	10,313	250	160	11,240
1986–7				1,629	2,229	11,538	15,396	362	10,000	1,448	285	12,095
1987–8[1]				3,301	2,757	7,444	13,502	222	10,700	105	150	11,177
1988–9[3]				2,325	4,867	3,600	10,792	242	9,250	50	0	9,542

[1] Preliminary. [2] Other disappearance represents cleaning loss, waste, and residual. [3] Forecasts. *Source: Agricultural Statistics Board, U.S.D.A.* T.235

U.S. Production of Flaxseed, By States In Thousands of Bushels

Crop Year	Minn-esota	North Dakota	South Dakota	Total	Crop Year	Minn-esota	North Dakota	South Dakota	Total
1981	1,300	4,250	2,249	7,289	1985	950	6,008	1,335	8,293
1982	1,650	5,873	2,755	10,278	1986	544	9,538	1,456	11,538
1983	938	4,600	1,365	6,903	1987[1]	224	6,518	702	7,444
1984	653	4,875	1,494	7,022	1988[1]				3,600

[1] Preliminary.   *Source: Agricultural Statistics Board, U.S.D.A.*   T.234

Average Price Received by Farmers for Flaxseed in the U.S.   In Cents Per Bushel

Year	July	Aug.	Sept.	Oct.	Nov.	Dec.	Jan.	Feb.	Mar.	Apr.	May	June	Average[1]
1980–1	655	702	717	710	723	759	754	748	725	735	765	747	720
1981–2	723	708	644	621	664	684	690	691	680	669	660	665	667
1982–3	625	535	537	511	495	468	486	470	460	454	469	492	517
1983–4	496	594	714	700	692	655	686	701	710	708	720	691	684
1984–5	625	607	572	567	595	605	659	664	618	667	694	654	609
1985–6	610	572	539	501	480	479	477	494	495	488	487	495	505
1986–7	439	380	369	346	339	341	318	313	304	315	335	344	344
1987–8	347	333	315	307	303	320	342	379	395	409	458	543	371
1988–9	629	720	767	785	809	807							

[1] Season average includes an allowance for unredeemed loans.   *Source: Agricultural Statistics Board, U.S.D.A.*   T.236

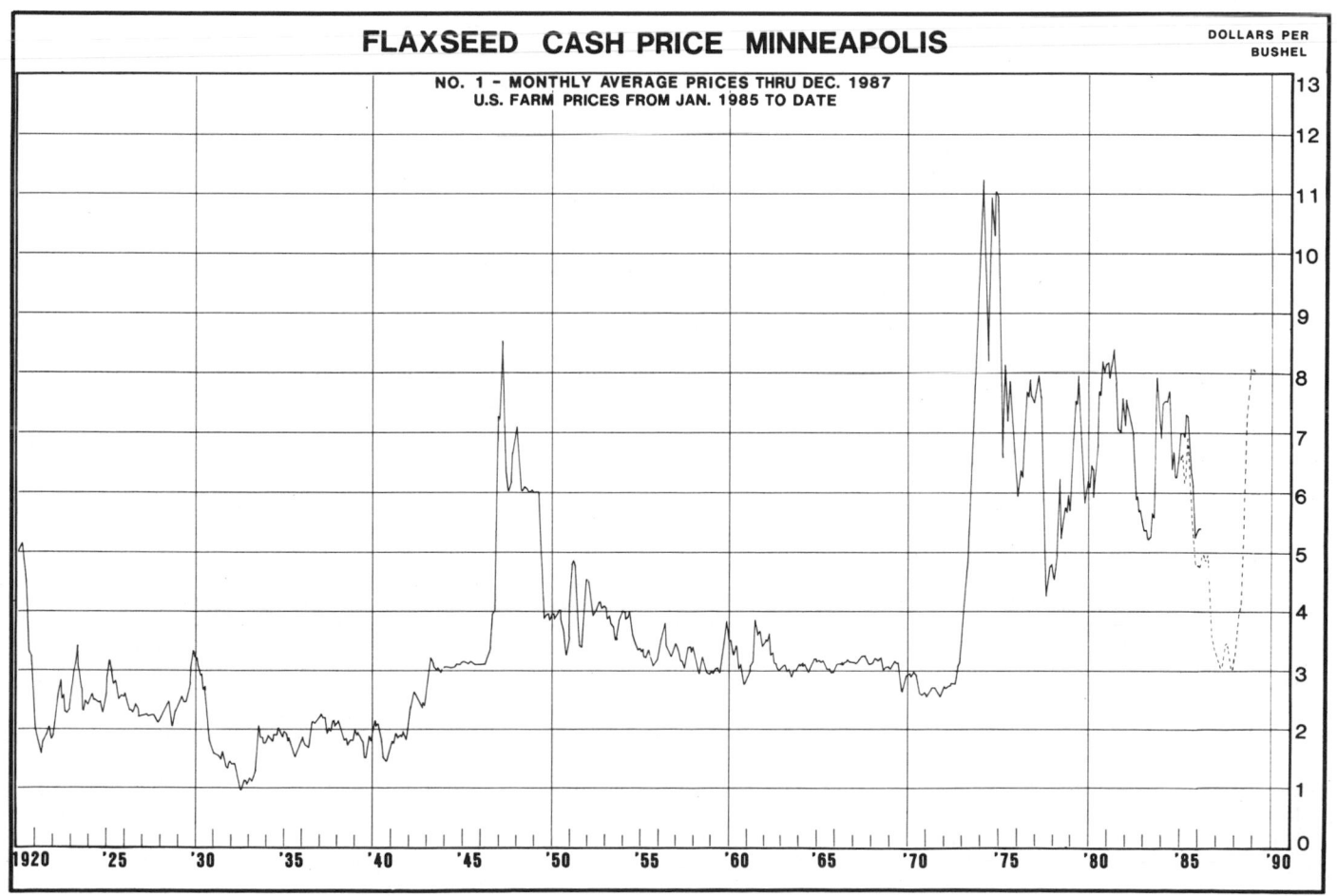

FLAXSEED CASH PRICE MINNEAPOLIS   DOLLARS PER BUSHEL

NO. 1 – MONTHLY AVERAGE PRICES THRU DEC. 1987
U.S. FARM PRICES FROM JAN. 1985 TO DATE

FLAXSEED AND LINSEED OIL

Supply and Distribution of Linseed Oil in the U.S. & World Production & Price   In Millions of Pounds

Year Beginning June	Supply Stocks June 1	Production	Total	Exports & Shipments	Paint & Varnish	Linoleum & Oilcloth	Resins & Plastics	Other Inedible	Total	Total World	Argentina	India	Japan	West Germany	U.S.	Price Rotterdam Ex-Tank $ Tonne
1982–3	50	182	232	21	50.1		20.4		176	650	221	108			88	456
1983–4	35	265	300	51	56.5		27.7		201	670	220	128	38	66	120	556
1984–5	48	194	242	15	113.5		26.3		194	640	185	146	35	87	88	639
1985–6	33	205	238	15	131.0		29.7		184	600	125	110	36	110	93	475
1986–7[1]	39	201	240	6	187.6				183	660	153	99	32	124	91	319
1987–8[2]	51	214	265	10					205	640	150	116	33	125	93	441
1988–9[2]	50	185	235	10					180	560						681

[1] Preliminary.   [2] Estimate.   [3] Oil production calculated from assumed extraction rates.   *Source: Economic Research Service, U.S.D.A.*   T.239

Factory Shipments of Paints, Varnish and Lacquer in the U.S.   In Millions of Dollars

Year	Jan.	Feb.	Mar.	Apr.	May	June	July	Aug.	Sept.	Oct.	Nov.	Dec.	Total
1982	486.9	509.1	616.1	633.4	664.3	736.0	631.6	671.5	653.8	545.2	479.8	419.7	6,988
1983	491.3	518.8	656.6	676.8	728.5	808.6	692.1	754.3	713.6	656.9	580.1	505.9	7,783
1984	624.5	672.4	760.7	754.3	839.2	839.9	785.1	833.0	744.4	765.3	633.0	566.5	8,818
1985	621.9	613.1	745.7	855.9	920.6	871.4	853.6	855.2	797.0	811.0	665.4	564.1	9,175
1986[1]	717.4	698.4	766.2	920.5	916.1	900.0	871.0	860.8	858.0	880.4	661.7	628.4	9,547
1987[1]	704.0	762.3	857.5	911.3	924.2	940.9	914.1	898.5	879.6	895.4	751.7	681.3	10,058
1988[1]	751.5	822.3	958.0	970.1	1,034.0	1,067.0	937.5	1,000.0	964.7				

[1] Preliminary.   *Source: Bureau of the Census*   T.246

Wholesale Price of Raw Linseed Oil at Minneapolis in Tank Cars   In Cents Per Pound

Year	July	Aug.	Sept.	Oct.	Nov.	Dec.	Jan.	Feb.	Mar.	Apr.	May	June	Average
1982–3	27.8	26.3	26.0	24.6	25.0	25.2	24.6	25.0	24.3	23.6	23.0	23.0	24.9
1983–4	22.8	25.5	31.6	34.0	31.5	32.0	32.0	32.0	31.8	32.0	33.0	34.5	31.1
1984–5	33.4	38.0	31.0	28.8	28.5	30.0	31.2	32.0	N.A.	N.A.	N.A.	N.A.	31.6
1985–6	34.6	33.3	33.0	30.0	30.0	27.6	30.0	30.0	30.0	30.0	30.0	29.4	30.7
1986–7	29.0	29.0	29.0	25.0	25.0	25.0	25.0	25.0	25.0	25.0	25.0	25.0	26.0
1987–8	25.00	25.00	25.00	22.75	24.25	25.00	25.00	25.00	25.00	24.75	24.75	28.20	25.0
1988–9	35.00	37.00	41.50										

Source: Department of Agriculture   T.240

U.S. Stocks of Linseed Oil (Crude & Refined) at Factories & Warehouses   In Millions of Pounds

Year	July 1	Aug. 1	Sept. 1	Oct. 1	Nov. 1	Dec. 1	Jan. 1	Feb. 1	Mar. 1	April 1	May 1	June 1
1982–3	37.4	33.9	30.5	44.6	43.0	26.8	39.0	34.1	41.8	41.6	27.1	35.1
1983–4	54.7	46.5	41.7	50.4	46.0	34.9	34.1	38.0	40.3	41.5	55.2	47.6
1984–5	50.7	40.8	24.9	48.3	41.3	36.1	39.3	38.3	34.1	30.1	35.1	33.4
1985–6	32.7	36.9	25.4	47.0	62.3	55.2	60.6	62.7	64.6	66.0	56.1	40.1
1986–7[1]	46.0	45.3	40.4	40.0	50.3	68.0	60.0	68.0	60.0	64.6	55.0	51.1
1987–8[1]	52.2	45.9	40.2	52.1	54.3	50.4	50.8	56.1	39.0	35.4	35.5	40.8
1988–9[1]	35.6	36.0	44.8	24.9	33.7							

[1] Preliminary.   *Source: Bureau of the Census*   T.245

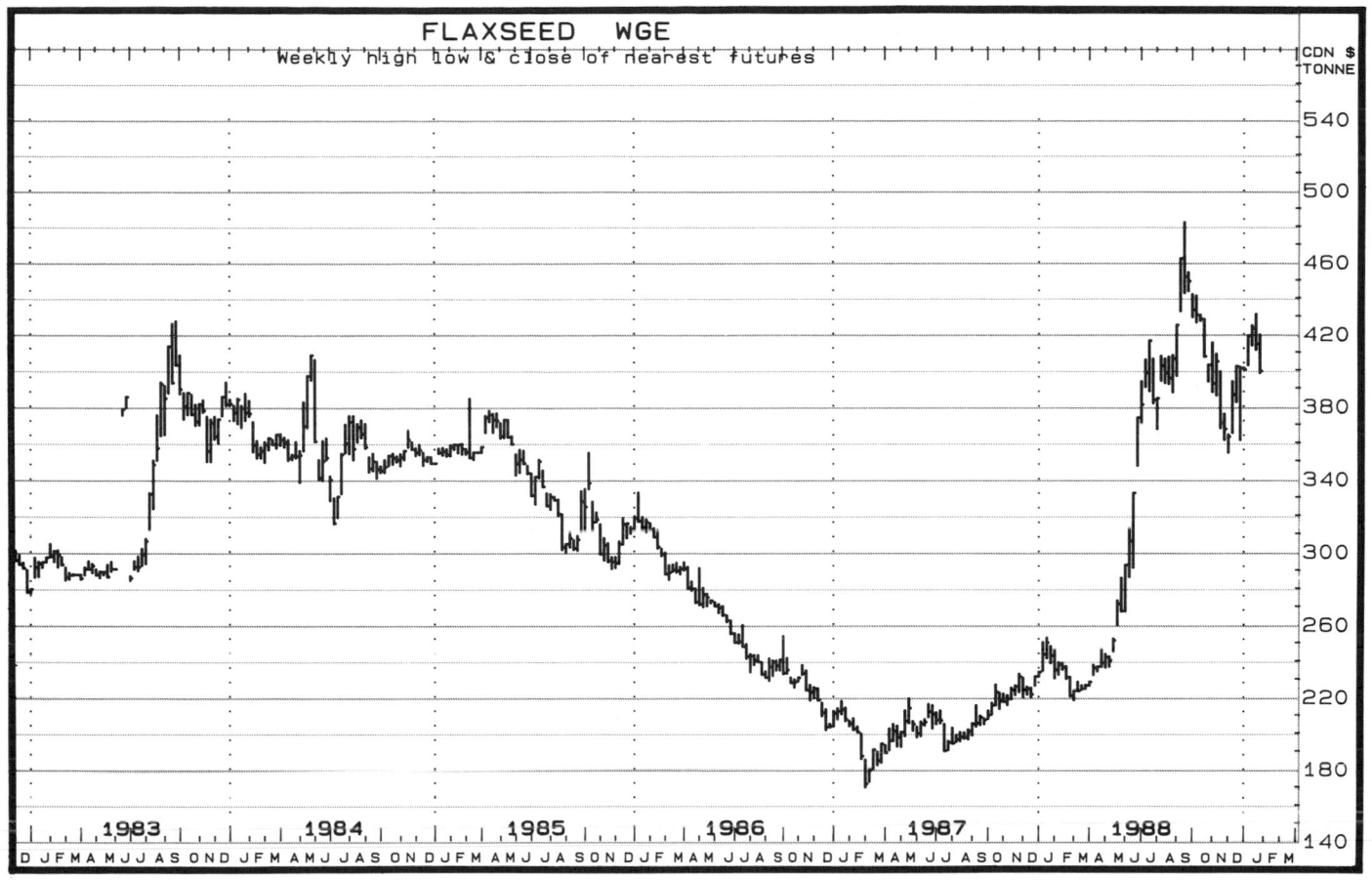

FLAXSEED WGE
Weekly high low & close of nearest futures

High, Low & Closing Prices of May Flaxseed Futures in Winnipeg   In Canadian Dollars per Tonne

Year of Delivery		June	July	Aug.	Sept.	Oct.	Nov.	Dec.	Jan.	Feb.	Mar.	Apr.	May	Life of Delivery Range
					Year Prior to Delivery						**Delivery Year**			
1986	High	375.0	373.1	353.9	340.0	349.0	313.0	333.0	334.0	319.3	300.5	293.5	282.0	378.5
	Low	374.2	350.3	318.2	318.0	316.0	303.5	309.1	317.0	295.3	290.3	270.1	269.0	269.0
	Close	366.0	350.3	324.4	328.5	317.5	308.5	325.0	318.0	295.5	293.5	290.4	269.5	—
1987	High	—	280.0	262.8	265.2	258.7	250.4	239.2	222.5	213.0	195.5	204.5	218.7	280.0
	Low	—	268.0	248.0	247.5	242.1	231.5	212.8	208.6	174.5	177.5	188.5	196.7	174.5
	Close	—	268.0	248.0	260.5	245.0	238.7	217.8	209.7	176.1	188.6	198.5	199.3	—
1988	High	237.6	235.0	218.8	230.2	244.2	246.0	242.5	260.0	244.8	233.8	245.8	285.5	285.5
	Low	231.0	214.0	214.0	217.6	227.3	228.8	231.0	236.0	224.8	223.8	231.9	236.5	214.0
	Close	234.0	217.0	218.0	228.0	230.8	242.5	239.6	241.0	226.1	230.0	241.8	275.0	—
1989	High	—	417.0	431.0	490.0	454.5	427.5	405.5						
	Low	—	406.0	410.0	435.0	403.0	371.0	366.5						
	Close	—	406.0	431.0	450.0	419.0	371.5	405.0						

Source: Winnipeg Commodity Exchange   T.243

Month–End Open Interest of Flaxseed Futures in Winnipeg   In Contracts

Year	Jan.	Feb.	Mar.	Apr.	May	June	July	Aug.	Sept.	Oct.	Nov.	Dec.
1984	6,509	6,964	5,100	5,944	4,509	3,943	5,140	6,164	5,853	4,490	5,618	5,162
1985	5,408	5,927	6,281	5,783	6,321	5,848	5,016	5,913	5,815	4,315	4,186	4,024
1986	5,037	5,600	5,204	6,586	6,137	6,487	5,561	6,626	7,147	3,955	5,618	4,247
1987	3,956	3,546	4,599	7,088	7,161	6,304	6,607	6,747	8,276	5,690	5,792	5,089
1988	6,179	6,972	5,787	6,920	6,191	8,431	6,101	7,232	8,078	9,874	10,695	7,228

Source: Winnipeg Commodity Exchange   T.244

Gas

Total U.S. natural gas consumption in 1988 was forecast at 17.7 trillion cubic feet, a 3 percent increase over 1987, but about 3 percent below previous estimates. The Department of Energy revised its consumption data in November 1988, after a study indicated that 43 industrial users had been consistently overstating their industrial consumption. The revised estimate of industrial natural gas consumption for the first half of 1988 was 3.1 trillion cubic feet, 6 percent higher than the same period in 1987. Data prior to the revision indicated a 26 percent increase in industrial use. For all of 1988, projected industrial use was 6.15 trillion cubic feet, 4 percent more than in 1987. Industrial demand for 1989 was forecast at 6.24 trillion cubic feet, based on expectations of a slowing rate of industrial growth.

For 1989, total demand was projected at 17.94 trillion cubic feet, up by over 1 percent from 1988. Consumption at electric utilities was expected to be flat, reflecting comparatively low prices for fuel oil and a recovery in hydroelectric power to replace some of the emergency gas-fired power generated during the 1988 summer drought. The American Gas Association was projecting a 3 percent increase in demand and a 7 percent rise in average prices.

The association also said that natural gas supplies were expected to be adequate to meet 1989 winter demand, although severely cold weather could cause tightness. In January 1988, a severe cold snap drove up prices across the country and forced some California utilities to cut off customers who could switch to alternative fuels.

The Federal Energy Regulatory Commission (FERC) announced in November 1988 that its Order 500 had produced 12 filings covering $5 billion in contracts. The order established rules for settlements of unprofitable take-or-pay contracts between pipelines and utilities that refused to accept the higher-priced gas contracted for during the 1977-1982 energy shortage. The FERC was also considering an experimental pipeline brokerage program that would allow pipelines to sell space on their systems to other shippers.

World Natural Gas Production (Marketed Production[3]) In Thousands of Terajoule[4]

Year	Argen-tina	Canada	China	France	Indo-nesia	West Germany	Iran	Italy	Mexico	Nether-lands	Poland	Romania	United Kingdom	United States	USSR	Vene-zuela	Aus-tralia
1976	268	2,820		279	115	676	788	600	515	3,422	243	1,384	1,491	20,552	11,194	497	231
1977	271	2,962		299	162	673	743	524	538	3,067	249	1,465	1,536	18,921	12,102	510	264
1978	256	2,856	535	307	353	720	668	524	701	3,048	244	1,475	1,458	18,846	12,967	528	274
1979	303	3,041	566	303	482	729	700	581	832	3,100	224	1,409	1,470	19,415	14,160	601	303
1980	327	2,790	558	289	607	632	279	476	1,036	3,012	193	1,455	1,379	19,256	15,168	643	351
1981	340	2,748	496	277	653	673	247	533	1,033	2,975	187	1,532	1,374	19,057	16,215	647	406
1982	393	2,825	464	257	646	580	257	583	1,044	2,533	167	1,640	1,483	17,655	17,414	682	432
1983	457	2,740	475	260	773	635	326	495	959	2,691	193	1,537	1,527	15,986	18,638	668	443
1984	478	2,969	478	247	940	617	327	525	706	2,717	190	1,526	1,494	17,341	20,469	741	470
1985	509	3,189	502	217	959	584	324	539	647	2,839	200	1,522	1,665	16,365	22,149	731	502
1986[1]	553	2,976	547	165	985	465	336	541	614	2,551	183	1,510	1,747	16,019	23,698	867	550
1987[2]	613	3,227	537	206	1,000	582		618	445	2,350	180		1,681	17,629	25,200	950	630

[1] Preliminary. [2] Estimate. [3] Comprises all gas collected & utilized as fuel or as a chemical industry raw material, including gas used in oilfields and/or gasfields as a fuel by producers. [4] Terajoule = 10^{12} Joule = approx. 10^9 BTU. *Source: United Nations* T.247

United States Recoverable Reserves and Deliveries of Natural Gas In Billions of Cubic Feet

Year	Recoverable Reserves of Natural Gas Dec. 31[3]	Residential	Commercial	Lease & Plant Fuel	Carbon Black	Petroleum Refineries	Used as Pipeline Fuel	Industrial	Other Consumers	Total Deliveries	Electric Utility Plants[2]
1976	216,026	5,051	2,668	1,634	28	919	548	6,964	285	17,764	3,081
1977	208,878	4,821	2,501	1,659	28		533	6,815	257	17,329	3,191
1978	200,302	4,903	2,601	1,648			530	6,757	291	17,449	3,188
1979	200,987	4,965	2,786	1,499			601	6,899	301	18,141	3,491
1980	199,021	4,752	2,611	1,026			635	7,172		18,216	3,682
1981	201,730	4,546	2,520	928			642	7,128		17,834	3,640
1982	201,512	4,633	2,606	1,109			596	5,831		16,295	3,226
1983	200,247	4,381	2,433	978			490	5,643		15,367	2,911
1984	197,463	4,555	2,524	1,077			529	6,154		16,345	3,111
1985	193,369	4,433	2,432	966			504	5,901		15,811	3,044
1986		4,314	2,318	923			485	5,579		14,814	2,602
1987[1]		4,315	2,414	1,149			519	5,895		15,468	2,844
1988[4]		3,700	2,200	1,000			500	5,750		15,000	2,700

[1] Preliminary. [2] Figures include gas other than natural (impossible to segregate); therefore, shown separately from other consumption. [3] Estimated proved recoverable reserves. [4] Estimated. *Source: U.S. Dept. of Energy* T.251

Gas Utility Sales in the United States by Types & Class of Service   In Trillions of BTU's[3]

Year	Total Utility Sales	No. of Cust. (Mil.)	Resi-dential	Com-mercial	Indus-trial	Electric Genera-tion	Other	Total	Resi-dential	Com-mercial	Indus-trial	Electric Genera-tion	Other
			Class of Service					Revenue—Mil. $					
1974	160,003	44.7	48,648	22,934	81,532		6,890	15,242	6,899	2,539	5,391		413
1975	148,629	44.8	49,910	23,868	68,371		6,480	19,101	8,445	3,303	6,745		608
1976	148,135	45.1	50,142	24,266	71,070		2,696	23,701	9,941	4,075	9,435		250
1977	143,409	45.7	49,463	24,094	67,107		2,746	28,303	11,541	4,980	11,455		328
1978[3]	14,748	46.0	5,107	2,500	6,932		211	32,150	12,939	5,696	13,139		377
1979	15,440	46.7	5,083	2,486	7,641		230	38,947	14,833	6,624	17,045		446
1980	15,413	47.4	4,826	2,453	7,957		177	48,303	17,432	8,183	22,215		473
1981	15,375	48.1	4,610	2,375	8,239		150	56,110	19,180	9,286	27,124		520
1982	14,183	48.5	4,770	2,471	6,794		147	63,200	23,700	11,666	27,200		634
1983	12,859	48.9	4,450	2,298	5,970		140	65,837	26,173	12,659	26,315		690
1984	13,162	49.5	4,628	2,396	5,991		146	67,496	27,485	13,205	26,093		713
1985	12,612	50.2	4,513	2,338	3,686	1,949	130	63,293	26,864	12,723	15,659	7,428	620
1986	11,126	51.0	4,380	2,238	2,892	1,449	167	51,194	24,750	11,268	10,554	3,949	673
1987[1]	10,115	51.8	4,350	2,132	2,158	1,306	169	44,828	23,390	10,065	7,204	3,569	600
1988[2]	12,000	53.0	6,000	2,700	2,200	1,000	170	53,000	28,000	12,000	7,100	2,500	610

[1] Preliminary.   [2] Estimate.   [3] Data prior to 1978 are in millions of therms.   *Source: American Gas Association*   T.253

Salient Statistics of Natural Gas in the United States

In Billions of Cubic Feet / Avg. Value Delivered to Consumers— $ Per Ths. Cu. Ft.

Year	Marketed Production	Storage Withdrawals	Import (Consumed)	Total Supply	Consumption	Exports	Stored	Extraction Loss	Unaccounted For	Total Disposition	Wellhead Price	Imports	Residential	Commercial	Industrial	Electric Utilities
1974	21,601	1,701	959	24,260	21,223	77	1,784	887	289	23,373	.30	N.A.	1.43	1.07	.67	.71
1975	20,109	1,760	953	22,821	19,538	73	2,104	872	235	21,949	.45	N.A.	1.71	1.35	.96	.77
1976	19,952	1,921	963	21,083	19,046	65	1,750	854	216	22,837	.58	N.A.	1.98	1.64	1.24	1.06
1977	20,025	1,750	1,011	21,924	19,521	56	2,307	863	41	22,786	.79	N.A.	2.35	2.04	1.50	1.32
1978	19,974	2,158	966	22,245	19,627	53	2,278	852	287	23,097	.91	2.21	2.56	2.23	1.70	1.48
1979	20,471	2,047	1,253	22,964	20,241	56	2,295	808	372	23,772	1.18	2.60	2.98	2.73	1.99	1.81
1980	20,180	1,972	985	22,515	19,877	49	1,949	777	640	23,292	1.59	4.42	3.68	3.39	2.56	2.27
1981	19,956	1,930	904	22,191	19,404	59	2,228	775	501	22,967	1.98	4.84	4.29	4.00	3.14	2.89
1982	18,520	2,165	933	21,000	18,001	52	2,472	762	475	21,762	2.46	4.94	5.17	4.82	3.87	3.48
1983	16,822	2,270	920	19,354	16,835	55	1,822	790	642	20,144	2.59	4.51	6.06	5.59	4.18	3.58
1984	18,230	2,098	843	20,443	17,951	55	2,295	838	143	20,443	2.66	4.08	6.12	5.55	4.22	3.70
1985	17,198	2,397	949	19,855	17,281	57	2,163	816	354	19,855	2.51	3.19	6.12	5.50	3.95	3.55
1986	16,791	1,837	750	18,692	16,221	61	1,984	800	427	18,692	1.94	2.53	5.83	5.08	3.23	2.43
1987[1]	17,349	1,905	992	19,534	17,137	54	1,911	812	432	19,534	1.67	2.14	5.54	4.78	2.94	2.32
1988[2]	16,800	1,700	1,200	20,000	16,800	58	2,300	820	−400	19,400	1.72	2.05	6.00	4.55	2.97	2.30

[1] Preliminary.   [2] Estimate.   [3] Total value of market production at the wellhead.   *Source: U.S. Dept. of Energy*   T.248

United States Marketed Production[1] of Natural Gas   In Billions of Cubic Feet

Year	Alaska	Arkansas	California	Kansas	Louisiana	Michigan	Mississippi	Montana	New Mexico	Ohio	Oklahoma	Pennsylvania	Texas	West Virginia	Wyoming
1974	129	124	365	887	7,754		79	55	1,245	92	1,639	83	8,171	202	327
1975	160	116	318	844	7,091	102	70	41	1,217	85	1,605	85	7,486	154	316
1976	166	110	354	829	7,007	119	71	43	1,231	89	1,727	89	7,192	153	329
1977	188	104	311	781	7,215	130	83	47	1,203	99	1,770	92	7,051	153	330
1978	203	107	311	854	7,476	148	107	47	1,174	114	1,774	98	6,548	149	357
1979	221	109	248	798	7,266	160	144	54	1,181	123	1,835	96	7,175	151	414
1980	231	112	310	735	6,639	159	175	52	1,150	139	1,892	97	7,116	157	410
1981	243	93	381	640	6,780	153	181	59	1,134	141	2,019	122	6,910	151	425
1982	264	125	384	430	6,172	153	167	57	991	138	1,934	121	6,469	151	425
1983[2]	277	128	415	435	5,332	139	151	52	895	151	1,730	118	5,939	130	444
1984	289	135	476	466	5,825	145	158	51	957	186	1,986	166	6,185	144	517
1985	34	155	491	513	5,014	132	144	52	905	182	1,936	150	6,053	145	417

[1] Comprises gas either sold or consumed by producers, including losses in transmission, quantities added to storage and increases of gas in pipelines.   [2] Preliminary.   *Source: U.S. Dept. of Energy*   T.250

Gasoline

U.S. gasoline demand remained strong in 1988, keeping prices high in spite of a sharp drop in crude oil prices. Through the first 11 months of 1988, demand for gasoline averaged 7.31 million barrels per day (bpd), up 1.5 percent from the first 11 months in 1987. Gasoline demand was expected to rise another 1.4 percent in 1989, enough to continue the strain on the domestic gasoline supply system that became evident in 1988.

The U.S. city average retail price for unleaded regular gasoline was 94.9 cents a gallon in November, virtually unchanged from the 1987 average of 94.8 cents. The average for regular gasoline was 90.4 cents in November, compared with the 1987 average of 89.7 cents. Higher gasoline taxes in several states absorbed some of the reduction in crude oil prices, which amounted to about $3 a barrel during the second and third quarters of 1988. But much of the firmness in prices at the pump went into an 8-cent per gallon increase in refiners' margins, the difference between the refiner or reseller price per barrel of petroleum product and the per barrel price of crude oil used to produce it.

Normally, an increase in refiners' margins would trigger extra production, which in turn would force producers to cut prices to move additional product. However, average utilization rates at operating refineries ranged from 91 percent to 95 percent during the second and third quarters. Furthermore, an explosion at a Shell refinery in May contributed to the production tightness, just when refineries were beginning to recover from an extremely cold winter that increased production of heating oil and residual fuel oil. Booming demand for chemical feedstocks, which require many of the components that are also used to make gasoline, also figured into the higher margins.

Usually, gasoline production shortfalls would be met by increasing imports, which did surge to 554,000 bpd in November. However, the 11-month average was 404,000 bpd, little changed from the 390,000 bpd for the first 11 months of 1987. Gasoline consumption also grew sharply in Europe, limiting availabilities for export during the peak driving season.

U.S. supply systems were affected by the drought, which lowered water levels in the Mississippi. In some cases, refineries had to import fresh water for use in their production operations, because tides were able to carry salt water far enough up the river to threaten their plant intakes. Also, barge traffic was severely limited, and many of the barges that were able to move had to carry reduced loads to avoid running into the bottom. Because pipelines were also booked to capacity, it became difficult to move product to where it was needed, forcing retailers who depend on the spot market to bid up prices of available supplies.

The switch to lower allowed lead content as part of the eventual phase-out of all lead in gasoline in the U.S. also reduced available supplies and raised production costs. Unleaded gas costs more to make because other octane boosters (such as methyl tertiary butyl ether) cost more than lead, because unleaded requires more extensive and complex refining processes, and because the yield per barrel of crude is lower. The market for high-octane unleaded gas expanded in 1988, growing from about one-fifth of total demand to about one-fourth, even though most new cars required octane ratings of as low as 87 or 88. Successful marketing efforts aimed at convincing buyers that higher octane means higher quality contributed to the growth.

The trend toward oil-exporting nations buying U.S. downstream operations continued in 1988, with Saudi Arabia agreeing to buy half of Texaco's Eastern U.S. refining and marketing operations. Venezuela, which owned half of a refinery in Corpus Christi, announced plans to buy the remaining interest and a share in a Chicago refining and marketing network.

Futures Market

Unleaded regular gasoline is traded on the New York Mercantile Exchange.

High, Low & Closing Prices of December Unleaded Regular Gasoline Futures In N.Y.   In ¢ Per Gallon

Year of Delivery		Yr. Prior to Delivery							Delivery Year[1]							Life of Delivery Range
	Oct.	Nov.	Dec.	Jan.	Feb.	Mar.	Apr.	May	June	July	Aug.	Sept.	Oct.	Nov.[1]	
1985 High	—	—	—	—	—	77.00	78.00	72.45	71.60	71.65	72.65	75.10	80.50	81.00	81.00
Low	—	—	—	—	—	72.75	72.00	70.75	67.65	69.45	70.00	68.70	73.80	78.25	67.65
Close	—	—	—	—	—	77.00	72.00	71.25	70.90	70.70	71.60	74.50	80.20	79.00	—
1986 High	—	—	—	61.00	52.50	43.50	40.65	42.60	39.60	35.30	43.55	46.40	43.90	43.00	61.00
Low	—	—	—	55.10	40.80	34.00	34.56	36.50	36.00	30.32	31.00	34.55	37.70	40.00	30.20
Close	—	—	—	55.10	41.75	34.00	36.08	38.25	36.00	31.30	43.18	40.24	41.53	41.28	—
1987 High	—	—	51.00	51.25	50.75	50.40	50.80	51.50	54.00	56.25	55.92	50.90	53.50	52.15	56.25
Low	—	—	49.25	48.65	45.90	46.70	47.70	49.30	51.00	52.86	47.10	48.10	50.10	47.85	45.90
Close	—	—	51.00	51.00	45.90	50.25	49.30	51.30	53.55	53.92	49.80	50.46	52.46	49.31	—
1988 High	—	—	—	—	—	—	48.80	47.70	47.70	44.80	43.90	42.16	46.92	49.70	49.70
Low	—	—	—	—	—	—	46.40	45.30	41.50	40.70	40.90	38.00	36.00	42.40	36.00
Close	—	—	—	—	—	—	46.80	47.38	41.53	43.68	41.80	38.74	44.33	49.05	—
1989 High	—	—	—												
Low	—	—	—												
Close	—	—	—												

[1] Contract expires the last business day of the previous calendar month quoted.   *Source: N.Y. Mercantile Exchange*   T.0575A

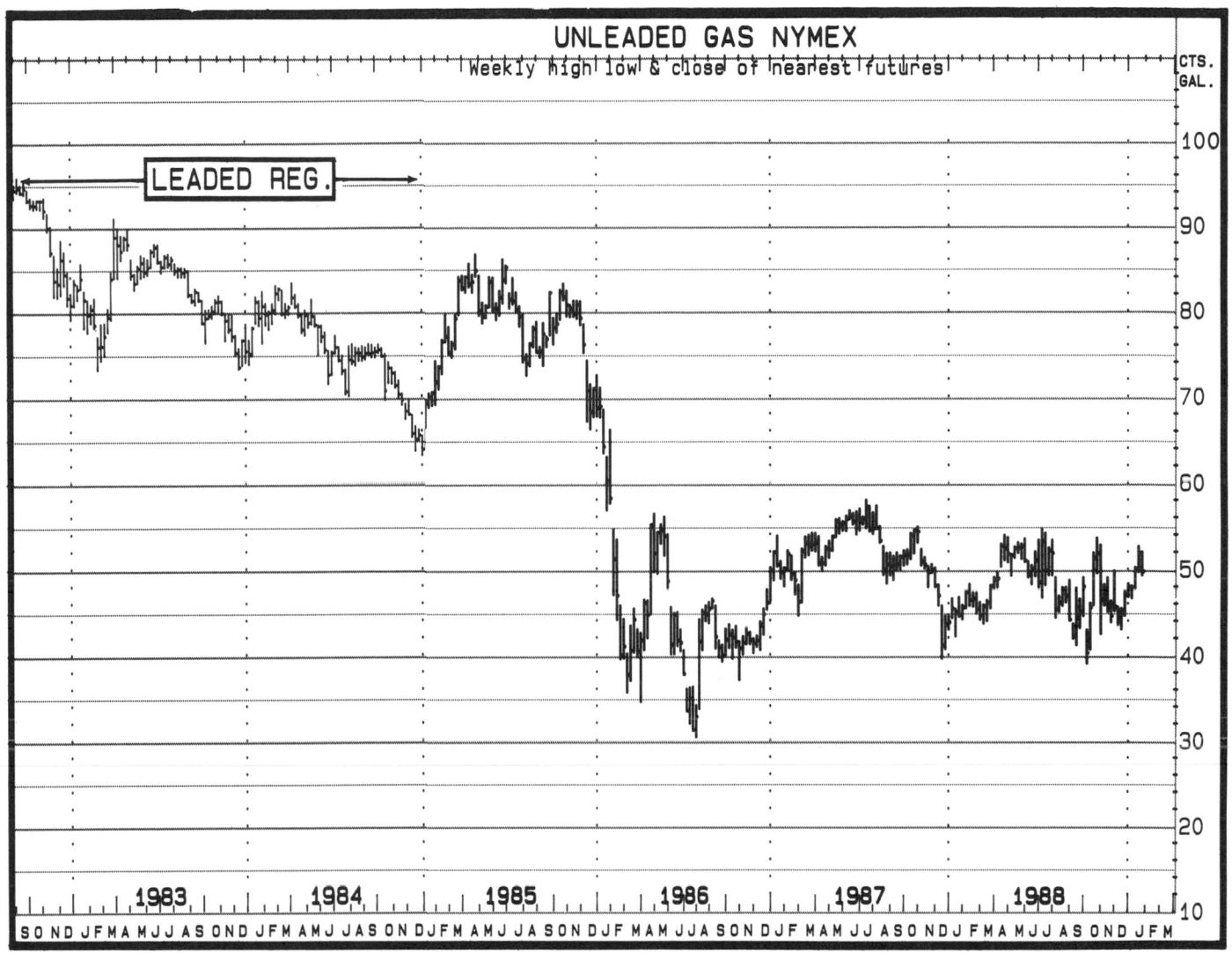

UNLEADED GAS NYMEX
Weekly high low & close of nearest futures

Month-End Open Interest of Unleaded Regular Gasoline Futures In New York   In Contracts

Year	Jan.	Feb.	Mar.	Apr.	May	June	July	Aug.	Sept.	Oct.	Nov.	Dec.
1984			FUTURES TRADING BEGAN DEC. 3, 1984									1,243
1985	2,429	1,464	3,411	4,977	4,406	4,923	5,685	4,599	3,910	4,921	3,922	3,150
1986	4,703	3,703	3,212	2,850	4,625	3,457	4,637	8,021	16,177	19,622	17,568	27,100
1987	30,693	36,605	44,056	36,397	35,408	32,109	30,398	27,244	26,501	31,192	35,262	38,968
1988	43,653	42,811	46,096	45,012	47,524	55,874	52,794	45,251	30,070	47,328	49,845	47,189

Source: N.Y. Mercantile Exchange   T.0576

Volume of Trading of Unleaded Regular Gasoline Futures in New York   In Contracts

Year	Jan.	Feb.	Mar.	Apr.	May	June	July	Aug.	Sept.	Oct.	Nov.	Dec.	Total
1985	9,042	4,045	7,848	10,093	10,853	12,219	19,532	16,403	10,604	15,808	8,427	7,737	132,611
1986	13,478	11,914	9,459	7,352	14,033	10,288	12,878	17,396	55,329	104,884	74,711	107,630	439,352
1987	135,208	139,885	211,590	214,982	178,735	175,585	182,661	154,685	155,352	166,365	152,176	190,014	2,056,238
1988	196,616	191,231	245,019	217,139	257,507	330,009	401,196	254,010	294,542	355,982	308,438	240,366	3,292,055

Source: N.Y. Mercantile Exchange   T.0576A

Gold

As 1988 began, gold prices were descending from a peak of $502.75/oz. at the December 14, 1987 London fix. The dollar slumped in late 1987, and the stock market was barely above its 1987 crash lows. However, 1988 began with central bank intervention to boost the dollar and with the oil market struggling to absorb excess OPEC production. The year avoided the recession many feared would be caused by the stock market crash, and inflation was relatively subdued. As a result, gold prices spent most of 1988 on the defensive, ending at $410.15 at the December 30 London fix.

Gold's best rally during 1988 came in sympathy with spring's bull market in grain prices caused by the drought. Sharp gains in the CRB Futures Price Index added to fears that inflation was increasing. Moreover, nickel, aluminum, steel scrap and zinc were in supply-driven bull markets, while copper was consolidating most of its 1987 gains (in a pause before soaring to all-time highs).

But unlike the industrial metals markets, each gold rally in 1988 was met by heavy producer selling. The mining boom that began in the early 1980s continued unabated. World mine production, excluding communist countries, was estimated at more than 1,300 tonnes for 1987 and was expected to top 1,500 tonnes by the mid-1990s, if not sooner. Much of the expansion was financed through gold loans. A mining company can borrow gold bullion from a bank, sell it on the open market, and pay back the gold with interest also paid in gold from the new production. This was cheaper for the borrower than a cash loan or an equity sale would have been--if the borrower could have raised cash in the first place in 1988's depressed market for new equity issues and junk bonds.

Since gold loans are private, the amount actually put on the market in 1988 is unknown. But several deals involving at least 1 million ounces were disclosed. In such a deal, the gold does not have to be sold all at once, though it may be hedged. Instead, the producer sells on rallies, or as the project needs cash. In 1988, producing nations, especially those whose debts had shut them out of the cash loan market, also were reported to be considering gold loans.

The U.S. Bureau of Mines estimated world above-ground gold stocks, excluding gold in industrial usage, at at 2.7 billion ounces at the end of 1987, of which 1.4 billion ounces were believed to be privately held as coins, bullion or jewelry.

Total gold supplies in 1987 topped 2,000 tonnes, including old scrap and toll-refined new industrial scrap. In 1987, world fabrication demand fell for the first time since 1983, according to Consolidated Goldfields, to 1,589 tonnes from 1,673 in 1986. After identifiable bar hoarding, the market was in surplus by 144 tonnes, compared with 81 tonnes in 1986. That gold was absorbed by investors.

Until the success of gold coins honoring Emperor Hirohito's 60th year on the throne in 1986, Japanese investment demand for gold was minor. But Japan was expected to import at least 150 tonnes of gold for investment purposes in 1988. Due to the falling dollar, gold prices in yen had been trending lower for several years, and the imposition of taxes on Japanese savings accounts boosted demand for hard assets.

However, the big story in the Far East was Taiwan, which imported a record 354.7 tonnes of gold, valued at $5.3 billion in 1988, including 249.6 tonnes for the central bank. Total Taiwanese imports were only 87 tonnes in 1987. About 146 tonnes of 1988's imports came from the U.S., strictly as a way to reduce Taiwan's trade surplus. But this was stopped in the summer, after U.S. complaints that gold purchases were not a substitute for importing other U.S. goods.

The Bureau of Mines projected 1988 U.S. mine output at 6.6 million ounces, up 32 percent from 5 million in 1987. The Gold Institute reported that the U.S. supplied 43 percent of its needs from new mine production in 1988, compared with only 17 percent in 1981. Further improvements toward self-sufficiency were expected.

Futures Markets

Gold futures and options on those futures are traded on the Commodity Exchange (COMEX) in New York. The Chicago Board of Trade, the Chicago International Monetary Market, and commodity exchanges in Winnipeg, Sydney, and Hong Kong also trade gold futures.

World Mine Production of Gold   In Thousands of Fine Ounces (Troy Ounces)

Year	Aus-tralia	Zaire (Congo)	Canada	China	Colom-bia	Ghana	India	Japan	Mexico	Nicara-gua	Papua N. Guinea	Philip-pines	Zim-babwe	South Africa	United States	USSR[1]	Total World[1]
1985	1,881	63	2,815	1,950	1,142	299	59	171	266	24	1,187	1,063	472	21,565	2,427	8,700	49,184
1986[2]	2,414	168	3,365	2,100	1,286	287	60	331	251	29	1,128	1,296	478	20,514	3,739	8,850	51,620
1987[1]	3,472	160	3,788	2,300	851	328	58	276	250	32	1,069	1,071	485	19,228	4,966	8,850	52,481

[1] Estimated. [2] Preliminary. *Source: U.S. Bureau of Mines*   T.258

U.S. Mine Production of Recoverable Gold   In Thousands of Troy Ounces

Year	Alaska	Arizona	Cali-fornia	Colorado	Idaho	Montana	Nevada	New Mexico	South Dakota	Utah	Other States	Total U.S.
1985	44.7	52.1	187.8	43.3	44.3	160.3	1,276.1	45.0	356.1	135.5	82.0	2,427.2
1986	48.3	[2]	425.6	120.3	70.4	[2]	2,099.0	39.9	[2]	[2]	929.8	3,739.0
1987[1]	86.5	95.2	602.6	178.8	97.8	234.4	2,679.5	[2]	[2]	[2]	991.6	4,966.4
1988[3]		150	700		70		3,500					6,500

[1] Preliminary. [2] Included in "Other States." [3] Estimate. *Source: Bureau of Mines*   T.262

SPOT GOLD   MONTHLY HIGH, LOW & CLOSE - N.Y. (HANDY & HARMAN)

Salient U.S. Gold Statistics   In Thousands of Troy Ounces

Year	Mine Produc-tion	Value Mil. $	Refinery Prod. Dom. & For-eign Ores	Secondary[2]	Exports (Excl. coinage)	Imports For Con-sumption	Treas. Dept.[5]	Futures Exch.	Ear-marked[6]	Industrial	Dental	Industrial[3]	Jewelry & Arts	Total	Price $ Per Troy Oz.[4]
1980	970	594.1			6,119	4,542	264.3	5.0	354.5	.9	341	1,287	1,505	3,215	612.56
1981	1,379	633.9			6,437	4,652	264.1	2.4	350.6	.6	314	1,210	1,730	3,276	459.64
1982	1,466	551.0	1,308	1,785	2,970	4,921	264.0	2.3	348.6	.8	358	1,102	1,994	3,463	375.91
1983	2,003	849.1	1,972	1,772	3,139	4,593	263.4	2.5	341.4	.6	360	1,032	1,706	3,101	424.00
1984	2,085	751.8	2,101	1,759	4,981	7,869	262.8	2.4	337.3	.8	363	1,084	1,709	3,164	360.66
1985	2,427	771.0	2,076	1,507	3,966	8,226	262.7	2.1	377.4	.6	380	1,027	1,585	2,999	317.66
1986[1]	3,733	1,374.7	2,431	1,522	4,613	15,749	262.0	2.8	332.7	.9	356	994	1,619	2,976	368.24
1987[1]	4,966	2,225	3,613	2,034	3,846	2,423	262.4	2.6	329.7	.7	223	1,108	1,894	3,228	447.95

[1] Preliminary. [2] Old Scrap. [3] Including space & defense. [4] Engelhard selling quotations. [5] Includes gold in Exchange Stabilization Fund. [6] Gold held for foreign & international official accounts at N.Y. Federal Reserve Bank. *Source: Bureau of Mines*   T.260

Commodity Exchange Inc. (COMEX) Depository Warehouse Stocks of Gold   In Thousands of Ounces

Year	Jan. 1	Feb. 1	Mar. 1	Apr. 1	May 1	June 1	July 1	Aug. 1	Sept. 1	Oct. 1	Nov. 1	Dec. 1
1982	2,366	2,339	2,267	2,196	2,198	2,181	2,047	1,980	1,982	1,971	1,985	2,137
1983	2,247	2,621	2,754	2,645	2,636	2,723	2,630	2,648	2,570	2,538	2,500	2,485
1984	2,481	2,472	2,408	2,452	2,412	2,426	2,376	2,395	2,387	2,391	2,349	2,366
1985	2,308	2,308	2,273	2,109	2,136	2,142	2,133	2,107	2,119	2,083	2,099	2,105
1986	2,109	2,352	2,580	2,593	2,567	1,986	1,992	1,621	1,664	1,726	1,787	2,193
1987	2,890	2,798	2,817	2,903	2,628	2,665	2,614	2,624	2,670	2,636	2,644	2,645
1988	2,624	2,605	2,586	1,596	1,566	1,675	1,834	2,099	2,189	1,949	1,629	1,267
1989	1,434											

Source: Commodity Exchange of N.Y. (COMEX)   T.263

GOLD

High, Low & Closing Prices of December Gold Futures on COMEX In Dollars per Ounce

Year of Delivery		Oct.	Nov.	Dec.	Jan.	Feb.	Mar.	Apr.	May	June	July	Aug.	Sept.	Oct.	Nov.	Dec.	Life of Delivery Range
		Year Prior to Deliv.								**Delivery Year**							
1984	High	450.0	452.0	443.5	419.7	434.0	439.5	416.5	414.0	422.0	389.8	369.0	356.3	355.8	353.5	332.6	608.0
	Low	419.5	412.1	411.0	393.0	405.0	414.0	399.5	392.0	385.5	345.0	349.0	341.6	333.5	325.0	304.7	304.7
	Close	411.1	445.1	421.4	404.9	426.9	416.4	401.1	410.4	391.6	350.3	358.0	351.3	336.0	329.1	312.1	—
1985	High	398.0	389.0	364.5	332.0	327.0	357.0	353.0	342.3	339.0	339.0	350.2	336.5	335.7	333.4	328.2	489.5
	Low	370.0	355.0	330.0	317.8	301.5	306.0	328.0	319.0	320.5	315.5	326.5	318.2	324.9	322.1	313.0	301.5
	Close	372.2	360.7	333.9	325.2	307.5	349.2	329.9	327.4	325.3	335.2	339.8	327.1	326.7	322.9	326.7	—
1986	High	363.6	358.5	352.3	392.0	375.0	375.0	361.0	358.0	362.2	371.3	404.5	446.0	446.5	443.8	400.0	446.5
	Low	350.5	347.5	336.5	348.5	347.5	344.0	341.0	347.5	342.0	349.3	364.0	392.0	400.0	376.5	383.0	336.5
	Close	352.4	348.5	351.4	369.7	356.6	345.3	357.7	353.9	354.0	369.7	393.3	429.8	405.0	390.9	389.3	—
1987	High	483.9	434.0	425.0	445.0	427.0	443.0	501.0	500.0	480.0	475.7	490.2	474.8	496.0	497.0	502.3	502.3
	Low	443.0	398.5	404.0	415.0	407.0	420.0	432.2	462.5	447.7	452.7	456.9	458.0	457.9	456.0	475.0	365.0
	Close	443.0	410.9	424.6	423.8	422.9	436.1	472.7	467.1	462.9	475.1	458.7	458.8	471.2	491.0	486.1	—
1988	High	546.0	536.0	542.0	520.5	482.0	478.0	479.0	477.1	485.0	461.0	448.6	439.7	419.0	428.9	433.5	546.0
	Low	498.8	491.5	508.0	473.5	441.3	443.0	461.5	458.0	442.5	435.5	433.0	395.5	398.1	412.6	412.0	395.5
	Close	508.8	529.1	519.6	478.5	448.8	472.0	466.5	469.9	448.1	447.3	439.9	399.2	415.1	424.8	413.9	—
1989	High	449.4	461.5	467.0													
	Low	429.5	444.8	436.5													
	Close	446.3	457.8	439.0													

Source: Commodity Exchange of N.Y. (COMEX)   T.266

Gold Total Open Interest at New York (COMEX) & Chicago IMM[1] In Thousands of Contracts

Year	Jan. 1	Feb. 1	Mar. 1	Apr. 1	May 1	June 1	July 1	Aug. 1	Sept. 1	Oct. 1	Nov. 1	Dec. 1	Jan. 1	Apr. 1	July 1	Oct. 1
				At New York (COMEX)									**At Chicago (IMM)[1]**			
1984	139.7	121.6	140.8	120.8	134.3	147.0	134.9	132.2	139.4	141.7	161.0	158.2	1.4	.6	.2	.2
1985	170.3	135.0	145.7	119.2	130.2	126.0	131.3	122.5	135.4	122.8	123.1	128.3	2.4	1.9	2.4	2.2
1986	132.8	141.3	144.4	139.9	134.3	114.0	122.4	127.0	143.8	128.9	149.5	132.2	1.3	1.6	1.2	2.4
1987	140.9	127.3	140.1	157.5	172.0	148.2	145.9	157.9	148.0	140.3	136.5	153.3	1.4	1.8	2.4	1.5
1988	150.5	153.2	159.3	147.6	155.1	141.4	150.6	139.1	140.7	158.7	160.3	144.1	1.0	1.8	1.1	.9
1989	155.4															

[1] Beginning Jan. 1, 1985 data are for "Kilo" gold at CBT. *Source: Commodity Exchange of N.Y. (COMEX), International Monetary Market of Chicago (IMM) & Chicago Board of Trade.*   T.261

Total Volume of Trading of Gold Futures at New York (COMEX) In Thousands of Contracts

Year	Jan.	Feb.	Mar.	Apr.	May	June	July	Aug.	Sept.	Oct.	Nov.	Dec.	Total
1984	749.3	786.5	829.8	563.2	833.7	737.8	1,006.9	791.3	753.2	671.3	814.9	577.7	9,122
1985	950.3	589.9	962.8	599.6	752.6	443.6	738.1	657.7	615.8	438.7	479.1	545.8	7,774
1986	1,126.2	574.2	703.9	617.9	482.2	451.6	527.6	711.1	1,054.7	846.9	724.3	579.6	8,400
1987	936.4	706.9	794.9	1,135.2	1,021.2	793.4	796.9	760.3	747.9	951.3	847.1	748.2	10,240
1988	815.0	778.7	965.0	637.7	866.2	946.3	884.2	587.5	790.9	694.5	895.5	634.9	9,496

Source: Commodity Exchange of N.Y. (COMEX)   T.265

U.S. Monetary Stock of Gold at End of Month In Billions of Dollars

Year	Jan.	Feb.	Mar.	Apr.	May	June	July	Aug.	Sept.	Oct.	Nov.	Dec.
1984	11.120	11.116	11.111	11.109	11.104	11.100	11.099	11.098	11.097	11.096	11.096	11.096
1985	11.095	11.093	11.093	11.091	11.091	11.090	11.090	11.090	11.090	11.090	11.090	11.090
1986	11.090	11.090	11.090	11.089	11.085	11.084	11.084	11.084	11.084	11.066	11.070	11.064
1987	11.062	11.085	11.081	11.076	11.070	11.069	11.069	11.068	11.075	11.085	11.082	11.078
1988	11.068	11.063	11.063	11.063	11.063	11.063	11.063	11.061	11.062			

Source: Federal Reserve Board   T.264

GOLD COMEX (WEEKLY)
Weekly high low & close of nearest futures

Monthly Average Gold Price (Handy & Harman at New York) $ Per Troy Ounce

Year	Jan.	Feb.	Mar.	Apr.	May	June	July	Aug.	Sept.	Oct.	Nov.	Dec.	Average
1980	675.4	665.5	553.6	516.8	513.9	600.7	643.3	627.5	675.8	660.3	622.5	594.8	612.51
1981	557.4	500.3	498.8	494.9	479.8	460.8	408.8	411.0	444.1	437.2	413.7	408.7	459.61
1982	384.1	374.1	330.3	350.0	334.4	315.0	340.1	366.0	435.6	421.8	414.1	445.4	375.94
1983	479.9	490.4	419.7	432.2	437.6	412.8	423.1	416.3	411.5	393.2	382.3	387.1	423.83
1984	370.9	386.0	394.4	381.7	377.3	377.7	346.4	347.7	340.9	340.1	340.9	319.0	360.23
1985	302.8	298.8	303.9	324.9	316.1	316.5	317.8	330.2	322.6	326.2	325.5	322.4	317.31
1986	345.5	339.3	345.4	340.6	340.5	342.8	348.9	376.9	419.0	423.6	398.8	391.2	367.70
1987	408.3	401.3	408.9	438.7	460.1	449.6	450.8	460.9	460.2	465.4	466.5	486.3	446.41
1988[1]	476.6	441.9	443.6	451.8	450.8	451.3	437.6	431.3	412.8	406.8	420.1	437.0	438.5

[1] Preliminary. *Source: U.S. Bureau of Mines; American Metal Market, Handy & Harman*

T.259

Grain Sorghum

World sorghum production in 1988/89 was projected by USDA at 55.6 million tonnes, the same as the year before. The U.S., the dominant producer, had a smaller crop. India was expected to produce 11 million tonnes, up 28 percent from 1987/88. Argentina, a major producer and exporter, planted less acreage, due to drought.

World exports were projected at 8.3 million tonnes, up 1 percent from 1987/88. The U.S. was projected to have an export market share of 64 percent. Australia and Argentina were also major exporters. Japan, by far the largest importer, was expected to purchase 3.8 million tonnes. Venezuela was next with projected imports of 1.4 million tonnes, followed by the USSR. World use of sorghum was expected to rise to 61.9 million tonnes, up 6 percent from a year earlier. World carryover stocks were forecast at 14 million tonnes, down 31 percent from the season before.

The U.S. crop was estimated at 578 million bushels, down 22 percent from a year earlier and the smallest since 1983's drought-damaged harvest. Harvested acreage was 9 million, down from 10.6 million in 1987/88. The national average yield of 64 bu./acre was 12 percent below the previous season's record. In Kansas, the major producing state, the crop was down 25 percent from the previous season. Other major producers were Texas and Nebraska.

U.S. beginning stocks in 1988/89 were 663 million bushels, 11 percent less than a year earlier. Total U.S. supplies were 1.24 billion bushels, 16 percent less than the previous year. Total use of sorghum, including exports, was forecast to fall 1 percent to 810 million bushels. Feed use was expected to account for 515 million bushels, 9 percent less than a year earlier. Projected exports of sorghum were 275 million bushels, up 19 percent.

Major markets for U.S. sorghum were Japan and Venezuela. The USSR was a large buyer in 1988/89. Additionally, Mexico and Israel have become important markets.

At the end of the 1988/89 season, U.S. stocks of sorghum were projected to be 430 million bushels, or 35 percent less than the previous season.

U.S. Government Program

The support loan rate in 1989 is $1.57/bu., down from $1.68 in 1988. The 1989 target price is $2.70/bu., compared with $2.78 in 1988. The 1989 acreage reduction requirement is 10 percent, compared to 20 percent a year earlier.

World Sorghum Supply and Demand   In Millions of Metric Tons

Crop Year	Exports Argentina	Exports Non-U.S.	Exports U.S.	Exports Total	Imports Japan	Imports U.S.S.R.	Imports Total	Total Production	Utilization China	Utilization Japan	Utilization Mexico	Utilization U.S.	Utilization Total	Stocks[3] Non-U.S.	Stocks[3] U.S.	Stocks[3] Total
1984–5	3.4	5.6	7.5	13.1	4.6	1.5	13.1	66.1	7.5	4.7	6.4	14.1	66.3	6.0	7.6	13.6
1985–6	2.2	4.6	4.1	8.7	5.1	.1	8.7	70.5	5.8	5.0	5.7	17.6	65.1	5.0	14.0	19.0
1986–7	1.0	2.8	5.1	8.0	4.2	.1	8.0	64.5	5.3	4.1	5.1	13.9	60.1	4.5	18.9	23.4
1987–8[1]	1.2	2.2	6.0	8.2	3.9	0	8.2	55.0	5.6	4.0	4.9	15.0	58.2	3.4	16.8	20.3
1988–9[2]	1.3	3.0	5.3	8.3	3.8	.2	8.3	55.6	5.4	3.8	4.8	14.4	61.9	2.7	11.3	14.0

[1] Preliminary.   [2] Estimate.   [3] End of crop year season.   *Source: Foreign Agricultural Service, U.S.D.A.*   T.272a

Salient Statistics of Grain Sorghum in the United States

Crop Year	Acreage Planted[2] for All Purposes 1,000 Acres	For Grain Acreage Harv. 1,000 Acres	For Grain Production 1,000 Bushels	For Grain Yield Per Harv. Acre Bushels	For Grain Price Cents Per Bushel	For Grain Produc. Value Million Dollars	For Silage Acreage Harv. 1,000 Acres	For Silage Production 1,000 Tons	For Silage Yield Per Harv. Acre Tons	U.S. Exports of Feed Grains Under Gov't. Programs Title I Sales (In Thousand Metric Tons)	Mutual Security (AID) (In Thousand Metric Tons)	Total All (In Thousand Metric Tons)
1984–5	17,254	15,355	866,241	56.4	239	2,055	609	6,472	10.6	364	793	1,618
1985–6	18,285	16,782	1,120,271	66.8	228	2,538	534	6,566	12.3	211	405	1,767
1986–7	15,336	13,859	938,124	67.7	136	1,316	500	5,898	11.8	124	445	701
1987–8[1]	11,804	10,604	740,869	69.9			424	5,157	12.2			
1988–9[1]	10,453	9,011	546,292	60.6								

[1] Preliminary.   [2] Grain and sweet sorghums for all uses including syrup.   *Source: Crop Reporting Board, U.S.D.A.*   T.267

Production of All Sorghum for Grain in the United States, by States   In Thousands of Bushels

Year	Alabama	Arizona	California	Colorado	Kansas	Missouri	Nebraska	New Mexico	North Carolina	Oklahoma	South Dakota	Texas	Arkansas
1984		1,360	3,936	15,910	216,750	91,770	121,600	15,400	3,025	18,000	18,565	209,350	42,480
1985	12,650	1,296	2,988	11,200	296,700	117,030	154,400	13,920	3,224	22,500	15,000	241,900	66,240
1986	4,000	1,044	2,210	11,700	311,250	92,340	136,170	10,350	1,400	23,030	14,030	213,750	40,920
1987	1,920	990	1,800	9,890	273,750	59,500	109,200	7,980	1,935	18,860	14,310	166,950	29,160
1988[1]	1,125	340	1,472	10,920	195,000	30,530	97,200	8,450	2,925	15,480	9,100	126,000	23,460

[1] Preliminary.   *Source: Crop Reporting Board, U.S.D.A.*   T.268

U.S. Grain Sorghum Quarterly Supply and Disappearance   In Millions of Bushels

Year & Period Beginning Sept. 1	Supply				Disappearance — Domestic Use				Ex-ports	Total	Ending Stocks		
	Begin. Stocks	Pro-duction	Im-ports	Total Supply	Food, Al-cohol & Industrial	Seed	Feed & Resid.	Total			Gov't. Owned[1]	Pri-vately Owned[2]	Total Stocks
1984–5	287.4	866.2	0.1	1,153.7	15.3	2.0	539.3	556.6	296.9	853.5	112.1	188.1	300.2
Sep.–May	287.4	866.2	0.1	1,153.7	12.4	1.5	542.2	556.7	236.8	792.9	111.1	249.7	360.8
June–Aug.	360.8	—	—	360.8	2.9	.5	-2.9	.5	60.1	60.6	112.1	188.1	300.2
1985–6	300.2	1,120.3	—	1,420.5	26.0	1.7	663.8	691.5	178.0	869.5	207.2	343.8	551.0
Sep.–May	300.2	1,120.3	—	1,420.5	22.1	1.2	626.9	650.2	140.3	790.5	181.4	447.5	630.0
June–Aug.	630.0	—	—	630.0	3.9	.5	36.9	41.3	37.7	79.0	207.2	343.8	551.0
1986–7	551.0	938.1	—	1,489.1	13.0	1.6	532.9	547.5	198.3	745.8	408.9	334.4	743.3
Sep.–May	551.0	938.1	—	1,489.1	11.0	1.0	487.3	499.3	154.8	654.1	400.4	434.6	835.0
June—Aug.	835.0	—	—	835.0	2.0	.6	45.6	48.2	43.5	91.7	408.9	334.4	743.3
1987–8[3]	743.3	740.9	—	1,484.2	12.6	1.4	576.1	590.1	231.4	821.5	463.6	199.1	662.7
Sep.–May	743.3	740.9	—	1,484.2	10.0	.8	480.2	491.0	185.4	676.4	511.4	296.4	807.8
June–Aug.	807.8	—	—	807.8	2.6	.6	95.9	99.1	46.0	145.1	463.6	199.1	662.7
1988–9[4]	662.7	546.3	—	1,209.0	——15.0——		550.0	565.0	200.0	765.0	37.5	69.0	444.0

[1] Uncommitted inventory. [2] Includes quantity under loan & farmer-owned reserve. [3] Preliminary. [4] Estimate. *Source: Economic Research Service, U.S.D.A.*
T.269

Average Price of Sorghum Grain, No. 2, Yellow at Kansas City   In Dollars Per 100 Pounds (Cwt.)

Year	Oct.	Nov.	Dec.	Jan	Feb.	Mar.	Apr.	May	June	July	Aug.	Sept.	Average
1980–1	5.65	5.91	5.82	5.79	5.52	5.46	5.49	5.38	5.23	5.29	4.58	4.16	5.48
1981–2	4.14	4.14	4.27	4.44	4.26	4.28	4.45	4.48	4.50	4.38	4.02	4.06	4.29
1982–3	3.85	4.25	4.37	4.37	4.54	5.08	5.30	5.37	5.37	5.32	5.69	5.55	4.80
1983–4	5.37	5.25	5.16	5.09	5.03	5.40	5.36	5.39	5.40	4.95	4.74	4.46	5.22
1984–5	4.25	4.28	4.32	4.48	4.33	4.58	4.76	4.74	4.74	4.50	4.06	3.56	4.46
1985–6	3.62	3.75	3.97	3.95	3.80	3.82	4.00	4.25	4.00	3.20	2.71	2.47	3.72
1986–7	2.60	2.70	2.62	2.50	2.57	2.80	2.85	3.10	3.20	2.80	2.55	2.64	2.73
1987–8[1]	2.75	2.90	2.95	3.05	3.24	3.27	3.16	3.21	4.58	4.79	4.28	4.27	3.40
1988–9	4.17	4.00											

[1] Preliminary. *Source: Economic Research Service, U.S.D.A.*
T.271

U.S. Exports of Grain Sorghum, by Country of Destination   In Thousands of Metric Tons

Yr. Beg. October	Poland	Belg. & Luxem.	Can-ada	Spain	W. Ger-many	Tai-wan	Venezu-ela	Israel	Japan	Sene-gal	Nether-lands	Nor-way	Mexico	South Africa	Total All Exports
1980–1	—	60.0			—	—	501	449.0	2,725.4	13.3	11.5	198.9	2,646.3	.3	7,701.6
1981–2	—	.4		790	.4	—	713	368.0	2,436.9	1.9	.4	201.2	544.2	—	6,289.8
1982–3	—	0		105		—	243	340.7	741.0	13.9	0	44.6	3,260.3	.2	5,402.6
1983–4	0	0		465	0	—	206	573.6	1,504.8	145.0	.2	0	2,758.4	.2	6,225.6
1984–5	0	.1	.4	45	.1	—	1,093	502.7	2,389.8	30.5	19.3	0	2,061.8	11.8	7,454.7
1985–6[1]	0	0	.1		.1	230	916	423.0	2,412.0	6.9	4.1	0	358.0	0	4,489.0
1986–7[1]							567	708	323.0	2,458.0				782.0		5,028.0

[1] Preliminary. *Source: Grain & Feed Division, U.S.D.A.*
T.270

Grain Sorghum Price Support Program & Market Prices

Year Beginning September	Price Support Operations (Million Cwt.)				Total Paym. to Part.-Mil.$	Support Loan	Target Price	No. 2 Yellow ($ Cwt.)			
	Put Under Price Support		Acquired By CCC	Owned by CCC Sept. 30		$ Per Cwt.		Kansas City	Texas High Plains	Los Angeles	Gulf Ports
	Quantity	% of Production									
1980–1	18.1	5.6	.1	21.4		3.82	4.46	5.48	5.97	7.31	6.27
1981–2	155.0	31.5	6.5	24.0		4.07	4.55	4.29	4.87	6.18	5.03
1982–3	134.5	28.8	41.0	92.4	67	4.32	4.64	4.80	5.19	6.56	5.41
1983–4	7.6	2.8	1.6	50.0	114	4.50	4.86	5.22	5.53	6.69	5.77
1984–5	36.4	7.5	36.4	67.6	158	4.32	5.14	4.46	5.04	6.08	4.90
1985–6	201.0	32.0	83.2	116.2	228	4.32	5.14	3.72	4.33	5.57	4.07
1986–7[1]	42.5	80.6	20.0	40.0	585	3.25	5.14	2.73	3.24		3.21
1987–8[2]					722	3.11	5.14	3.40	3.55		3.74
1988–9[2]						3.00	4.96				

[1] Preliminary. [2] Estimate. *Source: Economic Research Service, U.S.D.A.*
T.272

Hay

The USDA estimated that 130.2 million short tons of hay were harvested on 66.8 million acres in the U.S. in 1988. While acreage was up by 10 percent over the prior year, the crop was down 13 percent, due to the summer drought. In 1987, production was 149.14 million tons on 60.74 million harvested acres. Average yield was 1.95 tons per acre in 1988, compared with the prior year's 2.46 tons, and was the lowest since 1966.

Supplies were particularly critical in the drought-stricken North Central states. The sharpest year-to-year production declines occurred in Wisconsin, North Dakota, and Montana. Due to the drought, emergency haying and grazing of farm program set-aside acres was authorized in 43 states.

Stocks of hay on farms on May 1, 1988, the start of the 1988/89 season, were estimated at 27.3 million short tons, down 16 percent from a year earlier. The total hay supply was put at 157.5 million tons, down 13 percent from 1987/88 and the smallest since 1977/78.

Pasture and range conditions were rated at 59 percent on Nov. 1, 1988, compared with 71 percent a year earlier. Hay feeding started earlier than in 1987/88, when disappearance totaled 154.2 million tons.

Assuming 76.4 million roughage-consuming animal units, the 1988/89 per unit supply was estimated at 2.06 tons. This compares with 76.9 million roughage-consuming animal units and a per unit supply of 2.36 tons in the previous season.

Salient Statistics of All Hay in the United States

Year Beginning May	Acres Harvested 1,000 Acres	Yield Per Acre Tons	Production (Million Tons)	Carry-over May 1 (Million Tons)	Disappearance (Million Tons)	Supply Per Animal Unit (In Tons)	Disappearance Per Animal Unit (In Tons)	Animal Units Fed[2] Millions	Farm Price $ Per Ton	Farm Produc. Value Million $	Retail Price Paid by Farmers for Seed, April 15: Alfalfa (certified) (Dollars Per Cwt.)	Timothy	Red Clover	Sudan-Grass
1984–5	61,445	2.45	150.6	20.1	143.8	1.99	1.68	85.7	72.70	10,204	219.00	69.30	145.00	42.40
1985–6	60,423	2.46	148.6	26.9	148.8	2.11	1.79	83.1	67.60	9,437	219.00	58.80	121.00	43.50
1986–7	62,419	2.49	155.5	26.7	149.8	2.31	1.90	79.0	60.10	8,611	219.00	78.10	133.00	44.70
1987–8[1]	60,748	2.46	149.1	32.4	154.2	2.36	2.01	76.9	65.40	9,015	222.00	107.00	160.00	44.20
1988–9[1]	66,783	1.95	130.2	27.3		2.06		76.4			245.00	132.00	143.00	42.00

[1] Preliminary. [2] Roughage-consuming animal units fed annually. *Source: Economic Research Service, U.S.D.A.* T.275

Production of All Hay in the United States by Important States In Millions of Tons

Year	Calif.	Idaho	Ill.	Iowa	Mich.	Minn.	Mo.	No. Dak.	Nebr.	N.Y.	Ohio	Pa.	So. Dak.	Wis.	Texas
1983	7.4	4.9	2.7	5.9	4.5	8.3	5.4	4.5	7.6	5.3	3.2	4.6	7.6	12.2	7.5
1984	7.9	4.7	3.9	7.9	5.3	8.4	6.3	4.5	7.7	5.4	3.8	5.1	8.1	12.8	5.4
1985	8.0	4.1	4.1	7.1	5.7	8.0	6.5	3.8	6.8	5.3	4.6	5.3	4.8	11.1	8.2
1986	8.6	4.7	3.7	8.0	5.7	9.7	6.0	5.4	7.4	5.4	4.3	5.1	9.3	10.8	7.5
1987	9.0	4.5	3.2	6.9	4.4	7.8	6.2	4.8	6.5	5.3	4.4	5.2	7.1	8.9	7.9
1988[1]	8.8	3.9	2.9	7.3	4.4	7.7	4.7	1.8	6.6	4.8	3.8	5.0	5.8	5.0	5.5

[1] Preliminary. *Source: Crop Reporting Board, U.S.D.A.* T.277

U.S. Types of Hay Production & Farm Stocks In Millions of Short Tons

Crop Year	Production: Alfalfa & Mixtures	All Other	All Hay	Corn for Silage[1]	Sorghum[1] Silage	Farm Stocks: May 1	Dec. 1[3]
1983	82.2	58.6	140.8	96.3	6.6	28.1	104.0
1984	90.1	60.5	150.6	104.6	6.5	20.1	89.3
1985	85.0	63.6	148.6	102.8	6.6	26.9	100.6
1986	91.6	64.0	155.5	88.7	5.9	26.7	121.7
1987	84.6	64.6	149.1	85.6	5.2	32.4	119.7
1988[2]	69.6	60.6	130.2			27.3	

[1] Not included in all tame hay. [2] Preliminary. [3] Data prior to Dec. 1, 1986 are for Jan. 1. *Source: Crop Reporting Board, U.S.D.A.* T.276

Average Price Received by Farmers for All Hay (Baled) In Dollars Per Ton

Year	May	June	July	Aug.	Sept.	Oct.	Nov.	Dec.	Jan.	Feb.	Mar.	Apr.	Average[1]
1983–4	78.10	72.70	71.20	71.20	74.70	76.80	75.10	76.70	76.60	78.70	79.40	79.80	75.80
1984–5	82.50	76.10	72.40	70.40	70.70	73.10	71.40	73.40	73.00	73.10	72.20	72.50	72.70
1985–6	80.80	70.20	67.90	65.20	67.10	67.50	64.30	65.40	65.80	66.70	67.10	66.20	67.60
1986–7	70.30	61.50	58.40	58.10	57.80	56.90	56.00	56.80	56.10	58.50	59.20	64.10	60.10
1987–8[2]	73.40	63.20	61.80	61.80	65.50	64.70	62.10	65.00	62.80	65.50	66.20	72.90	65.40
1988–9[2]	80.90	76.80	83.10	83.10	85.50	86.80	87.50						

[1] Weighted average by sales. [2] Preliminary. *Source: Crop Reporting Board, U.S.D.A.* T.278

Heating Oil

From the end of the 1982 recession through 1987, distillate fuel oil demand grew at an average annual rate of 2.3 percent, the second fastest rate of growth of any petroleum product during that period. The two primary uses for distillate are heating oil and diesel fuel, of which heating oil is the more variable. In 1988, a very cold winter increased demand sharply, increasing total distillate usage by nearly 4 percent to an estimated 3.09 million barrels per day (bpd).

For 1989, the Department of Energy (DOE) was expecting distillate demand to grow by 3.2 percent, reflecting a return to a more typical winter weather pattern, continued strong demand in the rail and truck transportation sectors, and an increase in industrial fuel usage. Compared with the same period in 1987, diesel fuel demand grew an estimated 6.9 percent in the first seven months of 1988. For the 1988-89 heating season (October through March), heating oil demand was forecast at 3.4 million barrels per day, about 2 percent above the previous season's rate. Some of the expected gains came from an increase in homes heated by oil, the first in recent memory. The increases came largely in areas where there are no natural gas utilities, although, on a cost per BTU basis, oil was competitive in both 1987 and 1988.

Heating oil prices did not react to the decline in crude oil prices until the third quarter of 1988, and even then the declines were largely absorbed at the wholesale level. The average residential retail price for all of calendar year 1988 was 79 cents a gallon. Assuming an average number of heating degree days, DOE projected an average residential heating oil price of 75 cents for the fourth quarter of 1988 and 79 cents for the first quarter of 1989.

The primary distillate inventory at the start of the 1988-89 heating season was 133 million barrels, up slightly from 127 million a year earlier. DOE projected an ending inventory for March 31 of 97 million, compared with 89 million at the same date a year earlier.

U.S. refinery production of distillate was estimated at 2.89 million bpd for 1988 and was expected to rise to 2.96 million in 1989. Distillate accounts for about 22 percent of a refinery's yield. U.S. imports of crude oil averaged 280,000 bpd in 1988 and were expected to rise to about 300,000 bpd in 1989. Imports have become an increasingly important factor in the U.S. market, since it now takes about 10 days to move excess supplies from Europe to the U.S. East Coast. The availability of European oil helped keep a lid on prices during the 1987-88 heating season, preventing a repeat of the price bubble caused by a cold snap in 1984.

West Germany, Europe's largest user of distillate, imposed a distillate excise tax on January 1, 1989. Anticipatory purchases ahead of this date may have tightened overall supplies in Europe, but there was no apparent impact on spot market prices in either New York or Rotterdam ahead of the heating season. West Germany has large storage capacity, and inventory hoarding may have been completed at lower prices during the summer of 1988.

Futures Markets

Heating oil futures and options on those futures are traded on the New York Mercantile Exchange (NYMEX). In London, where the product is called gas oil, futures and options on those futures are traded on the International Petroleum Exchange.

High, Low & Closing Prices of January Heating Oil Futures (No. 2) in N.Y. In Cents per Gallon

Year of Delivery	Jan.	Feb.	Mar.	Apr.	May	Year Prior to Delivery[1] June	July	Aug.	Sept.	Oct.	Nov.	Dec.[1]	Life of Delivery Range
1983 High	—	—	85.00	95.75	100.40	98.75	93.60	96.65	101.95	104.20	99.20	90.60	104.20
Low	—	—	82.00	85.50	94.00	90.61	89.25	90.70	95.55	97.10	84.20	79.81	79.81
Close	—	—	85.00	94.40	97.00	91.08	90.80	96.30	99.79	98.29	86.52	82.81	—
1984 High	—	—	75.25	84.25	83.75	87.00	88.90	90.15	87.55	84.15	84.10	85.55	90.15
Low	—	—	68.70	78.50	79.25	81.80	85.25	86.30	82.00	80.20	77.10	75.80	68.70
Close	—	—	74.60	82.49	81.80	86.20	88.90	86.52	82.50	82.16	77.44	84.24	—
1985 High	—	—	83.75	84.40	87.45	87.40	83.25	84.05	86.10	85.45	81.05	79.25	87.45
Low	—	—	83.15	82.30	82.20	81.75	76.05	76.90	80.80	75.75	74.75	72.25	72.25
Close	—	—	83.75	83.00	86.87	83.00	76.30	82.55	84.80	79.98	76.61	72.40	—
1986 High	—	—	76.90	79.10	76.50	75.50	74.85	79.35	83.50	88.25	90.75	87.45	90.75
Low	—	—	76.70	75.50	74.10	70.00	70.35	73.15	76.55	80.30	85.15	74.80	70.00
Close	—	—	76.10	76.00	76.25	71.40	73.55	79.35	82.49	87.52	87.07	86.55	—
1987 High	57.60	54.00	46.15	44.65	47.10	44.45	40.70	47.80	49.00	46.25	46.75	49.20	57.60
Low	56.50	44.50	37.60	36.20	41.60	40.20	33.85	36.40	33.53	38.95	41.90	42.35	33.53
Close	56.50	44.50	37.60	41.33	41.60	41.33	36.20	47.36	44.57	43.08	42.89	48.90	—
1988 High	—	50.15	52.60	53.24	55.05	57.50	60.25	60.20	55.95	58.70	56.90	57.30	60.25
Low	—	49.02	48.75	50.85	52.70	54.35	56.50	50.75	52.00	55.10	52.80	46.60	46.60
Close	—	49.02	52.32	52.70	54.60	57.30	58.30	54.36	55.49	57.19	54.87	51.44	—
1989 High	—	47.00	48.60	51.89	50.73	50.85	48.65	47.90	45.64	45.35	48.60	53.90	53.90
Low	—	45.27	44.21	47.42	48.68	44.48	43.60	44.90	39.85	38.25	41.50	47.75	38.25
Close	—	45.65	48.02	50.59	50.41	44.48	47.28	45.10	40.02	42.48	48.24	53.48	—

[1] Contract expires the last business day of the previous calendar month quoted. *Source: N.Y. Mercantile Exchange*   T.281

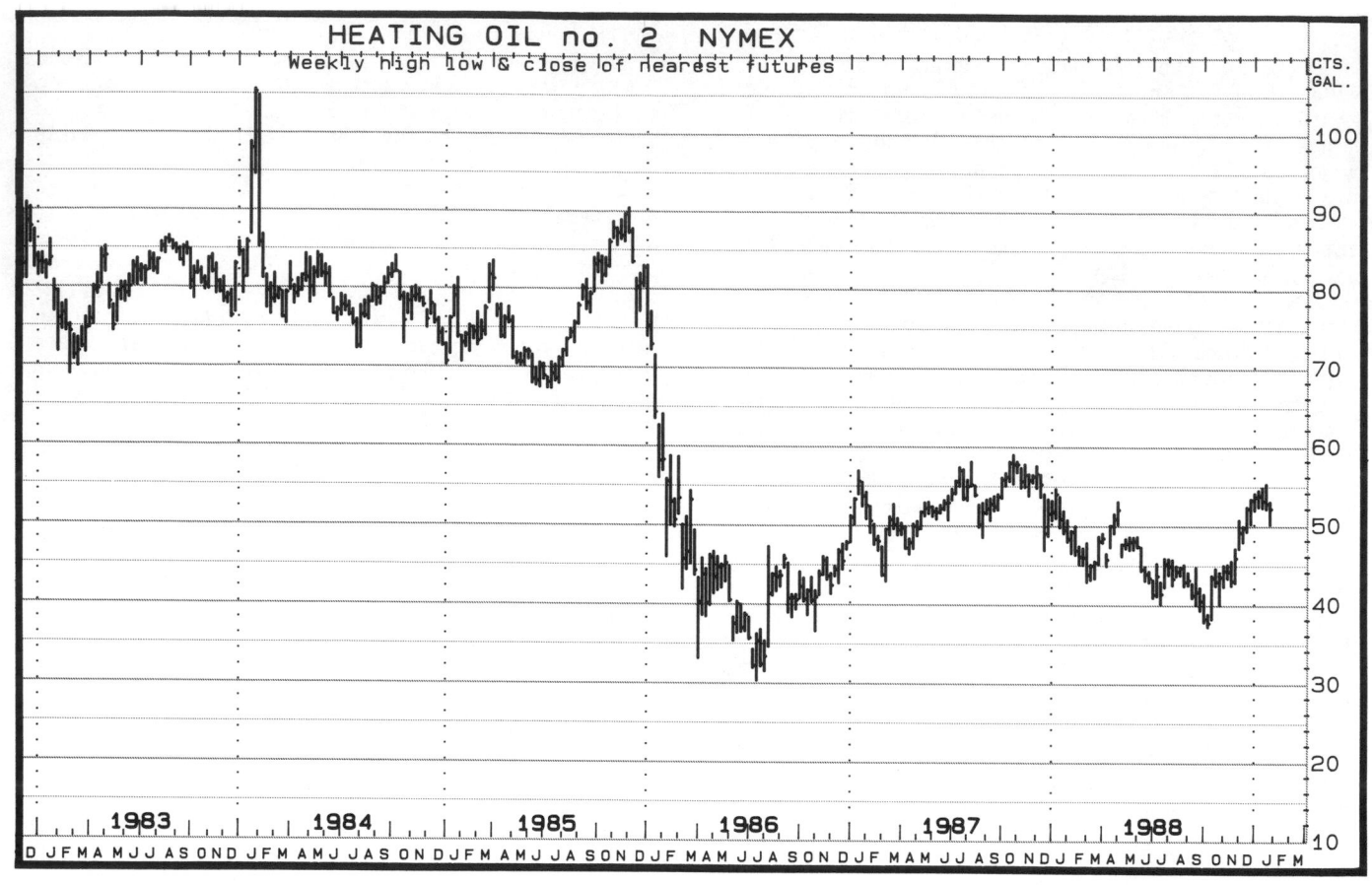

HEATING OIL no. 2 NYMEX
Weekly high low & close of nearest futures

Month-End Open Interest of Heating Oil Futures (No. 2) in New York   In Contracts

Year	Jan.	Feb.	Mar.	Apr.	May	June	July	Aug.	Sept.	Oct.	Nov.	Dec.
1980	2,186	2,590	2,032	2,324	2,622	2,948	3,286	5,889	8,365	11,884	13,519	11,556
1981	11,792	12,040	13,256	14,893	17,919	16,822	19,220	28,102	36,996	35,519	33,517	31,585
1982	22,042	15,655	21,121	18,502	19,248	21,277	21,676	20,815	22,500	29,614	24,486	21,848
1983	19,642	23,307	18,980	22,868	27,797	29,320	34,414	32,276	37,856	36,164	36,230	30,916
1984	32,596	18,900	17,738	16,617	18,343	18,109	19,813	20,290	28,995	27,200	26,798	25,371
1985	19,122	16,552	17,351	15,796	17,660	19,698	22,993	25,731	30,127	33,438	36,793	31,172
1986	29,066	31,685	33,377	33,760	40,977	55,945	67,625	64,450	74,104	82,224	70,196	72,564
1987	64,374	53,307	46,624	42,902	41,538	49,470	49,208	64,636	65,904	70,432	73,856	63,427
1988	55,136	48,366	44,201	46,143	52,477	74,926	72,297	84,564	88,956	96,150	82,868	74,797

Source: N.Y. Mercantile Exchange

T.279

Volume of Trading of Heating Oil Futures[1] in New York   In Contracts

Year	Jan.	Feb.	Mar.	Apr.	May	June	July	Aug.	Sept.	Oct.	Nov.	Dec.	Total
1980	8,512	8,427	5,146	4,798	3,421	5,923	6,074	11,564	27,430	40,525	53,098	63,366	238,284
1981	67,368	58,514	55,299	65,350	58,933	76,580	86,394	100,102	99,790	121,455	78,972	126,749	995,532
1982	165,079	148,794	176,373	146,821	98,440	135,181	107,102	118,496	120,830	167,439	177,832	183,139	1,745,526
1983	153,864	112,649	137,237	121,300	163,923	149,138	138,706	140,671	187,283	169,271	200,400	193,877	1,868,322
1984	254,788	209,802	144,326	144,041	161,689	144,182	120,668	153,913	137,011	281,183	182,005	163,938	2,091,546
1985	286,264	149,403	162,503	137,064	122,699	133,339	148,117	157,552	202,785	246,558	219,126	242,323	2,207,733
1986	274,057	221,156	214,501	207,748	223,943	247,552	309,662	282,636	285,246	387,054	271,497	349,992	3,275,044
1987	399,813	328,327	348,204	282,109	238,048	273,708	329,078	343,355	347,152	437,157	422,982	543,462	4,293,395
1988	506,182	377,379	403,181	267,233	286,365	380,550	431,231	363,276	441,939	578,648	475,675	423,356	4,935,015

[1] No. 2 heating oil.   *Source: N.Y. Mercantile Exchange*

T.280

U.S. Gross Input to Crude Oil Distillation Units   In Millions of 42-Gallon Barrels

Year	Jan.	Feb.	Mar.	Apr.	May	June	July	Aug.	Sept.	Oct.	Nov.	Dec.	Total
1974	373.2	326.5	368.7	371.6	400.4	398.8	414.1	409.1	380.0	398.3	386.0	404.9	4,632
1975	395.8	353.9	384.3	368.3	384.7	385.6	414.9	416.9	401.5	397.3	394.6	411.4	4,709
1976	403.6	388.1	412.2	396.4	413.4	457.9	446.1	446.3	425.3	428.0	437.3	457.0	5,081
1977	453.4	425.5	456.2	438.3	463.1	457.9	471.1	465.9	457.8	466.3	449.2	463.5	5,468
1978	450.1	401.4	448.3	426.6	472.4	451.5	470.5	483.8	462.2	475.9	470.6	487.6	5,501
1979	467.7	409.3	449.6	445.2	457.1	453.6	477.9	474.0	447.1	457.9	447.0	472.4	5,459
1980	453.6	421.7	433.8	413.5	423.4	421.7	422.5	412.3	408.2	402.9	403.4	432.4	5,049
1981	418.3	369.6	391.4	368.5	389.3	381.9	389.6	409.2	382.2	382.9	377.5	393.8	4,654
1982	371.5	325.1	361.4	353.1	379.1	388.1	399.6	378.0	376.7	376.8	364.4	368.8	4,443
1983	355.4	307.8	344.8	352.0	374.4	378.3	390.9	383.1	381.9	371.1	366.8	354.1	4,361
1984	364.8	356.0	374.2	362.3	385.5	372.5	377.5	388.6	374.2	376.7	367.7	371.0	4,471
1985	359.1	321.6	356.0	359.1	380.3	372.7	392.6	378.9	362.9	383.3	378.9	395.1	4,440
1986	390.1	337.9	364.5	378.1	412.7	400.4	403.3	415.2	395.7	395.3	387.8	400.3	4,681
1987[1]	392.8	346.6	378.1	377.9	397.3	399.2	422.0	419.3	399.8	399.8	392.2	414.9	4,746
1988[1]	408.3	374.3	410.5	399.9	422.5	411.1	427.9	432.2					

[1] Preliminary.   *Source: Bureau of Mines*   T.282

Average Price of Distillate (Middle) No. 2 Fuel Oil[1]   Index (1982^3 = 100)

Year	Jan.	Feb.	Mar.	Apr.	May	June	July	Aug.	Sept.	Oct.	Nov.	Dec.	Average
1974	194.8	234.1	251.8	257.9	269.2	279.7	288.9	294.8	298.8	297.9	296.0	300.1	272.0
1975	299.1	297.5	294.6	294.9	296.1	301.3	308.3	312.9	318.2	322.9	330.8	336.3	309.4
1976	336.7	339.3	335.3	331.8	328.5	329.2	332.2	336.2	338.9	341.2	344.3	349.8	337.0
1977	359.2	369.6	378.0	384.4	387.5	387.5	388.6	389.1	389.3	389.6	392.4	394.4	384.1
1978	396.7	398.6	394.8	393.3	393.3	393.3	393.2	393.6	394.0	400.0	407.6	418.0	398.0
1979	425.7	432.6	451.9	477.9	504.8	542.3	593.1	632.8	680.6	709.9	715.3	719.9	573.9
1980	739.3	793.5	837.7	858.9	964.8	860.9	870.2	875.6	873.2	868.4	873.4	891.1	850.6
1981	935.4	1,000.3	1,082.8	1,105.4	1,092.5	1,092.2	1,079.8	1,076.7	1,067.8	1,056.1	1,047.5	1,060.6	1,058.1
1982	1,067.8	1,058.2	1,029.3	953.6	928.7	974.6	1,024.0	1,022.2	998.8	999.2	1,041.5	1,054.5	1,012.7
1983	985.3	927.4	874.2	813.4	838.1	879.4	876.3	883.0	894.3	912.2	901.8	892.1	889.8
1984	871.4	924.4	952.1	874.9	881.9	895.2	893.4	859.6	837.8	854.4	868.9	851.4	880.5
1985	835.7	810.3	809.9	820.3	851.0	797.7	754.9	743.6	800.5	841.3	887.5	905.5	821.5
1986	830.2	631.6	519.1	504.3	476.4	452.9	369.0	406.5	469.0	436.0	440.7	461.8	499.8
1987[3]	51.4	53.1	49.7	52.2	53.3	55.1	56.3	59.4	56.8	59.3	61.2	58.1	55.5
1988[2]	54.8	51.5	49.7	53.3	54.3	50.6	46.9	46.8	45.9	42.3			

[1] Barge lots, f.o.b. refinery or terminal, excluding all fees & taxes.   [2] Preliminary.   [3] Data prior to 1987 are for 1967 = 100 index.   T.283
Source: Bureau of Labor Statistics (0573)

Average Wholesale Price of Kerosene (Light Distillate)—No. 1 Fuel   Index (1982^2 = 100)

Year	Jan.	Feb.	Mar.	Apr.	May	June	July	Aug.	Sept.	Oct.	Nov.	Dec.	Average
1974	154.3	184.8	198.7	209.4	217.6	233.2	241.7	250.2	256.8	254.7	261.4	257.9	226.7
1975	253.7	267.2	274.9	273.6	280.6	284.6	283.7	299.1	297.9	299.4	304.2	307.8	285.6
1976	310.5	316.6	313.9	311.2	306.7	303.8	305.4	309.2	311.5	316.0	320.2	323.2	312.3
1977	326.1	339.7	346.9	352.4	355.5	358.0	360.9	363.2	364.0	375.1	379.4	381.3	358.5
1978	383.0	388.2	388.4	387.9	390.7	391.4	393.1	394.4	395.8	397.6	398.4	403.0	392.7
1979	407.5	412.7	419.1	433.0	465.5	504.1	533.4	588.4	633.4	675.2	696.6	706.3	539.6
1980	733.9	776.9	834.6	862.5	870.5	878.4	892.7	903.1	903.2	896.3	896.8	911.4	863.4
1981	932.1	972.0	1,041.0	1,080.9	1,084.1	1,078.9	1,067.5	1,052.6	1,044.6	1,043.2	1,042.7	1,037.9	1,039.8
1982	1,044.3	1,034.3	1,027.9	1,009.1	975.9	974.7	984.4	983.0	976.3	969.7	985.9	992.1	996.4
1983	975.2	959.4	939.2	908.4	897.1	894.3	882.8	880.7	880.4	889.3	885.5	881.4	906.1
1984	872.2	885.8	903.5	879.2	876.8	876.5	874.3	863.0	853.2	854.4	857.1	847.5	870.3
1985	840.8	833.3	827.5	824.5	826.9	803.1	779.8	780.3	780.6	795.2	806.3	812.7	809.3
1986	795.6	750.2	684.6	584.8	523.8	504.4	452.7	413.3	426.8	423.9	419.4	429.1	534.0
1987[2]	45.4	49.0	48.8	50.4	51.4	53.2	55.3	57.9	58.1	60.0	60.8	58.3	54.1
1988[1]	55.2	55.1	53.7	52.4	53.7	53.0	51.1	50.0	49.1	46.9			

[1] Preliminary.   [2] Data prior to 1987 are for 1967 = 100 index.   *Source: Bureau of Labor Statistics (0572)*   T.284

HEATING OIL

Stocks of Distillate Fuel in the U.S., First of the Month   In Millions of Barrels

Year	Jan.	Feb.	Mar.	Apr.	May	June	July	Aug.	Sept.	Oct.	Nov.	Dec.	Residual Fuel Oil Stocks — Jan. 1	July 1
1978	250.3	213.3	165.7	137.9	136.2	144.6	157.3	180.5	200.2	220.7	233.1	233.2	90.0	72.0
1979	216.5	175.8	127.3	112.8	115.1	123.1	141.4	171.2	195.4	220.4	231.1	236.7	90.2	79.8
1980	228.7	212.4	191.7	177.9	177.2	183.4	196.6	213.8	226.3	232.4	225.7	222.4	95.6	87.8
1981	205.4	179.4	172.6	164.4	164.6	171.8	179.9	186.3	200.2	207.3	201.2	200.1	91.5	69.4
1982	191.5	164.4	147.4	126.3	108.0	113.6	123.7	148.2	158.7	161.2	170.1	185.6	78.0	60.7
1983	178.6	167.6	148.2	118.1	103.1	108.9	113.7	130.7	142.4	154.0	162.6	161.2	66.2	49.9
1984	140.3	119.3	132.2	109.6	97.7	98.1	112.8	124.4	133.3	142.9	152.2	161.0	48.5	46.9
1985	161.1	142.4	121.4	99.3	96.8	104.4	109.7	115.7	113.8	117.4	123.4	139.7	53.0	39.6
1986	143.7	136.5	112.4	98.8	95.9	98.9	107.9	118.9	137.7	152.4	151.6	158.3	50.4	42.8
1987[1]	155.1	141.4	123.5	110.0	100.4	101.8	104.4	114.6	124.7	126.8	121.0	128.0	47.4	41.3
1988[1]	134.5	127.2	109.6	89.3	94.3	104.5	110.7	119.4	125.2				47.4	42.1

[1] Preliminary. *Source: Bureau of Mines*   T.285

U.S. Production of Distillate Fuel Oil   In Millions of Barrels

Year	Jan.	Feb.	Mar.	Apr.	May	June	July	Aug.	Sept.	Oct.	Nov.	Dec.	Total
1978	95.1	82.7	93.5	88.8	100.8	93.3	96.8	102.2	95.6	102.3	101.0	104.2	1,156.1
1979	94.3	80.9	93.6	88.4	95.0	94.6	102.5	103.0	100.6	100.8	97.2	99.9	1,150.8
1980	93.4	80.2	79.3	73.8	76.7	79.4	83.4	76.3	80.6	80.3	81.1	89.6	974.1
1981	92.6	78.6	77.0	72.5	76.1	75.0	74.2	82.3	78.3	77.0	81.5	88.6	953.8
1982	80.3	67.9	70.9	70.7	81.2	81.9	84.8	77.7	79.7	88.0	85.8	82.3	951.3
1983	72.0	59.8	61.8	65.1	75.8	76.4	80.7	81.1	82.2	83.1	80.4	78.2	896.5
1984	80.3	83.1	76.8	70.3	81.3	86.4	84.3	82.5	81.2	83.4	84.8	86.7	981.2
1985	81.6	70.1	70.3	74.7	83.3	79.4	82.0	80.4	77.8	90.0	93.1	98.4	980.9
1986	89.9	71.8	81.9	83.6	88.6	81.9	84.0	90.6	86.0	84.2	87.5	91.2	1,021.2
1987[1]	86.0	72.1	73.9	76.6	79.5	80.7	83.7	83.9	82.4	86.2	91.1	100.5	996.6
1988[1]	93.2	77.8	84.3	86.1	90.9	86.8	86.3	88.2					

[1] Preliminary. *Source: Dept. of Energy*   T.286

U.S. Imports of Distillate Fuel Oil   In Millions of Barrels

Year	Jan.	Feb.	Mar.	Apr.	May	June	July	Aug.	Sept.	Oct.	Nov.	Dec.	Total
1978	6.1	5.9	6.0	3.0	3.9	4.4	4.6	4.4	4.9	5.5	6.7	7.9	63.3
1979	7.0	5.5	5.5	4.5	5.8	5.4	7.0	6.7	3.8	6.6	5.8	7.1	70.5
1980	5.5	6.9	6.0	4.6	3.9	3.2	3.6	2.4	3.0	3.6	4.0	5.2	51.9
1981	8.5	9.1	4.6	3.5	5.5	6.7	5.5	5.4	3.9	3.7	3.7	2.9	63.1
1982	3.0	3.7	1.5	1.8	2.3	3.1	3.9	2.5	1.8	2.8	4.4	3.4	34.0
1983	2.1	1.6	1.3	2.2	4.5	5.4	8.3	9.3	7.8	8.1	6.1	6.8	63.5
1984	9.3	13.2	3.6	6.6	7.8	7.7	6.2	8.0	8.7	13.0	9.5	5.9	99.4
1985	8.4	4.0	4.8	7.6	6.1	4.6	3.0	2.5	6.7	8.1	8.4	8.9	73.1
1986	10.1	4.7	6.7	4.4	4.6	5.1	9.7	11.5	7.8	7.5	7.6	10.5	90.3
1987[1]	6.1	6.4	7.8	5.5	6.2	7.4	11.7	6.6	6.6	7.3	5.6	11.7	93.2
1988[1]	11.0	9.6	7.5	6.3	7.1	6.3	6.4	8.4					

[1] Preliminary. *Source: Dept. of Energy*   T.287

U.S. Domestic Consumption of Distillate Fuel Oil   In Millions of Barrels

Year	Jan.	Feb.	Mar.	Apr.	May	June	July	Aug.	Sept.	Oct.	Nov.	Dec.	Total
1978	138.2	135.8	127.3	93.3	96.2	85.1	78.2	86.8	79.9	95.4	107.5	128.8	1,252.6
1979	142.0	134.7	113.6	90.5	92.9	81.2	79.4	85.6	79.4	96.7	97.4	114.9	1,208.5
1980	115.1	107.6	98.5	79.0	74.5	69.5	69.7	66.2	77.6	90.5	88.5	112.1	1,049.0
1981	127.4	94.5	90.0	76.0	74.7	73.9	73.7	74.0	75.4	86.9	86.4	99.6	1,032.5
1982	108.0	86.4	91.3	89.3	75.8	73.5	63.8	68.8	75.2	80.0	74.2	88.5	974.9
1983	86.7	77.8	91.4	80.9	73.0	75.7	70.4	77.3	77.3	80.9	86.2	104.3	981.9
1984	109.3	82.2	101.0	87.8	87.2	77.8	77.6	79.3	79.6	85.7	84.8	88.8	1,041.2
1985	107.4	93.2	95.9	83.9	80.8	77.8	75.5	81.7	77.3	89.9	82.4	100.9	1,046.8
1986	103.2	95.7	98.2	87.1	85.6	76.3	80.4	81.2	76.2	90.3	86.3	103.2	1,063.7
1987[1]	101.0	93.7	93.1	90.1	82.8	83.7	84.1	79.2	85.1	97.7	88.0	102.9	1,086.4
1988[1]	109.0	101.8	109.9	86.1	85.5	84.6	82.1	88.6					

[1] Preliminary. *Source: Dept. of Energy*   T.288

Hides and Leather

World hide production in 1988 was forecast to match the year-earlier level of 4.6 million tons. However, output was likely to decline in 1989, as cattle slaughter was expected to fall. Production of hides is dependent on the demand for meat. The U.S. continued to be the leading producer of hides in 1988, but the USSR was close behind and was expected to be the largest in 1989. The European Community was third.

The quantity of cattle hides from commercial slaughter in the U.S. was estimated at 34.9 million hogs in 1988, 2 percent less than a year earlier. This reflected the decline in cattle slaughter. Reduced demand for red meat has discouraged a build-up in cattle herds. As long as cattle slaughter remained low, supplies of leather products were expected to remain tight and prices firm.

About 58 percent of domestically produced cattle hide leather was consumed by the footwear industry. Production of sole leather in 1988 increased by about 4 percent, after a 10 percent decline in 1987. Output of shoe upper leather declined sharply, but demand for heavier leather for moccasins, boat shoes, and boots was strong. Automotive upholstery leather and furniture upholstery leather shipments both increased from 1987 levels.

U.S. exports of hides and skins were expected to fall to 600 million tons in 1988. This was attributed to the decline in cattle slaughter. The largest importers of U.S. cattle hides through the first half of 1988 were South Korea, which took 46 percent, Japan with 26 percent, and Taiwan with 11 percent. Although exports were expected to decline in quantity, their value was expected to be higher than in 1987, due to higher prices.

U.S. imports of leather in 1988 increased about 55 percent in value. Upholstery leather imports almost doubled in quantity to about 75 million square feet. Imports of cattle hide leather for uses other than upholstery increased 56 percent to 201 million feet. The largest overall supplier of leather to the U.S. was Argentina, accounting for 30 percent of U.S. imports by value. Italy and the United Kingdom were the largest EC suppliers, and had 10 percent each of the U.S. import market.

Cattle hide prices in 1988 reached record highs for the second consecutive year. The Department of Commerce cattle hide price index in 1988 was 205.9, compared with 179.7 in 1987 (using 1982 as a base year). Prices were expected to be higher in 1989, because of low slaughter levels and increased demand for leather for footwear and other uses.

World Production of Bovine Hides and Skins — In Thousands of Units of Metric Tons

Year	Argentina	Australia	Brazil	Canada	Colombia	France	Germany East	Germany West	Mexico	Italy	Poland	South Africa	Turkey	New Zealand	United Kingdom	United States	USSR
1981	333	142	291	96		EC-10 (683)						52		44		987	890
1982	293	155	308	98	92	179	44	149	138	96	75	53	56	46	106	1,019	867
1983	286	160	322	99	84	200	45	149	140	99	70	61	59	44	109	1,040	892
1984	297	129	310	94	87	190	45	164	145	101	73	60	60	37	113	1,066	917
1985	319	124	340	95	92	190	48	159	139	101	71		61	41	110	1,028	942
1986	332	131	324	94	92	186	48	161	120	95	85		62	36	104	1,164	1,022
1987[1]	308	143	355	88	91	193	50	162	122	93	76		62	54	105	1,113	1,060
1988[2]	297	132	370	86	90	184	50	151	144	91	73		63	45	98	1,083	1,075

[1] Preliminary   [2] Forecast.   *Source: Foreign Agricultural Service, U.S.D.A.*   T.289

Salient Statistics of Hides & Leather in the United States

Year	New Supply of Cattle Hides — Domestic Slaughter — Federally Inspected	Uninspected[4]	Total Production	Net Exports	Total New Supply	Wholesale Prices-¢ lb. Heavy Native Cows[2]	Heavy Native[3] Steers	Production All U.S. Tanning	Cattle-Hide	Upper & Lining Leather Exports Ths. Sq. Ft.	Wholesale Leather Indexes Upper Men — 1982 = 100 —	Women	Footwear Production[5] Mil. Pairs	Export
			Thousands of Equivalent Hides					In Ths. Equiv. Hides						
1981	32,819	2,134	34,953	18,701	16,252	46.1	44.2	19,184	15,520	192,193			372.0	9.7
1982	33,907	1,936	35,843	22,553	13,290	45.1	42.3	18,229	15,028	159,804			359.1	7.7
1983	34,816	1,833	36,649	21,205	15,444	53.5	50.2	18,610	15,430	155,808			339.2	6.2
1984	35,880	1,702	37,582	25,194	12,388	67.0	61.0	16,940	14,021	163,373			303.2	6.2
1985	34,765	1,528	36,293	24,398	11,895	57.55	54.69	15,230	12,550	131,505			265.1	9.2
1986[1]	35,913	1,375	37,288	26,522	10,766	68.06	64.09	14,460	12,497	160,888	107.2	104.3	240.9	10.3
1987[1]	34,468	1,179	35,647	24,007	11,640			14,800	12,846	194,152	111.4	107.2	225.9	14.7

[1] Preliminary.   [2] Heifers.   [3] Central U.S.   [4] Includes farm slaughter; diseased & condemned animals & hides taken off fallen animals.
[5] Other than rubber.   *Sources: Leather Industries of America; Bureau of Labor Statistics; Dept. of Commerce*   T.290

HIDES AND LEATHER

U.S. Exports of Upper & Lining Leather In Thousands of Square Feet

Year	Jan.	Feb.	Mar.	Apr.	May	June	July	Aug.	Sept.	Oct.	Nov.	Dec.	Total
1979	13,854	16,014	18,833	16,480	15,664	18,526	13,153	15,265	14,457	13,895	16,089	15,433	187,665
1980	15,769	16,873	18,710	13,024	12,652	15,483	15,481	15,215	15,818	19,051	20,880	13,641	192,597
1981	19,633	14,418	19,717	17,678	18,016	18,692	13,921	10,918	15,393	12,682	19,464	11,660	192,193
1982	10,849	10,343	13,696	15,534	17,449	18,610	18,486	12,065	10,417	11,842	9,726	10,786	159,804
1983	11,052	12,453	15,078	15,200	13,492	14,868	12,013	13,099	12,715	14,027	12,400	9,412	155,808
1984	13,624	13,015	17,787	14,772	19,514	14,294	12,907	14,046	11,219	11,533	10,231	10,431	163,373
1985	10,266	8,855	11,049	11,637	12,112	16,233	9,919	10,763	8,085	12,310	12,452	7,824	131,505
1986	12,032	10,849	13,050	13,652	14,560	13,945	11,902	16,769	11,502	13,043	14,003	15,581	160,888
1987[1]	12,172	15,625	19,865	18,874	18,818	19,585	15,455	15,015	14,806	13,557	15,703	14,677	194,152
1988[1]	16,033	18,431	18,430	14,647	19,273	17,623	15,023	13,967	21,022				

[1] Preliminary. *Source: Leather Industries of America* T.292

U.S. Production of All Footwear (Shoes, Sandals, Slippers, Athletic, Etc.) In Millions of Pairs

Year	Jan.	Feb.	Mar.	Apr.	May	June	July	Aug.	Sept.	Oct.	Nov.	Dec.	Total
1979	37.3	34.9	38.7	33.4	37.3	31.9	25.4	33.9	31.1	35.0	31.3	28.7	398.9
1980	34.9	33.2	33.9	32.9	34.1	32.5	27.3	30.7	32.5	36.2	29.5	28.6	386.3
1981	31.1	30.4	34.1	32.6	31.6	30.0	26.8	30.4	32.6	34.7	30.3	27.4	372.0
1982	29.4	30.2	34.4	30.0	31.0	31.0	26.1	30.7	31.4	31.2	28.4	25.3	359.1
1983	27.7	31.6	31.3	26.9	29.8	28.4	22.4	30.2	29.3	28.9	27.6	24.8	339.2
1984	27.3	29.1	30.2	27.7	28.6	24.6	20.7	26.0	21.9	25.2	22.3	19.6	303.2
1985	22.5	21.0	22.2	22.2	24.9	21.1	19.7	24.5	22.4	24.8	21.1	18.7	265.1
1986	22.5	21.6	21.3	21.2	20.8	18.4	18.4	20.9	19.8	21.5	18.4	16.6	240.9
1987[1]	17.3	18.4	19.4	19.0	18.4	20.0	15.6	19.9	20.6	20.3	18.0	14.8	225.9
1988[1]	15.3	19.0	19.8	17.5	18.3	17.9	13.6	18.9					

[1] Preliminary. *Source: U.S. Department of Commerce* T.295

U.S. Imports and Exports of All Cattle Hides In Thousands of Hides

| | Imports | | U.S. Exports—By Country of Destination | | | | | | | | | | | | | |
Year	Total	From Canada	Total	Canada	France	W. Germany	Japan	Mexico	Netherlands	Poland	Taiwan	Spain	Romania	Korea Repub.	Czech.	Italy
1979	673	643	23,731	1,248	691	454	7,396	2,428	324	513		892	1,317	2,526	682	2,248
1980	880	859	19,512	1,046	238	206	7,476	1,972	164	522		112	1,046	2,653	318	690
1981	1,028	881	19,703	1,212	137	319	7,512	2,485	94	203		394	680	3,579	334	486
1982	658	592	23,175	1,041	478	671	6,469	1,882	280	790		643	939	4,572	415	1,395
1983	665	570	21,281	1,235	332	343	6,413	1,296	174	303		246	1,318	4,635	489	823
1984	711	669	25,029	1,072	292	252	7,334	1,858	221	319	2,697	242	1,032	5,423	669	1,170
1985	1,044	883	24,956	729	215	110	6,824	2,287	71	402	2,797	214	1,168	6,441	418	1,134
1986	761	594	26,481	666	262	71	6,624	1,002	133	179	3,542	190	688	9,316	521	1,502
1987[1]	490	335	23,921	830	151	54	5,956	1,427	50	39	3,166	143	308	10,062	311	392

[1] Preliminary. *Source: Leather Industries of America* T.297

Average Factory Price of Footwear in the United States In Dollars Per Pair

Year	Jan.	Feb.	Mar.	Apr.	May	June	July	Aug.	Sept.	Oct.	Nov.	Dec.	Average
1979	9.73	9.84	9.68	10.23	10.00	10.48	11.74	10.31	10.30	10.46	11.15	11.47	10.60
1980	11.67	11.83	11.81	12.27	12.16	11.37	11.40	11.94	11.08	11.25	11.45	11.41	11.63
1981	11.67	11.93	12.52	12.72	13.09	13.16	13.01	13.14	13.22	12.90	12.67	12.58	12.52
1982	12.96	12.32	12.49	12.74	12.76	13.30	14.13	13.34	13.12	13.10	13.56	14.08	13.14
1983	12.88	13.72	13.18	13.54	14.20	13.57	12.91	14.14	14.06	15.02	14.69	15.55	13.96
1984	14.95	14.19	14.00	14.99	15.20	14.43	14.88	14.59	15.11	14.56	15.00	15.62	14.79
1985	15.24	14.97	14.10	14.87	14.86	15.35	14.24	14.55	14.12	13.71	13.56	15.13	14.56
1986	14.60	13.86	13.82	14.22	15.00	14.98	15.53	14.38	14.64	14.38	14.40	16.50	14.69
1987	15.09	14.58	14.05	15.15	15.89	15.63	16.47	15.60	15.63	15.23	15.89	17.96	15.60
1988[1]	18.38	16.42	15.39	17.39	15.28	16.02	19.16	16.56	16.99	17.20			

[1] Preliminary. *Source: Leather Industries of America* T.298

Wholesale Price of Hides (Packer Heavy Native Steers)—F.O.B. Chicago   In Cents Per Pound

Year	Jan.	Feb.	Mar.	Apr.	May	June	July	Aug.	Sept.	Oct.	Nov.	Dec.	Average
1980	496.7	409.3	331.5	320.5	283.6	321.0	369.0	448.0	361.4	412.9	455.9	420.6	385.9
1981	375.1	344.1	356.1	405.8	385.8	364.9	351.7	373.6	344.3	347.7	347.2	343.4	361.6
1982	353.6	346.0	325.8	339.3	353.5	342.1	342.1	349.7	343.5	336.4	324.7	312.9	339.1
1983	313.9	315.0	329.6	345.0	378.6	386.8	434.2	N.A.	447.5	450.2	469.9	489.6	396.4
1984[1]	54.8	56.0	62.0	61.7	64.5	64.7	66.5	69.2	68.9	61.7	52.5	47.9	60.9
1985	46.0	41.7	45.5	54.7	57.0	53.1	54.0	55.7	57.1	57.6	63.5	60.8	53.9
1986	57.7	58.4	57.7	63.1	68.6	68.7	68.3	69.9	64.5	65.9	65.2	61.8	64.2
1987	61.8	64.2	69.7	82.4	83.5	81.7	82.5	83.8	89.0	89.9	85.4	83.7	79.8
1988	82.9	86.3	97.4	100.0	99.2	87.6	84.2	93.7	87.3	80.5	77.1	76.7	87.7

[1] Data prior to 1984 are for the index 1967 = 100.   *Source: Bureau of Labor Statistics (0411–0111.99); Wall St. Journal; CRB.*   T.296

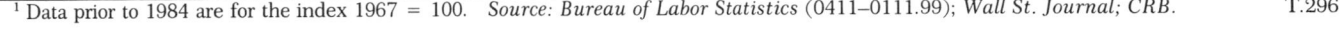

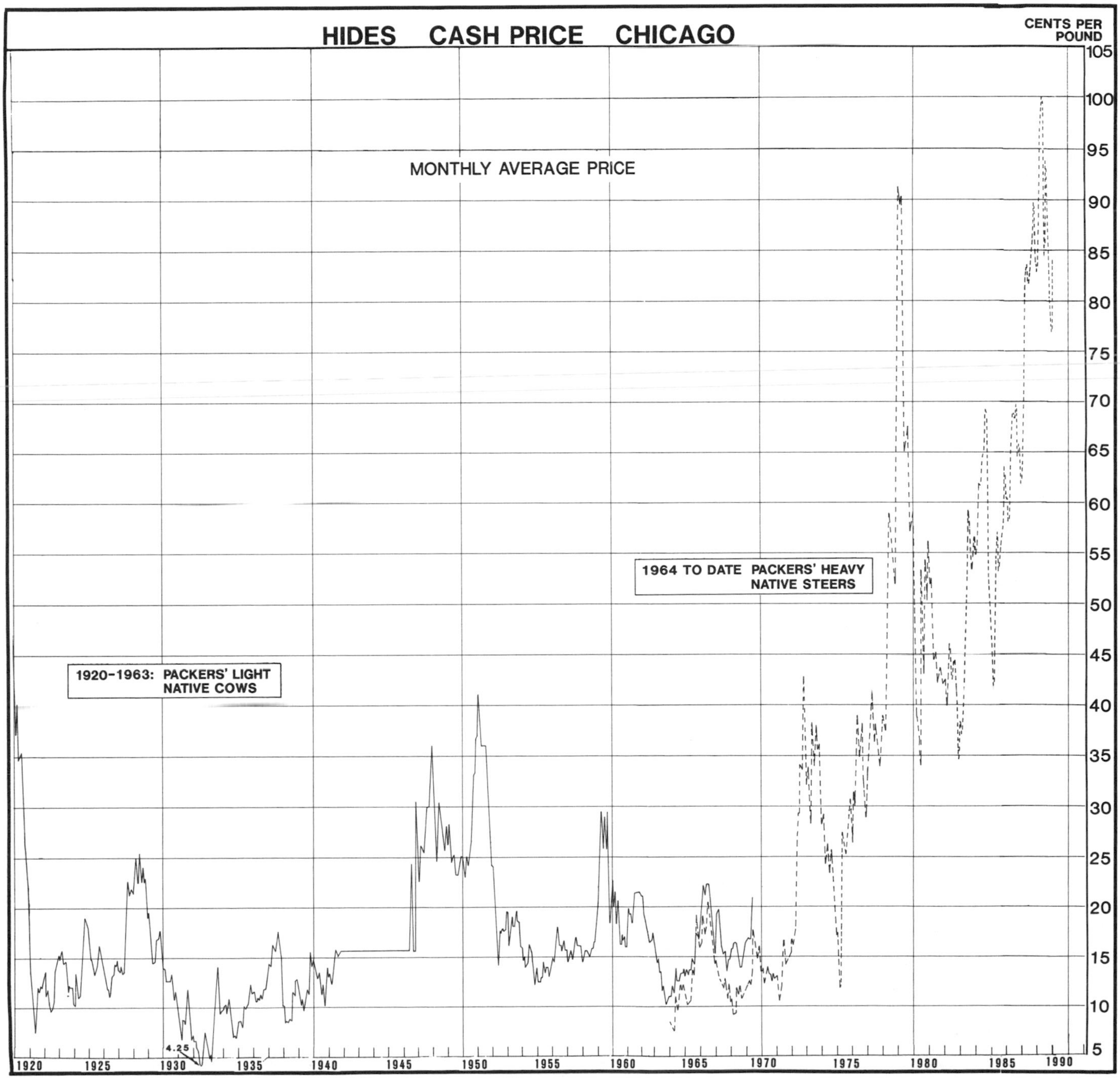

HIDES   CASH PRICE   CHICAGO

CENTS PER POUND

MONTHLY AVERAGE PRICE

1964 TO DATE PACKERS' HEAVY NATIVE STEERS

1920-1963: PACKERS' LIGHT NATIVE COWS

Hogs

Hogs kept for breeding on U.S. farms increased during the first half of 1988, extending a herd build-up that began in mid-1986. The June 1, 1988, breeding inventory of 7.5 million head was the largest since 1983. However, drought brought a sharp reduction in producers' returns, and excessive heat and humidity caused farrowing and conception problems in late spring and early summer. By September 1, the breeding inventory had dropped to 7.3 million, and the decline was to continue into late 1988. The inventory of all hogs and pigs on September 1, 1988, in the 10 quarterly estimating states was 45.1 million head, 5 percent above 1987 and the highest September inventory since 1983.

The June-August 1988 U.S. pig crop was 23.6 million head, 4 percent above 1987. Sows farrowing in that period totaled 3.09 million, 6 percent above a year earlier. Pigs saved per litter were 7.62, compared to 7.75 in the same 1987 period. Within this total, the 10-state June-August 1988 pig crop was 17.9 million head, 2 percent above 1987 and 11 percent more than in 1986. An estimated 2.34 million sows farrowed in June-August, up 4 percent from a year earlier and up 13 percent from 1986. U.S. hog producers intended to have 3.0 million sows farrow during September-November 1988, 5 percent above actual farrowings in the same 1987 period and 11 percent above 1986. Farrowing intentions for December 1988-February 1989 of 2.79 million sows were 3 percent above a year earlier.

As the large spring pig crop came to market, augmented by breeding herd liquidation, commercial pork production was expected to reach 4.35 billion pounds in 1988's fourth quarter, 7 percent above a year earlier.

In first quarter 1989, pork production was likely to be about 3 percent above a year earlier, due to an increase in the summer 1988 pig crop. Second quarter 1989 pork output was expected to be about the same as in 1988. Third and fourth quarter 1989 pork production was to be directly linked to the amount of herd liquidation in the second half of 1988. Moderate liquidation was anticipated, leading to a 3 percent annual decline in second-half 1989 production. Commercial slaughter in the third quarter was projected to be down 2 percent from the previous year, while the fourth quarter kill was likely to be down 5 percent.

U.S. pork imports were forecast to increase to 1,275 million pounds, carcass weight, in 1988, but to decline in 1989. Imports come mainly from Canada and Denmark. Because of a proposed reduction in the countervailing duty deposit rate on live hogs from Canada, more Canadian hogs were expected to be imported during 1988's last half and in 1989.

U.S. pork exports were forecast to reach 145 million pounds during 1988 and 130 million in 1989. Exports in second quarter 1988 were unusually heavy with additional sales to Japan. In that period, Japan increased imports from Denmark, Canada, and the U.S. to cover a temporary disruption in trade with Taiwan.

Futures Market

Live hog futures are traded on the Chicago Mercantile Exchange (CME) and the Mid America Commodity Exchange. Options are traded on the CME contract.

World Hog Numbers in Specified Countries as of January 1   In Millions of Head

Year	Brazil	Canada	Denmark	France	W. Germany	Hungary	Italy	Japan	Mexico	Philippines	Poland	Spain	China[3]	Un. Kingdom	United States	USSR	World
1982	33.5	10.0	9.8	11.8	22.3	8.3	9.0	10.0	16.2	7.6	19.1	10.7	293.7	7.9	58.7	73.3	693.5
1983	33.5	10.1	9.5	11.7	22.5	9.0	9.1	10.3	16.5	8.0	17.6	11.7	300.8	8.2	54.5	76.7	701.5
1984	30.0	10.3	9.0	11.3	23.4	9.8	9.2	10.4	13.1	7.6	15.9	15.0	298.5	7.8	56.7	78.7	703.4
1985	30.0	10.6	9.0	11.0	23.6	9.2	9.0	10.7	12.3	7.3	17.2	15.0	306.8	7.8	54.1	77.9	708.6
1986	30.5	10.0	9.1	11.0	24.3	8.3	9.1	11.1	13.1	7.3	19.2	15.8	331.4	7.9	52.3	77.8	735.2
1987	31.7	10.0	9.4	12.1	24.5	8.7	9.3	11.4	12.4	7.1	19.6	15.8	337.2	8.0	50.9	79.5	748.3
1988[1]	32.7	10.6	9.0	11.9	23.7	8.2	9.4	11.7	10.9	7.6	19.4	16.9	327.7	7.9	54.4	77.4	741.2
1989[2]	32.2	11.0	8.9	11.7	23.0	8.5	9.4	11.6	8.9	7.8	18.8	16.5	327.8	7.7	56.0	78.0	739.9

[1] Preliminary.   [2] Forecast.   [3] Mainland.   *Source: Foreign Agricultural Service, U.S.D.A.*   T.300

Salient Statistics of Pigs and Hogs in the U.S.

Year	Spring[2] Sows Farrowed	Pigs Saved	Fall[3] Sows Farrowed	Pigs Saved	Total Pig Crop	$ Per Head	Total Million $	Hog Marketings Ths. Head	Quantity Produced (Live Wt.) Mil. Lbs.	Value of Production Mil. $	Federally Inspected	Other	Total	Farm	Total
	In Thousands of Head										Hogs Slaughtered in Thousand Head — Commercial				
1982	5,664	41,575	5,884	43,614	85,189	89.90	4,903	86,972	19,658	10,297	79,328	3,861	82,190	655	82,845
1983	6,301	47,409	6,176	45,746	93,155	58.80	3,331	89,129	21,195	9,899	84,762	2,823	87,584	517	88,101
1984	5,694	42,403	5,857	44,183	86,586	75.00	4,056	87,344	20,196	9,498	82,478	2,690	85,168	473	85,641
1985	5,571	42,545	5,667	43,476	86,029	69.60	3,640	86,694	20,164	8,871	81,974	2,519	84,492	446	84,938
1986	5,246	40,392	5,423	41,997	82,389	91.90	4,679	82,608	19,363	9,532	77,290	2,309	79,598	358	79,956
1987[1]	5,538	43,135	5,775	44,676	87,811	76.20	4,097				78,913	2,168	81,081		
1988[4]	6,005	46,647	6,088	47,500	97,147						82,000	2,000	84,000		

[1] Preliminary.   [2] December–May.   [3] June–November.   [4] Estimate.   *Source: Statistical Reporting Service, U.S.D.A.*   T.302

Hogs and Pigs on U.S. Farms on December 1   In Thousands of Head

Year	Georgia	Illinois	Indiana	Iowa	Kansas	Kentucky	Minnesota	Missouri	Nebraska	No. Carolina	Ohio	South Dakota	Tennessee	Wisconsin	Total
1981	1,520	6,450	4,100	16,300	1,770	1,040	4,300	3,400	4,100	1,980	2,050	1,710	900	1,380	58,698
1982	1,450	5,600	4,400	14,400	1,670	960	4,000	3,500	3,800	2,150	1,920	1,580	750	1,220	54,534
1983	1,350	5,400	4,200	15,000	1,650	1,000	4,400	3,600	4,000	2,350	2,200	1,730	950	1,280	56,694
1984	1,200	5,400	4,300	14,200	1,600	880	4,300	3,450	3,700	2,300	1,970	1,600	1,100	1,300	54,073
1985	1,150	5,400	4,150	13,500	1,520	800	4,100	3,050	3,900	2,350	1,980	1,610	950	1,250	52,313
1986	1,100	5,000	4,150	12,600	1,420	880	4,260	2,850	3,950	2,360	2,000	1,520	770	1,300	50,920
1987[1]	1,175	5,300	4,600	13,800	1,450	900	4,350	2,950	4,000	2,500	2,150	1,520	800	1,280	53,795

[1] Preliminary.   *Source: Crop Reporting Board, U.S.D.A.*   T.301

Quarterly 10—U.S. State Hogs & Pigs Report   In Thousands of Head

Year[2]	Inventory[1]	Breeding[1]	Market[1]	Farrowings	Pig Crop	Year	Inventory[1]	Breeding[1]	Market[1]	Farrowings	Pig Crop
1985	42,420	5,348	37,072	8,831	67,648	1987[3]	39,690	5,110	34,580	8,783	68,417
I	42,420	5,348	37,072	1,935	14,690	I	39,690	5,110	34,580	1,916	14,840
II	39,680	5,220	34,460	2,420	18,762	II	38,370	5,215	33,155	2,352	18,601
III	41,650	5,397	36,253	2,191	16,941	III	40,880	5,325	35,555	2,257	17,481
IV	41,820	5,377	36,443	2,265	17,255	IV	43,075	5,300	37,775	2,259	17,503
1986	41,100	5,258	35,842	8,223	63,835	1988[3]					
I	41,100	5,258	35,842	1,863	14,254	I	42,845	5,465	37,380	2,103	16,331
II	38,210	4,948	33,262	2,161	16,878	II	41,145	5,500	35,645	2,552	19,968
III	38,075	4,870	33,155	2,074	16,164	III	44,040	5,625	38,415	2,343	17,877
IV	39,585	4,895	34,690	2,115	16,460	IV	45,070	5,470	39,600	2,345	

[1] Beginning of period.   [2] Quarters are Dec. preceding year—Feb. (I), Mar.–May (II), June–Aug. (III), & Sept.–Nov. (IV).   [3] Preliminary.   *Source: Crop Reporting Board, U.S.D.A.*   T.181a

U.S. Federally Inspected Hog Slaughter   In Thousands of Head

Week ended	1985	1986	1987	1988	Week ended	1985	1986	1987	1988
Jan. 1[1]	1,238	1,153	1,069		July 2	1,171	1,118	1,193	1,537
5	1,295	1,250	1,258		9	1,523	1,390	1,360	1,330
Jan. 9[1]	1,679	1,675	1,683	1,717	16	1,427	1,349	1,345	1,537
16	1,615	1,654	1,659	1,766	23	1,400	1,281	1,354	1,543
23	1,528	1,563	1,527	1,605	30	1,474	1,314	1,330	1,456
30	1,565	1,506	1,500	1,543	Aug. 6	1,556	1,338	1,372	1,525
Feb. 6	1,582	1,526	1,455	1,535	13	1,524	1,369	1,445	1,571
13	1,508	1,512	1,502	1,544	20	1,531	1,402	1,404	1,513
20	1,539	1,501	1,395	1,542	27	1,601	1,419	1,475	1,563
27	1,608	1,606	1,533	1,595	Sept. 3	1,429	1,257	1,548	1,608
Mar. 5	1,635	1,635	1,556	1,600	10	1,690	1,492	1,363	1,517
12	1,638	1,650	1,578	1,674	17	1,667	1,504	1,709	1,799
19	1,647	1,556	1,574	1,639	24	1,681	1,504	1,621	1,868
26	1,642	1,579	1,504	1,631	Oct. 1	1,644	1,521	1,658	1,802
Apr. 2	1,569	1,518	1,529	1,599	8	1,686	1,555	1,638	1,821
9	1,623	1,633	1,553	1,573	15	1,620	1,528	1,720	1,837
16	1,676	1,651	1,468	1,655	22	1,654	1,551	1,664	
23	1,662	1,619	1,393	1,659	29	1,668	1,580	1,763	
30	1,702	1,637	1,453	1,695	Nov 5	1,654	1,576	1,792	
May 7	1,699	1,607	1,475	1,653	12	1,654	1,537	1,778	
14	1,705	1,560	1,440	1,633	19	1,697	1,557	1,772	
21	1,580	1,518	1,448	1,577	26	1,328	1,308	1,463	
28	1,361	1,310	1,232	1,533	Dec. 3	1,656	1,530	1,845	
June 4	1,592	1,471	1,385	1,323	10	1,566	1,548	1,879	
11	1,561	1,459	1,372	1,489	17	1,655	1,503	1,728	
18	1,535	1,373	1,341	1,513	24	1,153	1,069	1,150	
25	1,476	1,330	1,356	1,510	31		1,258	1,458	

[1] Corresponding dates—1985: Jan. 12, 1985; 1986: Jan. 11, 1986; 1987: Jan. 10, 1987   *Source: Economic Research Service, U.S.D.A.*   T.181b

HOGS

Average Wholesale Price of Hogs, Average (All Weights) at Sioux City In Dollars Per 100 Pounds

Year	Jan.	Feb.	Mar.	Apr.	May	June	July	Aug.	Sept.	Oct.	Nov.	Dec.	Average
1984	50.14	46.68	47.36	48.69	48.22	50.04	54.25	52.57	47.86	45.01	48.55	49.03	49.03
1985	49.60	49.55	44.54	41.85	42.70	45.67	47.09	43.91	40.42	44.20	44.46	47.11	44.98
1986	45.60	43.80	41.08	40.59	46.43	54.95	61.59	63.66	59.59	54.86	54.44	52.02	50.73
1987	47.56	49.08	48.67	52.10	55.79	61.37	62.69	60.56	55.19	49.28	40.74	41.56	47.11
1988	44.59	47.45	43.19	42.28	47.75	48.26	45.60	45.98	41.28	38.92	36.52		

Source: Department of Agriculture

T.307

High, Low & Closing Prices of June Live Hogs Futures at Chicago In Cents per Pound

Year of Delivery		Apr.	May	June	July	Aug.	Sept.	Oct.	Nov.	Dec.	Jan.	Feb.	Mar.	Apr.	May	June	Life of Delivery Range
1985	High	53.75	55.20	55.40	54.40	53.15	53.25	51.10	53.67	54.95	54.95	54.22	52.90	49.97	49.20	50.10	55.40
	Low	52.62	53.65	52.60	50.10	50.80	48.65	48.40	50.70	50.25	53.05	50.65	49.05	46.15	44.40	46.70	44.40
	Close	53.60	54.32	54.15	51.00	52.70	48.77	50.95	52.95	54.57	53.85	51.65	49.57	46.30	47.95	49.35	—
1986	High	48.95	48.65	49.00	47.60	44.40	43.75	43.97	44.70	46.45	47.00	45.50	45.90	46.87	50.10	59.72	59.72
	Low	47.55	46.80	46.90	41.75	40.05	39.80	42.25	42.20	43.25	43.65	42.10	42.05	40.25	45.52	49.75	39.80
	Close	48.70	48.25	47.75	43.57	40.82	43.00	42.65	44.65	45.85	45.27	42.80	43.82	46.60	49.77	59.65	—
1987	High	43.30	44.75	46.67	48.00	49.50	59.20	49.40	48.70	49.10	47.85	48.25	48.85	54.80	58.85	64.10	64.10
	Low	39.90	39.90	43.80	46.10	41.20	46.00	45.45	45.50	44.90	44.60	45.60	46.45	52.60	57.85	37.50
	Close	40.97	40.85	44.95	47.45	47.45	48.25	46.70	48.47	45.62	47.82	45.50	47.82	53.47	58.17	64.00	—
1988	High	41.50	43.00	43.72	44.65	45.05	45.30	44.50	43.15	42.70	49.17	50.35	51.65	52.15	54.95	54.70	54.95
	Low	38.50	40.65	40.70	42.15	43.65	42.72	41.25	41.35	40.25	41.90	46.65	45.57	48.10	48.90	48.30	37.50
	Close	40.95	42.45	41.20	44.55	44.70	43.30	41.82	41.85	42.00	46.95	46.65	49.30	48.80	54.77	50.45	—
1989	High	44.60	46.80	56.25	54.80	50.10	49.90	49.35	48.95	50.50							
	Low	42.50	44.35	46.75	46.90	47.20	46.70	47.60	45.50	46.85							
	Close	44.40	46.70	54.20	47.52	47.27	49.10	48.40	47.05	49.57							

Source: Chicago Mercantile Exchange

T.308

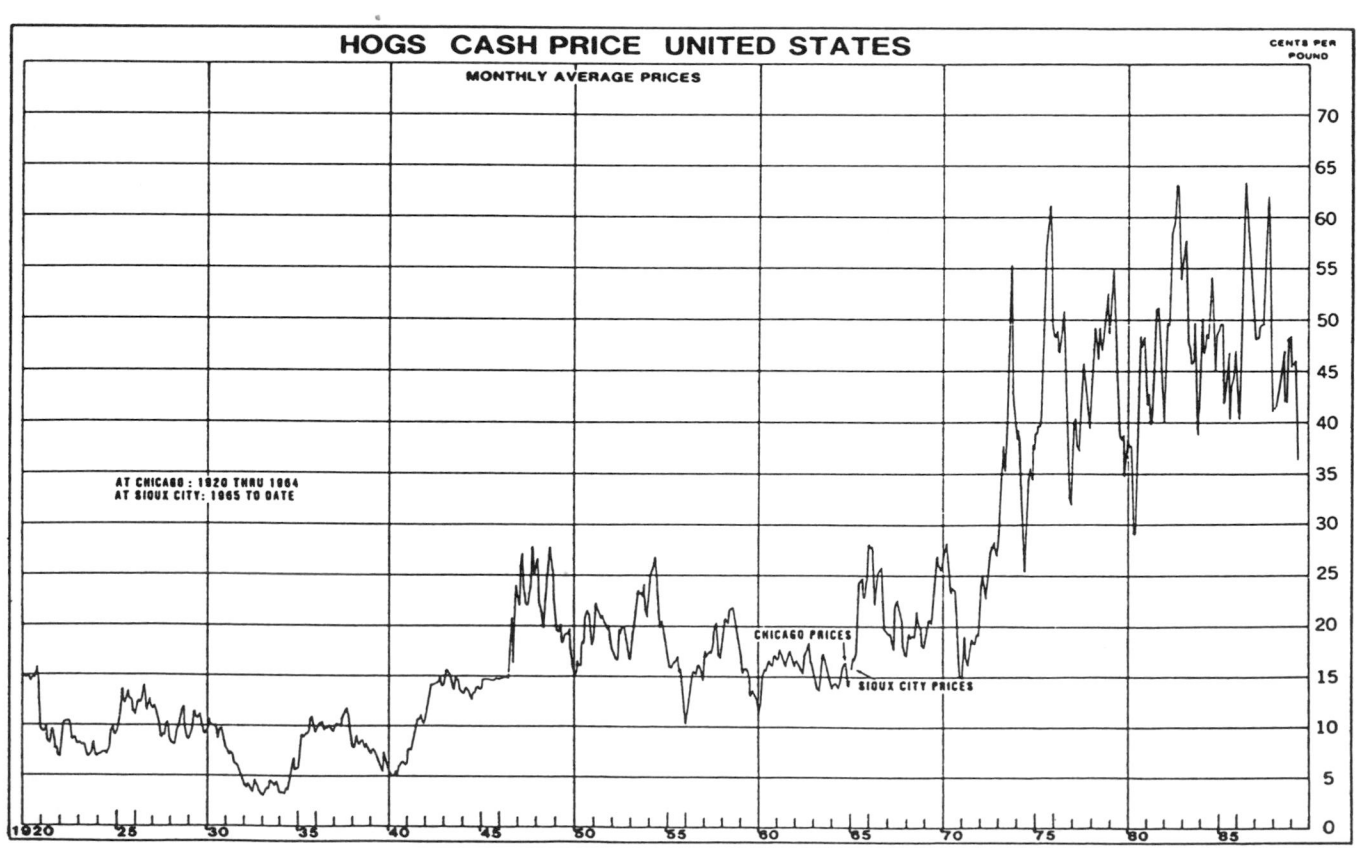

HOGS CASH PRICE UNITED STATES

MONTHLY AVERAGE PRICES

CENTS PER POUND

AT CHICAGO: 1920 THRU 1964
AT SIOUX CITY: 1965 TO DATE

CHICAGO PRICES

SIOUX CITY PRICES

Average Price Received by Farmers for Hogs in the U.S.   In Cents Per Pound

Year	Jan.	Feb.	Mar.	Apr.	May	June	July	Aug.	Sept.	Oct.	Nov.	Dec.	Average[1]
1984	48.40	45.40	45.80	47.50	47.20	49.00	52.00	50.50	46.30	43.60	47.00	48.60	47.61
1985	48.00	48.30	43.60	41.20	41.40	44.60	45.70	42.50	39.70	43.10	43.20	45.30	43.88
1986	44.30	42.80	40.40	39.70	45.80	52.60	59.00	62.10	58.30	53.10	52.80	50.60	50.10
1987[2]	47.20	48.20	47.40	50.80	54.40	59.20	59.60	58.60	54.30	48.90	40.60	40.30	50.93
1988[2]	43.00	45.80	42.20	41.90	46.30	47.10	44.10	44.70	40.70	38.70	36.20	40.50	50.79

[1] Weighted average by quantities sold.   [2] Preliminary.   *Source: Crop Reporting Board, U.S.D.A.*   T.306

Hog-Corn Price Ratio[1] at Omaha

Year	Jan.	Feb.	Mar.	Apr.	May	June	July	Aug.	Sept.	Oct.	Nov.	Dec.	Average
1984	16.0	15.3	14.5	14.5	14.3	14.8	16.6	16.8	16.0	16.4	18.4	19.6	16.1
1985[2]	18.8	18.7	16.4	15.2	15.7	16.9	17.9	18.2	17.1	19.5	19.3	19.8	17.8
1986[2]	19.0	19.0	17.6	17.2	19.5	22.4	30.3	39.3	42.9	39.0	34.7	33.4	27.8
1987[2]	32.7	35.1	32.6	32.7	31.6	34.3	38.4	41.3	36.3	31.0	24.3	23.8	32.8
1988[2]	25.0	25.7	23.0	22.5	24.3	18.9	16.8	17.8	15.9	14.9			

[1] Ratio computed by dividing average price packer and shipper purchases of barrows and gilts by average price No. 2 yellow corn both at Omaha. This ratio represents the number of bushels of corn required to buy 100 pounds of live hogs.   [2] Preliminary.   *Source: Economic Research Service, U.S.D.A.*   T.304

Cold Storage Holdings of Frozen Pork[1] in the U.S. on First of Month   In Millions of Pounds

Year	Jan.	Feb.	Mar.	Apr.	May	June	July	Aug.	Sept.	Oct.	Nov.	Dec.
1984	300.6	295.1	311.7	350.7	390.4	437.7	405.2	345.0	269.5	256.6	275.6	269.4
1985	274.3	291.9	286.3	314.1	368.2	410.3	385.0	343.1	294.7	277.0	277.5	265.0
1986[2]	229.4	235.4	239.1	253.5	282.0	275.6	247.7	214.9	184.7	185.9	215.8	206.2
1987[2]	197.1	217.7	228.5	221.8	217.8	218.8	189.2	181.1	175.1	186.2	212.2	251.7
1988[2]	285.5	287.2	308.1	346.1	396.3	388.6	362.6	336.7	287.0	288.0	320.9	363.9

[1] Excludes lard.   [2] Preliminary.   *Source: Crop Reporting Board, U.S.D.A.*   T.303

Federally Inspected Hog Slaughter in the United States   In Thousands of Head

Year	Jan.	Feb.	Mar.	Apr.	May	June	July	Aug.	Sept.	Oct.	Nov.	Dec.	Total
1984	6,947	6,591	7,578	6,953	7,153	6,392	5,806	6,628	6,439	7,908	7,354	6,729	82,478
1985	7,114	6,208	6,932	7,177	7,364	6,209	6,399	6,810	6,738	7,566	6,818	6,640	81,974
1986	6,968	6,158	6,662	7,160	6,703	5,894	5,918	5,799	6,323	7,083	6,064	6,558	77,290
1987[1]	6,723	5,886	6,786	6,492	5,916	5,987	6,019	6,018	6,855	7,519	7,121	7,583	78,913
1988[1]	6,803	6,519	7,505	6,929	6,713	6,715	6,199	7,101	7,534	7,887			

[1] Preliminary.   *Source: Statistical Reporting Service, U.S.D.A.*   T.305

Average Live Weight of All Hogs Slaughtered Under Federal Inspection   In Pounds Per Head

Year	Jan.	Feb.	Mar.	Apr.	May	June	July	Aug.	Sept.	Oct.	Nov.	Dec.	Average[1]
1984[2]	242	241	240	243	246	247	245	242	240	243	246	244	243.5
1985[2]	245	242	242	245	247	248	245	243	242	246	248	247	245.0
1986[2]	246	244	244	245	246	245	245	244	245	248	250	252	246.2
1987[2]	251	248	246	247	247	248	246	244	246	249	252	250	247.8
1988[2]	248	247	247	249	250	250	249	247	248				

[1] Average is weighted by federally inspected slaughter.   [2] Preliminary.   *Source: Department of Agriculture*   T.311

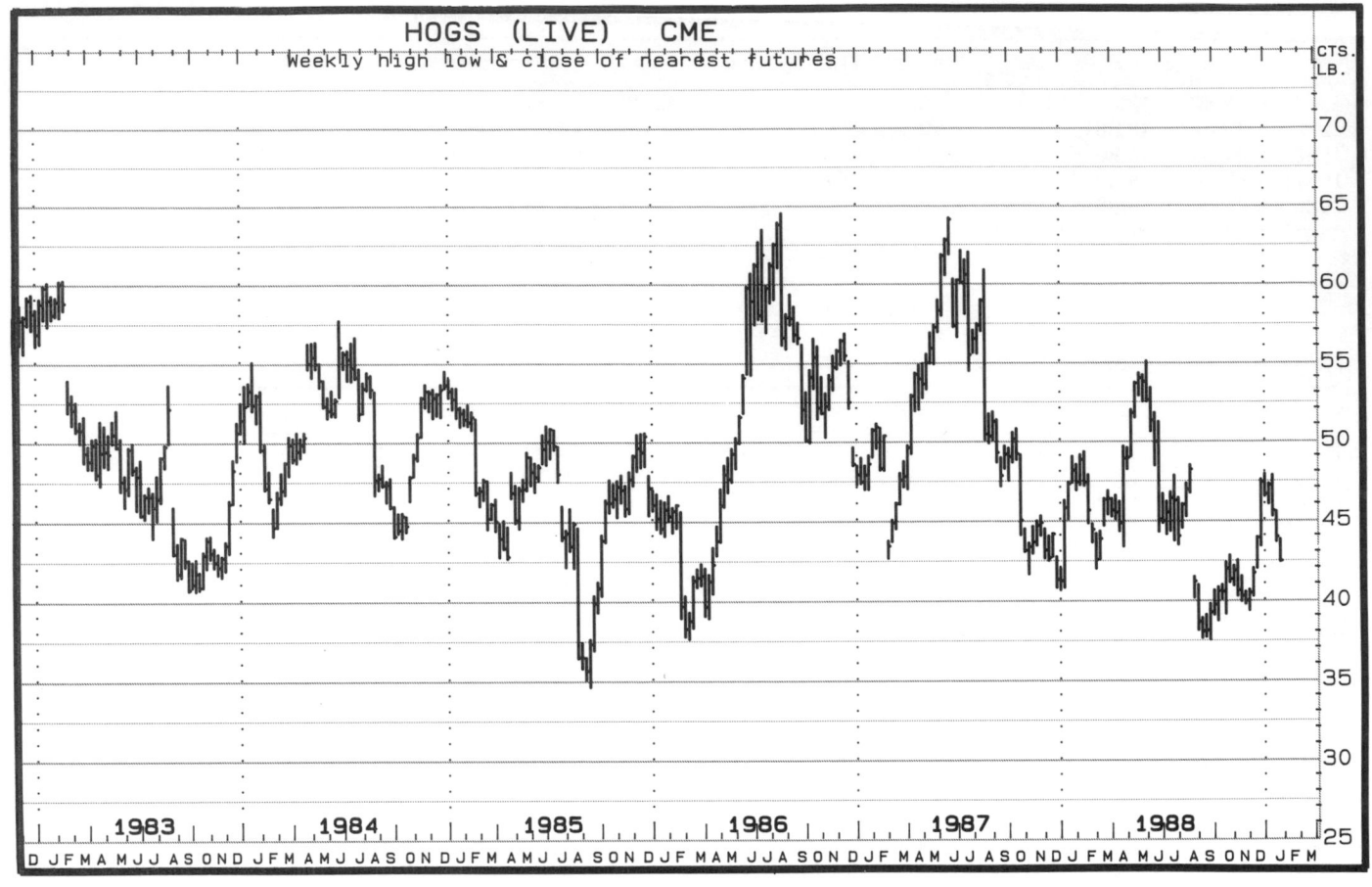

HOGS (LIVE) CME
Weekly high low & close of nearest futures

Month–End Open Interest of Live Hogs Futures at Chicago   In Contracts

Year	Jan.	Feb.	Mar.	Apr.	May	June	July	Aug.	Sept.	Oct.	Nov.	Dec.
1981	21,267	21,588	20,767	28,147	31,149	26,639	19,557	20,944	23,471	21,945	22,294	17,924
1982	27,528	29,960	43,387	51,056	63,760	46,002	42,884	51,530	48,263	48,751	47,067	43,791
1983	45,184	41,338	39,469	31,915	31,014	30,794	27,173	33,668	33,425	30.049	30,071	33,820
1984	33,049	35,159	35,289	33,122	34,148	30,517	23,579	24,061	21,048	20,689	26,975	24,037
1985	29,917	27,827	25,738	23,673	22,919	24,807	18,289	19,984	18,390	25,447	27,912	21,680
1986	22,125	21,639	17,123	19,037	25,497	26,878	32,704	32,643	32,479	27,447	30,980	23,620
1987	26,472	29,973	29,961	30,406	35,328	30,485	30,336	32,489	32,347	24,111	26,017	23,740
1988	29,251	30,540	29,212	27,844	35,073	26,335	23,986	28,228	27,402	33,330	33,762	33,064

Source: Chicago Mercantile Exchange   T.309

Volume of Trading of Live Hogs Futures at Chicago   In Thousands of Contracts

Year	Jan.	Feb.	Mar.	Apr.	May	June	July	Aug.	Sept.	Oct.	Nov.	Dec.	Total
1981	174.8	182.0	197.5	212.0	230.7	262.9	179.8	153.9	171.9	178.6	160.2	153.7	2,258.1
1982	178.7	195.6	262.6	222.6	288.0	408.3	300.1	344.5	347.2	383.4	324.9	305.1	3,561.0
1983	291.6	254.7	213.8	230.6	254.1	262.1	217.4	279.9	220.8	174.2	197.5	194.2	2,790.7
1984	232.2	212.7	243.8	172.3	211.0	192.6	189.2	143.9	109.1	140.7	181.0	140.5	2,169.0
1985	155.0	128.3	160.2	141.7	156.2	141.9	134.7	120.2	136.1	156.8	145.2	143.5	2,719.9
1986	156.3	108.5	113.7	153.6	157.4	160.8	224.3	168.8	196.5	183.4	171.0	142.5	1,936.7
1987	159.2	138.5	172.7	190.3	189.7	212.1	219.5	169.8	174.0	175.5	121.1	118.0	2,040.5
1988	172.9	143.0	172.4	137.6	169.6	267.0	171.4	140.3	160.7	150.3	166.8	156.7	2,008.8

Source: Chicago Mercantile Exchange   T.310

Honey

Honey output in selected producing countries in 1988 was forecast by USDA at 685,500 tonnes, down 3 percent from 1987. Total consumption showed a steady increase through 1987. However, total honey consumption in 1988 was forecast to fall by almost one percent. Because of the decline in total production, ending stocks were expected to fall from 109,258 tonnes in 1987 to 70,908 in 1988.

Total exports of honey declined in 1987 and were expected to stay around the same level in 1988. Argentine exports were expected to be down 9 percent in 1988. Australian shipments were forecast to rise. Chinese exports were likely to increase slightly from the 1987 level. Mexican exports were expected to decline, due to an 8 percent drop in domestic output. Dry conditions hurt output in the main producing states of Yucatan, Michoacan, Jalisco and Veracruz. Also, the Africanization of some beehives (producing bees that yielded less honey and were harder to manage) reduced production.

U.S. honey output in 1988 was forecast at about 82,000 tonnes, down 21 percent, due to poor flowering caused by the drought in most major producing states.

U.S. honey imports dropped 51 percent in 1987 and continued to be sluggish in 1988. The U.S. imported 16,101 tonnes of honey during the first eight months of 1988, versus 17,661 tonnes in the same 1987 period. In 1987, China supplied over 33 percent of U.S. honey imports. Other major suppliers included Canada, Argentina, and Mexico.

U.S. honey exports increased 34 percent from 4,181 tons in 1986 to 5,610 in 1987. West Germany took nearly 40 percent. Other major buyers included Saudi Arabia, Hong Kong, and Japan.

The price of honey is supported through a government loan program. The 1988 support price was 59.1 cents/lb. Loans on 1988-crop honey were available for extracted honey with a moisture content no greater than 18.5 percent.

A lower loan payback program was in effect for 1988-crop honey. This permitted repayment of honey loans at a rate which was below the loan rate. Payback rates are determined by market conditions and announced by USDA.

World Production of Honey   In Thousands of Metric Tons

Year	Argentina	Australia	Brazil	Canada	China (Mainland)	Ethiopia	France	West Germany	Japan	Mexico	Poland	Spain	Turkey	United States	U.S.S.R.	World Total
1977	22.0	14.9	14.0	25.4	60.0	19.0	8.2	20.0	6.2	60.0	10.0	12.0	21.7	81.0	208.0	798.3
1978	35.0	18.6	16.0	30.6	75.0	20.0	9.5	15.0	8.5	54.0	12.0	11.0	21.7	104.5	179.0	827.7
1979	30.0	25.0	18.0	32.9	110.0	20.0	14.4	9.9	7.5	52.0	13.0	12.0	23.7	107.8	189.0	880.1
1980	33.0	19.5	20.0	29.2	81.0	20.5	12.0	13.5	6.2	60.0	10.0	13.0	23.0	90.6	183.0	837.4
1981	30.0	24.8	24.0	32.9	110.0	21.0	10.0	14.0	6.0	60.0	10.0	13.0	23.0	84.3	184.0	873.8
1982	33.0	22.4	25.0	30.5	136.0		25.0	18.0	7.4	45.0				104.3	186.0	908.8
1983	30.0	25.0	25.0	38.8	143.3			19.0	6.9	68.0				93.0	210.0	970.0
1984	35.0	28.0	25.0	43.3	140.0			16.0	6.8	60.0				75.0	193.0	622.1[2]
1985	45.0	26.9	28.0	36.1	150.0			11.0	7.2	56.0				68.0	204.0	632.2[2]
1986	36.0	25.1	31.0	34.0	160.0			16.0	5.6	54.0				90.9	210.0	662.6[2]
1987[1]	40.0	28.0	30.5	40.6	204.0			16.0	6.0	47.9				103.0	190.0	706.0[2]
1988[1]	40.0	29.0	36.0	36.0	200.0			18.0	5.5	44.0				85.0	192.0	685.5[2]

[1] Preliminary.   [2] *Only for countries listed.*   *Source: Foreign Agricultural Service, U.S.D.A.*   T.312

Salient Statistics of Honey in the United States

Year	Number of Colonies Thous.	Yield Per Colony Lbs.	Total U.S.	California	Florida	Iowa	Minnesota	So. Dak.	Texas	Wisconsin	Domestic Disapp.	Imports For Consumption	Domestic Exports	Stocks Jan. 1	Producer Price ¢ Lb.	National Average Price Support ¢ Lb.	Per Capita Consumption Lbs.
					Honey Production; By States — In Millions of Pounds												
1977	4,346	41.0	178.1	13.7	14.4	6.1	12.0		9.0	9.6	240.8	63.9	5.5	34.3	46.9	32.7	1.09
1978	4,081	56.7	231.5	31.2	23.9	4.6	13.9		8.7	6.3	277.3	56.0	8.0	30.0	48.3	36.8	1.25
1979	4,155	57.4	238.7	17.1	27.3	6.6	15.8	17.3	11.4	8.8	282.7	58.6	8.8	32.2	53.1	43.9	1.26
1980	4,140	48.3	199.8	23.2	20.3	6.3	13.7	8.1	6.9	6.0	226.2	49.0	8.5	38.0	55.3	50.3	.99
1981	4,213	44.1	185.9	9.0	24.1	3.4	8.2	9.2	11.4	4.1	232.0	77.3	9.2	52.1	56.5	57.4	1.01
1982	4,250	54.1	230.0								250.8	92.0	8.5	74.1	56.8	60.4	1.08
1983	4,275	48.0	205.0								277.9	109.8	7.5	136.8	54.4	62.2	1.19
1984	3,200	38.4	165.0								251.8	124.0	7.6	194.8	49.5	65.8	1.0
1985	3,200	34.7	150.1								256.1	141.0	6.7	223.1	45.5	65.3	1.0
1986[1]	3,200	62.0	200.0	27.0	21.8	2.4	10.6	22.7	7.3	4.3	291.9	130.4	7.4	254.2	51.1	64.0	1.0
1987[2]	3,190	71.1	227.0	16.5	19.0	4.5	16.2	33.5	8.1	8.1	338.3	58.3	12.4	188.8	50.7	61.0	1.0
1988[2]	3,190		187.4								308.6	60.0	11.0	187.0			1.0

[1] Preliminary.   [2] Forecast.   *Source: Crop Reporting Board, U.S.D.A.*   T.313

Interest Rates

After the stock market crash in October 1987, Fed Chairman Greenspan relaxed his war on inflation to provide the banking system with the liquidity needed to avoid a financial panic. But mindful that its job is to "remove the punch bowl just when the party is becoming interesting," the Fed tightened credit slowly and steadily during the second half of 1988, forcing short-term rates to rise.

The M1 money supply (currency in circulation and checking accounts) grew at a 7.9 percent annual rate from December 1987 through April 1988. But discounts on new 3-month T-bills remained under 6 percent and yields on 30-year bonds stayed under 9 percent.

By April, when the Dow Jones Industrials broke away from the pattern established by the Dow in 1930 and the economy was showing signs of continued growth, the Fed began to focus on fears that the economy could be running into capacity constraints. Unemployment was near a 14-year low, commodity prices were rising, and the presidential election was approaching. In May, after the Commerce Department announced that the trade deficit shrank to $9.8 billion in March because of surging exports, interest rates rose across the yield curve, anticipating demand-pull inflation. Meanwhile, expectations of the adverse effects of a severe drought in the Midwest were driving grains and oilseeds prices sharply higher, reinforcing the inflationary psychology.

Since it was an election year, the Fed acted swiftly to avoid charges of playing politics with the economy. However, things were not so clear-cut that the Fed could act dramatically. Instead, the Open Market Committee gradually tightened credit, before raising the discount rate to 6.5 percent on August 9. It allowed the Fed funds rate to drift higher, as M1 growth slowed to an 0.5 percent annualized rate between July and November and ended the year up 4.2 percent. Meanwhile, M2 (which includes M1, money market accounts, and small time deposits) rose 5.4 percent in 1988, within its broad target range of 4 percent-8 percent growth. The Fed did not set a target for M1 in 1988, because it was unsure of the relationship between M1 growth and the economy.

As a result of the Fed's tightening, short-term interest rates began working steadily higher, but 30-year Treasury yields hardly budged, and the yield curve flattened. There were several explanations for the stability of the long bonds. First, there were expectations that the Fed would be able to control inflation over the long run, and long bonds yielded about double the underlying inflation rate. Also, investor demand for long bonds remained good, particularly for issues to be stripped into zeros for pension funds and for use to guarantee principal repayment for various government-backed loans, ranging from a Treasury-backed Mexican loan swap to the FSLIC bailout bonds issued by the newly created Financing Corporation (FICO). Then, it became evident that the Treasury was running out of authorization to sell bonds that paid coupons of more than 4.5 percent, and that the ceiling would not be raised in time for the November refunding.

Investors with the flexibility to switch to shorter maturities were able to take advantage of higher rates, but others who would have switched to corporate debt were restrained by fears of deteriorating credit quality. In November, the RJR Nabisco leveraged buy-out, which involved raising $25 billion (enough cash for a Treasury quarterly refunding), turned RJR Nabisco's AA bonds into junk-grade securities overnight, inflicting huge paper losses on their owners, including the state of North Carolina's public employee pension funds. Suddenly, it seemed unsafe to own anything except Treasuries.

The election of President Bush was anticipated by the debt markets, which expected a continuation of most of the Reagan Administration's fiscal policies in 1989.

U.S. Producer Commodity Price Index (Wholesale, All Commodities)   1982 = 100[2]

Year	Jan.	Feb.	Mar.	Apr.	May	June	July	Aug.	Sept.	Oct.	Nov.	Dec.	Average
1982	298.3	298.6	298.0	298.0	298.6	299.3	300.4	300.2	299.3	299.8	300.3	300.7	299.3
1983	299.9	300.9	300.6	300.6	301.5	302.4	303.2	304.7	305.3	306.0	305.5	306.1	303.1
1984	308.0	308.9	311.0	311.3	311.5	311.3	311.9	310.7	309.3	309.4	310.3	309.8	310.3
1985[2]	103.4	103.3	103.1	103.3	103.5	103.3	103.2	102.7	102.1	102.9	103.4	103.6	103.2
1986	103.2	101.7	100.3	99.6	100.0	99.9	99.4	99.3	99.4	99.7	99.8	99.7	100.2
1987	100.5	101.0	101.2	101.9	102.6	103.0	103.5	103.8	103.7	104.1	104.2	104.2	102.8
1988[1]	104.6	104.8	104.9	105.8	106.5	107.2	107.9	108.0	108.1	108.2	108.3		

[1] Preliminary.   [2] Data prior to 1985 are for the 1967 = 100 index.   *Source: Bureau of Labor Statistics*   T.315

U.S. Consumer Price Index   (Retail Price Index for All Items: Urban Consumers) 1982–84 = 100[2]

Year	Jan.	Feb.	Mar.	Apr.	May	June	July	Aug.	Sept.	Oct.	Nov.	Dec.	Average
1982	282.5	283.4	283.1	284.3	287.1	290.6	292.2	292.8	293.3	294.1	293.6	292.4	289.1
1983	293.1	293.2	293.4	295.5	297.1	298.1	299.3	300.3	301.8	302.6	303.1	303.5	298.4
1984	305.2	306.6	307.3	308.8	309.7	310.7	311.7	313.0	314.5	315.3	315.3	315.5	311.1
1985[2]	105.5	106.0	106.4	106.9	107.3	107.6	107.8	108.0	108.3	108.7	109.0	109.3	107.6
1986	109.6	109.3	108.8	108.6	108.9	109.5	109.5	109.7	110.2	110.3	110.4	110.5	109.6
1987	111.2	111.6	112.1	112.7	113.1	113.5	113.8	114.4	115.0	115.3	115.4	115.4	113.6
1988[1]	115.7	116.0	116.5	117.1	117.5	118.0	118.5	119.0	119.8	120.2	120.3		

[1] Preliminary.   [2] Data prior to 1985 are for the 1967 = 100 index.   *Source: Bureau of Labor Statistics*   T.316

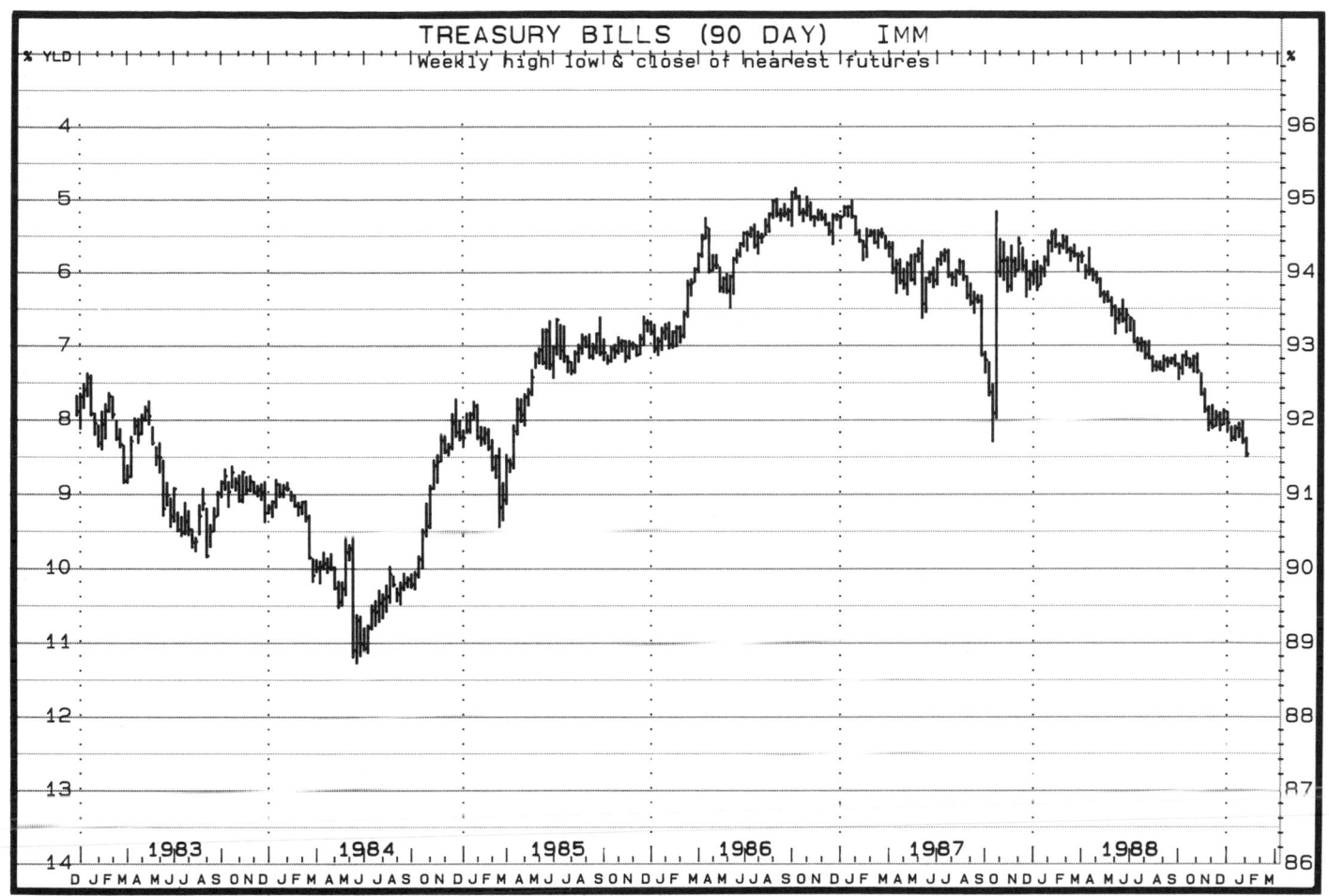

TREASURY BILLS (90 DAY) IMM
Weekly high low & close of nearest futures

Month–End Open Interest of 13 Wk.[1] Treasury Bill Futures in Chicago   In Thousands of Contracts

Year	Jan.	Feb.	Mar.	Apr.	May	June	July	Aug.	Sept.	Oct.	Nov.	Dec.
1980	30.2	25.0	28.5	28.2	24.7	25.2	22.9	23.1	21.4	24.2	39.2	42.9
1981	45.7	38.0	32.8	28.9	35.6	38.9	45.7	43.6	32.3	38.7	36.2	30.1
1982	33.9	33.0	36.5	43.9	52.5	41.4	52.2	59.6	51.1	45.8	50.1	49.0
1983	47.7	46.8	38.6	44.6	43.8	40.4	45.1	39.9	47.8	51.2	52.4	40.8
1984	48.7	50.8	48.8	55.8	52.4	47.5	43.4	44.9	36.8	47.8	45.7	40.7
1985	48.3	46.3	39.4	40.9	36.4	33.7	38.0	36.8	32.9	40.0	39.8	33.3
1986	37.9	47.6	49.2	47.6	39.9	39.0	40.7	39.6	35.0	37.0	37.6	37.6
1987	46.1	48.5	38.6	33.0	27.1	24.2	25.0	24.6	21.1	27.2	23.4	18.8
1988	23.2	23.2	22.6	28.0	22.4	20.5	23.2	21.4	20.9	26.2	27.0	26.9

[1] 90-day U.S. Treas. Bill.   *Source: International Monetary Market (Chicago)*   T.322

Volume of Trading of 13 Wk.[1] Treasury Bill Futures in Chicago   In Thousands of Contracts

Year	Jan.	Feb.	Mar.	Apr.	May	June	July	Aug.	Sept.	Oct.	Nov.	Dec.	Total
1980	237.5	245.4	290.3	350.1	321.2	250.7	224.4	204.9	231.1	274.3	287.7	401.1	3,338.8
1981	446.6	414.4	408.5	407.6	426.1	511.0	487.8	482.0	525.8	516.0	509.5	496.5	5,631.3
1982	503.5	465.5	638.7	529.1	595.4	546.0	615.2	738.4	628.6	521.4	442.4	374.7	6,598.8
1983	302.2	337.9	361.4	308.5	331.4	366.2	283.9	371.1	273.5	309.8	275.7	268.5	3,790.0
1984	200.0	213.4	304.9	300.2	489.1	342.8	315.1	242.5	201.6	203.6	264.0	215.5	3,293.0
1985	231.3	245.4	314.5	217.9	206.2	205.6	180.6	165.8	206.8	159.9	142.1	138.1	2,413.0
1986	175.0	215.4	149.5	212.8	169.7	152.9	117.8	135.7	160.8	114.2	106.3	105.1	1,815.2
1987	137.9	218.8	151.8	197.6	207.8	125.5	97.5	125.4	110.1	262.2	161.0	131.6	1,927.0
1988	103.2	111.6	129.2	125.6	163.4	105.3	84.3	117.9	97.9	101.6	129.1	104.5	1,373.6

[1] 90-day U.S. Treas. Bill.   *Source: International Monetary Market (Chicago)*   T.323

TREASURY BONDS CBOT
Weekly high low & close of nearest futures

Month–End Open Interest of Treasury Bond Futures in Chicago In Thousands of Contracts

Year	Jan.	Feb.	Mar.	Apr.	May	June	July	Aug.	Sept.	Oct.	Nov.	Dec.
1980	71.3	66.4	57.1	70.2	84.8	111.1	110.0	117.2	123.2	153.1	204.8	243.6
1981	240.7	223.6	226.1	230.4	241.3	290.9	315.1	295.4	240.5	257.7	248.7	221.7
1982	216.2	192.9	184.4	193.0	181.8	160.6	158.1	162.7	159.0	160.4	175.7	182.9
1983	177.6	142.9	147.5	142.1	130.3	144.5	165.1	142.5	150.0	172.9	193.4	183.7
1984	170.7	163.0	158.4	173.8	192.3	191.5	192.3	193.0	188.8	244.6	230.5	202.5
1985	208.3	224.2	214.1	220.2	210.8	197.6	223.1	215.8	234.5	309.1	306.3	300.6
1986	321.8	301.9	244.7	240.1	209.7	195.4	214.1	181.2	207.4	232.4	229.2	229.3
1987	283.7	253.3	235.1	327.2	238.3	255.1	290.8	320.2	352.3	366.5	296.4	262.3
1988	312.0	315.5	310.9	345.0	358.1	379.9	473.0	467.3	478.6	470.7	441.2	361.7

Source: Chicago Board of Trade   T.317

Volume of Trading of Treasury Bond Futures in Chicago In Thousands of Contracts

Year	Jan.	Feb.	Mar.	Apr.	May	June	July	Aug.	Sept.	Oct.	Nov.	Dec.	Total
1980	311.1	332.4	349.3	423.4	520.5	608.6	502.7	516.4	501.2	691.6	722.5	1,009.8	6,489.6
1981	846.7	868.6	975.9	998.9	1,178.1	1,094.4	1,081.8	1,191.5	1,313.7	1,289.1	1,691.5	1,377.9	13,908.0
1982	1,266.4	1,306.1	1,413.9	1,259.4	1,408.2	1,254.8	1,145.5	1,669.5	1,474.4	1,644.0	1,545.2	1,352.3	16,739.7
1983	1,333.9	1,447.8	1,600.4	1,262.9	1,679.2	1,704.8	1,579.0	2,312.7	1,605.7	1,839.4	1,687.0	1,497.8	19,551
1984	1,475.7	1,891.3	2,629.4	2,068.7	3,373.8	2,593.9	2,691.7	2,792.2	2,556.6	2,924.2	2,781.2	2,184.9	29,963
1985	2,974	3,250	2,906	2,272	3,339	3,755	3,308	3,409	3,149	3,558	4,118	3,965	40,448
1986	4,640	5,220	4,445	5,115	4,783	4,486	4,114	4,175	4,638	3,853	3,595	3,534	52,599
1987	4,188	4,308	4,128	7,110	6,120	5,518	4,839	6,185	7,769	7,388	4,861	4,428	66,841
1988	5,550	5,765	6,088	4,984	5,570	7,495	5,133	6,346	5,641	6,136	6,431	5,170	70,307

Source: Chicago Board of Trade   T.319

High, Low & Closing Prices of June 5-Yr. T-Notes Futures in New York   In 64ths of 100%

Year of Delivery	Year Prior to Delivery							Delivery Year						Life of Delivery Range
	June	July	Aug.	Sept.	Oct.	Nov.	Dec.	Jan.	Feb.	Mar.	Apr.	May	June	
1987 High												99–42	100–42	100–42
Low			Futures trading began May 7, 1987.									97–16	98–35	97–16
Close												99–03	100–22	—
1988 High	—	—	97–25	95–35	96–44	97–24	97–28	99–55	101–06	100–53	99–17	98–18	98–48	101–06
Low	—	—	95–37	93–17	91–02	96–04	95–42	96–48	99–42	98–62	98–01	96–28	96–58	91–02
Close	—	—	95–38	93–17	96–22	96–41	97–15	99–51	100–39	99–09	98–10	96–45	97–21	—
1989 High	—	—	95–54	96–16	97–22	97–24	96–30							
Low	—	—	94–05	94–27	96–55	95–17	95–07							
Close	—	—	94–24	96–16	97–22	96–07	95–32							

Source: N.Y. Cotton Exchange   T.326

Month–End Open Interest of 5-Yr. T-Notes Futures in New York   In Contracts

Year	Jan.	Feb.	Mar.	Apr.	May	June	July	Aug.	Sept.	Oct.	Nov.	Dec.
1987					2,559	5,508	4,883	3,903	5,312	2,250	6,618	2,590
1988	7,347	9,667	8,240	7,422	8,535	6,264	10,281	14,314	13,036	13,699	13,250	9,247

Source: N.Y. Cotton Exchange   T.325

Volume of Trading of 5-Yr. T-Notes Futures in New York   In Thousands of Contracts

Year	Jan.	Feb.	Mar.	Apr.	May	June	July	Aug.	Sept.	Oct.	Nov.	Dec.	Total
1987					30.9	43.9	38.5	52.3	73.4	59.8	45.9	37.8	383.6
1988	52.6	56.3	40.4	36.3	56.5	90.5	72.4	98.9	84.8	77.2	68.3	55.5	789.6

Source: N.Y. Cotton Exchange   T.324

High, Low & Closing Prices of June Treasury Bond Futures in Chicago   In 32nds of 100%

Year of Delivery	Year Prior to Delivery							Delivery Year						Life of Delivery Range
	June	July	Aug.	Sept.	Oct.	Nov.	Dec.	Jan.	Feb.	Mar.	Apr.	May	June	
1982 High	69–29	66–23	64–30	62–04	61–09	66–24	66–14	62–16	62–26	64–08	64–27	65–05	62–18	74–20
Low	65–28	62–28	59–04	56–08	56–12	58–30	60–20	58–05	57–10	60–22	61–05	62–15	59–01	56–08
Close	65–30	63–01	59–17	57–03	59–05	65–21	62–04	61–01	61–14	61–30	63–06	62–27	59–24	—
1983 High	63–30	65–06	69–29	71–05	77–04	77–20	76–24	77–04	77–13	78–08	79–02	80–00	76–29	80–00
Low	60–29	61–27	63–18	67–17	70–09	73–18	73–21	72–14	71–27	74–28	75–31	74–20	73–24	57–28
Close	62–19	64–01	67–20	70–27	75–11	73–28	76–00	72–21	76–22	75–31	78–30	74–21	73–27	—
1984 High	74–29	73–05	71–12	72–02	75–15	70–31	70–20	71–06	70–26	68–22	67–00	64–31	63–21	77–28
Low	72–00	67–26	66–28	68–09	69–18	68–23	68–05	68–30	67–22	65–22	64–17	59–16	60–11	58–28
Close	73–03	68–16	68–12	71–23	69–19	70–17	69–15	70–07	68–07	66–07	64–22	60–05	61–19	—
1985 High	61–16	63–10	65–04	67–20	70–03	72–05	72–00	73–07	70–14	69–24	72–17	77–14	80–11	80–11
Low	58–05	58–00	62–29	63–12	65–19	68–10	69–15	69–09	66–10	67–08	68–23	70–21	77–13	56–25
Close	58–07	63–01	64–06	66–05	69–14	70–10	70–11	72–03	66–15	69–23	70–24	77–11	79–18	—
1986 High	76–07	76–00	75–05	74–29	76–17	79–25	84–25	85–10	96–01	102–12	105–15	101–11	98–01	105–15
Low	72–10	71–09	71–19	71–26	72–04	75–15	78–04	80–20	82–26	92–06	97–29	93–19	90–22	56–29
Close	74–05	72–09	74–02	73–14	76–01	79–15	84–08	84–03	94–00	102–10	100–24	93–28	96–13	—
1987 High	97–10	99–07	100–03	99–23	96–24	98–24	99–30	101–02	100–25	101–19	98–16	93–19	94–07	102–05
Low	88–12	92–16	93–01	90–04	91–21	93–24	96–24	97–09	97–03	97–13	88–13	87–04	89–05	63–12
Close	97–06	95–10	99–29	94–21	96–06	97–25	97–06	98–25	100–14	98–15	93–02	92–02	93–08	—
1988 High	90–29	90–05	88–17	84–30	87–05	88–25	88–09	93–00	94–17	94–11	91–04	88–06	90–22	99–12
Low	85–29	86–12	84–02	79–19	75–00	84–19	82–16	85–09	91–14	89–14	87–17	85–03	86–05	66–16
Close	88–27	86–22	84–25	80–02	85–25	85–28	86–30	92–30	93–20	90–02	87–29	85–26	87–23	—
1989 High	87–09	86–29	85–26	88–02	90–11	90–12	89–26							
Low	83–08	83–04	82–02	84–05	87–16	86–09	86–27							
Close	86–09	84–04	84–12	87–24	90–10	87–23	88–26							

Source: Chicago Board of Trade   T.320

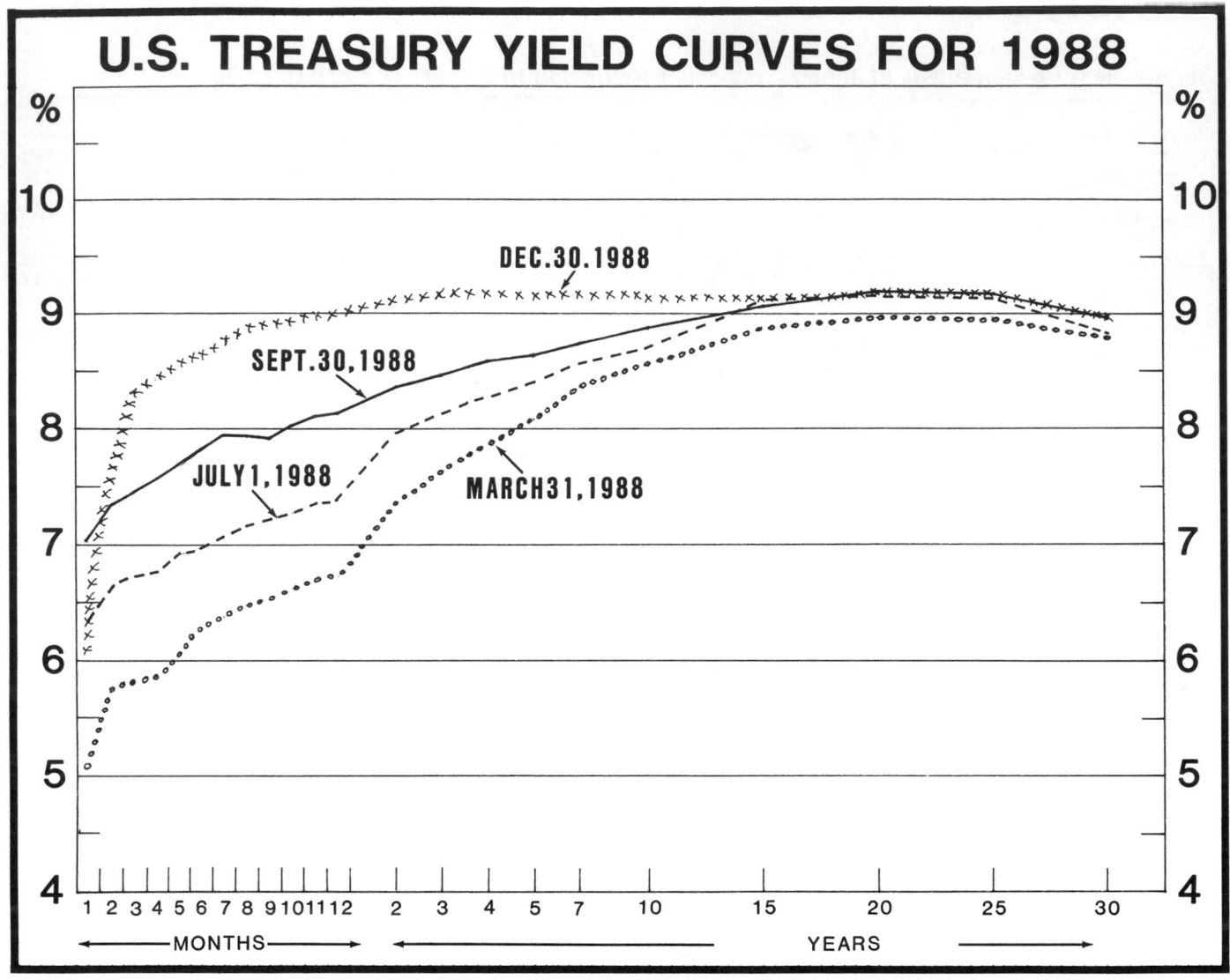

U.S. TREASURY YIELD CURVES FOR 1988

DEC.30,1988

SEPT.30,1988

JULY 1,1988

MARCH31,1988

←———MONTHS———→ ←——————————YEARS——————————→

U.S. Industrial Production Index[1] (Seasonally Adjusted) 1977 = 100

Year	Jan.	Feb.	Mar.	Apr.	May	June	July	Aug.	Sept.	Oct.	Nov.	Dec.	Average
1979	110.3	110.9	111.2	109.9	110.9	110.9	110.5	110.2	110.4	111.0	111.0	111.0	110.7
1980	111.3	111.4	111.4	109.1	106.2	105.0	104.8	106.3	107.7	108.5	110.7	111.0	108.6
1981	111.0	111.2	111.6	110.6	111.2	112.0	113.4	112.8	111.5	110.4	109.0	107.4	111.0
1982	105.4	107.0	105.8	104.5	103.6	103.0	102.5	102.0	101.3	100.5	100.6	100.5	103.1
1983	102.5	103.3	104.2	105.6	106.9	107.8	109.8	111.6	113.7	114.4	114.8	115.5	109.2
1984	118.5	119.3	119.9	120.5	121.0	121.9	122.8	123.0	122.4	122.1	122.7	122.7	121.8
1985	122.4	122.9	123.3	123.1	123.7	123.5	123.4	124.1	124.4	123.7	124.8	125.4	123.7
1986	126.4	125.5	123.9	124.7	124.3	124.1	124.8	124.9	124.5	125.3	125.7	126.8	125.1
1987[2]	126.2	127.1	127.4	127.4	128.2	129.1	130.6	131.2	131.0	132.5	133.2	133.9	129.8
1988[2]	134.4	134.4	134.7	135.4	136.1	136.5	138.0	138.5	138.6	139.3	139.9		

[1] Total Index of the Federal Reserve Index of Quantity Output.   [2] Preliminary.
Source: Federal Reserve System

T.318

High, Low & Closing Prices of June 13 Wk. Treasury Bill Futures in Chicago   In Points of 100%

| Year of Delivery | Year Prior to Delivery | | | | | | | | | Delivery Year | | | | | | Life of Delivery Range |
	Apr.	May	June	July	Aug.	Sept.	Oct.	Nov.	Dec.	Jan.	Feb.	Mar.	Apr.	May	June	
1980 High	90.91	91.55	92.59	92.50	92.30	91.65	91.41	91.22	91.01	90.50	89.05	86.40	89.94	92.73	93.97	93.97
Low	90.51	90.48	91.34	91.54	90.93	90.36	88.10	88.85	89.21	88.37	86.06	84.20	85.40	89.75	92.00	84.20
Close	90.62	91.46	92.32	91.89	91.11	91.03	89.29	90.55	90.17	88.84	86.49	85.82	89.90	92.30	92.12	—
1981 High	90.90	92.00	92.64	92.04	91.10	89.61	89.77	88.47	88.89	89.43	89.00	89.38	88.95	85.90	86.48	92.64
Low	87.51	90.60	91.15	90.65	88.45	87.66	87.47	87.08	85.40	87.31	86.36	86.64	85.52	83.35	84.34	83.35
Close	90.79	91.60	91.50	90.72	89.13	88.31	87.51	87.25	88.18	88.89	87.19	88.77	85.55	85.39	85.79	—
1982 High	89.20	87.81	88.47	87.86	87.52	87.00	87.61	89.54	89.42	87.85	87.48	88.32	88.16	88.94	88.46	91.26
Low	87.09	86.03	87.40	86.91	85.95	85.48	85.53	87.42	86.93	85.85	85.45	86.46	86.67	87.41	87.16	85.45
Close	87.10	87.73	87.92	87.21	86.08	85.60	87.55	89.19	87.76	86.90	86.92	86.83	87.88	88.57	87.18	—
1983 High	87.37	87.82	87.56	87.93	89.12	89.66	91.19	91.43	91.94	92.26	92.40	92.28	92.04	92.22	91.65	92.40
Low	86.45	87.00	86.32	86.75	87.63	87.95	89.29	90.57	90.67	91.41	91.26	91.12	91.20	91.28	91.12	85.83
Close	87.29	87.64	86.77	87.72	88.11	89.63	90.70	90.61	91.92	91.45	92.19	91.20	91.98	91.30	91.15	—
1984 High	91.23	91.47	90.60	90.44	90.06	90.51	90.66	90.57	90.47	90.82	90.78	90.48	90.18	90.36	90.37	91.47
Low	90.63	90.33	90.11	89.55	89.30	89.57	90.32	90.13	90.00	90.32	90.28	89.79	89.77	89.44	90.12	86.50
Close	91.23	90.34	90.39	89.60	89.59	90.46	90.39	90.39	90.44	90.72	90.38	89.97	89.94	90.18	90.28	—
1985 High	88.92	88.60	87.95	88.47	88.90	89.51	90.12	91.13	91.46	91.81	91.47	91.49	92.25	92.93	93.19	93.19
Low	88.46	87.16	87.14	87.17	88.28	88.53	89.09	89.45	90.69	91.14	90.78	90.39	91.26	91.98	92.95	87.14
Close	88.52	87.25	87.20	88.28	88.69	89.15	90.10	90.70	91.16	91.54	90.80	91.41	92.01	92.91	93.09	—
1986 High	90.64	91.68	92.24	92.41	92.17	92.32	92.59	92.91	93.30	93.18	93.53	94.07	94.71	94.20	93.74	94.71
Low	89.86	90.36	91.58	91.50	91.51	91.74	92.03	92.41	92.72	92.63	92.93	93.38	93.96	93.68	93.48	86.43
Close	90.37	91.66	91.89	91.62	91.93	92.19	92.51	92.91	93.14	93.13	93.39	94.07	94.11	93.71	93.49	—
1987 High	94.38	93.89	94.06	94.37	94.89	95.08	94.90	94.91	94.95	94.97	94.69	94.67	94.38	94.29	94.40	95.08
Low	93.55	93.17	92.94	93.91	94.22	93.46	94.50	94.55	94.62	94.58	94.18	94.20	93.68	93.66	94.13	90.41
Close	93.78	93.22	94.03	94.31	94.89	94.57	94.75	94.83	94.66	94.60	94.62	94.31	93.88	94.22	94.35	—
1988 High	94.06	93.05	93.40	93.58	93.38	92.84	94.10	93.59	93.79	94.20	94.45	94.40	94.30	93.88	93.51	94.45
Low	92.77	91.95	92.39	93.05	92.71	92.02	91.28	92.91	93.06	93.43	94.04	93.98	93.82	93.37	93.48	91.28
Close	92.98	92.70	93.29	93.11	92.82	92.07	93.04	93.58	93.70	94.18	94.35	94.19	93.87	93.47	93.49	—
1989 High	93.20	92.91	92.96	92.80	92.62	92.72	92.89	92.94	92.34							
Low	92.84	92.42	92.48	92.35	91.97	92.15	92.51	92.09	91.79							
Close	92.90	92.54	92.75	92.41	92.19	92.58	92.88	92.34	91.89							

Source: International Monetary Market (Chicago)   T.321

Volume of Trading of T-Note (10-Yr.) Futures in Chicago   In Thousands of Contracts

Year	Jan.	Feb.	Mar.	Apr.	May	June	July	Aug.	Sept.	Oct.	Nov.	Dec.	Total
1984	59.7	110.5	126.8	105.3	199.1	145.1	147.2	162.8	139.5	149.2	166.0	150.7	1,662
1985	171.8	216.0	215.9	175.8	274.9	266.9	219.4	282.9	212.7	234.3	297.5	292.5	2,860
1986	269.7	401.4	383.1	381.7	434.8	470.3	309.7	363.1	459.5	319.9	328.1	305.2	4,426
1987	304.9	358.3	347.6	643.8	541.3	405.1	269.6	446.0	512.9	662.0	369.4	392.8	5,254
1988	335.3	462.8	420.6	298.8	467.8	469.6	327.4	566.0	455.4	383.2	537.4	776.6	5,501

Source: Chicago Board of Trade   T.0565B

Volume of Trading of Eurodollar Futures in Chicago   In Thousands of Contracts

Year	Jan.	Feb.	Mar.	Apr.	May	June	July	Aug.	Sept.	Oct.	Nov.	Dec.	Total
1984	104.8	127.4	235.4	202.2	434.7	448.1	438.6	354.5	435.3	491.1	532.4	388.4	4,193
1985	524.7	723.6	877.2	764.7	753.7	891.5	798.0	697.5	769.1	694.3	695.4	710.7	8,901
1986	888.5	825.1	627.9	933.7	982.6	1,018.1	755.3	847.2	1,288.7	1,046.7	836.3	774.8	10,825
1987	1,072	1,472	1,197	2,562	1,825	1,760	1,292	1,514	2,495	2,849	1,202	1,177	20,416
1988	1,466	1,681	1,635	1,575	1,830	2,288	1,604	1,893	1,957	1,586	2,236	1,952	21,705

Source: International Monetary Market (IMM)—Chicago Mercantile Exchange   T.0564B

INTEREST RATES

Month-End Open Interest of Eurodollar Futures in Chicago   In Thousands of Contracts

Year	Jan.	Feb.	Mar.	Apr.	May	June	July	Aug.	Sept.	Oct.	Nov.	Dec.
1984	50.3	60.6	62.0	74.2	90.3	89.3	95.1	94.6	78.1	89.9	96.2	85.1
1985	105.5	105.5	98.4	110.0	130.7	116.3	128.9	131.4	122.0	144.2	165.3	121.5
1986	145.3	155.3	142.7	164.0	173.9	155.9	171.5	203.5	216.6	227.4	234.3	214.4
1987	256.6	255.6	236.0	281.5	294.7	253.0	301.9	344.2	361.0	369.7	354.3	292.3
1988	339.6	363.8	336.9	408.6	449.3	410.7	466.1	551.5	471.9	486.1	557.6	528.9

Source: International Monetary Market (IMM)—Chicago Mercantile Exchange

T.0564A

High, Low & Closing Prices of June Eurodollar Futures in Chicago   In Points of 100%

Year of Delivery		Apr.	May	June	July	Aug.	Sept.	Oct.	Nov.	Dec.	Jan.	Feb.	Mar.	Apr.	May	June	Life of Delivery Range
				Year Prior to Delivery									**Delivery Year**				
1986	High	89.44	90.47	91.15	91.16	90.98	91.14	91.55	91.93	92.34	92.19	92.55	93.04	93.69	93.42	93.02	93.69
	Low	88.34	88.93	90.38	90.17	90.25	90.40	90.83	91.40	91.59	91.53	91.76	92.39	92.95	92.81	92.82	86.73
	Close	88.94	90.46	90.79	90.31	90.72	90.97	91.46	91.82	92.14	92.02	92.39	93.03	93.25	92.93	93.00	—
1987	High	93.20	92.81	92.90	93.28	94.02	94.13	94.02	94.08	94.15	94.14	93.84	93.78	93.38	92.76	92.90	94.15
	Low	92.44	92.00	91.82	92.80	93.13	93.35	93.58	93.71	93.84	93.74	93.37	93.24	92.49	92.27	92.60	88.84
	Close	92.65	92.10	92.84	93.28	94.08	93.66	93.91	94.01	93.86	93.77	93.67	93.35	92.61	92.74	92.87	—
1988	High	92.93	91.78	92.10	92.21	92.01	91.48	93.80	92.16	92.32	92.79	93.14	93.10	92.70	92.50	92.40	93.80
	Low	91.44	90.60	91.13	90.95	91.36	90.65	89.79	91.54	91.60	92.00	92.71	92.58	92.37	92.19	92.24	89.79
	Close	91.78	91.47	91.89	91.76	91.46	90.74	91.74	92.03	92.20	92.76	93.00	92.72	92.41	92.23	92.38	—
1989	High	91.71	91.42	91.58	91.42	91.16	91.35	91.51	91.58	91.00							
	Low	91.35	90.97	91.08	90.93	90.50	90.66	91.15	90.67	90.50							
	Close	91.39	91.03	91.36	90.99	90.69	91.19	91.51	90.99	90.56							

Source: International Monetary Market (IMM)—Chicago Mercantile Exchange

T.0564

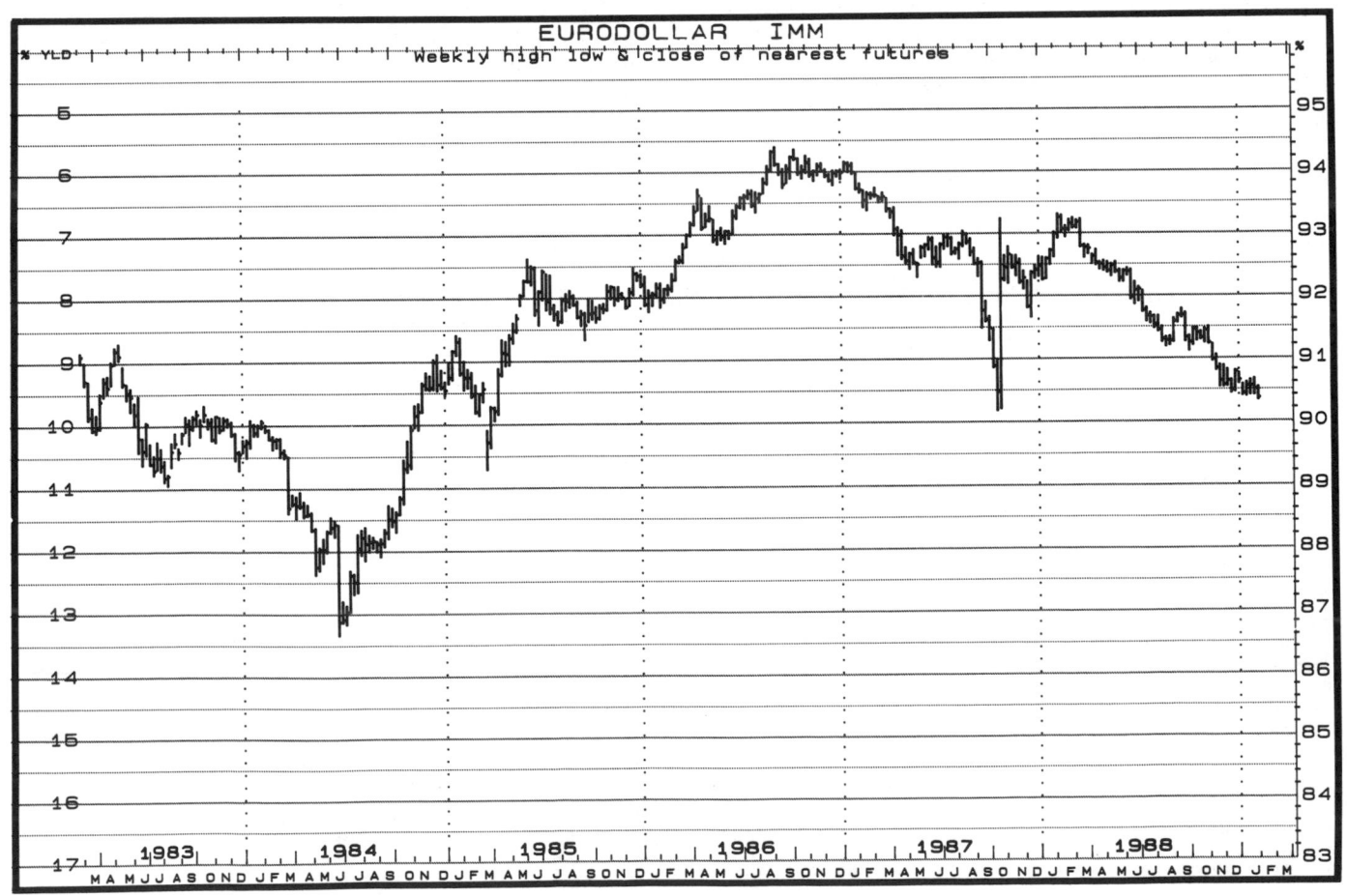

126

Month-End Open Interest of T-Note (10-Yr.) Futures in Chicago   In Thousands of Contracts

Year	Jan.	Feb.	Mar.	Apr.	May	June	July	Aug.	Sept.	Oct.	Nov.	Dec.
1985	41.4	48.7	43.9	45.1	50.7	49.4	62.1	57.7	57.2	70.5	64.5	70.5
1986	79.1	76.5	66.3	63.8	74.5	66.7	67.7	54.8	55.1	61.6	61.6	53.7
1987	57.6	50.8	56.0	66.9	64.0	65.6	72.3	78.0	79.0	82.6	73.7	76.2
1988	76.8	73.9	71.4	76.7	83.0	73.9	94.6	103.5	89.6	90.5	80.7	67.9

Source: Chicago Board of Trade

T.0565A

High, Low & Closing Prices of June T-Note Futures in Chicago   In 32nds of 100%

Year of Delivery		June	July	Aug.	Sept.	Oct.	Nov.	Dec.	Jan.	Feb.	Mar.	Apr.	May	June	Life of Delivery Range
				Year Prior to Delivery							Delivery Year				
1985	High	70–15	73–23	75–03	77–07	79–03	81–07	80–22	82–03	80–28	79–18	82–08	86–27	89–18	89–18
	Low	69–23	71–16	73–30	74–15	75–24	78–05	78–16	78–19	77–19	77–11	78–23	80–27	87–00	69–23
	Close	69–17	73–23	74–10	76–02	78–25	79–09	79–07	81–07	77–28	79–14	81–02	86–24	88–20	—
1986	High	85–17	84–29	84–24	84–15	86–10	88–19	92–17	92–21	100–03	102–26	105–08	102–13	101–02	105–08
	Low	81–15	81–00	81–14	82–18	82–31	85–23	87–22	89–05	91–00	97–05	100–18	97–12	95–19	74–30
	Close	82–30	81–27	83–27	83–26	85–28	88–11	92–02	92–07	98–15	102–24	102–08	97–23	100–06	—
1987	High	—	101–14	102–21	105–00	101–18	102–20	103–21	104–11	104–05	104–15	102–09	98–01	98–10	105–00
	Low	—	98–00	98–29	97–31	99–00	100–12	102–00	102–19	102–05	101–18	95–02	93–06	94–22	93–06
	Close	—	99–21	102–21	99–24	101–15	102–08	102–14	103–13	103–31	102–10	97–24	96–09	97–22	—
1988	High	—	—	92–25	90–23	92–17	93–14	93–10	97–04	98–04	98–09	95–31	94–00	95–15	98–09
	Low	—	—	90–29	87–19	83–30	91–04	89–25	91–24	96–05	94–27	93–20	91–15	92–10	83–30
	Close	—	—	91–00	87–19	91–24	91–23	92–26	97–03	97–23	95–13	93–29	92–02	93–00	—
1989	High	92–28	92–12	91–26	93–19	95–06	95–02	94–02							
	Low	89–31	90–15	89–24	90–30	93–17	92–05	92–03							
	Close	92–08	90–28	90–29	93–19	95–05	93–00	92–19							

Source: Chicago Board of Trade

T.0565

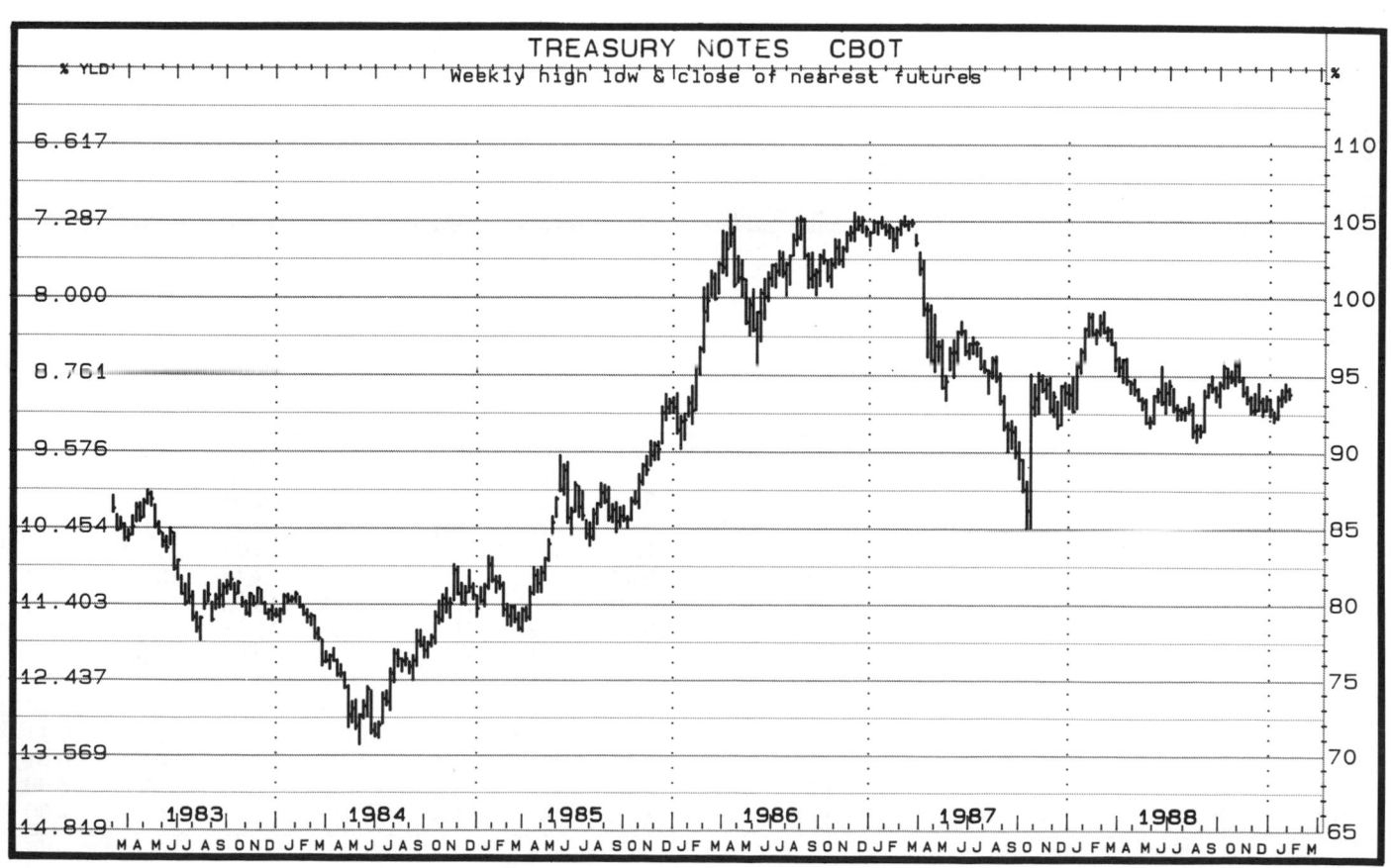

TREASURY NOTES   CBOT
Weekly high low & close of nearest futures

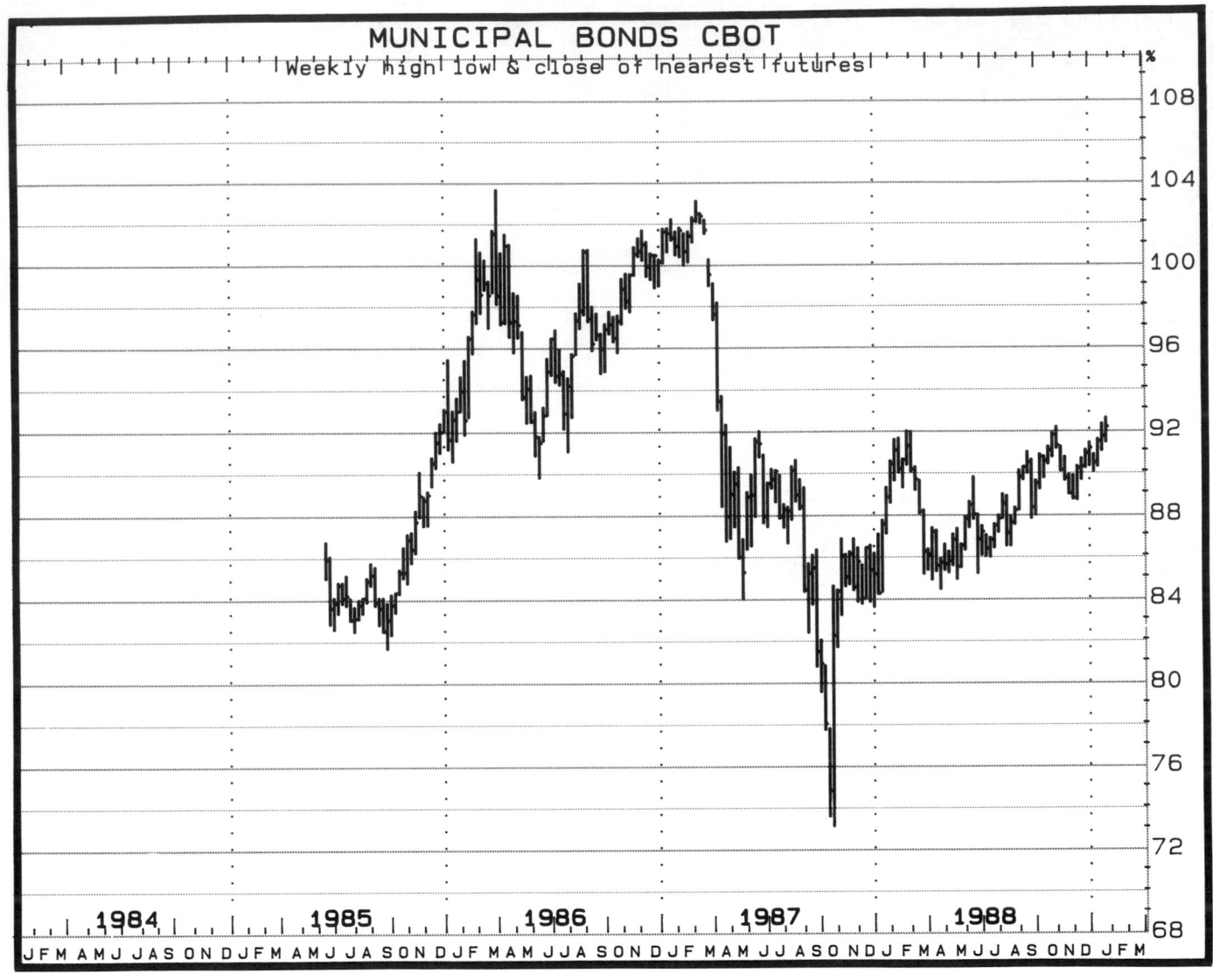

MUNICIPAL BONDS CBOT
Weekly high low & close of nearest futures

U.S. Federal Funds Rate   In Percent

Year	Jan.	Feb.	Mar.	Apr.	May	June	July	Aug.	Sept.	Oct.	Nov.	Dec.	Annual
1976	4.87	4.77	4.84	4.82	5.29	5.48	5.31	5.29	5.25	5.03	4.95	4.65	5.05
1977	4.61	4.68	4.69	4.73	5.35	5.39	5.42	5.90	6.14	6.47	6.51	6.56	5.54
1978	6.70	6.78	6.79	6.89	7.36	7.60	7.81	8.04	8.45	8.96	9.76	10.03	7.93
1979	10.07	10.06	10.09	10.01	10.24	10.29	10.47	10.94	11.43	13.77	13.18	13.78	11.19
1980	13.82	14.13	17.19	17.61	10.98	9.47	9.03	9.61	10.87	12.81	15.85	18.90	13.36
1981	19.08	15.93	14.70	15.72	18.52	19.10	19.04	17.82	15.87	15.08	13.31	12.37	16.38
1982	13.22	14.78	14.68	14.94	14.45	14.15	12.59	10.12	10.31	9.71	9.20	8.95	12.26
1983	8.68	8.51	8.77	8.80	8.63	8.98	9.37	9.56	9.45	9.48	9.34	9.47	9.09
1984	9.56	9.59	9.91	10.29	10.32	11.06	11.23	11.64	11.30	9.99	9.43	8.38	10.23
1985	8.35	8.50	8.58	8.27	7.97	7.53	7.88	7.90	7.92	7.99	8.05	8.27	7.41
1986	8.14	7.86	7.48	6.99	6.85	6.92	6.56	6.17	5.89	5.85	6.04	6.91	6.81
1987	6.43	6.10	6.13	6.37	6.85	6.73	6.58	6.73	7.22	7.29	6.69	6.77	6.66
1988	6.83	6.58	6.58	6.87	7.09	7.51	7.76	8.01	8.19	8.30	8.35	8.66	7.56

Source: U.S. Dept. of Commerce.

T.318a

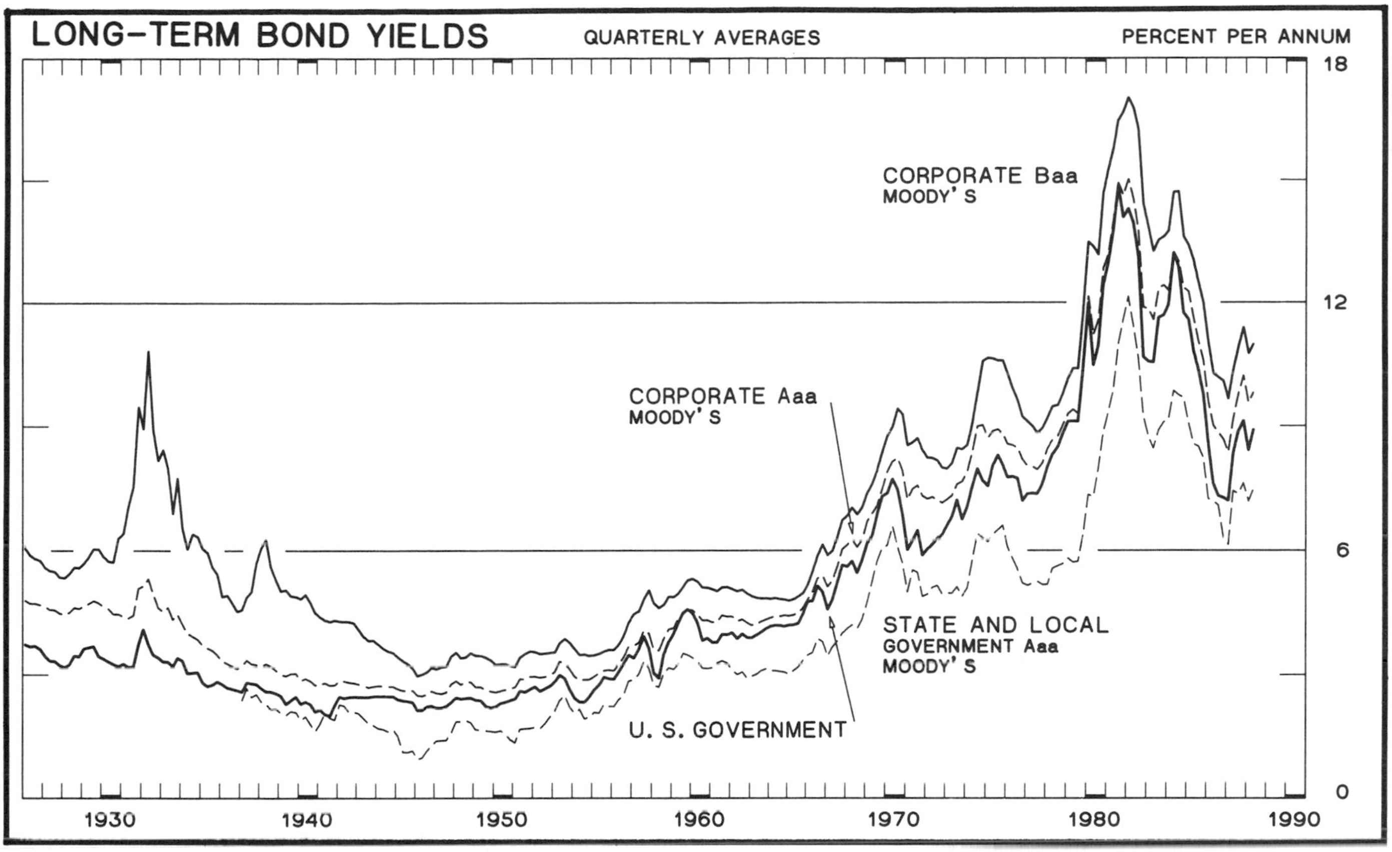

LONG—TERM BOND YIELDS   QUARTERLY AVERAGES   PERCENT PER ANNUM

CORPORATE Baa
MOODY'S

CORPORATE Aaa
MOODY'S

STATE AND LOCAL
GOVERNMENT Aaa
MOODY'S

U. S. GOVERNMENT

1930   1940   1950   1960   1970   1980   1990

18
12
6
0

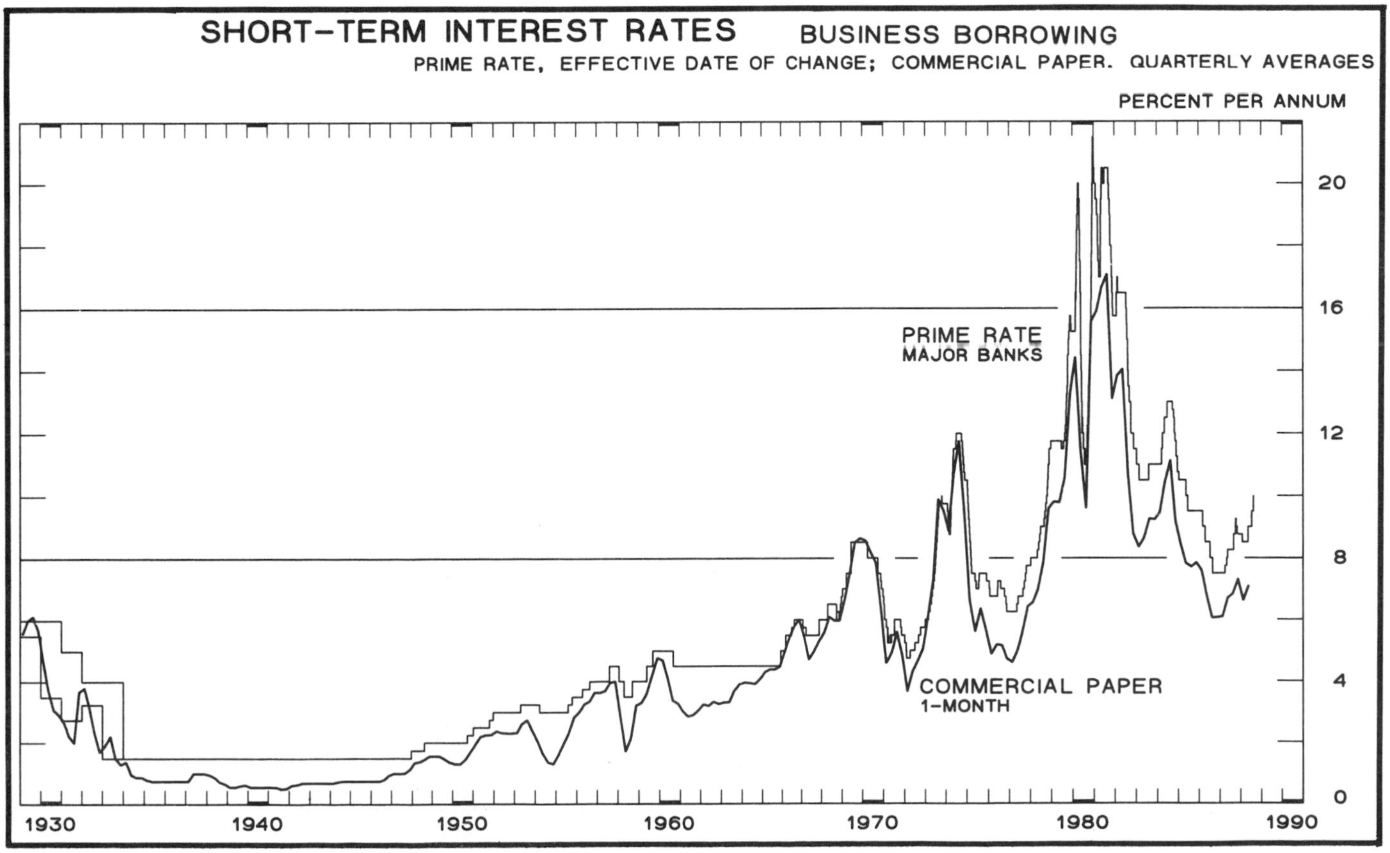

SHORT—TERM INTEREST RATES   BUSINESS BORROWING
PRIME RATE, EFFECTIVE DATE OF CHANGE; COMMERCIAL PAPER. QUARTERLY AVERAGES

PERCENT PER ANNUM

PRIME RATE
MAJOR BANKS

COMMERCIAL PAPER
1-MONTH

1930   1940   1950   1960   1970   1980   1990

20
16
12
8
4
0

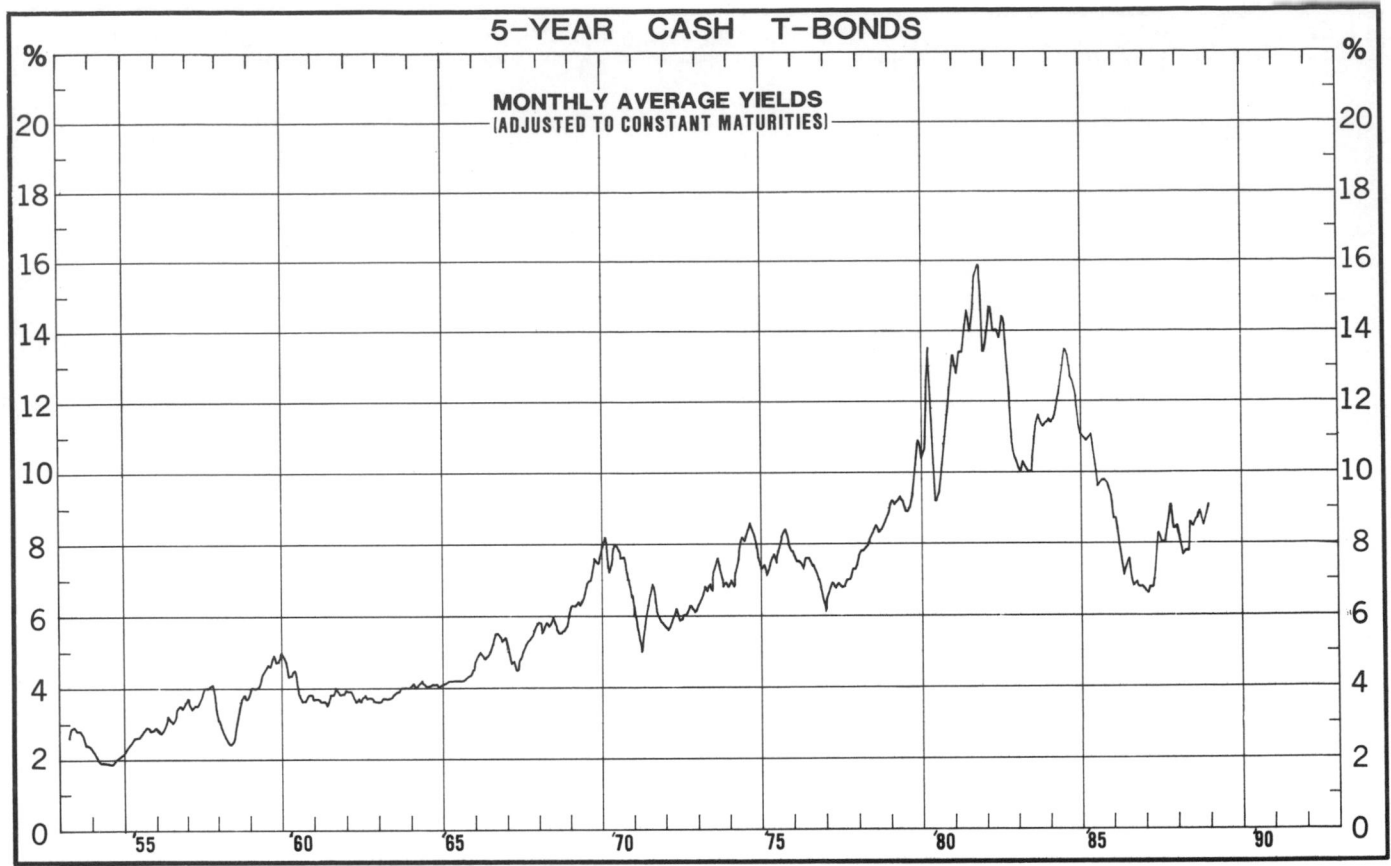

5-YEAR CASH T-BONDS
MONTHLY AVERAGE YIELDS
(ADJUSTED TO CONSTANT MATURITIES)

U.S. Money Supply M1 in 1982[2] Dollars   In Billions of Dollars

Year	Jan.	Feb.	Mar.	Apr.	May	June	July	Aug.	Sept.	Oct.	Nov.	Dec.	Average
1980	209.9	209.0	206.2	201.6	199.3	199.7	201.7	203.9	204.7	204.9	203.6	200.2	204.2
1981	200.5	200.0	200.3	202.0	199.9	198.2	197.1	196.5	194.9	194.3	194.8	196.4	197.8
1982	199.2	197.9	198.0	198.2	197.1	195.3	194.5	196.1	198.5	200.6	203.2	205.6	198.7
1983[2]	470.2	476.4	480.8	480.4	484.6	487.9	491.8	493.5	495.6	495.9	496.2	497.2	487.5
1984	496.4	497.1	498.9	498.7	499.8	502.8	501.7	500.5	502.4	499.2	501.9	505.4	500.4
1985	508.1	512.3	512.5	513.8	517.2	523.5	527.7	533.9	540.0	540.2	542.7	546.8	526.6
1986	546.8	551.3	562.1	569.4	577.7	583.2	591.5	599.0	603.5	609.0	618.0	633.0	587.0
1987[1]	633.8	631.0	630.8	637.0	636.4	631.0	630.7	630.5	629.2	634.4	629.9	627.2	631.8
1988[1]	631.8	631.3	631.0	633.8	631.8	634.9	637.1	634.6	632.5	630.8			

[1] Preliminary. [2] Data prior to 1983 are in 1972 dollars. *M1*—This measure is currency, travelers checks, plus demand deposits at commercial banks and interest-earning checkable deposits at all depository institutions. *Source: Federal Reserve System*
T.327

U.S. Money Supply M2 in 1982[2] Dollars   In Billions of Dollars

Year	Jan.	Feb.	Mar.	Apr.	May	June	July	Aug.	Sept.	Oct.	Nov.	Dec.	Average
1980	818.6	815.6	808.9	799.3	798.2	800.1	810.1	814.6	812.0	808.8	807.7	800.0	812.3
1981	787.2	786.3	788.3	793.8	790.9	788.5	784.9	786.4	784.2	787.9	792.0	798.6	789.1
1982	802.7	803.0	807.5	810.4	809.2	805.4	806.3	812.8	819.3	822.9	830.1	841.1	814.2
1983[2]	1,976	2,013	2,028	2,029	2,036	2,045	2,050	2,054	2,061	2,069	2,076	2,081	2,043
1984	2,079	2,087	2,093	2,097	2,103	2,110	2,112	2,115	2,123	2,126	2,140	2,165	2,113
1985	2,184	2,198	2,195	2,189	2,199	2,220	2,231	2,243	2,254	2,252	2,257	2,260	2,223
1986	2,262	2,278	2,308	2,334	2,351	2,361	2,384	2,399	2,409	2,424	2,435	2,450	2,366
1987[1]	2,450	2,441	2,435	2,436	2,429	2,425	2,424	2,423	2,425	2,428	2,424	2,424	2,430
1988[1]	2,436	2,449	2,455	2,462	2,463	2,467	2,464	2,459	2,453	2,445			

[1] Preliminary. [2] Data prior to 1983 are in 1972 dollars. *M2*—This measure adds to M1 overnight repurchase agreements (RP's) issued by commercial banks and certain overnight Eurodollars (those issued by Caribbean branches of member banks) held by U.S. nonbank residents, general purpose and broker/dealer money market mutual fund shares (MMMF), and savings and small-denomination time deposits.
Source: Federal Reserve System
T.328

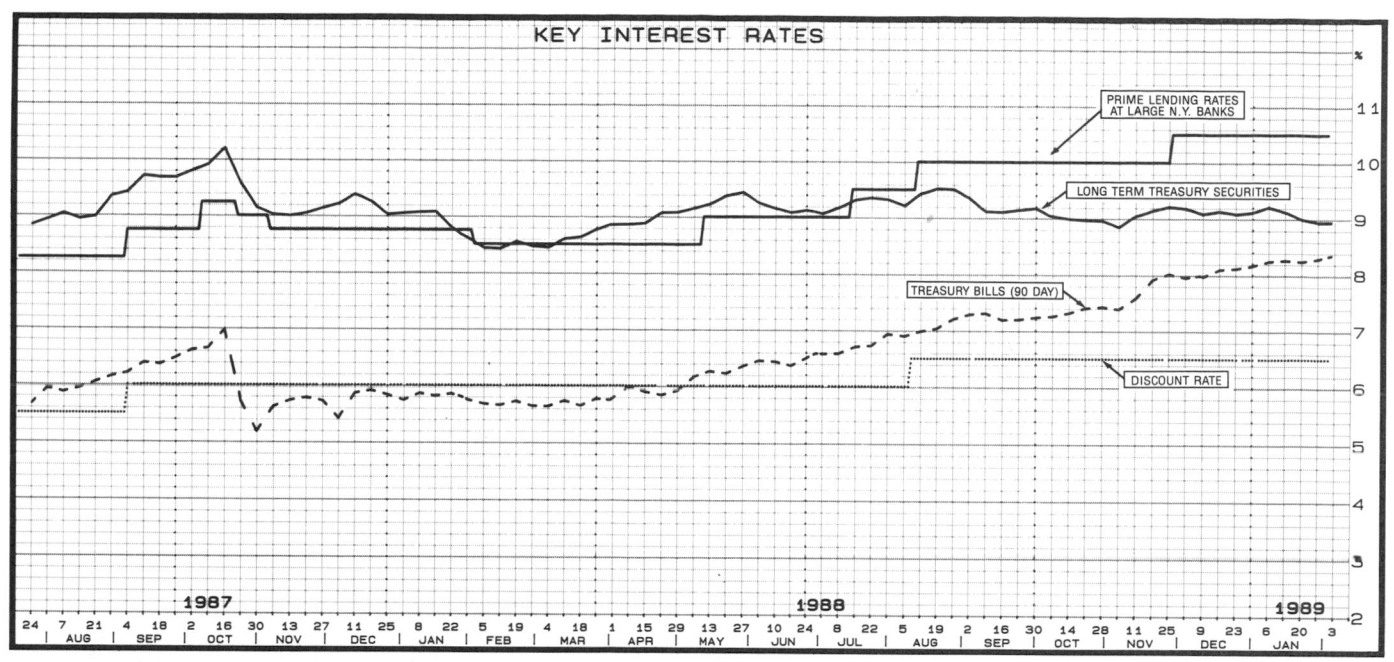

KEY INTEREST RATES

PRIME LENDING RATES AT LARGE N.Y. BANKS

LONG TERM TREASURY SECURITIES

TREASURY BILLS (90 DAY)

DISCOUNT RATE

1987　　1988　　1989

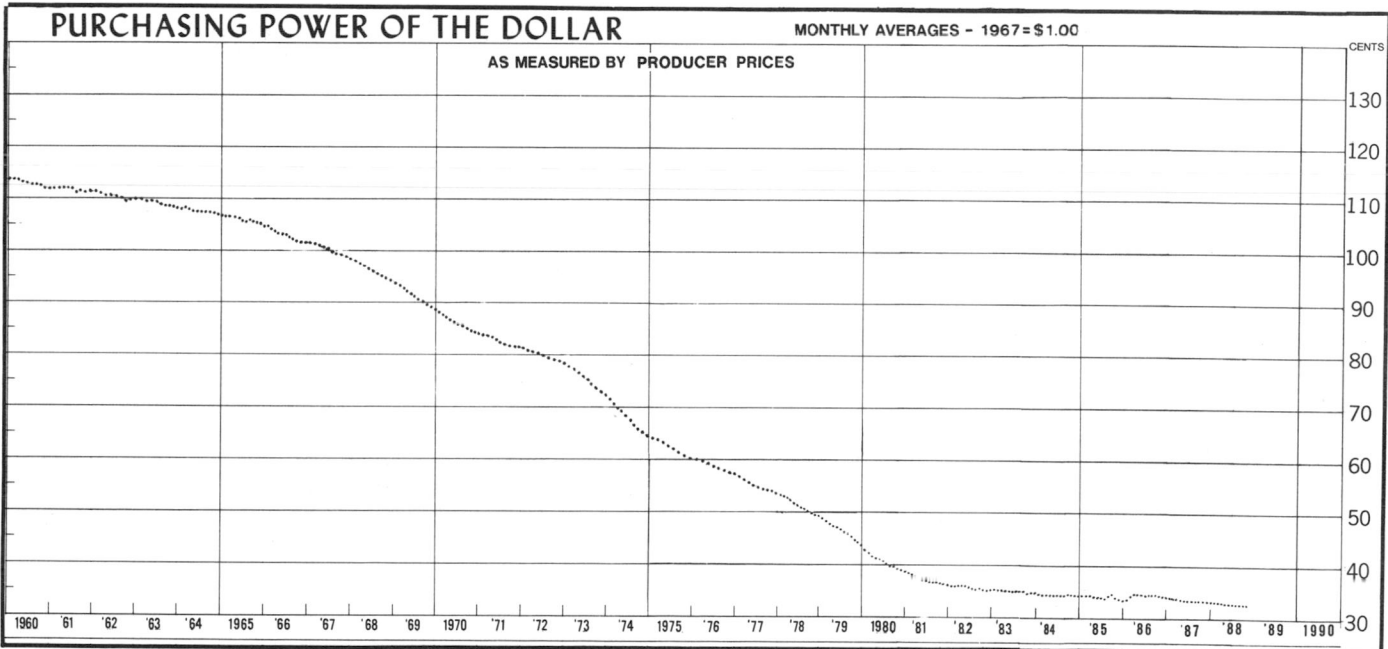

PURCHASING POWER OF THE DOLLAR   MONTHLY AVERAGES – 1967=$1.00

AS MEASURED BY PRODUCER PRICES

U.S. Gross National Product, National Income, and Personal Income   In Billions of Current Dollars[1]

Year	Gross National Product					National Income					Personal Income				
	I	II	III	IV	Annual Avg.	I	II	III	IV	Annual Avg.	I	II	III	IV	Annual Avg.
1981	2,979	3,018	3,100	3,114	3,053	2,388	2,415	2,483	2,487	2,444	2,441	2,485	2,568	2,591	2,521
1982	3,113	3,160	3,179	3,213	3,166	2,483	2,514	2,528	2,548	2,518	2,614	2,656	2,684	2,729	2,671
1983	3,266	3,367	3,444	3,546	3,406	2,599	2,686	2,742	2,852	2,720	2,753	2,813	2,847	2,942	2,839
1984	3,675	3,754	3,808	3,852	3,772	2,962	3,009	3,047	3,096	3,029	3,034	3,075	3,138	3,188	3,109
1985	3,926	3,979	4,047	4,108	4,015	3,162	3,209	3,252	3,313	3,234	3,263	3,308	3,332	3,399	3,325
1986[2]	4,180	4,208	4,268	4,305	4,240	3,379	3,422	3,451	3,497	3,437	3,461	3,517	3,547	3,600	3,531
1987[2]	4,392	4,484	4,568	4,663	4,527	3,573	3,632	3,708	3,802	3,679	3,676	3,736	3,801	3,907	3,780
1988[2]	4,725	4,824	4,909			3,851	3,929	3,996			3,951	4,022	4,092		

[1] Seasonally adjusted at annual rates.   [2] Preliminary.   [3] Forecast.   *Source: U.S. Dept. of Commerce*

T.329

Iron and Steel

The U.S. steel industry enjoyed a continued surge of prosperity in 1988, as earlier investments in more efficient production facilities fulfilled their promise. A good export pace for manufactured products and better-than-expected business and consumer spending combined to help steel demand in 1988.

Domestic raw steel production for January-June 1988 was 50.37 million tons, up 20 percent from the same 1987 period's 41.93 million tons. The share of total production from the electric arc furnace (EAF) process for the first six months of 1988 was 36 percent of the total, compared with 1987's 39 percent.

Through June 1988, continuous cast steel production was 60 percent of total raw steel production, the same as 1987's. Higher demand showed itself in increased capacity utilization. For the first six months, capacity utilization was estimated at 90 percent, up from 1987's same period figure of 75 percent, according to the U.S. Bureau of Mines.

According to analysts, the U.S. steel industry's international competitiveness has improved sharply in recent years. High rates of employment, efficient productivity (as measured in man-hours per ton), and low costs per ton shipped have put U.S. steelmakers in the forefront of the world's producers.

Although U.S. labor costs were estimated at $23.96 an hour, which are among the world's highest, these costs have been contained since 1984. In Japan, hourly rates were up to $24.50 an hour in 1988, while W. Germany's hourly wage was $22.48, Great Britain's $14.37, and France's $19.79.

Improved demand for pig iron, brought on by the resumption of production at strike-plagued USX Inc. in early 1987, gave the U.S. iron ore industry a needed shot in the arm. The U.S. Bureau of Mines reported that for the first six months of 1988 iron mine production was up 31 percent, and mine shipments gained 46 percent. Shipments from loading docks gained 29 percent, according to the Bureau. Imports rose 23 percent, and consumption put in a strong showing, gaining 22 percent in the period.

Total pig iron production in the first half of 1988 was 25.1 million tons, the largest semi-annual tonnage since 1984. In 1988, there were fifty blast furnaces in operation, a level which stayed steady throughout the entire year.

End-use distribution for domestic iron and steel consumption in recent years has been: construction, 30 percent; transportation, 27 percent; machinery, 18 percent; appliances, 8 percent, and other, 17 percent.

The price of No. 1 heavy melting steel scrap in Chicago was $100/ton in early 1988 and rose to $120 in July and August. At year's end, it had fallen to $111.

U.S. demand for steel was expected to soften somewhat in 1989, due to several economic factors. These included the possibility of higher interest rates, reduced construction activity, and slightly lower automotive demand.

World Production of Raw Steel (Ingots & Castings) In Millions of Short Tons

Year	Belgium	Brazil	Canada	Czechoslovakia	China	France	Italy	Japan	Rep. of Korea	Poland	Spain	South Africa	United Kingdom	United States	USSR	West Germany	World Total
1980	13.7	16.9	17.5	16.8	40.9	25.5	29.2	122.8	9.4	21.5	13.9	10.0	12.4	111.8	163.1	48.3	789.5
1981	13.6	14.6	16.3	16.8	39.2	23.4	27.3	112.1	11.9	17.3	14.2	9.9	17.2	120.8	163.6	45.9	778.9
1982	10.9	14.3	13.0	16.5	41.0	20.3	26.4	109.7	13.0	16.3	14.5	9.1	15.1	74.6	162.2	39.6	709.9
1983	11.2	16.2	14.1	16.6	44.0	19.4	23.9	107.1	13.1	17.9	14.0	7.9	16.5	84.6	168.1	39.4	730.6
1984	12.5	20.3	16.2	16.3	47.8	20.9	26.5	116.4	14.4	18.2	14.9	8.6	16.7	92.5	170.0	43.4	782.9
1985[1]	11.8	22.5	16.0	16.6	51.5	20.8	26.2	116.1	14.9	17.7	15.7	9.5	17.3	88.3	170.5	44.6	790.0
1986[2]	10.7	23.4	15.3	16.5	57.4	19.8	25.2	108.3	14.9	18.9	13.2	9.7	16.3	81.6	177.0	40.9	781.0
1987[2]					63			109						87	182		803

[1] Preliminary. [2] Estimate. *Source: Bureau of Mines* T.330

Average Wholesale Prices of Iron and Steel in the U.S. In Dollars Per Net Ton

Year	Pig Iron Bessemer Neville Isl., Pa.	Pig Iron Iron Age Composite	No. 2 F.O.B. Birmingham	Steel Billets Pitts.	No. 1 Heavy Melting Steel Scrap Pitts.	No. 1 Heavy Melting Steel Scrap Chicago	Tin Plate (¼ Lb.)	Hot Rolled Sheet[2]	Steel Bars Hot Rolled	Steel Bars Cold Finished	Hot Rolled Strip	Carbon Steel Plates	Cold Rolled Strip	Galvanized Sheets	Wire Rods-Chi. $Gr. Ton
1980	200.83	203.00	191.00	348.70	95.48	86.70	23.3–24.9	18.21	19.59	28.95	18.21	20.57	27.15	23.56	19.09
1981	209.67	204.66	205.33	358.00	100.57	91.76	24.9–26.7	20.13	16.95	29.45	20.13	23.04	30.23	26.05	20.27
1982	213.00	213.00	213.00	358.00	66.47	57.78	26.3–27.9	20.80	17.23	31.06	20.80	24.25	29.75	26.90	20.48
1983	213.00	213.00	213.00	358.00	76.99	72.42	27.7–29.3	22.16	20.25	28.50	22.39	25.45	33.45	28.23	20.48
1984	213.00	213.00	213.00	368.00	92.71	83.12	29.0–30.7	23.60	22.08	29.87	23.60	24.50	35.30	30.15	20.48
1985	213.00	213.00	213.00	378.00	77.43	72.89	30.7–31.9	23.60	24.10	32.00	23.49	24.50	37.24	30.15	20.48
1986	—	213.00	—	378.00	74.87	73.49	N.A.	21.15	24.10	32.00	23.30	18.27	37.24	27.89	20.48
1987[1]		213.00		378.00	90.58	87.22		21.92	17.12	21.23	22.50	19.29	37.24	29.97	20.48
1988[1]					113.78	113.47									

[1] Preliminary. [2] 10 gauge. *Source: American Metal Market* T.337

Salient Statistics of Steel in the United States   In Millions of Short Tons

Year	Value of (Million $) Exports	Value of (Million $) Imports	Finished Steel Composite Price ¢ Lb.	Production — Steel Ingots and Castings Basic Oxygen	Open Hearth	Electric[3]	Total	Alloy Steel[2] Stainless	Other	Total	Shipments of Steel Products Domestic Consumption	Export
1980	3,728	7,792		67.6	13.1	31.2	111.8	1.7	15.4	17.1	83.9	2.6
1981	3,649	11,286	24.22	73.2	13.5	34.1	120.8	1.7	17.6	19.3	88.5	1.8
1982	2,734	10,394	25.27	45.3	6.1	23.2	74.6	1.2	9.2	10.4	61.6	.8
1983	1,783	7,238	26.19	52.1	6.0	26.6	84.6	1.8	9.1	10.9	67.6	.5
1984	1,627	11,495	27.31	52.8	8.3	31.4	92.5	1.8	10.8	12.6	73.7	.4
1985	1,476	11,019	27.58	51.9	6.4	29.9	88.3	1.7	9.9	11.6	73.0	
1986[1]	1,404	9,348	24.79	47.9	3.3	30.4	81.6	1.7	8.5	10.2	70.3	
1987[4]			25.0	55.2		33.3	89.2	2.0			76.7	

[1] Preliminary.   [2] Included under total steel production.   [3] Includes crucible steels.   [4] Estimate.
Sources: American Iron & Steel Institute; U.S. Bureau of Mines   T.331

U.S. Production of Steel Ingots, Rate of Capability Utilization[1]   In Percent

Year	Jan.	Feb.	Mar.	Apr.	May	June	July	Aug.	Sept.	Oct.	Nov.	Dec.	Average
1980	82.7	85.3	88.4	83.0	69.6	58.4	53.1	54.4	62.6	72.2	79.5	77.8	72.8
1981	79.9	83.7	88.6	87.7	86.2	81.5	77.6	77.3	75.9	68.7	62.8	58.6	78.3
1982	59.3	60.9	61.7	55.2	50.9	47.7	43.8	42.4	41.9	40.2	35.9	34.0	48.4
1983	43.4	49.0	55.5	58.9	57.9	56.5	54.3	55.1	57.8	60.2	58.7	54.7	55.4
1984	69.6	76.0	79.1	80.8	79.8	71.4	65.3	60.5	57.7	58.4	57.8	52.4	68.4
1985	60.9	66.1	72.1	71.6	68.9	66.3	62.1	63.2	63.4	65.2	64.7	59.7	66.1
1986	69.4	71.8	71.9	73.5	69.5	63.5	59.2	52.8	54.3	56.8	56.5	54.9	63.8
1987[2]	65.5	69.5	77.3	80.3	80.2	79.7	77.3	79.1	83.9	84.4	85.2	82.8	79.5
1988[2]	88.1	89.7	92.2	91.4	93.1	87.4	88.0	86.6	90.1	87.7			

[1] Based on tonnage capability to produce raw steel for a full order book.   [2] Preliminary.   Source: American Iron and Steel Institute   T.332

United States Production of Steel Ingots   In Thousands of Short Tons

Year	Jan	Feb.	Mar.	Apr.	May	June	July	Aug.	Sept.	Oct.	Nov.	Dec.	Total
1980	10,701	10,332	11,439	10,658	9,226	7,501	6,796	7,018	7,767	9,442	10,057	10,180	111,835
1981	10,590	10,028	11,744	11,243	11,423	10,451	10,160	10,120	9,618	9,003	7,962	7,672	120,828
1982	7,737	7,178	8,049	7,006	6,678	6,050	5,719	5,538	5,299	5,262	4,546	4,456	74,577
1983	5,570	5,676	7,127	7,292	7,412	6,993	6,921	7,020	7,134	7,692	7,263	6,991	83,379
1984	7,970	8,142	9,056	8,997	9,174	7,945	7,460	6,915	6,378	6,703	6,422	6,013	92,528
1985	6,984	6,851	8,269	7,872	7,830	7,292	7,010	7,130	6,924	7,351	7,051	6,728	88,259
1986	7,665	7,171	7,947	7,787	7,616	6,730	6,352	5,668	5,644	6,087	5,860	5,877	81,606
1987[1]	6,248	5,992	7,375	7,402	7,641	7,349	7,324	7,494	7,694	8,073	7,882	7,916	89,151
1988[1]	8,380	7,984	8,763	8,398	8,832	8,031	8,313	8,181	8,237	8,332			

[1] Preliminary.   Source: American Iron and Steel Institute   T.333

Shipments of Steel Products[1] by Market Classifications in the United States   In Thousands of Net Tons

Year	Appliances, Utensils & Cutlery	Automotive	Containers, Packaging & Shipping Materials	Construction Includ. Maint.	Contractors Products	Electrical Mach. & Equipment	Export	Machinery, Industrial Equip. & Tools	Oil and Gas	Rail Transportation	Steel for Converting & Processing[2]	Steel Service Center & Distributors	All Other[3]	Total Shipments
1980	1,726	12,156	5,549	12,149	3,362	2,441	2,597	4,566	5,368	3,178	3,881	16,174	10,706	83,853
1981	1,775	13,154	5,292	8,446	3,230	2,600	1,844	4,624	6,238	2,162	3,338	17,637	16,672	87,014
1982	1,337	9,288	4,470	6,283	2,287	2,003	832	2,584	2,745	1,020	3,222	13,067	12,429	61,567
1983	1,618	12,320	4,532	7,271	2,703	2,335	544	2,486	1,296	937	1,211	16,710	13,621	67,584
1984	1,635	12,554	4,337	8,614	2,563	2,363	428	2,737	1,727	1,036	4,686	17,234	13,098	73,012
1985	1,182	12,725	4,069	6,407	2,663	1,845	494	2,129	1,745	1,059	4,971	17,548	15,861	72,698
1986	1,648	11,889	4,113	7,336	3,278	2,113	495	2,076	1,023	798	5,635	17,478	12,381	70,263
1987	1,633	11,343	4,372	7,681	3,337	2,373	515	2,277	1,489	758	7,195	19,840	13,844	76,654

[1] All grades including carbon, alloy & stainless steel.   [2] Net total after deducting shipments to reporting companies for conversion or resale.   [3] Includes agricultural; bolts, nuts, rivets & screws; forgings (other than automotive); shipbuilding & marine equipment; aircraft; mining, quarrying & lumbering; other domestic & commercial equipment machinery; ordnance & other direct military; & shipments of non-reporting companies.   Source: American Iron and Steel Institute   T.334

IRON AND STEEL

Net Shipments of Steel Products in the United States

(All Grades, Including Carbon, Alloy & Stainless Steel) In Thousands of Net Tons

Year	Cold Finished Bars	Rails & Accessories	Wire & Wire Products	Tin Mill Products	Plates	Sheets & Strip[3]	Hot Rolled Bars	Pipe & Tubing	Shapes & Steel Piling	Reinforcing Bars	Hot Rolled Sheets	Cold Rolled Sheets	Semi-Finished	Alloy	Stainless
1983	1,179	884	1,359	4,308	3,816	5,793	5,129	3,242	3,622	4,275	11,619	13,781	3,861	6,154	1,137
1984	1,158	1,239	1,222	4,062	4,342	8,357	5,791	4,276	3,983	4,315	13,133	13,664	4,314	7,482	1,248
1985	1,261	888	1,136	3,772	4,313	10,543	5,526	4,096	4,843	4,444	12,952	13,574	4,350	7,432	1,251
1986	1,257	640	1,080	3,802	3,565	11,269	5,648	2,836	4,528	4,299	12,167	13,250	4,954	6,556	1,187
1987[1]	1,361	515	1,105	3,988	4,048			3,570	5,120	4,918	13,048	13,859	5,456	7,275	1,623

[1] Preliminary. [2] Excludes Hot & Cold rolled sheets & strips. Shown elsewhere. *Source: American Iron & Steel Institute*   T.335

U.S. Foreign Trade of Iron & Steel Products   In Thousands of Short Tons

	U.S. Imports of Iron & Steel Pdts.						Exports of Iron & Steel Pdts. from U.S.						
Year	Steel Mill Pdts.	Other Steel Pdts.	Iron Pdts. & Ferro-alloys	Grand Total Quantity	Mil. $	Iron & Steel Scrap	Steel Mill Pdts.	Other Steel Pdts.	Iron Pdts. & Ferro-alloys	Grand Total Quantity	Mil. $	Iron & Steel Scrap
------	------	------	------	------	------	------	------	------	------	------	------	------
1983	17,034	804	125	17,964	7,238	641	1,199	247	144	1,589	1,783	7,520
1984	26,169	1,146	173	27,488	11,495	577	977	261	174	1,413	1,627	9,498
1985[1]	24,278	1,211	218	25,707	11,019	611	930	200	136	1,266	1,476	9,950
1986[2]	20,515	1,158	210	21,884	9,348	724	924	167	106	1,197	1,404	11,704

[1] Preliminary. [2] Estimate. *Source: U.S. Bureau of Mines; American Metal Market*   T.336

World Production of Pig Iron (Excludes Ferro-Alloys)   In Millions of Short Tons

Year	Australia	Belgium	Brazil	Canada	China	Czech.	France	W. Germany	India	Italy	Japan	Romania	Poland	Un. Kingdom	USSR	United States	World Total
1983	5.6	8.8	14.3	9.4	41.2	10.4	15.3	29.3	10.0	11.4	80.4	9.0	10.7	10.4	121.0	48.8	510.2
1984	5.9	9.9	19.0	10.6	44.1	10.5	16.6	33.3	10.3	12.8	88.6	10.5	11.0	10.5	121.6	52.0	546.8
1985	6.2	9.6	20.9	10.7	48.1	10.5	17.0	34.8	10.8	12.9	88.8	10.2	10.8	11.4	120.6	50.0	555.4
1986[1]	6.5	8.9	22.4	10.2	55.0	10.5	15.5	32.0	11.6	13.1	82.3	10.3	10.9	10.1	120.6	44.3	546.8
1987[2]	6.2	9.1		10.7	55.3	10.6	14.8	31.0	12.0	12.5	80.9	10.5	11.0	13.2	125.7	48.1	556.9

[1] Preliminary. [2] Estimated. *Source: Bureau of Mines*   T.338

U.S. Pig Iron Production (Excluding Production of Ferro-Alloys)   In Thousands of Short Tons

Year	Jan.	Feb.	Mar.	Apr.	May	June	July	Aug.	Sept.	Oct.	Nov.	Dec.	Total
1983	3,192	3,264	4,206	4,333	4,376	4,960	4,213	4,245	4,159	4,317	4,119	4,084	48,706
1984	4,310	4,497	5,083	5,077	5,166	4,565	4,329	4,057	3,473	3,739	3,817	3,694	51,904
1985	3,969	3,897	4,684	4,512	4,553	4,301	4,114	4,110	3,883	4,060	3,999	3,930	50,446
1986	4,297	4,002	4,341	4,341	4,284	3,697	3,526	2,966	2,982	3,161	3,097	3,146	43,952
1987[1]	3,214	3,069	3,891	4,048	4,256	4,079	4,235	4,165	4,208	4,407	4,351	4,447	48,137
1988[1]	4,683	4,443	4,842	4,699	4,932	4,497	4,762	4,584	4,612	4,646			

[1] Preliminary. *Source: American Iron and Steel Institute*   T.341

Salient Statistics of Ferrous Scrap & Pig Iron in the U.S.   In Millions of Short Tons

	Consumption: Ferrous Scrap & Pig Iron Charged To											Stocks—Dec. 31 Ferrous Scrap & Pig Iron at Consumers'		
	Mfg. of Pig Iron & Steel Ingots & Castings			Iron Foundries & Misc. Users			Mfg. of Steel Castings (Scrap)	All Uses			Imports of Scrap[2]	Exports of Scrap[3]			
Year	Scrap	Pig Iron	Total	Scrap	Pig Iron	Total		Ferr. Scrap	Pig Iron	Grand Total			Scrap	Pig Iron	Total Stocks
------	------	------	------	------	------	------	------	------	------	------	------	------	------	------	------
1983	49.0	49.0	98.0	11.4	1.0	12.4	1.5	61.8	50.1	111.9	.6	7.5	5.8	.3	6.2
1984	51.8	52.0	103.8	12.3	1.2	13.5	1.6	65.7	53.2	118.9	.6	9.5	5.3	.3	5.6
1985[1]	53.2	49.8	103.0	15.2	1.5	16.7	2.1	70.5	51.4	121.9	.6	10.0	5.1	.3	5.4
1986[4]	49.7	44.3	94.0	14.4	1.2	15.6	1.8	65.9	45.6	111.5	.7	11.7	4.3	.2	4.5
1987[4]								69.0	47.0	116.0	.8	10.5	4.4	.2	4.6

[1] Preliminary. [2] Including tinplate scrap. [3] Excluding tinplate circles, strips, cobbles, etc. [4] Estimate. *Source: Bureau of Mines*   T.342

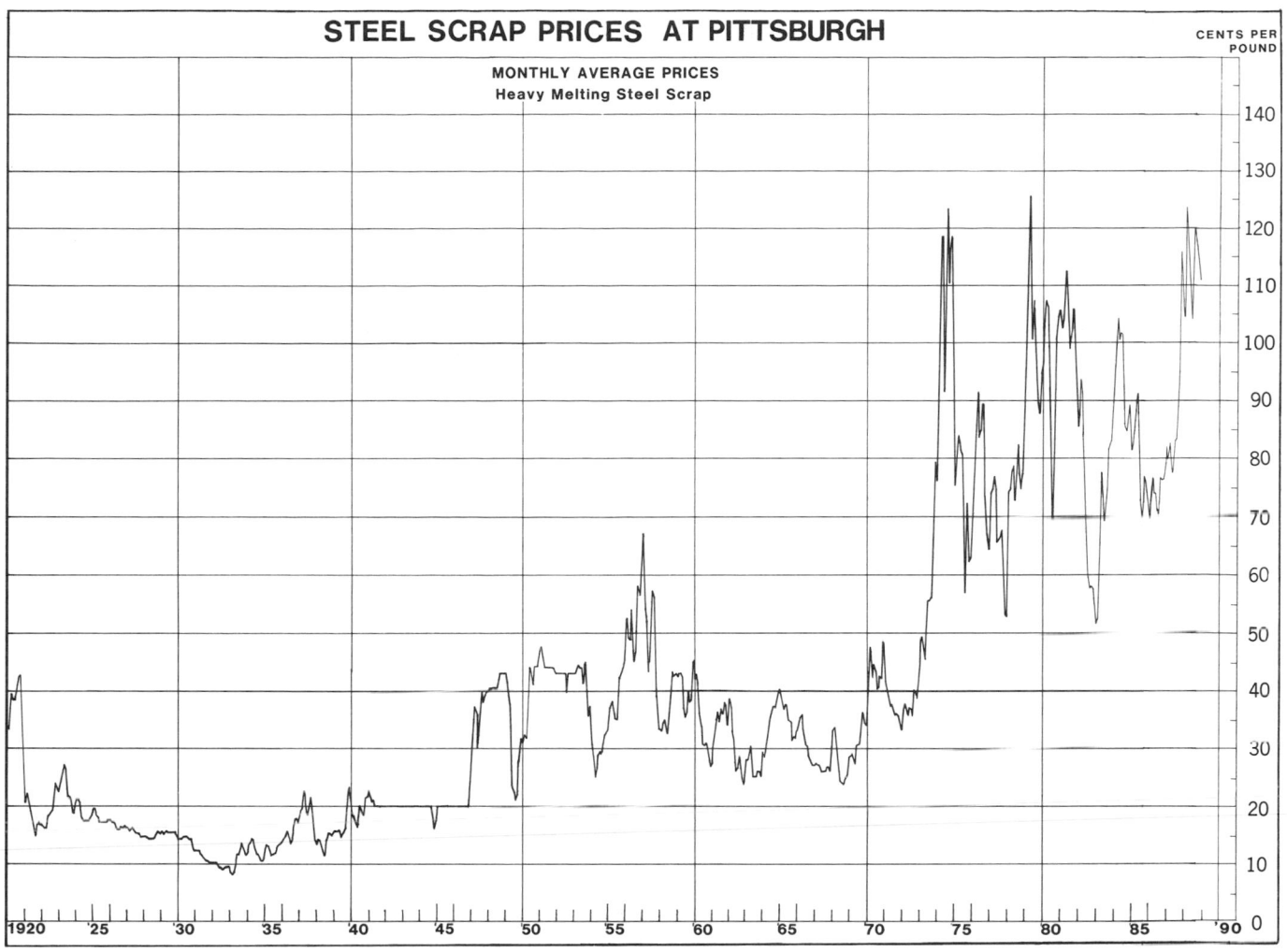

STEEL SCRAP PRICES AT PITTSBURGH

MONTHLY AVERAGE PRICES
Heavy Melting Steel Scrap

CENTS PER POUND

Consumption of Pig Iron in the U.S., by Type of Furnace or Equipment   In Thousands of Net Tons

Year	Open Hearth	Electric	Cupola	Basic Oxy. Consen.	Air & Other Furn.	Direct Casting	Total	Year	Open Hearth	Electric	Cupola	Basic Oxy. Conver.	Air & Other Furn.	Direct Castings	Total
1980	8,606	855	698	56,414	299	2,182	69,053	1984	5,720	368	469	45,551	92	1,002	53,202
1981	8,867	583	685	62,162	254	2,489	75,040	1985	4,737	503	501	44,515	56	1,100	51,411
1982	3,635	496	481	38,553	141	1,102	44,409	1986[1]	2,325	313	428	41,582	58	899	45,604
1983	3,918	341	425	44,330	91	965	50,070	1987[2]	1,180	428	366	46,995	51	780	49,800

[1] Preliminary.   [2] Estimate.   *Source: Bureau of Mines*   T.340

Wholesale Price of No. 1 Heavy Melting Steel Scrap at Chicago   In Dollars Per Gross Ton

Year	Jan.	Feb.	Mar.	Apr.	May	June	July	Aug.	Sept.	Oct.	Nov.	Dec.	Average
1979	93.00	103.00	121.73	110.10	91.91	106.62	98.62	89.96	86.00	86.22	91.00	91.28	96.69
1980	96.14	99.00	97.00	90.54	69.62	62.24	67.45	77.95	87.24	92.22	97.29	103.68	86.70
1981	95.00	91.11	105.14	107.55	97.50	88.00	88.45	97.76	92.52	82.64	75.00	74.41	91.76
1982	83.00	78.63	69.78	63.86	58.30	51.77	49.00	51.73	48.95	47.86	45.00	45.48	57.78
1983	56.14	67.00	77.70	70.33	65.00	70.52	70.08	74.00	78.00	78.00	78.30	84.00	72.42
1984	88.29	89.00	87.09	85.14	85.00	84.71	79.00	78.00	81.00	81.09	83.00	76.00	83.12
1985	78.86	82.16	84.76	79.59	68.00	62.00	64.24	73.00	72.00	71.87	69.00	69.19	72.89
1986	74.23	76.89	74.05	74.00	74.00	71.00	71.00	76.71	73.14	70.87	73.00	73.00	73.49
1987	78.00	78.00	73.00	72.00	74.15	77.00	78.73	84.00	96.52	116.00	115.47	103.73	87.22
1988	100.80	119.43	119.02	117.24	111.38	108.55	120.00	119.78	115.00	115.00	109.16	106.33	113.47

Source: American Metal Market   T.339

IRON AND STEEL

World Production of Iron Ore[3], by Specified Countries (Gross Weight)   In Millions of Long Tons

Year	Australia	South Africa	Brazil	Canada	Chile	China	France	Mauritania	India	Liberia	Spain	Sweden	Peru	United States	USSR[1]	Venezuela	World Total[1]
1978	81.8	23.1	83.6	41.1	6.7	68.9	32.9	6.8	38.2	17.7	8.4	21.1	4.8	81.6	242.5	13.3	833.3
1979	90.3	31.1	102.4	58.9	7.0	65.0	31.1	9.2	39.2	18.1	8.7	25.8	5.4	85.7	237.9	15.0	888.8
1980	94.0	25.9	112.9	48.0	8.5	67.0	28.5	8.8	41.3	17.9	9.1	26.8	5.6	69.6	240.8	15.8	877.2
1981	83.3	27.9	97.9	51.2	7.6	65.0	21.3	8.6	40.7	19.4	8.4	22.9	6.0	73.2	238.6	15.3	843.2
1982	86.3	24.2	91.7	35.0	6.4	68.0	19.1	8.1	40.3	17.9	8.2	15.9	5.7	35.4	240.6	11.0	768.6
1983	69.6	16.3	87.3	33.0	5.9	70.0	15.7	7.3	38.2	14.7	7.3	14.0	4.3	37.6	241.3	9.6	728.5
1984	92.9	24.3	110.3	40.4	7.0	74.0	14.6	9.4	40.4	14.9	7.1	17.8	4.0	51.3	243.2	12.8	821.9
1985	91.4	24.0	121.1	38.9	6.4	79.0	14.2	9.2	43.8	15.1	6.4	20.1	5.0	48.8	243.7	16.0	839.9
1986[2]	88.6	24.1	129.9	35.5	6.9	88.6	12.2	8.8	47.0	15.1	6.0	20.2	4.9	38.8	246.0	18.8	847.8
1987[1]	103.0	23.6	131.9	36.4	5.7	97.4	11.5	8.9	47.7	13.6	4.4	19.4	5.3	44.3	247.0	16.9	866.9

[1] Estimate. [2] Preliminary. [3] Iron ore, iron ore concentrates and iron ore agglomerates. *Source: Bureau of Mines*   T.344

Salient Statistics of Iron Ore[2] in the U.S.   In Millions of Long Tons

Year	Net Import Reliance % of Apparent Consumption	Production[3] Total[3]	Production Lake Superior	Production Northeast	Production Southeast	Production West	Shipments[4]	Value Mill. $ (at Mine)	Avg Value $ at Mine Per Ton	Stocks—Dec. 31 Mines	Stocks Consuming Plants	Stocks Lake Erie Docks	Imports	Exports	Consumption	Manganiferous Shipments[5]
1978	29	81.6	72.7		—8.9—		83.2	2,401.4	28.86	12.4	39.3	3.6	33.6	4.2	124.8	.3
1979	25	85.7	77.2		—8.6—		86.2	2,814.4	32.64	11.3	39.0	5.4	33.8	5.1	125.4	.2
1980	25	69.6	62.3		—7.3—		69.6	2,544.1	36.56	11.7	35.7	6.1	25.1	5.7	98.9	.2
1981	22	73.2	67.5		—5.7—		72.2	2,915.2	40.39	12.7	36.2	6.6	28.3	5.5	104.4	.2
1982	34	35.4	31.8		—3.6—		35.8	1,491.8	41.72	12.1	29.9	5.8	14.5	3.2	63.9	—
1983	37	37.6	35.6		—2.0—		44.6	1,945.0	43.61	4.1[6]	25.5	3.2	13.2	3.8	70.6	—
1984	19	51.3	49.7		—1.6—		50.9	2,247.7	44.17	5.3	24.0	2.9	17.2	5.0	72.5	.1
1985	21	48.8	47.4		—1.1—		49.4	2,076.7	42.03	6.0	21.3	2.4	15.8	5.0	70.6	—
1986[1]	33	38.8	37.6		—1.3—		41.3	1,472.5	35.63	3.3	17.2	2.0	16.7	4.5	61.1	—
1987[1]	28	46.9	46.2		—.7—		47.3			2.6	16.3	2.0	16.6	4.1	64.9	

[1] Preliminary. [2] Usable; less than 5% Mn. [3] Includes by-product ore. [4] Excludes by-product ore. [5] Iron ore; 5 to 35% Mn. [6] New classification. *Source: Bureau of Mines*   T.345

U.S. Imports (for Consumption) of Iron Ore from Principal Countries   In Thous. of Long Tons

Year	India	Venezuela	Australia	Brazil	Canada	Chile	South Africa	USSR	Liberia	Sweden	Peru	Norway	Total
1978	—	6,083	264	3,979	19,236	390	94	—	2,170	256	818	302	33,616
1979	54	4,563	183	3,095	22,602	245	106	—	2,190	171	456	44	33,776
1980	—	3,602	—	1,995	17,311	322	6	—	1,590	33	193	—	25,058
1981	—	5,071	—	1,738	18,845	342	—	—	2,160	87	77	—	28,328
1982	—	1,643	—	972	9,281	47	52	—	2,399	71	35	—	14,501
1983	—	1,333	—	1,276	8,832	—	—	—	1,732	68	—	—	13,246
1984	—	1,524	—	2,533	11,190	—	—	—	1,745	84	7	—	17,187
1985	—	2,068	—	2,540	8,557	164	—	—	2,206	65	121	—	15,771
1986[1]	—	2,309	—	3,693	8,696	93	—	—	1,487	104	91	—	16,743

[1] Preliminary. *Source: Department of Commerce*   T.346

Total[1] Iron Ore Stocks at End of Month in the U.S.   In Millions of Long Tons

Year	Jan.	Feb.	Mar.	Apr.	May	June	July	Aug.	Sept.	Oct.	Nov.	Dec.
1978	56.3	54.1	53.1	50.4	49.9	51.9	51.6	53.8	54.7	55.5	56.4	55.3
1979	53.0	50.7	47.8	46.7	46.6	48.0	51.0	51.5	52.0	54.2	55.2	55.8
1980	53.7	51.8	49.0	49.6	50.7	53.5	56.8	57.5	58.0	57.7	56.6	56.1
1981	54.5	53.2	50.8	49.8	51.4	53.7	56.4	58.8	59.6	60.4	60.1	60.2
1982	60.4	60.9	57.3	57.7	57.6	58.5	59.1	57.8	55.8	54.5	52.6	52.6
1983	45.5	42.6	39.6	37.5	37.2	37.4	37.0	35.3	35.7	34.7	33.8	32.6
1984	30.1	28.4	26.3	26.2	27.4	29.2	30.9	31.6	32.2	33.3	33.7	32.1
1985	30.4	28.9	28.1	28.0	29.0	29.8	29.6	30.7	31.2	30.6	29.9	29.4
1986	27.3	26.2	25.1	24.0	25.0	25.1	24.9	23.4	23.7	23.6	22.7	22.1
1987[2]	21.8	21.8	20.9	19.9	29.0	19.3	19.5	19.4	19.7	20.3	20.6	20.9
1988[2]	21.3	21.3	20.4	20.4	20.1	19.7						

[1] All stocks at mines, furnace yards and at U.S. docks. [2] Preliminary. *Source: American Iron Ore Association*   T.347

Lard

World lard production in 1987/88 (Oct.-Sept.) was forecast by *Oil World* at 5.17 million tonnes, up from 5.11 million the previous season. China was once again the largest producer, with an expected output of 1.26 million tonnes, down slightly from the previous season. Output in the USSR, the second largest producer of lard, was estimated at 835,000 tonnes, up from 808,000 tonnes the previous season.

World disappearance was forecast at 5.18 million tonnes, up from 5.09 million in 1986/87. The United Kingdom remained the largest importer of lard, while the USSR was expected to be the largest exporter. World ending stocks were projected to be 296,500

tonnes in 1987/88, down slightly from the year before.

U.S. production of lard was higher, due primarily to larger hog slaughter levels than the previous season. This ended seven consecutive seasonal declines in domestic lard production. Disappearance increased 6 percent and reflected higher factory usage of lard. U.S. exports during the 1987/88 season were estimated at 54,000 tonnes, up from 46,200 tonnes the previous season. Most of these exports went to Mexico.

Hog slaughter levels are expected to rise only slightly through 1989, and lard production is expected to increase only slightly.

Supply and Distribution of Lard in the United States   In Millions of Pounds

	Supply							Distribution						
	Production								Domestic Disappearance					
	Commercial							Total Disappearance	Domestic Disappearance			Direct Use as Lard		Per Capita
Year	Federally Inspected	Other	Total	Farm	Total Production	Stocks Jan. 1[2]	Total Supply	Exports			Shortening	Margarine	Civilian	Military	Lbs.
1983	952	20	972	7	979	37	1,015	89	977	888	277	30	487	1	2.1
1984	911	17	928	6	935	34	969	89	935	846	263	40	491	1	2.1
1985	906	17	923	6	929	34	963	105	931	826	289	62	425	1	1.8
1986	855	14	869	5	874	38	912	104	889	785	274		417	1	1.7
1987[1]	863	—	863	—	863	22	885	107	852	745	224		440	1	1.8

[1] Preliminary. [2] Factory & warehouse. *Source: Economic Research Service, U.S.D.A.*   T.348

Lard Exports[2] of the United States by Selected Country of Destination   In Thousands of Metric Tons

Year	Asia	Belgium & Lux.	Canada	Belize	Bolivia	Neth. Antilles	Colombia	West Germany	Haiti	Mexico	Ecuador	Netherlands	Poland	United Kingdom	Yugoslavia	Total
1982	1.1	1.0	11.4	1.4	0	.6	.1	—	2.1	24.6	—	—	0	.6	—	46.7
1983	5.4	1.0	7.3	1.5	—	.4	.1	—	1.5	19.7	—	—	—	.4	—	40.2
1984	.1	0	9.1	1.4	.1	.3	.1	—	.1	28.6	—	—	0	—	—	40.4
1985	—	0	5.6	.9	.1	.1	.1	—	3.5	35.6	—	—	—	—	—	47.4
1986[1]	.1	—	2.4	1.3	0	.1	—	—	2.0	41.6	—	—	—	0	—	47.8

[1] Preliminary. [2] Excludes exports for civilian relief & shipments by CARE. *Source: Foreign Agricultural Service, U.S.D.A.*   T.352

United States Commercial[1] Production of Lard   In Millions of Pounds

Year	Jan.	Feb.	Mar.	Apr.	May	June	July	Aug.	Sept.	Oct.	Nov.	Dec.	Total
1983	73.0	66.0	84.0	81.0	79.0	79.0	73.0	81.0	84.0	90.0	94.0	88.0	973
1984	79.0	74.0	86.0	79.0	81.0	72.0	66.0	76.0	74.0	90.0	84.0	78.0	939
1985	81.0	70.0	78.0	81.0	83.0	70.0	72.0	77.0	76.0	85.0	78.0	76.0	927
1986	80.0	68.0	76.0	81.0	76.0	67.0	67.0	66.0	71.0	80.0	69.0	75.0	876
1987	76.0	66.0	74.0	73.0	66.0	67.0	68.0	68.0	71.0	78.0	78.0	78.0	863
1988[2]	73.0	73.0	83.0	76.0	74.0	74.0	69.0	79.0	81.0	84.0			

[1] Includes "Rendered Pork Fat." [2] Preliminary. *Source: Department of Agriculture*   T.354

Consumption (edible & inedible) of Lard in the United States   In Millions of Pounds

Year	Jan.	Feb.	Mar.	Apr.	May	June	July	Aug.	Sept.	Oct.	Nov.	Dec.	Total
1983	25.4	27.2	29.3	32.2	41.9	37.1	30.1	34.4	31.7	33.8	38.9	38.3	400
1984	33.9	27.6	30.5	29.3	33.4	26.0	25.8	26.2	23.1	31.1	37.5	30.5	355
1985	34.1	29.6	30.0	30.1	31.2	29.3	27.9	30.8	36.4	44.5	43.0	33.4	400.3
1986	33.3	31.4	35.6	38.1	35.6	33.8	26.3	23.3	27.5	28.4	28.9	25.6	367.8
1987	20.2	22.1	25.9	21.3	18.5	28.0	26.8	22.3	33.0	27.4	26.3	32.4	304.2
1988[1]	25.6	27.7	31.1	29.3	28.5	27.4	25.9	28.0	37.9	40.0			

[1] Preliminary. *Source: Economic Research Service, U.S.D.A.*   T.349

LARD

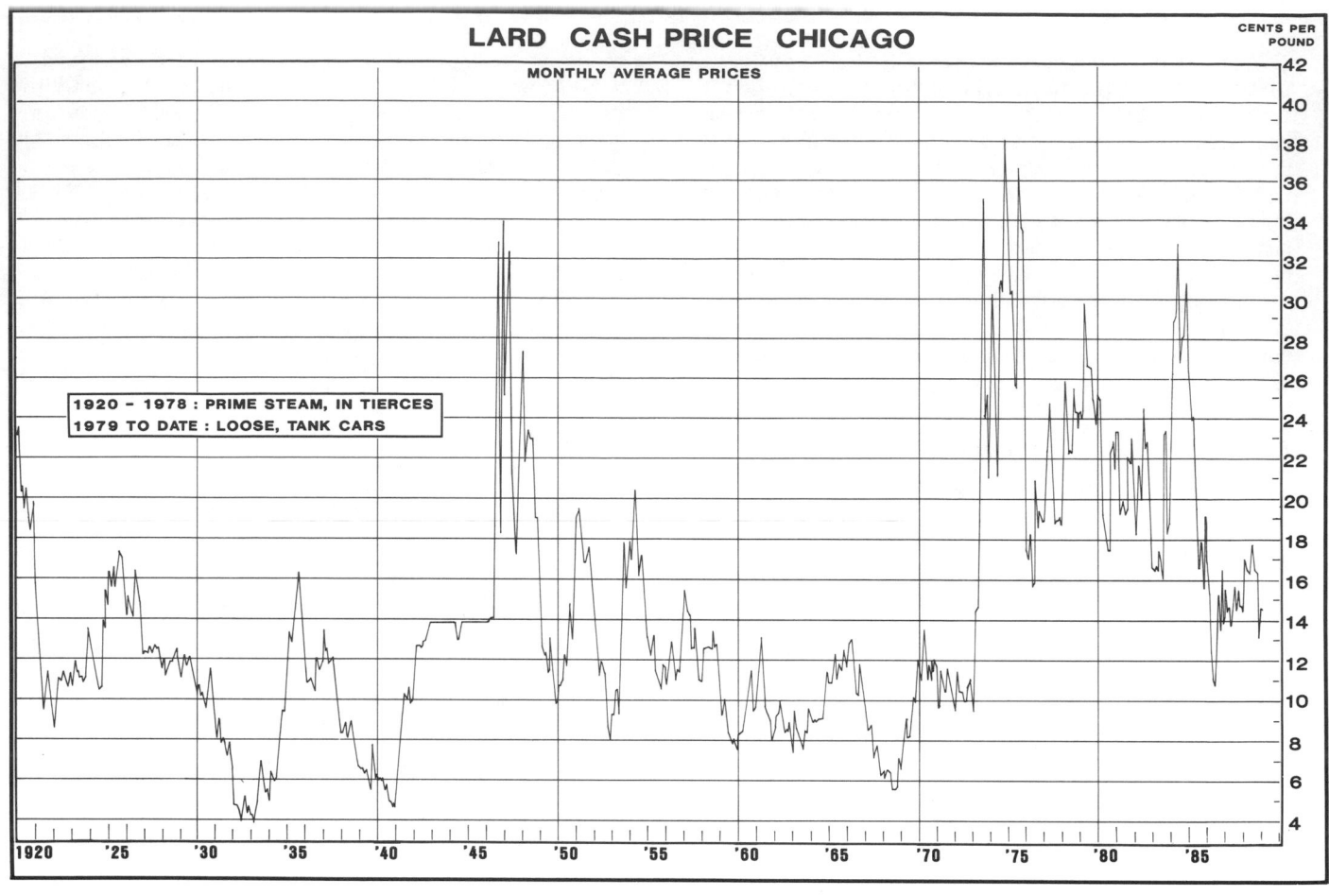

LARD CASH PRICE CHICAGO

MONTHLY AVERAGE PRICES

CENTS PER POUND

1920 – 1978 : PRIME STEAM, IN TIERCES
1979 TO DATE : LOOSE, TANK CARS

Average Wholesale Price of Lard—Loose, Tank Cars, Chicago   In Cents Per Pound

Year	Jan.	Feb.	Mar.	Apr.	May	June	July	Aug.	Sept.	Oct.	Nov.	Dec.	Average
1980	22.0	21.6	19.3	19.0	18.0	17.5	17.5	22.5	23.0	21.6	23.3	23.3	20.7
1981	20.0	19.0	19.6	19.9	19.4	19.6	22.0	21.8	22.8	21.5	21.0	18.4	20.3
1982	20.0	21.5	20.0	22.0	23.0	24.6	22.6	22.8	21.3	21.0	17.3	16.5	21.1
1983	16.4	16.7	16.4	17.4	17.1	16.4	16.1	23.2	23.4	18.3	18.7	18.8	18.2
1984	25.9	26.3	28.9	29.1	32.8	29.5	26.8	28.1	28.2	30.5	30.8	26.4	28.2
1985	24.6	24.0	24.1	22.7	20.0	18.1	16.9	17.8	15.8	15.4	19.2	16.5	19.6
1986	16.0	15.5	12.3	11.3	10.6	11.3	14.9	15.2	13.6	16.5	13.9	14.2	13.7
1987	15.5	14.4	14.6	13.7	14.7	14.9	15.7	14.5	15.5	14.7	14.7	14.4	14.8
1988	17.0	16.7	16.6	16.4	16.3	17.6	17.7	16.5	16.4	16.3	13.2	14.6	16.3

Source: Economic Research Service, U.S.D.A.; Wall St. Journal; CRB.   T.350

United States Cold Storage Holdings of all Lard[1], on First of Month   In Millions of Pounds

Year	Jan.	Feb.	Mar.	Apr.	May	June	July	Aug.	Sept.	Oct.	Nov.	Dec.
1980	49.9	54.4	61.3	62.5	57.9	51.7	59.1	57.1	55.0	43.5	44.6	48.7
1981	49.4	50.4	46.9	42.2	40.5	40.1	40.7	42.6	39.5	35.6	36.7	39.1
1982	37.0	35.3	32.5	34.0	32.7	31.8	31.4	25.5	32.2	24.2	29.5	39.0
1983	37.5	38.3	31.5	36.1	39.1	43.0	41.8	41.0	35.6	40.4	41.4	45.8
1984	34.2	34.1	28.5	29.1	31.2	38.1	34.4	32.9	33.1	29.9	37.8	33.1
1985	38.7	33.7	36.6	37.1	42.0	43.1	47.3	42.2	41.0	41.3	39.3	35.9
1986	35.4	37.6	36.4	40.8	39.8	35.5	27.3	32.1	28.3	21.6	30.6	28.9
1987	21.9	31.5	30.9	27.2	28.9	29.9	27.4	27.8	28.9	28.8	38.2	36.2
1988[2]	33.0	37.2	35.8	37.1	31.2	31.9	37.8	41.1	30.1	39.0	43.8	

[1] Stocks in factories & warehouses (except that in hands of retailers).   [2] Preliminary.   *Source: Bureau of the Census*   T.351

Lead

While demand for lead soared in 1987, pushing U.S. prices to a lofty 42 cents/lb., demand fell in 1988. Prices for the alchemist's metal retreated, and by mid-year were down to 27 cents/lb. on the London Metals Exchange. In July, LME prices were the lowest since October 1987's 27.1 cents/lb., when the spread between U.S. and LME prices reached an all-time high. That spread could widen in the future, as stringent environmental regulations in the Northern Hemisphere could cause producers to add anti-pollution measures to their costs.

In 1988, a U.S. Federal Court of Appeals decided that impounded primary lead smelter wastes must be listed as hazardous materials and treated as such under the Resource Conservation and Recovery Act (RCRA). Congressional hearings were held in the summer of 1988 on legislation passed in both houses of Congress to significantly lower the primary lead content in drinking water. The U.S. Evironmental Protection Agency (EPA) published a proposed rule to lower the allowable lead content in drinking water by 90 percent, which could have an impact on U.S. lead refiners and product manufacturers.

According to industry analysts, primary smelters have already raised their operating costs by 2.5 cents/lb. to meet these tighter environmental regulations and will have to increase them another 1.2 cents/lb. to meet new regulations.

However, lead, in its most important use, batteries of all sorts, is actually environmentally sound. Lead-acid batteries generate no fumes and can be used in enclosed spaces.

U.S battery sales were strong in the first half of 1988. However, battery production appears to have fallen sharply, following an inventory build-up in 1987. In the first seven months of 1988, consumption of lead, including oxides, for storage batteries totaled 350,547 tonnes; this was down sharply from 1987's pace, which put full-year consumption for batteries at 953,598 tonnes.

Total 1988 lead consumption was expected to fall some 40,000 tonnes from 1987's 1.23 million tonnes, according to U.S. industry analysts.

Imports for consumption lagged, as industry began to work off some of its more high-priced stock. In 1987, a grand total of 435,000 tonnes of lead was imported into the U.S., with 203,960 tonnes for domestic consumption. In the first seven months of 1988, total imports were 182,721 tonnes, with only 75,255 destined for consumption.

Futures Markets

Lead futures are traded on the London Metals Exchange (LME).

World Smelter (Primary & Secondary) Production of Lead   In Thousands of Metric Tons

Year	Aus- tralia[3]	Belgium[4]	Bul- garia	Canada[3]	China[2]	France	W. Ger- many	Japan	Mexico[3]	Peru[3]	Spain	United States	U.K.[3]	USSR	Yugo- slavia[3]	World Total
1978	356.0	76.5	120.0	245.9	160.0	151.4	305.0	293.9	215.4	74.3	122.2	1,337	253.4	620.0	140.4	5,133
1979	427.1	60.7	119.0	252.4	170.0	159.9	316.6	294.3	223.0	90.7	127.0	1,380	276.5	690.0	133.6	5,628
1980	393.9	83.9	119.0	234.6	175.0	162.5	301.4	315.6	189.0	84.9	120.7	1,224	241.4	700.0	124.7	5,397
1981	401.8	88.2	119.0	238.2	175.0	163.9	362.3	332.3	194.7	84.2	117.1	1,139	224.5	715.0	120.5	5,384
1982	428.7	80.9	118.0	238.9	175.0	140.4	350.4	311.9	179.4	73.8	131.6	1,088	209.3	730.0	109.0	5,265
1983	405.9	84.4	116.0	242.0	195.0	128.5	352.5	317.2	197.8	72.7	143.8	1,018	226.0	745.0	127.1	5,239
1984	399.8	101.5	116.0	252.0	195.0	131.4	357.2	337.1	204.8	75.2	160.0	1,029	227.4	755.0	130.0	5,439
1985[1]	398.9	75.3	116.0	239.5	195.0	145.8	356.3	351.6	234.0	86.8	156.1	1,103	215.1	765.0	150.0	5,587
1986[2]	356.5	80.0	115.0	250.0	195.0	152.5	365.9	348.0	232.0	71.3	133.0	981.1	200.0	770.0	150.0	5,413

[1] Preliminary.   [2] Estimated.   [3] Refined & bullion.   [4] Includes scrap.   *Source: Bureau of Mines*

T.355

Consumption of Lead in the United States by Products   In Thousands of Metric Tons

Year	Ammu- nition	Bear- ing Metals	Pipes, Traps & Bends[2]	Cable Cover- ing	Calking Lead	Casting Metals	Glass & Ceramic Pdt's.	Paints	Sheet Lead	Solder	Storage Battery Grids, Post, etc.	Storage Battery Oxides	Gaso- line Ad- ditives	Type- Metal	Brass and Bronze	Total Consump- tion
1978	55.8	9.5	10.5	13.9	9.9	3.6	—91.6—		12.6	68.4	412.6	466.7	178.3	10.8	16.5	1,432.7
1979	53.2	9.6	7.2	16.4	8.0	22.7	48.8	26.7	20.4	54.3	375.6	438.8	186.9	10.0	18.7	1,358.3
1980	48.7	7.8	8.6	13.4	5.7	19.0	45.4	20.7	19.8	41.4	302.2	343.1	127.9	9.0	14.0	1,070.3
1981	49.5	6.9	8.8	12.1	5.5	18.6	44.3	16.3	19.4	29.7	342.2	428.0	111.4	7.8	13.3	1,167.1
1982	44.2	6.1	8.6	15.2	4.1	25.1	34.5	13.4	15.2	28.5	312.6	391.7	119.2	2.8	11.4	1,075.4
1983	43.7	5.8	13.1	10.5	3.6	16.2	39.7	15.4	14.2	28.5	382.3	424.6	89.1	2.5	11.0	1,148.5
1984	47.8	4.7	13.7	12.3	4.0	15.8	46.1	17.4	14.7	24.4	426.3	439.2	78.9	2.2	7.0	1,207.0
1985	50.2	5.4	11.9	15.5	2.3	19.4	44.1	14.1	14.8	21.4	468.7	372.2	45.7	1.6	7.8	1,148.3
1986[1]	44.4	5.5	12.5	17.1	1.8	10.3	40.8	14.4	17.3	21.3	488.9	364.9	28.5	.3	8.4	1,124.8
1987[1]	46.8	5.3	11.5	22.0	1	16.6			17.4	19.8	—953.6—		52.3		9.9	1,230.4
1988[3]	55.0	4.5		17.0									40.0		7.0	1,350

[1] Preliminary.   [2] Building.   [3] Estimate.   *Source: Bureau of Mines*

T.358

139

LEAD

Salient Statistics of Lead in the United States   In Thousands of Metric Tons

Year	Net Import Reliance as a % of Apparent Consumption	Production of Refined Lead From — Domestic Ores[2]	Foreign Ores[2]	Total Primary	Secondary Sources	Total	Total Value of Refined Mil. $	Secondary Lead Recovered — As Refined Metal	In Antimonial Lead	In Other Alloys	Total	Total Value of Secondary Mil. $	Dec. 31 Stocks Producers' Stocks[3]	Consumers' Stocks	Avg. Price (¢ per Lb.) New York	London
1976	15	515.8	76.5	592.3	—	592.3	301.6	282.1	310.2	66.8	659.1	335.7	110.4	117.6	23.10	20.46
1977	13	486.7	62.0	548.7	.1	548.8	371.4	303.1	383.4	71.1	757.6	512.8	91.1	121.4	30.70	28.00
1978	12	501.6	63.5	565.2	1.2	566.4	419.3	282.6	409.9	76.5	769.2	570.7	98.7	125.2	33.65	29.86
1979	5	530.0	45.6	575.6	2.9	578.5	668.0	352.2	378.8	70.3	801.4	930.0	89.3	153.2	52.64	54.52
1980	5[5]	508.2	39.4	547.6	2.1	549.7	512.6	315.2	306.7	53.7	675.6	632.4	126.0	126.2	42.46	41.21
1981	1	440.2	55.1	495.3	1.7	497.1	398.9	282.2	304.4	54.6	641.1	516.3	140.2	123.2	36.53	33.30
1982	11	459.9	52.3	512.2	.7	512.8	288.4	240.5	284.4	46.4	571.3	321.7	125.5	97.2	25.54	24.66
1983	20	459.3	55.2	514.6	.6	515.2	245.9	189.6	271.6	42.3	503.5	240.7	106.7	100.8	21.68	19.27
1984	20	330.2	65.4	395.6	1.0	396.6	222.8	263.4	327.8	42.1	633.4	266.3	135.1	97.1	25.55	20.12
1985	13	416.1	71.4	487.4		488.0	204.9	273.7	299.3	42.7	615.7	258.9	128.0	93.1	19.07	17.84
1986[1]	20	344.2	22.1	366.2		400.0	178.0	280.5	290.1	44.3	614.9	298.9	87.0	83.8	22.05	18.43
1987[4]	15	311.3		373.6							695.7			88.6	35.94	26.99
1988[4]		390		400							600			65.0	37	28

[1] Preliminary.   [2] And base bullion.   [3] At primary smelters & refineries.   [4] Estimates.   [5] Net exporter.   *Source: Bureau of Mines*   T.357

U.S. Mine Production of Recoverable Lead   In Thousands of Metric Tons

Year	Arizona	California	Colorado	Idaho	Illinois	New York	Missouri	Montana	Nevada	New Mexico	Oklahoma	Utah	Virginia	Washington	Wisconsin	Total U.S.[2]
1976	.3	.1	24.3	48.7	N.A.	2.9	454.5	.1	.5	N.A.	N.A.	14.8	1.8	N.A.	N.A.	553.0
1977	.3	—	20.9	42.9	N.A.	2.5	453.8	.1	.7	N.A.	N.A.	9.7	2.0	1.1	N.A.	537.5
1978	.4	N.A.	15.2	44.8	N.A.	1.0	461.8	.1	.7	N.A.	—	2.5	1.8	N.A.	N.A.	529.7
1979	.4	N.A.	7.6	42.6	N.A.	.5	472.1	.3	—	N.A.	—	N.A.	1.6	—	N.A.	525.6
1980	.2	N.A.	10.3	38.6	N.A.	.9	497.2	.3	—	—	—	—	1.6	N.A.	—	550.4
1981	1.0	N.A.	11.4	38.4	N.A.	1.0	389.7	.2	N.A.	N.A.	—	1.7	1.6	—	—	445.5
1982	.4	N.A.	N.A.	N.A.	N.A.	1.1	474.5	.7	N.A.	N.A.	—	N.A.	—	N.A.	—	512.5
1983	.2	N.A.	N.A.	25.9	N.A.	1.3	409.3	1.2	—	.3	—	—	—	—	—	449.3
1984	N.A.	N.A.	N.A.	N.A.	N.A.	N.A.	278.3	N.A.	—	—	—	N.A.	—	—	—	322.7
1985	.6	—	N.A.	33.7	N.A.	N.A.	371.0	.8	—	N.A.	—	—	—	—	—	414.0
1986[1]	N.A.	—	N.A.	10.0	N.A.	N.A.	319.9	N.A.	—	N.A.	—	—	—	—	—	339.8
1987[1]							N.A.									311.3
1988[3]							320									370

[1] Preliminary.   [2] Includes Alaska.   [3] Estimate.   *Source: Bureau of Mines*   T.356

U.S. Foreign Trade of Lead   In Thousands of Metric Tons

Year	Exports Ore & Concentrate	Unwrought Lead[3]	Wrought Lead[4]	Scrap	Drosses, Etc.	Imports for Consumption Ores, Flue Dust or Fume & Mattes	Base Bullion	Pigs & Bars	Reclaimed Scrap, Etc.	Value Million $	General Imports From: Ore, Flue Dust & Matte Australia	Peru	Canada	Pigs & Bars Australia	Mexico	Peru	Canada
1977		4.3	4.7	77.5		88.8	7.3	230.1	3.5	196.9	16.6	6.6	16.0	19.9	71.8	30.4	75.4
1978		3.2	5.1	98.6		61.9	4.3	225.4	3.3	203.0	6.5	6.3	19.6	16.3	80.2	25.7	70.4
1979		7.4	3.3	119.7		44.4	1.7	182.6	4.0	248.3	1.9	12.4	12.8	17.3	73.6	17.9	
1980	27.6	156.5	8.0	119.7		29.6	.3	81.3	2.9	116.5	3.0	18.0	8.5	11.3	28.6	3.3	34.9
1981	33.0	16.8	6.5	59.4		27.2	.4	100.1	2.7	110.5	2.2	14.1	23.5	10.9	33.7	2.9	50.8
1982	29.1	51.0	4.6	51.8		18.9	—	94.9	4.8	69.9	7.7	14.5	4.8	7.3	23.5	8.3	49.8
1983	20.1	17.7	2.8	50.9		19.8	.1	134.4	4.2	89.9	10.0	22.7	6.1	10.9	34.9	10.1	72.7
1984	11.9	5.0	2.5	45.1	9.1	29.9	—	161.5	5.0	104.2	17.0	22.7	14.1	10.9	39.5	9.2	94.9
1985	10.0	25.4	2.0	59.9	10.0	2.6	.8	131.4	3.2	59.0	12.3	15.2	5.2	3.6	33.8	5.2	90.1
1986[1]	4.4	11.2	1.4	59.0	7.2	4.6	.1	140.2	3.3	63.9	11.5	8.4	62.9	—	29.5	1.1	105.3
1987[1]	8.8	— 10.1 —		52.8	3.5	.9	10.8	185.7	6.6		1.7	19.1	201.2	.1	42.6	.4	92.6
1988[2]	15.0	— 15.0 —		90.0	17.0	22.0	5.0	130.0	7.0		1.6	10.0	200.0		36.5		105.0

[1] Preliminary.   [2] Estimate.   [3] And lead alloys.   [4] Blocks, Pigs, etc.   *Source: Bureau of Mines*   T.359

Average Price of Pig Lead, U.S. Primary Producers (Common Corroding)[1] In Cents Per Pound

Year	Jan.	Feb.	Mar.	Apr.	May	June	July	Aug.	Sept.	Oct.	Nov.	Dec.	Average
1981	34.13	30.63	35.32	37.68	37.10	38.23	41.25	44.64	42.52	37.59	34.34	31.75	37.10
1982	29.90	28.89	27.98	26.57	26.50	25.89	27.88	27.45	26.64	23.12	21.48	20.12	26.03
1983	21.60	20.87	20.43	21.00	20.10	19.34	19.30	19.38	22.24	25.62	26.00	25.69	21.80
1984	26.38	26.00	26.45	27.00	26.55	29.00	32.14	30.13	25.68	24.04	26.42	23.11	26.91
1985	20.45	19.76	19.24	20.48	20.50	20.00	19.88	19.32	19.44	18.97	19.06	19.05	19.68
1986	18.70	18.41	18.55	18.93	19.58	22.41	22.63	22.52	23.43	25.53	27.93	28.37	22.25
1987	27.75	26.03	26.00	27.91	35.10	36.77	41.82	42.00	42.00	42.00	42.00	42.00	35.95
1988	38.00	34.83	34.00	34.00	34.67	36.59	37.00	37.04	38.81	39.58	40.75	42.04	37.28

[1] N.Y. Delivery.   *Source: American Metal Market*   T.360

Refiners Production[1] of Lead in the United States   In Thousands of Short Tons

Year	Jan.	Feb.	Mar.	Apr.	May	June	July	Aug.	Sept.	Oct.	Nov.	Dec.	Total
1981	58.0	53.6	58.2	52.7	35.0	24.4	33.0	45.1	43.7	46.1	39.4	44.0	533.2
1982	50.3	45.2	44.0	36.1	54.3	53.0	44.2	46.4	49.2	50.6	50.8	48.6	572.6
1983	57.0	50.9	52.8	48.9	47.2	42.0	39.5	45.3	41.2	50.0	50.9	46.4	572.3
1984	51.5	51.4	43.0	40.0	39.2	26.2	28.4	29.1	25.3	40.8	28.0	26.5	429.2
1985	43.1	50.3	56.3	52.7	53.4	50.9	32.5	46.6	44.9	39.3	30.1	44.5	544.5
1986	47.4	41.6	49.4	40.2	40.2	26.5	16.9	31.3	27.5	28.6	28.5	30.1	408.2
1987	38.8	33.6	36.0	33.2	34.2	29.5	28.8	30.9	33.4	37.6	39.5	36.3	411.8
1988	34.3	35.4	39.1	34.3	36.2	34.8	31.8	25.3	32.1	49.6	40.0	39.3	432.2

[1] Represents refined lead produced from domestic ores by primary smelters plus small amount of secondary material passing through these smelters. Includes GSA metal purchased for remelt.   *Source: American Bureau of Metal Statistics, Inc.*   T.362

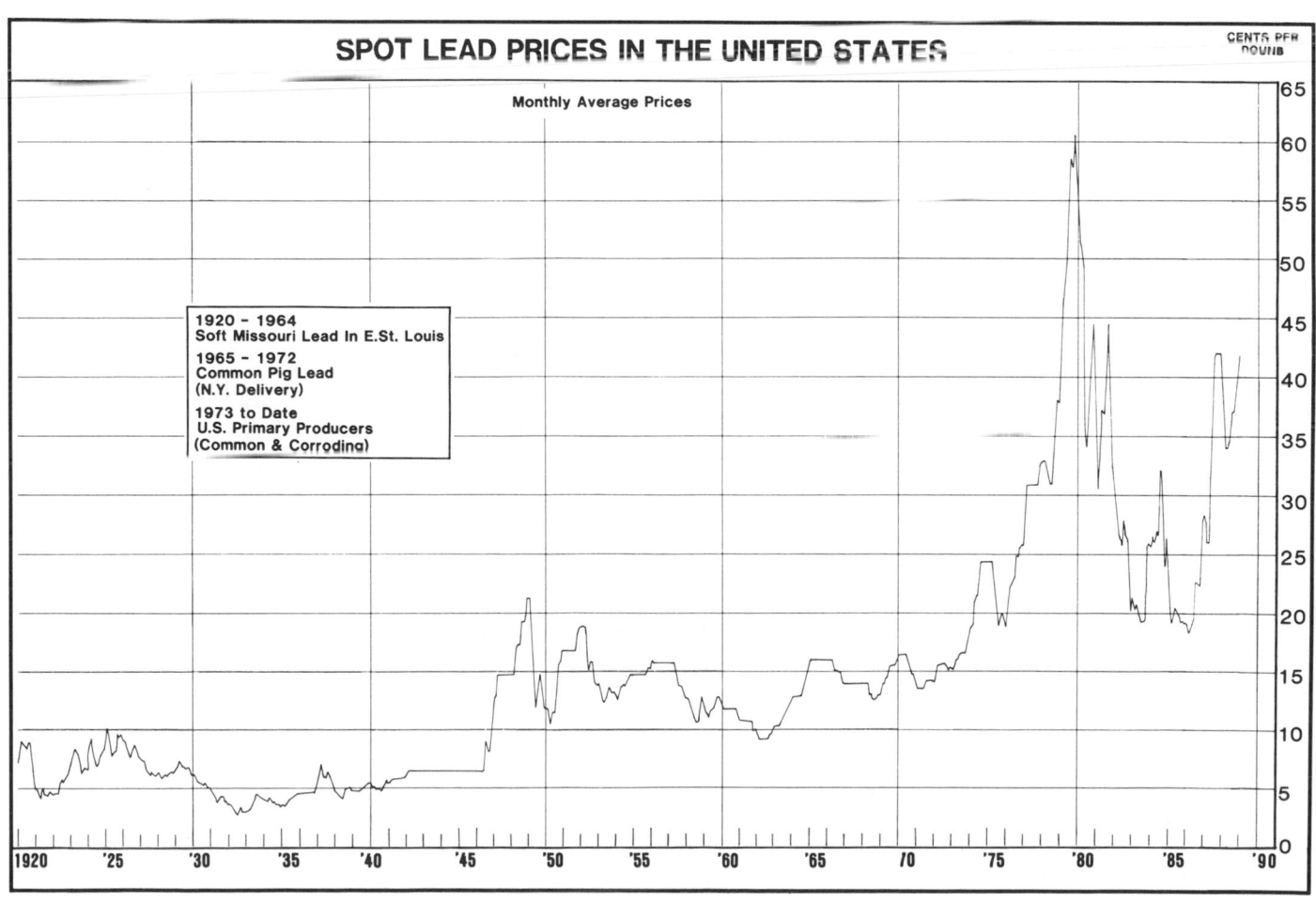

SPOT LEAD PRICES IN THE UNITED STATES

CENTS PER POUND

Monthly Average Prices

1920 – 1964
Soft Missouri Lead In E.St. Louis

1965 – 1972
Common Pig Lead
(N.Y. Delivery)

1973 to Date
U.S. Primary Producers
(Common & Corroding)

LEAD

U.S. Mine Production of Recoverable Lead   In Thousands of Metric Tons

Year	Jan.	Feb.	Mar.	Apr.	May	June	July	Aug.	Sept.	Oct.	Nov.	Dec.	Total
1981	42.6	40.9	43.4	26.7	27.8	17.4	31.8	38.2	48.0	47.5	39.8	41.3	445.5
1982	40.3	43.2	48.4	44.1	41.8	42.4	36.8	42.7	41.4	44.7	41.8	45.1	512.5
1983	44.9	39.6	37.5	36.7	35.9	28.4	35.3	43.2	37.4	37.1	38.3	34.9	449.2
1984	42.0	42.8	46.5	21.0	24.1	12.3	24.2	23.6	18.7	22.5	19.6	25.5	322.7
1985	31.8	33.3	37.6	39.3	37.1	32.5	34.5	34.8	30.9	36.9	32.5	33.0	414.0
1986	40.2	36.1	38.0	33.8	24.9	23.6	25.0	23.3	24.0	24.2	20.7	24.1	339.8
1987[1]	23.9	23.6	27.8	23.5	27.0	26.2	28.9	24.0	28.1	28.4	23.1	25.4	311.3
1988[1]	27.9	28.2	36.0	32.7	30.3	32.5	30.4	36.3	33.1				

[1] Preliminary.   *Source: Bureau of Mines*   T.359A

Total Stocks of Lead[1] in the United States at Refiners, at End of Month   In Thousands of Short Tons

Year	Jan.	Feb.	Mar.	Apr.	May	June	July	Aug.	Sept.	Oct.	Nov.	Dec.
1981	86.6	92.3	88.9	87.8	71.2	61.6	59.9	52.6	38.5	49.1	57.5	62.8
1982	65.4	67.2	65.9	60.1	65.1	73.2	70.8	64.9	71.4	72.9	78.0	79.0
1983	83.3	91.2	84.9	89.0	100.6	98.6	95.3	82.1	61.3	56.6	51.6	58.9
1984	63.3	70.3	76.1	81.5	84.2	83.5	84.9	78.4	64.8	66.2	53.0	49.7
1985	48.2	59.6	79.3	90.4	107.2	128.9	125.0	118.2	114.1	102.4	90.6	93.1
1986	96.1	104.1	116.4	115.8	116.7	105.9	89.1	81.0	57.8	41.9	30.0	22.5
1987	34.2	37.3	39.3	31.5	32.6	20.5	11.7	12.1	12.7	16.4	19.9	23.8
1988	24.7	30.5	30.2	31.8	26.5	16.6	16.2	6.6	5.1	11.6	13.1	17.0

[1] Stocks at own plant & elsewhere.   *Source: American Bureau of Metal Statistics, Inc.*   T.364

Total[1] Lead Consumption in the United States   In Thousands of Metric Tons

Year	Jan.	Feb.	Mar.	Apr.	May	June	July	Aug.	Sept.	Oct.	Nov.	Dec.	Total
1982	98.7	87.9	97.2	94.5	84.7	88.4	72.4	96.7	88.3	98.3	81.5	86.8	1,075
1983	91.5	74.0	83.1	85.9	83.8	96.3	79.3	102.6	115.7	112.3	102.7	121.4	1,149
1984	112.7	94.1	96.8	89.5	87.3	96.4	82.7	97.3	96.7	103.2	96.9	95.1	1,207
1985	87.3	101.5	100.7	90.1	86.0	77.0	67.8	101.8	100.4	106.3	90.7	82.4	1,148
1986	96.7	85.4	79.6	90.8	86.0	84.1	71.0	94.9	105.8	110.4	94.8	96.6	1,125
1987[2]	90.8	85.8	99.8	97.8	98.0	100.2	94.3	99.7	108.2	115.1	102.8	97.2	1,230
1988[2]	96.0	96.4	115.4	98.8	104.3	103.1	91.6	100.9	101.7				

[1] Represents total consumption of primary & secondary lead as metal, in chemicals, or in alloys.   [2] Preliminary.   *Source: Bureau of Mines* T.365

U.S. Lead Recovered from Scrap (Lead Content)   In Thousands of Metric Tons

Year	Jan.	Feb.	Mar.	Apr.	May	June	July	Aug.	Sept.	Oct.	Nov.	Dec.	Total
1981	46.5	43.9	43.8	42.5	44.1	46.7	46.4	49.1	52.5	50.9	52.2	48.7	641.1
1982	45.5	48.2	48.0	47.6	46.1	44.8	34.4	44.2	41.9	44.6	41.9	41.5	571.3
1983	41.3	37.4	41.0	41.3	42.5	37.3	37.2	39.6	43.4	48.9	48.4	45.7	503.5
1984	44.4	48.6	47.6	48.5	46.6	46.7	44.5	50.0	49.0	51.7	48.1	41.3	633.4
1985	41.3	43.2	46.4	43.9	44.7	34.9	41.1	45.5	50.8	53.9	54.2	43.4	594.2
1986	49.8	52.9	53.2	50.2	59.1	46.0	41.0	50.2	46.2	51.3	50.8	47.5	614.9
1987[1]	50.0	49.9	54.4	55.6	59.3	53.9	59.9	63.4	53.3	67.3	55.9	55.1	710.2
1988[1]	52.2	57.5	60.1	55.9	52.2	59.4	55.3	56.3	60.7				

[1] Preliminary.   *Source: Bureau of Mines*   T.366

Domestic Shipments[1] of Lead in the United States by Refiners   In Thousands of Short Tons

Year	Jan.	Feb.	Mar.	Apr.	May	June	July	Aug.	Sept.	Oct.	Nov.	Dec.	Total
1981	31.9	42.5	51.7	48.8	41.9	33.4	34.2	51.7	55.1	35.5	28.2	24.2	479.0
1982	39.3	35.8	37.0	30.7	40.9	37.8	41.9	48.1	42.6	46.7	39.8	39.7	480.4
1983	43.5	33.8	44.3	40.3	32.1	39.3	41.8	57.8	62.0	54.5	55.6	39.0	544.1
1984	46.6	43.8	36.6	34.6	36.4	26.7	26.9	35.5	38.5	39.1	40.8	29.6	435.2
1985	44.8	38.9	36.6	41.5	36.7	29.1	36.4	53.4	48.9	51.2	41.9	41.9	501.2
1986	44.5	33.5	37.1	40.9	39.3	37.3	33.7	39.3	50.7	44.6	40.4	37.6	478.8
1987	27.0	30.5	34.1	41.1	34.8	40.0	37.8	30.1	33.1	33.8	35.7	32.7	410.7
1988	33.5	29.5	39.2	33.0	41.4	44.7	32.0	34.7	33.7	43.0	38.5	35.5	438.7

[1] Includes GSA metal.   *Source: American Bureau of Metal Statistics, Inc.*   T.363

Lumber & Plywood

Despite an 8.2 percent drop in U.S. housing starts to 1.487 million dwelling units, the lowest since 1982, inflation-adjusted wood-products shipments were about flat in 1988 at an estimated $54.3 billion. They were expected to stay flat in 1989, in spite of forecasts of another 7 percent drop in housing starts in 1989. As in 1988, residential remodeling and repairs were expected to pick up the slack, while exports were expected to show modest growth.

U.S. loggers cut an estimated $10.7 billion of saw logs, veneer logs, pulpwood and other logs in 1988. Softwood logs, many from 1987 fire-killed timber in the Pacific Northwest, accounted for 42 percent of the industry's value of shipments. Softwood log output was estimated at 45.8 billion board feet (b.f.), down about 1 percent from 1987. A drought in the Northwest curtailed logging, as fires in Oregon and near Yellowstone National Park raised log prices and cut inventories. However, several strikes during contract negotiations in the summer had little impact on lumber prices.

Lawsuits by environmentalists, such as an injunction to block logging near northern spotted owl nests, lead to several cuts in harvest quotas in National Forests, contributing to rising stumpage fees. For the first 11 months of 1988, buyers of Western Washington and Western Oregon federal timber paid an average of $211 per 1,000 b.f. "on the stump." Since many larger, higher quality logs come from public lands, sawmills were squeezed between higher stumpage prices and generally flat cash lumber prices. Some Western mills announced closures and curtailments in late 1988; most let the volume of federal timber under contract fall, raising concerns about a shortage at some point in 1989.

The stumpage fee increases raised public appeals for the U.S. to ban, or at least allow the states to regulate, softwood log exports. However, no legislation was passed. The Reagan Administration's fiscal 1990 budget proposed Forest Service timber sales of 11.35 billion b.f. for $1.2 billion. Fiscal 1989 sales volume was estimated at 11.51 billion b.f.

Higher stumpage fees also hurt Canada, whose share of the U.S. softwood lumber market fell to under 29 percent in 1988 from nearly one-third in 1987. Under a U.S.-Canada Memorandum of Understanding, Canada had imposed a 15 percent export tax on softwood shipments to the U.S. to avoid U.S. countervailing duties. In early 1988, that tax was replaced by higher stumpage fees on government-owned timber in British Columbia, easing U.S. concerns about unfair export subsidies. Ontario's tax was cut to 8 percent after a smaller adjustment in its stumpage appraisal system. The 1988 U.S.-Canada Free Trade Treaty did not affect the Memorandum of Understanding.

In June 1988, the Occupational Health and Safety Administration proposed new sawdust abatement standards of 5 milligrams per cubic meter of air in softwood plants and 1 milligram per cubic meter in hardwood plants. In February 1989, exposure limits for most hardwood and softwood dusts of 5 milligrams per cubic meter were adopted, with a separate limit of 2.5 milligrams for Western Red Cedar. Industry estimated the cost of complying with the limit at $1.5 billion per year, including annualized initial capital investments of $4.5 billion.

The Western Wood Products Association (WWPA) estimated 1987 U.S. softwood lumber usage at 47.6 billion b.f., and demand was expected to slip to 45.3 billion in 1989. The American Plywood Association forecast that 1989 structural panel demand would fall to 26.5 billion square feet from 27.0 billion in 1988. Trade estimates for 1989 U.S. housing starts were between 1.37 million and 1.4 million dwelling units, with single-family starts at 975,000 to 1.02 million.

Between 1985 and 1988, the average size of a new one-family home grew from 1,785 square feet to 1,975 square feet. At 6.5 b.f. of lumber per square foot, the increase amounted to 1,235 b.f. per each new home. It also meant an extra 846 square feet of structural panels.

The WWPA forecast that 14.4 billion b.f. of lumber would be used in both residential and nonresidential repair and remodeling in 1989, compared with 14.86 billion b.f in 1988. Residential repair and remodeling expenditures were expected to rise about 5 percent in 1989 to $103 billion-$105 billion. However, those jobs were dependent on sales of existing homes, which were slowing as 1988 ended.

Canadian housing starts, which the Canada Mortgage and Housing Corp. said fell 9.5 percent in 1988 to 222,562 units, were projected at 200,000 units in 1989. Total North American lumber demand was privately projected to drop to about 53 billion b.f. in 1989 from 55.5 billion in 1988.

Futures Market

Random lengths lumber futures and options on those futures are traded on the Chicago Mercantile Exchange.

U.S. Housing Starts: Seasonally Adjusted Annual Rate   In Thousands   Total Is Actual Starts

Year	Jan.	Feb.	Mar.	Apr.	May	June	July	Aug.	Sep.	Oct.	Nov.	Dec.	Total
1982	843	866	931	917	1,025	902	1,166	1,046	1,144	1,173	1,372	1,303	1,062.2
1983	1,586	1,699	1,606	1,472	1,776	1,733	1,785	1,910	1,710	1,715	1,785	1,688	1,703.0
1984	1,897	2,260	1,663	1,851	1,774	1,843	1,732	1,586	1,698	1,590	1,689	1,612	1,749.5
1985	1,754	1,673	1,810	1,816	1,683	1,678	1,681	1,743	1,679	1,813	1,690	1,887	1,741.8
1986	2,004	1,923	1,887	1,945	1,848	1,842	1,786	1,800	1,689	1,657	1,637	1,837	1,805.4
1987	1,804	1,809	1,723	1,635	1,599	1,583	1,594	1,583	1,679	1,538	1,661	1,399	1,620.5
1988	1,382	1,519	1,529	1,584	1,393	1,454	1,477	1,461	1,467	1,542	1,563		

LUMBER

Salient Statistics of Lumber in the United States

Year	Industrial Roundwood Used for Production — Lumber	Pulp Products	Ply-wood & Veneer	Other Pdts.[2]	Total[2]	Total Imports	Total Ex-ports	Total Con-sumption	Fuel-wood Con-sump-tion	Con-sump-tion Consum. All Pdt's.	All Eastern Hard-woods	Doug-las Fir	South-ern Pine	West-ern Hemlock	Ponder-osa Pine	Maple Sugar
	In Million Cubic Feet												$ Per 1,000 Board Ft.			
1978	6,155	3,745	1,460	400	12,570	3,755	1,845	14,485	1,570	16,055	41.10	250.03	0134.50	113.60	164.70	60.50
1979	6,115	4,110	1,370	410	12,955	3,655	2,135	14,470	2,270	16,740	46.80	394.40	155.20	200.80	239.00	68.90
1980	5,300	4,390	1,175	390	12,090	3,250	2,350	12,995	3,190	16,185	52.40	432.20	155.40	212.70	206.10	70.10
1981	4,780	4,125	1,180	360	11,090	3,165	2,090	12,160	3,225	15,390	50.90	350.20	172.00	163.40	195.20	67.80
1982	4,635	3,970	1,135	345	10,825	3,015	1,995	11,840	3,480	15,320	56.40	118.20	127.20	44.50	66.90	71.10
1983	5,370	4,165	1,365	390	12,010	3,710	2,110	13,610	3,425	17,040	60.10	161.60	140.60	62.20	104.00	55.10
1984	5,770	4,355	1,400	410	12,685	4,165	2,060	14,790	3,635	18,425	90.10	132.90	139.40	61.80	122.70	80.50
1985[1]	5,640	4,165	1,410	400	12,420	4,335	2,065	14,690			65.40	126.20	90.70	50.50	101.40	70.00
1986[1]											69.90	160.70	103.60	74.70	156.60	66.20

[1] Preliminary. [2] Excludes fuelwood. Includes cooperage logs, poles & piling, fence posts, etc. *Sources: National Lumber Manufacturers Ass'n.: U.S. Dept. of Commerce; Forest Service*

T.367

United States Lumber Shipments   In Millions of Board Feet

Year	Jan.	Feb.	Mar.	Apr.	May	June	July	Aug.	Sept.	Oct.	Nov.	Dec.	Total
1979	2,813	2,756	3,279	3,107	3,329	3,087	3,128	3,408	3,106	3,224	2,777	2,589	38,263
1980	2,707	2,791	2,538	2,343	2,512	2,530	2,454	2,716	2,708	2,851	2,494	2,350	32,896
1981	2,424	2,379	2,752	2,755	2,633	2,765	2,395	2,431	2,260	2,382	2,045	1,989	30,834
1982	1,637	1,837	2,148	2,336	2,308	2,513	2,363	2,450	2,260	2,506	2,353	2,162	28,935
1983	2,435	2,290	2,632	2,683	2,775	2,764	2,537	2,669	2,737	2,795	2,404	2,445	35,239
1984	2,589	2,603	3,022	2,875	2,852	2,993	2,756	2,950	2,688	3,154	2,922	2,397	37,221
1985	2,666	2,602	3,013	3,496	3,349	3,031	2,944	3,294	3,162	3,221	2,828	2,809	37,023
1986	2,955	2,899	3,478	3,321	3,538	3,498	2,979	3,344	3,291	3,689	3,480	3,791	42,618
1987[1]	3,350	3,302	3,735	3,686	3,656	4,039	3,671	3,812	3,540	4,034	3,470	3,865	47,090
1988[1]	3,790	4,092	4,320	4,257	4,261	4,309	3,688	3,859					

[1] Preliminary. *Source: National Lumber Manufacturers' Association*

T.368

Stocks (Gross) of Lumber in the United States, Beginning of Month   In Millions of Board Feet

Year	Jan.	Feb.	Mar.	Apr.	May	June	July	Aug.	Sept.	Oct.	Nov.	Dec.
1979	4,852	4,811	4,932	4,964	4,975	4,868	5,003	4,893	4,843	4,875	5,063	5,207
1980	5,335	5,301	5,374	5,721	5,769	5,568	5,534	5,570	5,659	5,776	5,832	5,826
1981	5,800	5,883	6,065	6,098	6,123	6,213	6,015	6,103	6,232	6,284	6,285	6,075
1982	5,894	6,016	6,068	6,042	5,983	5,915	5,853	5,867	5,977	6,163	5,986	5,881
1983	5,809	5,770	5,950	5,997	5,924	5,824	5,772	5,817	5,858	5,870	5,862	5,964
1984	5,940	6,021	6,097	6,178	6,287	6,283	6,257	6,186	6,176	6,265	6,239	6,327
1985	6,155	6,299	6,415	6,488	6,282	6,198	6,445	6,535	6,555	6,603	6,770	6,792
1986	6,484	6,769	6,916	6,784	6,826	6,697	6,361	6,393	6,484	6,590	6,653	6,715
1987[1]	6,549	6,495	6,625	6,607	6,554	6,432	6,233	6,237	5,979	6,088	6,002	5,970
1988[1]	6,183	6,251	6,282	6,341	6,302	6,257						

[1] Preliminary. *Source: National Lumber Manufacturers' Association*

T.369

Lumber Production[1] in the United States   In Millions of Board Feet

Year	Jan.	Feb.	Mar.	Apr.	May	June	July	Aug.	Sept.	Oct.	Nov.	Dec.	Total
1979	2,877	2,877	3,306	3,119	3,219	3,143	3,018	3,355	3,131	3,412	2,914	2,631	38,746
1980	2,798	2,855	2,879	2,257	2,307	2,486	2,479	2,783	2,818	2,903	2,480	2,329	33,361
1981	2,523	2,542	2,818	2,780	2,651	2,588	2,483	2,554	2,307	2,379	1,831	1,765	30,928
1982	1,810	1,891	2,148	2,281	2,251	2,338	2,376	2,560	2,445	2,333	2,247	2,004	28,849
1983	2,484	2,481	2,682	2,623	2,645	2,718	2,585	2,714	2,748	2,787	2,504	2,345	35,370
1984	2,740	2,678	3,104	2,983	2,828	2,968	2,685	2,933	2,776	3,154	2,814	2,295	37,436
1985	2,727	2,718	3,085	3,296	3,256	3,101	3,034	3,299	3,196	3,387	2,851	2,649	37,352
1986	3,092	3,046	3,347	3,362	3,405	3,355	2,961	3,441	3,397	3,820	3,496	3,623	42,676
1987[2]	3,293	3,307	3,742	3,616	3,518	3,905	3,662	3,737	3,617	3,942	3,458	3,829	46,053
1988[2]	3,814	4,042	4,389	4,247	4,245	4,137	3,671	3,982					

[1] Adjusted with Census reports on lumber production. [2] Preliminary. *Source: National Lumber Manufacturers' Association*

T.374

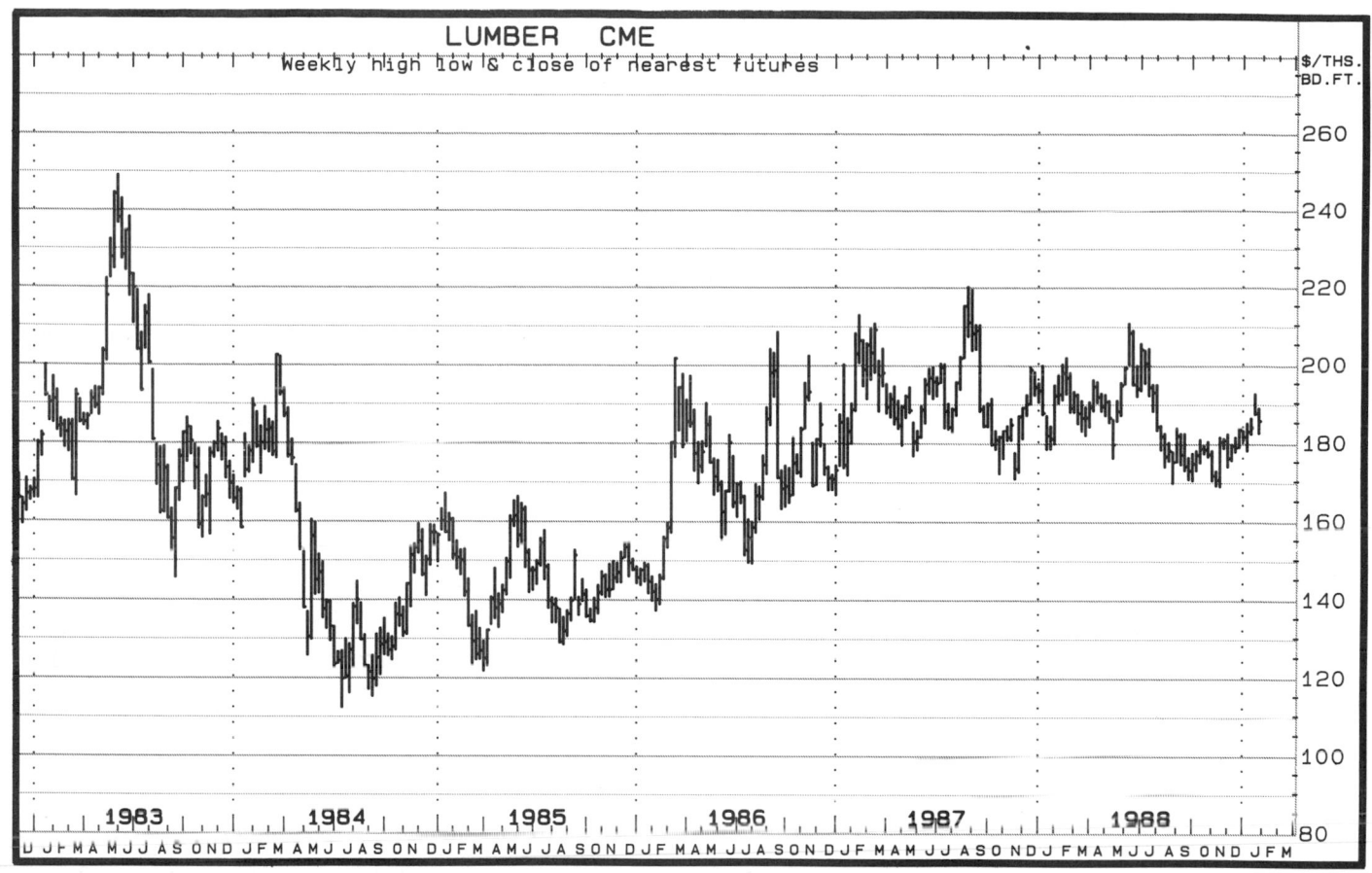

Month–End Open Interest of Lumber Futures at Chicago   In Contracts

Year	Jan.	Feb.	Mar.	Apr.	May	June	July	Aug.	Sept.	Oct.	Nov.	Dec.
1979	8,420	9,059	7,851	7,127	8,055	7,380	8,901	11,039	10,426	10,664	10,125	10,260
1980	10,839	10,587	9,948	10,130	11,452	11,736	12,461	11,644	13,734	14,251	12,829	9,338
1981	8,882	9,053	8,029	8,102	7,639	8,161	8,554	7,586	7,690	8,809	8,808	9,067
1982	9,328	8,982	6,990	7,460	6,578	5,648	4,629	5,789	6,088	8,282	10,490	9,915
1983	10,492	10,610	10,793	11,425	9,070	8,187	7,963	8,552	8,324	6,771	6,595	7,512
1984	8,673	8,614	8,973	8,810	7,487	7,631	7,519	8,157	7,757	8,955	9,374	9,949
1985	9,702	8,984	8,447	9,045	9,764	9,224	8,708	8,346	7,397	6,965	6,687	6,383
1986	5,783	6,936	9,571	9,471	6,342	5,519	5,039	6,356	4,784	5,673	5,646	5,844
1987	6,777	6,554	6,847	6,263	5,946	7,375	6,509	7,596	6,841	6,914	6,222	6,151
1988	6,356	6,213	5,963	6,192	5,125	5,424	6,003	6,111	5,323	6,100	5,437	6,872

Source: Chicago Mercantile Exchange

T.370

Volume of Trading of Lumber Futures at Chicago   In Contracts

Year	Jan.	Feb.	Mar.	Apr.	May	June	July	Aug.	Sept.	Oct.	Nov.	Dec.	Total
1979	60,964	57,594	52,316	43,097	46,530	50,265	56,421	62,923	56,421	71,581	63,777	39,980	649,478
1980	59,063	61,288	73,412	86,057	81,960	68,528	76,296	65,740	73,660	76,984	59,076	58,376	838,676
1981	57,173	45,937	54,295	60,517	51,007	58,879	49,427	49,428	45,592	57,021	55,044	51,614	635,934
1982	51,268	45,193	44,717	44,116	40,828	47,512	34,624	35,432	29,835	47,761	51,046	44,387	516,619
1983	54,976	56,706	51,520	48,327	77,107	73,554	62,053	76,322	68,019	68,228	44,266	49,925	731,003
1984	51,170	70,031	57,075	68,314	88,009	59,592	60,156	65,739	60,035	61,012	52,496	59,939	753,568
1985	71,719	55,737	56,718	65,762	62,766	57,422	43,525	39,151	36,517	34,703	29,556	27,972	581,548
1986	29,570	34,647	61,718	64,176	44,778	49,929	35,203	42,212	44,961	35,847	28,912	30,577	502,530
1987	40,351	49,167	40,504	39,211	27,954	33,505	31,345	38,876	34,039	39,437	32,052	30,648	437,089
1988	35,451	32,410	32,886	30,386	28,100	37,508	37,550	34,454	29,743	24,632	26,131	23,238	371,489

Source: Chicago Mercantile Exchange

T.371

LUMBER

Residential Construction Contracts Awarded (All Types) in U.S.   In Millions of Dollars

Year	Jan.	Feb.	Mar.	Apr.	May	June	July	Aug.	Sept.	Oct.	Nov.	Dec.	Total
1980	4,055	4,365	4,435	4,318	4,410	5,067	6,139	6,092	6,255	6,804	5,847	5,540	63,668
1981	4,227	4,167	5,957	6,617	5,855	5,805	5,810	4,726	4,704	4,718	3,648	3,677	60,164
1982	2,991	3,045	4,542	4,645	5,060	5,674	5,188	5,354	5,560	5,548	5,784	5,401	59,210
1983	5,080	4,942	7,945	7,859	8,594	10,223	8,532	9,113	8,698	8,223	7,604	6,596	93,567
1984	6,809	6,989	9,085	9,518	10,831	9,879	8,845	9,162	8,062	8,494	7,489	5,956	101,389
1985	6,684	6,192	9,884	10,111	10,523	9,595	10,240	9,971	9,465	9,878	8,295	7,542	108,662
1986[1]	7,443	7,208	10,002	12,416	12,033	11,923	11,463	10,145	9,950	10,636	8,361	8,034	122,896
1987[1]	7,350	7,920	11,228	11,276	10,260	10,986	11,279	10,919	10,445	10,290	8,229	7,827	119,915
1988[1]	6,610	7,846	10,898	10,326	11,004	11,888	9,912	11,119	10,117	9,996			

[1] Preliminary.   *Source: F. W. Dodge Co.*   T.372

United States Imports of Sawmill Products   In Millions of Board Feet

Year	Jan.	Feb.	Mar.	Apr.	May	June	July	Aug.	Sept.	Oct.	Nov.	Dec.	Total
1980	727	923	896	655	730	830	876	804	863	867	892	799	9,862
1981	756	848	966	980	992	934	842	465	660	755	728	591	9,517
1982	530	585	601	792	848	888	874	888	962	758	916	781	9,423
1983	879	933	1,055	885	1,153	1,099	1,048	1,090	1,057	1,118	1,092	885	12,294
1984	941	1,135	1,108	1,098	1,073	1,172	1,202	1,191	1,298	1,185	1,104	1,108	13,615
1985	967	1,190	1,212	420	1,431	1,445	1,318	1,308	1,307	1,395	1,146	1,039	14,178
1986	1,113	1,159	1,325	1,380	1,438	1,411	1,594	1,272	1,334	1,012	803	766	14,607
1987[1]	1,078	1,222	1,329	1,293	1,332	1,383	1,329	1,182	1,449	1,264	1,210	1,146	15,217
1988[1]	991	1,134	1,338	1,186	1,259	1,406	1,222	1,186	1,206				

[1] Preliminary.   *Source: Department of Commerce*   T.373

High, Low & Closing Prices of May Lumber Futures at Chicago   In Dollars per 1,000 Board Feet

Year of Delivery		Mar.	Apr.	May	June	July	Aug.	Sept.	Oct.	Nov.	Dec.	Jan.	Feb.	Mar.	Apr.	May	Life of Delivery Range
1980	High	—	—	—	215.0	217.0	227.0	239.5	241.0	227.5	230.2	244.4	242.2	219.3	183.0	160.0	244.4
	Low	—	—	—	208.5	211.0	214.0	222.0	197.7	201.2	216.5	215.3	215.0	181.5	153.1	146.5	146.5
	Close	—	—	—	212.7	214.6	222.7	233.5	206.3	222.8	218.4	234.1	216.3	185.5	161.5	152.2	—
1981	High	221.0	210.2	222.0	225.5	233.5	222.0	215.5	214.0	220.0	210.7	205.2	198.3	181.4	190.4	181.0	233.5
	Low	176.0	164.0	202.0	210.6	218.0	191.9	195.3	194.2	205.7	175.5	185.3	169.5	164.3	163.2	167.1	163.2
	Close	178.1	204.5	220.8	218.5	219.1	196.9	198.5	207.4	208.5	194.5	195.8	169.8	169.6	178.4	175.5	—
1982	High	—	—	—	220.3	214.3	201.5	186.0	183.0	182.8	180.0	166.5	153.1	151.9	145.2	127.5	220.3
	Low	—	—	—	204.6	199.0	183.3	160.0	157.1	162.4	163.4	147.6	142.7	137.5	120.6	115.5	115.5
	Close	—	—	—	211.0	199.3	184.0	163.2	164.8	179.2	169.1	154.0	142.9	142.4	126.8	122.6	—
1983	High	192.7	186.5	178.4	171.0	168.5	170.9	169.3	179.6	191.7	195.3	209.5	206.6	194.6	193.6	221.7	209.5
	Low	180.0	172.0	170.0	151.5	154.8	155.2	157.6	157.9	178.6	181.1	189.8	190.7	183.8	182.7	191.5	151.5
	Close	185.0	174.0	175.5	157.5	158.6	166.0	159.7	178.7	185.9	191.0	204.9	190.7	184.6	193.2	217.2	—
1984	High	237.1	240.1	245.5	234.5	231.0	221.5	213.7	217.6	209.4	205.0	194.3	199.7	201.9	188.2	150.4	245.5
	Low	228.8	228.6	222.9	221.0	214.0	200.4	195.3	198.5	196.8	189.5	184.0	182.0	186.0	148.2	125.1	125.1
	Close	231.8	239.5	230.6	228.5	214.8	207.4	213.0	199.3	202.8	194.2	185.7	197.0	186.7	148.6	130.8	—
1985	High	219.0	215.5	187.0	178.7	167.5	176.2	165.0	171.3	174.1	174.0	176.7	163.0	148.3	147.4	149.9	225.0
	Low	214.0	185.6	167.0	160.5	147.4	153.5	151.0	154.0	165.9	158.5	163.0	146.6	121.1	122.5	136.1	121.1
	Close	215.5	185.6	175.5	166.0	154.2	155.5	157.5	169.5	170.8	173.3	164.0	147.0	124.2	137.4	148.7	—
1986	High	164.5	173.0	176.4	176.0	170.5	158.7	154.9	158.2	160.5	161.9	156.6	161.9	197.0	196.5	189.5	197.0
	Low	153.0	154.0	162.0	165.5	154.5	145.2	145.6	147.7	153.0	155.0	143.3	140.0	159.1	169.0	175.1	140.0
	Close	155.0	163.0	171.1	168.1	156.9	150.3	152.7	157.4	157.9	158.1	144.3	159.9	183.9	177.4	180.6	—
1987	High	173.0	172.5	172.0	174.5	169.4	177.1	179.0	176.0	172.1	173.5	181.2	198.5	203.6	193.9	193.7	203.6
	Low	160.0	161.1	163.2	162.3	155.5	159.0	162.0	162.0	163.0	159.5	158.8	177.1	184.0	178.8	183.2	155.5
	Close	167.0	166.0	166.3	163.5	159.9	172.0	166.6	170.5	165.6	160.0	179.5	189.0	192.4	185.9	187.7	—
1988	High	—	—	—	171.0	170.8	184.5	183.0	179.5	176.8	188.3	192.0	197.9	190.3	195.7	190.3	197.9
	Low	—	—	—	164.5	168.0	169.5	172.1	165.6	166.5	173.7	177.6	184.3	181.5	186.6	175.7	164.5
	Close	—	—	—	169.0	169.9	181.5	172.1	168.4	174.6	181.8	189.1	185.4	188.6	190.1	179.1	—
1989	High	177.2	180.0	178.5	181.7	184.0	179.7	181.4	184.6	184.9	190.4						
	Low	170.1	175.0	175.1	176.0	176.6	174.2	175.1	177.3	178.5	179.8						
	Close	173.0	176.8	178.2	177.1	177.5	178.9	177.5	182.4	181.9	189.0						

Source: Chicago Mercantile Exchange   T.377

Average Index Price of Softwood Plywood, Western (Inland & Other Non-Southern)   1982 = 100[1]

Year	Jan.	Feb.	Mar.	Apr.	May	June	July	Aug.	Sept.	Oct.	Nov.	Dec.	Average
1980	293.8	308.0	302.3	256.9	275.4	301.7	324.5	346.2	324.0	324.2	330.3	343.3	310.9
1981	326.4	330.0	323.3	332.2	319.7	329.4	322.1	311.0	301.9	283.7	286.7	296.7	313.6
1982	291.3	288.4	288.7	283.5	279.2	287.6	282.3	278.8	274.9	272.5	276.5	284.6	282.4
1983	292.0	299.9	302.3	302.3	304.4	327.5	325.4	314.4	302.3	307.1	303.4	308.7	307.5
1984	312.4	320.1	318.0	308.7	289.7	288.8	290.3	308.6	305.2	307.2	302.4	302.4	304.5
1985	301.2	291.1	287.0	285.5	303.9	319.7	324.5	320.1	304.6	308.0	301.6	300.5	304.0
1986	300.1	298.2	312.2	329.5	321.1	311.0	310.1	307.7	311.2	309.9	308.4	304.4	310.3
1987[1]	109.0	113.2	114.2	109.8	107.4	107.0	108.3	112.8	120.5	111.3	112.7	110.7	111.4
1988	112.4	113.0	109.1	108.9	106.2	113.4	117.7	108.2	118.8	114.2			

[1] Data prior to 1987 are the index for 1967 = 100.   *Source: Bureau of Labor Statistics (0831–01)*   T.379

Average Index Price of Softwood Yellow Southern Pine (Dressed) Flooring (C & Better)   1982 = 100[1]

Year	Jan.	Feb	Mar	Apr.	May	June	July	Aug.	Sept.	Oct.	Nov.	Dec.	Average
1980	322.0	322.2	317.2	281.2	280.1	287.3	296.4	304.1	295.1	282.3	286.9	293.7	297.4
1981	291.9	292.2	294.7	308.4	313.9	309.5	297.0	291.6	279.4	273.6	267.0	279.7	291.6
1982	278.0	273.4	273.4	285.3	283.1	298.4	305.1	288.6	287.5	279.3	284.9	293.4	285.9
1983	303.0	314.8	319.3	321.3	325.5	334.9	330.0	323.4	308.3	313.5	316.2	328.2	319.9
1984	334.0	337.8	336.1	334.5	320.4	317.1	318.8	318.4	308.5	305.4	302.4	304.8	319.9
1985	303.4	294.2	295.8	292.4	326.4	347.0	321.1	297.1	288.0	283.4	279.6	279.5	300.7
1986	288.8	288.8	304.1	324.5	317.0	306.1	302.6	303.6	295.5	287.9	289.1	290.3	299.9
1987[1]	103.5	106.8	111.5	112.8	111.5	116.1	122.9	120.7	120.8	113.7	113.5	115.9	114.1
1988	118.1	119.6	118.4	118.6	115.7	115.2	114.9	106.5	101.6	102.7			

[1] Data prior to 1987 are the index for 1967 = 100.   *Source: Bureau of Labor Statistics (0811–02)*   T.381

Average Index Price of Rough Softwood Lumber—No. 2   1982 = 100[1]

Year	Jan.	Feb.	Mar.	Apr.	May	June	July	Aug.	Sept.	Oct.	Nov.	Dec.	Average
1982	97.1	96.8	97.2	96.2	95.3	94.9	95.5	94.2	94.1	93.7	92.1	91.7	94.9
1983	91.1	94.0	94.0	98.5	99.0	100.2	100.2	98.9	96.3	95.8	94.6	95.1	96.5
1984	95.9	97.5	97.8	97.6	94.9	94.8	91.5	90.4	89.9	89.2	89.8	89.1	93.2
1985	90.2	90.2	88.9	88.4	88.5	89.0	88.4	89.8	88.1	87.6	87.2	87.1	88.6
1986	86.2	86.7	87.9	89.4	90.0	90.2	90.3	90.6	90.5	90.7	91.2	92.0	89.6
1987[1]	97.8	98.4	100.4	101.7	103.1	103.0	104.2	105.8	108.7	106.6	106.3	105.6	103.5
1988	105.2	106.4	109.6	111.3	112.7	111.3	113.4	113.8	109.1	108.9			

[1] Data prior to 1987 are the index for Dec. 1980 = 100.   *Source: Bureau of Labor Statistics (0811–04)*   T.380

Average Index Price of Douglas Fir Softwood Lumber—Dressed   1982 = 100[1]

Year	Jan.	Feb.	Mar.	Apr.	May	June	July	Aug.	Sept.	Oct.	Nov.	Dec.	Average
1979	357.2	360.1	371.0	381.1	381.8	378.3	387.4	408.4	424.0	410.4	378.7	368.8	383.9
1980	363.3	367.1	358.8	327.1	329.6	353.2	358.7	360.0	357.1	354.5	352.9	353.4	353.0
1981	347.2	330.4	321.8	332.7	328.5	333.1	320.1	318.3	296.8	277.6	268.0	267.0	311.8
1982	266.4	259.4	258.5	265.6	262.1	271.8	277.8	268.9	269.6	261.8	259.9	272.5	266.2
1983	312.1	370.3	376.2	375.5	390.2	404.7	407.0	381.4	345.3	332.0	318.7	324.7	361.5
1984	322.8	351.7	369.7	364.3	335.8	322.8	307.8	309.2	312.5	301.6	312.8	325.8	328.1
1985	332.9	341.5	353.1	345.0	358.9	386.6	379.4	343.3	313.7	299.2	283.8	301.9	336.6
1986	314.2	303.6	316.1	348.0	358.2	331.1	341.4	339.3	345.4	333.5	329.4	317.6	331.5
1987[1]	118.2	122.6	122.4	122.7	121.3	121.5	124.6	127.6	138.2	128.2	126.1	127.7	125.1
1988	129.8	130.9	131.6	134.2	132.0	135.7	145.7	138.9	142.7	140.5			

[1] Data prior to 1987 are the index for 1967 = 100.   [2] Prices prior to 1979 are in $ per Ths. Board Feet.   *Source: Bureau of Labor Statistics (0811–01)*   T.382

Magnesium

Magnesium is generally a tame market with very few ripples. It's price performance in 1988 was unusual in that there were some things to report. The first price hike since early 1986 was implemented by Dow Chemical Corp., which saw fit to raise its primary magnesium price by five cents to $1.58 a pound. AMAX followed suit, and also boosted its price for diecasting alloy by five cents to $1.33 per pound.

Demand for the metal inched up, as second quarter 1988 magnesium metal shipments totaled 42,338 tons, five percent higher than the first quarter and 11 percent higher than fourth quarter 1987. Producers' metal stocks continued to decline, as they have since early 1986, and totaled only 17,861 tons at the end of the the first half of 1988.

U.S. imports through May 1988 were 32 percent higher than in the same period of 1987, while magnesium exports were 12 percent above those through May 1987.

In response to the shrinking supply situation, Dow Chemical Corp. announced that it would increase production at its Freeport, Texas plant to its full capacity of 96,000 tons a year. The production gain was expected to be fully implemented by June 1988. Capital improvements to the plant were expected to add increased capacity sometime in 1989.

Norsk Hydro A/S, a major European producer, was forced to shut down the remaining 6,600 tons of annual production at its 13,200 ton a year Heroeya plant, part of the large Porsgrunn primary magnesium production facility in Norway. The closure was the result of the Norway State Pollution Board's plan to impose fines totaling $237,000 a month, starting on September 1, 1988, for failure to meet mandated pollution levels. The board claimed that Norsk Hydro was emitting toxic organic chloride compounds into a nearby fjord.

Demand for lightweight, strong, and more fuel-efficient automobile engines, brought on by conservationist concerns, was having an undesirable pollution effect in various areas.

World Production of Magnesium (Primary and Secondary) In Short Tons

| | | | | Primary | | | | | United | | World | | Secondary Production | United | |
Year	Brazil	Canada	China	France	Italy	Japan	Norway	USSR	States	Yugoslavia	Total[1]	Japan	United Kingdom	United States	USSR
1976	—	6,715	5,500	8,857	9,740	12,335	42,778	69,000	119,957	—	274,882	8,379	3,000	30,553	N.A.
1977	—	8,414	5,500	9,570	9,663	10,379	42,070	72,000	125,958	—	283,554	8,360	3,000	32,684	N.A.
1978	—	9,159	6,600	9,370	10,668	12,304	43,166	77,000	149,463	0	317,755	12,057	3,000	36,228	N.A.
1979	—	9,937	6,600	9,968	9,653	12,531	48,697	79,000	162,464	0	338,850	18,058	3,000	37,222	8,000
1980	—	10,199	7,700	10,282	8,693	10,199	48,890	83,000	169,477	0	348,440	26,314	3,000	40,461	8,000
1981	—	9,370	7,700	8,006	11,900	6,247	52,472	86,000	153,782	4,254	339,731	31,345	2,100	46,256	9,000
1982	331	8,700	7,700	10,593	10,960	6,123	39,598	89,000	102,197	4,697	279,899	23,887	1,940	43,232	9,000
1983	551	6,600	7,700	12,208	8,473	6,643	32,897	91,000	115,431	5,252	286,755	14,343	1,900	46,329	9,000
1984	1,323	8,800	7,700	14,299	8,257	7,830	54,343	94,000	159,207	4,700	360,459	17,258	1,102	48,357	9,000
1985[2]	2,866	7,700	7,700	15,212	8,667	9,312	60,301	96,000	149,614	5,000	362,372	23,032	992	45,523	9,000
1986[1]	3,300	7,700	7,700	15,400	13,687	8,945	60,600	98,000	138,493	5,000	358,825	16,000	1,100	46,084	9,000
1987[1]	5,000	10,000	8,000	15,000	15,000	10,000	65,000	100,000	135,000	5,000	368,000			46,000	

[1] Estimate. [2] Preliminary. *Source: Bureau of Mines*   T.383

Salient Statistics of Magnesium in the United States In Short Tons

| | Primary | Production Secondary | | | | Imports | Consumer | $ | Domestic Consumption of Primary Magnesium | | | | | |
Year	(Ingot)	New Scrap	Old Scrap	Total	Exports[2]	for Consumption	Stocks Dec. 31[3]	Price per Pound[4]	Castings Structural	Wrought Products	Total	Alumin. Alloys	Other Uses[5]	Total
1976	119,957	19,024	11,529	30,553	13,444	14,907	17,295	.87–.92	7,051	10,241	17,292	54,320	32,841	104,453
1977	125,958	20,170	12,524	32,694	28,061	5,964	11,838	.96–.99	7,201	12,632	19,833	56,086	27,657	103,576
1978	149,463	22,135	14,093	36,228	41,807	6,668	12,583	.99–1.01	7,651	11,075	18,726	58,798	31,434	108,958
1979	162,464	23,340	13,882	37,222	54,280	4,754	13,901	1.01–1.09	7,460	11,562	19,022	60,549	29,273	108,844
1980	169,477	22,907	17,554	40,461	56,761	3,757	14,393	1.07–1.25	5,847	11,620	17,467	54,490	23,831	95,788
1981	153,782	22,073	24,183	46,256	34,855	6,897	11,367	1.25–1.34	4,951	10,376	15,327	50,518	25,616	91,461
1982	102,197	19,801	23,431	43,232	39,613	4,784	10,268	1.34	3,600	10,128	13,728	39,878	20,993	74,599
1983	115,431	21,591	24,738	46,329	46,690	6,350	11,329	1.38	3,341	11,435	14,776	46,026	21,174	81,976
1984	159,207	21,594	26,763	48,357	48,337	9,381	6,920	1.43–1.48	4,193	10,246	14,439	48,673	26,775	89,887
1985[6]	149,614	19,579	25,944	45,523	40,322	9,271	6,168	1.48–1.53	5,000	11,949	16,949	40,850	25,703	83,502
1986[1]	138,493	20,737	25,347	46,084	43,992	9,209	5,473	1.53	6,357	11,269	17,626	40,569	18,924	77,119
1987[1]	141,000				48,677	11,961	5,000	1.53						
1988[1]	150,000				51,000	12,000		1.58						

[1] Estimate. [2] Metal & alloys in crude form, & scrap. [3] Primary magnesium. Gov't. agencies continue to hold quantities of primary magnesium. [4] Magnesium ingots (99.8%) f.o.b. Valasco, Texas. [5] Distributive or sacrificial purposes. [6] Preliminary. *Source: Bureau of Mines* T.384

Manganese

One of the less publicized areas of U.S. foreign policy is the acquisition of strategic metals. The virtual absence of domestic manganese production has put South African ferromanganese on the list of ten strategic materials that are allowed entry into the U.S. under the 1986 Anti-Apartheid Act.

The fact that the other leading world producer is the Soviet Union hasn't made securing manganese supplies any easier, and there appears to be an effort on the part of U.S. fabricators to look towards other countries, such as Brazil and Australia, for their long-term needs.

At the end of June 1988, the GSA exercised its third year option with Elkem Metals Co. to upgrade manganese ore for national defense purposes. Throughout 1988 there were no sales from the strategic stockpile.

South Africa accounted for about 44 percent of total U.S. imports of high carbon ferromanganese, providing 89,651 tons out of a total 205,452 tons in 1988's first six months. France was second with 75,955 tons, and Australia was third with 13,897 tons. Mexico was by far our biggest supplier of medium carbon ferromanganese, and France was the major source for U.S. imports of low carbon ferromanganese.

U.S. steelmakers consume over 90 percent of all imported manganese, but have reduced their usage with advances in production metallurgy.

External reliance on manganese seems assured, as current environmental law will keep fabrication costs high. In 1988, manganese metal and chemical compounds of manganese were added to a list of toxic chemicals which, if released into the environment, must be reported annually to the Environmental Protection Agency.

One of the most important announcements in 1987 was the proposed joint venture between the Soviet Union and Brazilian firms to construct a ferromanganese plant that would produce 165,000 tons a year. The Soviets pledged a $50 million credit at 6 percent annual interest and were to receive half of the plant's output in the first twelve years. In May of 1988, Prometal Productos Metalurgicos S.A. disassociated itself from the Provale project, and instead proposed another project without Soviet involvement.

South Africa is estimated to have 3.3 million short tons of manganese reserves, out of a world total of 4.9 million tons, according to the Bureau of Mines. The USSR has manganese reserves of about 825,000 tons, followed by Gabon with 800,000 tons.

World Production of Manganese Ore (Gross Weight) In Thousands of Short Tons

Year	Australia[3] 37–53[5]	Brazil 38–50	Bulgaria 29	China 30	Gabon 50–53	Ghana 30–50	Hungary[4] 30–33	India 10–54	Japan 24–27	Mexico 27–50	Morocco 50–53	South Africa 30–48+	USSR 30–31	Yugoslavia 25–45	World Total
1980	2,204	2,515	54	1,760	2,366	275	91.0	1,865	87.7	492.9	144.8	6,278	10,750	33	29,086
1981	1,555	2,251	50	1,760	1,640	246	78.0	1,682	96	637	121	5,555	10,090	34	25,967
1982	1,238	2,580	50	1,760	1,667	176	91	1,642	86	561	106	5,750	10,830	30	26,701
1983	1,510	2,306	50	1,760	2,047	191	65	1,412	83	386	81	3,181	10,890	35	24,147
1984	2,038	2,969	50	1,760	2,336	296	74	1,246	68	525	65	3,361	11,100	30	26,106
1985	2,208	2,976	50	1,760	2,579	320	69	1,367	23	437	48	3,969	10,900	28	26,912
1986[1]	1,818	2,976	42	1,760	2,767	309	66	1,433	7	506	40	4,100	10,700	28	26,716
1987[2]	1,800	3,000		1,760	2,500			1,400		525		3,500	10,700		25,900

[1] Preliminary. [2] Estimated. [3] Metallurgical Ore. [4] Concentrate. [5] Ranges of percentage of manganese. *Source: Bureau of Mines* T.305

Salient Statistics of Manganese in the United States In Thousands of Short Tons (Gross Weight)

Year	Net Import Reliance as a % of Apparent Consumption	Manganese Ore (35% or More Mn) — Consumption by Use — Alloys and Metal	Pig Iron Steel	Dry Cells, Misc.	Imports For Consumption	Exports	Consumption	Stocks, Dec. 31[2]	Ferromanganese Domestic Production	Imports for Consumption	Exports	Consumption	Manganiferous Ore[3] Shipments	Value Mil. $[4]	Production	Silicomanganese Shipments	Exports	Imports
1980	98	727.5	131.5	211.7	698		1,071	1,030	189.5	605.7	11.7	789.1	173.9	2.4	188	162		
1981	98	744.8	147.8	184.0	639		1,077	1,036	192.7	671.2	14.9	820.9	174.8	2.9	173	173		
1982	99	412.3	83.9	112.6	238	29	609	751	119.0	492.7	10.3	439.2	31.5	.3	69	83	3.0	62.1
1983	99	274.5	105.5	150.9	368	19	531	617	86	341.6	8.4	446.3	33.5	.2	N.A.	63	6.4	139.7
1984	98	N.A.	117.0	N.A.	338	238	615	582	N.A.	409.3	6.8	492.2	88.4	9	N.A.	N.A.	5.3	138.5
1985	100	262.7	90.0	247.0	387	56	545	589	N.A.	366.9	6.9	466.0	20.0		N.A.	N.A.	3.1	165.5
1986[1]	100	197.6	74.0	193.5	463	42	500	455	N.A.	395.7	4.3	376	14				2.0	198.6
1987[5]	100				325	60	540	300		290	3	450						

[1] Preliminary. [2] Including bonded warehouses; excludes Gov't stocks; also excludes small tonnages of dealers' stocks. [3] 5 to 35% Manganese. [4] Combined value for total Manganese ore & Manganiferous ores. [5] Estimate. *Source: Bureau of Mines* T.386

MANGANESE

Manganese Ore (35% or More Mn) Imported[2] into the U.S.   In Thousands of Short Tons (Mn Content)

Year	Bel/ Lux.	Zaire	Brazil	Congo (Brazz.)	Canada	Ghana	Pan- ama	Mexico	Morocco	Gabon	Aus- tralia	Turkey	South Africa	Total	Value Mill. $
1978	—	13.2	52.1	9.5	—	—	—	18.4	14.5	127.0	32.6	—	11.0	278.2	33.6
1979	—	—	51.7	22.5	—	—	—	2.1	10.7	49.2	55.3	—	52.1	243.6	27.5
1980	—	—	33.6	—	—	—	—	18.6	5.3	79.9	106.0	—	86.4	329.8	46.4
1981	—	—	38.9	—	—	—	—	25.8	13.6	90.6	34.3	—	97.5	300.7	42.6
1982	—	—	3.0	—	1.7	—	—	1.5	5.0	23.2	18.8	—	57.9	111.1	16.2
1983	—	—	39.1	—	—	—	—	25.6	—	85.5	15.1	—	12.7	178.1	19.9
1984	—	—	44.3	—	—	—	—	16.3	—	66.1	21.0	—	17.3	165.0	16.0
1985	—	—	59.8	—	—	—	—	21.8	.1	64.1	43.1	—	—	188.8	22.6
1986[1]	.2	—	38.7	—	—	—	3.2	14.8	.2	119.1	35.5	—	14.0	225.6	23.1
1987[3]		29.7						3.7	—	96.5	48.7			178.7	

[1] Preliminary.   [2] Imported for consumption.   [3] Estimate.   *Source: Dept of Commerce*   T.387

United States General Imports[1] of Manganese Ore   In Thousands of Long Tons—Manganese Content

Year	Jan.	Feb.	Mar.	Apr.	May	June	July	Aug.	Sept.	Oct.	Nov.	Dec.	Total
1978	94	50	113	50	71	55	82	42	97	62	64	63	842
1979	62	50	60	57	85	122	61	34	85	53	105	76	850
1980	109	56	54	66	97	68	54	67	60	38	57	69	795
1981	22	76	55	70	111	78	68	55	72	51	67	49	775
1982	65	49	65	55	22	58	35	33	14	25	32	15	477
1983	61	29	37	20	38	45	50	28	46	56	39	35	483
1984	39	63	33	64	33	68	46	52	31	37	33	35	535
1985	43	66	81	130	35	63	80	53	41	61	97	50	828
1986	66	104	53	98	51	47	75	79	93	58	76	84	883
1987	30	31	46	64	57	95	57	58	62	85	116	101	801
1988	85	64	96	128	63	118	95	74	82				

[1] General imports of ore, concentrates manganiferous ore, manganese alloys & metals.   *Source: Department of Commerce*   T.388

Production of Ferromanganese in U.S., & Materials Used in Its Manufacture

| | Ferromanganese Produced | | Silico- Manga- nese Production (Gr. Wt.) Sh. Tns. | Materials Consumed (Short tons) | | Manganese Ore Used Per Ton of Ferro- manganese & Silico- manganese | Ferro- manganese ship- ments (Sh. Tons) |
| | | Manganese Contained | | Manganese Ore | | | |
Year	Short Tons	Per Cent	Short Tons		Foreign	Domestic		
1977	334,134	78.8	263,136	120,000	889,296	35,769	1.9	
1978	272,530	80.6	219,707	142,000	740,906	90,660	1.9	
1979	317,102	80.2	254,389	165,000	785,664	125,130	1.8	
1980	189,472	79.7	150,982	188,000	691,250	34,877	1.9	194
1981	192,690	80.0	154,156	173,000	684,857	57,722	2.0	188
1982	119,000	82.0	97,500	69,000	—— 412,000 ——		2.2	98
1983	86,000	81.0	109,000	N.A.	—— 283,000 ——		N.A.	109
1984	N.A.	82.0	N.A.	N.A.	—— N.A. ——		N.A.	N.A.
1985[1]	N.A.	81.0	N.A.	N.A.	—— N.A. ——		N.A.	N.A.

[1] Preliminary.   *Source: Bureau of Mines*   T.390

Average Price of Ferromanganese[1] (High Carbon[2]-F.O.B. Plant)   In Dollars Per Gross Ton—Carloads

Year	Jan.	Feb.	Mar.	Apr.	May	June	July	Aug.	Sept.	Oct.	Nov.	Dec.	Average
1976	432½	432½	432½	432½	432½	432½	432½	432½	432½	432½	425	417½	430.63
1977	417½	417½	417½	399½	399½	399½	399½	399½	399½	399½	399½	399½	404.00
1978	399½	399½	399½	399½	422.17	425	425	425	425	425	425	425	416.26
1979	440	440	440	465	490	490	490	490	490	493	510	510	479.04
1980	510	510	510	510	510	510	510	510	510	510	510	510	510.00
1981	510	510	510	510	510	510	510	510	510	510	510	510	510.00
1982	510	510	510	510	510	510	510	510	510	510	510	510	510.00
1983	510	510	510	510	510	510	510	510	510	510	510	510	510.00
1984	510	510	510	510	510	510	510	510	510	——No Quotes——			510.00
1987	——— No Quotes ———				326.25	331.88	339.50	345	355	358	363	373	348.95

[1] Domestic standard.   [2] Prior to May 1987 prices are for 78% Mn-F.O.B. plant.   *Source: American Metal Market.*   T.389

Meats

Total red meat and poultry production in the U.S. reached a record 60.4 billion pounds in 1988, up from 58.2 billion a year earlier. Red meat continued to be the largest category, with 1988 production of 39.8 billion pounds, 3 percent greater than a year earlier. Total poultry production was estimated at 20.6 billion pounds, up about 4 percent from a year earlier.

On a retail-weight basis, estimated U.S. red meat and poultry consumption in 1988 reached a record 220.1 pounds per capita. Beef consumption was expected to be 72.6 pounds per capita, down from 73.4 pounds the previous year. Pork consumption was estimated at 62.9 pounds per capita, up from 59.1 pounds in 1987. Total red meat consumption in 1988 was expected to be 138.4 pounds per capita, up about 2 percent from a year earlier.

U.S. chicken consumption in 1988 was estimated at 62.4 pounds per capita, up from 60.2 pounds in 1987, while turkey consumption was put at 16.7 pounds per capita, up 10 percent from a year earlier. Total poultry consumption was placed at 81.7 pounds per capita, up from 77.8 pounds a year earlier.

Pork supplies increased in 1988, due to the expansion of breeding herds a year earlier. Commercial pork production of 15.6 million pounds was the highest since 1981. Retail pork prices fell 3 percent, averaging $1.84 per pound. Pork imports through October were about 4 percent lower than in 1987, while exports were significantly higher, due to larger exports to Japan.

U.S. cattle slaughter fell nearly 2 percent in 1988, but the decline was offset by higher commercial dressed weights. The drought and higher feed costs led to delays in herd expansion, which kept beef production in line with 1987 levels. Retail prices for Choice beef rose almost 5 percent in 1988. The trade outlook for pork and beef was clouded by the emergence of the hormone-treated meat dispute between the U.S. and the EC.

Pork and beef production were both expected to decline in 1989, while chicken and turkey output were likely to increase again. Overall, total meat and poultry production was forecast to decline slightly from 1988's record.

World Total Meat[1] Production   In Millions of Metric Tons

Year	Argentina	Australia	China[3]	Canada	Czecho-slovakia	Denmark	France	West Germany	Japan	Italy	New Zealand	Poland	Brazil	South Africa	United Kingdom	United States	U.S.S.R.
1975	2.8	2.4		1.6	.8	1.0	3.4	3.8	1.3	1.7	1.0	2.1	3.0	.8	2.3	16.7	11.0
1976	3.2	2.7		1.7	.8	1.0	3.5	3.9	1.4	1.9	1.2	2.4	3.1	.8	2.1	18.1	10.0
1977	3.3	2.0		1.7	.9	1.0	3.4	3.9	1.5	2.0	1.1	2.3	3.4	.8	2.2	18.0	12.7
1978	3.5	2.8		1.7	1.3	1.1	3.5	4.1	1.7	2.0	1.1	2.7	3.1	.8	2.2	17.5	13.3
1979	3.5	2.5		1.7	1.3	1.2	3.7	4.2	1.8	2.1	1.1	2.7	3.0	.9	2.2	17.1	13.2
1980	3.3	2.3		1.9	1.3	1.2	3.7	4.3	1.9	2.2	1.1	2.6	3.2	.9	2.3	17.7	12.6
1981	3.4	2.2		1.9	1.3	1.2	3.7	4.3	1.9	2.2	1.2	2.0	3.2	.8	2.3	17.7	12.7
1982	2.7	2.5		1.9	1.2	1.2	3.5	4.2	1.9	2.2	1.1	2.3	3.4	.9	2.2	17.0	12.7
1983	2.5	2.1	13.2	1.9	1.3	1.3	3.5	4.2	1.9	2.3	1.2	2.2	3.4	.8	2.4	17.8	13.6
1984	2.7	2.0	14.4	1.9	1.3	1.3	3.7	4.4	2.0	2.4	1.1	2.1	2.9	.9	2.4	17.8	14.0
1985	2.8	2.2	17.0	1.9	1.3	1.3	3.6	4.4	2.1	2.3	1.2	2.3	3.0	.9	2.4	17.9	14.1
1986[2]	2.9	2.3	18.6	2.0	1.3	1.4	1.6	4.6	2.1	2.4	1.1	2.6	2.8	.8	2.3	17.8	14.5

[1] Production of beef & veal, mutton & lamb, goat meat, & pork. Horsemeat included from 1976.   [2] Preliminary.   [3] Predominately pork production.   *Source: Foreign Agricultural Service, U.S.D.A.*   T.395

Production and Consumption of Red Meats in the United States (*Carcass Weight*)

	Beef			Veal			Lamb & Mutton			Pork (Excluding Lard)			All Meats		
	Comm. Produc-tion	Consumption		Comm. Produc-tion	Consumption		Comm. Produc-tion	Consumption		Comm. Produc-tion	Consumption		Produc-tion	Consumption	
Year	Total	Total	Per Capita Lb.	Total	Total	Per Capita Lb.	Total	Total	Per Capita Lb.	Total	Total	Per Capita Lb.	Total	Total	Per Capita Lb.
	— Mil. Lbs. —			— Mil. Lbs. —			— Mil. Lbs. —			— Mil. Lbs. —			— Mil. Lbs. —		
1978	24,242	25,998	117.9	599	645	2.9	301	343	1.6	13,393	13,293	60.3	38,119	40,279	182.7
1979	21,262	23,522	105.5	411	450	2.0	282	332	1.5	15,270	15,353	68.8	37,225	39,657	177.8
1980	21,469	23,320	103.4	379	410	1.8	310	345	1.5	16,431	16,574	73.5	38,590	40,648	180.2
1981	22,214	23,756	104.3	415	438	1.9	327	360	1.6	15,719	15,927	69.9	38,675	40,481	177.8
1982	22,366	23,998	104.3	423	457	1.99	356	381	1.65	14,121	14,425	62.6	37,266	39,261	170.5
1983	23,060	24,710	106.2	428	457	1.97	367	388	1.67	15,117	15,369	66.1	38,972	40,924	175.9
1984	23,418	24,900	106.1	479	503	2.14	371	398	1.70	14,720	15,396	65.6	38,988	41,197	175.5
1985	23,557	25,342	106.9	499	527	2.22	352	386	1.63	14,728	15,651	66.0	39,136	41,903	176.8
1986	24,213	25,935	107.4	509	550	2.3	331	375	1.6	13,998	15,008	62.1	39,051	41,868	173.3
1987[1]	23,405	25,205	103.3	416	449	1.8	309	360	1.5	14,312	15,237	62.5	38,442	41,251	169.1
1988[2]	23,291	25,141	102.2	398	426	1.7	328	386	1.6	15,611	16,480	66.9	39,628	42,433	172.4

[1] Preliminary.   [2] Estimate.   *Source: Economic Research Service, U.S.D.A.*   T.400

MEATS

Total Red Meat Imports (Carcass Weight Equivalent[2]) of Importing Countries In Thous. of Metric Tons

Year	Belgium & Lux.	Canada	Czecho-slovakia	France	Rep. of Korea	W. Ger-many	Greece	Hong Kong	Italy	Is-rael	Japan	Nether-lands	Spain	Switz-erland	Un. King-dom	United States	USSR
1977	121.2	194.3	21.4	556.2		627.0	110.9		612.9	30	649.0	175.3	59.2	26.0	1,280	1,100	496.2
1978	143.9	172.9	21.0	630.4		633.0	142.0		632.1	37	665.4	187.5	112.3	33.8	1,276	1,296	132.0
1979	99	140	21	541	108	648	140		684	71	610	149	124	25	1,245	1,348	469
1980	91	111	21	590	15	700	134		722	33	486	168	27	23	1,122	1,210	706
1981	88	110	21	579	45	687	80		690	55	612	146	16	31	1,072	1,058	786
1982	79	112	29	618	82	692	157	68	824	56	546	119	28	25	1,137	1,175	679
1983	107	121	25	676	78	728	216	82	832	46	599	108	26	27	1,072	1,212	779
1984	79	130	15	711	39	796	194	238	823	43	636	105	36	21	1,015	1,280	691
1985	79	132	15	760	19	843	208	259	948	47	647	116	36	15	955	1,476	587
1986[1]	78	116	15	869	14	722	221	263	943	46	665	126	55	14	955	1,482	570

[1] Preliminary. [2] Excludes fat, offals & live animals. *Source: Foreign Agricultural Service, U.S.D.A.* T.397

Total Red Meat Exports (Carcass Weight Equivalent[2]) of Principal Countries In Thousands of Metric Tons

Year	Argen-tina	Aus-tralia	Brazil	Canada	China	Den-mark	France	Ire-land	Rom-ania	Nether-lands	N. Zea-land	Poland	United States	Un. King-dom	USSR	Uru-guay	Yugo-slavia
1977	669.6	1,335	240.0	112.1		695.6	312.2	363.8		697.2	790.9	131.8	236.0	185	49.2	134.6	88.0
1978	823.7	1,377	178.1	117.1		753.4	267.2	359.3		751.6	724.7	141.0	256.6	177	38.0	118.8	113.4
1979	728	1,306	111	133		832	306	342		785	783	155	211	179	33	84	82
1980	487	1,087	170	182		857	362	453	208	843	796	141	195	228	35	128	98
1981	508	966	281	207		905	415	324	245	932	817	60	240	243	53	185	72
1982	546	1,184	361	247	230	909	401	311	160	879	846	52	213	194	32	182	107
1983	438	947	404	242	264	945	387	341	185	957	938	93	225	296	25	236	83
1984	266	747	483	280	273	952	489	301	177	1,066	815	68	227	344	27	142	98
1985	271	860	540	313	263	958	503	370	270	1,158	876	80	210	284	30	131	97
1986[1]	230	922	435	328	292	1,028	523	460	225	1,218	784	100	284	290	35	151	83

[1] Preliminary. [2] Excludes fat, offals & live animals. *Source: Foreign Agricultural Service, U.S.D.A.* T.398

United States Meat Exports by Type of Product In Metric Tons

Year	Beef and Veal Fresh or frozen	Beef and Veal Canned	Beef and Veal Pick-led or cured	Goat, lamb mut-ton, fresh or frozen	Pork Fresh or frozen	Pork Hams & shoul-ders, cured or cooked	Pork Bacon	Pork Other pork, pickled, salted or other-wise cured	Pork Other pork, canned	Sau-sage, bolo-gna, frank-furters	Variety meats fresh or fro-zen[1]	Other meats[2]	Total
1977	40,982		517	1,755	116,282	2,941	1,216	2,919	1,810	3,426	173,060	8,198	353,106
1978	51,710	2,296	1,263	1,375	84,120	3,934	1,655	7,524	2,932	3,653	185,831	6,801	353,095
1979	53,823	1,625	1,955	562	83,058	3,380	912	8,912	1,123	3,003	163,930	4,664	331,946
1980	55,003	1,995	2,505	595	69,966	3,327	820	8,438	1,667	3,296	200,417	7,427	355,454
1981	68,608	2,826	3,235	972	86,652	2,363	1,079	9,130	1,662	3,819	209,981	7,949	397,870
1982	78,781	3,028	3,858	676	58,541	1,358	774	7,514	1,289	3,404	230,344	5,291	394,857
1983	86,962	1,584	4,500	632	62,141	1,794	601	5,581	695	3,139	218,311	3,795	389,735
1984	105,995	1,936	3,598	878	46,098	1,474	621	3,837	513	2,603	217,019	3,605	388,177
1985	105,792	1,134	2,603	460	34,394	1,175	450	4,066	638	2,908	247,582	4,383	405,585
1986[3]	179,434	918	4,052	558	20,969	650	474	4,796	349	3,214	249,460	4,214	469,088

[1] Edible animal organs. [2] Includes sausage ingredients, cured (excluding canned); meat and meat products canned (n.e.s.); and baby food, canned. [3] Preliminary. *Source: Foreign Agricultural Service. Compiled from reports of the U.S. Department of Commerce* T.399

U.S. Imports of Meats and Meat Preparations   In Millions of Pounds

Year	Jan.	Feb.	Mar.	Apr.	May	June	July	Aug.	Sept.	Oct.	Nov.	Dec.	Total
1980	196	152	166	134	173	154	208	170	133	207	167	191	2,052
1981	171	167	131	155	140	153	162	168	180	167	120	118	1,832
1982	127	106	160	169	167	215	158	234	246	194	124	114	2,015
1983	208	177	170	178	187	176	189	181	171	169	123	104	2,030
1984	180	167	171	198	161	128	209	198	189	226	175	159	2,160
1985	193	179	207	213	214	221	230	232	226	198	196	201	2,511
1986	225	196	197	179	180	213	260	232	232	223	237	168	2,544
1987[1]	211	218	236	240	222	268	277	244	249	244	191	156	2,755
1988[1]	290	238	280	247	230	276	219	252	200				

[1] Preliminary.   *Source: Dept. of Commerce*   T.401

United States Meat Imports by Type of Product   In Metric Tons

	Beef and Veal				Pork								
Year	Fresh or frozen[1]	Canned, including sausage	Other prepared or preserved[2]	Lamb, Mutton, & goat, except canned	Fresh and frozen	Canned[3]	Other prepared or preserved[2]	Sausage, all types[4]	Mixed sausage	Other meats n.s.p.f.[5]	Variety meats, fresh or frozen	Total
------	------	------	------	------	------	------	------	------	------	------	------	------
1980	642,268	42,729	17,799	15,482	93,143	98,529	1,990	2,929	2,230	5,957	4,562	927,618
1981	544,610	34,932	23,303	14,384	98,226	94,102	1,496	1,935	2,103	7,896	3,560	826,547
1982	607,184	37,747	17,402	8,649	125,282	96,831	1,547	2,372	2,242	7,373	2,823	909,452
1983	565,997	59,073	16,766	8,752	121,707	125,593	2,300	2,176	1,911	8,396	3,935	916,604
1984	516,960	57,863	19,864	8,693	207,703	142,423	3,372	2,243	2,121	7,129	5,707	974,078
1985	594,476	64,277	18,314	15,565	254,538	160,802	6,312	2,192	2,672	9,163	5,622	1,133,933
1986[6]	637,717	45,780	20,778	16,596	263,487	151,730	8,221	2,640	2,849	8,512	6,476	1,164,786

[1] Includes prepared items.   [2] Includes pickled and cured.   [3] Includes canned hams, shoulders, and bacon.   [4] Includes fresh and cured sausages.   [5] Mostly mixed luncheon meats.   [6] Preliminary.   *Source: Foreign Agricultural Service. Compiled from reports of the U.S. Department of Commerce.*   T.402

U.S. Exports of Meat and Meat Preparations   In Millions of Pounds

Year	Jan.	Feb.	Mar.	Apr.	May	June	July	Aug.	Sept.	Oct.	Nov.	Dec.	Total
1980	101	108	144	132	139	164	145	129	136	165	144	154	1,663
1981	143	141	169	148	189	180	128	144	123	174	154	153	1,847
1982	129	147	124	131	167	147	111	108	112	133	143	115	1,566
1983	114	104	136	133	115	118	121	99	130	127	134	119	1,449
1984	112	104	134	106	114	103	128	119	123	139	121	119	1,422
1985	119	110	118	112	116	116	130	139	118	139	122	123	1,461
1986	124	123	123	132	139	121	125	147	159	188	170	171	1,722
1987[1]	151	133	151	157	176	167	177	178	180	176	191	181	2,017
1988[1]	159	153	165	179	191	198	205	229	219				

[1] Preliminary.   *Source: Dept. of Commerce*   T.403

Average Wholesale Prices of Meats   In Cents Per Pound

Year	Composite Retail Price of Beef Grade 3 (Choice)	Composite Retail Price of Pork[3]	Net Farm Value of Pork[5]	Canner & Cutter Cow Beef Midwest	Choice, Steer Beef Carcass, Centr. U.S. (600–700 Lb.)	Fresh Beef, Steer Carcasses Choice, E. Coast	Lamb Carcasses Choice & Prime (55-65 Lb.) East Coast	Pork, Fresh Loins, (8-14 lbs.) N.Y.	Hams Midwest Skinned, Smoked 14-17 Lb.	Pork[1] Bellies 12-14 lbs. Midwest	Live Broilers Georgia
1980	237.6	139.4			104.44	104.4	134.98	101.14	88.99	67.01	27.0
1981	238.7	152.4			99.84	99.8	127.67	113.70	95.55	68.38	26.5
1982	242.5	175.4	88.0		101.31	101.3	122.15	127.66	111.98	78.19	25.0
1983	238.1	169.8	76.5	78.48	97.83	97.8	125.86	115.90	75.60	60.58	27.0
1984	239.6	162.0	77.4	74.70	98.01	100.1	131.89	115.73	78.22	60.08	32.0
1985	232.6	162.0	71.4	74.13	90.76	91.3	145.93	113.60	67.50	59.50	28.0
1986[2]	230.7	78.4	82.4	71.31	88.98	89.0	139.89	128.50	80.01	65.82	32.5
1987[2]	242.5	188.4	82.7	83.70	97.21	97.2	150.41	126.50	80.96	63.11	26.5
1988[4]	253.1	184.9	71.9	88.04	102.75	102.8	139.50	120.70	70.05	43.54	32.1

[1] Prior to 1983 prices are for cured pork cuts, picnics at N.Y. (4-8 lb).   [2] Preliminary.   [3] Sold as retail cuts (ham, bacon, loin, etc.).   [4] Estimate.   [5] Gross farm value minus by-product allowance.   *Sources: Bureau of Labor Statistics; Department of Agriculture*   T.404

MEATS

Average Wholesale Price of Steer Beef Carcass, Choice[1], at Midwest Markets   In Cents per Pound

Year	Jan.	Feb.	Mar.	Apr.	May	June	July	Aug.	Sept.	Oct.	Nov.	Dec.	Average
1979	93.57	97.47	104.59	108.61	108.64	103.56	99.85	94.13	101.91	98.32	103.22	105.53	101.62
1980	102.26	103.70	103.15	99.41	102.00	105.18	110.11	111.96	107.97	105.49	101.44	100.57	104.40
1981	99.80	96.10	94.32	99.68	103.32	106.52	107.20	103.90	102.96	96.02	94.56	93.70	99.80
1982	97.40	101.20	103.80	109.50	115.10	111.20	102.60	100.80	95.50	93.00	92.90	92.62	101.30
1983	93.90	96.55	100.62	107.76	105.00	102.47	97.72	95.01	92.10	91.24	91.57	99.82	97.83
1984	105.74	102.86	105.14	103.50	99.62	98.54	101.26	97.61	94.37	92.38	99.08	101.22	100.11
1985	99.50	97.42	92.00	89.20	89.52	88.48	82.22	80.02	81.14	91.11	99.68	98.84	90.76
1986	92.26	86.82	85.04	83.34	86.42	83.58	89.25	90.98	90.50	91.80	95.70	92.04	88.98
1987	89.70	91.69	92.86	100.56	107.80	105.71	99.29	95.45	96.87	96.80	95.34	94.50	97.21
1988	97.15	99.50	103.47	105.25	111.70	106.38	97.09	101.04	103.15	104.40			

[1] 500–600 pounds.   *Source: Economic Research Service, U.S.D.A.*   T.405

Production[2] (Commercial Slaughter) of All Meats[1] in the U.S.   In Millions of Pounds—Carcass Weight

Year	Jan.	Feb.	Mar.	Apr.	May	June	July	Aug.	Sept.	Oct.	Nov.	Dec.	Total
1979	3,280	2,756	3,090	2,879	3,130	2,990	2,958	3,329	2,876	3,556	3,306	3,074	37,225
1980	3,398	3,050	3,099	3,315	3,311	3,089	3,070	3,016	3,221	3,577	3,097	3,349	38,590
1981	3,417	3,014	3,389	3,299	3,071	3,118	3,041	3,044	3,247	3,433	3,185	3,417	38,675
1982	3,152	2,894	3,296	———— 9,097 ————			———— 9,165 ————			———— 9,659 ————			37,266
1983	3,151	2,787	3,269	3,051	3,163	3,299	3,002	3,440	3,435	3,523	3,472	3,383	38,974
1984	3,219	3,092	3,349	3,079	3,411	3,205	3,045	3,362	3,111	3,672	3,324	3,119	38,987
1985	3,421	2,938	3,162	3,295	3,488	3,085	3,277	3,402	3,252	3,544	3,123	3,145	39,131
1986	3,482	2,942	3,133	3,477	3,388	3,156	3,281	3,180	3,259	3,506	2,986	3,261	39,050
1987[3]	3,410	2,817	3,198	3,160	2,975	3,102	3,157	3,135	3,331	3,521	3,197	3,378	38,442
1988[3]	3,242	3,070	3,354	3,158	3,206	3,317	3,170	3,505	3,462	3,510	3,397		

[1] Except for pork production & lard.   [2] Represents the total dressed carcass weight of livestock slaughtered under Federal inspection, exclusive of meats from condemned animals.   [3] Preliminary.   *Source: Agricultural Marketing Service, U.S.D.A.*   T.406

Cold Storage Holdings of All[1] Meats in the United States, at End of Month   In Millions of Pounds

Year	Jan.	Feb.	Mar.	Apr.	May	June	July	Aug.	Sept.	Oct.	Nov.	Dec.
1979	728.4	710.9	762.5	783.4	797.0	755.0	685.6	580.7	549.1	604.5	656.9	706.2
1980	735.3	712.6	695.4	715.5	706.5	641.9	578.5	514.3	510.0	584.2	678.6	749.6
1981	790.3	782.9	775.9	817.2	795.2	716.6	628.6	538.9	508.6	546.8	552.2	578.2
1982	553.4	524.2	536.0	—	—	503.9	—	—	473.9	—	—	553.8
1983	573.4	571.0	576.3	607.6	619.2	595.5	569.8	543.3	535.3	576.7	667.6	679.3
1984	692.9	707.7	738.1	777.5	818.9	776.3	713.8	627.6	646.2	674.9	681.4	696.0
1985	735.0	702.9	721.2	772.7	784.9	758.6	738.2	677.1	654.2	645.2	633.0	607.4
1986	616.8	615.3	622.5	658.2	667.2	638.8	618.6	572.0	541.1	572.4	564.3	566.2
1987[2]	597.6	599.0	598.2	590.8	560.2	498.7	515.6	495.9	523.0	575.6	613.8	622.9
1988[2]	656.4	693.5	715.7	757.7	719.6	668.9	665.8	629.9	645.9	664.1	703.8	

[1] Includes beef and veal, mutton and lamb, pork and products, rendered pork fat, and miscellaneous meats. Excludes lard.   [2] Preliminary.   *Source: Crop Reporting Board, U.S.D.A.*   T.407

Cold Storage Holdings of Frozen Beef[1] in the United States   In Millions of Pounds

Year	Jan. 1	Feb. 1	Mar. 1	Apr. 1	May 1	June 1	July 1	Aug. 1	Sept. 1	Oct. 1	Nov. 1	Dec. 1
1979	405.4	423.7	405.0	427.4	410.1	411.9	395.7	369.6	324.2	296.7	308.2	321.9
1980	350.3	367.3	357.6	335.1	296.6	277.9	256.5	242.5	228.6	219.7	243.8	279.0
1981	328.2	361.3	347.8	341.5	339.4	328.6	297.5	272.6	245.2	234.9	244.6	232.2
1982	256.7	249.1	223.3	211.9	—	—	189.7	—	—	247.7	—	—
1983	294.4	303.1	307.0	299.1	277.3	265.2	254.0	252.3	267.4	268.2	278.0	316.0
1984	325.0	338.0	332.5	325.7	324.6	312.8	303.2	301.7	290.0	319.6	326.0	340.1
1985	357.7	375.1	347.0	334.0	328.0	300.9	292.5	319.7	310.6	308.4	294.9	302.3
1986	317.4	318.4	302.3	297.1	301.2	318.5	321.6	337.0	319.4	291.6	292.3	297.5
1987[2]	310.6	320.6	306.0	311.1	312.3	280.1	252.7	278.7	269.3	286.5	307.6	304.3
1988[2]	288.6	312.4	327.7	312.9	304.3	273.5	246.8	265.3	291.0	307.3	296.5	300.4

[1] Includes frozen beef, cured beef, and beef in process of cure.   [2] Preliminary.   *Source: Crop Reporting Board, U.S.D.A.*   T.408

Mercury

The U.S. has only one mercury-producing mine, located in Nevada. The mine was closed during most of 1987 and into early 1988. Although production data are not disclosed, estimated 1988 output, following the mine's reopening in March 1988, was 12,000 to 14,000 flasks. Mercury is obtained as a by-product in gold production, but this adds relatively little to domestic mercury output, which has been declining for much of the 1980s. There is little sign of a change in this pattern. U.S. mercury needs are met mostly by imports, largely from Spain and also from China in the past few years.

The USSR provides about one-third of the world's annual production, which apparently peaked in the mid-1980s near 200,000 flasks. Spain, which has the world's largest mercury mine, produces about 43,000 flasks annually. Thus, two countries provide more than half the world's output. Algeria, China, and Mexico account for another 30 percent or so. In mid-1988, Spanish mercury reportedly became available in one-tonne containers, in addition to the traditional 76-pound flask.

Demand for mercury has been declining, largely reflecting the metal's adverse and well-publicized effects on the environment and broadening demand for pollution controls. In the U.S., demand for mercury in paints and batteries, which has more than offset small gains in electrical applications, has been dropping steadily. Improved technology has helped trim mercury's use in batteries. However, on a worldwide basis, increasing numbers of vehicles could help maintain mercury's use. Efforts to phase out mercury in some industrial applications, as in the manufacture of chlorine and caustic soda, appear to be under way. In the mid-1980s, Japan eliminated mercury's use in the manufacture of those chemicals.

U.S. mercury consumption during the first half of 1988 totaled 22,616 flasks, versus 41,939 during the year 1987. Battery use, the largest consumer, totaled 6,455 flasks during the first half of 1988, versus 15,462 flasks for all of 1987. The manufacture of chlorine and caustic soda has recently consumed about 9,000 flasks annually. Wiring devices and measuring instruments have helped offset some of the slippage in mercury usage.

The U.S. government maintains a mercury stockpile. In February 1988, the Secretary of Defense was designated as manager of the national stockpile. The General Services Administration (GSA) held monthly auctions during second quarter 1988, selling 500 flasks of primary mercury from the defense stockpile and 771 flasks of secondary mercury from the Department of Energy's stocks. In 1987, the government sold 3,700 flasks of primary mercury from the Defense stockpile, and 3,404 flasks were released by the Department of Energy.

Mercury prices have been volatile in the 1980s. The New York price averaged $416 a flask in 1981 and $243 in 1986. Prices have since rebounded, averaging almost $290 in 1987 and about $350 for much of 1988. At 1988's end, prices had slipped about $40/flask from the summer high.

World Mine Production of Mercury   In Flasks of 34.5 Kilograms (76 Pounds)

Year	Algeria	China[1]	Czecho-slovakia	Dom. Rep.	Fin-land	Italy	Mexico	Spain	Turkey	United States	USSR[1]	W. Germany	Yugo-slavia	World Total
1982	11,000	20,000	4,380	49	2,068	4,612	8,558	48,808	7,129	25,760	64,000	1,537	—	197,901
1983	10,000	20,000	4,177	60	1,857	—	6,411	41,075	4,680	25,070	64,000	2,005	1,500	180,835
1984	23,000	20,000	4,409	80	2,292	—	11,140	44,090	5,272	19,048	64,000	—	2,000	195,331
1985[1]	23,000	20,000	4,400	14	2,300	—	11,430	45,042	6,000	16,530	65,000	—	2,000	195,823
1986[2]	23,000	20,000	4,400	120	2,300	—	10,000	42,000	6,000	N.A.	66,000	—	2,000	175,820
1987[2]	20,000						10,000	42,000	7,000		66,000			174,000

[1] Estimate.   [2] Preliminary.   *Source: Bureau of Mines*   T.409

Salient Statistics of Mercury in the United States   In Flasks (76 Pounds Each)

Year	Net Import Reliance as a % of Apparent Consumption	Ore Treated (1,000 Short Tons)	Mercury Produced[2] Flasks	Pounds per Ton of Ore	Production Mine	Second-ary	Stocks, Dec. 31 Producers	Consumers & Dealers	Total	Ex-ports	U.S. Imports (For Consumption) From: Total	Alg-eria	Canada	Tur-key	Mex-ico	Spain	Japan
1982	32	301.0	25,704	6.5	25,760	4,473	13,598	15,229	28,827	—	8,916	—	5	—	182	1,404	4,345
1983	30	335.4	25,033	5.7	25,070	13,751	18,323	12,695	31,018	—	12,786	1,795	4	—	1,590	3,408	511
1984	58	216.2	19,014	6.7	19,048	5,673	19,964	7,291	27,255	—	25,327	8,201	14	2,002	21	11,749	500
1985	57	182.4	16,337	6.8	16,530	5,358	19,398	8,587	27,985	—	18,890	1,938	5	3,012	214	7,955	2,502
1986[1]	50	N.A.	N.A.	N.A	N.A.	6,362	N.A.	7,189	N.A.	—	20,187	1,251	10	4,328	655	5,824	2,202
1987[3]	N.A.					7,692		9,287			18,451	—	155	—	10	5,002	1,000
1988[3]						8,000		11,000			10,000						

[1] Preliminary.   [2] Excludes mercury produced from placer operation & from clean-up activity at furnaces & other plants.   [3] Estimate.
Source: Bureau of Mines   T.412

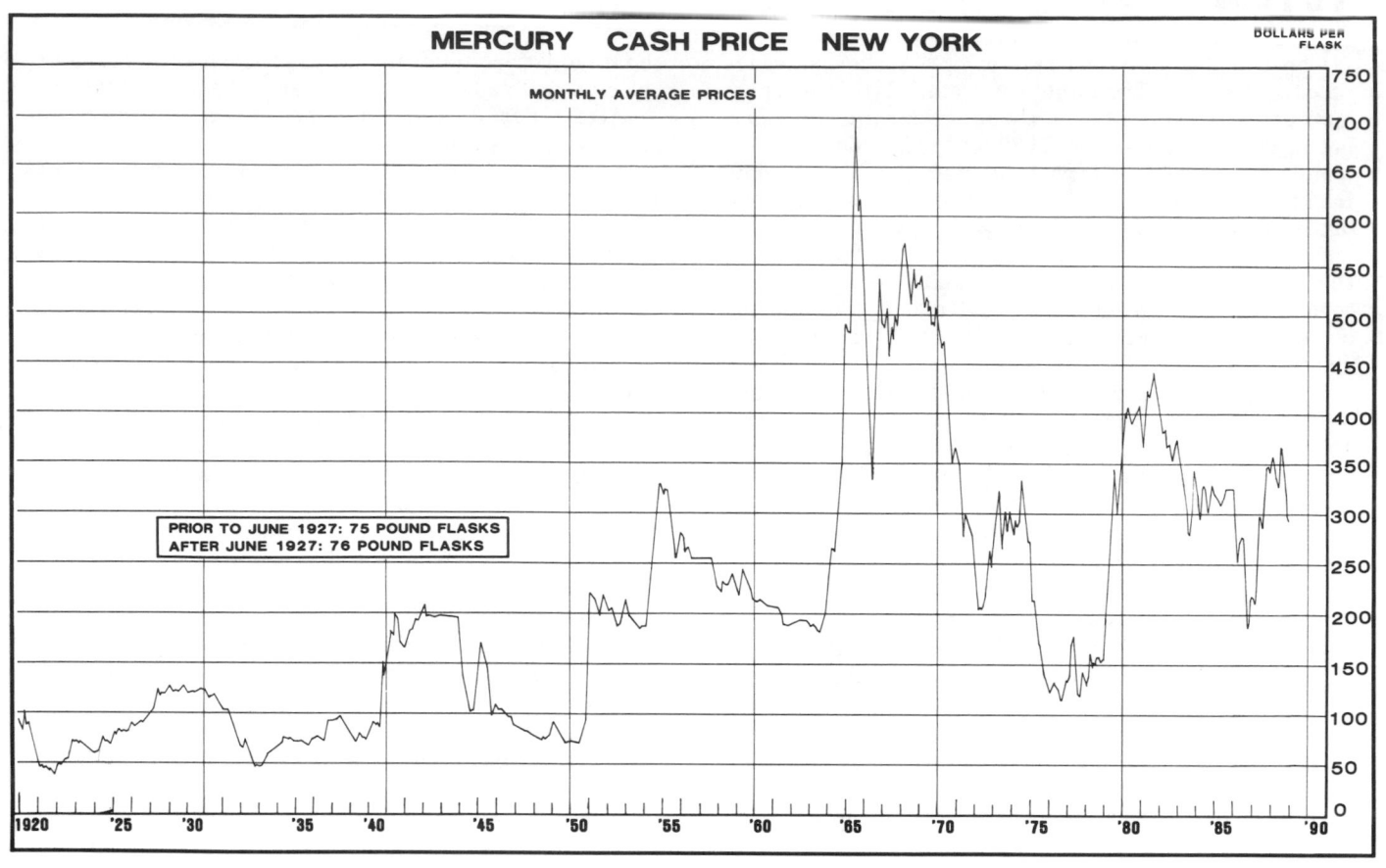

MERCURY CASH PRICE NEW YORK

MONTHLY AVERAGE PRICES

DOLLARS PER FLASK

PRIOR TO JUNE 1927: 75 POUND FLASKS
AFTER JUNE 1927: 76 POUND FLASKS

Average Price of Mercury in New York   In Dollars Per Flask of 76 Pounds

Year	Jan.	Feb.	Mar.	Apr.	May	June	July	Aug.	Sept.	Oct.	Nov.	Dec.	Average
1980	383.75	399.90	420.00	406.81	398.33	389.57	397.11	397.26	402.62	407.83	404.56	376.19	396.72
1981	366.00	386.79	411.18	423.41	418.50	423.07	433.75	441.14	436.55	425.91	421.84	413.07	416.77
1982	405.00	380.92	390.76	384.32	365.88	367.50	364.29	343.30	352.55	373.21	373.75	374.29	372.98
1983	366.67	346.18	338.91	327.62	316.31	300.23	282.25	279.02	299.05	339.29	344.50	331.69	322.64
1984	318.67	295.68	300.45	324.26	328.27	325.48	314.64	302.09	317.18	329.07	327.13	320.08	316.92
1985	317.30	315.00	314.38	309.34	297.27	309.05	316.74	324.61	325.00	325.00	325.00	325.00	316.98
1986	285.68	261.97	252.44	272.05	277.50	276.07	260.00	218.10	181.91	193.80	215.19	219.43	242.85
1987	216.70	211.03	223.73	260.00	297.63	297.73	286.82	306.55	337.86	345.91	348.95	342.27	289.60
1988	354.00	357.00	350.00	337.14	326.90	352.28	367.13	360.43	349.29	322.74	299.34	293.45	339.14

Source: American Metal Market

T.410

Mercury Consumed in the United States   In Flasks

Year	Bat- teries	Chlo- rine & Caustic Soda	Cata- lysts Misc.	Dental Equip.	Elec- trical Light- ing	Gen- eral Lab. Use	Meas- uring Control Instrum.	Other Instru- ments + Relat.	Paints	Wiring Devices & Switches	Other Uses	Grand Total
1980	27,829	9,470	765	1,779	1,036	363	3,049	190	8,621	3,062	790	58,983
1981	29,441	7,323	815	1,613	1,043	328	5,671	253	7,049	2,641	242	59,244
1982	24,880	6,243	499	1,019	826	281	3,064	194	6,794	2,004	984	48,943
1983	23,350	8,054	484	1,597	1,273	280	2,465	N.A.	6,047	2,316	1,356	49,138
1984	29,700	7,347	359	1,432	1,487	269	2,856	N.A.	4,651	2,730	1,404	54,669
1985	27,622	6,804	488	1,444	1,147	413	2,300	N.A.	4,892	2,762	267	49,846
1986[1]	21,764	7,548	536	1,507	1,197	568	1,814	N.A.	5,006	2,981	309	45,946
1987[1]	15,462	9,014	402	1,613	1,299	571	1,717	N.A.	5,755	3,811	420	41,939
1988[2]	13,000	12,000		1,500	900	650	2,000		5,000	6,000	700	45,000

[1] Preliminary.   [2] Estimate.   *Source: Bureau of Mines*

T.413

Milk

U.S. milk production in the July-September 1988 quarter rose 1.5 percent from a year earlier, similar to the increase in the second quarter. Output in late 1987 and early 1988 was in the range of 3 percent. The major development in the dairy industry in recent years has been the Dairy Termination Program. From April 1986-August 1987, the program removed the capacity for producing over 12 billion pounds of milk. Still, milk production in 1987 declined by less than 1 percent from levels in 1985 and 1986. During the first quarter of 1987, milk output was more than 3 percent below a year earlier. It moved above 1986 levels about mid-year. By October-December 1987, production was 3 percent larger than a year earlier. In 1987, there were declining cow numbers, but good increases in yield per cow.

During the third quarter of 1988, the average number of cows on farms fell by almost 1 percent from a year earlier. At the same time, milk output per cow posted a 2 percent increase. During the July-September period, the average number of cows was 8.58 million, compared with 8.65 million in July-September 1987. In the same quarter of 1986, the average cow population was 8.95 million.

While the number of cows was smaller, the output or yield per cow had risen. Improving genetic potential, better management, more feeding of concentrates, and improved formulation of rations accounted for higher yields. There had also been improvements in the quality of forage feed. The Dairy Termination Program eliminated many low-yielding cows and herds.

In the 21 major states, the milk output per cow for the July-September 1988 period averaged 1,192 pounds, compared to 1,166 in the same quarter of 1987. By comparison, the same quarter yield in 1986 was 1,122 pounds, while in 1985 it was 1,117. The milk-feed ratio in the first 8 months of 1988 dropped from a year earlier, due partly to the drought. The July-September milk-feed ratio fell to the lowest level since the mid 1970s. In addition to higher feed prices, there were problems with feed quality. Due to the drought, more

forage was expected to be fed to milking herds than would normally be the case. The drought reduced alfalfa yields in the Midwest, though rains helped later cuttings. Alfalfa hay prices in September reached record levels, and were about $20/ton higher than a year earlier. There was some concern with corn aflatoxin contamination. The main impact of the drought was that milk yield per cow was likely to decline in 1989.

Milk production in the 21 major states during the July-September quarter averaged 10.22 billion pounds per month, compared to 10.08 billion in the same period of 1987. In the first quarter of 1988, milk production was up 3.8 percent from a year earlier. Increased production was due partly to a reduction in the number of low-yielding cows. In the 21 states, the number of dairy cows fell by about 84,000 between January and September. For the year, milk production was expected to increase by about 1 percent. With higher feed costs, milk production in the final months of 1988 was likely to tail off. The year 1989 was expected to get started on a weak note. Cow numbers were likely to decline some, while yield increases were expected to be small. If the price of feed declined with improving new crop prospects, it was possible that milk production would recover.

June-August 1988 milk marketings were 1 percent above a year earlier. Butter and cheese production absorbed most of the increase in supplies.

The U.S. is an exporter of dairy products, though shipments were expected to fall in 1988. Much of the exports are butter, cheese, and non-fat dry milk from Commodity Credit Corporation (CCC) stocks as export sales or donations. Smaller CCC supplies meant lower exports, but commercial exports of non-fat dry milk were to rise. Over May-June 1988, dairy exports were 321 million pounds in milk-equivalent, down about 35 percent from a year earlier. Imports of dairy products over the same period were the equivalent of 544 million pounds, off slightly from a year earlier.

World Fluid Milk Production (Cow's Milk)   In Millions of Metric Tons

Year	Australia	Brazil	Canada	Czecho-slovakia	Den-mark	Fin-land	West Germany	USSR	India	Nether-lands	New Zealand	France	Poland	Switzerland	United Kingdom	United States
1984	6.1	10.8	8.1	6.8	5.2	3.2	26.2	97.9	17.1	12.8	7.6	27.6	16.8	3.9	16.6	61.4
1985	6.3	10.7	7.9	6.9	5.1	3.1	25.7	98.6	19.0	12.6	7.9	26.8	16.6	3.8	16.3	64.9
1986	6.2	11.6	7.9	6.9	5.1	3.1	26.4	102.2	19.5	12.7	8.2	28.1	15.7	3.8	16.2	65.4
1987[1]	6.4	13.3	8.0	6.9	4.9	2.9	24.4	103.4	21.2	11.7	7.3	27.1	15.5	3.8	15.4	64.6
1988[3]	6.3	13.2	8.2	6.9	4.7	2.8	23.6	105.5	22.5	11.2	7.9	26.1	15.0	3.8	14.6	65.9

[1] Preliminary.   [2] Estimate.   *Source: Foreign Agricultural Service, U.S.D.A.*   T.414

U.S. Milk-Feed Price Ratio[1]   In Pounds

Year	Jan.	Feb.	Mar.	Apr.	May	June	July	Aug.	Sept.	Oct.	Nov.	Dec.	Average
1984	1.33	1.33	1.34	1.32	1.32	1.32	1.35	1.40	1.48	1.56	1.62	1.59	1.41
1985	1.57	1.57	1.55	1.51	1.47	1.45	1.44	1.47	1.51	1.56	1.55	1.53	1.52
1986	1.48	1.50	1.48	1.48	1.46	1.45	1.51	1.55	1.61	1.75	1.77	1.77	1.57
1987	1.74	1.69	1.63	1.62	1.58	1.57	1.56	1.58	1.65	1.65	1.65	1.63	1.63
1988[2]	1.52	1.48	1.43	1.40	1.37	1.36	1.15	1.19	1.25	1.32	1.34		

[1] Pounds of 16% protein mixed dairyfeed equal in value to one pound of milk.   [2] Preliminary.   *Source: National Agricultural Service, U.S.D.A.*   T.420

MILK

Milk Cows & Cattle and Milk Production in the U.S.

Year	Number of Milk Cows on Farms[2] (Thousands)	Production Per Milk Cow[3] Milk Pounds	Milk Fat	Total Milk Production[3] Quantity Billion Pounds	% of Fat in All Milk Produced	Milk Fat Mil. Lbs.	Milk Sold to Plants & Dealers Quantity Billion Pounds	$ Per 100 Lbs.	Milk Sold Directly to Consumers Quantity Million Quarts	¢ Per Quart	Milk Utilized Bill. Lbs.	Farm Value of All Milk Produced Mill. $	Exports Mill. Lbs.	Per Capita Consump. Fluid Milk[4] In Lbs.
1981	10,898	12,183	444	132.8	3.64	4,836	129.0	13.77	684.7	48.3	130.5	18,415	3,197	222
1982	11,011	12,306	450	135.5	3.65	4,950	131.9	13.61	597.8	48.1	133.1	18,559	5,095	216
1983	11,098	12,585	460	139.7	3.66	5,105	136.1	13.58	563.4	48.4	137.3	19,081	3,188	215
1984	10,833	12,506	458	135.5	3.66	4,964	131.4	13.46	530.8	49.2	132.5	18,341	3,600	217
1985	11,016	12,994	476	143.1	3.67	5,249	139.4	12.75	583.9	48.7	140.7	18,379	4,805	220
1986[1]	10,813	13,260	487	143.4	3.67	5,284	140.3	12.51	564.8	48.4	141.5	18,147	1,970	221
1987[1]	10,334	13,786		142.5									2,434	220
1988[5]	10,250	14,000		145.0										

[1] Preliminary. [2] Average number on farms during year excluding heifers not yet fresh. [3] Excludes milk sucked by calves & milk produced by cows not on farms. [4] And cream (milk fat basis). [5] Estimate. *Source: Crop Reporting Board, U.S.D.A.* T.415

Utilization of Milk in the United States   In Millions of Pounds (Milk Equivalent)

Year	Butter from Whey Cream	Creamery Butter[1]	Cheese[6]	Cottage Cheese (Creamed)	Condensed Whole Milk	Evaporated Milk[5]	Dry Whole Milk Products	Ice Cream & Other	Frozen Dairy Products[2]	Fluid Consumption Nonfarm	Farm[5]	Fed to Calves	Other Mfg. Products[4]
1981	3,192	24,614	36,546	977	639	1,669	686	14,080	11,964	50,215	886	1,418	821
1982	3,365	24,987	38,903	950	704	1,490	758	14,268	12,135	49,346	839	1,521	656
1983	3,554	25,788	41,006	941	648	1,525	823	14,720	12,598	49,705	842	1,527	663
1984	3,406	21,471	38,718	932	724	1,419	880	14,783	12,660	50,605	804	2,134	488
1985	3,694	24,385	41,700	917	817	1,509	877	15,021	12,855	52,014	709	1,757	477
1986[3]	3,799	23,274	42,239	914	835	1,278	901	15,451	13,226	52,674	690	1,869	559

[1] Excludes whey butter. [2] From milk and cream only. [3] Preliminary. [4] Includes dry cream, malted milk, dry part skim milk, dry ice cream mix. [5] Used for farm-churned butter. [6] American & other. *Source: Crop Reporting Board, U.S.D.A.* T.416

Milk Production on Farms in the United States   In Millions of Pounds

Year	Jan.	Feb.	Mar.	Apr.	May	June	July	Aug.	Sept.	Oct.	Nov.	Dec.	Total
1982	11,106	10,361	11,700	11,607	12,191	11,781	11,618	11,370	10,939	11,053	10,644	11,135	135,505
1983	11,443	10,707	12,029	11,956	12,616	12,261	12,046	11,672	11,218	11,400	10,979	11,345	139,672
1984	11,373	10,856	11,713	11,660	12,219	11,710	11,487	11,205	10,784	10,913	10,524	11,006	135,450
1985	11,276	10,485	11,874	12,028	12,869	12,506	12,553	12,342	11,790	11,986	11,520	11,918	143,147
1986	12,211	11,276	12,565	12,517	13,127	12,509	12,272	11,899	11,288	11,360	10,963	11,393	143,381
1987[1]	11,668	10,396	12,250	12,248	12,860	12,291	12,207	11,888	11,417	11,665	11,264	11,808	142,462
1988[1]	12,042	11,493	12,563	12,482	13,010	12,348	12,356	12,086	11,606				

[1] Preliminary. *Source: Crop Reporting Board, U.S.D.A.* T.417

Average Price Received by U.S. Farmers for All Milk[2] (Sold to Plants)   In Dollars Per Cwt.

Year	Jan.	Feb.	Mar.	Apr.	May	June	July	Aug.	Sept.	Oct.	Nov.	Dec.	Average[1]
1983	13.90	13.80	13.60	13.60	13.30	13.20	13.20	13.30	13.50	13.80	13.90	13.70	13.58
1984	13.60	13.40	13.30	13.10	13.00	12.90	13.00	13.20	13.60	14.00	14.30	14.00	13.46
1985	13.90	13.70	13.30	12.90	12.50	12.20	12.10	12.10	12.30	12.60	12.60	12.60	12.75
1986	12.50	12.40	12.20	12.10	12.00	11.90	12.00	12.30	12.80	13.20	13.40	13.40	12.50
1987[3]	13.20	12.90	12.50	12.20	12.00	11.90	12.00	12.20	12.70	12.90	12.90	12.70	12.54
1988[3]	12.50	12.30	11.90	11.60	11.40	11.30	11.40	11.80	12.20	13.00	13.20		

[1] Weighted average. [2] Adjusted for seasonal variation. [3] Preliminary. *Source: Crop Reporting Board, U.S.D.A.* T.418

Farm Price of Milk[1] Eligible for Fluid Market   In Dollars Per Hundred Pounds

Year	Jan.	Feb.	Mar.	Apr.	May	June	July	Aug.	Sept.	Oct.	Nov.	Dec.	Average
1983	14.00	14.00	13.80	13.70	13.50	13.30	13.30	13.50	13.70	13.90	14.10	13.90	13.75
1984	13.80	13.50	13.40	13.20	13.10	13.00	13.10	13.30	13.80	14.20	14.40	14.10	13.61
1985	14.10	13.90	13.50	13.00	12.70	12.30	12.30	12.30	12.40	12.70	12.70	12.70	12.90
1986	12.70	12.60	12.40	12.20	12.10	12.00	12.10	12.40	12.90	13.30	13.50	13.50	12.62
1987	13.40	13.10	12.70	12.40	12.10	12.10	12.20	12.40	12.90	13.00	13.00	12.90	12.68
1988	12.70	12.40	12.10	11.80	11.50	11.40	11.60	11.80	12.50	13.10	13.30		

[1] MILK, Standard Grade, 3.5% milkfat. Weighted average price per 100 pounds (f.o.b. city). *Source: Crop Reporting Board, U.S.D.A.* T.419

Molasses

World molasses production in 1988/89 was estimated at 34.7 million tonnes, compared with 34.9 million the previous season and 33.4 million in 1986/87.

Output by Brazil, the world's major producer, was placed at 4 million tonnes in 1988/89, unchanged from the year before. The USSR's output was forecast to be 2.95 million tonnes, up 4 percent from 1987/88. India's output was expected to be about 8 percent lower at 3.5 million tonnes. China's production has remained at around 1.9 million tonnes since 1986/87.

U.S. production in 1988/89 was projected at 2.01 million tonnes, compared with 2.05 million in 1987/88 and 2.02 million in 1986/87.

The average price of blackstrap molasses (cane) at New Orleans in the first four months of 1988 was higher than the average for 1987. The 1987 average was $53.23/ton, while the price for the first four months of 1988 averaged $59.96. However, in sympathy with other foodstuffs after 1988's summer drought, molasses ended 1988 at $66.25, up almost 21 percent on the year.

Total U.S. molasses supplies in 1987 were estimated at 534.5 million gallons, including 200.2 million gallons of domestic beet molasses. Total mainland production was placed at 357.5 million gallons. Shipments from Hawaii were 52 million gallons. U.S. imports amounted to 187.6 million gallons.

World Production of Molasses (Industrial)   In Thousands of Metric Tons

Crop Year	Argentina	Brazil	Cuba[2]	France	W. Germany	India	Italy	Mexico	Philippines	Poland	Australia	Thailand	China	United States	USSR	World Total
1978–9	818	5,000	1,296	952	685	2,564	365	1,410	818	657	577			2,148	3,306	32,688
1979–0	789	4,800	1,185	958	653	1,582	390	1,260	818	653	598			2,054	3,062	30,052
1980–1	654	5,400	1,111	1,013	657	2,129	410	1,145	860	430	713			2,012	2,669	30,941
1981–2	565	4,520	1,200	1,404	836	3,400	500	1,373	941	665	719	1,736		2,051	2,385	34,384
1982–3	541	5,110	1,050	1,364	807	3,700	370	1,270	957	758	726	1,316		1,900	2,530	35,139
1983–4	560	5,130	1,150	1,072	605	2,500	380	1,390	928	816	718	1,230	1,275	2,015	2,723	32,981
1984–5	702	4,800	1,150	1,165	640	2,500	380	1,400	744	708	736	1,356	1,130	2,012	3,200	33,755
1985–6	854	3,986	2,000	1,126	751	2,850	486	1,608	551	636	658	1,194	1,909	1,848	2,900	33,852
1986–7	950	2,587	1,750	998	715	3,660	530	1,552	490	638	693	1,206	1,875	2,027	2,950	33,429
1987–8[1]	880	4,000	1,750	1,050	600	3,800	539	1,560	490	635	730	1,215	1,870	2,056	2,850	34,866
1988–9[3]	850	4,000	1,750	1,000	600	3,500	490	1,560	490	635	740	1,275	1,875	2,010	2,950	34,717

[1] Preliminary.   [2] Includes hi-test molasses.   [3] Estimate.   *Source: Foreign Agricultural Service, U.S.D.A.*   T.421

U.S. Annual Average Prices of Molasses, by Types (F.O.B. Tank Car or Truck)   In Dollars Per Ton[1]

Year	Blackstrap New Orleans	Blackstrap South Florida	Blackstrap Baltimore	Blackstrap Minneapolis	Blackstrap Omaha	Blackstrap Calif. Ports	Beet Molasses Colorado	Beet Molasses Wyo. & Montana	Beet Molasses Ore., Utah & Idaho	Citrus Molasses Florida
1977	40.55	42.45	47.00	54.35	58.75	42.90	41.45	45.20	55.10	50.65
1978	51.50	52.40	59.25	67.30	72.55	54.00	60.40	58.35	60.95	61.05
1979	82.95	85.50	91.20	107.90	107.75	84.05	85.30	82.65	N.A.	79.40
1980	96.50	96.80	106.75	124.45	128.85	101.70	95.60	96.55	N.A.	103.65
1981	84.90	90.00	99.30	111.20	119.40	89.20	85.30	95.20	N.A.	103.10
1982	48.00	56.55	64.15	70.85	81.90	60.50	69.40	63.70	44.50	86.90
1983	56.50	63.10	73.05	76.90	91.90	70.40	79.45	65.95	60.55	89.20
1984	61.50	71.00	77.65	81.00	94.45	71.95	82.50	79.15	70.65	97.50
1985	50.28	59.79	64.66	72.83	85.00	61.89	N.A.	67.50	57.33	N.A.
1986	69.61	78.10	83.05	92.03	N.A.	73.26	80.33	86.75	68.44	N.A.
1987[2]	53.23	61.96	72.83	80.05	N.A.	67.17	60.31	54.69	62.22	N.A.

[1] Per ton prices are based on 171 gallons for blackstrap, beet and corn molasses and on 175 gallons for citrus molasses. Prices represent sales F.O.B. terminal to the general feed trade and do not include sales made under various pricing arrangements above or below prices generally available to the ultimate user. Ton—2,000 lbs. Gallon—U.S. gallon. Prices are now rounded off to the nearest 5 cents.   [2] Preliminary.   *Source: Molasses Market News, Annual Summary, AMS, U.S.D.A. Denver Colorado, and Molasses Market News, Weekly, various issues*   T.423

MOLASSES

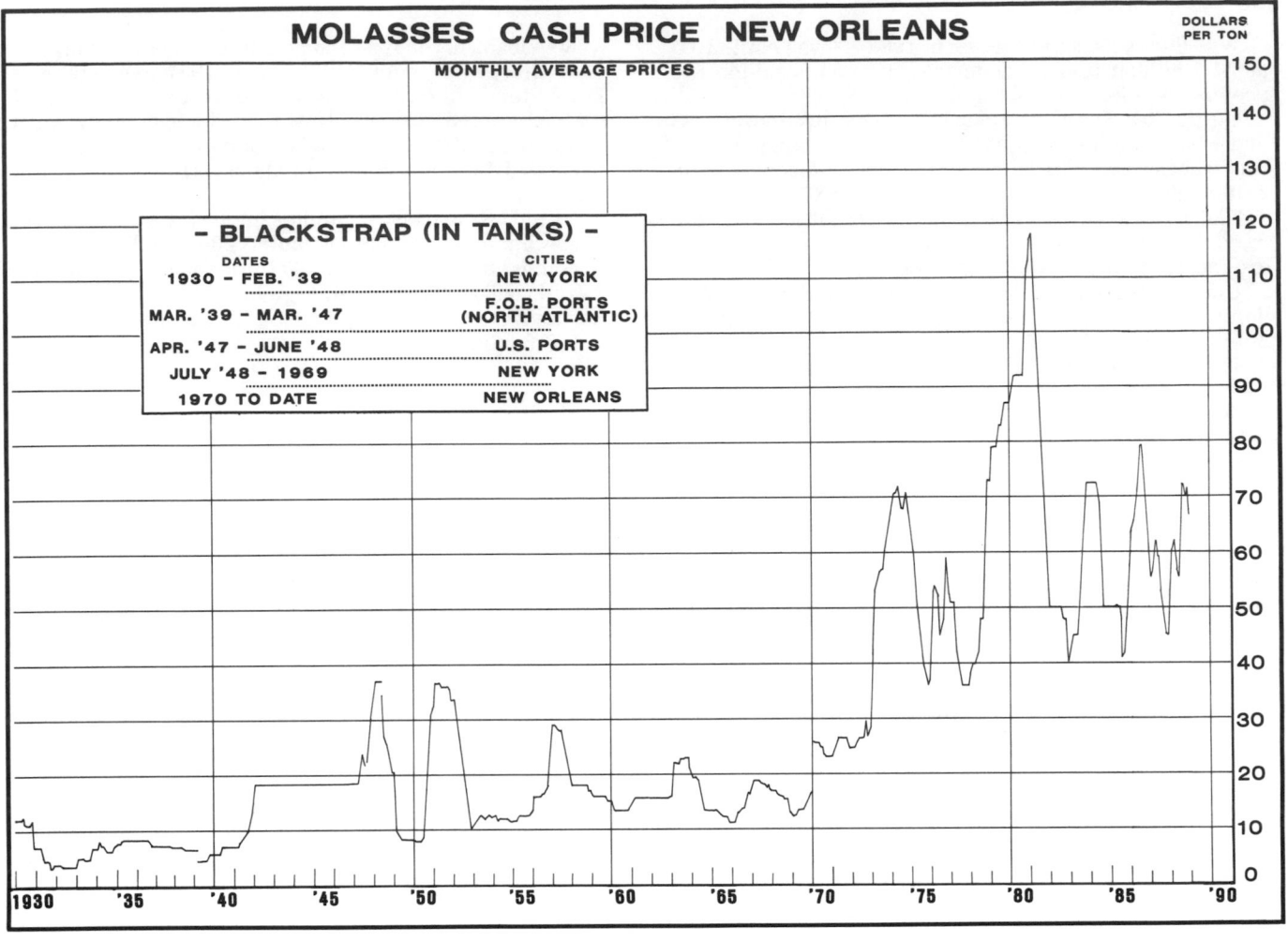

MOLASSES CASH PRICE NEW ORLEANS
MONTHLY AVERAGE PRICES

- BLACKSTRAP (IN TANKS) -

DATES	CITIES
1930 - FEB. '39	NEW YORK
MAR. '39 - MAR. '47	F.O.B. PORTS (NORTH ATLANTIC)
APR. '47 - JUNE '48	U.S. PORTS
JULY '48 - 1969	NEW YORK
1970 TO DATE	NEW ORLEANS

Salient Statistics of Molasses in the United States   In Thousands of Gallons

Year	Mainland cane	Domestic beet	Refiners blackstrap	Total[2]	In ship-ments from Hawaii	Imports	Exports	Total U.S. supply
1982	126,956	170,781	38,189	350,337	49,109	206,291	47,247	558,490
1983	123,007	162,762	31,549	331,027	54,354	312,279	48,643	649,017
1984	118,993	170,426	34,598	330,284	50,029	260,724	26,371	614,666
1985	132,544	165,071	25,574	323,186	44,316	313,215	25,598	655,119
1986	137,285	192,565	23,922	353,772	51,395	249,760	72,545	582,382
1987[1]	136,496	200,182	20,844	357,482	52,000	187,587	62,582	534,487

[1] Preliminary.   [2] Starting 1984 totals are adjusted to reflect omission of citrus and hydrol production.   NA = not available.
Source: Molasses Market News, AMS, USDA.

Wholesale Price of Blackstrap Molasses (Cane) at New Orleans   In Dollars Per Ton

Year	Jan.	Feb.	Mar.	Apr.	May	June	July	Aug.	Sept.	Oct.	Nov.	Dec.	Average
1982	50.00	50.00	50.00	50.00	50.00	50.00	50.00	48.00	48.00	44.00	40.00	41.00	47.60
1983	44.00	45.00	45.00	45.00	47.50	49.40	53.75	61.50	68.75	72.50	72.50	72.50	56.45
1984	72.50	72.50	72.50	72.50	70.70	68.75	59.00	50.00	50.00	50.00	50.00	50.10	61.55
1985	50.00	50.00	50.00	50.00	50.00	47.75	41.00	41.90	48.00	53.75	57.50	63.50	50.28
1986	65.00	65.60	68.50	71.00	73.75	79.00	79.13	76.60	72.30	68.10	60.25	55.50	69.56
1987	56.25	59.40	62.00	59.40	59.10	53.00	50.60	48.60	45.30	45.00	47.00	53.10	53.23
1988	60.30	62.00	60.60	56.90	55.50	62.50	72.50	72.50	70.00	71.50	67.50	66.90	64.89

Source: Economics Service, U.S.D.A.

T.424

Molybdenum

Consumption of molybdenum ran at a strong pace in early 1988, and industrial inventories were reduced. World production in 1988 was forecast at 175 million pounds, and consumption was placed at 180 million pounds. The leading producers are the U.S., Chile, Canada, and Mexico.

In April 1988, U.S. dealer prices of molybdenum oxide dropped from a high of $4.25/lb. to $3.65, while the large mine operators, Amax and Cyprus Mines, left prices at $3.65.

Two U.S. mines produce molybdenum ore, and seven mines recover molybdenum as a by-product or co-product from copper. In 1987, total U.S. molybdenum concentrate production was 75.1 million pounds. For the first seven months of 1988, production was 51.7 million pounds, for an implied annual total of more than 88.0 million pounds, or about a 17 percent gain.

U.S. gross output of molybdenum products totaled 34.65 million pounds in 1987. For the first seven months of 1988, the total was 30.17 million pounds, for an implied annual 51.42 million pounds, a possible gain of 48 percent.

The largest area of U.S. molybdenum consumption is full-alloy molybdenum steel, which accounts for about a quarter of total usage. Next is stainless and heat resistant steel, which is a large user of molybdic oxides.

Another major area of use is mill products made from molybdenum metal powder. For the first seven months of 1988, consumption was 20.39 million pounds, compared with total 1987 consumption of 32.62 million.

In 1988, there appeared to be a drop in the amount of molybdenum imported into the U.S. In 1987, the total amount of molybdenum in all imports was 12.35 million pounds, valued at $47.71 million. For the first seven months of 1988, this total was 4.48 million pounds with a value of $21.83 million.

Increased production in the U.S. may have been responsible for the decline in imported material. In recent years, the largest suppliers of molybdenum to the U.S. have been Chile, Canada, Mexico, China and Peru.

Identified molybdenum resources are about 19 billion pounds in the U.S. and around 46 billion pounds in the world. Resources are more than adequate to supply foreseeable demand.

There are few substitutes for molybdenum in steel alloy making. Due to it's usefulness and availability, industry is looking for more ways to utilize the metal. One recent discovery involves the use of molybdenum treatment on lumber as an environmentally acceptable method of combating termites.

World Mine Production of Molybdenum   In 1,000 Pounds (Contained Molybdenum)

Year	Bulgaria	Canada[3]	Chile	China	Japan	Mexico	Mongolia	Niger	Peru	Philippines	South Korea	United States	USSR	World Total
1979	330	24,634	29,895	4,400	154	105			2,637	311	417	143,967	22,500	229,350
1980	330	26,892	30,133	4,400	123	163	1,070	269	5,926	201	661	150,686	22,900	243,754
1981	330	28,329	33,863	4,400	163	994	1,460	249	5,485	207	1,023	139,900	23,600	240,003
1982	375	30,779	44,198	4,400	214	11,442	1,830	93	6,427	150	796	84,381	24,300	209,385
1983	420	22,474	33,651	4,400	214	12,932	2,120	88	5,825	86	313	33,593	24,500	140,616
1984	420	25,479	37,172	4,400	324	8,938	2,200	73	6,557	—	348	103,664	24,700	214,275
1985[1]	420	17,311	40,541	4,400	215	8,292	2,200	44	8,898	—	734	108,409	24,900	216,364
1986[2]	400	28,440	35,971	4,000	—	7,720	2,200	44	7,681	—	660	93,976	25,100	206,192
1987[2]		25,000	40,000			8,000			8,000			65,000		179,000

[1] Preliminary.   [2] Estimate.   [3] Shipments.   *Source: Bureau of Mines*   T.425

U.S. Salient Statistics of Molybdenum   In 1,000 Pounds (Contained Molybdenum)

Year	Production	Concentrate Total (Includes Exports)	Concentrate Shipments Value Mill. $	Concentrate For Exports	Con-sumption	Imports for Con-sump-tion	Stocks Dec. 31[2]	Grand Total	Net Production Molyb-dic Oxide[4]	Net Production Molyb-denum Metal Powder	So-dium Molyb-date	Primary Products[3] Shipments To Do-mestic Destina-tions	Primary Products[3] Shipments Oxide For Ex-ports	Con-sump-tion	Pro-ducers' Stocks Dec. 31
1979	143,967	143,504	871.1	36,405	103,152	2,329	9,520	101,752	79,035	4,946	1,541	109,419	35,773	60,388	8,502
1980	150,686	149,311	1,344	35,026	108,206	1,825	18,101	106,284	84,554	4,904	1,142	95,391	35,557	53,265	27,007
1981	139,900	118,916	945.5	32,735	80,725	1,988	35,043	105,824	59,645	3,513	96	64,368	20,004	50,189	44,961
1982	84,381	76,135	504.1	21,870	49,444	3,115	38,510	65,381	35,354	3,304	121	47,884	23,375	27,665	49,402
1983	33,593	48,805	166.6	18,979	27,014	1,673	11,637	37,533	11,148	3,667	191	50,562	19,877	27,225	28,352
1984	103,664	102,405	326.8	41,687	54,843	28	12,450	79,689	40,186	4,302	N.A.	65,527	24,553	34,792	22,155
1985	108,409	111,936	347.8	38,646	N.A.	112	9,322	87,436	48,750	3,734	N.A.	73,861	36,268	33,451	21,014
1986[1]	93,976	95,006	240.5	18,267	53,061	1,120	8,715	41,490	6,147	4,256	N.A.	57,855	21,325	31,898	20,699
1987[5]	75,117	69,867		18,587	37,442	1,264	15,082	34,659				40,668			22,168
1988[5]	77,000	90,000		21,000				42,000				45,000			

[1] Preliminary.   [2] At mines & at plants making molybdenum products.   [3] Comprises ferromolybdenum, molybdic oxide, & molybdenum salts & metal.   [4] Includes molybdic oxide briquets, molybdic acid, & molybdenum trioxide.   [5] Estimate.   *Source: Bureau of Mines*   T.426

Nickel

In 1988, nickel was marked by turbulent price action, which drove the market from about $2.50 a pound in January to just over $8.00 by March. There was some later price weakness, but the year was undoubtedly one of the more exciting that we've seen in this usually stable and well controlled market.

The cause and effect of the spectacular price action was similar to that seen in other industrial metals. Years of low prices, which in the case of nickel had hovered around the $2.00 a pound level, forced mine operators and refiners to institute production cuts or shut down entirely. The resulting production loss was cushioned by large stocks which had built up when the industry was operating at a higher capacity rate. As value-conscious users became aware of the developing situation around mid-1987, they began to bid up prices of available supplies.

In June 1987, the nickel market broke up above $2.00 a pound and climbed steadily to $4.00 in January 1988. In eight months, prices had doubled. It then took just three months for the market to double again from $4.00 to $8.00. Stocks on the London Metal Exchange (LME) went from just over 20 million pounds in June 1987 to about 5 million pounds in May 1988.

For the first six months of 1988, U.S. nickel consumption in all forms was estimated at 114.7 million pounds, compared with 1987's 111.0 million pounds in the same period. Stainless steel was the biggest single consumer use of nickel, with Jan.-June 1988 usage of 39.88 million pounds. Use of nickel for other alloys and as nickel in its own right totaled 21.16 million pounds in the same period, and electroplating use totaled 23.83 million.

Canada, home to two of the world's largest nickel mining companies, Inco Ltd. and Falconbridge Ltd., was the biggest exporter to the U.S., supplying a total of 102.2 million pounds in Jan.-June 1988. Norway and the Dominican Republic followed with much smaller amounts. Total U.S. nickel imports during the first six months of 1988 totaled 168.2 million pounds, compared with 149.1 million in the same period of 1987.

Identified world resources of one percent or better nickel are estimated at 143 million short tons, with substantially more in low-grade deposits. Also, extensive deposits of nickel in the form of manganese nodules cover large areas of the Pacific Ocean floor and, to a lesser extent, the Atlantic Ocean.

Futures Market

Nickel futures are traded on the London Metal Exchange (LME).

World Mine Production of Nickel   In Thousands of Short Tons of Contained Nickel

Year	Australia[3]	Bots-wana	Brazil	Canada	Cuba	Domin. Repub.	Finland[3]	Greece	Indo-nesia	New Caledonia	Philip-pines	South Africa	United States	USSR	Zim-babwe	World Trade
1979	76.8	17.8	3.3	139.4	34.3	27.7	6.4	22.2	41.1	88.2	36.7	33.3	15.1	166.0	16.1	756.5
1980	81.9	17.0	2.5	203.7	40.3	18.0	7.2	16.8	58.7	95.5	51.9	28.3	14.7	170.0	16.6	858.9
1981	82.0	18.2	7.2	176.6	42.5	20.6	7.6	17.2	53.8	86.1	32.2	29.1	12.1	174.0	14.4	800.0
1982	96.5	19.6	15.9	97.6	39.8	5.9	7.0	5.5	50.6	66.3	21.6	24.3	3.2	182.0	17.4	685.0
1983	84.5	20.1	17.2	141.2	41.5	21.6	5.9	18.5	54.4	50.9	15.3	22.6	—	187.0	13.3	743.7
1984	84.8	20.5	25.9	192.0	35.1	26.4	7.6	18.4	52.5	64.3	15.0	27.6	14.5	192.0	13.4	848.9
1985[1]	94.5	21.6	22.4	187.4	35.7	28.0	8.7	20.6	44.8	80.4	31.0	27.6	6.1	198.0	12.3	884.3
1986[2]	77.0	22.0	25.4	199.1	36.0	24.3	7.2	19.3	48.3	71.7	15.0	27.6	1.2	205.0	12.1	864.1
1987[2]	75.0	25.0	30.0	220.0		27.0	7.0	9.0	48.0	71.0	11.0	27.0		205.0	12.0	874.0

[1] Preliminary. [2] Estimate. [3] Content of nickel sulfate and concentrates. *Source: Bureau of Mines*   T.427

Salient Statistics of Nickel in the United States   In Short Tons

Year	Net Import Reliance as a % of Apparent Consumption	Production Plant[4]	Production Secondary[3]	Alloy Steels	Cast Irons	Copper Base Alloys	Electroplating Anodes	Nickel Alloys	Stainless & Heat Resisting Steels	Super Alloys	Chemicals	Total	Stocks Dec. 31 At Consumers' Plants	Stocks Dec. 31 At Producer Plants	Nickel & Pdt's Imports (Gross Weight)	Nickel & Pdt's Exports (Gross Weight)	Avg. N.Y. Cathode Price Free Mkt. $ Lb.
1979	75	44,181	57,404	20.2	4.7	8.5	28.5	41.1	69.6	17.6	1.2	196,293	19,518	28,500	177,205	50,810	
1980	76	44,225	49,291	16.9	4.0	8.8	18.8	27.4	54.7	19.2	1.5	156,299	15,231	60,000	189,188	56,675	2.85
1981	75	48,805	52,076	16.5	3.7	10.6	22.3	10.6	50.6	13.5	2.0	144,851	22,508	100,000	209,008	46,836	2.65
1982	76	44,956	42,968	10.0	1.9	4.3	20.9	17.9	32.2	11.0	2.0	103,981	18,853	62,000	129,787	57,029	2.24
1983	75	33,400	49,852	9.8	1.1	6.3	22.6	24.9	47.0	11.5	2.0	127,845	20,448	38,500	152,333	43,913	2.20
1984	69	44,933	55,167	11.9	1.5	6.7	24.8	29.4	45.8	12.9	2.2	136,861	20,934	37,300	176,715	58,525	2.22
1985	73	36,382	53,645	9.6	3.1	14.9	24.9	25.3	68.0	13.6	2.1	119,907	19,106	17,400	157,690	51,429	2.26
1986[2]	75	N.A.	43,726	8.2	2.6	10.6	21.0	19.9	60.2	12.7	1.9	107,062	16,557	10,300	129,094	23,269	1.86
1987[2]	74		55,000									140,000	9,857	11,000	150,000		2.15

[1] Exclusive of scrap. [2] Preliminary. [3] From purchased scrap (ferrous & nonferrous). [4] Smelter & refinery. *Source: Bureau of Mines*   T.428

Oats

U.S. oats production in 1988/89 was only 219 million bushels, down 41 percent from the 1987/88 season and the smallest crop in many years. As recently as 1985, oats production was 521 milliion bushels. Oats are grown primarily in the Northern states of Minnesota, the Dakotas, and Iowa. This area was gripped by a severe drought during the spring and summer of 1988, which resulted in sharply reduced yields. The national average oats yield was only 39 bu./acre, or 28 percent less than the previous year's 54 bushels.

Acreage devoted to oats has been shrinking. With the long decline in farm animal numbers due to mechanization, the need to grow oats has been reduced. Additionally, the price support loan programs for feed grains like barley and corn for some time encouraged production of those crops over oats. Consequently, oats are now being imported. The USDA has begun to implement policies to encourage more oats production. This may be accomplished partly by lowering the acreage set-aside requirement in the government oats program.

Harvested acreage of oats in 1988/89 was estimated at 5.4 million acres, down from 6.9 million in 1987/88. Despite adjustments in the government program that allowed more oats to be seeded, producers did not respond. This was due in part to the potential for much higher corn yields under favorable weather conditions, as was seen in 1986 and 1987. As in recent seasons, there was concern about the availability of high-quality oats for use in food. Much of the oats crop is grown for use on the farm by animals, and there was less movement of oats into the cash market. Supply tightness resulted in higher prices and increasing imports, especially from Canada. With the reduction in U.S. supplies due to the drought, Canadian oats exports to the U.S. rose sharply.

U.S. beginning stocks of oats in 1988/89 were estimated at 112 million bushels, 16 percent less than the previous season. With the smaller crop and imports of 60 million bushels, total availability of oats was estimated by USDA to be 391 million bushels, 29 percent less than a year earlier.

Total season's use was projected to be 302 million bushels, or 32 percent less than the previous year. Feed use of oats was placed at 215 million bushels, down from 361 million bushels in 1987/88. On the basis of relative feed value, corn can be substituted for oats in many feeding situations. Use of oats for food, seed and industrial purposes was forecast to total 86 million bushels, or 9 percent more than the previous year. Higher food use has been related to consumer concerns about serum cholesterol. Ending stocks of oats in 1988/89 were projected by the USDA at only 89 million bushels, or 21 percent less than the previous season.

For 1989-crop oats, the price support loan rate is 85 cents/bu., compared with 90 cents the year before. In 1989, the acreage reduction requirement is 5 percent, the same as in 1988.

Futures Markets

Oats futures are traded on the Chicago Board of Trade, the Minneapolis Grain Exchange, and the Winnipeg Commodity Exchange.

World Production of Oats   In Thousands of Metric Tons

Crop Year	Argentina	Aus- tralia	Canada	China	Den- mark	France	Nether- lands	Poland	Spain	Swe- den	Tur- key	United States	USSR	Un. King.	West Germany	World Total
1975–6	433	1,141	4,466		367	1,948	158	2,920	609	1,345	390	9,551	12,495	795	3,445	47,044
1976–7	530	1,073	4,831		256	1,402	103	2,695	505	1,251	400	7,930	18,113	764	2,497	48,744
1977–8	570	991	4,303	1,515	288	1,928	94	2,561	421	1,416	370	10,901	18,407	790	2,714	51,508
1978–9	676	1,763	3,621	1,500	206	2,203	140	2,492	553	1,550	370	8,730	18,507	706	4,049	51,753
1979–0	522	1,411	2,978	1,600	163	1,845	109	2,186	456	1,524	370	7,643	15,200	542	3,697	45,165
1980–1	433	1,128	3,028	1,800	160	1,927	94	2,245	680	1,567	355	6,652	15,544	601	3,249	44,543
1981–2	339	1,617	3,188	1,700	176	1,774	115	2,731	445	1,816	325	7,391	15,000	620	3,200	45,343
1982–3	637	848	3,637	1,660	178	1,802	136	2,608	443	1,663	330	8,602	15,500	575	3,777	47,866
1983–4	593	2,296	2,773	1,650	86	1,374	61	2,377	464	1,268	310	6,923	17,000	465	2,489	45,115
1984–5	610	1,367	2,670	780	150	1,892	58	2,604	780	1,904	300	6,875	19,200	516	2,973	48,391
1985–6	400	1,339	2,997	664	152	1,803	58	2,682	719	1,668	314	7,559	20,500	615	3,278	50,062
1986–7[1]	400	1,600	3,300	700	111	1,000	40	2,500	422	1,500	316	5,582	21,900	505	2,700	47,500
1987–8[2]	700	1,700	3,000	700	93	1,000	47	2,500	502	1,400		5,429	18,500	440	2,400	43,700
1988–9[2]	700	1,900	2,900	700	130	1,000	27	2,200	580	1,400		3,059	16,500	685	2,500	39,200

[1] Preliminary.   [2] Estimated.   *Source: Foreign Agricultural Service, U.S.D.A.*   T.434

United States Official Oat Crop Production Reports   In Thousands of Bushels

Year	July 1	Aug. 1	Sept. 1	Oct. 1	Dec.	Final	Year	July 1	Aug. 1	Sept. 1	Oct. 1	Dec.	Final
1980	449,504	440,655	450,660	—	457,593	458,263	1985	498,953	519,028	537,443	—	518,626	520,800
1981	528,118	522,408	509,457	—	508,083	509,167	1986	—	443,183	413,025	—	383,553	384,356
1982	580,288	591,478	599,008	—	616,981	620,509	1987	—	392,843	—	—	—	374,000
1983	519,002	504,201	472,541	—	477,303	476,961	1988	—	206,330	206,330	210,766	—	
1984	454,747	455,190	472,460	—	471,921	473,661	1989						

Source: Crop Reporting Board, U.S.D.A.   T.431

OATS

Production of Oats in the United States, by States   In Millions of Bushels

Year	Illinois	Indiana	Iowa	Michigan	Minnesota	Missouri	Nebraska	New York	No. Dakota	Ohio	Oregon	Pennsylvania	So. Dakota	Texas	Wisconsin	California
1979	15.6	6.4	63.0	18.9	84.9	2.0	21.2	18.0	37.0	20.3	4.0	18.4	94.4	16.8	55.9	4.1
1980	14.0	5.9	62.0	20.1	82.7	2.0	15.6	17.9	13.5	19.4	4.1	19.0	66.0	12.6	58.7	4.3
1981	13.5	5.5	59.5	21.1	90.1	4.6	15.8	17.9	44.2	17.0	4.6	20.0	70.5	18.9	52.6	3.6
1982	11.8	6.7	54.2	28.4	97.9	3.3	26.7	18.2	55.7	23.5	6.4	19.8	123.5	10.7	49.3	3.4
1983	12.6	4.6	38.3	15.6	77.0	2.5	13.6	11.4	63.6	15.4	6.0	16.2	79.2	24.0	45.1	2.9
1984	11.4	5.0	47.4	21.7	78.0	1.6	15.7	10.6	50.0	13.9	6.6	16.0	86.8	8.8	53.3	3.5
1985	12.5	7.6	57.8	26.1	77.0	5.8	25.6	17.7	44.5	26.4	9.2	21.0	79.5	15.0	51.5	3.0
1986	14.4	6.4	39.1	17.0	43.4	5.0	21.2	12.9	38.5	12.2	7.6	16.1	46.2	8.4	52.7	3.2
1987	13.1	6.4	35.8	17.1	45.6	3.4	17.6	12.0	36.4	17.5	5.2	14.8	52.9	9.9	43.2	2.8
1988[1]	9.2	3.0	26.4	6.0	18.2	1.4	12.2	7.5	7.2	9.0	6.0	13.0	20.0	9.0	19.7	2.5

[1] Preliminary.   Source: Crop Reporting Board, U.S.D.A.   T.437

Oats Supply and Utilization in the United States

Year June–May	Acreage		Yield	Production	Imports	Total supply	Feed & residual	Food & industrial	Seed	Exports	Total use	Ending stocks	Farm price	Nat. avg. supp. rate
	Planted	Harvested												
	— Mil. acres —		Bu/acre					Mil. bu						—$/bu.—
1980/1	13.4	8.7	53.0	459	1.3	697	432	41.0	33.0	13.3	520	177	1.79	1.16
1981/2	13.6	9.4	54.2	510	1.6	688	453	41.2	35.4	6.6	536	152	1.89	1.24
1982/3	14.0	10.3	57.8	592.6	3.9	748.4	440.6	41.7	43.3	3.0	528.6	219.8	1.49	1.31
1983/4	20.3	9.1	52.6	477.0	30.1	726.9	470.9	40.9	31.9	2.1	545.8	181.1	1.62	1.36
1984/5	12.4	8.2	58.0	473.7	34.0	688.8	432.0	41.0	34.6	1.3	508.9	179.9	1.67	1.31
1985/6	13.3	8.2	63.7	520.8	27.5	728.2	459.9	44.0	38.4	2.2	544.5	183.7	1.23	1.31
1986/7	14.7	6.9	56.3	386.4	33.3	603.4	392.4	45.0	31.5	2.8	470.7	132.7	1.21	.99
1987/8[1]	18.0	6.9	54.0	374.0	46.3	553.0	360.0	46.0	33.0	1.0	441.0	112.0	1.56	.94
1988/9[2]	13.9	5.4	39.1	210.8	60.0	382.8	214.8	— 86.0 —		1.0	301.8	81.0	2.73	.90

[1] Preliminary.   [2] Estimate.   Source: Economic Research Service, U.S.D.A.   T.430

Volume of Trading in Oats Futures at Chicago Board of Trade   In Millions of Bushels

Year	July	Aug.	Sept.	Oct.	Nov.	Dec.	Jan.	Feb.	Mar.	Apr.	May	June	Total
1978–9	103.8	121.3	120.0	149.0	141.0	67.7	59.3	93.9	51.6	95.4	87.1	135.7	1,225.3
1979–0	127.8	111.6	76.1	98.6	96.0	47.1	56.9	85.3	53.8	81.1	131.5	144.8	1,110.6
1980–1	200.4	183.9	199.6	197.1	167.9	151.0	124.8	170.2	129.2	136.4	120.5	162.2	1,943.2
1981–2	125.3	134.6	117.0	144.5	264.9	221.0	166.7	184.7	204.3	223.6	196.5	247.9	2,231.0
1982–3	221.0	218.9	151.2	113.2	127.6	82.5	121.1	154.0	141.3	213.6	159.1	159.7	1,863.2
1983–4	160.1	254.5	180.4	95.1	102.4	57.9	58.9	91.9	77.1	89.8	59.8	76.6	535.0
1984–5	64.7	88.7	38.5	41.0	48.8	39.5	46.1	38.1	33.7	33.7	30.9	31.2	534.9
1985–6	42.6	55.6	37.2	57.0	53.9	35.2	54.7	41.7	41.9	62.0	59.2	62.3	603.3
1986–7	42.0	45.6	47.0	47.2	93.6	107.6	94.0	138.3	120.6	106.2	121.3	117.0	1,080.4
1987–8	103.7	153.6	109.4	135.4	139.4	116.6	92.1	121.2	146.6	162.1	162.6	267.1	1,709.8
1988–9	160.3	121.1	107.6	108.1	183.0	141.1							

Source: Chicago Board of Trade   T.440

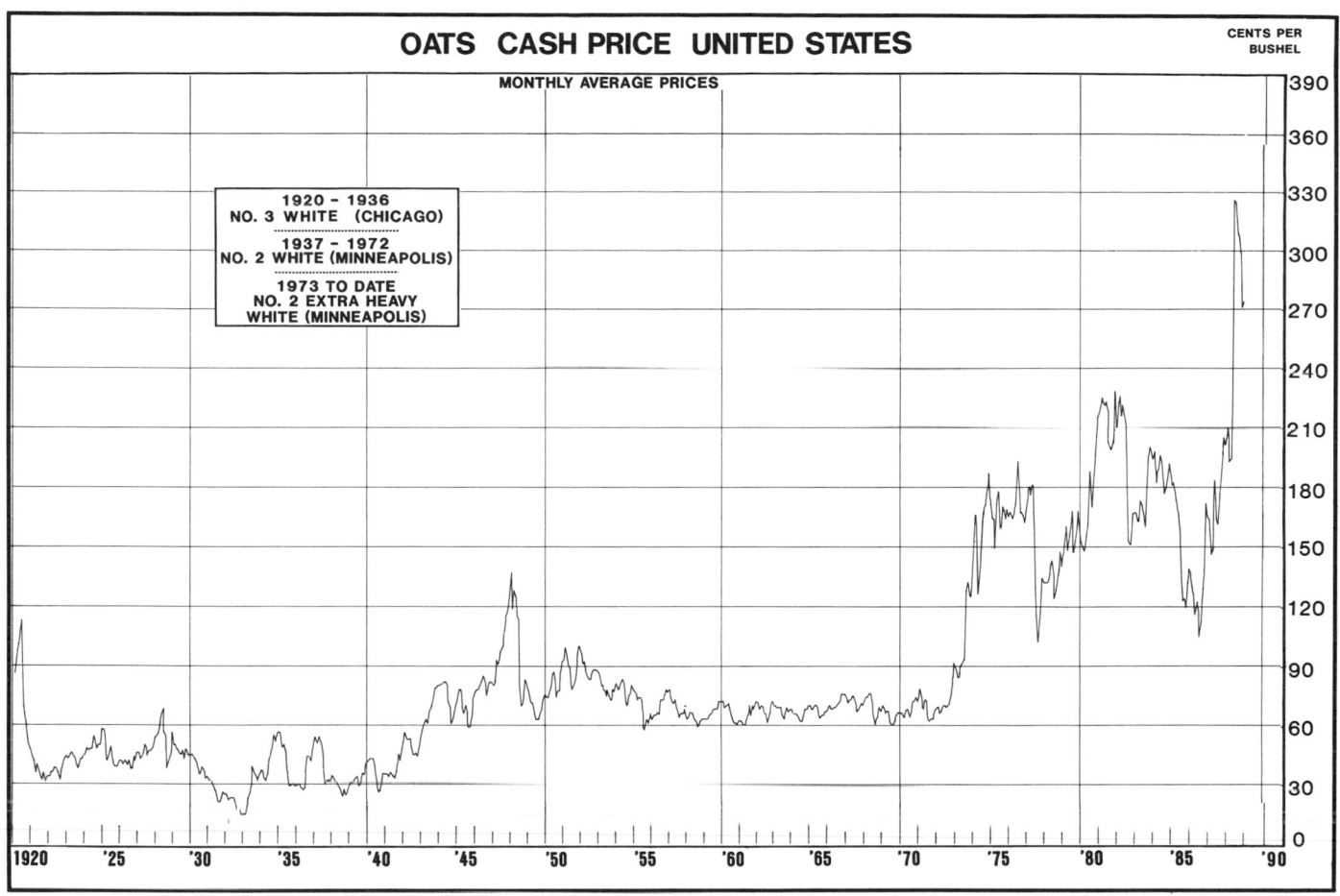

OATS CASH PRICE UNITED STATES

MONTHLY AVERAGE PRICES

CENTS PER BUSHEL

1920 – 1936
NO. 3 WHITE (CHICAGO)
1937 – 1972
NO. 2 WHITE (MINNEAPOLIS)
1973 TO DATE
NO. 2 EXTRA HEAVY
WHITE (MINNEAPOLIS)

Average Cash Price[1] of No. 2 Heavy White Oats at Minneapolis In Cents Per Bushel

Year	June	July	Aug.	Sept.	Oct.	Nov.	Dec.	Jan.	Feb.	Mar.	Apr.	May	Average[1]	No. 2 Heavy White, Portland	Toledo
1977–8	138	115	102	111	117	134	132	132	132	133	140	143	127	144	136
1978–9	136	124	128	136	139	147	140	147	154	160	148	155	143	179	137
1979–0	168	160	147	155	165	167	159	152	150	148	152	162	157	187	160
1980–1	188	180	170	186	196	215	216	220	225	223	221	223	204	242	217
1981–2	218	202	199	202	209	228	210	223	226	216	221	216	214	236	223
1982–3	212	187	153	151	151	167	167	167	163	163	173	171	169	218	155
1983–4	167	160	179	194	200	197	194	198	182	188	189	196	187	195	201
1984–5	192	184	177	179	184	192	187	181	182	179	173	165	181	212	192
1985–6	159	144	123	124	119	132	139	137	130	127	116	122	131	160	108
1986–7	118	105	112	129	139	172	166	164	156	146	159	183	146	153	120
1987–8	164	161	177	185	197	205	202	210	206	193	194	212	196		168
1988–9[2]	326	325	309	307	299	271									

[1] Weighted average of reported daily cash sales.   [2] Preliminary.   *Source: Economic Research Service, U.S.D.A.*   T.435

OATS

Month-End Open Interest of Oats at the Chicago Board of Trade & Winnipeg Commodity Exchange

Year	Jan.	Feb.	Mar.	Apr.	May	June	July	Aug.	Sept.	Oct.	Nov.	Dec.	Mar.	June	Sept.	Dec.
					Chicago (In Millions of Bushels)								Winnipeg (In Contracts)			
1979	31.1	32.8	24.4	29.8	25.4	28.8	27.0	32.2	29.2	28.6	26.2	25.8	2,515	2,778	3,085	2,635
1980	23.8	23.2	17.5	23.2	21.2	25.8	35.3	41.3	41.6	39.5	37.6	27.6	2,827	2,315	3,178	3,598
1981	36.2	36.7	27.0	25.2	27.8	29.7	25.3	23.9	29.0	45.6	42.4	34.6	3,295	2,625	2,203	1,863
1982	36.5	39.6	40.5	40.5	43.4	45.8	43.4	32.6	30.5	31.4	23.7	21.5	1,298	1,185	1,155	1,225
1983	30.8	35.8	43.3	45.1	48.8	42.5	49.8	48.2	41.8	36.7	26.0	22.1	1,202	1,313	3,170	1,978
1984	21.8	24.3	23.7	21.5	21.0	21.5	24.2	23.1	23.3	22.4	20.8	18.7	1,529	3,127	3,551	1,073
1985	19.4	19.0	16.5	16.2	14.5	14.9	16.7	16.6	15.8	21.3	19.3	19.3	1,028	1,248	1,581	1,028
1986	18.5	18.7	20.8	19.3	16.5	14.9	15.3	16.8	13.7	18.9	25.2	30.3	421	513	607	1,700
1987	35.4	35.7	31.9	29.2	26.2	24.5	30.4	36.3	33.2	30.4	28.1	30.6	1,533	1,417	1,427	1,784
1988	40.0	39.7	41.1	44.6	42.8	46.2	36.4	33.8	34.5	39.1	43.4	48.8	2,145	2,709	2,576	1,724

Source: Chicago Board of Trade & Winnipeg Commodity Exchange

T.438

High, Low & Closing Prices of May Oats Futures at the Chicago Board of Trade   In Cents per Bushel

Year of Delivery		Year Prior to Delivery							Delivery Year					Life of Delivery Range
	May	June	July	Aug.	Sept.	Oct.	Nov.	Dec.	Jan.	Feb.	Mar.	Apr.	May	
1982 High	231½	230	222½	217	194½	207	222½	212	209½	213¼	206	221¾	215	231½
Low	226¼	212½	210	193	180½	185¼	197¾	177½	193¾	191½	186	202¾	200¼	177½
Close	229¼	215	216	194½	185¾	205¾	206	200¼	207¾	199	203¼	208	207	—
1983 High	196	185	182½	177½	175	172¼	184½	179¾	181¼	175½	169	172½	163½	196
Low	188½	173½	164	158½	163½	161	165½	172	172¼	149	151	151¾	154	149
Close	189	176½	167¾	171	170¼	164	177½	174½	174½	149¼	160¼	155¾	157¼	—
1984 High	185	183½	200	226	220	206	199½	192¼	188	181½	185½	189¼	193	226
Low	179½	177	181	189½	199¼	193	184½	180½	178	163	169	169¾	171½	163
Close	179½	181½	197½	200	206	193	184½	188¾	180	168¾	185½	171	193	—
1985 High	—	191	185¾	181½	175	179¾	180¾	179¾	177½	174½	173¼	170	164	191
Low	—	181	175	171	171	173	176	172½	169¼	167½	167¼	160¼	156¾	156¾
Close	—	190	178½	172¼	173½	179	179	176¾	172¼	170¼	167¾	160½	160½	—
1986 High	163	161	150½	135	135¾	138¾	141¾	143½	142	129	122½	109	119	163
Low	160	149¾	133½	127½	128	130½	134¾	133½	121½	118	106¾	94¼	101½	94¼
Close	161	150¾	133¾	130	135	138½	135¼	142¼	124¼	120	108¼	109	108½	—
1987 High	116½	119	117½	123	128¾	135¼	150¾	155¾	157	162	147½	166¾	190½	190½
Low	116¼	112½	110	115	120½	126	134¼	136	151¾	144	130½	141½	167¼	110
Close	116¼	115½	113¼	122¾	128	133¾	146	155¾	154½	149½	140½	166¾	183¼	—
1988 High	159	174	170½	188½	188	190	194½	191½	187	184¼	182	169¾	170	194½
Low	150¾	147	155½	162¾	176	167½	162	173	175	176¼	158½	157	155	147
Close	150¾	160	170	179	180	169¼	189	175½	185	181	161½	159¼	166	—
1989 High	197½	340	325	286½	281	259	241	243						
Low	186¾	194	247	249	247	238	205½	206						
Close	197½	310	267	261¾	247¼	242	211¼	242¼						

Source: Chicago Board of Trade   T 439

Average Price Received by U.S. Farmers for Oats   In Cents Per Bushel

Year	June	July	Aug.	Sept.	Oct.	Nov.	Dec.	Jan.	Feb.	Mar.	Apr.	May	Average[1]
1979–0	135	133	124	129	131	141	131	139	137	134	138	143	136
1980–1	148	150	153	163	165	184	192	198	201	208	205	205	179
1981–2	199	184	172	174	178	188	194	197	199	202	199	199	189
1982–3	188	157	139	135	132	140	144	146	148	149	154	154	149
1983–4	151	146	145	155	162	167	173	181	188	181	182	184	162
1984–5	180	168	162	160	169	164	172	174	169	168	168	160	167
1985–6	159	131	116	110	108	117	120	118	116	114	113	121	123
1986–7	110	90	86	99	111	132	144	146	147	145	150	157	121
1987–8	152	129	141	149	161	162	176	178	185	178	182	184	156
1988–9	268	286	254	256	256	240							

[1] Weighted average by sales.   *Source: Crop Reporting Board, U.S.D.A.*   T.433

Oats Under Price Support Through the End of the Month
(Cumulative Total from Current Season's Crop)   In Millions of Bushels

Year	July	Aug.	Sept.	Oct.	Nov.	Dec.	Jan.	Feb.	Mar.	Apr.	May	June	Total
1978–9	.5	8.2	14.9	18.5	21.2	22.4	23.9	24.2	24.5	24.7	24.8	24.8	24.8
1979–0	—	2.2	5.0	7.1	8.7	9.5	10.5	11.0	11.6	12.1	12.2	12.2	12.2
1980–1	—	1.8	3.4	4.4	4.9	5.7	6.0	6.1	6.2	6.3	6.3	6.3	6.3
1981–2	.6	3.4	6.1	7.4	8.0	8.7	9.3	9.5	9.6	9.6	9.6	9.6	9.6
1982–3	.1	1.2	4.0	5.8	6.9	7.7	8.3	8.5	8.8	9.0	9.1	9.1	9.1
1983–4	.1	1.0	1.4	2.8	3.1	3.2	3.4	3.5	3.5	3.6	3.6	3.6	3.6
1984–5	—	.9	2.1	2.6	2.8	3.0	3.1	3.1	3.1	3.1	3.1	3.1	3.1
1985–6	.1	1.0	2.3	3.6	4.0	4.3	4.6	4.8	4.9	5.2	5.3	5.3	5.3
1986–7	.2	1.8	4.1	5.9	6.7	7.2	7.4	7.6	7.7	7.7	7.7	7.7	7.8
1987–8		.1	1.4	2.1	2.5	2.6	2.6	2.8	2.9	2.9	2.9	2.9	2.9
1988–9	—	.4	.6	.7									

Source: U.S. Department of Agriculture   T.432

Olive Oil

World olive oil production in 1988/89 was projected by the USDA to fall 13 percent to 1.54 million tonnes. Olive oil comprises only 3 percent of world vegetable and marine oil output, and is quite cyclical. After a season with a large crop, output is normally lower the following year. As usual, the major olive oil producers were Italy, Spain, Greece and Tunisia.

The olive harvest begins in mid-November in the northern Mediterranean producing areas and then moves into the more southern regions. Normally, the harvest is completed by March.

With a smaller world crop in 1988/89, the USDA projected world olive oil exports at 480,000 tonnes, down about 4 percent from a year earlier. Although the European Community (EC) heavily subsidizes olive oil production, output had been increasing slowly because of declines in Italy.

Italy, a major consumer, was expected to further increase imports from Spain and Greece in 1988/89. The U.S. was also a major importer. For the first ten months of the 1987/88 season, the Census Bureau estimated U.S. imports at 61,000 tonnes, 20 percent more than in the same period the previous season.

Global olive oil consumption in 1988/89 was projected at 1.77 million tonnes, the same as a year earlier. Olive oil use was showing little growth, reflecting competition from less expensive cooking oils. The EC, by far the largest consumer, used 1.3 million tonnes of olive oil, about 72 percent of the world's total. Italy, Spain, and Greece were the largest individual consumers. World olive oil consumption was expected to exceed production in 1988/89; and ending stocks were forecast to fall 24 percent to 510,000 tonnes.

World Production of Olive Oil (Pressed Oil)[2] In Thousands of Metric Tons

Crop Year[2]	Al-geria	Greece	Italy	Jordan	Leba-non	Argen-tina	Moroc-co	Portu-gal	Spain	Syria	Tunisia	Turkey	Libya	Israel	World Total
1978–9	14	240	419	7	6	15	20	40	500	66	83	160	5	0	1,590
1979–0	10	203	626	1	15	22	39	66	433	42	85	52	4	5	1,599
1980–1	18	321	606	10	2	11	23	32	479	83	145	170	8	2	1,921
1981–2	15	229	515	5	12	14	34	23	300	44	70	60	8	4	1,350
1982–3	16	324	430	7	8	16	23	79	666	97	55	170	7	3	1,908
1983–4	13	230	824	10	15	13	28	9	258	31	150	40	8	4	1,644
1984–5	12	185	343	4	9	16	27	47	689	63	105	80	7	5	1,600
1985–6[1]	12	340	641	7	9	16	28	33	397	32	105	60	7	4	1,630
1986–7[3]	15	230	355	14	6	7	35	41	491	73	120	120	7	3	1,560
1987–8[3]	10	225	600	4	5	9	38	37	691	32	95	60	9	1	1,770
1988–9[3]	10	260	480	10	7	8	30	23	360	80	61	150	6	2	1,370

[1] Preliminary. [2] Total pressed oil in marketing year beginning Nov. 1; excludes sulfur oil extracted from residues. [3] Forecast.
Source: Foreign Agricultural Service, U.S.D.A.; Oil World.   T.441

Average Unit Value of U.S. Olive Oil Imports In Thousand Dollars Per Metric Ton

Year	Jan.	Feb.	Mar.	Apr.	May	June	July	Aug.	Sept.	Oct.	Nov.	Dec.	Average
1984	1,336	1,313	1,301	1,307	1,424	1,357	1,379	1,342	1,438	1,361	1,397	1,284	1,353
1985	1,256	1,169	1,215	1,235	1,256	1,249	1,251	1,257	1,308	1,333	1,292	1,338	1,263
1986	1,402	1,400	1,402	1,469	1,492	1,495	1,587	1,554	1,751	1,572	1,732	1,589	1,537
1987	1,690	1,763	1,652	1,726	1,635	1,577	1,588	1,608	1,563	1,646	1,609	1,696	1,646
1988	1,682	1,694	1,736	1,699	1,701	1,669	1,465	1,562	1,691				

Source: U.S. Bureau of the Census

World Olive Oil Supply and Distribution In Thousands of Metric Tons

Crop Year	Production	Exports	Imports	Consumption	Ending Stocks
1980–1	1,921	267	260	1,663	864
1981–2	1,337	204	296	1,593	700
1982–3	1,908	360	401	1,627	1,022
1983–4	1,644	296	338	1,810	908
1984–5	1,601	480	504	1,730	792
1985–6	1,620	370	490	1,720	830
1986–7	1,550	520	560	1,730	690
1987–8[1]	1,768	501	495	1,748	674
1988–9[2]	1,539	475	518	1,744	512

[1] Preliminary. [2] Forecast. *Source: Foreign Agricultural Service, U.S.D.A.*

Onions

Salient Statistics of Onions in the United States

Crop Year	Jan. 1 Stocks Frozen	Annual Pack Frozen	Imports Canned	Acres Harvested	Yield Per Acre	Production	Price Per Cwt.	Farm Value	Domestic Exports (Fresh)	Imports (Fresh)	Per Capita[2] Utilization (Lbs.)	Frozen
	Million Pounds			Acres	Cwt.	1,000 Cwt.	Dollars	$1,000	Million Pounds			
1979	24.4	167.2	9.0	123,910	312	38,602	6.98	237,432	156.7	157.4	14.7	.74
1980	26.7	156.1	7.9	113,160	296	33,526	11.40	347,054	256.6	132.8	13.7	.68
1981	28.0	159.9	8.3	112,030	314	35,155	14.70	475,470	420.1	136.1	13.1	.7
1982	28.4	182.3	8.7	125,920	332	41,861	8.24	307,501	140.7	165.7	15.2	.8
1983	31.9	139.6	9.5	123,040	315	38,762	12.40	431,906	183.2	204.9	15.3	.6
1984	28.8	156.5	12.1	129,350	338	43,657	10.60	422,538	273.9	267.2	16.1	.7
1985	23.4	142.0	14.0	122,760	367	45,059	9.08	347,247	121.6	263.6	16.5	
1986[1]	27.4	185.5	12.3	115,340	375	43,301	10.90	427,669	164.4	247.7	17.9	
1987[1]	35.7	188.0	13.0	123,720	364	44.997	12.50	503,666	195.8	371.2	16.3	
1988[1]	29.6			124,830	363	45,288						

[1] Preliminary. [2] Includes fresh and processing. Source: Economic Research Service, U.S.D.A.

T.443

Production of Onions in the United States   In Thousands of Hundredweight (Cwt.)

Year	Spring Texas	California	Arizona	Total (All)	Summer New Mexico	Texas	California	Colorado	Idaho	Michigan	Minnesota	New York	Oregon	Total (All)	Grand Total
1981	2,700	2,160	512	5,372	1,242	1,488	7,025	2,925	2,625	2,446	199	3,933	4,460	29,649	35,021
1982	3,492	2,805	876	7,173	1,643	1,544	10,395	3,255	2,475	2,336	168	4,550	4,821	34,464	41,637
1983	3,800	2,166	656	6,622	1,248	1,643	9,179	3,432	2,475	2,573	158	2,793	5,292	32,140	38,762
1984	3,348	2,734	805	6,887	1,365	1,560	9,819	4,636	2,323	2,933	156	3,384	6,785	36,770	43,657
1985	3,230	3,510	564	7,304	1,463	943	9,250	5,355	3,740	2,535	194	3,960	6,785	37,755	45,059
1986	3,600	2,886	660	7,146	1,810	1,537	9,953	4,590	3,710	1,653	208	3,456	5,945	36,155	43,301
1987	2,750	3,198	585	6,533	2,106	799	9,860	4,688	4,620	1,900	195	3,132	7,032	38,464	44,997
1988[1]				6,805			9,975	5,535		2,000	150	2,530		38,483	45,288

[1] Preliminary.   Source: Crop Reporting Board, U.S.D.A.

T.444

Cold Storage Stocks of Fresh Onions in the United States   In Thousands of Pounds

Year	Jan. 1	Feb. 1	Mar. 1	Apr. 1	May 1	June 1	July 1	Aug. 1	Sept. 1	Oct. 1	Nov. 1	Dec. 1
1981	7,777	6,972	4,422	3,730	1,247	591	1,828	649	143	719	665	3,219
1982	3,474	3,963	3,319	1,813	—	—	275	—	—	952	—	—
1983	4,183	4,407	4,116	2,988	1,042	235	325	724	385	785	1,348	8,826
1984	8,648	7,006	2,527	343	1,230	556	527	1,212	5,270	5,618	5,354	6,949
1985	7,465	5,518	4,454	2,248	810	4,806	2,804	1,280	6,205	6,526	5,890	6,128
1986	5,171	5,325	2,572	1,573	545	1,769	1,627	1,001	346	2,116	4,693	7,784
1987	6,773	5,330	2,710	1,883	1,560	2,403	1,181	137	1,276	2,500	3,823	6,641
1988[1]	4,406	1,982	192	35	575	2,551	1,587	268	3,508	7,453	10,499	

[1] Preliminary.   Source: Crop Reporting Board, U.S.D.A.

T.445

Average Price Received by Growers for Onions in the U.S.   In Dollars Per Hundred Pounds (Cwt.)

Year	Jan.	Feb.	Mar.	Apr.	May	June	July	Aug.	Sept.	Oct.	Nov.	Dec.	Average[2]
1981	15.40	17.20	23.60	26.10	22.40	18.10	17.70	15.40	11.50	12.80	14.80	14.60	14.70
1982	17.60	17.40	13.20	12.70	12.60	9.43	11.90	12.60	7.83	7.12	6.90	6.35	8.24
1983	5.13	6.35	7.59	10.70	10.60	9.62	10.70	10.90	10.80	11.00	12.90	18.30	12.40
1984	17.30	19.40	25.20	25.30	13.90	11.00	14.00	13.60	11.00	9.52	10.30	11.90	10.60
1985	10.20	8.91	7.95	9.12	13.00	10.90	19.20	11.20	7.61	6.40	6.97	8.19	9.08
1986	7.70	7.01	7.07	9.37	9.31	10.70	11.30	9.78	10.90	12.00	10.60	11.80	10.90
1987	16.20	17.60	19.90	26.30	22.40	16.80	14.90	10.60	9.70	8.76	9.37	10.50	12.50
1988[1]	15.30	13.80	12.50	15.10	9.10	8.49	11.50	8.09	10.40	9.02	9.37		

[1] Preliminary.   [2] Seasonal Average.   Source: Crop Reporting Board, U.S.D.A.

T.448

Orange Juice

The U.S. orange crop continued to recover from the freeze-ravaged conditions of the early 1980s. Total U.S. production for the 1988/89 (Dec.-Nov.) season was forecast at just under 215 million boxes, up from 198 million in 1987/88. Florida orange production was forecast at 150 million boxes in the 1988/89 season, up from the previous season's 138 million. FCOJ production in the state was expected to be 170 million gallons, or about 18 percent over the previous season. Florida's average FCOJ yield was forecast at 1.52 gallons per box, down from the previous season's record yield of 1.55.

Total pack for the 1987/88 season was estimated at about 170 million gallons, compared with 145 million the previous season. Total movement was expected to be about 225 million gallons, up slightly from the previous season, despite sluggish movement later in the year. Total U.S. imports of FCOJ through November 1988 were 23 percent less than the 1987 level, while the average import price was 55 percent higher than a year earlier.

The orange crop in Brazil in 1988/89 (June-May) was forecast at 215 million boxes , slightly less than the previous season's crop, as dry weather plagued the Brazilian citrus areas in the first half of the season.

Prices for FCOJ were relatively high in 1988 because of tight world supplies, but were expected to drop in 1989, due to increased production and sluggish demand. The average U.S. price for all forms of orange juice was up to $3.70 per gallon by late summer 1988, compared with an average price of $3.41 for all of 1987.

Futures Market

FCOJ futures are traded on the Citrus Associates of the New York Cotton Exchange (NYCE).

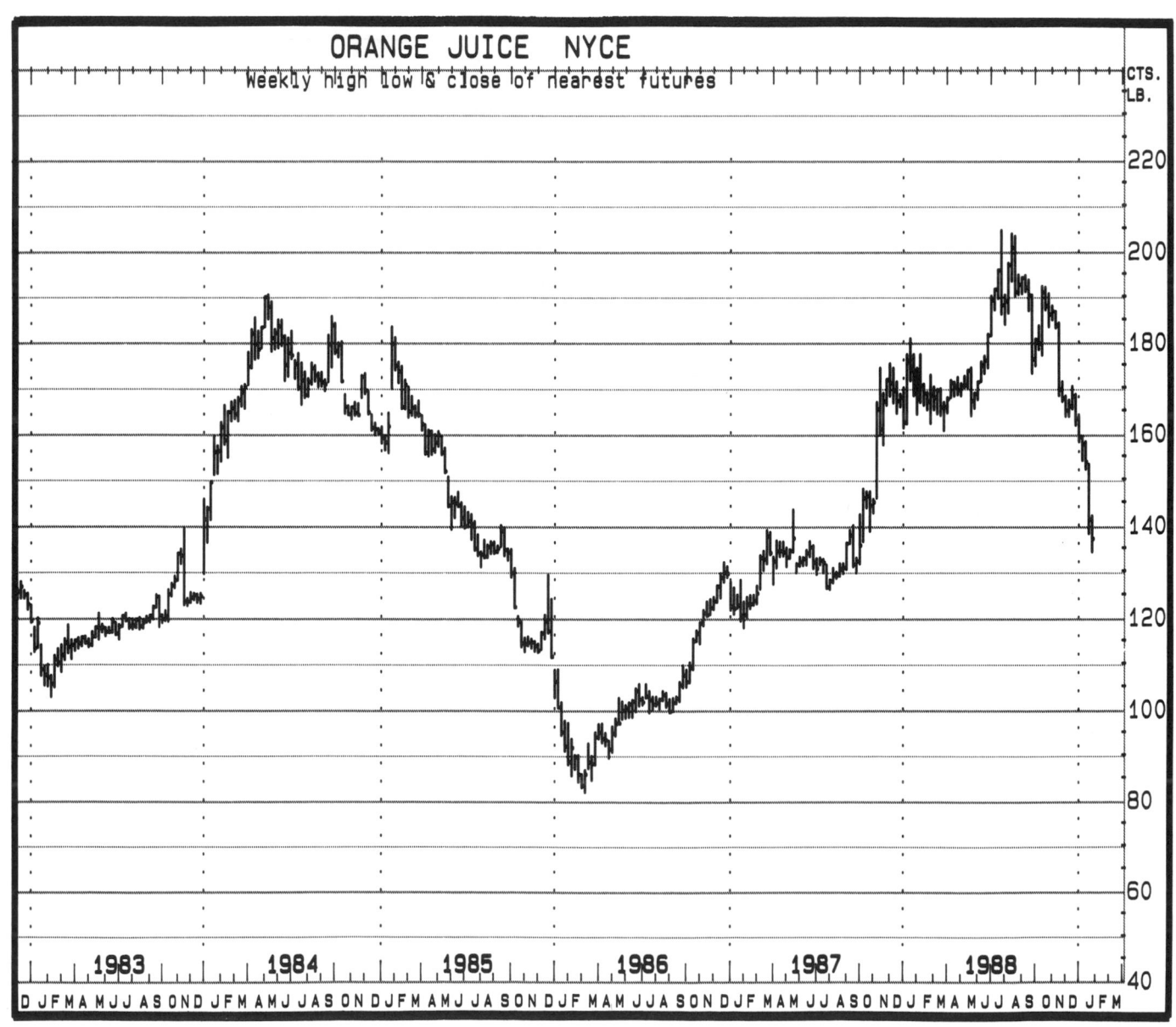

ORANGE JUICE NYCE
Weekly high low & close of nearest futures

World Production of Oranges[3] In Thousands of Metric Tons

Season	Argentina	Australia	Brazil	Cuba	Egypt	Greece	Israel	Italy	Japan	Mexico	Morocco	South Africa	Spain	Turkey	United States	World Total[3]
1978–9	925	451	6,471		928	506	992	1,959	3,637	1,398	827	600	2,526	806	8,310	24,050
1979–0	921	448	9,282		1,148	360	943	2,104	3,945	1,810	1,024	565	2,597	835	10,734	38,502
1980–1	905	381	9,872	386	991	561	812	2,057	3,229	1,600	965	569	2,605	862	9,514	36,725
1981–2[3]	606	421	9,942	360	895	704	1,105	1,752	37	1,650	695	546	1,629	675	7,025	28,666
1982–3	639	392	9,210	400	1,201	665	889	1,498	52	1,380	670	510	1,652	656	8,827	29,294
1983–4	500	488	9,588	385	1,243	691	962	2,299	60	1,300	747	512	2,077	730	6,691	28,927
1984–5	653	489	1,715	390	1,182	775	941	1,960	59	1,000	686	486	1,365	760	6,109	29,355
1985–6[1]	560	519	10,792	390	1,168	554	706	2,257	63	1,410	841	496	1,942	550	6,792	29,849
1986–7[2]	700	508	11,925	390	1,170	800	840	2,260	65	1,425	635	515	2,100	600	7,019	31,763
1987–8[2]															8,426	

[1] Preliminary. [2] Estimate. [3] Data prior to 1981–82 include tangarines. *Source: Foreign Agricultural Service, U.S.D.A.* T.449

U.S. Salient Statistics of Oranges & Orange Juice

Season	Production[2] California Million Boxes	Florida	Total U.S.	Farm Price $ Per Box	Farm Value Million $	Frozen Concentrated Orange Juice—Florida Carry-in	Pack (in Million Gallons)	Total Supply	Total Season Movem.	Florida Crop Processed Frozen Concentrates (Million Boxes)	Juice	Total Processed	Yield Per Box (Gall.)	U.S. Imports of Frozen Concentrated Orange Juice Brazil	Others	Total (In Million Gallons[4])
1977–8	42.6	167.8	220.1	5.45	1,198.7	29.1	185.0	200.8	185.1	132.2	25.3	166.0	1.23	139.5	11.3	150.7
1978–9	37.3	164.0	210.6	6.15	1,296.0	33.5	206.2	221.9	206.1	130.2	22.8	159.8	1.34	152.3	7.7	160.0
1979–0	59.4	206.7	273.6	4.76	1,304.2	37.4	256.4	293.8	239.0	174.9	24.4	206.6	1.34	97.7	2.3	100.0
1980–1	65.3	172.4	244.6	4.85	1,327.7	57.3	249.6	306.9	240.6	145.3	19.6	171.5	1.21	203.1	11.1	214.2
1981–2	41.9	125.8	176.7	5.30	1,295.3	69.0	214.9	283.9	230.5	105.2	16.3	126.1	1.28	374.0	22.1	396.1
1982–3	76.1	139.6	225.2	6.61	1,167.8	53.4	228.4	281.8	239.0	114.6	18.1	135.5	1.48	337.2	27.6	364.8
1983–4	48.5	116.7	169.5	5.85	1,317.1	42.8	239.9	282.7	228.3	94.5	17.0	114.4	1.29	510.1	23.5	533.6
1984–5	52.4	103.9	158.8	7.69	1,304.3	54.4	209.6	264.0	215.7	86.1	14.9	102.9	1.38	578.2	18.5	596.3
1985–6	53.9	119.2	175.7	9.19	1,459.3	48.3	215.1	263.5	226.5	96.1	17.3	114.7	1.38	500.5	45.7	546.2
1986–7[1]	57.9	119.7	181.2	6.18	1,092.2	37.0	228.1	264.9	225.1	96.2	19.7	116.8	1.51	505.0	51.1	556.1
1987–8[3]	56.5	138.0	197.7	7.00	1,322.6	39.8				110.2	23.3	134.4	1.55			
1988–9[3]	61.0	152.0	217.1		1,701.5								1.52			

[1] Preliminary. [2] Fruit ripened on trees, but destroyed prior to picking is not included. [3] Estimate. [4] Single strength.
Source: Economic Research Service, U.S.D.A. Florida Citrus Processors Assoc. T.450

U.S. Cold Storage Stocks of Orange Juice Concentrate[2] In Millions of Pounds

Year	Jan. 1	Feb. 1	Mar. 1	Apr. 1	May 1	June 1	July 1	Aug. 1	Sept. 1	Oct. 1	Nov. 1	Dec. 1
1981	722.4	907.1	1,053.2	1,180.1	1,264.4	1,502.2	1,491.3	1,307.8	1,178.8	1,022.2	892.2	759.1
1982	753.1	957.0	1,172.3	1,300.7	—	—	1,406.2	—	—	846.5	—	—
1983	835.9	1,028.1	1,016.2	963.3	1,187.0	1,408.0	1,318.6	1,192.4	960.8	810.7	684.8	595.0
1984	631.1	785.7	956.3	976.3	920.1	998.2	903.2	780.4	707.0	595.8	557.3	564.8
1985	651.6	883.4	1,050.6	1,102.7	1,188.6	1,229.5	1,063.7	1,036.1	912.4	882.2	778.8	656.0
1986	679.2	888.4	966.8	911.5	1,031.6	1,047.5	1,056.9	920.3	855.3	715.4	577.8	524.8
1987	621.2	874.8	1,012.7	933.8	999.0	1,109.1	1,105.1	942.1	792.6	840.0	652.8	569.0
1988[1]	662.4	980.5	1,073.1	969.4	1,018.7	1,120.1	1,154.7	1,001.8	862.5	693.1	642.8	

[1] Preliminary. [2] Adjusted to 42° BRIX basis (9.896 lbs./gal.) *Source: Crop Reporting Board, U.S.D.A.* T.451

Month–End Open Interest of Frozen Concentrated Orange Juice Futures In Thousands of Contracts

Year	Jan.	Feb.	Mar.	Apr.	May	June	July	Aug.	Sept.	Oct.	Nov.	Dec.
1980	7,612	6,501	6,126	6,390	6,210	5,923	6,186	6,920	8,046	9,063	9,239	9,582
1981	7,980	10,787	12,018	11,354	11,667	11,925	10,675	9,751	9,454	7,991	7,654	8,037
1982	9,519	8,634	6,580	6,238	6,227	5,808	6,007	6,395	5,666	5,775	7,106	9,359
1983	9,720	7,136	6,229	6,267	6,225	6,264	5,969	6,413	6,487	6,155	5,732	7,186
1984	8,873	10,650	11,676	11,733	11,295	12,965	11,646	10,350	10,039	9,356	9,339	8,542
1985	7,854	6,680	6,452	6,373	5,885	5,504	4,895	4,300	4,756	5,701	7,156	12,951
1986	8,763	7,782	7,827	6,469	7,013	7,295	6,908	6,682	7,470	8,774	9,460	11,290
1987	9,916	11,336	9,318	9,265	8,249	7,650	6,557	6,496	7,925	8,097	9,798	10,562
1988	12,529	16,641	15,863	13,403	11,396	10,780	11,139	10,554	8,942	8,172	9,253	7,905

Source: Citrus Assoc. of the N.Y. Cotton Exchange T.456

ORANGES AND ORANGE JUICES

High, Low & Closing Prices of May Orange Juice[1] Futures at New York   In Cents per Pound

| Year of Delivery | Year Prior to Delivery | | | | | | | | | | Delivery Year | | | | | Life of Delivery Range |
	Mar.	Apr.	May	June	July	Aug.	Sept.	Oct.	Nov.	Dec.	Jan.	Feb.	Mar.	Apr.	May	
1984 High	106.90	104.95	104.30	108.50	110.00	111.30	114.25	121.00	122.50	149.00	159.50	167.20	177.40	186.40	190.00	190.00
Low	104.00	100.50	101.40	103.30	106.90	109.20	110.85	109.00	119.70	121.10	141.00	155.00	160.00	174.10	177.75	100.50
Close	104.80	102.05	103.70	106.60	108.80	110.95	112.45	120.50	121.75	146.00	156.75	163.00	174.20	186.15	177.75	—
1985 High	170.00	176.00	181.50	179.50	168.50	172.00	185.00	181.75	172.90	170.00	183.50	178.00	170.35	161.40	159.90	185.00
Low	155.00	166.50	174.50	167.00	164.90	167.00	167.50	166.50	166.80	162.40	159.20	166.60	160.30	154.70	151.00	114.90
Close	165.60	176.00	178.65	168.00	166.90	169.70	181.20	166.90	169.90	163.90	178.60	168.10	161.60	158.20	151.20	—
1986 High	166.25	160.50	152.45	140.90	133.45	127.00	128.90	128.10	116.60	131.50	113.25	92.95	95.70	96.40	101.00	178.40
Low	160.35	152.50	136.70	133.10	124.00	122.95	122.65	111.95	113.00	107.25	88.30	83.50	82.60	89.00	93.10	82.60
Close	161.30	152.50	140.00	133.15	124.65	122.95	128.50	114.45	114.55	108.15	89.00	84.30	95.60	92.75	96.55	—
1987 High	91.40	94.75	101.85	109.95	110.00	108.70	109.50	120.20	123.70	134.80	128.80	127.85	138.50	136.25	143.00	143.00
Low	84.50	90.50	92.95	100.40	101.10	105.80	106.80	108.00	119.50	123.95	118.60	120.85	127.00	128.10	132.25	84.45
Close	91.40	92.75	100.80	108.25	107.70	106.20	108.25	119.70	123.65	125.10	121.20	126.80	128.90	132.25	130.80	—
1988 High	130.05	126.50	126.95	123.90	124.25	128.10	132.00	145.25	171.00	174.00	176.70	173.65	167.50	172.00	174.10	176.70
Low	123.40	123.40	124.15	119.25	120.15	122.90	128.50	132.20	146.00	164.50	165.00	156.25	156.50	167.70	167.15	
Close	123.40	125.00	124.20	120.50	122.85	128.10	132.00	145.25	167.50	165.70	166.85	159.00	167.25	170.15	167.15	—
1989 High	152.45	155.50	155.25	168.50	172.00	173.50	170.50	172.50	173.00	166.60						
Low	144,85	148.50	151.05	151.70	167.00	167.00	162.20	166.25	163.50	156.60						
Close	148.95	154.80	151.40	168.45	171.65	169.25	167.25	172.00	164.50	157.90						

[1] Frozen concentrated orange juice.   Source: Citrus Associates of the N.Y. Cotton Exchange, Inc.   T.455

Volume of Trading of Frozen Concentrated Orange Juice Futures   In Contracts

Year	Jan.	Feb.	Mar.	Apr.	May	June	July	Aug.	Sept.	Oct.	Nov.	Dec.	Total
1981	35,041	32,755	49,107	39,785	32,611	35,459	32,944	29,979	22,927	25,435	19,747	31,392	387,182
1982	28,968	25,524	27,139	17,038	12,206	21,501	14,577	14,242	8,424	9,606	8,647	19,188	207,070
1983	28,122	20,345	11,754	6,704	7,614	7,823	4,881	4,531	5,621	9,690	6,409	10,773	124,267
1984	33,189	36,206	34,643	32,774	26,882	30,273	23,803	15,246	36,508	23,693	11,737	12,410	317,364
1985	28,768	20,572	8,135	11,529	9,514	10,011	8,238	7,893	9,395	16,320	11,115	49,268	190,758
1986	39,756	24,971	21,413	13,209	13,909	14,979	10,469	9,887	10,940	17,513	9,551	24,946	211,543
1987	28,566	24,342	27,999	19,569	10,651	15,470	8,805	10,710	12,330	20,321	20,724	26,758	266,641
1988	40,976	42,153	37,295	28,937	22,931	36,877	23,752	27,118	26,228	26,922	19,399	25,451	358,039

Source: Citrus Assoc. of the N.Y. Cotton Exchange   T.452

Wholesale Index Price of Frozen Orange Concentrate[1]   1982 = 100[2]

Year	Jan.	Feb.	Mar.	Apr.	May	June	July	Aug.	Sept.	Oct.	Nov.	Dec.	Average
1982	312.9	337.7	334.5	326.5	315.4	308.4	308.7	307.1	307.8	307.7	307.5	303.2	315.5
1983	304.0	300.8	299.6	299.1	302.3	300.7	301.1	300.8	302.4	302.5	303.8	303.9	301.8
1984	316.4	361.6	373.3	380.3	385.2	395.0	387.7	392.4	403.7	410.2	408.3	407.8	385.2
1985[2]	127.3	133.1	133.2	132.9	133.5	132.4	130.5	126.0	123.9	119.3	114.9	112.8	126.7
1986	104.4	102.2	97.6	94.4	94.1	94.3	94.2	94.2	93.7	96.0	98.6	101.4	97.1
1987	106.9	106.9	107.4	109.5	109.7	110.0	110.1	111.0	110.6	110.6	117.2	129.9	111.7
1988	132.1	140.5	142.4	140.5	142.0	141.1	141.6	142.0	141.7	141.7			

[1] Packer to wholesale distributor, or retail chain store, f.o.b. plant.   [2] Data prior to 1985 are for 1967 = 100.   Source: Bureau of Labor Statistics (0242–0301)   T.454

Wholesale Price of Oranges (California) F.O.B. Packed Fresh   In Dollars Per Box

Year	Jan.	Feb.	Mar.	Apr.	May	June	July	Aug.	Sept.	Oct.	Nov.	Dec.	Average
1981	11.00	10.90	10.20	9.78	10.00	12.10	14.10	12.80	12.60	11.70	11.50	12.70	11.62
1982	13.50	13.80	13.50	14.20	17.20	17.50	18.70	20.30	28.30	28.40	16.50	12.80	17.89
1983	10.80	10.40	10.50	10.30	9.85	10.60	11.70	11.30	10.20	9.30	12.90	13.00	10.90
1984	13.10	12.00	11.60	12.60	19.20	22.40	22.50	23.30	24.40	24.40	19.30	18.50	18.61
1985	18.70	17.50	16.20	17.00	17.40	16.50	15.90	15.40	15.00	13.70	15.60	16.20	16.26
1986	15.10	13.70	13.80	12.90	13.10	12.10	13.30	14.60	14.00	14.30	13.90	13.70	13.71
1987	13.20	14.90	15.00	15.80	14.30	16.80	17.10	15.60	14.80	17.00	24.30	15.10	16.16
1988	14.70	13.90											

Source: Economic Research Service, U.S.D.A.   T.453

Palm Oil

Palm oil is the world's second leading vegetable oil, accounting for over 15 percent of total vegetable oil output. The USDA forecast 1988/89 world palm oil production at 9.09 million tonnes, 6 percent more than a year earlier. Malaysia, the largest producer, accounted for most of the increase. The country's output was projected at 5.3 million tonnes, 58 percent of the world's total. Malaysian output has nearly doubled since 1980, when it was 2.7 million tonnes. Indonesia was the second largest producer.

Global palm oil consumption in 1988/89 was forecast at 9.08 million tonnes, 5 percent more than in 1987/88. Palm oil was expected to account for 17 percent of total world vegetable and marine oil usage of 53.3 million tonnes. The major consumers of palm oil were India, Indonesia, Malaysia, Nigeria, and China. While consumption remained concentrated in Asia, other nations, including the USSR and the U.S., used larger amounts. In 1987/88, prices of competitive oils like soybean, cottonseed, sun and rapeseed increased more than palm oil. Moreover, the proximity of Malaysia and Indonesia to importers with large populations, like India and Pakistan, has kept transportation costs down.

China has shown the most potential for expanded use. Chinese palm oil consumption more than tripled from 1983/84 to 500,000 tonnes in 1987/88. Soviet imports have held steady at about 200,000 tonnes. U.S. palm oil imports, however, were expected to decline by about a third in 1988/89, because of ample soybean oil supplies.

World palm oil exports in 1988/89 were estimated at 5.87 million tonnes, up 8 percent from 1987/88. Malaysia was the largest shipper, with projected exports of 4.5 million tonnes, up 11 percent. Palm oil is the most widely traded vegetable oil, having an estimated 1988/89 export market share of 33 percent, compared with soybean oil's 22 percent.

Ending palm oil stocks in 1988/89 were estimated at 1.51 million tonnes, down marginally from a year earlier.

World Palm Oil Statistics   In Thousand Metric Tons

Crop Year	Malaysia	Colombia	China	Indonesia	Ivory Coast	Papua N. Guin.	Zaire	Nigeria	World Total	Malaysia	Indonesia	Ivory Coast	E.C. 12	Singapore	Zaire	Papua N. Guin.	World Total
1982–3	3,179	104	115	983	162	85	159	530	5,902	2,871	407	58	146	420	5	80	3,681
1983–4	3,324	118	110	1,150	167	110	157	540	6,290	2,819	247	56	136	608		105	3,542
1984–5	3,817	120	110	1,185	164	120	160	550	6,920	3,258	652	56	163	677		115	4,440
1985–6	4,773	141	110	1,300	217	125	160	600	8,170	4,098	684	94	169	719		115	5,290
1986–7[1]	4,560	148	110	1,300	227	145	160	625	8,100	3,977	550	91	181	563		135	5,200
1987–8[2]	4,850	176	110	1,400	235	145	160	650	8,580	4,026	700	89	183	620		135	5,440
1988–9[2]	5,300								9,320	4,400							5,910

[1] Preliminary. [2] Projected. *Source: Economic Research Service, U.S.D.A.*   T.457

Palm Oil—U.S. Supply & Distribution   In Millions of Pounds

Year Begin. Oct.	Imports	Supply Stocks Oct. 1	Total Supply	Shortening	Margarine	Salad or Cooking Oil	Other	Total	Non–Food Uses	Total Disappearance	Exports (& Shipments)	Palm Kernel Oil ¢ Per Pound	U.S. Ports C.I.F. ¢ Lb.	Malaysia[2] U.S. $ Metric Ton
1982–3	282	47	329	206				272		286	4		20.8	406
1983–4[1]	413	69	482	215				287		402	29		24.6	767
1984–5[1]	373	51	424	226				270		370	0		33.3	569
1985–6[1]	610	53	663	304				364		590	0		27.2	274
1986–7[3]	747	73	820	247				249		507	0		14.4	310
1987–8[3]	386	40	426	180				200		386	0		17.3	402
1988–9[3]	495	40	535							485	0			397

[1] Preliminary. [2] Malaysia FOB; RBD. [3] Estimate. *Source: Economic Research Service, U.S.D.A.*   T.458

Average Wholesale Palm Oil Prices, CIF, Bulk, U.S. Ports   In Cents Per Pound

Year	Jan.	Feb.	Mar.	Apr.	May	June	July	Aug.	Sept.	Oct.	Nov.	Dec.	Average
1982	N.A.	N.A.	24.0	23.7	24.4	22.3	18.9	18.6	19.3	18.0	19.0	20.0	20.8
1983	19.5	19.0	18.8	19.8	20.7	19.5	20.6	26.2	30.6	31.1	32.0	37.5	24.6
1984	40.5	38.2	36.6	37.0	43.0	36.3	28.2	28.4	30.3	28.3	32.4	29.8	33.3
1985	28.3	29.0	29.5	34.3	34.6	31.6	28.7	25.1	23.5	21.7	19.9	19.7	27.2
1986	18.4	15.6	13.3	14.3	14.1	14.1	13.2	12.1	11.7	14.6	16.1	15.3	14.4
1987	17.0	17.6	16.9	17.0	16.9	17.1	16.0	16.1	17.2	17.3	17.8	21.1	17.3
1988	24.71	22.56	19.36	19.93	20.67	22.83	24.21	20.95	20.34				

Source: Economic Research Service, U.S.D.A.   T.459

Paper

With continued growth in domestic and foreign demand, U.S. paper and paperboard production rose by almost 6 percent to a record 77 million tons. Operating rates averaged 95 percent at paper mills and close to 98 percent at paperboard mills. Tonnage allocations, which became common in some paper and board grades in 1987, spread in 1988. Some end users, such as paperback book publishers (who use special groundwood papers) became concerned about the availability of supplies, and mills frequently turned away spot orders on many grades during 1988.

U.S. coated paper production rose an estimated 13 percent in 1988, while uncoated printing and writing paper output increased about 8 percent from 1987 levels. Kraft linerboard production, which accounted for nearly 25 percent of the total output of all U.S. paper and paperboard mills, increased nearly 7 percent from 1987, surpassing the planned expansion in liner-board capacity. The extra output came as swing machines capable of producing either kraft paper or board were switched to board. Most of the increased linerboard output went into domestic boxes. Kraft board exports matched 1987 levels, but total paperboard exports rose by nearly 19 percent, gaining from the long-run impact of a lower dollar.

U.S. paper and paperboard prices increased an average of 10 percent in 1988, and the industry's practice of discounting from list price was frequently abandoned.

Based on strong order files through the third quarter of 1988, shipments from paper and paperboard mills were expected to rise by 3 percent in 1989. Paper makers were planning to add 6.1 million tons of capacity between 1988 and 1990, primarily in kraft paperboard, free-sheet papers, and newsprint.

Shipments of (Paper Products) Shipping Containers[1] In Millions of Square Feet Surface Area

Year	Jan.	Feb.	Mar.	Apr.	May	June	July	Aug.	Sept.	Oct.	Nov.	Dec.	Total
1985	22,918	20,230	22,028	22,871	22,595	21,545	22,257	23,441	22,300	25,838	21,003	19,889	267,453
1986	24,531	21,700	22,479	25,290	23,340	23,495	23,949	23,726	24,390	27,132	21,406	22,030	283,921
1987[2]	24,708	22,811	24,755	25,591	23,637	25,490	25,341	24,977	25,925	27,755	23,281	23,141	297,430
1988[2]	24,782	24,679	27,222	26,053	24,986	25,830	24,470	26,878	26,059	27,797			

[1] Corrugated & solid fiber.   [2] Preliminary.   *Source: National Paperboard Association*   T.463

Index Price of Coated Printing Paper, No. 3   (Dec. 1982 = 100)[2]

Year	Jan.	Feb.	Mar.	Apr.	May	June	July	Aug.	Sept.	Oct.	Nov.	Dec.	Average
1985	234.2	234.6	234.6	234.6	234.6	234.6	234.6	234.6	234.6	234.6	234.6	234.2	234.5
1986	234.2	233.8	233.8	233.8	233.8	233.2	233.2	233.2	233.2	233.8	234.8	235.2	233.8
1987[2]	116.1	116.1	116.4	115.7	115.5	115.5	115.5	115.9	116.1	119.9	120.4	120.2	116.9
1988[1]	120.9	121.2	122.2	121.8	122.0	122.3	124.0	126.8	127.3	127.4	127.8		

[1] Preliminary.   [2] Data prior to 1987 are for Dec. 1973 = 100.   *Source: Bureau of Labor Statistics (0913–0113)*   T.470

Salient Statistics of Newsprint in the United States and Canada   In Thousands of Metric[3] Tons

| | United States | | | | | | | | | | | | | Canada | | |
| | | | Imports[3] By Countries of Origin | | | | | | | | | Stocks, Dec. 31 | | | | Stocks |
Year	Pro-duction	Ex-ports	Canada	Finland	Italy	Nor-way	Swe-den	U.K.	South Africa	Total	Con-sumption	At Mills	At Pub-lishers[2]	Pro-duction	Ex-ports	At Mills
1984	5,025	258	7,688	31		63	86			7,899	11,431	60	874	9,013	8,133	298
1985	4,924	279	6,674	42	23	71	119	17	34	8,472	11,587	57	910	8,988	7,964	290
1986	5,107	337	6,735	24	1	80	135	11	39	8,589	11,937	49	849	9,289	8,181	277
1987[1]	5,300	284	7,087	22	14	57	221	26	21	8,975	12,322	36	900	9,673	8,574	193
1988[1]	5,427	381	7,087								12,376	48	918	9,969	8,640	290

[1] Preliminary.   [2] Reporting only to A.N.P.A.; group represents about 75%.   [3] Data for imports are in thousands of short tons.
Source: Newsprint Service Bureau, A.P.I.   T.464

Producer Price Index of Standard Newsprint   (1982 = 100)[2]

Year	Jan.	Feb.	Mar.	Apr.	May	June	July	Aug.	Sept.	Oct.	Nov.	Dec.	Average
1984	309.6	309.6	316.0	314.8	314.8	314.8	334.5	331.2	331.2	332.5	334.9	333.2	323.1
1985	334.3	332.4	332.4	332.6	332.9	333.7	333.0	334.9	333.9	329.3	329.8	330.2	332.5
1986	324.1	324.5	324.3	324.1	324.1	323.1	323.5	322.2	322.3	333.6	333.8	333.6	326.1
1987[2]	107.9	108.6	108.4	108.5	108.7	108.7	112.7	116.3	116.9	116.9	117.1	117.0	112.3
1988[2]	127.1	127.9	127.9	127.7	127.9	127.9	127.8	127.3	127.3	127.3	127.1		

[1] Preliminary.   [2] Data prior to 1987 are for 1967 = 100.   *Source: Bureau of Labor Statistics (0913–0291)*   T.468

U.S. Production & Consumption & Foreign Trade of Woodpulp   In Thous. of Short Tons[6]

Year	Dissolving Pulp	Woodpulp Production Sulfate Bleached	Woodpulp Production Sulfate Paper Grades[2]	Woodpulp Production Sulfate Unbleached	Ground-wood	Semi-Chemical	Total Wood Pulp	Consumption in the Manufacture of Paper and Board Wood Pulp[4]	Consumption in the Manufacture of Paper and Board Waste Paper[5]	Consumption in the Manufacture of Paper and Board Pulp-wood[6]	All Grades Woodpulp Exports	All Grades Woodpulp Imports	Inventories—Dec. 31 Pulp-Wood	Inventories—Dec. 31 Waste Paper	Inventories—Dec. 31 Woodpulp At Pulp Mills	Inventories—Dec. 31 Woodpulp At Paper & Board Mills
1982	1,093	—	39,478	—	5,063	3,700	49,333	13,565	79,039	3,395	3,893	5,426	1,017	614	492
1983	1,261	—	42,358	—	5,067	3,851	52,537	14,696	85,442	3,674	4,095	5,229	923	554	550
1984	1,206	—	44,690	—	5,506	4,069	55,470	15,926	87,646	3,694	4,490	5,574	1,053	759	545
1985	1,174	—	43,696	—	5,251	4,027	54,147	15,623	85,744	3,794	4,466	5,046	969	650	492
1986	1,258	—	46,081	—	5,476	4,191	57,005	17,285	91,434	4,308	4,340	4,794	838	458	496
1987[1]	1,312	—	48,293	—	5,702	4,246	59,552	18,296	93,946	5,047	4,974	5,096	920	394	529

[1] Preliminary. [2] Chemical pulp. [3] Or exploded. [4] Does not include wood pulp consumption by plants classified outside paper & board industries. [5] Waste paper; straw; rags; cotton fibre; manila stock; etc. [6] Data for pulpwood expressed in thousands of cords of 128 cu. ft.—roughwood basis. Pulpwood includes slabs, chips, & millwaste. *Sources: Bureau of the Census; American Paper Institute.*   T.465

Paper and Board Production in the United States   In Thousands of Short Tons

Year	News-print[5]	Paper Coated (Shipments)	Tissue Paper	Uncoated Free Sheet (Shipments)	Ground-wood Paper Uncoated[2]	Packaging & Industrial Converting[4] (Shipments)	All Paper Total	Other Bleached Paper-board	Corru-gating Material	Unbleac. Kraft	All Paper-board Total	Con-struc-tion (Paper)	All Con-struction Total	Total All Types
1981	4,752	4,940	4,518	8,234	1,463	3,880	31,030	1,900	6,000	14,800	31,232	1,200	3,847	66,440
1982	4,574	4,974	4,438	8,184	1,471	3,688	30,422				29,065			
1983	4,688	5,716	4,789	9,060	1,531	3,666	32,823				32,177			
1984	5,025	6,249	4,921	9,510	1,565	3,666	34,447				34,039			
1985	4,924	5,875	4,941	9,952	1,521	3,403	33,996				33,034			
1986	5,107	6,263	5,095	10,681	1,540	3,303	35,510				35,379			
1987[1]	5,300	6,860	5,301	11,228	1,485	3,079	36,994				37,439			

[1] Preliminary. [2] Shipments. [3] Paper & board. [4] Unbleached kraft. *Source: Bureau of the Census*   T.467

Index Price of Wood Pulp, Bleached Sulphate Softwood   1982 = 100[1]

Year	Jan.	Feb.	Mar.	Apr.	May	June	July	Aug.	Sept.	Oct.	Nov.	Dec.	Average
1984	354.8	385.0	387.8	417.8	439.2	440.2	439.1	437.3	434.3	431.1	423.4	404.5	416.2
1985	385.4	366.0	352.1	337.6	331.8	330.7	332.2	328.9	323.3	320.7	317.2	316.3	336.8
1986	318.2	321.1	318.8	345.0	354.6	363.1	386.5	385.6	393.4	398.9	410.7	416.5	367.7
1987[1]	114.5	116.7	118.3	122.5	124.3	124.1	125.1	125.5	125.7	130.1	132.4	132.9	124.3
1988	138.6	143.7	144.4	148.3	151.0	149.3	159.9	161.3	161.5	165.9	166.0		

[1] Data prior to 1987 are for 1967 = 100. *Source: Bureau of Labor Statistics (0911–0211)*   T.469

Index Price of Shipping Sack Paper[1]   1982 = 100[2]

Year	Jan.	Feb.	Mar.	Apr.	May	June	July	Aug.	Sept.	Oct.	Nov.	Dec.	Average
1984	231.8	238.8	247.2	247.2	247.8	247.8	241.1	241.1	241.1	241.1	241.1	233.0	240.3
1985	233.0	233.0	225.7	223.9	227.5	222.7	211.0	211.0	211.0	211.0	211.0	211.0	219.3
1986	211.0	211.0	211.0	218.0	218.0	218.0	218.0	218.0	218.0	226.8	234.9	234.0	219.7
1987[2]	110.1	113.2	114.0	117.3	117.3	117.3	117.3	117.3	120.4	121.7	125.0	125.4	118.0
1988	125.4	125.4	129.2	130.4	133.2	133.2	133.2	133.2	133.2	133.2	133.2		

[1] Unbleached kraft. [2] Data prior to 1987 are for Dec. 1973 = 100. *Source: Bureau of Labor Statistics (0913–0304)*   T.471

Index Price of Paperboard   1982 = 100[1]

Year	Jan.	Feb.	Mar.	Apr.	May	June	July	Aug.	Sept.	Oct.	Nov.	Dec.	Average
1985	287.2	285.9	285.7	284.2	280.4	273.7	267.8	265.8	266.0	265.8	266.4	266.7	274.6
1986	264.6	265.7	267.0	267.6	269.0	268.5	272.2	274.9	274.9	276.2	278.1	280.8	271.6
1987[1]	113.9	115.5	115.5	116.2	115.8	115.9	116.1	119.8	121.3	122.1	122.5	123.1	118.1
1988	126.6	127.1	130.5	132.6	133.4	134.0	134.3	134.5	136.3	136.5	136.5		

[1] Data prior to 1987 are for 1967 = 100. *Source: Bureau of Labor Statistics (0914)*

Peanuts and Peanut Oil

World peanut production in 1988/89 was projected by USDA at 21.61 million tonnes, 9 percent more than the previous year. The main reason for the larger output was a rebound in the Indian crop, which had been damaged by drought in 1987/88. India's 1988/89 crop was forecast at 6.8 million tonnes, up from 4.8 million. With a rebound in the peanut crop, India was expected to reduce imports of vegetable oils like palm and soy.

Output in China was projected to decline 6 percent to 5.8 million tonnes. India and China were the leading peanut producers, followed by the U.S. and Senegal. In 1988/89, Senegal was expected to produce 800,000 tonnes, down 17 percent. Indonesia, Burma, Nigeria, and Sudan were also major producers.

The 1988/89 world peanut crush was forecast at 11.56 million tonnes, 13 percent more than a year earlier. World peanut meal production was expected to be 4.70 million tonnes, above 4.15 million the previous season. World peanut oil production was estimated at 3.31 million tonnes, 13 percent more than a year earlier.

With larger world production, trade in peanuts was expected to increase. The USDA pegged 1988/89 world exports at 1.29 million tonnes, 7 percent more than a year earlier. The leading exporters were the U.S., China, and Argentina.

Total peanut meal exports were estimated at 665,000 tonnes, down 5 percent from 1987/88. The major meal exporters were India and Senegal. World peanut oil exports were estimated to be 302,000 tonnes, compared to 361,000 tonnes a year earlier.

World ending stocks of peanuts in 1988/89 were projected to rise 7 percent to 565,000 tonnes. The U.S. held the bulk of these stocks.

The 1988/89 U.S. peanut crop was estimated by USDA at 4.26 billion pounds, up almost 18 percent from the previous drought-damaged crop. Harvested acreage was 1.64 million acres, up 6 percent from 1987/88 and the largest since 1955. Acreage in the Southeast rose almost 9 percent, and in the Southwest it expanded 2 percent. The national acreage yield was 2,590 pounds per acre, 10 percent above a year earlier. Yields in the Southeast rose sharply, while the Southwest's average yield was lower. Carry-in stocks were 833 million pounds, and the 1988/89 peanut supply was estimated at 5.1 billion pounds.

With the larger supply, the 1988/89 crush was estimated to be 800 million pounds, up from 560 million in 1987/88. This was expected to result in peanut oil output of 250 million pounds, compared to the previous season's 175 million pounds. Peanut meal production was forecast to be 165,000 tons, up 40 percent from 1987/88. The U.S. is a leading exporter of both peanut meal and oil.

The U.S. also sells large amounts of peanuts, trailing only India and China. U.S. exports were forecast at 725 million pounds, compared to 618 million a year earlier. The primary buyers were Canada, Japan, and European countries. As a part of the Food Security Act of 1985, the USDA was given the authority to use Commodity Credit Corporation funds or commodities to offset the adverse effects of unfair trade practices on U.S. agricultural exports. The National Peanut Council has been a significant recipient of funds under the Targeted Export Assistance program.

Domestic food use of peanuts in 1987/88 was 2.07 billion pounds, virtually the same as the previous year. That was the first time since 1980/81 that domestic food use showed no increase. This was partly due to higher prices, which were 5 cents/lb. above 1986/87's.

A number of primary products are made from shelled edible peanuts. In 1987/88, the major product was peanut butter, which used 701 million pounds or 47 percent of the total. Salted peanuts used 374 million pounds, while peanut candy consumed 325 million.

With the total U.S. supply of peanuts forecast at 5.1 billion pounds, and usage estimated to be 4.1 billion, stocks of peanuts were projected to reach one billion pounds. This was 20 percent more than a year earlier.

Over the October 1987-September 1988 period, prices of peanuts in Rotterdam averaged $990/tonne, the highest since 1980/81. During the same period in 1986/87, peanut prices averaged $836.

U.S. Government Program.

The USDA indicated that the 1989 peanut crop would have a national poundage quota of 1.44 million short tons, 2.7 percent above 1988's. The national support price in 1989 was to be announced in February 1989. The 1988 support price was $615.27 per short ton.

World Production of Peanuts (in the Shell)   In Thousands of Metric Tons

Crop Year	Argentina	Brazil	Burma	China (mainland)	India	Indonesia	Mali	Nigeria	South Africa	Senegal	Sudan	Taiwan	Thailand	United States	Zaire (Congo)	World Total
1979–0	337	545	337	2,822	5,768	783	57	377	348	673	852	86	122	1,800	295	17,339
1980–1	243	310	431	3,600	5,005	791	92	560	309	521	707	82	130	1,045	320	16,301
1981–2	270	305	564	3,826	7,223	728	80	610	116	878	740	83	146	1,806	310	20,014
1982–3	250	250	541	3,916	5,282	795	80	580	89	1,109	497	63	145	1,560	310	17,619
1983–4	329	220	532	3,951	7,086	747	90	591	72	568	413	98	147	1,495	367	18,727
1984–5	270	337	667	4,815	6,436	755	90	500	196	560	390	88	172	1,998	375	19,682
1985–6	439	218	560	6,664	5,120	780		400	111	587	275	90	171	1,870	375	19,935
1986–7	518	200	544	5,882	6,060	750		400	130	842	450	69	178	1,679	380	20,452
1987–8[1]	450	170	559	6,170	4,800	784		475	210	960	400			1,642	380	19,761
1988–9[2]	400	150	575	5,800	7,300	790		400	220	800	400			1,869	380	22,050

[1] Preliminary.   [2] Estimated.   *Source: Foreign Agricultural Service, U.S.D.A.*   T.474

Salient Statistics of Peanuts in the United States

Crop Year	Acreage Planted —— (1,000 Acres) ——	Acreage Harvested For Nuts	Average Yield Per Acre In Lbs.	Production Picked and Threshed 1,000 Lbs.	Season Farm Price ¢ Lb.	Farm Value Million Dollars	Thousand Pounds (Yr. Beg. Aug.) Exports Unshelled	Exports Shelled	Imports Unshelled	Imports Shelled
1976–7	1,549	1,518	2,464	3,739,190	20.0	746,675	24,765	580,496	432	66
1977–8	1,545	1,512	2,456	3,715,055	21.0	780,869	64,284	705,032	413	148
1978–9	1,541	1,509	2,619	3,952,384	21.1	833,885	94,612	783,236	413	139
1979–0	1,546	1,520	2,611	3,968,485	20.6	819,276	64,810	745,828	424	140
1980–1	1,521	1,400	1,645	2,302,762	25.1	578,635	33,071	353,683	3,597	300,710
1981–2	1,514	1,489	2,675	3,981,850	26.9	1,069,526	77,998	374,812	6	4,632
1982–3	1,311	1,277	2,693	3,440,255	25.1	862,686	51,321	473,416	844	1,323
1983–4	1,411	1,374	2,399	3,295,530	24.7	814,579	39,509	529,949	298	1,715
1984–5	1,563	1,531	2,878	4,405,745	27.9	1,230,720	72,907	592,333	82	2,167
1985–6	1,490	1,467	2,810	4,122,787	24.4	1,003,412	83,747	721,690	1,495	1,942
1986–7	1,573	1,537	2,407	3,700,745	29.2	1,074,487				
1987–8[1]	1,567	1,546	2,341	3,619,440	27.7	1,015,658				
1988–9[2]	1,680	1,644	2,507	4,120,800	27.4	1,129,099				

[1] Preliminary. [2] Estimate. *Source: Economic Research Service, U.S.D.A.* T.475

Peanuts Supply & Disposition (Farmers' Stock Basis) & Support Program in the United States

Crop Year Begin. Aug. 1	Supply Production[3]	Imports	Stocks Aug. 1	Total	Disposition Exports & Shipments — Million Pounds —	Crushed for Oil	Seed, Loss & Residual	Food Use Military	Food Use Civilian	Total Disappear.	Support Price — ¢ per lb. —	Additional	Amount Put under Support Quantity Mil. Lbs.	% of Prod.	Owned by CCC July 31 Mil. Lbs.
1976–7	3,739	1	1,060	4,800	783	1,108	666	—	1,635	4,192	20.70		854	22.8	0
1977–8	3,715	1	608	4,324	1,025	487	556	—	1,675	3,743	21.50		535	14.4	2
1978–9	3,953	1	581	4,534	1,141	527	521	—	1,759	3,948	21.00	12.5	515	12.9	—
1979–0	3,968	1	586	4,555	1,057	571	522	—	1,777	3,927	21.00	15.0	709	17.9	—
1980–1	2,303	401	628	3,332	503	446	505	—	1,465	2,919	22.75	12.5	337	14.6	—
1981–2	3,982	2	413	4,397	576	573	795	—	1,696	3,640	22.75	12.5	835	20.9	2
1982–3	3,440	2	757	4,199	681	342	463	—	1,849	3,335	27.50	10.0	539	15.7	—
1983–4	3,296	2	864	4,162	744	387	564	—	1,856	3,551	27.50	9.3	367	11.1	—
1984–5	4,406	2	611	5,019	860	625	199	—	1,911	3,595	27.50	9.3	1,370	30.9	—
1985–6	4,123	2	1,424	5,549	1,043	812	826	—	2,023	4,704	27.95	7.4	1,359	33.0	—
1986–7	3,701	2	845	4,548	663	514	295	—	2,073	3,545	30.37	7.5	290	7.8	—
1987–8[1]	3,619	2	1,003	4,624	618	560	542	—	2,071	3,791	30.37	7.5			
1988–9[2]	4,257	2	833	5,092	725	800	444	—	2,123	4,092	30.79	7.5			

[1] Preliminary. [2] Estimate. [3] Production is on a net weight basis. *Source: Economic Research Service, U.S.D.A.* T.476

U.S. Production of Peanuts (Harvested for Nuts) by States In Millions of Pounds

Crop Year	Alabama	Arkansas	Florida	Georgia	Louisiana	Mississippi	New Mexico	No. Car.	Oklahoma	So. Car.	Tennessee	Texas	Virginia	U.S. Total
1976	513.6	—	165.0	1,554.3	—	12.3	21.7	440.7	246.0	24.6	—	463.6	309.0	3,739
1977	589.1	—	170.5	1,499.1	—	11.6	25.4	444.1	267.6	31.2	—	394.5	293.0	3,715
1978	551.8	—	182.1	1,725.3	—	13.1	24.1	465.4	207.0	35.7	—	436.5	311.6	3,952
1979	584.9	—	179.9	1,704.8	—	12.4	25.3	378.5	264.0	32.3	—	533.0	253.5	3,968
1980	265.0	—	143.0	994.6	—	7.5	22.4	291.3	140.2	14.3	—	293.3	129.8	2,303
1981	602.7	—	178.0	1,655.5	—	12.7	24.9	555.6	189.3	39.0	—	393.3	330.8	3,982
1982	522.2	—	153.0	1,517.5	—	—	25.2	417.2	174.6	30.0	—	325.1	275.5	3,440
1983	454.5	—	166.8	1,568.0	—	—	25.6	318.3	176.5	25.0	—	362.3	198.6	3,296
1984	648.6	—	246.4	2,160.0	—	—	32.2	449.5	189.0	39.2	—	371.3	269.7	4,406
1985	590.0	—	216.0	1,921.3	—	—	32.0	452.0	171.0	34.2	—	422.6	283.7	4,123
1986	494.9	—	233.2	1,632.6	—	—	28.7	440.4	184.5	25.5	—	385.0	275.9	3,701
1987	465.3	—	215.8	1,575.0	—	—	33.5	392.2	222.5	31.2	—	441.0	243.0	3,619
1988[1]	618.8		226.2	1,863.0			35.1	428.4	220.5	34.3		412.5	282.0	4,121

[1] Preliminary. *Source: Crop Reporting Board, U.S.D.A.* T.477

PEANUTS AND PEANUT OIL

Disappearance and Reported Uses of Peanuts and Products in the U.S.   In Millions of Pounds

Year Begin. Aug. 1	Apparent Disappear.[2] (Milled Peanut Prod.) — Shelled Peanuts — Edible Grades	Oil Stock[3]	Total All Grades	Cleaned (In Shell)	Crude Peanut Oil[4]	Cake & Meal[4]	Reported Used (Shelled Peanuts—Raw Basis) Edible Grades Used in — Peanut — Candy	Salted	Sand-wich Spread	Butter[5]	Other Products	Roast-ing Stocks	Total	Oil Stock Crushed For Oil, Cake & Meal	Total All Grades
1977–8	1,895	461.2	2,356	190.6	179.1	208.9	235.2	274.2	28.2	623.8	18.7	126.7	1,180	366.2	1,546
1978–9	1,955	426.9	2,382	210.9	161.6	227.9	268.4	291.6	28.1	664.9	19.1	116.7	1,272	396.0	1,668
1979–0	1,979	503.9	2,483	201.4	175.3	228.4	258.4	284.9	30.3	700.0	19.3	137.1	1,293	429.1	1,722
1980–1	1,097	306.0	1,403	120.3	143.5	189.6	237.9	205.5	24.1	588.6	19.7	90.8	1,076	335.5	1,411
1981–2	1,096	377.6	2,283	200.7	155.7	233.7	255.9	278.0	22.7	653.7	15.3	122.7	1,225	431.5	1,657
1982–3				206.4		145.5	284.2	308.1	21.9	677.6	17.0	155.9	1,309	256.4	1,565
1983–4				173.0		149.9	298.1	302.0	24.3	671.4	15.5	133.8	1,311	291.1	1,602
1984–5				211.9			290.3	309.1	26.2	697.1	19.2	139.1	1,342	470.3	1,812
1985–6[1]				234.6			313.8	358.5	24.6	701.3	23.5	152.3	1,422	610.9	2,033
1986–7[1]							321.0	384.0	34.0	679.0	41.0		1,460		
1987–8[1]							325	374	46	701	38		1,484		

[1] Preliminary.   [2] Includes in transit, exports and domestic use, except for oil stock for which disappearance is assumed to equal crushings.   [3] Graded & ungraded oil stock only.   [4] Relates to peanut oil mills only.   [5] Peanuts used in peanut butter by mfrs. for own use in candy is included under peanut candy.   *Source: Statistical Reporting Service, U.S.D.A.*   T.481

World Peanut Oil Salient Statistics   In Thousands of Metric Tons

Crop Year	Production — Bur-ma	China	India	Total	Imports — EC–12	Total	Exports — Arg-entina	China	Sen-egal	Total	Consumption — Bur-ma	China	EC–12	India	Total	Ending Stocks Total
1983–4	136	490	1,608	2,926	279	343	30	49	92	295	136	441	254	1,608	2,970	46
1984–5	171	632	1,520	3,035	244	313	28	40	42	274	171	592	226	1,520	3,085	35
1985–6	143	871	1,221	2,942	238	297	33	80	81	330	143	791	212	1,221	2,873	70
1986–7	139	754	1,404	3,117	260	324	77	80	100	353	139	674	233	1,404	3,093	65
1987–8[1]	143	805	1,119	2,927	269	334	55	60	136	361	143	745	239	1,119	2,916	49
1988–9[2]	147	747	1,573	3,306	256	316	40	60	100	302	147	687	228	1,573	3,317	52

[1] Preliminary.   [2] Forecast.   *Source: Foreign Agricultural Service, U.S.D.A.*   T.482

Production, Consumption, Stocks and Foreign Trade of Peanut Oil in the U.S.   In Millions of Pounds

Crop Yr. Begin. Oct.	Production Crude	Refined	Consumption In Refining	In End pdt's.	Stocks—Sept. 30 Crude	Refined	Imports for Con-sumption	Exports Crude	Refined
1977	252.0	249.7	257.2	243.9	91.5	7.6	—	71.8	9.7
1978	145.2	171.9	178.0	169.0	7.3	4.7	—	32.9	7.6
1979	183.0	130.1	134.3	120.4	22.6	7.3		14.4	1.2
1980	182.4	170.6	166.7	165.3	7.5	4.3		46.0	1.6
1981	141.6	122.8	133.5	115.3	12.9	5.2		38.1	2.7
1982–3[1]	N.A.	168.8	183.9	174.0	N.A.	3.9	3.8	4.5	.5
1983–4	N.A.	139.6	148.4	132.9	17.9	4.0	1.9	5.1	.4
1984–5	138.2	119.9	124.6	N.A.	9.6	4.8	.9	33.4	1.5
1985–6	N.A.	139.7	145.7	N.A.	64.9	4.0	.5	78.0	—
1986–7	144.2	160.0	169.0	153.2	17.0	3.6	2.4	5.5	.8

[1] Data prior to 1982–83 are for the calendar years.   *Source: Bureau of Census*   T.483

Utilization of Peanut Oil in the United States   In Thousands of Pounds

Year Begin. Aug.	Shortening	Margarine	Cooking and Salad Oils	Other Edible	Total Food Uses	Non-Food Uses	Factory Consumption	Foots & Loss	Domestic Disappearance
1977–8	20,000	—	211,000	−47,000	183,000	11,000		8,000	194,000
1978–9	16,000		96,000						120,000
1979–0[1]			148,000						193,000
1980–1[2]			100,000						150,000
1981–2[2]			136,000		139,000				
1982–3[2]			157,000		174,000				
1983–4[2]			119,000		131,000				
1984–5[2]			110,000		118,405				
1985–6[2]			136,000		137,383				
1986–7[2]			149,500		151,100				

[1] Preliminary.   [2] Estimate.   *Source: Bureau of the Census*   T.484

Average Price Received by Producers in U.S. for Peanuts in the Shell   In Cents Per Pound

Year	Aug.	Sept.	Oct.	Nov.	Dec.	Jan.	Feb.	Mar.	Apr.	May	June	July	Average[1]
1978–9	21.2	20.8	21.4	21.0	20.8	21.2	—	—	—	—	—	—	21.1
1979–0	—	21.4	20.3	20.4	20.4	20.4	—	—	—	—	—	—	20.6
1980–1	—	22.5	23.2	27.9	37.3	47.7	—	—	—	—	—	—	25.1
1981–2	25.7	28.9	26.7	25.1	25.8	24.9	—	—	—	—	—	—	26.9
1982–3	27.1	25.1	24.9	25.3	26.1	22.9	—	—	—	—	—	—	25.1
1983–4	—	25.2	24.3	24.5	26.0	27.8	—	—	—	—	—	—	24.7
1984–5	24.7	29.9	27.1	25.6	26.3	—	—	—	—	—	—	—	27.9
1985–6	29.6	24.4	24.3	24.6	23.3	20.6	—	—	—	—	—	—	24.4
1986–7	29.7	27.0	28.8	29.8	32.5	24.5	—	—	—	—	—	—	29.2
1987–8[2]	20.0	29.2	27.8	27.1	26.2	22.9	—	—	—	—	—	—	27.7
1988–9[2]		29.0	26.9	25.6	24.7								

[1] Weighted average by sales.   [2] Preliminary.   *Source: Crop Reporting Board, U.S.D.A.*   T.479

Crude Peanut Oil Produced[2] in the United States   In Millions of Pounds

Year	Jan.	Feb.	Mar.	Apr.	May	June	July	Aug.	Sept.	Oct.	Nov.	Dec.	Total
1979	11.7	14.2	22.5	18.6	23.0	15.5	8.2	10.8	4.5	4.5	6.1	7.7	183.0
1980	6.2	15.1	16.7	25.9	30.7	22.9	23.5	21.2	5.9	2.1	6.3	5.9	182.4
1981	6.1	6.0	10.5	17.3	19.1	19.5	13.6	9.8	5.3	9.7	12.0	12.7	141.6
1982	11.3	11.1	19.4	26.3	22.3	19.0	15.0	11.8	N.A.	N.A.	N.A.	N.A.	N.A.
1983	N.A.	N.A.	N.A.	N.A.	N.A.	N.A.	N.A.	N.A.	N.A.	N.A.	N.A.	N.A.	N.A.
1984	12.1	13.3	10.8	12.5	10.1	8.9	5.1	5.3	4.3	9.9	8.6	7.3	108.2
1985	9.8	13.9	15.8	15.5	14.5	12.4	10.4	10.0	10.1	9.2	10.2	14.9	146.7
1986	19.2	21.1	19.9	20.8	24.0	26.4	14.2	9.6	N.A.	4.1	11.9	10.7	181.9
1987	9.8	13.6	20.5	11.0	17.8	15.8	14.5	9.7	4.2	7.5	13.7	13.1	151.8
1988[1]	13.8	14.9	10.1	8.3	19.5	12.5	17.0	11.4	2.8	9.7			

[1] Preliminary.   [2] Not seasonally adjusted.   *Source: Statistical Reporting Service, U.S.D.A.*   T.473

Average Price of Domestic Crude Peanut Oil (in Tanks) F.O.B. Southeast Mills   In Cents Per Pound

Year	Oct.	Nov.	Dec.	Jan.	Feb.	Mar.	Apr.	May	June	July	Aug.	Sept.	Average
1979–0	34.4	31.1	29.5	25.9	25.8	22.9	20.5	22.4	23.1	26.9	33.2	36.0	27.6
1980–1	35.8	48.7	49.1	47.7	39.3	34.1	34.0	37.1	38.0	38.1	43.2	40.3	40.5
1981–2	34.5	34.5	30.9	27.3	31.4	23.3	29.1	29.9	26.2	24.7	22.7	22.5	28.1
1982–3	22.9	25.2	26.1	25.6	25.7	24.1	25.1	26.4	26.4	26.7	30.7	50.5	28.0
1983–4	50.7	48.8	48.1	47.3	46.5	48.4	52.6	58.2	59.1	57.7	54.8	39.2	47.3
1984–5	36.7	41.2	41.4	39.2	38.8	40.3	49.6	46.2	40.7	39.7	37.6	33.9	40.4
1985–6	38.3	42.2	36.1	29.5	22.6	21.5	24.4	27.6	28.0	27.5	30.5	28.3	29.7
1986–7	27.80	29.80	26.50	25.10	25.00	23.75	24.00	26.15	25.68	25.27	24.61	26.74	25.87
1987–8	33.48	31.50	32.10	35.73	32.40	29.61	29.50	30.02	34.00	39.80	37.86	36.00	33.50

Source: Agricultural Marketing Service, U.S.D.A.   T.485

Pepper

As had been the case for several years, world consumption exceeded production in 1987/88. The major producers were Indonesia, India, Brazil, and Malaysia. Singapore was an important importer and re-exporter.

USDA indicated that pepper output in the major producing countries in 1987 was disappointing, given early-season forecasts that production would rebound. Low prices prior to 1984 apparently discouraged growers from expanding output or even continuing good cultural practices. While high prices tend to boost output, it takes three to four years for new plants to come into production. India's crop in 1987/88 was expected to be larger, though impacted by drought in 1987. In Malaysia, pepper producers shifted some area into alternative crops like cocoa. Brazilian producers have also been hesitant to expand output, since pepper requires a larger investment than competing crops.

With disappointing crops in 1987, exports of pepper were lower. Brazil's exports were 17,000 tonnes, 20 percent less than in 1986. Brazil had record exports in 1981 of almost 46,900 tonnes. Malaysia's 1987 exports were about 14,200 tonnes, somewhat smaller than in 1986, and less than half of the amount exported a decade earlier. Indonesia's 1987 exports were ex-

pected to exceed the 1986 level of 29,600 tonnes. With a larger crop, India could be expected to increase exports. However, the Food and Drug Administration (FDA) in late July of 1987 "blocklisted" Indian pepper. This meant that all shipments were to be detained for FDA inspection at U.S. ports.

U.S. imports of black pepper in 1987 were 31,374 tonnes, down 18 percent, due to a sharp decline in purchases from India. Brazil emerged as the major supplier, providing almost 12,000 tonnes to the U.S. Indonesia supplied almost 7,000 tonnes, and Malaysia nearly 1,700 tonnes.

U.S. imports of white pepper in 1987 were 4,530 tonnes, up almost 27 percent from 1986. Indonesia supplied 93 percent.

Pepper prices have been climbing since 1984. The New York spot price for Brazilian black pepper in 1984 averaged over 96 cents/lb. In 1987, prices averaged almost $2.36, reaching a high of $2.51 in September 1987. By March 1988, prices had pulled back to $2.10.

In 1984, spot prices for Indonesia Muntok white pepper in New York averaged almost $1.54/lb. In 1987, prices averaged almost $2.68, and by March 1988 they were over $2.77.

World Exports of Pepper (Black & White) and Prices

| | Exports (metric tons) | | | | | | | New York Spot Prices (¢ per pound) | | | | | |
| | | | | | | | | Indonesian | | Brazilian | | Indian | |
Year	Brazil	India	Indonesia	Singapore[2]	Madagascar	Sarawak	Sri Lanka	Lampong Black	Muntok White	Black	White	Malabar Black	Telli-cherry[3]
1976	19,986	17,813	29,481		2,958	34,850	10						
1977	17,099	25,892	30,856		3,748	26,795	635						
1978	29,505	19,370	37,090	40,904	1,566	30,780	1,205						
1979	25,186	20,545	24,986	38,395	1,894	36,118	876	93.7	132.6	91.9	129.7	93.9	112.2
1980	31,964	26,795	29,345	33,233	1,674	30,709	945	87.6	120.9	83.3	116.3	87.6	102.5
1981	46,895	18,636	33,996	30,098	1,440	28,696	2,042	68.8	101.5	62.3	100.0	80.4	103.8
1982	44,539	20,454	36,327	26,459	1,796	25,010	1,238	66.3	84.8	62.1	84.7	69.2	83.7
1983	30,363	27,982	45,061	N.A.	3,231	23,481	1,120	72.1	96.7	65.5	96.2	76.0	86.5
1984	36,499	28,381	33,817		2,804	16,502	2,202	98.6	153.9	96.5	152.8	98.9	115.2
1985	24,676	19,538	26,202		2,618	19,070	1,260	169.6	190.6	167.4	190.4	169.6	185.3
1986[1]	22,069	49,807	29,566		2,500	15,380	1,286	215.0	275.3	212.5	275.3	214.6	235.1
1987[1]								237.1	267.7	235.9	267.7	236.0	262.8

[1] Preliminary.   [2] Reexports.   *Source: Foreign Agricultural Service, U.S.D.A.*

T.486

United States Imports of Pepper from Specified Countries   In Metric Tons

| | Black Pepper | | | | | | | | | | White Pepper | | | | | | |
Year	Brazil	Mexico	Sri Lanka (Ceylon)	Spain	India	Indonesia	Malaysia	Singapore	China	Total	Brazil	China	W. Germany	Indonesia	Malaysia	Singapore	Total
1976	6,609		—		359	11,774	4,037	1,321	3	24,128	53	—		2,118	56	128	2,362
1977	5,282		157		4,890	9,466	3,140	478	—	23,540	40			2,765	42	63	2,920
1978	10,472		186		1,880	10,595	2,293	604	6	26,142	285	—		1,994	64	28	2,382
1979	9,704		281	—	627	10,898	2,644	156	61	24,482	414	10	—	2,159	51	94	2,756
1980	10,075	131	3,194														
1981	14,716	75	2,503														
1982	14,887	10	172	—	848	11,620	172	63	3	27,811	423	1	5	2,194	—	95	2,721
1983	13,047	—	256	—	2,498	12,327	25	120	3	28,346	571	17	6	2,460	—	65	3,130
1984	10,369	3	158	34	4,024	9,814	131	322	378	27,421	246	260	10	3,805	100	100	4,762
1985	12,227	3	158	34	4,024	9,814	131	322	378	27,421	246	260	10	3,805	100	100	4,762
1986	9,416	7	255	1	20,976	5,980	634	120	243	38,063	134	171	7	2,846	65	140	3,578
1987[1]	11,981	23	388	—	9,343	6,958	1,667	379	107	31,374	65	6	1	4,238	22	110	4,533

[1] Preliminary.   *Source: Foreign Agricultural Service, U.S.D.A.*

T.487

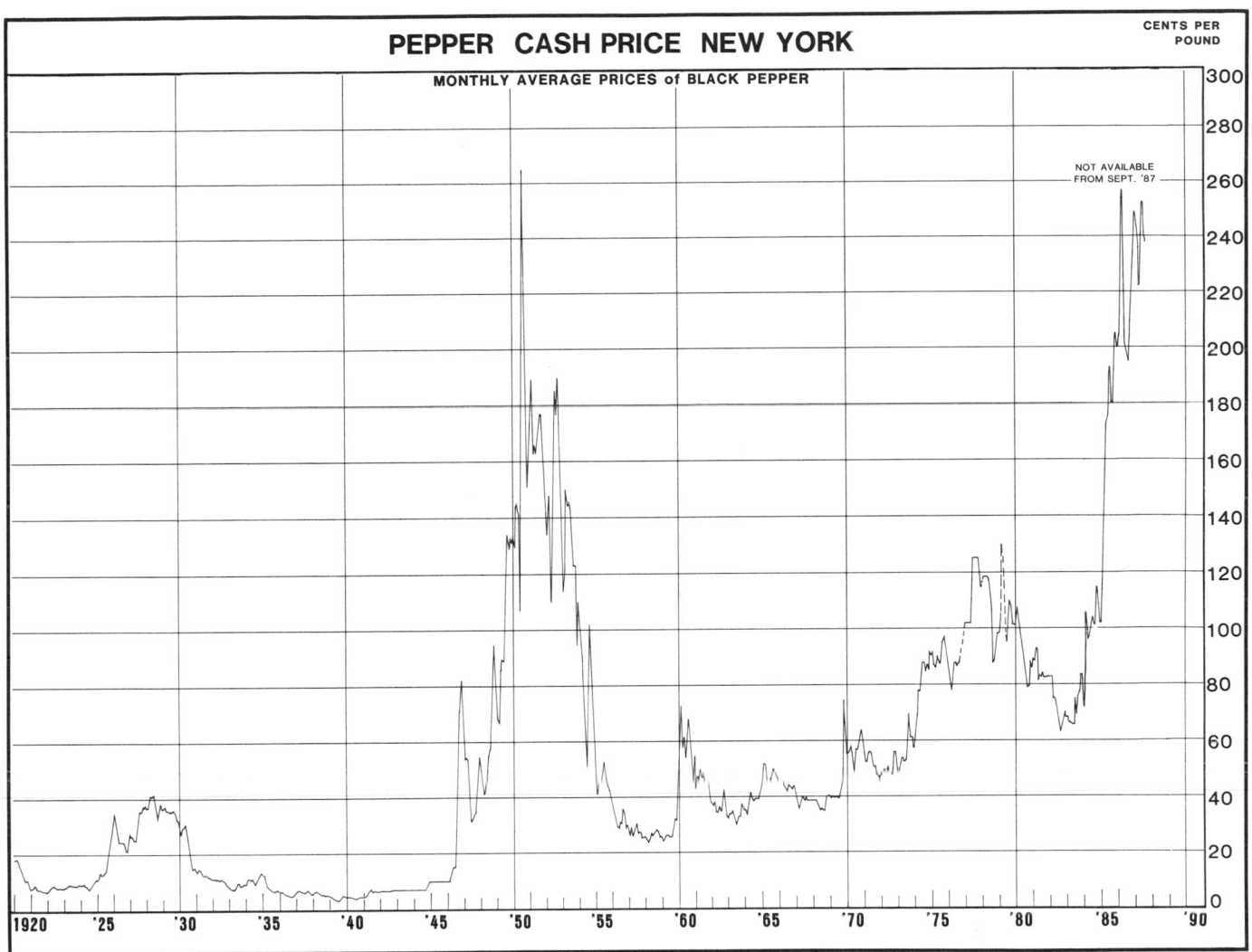

PEPPER CASH PRICE NEW YORK

CENTS PER POUND

MONTHLY AVERAGE PRICES of BLACK PEPPER

NOT AVAILABLE FROM SEPT. '87

Average Black Pepper Prices in New York   In Cents Per Pound

Year	Jan.	Feb.	Mar.	Apr.	May	June	July	Aug.	Sept.	Oct.	Nov.	Dec.	Average
1973	49.3	52.0	54.0	53.0	52.5	53.0	65.0	70.0	61.0	61.0	57.5	61.0	57.4
1974	64.0	70.0	78.0	78.0	85.0	88.0	88.0	85.0	87.5	85.5	92.0	91.0	82.7
1975	91.5	87.0	86.0	90.0	89.0	87.5	88.5	95.0	97.0	94.0	87.5	85.0	89.8
1976	81.0	79.0	77.5	88.0	88.0	87.0	87.5	87.5	N.A.	N.A.	N.A.	102.0	86.4
1977	102.0	102.0	102.0	102.0	125.0	125.0	125.0	125.0	125.0	125.0	114.5	N.A.	115.7
1978	118.5	118.5	118.5	118.5	117.5	109.0	107.5	88.0	88.5	95.5	98.5	98.5	106.4
1979	105.0	N.A.	130.0	N.A.	N.A.	95.0	97.0	110.0	108.0	108.0	102.0	101.3	106.3
1980	108.0	101.0	96.3	93.0	87.0	84.3	82.8	79.0	79.0	88.0	86.5	89.3	89.5
1981	88.5	93.3	92.0	81.0	83.0	82.3	84.0	82.5	82.3	82.3	82.5	82.5	84.7
1982	82.5	82.5	75.0	75.0	70.0	69.0	67.0	63.0	69.0	70.5	68.5	68.3	71.7
1983	68.3	66.5	66.3	65.5	65.5	65.5	75.0	69.3	76.3	77.3	83.5	83.5	71.9
1984	105.7	102.0	95.7	97.0	100.7	102.0	103.7	101.3	109.0	115.3	107.3	102.3	103.5
1985	114.0	124.3	145.0	173.3	175.7	190.7	192.7	180.0	180.0	193.0	205.0	200.0	172.8
1986	208.0	217.0	257.0	226.0	201.0	199.0	197.0	195.0	210.0	231.0	233.0	249.0	218.6
1987	243.5	235.5	222.0	240.5	253.2	252.2	240.8	234.4	N.A.	N.A.	N.A.		

Source: Bureau of Labor Statistics (0289–0131);   N.Y. Wall St. Journal; CRB   T.488

Petroleum

Global free-market petroleum demand was projected to reach at least 49.8 million barrels per day (bpd) in 1988, an increase of almost 2 percent from the 1987 level, according to preliminary estimates by the U.S. Department of Energy (DOE). Demand was expected to increase by some 670,000 bpd to 50.5 million in 1989, with about one-third of the growth coming from developing industrialized countries like South Korea.

World oil production through the first three quarters of 1988 averaged 57 million bpd, up 3 percent from the same period a year earlier. Total 1988 production was forecast to be up 3 percent from 1987. Supplies available to countries that are market economies were forecast at about 50.6 million bpd in 1988, compared with 48.7 million a year earlier. Closing 1988 stocks were forecast at 5.45 billion barrels of crude or petroleum products, up from 5.09 billion a year earlier.

OPEC oil production was estimated to have averaged about 21 million bpd, above the 1987 rate of 19.6 million. However, OPEC output may have averaged as much as 22.7 million bpd during the fourth quarter of 1988. These figures were well in excess of OPEC's stated quotas.

OPEC meetings in April and June failed to resolve deep differences among the 13 member nations. Early in the year, it became apparent that Saudi Arabia and the United Arab Emirates had abandoned attempts to support the official OPEC bench mark price of $18/barrel. The OPEC production quota of 15.06 million bpd did not include Iraq at that time, a concession to the fact that Iraq had been ignoring its quota since mid-1986. Iraq's production in the summer of 1988 was estimated at 3 million bpd, very close to its capacity.

Iran agreed on July 18 to accept a cease-fire sponsored by the United Nations, raising fears that the shooting war with Iraq would be replaced by an oil production and price war.

Following a string of uneventful OPEC committee meetings in the fall, a series of compromises was worked out at OPEC's November ministerial meeting. The producton quota for the first half of 1989 was raised to 18.5 million bpd, and Iraq agreed to rejoin the fold after Iran agreed to accept parity with Iraq at a quota of 2.64 million bpd. At the time, industry analysts predicted that first-quarter 1989 demand for OPEC oil would be no more than 18.2 million bpd. However,

prices began advancing almost immediately, and the price strength continued through the remainder of 1988. The January 1989 crude oil futures contract expired on December 20, 1988, at $17.73/barrel, having traded as high as $18.20 that day. In early 1989, it appeared that actual first-quarter demand for OPEC oil would be above 20 million bpd, or about what OPEC was likely to be producing.

Total 1988 U.S. demand for petroleum and petroleum products was expected to top 17 million bpd for the first time since 1980, partly because of extreme weather conditions. Heating oil demand surged early in 1988 because of very cold weather and held up well into the spring. Temperatures stayed unseasonably low in the Northeast into early June, only to be followed almost immediately by a severe heat wave. Meanwhile, in the Midwest and the Far West, a severe drought boosted demand for electricity from oil-fired standby generators, as hydroelectric supplies, including imports from Canada, became unavailable. Demand also grew because of the economy's surprising growth. The recession feared after the 1987 stock market crash did not develop, and the U.S. economy was relatively strong during 1988 and into 1989.

Assuming that the U.S. economy would grow at a 2.9 percent annual rate in 1989, U.S. petroleum demand was expected to rise to 17.46 million bpd for the first quarter and settle back to an average of 17.21 million for the year.

The DOE's Economic Regulatory Administration, responsible for price-control regulations in effect between 1974 and 1982, closed its casebook to new claims on September 30, 1988, and officially went out of business on November 15. However, existing cases involving overcharges for oil were expected to be processed through 1989.

Futures Markets

Futures contracts on crude oil, heating oil, and unleaded regular gasoline are traded on the New York Mercantile Exchange (NYMEX), along with options on heating oil and crude oil. Heating oil is traded on the London International Petroleum Exchange, where it is called gas oil. London also trades Brent crude oil futures and options on gas oil.

World Production of Crude Petroleum, by Specified Countries   In Thousand Barrels Per Day

Year	Algeria	Canada	China	Libya	Iran	Iraq	Kuwait	Nigeria	Mexico	Indo-nesia	United Kingdom	USSR	Saudi Arabia	United States	Vene-zuela	World Total
1978	1,231	1,316	2,082	1,983	5,242	2,563	2,131	1,897	1,209	1,635	1,082	10,950	8,301	8,707	2,165	60,003
1979	1,224	1,500	2,122	2,092	3,168	3,477	2,500	2,302	1,461	1,591	1,568	11,187	9,532	8,552	2,356	62,477
1980	1,106	1,435	2,114	1,787	1,662	2,514	1,656	2,055	1,936	1,577	1,622	11,460	9,900	8,597	2,168	59,353
1981	1,002	1,285	2,012	1,140	1,380	1,000	1,125	1,433	2,313	1,605	1,811	11,552	9,815	8,572	2,102	55,778
1982	987	1,271	2,045	1,150	2,214	1,012	823	1,295	2,748	1,339	2,065	11,615	6,483	8,649	1,895	53,184
1983	968	1,356	2,120	1,105	2,440	1,005	1,064	1,241	2,689	1,343	2,291	11,684	5,086	8,688	1,801	52,967
1984	1,014	1,438	2,296	1,087	2,174	1,209	1,157	1,388	2,780	1,412	2,480	11,576	4,663	8,879	1,798	54,203
1985	1,037	1,471	2,505	1,059	2,250	1,433	1,023	1,495	2,745	1,325	2,530	11,250	3,388	8,971	1,677	53,646
1986	945	1,474	2,620	1,034	2,035	1,690	1,419	1,484	2,435	1,390	2,539	11,540	4,870	8,680	1,787	55,889
1987[2]	985	1,533	2,690	972	2,426	2,079	1,361	1,340	2,540	1,311	2,476	11,690	4,186	8,349	1,751	56,096
1988[1]	982	1,594	2,710	994	2,164	2,618	1,326	1,406	2,534	1,289	2,363	11,681	4,547	8,213	1,786	57,045

[1] Estimate. [2] Preliminary. *Source: Energy Information Administration*

T.489

United States Production of Gasoline[1] (Includes Aviation)   In Millions of Barrels

Year	Jan.	Feb.	Mar.	Apr.	May	June	July	Aug.	Sept.	Oct.	Nov.	Dec.	Total
1982	191.8	165.7	186.5	183.4	196.7	203.5	210.7	200.1	196.5	194.9	188.9	203.2	2,322
1983	188.7	164.3	183.7	186.7	199.0	200.6	208.8	203.7	199.3	192.7	199.7	196.1	2,323
1984	187.7	184.1	197.6	196.4	207.0	199.6	200.9	199.5	196.2	198.7	202.1	201.4	2,371
1985	184.2	166.2	189.0	191.1	204.3	204.2	211.5	212.3	189.8	197.8	195.2	206.7	2,352
1986	202.8	177.3	188.6	195.8	220.9	214.1	216.8	221.2	208.7	206.0	207.5	216.5	2,476
1987[2]	208.2	179.0	204.0	206.5	217.5	213.7	219.2	215.9	208.6	207.5	207.7	218.1	2,506
1988[2]	209.1	195.8	208.2	207.9	213.2	210.3	222.9	224.3					

[1] Gasoline and naphtha from crude petroleum and natural gasoline used at refineries.   [2] Preliminary.   *Source: Bureau of Mines*   T.502

United States Domestic Consumption of Gasoline   In Millions of Barrels

Year	Jan.	Feb.	Mar.	Apr.	May	June	July	Aug.	Sept.	Oct.	Nov.	Dec.	Total
1982	185.5	174.0	201.2	207.7	207.1	206.1	211.4	206.1	196.9	198.8	197.6	203.6	2,396
1983	187.8	168.9	212.5	194.4	205.8	210.8	210.7	216.0	202.8	205.2	198.8	212.9	2,427
1984	194.6	181.4	202.8	201.1	214.7	214.1	212.5	220.9	198.3	209.2	204.7	203.7	2,458
1985	197.5	185.0	207.4	209.6	219.7	210.8	218.3	225.6	199.8	214.6	203.7	211.4	2,503
1986	202.2	181.7	216.5	214.1	221.4	217.3	231.6	231.7	207.8	225.6	207.1	222.1	2,579
1987[1]	201.2	189.1	215.5	220.5	232.5	227.1	235.9	228.4	216.9	227.2	215.1	225.3	2,639
1988[1]	207.8	203.8	226.0	222.2	226.4	236.1	232.7	233.7					

[1] Preliminary.   *Source: Bureau of Mines*   T.503

Stocks of Finished Gasoline[2] on Hand in the United States, at End of Month   In Millions of Barrels

Year	Jan.	Feb.	Mar.	Apr.	May	June	July	Aug.	Sept.	Oct.	Nov.	Dec.
1982	215.9	211.2	200.7	181.0	175.6	179.5	185.0	187.6	193.3	194.6	191.9	196.8
1983	210.0	209.2	185.4	185.4	188.0	185.4	192.3	187.4	191.8	189.5	198.4	187.8
1984	188.0	199.3	204.8	209.7	212.7	206.5	202.2	188.3	196.5	195.5	201.2	207.9
1985	200.9	191.8	188.2	184.2	183.4	188.5	194.4	190.4	189.7	182.3	185.6	192.4
1986	203.2	207.8	186.2	176.0	189.8	197.8	192.0	189.7	198.5	187.0	193.0	196.4
1987[1]	211.7	209.6	208.1	203.4	197.7	194.5	190.8	189.9	193.4	184.1	190.2	191.1
1988[1]	202.3	204.4	195.9	191.5	190.4	175.6	179.7	184.3				

[1] Preliminary.   [2] Includes aviation.   *Source: Bureau of Mines*   T.504

United States Crude Oil[1] Supply & Disposition

Yearly Average	Field Production — Total Domestic	Alaskan	Imports Total	SPR[4]	Other	Stock Withdrawal[3] SPR[4]	Other	Unaccounted for Crude Oil	Disposition — Refinery Inputs	Exports	Ending Stocks[2] Total	SPR[5]	Other Primary
					Thousands barrels PER DAY						Million barrels		
1984	8,879	1,722	3,426	197	3,229	−195	− 4	185	12,044	181	796	451	345
1985	8,971	1,825	3,201	118	3,083	−117	67	145	12,002	204	814	493	321
1986	8,680	1,867	4,178	48	4,130	− 50	− 28	139	12,716	154	843	512	331
1987	8,349	1,962	4,674	73	4,601	− 80	− 49	145	12,854	151	890	541	349
1988[6]	8,170	2,021	5,008	52	4,957	− 52	23	334	13,283	162	897	556	341
Aug.	8,063	2,009	5,039	26	5,013	− 26	521	385	13,797	155	885	552	333
Sept.	7,800	2,020	5,183	84	5,099	− 84	157	313	13,309	122	883	555	328
Oct.	8,085	2,044	5,329	60	5,269	− 60	−449	389	13,095	170	897	556	341

[1] Includes lease condensate.   [2] Stocks are totals as of end of period.   [3] A negative number indicates an increase in stocks and a positive number indicates a decrease.   [4] Strategic Petroleum Reserve.   [5] Stocks of Alaskan crude oil in transit were included beginning in January 1981. Stock withdrawals are calculated using new basis levels.   [6] Preliminary.   *Source: Energy Information Administration*   T.489a

PETROLEUM

Crude Petroleum Refinery Operations Ratio[1]   In Percent of Capacity

Year	Jan.	Feb.	Mar.	Apr.	May	June	July	Aug.	Sept.	Oct.	Nov.	Dec.	Average
1982	67	65	66	66	69	75	75	71	74	71	71	70	70
1983	68	65	66	70	72	75	75	74	78	73	75	70	72
1984	73	76	75	75	77	77	76	78	78	76	77	76	76
1985	74	74	74	76	78	79	81	78	77	79	80	81	78
1986	81	78	76	82	86	86	84	87	86	83	84	84	83
1987[2]	81	79	78	80	82	85	87	87	86	83	82	84	83
1988[2]	83	81	84	84	86	86	86	87					

[1] Based on the ratio of the daily avg. crude runs to stills to the rated capacity of refineries per day.   [2] Preliminary.   *Source: Bureau of Mines*
T.496

Production of Major Refined Petroleum Products in Continental U.S.   In Millions of Barrels

Year	As-phalt[2]	Avia-tion Gasol.	Fuel Oil Dis-tillate	Fuel Oil Resid-ual	Gaso-line[4]	Petro-Chemical Feedstocks	Special Naph-thas	Miscel. pdt's.	Jet Fuel	Kero-sene	Liquified Gases[7] (For Fuel)	Lubri-cants	Liquefied Gases[3] Total	Liquefied Gases[3] at L.P.G.[5]	Liquefied Gases[3] at L.R.G.[6]
1983	135.7	9.2	896.5	310.9	2,323				373.2	40.0		53.8	599.2	479.6	119.6
1984	141.3	9.1	981.2	326.2	2,371				414.3	41.8		58.3	620.9	488.2	132.7
1985	146.3	9.3	980.9	322.0	2,352				433.9	34.5		53.1	622.0	479.3	142.6
1986	149.7	11.7	1,021.2	324.3	2,476				472.0	32.6		58.2	618.5	466.2	152.3
1987[1]	158.4	9.1	996.6	323.2	2,506				490.1	28.7		60.9	638.2	474.5	163.7

[1] Estimated.   [2] 5.5 barrels = 1 short ton.   [3] Includes ethane & ethylene.   [4] Finished (includes aviation).   [5] Gas processing plants.   [6] Refineries.   [7] Liquified refinery gases.   *Source: Bureau of Mines*
T.490

Stocks of Petroleum & Products in the United States on January 1   In Millions of Barrels

Year	Crude Petro-leum	Strate-gic Reserve	Total	As-phalt[2]	Avia-tion Gasol.	Fuel Oil Distil-late	Fuel Oil Resid-ual	Finished Gasoline[6]	Petro-Chemical Feedstocks	Jet Fuel	Kero-sene	Liquefied Gases[3]	Lubri-cants	Road Oil	Wax[4]	Unfinished Oils (Net)[5]
1983	643.6	293.8	628.3	15.9	2.3	178.6	66.2	196.8		36.8	10.4	94.0	12.5			158.1
1984	722.9	379.1	569.2	18.8	2.3	140.3	48.5	187.8		38.6	7.9	100.6	12.1			161.5
1985	795.9	450.5	620.6	17.2	2.7	161.1	53.0	207.9		42.0	11.9	100.8	12.7			139.8
1986	814.2	493.3	556.6	21.2	2.1	143.7	50.4	192.4		40.5	7.5	73.5	11.8			148.0
1987	842.8	511.6	609.4	17.7	2.2	155.1	47.4	196.4		49.7	8.4	102.7	14.2			140.4
1988[1]	889.6	540.6	579.5	18.8	2.3	134.5	47.4	191.1		49.9	8.4	97.1	13.3			138.3

[1] Preliminary.   [2] 5.5 bbls. = 1 s. ton.   [3] Includes ethane & ethylene at plants & refineries.   [4] 1 bbl. = 280 lbs.   [5] And misc. products.   [6] Includes aviation.   *Source: Bureau of Mines*
T.493

Stocks of Crude Petroleum[1] in the United States at Beginning of Month   In Millions of Barrels

Year	Jan.	Feb.	Mar.	Apr.	May	June	July	Aug.	Sept.	Oct.	Nov.	Dec.
1983	643.6	660.4	669.4	666.8	678.9	679.4	683.0	675.8	700.5	707.7	716.2	712.7
1984	722.9	733.1	727.4	728.2	742.5	763.5	766.6	771.8	764.1	756.3	779.8	786.9
1985	795.9	793.5	781.6	791.2	806.8	828.6	820.6	810.5	805.6	806.6	803.6	812.4
1986	814.2	826.1	827.1	837.8	836.6	828.5	828.4	845.2	837.7	844.2	851.4	848.6
1987[2]	842.8	848.7	853.0	853.0	850.5	857.0	854.8	853.8	864.4	871.1	891.5	902.2
1988[2]	889.6	888.2	892.0	898.6	904.4	905.7	909.1	900.7	885.3			

[1] Total gasoline-bearing in the U.S.   [2] Preliminary.   *Source: Bureau of Mines*
T.501

U.S. Production of Residual Fuel Oil and Distillate Fuel Oils   In Millions of Barrels

Year	Jan.	Feb.	Mar.	Apr.	May	June	July	Aug.	Sept.	Oct.	Nov.	Dec.	Total
1983	102.1	83.8	87.7	93.3	104.8	101.2	104.5	103.1	107.0	108.1	105.8	106.0	1,207
1984	110.1	112.2	104.4	95.7	107.4	111.9	108.2	107.3	106.7	111.5	112.6	119.3	1,307
1985	112.7	99.2	100.1	102.1	107.9	100.4	104.7	103.4	102.0	118.3	121.1	131.1	1,303
1986	119.0	95.8	107.1	111.6	116.9	106.5	110.3	118.4	111.6	109.8	116.7	121.8	1,346
1987[1]	114.5	95.4	100.8	101.5	104.7	106.6	111.7	111.2	109.5	113.7	118.9	131.5	1,320
1988[1]	124.5	106.7	113.6	114.6	117.7	113.2	114.6	115.0					

[1] Preliminary.   *Source: Bureau of Mines*
T.505

Production[1] of Crude Petroleum in the United States   In Millions of Barrels of 42 Gallons

Year	Jan.	Feb.	Mar.	Apr.	May	June	July	Aug.	Sept.	Oct.	Nov.	Dec.	Total
1982	263.8	243.7	268.7	257.7	269.2	259.4	268.4	267.6	261.0	269.7	260.9	266.5	3,157
1983	269.6	245.2	269.7	263.3	267.6	260.0	267.7	269.1	263.5	271.9	263.1	260.3	3,171
1984	274.9	257.4	268.8	265.9	277.6	265.6	275.4	273.1	269.8	276.1	269.4	275.8	3,250
1985	270.9	252.7	281.9	271.3	283.1	270.7	277.4	272.9	268.6	278.1	267.1	279.9	3,275
1986	283.2	256.9	279.4	265.9	274.0	258.7	268.4	259.6	249.8	261.0	252.4	258.9	3,168
1987[2]	262.8	232.9	258.8	252.8	257.5	248.4	255.8	254.5	246.2	259.3	251.9	257.8	3,047
1988[2]	255.6	242.9	258.8	248.0	254.3	244.7	249.8	250.0					

[1] Represents oil transported from producing properties, plus that remaining on properties & consumed on leases.   [2] Preliminary.
Source: Bureau of Mines   T.500

U.S. Foreign Trade[3] of Petroleum and Products   In Thousands of Barrels (42 gallons)

Year	Exports		Imports			
	Crude Oil	Refined Products	Crude Oil Unfin. Oil	Refined Products	Distillate Fuel Oil	Residual Fuel Oil
1980	104,908	94,289	1,946,200	582,500	51,900	343,600
1981	83,200	133,900	1,654,200	534,200	63,100	292,100
1982	86,300	211,200	1,352,400	514,000	34,000	283,100
1983	59,900	209,900	1,317,800	525,900	63,500	255,200
1984	66,200	196,900	1,368,800	620,200	99,400	249,200
1985	74,500	209,900	1,308,600	540,300	73,100	186,300
1986	56,200	229,300	1,642,700	628,000	90,300	244,200
1987[1]	55,000	223,000	1,837,300	599,400	93,200	206,100
1988[2]	60,600	244,200	1,963,200	600,000	94,000	200,000

[1] Preliminary.   [2] Estimate.   [3] Includes shipments to & from noncontiguous territories.
Source: Energy Information Administration

Domestic First Purchase Price of Crude Petroleum at Wells[1]   In Dollars per Barrel

Year	Jan.	Feb.	Mar.	Apr.	May	June	July	Aug.	Sept.	Oct.	Nov.	Dec.	Average
1984	25.93	26.06	26.05	25.93	26.00	26.09	26.11	26.02	25.97	25.92	25.44	25.05	25.88
1985	24.26	23.64	23.89	24.19	24.18	24.07	24.04	23.99	23.96	24.10	24.27	24.51	24.09
1986	23.12	17.65	12.62	10.68	10.75	10.68	9.25	9.77	11.09	11.00	11.05	11.73	12.51
1987	13.89	14.50	14.53	14.95	15.29	15.95	16.88	17.06	16.29	15.95	15.46	14.27	15.41
1988[2]	13.64	13.41	12.95	13.91	14.11	13.57	12.36	12.20					

[1] Buyers posted prices.   [2] Preliminary.   *Source: Bureau of Labor Statistics Energy Inform. Administration*   T.497

Refiner Sales Prices of Finished Motor Gasoline to End Users (Excludes Tax)   ¢ per Gallon

Year	Jan.	Feb.	Mar.	Apr.	May	June	July	Aug.	Sept.	Oct.	Nov.	Dec.	Average
1984	90.6	90.2	90.7	92.9	93.4	92.5	90.4	89.2	89.7	90.5	89.9	88.0	90.7
1985	84.6	83.6	87.1	92.4	94.4	95.2	95.4	94.0	91.9	90.8	91.7	91.9	91.2
1986	89.3	80.5	65.4	59.1	63.8	64.9	58.0	55.5	56.2	53.2	53.2	54.2	62.4
1987	59.3	61.7	62.4	64.5	65.8	67.0	68.8	70.9	69.7	69.2	68.8	66.9	66.2
1988[2]	64.3	62.8	62.4	66.0	68.4	68.1	66.9	71.8					

[1] Excludes aviation.   [2] Preliminary.   *Source: Bureau of Labor Statistics Energy Inform. Administration*   T.498

Volume of Trading of Crude Oil Futures in New York   In Thousands of Contracts

Year	Jan.	Feb.	Mar.	Apr.	May	June	July	Aug.	Sept.	Oct.	Nov.	Dec.	Total
1984	108.7	130.7	121.5	106.2	136.4	134.5	154.9	200.4	111.2	243.3	174.7	217.7	1,840.3
1985	385.3	263.3	298.5	272.6	290.1	342.2	329.8	269.7	339.8	365.9	337.9	386.8	3,980.9
1986	520.1	490.9	560.0	691.4	677.0	612.7	860.5	701.6	666.7	986.4	604.4	941.8	8,313.5
1987	873.2	968.4	1,199	1,059	937.3	1,196	1,412	1,505	1,126	1,205	1,287	1,813	14,582
1988	1,626	1,336	1,809	1,352	1,205	1,507	1,754	1,216	1,956	2,040	1,609	1,450	18,859

Source: N.Y. Mercantile Exchange   T.502c

PETROLEUM

Month–End Open Interest of Crude Oil Futures in New York In Contracts

Year	Jan.	Feb.	Mar.	Apr.	May	June	July	Aug.	Sept.	Oct.	Nov.	Dec.
1984	23,168	27,650	28,142	26,647	23,970	28,635	37,349	32,245	32,236	37,613	39,896	49,201
1985	63,458	57,479	44,532	45,875	50,450	57,820	52,134	53,743	64,731	64,981	58,099	61,161
1986	66,522	64,007	72,083	92,863	98,292	102,404	131,234	97,455	100,805	114,505	100,041	121,248
1987	134,716	147,632	158,154	147,705	138,707	167,392	178,226	193,788	188,337	156,013	159,115	208,259
1988	201,833	198,951	196,192	180,557	174,306	192,860	166,719	182,877	235,823	195,360	198,923	185,218

Source: N.Y. Mercantile Exchange

T.502b

High, Low & Closing Prices of December Crude Oil Futures in New York In Dollars Per Barrel

Year of Delivery		Year Prior to Delivery		Delivery Year											Life of Delivery Range
	Oct.	Nov.	Dec.	Jan.	Feb.	Mar.	Apr.	May	June	July	Aug.	Sept.	Oct.	Nov.	
1984 High	—	29.75	29.55	29.60	30.50	30.56	30.42	31.60	30.89	30.34	30.29	30.02	29.92	28.87	31.60
Low	—	28.60	27.50	28.20	28.85	30.05	30.15	30.10	29.62	28.01	28.31	29.23	26.93	28.30	26.93
Close	—	29.00	28.20	29.15	30.03	30.35	30.15	30.85	30.25	28.19	29.72	29.89	28.46	28.44	—
1985 High	29.50	27.93	27.20	25.95	26.50	27.60	28.60	26.65	26.25	26.49	27.68	28.65	30.40	31.82	31.82
Low	26.99	26.56	25.91	23.90	25.00	25.90	26.55	26.10	24.58	24.93	25.60	26.12	27.84	29.93	23.90
Close	27.66	26.72	25.91	25.35	25.45	27.42	26.77	26.50	25.50	25.66	27.40	28.63	30.38	31.72	—
1986 High	25.60	26.45	25.66	22.05	19.23	15.85	14.85	15.30	13.80	12.70	15.92	16.52	15.85	15.83	26.45
Low	23.80	24.74	22.18	19.15	15.05	11.69	11.20	13.00	12.70	10.40	11.28	13.90	13.52	14.68	10.40
Close	25.33	24.74	22.21	19.19	15.44	11.69	12.82	13.56	12.82	11.28	15.85	14.93	15.27	15.08	—
1987 High	—	—	—	18.15	18.10	18.08	18.14	18.94	20.31	21.39	21.65	19.59	20.52	19.83	21.65
Low	—	—	—	16.68	16.40	16.42	17.33	17.79	18.75	19.99	18.10	18.54	19.30	18.05	16.40
Close	—	—	—	18.03	16.58	17.97	17.77	18.80	20.05	20.71	19.43	19.48	19.96	18.93	—
1988 High	—	18.15	18.00	16.90	16.72	16.78	18.35	18.07	18.00	16.80	16.57	15.28	14.96	14.38	18.35
Low	—	17.94	14.99	15.55	15.40	15.13	16.31	16.80	15.65	15.00	15.21	13.00	12.13	13.23	12.13
Close	—	17.94	15.97	16.14	15.55	16.65	17.71	17.91	15.68	16.64	15.23	13.02	13.58	13.60	—
1989 High	—	15.15	15.85												
Low	—	12.70	14.84												
Close	—	15.05	15.36												

Source: N.Y. Mercantile Exchange

T.502a

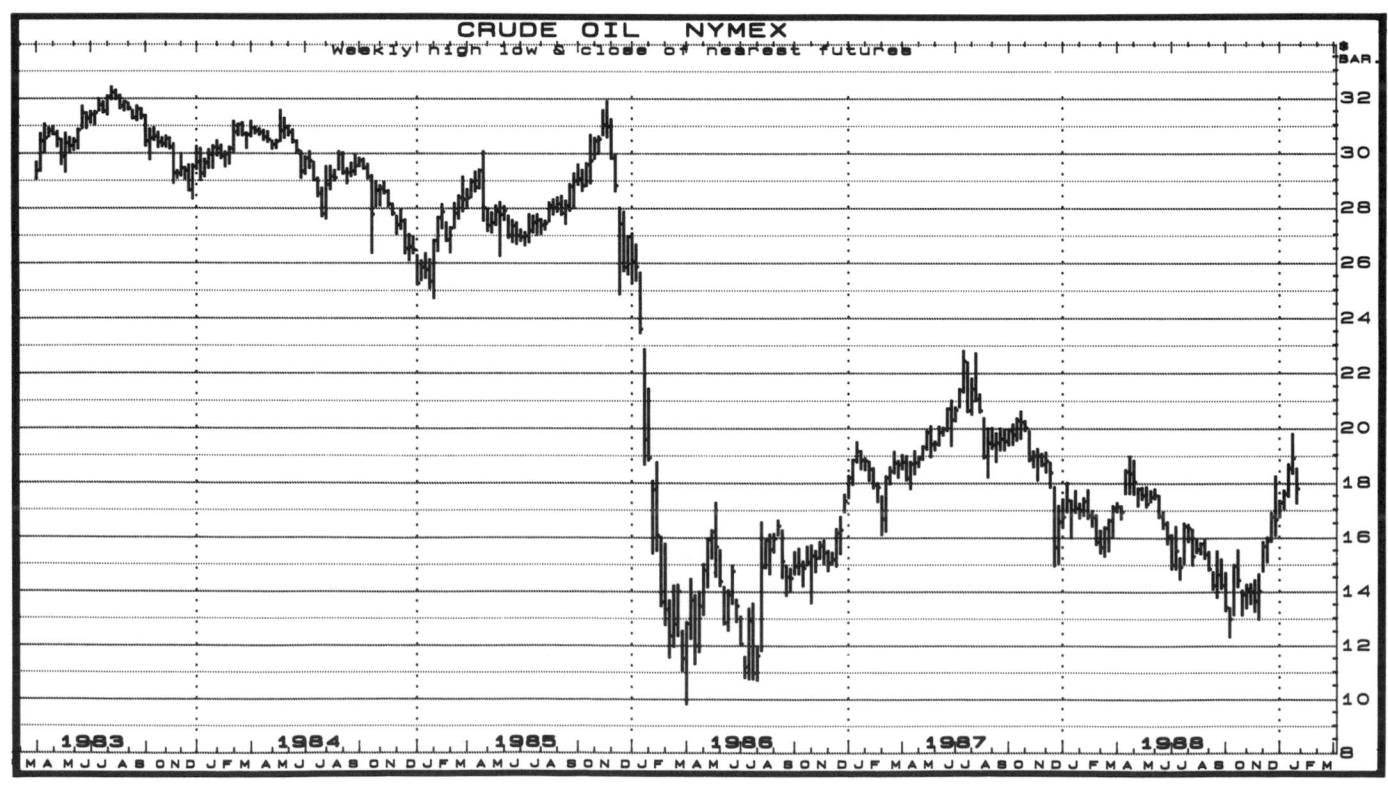

186

Plastics

U.S. plastic resin production was forecast at 59.4 billion pounds in 1988, up 7 percent from 55.1 billion in 1987, according to the Society of the Plastics Industry (SPI). The forecast was based on SPI data for the first three quarters of 1987, which showed actual output for the period of 38.98 billion pounds, up 7 percent from the same period in 1987. Polypropylene production was projected to rise 9 percent to 7.25 billion pounds from 6.5 billion in 1987, while polystyrene production was expected to rise 7 percent to 5.1 billion pounds.

Production of polyethylene, the highest volume plastic resin, was expected to rise 6 percent to 10.1 billion pounds. U.S. capacity for linear low-density polyethylene, estimated at 4.2 billion pounds in 1987, was projected to grow 6 percent annually through 1992. Capacity for high-density material, estimated at 7 billion pounds in 1987, was projected to rise at a 6 percent rate.

Polyvinyl chloride production increased an estimated 4 percent to 8.2 billion pounds, after rising 8 percent the previous year. U.S. PVC capacity was 8.5 billion pounds in 1987 and was expected grow nearly 4 percent a year through 1992. Demand for vinyls exceeded forecasts in the 1980s, because of lower prices for petroleum feedstocks. But production was hindered during 1988 by problems at several refineries, including a fire in a Louisiana plant, which resulted in extremely tight supplies. PVC prices peaked in both the U.S. and Europe during the summer because of the tightness. But while many customers in Europe were put on alloca-

tion, price increases were moderated by concern about the additional capacity that was coming on line later in the year. In fact, there were concerns that the number of large additions to resin capacity scheduled to come on line through 1990 would cause a temporary resin production glut, especially if U.S. economic growth began to slow.

Recycling became more common in 1988, and with plastic container demand expected to continue growing at 5 percent annually through 1992, recycling was expected to intensify. One firm was scheduled to open a polystyrene recycling plant in early 1989. It was expected to be able to turn 3 million pounds of plastic cups, trays, and cutlery into pellets used to make insulation and other products not used with food (avoiding the danger of contamination). Suffolk County, N.Y., and several other municipalities had already banned styrofoam food packaging.

Also, photo-degradable and biodegradable garbage bags were being tested. However, biodegradation poses the risk of leachate from the bags contaminating groundwater, while nondegradable bags are chemically inert.

One pilot plant in Michigan was recycling the two most common packaging plastics: polyethylene terephthalate (PET) used in soft drink bottles and high-density polyethylene. Plans called for the PET to be recycled into new bottles. A commercial plant with a capacity of 50 million pounds a year was expected to be in operation in 1990.

World Production of Plastics and Resins[3] (Condensation, Polymerization, Etc.)   In Thous. of Metric Tons

Year	Australia	Austria	Czecho-slovakia	France	Germany East	Germany West	Italy	Japan	Netherlands	Poland	Belgium	Hungary	USSR	United Kingdom	United States
1976	407	404	580	1,769	679	7,088	2,266	4,952	1,723	559	824	186	3,216	2,556	13,261
1977	480	430	738	1,834	734	6,270	2,538	4,978	1,783	583	1,471	144	3,300	2,710	11,232
1978	522	434	810	1,885	762	6,703	2,466	5,882	1,962	596	1,682	209	3,516	2,621	12,380
1979	618	437	853	2,220	779	7,255	2,562	6,964	2,012	571	1,969	289	3,504	2,647	13,866
1980	709	487	894	2,052	859	6,710	2,464	6,422	1,975	667	1,835	324	3,636	2,260	12,418
1981	700	504	913	2,480	998	6,600	2,154	5,936	2,393	588	1,940	307	3,696	2,051	13,664
1982	715	454	961		989	6,275	2,142	5,986	2,502	600	2,023	322	4,057	1,966	13,009
1983	776	550	1,004	2,650	1,045	7,031	2,436	6,504	2,777	526	2,246	337	4,392	1,800	14,790
1984		613	1,034	2,694	1,056	7,409	2,718	7,424	2,641	600	2,374	377	4,500	1,900	15,505
1985[1]		606	1,100	2,756	1,048	7,553	2,640	7,301	2,500	604	2,498	382	4,700	1,800	15,762
1986[2]		590	1,140	3,050	1,045	7,841	2,662	7,334		631	2,770	415	5,500	1,850	16,730

[1] Preliminary.   [2] Estimate.   [3] Refers to production of thermoplastic & thermosetting resins & plastic materials obtained by chemical transformation of natural organic substances or by chemical synthesis.   *Source: United Nations*

T.506

Production of Important Synthetic Plastics & Resin Materials in the U.S.   In Millions of Pounds

Year	Phenolic Resins	Polyethlene & Copolymers	Poly-propylene	Polystyrene & Copolymers	Polyvinyl Chloride & Copolymers	Year	Phenolic Resins	Polyethlene & Copolymers	Poly-propylene	Polystyrene & Copolymers	Polyvinyl Chloride & Copolymers
1979	1,779	12,408	3,824	6,327	6,211	1984	1,656	14,621	5,216	6,857	6,828
1980	1,745	11,720	3,699	5,540	5,485	1985	1,714	15,318	5,654	7,229	6,668
1981	1,688	12,604	4,008	5,915	5,618	1986	1,814	15,983	6,257	7,078	7,284
1982	1,398	12,548	3,515	5,609	5,397	1987[1]	N.A.	17,676	6,634	N.A.	7,986
1983	1,460	13,890	4,457	6,254	6,256	1988[2]	N.A.	18,100	7,000	N.A.	9,000

Note: Data included in the table does not cover all Plastics production. Various types of Plastics production of lesser importance are not included because statistics are not available on a consistent basis. Also, many individual firms do not make their production figures known.   [1] Preliminary.
[2] Estimate.   *Sources: U.S. Tariff Commission, Bureau of Census*

T.507

PLASTICS

Average Producer Price Index of Plastic Materials in the United States (1982 = 100) [1]

Year	Jan.	Feb.	Mar.	Apr.	May	June	July	Aug.	Sept.	Oct.	Nov.	Dec.	Average
						Plastic Resins and Materials (066)							
1980	270.4	272.1	274.5	287.6	288.4	287.6	285.7	281.5	276.5	276.1	276.2	274.1	279.2
1981	274.7	276.1	279.4	285.1	287.9	290.0	295.9	297.5	296.8	299.5	293.2	294.2	289.2
1982	286.1	297.3	285.5	286.0	283.2	282.1	280.9	282.2	281.6	281.6	281.4	281.4	284.1
1983	283.8	283.1	282.1	285.4	288.0	289.1	291.3	293.7	302.6	299.1	297.9	301.5	291.5
1984	305.2	305.0	306.2	307.8	310.6	311.1	310.6	310.3	311.8	309.4	309.0	306.2	308.6
1985	305.2	306.9	306.3	306.1	305.4	307.1	307.5	306.4	305.1	300.7	300.3	299.3	304.7
1986	300.9	302.4	301.8	296.6	295.6	295.2	296.7	294.4	290.1	292.9	295.0	290.3	296.0
1987[1]	102.6	102.4	103.2	106.3	107.0	109.7	112.8	113.1	114.2	116.8	117.4	117.7	110.3
1988	121.5	123.5	124.4	127.6	130.1	130.5	134.8	137.0	138.9	139.8	140.3		
1989													
						PE Resin, Low, Film & Sheeting (0662-0301.99)							
1980	257.2	260.9	N.A.	275.1	270.8	264.0	259.4	254.4	249.4	249.3	251.8	250.9	258.5
1981	251.5	251.2	252.5	263.0	263.0	263.7	280.7	N.A.	279.8	279.9	N.A.	247.3	263.3
1982	207.5	208.1	209.7	224.5	202.1	197.2	184.3	185.3	184.2	183.9	184.7	184.7	196.4
1983	204.9	205.2	193.9	215.4	215.4	N.A.	236.2	236.2	237.8	251.6	250.9	250.9	227.1
1984	272.1	272.6	272.1	272.1	272.1	272.1	272.1	272.1	272.1	272.1	272.1	272.1	272.1
1985	272.1	272.1	272.1	272.1	272.1	272.1	272.1	272.1	272.1	206.8	206.8	206.8	255.8
1986	224.7	224.7	224.7	224.7	224.7	224.7	224.7	224.7	N.A.	224.0	222.5	224.5	224.4
1987[1]	112.3	113.1	110.5	113.9	114.6	121.5	123.9	127.8	127.9	131.9	138.8	140.7	123.1
1988	145.9	150.3	153.8	157.9	171.4	171.4	178.3	190.9	201.2	203.5	202.7		
1989													
						Thermoplastic Resins (0662)							
1981	100.2	101.0	102.6	104.6	105.8	106.6	109.3	110.1	109.7	110.5	107.2	107.6	106.3
1982	103.5	104.2	103.2	103.5	102.1	101.5	100.9	101.5	101.3	101.3	101.3	101.1	102.1
1983	102.4	102.1	101.5	103.4	104.7	105.2	106.3	107.3	111.6	109.6	108.8	110.6	106.1
1984	112.3	112.0	112.5	112.8	113.4	114.0	113.8	113.6	114.4	113.2	113.0	111.7	113.1
1985	111.1	112.0	111.7	111.5	111.3	111.9	111.9	111.4	110.6	108.3	108.1	107.8	110.6
1986	108.7	109.4	109.0	106.9	106.3	105.9	106.7	105.7	103.6	105.2	106.2	103.9	106.5
1987[2]	102.3	102.1	103.1	107.3	107.9	111.1	113.9	114.1	115.3	118.5	119.3	119.7	111.2
1988	124.4	126.7	127.8	131.1	133.7	134.0	139.0	141.2	143.4	144.4	144.6		
1989													
						Styrene Plastics Materials (0662–06)							
1987[1]	96.0	96.1	101.3	108.3	110.0	116.8	119.6	115.4	117.6	116.6	119.5	119.7	111.4
1988	122.2	125.2	127.0	128.9	129.0	129.1	133.3	134.1	134.1				
1989													
						Thermosetting Resins (0663)							
1981	101.4	101.1	101.4	104.0	104.5	105.4	106.6	106.5	106.6	107.7	107.6	108.2	105.1
1982	108.0	107.9	108.1	108.1	108.0	108.6	108.7	108.8	108.9	108.8	108.9	109.2	108.4
1983	109.0	108.8	108.9	108.5	108.4	108.6	108.7	109.4	110.1	110.8	111.5	111.5	109.5
1984	112.2	112.7	113.1	113.3	116.1	114.6	114.4	114.6	114.5	114.4	114.2	114.2	114.0
1985	114.1	114.1	114.2	114.1	114.0	114.6	114.9	115.0	115.3	115.7	115.7	115.1	114.7
1986	114.9	115.0	115.1	113.7	113.5	114.0	114.0	113.4	113.3	112.7	112.8	112.7	113.8
1987[2]	101.5	101.4	101.9	102.2	103.6	105.5	110.6	111.1	111.8	111.8	111.3	111.0	107.0
1988	110.2	110.4	110.7	113.5	115.4	115.7	116.8	119.2	119.7	120.1	122.2		
1989													
						Phenolic Molding Compounds (0663–0201)							
1980	239.7	239.7	244.3	249.9	251.3	251.3	250.4	240.2	240.2	240.2	240.2	240.2	244.0
1981	N.A.	N.A.	N.A.	N.A.	N.A.	N.A.	254.2	254.2	254.2	254.2	254.2	254.2	254.2
1982	254.2	254.2	254.2	254.2	254.6	254.6	254.6	254.5	254.5	254.5	254.5	254.5	254.4
1983	249.6	245.7	245.7	245.7	245.7	245.7	245.7	245.9	246.0	246.0	245.6	245.7	246.1
1984	245.6	245.8	246.3	252.1	259.5	260.2	259.4	259.4	259.7	259.6	259.2	259.2	255.5
1985	259.2	259.2	259.2	259.2	259.2	259.2	259.2	268.1	268.1	268.1	268.1	268.1	262.9
1986	267.3	267.3	267.3	259.2	252.4	252.4	252.4	252.4	252.4	252.4	252.4	252.4	256.7
1987[1]	100.8	99.2	99.2	101.1	112.0	112.1	112.1	114.8	114.8	114.8	114.8	114.8	109.2
1988	114.8	114.8	115.4	115.4	122.1	123.8	122.3	122.3	122.3	123.6	128.2		
1989													

[1] Data prior to 1987 are for 1967 = 100.   [2] Data prior to 1987 are for Dec. 1980 = 100.   *Source: Bureau of Labor Statistics*

T.508

Platinum-Group Metals

World 1988 mine production of all platinum-group metals (palladium, iridium, osmium, rhodium, and ruthenium) was estimated at 8.9 million ounces, up 200,000 from 1987, by the Bureau of Mines (BOM). South Africa remained the largest producer with 4.5 million ounces, up 7 percent from 4.22 million in 1987. Soviet output was estimated at 3.9 million ounces, unchanged from 1987.

World 1988 mine production of platinum outside the USSR was put at 2.77 million ounces by Johnson Matthey, up 70,000 ounces from the firm's 1987 estimate. Soviet sales, used as a proxy for Soviet output, were estimated at 400,000 ounces, unchanged from 1987. Mine production of palladium outside the USSR rose 14 percent in 1988 to 1.55 million ounces. Soviet sales fell to 1.76 million ounces from 1.79 million.

While small amounts of PGM are recovered from copper refined in Utah and Texas, the only U.S. PGM mine in 1988 was the Stillwater Complex in Montana, some 30 miles north of Yellowstone National Park. The mine yielded about 36,000 ounces of platinum and 124,000 of palladium in 1988, according to Chevron Resources Company, which owns the mine with Manville Corp. and Lac Resources. It also produced between 600 and 700 ounces of rhodium in 1988; this was a bonus in light of rhodium's 1988 average producer price of $1,275/oz.

Expansions at Stillwater were expected to raise 1989 output to 267,000 ounces, including 60,000 of platinum and 207,000 of palladium. But while the mine yielded about 3.5 ounces of palladium to each ounce of platinum, revenues were split about 50-50 because of platinum's higher price. The mine sent its concentrates to Belgium for toll refining and sale on the world market. Unlike the by-product production from nickel that yields most Soviet and Canadian PGM, Stillwater requires a more expensive refining process, similar to the one used for South African ores.

Development of a second PGM mine near Stillwater was expected to move to tunneling in 1989, with production to begin by 1991. An on-site smelter also was planned, with a goal of operating by 1990. Still, the U.S. will remain almost totally dependent on imports for its PGM. The BOM estimated net import reliance as a percent of consumption at 93 percent in 1988, little changed from previous years. The State Department has certified the PGM as strategic minerals, and exempts South African output from import bans under the Comprehensive Anti-Apartheid Act of 1986.

World PGM demand grew in 1988, reflecting the continued health of the industrialized economies. Johnson Matthey estimated world free-market demand at 3.615 million ounces of platinum and 3.35 million ounces of palladium, up 10 percent and 4 percent, respectively, from 1987 usage. Meeting the demand required inventory drawdowns of 465,000 ounces of platinum and 35,000 ounces of palladium. Nevertheless, the average New York dealer price fell, with platinum averaging $531/oz., versus $555 in 1987. However, the metal ended 1988 at $520.50, up 4 percent from its close a year earlier.

Platinum's price performance would have been stronger if not for the market's reaction to a December announcement that Ford Motor Co. was testing a catalytic converter that did not use platinum. The converter apparently used palladium, rhodium and alloys of some rare earths, and would be vulnerable to contamination from any lead remaining in the gasoline distribution system. Palladium rallied on the news, though large-scale use of the new converter was years away.

According to the BOM, the average 1986 model car's catalytic converter used only 0.057 ounce of platinum, 0.015 ounce of palladium, and 0.006 ounce of rhodium. That adds up when millions of autos and light trucks are built, and autocatalysts accounted for 45 percent of U.S. PGM consumption in 1988. Electrical and electronic industries used 22 percent; dental and medical, 12 percent; chemical, 6 percent; and others, 15 percent.

PGM investment demand grew in 1988, particularly in Japan, where the yen price of platinum remained low. Japan imported an estimated 70 tonnes of platinum in 1988, including some 12 tonnes for investment holdings. Japanese platinum jewelry demand was expected to exceed 1975's record of 1.06 million ounces. In June, almost 40 percent of the platinum jewelry on the Japanese market was priced below the commodity-tax threshold of 37,500 yen.

Investor interest was raised by the September 1988 introduction of Australia's Koalas, platinum legal tender bullion coins weighing 1 oz., 1/2 oz., 1/4 oz. and 1/10 oz. More than 100,000 ounces of Koalas were sold to dealers in the coin's first two months on the market. Koalas were minted in Perth from Soviet platinum made into coin blanks in Japan. Canada also lauched its platinum Maple Leaf in 1988, and the USSR and the Isle of Man issued platinum coins.

Futures Markets

Platinum and palladium futures are traded on the New York Mercantile Exchange (NYMEX). The Tokyo Commodity Exchange for Industry trades platinum futures, and Johnson Matthey estimated that up to 8 tonnes of platinum may have been delivered into Tokyo warehouses in 1988.

World Mine Production of Platinum-Group Metals   In Troy Ounces

Year	Australia	Zimbabwe	Finland	Canada	Colombia[3]	Ethiopia	Japan	South Africa	USSR	United States	Yugo-slavia	World Total[1]
1983	13,900	4,090	4,469	223,925	10,303	125	58,582	2,600,000	3,600,000	6,257	3,119	6,524,770
1984	13,900	1,994	2,154	348,216	10,106	125	53,325	3,500,000	3,700,000	14,635	3,300	7,647,755
1985	16,000	1,576	2,200	337,088	11,650	125	65,919	3,700,000	3,800,000	N.A.	3,550	7,938,108
1986[2]	16,000	1,500	2,000	281,000	12,000	125	68,011	3,600,000	3,850,000	N.A.	3,200	7,833,836
1987[1]				300,000				3,700,000	3,850,000			8,000,000

[1] Estimate.   [2] Preliminary.   [3] Placer platinum.   *Source: Bureau of Mines*   T.509

PLATINUM CASH PRICE NEW YORK

Monthly Average Producer Prices Prior to 1982
Merchant Prices From 1982 to Date

DOLLARS PER TROY OUNCE

Platinum-Group Metals Sold to Consuming Industries in the United States   In Thousands of Troy Ounces

Year	Automotive Platinum	Automotive Others[2]	Chemical Platinum	Chemical Others[2]	Electrical Platinum	Electrical Others[2]	Dental & Medical Platinum	Dental & Medical Others[2]	Jewelry & Decorative Platinum	Jewelry & Decorative Others[2]	Petroleum Platinum	Petroleum Others[2]	All PGM Platinum	All PGM Palladium	All PGM Other[2] Metals	Total
1979	803.2	248.3	98.6	264.9	115.8	457.4	27.1	244.9	27.7	21.6	170.0	27.9	1,408.9	1,132.6	214.5	2,756.0
1980	517.1	214.2	119.0	165.6	150.1	376.1	25.8	245.4	51.0	22.6	144.0	26.7	1,118.2	912.0	175.7	2,205.9
1981	446.7	160.6	78.1	152.4	111.7	388.3	18.7	255.8	27.6	19.6	88.3	22.9	872.6	889.2	158.8	1,920.7
1982	477.8	144.8	63.6	200.6	90.0	348.4	22.8	312.1	16.0	12.7	21.6	21.7	780.1	926.3	166.8	1,873.3
1983	508.5	191.8	65.4	99.8	74.7	404.8	16.7	261.7	10.3	10.6	38.0	51.1	796.7	921.8	195.4	1,914.0
1984	569.0	232.3	73.5	108.7	99.2	452.8	18.6	349.0	9.5	11.0	28.0	92.7	876.2	1,150.5	173.1	2,199.8
1985	619.0	250.3	85.2	87.4	115.8	359.1	24.5	340.1	16.0	12.8	28.8	81.0	1,025.8	1,060.3	185.4	2,271.5
1986	625.0	233.2	77.7	75.4	103.5	386.3	22.6	403.5	11.9	11.5	30.6	61.0	983.4	1,056.3	210.0	2,249.7
1987[1]	605.0	223.1	61.7	41.3	58.5	349.8	15.4	338.4	5.7	15.4	23.8	41.3	825.2	995.3	123.9	1,944.4
1988[3]	650	240	42	86	76	356	9	233	9	9	37	13	894	932	158	1,984

[1] Preliminary.   [2] Palladium, iridium, osmium, rhodium, & ruthenium.   [3] Estimate.   *Source: Bureau of Mines*   T.512

Salient Statistics of Platinum and Allied Metals in the U.S.   In Troy Ounces

Year	Net Import Reliance as a % of Apparent Consump.	Production Crude[5]	Refinery New Metal	Refinery Secondary Metal	Stocks as of Dec. 31[1] Platinum	Stocks as of Dec. 31[1] Palladium	Stocks as of Dec. 31[1] Other	Total	Imports for Consumption	Value of Imports Mil. $	Exports Platinum	Exports Other Groups[3]	Exports Other[4]
1979	89	7,300	8,392	309,022	305,605	323,865	131,812	761,282	3,479,128	840.5	207,832	522,195	189,218
1980	87	3,348	2,300	330,923	502,185	353,002	118,074	973,261	3,501,782	1,177	289,454	302,457	173,053
1981	83	7,318	5,607	391,637	401,389	398,933	117,856	918,178	2,849,617	800.3	391,194	258,745	213,426
1982	81	8,033	7,078	344,160	604,632	384,184	117,812	1,106,628	2,493,706	553.9	175,805	262,764	397,307
1983	89	6,257	5,884	303,165	433,457	412,178	97,513	943,148	3,218,022	752.8	184,599	261,188	782,967
1984	89	15,000	14,433	339,526	648,130	524,924	145,593	1,318,647	4,474,106	1,118.1	220,885	377,802	563,345
1985	92	N.A.	3,987	258,597	571,725	454,999	101,955	1,128,679	3,989,594	1,025.7	187,013	339,254	362,384
1986[2]	92	N.A.	4,355	231,031	948,468	638,746	167,239	1,754,453	4,477,177	1,346.7	104,155	277,772	368,748
1987[2]	88		5,000	240,000	522,436	477,420	235,131	1,234,987	3,806,547	1,240.0	90,208	349,221	276,727

[1] In hands of refiners, importers, & dealers.   [2] Preliminary.   [3] Palladium, rhodium, iridium, osmium, ruthenium & osmium metals & balloys.   [4] Ore & concentrates, waste, scrap & sweepings.   [5] From crude platinum placers & byproduct platinum-group metals.
Source: Bureau of Mines   T.513

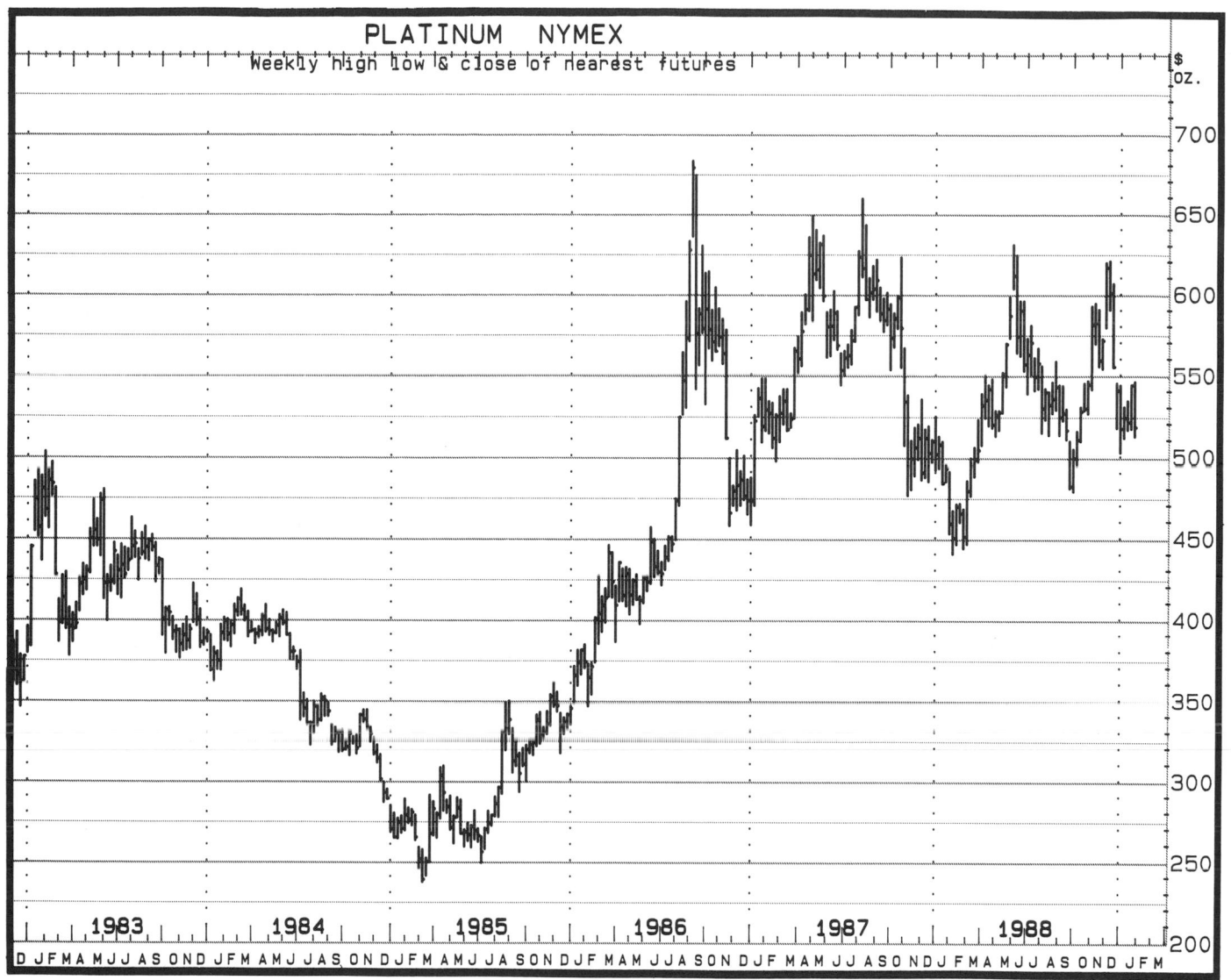

PLATINUM NYMEX
Weekly high low & close of nearest futures

Average Merchant's Prices of Platinum in New York   In Dollars Per Troy Ounce

Year	Jan.	Feb.	Mar.	Apr.	May	June	July	Aug.	Sept.	Oct.	Nov.	Dec.	Average
1974	162.68	172.50	172.50	172.50	174.55	195.00	195.00	195.00	195.00	195.00	195.00	195.00	184.98
1975	195.00	180.53	175.00	163.06	160.00	160.00	162.73	175.00	175.00	172.17	160.00	160.00	169.87
1976	160.00	160.00	160.00	160.00	160.00	163.54	175.60	182.50	182.50	182.50	167.00	167.00	168.39
1977	167.00	167.00	167.00	167.00	167.00	167.00	167.00	167.00	167.00	167.00	167.65	174.81	167.71
1978[1]	186.55	206.58	217.07	220.00	220.00	227.73	237.89	241.74	250.23	253.18	284.00	300.00	237.08
1979	303.41	325.00	325.00	327.38	350.00	350.00	350.00	357.83	380.00	380.00	380.00	393.33	351.83
1980	420.00	420.00	420.00	420.00	420.00	420.00	420.00	425.24	475.00	475.00	475.00	475.00	436.77
1981	475.00	475.00	475.00	475.00	475.00	475.00	475.00	475.00	475.00	475.00	475.00	475.00	475.00
1982	369.26	361.95	322.46	338.95	314.43	278.26	286.90	290.41	334.98	324.58	346.65	370.95	328.32
1983	441.07	468.34	400.17	410.38	446.69	420.23	431.63	438.30	431.93	399.87	389.33	399.70	423.14
1984	375.11	391.38	398.47	395.17	388.95	386.31	345.55	336.03	327.36	324.65	328.45	309.11	358.83
1985	275.76	274.37	255.36	287.23	273.24	267.94	269.52	303.91	304.59	321.73	334.53	327.75	291.33
1986	362.77	377.74	412.48	422.93	415.52	431.23	436.50	526.52	597.92	578.50	524.65	480.14	463.91
1987	520.08	518.30	533.27	587.38	607.08	569.14	573.57	610.12	590.55	568.65	500.02	479.29	554.79
1988[2]	494	459	496	527	549	580	549	532	512	526	576	570	531

[1] Prior to 1978 prices are for *producer* prices.   [2] Preliminary.   *Source: American Metal Market*

T.511

PLATINUM–GROUP METALS

Month–End Open Interest of Platinum Futures in New York   In Contracts

Year	Jan.	Feb.	Mar.	Apr.	May	June	July	Aug.	Sept.	Oct.	Nov.	Dec.
1980	8,200	8,409	6,209	5,434	6,369	7,943	7,797	8,286	14,239	12,140	12,026	11,911
1981	9,410	8,946	9,441	7,709	8,130	7,891	5,520	6,446	8,421	7,055	8,601	7,839
1982	6,278	7,524	8,686	8,302	10,326	9,337	11,137	12,853	14,141	13,002	15,547	15,620
1983	19,927	23,506	15,197	15,878	18,375	15,918	16,934	15,671	15,413	12,450	13,227	13,384
1984	12,692	13,912	13,805	15,244	15,852	17,254	15,775	15,766	17,288	14,826	14,753	15,525
1985	15,210	14,131	13,256	12,096	11,668	11,371	11,677	16,492	13,149	13,068	17,969	14,853
1986	18,163	20,490	19,938	15,768	16,582	18,748	18,749	25,939	23,364	19,152	18,204	17,707
1987	16,490	16,741	19,771	19,699	17,981	17,362	20,947	22,280	26,233	22,188	20,141	17,764
1988	20,135	19,217	17,534	15,535	23,062	21,102	18,396	17,737	21,333	18,106	25,030	19,919

Source: N.Y. Mercantile Exchange

T.515

Volume of Trading of Platinum Futures in New York   In Thousands of Contracts

Year	Jan.	Feb.	Mar.	Apr.	May	June	July	Aug.	Sept.	Oct.	Nov.	Dec.	Total
1980	35.2	28.5	41.7	21.4	26.6	37.6	40.8	26.7	59.7	41.0	34.8	35.9	429.7
1981	36.5	29.7	56.1	36.7	30.8	44.7	37.9	39.1	63.9	35.4	33.2	46.6	490.5
1982	32.5	29.5	48.4	42.4	33.1	46.6	55.8	76.9	84.8	70.8	70.0	78.1	669.0
1983	126.0	117.0	107.9	71.9	106.2	115.4	75.9	77.0	79.2	61.5	57.2	57.9	1,035.4
1984	44.7	43.7	68.9	54.5	44.9	53.8	55.2	38.4	52.2	35.9	38.3	40.7	571.1
1985	41.0	26.2	53.5	48.8	43.1	42.2	40.3	98.1	82.7	68.6	64.8	84.0	693.3
1986	101.3	114.7	139.8	100.3	77.0	122.2	75.4	189.8	289.4	164.8	136.6	113.3	1,624.6
1987	117.2	85.7	134.1	149.3	110.8	116.5	87.1	133.2	122.7	127.2	88.6	89.2	1,361.5
1988	82.8	77.6	119.2	74.3	123.3	182.2	111.5	105.8	125.1	114.6	164.8	179.2	1,460.5

Source: N.Y. Mercantile Exchange

T.516

High, Low & Closing Prices of April Platinum Futures in New York   In Dollars per Ounce

Year of Delivery		Feb.	Mar.	Apr.	May	June	July	Aug.	Sept.	Oct.	Nov.	Dec.	Jan.	Feb.	Mar.	Apr.	Life of Delivery Range
						Year Prior to Delivery								Delivery Year			
1983	High	429.6	390.0	400.0	356.0	329.5	333.0	358.1	415.0	392.0	385.0	405.0	499.3	502.0	428.0	433.0	502.0
	Low	388.0	342.6	352.0	318.0	263.0	280.5	271.5	291.0	285.2	320.0	352.0	393.0	396.3	376.5	393.0	263.0
	Close	395.0	357.2	352.0	315.2	306.4	303.3	333.1	294.4	355.1	384.3	392.6	498.7	396.3	392.6	424.0	—
1984	High	526.0	461.0	459.5	495.0	465.0	474.0	470.0	464.5	421.0	426.0	422.0	398.5	410.0	417.5	407.2	528.0
	Low	423.3	410.0	433.5	458.0	422.0	439.0	439.5	404.0	382.0	380.0	389.5	369.0	382.0	388.0	384.0	364.3
	Close	423.3	425.6	453.4	468.5	441.5	457.7	453.6	415.8	383.0	417.2	399.5	391.3	403.8	392.2	397.0	—
1985	High	438.5	447.5	440.0	427.5	433.5	402.0	370.5	352.2	345.0	350.0	328.0	289.5	282.0	290.0	308.0	447.5
	Low	415.0	422.0	414.0	411.5	401.0	343.0	350.5	335.0	327.8	322.0	291.0	265.5	244.5	236.0	263.5	236.0
	Close	433.5	426.0	417.4	426.2	402.9	349.7	361.3	336.1	331.7	323.0	293.0	280.5	249.3	281.4	281.5	—
1986	High	—	308.5	329.8	303.9	293.9	298.5	357.0	333.0	345.0	362.5	356.0	385.0	425.8	444.5	434.0	444.0
	Low	—	279.5	290.5	273.0	275.5	261.2	287.0	297.5	311.0	326.5	321.0	340.0	345.2	391.2	385.0	261.2
	Close	—	307.3	290.5	281.5	278.6	297.7	338.9	309.5	327.9	349.0	346.2	372.7	402.3	399.1	426.9	—
1987	High	430.0	448.5	446.0	434.5	463.3	475.0	620.1	689.5	622.0	586.0	506.7	553.7	536.0	573.0	647.5	689.5
	Low	361.0	400.0	398.0	404.0	425.5	432.0	471.0	546.4	564.5	459.5	462.0	472.0	496.2	515.0	551.5	361.0
	Close	409.4	412.9	430.3	433.1	441.9	473.6	620.1	558.6	576.2	481.7	476.2	527.7	525.6	555.8	602.8	—
1988	High	546.5	590.0	670.8	657.0	622.5	639.1	669.0	635.0	637.0	546.0	531.5	518.8	475.0	538.0	549.0	670.8
	Low	516.0	533.6	573.0	588.0	565.0	572.0	600.0	580.0	516.0	484.3	493.0	452.1	439.5	462.0	512.0	439.5
	Close	542.6	574.8	629.7	600.4	574.0	636.5	612.1	582.6	541.1	527.8	507.6	457.9	475.0	530.7	516.1	—
1989	High	493.0	555.0	565.4	630.4	648.7	599.0	565.9	551.0	552.0	605.0	607.0					
	Low	467.1	482.0	537.9	536.6	570.0	530.0	528.0	489.0	505.0	549.5	501.0					
	Close	493.0	552.4	544.6	630.4	577.8	542.9	544.9	511.0	549.6	604.7	515.6					

Source: N.Y. Mercantile Exchange

T.514

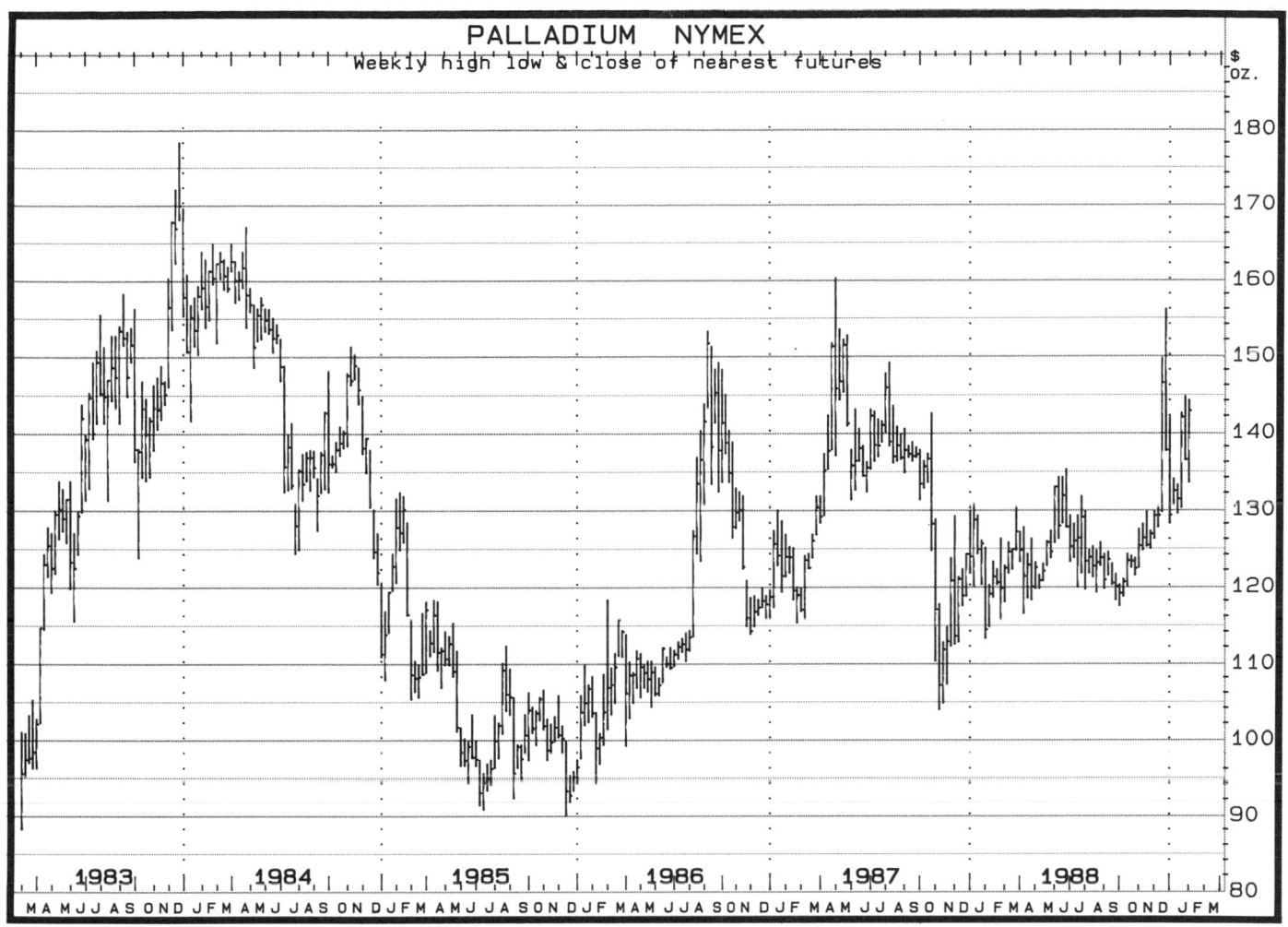

PALLADIUM NYMEX
Weekly high low & close of nearest futures

Average Dealer[1] Price of Palladium in the United States   In Dollars Per Troy Ounce

Year	Jan.	Feb.	Mar.	Apr.	May	June	July	Aug.	Sept.	Oct.	Nov.	Dec.	Average
1976	42.00	39.62	37.56	38.50	41.58	48.50	55.75	50.28	53.25	52.99	59.20	52.38	47.63
1977	54.06	58.10	57.82	55.20	52.97	45.18	44.90	42.36	42.20	43.07	48.83	51.97	49.72
1978	55.10	64.86	64.18	59.33	60.82	60.42	59.53	61.86	60.09	71.58	70.74	73.25	63.48
1979	76.14	103.35	95.56	93.97	105.53	124.33	121.40	117.45	136.94	143.63	141.95	163.42	118.62
1980	220.00	262.80	259.83	194.79	169.74	169.56	199.55	203.88	212.74	204.72	185.85	155.69	203.10
1981	134.38	112.18	117.82	110.42	102.90	94.76	83.61	85.86	85.50	79.08	72.13	69.51	95.68
1982	67.70	67.53	66.99	69.43	68.51	59.27	57.35	57.76	64.50	59.99	74.03	86.14	66.60
1983	116.05	124.33	99.55	114.67	130.60	128.66	143.83	147.65	152.21	145.35	147.71	160.69	134.28
1984	157.30	161.10	159.26	161.03	156.25	154.07	140.98	135.83	136.94	140.07	146.47	136.72	148.84
1985	120.87	127.88	114.45	114.77	108.67	99.15	94.79	102.49	97.25	101.55	101.32	94.50	106.48
1986	101.83	103.18	110.62	110.64	109.23	110.40	112.00	127.05	142.30	136.68	125.36	118.15	117.29
1987	124.13	121.32	122.74	136.58	146.55	140.00	141.34	143.32	137.93	132.72	113.42	121.99	131.84
1988[2]	124	120	122	123	123	128	126	124	121	122	126	132	124

[1] Based on wholesale quantities, prompt delivery.   [2] Estimate.   *Source: American Metal Market*   T.510

Pork Bellies

Pork bellies are used for bacon, which is sliced from the layer of meat and fat from the underside of the hog. A hog has two bellies, each weighing 8-18 pounds, depending on the animal's slaughter weight (typically 230-240 pounds). Bellies generally account for about 12 percent of a hog's live weight and a somewhat larger percentage of the total cut-out value of all pork products, including ham and loins.

Even when the overall cut-out value is profitable, the price of any one product may be weak because of seasonal drops in demand or other reasons. Typically, retail bacon demand is strongest during the summer when lighter foods are preferred. However, at times, futures have been under pressure and have set contract lows during the summer, as in 1988.

There are no futures contracts available between the August and the following February deliveries, which can distort the weekly futures continuation chart, accompanying this article, with sharp price spikes in mid-August. This isn't a reflection of cash market conditions as of mid-August, but represents what traders think they will be six months later.

During the course of a year, belly prices are sensitive to the inventory in cold storage and to net movement in or out (which reflects demand, although a better measure is the amount of bellies being sliced into bacon). The USDA's monthly cold storage reports showed belly stocks in 1988 consistently over year-earlier levels, reflecting the 1987 expansion in hog production. Bellies in storage prior to November 1, however, are not deliverable against the February futures contract, which means that a high level of stocks in late summer-early fall is not necessarily a bearish factor.

Typically, belly futures are at a premium to cash prices during the Oct.-Dec. period, which encourages storage in the fourth quarter. The premium tends to average more than 10 percent, but it narrows during periods of hog crop expansion.

Futures prices trended lower during 1988, owing to large storage supplies, and were around 44 cents/lb. late in the year. Futures averaged nearly 60 cents early in the year. The average monthly cash price was 51.82 cents (12-14 pounds) in January, and fell to around 35 cents in December. Retail bacon prices during the first half of 1988 averaged $1.92/lb., versus $2.15 for all of 1987. Cash belly prices were expected to remain under pressure during early 1989. Although bacon demand shows strong seasonal traits, it also responds to the economy's health, and falls if retail prices are high when income is static or declining.

Futures Markets:

Pork belly futures and options are traded on the Chicago Mercantile Exchange (CME).

United States Quarterly Sliced Bacon Production[1] In Millions of Pounds

Year	Retail	Commercial	Total	Year	Retail	Commercial	Total
1982	1,000.7	500.8	1,501.5	1984[2]	1,038.0	693.6	1,754.0
I	246.3	120.9	367.2	I	253.6	176.4	430.0
II	247.2	128.0	375.3	II	246.8	162.2	409.0
III	273.5	129.2	402.6	III	268.8	166.4	435.2
IV	233.7	122.7	356.4	IV	268.8	188.6	457.4
1983	1,113.6	562.8	1,676.4	1985[2]			1,672.5
I	248.6	127.7	376.2				
II	250.8	140.8	391.6				
III	260.6	152.1	412.8				
IV	353.6	142.2	495.7				

[1] Smoked, dried or cooked. Under Federal Inspection. [2] Preliminary. *Source: Agricultural Marketing Service, USDA*   T.517a

U.S. Frozen Pork Belly Storage Stocks (In Thousand Pounds, as of First of the Month)

Year	Jan.	Feb.	Mar.	Apr.	May	June	July	Aug.	Sept.	Oct.	Nov.	Dec.
1978	23,747	19,013	15,738	39,631	70,976	82,343	75,027	44,787	21,015	7,482	20,013	40,964
1979	54,367	39,432	37,172	57,744	69,689	86,065	78,935	53,373	21,800	11,077	17,739	42,156
1980	70,201	69,635	67,800	85,444	98,163	106,869	96,967	68,616	34,410	21,867	42,186	72,127
1981	97,365	90,181	94,661	104,357	125,469	132,568	117,795	72,998	36,094	16,228	18,060	35,058
1982	54,639	46,167	41,855	66,061	—	—	72,593	—	—	7,558	—	—
1983	31,292	33,592	33,400	44,304	54,510	64,671	63,468	48,409	26,642	15,672	20,047	52,924
1984	78,648	71,568	78,169	95,009	112,205	127,527	115,034	85,630	43,626	22,321	24,048	38,333
1985	57,361	53,623	51,633	68,315	83,836	96,040	88,367	61,397	35,764	20,158	29,787	47,427
1986	51,314	47,633	51,218	62,508	68,325	65,895	61,547	40,333	20,797	12,941	17,022	24,528
1987	37,771	34,900	34,717	41,821	50,482	58,245	47,367	28,649	18,938	12,620	14,850	35,487
1988[1]	62,089	62,996	66,993	67,035	102,543	111,484	103,401	73,201	42,623	31,054	49,550	95,750

[1] Preliminary. *Source: Crop Reporting Board, U.S.D.A.*   T.517

Weekly Pork Belly Storage Movement

1986 Week Ending	Stocks[1] in Thousands of Pounds			Net Move-ment	1987 Week Ending	Stocks[1] in Thousands of Pounds			Net Move-ment
	In	Out	On Hand			In	Out	On Hand	
Jan. 4	1,178	1,209	43,120	− 31	Jan. 3	1,767	363	33,134	+ 1,404
11	960	1,864	42,216	− 904	10	1,419	1,357	33,196	+ 62
18	523	1,101	41,638	− 578	17	796	1,115	32,877	− 319
25	957	1,327	41,268	− 370	24	994	646	33,225	+ 348
Feb. 1	461	1,553	40,176	−1,092	31	231	2,599	30,857	−2,368
8	1,115	474	40,817	+ 641	Feb. 7	277	1,684	29,450	−1,407
15	1,461	730	41,547	+ 731	14	809	884	29,375	− 75
22	695	840	41,402	+ 145	21	795	773	29,397	− 22
Mar. 1	1,517	1,370	41,549	+ 147	28	545	432	29,510	− 113
8	1,941	769	42,991	+1,172	Mar. 7	442	294	29,658	+ 148
15	3,330	376	45,675	+2,954	14	741	573	29,826	+ 168
22	3,886	623	48,938	+3,263	21	1,742	241	31,327	+1,501
29	2,111	542	50,507	+1,569	28	2,825	466	33,686	+2,359
Apr. 5	1,930	249	52,188	+1,681	Apr. 4	2,810	218	36,278	+2,592
12	2,061	360	53,889	+1,701	11	2,590	115	38,753	+2,475
19	2,011	327	55,573	+1,684	18	3,045	482	41,316	+2,563
26	1,708	452	56,829	+1,256	25	1,242	647	41,911	+ 595
May 3	1,169	273	57,725	+ 896	May 2	779	479	42,211	+ 300
10	306	1,055	56,976	− 749	9	2,559	246	44,524	+2,313
17	564	630	56,910	− 66	16	1,957	271	46,210	+1,686
24	426	1,060	56,276	− 634	23	1,992	397	47,805	+1,595
31	286	48	56,080	− 196	30	1,508	391	48,922	+1,117
June 7	541	340	56,281	+ 201	June 6	537	626	48,833	− 89
14	585	450	56,416	+ 135	13	206	2,534	46,505	−2,328
21	476	524	56,369	− 48	20	199	3,158	43,546	−2,959
28	131	2,939	53,561	−2,808	27	164	2,333	41,377	−2,169
July 5	65	3,165	50,461	−3,100	July 4	384	2,701	39,060	−2,317
12	52	3,215	47,298	−3,163	11	124	3,224	35,960	−3,100
19	190	3,142	44,346	−2,952	18	205	3,482	32,683	−3,277
26	86	3,375	41,057	−3,289	25	137	3,851	28,969	−3,714
Aug. 2	97	4,700	36,454	−4,603	Aug. 1	83	4,787	24,265	−4,704
9	167	5,959	30,662	−5,792	8	222	3,282	21,205	−3,060
16	174	4,204	26,632	−4,030	15	70	2,622	18,653	−2,552
23	72	4,327	22,377	−4,255	22	440	2,240	16,853	−1,800
30	144	4,637	17,919	−4,458	29	409	2,090	15,172	−1,681
Sept. 6	26	2,957	14,988	−2,931	Sept. 5	253	1,846	13,579	−1,593
13	309	3,913	11,384	−3,604	12	50	1,249	12,380	−1,199
20	480	1,690	10,174	−1,210	19	114	1,162	11,332	−1,048
27	982	1,224	9,932	− 242	26	590	1,732	10,190	−1,142
Oct. 4	1,257	438	10,751	+ 819	Oct. 3	134	1,345	8,979	−1,211
11	2,370	302	12,819	+2,068	10	15	625	8,369	− 610
18	1,660	358	14,121	+1,302	17	27	224	8,172	− 197
25	648	995	13,774	− 347	24	1,076	170	9,078	+ 906
Nov. 1	773	808	13,739	− 35	31	1,514	238	10,354	+1,276
8	1,622	843	14,518	+ 779	Nov. 7	3,454	98	13,710	+3,356
15	2,456	231	16,743	+2,225	14	4,856	249	18,313	+4,607
22	1,652	200	18,195	+1,452	21	5,964	153	24,124	+5,811
29	1,671	214	19,652	+1,457	28	5,082	55	29,151	+5,027
Dec. 6	3,036	83	22,605	+2,953	Dec. 5	7,553	63	36,641	+7,490
13	3,257	43	25,819	+3,214	12	7,133	64	43,710	+7,069
20	3,442	186	29,075	+3,256	19	5,039	238	48,511	+4,801
27	3,144	489	31,730	+2,655	26	4,423	76	52,858	+4,347

[1] Total approved Chi. Merc. Exch. warehouses. [2] Preliminary. *Sources: U. S. Department of Agriculture; Chicago Mercantile Exchange* T.518

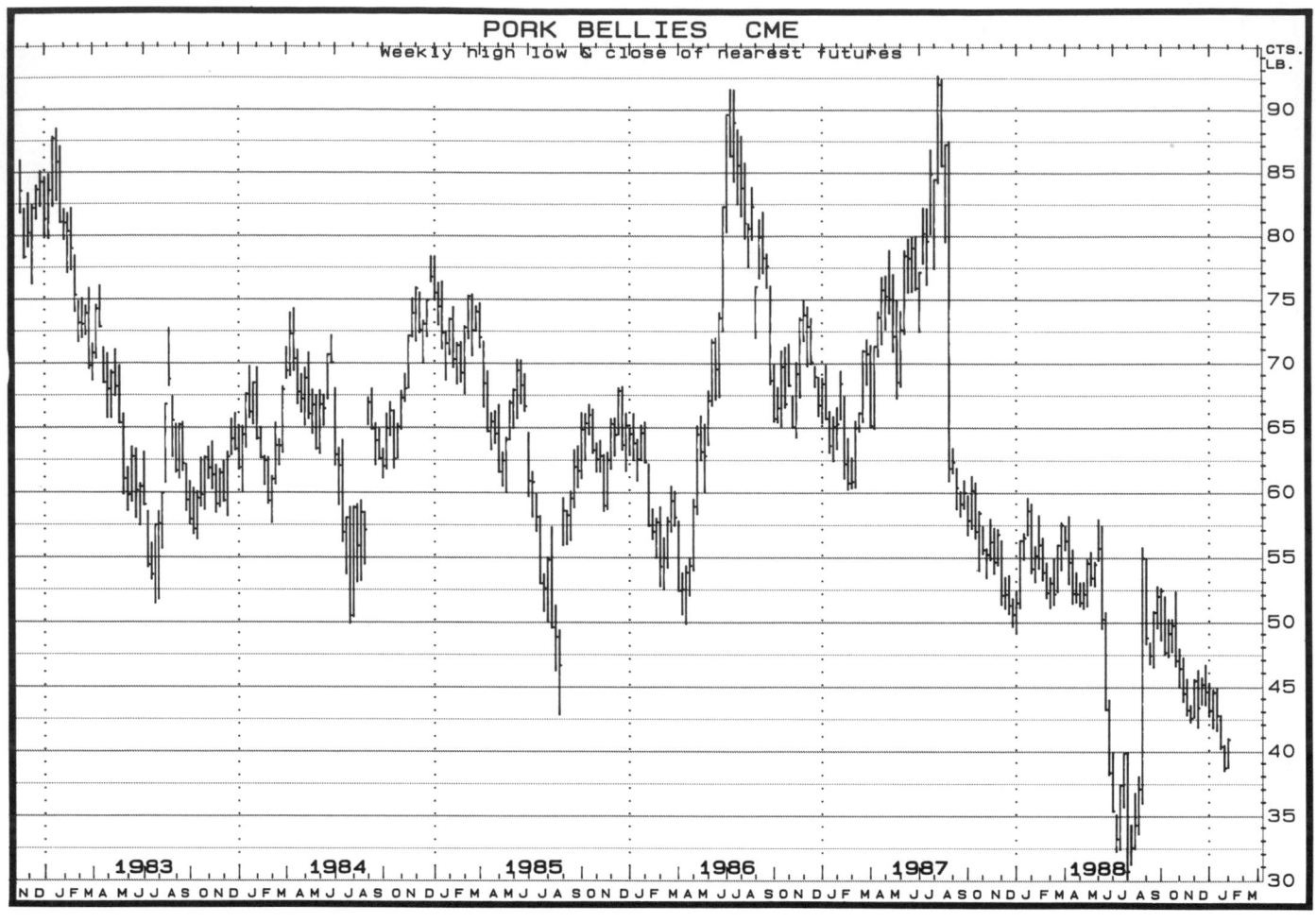

PORK BELLIES CME
Weekly high low & close of nearest futures

Month-End Open Interest of Pork Bellies Futures at Chicago In Contracts

Year	Jan.	Feb.	Mar.	Apr.	May	June	July	Aug.	Sept.	Oct.	Nov.	Dec.
1981	15,687	12,471	12,821	16,714	15,825	18,911	11,550	10,058	10,424	14,088	16,425	13,643
1982	21,542	21,666	21,048	28,063	25,765	17,940	14,203	14,799	16,090	19,063	18,596	18,521
1983	19,654	16,510	17,563	16,850	16,870	17,242	12,162	12,268	16,042	16,976	20,242	20,247
1984	18,836	17,434	19,114	18,332	17,379	17,250	9,453	7,387	8,925	9,763	13,265	13,507
1985	14,452	14,784	12,561	12,580	11,355	10,731	8,452	6,590	6,914	7,904	9,134	8,103
1986	7,821	7,826	7,145	8,987	10,530	10,838	8,567	7,698	7,915	9,432	11,453	11,057
1987	10,911	9,964	11,939	15,813	12,506	11,253	11,549	6,882	8,829	9,593	10,554	12,386
1988	10,499	12,944	13,039	17,532	17,847	16,467	12,491	12,172	14,613	17,685	20,660	19,362

Source: Chicago Mercantile Exchange   T.520

Volume of Trading of Pork Bellies Futures at Chicago In Contracts

Year	Jan.	Feb.	Mar.	Apr.	May	June	July	Aug.	Sept.	Oct.	Nov.	Dec.	Total
1981	176,243	154,438	135,527	179,503	157,342	199,013	187,785	131,619	139,272	171,480	194,561	170,944	1,997,697
1982	196,040	216,333	263,431	265,863	301,763	248,825	217,434	229,207	188,129	224,449	227,482	232,688	2,811,674
1983	276,556	229,198	207,543	225,034	226,617	227,522	218,813	169,113	132,894	154,642	159,982	175,363	2,403,277
1984	221,795	182,080	186,817	159,774	207,820	173,066	187,619	119,469	77,028	121,926	148,940	121,711	1,908,045
1985	173,488	137,334	133,509	148,489	149,809	135,319	136,026	89,784	77,326	99,291	85,377	91,634	1,457,386
1986	92,033	81,768	75,830	96,642	106,958	100,331	109,981	78,967	91,470	87,712	91,779	86,868	1,100,339
1987	104,134	95,108	92,707	118,107	112,112	120,598	118,996	89,564	60,670	66,423	53,903	64,688	1,097,010
1988	70,150	76,741	85,947	99,754	116,780	179,505	112,356	90,371	79,667	94,646	84,236	96,446	1,186,599

Source: Chicago Mercantile Exchange   T.521

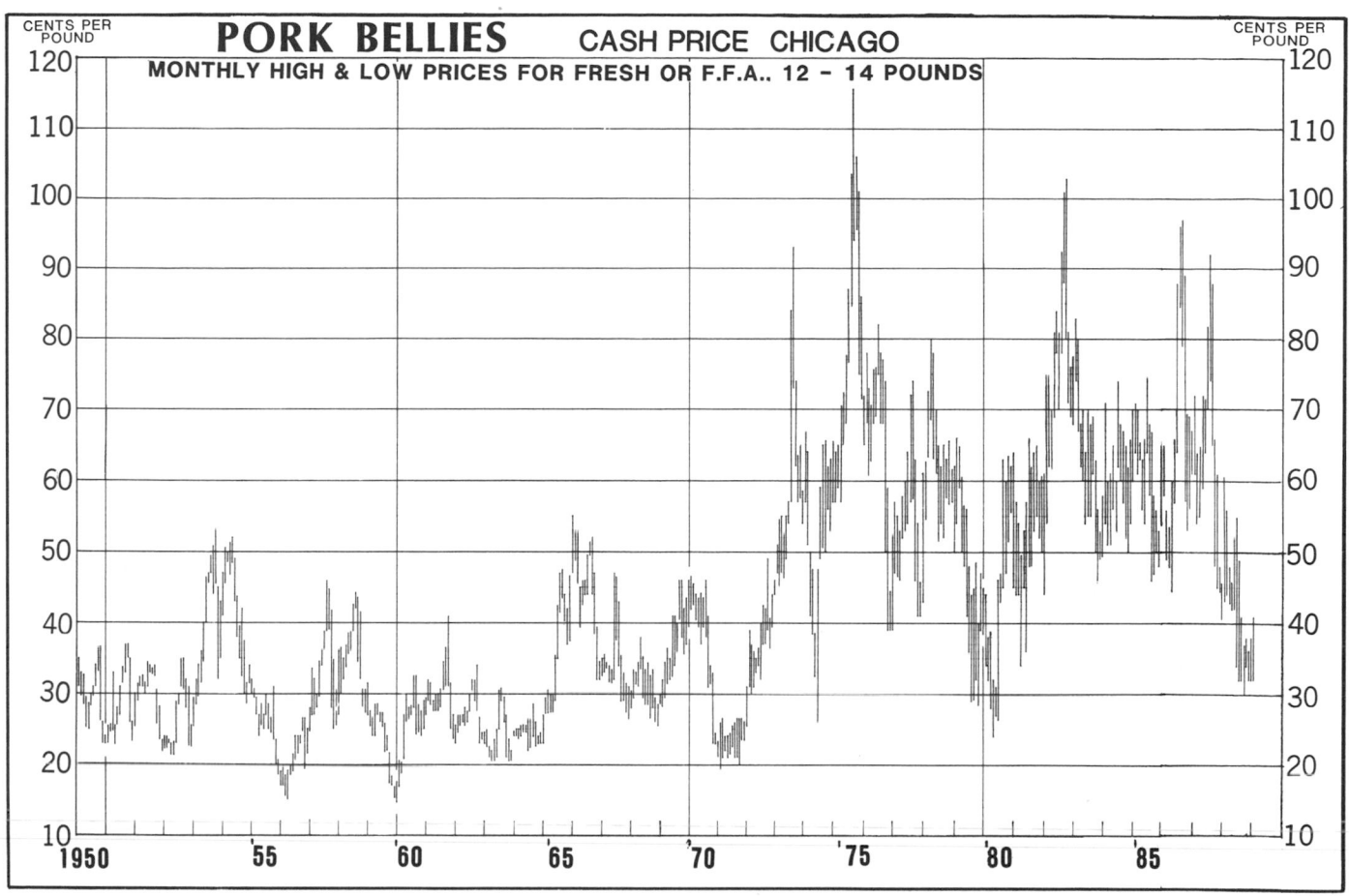

PORK BELLIES   CASH PRICE   CHICAGO
MONTHLY HIGH & LOW PRICES FOR FRESH OR F.F.A.. 12 - 14 POUNDS

High, Low & Closing Prices of May Pork Bellies Futures at Chicago   In Cents per Pound

Year of Delivery		Mar.	Apr.	May	June	July	Aug.	Sept.	Oct.	Nov.	Dec.	Jan.	Feb.	Mar.	Apr.	May	Life of Delivery Range
					Year Prior to Delivery									Delivery Year			
1982	High	69.15	75.50	72.70	75.90	69.40	72.10	72.50	70.22	71.40	63.75	73.55	75.80	77.85	85.10	91.50	91.50
	Low	54.50	70.15	63.00	64.10	61.75	64.12	62.70	62.95	59.25	51.90	61.12	67.55	69.00	74.75	84.15	51.90
	Close	69.15	70.15	72.70	64.10	65.15	64.95	65.15	68.85	61.05	62.70	73.55	70.37	75.15	84.92	84.95	—
1983	High	73.85	77.95	79.20	77.00	75.00	82.90	85.45	82.05	83.10	83.30	86.30	81.55	76.40	75.90	70.90	86.30
	Low	70.20	71.65	74.00	65.25	67.25	69.02	75.37	75.80	74.25	74.35	78.15	74.25	68.50	65.60	64.45	64.45
	Close	72.60	77.55	79.00	72.72	74.35	82.10	82.40	77.80	80.75	79.70	79.70	74.25	70.60	67.80	65.05	—
1984	High	65.40	65.95	65.90	61.90	64.75	71.55	66.80	64.10	65.60	67.40	71.30	68.10	71.07	74.10	70.65	74.10
	Low	61.25	62.80	60.00	56.00	54.70	61.50	59.50	58.35	60.32	60.40	62.12	59.25	60.55	65.50	64.35	54.70
	Close	64.90	64.72	61.00	57.15	61.90	65.37	59.37	64.22	62.30	63.62	67.27	60.70	69.22	65.82	65.42	—
1985	High	79.95	80.50	79.00	82.47	77.70	69.50	67.70	68.52	76.50	79.00	79.15	74.90	75.40	71.52	66.30	82.47
	Low	67.00	74.95	73.80	75.40	63.70	63.15	61.05	62.50	67.90	70.75	70.75	67.47	70.20	63.10	59.80	59.80
	Close	78.50	75.30	74.65	77.75	64.75	66.80	62.62	68.15	76.40	78.52	72.75	70.72	71.82	65.65	65.65	—
1986	High	75.60	75.25	74.57	75.27	70.00	64.35	64.85	67.52	66.65	67.80	66.90	63.45	61.67	58.55	65.75	75.60
	Low	69.00	70.55	69.80	69.70	59.50	57.05	57.25	62.35	60.00	63.00	62.35	54.40	54.37	49.65	57.65	49.65
	Close	75.35	73.70	74.12	70.30	62.95	59.65	64.85	63.65	66.45	64.90	63.50	55.85	55.87	58.55	59.85	—
1987	High	63.15	63.20	62.50	72.80	78.20	76.40	79.87	69.70	72.95	72.20	68.22	66.85	71.25	76.70	78.72	79.87
	Low	61.50	58.40	59.20	58.20	64.92	69.85	66.37	63.90	63.00	65.20	61.90	58.35	61.20	64.75	70.70	58.40
	Close	62.77	62.20	61.10	66.92	75.40	73.85	66.45	66.25	71.62	65.77	64.45	61.40	68.97	75.10	72.00	—
1988	High	56.25	59.95	75.60	64.85	66.55	67.75	62.50	60.65	58.75	56.00	61.40	60.20	57.55	58.05	55.27	75.60
	Low	54.40	51.00	57.80	59.00	58.50	60.95	56.45	54.40	54.45	51.10	52.27	52.92	52.10	51.10	50.90	50.90
	Close	54.50	59.45	60.20	59.00	66.55	61.90	57.10	56.90	55.70	52.35	55.75	53.27	56.12	51.35	54.02	—
1989	High	—	—	62.00	65.50	59.70	57.25	54.50	54.25	49.85	48.25						
	Low	—	—	59.25	57.15	52.55	50.97	48.50	48.47	44.25	44.25						
	Close	—	—	62.00	60.27	52.90	50.97	54.40	48.67	47.02	45.50						

Source: Chicago Mercantile Exchange

T.519

Potatoes

U.S. potato production is classified by seasonal group: winter (January-March), spring (April-June), summer (July-September), and fall (October-December).

Potato production declined in 1988, despite strong winter and spring output. Drought and reduced harvested area cut summer potato output by 13 percent. Excessive heat also hurt the all-important fall crop by reducing potato size and yields. The fall crop accounted for about 88 percent of U.S. production. The 1988 crop totaled 350 million cwt., versus 385 million in 1987, and was the smallest since 1983.

While accounting for just 6 percent of total potato output, the summer crop is an important supply bridge between the previous year's fall storage crop and the next fall crop. Despite the drought, irrigation and timely rains in some states allowed the summer crop to match that of the spring.

Total 1988 acreage harvested for all seasonal groups of 1.2 million acres was down 3 percent from 1987. The winter crop was the only seasonal group with higher harvested area.

Acreage planted to round white potatoes increased to 27 percent from 26 percent in 1987. This reversed a trend of whites losing ground to russets and, to some extent, reds. In 1988, the shift occurred at the expense of russet varieties. Maine's plantings of whites accounted for 80 percent of the state's potato area, up sharply from a year earlier. The change was due partly to the success of programs promoting Maine white potatoes.

Fresh potato exports to Canada, the primary U.S. export market for fresh potatoes, declined by 39 percent. But the country still accounted for 93 percent of U.S. fresh exports. Canada's 1987/88 crop was near record at 65.9 million cwt. U.S. imports of fresh potatoes (for food and seed) dropped 13 percent during the first half of 1988 to 3.2 million cwt.

Prices received by U.S. potato growers averaged above a year earlier, because of reduced stocks and stronger competition for supplies from processors and table-stock users. Prices remained fairly static from March-June 1988, hovering around $4.00/cwt. However, with the summer drought, prices moved to $6.30/cwt. in August 1988. Retail prices were expected to rise, reflecting the tighter supply/demand picture.

U.S. exports of frozen potatoes (mostly French fries) continued their rise through the first half of 1988, increasing 29 percent from 1987's first half. Japan continued to be the primary destination for frozen potato products, accounting for 86 percent of first-half 1988 export volume. So. Korea could prove to be a strong market for U.S. frozen fries in the future.

Salient Statistics of Potatoes in the United States

Year	Acreage Planted — 1,000 Acres	Acreage Harvested — 1,000 Acres	Yield Per Harv. Acre Cwt.	Total Production Mil. Cwt.	Seed & Feed Million Cwt.	Shrinkage & Loss Million Cwt.	Sold[3]	Farm Price $ Cwt.	Value of Prod.[2] Million $	Value of Sales Million $	Stocks on Jan. 1[4] 1,000 Cwt.	Dom. Exports Ths. Cwt.	Im-ports Ths. Cwt.	Fresh In Lbs.	Pro-cessed
1980	1,182	1,148	265	303.9	6.4	23.4	273.1	6.55	1,979	1,788	176,020	1,996	1,407	51.0	63.9
1981	1,263	1,232	276	340.6	6.0	26.1	306.5	5.41	1,819	1,660	147,010	2,807	2,470	45.7	67.4
1982	1,303	1,267	280	355.1	7.3	31.0	316.8	4.45	1,563	1,411	164,380	2,256	3,484	46.6	69.3
1983	1,272	1,243	269	333.9	6.0	24.7	303.3	5.82	1,936	1,765	178,980	1,957	2,702	49.9	67.6
1984	1,337	1,301	279	362.6	5.7	30.1	326.7	5.69	2,046	1,858	165,330	1,484	3,738	48.8	71.3
1985	1,409	1,361	299	407.1	8.1	52.8	346.2	3.92	1,571	1,357	173,380	1,026	2,991	46.6	74.7
1986	1,257	1,220	296	361.5	6.3	28.3	326.9	5.03	1,808	1,643	202,800	874	2,816	49.6	74.5
1987[1]	1,302	1,279	301	385.5	5.6	31.7	348.2	4.35	1,657	1,514	180,800	1,076	4,028	47.0	76.4
1988[1]	1,269	1,243	283	352.1							195,750				

Note: 60 pounds equals one bushel. [1] Preliminary. [2] Farm weight basis. Excludes canned & frozen potatoes. [3] For all purposes, including food, seed processing livestock feed. [4] Merchantable stocks held by growers & local dealers.
Source: National Agricultural Statistics Service, U.S.D.A. T.522

U.S. Cold Storage Stocks of All Frozen Potatoes (First of Month)   In Millions of Pounds

Year	Jan.	Feb.	Mar.	Apr.	May	June	July	Aug.	Sept.	Oct.	Nov.	Dec.
1983	767.3	800.1	879.9	899.8	958.0	986.6	1,015.3	823.2	603.8	637.2	775.2	817.4
1984	773.0	754.8	783.9	827.6	808.2	843.3	840.4	626.8	516.5	635.3	821.3	884.2
1985	892.3	900.0	943.4	1,003.3	1,023.6	1,081.6	1,058.4	828.2	735.4	861.4	1,014.2	1,020.2
1986	1,012.3	907.0	950.4	1,017.3	1,075.7	1,126.5	1,096.9	958.1	733.4	771.2	904.1	941.2
1987	894.1	786.7	795.9	856.6	886.7	962.9	1,003.3	816.4	675.5	774.2	947.5	966.1
1988[1]	881.8	898.2	975.5	964.2	942.5	955.0	992.6	882.4	835.0	917.6	1,054.8	
1989												

[1] Preliminary. *Source: Crop Reporting Board, U.S.D.A.* T.529

Potato Crop Production Estimates, Stocks & Disappearance in the U.S.   In Millions of Cwt.

Year	Crop Production Estimates — Total Crop Oct. 1	Nov. 1	Dec.	Fall Crop Oct. 1	Nov. 1	Dec. 1	Total Storage Stocks[2] — Following Year Dec. 1	Jan. 1	Feb. 1	Mar. 1	Apr. 1	May 1	Disappearance of Previous Fall Crop Until Following Year Dec. 1	Jan. 1	Feb. 1	Mar. 1	Apr. 1
1980	296.9	296.9	301.0	260.7	260.7	264.6	172.0	147.0	122.1	97.7	72.7	44.5	84.1	110.0	135.0	160.0	186.0
1981	329.9	329.9	333.7	287.1	287.1	290.7	193.6	164.4	137.8	111.8	82.3	50.8	93.6	121.0	149.0	175.0	204.0
1982	350.0	350.0	349.3	306.9	308.9	305.0	206.5	179.0	150.2	122.5	90.1	57.3	92.3	121.0	149.0	178.0	209.0
1983	329.8	329.8	325.7	292.7	292.7	325.7	192.5	165.3	138.9	112.7	81.7	50.4	90.7	117.0	143.0	169.0	200.1
1984	358.8	358.8	361.6	310.0	310.0	312.2	201.4	173.4	144.8	118.4	86.4	52.5	130.0	159.0	187.0	217.0	251.0
1985	—	400.4	404.1	—	346.1	340.8	235.5	202.8	171.5	138.7	104.5	65.4	139.0	171.0	203.0	238.0	277.0
1986	—	352.3	352.3	—	307.5	301.0	209.3	180.8	154.5	128.7	95.1	59.8	96.8	124.0	150.0	176.0	209.0
1987[1]	—	361.5		—	342.7		224.6	195.8	166.7	138.4	105.8	70.0	110.0		166.0	195.0	
1988[1]		352.1			309.9												

[1] Preliminary.   [2] Held by growers & local dealers in the fall producing areas.   *Source: Crop Reporting Board, U.S.D.A.*   T.525

United States Potato Production by Seasonal Groups   In Millions of 96.8 Cwt.

Year	Winter	Spring Florida	Calif.	Total Spring	Summer Va.	Total	Fall Maine	Wisc.	Minn.	Colo.	No. Dak.	Wash.	Idaho	Oregon	Total Fall
1980	2.4	3.6	8.8	17.1	1.5	17.0	25.0	16.0	9.9	11.0	15.7	43.9	79.8	19.7	266.4
1981	2.2	5.3	10.3	20.8	2.3	20.0	26.5	18.2	13.3	11.6	20.1	52.9	84.5	21.7	295.6
1982	2.3	5.7	9.6	21.0	2.5	22.8	27.0	22.6	11.5	12.8	17.3	52.8	91.8	21.1	309.1
1983	2.2	5.1	8.3	18.3	1.0	18.7	22.6	18.9	10.3	14.0	20.5	54.1	86.0	20.7	294.7
1984	2.6	6.7	11.1	23.8	1.5	23.1	21.4	21.4	13.8	17.2	20.6	56.9	86.6	23.5	313.1
1985	2.7	6.6	10.6	23.0	3.3	27.8	28.2	24.1	14.1	17.9	23.6	63.6	102.5	26.9	353.6
1986	3.0	7.0	7.6	19.8	1.1	20.9	21.9	20.1	13.7	18.8	21.6	62.0	90.2	23.2	317.8
1987	2.5	4.9	7.9	17.7	2.0	22.8	23.2	21.9	16.3	19.5	23.1	67.0	99.7	25.9	342.5
1988[1]	2.6	6.8	7.5	19.8	2.4	19.8	22.6	20.0	12.9	19.3	14.4	63.3	99.5	20.7	309.9
1989															

[1] Preliminary, December estimate.   *Source: Crop Reporting Board, U.S.D.A.*   T.524

Utilization of Potatoes in the United States   In Millions of Cwt.

Crop Year	Table Stock	Sales — Chips, Shoestrings	For Processing For dehydration	Frozen French Fries	Other Frozen Pdt's	Canned Potatoes	Other Canned Pdt's[2]	Starch & Flour	Other Sales Livestock Feed	Seed	Total Sales	Non-sales Used on Farms Where Grown	Shrinkage & Loss	Total Non-sales	Total
1980	96.8	37.9	28.2	67.2	13.7	2.1	2.0	2.2	3.9	19.2	273.1	5.0	23.2	29.6	302.9
1981	112.0	39.3	29.9	79.8	16.8	2.5	1.7	2.3	3.6	20.4	308.3	4.5	26.3	32.3	340.6
1982–3	120.3	40.7	27.7	76.0	17.3	2.7	1.8	4.6	6.2	19.5	316.8	4.7	31.0	38.3	355.2
1983–4	107.3	43.3	26.8	74.4	19.7	2.1	2.0	3.0	3.8	20.9	303.3	4.6	24.7	30.6	333.9
1984–5	113.8	42.3	27.8	87.4	20.3	2.6	1.8	3.4	4.7	22.6	326.7	4.4	30.1	35.9	362.6
1985–6	125.3	42.2	30.0	94.7	17.9	3.0	1.6	3.5	8.1	20.0	346.2	5.1	52.8	60.9	407.1
1986–7	109.3	45.8	28.4	96.2	15.7	2.8	1.3	2.8	4.0	20.5	326.9	5.1	28.3	34.6	361.5
1987–8[1]	26.3	40.5	30.8	102.6	16.6	3.0	1.6	2.2	3.8	20.8	348.2	4.5	31.7	37.3	385.5
1988–9															

[1] Preliminary.   [2] Hash, stews, soups.   [3] Includes 12.0 sold for livestock feed & starch under the U.S.D.A. diversion program.
Source: Crop Reporting Board, U.S.D.A.   T.531

POTATOES

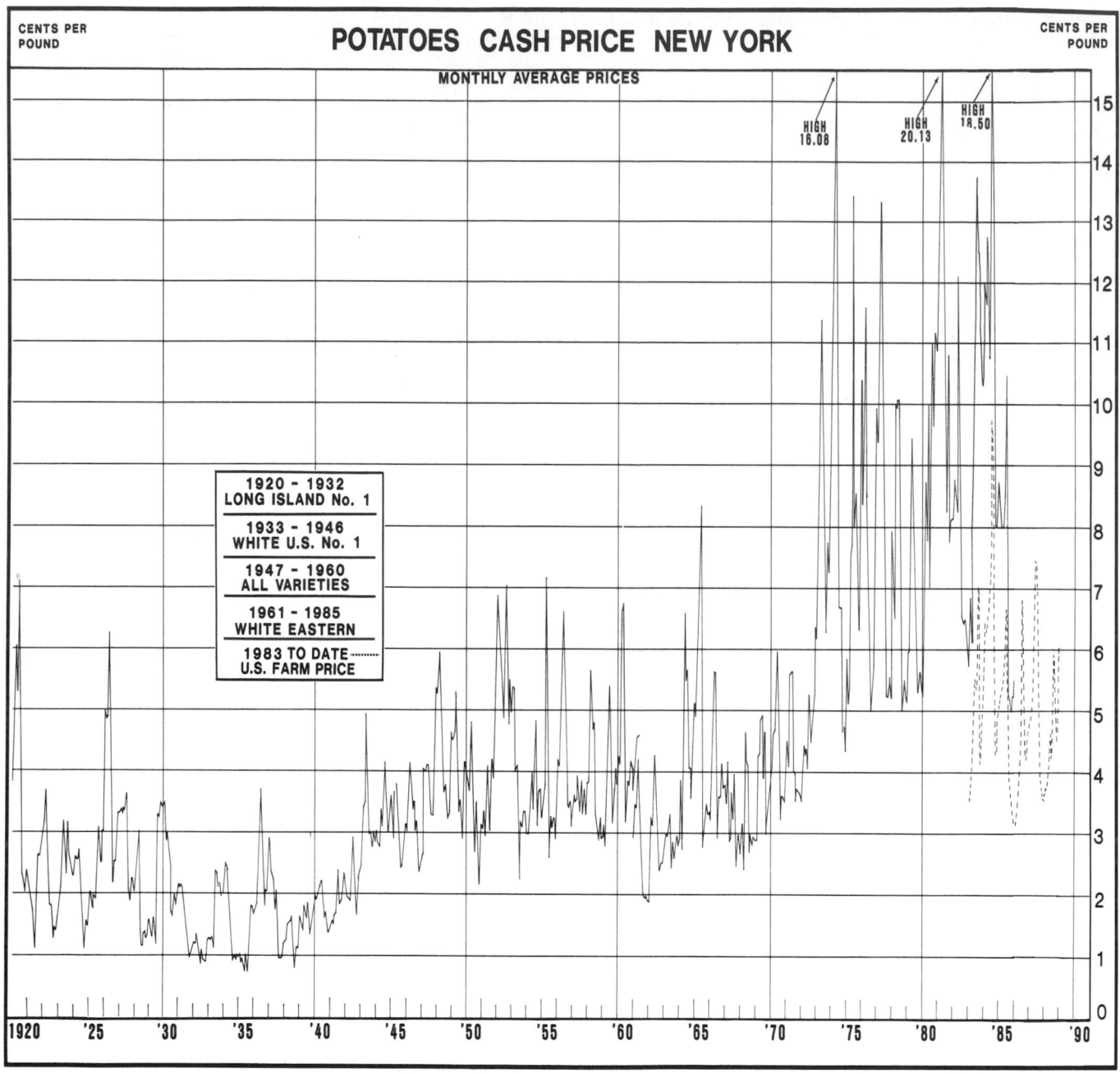

POTATOES CASH PRICE NEW YORK

CENTS PER POUND

MONTHLY AVERAGE PRICES

HIGH 16.08

HIGH 20.13

HIGH 18.50

1920 - 1932
LONG ISLAND No. 1

1933 - 1946
WHITE U.S. No. 1

1947 - 1960
ALL VARIETIES

1961 - 1985
WHITE EASTERN

1983 TO DATE
U.S. FARM PRICE

U.S. Average Price Received by Farmers for Potatoes   In Dollars Per Cwt.

Year	Jan.	Feb.	Mar.	Apr.	May	June	July	Aug.	Sept.	Oct.	Nov.	Dec.	Avg.[1]
1981	7.38	7.51	8.12	8.41	8.22	9.13	9.67	7.06	4.84	4.01	4.44	4.65	5.42
1982	4.71	4.78	5.03	5.59	6.21	7.11	6.52	5.80	4.25	3.78	3.73	3.71	4.45
1983	3.53	3.69	4.07	4.65	5.52	5.33	6.36	7.03	4.94	4.14	4.87	5.46	5.82
1984	6.43	6.29	6.55	6.69	7.04	7.52	9.72	8.75	4.87	4.26	4.60	4.90	5.69
1985	5.22	5.31	5.40	5.80	6.44	6.67	5.84	3.83	3.56	3.51	3.46	3.26	3.92
1986	3.12	3.35	3.50	3.99	4.39	4.79	6.91	5.68	4.28	4.20	4.63	4.78	5.03
1987	5.01	4.93	5.05	5.66	7.23	6.94	7.06	4.52	3.89	3.74	3.62	3.63	4.35
1988[2]	3.75	3.73	4.00	4.09	4.66	4.23	5.70	5.92	4.97	4.50	5.50		

[1] Annual weighted average by sales.   [2] Preliminary.   *Source: Statistical Reporting Service, U.S.D.A.*   T.530

United States Potatoes Processed[1], Eight States In Thousands of Cwt.

States	Storage Season	to Dec. 1	to Jan. 1	to Feb. 1	to Mar. 1	to Apr. 1	to May 1	Entire Season
Idaho and	1983–4	15,755	20,445	24,785	29,540	35,155	40,640	53,810
Malheur Co.,	1984–5	19,000	24,310	29,200	34,010	39,510	44,650	57,410
Oregon	1985–6	17,830	22,980	26,660	32,170	37,910	43,240	55,220
	1986–7	13,200	17,980	21,910	27,070	33,360	38,970	55,470
	1987–8	18,260	23,320	28,680	34.340	40,380	46,440	64,495
	1988–9							
Maine[2]	1983–4	1,160	1,745	2,260	2,780	3,370	3,970	5,125
	1984–5	1,820	2,410	3,015	3,520	4,330	5,185	6,830
	1985–6	2,215	2,935	3,845	4,630	5,540	6,280	8,660
	1986–7	2,100	2,835	3,345	3,865	4,500	5,195	6,995
	1987–8	1,770	2,440	3,145	3,745	4,410	4,865	6,745
	1988–9							
Wash. and other	1983–4	16,245	19,920	23,690	28,250	33,280	37,455	45,800
areas, Oregon	1984–5	20,745	24,690	29,345	33,560	38,815	43,380	51,670
	1985–6	21,725	25,665	29,450	34,450	39,990	45,110	57,430
	1986–7	21,530	25,510	28,530	33,595	39,610	44,865	56,910
	1987–8	22,265	25,950	30,790	35,800	40,900	44,925	58,085
	1988–9							
Other States[3]	1983–4	4,305	6,005	7,755	9,600	11,615	13,400	16,320
	1984–5	5,695	7,510	9,210	10,930	12,745	14,715	21,005
	1985–6	6,470	7,990	9,900	12,020	13,860	16,095	22,245
	1986–7	6,240	8,405	10,330	12,320	14,690	16,750	20,975
	1987–8	5,750	7,370	9,200	11,250	13,305	15,270	20,155
	1988–9							
Total	1983–4	37,465	48,115	58,490	70,170	83,420	95,465	121,055
	1984 5	47,260	58,920	70,770	82,020	95,400	107,930	136,915
	1985–6	48,240	59,570	69,855	83,270	97,300	110,725	143,555
	1986–7	43,070	54,730	64,115	76,850	92,160	105,780	140,350
	1987–8	48,045	59,080	71,815	85,135	98,995	111,500	149,480
	1988–9							

[1] Total quantity received and used for processing regardless of the state in which the potatoes were produced. Does not include quantities used for potato chips in Maine, Mich., Minn., N. Dak. or Wis. [2] Includes Maine grown potatoes only. [3] Mich., Minn., N. Dak. and Wis.
Source: Crop Reporting Board, U.S.D.A. T.524a

Potatoes U.S. Total Per Capita Utilization In Pounds

Year	Total	Fresh	Freezing	Chips[2]	Other[3]
1981	113.1	45.7	38.2	16.8	12.4
1982	115.9	46.6	40.1	17.2	12.0
1983	117.5	49.9	38.1	17.9	11.6
1984	120.1	48.8	41.4	18.1	11.8
1985	121.3	46.6	44.0	17.7	13.0
1986	124.1	49.6	44.0	18.2	12.3
1987[1]	123.4	47.0	46.5	17.7	12.2
1988					

[1] Preliminary. [2] Includes shoestrings. [3] Includes canning and dehydrating. *Source: Economic Research Service, U.S.D.A.*

Rapeseed

World rapeseed (canola) production in 1988/89 was projected by USDA at 21.8 million tonnes, down 6 percent from the previous season. China's crop of 5.7 million tonnes was off 15 percent, due to a dry spring and switching of acreage into wheat. The European Community's production was projected at 5.3 million tonnes, down 10 percent. Britain's crop was down 26 percent, while France's was off 5 percent and W. Germany's was down 7 percent. Nonetheless, EC production has grown rapidly, due to subsidies. India's crop was projected at 2.9 million tonnes, the same as a year earlier. In Canada, acreage expanded by over 30 percent, but severe drought affected the crop. It was forecast at a record 4 million tonnes, 4 percent more than a year earlier. Poland's crop was forecast at 1.1 million tonnes, down 5 percent. Rapeseed comprised about 11 percent of world oilseed production in 1988.

World exports in 1988/89 were put at 4.7 million tonnes, off marginally from a year earlier. The EC was a net importer. Canada was the largest exporter, with shipments projected at 1.95 million tonnes, up 8 percent. Poland's shipments of 340,000 tonnes were down from 400,000 tonnes the year before. Japan, the largest importer, was projected to purchase 1.7 million tonnes, mostly from Canada. Mexico's imports were expected to be 250,000 tonnes, the same as a year earlier.

The world rapeseed crush was projected at 19.6 million tonnes, down 4 percent from a year earlier. The major processor was the EC, followed by China. With the smaller crop, world ending stocks of rapeseed were expected to fall slightly to 1.2 million tonnes.

World rape meal production in 1988/89 was placed at 11.8 million tonnes, 5 percent less than a year earlier. China was the leading meal producer, followed by the EC. Meal exports worldwide were projected at 1.7 million tonnes, down 7 percent. The EC, China, and Canada were the dominant exporters. Major meal importers included the U.S. and Japan. World consumption of rape meal was put at 11.9 million tonnes, down 4 percent. The EC was the largest meal consumer, followed by China, India, and Japan. Ending stocks of rapeseed meal were projected at 362,000 tonnes, down 4 percent.

World rape oil production was estimated to be 7.3 million tonnes, down 3 percent from the season before. Rape oil now ranks fourth in the world behind soy, palm, and sunflowerseed, and comprises almost 14 percent of world vegetable and marine oil output. The EC is the largest rape oil producer, with output estimated at just over 2 million tonnes. The EC is producing more low erucic acid rapeseed, which contains less indigestible glucosinolates and can be used more extensively in food. The low acid varieties tend to have lower yields, but receive much higher subsidies. All the rapeseed grown in W. Germany and Denmark is low erucic, while France and Britain are rapidly converting to these varieties. By 1991/92, the Community will pay crushing subsidies only for low erucic acid varieties.

China's rape oil output is expected to be 1.7 million tonnes, down 16 percent from a year earlier. China has emerged as a major importer of rape oil. Its imports in 1988/89 were projected to be 225,000 tonnes, almost double the previous season. Other important producers of rape oil include India, Canada, and Japan.

World rape oil exports were projected at 1.7 million tonnes, down 1 percent. The EC and Canada were the leading exporters. Since the U.S. Food and Drug Administration declared that low erucic acid rape oil was generally safe in food, Canadian exports to the U.S. have increased from 4,000 tonnes in 1984 to 150,000 tonnes in 1988/89. Free trade with Canada may mean that more rape oil will be sold in the U.S. All Canadian rapeseed is of the low erucic acid variety.

China, the EC, and India are the major consumers of rape oil. World ending stocks of rape oil were estimated to be 470,000 tonnes, down slightly from a year earlier.

Futures Market

Rapeseed futures are traded on the Winnipeg Commodity Exchange.

World Production of Rapeseed (In Thousands of Metric Tons)

Year[2]	Canada	China	Czecho-slovakia	Denmark	France	East Germany	West Germany	India	United Kingdom	Bangla-desh	Pakistan	Poland	Sweden	Yugo-slavia	World Total
1974	1,207	1,075	85	112	690	200	301	1,692		107	293	523	351		7,022
1975	1,163	1,090	115	115	532	250	194	2,300		110	305	726	327		7,989
1976	1,749			90	561							980	279		
1977	1,973	1,180	162	77	388	308	282	1,650	142	134	236	708	236	40	7,890
1978	3,497	1,868	166	91	568	318	331	1,860	155	137	248	691	289	73	10,721
1979	3,411	2,402	80	150	510	201	321	1,428	198	118	247	233	264	93	10,080
1980	2,484	2,384	214	225	1,103	277	377	2,002	300	122	252	572	285	68	11,104
1981	1,849	4,065	200	290	990	284	363	2,382	325	123	238	496	282	65	12,345
1982	2,225	5,656	178	335	1,147	307	535	2,207	580	120	246	433	320	79	14,804
1983	2,609	4,287	314	309	906	260	599	2,608	565	131	217	554	318	103	14,259
1984	3,412	4,205	300	474	1,305	305	662	3,073	925	140	234	911	327	124	16,935
1985	3,498	5,607	285	544	1,340	381	803	2,681	895	133	250	1,073	320	126	18,574
1986	3,787	5,881	306	618	1,068	370	969	2,635	940	119	217	1,298	321	131	19,463
1987[1]	3,846	6,610	337	592	2,641	390	1,239	3,100	1,353	140	200	1,200	253	68	22,950
1988[3]	4,240	5,700	350	570	2,500	400	1,150	3,000	1,000	125	235	1,140	302	62	21,760

[1] Preliminary. [2] Harvest generally occurs in the first half of the calendar year given in all major producing countries except Canada.
[3] Estimate. *Source: Foreign Agricultural Service, U.S.D.A.*

T.533

RAPESEED WGE
Weekly high low & close of nearest futures

World Supply & Distribution of Rapeseed & Products   In Thousands of Metric Tons

Crop Year	Rapeseed					Rapeseed Meal					Rapeseed Oil				
	Pro-duction	Exports	Imports	Crush	Ending Stocks	Pro-duction	Exports	Imports	Con-sumption	Ending Stocks	Pro-duction	Exports	Imports	Con-sumption	Ending Stocks
1979–80	10,081	2,102	2,403	8,714	1,708	5,206	520	640	5,316	149	3,365	643	571	3,295	159
1980–81	11,104	2,305	2,366	10,477	1,489	6,297	808	636	6,075	199	3,933	814	756	3,914	210
1981–82	12,345	2,142	2,216	11,959	911	7,331	845	683	7,182	186	4,383	824	775	4,404	140
1982–83	14,804	2,469	2,540	13,826	740	8,449	768	871	8,500	238	4,991	841	790	4,925	155
1983–84	14,263	2,537	2,704	13,312	647	8,130	1,198	1,303	8,206	267	4,856	984	980	4,827	180
1984–85	16,935	3,153	3,291	15,369	1,033	9,419	1,463	1,451	9,454	220	5,602	1,298	1,199	5,497	186
1985–86	18,574	3,632	3,646	16,865	1,267	10,188	1,824	1,708	10,007	285	6,192	1,313	1,205	5,939	331
1986–87	19,463	4,579	4,919	18,375	1,027	11,076	1,692	2,217	11,524	362	6,784	1,662	1,444	6,487	410
1987–88[1]	22,950	4,620	4,340	20,640	1,200	12,480	1,700	1,880	12,640	390	7,570	1,760	1,500	7,170	540
1988–89[1]	21,760	4,580	4,280	19,690	1,140	11,880	1,610	1,750	12,080	320	7,270	1,680	1,480	7,130	480

[1] Preliminary.   Source: Foreign Agricultural Service, U.S.D.A.

T.534a

RAPESEED

Wholesale Price of Rapeseed Oil, Refined (Denatured), in Tanks at N.Y. In Cents Per Pound

Year	Jan.	Feb.	Mar.	Apr.	May	June	July	Aug.	Sept.	Oct.	Nov.	Dec.	Average
1976	46.0	46.0	46.0	46.0	46.0	46.0	46.0	44.2	39.0	39.0	39.0	39.0	43.5
1977	39.0	39.0	39.0	39.0	39.0	39.0	39.0	39.0	39.0	39.0	39.0	39.0	39.0
1978	39.0	39.0	39.0	39.0	39.0	39.0	39.0	39.0	39.0	39.0	39.0	39.0	39.0
1979	39.0	39.0	39.0	39.0	39.0	39.0	39.0	39.0	39.0	39.0	39.0	39.0	39.0
1980	47.0	47.0	47.0	47.0	47.0	47.0	47.0	46.0	46.0	46.0	46.0	46.0	46.6
1981	56.4	59.0	59.0	59.0	59.0	59.0	59.0	59.0	59.0	59.0	59.0	59.0	58.8
1982	57.0	55.0	56.8	57.5	56.0	56.0	56.0	56.0	55.7	55.3	55.3	55.3	50.0
1983	55.3	55.3	55.3	55.3	55.3	55.3	55.3	55.3	55.3	55.3	55.3	55.3	55.3
1984	55.3	55.3	55.3	55.3	55.5	55.5	55.2	55.2	55.2	55.2	55.2	55.2	55.3
1985	55.2	55.2	55.2	N.A.	N.A.	68.3	67.9	64.0	62.5	62.5	62.5	60.5	61.4
1986	60.0	60.0	60.0	60.0	60.0	60.0	60.0	60.0	60.5	60.5	60.5	60.5	60.1
1987	60.50	62.00	62.50	62.50	64.25	69.50	69.50	65.00	63.50	63.50	63.50	63.50	64.15
1988	63.56	63.50	63.50	63.50	63.50	63.50	63.50	63.50	63.50				

Source: Economic Research Service, U.S.D.A.

T.534

Month–End Open Interest of Rapeseed Futures in Winnipeg In 20–Tonne Units

Year	Jan.	Feb.	Mar.	Apr.	May	June	July	Aug.	Sept.	Oct.	Nov.	Dec.
1979	15,288	15,164	16,338	15,593	12,993	14,209	12,950	13,596	15,001	21,300	21,827	21,966
1980	15,718	17,516	13,392	14,285	17,722	17,254	17,126	17,108	18,827	22,036	21,911	20,504
1981	15,376	15,326	18,028	18,764	18,000	15,332	14,948	15,316	15,755	16,064	16,260	12,911
1982	13,532	14,970	9,952	12,230	15,997	11,554	12,623	16,948	13,904	15,503	17,992	20,555
1983	16,288	17,964	18,266	16,681	15,327	13,834	18,249	22,681	20,481	18,778	18,302	17,554
1984	14,170	16,807	13,980	13,743	15,220	14,025	14,348	15,822	17,967	15,893	18,046	19,361
1985	20,883	22,483	22,144	19,666	19,617	16,639	18,019	18,962	13,924	15,894	15,213	18,832
1986	15,083	21,017	19,412	21,161	23,154	17,457	17,478	24,836	22,087	32,220	28,293	27,989
1987	27,324	36,769	33,374	31,589	28,664	29,409	23,210	23,937	27,953	23,857	21,953	29,265
1988	30,901	34,534	32,538	34,064	33,518	32,020	29,639	28,000	26,751	31,230	26,380	28,779

Source: Winnipeg Commodity Exchange

T.535

High, Low & Closing Prices of June Rapeseed Futures in Winnipeg In Dollars per Tonne

Year of Delivery		Apr.	May	June	July	Aug.	Sept.	Oct.	Nov.	Dec.	Jan.	Feb.	Mar.	Apr.	May	June	Life of Delivery Range
					Year Prior to Delivery								Delivery Year				
1982	High	—	—	—	396.0	391.0	378.3	371.8	366.5	353.0	344.0	340.8	333.5	342.8	340.8	331.7	396.0
	Low	—	—	—	384.0	375.5	355.0	358.8	341.6	334.6	331.0	328.0	319.8	327.3	329.7	321.0	319.8
	Close	—	—	—	391.0	375.5	360.3	365.4	344.8	335.1	334.5	332.7	327.0	334.1	332.7	330.0	—
1983	High	—	—	—	—	361.0	366.3	345.5	349.1	340.0	335.9	329.0	321.0	329.3	328.1	308.5	366.3
	Low	—	—	—	—	346.0	332.0	332.6	339.6	322.3	323.1	311.5	311.8	311.0	309.5	292.8	292.8
	Close	—	—	—	—	354.2	337.0	342.5	340.3	325.6	329.1	311.7	316.0	324.7	309.9	297.2	—
1984	High	—	—	—	359.5	434.0	467.4	452.5	435.2	424.5	431.4	412.0	426.5	502.2	724.0	724.0	724.0
	Low	—	—	—	330.0	364.5	415.5	409.0	406.1	397.3	406.5	382.9	403.0	426.0	507.5	577.0	330.0
	Close	—	—	—	350.5	423.6	447.5	409.7	407.8	421.5	410.2	403.5	426.5	502.2	704.0	577.0	—
1985	High	—	—	—	443.9	434.5	417.5	424.1	427.9	417.5	408.8	404.5	402.5	429.2	422.0	389.7	443.9
	Low	—	—	—	409.5	413.5	406.5	414.9	415.3	389.8	388.0	395.5	391.4	393.2	361.5	379.0	361.5
	Close	—	—	—	413.0	413.7	416.5	417.7	416.8	390.5	397.4	397.4	397.5	408.6	367.0	381.9	—
1986	High	422.5	424.0	409.5	400.4	370.0	357.0	351.5	315.5	347.3	346.7	329.8	316.7	306.5	295.0	277.5	424.0
	Low	421.5	402.5	388.0	364.5	348.0	342.5	328.4	325.5	330.7	328.6	296.1	298.8	271.0	274.0	261.3	261.3
	Close	421.5	403.2	388.0	368.5	352.8	342.5	328.4	333.6	342.2	329.5	300.6	305.7	291.5	275.8	267.7	—
1987	High	—	—	—	290.7	270.0	284.0	277.0	278.0	269.4	260.5	253.7	234.0	233.4	259.9	272.7	290.7
	Low	—	—	—	290.2	254.0	255.0	258.5	266.8	256.5	251.0	224.1	216.0	218.8	229.1	240.7	216.0
	Close	—	—	—	270.2	258.6	279.8	270.8	268.6	258.1	253.8	226.1	221.5	229.7	245.0	265.7	—
1988	High	—	—	—	285.0	262.5	273.6	284.0	300.4	307.0	323.5	309.9	303.4	317.8	378.3	431.0	431.0
	Low	—	—	—	257.0	253.0	254.8	268.7	265.3	284.5	298.0	298.0	288.0	305.3	310.0	371.3	253.0
	Close	—	—	—	265.2	257.3	270.5	269.6	292.8	306.2	300.2	301.7	301.6	317.6	376.2	431.0	—
1989	High	339.0	402.4	490.0	480.0	426.0	424.0	392.7	376.5	367.5							
	Low	322.2	338.0	397.0	380.0	393.5	387.5	355.5	339.3	344.5							
	Close	339.0	397.0	470.0	391.0	407.5	389.5	364.5	345.8	362.5							

Source: Winnipeg Commodity Exchange

T.536

Rayon and Other Synthetic Fibers

Worldwide Cellulosic Fiber Production In Thousands of Metric Tons

Year	Austria	Brazil	China	Finland	Germany East	Germany West	India	Japan	Poland	Romania	Taiwan	Un. Kingdom	United States	USSR	Yugoslavia	Total
1980	115.9	51.3	170.0	47.8	168.5	111.2	132.4	397.3	86.4	63.5	78.3	146.0	365.6	650.0	73.0	3,242
1981	123.5	46.3	185.0	46.6	169.0	115.0	150.4	392.2	63.9	64.6	99.7	129.4	349.3	645.5	73.0	3,204
1982	114.6	45.0	185.0	53.1	161.8	111.5	101.4	379.3	64.4	58.2	92.8	113.2	264.6	634.9	68.0	2,946
1983	121.1	40.4	130.4	57.6	165.1	114.0	116.1	387.8	69.4	59.5	101.5	140.2	290.3	599.9	72.0	2,929
1984	123.8	46.7	153.0	58.0	170.2	116.0	141.8	377.4	75.5	59.5	128.0	127.2	285.1	602.0	69.0	3,002
1985	123.9	46.6	180.0	60.0	167.8	119.0	141.9	387.9	71.1	61.8	121.9	78.2	253.0	586.0	69.9	2,929
1986	123.0	50.4	190.0	55.0	127.7	119.0	140.0	320.0	72.0	64.0	119.9	58.0	280.7	589.0	71.1	2,839
1987[1]	120.0	48.9	210.0	54.0	128.5	118.0	145.8	300.5	72.8	66.0	119.6	55.0	274.6	591.5	63.3	2,833

[1] Preliminary. *Source: Textile Economics Bureau, Inc.* T.537

Worldwide Noncellulosic Fiber Production (Except Olefin) In Thousands of Metric Tons

Year	Brazil	China	France	W. Germany	India	Italy/Malta	Japan	Korea Rep.	Mexico	Romania	Spain	Taiwan	Un. Kingdom	United States	USSR	Total
1980	231.4	248.0	192.0	720.1	70.5	354.8	1,357	536.4	239.4	136.0	201.7	557.8	287.6	3,242	550.0	10,476
1981	201.8	347.0	201.2	752.2	90.7	435.3	1,329	610.4	244.0	154.0	241.2	587.0	249.3	3,276	572.8	10,827
1982	198.1	384.0	190.1	669.0	106.2	428.7	1,302	612.5	232.5	153.0	231.4	630.9	204.3	2,602	587.8	10,145
1983	185.3	386.2	192.2	732.2	128.0	458.6	1,318	664.1	269.5	153.0	247.8	738.1	223.8	3,009	622.0	11,076
1984	215.8	559.4	191.7	731.0	162.3	527.8	1,369	746.5	300.2	174.4	260.4	871.8	240.0	2,937	658.3	11,851
1985	217.5	732.0	182.7	762.0	193.7	563.6	1,403	811.6	305.9	196.8	274.9	1,024	242.7	2,864	712.8	12,499
1986	239.7	801.0	167.2	742.0	223.4	572.0	1,356	862.2	296.3	199.7	270.9	1,232	208.2	2,919	757.8	12,994
1987[1]	248.0	910.0	159.0	764.0	231.9	564.0	1,341	969.3	336.0	201.9	263.0	1,391	203.0	3,094	836.0	13,759

[1] Preliminary. *Source: Textile Economics Bureau, Inc.* T.538

World Production of Rayon & Other Synthetic Fibers In Thousands of Metric Tons

Year	Noncellulosic Fiber Production (Except Olefin) — By Fibers — Acrylic & Mod-Acrylic	Nylon & Aramid	Polyester	Other Fibers[3]	World Total — Yarn & Monofilaments	Staple & Tow & Fiberfil	Total	Glass Fiber Production — Europe[3]	United States	Other Americas	Japan	Other[4]	This Total	P.R.C. China	USSR	Cigarette Tow Production
1980	2,060	3,151	5,127	138	4,732	5,744	10,476	300	393	30	167	13	903	N.A.	N.A.	335
1981	2,090	3,139	5,465	133	4,809	6,018	10,827	277	472	31	174	14	968	N.A.	N.A.	349
1982	2,058	2,853	5,106	129	4,480	5,666	10,146	250	408	35	198	12	903	30	65	339
1983	2,221	3,196	5,535	124	4,867	6,209	11,076	290	530	37	206	14	1,077	30	65	334
1984	2,298	3,354	6,053	145	5,225	6,625	11,850	300	632	39	249	14	1,234	40	75	314
1985	2,382	3,442	6,511	165	5,579	6,921	12,500	320	610	32	273	28	1,263	50	85	337
1986	2,443	3,497	6,912	141	5,752	7,241	12,993	364	630	35	240	30	1,299	50	100	362
1987[1]	2,511	3,637	7,464	146	6,095	7,663	13,758	407	725	50	261	35	1,478	55	110	400

[1] Preliminary. [2] Alginate, Azion, Spandex, Saran, etc. [3] West & East (excluding USSR). [4] Except USSR & China (P.R.C.)
Source: Textile Economics Bureau, Inc. T.539

Man-Made Fiber Production in the United States In Millions of Pounds

Year	Rayon Yarn Indust.	Rayon Yarn Textile	Acet. Yarn	Total Yarn	Staple & Tow Rayon	Staple & Tow Acetate	Total	Total (Rayon & Acetate)	Non-Cellulosic Yarn	Non-Cellulosic Staple	Total	Total Ray. & Acet. & Non-Cel.	Textile Glass Fiber	Total Man-made Fiber	Producers' Waste Shipments Rayon	Producers' Waste Shipments Non-Cell.
1979	41.7	15.1	316.6	373.4	549.4	7.0	556.4	929.8	4,154.3	4,282.3	8,436.6	9,336.4	1,014.4	10,380.8	17.2	238.6
1980	32.2	15.0	308.5	355.7	443.3	7.0	450.3	806.0	3,744.3	4,148.2	7,892.5	8,698.5	867.3	9,565.8	13.5	170.2
1981	33.4	15.1	257.0	305.5	460.6	4.0	464.6	770.1	3,814.8	4,191.1	8,005.9	8,776.0	1,041.1	9,817.1	15.3	174.2
1982	20.8	12.4	195.2	228.4	355.0	1.0	356.0	584.4	3,057.4	3,402.5	6,459.9	7,044.3	899.2	7,943.5	10.7	173.2
1983	25.0	11.2	227.6	263.8	374.8	1.4	376.2	640.0	3,568.0	3,971.0	7,538	8,178	1,167.2	9,335.9	9.4	214.1
1984	28.8	12.1	198.2	239.1	389.2	.4	389.6	628.7	3,524	3,947	7,472	8,100	1,394.0	9,494	11.4	216.9
1985	N.A.			204.6	352.7	.5	353.2	557.8	3,790	3,773	7,564	8,121	N.A.		8.8	260.2
1986	N.A.			214.8	403.7	.5	404.2	619.0	3,836	3,992	7,828	8,447	N.A.		10.4	261.5
1987[1]	N.A.			191.1	415.5	.5	416.0	607.1	4,010	4,306	8,316	8,923	N.A.		9.6	221.3

[1] Preliminary. *Source: Textile Organon* T.543

RAYON AND OTHER SYNTHETIC FIBERS

U.S. Rayon and Acetate Distribution   In Millions of Pounds

	Yarn & Monofilaments								Staple & Tow & Fiber Fill						
	Producers' Shipments								Producers' Shipments						
	To Domestic Consumers							Domestic	Domestic Consumers						Domestic
Year	Industrial	Textile	Acetate	Total	Export	Total	Import	Consump.	Rayon	Acetate	Total	Export	Total	Import	Consump.
1982	—30.1—		169.0	199.1	29.8	228.9	7.0	206.1	293.7	1.0	294.7	66.5	361.2	13.4	308.1
1983	—35.5—		197.6	233.1	28.2	261.3	8.7	241.8	333.5	1.4	334.9	43.9	378.8	13.6	348.5
1984	—38.2—		180.1	218.3	18.2	236.5	10.0	228.3	331.9	.4	332.3	52.1	384.4	17.0	349.3
1985	—N.A.—			187.1	23.0	210.1	13.9	201.0	323.7	.5	324.2	35.0	359.2	12.3	336.5
1986	—N.A.—			192.1	20.2	212.3	17.0	209.1	373.0	.5	373.5	30.8	404.3	17.4	390.9
1987[1]	—N.A.—			166.8	24.9	191.7	12.8	179.6	383.1	.5	383.6	32.4	416.0	13.8	397.4

[1] Preliminary.   *Source: Textile Organon*   T.540

U.S. Domestic Shipments of Synthetic Fibers   In Millions of Pounds

	Yarn & Monofilaments							Staple & Tow						
	Cellulosic			Non-Cellulosic						Non-Cellulosic				
						Polyester &		Cellulosic		Acrylic & Mod	Olefin &			Textile Glass
Year	Rayon	Acetate	Total	Nylon	Olefin[2]	Other	Total[3]	Rayon	Nylon	Acrylic	Vinyon	Polyester	Total	Fiber
1982	30.1	169.0	199.1	1,166	577.0	1,135	2,894	293.7	673.3	457.9	138.9	1,768	3,038	904.4
1983	35.5	197.6	233.1	1,392	698.6	1,294	3,385	333.5	897.1	492.2	183.4	2,099	3,672	1,184
1984	38.2	180.1	218.3	1,438	725.6	1,145	3,309	331.9	814.4	446.7	240.9	1,992	3,494	1,309
1985	—N.A.—		187.1	1,417	937.6	1,204	3,559	323.7	830.3	458.7	279.7	1,873	3,441	1,260
1986	—N.A.—		192.1	1,480	1,049	1,092	3,621	373.0	894.9	531.2	312.7	1,999	3,737	1,339
1987[1]	—N.A.—		166.8	1,554	1,136	1,113	3,803	383.1	966.0	479.3	341.1	2,201	3,987	1,513

[1] Preliminary.   [2] Includes film fiber.   [3] Includes Saran & Spandex.   *Source: Textile Organon*   T.541

U.S. Mill Consumption of Fiber & Products & Per Capita Consumption

| | Mill Consumption (Million Pounds) | | | | | | | | | | | Per Capita[4] Consumption (Pounds) | | | | |
Year	Yarn & Monofilaments	Staple & Tow	Total R. & A.[2]	Noncellulosic Fiber	Textile Glass Fiber	Waste	Total Manmade[3]	Cotton	Wool	Silk	Grand Total	Non-cell. Man-made Fibers	Rayon & Acetate	Cotton	Wool	Total All Fibers
1982	206.1	308.1	514.2	6,131	875.6	183.9	6,654	2,479	129.5	2.0	9,264	26.9	2.2	13.5	.9	40.5
1983	241.8	348.5	590.3	7,396	1,166.1	223.5	7,995	2,796	162.5	1.6	10,954	32.4	2.5	15.9	1.2	47.5
1984	228.3	349.3	577.6	7,202	1,273.8	228.3	7,790	2,668	163.2	1.4	10,622	31.2	2.4	16.8	1.4	45.7
1985	201.0	336.5	537.5	7,490	N.A.	269.0	8,036	2,796	134.7	1.5	10,968	31.9	2.3	17.7	1.5	46.6
1986	209.1	390.9	600.0	7,846	N.A.	271.9	8,454	3,302	164.5	1.0	11,921	— 35.8 —		20.2	1.6	49.9
1987[1]	179.6	397.4	577.0	8,258		230.9	8,844	3,743	167.6	1.0	12,755	— 37.1 —		23.9	1.6	53.2

[1] Preliminary.   [2] Rayon and acetate.   [3] Man-made fiber data include only glass fiber for textile end uses.   [4] Mill consumption adjusted for raw fiber equivalent of net U.S. trade in textile mfg.   *Source: Textile Economics Bureau; Economic Research Service, U.S.D.A.*   T.542

United States Imports of Manmade Fiber Manufactures   In Millions of Pounds

Year	Jan.	Feb.	Mar.	Apr.	May	June	July	Aug.	Sept.	Oct.	Nov.	Dec.	Total
1982	53.18	48.07	47.74	40.14	67.85	91.93	77.34	100.05	82.75	70.14	68.76	59.16	807.10
1983	79.98	71.92	76.53	73.20	86.99	105.55	98.14	108.25	98.34	106.84	85.83	77.93	1,069.5
1984	100.34	118.86	110.21	110.50	114.35	122.45	169.47	127.72	114.80	98.79	80.51	74.56	1,342.6
1985	96.06	116.00	115.84	97.15	130.83	133.94	146.30	127.64	158.29	132.32	122.32	114.33	1,491.0
1986	142.31	130.04	132.47	125.18	147.02	159.71	179.65	162.82	135.95	135.27	134.26	118.27	1,703.0
1987[1]	136.8	149.9	137.7	148.1	162.0	178.3	190.7	174.1	145.6	147.6	114.0	120.7	1,805.4
1988[1]	142.0	135.0	125.5	123.2	148.8	171.3	169.9	174.4	146.0				

[1] Preliminary.   *Source: Department of Commerce*   T.544

Producer Price Index of Gray Synthetic Broadwovens   (1982 = 100)

Year	Jan.	Feb.	Mar.	Apr.	May	June	July	Aug.	Sept.	Oct.	Nov.	Dec.	Average
1985	149.4	148.1	147.3	147.0	148.0	147.2	146.4	146.1	146.2	146.6	147.0	147.1	147.2
1986	147.1	147.3	147.2	147.9	147.2	147.4	147.5	145.9	144.1	145.1	145.0	145.1	146.3
1987[2]	101.9	101.9	102.2	103.4	103.9	105.3	106.4	106.9	107.9	108.6	109.0	109.2	105.6
1988[1]	110.0	111.1	111.6	111.8	112.2	113.0	113.4	113.7	113.2	113.7	113.7		

[1] Preliminary.   [2] Data prior to 1987 are for Dec. 1975 = 100.   *Source: Bureau of Labor Statistics. (0337-03)*   T.545

Rice

Tight supplies and higher prices in 1987/88 set the stage for increased rice production in 1988/89. U.S. rice output was put at 7.1 million tonnes, up 23 percent, and foreign production at 475 million tonnes, up 5 percent. Global trade and consumption were expected to rise substantially. While the U.S. stood to benefit from growth in trade, competition was keen. Major world exporters were Thailand, Burma, and Pakistan; major importers included Hong Kong, Indonesia, Middle Eastern countries, Nigeria, and the European Community.

Asian farmers were expected to expand 1988/89 production, assuming normal weather. Farmers in Thailand increased dry-season area planted to rice. Heavy rains and water from new wells improved dry-season crop prospects.

Demand for rice remained strong. India, for example, bought 500,000 tonnes from Thailand in mid-1988. The Philippines was expected to import 130,000 tonnes of rice from the U.S. under the PL 480 program in late 1988. China and Burma were unlikely to export as much as previously forecast, choosing instead to satisfy growing domestic demand and to increase stocks.

U.S. food use of rice was projected to rise by 1.5 million cwt. and brewers' use by 1 million. Rising preferences for grain-based foods, aggressive marketing, and more easy-to-prepare rice products have boosted consumption. Growth in the Asian and Hispanic populations and the popularity of Oriental and Spanish foods have helped. Brewers' use of rice shows year-to-year increases.

U.S. long grain production rose by 29 percent in 1988, while medium/short fell by 10 percent. Under the 1988 rice program, producers were allowed to plant up to 75 percent of their base acreage, compared with 65 percent in the previous three years. The 1988 program cut the target price to $11.15/cwt. from $11.66 in 1987. The loan rate was $6.63/cwt., compared with $6.84 in 1987.

A reduction in U.S. carry-in stocks nearly offset a production increase in 1988/89. Ending stocks were projected to remain at a low level of about 32 million cwt.

In early 1988, U.S. cash prices moved well above world prices, but eased when importers resisted the higher priced rice. Forecasts for increased Thai exports dampened world prices. U.S. prices in 1988/89 should be $5.00-$7.00/cwt., down from 1987/88, but much higher than two years ago.

Futures Market

Rough rice futures are traded on the Chicago Rice and Cotton Exchange.

World Rice[3] Supply & Distribution   In Millions of Metric Tons

Year	Production U.S.	Production Non-U.S.	Production Total	Exports U.S.	Exports Non-U.S.	Exports Total	Imports U.S.	Imports Non-U.S.	Imports Total	Utilization U.S.	Utilization Non-U.S.	Utilization Total	Stocks (End) U.S.	Stocks (End) Non-U.S.	Stocks (End) Total
1984	4.5	449.3	453.8	2.1	10.4	12.6	—	12.6	12.6	1.8	306.8	308.6	1.5	45.3	46.7
1985	6.3	461.9	468.2	1.9	9.6	11.5	—	11.5	11.5	1.9	308.7	310.6	2.1	52.8	54.9
1986	6.1	464.3	470.4	2.4	10.4	12.8	—	12.8	12.8	2.1	318.7	320.8	2.5	51.7	54.1
1987	6.0	461.7	467.7	2.4	10.3	12.7	—	12.7	12.7	2.5	320.1	322.5	1.6	48.3	49.9
1988[1]	5.8	447.3	453.1	2.2	9.0	11.2	—	11.2	11.2	2.5	313.9	316.4	1.0	41.3	42.3
1989[2]	7.1	462.9	470.0	2.6	9.8	12.4	—	12.4	12.4	2.6	319.6	322.2	1.0	38.9	39.9

[1] Preliminary.   [2] Forecast.   [3] Production is on rough basis; the rest are on milled basis.   *Source: Foreign Agricultural Service, U.S.D.A.*   T.547a

World Production of Rough Rice   In Millions of Metric Tons

Crop Year	Brazil	Burma	China	Vietnam	India	Japan	Indonesia	Rep. of Korea	Bangladesh	Philippines	Pakistan	Taiwan	Thailand	United States	World Total
1984–5	9.0	14.3	178.3	15.4	87.5	14.8	38.1	5.2	21.9	8.2	5.0	2.9	19.9	6.3	468.2
1985–6	10.3	13.3	168.6	15.0	95.7	14.6	39.0	5.3	22.6	8.7	4.4	2.9	20.3	6.1	470.4
1986–7	10.4	12.5	172.2	15.5	90.6	14.6	39.0	5.6	23.1	9.4	5.2	2.5	18.9	6.0	467.7
1987–8[1]	11.0	12.2	174.4		79.5	13.3	38.7	5.6	23.0		4.8		17.3	5.8	453.1
1988–9[2]	10.1	14.0	171.0		94.5	12.5	38.7	5.6	21.9		5.0		20.5	7.1	470.0

[1] Preliminary.   [2] Estimate.   *Source: Foreign Agricultural Service, U.S.D.A.*   T.547

World Exports of Rice (Milled Basis), by Country of Origin   In Thousands of Metric Tons

Year	Australia	Argentina	Guyana	Burma	P.R. China	Egypt (U.A.R.)	Uruguay	Pakistan	EC-12	Indonesia	India	Taiwan	Thailand	United States	World Total
1984	370	115	47	727	1,168	50	155	1,050	763	0	200	210	4,528	2,129	12,558
1985	450	165	35	450	1,010	16	231	962	885	392	200	40	3,993	1,906	11,465
1986	400	150	35	636	950	92	246	1,146	1,136	220	200	169	4,338	2,401	12,752
1987[1]	350	150	35	467	1,000	105	190	1,226	981	100	350	240	4,345	2,444	12,714
1988[2]	500	160	35	100	700	100	200	1,000	1,065	0	200	125	4,100	2,200	11,165

[1] Preliminary.   [2] Estimate.   *Source: Foreign Agricultural Service, U.S.D.A.*   T.552

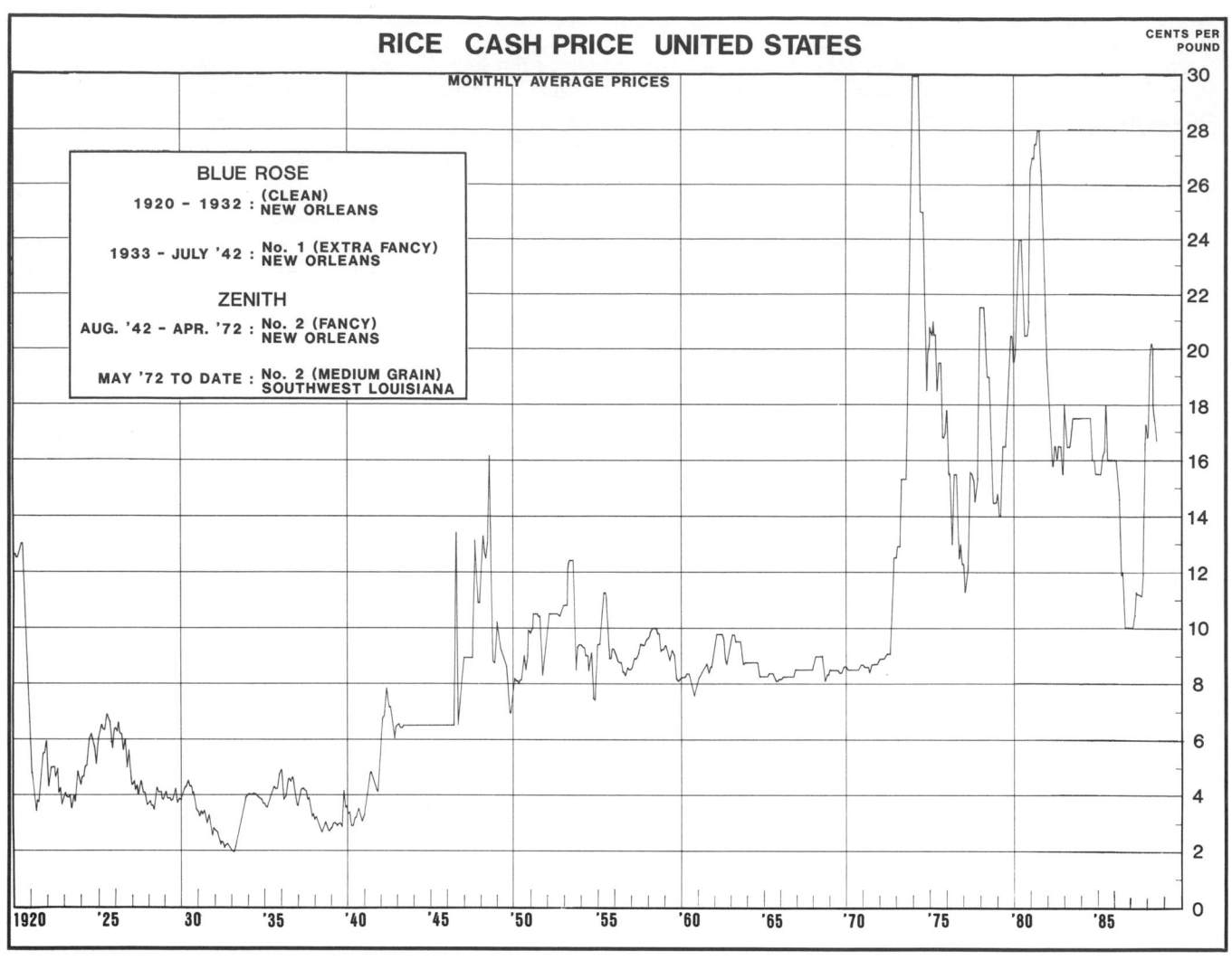

RICE CASH PRICE UNITED STATES

CENTS PER POUND

MONTHLY AVERAGE PRICES

BLUE ROSE
1920 - 1932 : (CLEAN) NEW ORLEANS

1933 - JULY '42 : No. 1 (EXTRA FANCY) NEW ORLEANS

ZENITH
AUG. '42 - APR. '72 : No. 2 (FANCY) NEW ORLEANS

MAY '72 TO DATE : No. 2 (MEDIUM GRAIN) SOUTHWEST LOUISIANA

Average Wholesale Price of Rice No. 2 (Medium Grain)[1] Southwest Louisiana   Dollars per cwt. bagged

Year	Aug.	Sept.	Oct.	Nov.	Dec.	Jan.	Feb.	Mar.	Apr.	May	June	July	Average
1979–0	19.0	20.0	20.5	20.5	19.5	20.0	22.0	23.5	24.0	24.0	22.0	21.0	21.3
1980–1	20.5	20.8	21.6	24.4	26.4	27.0	27.1	27.5	27.6	28.0	28.0	27.8	25.6
1981–2	26.4	24.2	22.9	21.2	20.0	18.8	17.8	16.1	16.0	16.4	16.2	16.0	19.3
1982–3	16.5	16.5	16.5	16.7	17.8	17.3	16.5	16.5	16.5	17.1	17.5	17.5	16.9
1983–4	17.5	17.5	17.5	17.5	17.5	17.5	17.5	17.5	17.5	17.5	17.5	17.5	17.5
1984–5	16.0	16.0	15.5	15.5	15.5	15.5	15.5	16.0	16.2	16.3	18.0	16.2	16.0
1985–6	16.0	16.0	16.0	16.0	16.0	16.0	15.67	15.5	14.57	11.92	12.0	11.33	14.75
1986–7	10.0	10.0	10.0	10.0	10.0	10.0	10.0	10.49	11.25	11.15	11.22	11.18	10.45
1987–8[2]	11.1	12.0	16.6	17.3	16.8	18.5	19.8	20.15	20.00	18.0	17.4	16.7	17.00

[1] U.S. No. 2—Broken not to exceed 4%.   [2] Preliminary.   *Source: Bureau of Labor Statistics (0213–0101)*   T.549

U.S. Rice (Rough) Production by Type and Variety   In Thousands of Cwt.

Year	Long Grain	Medium Grain	Short Grain	Total	Year	Long Grain	Medium Grain	Short Grain	Total
1983	64,318	27,388	8,014	99,720	1986	96,773	32,239	4,344	133,356
1984	96,029	35,304	7,477	138,810	1987	88,912	34,996	3,817	127,725
1985	100,367	28,464	6,082	134,913	1988[1]	115,085	38,571	3,014	156,670

[1] Preliminary.   *Source: Crop Reporting Board, U.S.D.A.*   T.548

Salient Statistics of Rice, Rough & Milled (Rough Equivalent) in the United States   In Millions of Cwt.

Year Beginning August	Supply				Disappearance						Total Disappearance	Owned By CCC July 31	Put Under Price Support	Government Support Program Loan Rate ($ CWT.)			
	Stocks Aug. 1	Pro-duction	Im-ports[2]	Total Supply	Domestic				Exp-orts	Res-id-ual				Rough		Milled Long	All Classes
					Food[3]	Brew-ers	Seed	Total						Long	Med & Short		
1982–3	49.0	153.6	.7	203.3	37.3	13.5	3.2	54.0	68.9	8.9	131.8	22.3	65.8	8.86	7.74	14.75	8.14
1983–4	71.5	99.7	.9	172.1	33.2	12.8	3.3	49.3	70.3	5.6	125.2	25.0	40.0	9.12	7.58	14.96	8.14
1984–5	46.9	138.8	.6	187.3	35.8	13.9	2.8	52.5	62.1	8.0	122.6	44.3	57.8	9.12	6.80	14.96	8.00
1985–6	64.7	134.9	2.2	201.8	45.6	14.1	2.6	62.3	58.7	3.5	124.5	43.6	75.0	8.86	6.60	14.53	8.00
1986–7	77.3	133.4	2.6	213.3	53.1	15.0	2.6	70.7	84.2	7.0	161.9	8.7	132.0	7.57	6.45	12.44	7.20
1987–8[4]	51.4	127.7	3.0	182.3	53.4	15.4	3.0	71.8	72.2	6.7	150.7	0		7.04	6.48	11.36	6.84
1988–9[4]	31.4	156.7	3.2	191.3	56.0	16.0	3.2	75.2	77.0	7.0	159.2	0		6.75	6.19	10.89	6.63

[1] Preliminary.   [2] Consists mostly of broken rice.   [3] Includes shipments to territories and military food use.   [4] Projected.   *Source: Economic Research Service, U.S.D.A.*
T.551

Acreage, Yield, Production, and Prices of Rice in the United States

Crop Year	Acreage Harvested (1,000 Acres)			Yield Per Harvested Acre (In Lbs.)		Production 1,000 Cwt.			Farm Value of Pro-duction $1,000	Wholesale Prices ($ Per Cwt.)		$ Per Tonne Milled Rice Average C.I.F. At Rotterdam		
	Southern States	California	United States	California	United States	Southern States	California	United States		Arkansas[2]	Houston[3]	U.S. No. 2[4]	Thai "A"[5]	Thai "B"[5]
1982–3	2,727	535	3,262	6,700	4,710	117,740	35,848	153,637	1,246,608	16.80	18.70	488	367	336
1983–4	1,841	328	2,169	7,040	4,598	76,631	23,089	99,720	874,004	17.35	19.88	527	369	328
1984–5	2,352	450	2,802	7,120	4,954	106,750	32,060	138,810	1,119,373	16.23	18.69	495	300	267
1985–6	2,102	390	2,492	7,300	5,414	106,445	28,468	134,913	893,377	15.22	16.84	418	276	236
1986–7	2,000	360	2,360	7,700	5,651	105,629	27,727	133,356	500,000	12.22	11.59	260	279	232
1987–8[1]	1,963	367	2,330	7,100	5,482	101,668	26,057	127,725	887,500	17.80	19.85	408	359	318
1988–9[1]	2,436	420	2,856	7,100	5,486	126,850	29,820	156,670	940,200					

[1] Preliminary.   [2] F.O.B. mills, Arkansas, medium.   [3] Houston, Texas (long grain).   [4] Milled, 4%, Bagged.   [5] SWR 100% Bagged.   *Source: Economic Research Service, U.S.D.A.*
T.550

U.S. Exports of Milled Rice[1] by Country of Destination   In Thousands of Metric Tons

Crop Year	Belg.-Lux.	South Africa	Cana-da	United Kingd.	South Korea	Niger-ia	Indo-nesia	Italy	Bangla-desh	Liberia	Saudi Arabia	Switzer-land	Iraq	Iran	Total Exports
1981–2	118.4	114.1	101.0	30.5	281.6	412.8	15.8	201.4	22.6	88.4	277.7	91.1	221.1	147.2	2,682
1982–3	114.9	109.3	100.6	26.2	187.8	168.7	63.4	11.6	67.3	91.3	279.1	57.2	279.2	—	2,219
1983–4	135.3	154.5	94.1	4.2	98.9	82.7	81.6	51.0	55.7	83.5	285.7	65.1	274.8	0	1,644
1984–5	133.1	83.6	97.6	9.4	.1	.5	3.0		80.3	52.5	240.8	55.4	380.4	0	1,961
1985–6[2]	94.4	61.4	82.9	15.4	.1	—	2.0		0	81.1	174.3	41.3	455.8	0	1,881

[1] No adjustment of brown & parboiled rice has been made; treated as milled rice.   [2] Preliminary. *Source: Bureau of the Census, Dept. of Commerce*
T.553

Exports of Rice from the United States   In Millions of Pounds[1] (Clean Basis)

Year	Aug.	Sept.	Oct.	Nov.	Dec.	Jan.	Feb.	Mar.	Apr.	May	June	July	Total
1984–5	384	567	331	343	307	236	292	411	315	355	296	336	4,173
1985–6	380	489	417	290	283	277	163	249	208	212	450	603	4,021
1986–7	778	835	565	446	323	343	411	365	399	560	254	582	5,861
1987–8	474	439	556	517	349	409	299	411	333	486	278	373	4,924

[1] 162 pounds rough—100 pounds clean.   *Source: Department of Commerce*
T.554

Average Price Received by Farmers for Rice (Rough) in the U.S.   In Dollars Per 100 Pounds (Cwt.)

Year	Aug.	Sept.	Oct.	Nov.	Dec.	Jan.	Feb.	Mar.	Apr.	May	June	July	Average[1]
1982–3	7.31	7.75	7.73	7.78	8.06	8.05	8.26	7.99	8.23	8.23	7.88	7.95	7.91
1983–4	8.41	8.48	8.80	8.80	8.66	8.57	8.85	8.63	8.49	8.24	8.20	8.18	8.57
1984–5	8.22	8.17	8.08	8.13	8.08	8.09	7.72	8.17	8.20	7.91	7.83	7.54	8.04
1985–6	7.86	7.55	7.73	7.84	7.71	7.90	7.86	7.60	5.32	4.52	4.04	3.86	6.53
1986–7	3.95	3.82	3.89	3.91	3.76	3.61	3.80	3.68	3.64	3.74	3.68	3.65	3.75
1987–8[2]	3.74	4.32	5.88	7.08	7.37	7.70	8.97	8.79	8.33	7.71	7.29	7.51	6.95
1988–9[2]	7.42	6.82	7.15										

[1] Weighted average by sales.   [2] Preliminary.   *Source: Crop Reporting Board, U.S.D.A.*
T.555

Rubber

World natural rubber output averaged nearly 4 million tonnes a year in the first half of the 1980s, but the second-half average was likely to be much higher. Production was 4.7 million tonnes in 1987 and was expected to rise about 5 percent in 1988. However, the Malaysian Rubber Exchange and Licensing Board said 1988 output would be about 150,000 tonnes below estimated demand of 5.14 million tonnes. The shortfall was met by sales from the International Rubber Agreement's stockpile.

Malaysia, the largest producer, accounted for about 35 percent of world output in 1987 and 1988. Indonesia produced about 20 percent, and Thailand about 17 percent. This ranking was expected to persist, although Thailand was slowly closing in on Indonesia. India and China have shown steady production growth, but their combined output was well under Thailand's. Output was slowly rising in parts of West Africa.

Producers exported more than 80 percent of their natural rubber crops in 1988. Also, they expanded domestic production of rubber gloves and other items to meet surging demand caused by the AIDS epidemic. Indonesia alone was building 20 rubber glove factories in 1988; they were expected to produce 787 million pairs by 1990. Synthetics cannot compete with natural latex in medical applications.

The U.S., which produces no natural rubber, was the largest importer, taking about 750,000 tonnes a year during the mid-1980s. U.S. imports in the first half of 1988 ran ahead of the 1987 pace, which for the full year was 769,000 tonnes. Japan was the second largest importer. Collectively, however, Western Europe imports more natural rubber than the U.S. does.

Synthetic rubber production, which was about double natural rubber output during the mid-1980s, was accelerating as 1988 ended. World synthetic rubber output in 1987 was 9.5 million tonnes. It was forecast to be near 9.8 million tonnes in 1988. The USSR was the largest synthetic rubber producer, followed by the U.S. and Japan; together, they produced about 61 percent of the world's output in 1987 and a bit more in 1988. The U.S., which outproduced Western Europe, exported 15-20 percent of its production. The USSR consumed most of its output.

Natural rubber consumption generally is separated into tires and general rubber products (GRP) groupings. However, about half the GRP consumed in the non-communist world also ends up in automobiles. In the 1980s, an increasing percentage of natural rubber went into tires to meet rising demand for radials, especially outside of Western Europe, while synthetic rubber gained market share in the GRP sector.

The International Institute of Synthetic Rubber Producers forecast North American synthetic rubber usage in 1988 at 2.655 million tonnes, above 2.583 million in 1987. Due to the dollar's softness, U.S. exports of manufactured items rose, boosting demand for synthetic rubber.

U.S. tire production, which averaged about 160 million tires a year in the mid-1980s, was 168 million in 1987 and ran above the year-earlier level in the first half of 1988. Radials, which require more natural rubber than bias-ply tires, had steadily gained passenger car market share. They rose from about 68 percent of production in 1982 to almost 90 percent in 1987. Truck and bus radial production also grew. On a GRP basis, U.S. output in 1987 was about 26 percent over 1982 levels. First-half 1988 output was about 35 percent higher than 1982's rate. In contrast, Japan's GRP production was flat during the 1980s. Using 1980 as a base of 100, Japan's 1987 GRP was at 98.7.

Natural rubber prices soared in the first half of 1988, reaching $1,557/tonne for no. 1 smoked sheets at midyear. The 1987 average was $1,113. World rubber prices also made 8-year highs in 1988. But as 1988 was ending, prices had retreated to levels prevailing earlier in the year. For 1989, some price slippage was expected, assuming a slowing economy in the U.S.--if not in other key consuming nations--and increased world production.

The U.S. joined the second International Rubber Agreement on November 9, 1988. The agreement uses a stockpile system to stabilize world rubber prices. The previous pact had expired on October 1.

Futures Markets

Rubber futures are listed for trading in Kuala Lumpur, Tokyo, and Singapore.

U.S. Imports of Natural Rubber (Includes Latex & Guayule) In Thousands of Long Tons

Year	Jan.	Feb.	Mar.	Apr.	May	June	July	Aug.	Sept.	Oct.	Nov.	Dec.	Total[1]
1981	30.06	86.64	53.38	67.62	66.36	50.47	41.59	43.40	62.76	69.42	56.23	49.13	662.4
1982	50.99	59.33	45.71	53.86	56.19	63.39	38.67	54.35	40.60	54.36	51.37	49.45	618.3
1983	33.01	49.63	48.54	62.11	63.44	65.20	50.41	31.90	44.22	67.83	71.06	54.71	642.1
1984	87.84	57.82	75.45	69.18	70.25	41.45	73.81	56.23	67.46	61.95	62.36	62.21	786.0
1985	71.64	71.68	88.04	63.98	84.66	48.09	59.97	45.30	40.73	69.44	71.81	64.49	779.8
1986	63.64	70.32	76.62	83.12	47.64	54.01	68.96	44.47	62.91	72.34	53.13	55.83	753.0
1987[2]	55.0	89.9	80.7	32.7	63.6	58.0	63.2	46.8	58.5	56.8	62.9	77.7	745.7
1988[2]	81.9	68.5	85.7	67.5	66.2	63.8	48.7	81.9	58.2	68.2			

[1] Includes latex and guayule. [2] Preliminary. *Source: Department of Commerce* T.560

World Rubber Production[1]   In Thousands of Metric Tons

Year	Sri Lanka	India	Indonesia	Malaysia	Philippines	Thailand	Liberia	Brazil	China	World Total	Canada	West Germany	Japan	United States	United Kingdom	USSR	World Total
					Natural								Synthetic				
1980	133.2	155.4	1,020	1,530	69.9	501.1	77.5	27.8	113.0	3,850	252.8	389.9	1,094	2,215	211.8	2,040	8,695
1981	123.9	150.7	867.5	1,510	75.3	504.0	77.5	30.3	127.7	3,705	263.3	396.8	1,010	2,225	226.2	2,000	8,545
1982	126.2	165.9	880.0	1,494	74.2	552.2	68.0	32.8	152.6	3,750	181.7	383.8	930.7	1,817	207.6	1,950	7,825
1983	140.0	168.0	997.2	1,564	69.9	587.2	76.5	35.2	172.4	4,030	182.0	418.0	1,003	1,987	219.5	1,970	8,275
1984	141.9	183.9	1,116	1,531	76.6	628.6	86.4	36.0	188.8	4,250	217.8	437.6	1,161	2,219	237.2	2,085	9,055
1985	137.5	198.3	1,130	1,470	85.3	725.7	84.4	40.4	187.9	4,335	209.2	447.6	1,158	2,026	232.6	2,125	8,955
1986[2]	137.8	219.0	1,034	1,539	89.0	782.1	88.7	32.6	211.0	4,435	187.1	452.5	1,150	2,119	249.2	2,320	9,205
1987[3]	121.8	227.4	1,190	1,581	83.0	810.0	84.0	26.6	140.0	4,705	179.8	468.4	1,192	2,182	257.0	2,370	9,460

[1] Including rubber in the form of latex.   [2] Preliminary.   [3] Estimate.   *Source: Rubber Study Group*   T.556

World Consumption of Natural and Synthetic Rubber   In Thousands of Metric Tons

Year	Australia	Brazil	Canada	France	West Germany	Japan	United Kingdom	United States	World Total	Canada	France	West Germany	Japan	United Kingdom	United States	World Total
					Natural							Synthetic				
1980	42.2	81.1	80.0	187.7	179.7	427.0	130.8	585.0	3,760	200.0	341.9	421.3	885.0	248.2	1,980	8,785
1981	41.9	74.4	82.0	169.0	169.1	436.0	120.0	635.0	3,700	210.0	303.4	396.2	851.0	247.0	2,022	8,565
1982	36.4	67.8	76.0	158.0	171.2	439.0	118.0	585.0	3,655	182.0	265.2	386.9	797.0	232.0	1,765	8,035
1983	30.9	70.2	87.0	163.0	179.5	504.0	120.0	665.0	3,990	195.0	276.6	395.8	851.0	228.0	1,883	8,360
1984	35.9	88.7	102.0	162.0	190.0	525.0	118.0	750.7	4,230	280.0	287.0	403.0	915.0	247.0	2,062	9,030
1985	35.8	97.6	95.0	156.0	202.2	539.5	126.0	764.0	4,345	173.0	311.8	411.3	947.5	238.0	1,999	9,045
1986[1]	30.6	105.6	86.0	158.7	198.7	535.0	130.0	743.0	4,420	178.0	301.6	423.2	910.0	231.3	2,075	9,175
1987[2]	35.5	121.0	98.0	170.0	198.5	568.0	134.0	789.0	4,760							

[1] Preliminary.   [2] Estimate.   *Source: Rubber Study Group*   T.557

World Stocks[1] of Natural Rubber, January 1   In Thousands of Metric Tons

Year	Brazil	Vietnam	Sri Lanka	Indonesia	Malaysia (Peninsular)	Singapore	Thailand	Total	Australia	Canada	China	France	West Germany	India	Japan	United Kingdom	United States	Total
			In Producing Countries								In Consuming Countries (Commercial Stocks)							
1980	20.8	4.0	61.3	75.0	240.1	51.1	44.7	515	3.8	7.3	135.0	20.3	13.5	54.6	76.5	27.6	144.6	735
1981	20.8	4.0	58.5	75.0	254.8	46.3	61.0	535	3.2	6.0	150.0	19.6	13.5	40.1	106.9	21.4	126.7	770
1982	19.6	4.0	33.7	75.0	286.3	43.8	60.0	535	2.7	9.9	140.0	16.8	14.5	45.9	116.9	20.0	131.9	835
1983	18.5	4.0	11.3	75.0	266.0	26.9	36.6	570	4.2	6.9	137.5	9.5	14.5	60.6	90.8	17.8	95.4	860
1984	15.3	4.0	9.6	75.0	254.9	32.2	39.6	545	1.8	7.4	185.0	9.0	14.5	47.4	81.0	16.8	80.8	870
1985	11.2	5.0	10.2	95.0	228.8	36.8	41.3	545	2.8	8.5	187.5	4.0	15.0	58.0	70.7	15.8	96.4	910
1986	13.5	6.0	12.2	90.0	191.8	22.0	47.1	515	2.6	9.0	122.5	4.0	15.0	58.2	70.7	10.0	95.2	875
1987[2]	13.3	6.0	23.6	72.5	207.3	21.6	32.5	515	2.6	12.0	105.0	3.0	15.0	85.5	61.9	10.5	73.0	865
1988[3]	13.5	6.0	20.0	72.5	208.5	21.6	40.0	470	2.5	12.5	85.0	6.0	15.0	77.6	63.6	10.5	72.5	800

[1] Exclusive of "Stock Afloat" and unreported gov't. stockpiles.   [2] Preliminary.   [3] Estimate.   *Source: Rubber Study Group* (London)   T.558

Net Exports of Natural Rubber from Producing Areas   In Thousands of Metric Tons

Year	Burma	Kampuchea	Sri Lanka (Ceylon)	Indonesia	Malaysia (Peninsular)	Sabah	Sarawak	Thailand	Vietnam	Other Asia	Liberia	Nigeria	Other Africa	Papua New Guinea	World Total
1980		—	120.9	976.1	1,416	30.9	35.2	456.8	33.3	30.5	76.5	14.6	59.2	4.0	3,270
1981		4.0	132.5	808.7	1,402	25.5	28.2	476.0	33.7	30.8	76.9	23.6	57.5	4.5	3,110
1982		7.5	131.3	801.4	1,317	21.7	15.9	546.7	32.3	24.2	60.1	26.8	57.8	2.3	3,065
1983		10.0	125.2	938.0	1,498	21.5	18.9	552.5	35.8	19.0	73.6	28.8	62.0	2.7	3,370
1984		12.0	126.2	1,010	1,486	25.2	18.0	595.2	35.0	19.0	87.9	28.8	65.5	3.0	3,515
1985		14.0	120.4	1,001	1,426	22.0	17.4	685.3	35.5	24.7	87.2	29.1	69.0	5.1	3,605
1986[1]		20.0	110.0	958.7	1,444	24.6	16.3	755.2	35.0	30.3	90.4	34.4	78.0	4.9	3,615
1987[2]		20.0	106.0	1,093	1,529	29.5	19.9	900.0	48.0	24.3	84.0	36.5	94.0	4.0	3,965

[1] Preliminary.   [2] Estimate.   *Source: Rubber Study Group* (London)   T.559

RUBBER

Average Spot Crude Rubber Prices (Smoked Sheets[1]) in New York   In Cents Per Pound

Year	Jan.	Feb.	Mar.	Apr.	May	June	July	Aug.	Sept.	Oct.	Nov.	Dec.	Average
1981	71.3	69.0	65.0	59.0	58.0	57.0	56.0	54.0	50.4	—	45.6	48.3	57.6
1982	48.8	46.5	47.0	45.3	45.3	46.1	46.5	46.8	44.5	42.6	42.1	41.8	45.3
1983	44.0	48.5	57.8	57.8	56.8	54.5	58.3	59.3	60.5	60.5	58.3	—	56.0
1984	57.3	58.3	58.0	56.8	51.8	47.0	46.0	46.0	46.0	43.0	42.8	42.0	49.6
1985	42.3	42.3	41.8	42.3	40.8	42.0	40.3	41.8	41.8	43.8	42.5	39.8	41.8
1986	40.7	42.8	42.0	39.2	40.1	41.0	43.5	43.5	45.3	46.9	44.7	44.7	42.9
1987	45.9	46.5	43.8	47.4	49.1	50.6	53.5	53.7	54.2	53.8	53.1	54.0	50.5
1988	54.6	53.8	54.9	55.7	58.6	67.6	66.1	63.8	60.1	55.2	53.0	54.1	58.1

[1] No. 1, ribbed, plantation rubber.   *Source: Bureau of Labor Statistics (07–11–02.01); Wall St. Journal; CRB.*

T.561

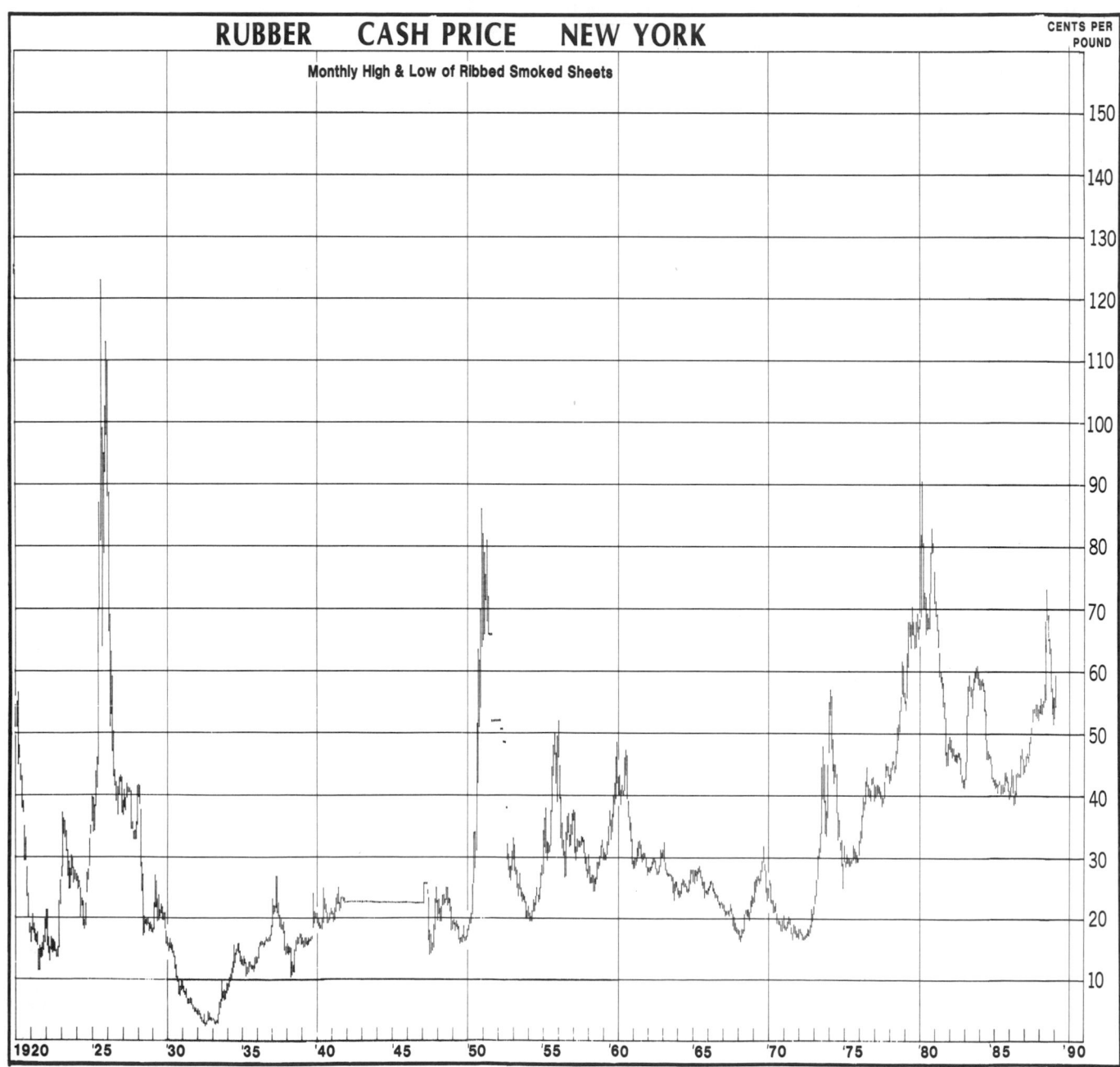

RUBBER   CASH PRICE   NEW YORK

CENTS PER POUND

Monthly High & Low of Ribbed Smoked Sheets

Consumption of Natural Rubber in the United States In Thousands of Metric Tons

Year	Jan.	Feb.	Mar.	Apr.	May	June	July	Aug.	Sept.	Oct.	Nov.	Dec.	Total
1979	68.3	66.6	74.5	61.8	60.2	59.0	57.9	63.2	57.7	65.2	55.6	47.9	739.00
1980	63.0	57.3	55.7	46.9	42.3	41.3	38.8	43.2	49.4	49.5	50.3	48.7	586.15
1981	49.0	52.6	55.4	55.1	53.9	59.5	56.4	51.1	52.1	57.3	49.7	42.6	634.67
1982	55.3	59.9	50.2	57.8	63.3	68.9	32.7	65.6	48.8	53.3	48.9	56.0	660.61
1983	64.5	44.5	55.3	55.3	56.9	67.0	48.8	39.2	50.2	75.3	69.7	49.6	676.27
1984	73.8	56.8	83.1	68.2	65.1	42.4	73.9	56.1	63.7	58.3	55.4	54.1	750.74
1985	71.8	65.7	91.5	51.7	89.0	45.2	55.4	47.3	68.1	47.2	65.7	52.4	774.69
1986	59.4	71.8	71.3	81.9	45.5	54.6	69.9	49.9	57.0	80.3	50.8	51.2	743.56
1987[1]	49.9	85.4	81.3	62.3	62.6	56.3	67.4	61.4	61.9	57.4	60.6	69.4	775.38
1988[1]	79.1	65.2	88.1	58.7	65.7	60.5	49.1	76.8	61.1				

[1] Preliminary. *Source: Rubber Manufacturers' Association*   T.562

Stocks of Natural Rubber in the United States, Beginning of Month In Thousands of Metric Tons

Year	Jan.	Feb.	Mar.	Apr.	May	June	July	Aug.	Sept.	Oct.	Nov.	Dec.
1979	125.6	121.4	115.6	116.1	136.6	130.2	137.7	146.0	144.4	135.6	135.0	124.5
1980	132.1	131.4	135.3	141.4	152.4	145.7	147.4	149.9	138.5	132.9	129.5	123.1
1981	126.7	128.0	125.4	122.8	127.6	124.1	119.5	113.5	111.2	114.4	123.0	130.5
1982	142.4	127.1	126.5	121.3	116.6	110.8	105.4	110.2	97.7	89.0	90.2	95.4
1983	95.4	91.8	95.0	87.4	93.8	100.0	97.9	99.2	90.7	83.3	74.8	75.9
1984	80.8	95.2	95.7	87.7	87.8	91.4	88.5	87.0	84.8	86.2	87.3	91.3
1985	96.4	94.3	97.3	91.4	101.9	95.9	95.6	97.9	93.9	84.9	81.1	85.1
1986	95.2	97.0	96.9	100.4	98.6	98.6	96.7	93.8	86.4	91.6	75.3	78.2
1987[1]	38.5	76.7	78.8	70.2	80.2	79.5	79.0	82.5	77.0	70.6	65.9	65.5
1988[1]	72.5	74.9	75.3	70.7	74.6	72.9	71.6	68.7	71.0	63.7		

[1] Preliminary. *Source: Rubber Manufacturers' Association*   T.563

Stocks of Synthetic Rubber in the United States, Beginning of Month In Thousands of Metric Tons

Year	Jan.	Feb.	Mar.	Apr.	May	June	July	Aug.	Sept.	Oct.	Nov.	Dec.
1978	426.8	441.0	427.9	434.5	446.9	441.4	433.1	456.5	445.1	435.8	425.3	419.9
1979	424.1	407.1	400.0	393.6	398.9	391.5	401.3	411.3	402.2	402.8	389.9	402.1
1980	402.9	439.9	436.2	427.6	452.2	445.1	429.2	391.2	372.3	339.7	325.4	328.9
1981	341.8	364.5	354.6	347.0	365.9	368.3	359.8	369.4	353.4	351.9	352.6	364.4
1982	349.0	333.3	336.8	349.2	358.3	364.4	352.9	342.8	326.6	304.3	318.8	294.6
1983	269.7	281.0	284.8	283.5	283.8	294.3	290.8	304.8	269.8	256.2	250.7	276.9
1984	277.9	284.1	277.2	277.0	294.6	305.0	302.3	309.3	300.6	312.0	301.4	285.9
1985	272.1	281.2	271.8	288.6	294.0	398.0	247.8	295.8	413.5	397.3	374.9	367.0
1986	213.9	352.8	217.5	397.7	403.0	238.6	247.5	239.9	233.4	236.5	231.1	224.6
1987[1]	235.6	247.0	249.4	242.6	240.3	242.2	241.8	251.9	240.6	222.8	213.6	213.8
1988[1]	220.7	237.8	235.1	229.6	237.5	246.2	249.6	261.0	259.6	257.9		

[1] Preliminary. *Source: Department of Commerce*   T.564

Production of Synthetic Rubber in the United States In Thousands of Metric Tons

Year	Jan.	Feb.	Mar.	Apr.	May	June	July	Aug.	Sept.	Oct.	Nov.	Dec.	Total
1978	198.2	193.8	210.3	214.9	211.2	194.4	195.9	205.7	207.4	212.3	212.1	219.1	2,475
1979	207.9	200.8	232.1	216.7	223.3	210.7	202.9	202.8	210.0	213.8	206.0	207.6	2,535
1980	195.6	194.7	206.8	192.4	159.6	129.6	110.3	123.7	149.8	174.6	178.5	193.7	2,015
1981	193.5	169.7	200.4	180.9	175.9	158.2	161.5	159.7	168.4	170.0	157.7	125.5	2,021
1982	155.6	162.3	187.9	171.7	171.1	156.8	139.7	145.5	147.9	154.4	122.4	116.5	1,829
1983	155.2	153.9	170.1	160.5	171.1	164.6	154.4	146.7	159.6	174.5	189.4	160.2	1,936
1984	183.3	173.0	190.3	193.2	191.4	183.7	166.7	178.4	173.0	179.7	158.3	147.5	2,156
1985	169.9	161.6	182.1	166.0	154.2	139.5	150.4	154.2	160.3	153.6	149.2	131.8	1,838
1986	166.5	156.7	189.1	178.6	167.8	164.9	155.3	170.5	178.6	186.7	145.6	174.7	2,013
1987[1]	187.1	177.5	193.6	174.1	179.8	175.0	186.2	164.2	176.0	191.0	182.9	194.8	2,184
1988[1]	187.0	179.1	201.2	193.7	205.4	197.4	187.4	200.4	189.6				

[1] Preliminary. *Source: Department of Commerce*   T.565

RUBBER

Consumption of Synthetic Rubber in the United States   In Thousands of Metric Tons

Year	Jan.	Feb.	Mar.	Apr.	May	June	July	Aug.	Sept.	Oct.	Nov.	Dec.	Total
1978	193.7	193.2	206.2	197.5	212.7	194.7	170.6	213.9	211.7	220.3	212.1	209.8	2,436
1979	226.0	201.4	224.4	201.5	212.0	179.6	176.5	202.3	187.9	202.8	174.5	163.3	2,341
1980	170.8	176.1	191.1	148.9	135.7	120.1	131.0	133.7	166.0	167.9	157.7	155.1	1,854
1981	153.0	166.7	194.0	144.9	167.1	154.1	144.7	165.0	163.5	163.8	141.1	131.9	1,890
1982	153.3	140.7	154.3	145.3	148.5	154.5	135.8	150.5	158.1	131.0	136.8	136.1	1,757
1983	131.7	140.2	158.2	146.3	146.2	156.7	135.6	170.3	170.5	180.4	158.2	147.2	1,828
1984	177.5	175.4	180.5	166.7	167.1	171.0	147.1	173.9	151.5	184.1	166.3	147.2	2,062
1985	155.8	169.5	159.6	154.8	163.6	137.9	139.8	150.6	171.6	174.3	154.0	140.3	1,802
1986	160.7	145.0	175.7	157.6	163.9	148.0	151.5	168.5	160.6	177.5	145.8	155.7	1,895
1987[1]	162.8	166.1	182.8	160.5	163.1	157.8	161.9	163.6	172.2	185.1	167.6	174.1	2,017
1988[1]	158.5	166.8	186.8	163.1	172.1	166.3	160.9	171.4	162.5				

[1] Preliminary.   *Source: Department of Commerce*   T.566

Exports of Synthetic Rubber from the United States   In Thousands of Long Tons

Year	Jan.	Feb.	Mar.	Apr.	May	June	July	Aug.	Sept.	Oct.	Nov.	Dec.	Total
1978	16.94	18.86	22.55	19.48	24.90	22.28	19.35	20.04	20.77	22.22	23.81	23.77	254.97
1979	23.62	22.29	27.74	29.43	28.74	34.61	34.51	39.37	34.90	38.61	36.53	34.76	385.11
1980	31.46	34.48	41.98	41.68	46.88	37.33	36.54	30.46	25.51	33.45	30.72	32.31	422.80
1981	31.21	31.65	38.73	31.77	32.00	28.55	26.27	21.97	24.40	23.94	22.49	21.65	334.63
1982	27.76	23.46	31.18	26.53	24.73	25.23	20.40	22.04	22.83	21.13	20.47	18.86	284.62
1983	20.24	18.61	24.44	24.91	31.66	24.37	20.15	21.08	22.01	20.14	23.75	23.67	275.03
1984	24.12	22.22	28.09	29.13	29.42	28.02	29.58	30.24	29.95	25.54	25.92	25.68	327.91
1985	23.86	22.68	28.88	26.23	30.38	27.25	22.21	24.95	27.60	25.33	22.13	25.44	306.94
1986	23.49	27.66	24.00	35.39	25.71	25.04	26.34	31.77	34.24	30.39	27.78	27.04	338.85
1987[1]	31.91	32.69	35.49	36.48	38.79	36.34	33.56	32.75	38.23	32.93	36.94	36.53	422.65
1988[1]	39.07	36.76	41.11	41.02	39.79	40.47	29.29	43.34	38.01	36.59			

[1] Preliminary.   *Source: Department of Commerce*   T.567

Production of Auto. Pneumatic Casings[2] & Truck & Bus Retail Sales[1] in the U.S.   In Ths. of Casings

Year	Jan.	Feb.	Mar.	Apr.	May	June	July	Aug.	Sept.	Oct.	Nov.	Dec.	Total	Retail Sales[1]
1978	18,290	18,319	18,987	18,828	19,148	18,946	15,108	19,245	19,155	20,497	18,299	18,869	223,406	3,921
1979	20,352	19,592	21,807	18,609	18,544	15,603	14,904	16,911	15,985	17,775	14,480	12,340	206,687	3,120
1980	15,188	15,059	15,082	13,678	11,370	10,716	10,206	12,057	13,911	15,790	12,861	13,346	159,263	2,003
1981	15,434	15,614	16,805	15,438	15,157	15,447	14,321	15,443	15,894	16,604	13,750	11,855	181,762	1,808
1982	14,866	15,387	17,051	15,077	14,856	15,669	12,293	14,835	15,528	15,381	13,585	13,972	178,500	2,152
1983	15,497	14,992	15,370	16,325	15,653	15,473	12,570	16,440	16,360	16,734	15,136	15,483	186,923	2,654
1984	16,749	17,498	19,122	16,988	18,043	18,557	15,546	18,078	17,333	19,136	16,645	15,682	209,375	3,485
1985	18,381	17,375	18,704	17,388	16,781	15,216	12,989	16,635	16,844	17,626	15,198	13,786	196,923	3,913
1986	16,306	15,966	16,968	16,037	15,003	14,647	14,203	16,112	16,540	18,180	15,144	15,183	190,289	3,947
1987[3]	16,879	16,593	17,733	16,680	16,982	16,548	15,796	16,723	17,204	18,956	16,455	16,428	202,978	4,088
1988[3]	17,345	18,027	19,305	17,642	17,403	17,941	15,022	18,058	18,115					

[1] Domestic & imports, in thousands.   [2] Passenger cars, buses, trucks & motorcycle tires.   [3] Preliminary.
Sources: Rubber Manufacturers' Association; Motor Vehicle Manufacturing Association   T.568

Stocks of Auto. Pneumatic Casings & Passenger[1] Car Retail Sales in the U.S.   In Ths. of Casings

Year	Jan. 1	Feb. 1	Mar. 1	Apr. 1	May 1	June 1	July 1	Aug. 1	Sept. 1	Oct. 1	Nov. 1	Dec. 1	Retail Sales[1]
1978	47,181	51,523	54,621	51,986	50,006	49,277	46,293	44,280	44,057	41,796	40,135	40,394	11,164
1979	43,472	47,212	51,284	52,223	53,540	53,033	46,362	49,397	48,422	46,002	44,357	44,546	10,559
1980	44,873	46,760	49,993	50,471	49,220	46,972	42,817	40,079	37,057	33,730	32,112	32,363	8,979
1981	33,298	41,226	44,402	45,217	44,713	43,480	41,445	39,998	39,601	38,986	39,487	41,112	8,535
1982	40,863	42,904	46,254	47,817	46,583	45,337	43,475	40,763	40,192	38,685	38,116	38,436	7,980
1983	39,955	43,839	45,483	50,287	51,921	42,395	39,622	36,989	35,541	32,854	31,530	31,676	9,179
1984	33,340	35,450	37,615	38,529	38,026	37,693	37,678	36,365	37,199	37,685	37,277	37,995	10,394
1985	39,623	41,948	45,905	48,875	49,168	49,063	46,909	44,349	43,553	41,514	40,425	40,023	11,039
1986	39,823	40,717	43,499	45,359	44,519	44,741	40,009	38,036	36,836	34,890	34,130	33,681	11,450
1987[2]	34,286	36,323	38,341	40,673	39,962	40,312	37,872	37,344	37,501	36,234	34,539	33,702	10,278
1988[2]	34,338	37,047	39,904	40,737	41,149	40,159	37,976	37,355	36,064	34,771			

[1] Domestic & imports, in thousands.   [2] Preliminary.   *Sources: Rubber Manufacturers' Association; Motor Vehicle Mfg. Association*   T.569

Rye

Rye is used for bread, as a feedstuff for animals, and as an ingredient in whiskey and gin. U.S. production in 1988 was reduced by drought and was estimated by the USDA at 15.1 million bushels, compared with 19.8 million in 1987 and 19.5 million in 1986. Planted area in 1988 was pegged at 2.44 million acres, versus 2.50 million in 1987 and 2.38 million in 1986.

The carryover, which jumped from 11.3 million bushels in 1983/84 to 21.9 million in 1985/86, had been burdensome. In 1988/89, it was expected to fall to 14.7 million bushels from 18.9 million in 1987/88.

On the demand side, feed consumption had grown rapidly. From 8.2 million bushels in 1981/82, feed (and residual) use rose to 14.6 million in 1984/85. However, feed usage was put at 10.5 million in 1988/89, down from 10.9 million in 1987/88. Total domestic use in 1988/89

should amount to 19.8 million bushels, compared with 20.2 million in the prior year.

Exports were forecast at 500,000 bushels in 1988/89, unchanged from 1987/88.

North Dakota produced 1.35 million bushels of rye in 1988, and South Dakota's output amounted to 2.25 million. Both states were severely affected by drought.

The support loan rate for 1988 was $1.50 per bushel, down 5 cents from the previous year. The season's average price was projected by USDA at $2.25 per bushel, up from $1.51 in 1987/88.

Futures Market

Rye futures are traded on the Winnipeg Commodity Exchange (WCE).

RYE WPG
Weekly high low & close of nearest futures

World Production of Rye   In Thousands of Metric Tons

Crop Year	Argentina	Austria	Canada	Czechoslovakia	Denmark	France	Germany West	Germany East	Hungary	Netherlands	Poland	Spain	Turkey	USSR	United States	World Total
1980–1	155	383	448	575	199	405	2,184	1,917	139	39	6,566	284	525	10,205	419	25,268
1981–2	149	320	927	544	208	342	1,793	1,797	116	29	6,731	212	520	9,500	478	24,373
1982–3	148	348	933	583	235	327	1,703	2,119	120	26	7,792	169	430	14,000	496	30,108
1983–4	130	348	827	751	315	278	1,646	2,092	138	26	8,781	253	380	14,000	689	31,407
1984–5	140	380	664	710	608	321	1,983	2,510	192	25	9,540	325	360	13,400	827	33,398
1985–6	100	339	598	620	565	283	1,877	2,500	163	19	7,600	295	350	14,000	664	32,231
1986–7[1]	110	284	600	500	500	225	1,800	2,400	169	19	7,300	220	360	15,200	496	31,000
1987–8[2]			500	500	500		1,600	2,400			7,800			18,100	503	34,000
1988–9[2]			300	500	400		1,600	1,800			7,100			16,500	383	30,800

[1] Preliminary.   [2] Estimate.   Source: Foreign Agricultural Service, U.S.D.A.   T.570

Salient Statistics of Rye in the United States

Year Begin. June 1	Supply — Stocks, June 1 — Privately Owned[2]	Gov't.[3]	Total Stocks	Production	Imports	Total Supply	Disappearance — Domestic Use — Food	Industry	Seed	Feed[5]	Total	Exports	Total Disappearance	Acreage — Planted	Harvested for Grain	Yield Per Harvested Acre Bushels
						Thousands of Bushels								Mil.		
1980–1	12,000	192	12,192	16,483	10	28,685	3,515	2,050	4,150	6,700	16,400	7,494	23,900	2,488	650	24.6
1981–2	4,000	145	4,030	18,187	432	22,600	3,458	2,242	4,160	8,200	18,100	1,529	19,600	2,566	685	26.6
1982–3			3,012	19,533	3,043	25,600	3,315	2,256	4,300	9,600	19,500	194	19,700	2,533	677	28.9
1983–4			5,822	27,116	1,600	34,500	3,500	2,100	4,700	11,900	22,200	1,000	23,200	2,707	896	30.3
1984–5			11,300	32,463	600	44,400	3,500	2,000	4,100	14,600	24,200	400	24,600	2,971	981	33.1
1985–6			19,800	20,637	2,200	42,600	3,500	2,100	3,800	11,200	20,500	200	20,800	2,563	717	28.8
1986–7			21,900	19,522	1,000	42,400	3,500	2,000	3,700	14,100	23,300	500	23,800	2,384	677	28.8
1987–8[1]			18,600	19,818	2,000	39,600	3,500	2,000	3,800	10,900	20,200	500	20,700	2,498	683	29.0
1988–9[4]			20,800	15,062	1,000	35,000	3,500	2,000	3,800	10,500	19,800	500	20,300	2,444	607	24.8

[1] Preliminary.   [2] Includes total loans.   [3] Uncommitted, gov't only.   [4] Forecast.   [5] Includes residual; approximates total feed use.
Source: Economics Research Service, U.S.D.A.   T.571

Production of Rye in the United States   In Thousands of Bushels

Year	Illinois	Indiana	Kansas	Michigan	Minnesota	Georgia	Nebraska	No. Dakota	Ohio	Oklahoma	Oregon	So. Dakota	Virginia	Texas	Wisconsin	So. Carolina
1979	391	208	504	625	2,275	2,310	770	4,200	155	910	144	5,700	384	513	368	609
1980	368	182	210	504	1,900	1,995	666	1,470	231	816	150	4,030	325	494	368	616
1981	336	234	252	532	2,883	2,730	924	2,560	150	680	150	3,220	364	475	408	726
1982	299	260	240	522	3,300	1,470	1,269	2,400	155	736	116	4,680	364	504	300	621
1983	336	270	220	600	4,960	1,470	1,265	4,320	210	780	100	8,740	312	450	300	320
1984	308	336	312	588	6,650	1,760	1,392	5,400	175	704	140	10,800	378	240	216	546
1985	256	308	300	651	3,300	2,070	1,242	2,640	172	828	111	4,440	312	400	234	532
1986	210	280	210	713	1,600	1,785	1,035	4,250	175	840	200	4,440	364	190	168	391
1987	144	297	270	640	1,200	1,540	1,150	5,115	180	360	120	5,040	435	150	100	528
1988[1]	140	330	130	650	920	1,890	1,375	1,350	185	720	90	2,250	560	150	120	720

[1] Preliminary.   Source: Crop Reporting Board, U.S.D.A.   T.572

Month-End Open Interest of Rye Futures in Winnipeg   In 20 Tonne Units

Year	Jan.	Feb.	Mar.	Apr.	May	June	July	Aug.	Sept.	Oct.	Nov.	Dec.
1980	4,648	5,028	5,379	6,172	3,313	5,229	5,348	4,839	5,814	6,106	4,250	3,428
1981	3,876	4,811	3,704	3,640	2,948	3,368	5,028	6,440	5,251	2,516	4,404	3,828
1982	3,739	3,622	3,219	3,583	4,426	3,008	2,268	4,286	5,250	4,052	3,773	3,244
1983	3,227	3,628	3,097	4,625	4,834	4,935	7,883	7,915	3,665	4,494	3,110	3,054
1984	2,224	4,566	3,980	3,883	3,731	3,023	2,888	5,430	7,098	6,320	5,894	4,158
1985	4,267	4,826	4,175	4,227	3,893	3,919	4,031	5,022	4,872	5,478	4,289	3,786
1986	4,287	4,335	3,302	4,211	3,039	2,553	2,900	3,447	3,377	2,862	2,437	2,032
1987	2,463	1,906	2,084	3,006	4,441	3,853	2,595	4,139	3,518	3,542	2,876	2,437
1988	2,456	2,833	2,919	2,211	2,738	3,969	3,463	3,650	3,533	3,231	2,500	2,189

Source: Winnipeg Commodity Exchange   T.577

U.S. Rye Crop Production Reports and CCC Operations   In Thousands of Bushels

Year Begin. June 1	Official Crop Reports				National Average Support Rate		Placed Under Loan	Direct Purchases	Placed Under Loan Total	Acquired by CCC	Total Stocks Ending June 30		Privately Owned[3]	
	July 1	Aug. 1	Dec. 1	Final	$ Per Bushel	% of Parity					Ending Carry-over[1]	CCC Owned	Under Loan[4]	Other
1978–9	28,518	28,567	26,160	24,065	1.70	56	—	—	3,000	—	4,137	—	—	—
1979–0	23,638	23,736	24,549	21,887	1.79	49			1,900	—	8,973		—	
1980–1	15,784	16,189	16,265	15,958	1.91	51			450	—	11,970		—	
1981–2	16,743	17,083	18,621	18,187	2.04	48			500	—	4,030			
1982–3	20,119	19,924	20,817	19,533	2.17	48			1,700	1,400	3,012	—		
1983–4	26,058	25,698	28,152	27,116	2.25	47			5,300	4,900	5,822	1,200		
1984–5	29,903	30,184	32,392	32,463	2.17	45			10,100	9,800	11,300	5,100		
1985–6	19,255	19,298	20,637	20,637	2.17	47			4,100	2,800	19,800	16,000		
1986–7[2]		17,892	19,498	19,522	1.63	38			5,800		21,900	16,500		
1987–8[2]	—	19,098	19,718	19,818	1.55						18,600			
1988–9[2]		15,062			1.50						20,800			

[1] Old-crop rye under loan at end of crop year.   [2] Preliminary.   [3] Derived by subtracting CCC stocks & loans outstanding from ending carryover.   [4] Includes previous crops under reseal.   *Source: Economic Research Service, U.S.D.A.*   T.573

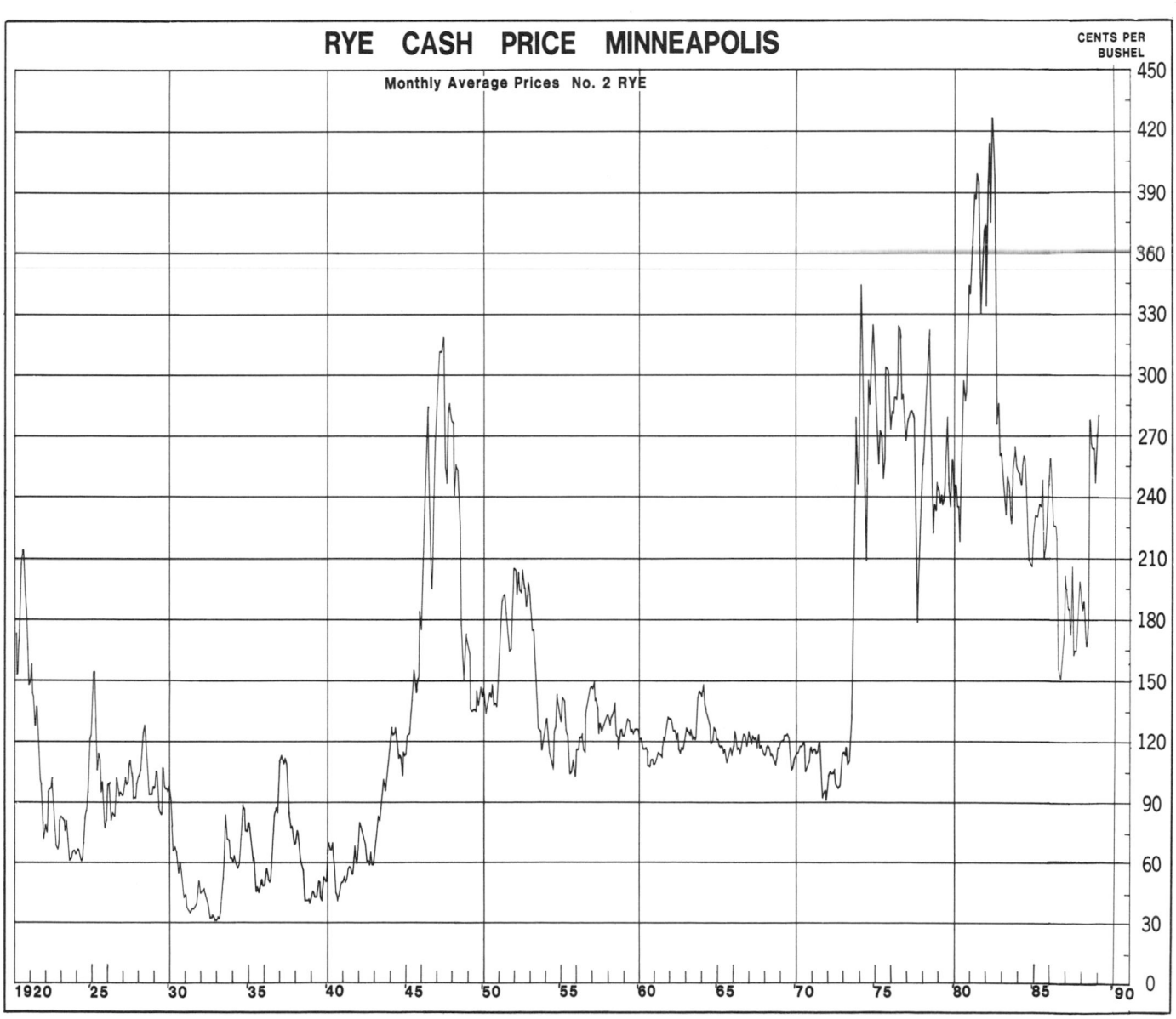

RYE CASH PRICE MINNEAPOLIS

Monthly Average Prices No. 2 RYE

CENTS PER BUSHEL

RYE

Average Price of Cash Rye No. 2 at Minneapolis   In Cents per Bushel

Year	July	Aug.	Sept.	Oct.	Nov.	Dec.	Jan.	Feb.	Mar.	Apr.	May	June	Average
1980–1	297	287	292	307	344	340	352	363	389	387	396	394	346
1981–2	352	330	356	371	374	334	394	414	375	426	410	397	378
1982–3	342	276	286	260	261	256	251	246	231	250	244	232	261
1983–4	227	256	265	256	254	252	251	245	250	260	258	244	252
1984–5	227	209	207	206	221	227	231	230	235	236	235	248	226
1985–6	210	215	223	233	248	259	246	228	226	226	219	178	226
1986–7	156	151	160	168	173	202	195	185	185	173	196	163	176
1987–8	165	165	175	198	199	189	185	189	175	167	181	278	189
1988–9	266	264	264	247	269	280							

Source: Economic Research Service, U.S.D.A.   T.575

High, Low & Closing Prices of May Rye Futures in Winnipeg   In Canadian Dollars per Tonne

Year of Delivery		Year Prior to Delivery						Delivery Year					Life of Delivery Range
	June	July	Aug.	Sept.	Oct.	Nov.	Dec.	Jan.	Feb.	Mar.	Apr.	May	
1981 High	193.50	205.90	194.50	205.70	231.00	250.50	244.00	242.00	244.50	242.50	232.50	199.50	250.50
Low	170.50	189.00	182.10	192.00	201.80	228.00	216.50	223.00	225.50	223.40	176.00	186.70	170.50
Close	192.90	194.00	194.20	203.00	230.00	242.80	237.00	225.50	244.50	230.20	189.50	194.00	—
1982 High	167.00	181.50	215.90	233.50	218.00	195.60	187.00	185.20	187.30	171.00	178.00	180.90	233.50
Low	151.20	154.90	183.50	211.20	193.00	181.50	169.80	168.70	169.50	158.50	160.00	163.40	151.20
Close	151.20	181.50	215.90	217.70	194.20	183.40	171.00	182.00	169.50	160.30	170.00	165.50	—
1983 High	162.00	162.00	152.50	150.50	139.50	140.20	133.00	126.30	123.20	123.00	130.00	126.00	162.00
Low	162.00	152.00	138.00	133.80	128.00	129.00	121.00	119.80	116.40	115.30	118.10	116.50	115.30
Close	162.00	152.50	145.00	133.80	128.20	130.20	121.00	123.10	120.50	122.70	118.70	122.50	—
1984 High	—	—	174.00	176.00	173.30	165.80	158.30	150.00	141.00	140.00	139.30	157.00	176.00
Low	—	—	154.40	169.50	154.40	156.60	146.00	140.70	125.10	129.20	134.00	131.50	125.10
Close	—	—	170.10	170.50	162.50	157.70	148.90	141.00	129.30	138.20	135.50	151.50	—
1985 High	—	—	156.00	158.70	156.90	157.20	154.80	145.40	142.30	134.60	133.80	128.80	158.70
Low	—	—	152.20	152.90	152.20	153.00	145.20	143.00	132.00	132.30	128.30	122.80	122.80
Close	—	—	153.00	157.70	152.70	154.10	145.20	143.00	132.60	133.70	128.30	122.80	—
1986 High	—	—	131.70	130.80	128.00	132.50	134.00	126.90	118.40	107.00	102.20	116.00	131.70
Low	—	—	121.50	124.50	121.40	125.00	126.30	119.50	106.60	100.70	91.70	96.30	91.70
Close	—	—	128.30	124.50	125.00	132.10	126.30	119.70	107.50	102.50	100.50	107.20	—
1987 High	—	—	101.00	102.50	105.00	104.50	103.00	98.70	96.00	89.50	88.20	101.20	105.00
Low	—	—	100.50	97.40	99.50	100.80	96.00	94.20	82.70	83.00	82.30	85.50	82.30
Close	—	—	101.00	100.40	101.00	103.10	98.20	95.70	84.70	84.50	85.40	97.50	—
1988 High	—	—	106.50	107.00	107.50	104.70	104.70	108.40	110.30	111.00	107.50	160.00	160.00
Low	—	—	98.00	104.00	100.00	99.40	102.00	103.00	104.20	104.50	103.50	103.40	98.00
Close	—	—	106.50	104.80	101.20	103.80	103.00	104.20	110.10	106.50	103.50	160.00	—
1989 High	—	—	168.50	171.00	162.80	165.00	160.50						
Low	—	—	156.00	157.00	157.00	156.00	157.50						
Close	—	—	157.50	159.90	161.50	158.80	158.80						

Source: Winnipeg Commodity Exchange   T.576

Rye Under Price Support Through the End of the Month
(Cumulative Total from Current Season's Crop)   In Thousands of Bushels

Year	July	Aug.	Sept.	Oct.	Nov.	Dec.	Jan.	Feb.	Mar.	Apr.	May	June	Total
1980–1	—	97	240	297	348	384	396	399	402	406	406	406	
1981–2	36	264	359	398	424	439	448	456	456	456	456	456	
1982–3	7	344	771	1,008	1,096	1,193	1,324	1,369	1,588	1,709	1,711	1,712	
1983–4	83	1,819	2,228	3,533	3,885	4,199	4,577	4,862	5,141	5,228	5,254	5,256	
1984–5	68	3,581	6,661	8,224	8,653	8,911	9,655	9,830	9,996	10,078	10,066	10,070	
1985–6	567	1,769	2,836	3,516	3,728	3,816	3,955	3,996	4,012	4,060	4,074	4,078	
1986–7	147	1,337	3,249	4,627	5,022	5,140	5,383	5,594	5,722	5,879	5,878	5,888	5,892
1987–8	—	1,237	4,472	5,621	6,498	6,690	7,282	8,164	8,485	8,579	8,605	8,607	8,604
1988–9	—	158	225	239									

Source: U.S. Department of Agriculture   T.578

Salt

U.S. salt production was estimated at 37.8 million short tons in 1988, up slightly from 36.9 million in 1987. The Bureau of Mines estimated that producers either sold or consumed in their own chemical processes 37.5 million tons in 1988, up 1 million from 1987. Apparent consumption increased to 42.5 million tons from 41.7 million. Net imports of about 5 million tons and changes in inventories made up the difference between 1988 production and consumption. Domestic salt production in 1989 was forecast at 37.5 million tons, and apparent consumption was projected at 42.3 million.

The chemical industry took about 48 percent of the salt used in the U.S. in 1988. Production of chlorine and caustic soda, its by-product, accounted for about 95 percent of the chemical sector's demand. Besides bleach, chlorine is used in the production of pulp and paper and alumina, which had strong markets in 1988. However, oil refinery problems reduced the available supplies of ethylene, which is mixed with chlorine to make PVC pipes and other plastic products. This reduced domestic chlorine demand and forced some producers to cut prices to sell the surplus on the export market. Strong demand and rising prices for caustic soda, which has numerous industrial uses, kept chlorine plants operating at close to capacity.

About 25 percent of 1988 use was for highway deicing. Other major markets for salt included agriculture, food processing and water treatment.

World salt production was estimated at 197 million tons in 1988, compared with 195.6 million in 1987.

World Production of All Salt In Thousands of Short Tons

Year	Brazil	Canada	China	France	West Germany	India	Italy	Japan	Mexico	Nether- lands	Poland	Spain	United Kingdom	United States	USSR	World Total
1981	3,974	7,981	20,194	7,315	13,824	9,845	5,039	1,105	8,767	3,944	4,708	4,072	7,408	38,907	16,755	189,198
1982	4,105	8,752	18,060	7,389	12,951	7,763	4,920	1,065	6,130	3,517	4,251	3,626	8,418	37,910	17,416	181,071
1983	4,615	9,482	17,780	7,661	11,980	7,730	4,618	1,015	6,287	3,444	3,996	3,481	6,957	34,605	17,857	175,099
1984	4,990	11,282	17,950	7,880	13,461	8,520	4,385	1,053	6,798	4,050	5,193	3,735	7,856	39,256	18,200	190,070
1985	3,008	11,117	15,924	7,841	14,407	10,889	4,129	1,300	7,129	4,579	5,363	3,571	7,877	40,102	17,747	191,628
1986[1]	3,900	11,389	19,070	7,808	14,443	11,153	4,444	1,510	6,533	4,148	6,006	3,400	7,800	36,703	17,700	194,720
1987[2]	3,900	11,000	19,800	7,890	14,500	12,102	4,240	1,540	6,600	4,380	6,799	3,400	7,800	36,592	17,700	195,594

[1] Preliminary. [2] Estimate. *Source: Bureau of Mines*   T.581

Salient Statistics of the Salt Industry in the United States In Thousands of Short Tons

Year	Net Import Reliance as a % of Apparent Consumption	Avg. Value F.O.B. Mine Vacuum & Open Pan $ Ton	Evaporated (Mfg.) Bulk Open Pan Vacuum Pans	Solar	Pressed Blocks	Total Evaporated	Rock Salt Bulk	Pressed Block	Total Salt Rock	Salt in Brine	Total Salt	Value[3] Million $	Imports for Consumption	Exports Total	Exports To Canada	Apparent Consumption
1981	8	79.68	3,500	2,298	404	6,201	11,809	62	11,871	20,835	38,907	637.6	4,319	1,046	1,011	42,180
1982	11	86.72	3,379	2,478	447	6,305	13,431	72	13,503	18,086	37,894	671.4	5,451	1,001	957	42,344
1983	18	87.39	3,309	1,962	408	5,680	9,867	73	9,941	18,952	34,573	597.1	5,997	517	475	40,053
1984	15	92.78	3,322	2,345	542	6,209	13,276	71	13,348	19,669	39,225	675.1	7,545	820	792	45,950
1985	14	92.66	3,604	2,666	455	6,725	14,000	70	14,690	19,107	40,067	739.6	6,207	904	883	45,370
1986[1]	12	91.27	3,583	2,562	465	6,610	11,927	67	12,598	17,920	36,663	665.4	6,665	1,165	1,091	42,163
1987[2]	12	93.00	3,776	2,627	487	6,890	11,331	73	11,965	18,124	36,493	684.2	5,716	541	477	41,668

[1] Preliminary. [2] Estimate. [3] Values are f.o.b. mine or refinery & do not include cost of cooperage or containers. [4] Or Grainers. *Source: Bureau of Mines*   T.582

Salt Sold or Used by Producers in the U.S. by Classes & Consumers or Uses In Thousands of Short Tons

Year	Chemical[4]	Tanning Leather	Textile & Dyeing	Meat Packers[2]	Canning	Baking	Agri-Distribution	Feed Dealers	Feed Mfgs.	Rubber	Oil	Paper & Pulp	Metal Process ing	Water Treatment	Grocery Stores	Water Conditioning Distal.	Ice Control &/or Stabilization
1981	22,241		180	491	230	109		1,147	646	113	820	246			1,021		
1982	18,861		165	550	204	109		967	699	51	1,035	209			1,053		
1983	19,950		171	531	211	114		977	628	45	918	274			987		
1984	19,701		135	436	242	124		923	590	41	860	307			859		
1985	21,204	137	186	415	263	126	387	863	412	36	965	311	382	553	901	888	11,180
1986	19,801	152	226	436	271	134	286	940	388	133	627	307	304	525	946	1,028	10,541
1987[1]	18,715	124	237	452	296	158	302	995	416	145	597	387	311	392	1,007	1,063	9,878

[1] Preliminary. [2] Prior to 1984, data also includes tanners & casing mfg. [3] Also service companies. [4] Chloralkali producers & other chemical.
Source: Bureau of Mines   T.583

Sheep & Lambs

In 1988, sheep numbers in the 28 major raising countries were preliminarily estimated by USDA at 693 million head, down from 696 million in 1987. Australian sheep numbers expanded by nearly four percent to 165 million, while New Zealand's fell by 7 percent to 64 million. Australia raises sheep primarily for wool, while New Zealand raises them for meat.

Australia's production of lamb, mutton, and goat meat was put at 619,000 tonnes in 1988, above 589,000 in 1987. New Zealand's output was forecast at 536,000 tonnes, versus 572,000 in 1987. The export market continued to be dominated by Australia and New Zealand. Australia's share of the export market was expected to increase slightly to 24 percent in 1988, while New Zea-

land's was likely to decline to 45 percent. The EC and Japan continued to absorb more than 80 percent of the lamb, mutton, and goat meat traded internationally.

U.S. commercial liveweights for the first three quarters of 1988 were 4 percent above the same period in 1987, while production was up only 1 percent. Fourth-quarter production was expected to be 2 percent above 1987 levels.

U.S. lamb production in 1989 was expected to increase by 2 percent to 335 million pounds, from 328 million in 1988. Meat output was expected to be largest in the first quarter, as spring's religious holidays fell then.

U.S. per capita consumption of lamb and mutton was expected to remain below 1.5 pounds again in 1989.

World Sheep Numbers in Specified Countries   In Millions of Head

Year	Argentina	Australia	Bulgaria	China[4]	France	India	Italy	New Zealand	Romania	Spain[2]	South Africa	Turkey	United Kingdom	United States	Uruguay	USSR	World
1981	30.0	134.4		187.0		40.7		68.8		16.5	33.8	48.6	21.6	12.9	24.1	141.6	657
1982	29.0	138.0			13.1	48.0		69.9		17.1	33.6	49.6	22.2	13.0	23.2	142.4	671
1983	33.5	133.2	10.8		12.1	49.5	9.3	70.3	16.9	17.5	32.0	47.5	22.9	12.1	23.3	142.2	669
1984	33.9	139.2	11.0		11.9	51.1	10.7	70.3	18.5	17.6	31.3	47.7	23.3	11.5	23.3	145.3	681
1985	29.4	149.7	10.5		11.6	52.8	11.1	69.7	18.6	17.5	30.3	47.8	23.9	10.4	22.8	142.9	686
1986	29.2	155.6	9.7		11.2	54.5	11.3	67.9	18.6	17.3	29.5	47.0	24.5	10.0	24.8	140.9	690
1987	29.0	158.8	9.6		10.6	55.5	11.5	69.2	18.8	17.6	29.7	43.5	26.0	10.3	25.7	142.2	696
1988[1]	29.2	164.6	8.9		10.4	51.7	11.5	64.2	18.9	17.9	29.6	40.0	27.8	10.8	27.4	140.8	693
1989[3]	29.5	171.3	9.0		10.0	51.0	11.5	64.8	19.4	18.0	30.2	36.5	29.0	11.0	28.4	142.0	701

[1] Preliminary.   [2] One year old & older.   [3] Estimate.   [4] Mainland.   *Source: Foreign Agricultural Service, U.S.D.A.*   T.584

Salient Statistics of Sheep & Lambs in the United States   Avg. Lv. Weight

Year	On Hand Jan. 1 — Mil. Head —	Lambs Saved — Mil. Head —	In Shipments	Market-ings[2] Ths. Head	Slaughter Farm	Slaughter Total[4]	Production Mil. Lbs.	SH.&LM. Federally Inspected in Ths.	Value of Production	Cash Receipts[3]	Value of Home Consumption — Millions of Dollars —	Gross Income	Farm Value (1/1) All	Farm Value (1/1) $ per Head
1981	12.9	8.8	1,885	8,613	189	6,197	772.4	5,789	359.1	416.1	12.3	428.4	903.3	69.80
1982	13.0	8.6	2,115	9,482	195	6,644	785.4	6,273	355.7	445.1	13.0	458.1	739.6	57.00
1983	12.1	8.2	1,838	8,924	171	6,790	767.6	6,412	356.7	426.4	10.6	437.0	628.6	51.80
1984	11.5	7.8	1,859	8,828	141	6,900	694.1	6,549	376.5	466.5	11.1	477.7	598.9	58.10
1985	10.4	7.4	1,693	8,066	135	6,300	694.2	5,976	427.8	503.2	12.8	516.0	637.9	61.10
1986[1]	10.0	7.3	1,781	7,385	127	5,762	720.7	5,464	443.6	483.5	12.5	496.0	673.0	67.40
1987[1]	10.3	7.2				5,312		5,042					782.1	75.70
1988[5]	10.8							5,150					968.9	89.90

[1] Preliminary.   [2] Excludes interfarm sales.   [3] Includes receipts from marketings & from sales of farm slaughter meats.   [4] Includes all commercial & farm.   [5] Estimate.   *Source: Crop Reporting Board, U.S.D.A.*   T.585

Sheep and Lambs on Farms in the United States, January 1   Thousands of Head

Year	Minnesota	California	Colorado	Idaho	Missouri	Montana	New Mexico	Ohio	South Dakota	Texas	Utah	Wyoming	Iowa	Total[2]	Total[1] Stock
							All Sheep and Lambs[2]								
1981	295	1,205	810	512	138	595	650	310	780	2,360	650	1,110	437	12,947	11,298
1982	335	1,210	710	498	133	616	615	313	750	2,400	636	1,130	485	12,997	11,433
1983	300	1,115	750	429	126	560	610	295	680	2,225	590	1,060	457	12,140	10,479
1984	225	1,115	690	383	128	564	589	265	740	1,970	568	1,090	425	11,487	9,769
1985	255	1,065	675	313	123	515	538	265	639	1,810	515	860	360	10,443	8,847
1986	213	1,065	600	320	101	423	525	275	540	1,810	484	819	350	9,983	8,491
1987[3]	237	980	690	314	110	523	480	300	605	1,930	464	775	375	10,334	8,826
1988[3]														10,774	8,993

[1] Stock sheep & lambs; does not include sheep & lambs on feed for market.   [2] Includes sheep & lambs on feed for market and stock sheep & lambs.   [3] Preliminary.   *Source: Crop Reporting Board, U.S.D.A.*   T.586

Average Wholesale Price of Lambs at Omaha   In Dollars Per 100 Pounds

Year	Jan.	Feb.	Mar.	Apr.	May	June	July	Aug.	Sept.	Oct.	Nov.	Dec.	Average
1981	50.00	53.50	55.25	59.25	65.00	66.42	57.33	54.10	48.53	49.86	45.27	45.10	52.23
1982	48.92	51.58	58.52	58.67	62.56	60.28	56.16	50.71	48.93	46.92	45.46	47.62	53.03
1983	53.50	58.50	59.75	58.75	59.00	53.00	51.12	49.25	48.50	51.75	56.00	57.75	54.74
1984	60.50	58.75	58.75	60.50	62.25	61.75	61.50	62.76	63.58	63.35	62.98	60.08	61.39
1985	62.13	66.92	67.75	69.50	74.25	72.56	71.98	71.42	68.94	63.32	62.50	60.62	68.41
1986	61.75	68.50	67.00	68.00	80.75	74.71	70.50	66.16	62.45	57.23	65.17	72.70	67.54
1987[1]	77.25	74.62	82.50	85.50	89.94	85.42	74.02	70.86	67.14	66.00	63.50	72.44	75.77
1988[1]	78.17	79.38	79.50	N.A.	75.17	58.80	57.55	54.90	58.35	60.44	61.90		

[1] Preliminary.   *Source: Economic Research Service, U.S.D.A.*   T.587

Federally Inspected Slaughter of Sheep & Lambs in the United States   In Thousands of Head

Year	Jan.	Feb.	Mar.	Apr.	May	June	July	Aug.	Sept.	Oct.	Nov.	Dec.	Total
1981	488	426	488	512	426	440	439	467	546	558	476	522	5,789
1982	510	490	570	———	1,493	———	———	1,577	———	———	1,634	———	6,273
1983	509	457	616	509	508	508	497	585	595	580	510	536	6,412
1984	540	548	586	592	558	500	511	561	528	588	524	514	6,549
1985	544	473	564	512	494	423	485	496	480	554	460	490	5,976
1986	507	441	524	477	417	406	432	426	495	495	401	442	5,464
1987[1]	418	390	432	477	363	407	411	400	459	446	399	439	5,042
1988[1]	380	408	535	388	414	413	387	442	452	437			

[1] Preliminary.   *Source: Economic Research Service, U.S.D.A.*   T.588

Cold Storage Holdings of Lamb and Mutton, on 1st of Month   In Thousands of Pounds

Year	Jan.	Feb.	Mar.	Apr.	May	June	July	Aug.	Sept.	Oct.	Nov.	Dec.
1981	9,142	8,997	7,843	7,823	10,196	10,403	12,297	12,564	13,694	13,311	12,676	11,362
1982	10,540	9,569	8,449	8,783	—	—	8,200	—	—	8,571	—	—
1983	8,653	7,682	7,673	8,218	8,331	8,839	8,691	7,717	8,815	8,622	9,092	10,270
1984	10,701	8,312	7,542	8,057	9,123	8,839	8,678	8,404	8,026	8,889	8,403	7,890
1985	7,066	7,339	6,840	6,547	7,644	8,068	8,931	9,193	9,541	9,237	10,033	12,525
1986	12,766	11,615	13,813	11,615	12,754	12,742	14,068	14,318	15,459	14,450	14,641	13,843
1987	12,603	11,550	13,565	13,595	13,248	13,997	12,007	9,311	8,468	6,978	7,036	8,637
1988[1]	7,949	8,069	7,852	7,108	7,639	7,977	8,686	8,537	7,052	6,770	6,396	5,937

[1] Preliminary.   *Source: Crop Reporting Board, U.S.D.A.*   T.589

Average Price Received by Farmers for Sheep in the U.S.   In Dollars per 100 Pounds

Year	Jan.	Feb.	Mar.	Apr.	May	June	July	Aug.	Sept.	Oct.	Nov.	Dec.	Average[1]
1981	27.40	29.00	26.10	23.40	19.50	20.30	23.00	20.40	20.30	19.70	19.10	19.20	21.20
1982	25.10	21.30	27.20	22.20	21.00	22.00	21.00	18.60	16.50	15.20	15.30	16.80	19.50
1983	21.30	21.90	20.80	17.40	15.20	14.50	16.20	15.50	12.80	13.80	15.10	17.00	15.70
1984	18.20	19.80	18.70	16.30	13.00	13.80	16.80	17.30	15.90	15.20	18.10	24.30	16.40
1985	26.50	26.50	26.20	24.70	23.00	22.00	27.20	26.10	25.30	21.50	23.60	26.60	23.90
1986	29.90	26.10	22.80	24.90	24.10	25.90	26.70	26.40	27.30	25.50	26.10	29.30	25.60
1987[2]	31.60	32.20	30.70	28.60	28.30	25.70	28.50	32.00	32.50	31.50	30.90	32.30	29.50
1988[2]	34.70	30.10	29.70	26.00	26.10	23.20	25.00	25.30	25.90	25.30	27.80	27.10	27.20

[1] Weighted average by quantities sold.   [2] Preliminary.   *Source: Crop Reporting Board, U.S.D.A.*   T.590

Average Price Received by Farmers for Lambs in the U.S.   In Dollars per 100 Pounds

Year	Jan.	Feb.	Mar.	Apr.	May	June	July	Aug.	Sept.	Oct.	Nov.	Dec.	Average[1]
1981	54.10	55.40	56.50	58.80	63.10	65.00	59.50	56.20	50.40	50.60	47.40	47.50	54.90
1982	50.40	53.30	60.30	61.50	63.50	57.80	56.30	52.90	50.90	49.10	47.70	50.90	53.10
1983	55.50	60.50	63.20	61.50	59.60	54.20	49.80	48.30	47.50	50.90	55.80	58.90	53.90
1984	60.00	59.20	58.20	60.60	59.50	57.50	58.60	61.00	61.80	62.40	63.30	61.90	60.10
1985	63.40	66.70	68.00	68.40	72.40	69.70	70.80	70.80	70.20	67.80	66.00	62.70	67.70
1986	63.90	67.00	64.90	69.10	76.30	74.00	71.90	69.50	67.60	62.50	69.30	73.20	69.00
1987[2]	76.60	76.00	80.80	86.10	90.10	83.50	78.70	76.10	76.80	71.90	65.70	72.80	77.60
1988[2]	80.70	80.40	80.20	74.80	72.60	60.20	60.00	59.80	64.30	66.20	66.30	68.30	69.50

[1] Weighted average by quantities sold.   [2] Preliminary.   *Source: Crop Reporting Board, U.S.D.A.*   T.591

Silver

U.S. mine production of silver increased an estimated 13 percent in 1988 to 45 million ounces, according to the Bureau of Mines. The gains resulted from the reopening of higher-cost mines in Idaho in 1987 and from a surge in gold mining. Many of the new gold mines, such as the McCoy/Cove mine in Nevada, were open-pit, heap-leach operations yielding far more silver than gold.

While McCoy/Cove was exceptionally rich in silver, its economics were typical. It was expected to produce about 100,000 ounces of gold and 700,000 ounces of silver in 1988. Its owner, Echo Bay Mines Ltd., estimated its cash production costs at $230 per ounce of gold or gold equivalent (equating 70 ounces of silver to one of gold). The mine was expected to produce 225,000 ounces of gold and 2.7 million ounces of silver in 1989 and more than 330,000 ounces of gold and 6.5 million ounces of silver in 1990. Yet, it was still primarily a gold mine. Echo Bay said three-quarters of its revenues would come from the gold.

By-product silver also is produced in numerous copper mining operations and is often associated with lead and zinc deposits. Given the strong prices for copper and zinc in 1988, and expectations that demand for those base metals would continue strong through most of 1989, further large increases in silver by-product production were expected in 1989.

World silver production was estimated at 430 million ounces in 1988, little changed from 429.1 million a year earlier. Labor problems in Peru, where mines were shut repeatedly by strikes, reduced that major exporter's output from an estimated 62 million ounces in 1987. In the summer of 1988, while its mines were closed by a two-month strike, Peru announced plans to stockpile silver until prices rose. These developments occurred near 1988's drought-inspired rally in commodities, and speculative buying briefly drove silver prices over $8/oz. Yet there was skepticism that a government as bankrupt as Peru's could halt exports of one of its leading sources of foreign exchange. Talk of an impending silver shortage, echoing the situation in base metals, was quickly ended by heavy hedge selling at the market's top.

For the year, the average cash price slipped to $6.55/oz. from $7.20 in 1987. And as 1988 ended, the Handy and Harman cash price was $6.02, down 10 percent from $6.695 at the end of 1987.

The Bureau of Mines estimated 1988 U.S. industrial silver consumption at 120 million ounces, virtually unchanged from 1987's usage. In September 1987, the Bureau of Mines announced that there were problems with its silver consumption data, largely because of inaccurate reporting by end users. This continued in 1988, and reliable consumption data for individual industries were not available. But the trend in warehouse stocks argued against either a boom in demand or a supply shortfall. Estimated ending stocks available to industry--including COMEX and CBT deliverable stocks--jumped by 20 million ounces in 1988 to 205 million. U.S. silver coinage was not included in the forecasts above, because the estimated 6 million ounces that went into coins in 1988 (including American Eagle bullion coins) came from excess silver in the defense stockpile, as required by federal law. At the end of 1988, there were still nearly 100 million ounces in the defense stockpile, and the Treasury was holding 42.9 million ounces of surplus silver.

The Treasury Department's fiscal 1989 appropriations bill required the Treasury to sell 2.5 million ounces of its silver in each of the following three years. Both the timing and the sales procedures were to be determined by the Treasury.

About 25 million ounces of silver were recovered from old scrap in the U.S. in 1988, approximately 21 percent of industrial usage. Another 45 million ounces were recovered from new scrap generated during fabrication processes. Silver imports were estimated to have increased by 22 percent to 100 million ounces.

Futures Markets

Silver is traded on the New York Commodity Exchange (COMEX), the Chicago Board of Trade, the Mid-America Exchange, the London Metal Exchange, and in Winnipeg.

World Mine Production of Silver, by Selected Countries — In Millions of Fine Ounces (Troy Ounces)

Year	Argentina	Australia	Bolivia[1]	Canada	West Germany	Honduras	Japan	Mexico	Morocco	Peru	Poland	United States	USSR[2]	Yugoslavia	Zaire (Congo)	World Total[2]
1976	2.25	25.03	5.34	41.20	1.03	3.18	9.30	42.64	2.05	35.58	17.8	34.33	44.0	4.63	2.47	316.4
1977	2.45	27.53	5.81	42.24	1.06	2.82	9.60	47.03	2.82	39.73	20.7	38.17	45.0	4.68	2.73	331.3
1978	2.16	26.12	6.29	40.73	.80	2.79	9.66	50.78	3.13	37.02	21.9	39.39	46.0	5.13	4.39	345.0
1979	2.21	26.76	5.74	36.87	1.04	2.43	8.68	52.17	3.28	39.25	22.6	37.90	46.0	5.21	3.89	348.1
1980	2.36	24.65	6.10	33.34	1.06	1.77	8.60	50.05	3.15	44.42	24.63	32.33	46.0	4.79	2.73	342.8
1981	2.52	23.91	6.39	36.30	1.13	1.82	9.01	52.92	2.12	46.94	20.58	40.68	46.5	4.44	2.58	361.6
1982	2.68	29.16	5.47	42.25	1.28	2.10	9.84	59.18	2.64	41.96	21.12	40.25	46.9	3.34	1.75	371.2
1983	2.50	33.21	6.03	35.56	1.17	2.59	9.88	63.61	2.85	50.48	21.80	43.43	47.2	3.99	1.29	387.7
1984	1.98	31.26	4.56	42.66	1.23	2.70	10.40	75.34	2.41	53.08	23.92	44.59	47.4	4.05	1.23	413.9
1985	2.17	34.91	3.58	38.48	1.09	2.77	10.92	73.17	2.73	58.23	26.72	39.43	47.9	5.02	1.52	422.1
1986[3]	2.13	32.88	3.06	34.98	.88	2.75	11.29	75.20	1.57	61.92	26.65	34.52	48.2	5.69	1.50	415.9
1987[2]	2.00	32.76	3.80	40.18	1.74	2.00	9.04	75.00	1.41	66.00	26.50	39.79	48.2	4.85	1.40	429.1
1988[2]												50.0				

[1] Exports. [2] Estimate. [3] Preliminary. *Source: Bureau of Mines*

T.594

SILVER CASH PRICE NEW YORK
HANDY & HARMAN MONTHLY AVERAGE PRICES
HIGH JAN. 38.27 FEB. 35.09

Average Price of Silver in New York (Handy & Harman)   In Cents per Troy Ounce (.999 Fine)

Year	Jan.	Feb.	Mar.	Apr.	May	June	July	Aug.	Sept.	Oct.	Nov.	Dec.	Average
1973	201.7	223.6	230.9	220.7	240.1	262.1	270.6	263.7	267.5	288.6	286.0	313.7	256.0
1974	363.7	535.9	532.6	503.6	543.2	489.6	441.6	443.1	404.9	483.0	469.4	439.1	470.8
1975	419.3	437.0	434.5	420.9	453.8	448.9	470.5	492.5	451.6	432.9	433.2	408.5	442.0
1976	406.3	408.6	418.9	435.1	448.9	481.2	478.0	423.7	429.5	422.5	437.3	434.7	435.4
1977	440.9	452.7	484.2	477.7	469.2	444.3	449.8	444.4	453.9	476.3	482.8	470.6	462.3
1978	493.4	493.6	526.8	511.6	512.0	531.6	533.1	549.5	557.5	591.8	586.5	593.0	540.0
1979	625.5	741.7	745.4	749.3	836.6	853.8	913.5	933.4	1,395.9	1,678.1	1,655.3	2,179.3	1,109.0
1980	3,827.2	3,508.5	2,413.3	1,384.1	1,253.3	1,574.8	1,606.0	1,589.7	2,014.4	2,018.1	1,864.8	1,639.3	2,063.3
1981	1,475.2	1,306.5	1,236.9	1,091.7	1,084.8	1,000.1	863.1	892.3	1,003.6	925.1	854.7	843.2	1,048.1
1982	803.1	826.8	721.3	731.1	667.4	557.8	649.7	713.6	872.5	948.8	991.8	1,058.6	795.0
1983	1,239.6	1,396.4	1,061.9	1,169.4	1,295.3	1,174.9	1,208.8	1,209.6	1,191.5	984.1	883.7	912.1	1,143.9
1984	818.2	912.7	965.1	922.1	897.2	874.4	741.6	761.3	726.3	731.7	748.9	669.4	814.1
1985	609.8	607.0	601.4	645.8	628.1	617.2	610.4	624.7	605.4	618.8	613.4	588.8	614.2
1986	605.3	587.4	503.9	522.9	511.5	515.3	504.9	521.8	568.3	566.7	559.6	536.4	547.0
1987	552.9	548.8	568.2	742.8	843.9	741.1	767.8	784.7	759.1	755.8	666.2	679.0	700.9
1988	673.3	632.5	641.3	647.8	654.3	703.7	714.7	670.8	636.5	628.5	627.5	610.8	653.5

Source: Handy & Harman

T.595

SILVER

World[2] Silver Consumption   In Millions of Troy Ounces

| | | | Industrial Uses | | | | | | | Coinage | | | | | | |
Year	Canada	France	W. Ger-many	India	Italy	Japan	Un. King-dom	United States	World Total	Cana-da	France	W. Ger-many	Aus-tria	Mex-ico	United States	World Total	World Total
1973	8.6	14.3	64.7	13.0	41.5	69.0	31.0	195.9	477.8	1.4	.1	9.5	6.6		.9	29.2	507.0
1974	9.6	15.5	59.9	15.0	38.6	46.5	25.0	177.0	409.4	8.9	.1	8.8	5.6		1.0	27.9	436.9
1975	10.6	21.2	38.9	13.0	28.9	46.4	28.0	157.7	376.8	10.4	5.2	4.3	13.4	—	2.7	38.8	415.6
1976	9.5	19.0	50.8	18.0	32.1	60.7	28.0	170.5	437.5	8.4	6.7	2.9	6.9	—	1.3	29.7	467.2
1977	8.8	20.6	59.5	17.6	33.8	63.2	32.2	153.6	433.6	.3	6.9	2.6	3.0	4.2	.4	23.4	457.0
1978	9.0	22.2	47.2	20.0	41.8	64.8	29.0	160.2	442.6	.3	11.1	3.6	4.5	6.3	.1	36.3	478.9
1979	8.1	21.5	46.1	19.0	31.1	66.4	26.5	157.2	434.2	.3	7.7	3.7	5.0	5.0	.1	27.8	462.0
1980	8.7	20.2	29.1	19.0	21.8	61.7	20.5	124.7	354.5	.2	—	—	4.3	6.1	.1	13.7	368.2
1981	9.4	20.6	33.8	19.0	12.9	59.8	18.5	116.6	344.0	.2	—	—	3.0	—	—	9.0	353.0
1982	9.0	18.6	35.9	16.1	9.6	63.2	20.0	118.8	345.4	.3	—	—	4.0	—	2.5	12.8	358.2
1983	8.9	18.6	30.3	12.9	9.0	71.5	18.0	116.3	340.7	.4	—	—	2.0	—	11.2	18.2	358.9
1984	9.0	17.0	30.1	16.1	11.6	78.7	19.0	114.8	353.3	.3	—	—	—	2.0	3.4	8.7	362.0
1985	9.1	18.0	31.7	20.9	4.6	75.3	19.0	118.6	357.2	.3	—	—	—	3.0	4.4	12.7	369.9
1986	9.6	16.4	36.9	16.1	14.5	84.7	20.5	118.9	380.7	2.0	—	—	1.0	1.7	7.4	26.0	406.7
1987[1]	10.4	19.6	40.5	16.1	10.0	86.8	21.5	115.3	384.6	3.2			2.0	.5	13.2	31.1	415.7

[1] Preliminary.   [2] Non-communist areas only.   *Source: Handy & Harman*   T.597

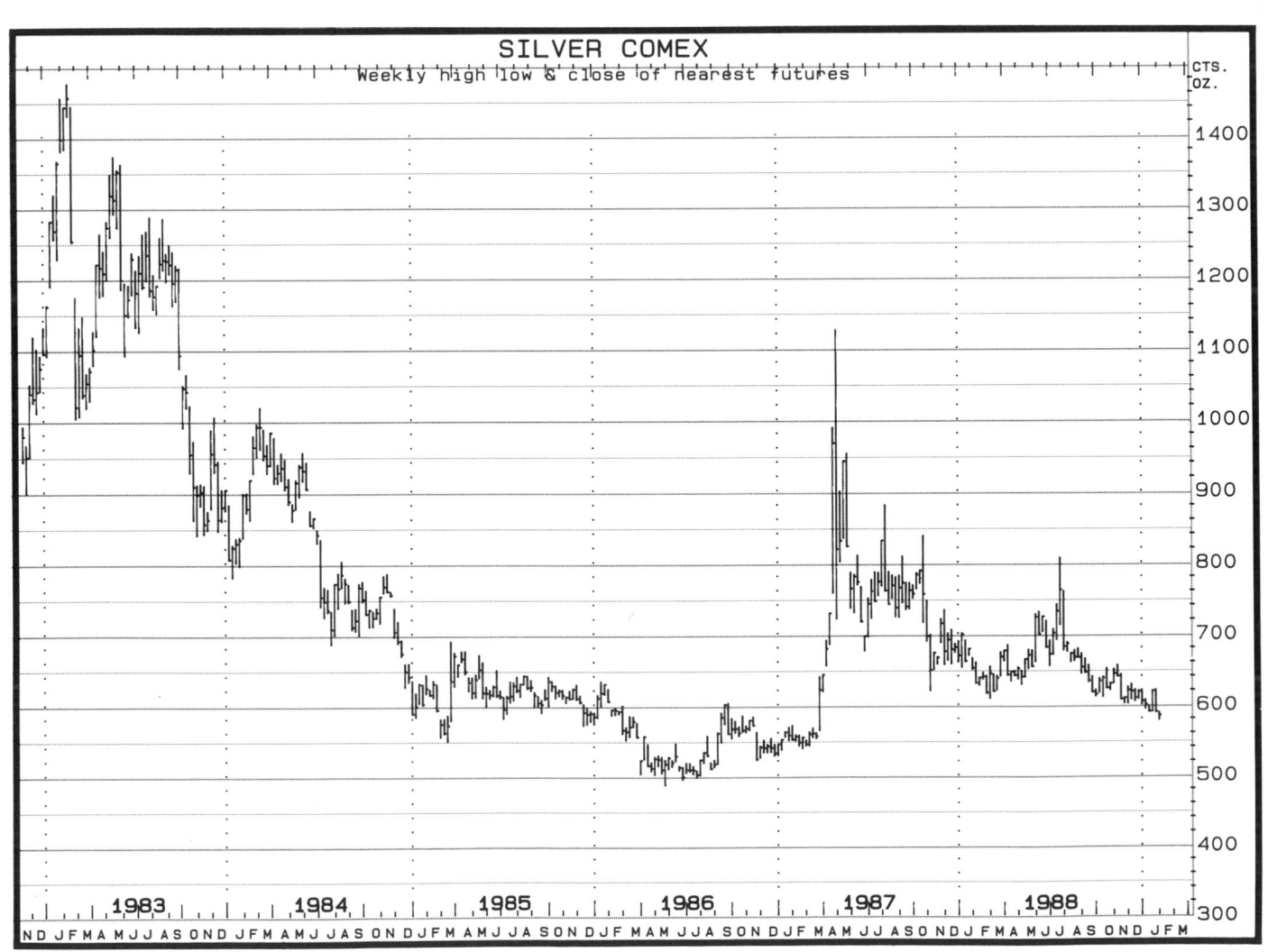

SILVER COMEX

Weekly high low & close of nearest futures

U.S. Mine Production of Recoverable Silver   In Thousands of Troy Ounces

Year	Ari-zona	Cali-fornia	Colo-rado	Idaho	Ore-gon	Mis-souri	Mon-tana	Nevada	New Mexico	New York	Ten-nessee	So. Dakota	Utah	Alaska	Total
1979	7,479	64	2,809	17,144	2	2,201	3,302	560	N.A.	11	N.A.	58	2,454	N.A.	37,896
1980	6,268	49	2,987	13,695	1	2,357	2,024	940	N.A.	21	N.A.	51	2,203	8	32,329
1981	8,055	53	3,009	16,546	7	1,837	2,989	3,039	1,632	29	N.A.	56	2,883	2	40,683
1982	6,309	34	1,934	14,830	—	2,241	6,169	3,142	805	27	N.A.	26	4,343	2	40,248
1983	4,492	27	2,146	17,684	1	2,021	5,708	5,179	N.A.	33	N.A.	62	4,567	4	43,431
1984	4,247	N.A.	2,200	18,869	N.A.	1,401	5,653	6,477	N.A.	N.A.	N.A.	50	N.A.	N.A.	44,592
1985	4,885	115	549	18,828	—	1,635	4,010	4,947	N.A.	N.A.	N.A.	63	N.A.	N.A.	39,433
1986	4,506	155	645	11,207	—	1,459	4,773	6,409	N.A.	N.A.	N.A.	N.A.	N.A.	N.A.	34,524
1987[1]	3,667	122	861	N.A.	N.A.	1,181	5,837	12,190	N.A.	N.A.	N.A.	N.A.	N.A.	10	39,790
1988[2]	4,000	470	800	10,500		1,500	6,000	16,000							

[1] Preliminary.   [2] Forecast.   *Source: Bureau of Mines*   T.599

U.S. Consumption of Silver, by End Use   In Thousands of Troy Ounces

Year	Bear-ings	Brazing Alloys & Solders	Cata-lysts	Dental & Medical	Electro-plated Ware	Electrical & Electronic Products Batteries	Contacts & Con-ductors	Jewelry	Mirrors	Photo-graphic Ma-terials	Ster-ling Ware	Coins, Medal-lions[2]	Total Net Industrial Consump-tion	Coinage	Total Consump-tion
1979	332	10,912	5,637	2,295	8,065	4,583	33,506	5,358	1,850	65,978	13,088	4,676	157,258	168	157,426
1980	649	8,508	3,035	2,212	4,350	5,976	27,796	5,893	672	49,825	9,082	4,693	124,694	72	124,766
1981	297	7,718	3,830	1,709	3,904	3,803	26,411	5,368	581	51,025	4,407	2,622	116,670	179	116,849
1982	228	7,384	2,418	1,688	3,254	4,167	27,730	6,260	970	51,769	6,579	1,832	118,840	1,846	120,686
1983	170	5,837	2,424	1,532	3,154	2,800	26,298	6,861	970	51,827	7,022	2,979	116,440	2,128	118,568
1984	260	5,889	2,448	1,569	3,542	2,671	25,633	5,773	970	55,322	3,638	2,564	114,841	2,665	117,506
1985	190	5,593	2,409	1,480	3,660	2,470	27,509	5,779	970	57,895	3,527	2,514	118,555	362	118,917
1986	375	6,467	2,313	1,474	3,724	3,309	27,429	4,666	970	58,554	3,935	3,957	121,743	7,535	129,278
1987[1]	317	5,591	2,474	1,400	3,010	2,413	23,457	4,514	1,000	61,377	3,897	4,194	118,500	15,074	133,574

[1] Preliminary.   [2] Includes commemorative objects.   [3] Estimate.   *Source: Bureau of Mines*   T.598

Commodity Exchange, Inc. (COMEX) Warehouse Stocks of Silver   In Millions of Ounces

Year	Jan. 1	Feb. 1	Mar. 1	Apr. 1	May 1	June 1	July 1	Aug. 1	Sept. 1	Oct. 1	Nov. 1	Dec. 1
1979	58.2	52.0	51.8	49.2	50.3	55.5	54.1	48.9	47.3	51.8	60.3	70.2
1980	74.8	76.0	77.8	83.1	84.2	82.3	82.0	81.7	82.6	82.2	87.1	86.1
1981	86.9	86.8	85.4	84.6	85.7	85.1	86.6	85.4	78.8	78.1	76.0	77.3
1982	77.6	76.3	78.5	77.1	79.9	78.0	72.4	66.2	60.0	60.7	59.2	80.6
1983	91.2	90.9	106.4	96.8	91.3	69.8	91.1	93.7	113.6	129.3	129.4	129.6
1984	127.4	123.7	116.8	117.2	115.3	114.3	121.8	120.3	116.2	115.0	113.4	115.4
1985	118.9	121.5	122.3	106.6	106.0	104.2	133.7	140.8	141.0	143.6	149.2	153.7
1986	155.2	142.3	145.9	151.3	154.9	144.6	151.9	150.7	158.6	156.8	138.1	145.1
1987	144.9	150.2	160.0	157.9	157.7	156.1	152.5	151.9	158.6	155.7	154.8	155.8
1988	156.3	156.3	156.9	155.8	161.3	164.3	167.1	169.7	175.6	178.8	175.3	178.5
1989	174.4	179.2										

Source: Commodity Exchange of New York (COMEX)   T.600

United States Production[1] of Refined Silver from All Sources   In Thousands of Troy Ounces

Year	Jan.	Feb.	Mar.	Apr.	May	June	July	Aug.	Sept.	Oct.	Nov.	Dec.	Total
1979	10,592	10,888	13,070	11,451	11,938	11,600	12,433	9,837	9,118	12,476	12,221	17,008	155,723
1980	18,088	17,548	17,673	16,941	10,400	14,800	6,676	11,583	10,785	10,603	10,578	14,553	166,326
1981	12,889	12,000	11,352	11,889	10,402	11,500	10,433	10,114	10,533	9,954	8,105	11,589	130,783
1982	9,043	8,407	10,300	8,856	9,095	8,840	7,781	8,518	7,872	8,307	9,607	11,655	108,252
1983	9,121	8,533	9,063	9,653	7,663	10,210	8,579	8,342	7,886	8,738	9,880	12,058	112,200
1984	7,094	8,414	8,446	9,827	10,423	8,921	8,879	11,226	8,971	8,386	10,200	13,920	116,400
1985	8,414	7,930	8,645	9,238	9,344	9,850	8,578	9,885	8,191	8,429	8,987	11,467	109,000
1986	7,897	7,835	7,340	8,727	7,547	7,129	3,988	6,404	6,932	7,869	8,216	10,197	90,081
1987	8,170	6,098	7,047	7,946	8,473	7,839	8,777	7,731	7,703	6,692	6,955	9,024	92,455
1988	7,852	7,264	9,453	7,956	7,891	9,453	10,562	9,903	7,374	8,074			

[1] Output of commercial bars .999 fine, including U.S. Mint purchases of crude. Production is from both foreign and domestic silver.
Sources: American Bureau of Metal Statistics; The Silver Institute, Inc.   T.603

SILVER

Highest and Lowest Prices of December Silver Futures at New York (Comex)   In Dollars per Ounce

Year of Delivery	Yr. Prior to Delivery Nov.	Dec.	Delivery Year Jan.	Feb.	Mar.	Apr.	May	June	July	Aug.	Sept.	Oct.	Nov.	Dec.	Life of Delivery Range
1981 High	23.525	22.615	18.800	15.900	14.670	13.580	12.700	11.840	9.780	10.260	11.800	10.050	9.410	9.050	43.750
Low	20.875	17.190	14.600	13.750	12.800	11.900	11.210	9.080	8.770	8.730	8.490	9.000	7.870	7.980	7.970
Close	22.015	18.190	15.165	13.720	13.135	12.205	11.685	9.180	9.032	9.720	9.380	9.250	8.205	7.985	—
1982 High	10.700	10.150	9.490	9.860	8.820	8.390	7.540	6.680	7.720	8.660	9.975	10.070	11.010	11.180	17.975
Low	9.110	9.040	8.730	8.650	7.600	7.350	6.670	5.110	5.800	6.320	7.700	8.020	8.950	10.020	5.110
Close	9.280	9.185	9.182	8.622	7.870	7.470	6.675	6.406	6.965	8.040	8.240	10.090	10.090	11.140	—
1983 High	11.900	12.350	15.238	16.070	12.180	13.380	14.420	13.320	13.110	13.250	12.740	10.780	9.860	10.040	16.070
Low	9.900	11.070	11.840	12.666	10.710	11.440	12.680	11.513	11.720	11.750	11.010	8.630	8.320	8.440	6.146
Close	11.090	11.910	15.238	12.666	11.382	12.715	13.640	12.055	12.225	12.410	11.070	8.630	9.620	8.810	—
1984 High	10.860	11.100	9.780	10.730	10.970	10.490	9.970	10.130	8.739	8.390	7.900	7.865	7.900	17.165	17.550
Low	9.220	9.400	8.470	9.290	9.930	9.465	9.110	8.700	7.060	7.200	7.120	7.120	6.950	6.245	6.245
Close	10.649	9.867	9.329	10.420	10.541	9.555	9.835	8.817	7.274	7.660	7.620	7.280	7.019	6.573	—
1985 High	8.745	7.850	6.930	6.850	7.250	7.200	7.015	6.740	6.615	6.630	6.320	6.530	6.318	6.120	12.300
Low	7.700	6.800	6.300	5.930	5.900	6.440	6.180	6.200	5.990	6.230	5.960	6.075	6.040	5.700	5.700
Close	7.736	6.860	6.832	6.059	7.106	6.480	6.392	6.309	6.460	6.370	6.095	6.125	6.077	5.865	—
1986 High	6.840	6.650	6.830	6.450	6.140	5.795	5.495	5.660	5.295	5.780	6.120	5.900	5.870	5.515	7.990
Low	6.540	6.130	6.070	5.930	5.370	5.170	5.030	5.100	5.060	5.150	5.240	5.470	5.200	5.270	5.030
Close	6.609	6.263	6.443	5.968	5.395	5.342	5.434	5.256	5.214	5.230	5.625	5.680	5.389	5.290	—
1987 High	6.210	5.850	6.030	5.880	6.675	10.148	9.900	8.370	8.585	9.100	8.240	8.620	7.330	7.060	10.148
Low	5.520	5.580	5.670	5.635	5.695	6.490	7.600	6.850	7.390	7.370	7.370	6.700	6.240	6.560	5.435
Close	5.717	5.714	5.791	5.707	6.466	8.320	7.920	7.555	8.511	7.530	7.610	6.990	7.037	6.713	—
1988 High	8.000	7.665	7.600	7.070	7.130	7.200	7.080	7.740	8.340	7.150	6.780	6.545	6.590	6.280	
Low	6.697	7.120	6.830	6.450	6.510	6.620	6.600	6.800	6.850	6.600	6.160	6.196	5.980	6.040	
Close	7.656	7.203	6.922	6.600	7.085	6.805	6.889	6.918	7.011	6.710	6.225	6.348	6.136	6.088	
1989 High	7.210	6.850													
Low	6.570	6.540													
Close	6.756	6.598													

Source: Commodity Exchange of N.Y. (COMEX)   T.596

Month–End Total Open Interest of Silver Futures at New York (COMEX) & Chicago   In Thous. of Contracts

Year	At New York (COMEX) Jan. 1	Feb. 1	Mar. 1	Apr. 1	May 1	June 1	July 1	Aug. 1	Sept. 1	Oct. 1	Nov. 1	Dec. 1	At Chicago (1,000 oz.[1]) Jan. 1	Apr. 1	July 1	Oct. 1
1981	32.0	27.6	24.3	25.7	26.1	28.8	29.4	31.0	31.0	29.9	32.3	27.5	28.0	21.2	29.8	16.3
1982	27.6	27.5	25.0	29.3	28.3	27.0	27.3	29.0	27.2	24.6	30.0	31.0	7.1	8.6	7.0	12.5
1983	33.9	44.6	54.3	45.9	50.1	57.1	42.8	42.7	48.1	53.0	51.7	55.4	19.4	32.6	35.8	35.1
1984	59.9	62.0	64.3	71.6	64.5	66.5	58.2	64.8	61.3	64.1	73.2	76.2	32.0	37.8	42.7	35.0
1985	81.5	84.3	76.1	74.3	70.1	77.3	73.5	72.5	70.1	76.1	86.6	85.3	27.1	23.2	25.1	21.4
1986	86.7	82.2	79.5	78.9	73.0	75.6	66.6	72.3	69.4	69.8	92.0	90.5	18.5	16.6	12.9	12.9
1987	89.4	94.5	89.0	105.3	105.7	92.0	79.1	90.4	82.0	80.7	83.2	69.7	12.4	12.8	15.2	13.5
1988	75.5	78.9	70.9	69.5	61.2	73.0	76.9	84.1	80.5	83.3	86.8	87.7	10.3	10.1	11.8	12.6
1989	92.8												12.0			

[1] 1,000 oz. contract from 1/82. Prior data are for 5,000 oz. contract.   *Source: Commodity Exchange of N.Y. (COMEX); Chicago Board of Trade*   T.601

Volume of Trading in Silver Futures at New York (COMEX)   In Thousands of Contracts

Year	Jan.	Feb.	Mar.	Apr.	May	June	July	Aug.	Sept.	Oct.	Nov.	Dec.	Total
1981	70.7	71.0	74.9	72.6	58.0	97.4	77.4	116.0	171.9	121.4	136.6	172.8	1,241
1982	112.8	193.9	211.5	192.9	99.7	217.4	263.1	317.2	258.0	288.9	350.6	372.8	2,869
1983	502.7	601.4	446.6	452.9	516.1	623.7	454.3	656.5	492.0	569.0	596.9	512.7	6,433
1984	570.8	698.8	695.7	629.9	626.7	587.4	554.7	601.5	431.3	449.2	534.2	362.3	6,698
1985	531.8	488.0	518.4	449.8	424.8	377.9	377.7	388.5	267.7	314.0	332.8	349.9	4,821
1986	394.0	368.9	277.6	438.8	280.1	336.1	187.9	317.8	454.6	286.7	338.9	168.2	3,850
1987	247.3	248.0	343.2	932.7	438.6	486.4	378.7	502.7	390.3	468.1	355.9	263.7	5,056
1988	274.1	301.1	348.9	313.9	341.1	726.9	638.9	411.7	299.9	268.4	475.4	264.4	4,665

Source: Commodity Exchange of N.Y. (COMEX)   T.602

Soybean Meal

World soymeal production in 1988/89 was estimated by USDA at 65.35 million tonnes, 3 percent less than a year earlier. Soymeal accounted for 58 percent of world protein meal output. Soymeal's share of protein meal production has stayed relatively constant recently, while rapeseed meal's has grown significantly. The U.S. was the world's largest soymeal producer, followed by Brazil and Argentina.

Soymeal consumption worldwide was forecast at 65.4 million tonnes, 4 percent less than a year earlier. U.S. use was put at 18.14 million tonnes, almost 28 percent of world consumption. The European Community was expected to consume almost 17 million tonnes. The USSR has become an important soymeal importer in an effort to raise more livestock. The Soviets were actively buying soymeal from Argentina and the U.S. China, Taiwan, and South Korea were using more soymeal to upgrade diets and to make feed rations efficient. In France and W. Germany, soymeal use was slowing, due to competition from domestically produced feeds like rapeseed meal.

World soymeal exports were projected at 25.72 million tonnes, 5 percent more than a year earlier. Brazil is by far the major exporter, and with another large crop expected, was forecast to export 9.2 million tonnes, up 26 percent from a year earlier. Argentina's soybean crop was also expected to be larger. With a system of differential export taxes that encourages sales of soymeal and a large capacity to process oilseeds, Argentina was projected to export 5.8 million tonnes of soymeal, 40 percent above a year earlier.

EC imports were projected to reach 12.5 million tonnes, up 2 percent from 1987/88. The USSR was expected to import 3 million tonnes, compared to 2.8 million a year earlier. Eastern European countries were also major buyers.

U.S. soymeal production in 1988/89 was estimated at 24.25 million short tons, down 14 percent. With carry-in stocks of 250,000 tons, the U.S. soymeal supply was put at 24.5 million tons, 13 percent less than a year earlier. Processing margins were very profitable, and demand appeared to be good. While processors responded to soymeal demand, the large soyoil inventory kept a lid on meal production. Domestic use was projected to be 20 million tons, or 6 percent less than a year earlier. Despite the summer drought, livestock producers decided to go ahead with most expansion plans. This was expected to keep demand for soymeal fairly strong.

U.S. soymeal exports in 1988/89 were forecast to be 4.2 million tons, down 38 percent. An expected rise in soybean production in Brazil and Argentina was likely to mean significant export competition. The leading markets for U.S. soymeal were the USSR, the Netherlands, Venezuela, Canada and Italy. In 1988/89, the Soviets bought large amounts of U.S. soymeal. As the USSR continued to increase livestock production, its demand for soymeal was expected to trend higher. Venezuela and Canada expanded their purchases, while the Netherlands reduced theirs.

Total U.S. soymeal use was put at 24.3 million tons, down 13 percent from a year earlier. Ending stocks of soymeal were forecast at 300,000 tons, 50,000 tons above a year earlier.

Futures Market

Soybean meal futures and options are traded on the Chicago Board of Trade.

World Soybean Meal Supply & Distribution In Thousands of Metric Tons

Season Year	Production Brazil	China	EC-12	United States	Total	Exports Brazil	United States	Total	Imports France	Total	Consumption EC-12	United States	Total	Stocks Brazil	United States	Total
1983–4	9,702	1,430	10,120	20,646	55,310	7,706	4,862	21,440	3,399	22,400	17,270	15,983	55,750	984	231	3,060
1984–5	10,190	1,410	9,790	22,252	58,200	8,440	4,460	22,310	3,290	22,850	17,970	17,672	59,010	720	351	2,780
1985–6	9,690	2,020	10,220	22,635	60,900	7,380	5,476	23,120	3,670	23,900	18,730	17,318	61,610	610	192	2,860
1986–7[1]	11,280	2,510	10,750	25,182	66,780	8,370	6,061	25,890	3,660	26,310	19,240	18,195	66,950	520	218	3,110
1987–8[1]	9,830	2,880	10,320	25,456	66,470	7,350	6,233	24,800	3,110	26,020	18,060	19,302	67,570	830	139	3,230
1988–9[2]	11,730	2,550	9,200	22,223	65,500	9,000	3,946	25,580	2,800	25,860	17,200	18,144	65,810	850	272	3,200

[1] Preliminary. [2] Forecast. *Source: Foreign Agricultural Service, U.S.D.A.*   T.607a

Supply and Distribution of Soybean Meal in the United States In Thousands of Short Tons

Year Begin. Oct.	For Stocks Oct. 1	Supply Production Total	For Animal Feed	For Edible Protein Pdt's.	Total Supply	Distribution Domestic Feed[2]	Exports	Total	$ Ton Decatur 44% Solvent	$ Tonne Decatur 44% Solvent	$ Tonne Brazil FOB 45–46% Protein
1983–4	474	22,756			23,230	17,615	5,360	22,975	188.21	207	203
1984–5	255	24,529			24,784	19,480	4,917	24,397	125.46	138	141
1985–6	387	24,951			25,338	19,090	6,036	25,126	154.88	171	175
1986–7	212	27,758			27,970	20,387	7,343	27,730	162.70	172	185
1987–8[1]	240	28,060			28,300	21,300	6,750	28,050	222.00	245	239
1988–9[3]	250	24,250			24,500	20,000	4,200	24,200	262.50	285	272

[1] Preliminary. [2] Includes small quantities used for industrial purposes, estimated at 30,000 tons annually. [3] Estimate.
Source: Economic Research Service, U.S.D.A.   T.606

SOYBEAN MEAL CBOT
Weekly high low & close of nearest futures

Stocks (at Oil Mills) of Soybean Cake & Meal in the United States In Thousands of Short Tons

Year	Oct. 1	Nov. 1	Dec. 1	Jan. 1	Feb. 1	Mar. 1	April 1	May 1	June 1	July 1	Aug. 1	Sept. 1
1976–7	354.9	423.5	427.7	353.9	384.7	429.9	412.6	449.0	408.3	390.7	399.0	270.4
1977–8	228.3	270.0	239.8	245.1	251.7	239.7	227.3	308.2	263.3	191.1	262.6	234.1
1978–9	242.9	210.4	178.2	260.5	215.1	198.4	210.4	231.6	207.4	205.3	232.2	140.3
1979–0	224.3	204.1	164.2	207.7	158.7	160.6	219.1	193.9	265.0	262.0	232.4	225.1
1980–1	189.7	211.1	350.0	221.8	209.7	214.4	232.2	184.4	254.0	209.7	156.1	199.7
1981–2	233.8	309.2	314.8	279.4	315.7	324.9	190.3	172.1	309.3	224.9	209.1	189.7
1982–3	175.2	342.8	349.6	332.3	400.2	422.8	341.0	356.1	341.5	272.3	365.2	378.5
1983–4	474.1	419.3	466.8	391.1	475.8	446.7	460.7	418.6	427.2	391.2	355.5	242.7
1984–5	255.4	236.1	285.7	336.8	319.6	334.1	444.6	429.8	495.8	569.6	562.5	458.0
1985–6	386.9	318.4	369.2	358.4	372.4	281.3	386.6	300.8	282.4	278.7	250.6	298.3
1986–7	211.7	218.0	387.3	240.3	311.2	277.5	235.8	244.0	321.7	261.3	292.9	301.3
1987–8[1]	240.2	267.6	311.8	296.2	390.4	304.9	243.7	299.5	255.6	294.4	437.4	264.6
1988–9[1]	153.7											

[1] *Preliminary.* *Sources: Economic Research Service, U.S.D.A.; Bureau of the Census*

T.613

U.S. Exports of Soybean Cake & Meal by Country of Destination   In Thousands of Metric Tons

Yr. Beg. Oct. 1	Egypt	Venezuela	Canada	Mexico	France	West Germany	Spain	Ireland	Italy	Netherlands	Philippines	Poland	United Kingdom	Yugoslavia	Total
1982–3	22.5	464.0	401.4		3.7	1,073	28.6	21.2	953.5	2,066	82.5	57.1	72.7	80.1	6,449
1983–4	14.3	527.2	427.6	0	0	1,154	63.0	4.6	493.0	693.1	293.8	278.5	2.5	8.1	4,862
1984–5	87.0	686.5	489.9	105.8	0	195.9	73.5	16.2	499.0	905.0	195.6	117.2	56.2	51.3	4,457
1985–6	200.0	566.8	607.3	81.5	15.0	576.0	74.5	4.7	658.2	1,221	164.0	0	59.7	128.8	5,476
1986–7	274.9	628.1	835.1	102.5	53.7	803.5	189.5	40.6	979.7	926.4	124.9	—	73.4	124.7	6,661
1987–8[1]	182.0	680.4	704.6	184.0	33.3	177.3	67.7	32.4	554.7	587.0	93.0	26.9	41.6	88.6	6,233

[1] Preliminary.   *Source: Bureau of the Census, U.S. Dept. of Commerce*   T.607

Average Price of Soybean Meal[1] (44% Solvent) at Decatur   In Dollars per Short Ton (Bulk)

Year	Jan.	Feb.	Mar.	Apr.	May	June	July	Aug.	Sept.	Oct.	Nov.	Dec.	Average
1982	191.00	191.00	183.60	190.25	192.40	183.60	181.90	169.00	160.80	157.00	173.40	178.50	179.37
1983	179.75	177.10	177.30	186.75	185.75	175.50	189.30	232.80	233.60	228.60	224.70	216.60	200.64
1984	201.90	184.40	196.40	190.00	187.40	174.40	157.60	151.60	144.90	141.60	135.20	136.75	166.84
1985	135.25	125.20	125.90	117.90	111.50	110.25	144.00	121.40	130.60	138.30	142.50	145.00	126.43
1986	153.25	152.25	163.70	157.00	157.90	158.90	161.00	163.50	165.20	151.90	154.00	149.60	157.35
1987	146.80	154.40	146.60	159.00	174.90	185.80	181.25	169.90	177.20	185.50	206.60	214.80	175.23
1988	193.75	183.00	191.80	200.40	223.50	287.80	255.60	255.10	264.90	259.75	248.20		

Source: Consumer Marketing Service, U.S.D.A.   T.608

Production of Soybean Cake & Meal in the U.S.   In Thousands of Short Tons

Crop Year	Oct.	Nov.	Dec.	Jan.	Feb.	Mar.	April	May	June	July	Aug.	Sept.	Total	Meal in Form of Soybeans[2]
1982–3	2,386	2,581	2,670	2,628	2,221	2,259	1,950	1,993	1,956	1,934	2,053	2,075	26,714	
1983–4	2,288	2,049	2,123	2,220	1,872	2,029	1,760	1,872	1,665	1,629	1,690	1,559	22,756	
1984–5	2,108	2,326	2,381	2,226	1,887	2,024	1,958	2,101	1,953	1,934	1,832	1,802	24,530	
1985–6	2,218	2,288	2,380	2,344	1,925	2,160	2,008	2,037	1,879	1,977	1,863	1,872	24,951	
1986–7	2,521	2,563	2,527	2,590	2,410	2,489	2,256	2,246	2,135	2,185	1,949	1,888	27,759	
1987–8[1]	2,439	2,668	2,649	2,554	2,377	2,573	2,450	2,340	2,129	2,110	1,873	1,898	28,060	
1988–9[1]	2,111													

[1] Preliminary.   [2] Calculated at 47.5 lbs of meal per bushel.   *Sources: Economic Research Service, U.S.D.A.; Bureau of Census.*   T.609

Month–End Open Interest of Soybean Meal Futures at the Chicago Board of Trade   In Contracts

Year	Jan.	Feb.	Mar.	Apr.	May	June	July	Aug.	Sept.	Oct.	Nov.	Dec.
1982	41,034	39,700	43,830	45,035	45,481	45,877	47,094	50,823	46,833	44,740	47,300	46,016
1983	50,744	44,808	52,979	46,653	42,893	40,900	50,340	66,826	64,266	64,124	63,461	60,248
1984	55,566	54,875	64,511	58,259	74,576	61,051	48,893	48,410	43,264	47,877	46,919	37,167
1985	39,110	43,110	45,164	48,579	54,103	53,405	41,451	44,260	40,703	46,091	42,925	46,875
1986	43,681	48,404	49,219	49,060	46,708	53,813	50,539	51,857	50,791	56,566	57,794	56,475
1987	64,057	70,403	63,315	67,482	64,661	60,709	51,454	46,696	57,538	63,850	82,040	68,170
1988	62,315	61,246	61,276	70,676	72,303	72,411	73,233	76,836	75,458	77,085	73,688	71,884

Source: Chicago Board of Trade   T.610

Volume of Trading of Soybean Meal Futures at the Chicago Board of Trade   In Thousands of Contracts

Year	Jan.	Feb.	Mar.	Apr.	May	June	July	Aug.	Sept.	Oct.	Nov.	Dec.	Total
1982	219.6	238.1	258.6	279.7	197.3	244.0	229.9	225.1	198.8	241.0	233.4	218.9	2,784
1983	269.2	248.0	252.7	272.9	238.6	259.5	320.5	528.2	447.6	349.4	413.1	271.8	3,872
1984	298.8	283.3	299.6	355.5	449.0	424.0	382.2	307.5	271.2	246.3	266.7	237.3	3,822
1985	252.1	232.6	244.5	283.9	285.0	277.3	420.9	250.7	268.5	287.5	292.3	243.9	3,339
1986	260.2	252.9	218.2	289.3	260.6	242.1	292.5	274.6	222.7	292.3	209.3	234.8	3,049
1987	260.4	211.6	222.6	305.3	353.3	430.1	307.8	247.1	334.7	388.7	385.5	350.9	3,798
1988	393.7	371.5	350.4	396.3	497.3	584.3	419.0	427.7	449.6	446.3	553.1	424.0	5,313

Source: Chicago Board of Trade   T.611

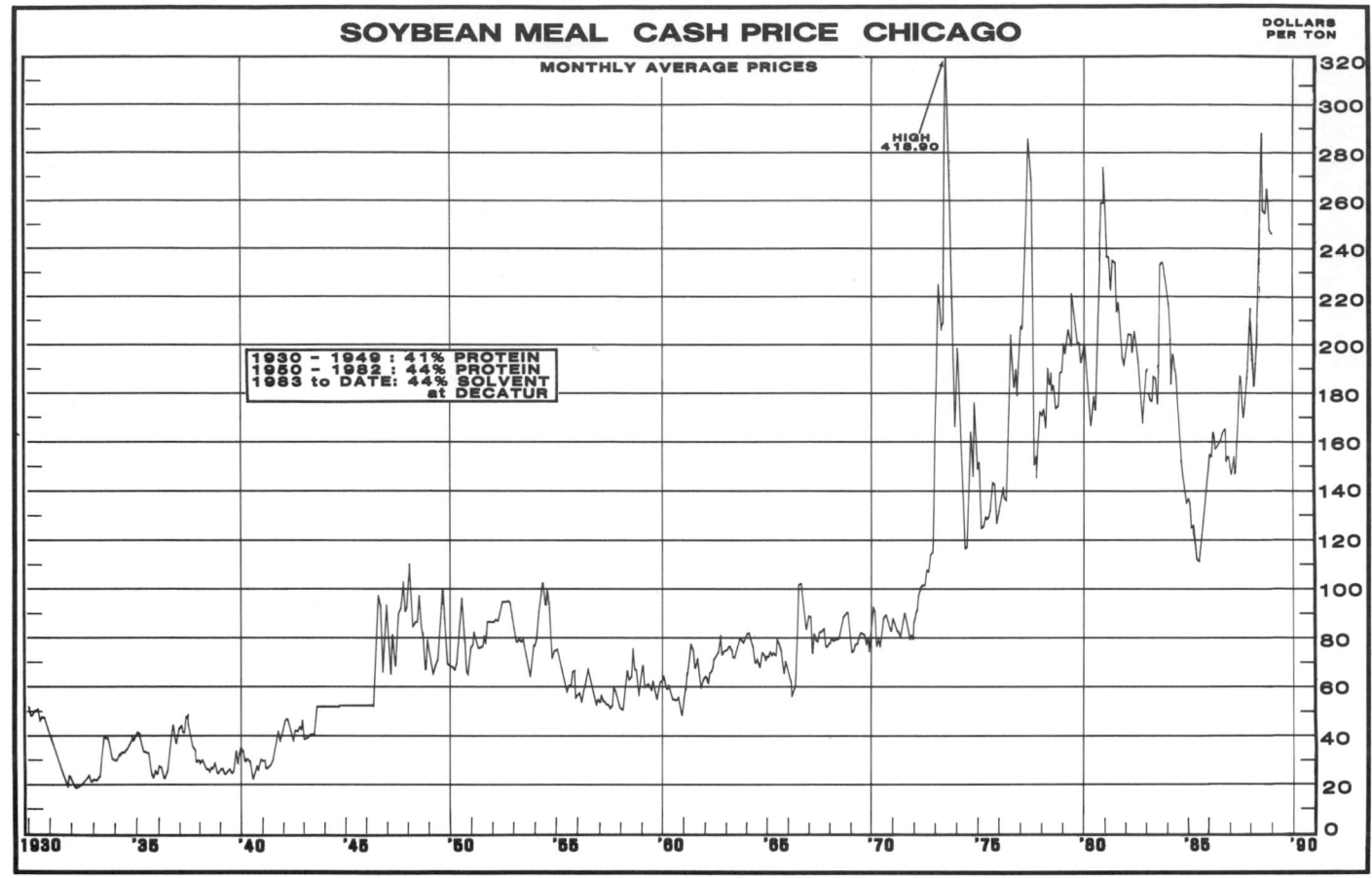

SOYBEAN MEAL CASH PRICE CHICAGO

MONTHLY AVERAGE PRICES

DOLLARS PER TON

1930 – 1949 : 41% PROTEIN
1950 – 1982 : 44% PROTEIN
1983 to DATE: 44% SOLVENT
at DECATUR

HIGH 418.90

High, Low & Closing Prices of May Soybean Meal Futures on the Chicago Board of Trade $ per Ton

Year of Delivery		Mar.	Apr.	May	Year Prior to Delivery							Delivery Year					Life of Delivery Range
					June	July	Aug.	Sept.	Oct.	Nov.	Dec.	Jan.	Feb.	Mar.	Apr.	May	
1982	High	—	261.5	252.0	242.0	241.0	230.0	218.0	210.5	206.5	203.5	197.0	197.7	188.5	196.0	196.5	261.5
	Low	—	248.5	234.5	221.0	223.0	207.0	203.5	201.8	194.1	181.5	187.8	182.7	178.4	186.2	188.0	181.5
	Close	—	249.5	239.0	225.0	231.5	209.0	206.5	203.5	197.3	188.3	195.9	186.1	187.7	190.9	189.0	—
1983	High	—	215.0	210.0	205.5	199.0	195.5	176.0	169.0	180.5	178.5	186.0	186.1	192.8	193.3	190.3	215.0
	Low	—	203.0	201.5	197.0	189.5	171.0	165.3	160.3	166.5	171.3	174.1	170.6	172.5	183.3	176.1	160.3
	Close	—	209.5	201.5	197.7	192.0	174.0	166.5	166.0	178.0	175.2	185.6	171.4	189.7	189.4	181.3	—
1984	High	219.5	217.5	213.0	198.0	229.0	267.5	261.0	246.0	249.6	229.5	221.5	201.5	210.0	205.4	199.0	267.5
	Low	213.5	207.5	194.2	185.0	194.0	218.8	229.0	229.5	220.0	212.2	193.2	188.9	200.5	182.5	183.0	182.5
	Close	215.2	211.5	194.2	195.0	216.2	244.0	240.0	232.0	226.7	225.0	197.4	200.7	202.9	183.8	198.4	—
1985	High	—	204.5	195.7	201.0	197.0	180.0	172.0	175.0	173.3	165.5	154.0	147.0	141.5	137.0	124.9	204.5
	Low	—	196.0	190.5	188.2	169.5	167.5	160.0	160.5	163.0	150.1	145.6	129.5	130.1	120.1	118.5	118.5
	Close	—	196.0	198.0	200.5	171.3	171.0	162.0	169.7	164.8	151.1	147.6	130.3	138.1	120.5	118.6	—
1986	High	—	162.5	154.3	151.5	158.0	139.5	145.2	151.9	152.5	157.0	160.5	161.5	163.9	159.5	156.5	163.9
	Low	—	152.8	145.0	143.0	135.5	132.5	134.0	139.0	136.0	141.5	150.0	150.3	153.5	150.5	144.3	132.5
	Close	—	152.8	146.2	143.7	137.0	135.5	141.0	151.0	145.0	153.4	154.0	161.2	153.7	157.2	149.6	—
1987	High	—	165.5	169.7	154.0	158.5	155.4	157.1	155.5	151.8	149.0	145.8	143.3	143.5	161.9	179.5	179.5
	Low	—	149.7	152.0	146.5	143.0	148.0	152.1	148.7	148.6	141.5	139.2	135.6	135.8	143.6	158.8	135.6
	Close	—	165.2	153.2	146.5	154.7	155.3	155.0	151.8	149.0	145.5	140.0	136.9	143.1	160.9	168.0	—
1988	High	—	163.5	188.0	199.0	170.0	156.5	167.5	171.0	195.5	196.5	189.5	191.9	195.2	203.7	249.0	249.0
	Low	—	155.0	162.0	168.0	157.0	148.0	154.0	157.2	163.3	177.0	175.5	174.5	179.8	193.5	202.0	148.0
	Close	—	163.5	173.0	169.5	160.2	152.9	163.7	167.2	192.2	185.2	178.1	188.6	193.8	203.5	246.5	—
1988	High	204.5	215.5	241.7	304.0	280.0	260.0	274.0	258.0	262.0	264.0						
	Low	200.5	204.0	209.5	239.0	221.5	236.0	245.5	239.0	232.5	236.5						
	Close	203.5	214.2	241.7	275.0	233.2	254.0	249.7	247.5	245.7	263.5						

Source: Chicago Board of Trade

T.612

Soybean Oil

World soyoil production in 1988/89 was pegged by the USDA at 14.86 million tonnes, down 2 percent from 1987/88. Soyoil was expected to amount to almost 28 percent of total world output of vegetable and marine oils, followed by palm oil with 17 percent.

The U.S. is the major soyoil producer, accounting for 34 percent of world output in 1988/89. Brazil and Argentina were expected to increase production, and part of the U.S. market share was being lost to them.

World soyoil consumption in 1988/89 was put at 14.8 million tonnes, near the previous season. Consumption has been rising, due to population growth, higher incomes, and better diets. In Asia, particularly Pakistan and Bangladesh, it has grown rapidly. In Europe and the USSR, usage is steady or declining.

Global soyoil exports in 1988/89 were put at 3.8 million tonnes, up almost 2 percent from a year earlier. While U.S. shipments were likely to fall, Brazilian exports were expected to rise to 900,000 tonnes from 620,000 tonnes the previous season. Argentina was emerging as the largest exporter with projected shipments of 1.2 million tonnes, above the previous year's 840,000 tonnes. The EC was expected to export 1 million tonnes, down 22 percent from a year earlier. Major importers were the USSR, Iran, China, Japan, India and Mexico.

World ending stocks of soyoil were pegged at 1.9 million tonnes in 1988/89, down 15 percent from a year earlier. U.S. stocks were forecast to fall, while those in Brazil and Argentina were expected to rise.

U.S. soyoil production in 1988/89 was estimated at 11.3 billion pounds, down 13 percent from a year earlier. With beginning stocks a burdensome 2.15 billion pounds and projected imports of 200 million pounds, total supplies were put at 13.65 billion. This was down 9 percent from the previous season, but still large.

There was continued concern about U.S. soyoil imports. Soyoil is often brought into southern ports, refined, and reexported to Caribbean countries. Price differentials which make U.S. soyoil prices higher than South American oil cause this to occur.

Domestic use of soyoil was projected at 11.05 billion pounds, up only 1 percent from 1987/88. With rising incomes and higher employment, more consumers were eating away from home, boosting soyoil consumption.

U.S soyoil exports in 1988/89 were expected to fall 29 percent to 1.35 billion pounds. High U.S. prices and competition from South American soyoil and other oils underscored the decline. In particular, palm oil production was at record levels, and its price had not risen as much as soyoil. Since U.S. soyoil is sold to Asian countries like Pakistan, Malaysian palm oil exports provide significant competition.

Some U.S. soyoil is sold under the Export Enhancement Program, which subsidizes sales. The program was expected to be needed in 1988/89, since larger crops were forecast for Brazil and Argentina. U.S. exports were expected to face especially strong competition in spring and summer of 1989 from Argentina.

U.S. ending stocks in 1988/89 were projected at 1.25 billion pounds, down 42 percent from a year earlier.

Futures Market

Soybean oil futures and options are traded on the Chicago Board of Trade.

World Supply & Demand of Soybean Oil   In Thousands of Metric Tons

Crop Year	Production Brazil	Production EC-12	Production United States	Production Total	Exports Brazil	Exports United States	Exports Total	Imports India	Imports Total	Consumption Brazil	Consumption EC-12	Consumption India	Consumption United States	Consumption Total	Stocks[3] United States	Stocks[3] Total
1982–3	2,564	2,580	5,462	13,570	1,020	918	3,810	537	3,650	1,612	1,550	540	4,472	13,230	572	1,540
1983–4	2,350	2,260	4,932	12,770	987	827	3,970	810	3,890	1,510	1,350	760	4,350	12,960	327	1,270
1984–5	2,460	2,210	5,202	13,340	990	753	3,630	400	3,510	1,550	1,400	580	4,498	13,130	287	1,360
1985–6	2,350	2,250	5,269	13,820	450	570	3,150	260	3,060	1,940	1,380	470	4,560	13,440	430	1,650
1986–7[1]	2,730	2,360	5,798	15,130	950	538	3,840	360	3,710	1,930	1,450	440	4,915	14,640	782	2,010
1987–8[1]	2,370	2,240	5,885	15,000	620	850	3,770	400	3,620	1,860	1,420	610	4,957	14,810	949	2,000
1988–9[2]	2,820	2,020	5,202	14,900	800	590	3,700	180	3,510	1,980	1,400	410	5,035	14,940	662	1,820

[1] Preliminary.   [2] Forecast.   [3] End of season.   *Source: Foreign Agricultural Service, U.S.D.A.*   T168b

Supply & Distribution of Soybean Oil in the U.S.   In Millions of Pounds

Year Begin. Oct.	Production	Imports	Stocks Oct. 1	Exports & Shipments	Total Domestic	Food Shortening	Food Margarine	Food Cooking & Salad Oils	Other Edible	Total Food	Non-Food Paint & Varnish	Non-Food Resins & Plastics	Fatty Acids	Total Non-Food	Total Disappearance
1982–3	12,040	0	1,103	2,025	9,857	2,944	1,615	4,668	58	9,284	38	96		205	11,882
1983–4	10,872	0	1,261	1,824	9,588	3,207	1,494	4,442	101	9,245	39	110		231	11,412
1984–5	11,468	20	721	1,660	9,917	3,655	1,589	4,800	129	10,172	52	93	29	252	11,577
1985–6	11,617	8	632	1,257	10,053	3,440	1,735	4,686	138	10,004	60	99	32	280	11,310
1986–7	12,783	15	947	1,187	10,833	3,359	1,661	5,054	138	10,213	63	109	33	300	12,020
1987–8[1]	12,974	196	1,725	1,873	10,930	3,520	1,610	5,100	140	10,600					12,803
1988–9[2]	11,468	300	2,092	1,300	11,100										12,400

[1] Preliminary.   [2] Forecast.   *Source: Economic Research Service, U.S.D.A.*   T.623

231

SOYBEAN OIL

Salient Statistics of Soybean Oil in the U.S.   In Millions of Pounds

Crop Year Begin. Oct.	Production Crude	Production Refined	Consumption In Refining	Consumption In End Pdt's.	Stocks Sept. 30 Crude	Stocks Sept. 30 Refined	Imports for Consumption	Exports Crude	Exports Refined	$ Tonne S.B. Oil Brazil FOB Bulk
1982–3	12,040	9,714	10,075	9,485	959.4	301.6	66.8	1,725	17.0	444
1983–4	10,872	9,475	9,827	9,477	435.5	285.0	0	1,398	22.9	685
1984–5	11,470	9,937	10,284	10,515	341.3	291.2	20.4	1,255	16.4	609
1985–6	11,617	9,719	10,088	10,283	652.6	294.0	7.7	833.3	32.8	342
1986–7	12,798	10,400	10,751	10,512	1,451	274.0	1.1	903.0	38.8	302
1987–8										400

Source: Bureau of Census   T.614

U.S. Exports of Soybean Oil,[1] by Country of Destination   In Thousands of Metric Tons

Yr. Beg. Oct. 1	Australia	Colombia	Canada	Venezuela	Ecuador	Ethiopia	Haiti	Peru	India	Israel	Mexico	Morocco	Pakistan	Panama	Egypt	Grand Total
1979–0	16.4	82.6	14.8		35.3		22.8	36.2	427.7	9.6	31.4	2.3	147.4	17.9	6.0	1,220
1980–1	16.5	60.3	7.8		38.6		22.4	41.2	61.8	5.2	21.6	5.0	125.7	14.7	3.4	740
1981–2	22.6	77.4	5.4	42.7	36.2		8.8	46.8	68.4	.3	91.1	9.7	259.9	21.7	6.9	942
1982–3	5.0	69.5	7.5	55.9	50.4		20.4	70.2	54.9	.4	16.3	9.0	236.7	16.4	3.5	918
1983–4	.3	24.8	9.8	50.5	41.1		12.5	24.9	169.4	.5	68.1	2.5	216.1	15.7	3.6	827
1984–5	.2	22.2	12.9	51.9	44.7	24.0	16.1	11.4	62.8	.9	45.4	3.8	168.4	8.0	3.9	753
1985–6	.2	8.9	6.1	17.1	16.7	17.3	9.5	1.6	37.6	.4	49.1	3.2	274.9	2.8	4.9	570
1986–7	.4	.5	6.9	18.7	18.8	.6	15.3	1.3	47.1		21.9	59.5	146.7	3.0	1.9	538.5
1987–8[2]	—	.3	7.3	4.9	19.1	17.6	3.4	1.1	151.6		11.5	35.8	396.7	3.7	.7	650.0

[1] Crude & refined oil combined as such.   [2] Preliminary.   *Source: The Bureau of the Census, U.S. Dept. of Commerce.*   T.615

U.S. Production of Crude Soybean Oil   In Millions of Pounds

Year	Oct.	Nov.	Dec.	Jan.	Feb.	Mar.	Apr.	May	June	July	Aug.	Sept.	Total
1979–0	1,020	1,068	1,102	1,115	1,065	1,098	993.7	1,010	901.6	927.8	913.8	890.1	12,105
1980–1	1,080	1,078	1,024	1,011	887.8	991.3	954.2	914.9	830.7	815.8	827.2	855.6	11,271
1981–2	1,125	1,018	1,070	995.6	917.7	912.1	866.8	930.2	828.4	765.6	732.0	818.3	10,979
1982–3	1,079	1,145	1,191	1,167	997.0	1,015	881.3	908.9	891.3	888.0	930.2	945.3	12,040
1983–4	1,081	957.7	990.9	1,053	896.9	972.7	846.7	906.3	803.5	788.8	819.4	755.9	10,872
1984–5	995.5	1,072	1,096	1,027	879.0	946.0	917.6	983.3	918.9	912.6	868.8	853.4	11,470
1985–6	1,040	1,053	1,096	1,086	894.8	1,005	935.4	953.3	881.9	909.5	875.3	886.7	11,618
1986–7	1,163	1,172	1,152	1,186	1,110	1,149	1,047	1,038	980.9	1,014	891.3	881.4	12,783
1987–8[1]	1,120	1,207	1,208	1,170	1,092	1,187	1,133	1,087	996.4	994.2	878.6	901.3	12,975
1988–9[1]	1,047												

[1] Preliminary.   *Source: Bureau of the Census*   T.618

U.S. Production of Refined Soybean Oil   In Millions of Pounds

Year	Oct.	Nov.	Dec.	Jan.	Feb.	Mar.	Apr.	May	June	July	Aug.	Sept.	Total
1979–0	805.9	797.6	760.3	801.9	760.5	767.7	687.1	712.8	669.0	720.3	760.7	764.5	9,038
1980–1	784.1	760.5	763.1	741.6	706.3	833.9	741.2	754.9	812.9	765.4	813.3	812.1	9,289
1981–2	833.6	840.9	805.2	768.7	767.6	866.4	754.5	817.3	866.3	775.4	811.7	794.0	9,702
1982–3	824.6	827.8	795.1	784.1	727.1	841.8	800.9	843.1	824.0	778.7	837.7	828.8	9,714
1983–4	839.2	747.2	737.1	797.9	813.2	841.8	763.8	859.5	794.6	767.9	752.2	760.9	9,475
1984–5	907.6	835.5	821.2	838.7	796.1	835.5	865.0	899.5	773.1	763.9	806.2	794.4	9,937
1985–6	865.7	834.8	790.0	804.2	751.1	819.5	783.0	808.5	816.8	780.2	830.1	834.8	9,719
1986–7	911.3	848.1	850.0	790.2	763.6	900.7	871.2	826.9	871.3	921.8	898.6	946.5	10,400
1987–8[1]	975.5	925.8	902.5	880.3	843.4	925.6	843.5	894.1	890.1	947.4	903.6	838.7	10,771
1988–9[1]	904.8												

[1] Preliminary.   *Source: Bureau of the Census*   T.617

Soybean Oil Consumption in End Products in the U.S.   In Millions of Pounds

Year	Jan.	Feb.	Mar.	Apr.	May	June	July	Aug.	Sept.	Oct.	Nov.	Dec.	Total
1978	664.1	648.8	771.7	686.5	662.4	640.5	596.2	699.8	672.5	715.9	709.3	707.5	8,175
1979	695.1	636.2	755.3	682.4	775.0	701.6	711.4	744.8	700.9	781.4	742.2	730.1	8,656
1980	750.7	719.4	762.9	671.6	693.6	683.7	671.2	754.5	737.1	719.1	682.6	738.7	8,585
1981	698.7	680.7	775.1	722.3	728.7	774.0	741.1	755.1	796.4	796.8	783.6	749.3	9,002
1982	740.0	737.7	809.6	715.2	761.0	834.6	775.2	811.9	820.5	799.9	763.1	733.2	9,302
1983	761.6	702.2	827.3	765.9	814.9	830.3	745.1	847.0	894.3	812.7	711.4	705.2	9,418
1984	827.6	821.7	837.8	781.1	857.4	824.4	744.7	772.2	780.6	932.0	883.4	856.1	9,919
1985	989.0	804.0	867.1	885.9	940.8	810.5	825.9	856.1	863.7	922.4	864.2	851.6	10,481
1986	836.7	794.0	889.7	849.1	850.3	856.8	835.1	843.1	890.3	927.6	840.6	891.2	10,305
1987[1]	800.9	789.7	862.0	869.6	826.4	918.9	932.7	902.9	949.6	961.4	876.0	891.5	10,582
1988[1]	906.4	820.5	930.0	839.9	870.5	937.9	936.5	907.3	829.1	925.7			

[1] Preliminary.   *Source: Bureau of the Census*   T.624

U.S. Exports of Soybean Oil (Crude & Refined)   In Millions of Pounds

Year	Jan.	Feb.	Mar.	Apr.	May	June	July	Aug.	Sept.	Oct.	Nov.	Dec.	Total
1978	113.1	141.8	252.6	218.9	176.4	147.2	165.5	108.8	193.4	96.8	154.8	175.4	1,945
1979	219.1	249.8	199.0	185.6	107.3	299.0	166.2	187.4	159.1	127.8	208.5	261.9	2,371
1980	173.4	250.0	325.4	269.6	327.3	194.6	109.7	175.7	171.2	112.5	84.7	120.5	2,315
1981	116.0	113.8	202.8	76.1	109.6	108.8	93.1	291.7	97.9	187.2	146.6	184.3	1,698
1982	43.9	176.7	126.5	148.5	103.3	208.0	270.2	237.4	244.1	181.1	174.9	142.0	2,057
1983	124.0	225.9	90.4	305.7	127.5	94.1	208.9	125.1	225.1	55.1	54.7	95.5	1,732
1984	161.3	289.9	258.9	163.3	208.3	157.3	140.0	73.0	156.3	200.3	214.6	189.6	2,068
1985	66.7	198.3	184.9	66.9	52.4	138.8	174.4	70.1	102.8	125.4	38.1	74.3	923.3
1986	80.6	100.7	92.8	124.0	50.7	115.1	44.6	187.7	223.4	118.2	27.4	22.8	1,188
1987	67.9	74.0	52.1	28.2	47.4	85.0	175.6	261.0	224.8	100.1	139.0	134.0	1,389
1988[1]	25.7	281.0	273.7	87.7	138.6	269.0	157.2	78.9					

[1] Preliminary.   *Source: Dept. of Commerce*   T.619

U.S. Stocks of Soybean Oil (Crude & Refined) at Factory & Warehouses   In Millions of Pounds

Year	Oct. 1	Nov. 1	Dec. 1	Jan. 1	Feb. 1	Mar. 1	April 1	May 1	June 1	July 1	Aug. 1	Sept. 1
1978–9	728.6	813.4	837.1	970.6	932.2	942.8	1,004	987.3	1,043	922.9	915.4	815.1
1979–0	775.8	819.8	867.3	1,030	1,155	1,205	1,176	1,184	1,145	1,226	1,305	1,263
1980–1	1,210	1,428	1,677	1,738	1,900	1,976	2,017	2,119	2,166	2,139	2,024	1,783
1981–2	1,736	1,790	1,884	2,024	2,160	2,141	2,141	2,112	2,018	1,889	1,647	1,398
1982–3	1,103	1,208	1,305	1,587	1,713	1,700	1,842	1,600	1,552	1,546	1,411	1,408
1983–4	1,261	1,453	1,661	1,919	1,907	1,583	1,520	1,380	1,203	1,012	989.6	871.0
1984–5	720.5	597.2	580.1	777.1	883.6	723.9	715.6	666.0	706.7	731.9	724.2	715.7
1985–6	632.4	636.1	810.4	969.4	1,167	1,181	1,247	1,219	1,360	1,225	1,321	1,152
1986–7	946.6	963.6	1,269	1,507	1,837	2,017	2,352	2,344	2,416	2,339	2,184	1,979
1987–8[1]	1,725	1,661	1,834	2,050	2,391	2,239	2,343	2,385	2,570	2,361	2,203	2,212
1988–9	2,092	2,063										

[1] Preliminary.   *Source: Bureau of the Census*   T.616

Average Prices of Crude Domestic Soybean Oil (in Tank Cars) F.O.B. Decatur   In Cents per Pound

Year	Oct.	Nov.	Dec.	Jan.	Feb.	Mar.	Apr.	May	June	July	Aug.	Sept.	Average
1978–9	26.7	23.7	25.8	25.8	27.3	26.9	26.7	27.8	27.4	29.1	29.2	30.0	27.2
1979–0	27.9	27.8	26.2	23.6	23.4	22.1	20.3	20.8	21.6	26.2	25.9	26.1	24.3
1980–1	25.1	26.7	23.7	23.0	22.0	23.1	23.4	21.6	21.3	22.8	20.8	19.4	22.7
1981–2	19.7	19.9	18.9	18.4	18.2	18.5	19.7	20.6	19.4	19.0	17.9	17.4	19.0
1982–3	17.4	17.6	16.6	16.4	17.3	17.7	19.3	19.8	19.4	21.6	30.2	34.3	20.6
1983–4	30.7	28.1	27.3	28.3	27.2	30.1	32.1	39.0	36.0	31.0	29.0	28.0	30.6
1984–5	30.6	31.9	28.4	28.0	29.6	31.3	33.6	32.5	32.5	29.1	24.1	22.6	29.5
1985–6	20.7	20.6	21.4	20.6	18.6	17.6	17.7	17.8	16.8	16.2	14.3	13.9	18.0
1986–7	14.63	14.88	14.94	15.60	15.40	15.21	15.31	16.22	15.96	15.41	15.16	15.58	15.36
1987–8	17.03	17.55	19.00	21.98	20.94	20.22	21.67	26.55	27.68	29.65	27.16	25.55	22.92
1988–9[1]	23.16	21.31											

[1] Preliminary.   *Source: Bureau of Labor Statistics*   T.620

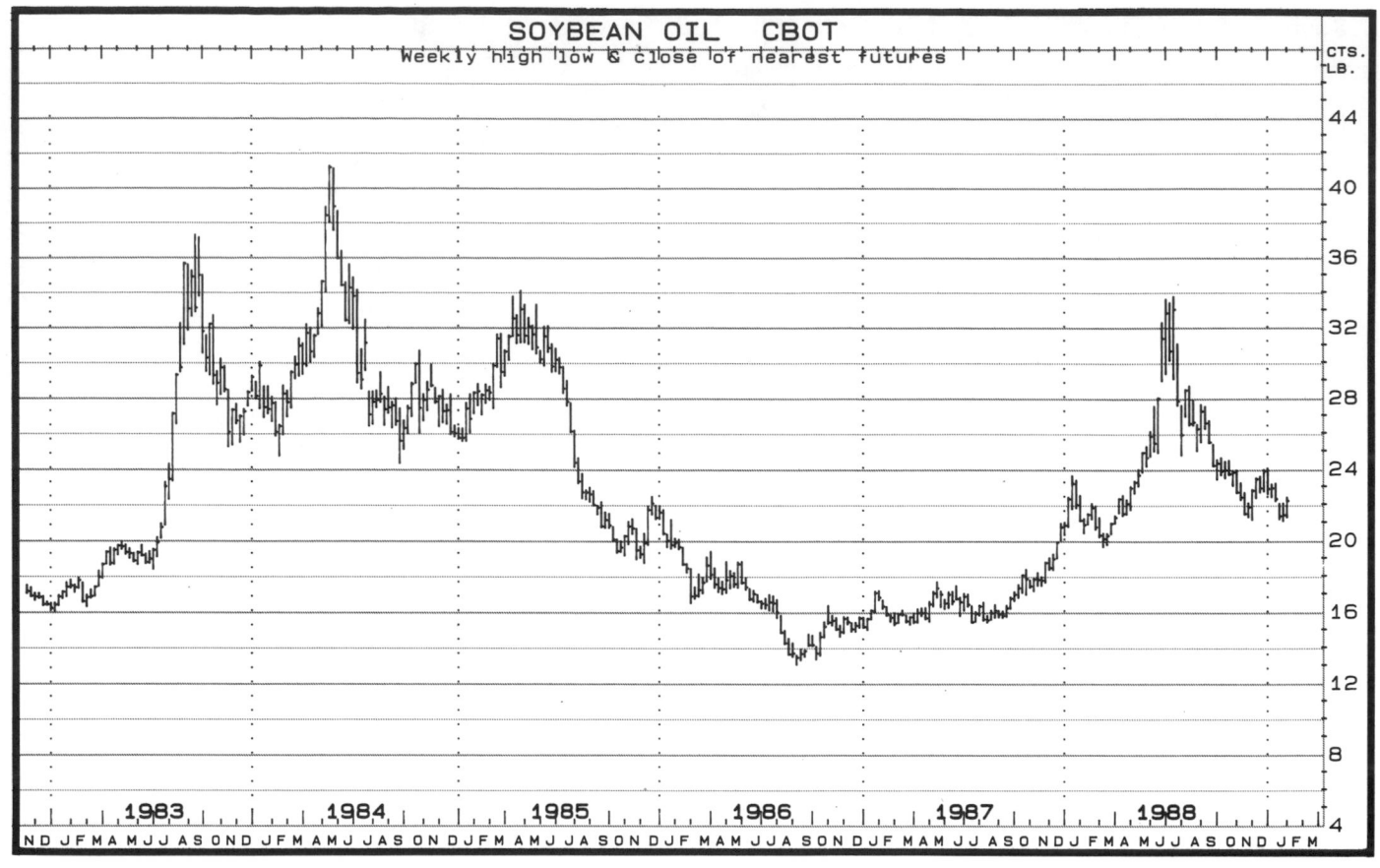

High, Low & Closing Prices of May Soybean Oil Futures on the Chicago Board of Trade ¢ per lb.

Year of Delivery		Mar.	Apr.	May	June	July	Aug.	Sept.	Oct.	Nov.	Dec.	Jan.	Feb.	Mar.	Apr.	May	Life of Delivery Range
						Year Prior to Delivery								**Delivery Year**			
1982	High	28.60	29.02	28.10	26.50	27.90	25.90	24.50	24.25	23.25	21.85	21.01	21.08	19.45	20.25	20.90	29.02
	Low	27.13	27.75	26.30	24.70	24.85	23.50	22.52	22.45	21.20	19.65	19.70	18.72	18.26	18.88	19.70	18.26
	Close	28.60	27.75	26.35	25.02	25.90	23.60	22.87	23.00	21.21	19.76	20.88	19.13	18.88	19.83	20.72	—
1983	High	—	—	22.90	21.65	20.42	19.90	19.35	18.60	18.40	17.75	17.96	18.30	18.59	19.64	19.85	22.90
	Low	—	—	21.66	20.30	19.73	18.15	18.00	17.50	17.25	16.91	16.61	16.65	16.80	18.54	18.92	16.61
	Close	—	—	21.66	20.32	19.73	18.85	18.00	17.60	17.48	16.91	17.91	16.74	18.56	19.61	19.29	—
1984	High	—	21.60	21.60	20.75	25.25	34.00	35.85	22.60	30.70	30.10	30.60	28.82	31.55	33.70	41.15	41.15
	Low	—	20.75	19.27	19.75	20.50	25.05	29.90	28.35	26.20	26.50	27.00	25.05	27.72	29.70	31.97	19.27
	Close	—	21.53	20.20	20.75	24.30	32.75	31.00	28.88	27.74	30.08	27.68	28.25	29.82	32.47	39.87	—
1985	High	—	—	29.95	30.10	27.15	27.45	26.50	25.75	26.10	25.60	27.20	27.70	30.60	34.00	33.27	34.00
	Low	—	—	28.10	26.92	23.15	24.35	22.80	23.85	23.78	23.95	24.40	26.30	26.15	30.05	30.65	22.80
	Close	—	—	28.88	27.92	24.35	26.70	23.80	25.07	24.55	24.61	26.67	27.26	30.52	32.53	32.93	—
1986	High	24.40	27.85	27.45	25.80	25.40	24.20	22.65	22.15	21.60	23.04	22.50	20.30	19.27	19.25	18.50	27.85
	Low	24.40	24.40	24.40	24.20	23.90	22.30	21.45	20.02	19.25	19.30	19.91	16.76	16.96	16.90	17.22	16.76
	Close	24.40	27.20	24.53	24.86	24.25	22.60	22.20	20.92	19.60	22.01	20.14	17.06	18.65	17.50	—
1987	High	20.60	20.90	19.75	18.71	18.40	17.35	15.80	16.75	16.35	16.30	17.38	17.20	16.30	16.14	17.60	20.90
	Low	18.38	18.48	18.50	17.65	17.20	14.75	14.40	14.60	15.27	15.50	15.45	15.84	15.21	15.30	15.95	14.40
	Close	20.60	19.95	18.68	17.65	17.20	14.90	15.43	15.95	16.19	15.76	17.00	15.91	15.59	15.92	16.56	—
1988	High	—	—	19.25	19.00	18.40	17.50	18.04	19.30	19.55	21.55	23.70	22.33	21.50	22.95	24.80	24.80
	Low	—	—	17.77	17.50	16.85	16.50	16.80	17.81	17.86	19.00	21.32	20.66	19.86	21.32	22.58	16.50
	Close	—	—	17.82	18.15	17.38	16.95	17.75	18.08	19.30	21.41	21.33	21.57	21.21	22.86	24.64	—
1989	High	—	24.25	27.15	33.00	32.90	29.43	29.10	26.15	25.07	24.95						
	Low	—	22.42	24.20	25.80	25.90	26.70	25.20	24.22	22.45	22.90						
	Close	—	24.25	27.10	31.50	26.90	28.65	25.77	24.72	23.17	23.95						

Source: Chicago Board of Trade

T.622

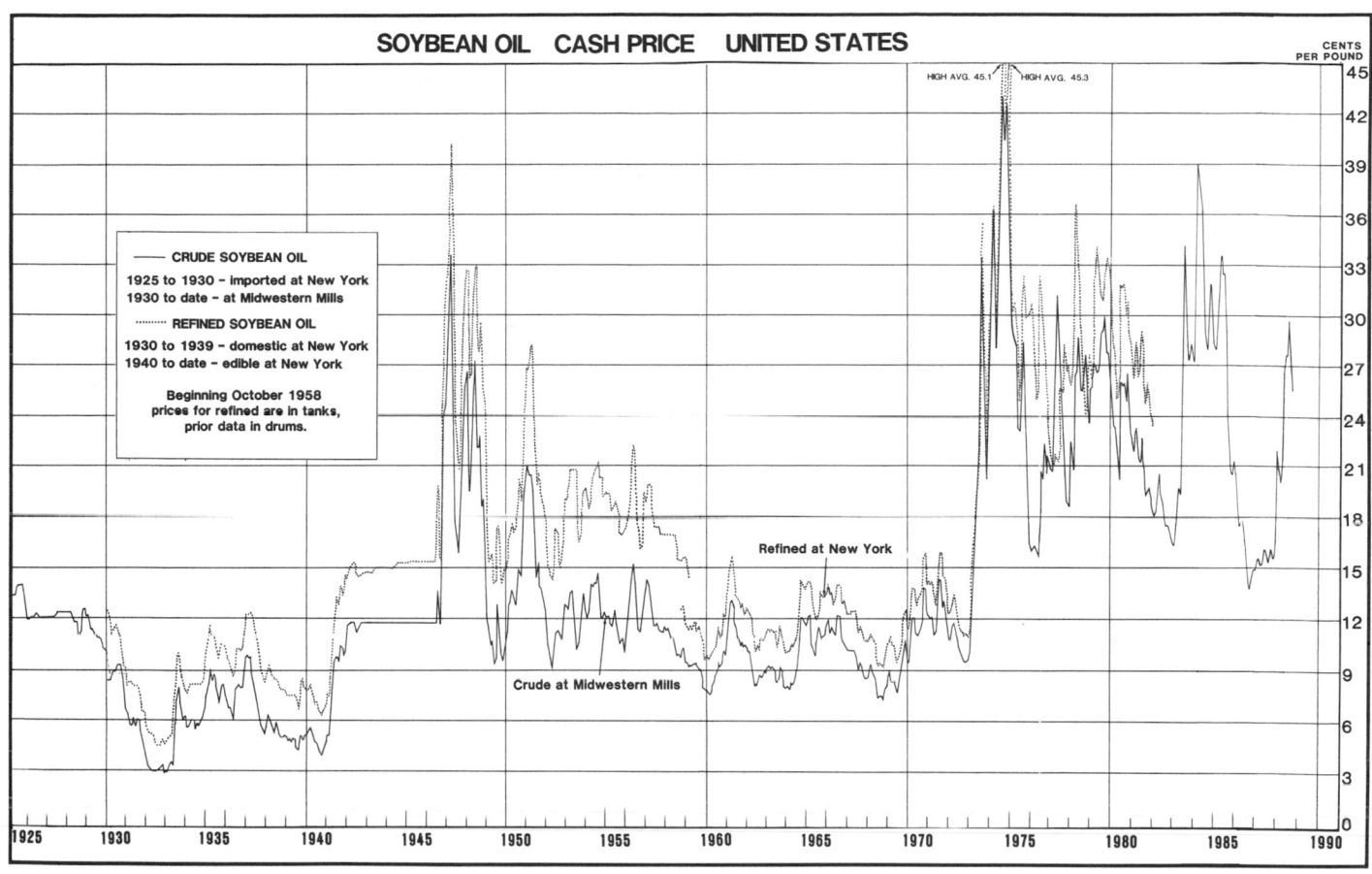

SOYBEAN OIL   CASH PRICE   UNITED STATES

CENTS PER POUND

CRUDE SOYBEAN OIL
1925 to 1930 – imported at New York
1930 to date – at Midwestern Mills
REFINED SOYBEAN OIL
1930 to 1939 – domestic at New York
1940 to date – edible at New York

Beginning October 1958
prices for refined are in tanks,
prior data in drums.

Refined at New York

Crude at Midwestern Mills

Month–End Open Interest of Soybean Oil Futures of the Chicago Board of Trade   In Contracts

Year	Jan.	Feb.	Mar.	Apr.	May	June	July	Aug.	Sept.	Oct.	Nov.	Dec.
1979	50,713	57,729	57,893	55,657	57,820	64,671	58,852	58,258	60,854	67,778	65,893	64,374
1980	62,515	63,472	59,707	52,805	61,089	65,949	64,710	63,908	66,723	75,815	91,407	71,527
1981	58,671	65,580	57,956	67,241	56,968	63,400	54,007	56,847	49,411	50,786	54,232	48,295
1982	53,029	53,375	49,824	53,395	57,366	58,151	56,863	50,574	44,091	41,930	45,976	50,290
1983	49,329	49,360	57,446	59,894	58,635	55,678	53,842	71,341	73,946	79,303	74,817	67,695
1984	58,227	54,536	53,081	60,190	65,570	58,857	49,323	46,848	41,617	40,386	43,856	40,264
1985	38,534	44,803	48,093	60,717	58,629	59,856	41,451	56,313	48,963	45,951	44,186	48,361
1986	50,584	55,010	57,640	57,825	54,035	61,808	62,011	59,429	53,720	66,372	72,037	63,797
1987	85,826	77,627	73,653	77,508	81,405	88,656	77,028	68,039	66,938	69,040	80,398	70,229
1988	85,655	87,700	85,335	91,026	86,679	91,569	91,579	86,498	83,108	81,549	82,576	72,108

Source: Chicago Board of Trade   T.625

Volume of Trading of Soybean Oil Futures at the Chicago Board of Trade   In Thousands of Contracts

Year	Jan.	Feb.	Mar.	Apr.	May	June	July	Aug.	Sept.	Oct.	Nov.	Dec.	Total
1979	215.0	291.5	233.8	254.4	212.3	321.7	313.0	252.5	262.0	311.6	222.3	191.6	3,082
1980	200.7	210.3	177.1	185.0	198.2	216.9	361.8	284.8	329.9	332.6	327.0	343.7	3,168
1981	243.8	231.1	237.9	254.0	221.7	274.8	355.1	233.7	240.2	235.0	228.1	292.1	3,047
1982	219.1	245.6	239.8	272.2	277.7	270.7	264.5	294.9	260.5	195.4	307.4	221.6	3,049
1983	273.6	244.1	264.4	273.2	233.1	288.9	332.6	452.3	445.4	378.7	355.5	316.7	3,859
1984	358.3	346.5	337.7	360.0	513.7	436.7	353.6	280.8	244.2	269.5	288.0	220.5	4,010
1985	264.2	256.0	311.6	405.0	416.4	308.7	341.1	281.5	233.0	270.0	281.5	278.4	3,647
1986	263.1	235.9	254.0	311.7	273.8	262.0	296.0	237.9	202.7	324.8	261.4	259.6	3,183
1987	347.3	304.8	267.7	303.4	374.2	363.9	356.3	267.6	301.1	349.8	315.1	361.2	3,912
1988	437.0	390.7	346.8	442.7	399.2	580.2	461.4	403.6	390.0	303.1	377.3	364.2	4,896

Source: Chicago Board of Trade   T.626

Soybeans

Soybeans accounted for about 47 percent of world oilseed production in 1988/89, followed by cottonseed and peanuts. World soybean output was forecast at 93 million tonnes, below 103 million in 1987/88.

Even with a drought-reduced crop, the U.S. provided 45 percent of the world's soybean output. In response to higher world prices, Brazil, Argentina, and Paraguay expanded acreage and were to provide 32 percent of world output, versus 28 percent the previous season. Brazil's crop was put at 20 million tonnes, up 12 percent from the large 1987/88 crop. High world prices caused Brazilian producers to switch area into soybeans, despite government efforts to encourage more corn planting. Acreage was also moved from cotton into soybeans. The only constraint on more soybean acreage was a shortage of high-quality seed. Some of Brazil's major soybean areas were initially dry, but later received needed rains. Argentina's crop was estimated at 9 million tonnes, 9 percent below a year earlier because of dry weather. While acreage expanded, yields were likely to fall. Paraguay's crop was placed at 1.2 million tonnes, up from 1 million.

World trade in soybeans was expected to decline 16 percent due to lower U.S. exports. Global exports were put at 24.9 million tonnes, below 1987/88's active trade of 29.8 million tonnes. U.S. shipments fell by 30 percent, but accounted for 62 percent of world trade.

The South American producers boosted their exports. In recent years, Brazil and Argentina have concentrated on using their extensive crushing capacity to process soybeans and to export the value-added products, soyoil and soymeal. Brazil, in particular, is an active crusher, exporting large amounts of soymeal, while keeping soyoil in the domestic market. Brazil's soybean exports were estimated at 3.9 million tonnes in 1988/89, up from 2.6 million. Argentina has developed a large capacity to process oilseeds, due to an expanding sunflower industry. Additionally, Argentina uses a tax system whereby export taxes on soybeans are higher than on soyoil and soymeal. Crushing is thus encouraged and exports of soybeans discouraged. Still, Argentina's soybean exports were projected to be 2.5 million tonnes, 20 percent more than in 1987/88.

The major soybean importers are the European Community (EC), particularly the Netherlands and West Germany. Japan is a large importer, with 1988/89 purchases projected at 4.75 million tonnes.

The 1988/89 world soybean crush was projected at 81.9 million tonnes, below the previous season. The leading soybean processors were the U.S., Brazil, Argentina, the EC, and Asian countries like Japan. The U.S. share of the world crush was put at 34 percent, while the South American countries accounted for 32 percent. The U.S. share was declining, while the South American portion was expanding. Soybean processing in the EC was on the decline. World ending stocks of soybeans were estimated at 14 million tonnes, down 30 percent from 1987/88, due to the smaller U.S. crop.

The 1988 U.S. soybean crop was put at 1.54 billion bushels, 20 percent less than a year earlier. While harvested acreage was 57.4 million, yields fell to 27 bu./acre, compared to 34 bushels the year before. Drought enveloped most of the Corn Belt by spring, while the Atlantic Coast and Delta were largely spared. While there was some relief in late July and August, yield potential had been damaged by low subsoil moisture. Soybeans that were planted late benefited from timely rains and more normal conditions in August.

U.S. carry-in stocks in 1988/89 were 302 million bushels, down 31 from a year earlier. The smaller carry-in and drought-reduced crop put total supplies of soybeans at 1.84 billion bushels, 22 percent less than the previous season.

With sharply higher prices in 1988/89, usage was expected to be lower. The crush was projected at 1.04 billion bushels, down 11 percent. Similar to a year earlier, processing margins remained quite profitable, but crushers were disciplined. While demand for soymeal was good, large supplies of soyoil discouraged processors from adding to stocks.

U.S. soybean exports in 1988/89 were put at 565 million bushels, down 30 percent. The major U.S. markets were Japan and the EC, especially the Netherlands. High prices and large competitor supplies worked against larger sales. Importers were reluctant to buy soybeans for processing, given the world surplus of soyoil, and were inclined to purchase soymeal. The large Brazilian crop was expected to keep buyers sidelined, until those soybeans were harvested.

Total U.S. soybean use was projected to be 1.7 billion bushels, 17 percent less than a year earlier. Stocks at the end of 1988/89 were forecast at 140 million bushels, well below 302 million in 1987/88.

The price support loan rate for 1988-crop soybeans was $4.77/bu., the same as a year earlier.

Futures Markets

Soybeans futures and options are traded on the Chicago Board of Trade.

World Production of Soybeans In Thousands of Metric Tons

Crop[3] Year	Argentina	Brazil	Canada	China	Colombia	India	Indonesia	Japan	Rep. of Korea	Mexico	Romania	Paraguay	Thailand	United States	USSR	World Total
1983	7,000	15,541	735	9,760	85	614	625	217	226	600	259	550	179	44,518	560	83,160
1984–5	6,750	18,278	917	9,700		955	870	238	254	550	407	950	246	50,644	469	93,140
1985–6	7,300	14,100	1,012	10,510		982	890	228	234	710	317	600	309	57,113	458	97,030
1986–7[1]	7,000	17,300	960	11,610		1,100	980	245	199	610	375	950	320	52,801	703	97,910
1987–8[1]	9,900	17,800	1,267	12,180								1,000		52,329	487	102,860
1988–9[2]	11,000	20,000	1,100	11,000								1,200		41,147	472	94,250

[1] Preliminary. [2] Projected. [3] Split year includes Northern Hemisphere crops harvested in the late months of the first year shown combined with Southern Hemisphere crops harvested in the early months of the following year. *Source: Foreign Agricultural Service, U.S.D.A.* T.627

Supply and Distribution of Soybeans in the United States In Millions of Bushels

Crop Year Begin. Sept. 1	Supply					Distribution					Total Distri- bution
	Stocks, Sept. 1										
	Farms	Mills, Elevators[2]	Total	Production	Total Supply	Crushings	Exports	Seed	Feed	Residual	
1977–8	32.7	70.2	102.9	1,767.3	1,870.2	926.7	700.5	68.0	1.0	13.0	1,703.6
1978–9	59.0	102.0	161.0	1,868.8	2,029.8	1,018	739.0	75.0	1.0	23.0	1,856.0
1979–0	61.5	112.6	174.1	2,260.7	2,437	1,123	875.0	———81———			2,079
1980–1	128.6	229.9	358.5	1,797.5	2,156	1,020	724.0	———99———			1,843
1981–2	153.6	159.4	313.0	1,989.1	2,302	1,030	929.0	———89———			2,048
1982–3	117.7	136.7	254.5	2,190.3	2,444	1,108	905	———86———			2,099
1983–4	118.6	226.1	344.6	1,635.8	1,981	983	743	———79———			1,805
1984–5	67.9	107.8	175.7	1,860.9	2,037	1,030	598	———93———			1,721
1985–6	143.2	172.8	316.1	2,098.5	2,415	1,053	740	———86———			1,879
1986–7	167.1	369.3	536.4	1,940.1	2,476	1,179	757	———104———			2,040
1987–8[1]	108.0	328.5	436.4	1,922.8	2,359	1,174	800	———83———			2,057
1988–9[3]	105.1	197.4	302.5	1,511.9	1,803	1,020	565	———93———			1,678

[1] Preliminary. [2] Also warehouses. [3] Estimates. *Source: Economic Research Service, U.S.D.A.* T.632

U.S. Soybean Price Support Program & Official Crop Production Reports In Millions of Bushels

Crop Year Begin. Sept.	Quantity Put Under Support	Deliveries to C.C.C.	Sept. 1 Stocks		National Avg. Support		(In Thousands of Bushels) Crop Production Reports					
			Total	Gov't. Owned	% of Parity	$ Per Bu.	August 1	September 1	October 1	November 1	December 1	Final
1977	97.5	—	102.9	—	46	3.50	1,602,065	1,644,220	1,647,315	1,682,705	1,761,755	1,767,267
1978	64.2	—	161.0	—	51	4.50	1,765,024	1,772,364	1,792,064	1,810,389	1,870,181	1,868,754
1979	122.1	—	174.1	—	45	4.50	2,129,254	2,174,179	2,213,289	2,235,869	2,267,647	2,260,655
1980	133.2	—	358.5	.1	43	5.02	1,880,342	1,831,172	1,757,272	1,774,742	1,817,097	1,797,543
1981	221.5	—	313.0	.5	40	5.02	2,017,468	2,089,418	2,106,568	2,076,998	2,030,452	1,989,110
1982	396.6	—	254.5	20.9	39	5.02	2,293,420	2,313,880	2,300,345	2,299,520	2,276,976	2,190,297
1983	101.2	—	344.6	.7	39	5.02	1,843,459	1,534,969	1,517,019	1,536,519	1,595,437	1,635,772
1984	278.3	—	175.7	4.4	39	5.02	2,035,370	2,027,565	1,971,700	1,901,565	1,860,783	1,860,863
1985	516.9		316.1	131.3	40	5.02	1,959,439	2,062,889	2,108,379	2,129,034	2,098,531	2,098,531
1986[1]	325.0	—	536.4		39	4.77	1,979,773	1,979,773	1,991,763	2,009,333	2,007,033	1,940,101
1987[1]			436.4			4.77	2,000,349	1,956,859	1,968,069	1,959,949	1,904,712	1,922,762
1988[1]			302.5			4.77	1,473.986	1,472,376	1,501,381	1,511,876		

[1] Preliminary. *Source: Crop Reporting Board, U.S.D.A.* T.628

Soybean Stocks in the United States In Millions of Bushels

Year	On Farms				Off Farms				Total Stocks			
	Mar. 1	June 1	Sept. 1	Dec. 1	Mar. 1	June 1	Sept. 1	Dec. 1	Mar. 1	June 1	Sept. 1	Dec. 1
1985	N.A.	326.6	143.2	1,030.9	N.A.	281.8	172.8	929.0	N.A.	608.4	316.1	1,959.8
1986	699.3	411.7	167.1	1,061.0	671.9	437.2	369.3	895.6	1,371.3	848.9	536.4	1,956.6
1987	589.0	282.1	108.0	865.3	750.0	554.7	328.5	890.2	1,339.0	836.8	436.4	1,755.5
1988[1]	551.5	303.9	105.1		594.4	351.4	197.4		1,145.9	655.3	302.5	

[1] Preliminary. *Source: Crop Reporting Board, U.S.D.A.* T.629

U.S. Commercial Stocks of Soybeans on the First of the Month In Millions of Bushels

Year	Jan.	Feb.	Mar.	Apr.	May	June	July	Aug.	Sept.	Oct.	Nov.	Dec.
1977	46.8	49.5	51.1	52.3	55.4	50.0	38.7	19.6	8.5	10.9	43.6	50.9
1978	46.2	44.3	41.8	49.1	47.9	42.7	30.6	23.0	10.7	13.0	58.3	63.2
1979	60.9	57.6	62.0	60.8	52.5	40.7	37.6	31.2	19.3	11.5	77.6	84.9
1980	76.5	71.5	73.2	72.3	56.5	52.6	53.2	51.8	44.8	51.5	80.6	79.5
1981	73.1	71.1	69.0	53.1	45.3	35.7	24.7	19.0	11.2	12.6	40.7	51.7
1982	50.6	50.4	41.1	39.9	34.7	67.4	21.5	18.4	11.5	12.8	43.9	53.5
1983	53.6	58.2	57.5	55.7	55.9	44.7	34.9	35.8	42.5	47.0	78.8	83.0
1984	77.2	74.4	65.2	58.6	49.2	41.1	35.4	20.8	7.9	6.7	23.3	41.7
1985	41.1	44.0	38.2	33.3	22.8	14.7	12.7	11.3	6.9	9.6	47.6	60.9
1986	61.7	63.9	57.3	53.6	40.2	30.5	24.9	24.5	24.8	30.1	52.5	61.5
1987	62.0	61.4	56.9	52.5	49.4	46.3	38.4	26.0	16.6	21.3	56.5	57.1
1988	63.0	66.9	63.6	61.2	54.6	51.7	53.2	54.5	46.0	41.6	74.7	80.9

Source: Foreign Agricultural Service, U.S.D.A. T.630

SOYBEANS

Salient Statistics of Soybeans in the United States

Crop Year	Planted Alone — 1,000 Acres	Acreage Harvested — 1,000 Acres	Yield Per Acre (Bus.)	Farm Price ($ Bu.)	Farm Value (Million Dollars)	Pounds Per Bushel Crushed — Yield of Oil	Yield of Meal	U.S. Exports of Soybeans Crop Year (Sept.-Aug.) (Ths. Metric Tons[2]) — Grand Total	Bel.-Luxem.	Spain	Canada	W. Germany	Japan	Netherlands	Taiwan	U.S.S.R.
1975–6	54,550	53,617	28.9	4.92	7,622	10.94	47.27	555.1	17.7		28.0	45.6	118.1	130.5	32.8	11.4
1976–7	50,226	49,401	26.1	6.81	8,776	11.09	47.81	15,351	411	1,030	462	1,520	3,219	3,007	697	825
1977–8	58,760	57,830	30.6	5.88	10,383	10.39	47.34	19,061	475	1,532	264	1,521	3,636	4,086	854	744
1978–9	64,708	63,663	29.4	6.66	12,450	11.07	47.63	20,117	420	1,475	352	1,486	3,865	4,012	1,271	1,178
1979–0	71,632	70,343	32.1	6.28	14,204	10.74	48.01	23,818	584	2,203	392	1,318	3,868	6,035	780	813
1980–1	70,037	67,813	26.5	7.57	13,601	11.09	47.93	19,712	670	1,383	345	1,791	3,816	3,839	1,063	
1981–2	67,810	66,163	30.1	6.04	12,005	10.72	47.86	25,285	1,404	3,855	310	2,135	4,196	5,349	1,059	683
1982–3	70,884	69,442	31.5	5.65	12,463	10.76	47.88	24,634	1,259	2,313	324	1,813	4,580	4,648	1,300	199
1983–4	63,779	62,525	26.2	7.83	12,775	11.26	47.36	20,215	882	1,800	248	967	4,394	2,988	1,382	408
1984–5	67,755	66,113	28.1	5.84	10,748	11.05	47.15	16,279	658	1,084	140	718	3,828	2,857	1,389	0
1985–6[1]	63,130	61,584	34.1	5.05	10,597	11.01	47.27	20,158	784	1,519	114	934	4,293	3,056	1,506	1,519
1986–7[3]	61,480	58,292	33.3	4.78	9,312	10.86	47.08	20,600	888	1,775	206	1,393	4,024	3,540	1,968	71
1987–8[3]	57,955	56,977	33.7	5.02	9,263	11.04	47.76	21,165	758	1,505	154	1,331	3,778	4,150	1,820	803
1988–9[3]	58,830	56,818	26.6	6.15	10,560											

[1] Preliminary.   [2] Data prior to 1976–7 are in millions of bushels.   [3] Forecast.   *Source: Crop Reporting Board, U.S.D.A.*   T.631

Production of Soybeans for Beans in the U.S., by Selected States   In Millions of Bushels

Year	Ark.	So. Car.	Ill.	Ind.	Iowa	La.	Mich.	Minn.	Miss.	Mo.	N. Car.	Ohio	Tenn.	Nebr.	Ky.
1975	117.5	30.4	299.5	121.6	237.0	48.0	15.9	98.6	70.2	113.6	33.4	102.3	46.3	32.4	29.7
1976	82.1	21.4	249.5	111.5	200.0	63.0	11.6	66.4	71.5	84.0	24.6	95.0	40.5	19.6	28.9
1977	105.8	26.7	336.3	144.3	251.3	63.0	21.6	133.8	78.5	148.8	29.0	120.0	52.2	40.7	40.9
1978	115.2	32.3	309.5	144.2	283.1	76.0	21.6	146.2	81.7	155.0	40.3	127.7	56.9	42.5	40.8
1979	144.2	39.8	379.1	159.1	306.4	93.8	30.3	162.6	118.9	183.6	45.8	144.8	70.7	54.7	54.0
1980	65.3	20.8	309.9	157.7	318.4	67.0	30.4	149.9	61.6	135.5	34.7	135.4	45.9	53.1	36.0
1981	99.0	31.0	351.5	151.8	326.0	64.2	29.1	139.2	75.6	155.6	46.3	99.8	61.1	78.7	47.9
1982	105.6	39.6	354.2	173.3	306.6	75.4	35.3	169.1	92.3	171.0	52.5	133.2	61.0	78.8	51.3
1983	70.3	23.6	267.0	122.5	278.6	68.1	33.8	151.8	58.9	103.0	33.0	105.0	31.5	59.0	24.5
1984	101.4	29.8	284.1	150.1	264.6	66.8	32.1	172.9	76.8	108.7	46.5	137.6	48.1	66.3	42.3
1985	98.1	24.6	382.5	185.1	309.7	44.1	34.6	160.0	70.7	180.4	39.1	160.6	45.3	85.0	41.8
1986	66.0	13.7	360.0	157.3	350.7	35.0	28.8	162.8	41.7	170.6	36.7	146.6	35.5	93.1	35.8
1987	71.5	15.7	330.6	174.0	343.7	38.8	38.2	181.4	47.8	154.6	32.8	147.3	28.8	83.4	24.0
1988[1]	78.8	17.2	234.9	117.6	235.5	43.4	33.9	117.5	50.6	109.2	41.2	103.6	34.8	69.0	25.7

[1] Preliminary.   *Source: Crop Reporting Board, U.S.D.A.*   T.633

Soybean Stocks at U.S. Mills on First of Month   In Millions of Bushels

Crop Year	Sept.	Oct.	Nov.	Dec.	Jan.	Feb.	Mar.	Apr.	May	June	July	Aug.
1978–9	37.9	31.9	138.4	149.4	127.3	112.4	124.0	120.9	96.7	71.1	73.0	55.6
1979–0	37.5	39.2	166.5	184.5	163.3	145.4	130.7	118.6	95.8	79.7	75.7	73.9
1980–1	56.9	80.4	166.0	172.0	138.7	125.9	105.4	97.2	84.4	67.8	49.2	43.9
1981–2	33.4	31.5	105.8	135.2	114.5	99.8	84.6	79.2	72.2	60.8	51.2	43.6
1982–3	30.0	29.0	114.2	145.5	125.1	116.2	98.5	96.2	84.6	69.8	62.0	55.4
1983–4	58.6	63.9	124.5	142.3	124.0	125.3	114.8	105.3	94.2	101.7	83.4	57.7
1984–5	35.3	19.7	53.9	116.4	98.4	85.9	65.8	69.7	65.2	53.4	47.6	36.0
1985–6	26.7	25.7	92.8	113.4	119.9	124.6	97.5	84.9	67.6	53.2	40.7	40.2
1986–7	28.5	38.3	108.1	127.4	117.2	113.1	105.4	90.2	85.2	72.9	63.6	49.8
1987–8[1]	31.2	65.7	158.5	155.5	145.0	141.8	139.3	133.8	113.9	95.4	90.1	66.2
1988–9[1]	59.7	61.4	136.6									

[1] Preliminary.   *Sources: Economic Research Service, U.S.D.A.*   T.635

Soybean Exports from the United States   In Millions of Bushels

Year	Sept.	Oct.	Nov.	Dec.	Jan.	Feb.	Mar.	Apr.	May	June	July	Aug.	Total
1978–9	38.0	87.6	101.7	70.6	77.0	53.2	83.5	67.7	46.8	40.9	32.7	39.7	739.2
1979–0	40.9	88.9	118.1	78.3	85.8	73.0	69.4	81.3	74.2	58.7	49.1	57.7	875.2
1980–1	41.4	60.3	75.0	74.5	71.7	55.5	103.2	60.0	69.6	41.8	29.6	41.8	724.3
1981–2	50.9	100.8	103.7	73.6	84.3	89.4	79.0	85.7	90.6	59.8	53.8	57.5	929.1
1982–3	58.0	94.4	93.6	90.1	86.3	87.2	84.4	73.3	58.5	67.7	51.6	60.2	905.2
1983–4	53.9	67.6	69.2	74.5	80.4	79.7	78.8	68.5	56.8	41.1	39.2	30.7	686.6
1984–5	19.0	40.9	93.5	84.8	70.3	72.6	59.8	60.4	33.1	18.2	19.2	26.3	598.2
1985–6	31.5	55.3	79.6	94.1	84.7	92.1	89.9	80.4	57.2	28.7	26.6	20.4	740.7
1986–7	30.2	89.7	96.6	89.0	71.7	73.8	67.8	53.9	37.6	37.9	54.3	54.5	756.9
1987–8[1]	56.7	97.9	98.1	76.7	77.0	97.0	74.8	65.1	39.7	29.3	29.5	35.8	777.7

[1] Preliminary.   *Source: Bureau of the Census*   T.636

High, Low & Closing Prices of May Soybean Futures at the Chicago Board of Trade   In Cents per Bushel

Year of Delivery		Mar.	Apr.	May	June	July	Aug.	Sept.	Oct.	Nov.	Dec.	Jan.	Feb.	Mar.	Apr.	May	Life of Delivery Range
					Year Prior to Delivery							Delivery Year					
1982	High	894	922	883	832½	853½	807	751	739	721	696¼	677	683	642	670¾	669½	922½
	Low	859	872	820	772	787	722	703½	705	670	619	637	617½	605½	639½	647	605
	Close	888½	873	829	788½	812½	730	715¼	714¼	678¼	641¼	674½	632¾	640	651¾	666	—
1983	High	713	729½	723½	704½	678½	664½	611½	588	607¾	595½	620	622	643¾	655½	643	746
	Low	667½	698	687½	670	651	593½	572½	558½	570½	576¼	577	572½	577½	620¼	610¼	558½
	Close	696	716½	687½	671	654¾	601	574¼	568¼	594	581¾	618½	575½	637	640¼	621½	—
1984	High	718	732	720	678	794	984	996	927	903½	853	825	768	815	813	894	996
	Low	645	695½	659	630	657½	760	859½	831	791	775½	738	706	762	765	768½	630
	Close	714	719	659½	660	761	930	800	851	822	843½	747½	765	789	771	888	—
1985	High	773	777	784	797	764	700	675	678	676½	640½	624	619½	614	609¾	590¾	797
	Low	753	737	744½	736	940	643½	601	623	623	597¼	581¾	572	570¾	585	568	568
	Close	768½	737	777	761	646½	675	627	659¾	634¼	599	613¼	573	605½	588	568	—
1986	High	645	650	637	616	618	560½	560½	551½	557	567	566½	545	548	563	549	650
	Low	608½	631	583½	577	547	531¼	532	534¼	549	504	537	523¼	527¼	519½	527	504
	Close	643½	636½	590½	583	555¼	541	547½	548¾	513	554	542½	529¾	541½	544	534½	—
1987	High	554	574	574	536	541½	529½	513¾	514	512	511¼	502¼	500¾	498	536	584	584
	Low	535½	522	529½	509½	504½	492	491¾	493¼	501	489	489	478½	482½	496½	531¼	478½
	Close	544¾	564½	529½	510	525	502	508½	509	510½	498¼	498¾	483	496½	534½	549½	—
1988	High	505½	554	634	650	577	539	554¼	576	626½	629½	651	656	656	690	784	784
	Low	488	509	549½	566	532	509	520½	540½	538½	592¼	610	603½	608	656	682	476
	Close	504	554	579	575	547½	521¾	550½	549½	618½	622	616½	642½	653½	689½	777	—
1989	High	693	735	828	1003	960	882	912	843	826	828						
	Low	647	702½	727	814	747	806	816½	782	748	767½						
	Close	693	735	828	935½	795	870	826¾	802¼	779½	827¼						

Source: Chicago Board of Trade   T.634

Volume of Trading in Soybean Futures at the Chicago Board of Trade   In Millions of Bushels

Year	Jan.	Feb.	Mar.	Apr.	May	June	July	Aug.	Sept.	Oct.	Nov.	Dec.	Total
1979	3,701	5,038	4,123	3,856	3,686	5,485	4,184	2,843	2,920	3,946	3,115	2,674	45,572
1980	3,222	2,916	2,808	3,035	2,911	3,602	6,803	5,226	6,562	7,706	7,025	7,024	58,841
1981	5,808	4,074	4,796	4,585	3,917	4,737	4,821	3,897	3,626	4,087	3,765	4,337	52,450
1982	3,120	3,497	4,478	4,484	3,517	4,245	4,017	3,822	3,197	4,014	4,282	3,198	45,828
1983	3,942	3,820	4,247	4,375	4,259	4,409	6,224	8,799	7,852	8,071	6,793	5,609	68,402
1984	5,550	5,247	6,008	4,945	7,300	6,323	5,314	4,045	2,505	3,687	3,427	2,463	56,813
1985	3,315	2,749	2,657	2,821	2,766	3,309	3,779	2,581	2,525	3,364	3,881	3,213	36,961
1986	3,692	2,484	2,435	2,976	2,546	2,199	2,925	2,049	1,812	3,266	2,473	1,811	30,668
1987	2,174	1,816	1,794	3,118	3,969	4,356	3,785	1,935	2,305	4,109	3,674	3,859	36,894
1988	4,436	4,252	4,284	4,822	6,339	7,975	5,574	5,214	4,516	5,235	5,001	4,777	62,485

Source: Commodity Futures Trading Commission   T.638

Month–End Open Interest of Soybean Futures at Chicago Board of Trade   In Millions of Bushels

Year	Jan.	Feb.	Mar.	Apr.	May	June	July	Aug.	Sept.	Oct.	Nov.	Dec.
1978	470.3	438.0	499.4	483.9	553.5	491.8	452.8	485.8	562.2	726.6	720.1	775.1
1979	613.9	719.0	642.0	576.1	562.2	584.4	514.4	477.1	534.9	564.7	630.4	704.3
1980	533.2	540.0	502.2	449.6	513.5	615.0	703.5	784.4	880.4	1,069.6	1,102.7	1,056.4
1981	645.7	586.9	565.0	551.4	523.3	513.6	470.3	455.7	449.1	523.2	491.4	426.6
1982	400.8	391.6	435.2	422.1	399.1	377.0	400.2	353.7	357.7	422.9	433.3	424.7
1983	465.3	413.9	485.7	507.5	428.5	401.2	547.5	714.3	745.7	684.1	648.2	603.2
1984	548.3	548.9	556.2	494.5	577.1	428.7	316.2	275.1	287.0	339.4	351.2	343.2
1985	359.5	359.2	327.9	311.9	320.2	321.5	329.9	331.6	307.9	390.1	370.5	386.4
1986	373.3	376.5	385.4	371.7	328.7	323.2	287.7	296.3	309.7	426.5	408.7	392.2
1987	383.7	363.7	414.2	445.5	452.1	432.4	368.0	354.9	426.4	485.8	621.1	550.4
1988	580.0	615.7	636.4	701.7	802.9	725.1	561.3	576.0	601.3	561.3	583.6	604.4

Source: Chicago Board of Trade

T.642

Soybeans Under Price Support Through the End of the Month
(Cumulative Total from Current Season's Crop)   In Thousands of Bushels

Year	Sept.	Oct.	Nov.	Dec.	Jan.	Feb.	Mar.	Apr.	May	June	July	Aug.
1978–9	0	6,403	31,008	43,015	58,278	61,489	62,365	63,146	63,508	65,087	—	—
1979–0	11	9,507	39,559	67,372	101,052	106,135	113,638	119,860	121,684	122,013	—	—
1980–1	22	11,705	28,541	67,744	100,809	116,167	125,480	130,236	132,346	133,160	—	—
1981–2	1,044	26,019	81,377	138,202	191,386	208,285	216,412	219,743	144,165	221,303		
1982–3	861	50,145	203,031	311,105	363,696	382,536	391,432	393,567	394,727	395,893		
1983–4	0	9,098	32,869	62,736	84,526	92,974	98,945	100,030	100,656	100,817		
1984–5	0	46,349	99,437	174,002	242,526	258,174	268,812	271,353	274,051	275,687		
1985–6	1,056	86,633	265,929	408,793	482,658	499,223	506,818	511,462	513,089	513,954	—	—
1986–7	313	34,971	154,207	240,072	299,018	316,598	321,327	327,233	329,094	329,766	329,971	—
1987–8	4,383	58,666	165,997	209,121	259,010	211,856	272,632	274,046	274,774	274,952	274,929	—
1988–9	896	16,805										

Source: U.S. Department of Agriculture

T.639

Soybeans Crushed (Factory Consumption) in the U.S.   In Millions of Bushels—One Bushel = 60 Pounds

Year	Sept.	Oct.	Nov.	Dec.	Jan.	Feb.	Mar.	Apr.	May	June	July	Aug.	Total
1978–9	71.4	89.3	89.6	96.4	90.6	81.5	89.0	83.3	86.9	82.8	80.6	76.4	1,018
1979–0	75.9	95.8	101.4	104.4	106.6	100.0	102.2	92.0	93.8	82.7	84.9	83.7	1,123
1980–1	81.0	97.8	98.6	94.1	92.2	79.6	88.7	85.4	82.3	73.4	72.3	74.6	1,020
1981–2	75.4	104.5	97.6	102.5	94.9	86.7	85.1	81.0	86.6	77.1	70.6	67.8	1,030
1982–3	76.0	100.2	108.1	111.9	110.0	93.0	94.6	81.8	83.7	81.5	81.6	85.7	1,108
1983–4	86.6	96.4	86.6	89.4	93.8	79.2	86.0	74.6	79.4	70.6	69.0	71.1	982.7
1984–5	65.5	89.2	98.9	101.1	94.5	80.8	85.6	83.2	89.3	82.7	82.0	77.5	1,030
1985–6	76.5	94.3	96.7	100.8	99.6	81.4	91.6	84.4	86.3	79.6	83.1	78.4	1,053
1986–7	79.4	107.0	109.4	107.6	110.3	102.3	106.0	95.9	95.3	90.6	92.6	82.4	1,179
1987–8[1]	79.7	102.5	111.2	110.8	106.7	99.8	107.6	102.6	98.0	89.2	88.0	78.3	1,174
1988–9[1]	79.9	94.4											

[1] Preliminary.   *Source: Bureau of the Census*

T.641

Average Price Received by Farmers for Soybeans in the U.S.   In Cents Per Bushel

Year	Sept.	Oct.	Nov.	Dec.	Jan.	Feb.	Mar.	Apr.	May	June	July	Aug.	Average
1978–79	620	626	641	649	658	699	716	706	706	736	736	707	666
1979–80	681	635	630	627	639	620	594	563	576	591	675	718	628
1980–81	759	768	818	780	780	750	759	760	740	705	713	671	757
1981–82	621	606	603	600	613	604	604	617	627	612	599	559	604
1982–83	522	506	534	546	556	566	582	609	606	590	627	757	565
1983–84	828	796	780	774	785	728	768	783	812	799	695	650	783
1984–5	609	608	602	582	591	577	588	588	570	562	542	510	584
1985–6	499	485	492	500	516	518	523	523	525	519	511	499	505
1986–7	485	455	464	467	470	469	473	490	520	536	525	502	478
1987–8	502	504	536	563	573	596	605	639	698	818	850	833	615
1988–9	794	753	743	748									

Source: Crop Reporting Board

T.637

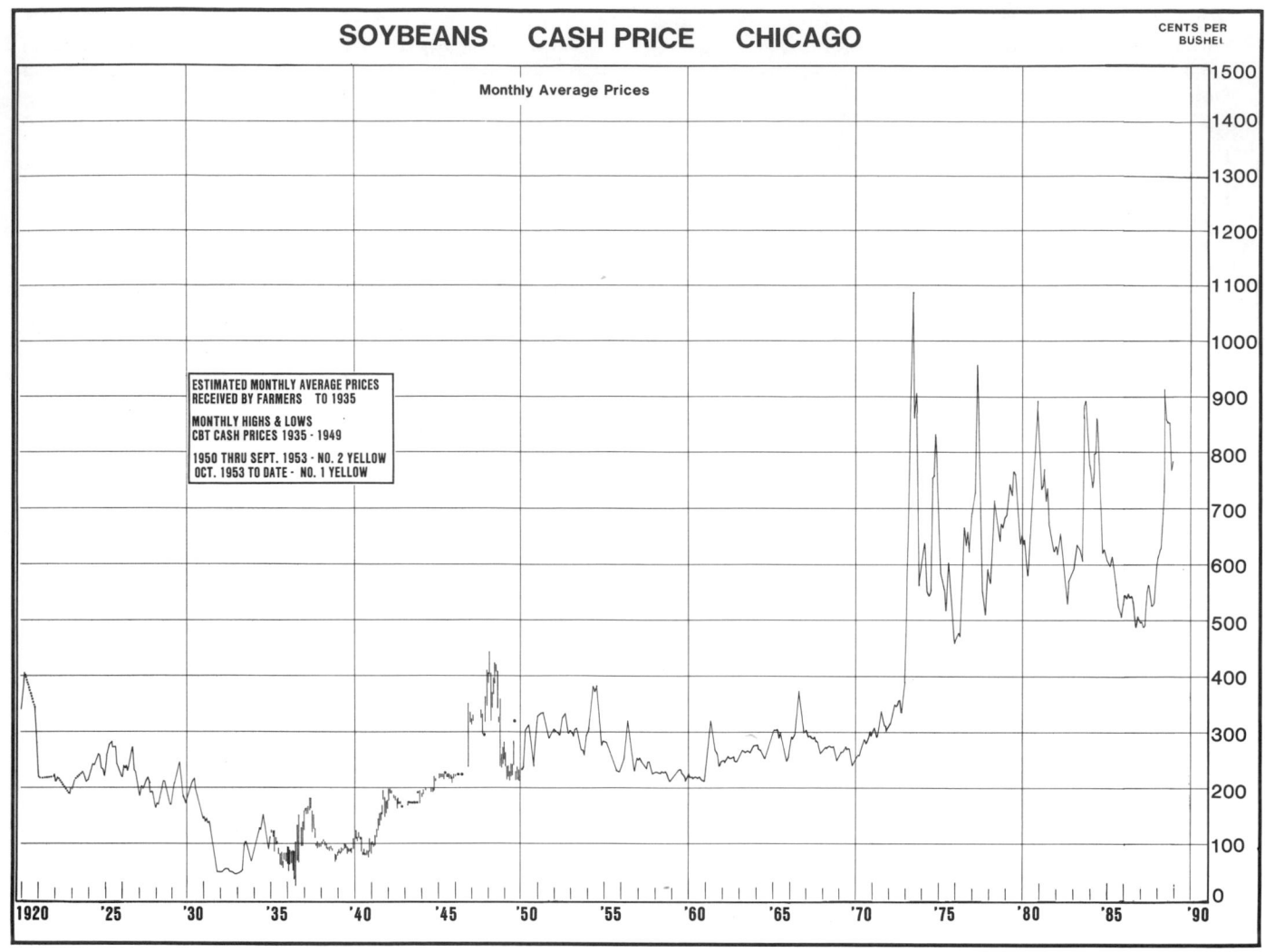

SOYBEANS CASH PRICE CHICAGO

Monthly Average Prices

CENTS PER BUSHEL

ESTIMATED MONTHLY AVERAGE PRICES
RECEIVED BY FARMERS TO 1935

MONTHLY HIGHS & LOWS
CBT CASH PRICES 1935 - 1949

1950 THRU SEPT. 1953 - NO. 2 YELLOW
OCT. 1953 TO DATE - NO. 1 YELLOW

Average Cash Price of No. 1 Yellow Soybeans at Illinois Processor In Cents per Bushel

Year	Sept.	Oct.	Nov.	Dec.	Jan.	Feb.	Mar.	Apr.	May	June	July	Aug.	Average
1976–7	516	622	655	686	706	726	825	960	942	825	640	549	721
1977–8	642	507	584	594	573	565	658	681	701	676	662	647	624
1978–9	704	672	668	681	689	728	745	727	721	768	764	728	716
1979–0	813	656	652	653	636	642	607	580	604	610	722	745	660
1980–1	644	827	891	773	757	734	737	772	758	713	736	694	753
1981–2	540	630	628	623	630	624	616	642	656	631	620	573	618
1982–3	893	526	570	573	581	586	598	635	627	606	659	846	640
1983–4	621	846	820	777	767	737	797	798	861	791	685	663	786
1984–5	519	627	625	607	604	597	608	613	595	588	565	528	598
1985–6	496	505	519	532	545	538	547	540	544	543	533	500	530
1986–7	527	489	508	496	495	489	492	512	552	563	547	528	514
1987–8	852	532	564	594	617	621	630	671	731	913	859	852	676
1988–9	792	767											

Source: Agricultural Marketing Service, U.S.D.A.

T.643

Stock Index Futures

For the sixth straight year, the stock market closed higher in 1988, much to everyone's relief. After Black Monday (October 19, 1987), many pundits said 1988 would be a repeat of 1930. This fear continued until mid-May, when the Dow Jones Industrials broke from closely tracking the pattern established by the 1929 crash. Nonetheless, the recovery did not end the malaise that kept many investors out of stocks.

The Dow Jones Industrials ended 1988 at 2168.57, up 11.8 percent. Including dividends, the total return was 16.6 percent. The Dow yielded 3.7 percent, versus 3.57 percent a year earlier. But others also soared. The S&P 500 closed at 277.72, up 12.4 percent; its total return was 17.07 percent. The S&P 500 also yielded 3.7 percent. The Wilshire 5000 Index returned 17.92 percent, including price gains of 13.3 percent, which was in line with the capital gains by other broad-based indices. The New York Stock Exchange Composite gained 13 percent, and the Value Line gained 15.4 percent.

The best-performing widely followed index was the Dow Jones Transportation Index, which rose 29.5 percent and closed just below its 1988 high of 973.61. The index benefited from higher air fares, lower oil prices, and the continued economic expansion.

The major laggard was the Dow Utilities Index, which hit its 1988 peak of 190.02 on January 29 and hung on to close at 186.28, up 6.4 percent for the year. Utilities were pressured by rising interest rates, nuclear power plant woes, and the summer drought and heat wave, which reduced supplies of hydroelectric power and forced the use of expensive backup generators. Fears of rising inflation also hurt the utilities, which are viewed as bond substitutes.

Takeovers and leveraged buy-outs contributed to the 1988 bull market. One deal, the RJR Nabisco buy-out, cost $25 billion, roughly the size of a U.S. Treasury quarterly refunding. An estimated $100 billion in common stock was removed from the market by deals in 1988. Some of the proceeds went into junk bonds; others were parked in T-bills, yielding almost 9 percent as 1988 ended. However, bulls hoped that much of the sidelined cash would reenter the market in 1989.

Daily trading volume shrank in 1988, reflecting lingering damage from the crash. Brokers mourned the vanished small investors, who also switched from stock mutual funds into money market funds. Nevertheless, returns on diversified equity portfolios were significantly higher than fixed-income returns--and better than the long-run total return of 10-12 percent expected on stocks.

As 1989 began, fears of higher interest rates continued. However, the spread between the yield on the Dow Industrials and highest-quality corporate debt (if such a thing still existed, after the RJR Nabisco deal turned its bonds into junk issues overnight) narrowed to 5.85 points from 6.13 points a year earlier. Despite rising interest rates, moderate economic growth was expected to continue in 1989, although corporate profits were expected to increase at a slower rate than earlier in the economic expansion.

The world's strongest stock market in 1988 was Tokyo's. Despite P/Es over 70 (versus 12 for the Dow), the Nikkei index of 225 Japanese stocks ended 1988 at a record 30,159, up 39.9 percent, and the broader Topix index gained 36.6 percent to close at a record 2,357.03. The total market value of the companies listed on the Tokyo exchange dwarfed the U.S. stock market's capitalization.

Month–End Open Interest of NYSE Composite Stock Index Futures   at New York in Contracts

Year	Jan.	Feb.	Mar.	Apr.	May	June	July	Aug.	Sept.	Oct.	Nov.	Dec.
1984	9,348	9,874	8,571	8,454	9,376	7,957	7,918	10,968	9,710	9,181	7,745	7,149
1985	11,062	10,884	9,804	9,438	13,672	9,677	12,102	10,388	7,218	7,011	8,131	9,381
1986	10,164	13,992	15,320	13,809	15,902	10,503	11,662	11,883	21,880	18,816	20,740	9,306
1987	11,893	13,228	13,007	14,682	11,000	9,115	13,059	18,768	12,819	9,431	8,887	5,106
1988	5,365	6,033	6,800	6,968	9,534	6,958	6,410	7,579	6,408	7,269	7,246	5,276

Source: New York Futures Exchange   T.643E

Month–End Open Interest of KC Value Line Stock Index Futures   at Kansas City in Contracts

Year	Jan.	Feb.	Mar.	Apr.	May	June	July	Aug.	Sept.	Oct.	Nov.	Dec.
1984	4,019	5,032	3,241	3,235	3,669	3,041	3,811	5,305	3,000	4,195	5,244	3,888
1985	7,563	7,332	5,741	6,197	8,634	6,556	11,707	10,695	7,576	7,765	11,926	16,844
1986	16,536	19,310	15,129	15,568	14,607	8,603	7,941	7,442	6,478	6,625	6,543	8,735
1987	10,822	11,323	7,118	7,133	6,461	4,645	5,320	5,596	3,447	3,701	2,851	1,524
1988	1,451	1,804	2,990	3,110	3,367	1,637	1,520	1,346	1,301	1,165	1,840	1,531

Source: Kansas City Board of Trade   T.643F

Month–End Open Interest of Maxi Major Market Stock Index Futures   at Chicago (CBT) in Contracts

Year	Jan.	Feb.	Mar.	Apr.	May	June	July	Aug.	Sept.	Oct.	Nov.	Dec.
1986	4,350	5,973	7,760	5,028	7,290	8,765	8,407	7,524	8,351	7,558	7,268	4,713
1987	7,389	6,671	6,137	12,882	5,614	6,029	8,579	12,079	8,866	4,244	3,074	2,233
1988	2,030	3,000	6,168	6,224	7,433	3,086	2,740	3,005	4,125	4,714	4,894	6,387

Source: Chicago Board of Trade   T.643H

STOCK INDEX FUTURES

High, Low & Closing Prices of the December S&P 500 Stock Index Futures   at Chicago IMM

Year of Delivery	Yr. Prior to Del. Dec.	Jan.	Feb.	Mar.	Apr.	May	June	July	Aug.	Sept.	Oct.	Nov.	Dec.	Life of Delivery Range
1984 High	175.00	177.30	171.50	166.75	166.20	167.70	160.55	158.90	173.95	174.60	174.40	172.90	169.50	179.20
Low	169.95	170.65	158.60	154.60	159.70	153.90	153.95	150.70	155.40	166.30	162.75	163.90	161.55	150.70
Close	173.85	171.00	162.50	165.35	166.00	155.60	157.35	154.90	170.20	170.10	168.60	164.55	165.51	—
1985 High	181.05	191.25	194.90	196.50	191.90	198.00	199.10	200.85	195.75	191.40	190.45	204.50	213.85	213.85
Low	178.40	175.40	188.75	187.00	186.20	185.35	191.55	192.20	188.75	180.65	182.10	189.10	200.40	175.40
Close	178.40	189.75	193.55	190.20	187.20	186.40	196.65	193.85	189.90	182.80	189.25	202.40	210.90	—
1986 High	220.90	223.30	237.20	249.50	252.10	254.80	255.30	257.25	256.85	256.40	244.80	249.95	256.05	257.25
Low	215.70	209.50	218.00	230.20	232.40	235.60	241.20	234.40	232.95	226.10	229.80	235.20	244.75	209.50
Close	219.30	220.50	234.90	247.30	239.55	252.20	254.25	237.55	254.35	230.60	244.70	248.65	249.60	—
1987 High	251.40	286.50	293.00	309.20	310.00	305.30	315.90	322.90	342.35	336.20	333.00	258.20	248.90	342.35
Low	243.20	248.10	278.00	287.10	278.50	281.70	291.50	306.30	317.30	311.30	181.00	225.00	220.80	181.00
Close	244.55	277.80	287.75	294.95	293.10	293.75	305.95	322.80	333.80	325.85	259.35	232.00	243.15	—
1988 High	—	262.20	273.00	277.50	277.30	267.40	282.10	281.20	278.35	277.70	285.75	282.00	279.80	285.75
Low	—	258.00	252.60	259.70	257.60	252.20	266.50	265.00	258.90	259.25	270.50	263.50	270.70	252.20
Close	—	261.60	271.35	262.20	264.50	266.40	277.60	275.70	264.10	276.40	279.10	273.05	274.35	—

Source: Chicago Mercantile Exchange, International Monetary Market.   T.643B

High, Low & Closing Prices of the December NYSE Composite Stock Index Futures   at N.Y. Futures Exch.

Year of Delivery	Yr. Prior to Delivery Nov.	Dec.	Jan.	Feb.	Mar.	Apr.	May	June	July	Aug.	Sept.	Oct.	Nov.	Dec.	Life of Delivery Range
1984 High	102.25	101.15	102.65	99.30	95.90	95.45	96.20	92.55	91.50	100.40	100.85	100.90	9.85	97.90	103.55
Low	98.25	98.50	98.70	91.00	91.90	91.80	88.55	88.80	86.70	89.35	95.85	93.80	94.45	93.20	86.70
Close	100.95	99.85	99.00	93.90	95.15	95.35	89.55	90.70	89.00	98.30	98.05	97.40	94.90	95.56	—
1985 High	—	104.15	110.90	112.95	113.75	111.55	115.15	115.50	117.20	115.45	111.05	110.05	117.95	123.25	123.25
Low	—	103.20	101.20	109.60	108.55	108.05	107.60	111.80	111.55	109.60	104.45	105.15	109.20	115.65	101.20
Close	—	103.55	110.25	112.25	110.85	108.70	114.30	114.40	112.55	110.20	105.70	109.35	116.75	121.30	—
1986 High	—	127.05	129.10	136.30	144.20	145.35	146.55	146.70	148.00	147.65	146.65	141.05	143.30	146.50	148.00
Low	—	124.85	121.00	126.90	133.55	134.60	135.60	139.00	133.90	133.90	128.00	131.80	135.15	139.90	121.00
Close	—	126.45	127.15	134.90	142.60	138.15	144.70	145.95	136.55	145.95	132.60	140.95	142.35	142.65	—
1987 High	—	144.50	163.00	166.50	175.25	175.45	171.45	177.15	181.20	191.45	188.15	186.35	144.70	140.00	191.45
Low	—	139.70	143.00	158.25	164.00	157.75	159.00	164.10	172.25	178.25	174.45	103.00	126.35	124.10	103.00
Close	—	139.70	158.80	163.95	167.60	165.35	164.80	172.25	181.05	186.80	182.65	144.35	130.40	139.20	—
1988 High	—	144.95	150.15	153.40	155.50	156.60	150.60	159.20	159.00	156.95	156.85	160.75	158.80	157.25	160.75
Low	—	140.40	137.95	142.55	147.50	145.50	143.30	151.00	149.95	146.70	147.00	152.95	148.45	152.50	137.95
Close	—	140.75	147.05	152.95	148.50	149.55	150.60	156.90	156.00	149.85	156.15	157.05	153.65	154.15	—
1989 High	—	163.40													
Low	—	162.00													
Close	—	163.40													

Source: New York Futures Exchange.   T.643C

High, Low & Closing Prices of the December Value Line Stock Index Futures   at K.C. Board of Trade

Year of Delivery	Nov.	Dec.	Jan.	Feb.	Mar.	Apr.	May	June	July	Aug.	Sept.	Oct.	Nov.	Dec.	Life of Delivery Range
1985 High	—	—	—	211.55	215.45	209.15	213.00	210.50	217.05	209.80	202.60	196.00	209.70	216.65	216.65
Low	—	—	—	209.50	204.70	201.80	200.30	202.00	205.20	200.80	188.80	188.60	194.60	205.30	188.60
Close	—	—	—	211.40	207.30	201.80	209.10	207.70	206.95	202.20	190.20	194.85	207.55	213.70	—
1986 High	—	226.25	228.35	235.30	250.00	251.90	251.60	247.65	250.10	237.60	240.00	231.00	233.60	235.60	251.90
Low	—	219.00	217.50	224.20	235.20	236.00	237.00	240.70	221.30	218.70	210.80	215.50	220.90	226.50	210.80
Close	—	222.00	223.65	235.30	246.90	240.30	248.00	245.80	222.45	235.15	218.80	230.65	230.00	231.00	—
1987 High	—	—	242.50	258.60	272.40	272.10	263.70	270.70	278.70	288.50	285.60	281.70	207.25	202.10	288.50
Low	—	—	240.00	246.70	258.15	245.80	246.00	255.10	264.30	274.30	266.00	170.00	182.50	179.20	170.00
Close	—	—	241.85	258.10	261.80	255.90	255.30	263.70	278.00	283.65	278.15	198.00	188.25	201.95	—
1988 High	—	—	—	—	242.65	245.75	239.55	253.80	255.60	251.60	248.90	251.50	245.90	242.90	255.60
Low	—	—	—	—	230.80	231.55	227.25	240.70	244.40	236.60	237.00	243.80	230.80	236.50	227.25
Close	—	—	—	—	234.25	238.70	237.10	253.80	251.20	240.90	247.80	245.10	237.30	241.12	—

Source: Kansas City Board of Trade.   T.643A

Month-End Open Interest of S&P 500 Stock Index Futures at Chicago IMM in Contracts

Year	Jan.	Feb.	Mar.	Apr.	May	June	July	Aug.	Sept.	Oct.	Nov.	Dec.
1984	34,012	38,441	27,931	33,389	34,200	28,395	33,971	31,973	31,610	46,104	53,530	42,191
1985	58,332	62,142	57,664	58,131	72,642	58,890	60,612	60,718	53,629	65,568	74,909	62,879
1986	63,660	86,224	78,431	73,268	99,371	83,100	112,015	107,016	125,304	138,262	144,347	95,433
1987	107,929	123,021	97,673	121,860	128,356	109,452	115,389	129,539	114,182	152,340	139,887	107,973
1988	118,583	122,741	110,129	116,738	134,175	98,175	114,248	119,496	114,434	125,889	141,766	120,511

Source: *International Monetary Market* (Chicago)   T.643D

High, Low & Closing Prices of the September Major Market Maxi Stock Index Futures at Chicago BOT

Year of Delivery		Jan.	Feb.	Mar.	Apr.	Delivery Year May	June	July	Aug.	Sept.	Life of Delivery Range
1986	High	287.00	299.00	272.60	353.50	362.10	365.70	366.90	368.80	368.00	368.80
	Low	272.60	272.60	272.60	272.60	333.90	348.60	336.00	336.00	335.00	272.60
	Close	272.60	272.60	272.60	340.70	357.40	363.65	342.75	364.20	336.65	—
1987	High	—	—	—	477.50	472.00	486.60	500.60	543.30	535.50	543.30
	Low	—	—	—	439.00	436.50	450.00	476.30	494.30	495.70	436.50
	Close	—	—	—	452.00	453.60	476.90	499.75	530.40	497.18	—
1988	High	—	—	392.50	416.50	401.20	422.00	422.20	419.10	413.90	422.20
	Low	—	—	386.50	387.50	377.70	398.50	398.50	387.40	388.50	377.70
	Close	—	—	391.00	398.00	397.90	416.20	414.30	395.90	409.66	—

Source: *Chicago Board of Trade*   T.643G

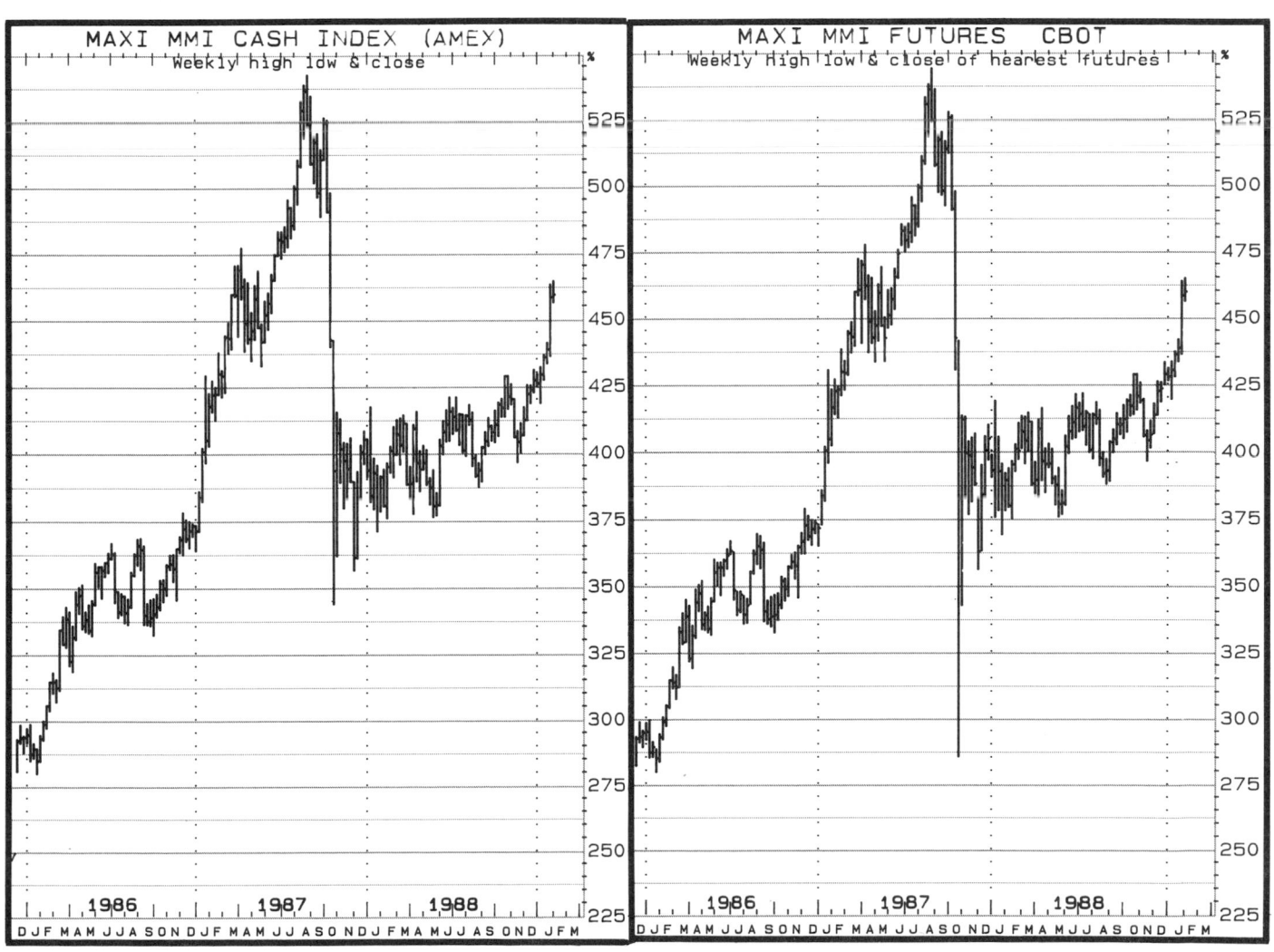

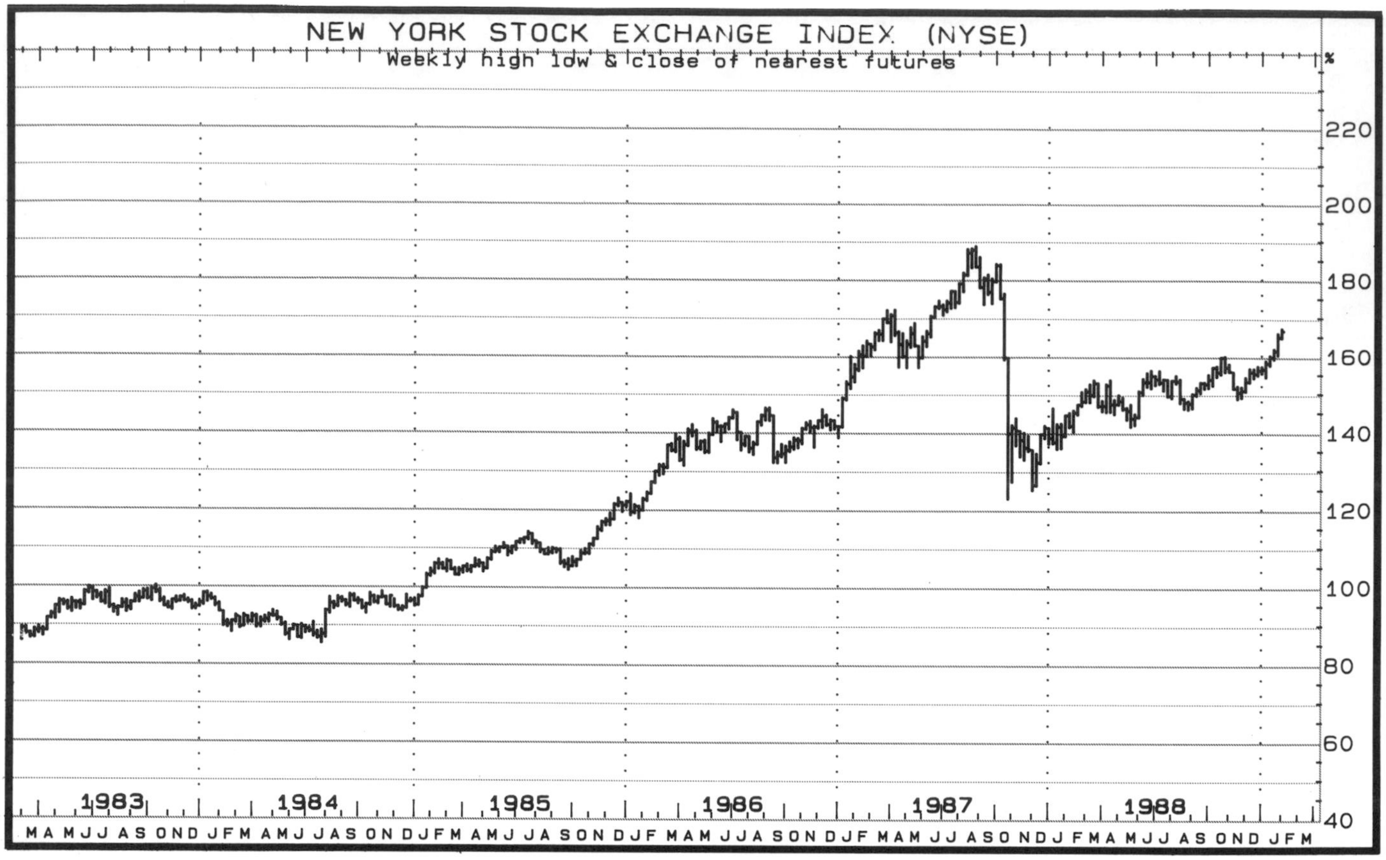
NEW YORK STOCK EXCHANGE INDEX (NYSE)
Weekly high low & close of nearest futures
%
220
200
180
160
140
120
100
80
60
40
1983
1984
1985
1986
1987
1988
M A M J J A S O N D J F M A M J J A S O N D J F M A M J J A S O N D J F M A M J J A S O N D J F M A M J J A S O N D J F M A M J J A S O N D J F M

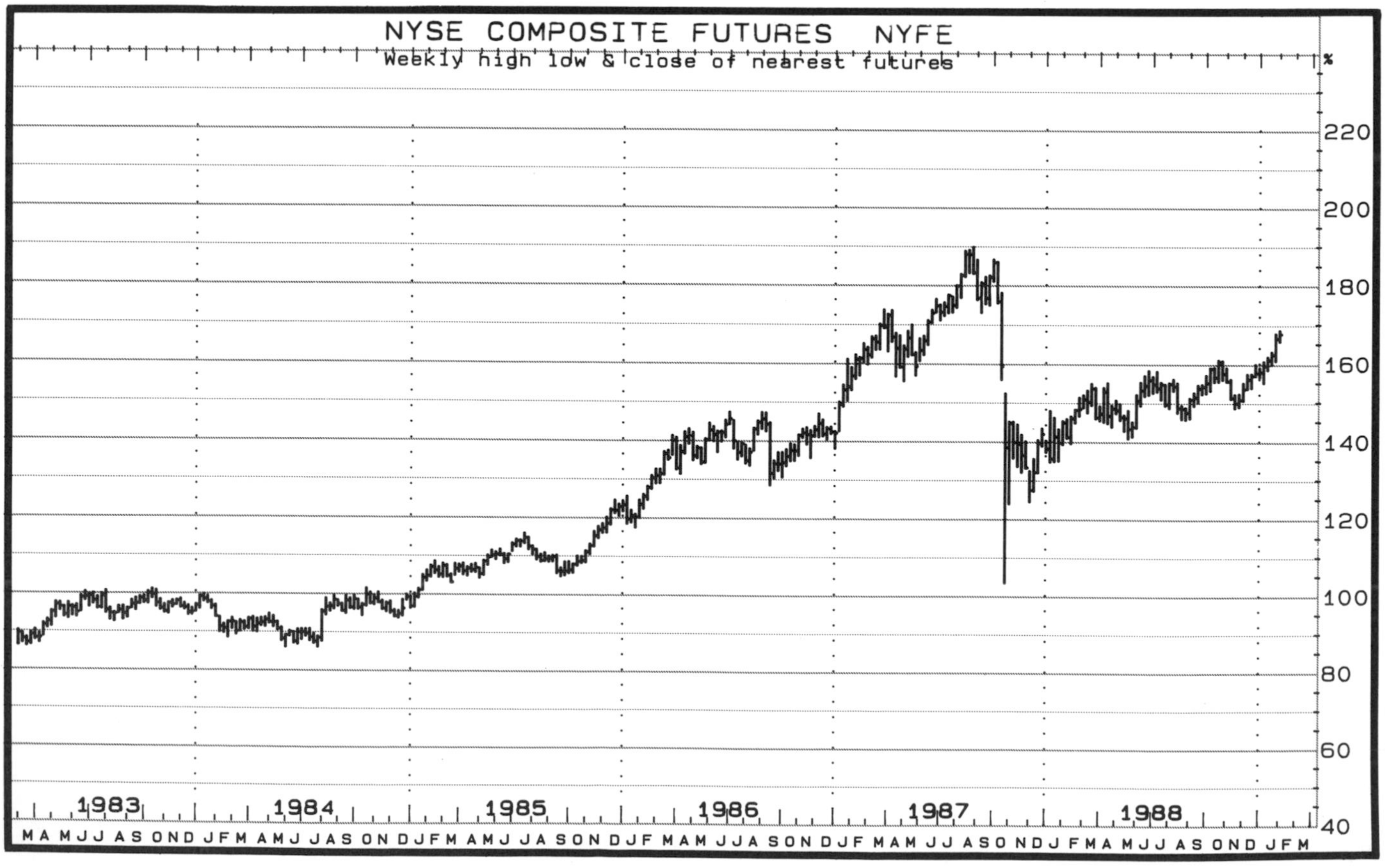
NYSE COMPOSITE FUTURES NYFE
Weekly high low & close of nearest futures
%
220
200
180
160
140
120
100
80
60
40
1983
1984
1985
1986
1987
1988
M A M J J A S O N D J F M A M J J A S O N D J F M A M J J A S O N D J F M A M J J A S O N D J F M A M J J A S O N D J F M A M J J A S O N D J F M

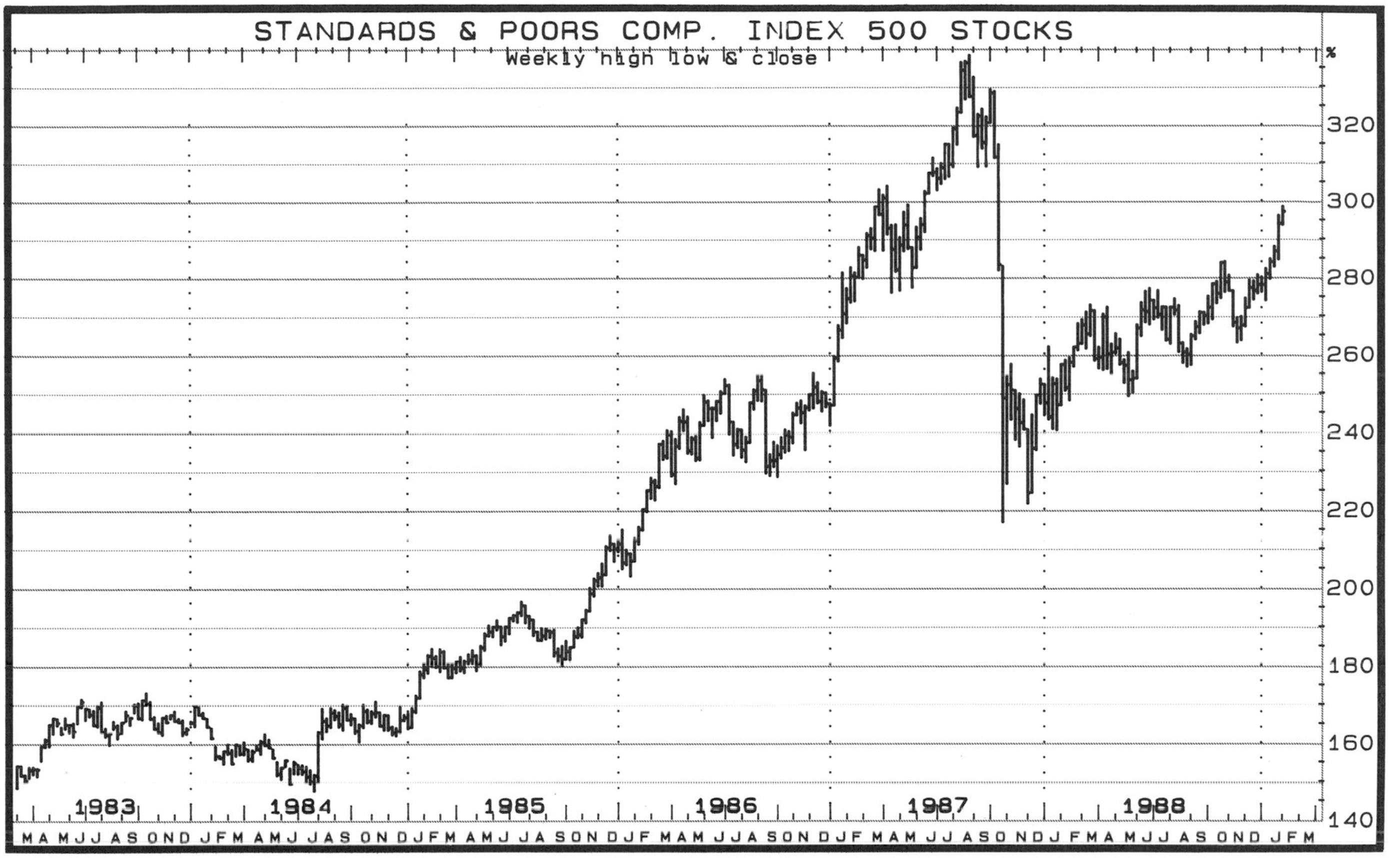
STANDARDS & POORS COMP. INDEX 500 STOCKS
Weekly high low & close
%
320
300
280
260
240
220
200
180
160
140
1983
1984
1985
1986
1987
1988
M A M J J A S O N D J F M A M J J A S O N D J F M A M J J A S O N D J F M A M J J A S O N D J F M A M J J A S O N D J F M A M J J A S O N D J F M

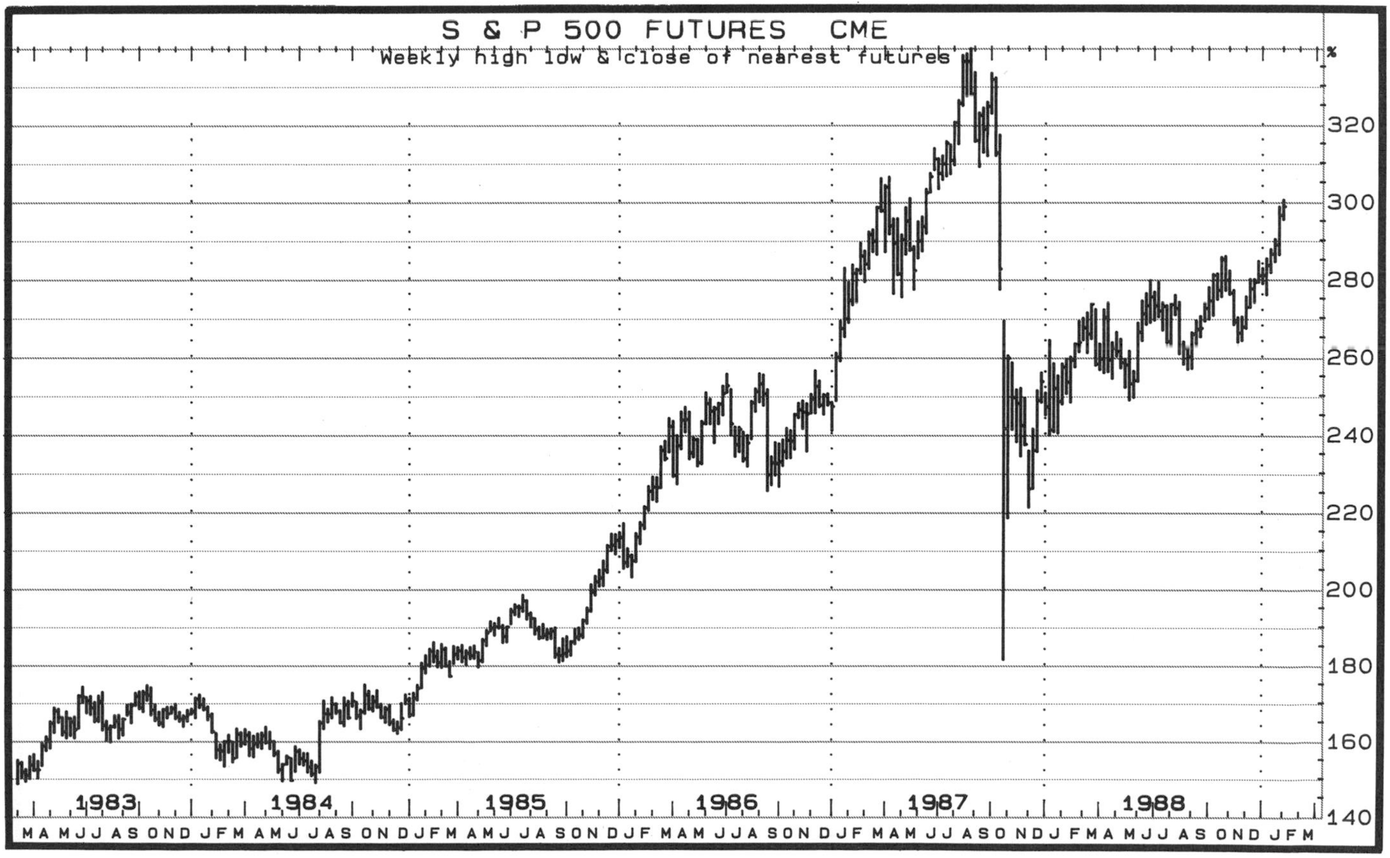
S & P 500 FUTURES CME
Weekly high low & close of nearest futures
%
320
300
280
260
240
220
200
180
160
140
1983
1984
1985
1986
1987
1988
M A M J J A S O N D J F M A M J J A S O N D J F M A M J J A S O N D J F M A M J J A S O N D J F M A M J J A S O N D J F M A M J J A S O N D J F M

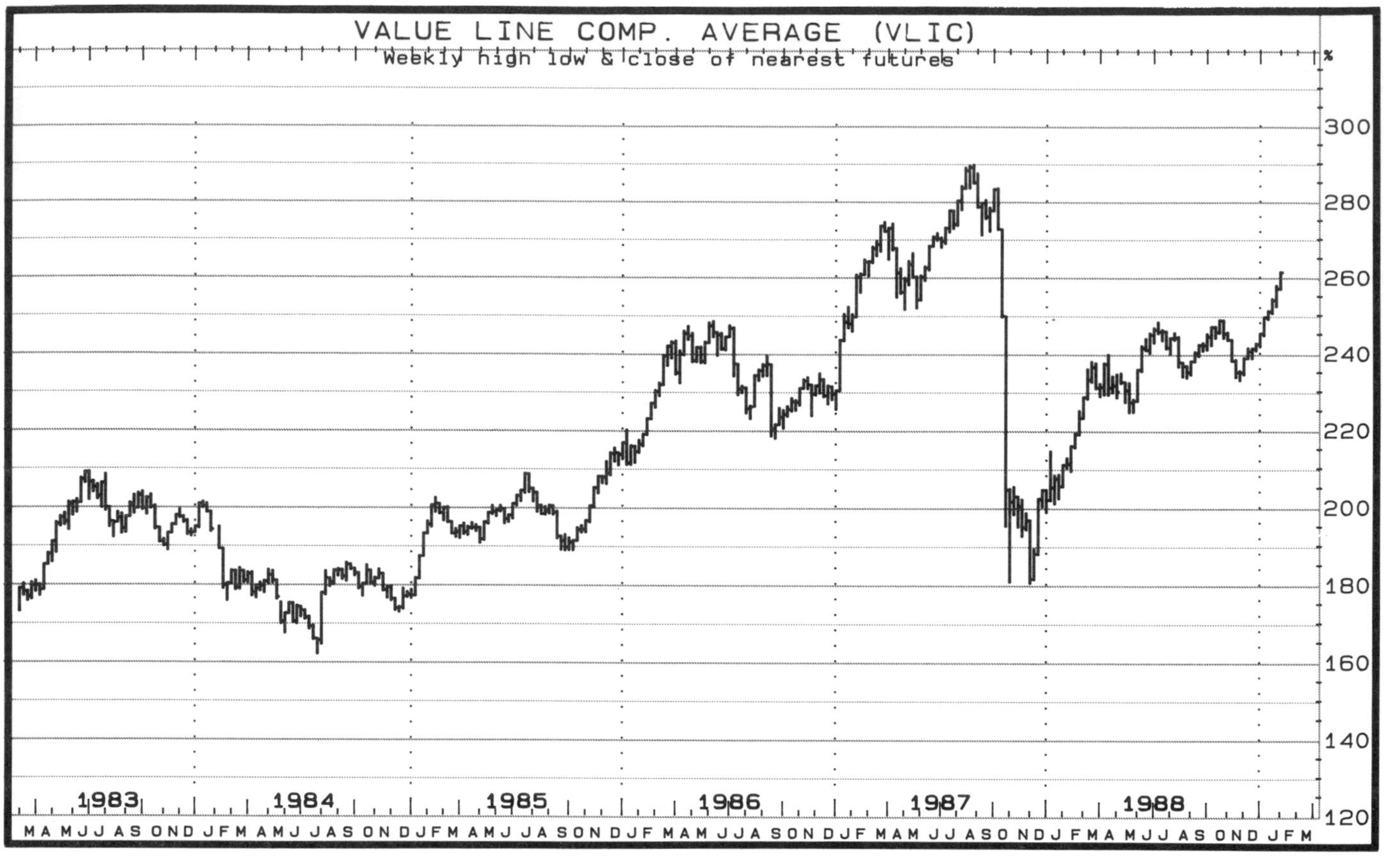
VALUE LINE COMP. AVERAGE (VLIC)
Weekly high low & close of nearest futures
%
300
280
260
240
220
200
180
160
140
120
1983
1984
1985
1986
1987
1988
M A M J J A S O N D J F M A M J J A S O N D J F M A M J J A S O N D J F M A M J J A S O N D J F M A M J J A S O N D J F M A M J J A S O N D J F M

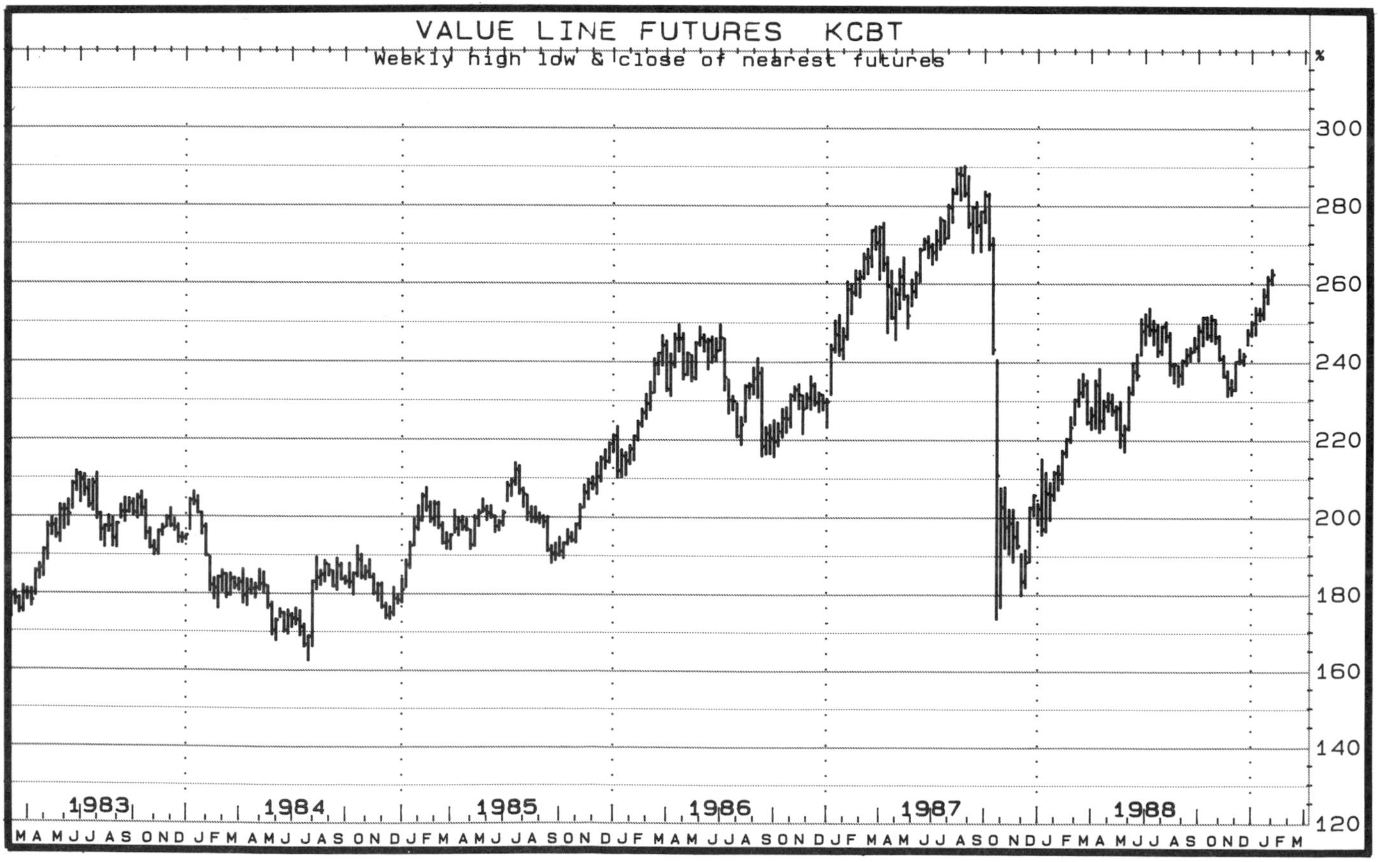
VALUE LINE FUTURES KCBT
Weekly high low & close of nearest futures
%
300
280
260
240
220
200
180
160
140
120
1983
1984
1985
1986
1987
1988
M A M J J A S O N D J F M A M J J A S O N D J F M A M J J A S O N D J F M A M J J A S O N D J F M A M J J A S O N D J F M A M J J A S O N D J F M

Sugar

World sugar production in 1988/89 was expected to reach a record for the third year in a row. The USDA's forecast of 106.8 million tonnes (raw value) was more than 3 percent above 1987/88. Consumption was also expected to be a record at 107.0 million tonnes, 2 percent above 1987/88.

In 1988/89, there were dramatic gains in sugar output in the EC and India; sizable increases in Thailand, Cuba, China, and the USSR; and drought-induced losses in the U.S., Eastern Europe, and Indonesia.

Since the early 1980s, cane sugar production, which accounts for just under two-thirds of world sugar output, has increased 26 percent, while beet sugar production has risen 15 percent. These gains were achieved in different ways--beet sugar by yield advances and cane by area expansion. From average 1978/79-1980/81 levels, beet sugar yields have risen 17 percent, and cane area has expanded by almost a third.

Beets are grown in temperate climates, mostly in the Northern Hemisphere, where agricultural systems are relatively mature and capital intensive. Yield gains are the result of research on seed varieties and investment in efficient refining technology. Beet industries in the EC, U.S., USSR, and Eastern Europe have been shielded from drops in world sugar prices by government policies. Cane is grown in semitropical and tropical regions, where, with the exception of the U.S., Australia, and South Africa, production tends to be less capital intensive and more vulnerable to world price gyrations than beet production. Most of the increase in world cane area occurred in the early 1980s, after prices averaged over 20 cents in 1979-81. Cane sugar yields have failed to reach earlier peaks.

Brazil and India are the world's largest cane producers. In Brazil, more than half the available cane is distilled for ethanol. In India, 40-50 percent of cane is ground into locally consumed non-milled sugars, such as gur and khandsari. High world sugar prices quickly divert some cane from ethanol or the local markets and into milled sugar production and commercial markets.

In 1988/89, Brazil's crop was forecast at 8.7 million tonnes, up 200,000 tonnes. Cuba's crop was expected to rise by 500,000 tonnes to 7.75 million, as a three-year drought appeared to have broken.

Sugar production in the USSR rose by almost a fourth during the 1980s, despite a 9 percent drop in area. An increase of over a third in sugar yields was accomplished by equal gains in beet yields and recovery rates. Chinese sugar output rose by 7 percent to 5.1 million tonnes in 1988/89, still below 1986/87's record.

In the U.S., 1988/89 cane sugar output was expected to be about the same as a year earlier, but drought and disease cut beet production sharply from 1987/88's huge harvest. Still, 1988/89 total cane and beet output of 6.1 million tonnes was the second best of the decade.

World sugar consumption has grown at a pace of about 2 percent annually over the past decade. The 1988/89 forecast of 107 million tonnes was up by over 7 million tonnes from 1985/86. Over half that increase has occurred in Asia, led by China and India, where per capita consumption remains among the world's lowest. India's production successes have enabled it to boost consumption, while virtually eliminating imports. India moved from being a leading importer in the mid-1980s to a potentially significant exporter in 1988/89. China achieved consumption gains, despite production problems and sugar rationing, by more than doubling its imports in the past four years. China's sugar import decisions have been a major factor in the world market.

Consumption in the USSR has risen by about 1 million tonnes since 1985/86. Yet, it has remained the largest importer, sometimes making surprisingly large purchases. Cuba normally provides the Soviets with three quarters of their imports, but Cuba's extended drought problems have forced the Soviets to look to other suppliers. An important, if somewhat elusive, factor in anticipating Soviet sugar demand has been the government's anti-alcohol policy. Restrictions on alcohol production and sales drove up sugar demand to the point that sugar hoarding and rationing occurred.

Sugar consumption in the developed world has been fairly flat in recent years. Per capita consumption is near saturation levels, and corn sweeteners have cut into sugar's market share. U.S. consumption has risen modestly, as the decade-long substitution of corn sweeteners for sugar in beverages has run its course.

The world sugar stocks-to-use ratio was projected to slip below 20 percent in 1988/89 for the first time since 1980/81. Structural changes in the market over the past decade suggested the relationship between the ratio and prices may have shifted. Sugar consumers were unlikely to bid prices up to previous peaks because of lower revenues in oil-exporting countries, debt problems in developing countries that import sugar, and increased availability of alternative sweeteners, mainly corn fructose, in developed countries.

Futures and Options Markets

World (raw and white) and domestic raw sugar futures are traded on the New York Coffee, Sugar and Cocoa Exchange (CSCE). World raw and white sugar futures are listed on the London United Terminal Sugar Market. White sugar futures are traded on the Paris International Sugar Market and the London Terminal. Options on the No. 11 contract are traded on the CSCE, and options are traded on the London Futures and Options Exchange.

United States Foreign Trade of Sugar (Raw & Refined)   In Thousands of Short Tons

Year		Jan.	Feb.	Mar.	Apr.	May	June	July	Aug.	Sept.	Oct.	Nov.	Dec.	Total
1987[1]	Exports	84	50	63	85	87	34	53	28	27	33	33	41	618
	Imports	33	129	140	146	116	74	167	65	139	87	128	51	1,275
1988[1]	Exports	11	25	14	25	10	46	40	31	25	42			
	Imports	78	104	78	84	106	68	123	159	109	181			

[1] Preliminary.   *Source: Bureau of the Census*

SUGAR

United States Sugar (Cane & Beet) Supply and Utilization   In Thousands of Short Tons (Raw Value)

		Supply		Offshore Receipts						Utilization			Domestic Disappearance Military & Civilian	
Year	Cane	Production Beet	Total	For-eign	Terri-tories	Total	Begin-ning Stocks	Total Supply	Total Use	Ex-ports	Net Changes in Invisible Stocks	Refin. Loss Adjust.[3]	Imp. Blends & Mix-tures	Total	Per Capita
1977	2,666	3,423	6,089	6,138	102	6,240	3,498	15,827	11,336	22	201	14	—	11,099	94.2
1978	2,535	3,067	5,602	4,683	52	4,735	4,491	14,828	11,074	48	29	108	—	10,889	91.4
1979	2,727	3,066	5,793	5,027	47	5,074	3,754	14,621	10,921	73	−12	103	—	10,756	89.3
1980	2,684	3,052	5,736	4,495	178	4,673	3,701	14,110	11,028	689	72	78	—	10,189	83.6
1981	3,043	3,182	6,225	5,025	48	5,073	3,082	14,380	10,919	1,191	−94	53	—	9,769	79.4
1982	2,776	3,160	5,936	2,964	80	3,044	3,461	12,441	9,327	137	30	53	—	9,153	73.6
1983	3,094	2,588	5,682	3,186	67	3,253	3,068	12,003	9,327	300	143	72	—	8,812	70.2
1984	2,831	3,059	5,890	3,559	24	3,583	2,570	12,043	8,923	429	−18	58	8	8,428	66.5
1985	3,100	2,869	5,969	2,797	36	2,833	3,005	11,807	8,681	464	−67	122	15	7,997	62.5
1986	3,056	3,201	6,257	2,223	31	2,254	3,126	11,637	8,412	556	42	28	30	7,711	59.7
1987[1]	3,410	3,899	7,309	1,546	12	1,558	3,225	12,092	8,897	742	−30	18	30	8,037	61.6
1988[2]	3,320	3,620	6,940	1,387	20	1,407	3,195	11,542	8,570	355	—	—	30	8,085	61.5
1989[4]	3,375	3,730	7,105	1,495	20	1,515	2,972	11,590	8,520	220	—	20	30	8,170	61.7

[1] Preliminary.   [2] Estimate.   [3] Residual.   [4] Forecast.   *Source: Agricultural Marketing Service, U.S.D.A.*   T.645

Sugar Cane for Sugar & Seed and Production of Cane Sugar and Molasses in the United States

	Acreage Har-vested 1,000 Acres	Yield of Cane per Har. Acre Tons	Production for Sugar 1,000 Tons	Production for Seed 1,000 Tons	Total 1,000 Tons	Sugar Yield per Acre Sh. Tons	Farm Price $ per Ton	Farm Value of Cane used for Sugar 1,000 Dollars	Farm Value of Cane used for Sugar & Seed 1,000 Dollars	Sugar Production Raw Value Total 1,000 Tons	Sugar Production Raw Value Per Ton of Cane Lbs.	Sugar Production Refined Basis 1,000 Tons	Molasses Made Edible 1,000 Gallons	Molasses Made Total 1,000 Gallons
Year														
1977	759	35.3	25,730	1,100	26,830		18.50	454,217	474,257	2,684	209	2,508	2,538	164,894
1978	744	35.0	24,821	1,176	25,997		19.40	483,905	507,069	2,612	210	2,441	2,750	161,810
1979	733	36.2	25,410	1,122	26,532		26.00	661,212	690,544	2,700	213	2,524	2,900	164,581
1980	733	36.8	25,582	1,381	26,963		38.50	984,559	1,035,990	2,728	213	2,550	1,900	163,341
1981	755	36.3	26,165	1,243	27,408	3.96	24.90	650,721	681,983	2,833	217	2,647	2,100	182,656
1982	742	40.1	28,450	1,321	29,770	4.37	26.50	755,038	789,896	3,063	215	2,863	1,550	177,041
1983	768	36.7	27,201	960	28,161	4.00	27.80	755,574	781,393	2,930	215	2,739	1,850	175,875
1984	747	36.6	26,008	1,332	27,340	4.29	28.20	734,026	769,934	3,007	231	2,811	2,070	175,573
1985	770	36.6	26,877	1,336	28,213	4.20	26.70	717,690	751,550	3,033	226	2,835	1,650	178,539
1986[1]	796	38.1	28,936	1,375	30,311	4.37				3,281	227	3,066	1,800	187,670
1987[1]	824	35.5	28,026	1,192	29,218	4.28				3,368		3,148		191,491
1988[2]	841	37.0	29,910	1,205	31,115	4.19								

[1] Preliminary.   [2] Estimate.   *Source: Statistical Reporting Service, U.S.D.A.*   T.646

U.S. Sugar Beets, Beet Sugar, Pulp, & Molasses Produced from Sugar Beets & Raw Sugar Spot Prices

Year of Harvest	Acreage Planted 1,000 Acres	Acreage Harv. 1,000 Acres	Yield Per Har. Acre Tons	Production 1,000 Tons	Sugar Yield per Acre Sh. Tons	Price[1] Dollars	Farm Value $1,000	Sugar Production Refined Basis 1,000 Sh. Tons	Sugar Production Equivalent "Raw Value"[2] 1,000 Sh. Tons	Raw Sugar Prices World[4] Intern. Agreem. Cents Per Lb.	Raw Sugar Prices Cof., Sugar Exch. World Cents Per Lb.	Raw Sugar Prices Cof., Sugar Exch. N.Y. Duty Paid Cents Per Lb.	Whole-sale List Price HFCS (42%) Nor. East
1977	1,273	1,216	20.6	25,007		24.20	604,399	2,905	3,108	8.10	8.11	11.00	13.05
1978	1,305	1,269	20.3	25,788		25.20	649,846	3,074	3,289	7.81	7.82	13.93	12.32
1979	1,161	1,120	19.6	21,996		33.90	745,273	2,691	2,879	9.65	9.66	15.56	13.54
1980	1,231	1,190	19.8	23,502		47.20	1,108,974	2,943	3,149	28.66	29.02	30.11	24.27
1981	1,252	1,228	22.4	27,538	2.76	29.20	803,569	3,166	3,388	16.89	16.93	19.73	21.94
1982	1,054	1,027	20.3	20,894	2.67	35.40	740,342	2,558	2,737	8.40	8.42	19.92	16.82
1983	1,081	1,056	19.9	20,992	2.56	37.00	777,718	2,522	2,699	8.46	8.49	22.04	18.47
1984	1,124	1,096	20.2	22,134	2.65	33.90	750,162	2,715	2,905	5.21	5.18	21.74	20.41
1985	1,125	1,103	20.4	22,529	2.72	33.80	761,236	2,804	3,000	4.06	4.04	20.34	19.38
1986	1,232	1,191	21.1	25,162	2.87			3,193	3,416	6.04	6.05	20.95	19.30
1987[3]	1,266	1,251	22.3	27,937	3.16			3,698	3,957	6.75	6.71	21.83	17.72
1988[5]	1,320	1,301	19.3	25,120	2.61					10.10	10.00	22.10	18.50

[1] Includes support payments, but excludes Sugar beet payments.   [2] Refined sugar multiplied by factor of 1.07.   [3] Preliminary.   [4] International Sugar Agreement, World Price.   [5] Estimate.   *Source: Statistical Reporting Service, U.S.D.A.*   T.647

Raw Sugar N.Y. Spot Price (C.I.F., Duty/Fee Paid, Contract #12 & #14)   In Cents per Pound

Year	Jan.	Feb.	Mar.	Apr.	May	June	July	Aug.	Sept.	Oct.	Nov.	Dec.	Average
1982	18.16	17.77	17.13	17.89	19.57	21.03	22.15	22.45	20.88	20.44	20.79	20.83	19.92
1983	21.23	21.76	21.86	22.43	22.60	22.54	22.09	22.55	22.20	21.94	21.83	21.47	22.04
1984	21.51	21.90	22.00	22.03	22.01	22.06	21.89	21.72	21.70	21.56	21.40	21.10	21.74
1985	20.72	20.38	20.91	20.97	21.09	21.27	21.23	20.59	19.51	18.68	18.89	19.89	20.34
1986	20.67	21.01	20.95	20.85	20.88	20.99	20.97	20.87	20.87	21.08	21.17	21.12	20.95
1987	21.50	21.76	21.76	21.81	22.01	22.06	22.07	21.88	21.88	21.69	21.75	21.76	21.83
1988	21.83	22.11	22.16	22.16	22.13	22.54	23.43	21.90	21.77	21.74	21.70		

Sources: Economic Research Service, U.S.D.A.; N.Y. Coffee & Sugar Exchange   T.648

World Production of Sugar (Centrifugal Sugar–Raw Value)   In Thousands of Metric Tons

Crop Year	Australia Cane	Brazil Cane	Mainland China	Cuba Cane	South Africa Cane	India Cane	Indonesia Cane	Philippines Cane	Poland Beet	West Germany	Thailand	United States	USSR Beet	Mexico	France	World All
1982–3	3,535	9,300	4,132	7,200	2,256	9,508	1,731	2,521	2,009	3,591	2,305	5,359	7,392	3,078	4,833	101,342
1983–4	3,414	9,400	3,825	8,330	1,462	7,042	1,762	2,381	2,141	2,726	2,305	5,275	8,700	3,242	4,153	96,542
1984–5	3,548	9,300	4,627	8,100	2,514	7,071	1,709	1,767	1,878	3,146	2,533	5,289	8,587	3,436	4,301	100,183
1985–6	3,404	8,100	5,535	7,200	2,247	7,983	1,728	1,561	1,811	3,430	2,586	5,473	8,260	3,928	4,297	98,938
1986–7	3,457	8,525	5,774	7,220	2,170	9,474	2,024	1,373	1,891	3,469	2,639	6,075	8,696	3,970	3,707	103,398
1987–8[2]	3,528	8,500	4,763	7,250	2,120	10,000	2,100	1,250	1,823	2,963	2,704	6,610	9,560	3,830	3,966	103,545
1988–9[1]	3,650	8,700	5,100	7,750	2,175	10,650	1,800	1,425	1,800	3,400	3,300	6,110	10,000	3,850	4,295	106,849

[1] Estimated.   [2] Preliminary.   *Source: Foreign Agricultural Service, U.S.D.A.*   T.644

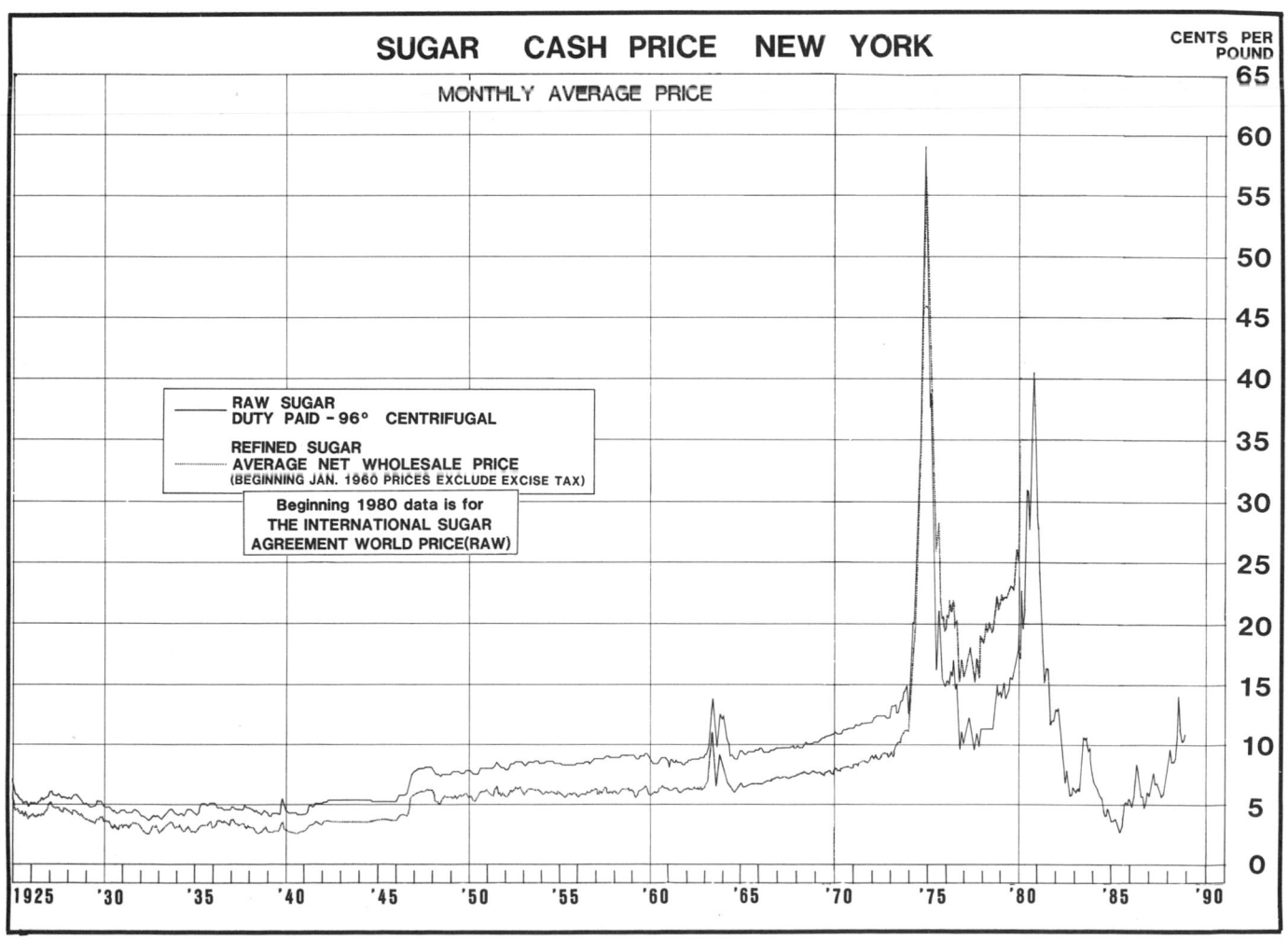

SUGAR   CASH   PRICE   NEW   YORK

CENTS PER POUND

MONTHLY AVERAGE PRICE

RAW SUGAR
DUTY PAID - 96° CENTRIFUGAL

REFINED SUGAR
AVERAGE NET WHOLESALE PRICE
(BEGINNING JAN. 1960 PRICES EXCLUDE EXCISE TAX)

Beginning 1980 data is for
THE INTERNATIONAL SUGAR
AGREEMENT WORLD PRICE (RAW)

United States Production & Imports of Edible Syrups   In Thousands of Gallons

Year	Production[2] Corn	Syrups Maple	Refiners'	Edible Molasses	Honey	Total	Imports Maple Syrup	Edib. Molas. & Cane Syrup	Honey	Total
1980	941,056	973	1,983	1,900	16,871	962,783	856	3,422	4,143	8,420
1981	1,073,933	1,410	1,446	2,100	15,703	1,094,592	1,046	2,040	6,530	9,616
1982	1,212,759	1,292	1,003	1,550	18,666	1,235,270	1,154	2,566	7,767	11,487
1983	1,334,557	1,150	1,000	1,850	17,314	1,355,871	1,288	2,336	9,277	12,900
1984	1,501,377	1,366	950	2,070	13,936	1,519,699	1,248	3,495	10,869	15,612
1985	1,721,980	1,325	1,100	1,650	12,669	1,738,724	1,323	4,164	11,676	17,163
1986[1]	1,726,348	937	900	1,800	16,925	1,746,910	1,672	8,095	10,000	19,767
1987[3]							1,493	6,905		

[1] Preliminary. [2] Production of cane syrup, sorghum syrup, & edible molasses is of the fall of the preceding year. [3] Estimate.
Source: Agricultural Marketing Service, U.S.D.A.   T.652

U.S. Exports & Domestic Consumption of Edible Syrups, Corn Sugar & Sugar   In Thousands of Gallons

Year	Exports Corn Syrup	Honey	Total	Indicated Domestic Consumption Syrups Corn	Maple	Cane & Refin. & Edib. Mol.	Honey	Total	Per Capita Consumption in Pounds Corn Sweet-ners[2]	Cal-oric Sweet-eners	Aspar-tame	Sacc-harin	Sugar U.S. Grown	Cane	Total	Total All Sweet-eners
1980	3,498	722	4,220	937,558	1,828	7,620	20,292	967,298	40.2	125.1	0	7.7	51.2	56.7	83.6	132.8
1981	2,916	777	3,693	1,071,017	2,456	5,586	21,456	1,100,515	44.5	125.1	.2	8.0	47.1	53.8	79.4	133.3
1982	791	721	1,512	1,211,968	2,446	5,119	25,712	1,245,245	48.2	123.2	1.0	8.4	48.8	48.3	73.7	132.6
1983	1,223	630	1,853	1,333,334	2,437	5,186	25,961	1,366,918	52.2	124.6	3.5	9.5	48.0	47.1	71.1	137.6
1984	656	627	1,283	1,500,721	2,614	6,515	24,178	1,534,028	57.8	126.7	5.8	10.0	42.7	45.0	67.6	142.5
1985	534	549	1,083	1,721,446	2,648	6,914	23,796	1,754,804	66.5	131.2	12.0	6.0	44.0	38.6	63.3	142.4
1986[1]	638	778	1,416	1,725,710	2,609	10,795	26,147	1,765,261	67.1	129.3	13.0	5.5	46.4	35.6	60.8	148.9
1987[3]					2,047				68.8	132.6	13.5	5.5	53.9	33.6	62.4	147.2
1988[3]									70.3	133.9	14.0	6.0			62.2	152.4

[1] Preliminary. [2] Corn syrup & dextrose. [3] Estimate. *Source: Agricultural Marketing Service, U.S.D.A.*   T.653

Sugar Deliveries and Stocks in the United States   In Thousands of Short Tons, Raw Value

Year	Deliveries by Primary Distributors Cane[1] Sugar Re-fineries	Beet Sugar Fac-tories	Importers of Direct Consump-tion Sugar	Cane Sugar Mills[1]	Total	Sales of Refined Sugar For Export	Total Domestic Consump-tion[2]	Stocks (January 1) Cane Sugar Re-fineries	Beet Sugar Fac-tories	Comm. Credit Corp.	Re-finers' Raws	Main-land Cane Mills	Total
1981	6,618	3,151	17	24	9,770	1,191	9,769	315	1,286	20	691	658	2,970
1982	6,127	3,026	46	24	9,153	137	9,153	272	1,277	20	844	931	3,344
1983	5,910	2,902			8,812	300	8,812	262	1,417	—	517	701	2,897
1984	5,722	2,732			8,454	429	8,428	225	1,103	—	528	592	2,448
1985	4,973	3,062			8,035	464	7,997	214	1,430	—	473	762	2,879
1986	4,667	3,120			7,786	556	7,711	197	1,189	220	523	834	2,964
1987	4,512	3,655			8,167	742	8,037	211	1,304	177	516	830	3,038
1988[4]								184	1,546	—	401	996	3,128

[1] Sugar for direct consumption only. [2] Includes deliveries for U.S. military forces at home and abroad. [3] Preliminary [4] Estimate.
Source: Department of Agriculture   T.654

Sugar, Refined—Deliveries by Type of Product of Buyer in the U.S.   In Thousands of Short Tons

Year	Bakery & Cereal Pdts.	Bever-ages	Confec-tionery[3]	Insti-tutions	Dairy Products	Proc-essed Foods	Other Food Uses	Retail Gro-cers[4]	Whole-sale Grocers[5]	Other Uses[e]	Total De-liveries	In Con-sumer Size Pckgs.	To Indus-trial Users
1981	1,306	1,852	983	259	459	484	581	1,161	2,001	126	9,212	2,425	737
1982	1,296	1,583	940	177	404	450	526	1,086	1,951	106	8,519	2,310	727
1983	1,387	1,248	1,087	195	385	454	431	1,168	1,713	131	8,199	2,314	567
1984	1,404	908	1,115	209	408	433	416	1,100	1,744	127	7,864	2,274	570
1985	1,494	340	1,059	204	456	428	441	1,045	1,874	131	7,472	2,185	734
1986	1,432	266	1,051	142	447	387	443	1,066	1,867	138	7,239	2,298	635
1987[1]	1,513	212	1,146	163	449	398	534	996	2,040	149	7,600	2,144	892
1988[6]	1,580	240	1,120	170	425	350	500	940	2,200	140	7,800	1,900	950

[1] Preliminary. [2] Used largely for pharmaceuticals & some tobacco. [3] And related products. [4] Chain stores, supermarkets. [5] Jobbers, sugar dealers. [6] Forecast. *Source: Stat. Rep. Serv., U.S.D.A.*   T.649

World Stocks of Centrifugal Sugar as of Sept. 1   In Thousands Metric Tons (Raw Value)

Sugar-Making Season	Australia	Brazil	France	West Germany	India	Italy	Japan	Mexico	Netherlands	Philippines	Sweden	Iran	United Kingdom	U.S. & Insular	World Total
1977–8	534	1,286	706	202	732	562	104	198	199	1,607	127	304	253	2,718	12,820
1978–9	383	1,516	947	305	1,448	859	350	134	207	1,290	140	364	234	3,375	15,843
1979–0	687	3,008	962	537	1,934	758	421	138	222	1,214	108	354	455	3,549	19,122
1980–1	555	1,959	899	535	386	833	497	192	196	727	93	325	625	2,904	14,353
1981–2	499	2,234	415	300	706	663	212	167	181	158	75	275	706	2,508	12,322
1982–3	364	918	1,212	416	3,354	570	377	587	128	269	317	151	503	1,399	14,253
1983–4	486	918	1,566	558	4,999	479	340	1,112	178	375	281	201	204	1,277	18,508
1984–5	603	1,825	729	407	2,457	467	296	1,439	92	768	340	251	159	1,461	16,249
1985–6	603	1,386	1,016	566	1,803	350	216	1,394	149	229	329	151	124	1,596	27,242
1986–7	348	496	1,073	692	2,166	256	227	1,620	270	283	368	221	420	1,499	25,284
1987–8[1]	310	601	1,089	707	2,960	439	194	1,485	233	209	264	221	397	1,358	23,892

[1] Preliminary.   *Source: Foreign Agricultural Service, U.S.D.A.*   T.650

Month–End Open Interest of World Sugar (#11) Futures at New York   In Contracts

Year	Jan.	Feb.	Mar.	Apr.	May	June	July	Aug.	Sept.	Oct.	Nov.	Dec.
1979	35,004	34,529	36,200	31,824	36,521	39,646	44,938	58,184	61,442	73,701	87,182	92,007
1980	103,041	87,843	68,667	61,126	69,666	68,554	68,996	70,993	71,316	79,313	76,754	64,740
1981	61,522	57,087	59,025	54,898	62,330	61,022	66,730	64,604	52,740	60,761	66,399	72,326
1982	76,623	60,990	65,457	57,719	61,332	51,267	54,706	51,737	42,363	50,682	61,916	64,406
1983	78,889	76,429	83,851	88,011	99,100	94,091	94,216	94,245	80,360	81,261	83,302	84,059
1984	81,806	73,634	92,503	84,925	92,769	89,393	90,897	98,425	76,056	85,413	86,508	80,550
1985	91,973	81,892	84,390	78,336	94,570	81,969	91,489	92,291	85,946	84,583	97,145	93,355
1986	96,382	85,112	118,580	111,625	95,088	86,064	85,427	91,764	82,851	84,290	84,340	92,574
1987	105,733	95,869	90,775	95,034	92,870	93,889	98,898	102,111	96,033	95,197	115,200	135,754
1988	155,823	132,682	137,240	123,493	150,872	162,044	140,856	136,770	121,312	117,924	137,049	143,241

Source: Coffee, Sugar & Cocoa Exch., Inc., N.Y.   T.660

Volume of Trading of World Sugar (#11) Futures at New York   In Contracts

Year	Jan.	Feb.	Mar.	Apr.	May	June	July	Aug.	Sept.	Oct.	Nov.	Dec.	Total
1979	72,961	107,951	76,267	82,804	64,224	132,200	121,474	142,006	192,200	255,858	278,458	256,919	1,783,342
1980	381,805	354,441	338,118	245,233	309,417	277,846	271,884	279,149	317,170	295,673	250,627	255,379	3,576,702
1981	233,217	237,286	212,519	240,420	212,708	241,736	192,142	203,404	247,160	138,529	137,768	183,438	2,470,327
1982	166,913	209,386	199,263	217,689	138,377	177,657	176,641	144,980	151,639	140,262	160,656	154,657	2,037,020
1983	207,678	249,392	198,034	261,939	396,435	396,267	272,150	329,129	283,827	214,897	231,757	160,436	3,201,941
1984	192,451	205,499	252,489	227,150	175,268	213,491	163,955	228,279	263,419	234,008	154,735	124,579	2,449,549
1985	273,316	265,967	215,540	210,046	193,527	237,904	263,842	338,816	323,387	224,856	216,340	249,398	3,012,929
1986	308,044	268,053	382,053	519,027	343,746	289,900	281,124	235,555	328,830	258,744	173,612	195,126	3,583,814
1987	387,630	381,393	323,047	381,972	278,857	313,001	248,133	235,263	367,074	331,052	268,226	337,851	3,853,499
1988	603,565	605,773	348,510	391,971	474,693	705,498	807,381	442,101	450,116	276,010	322,463	381,040	5,819,121

Source: Coffee, Sugar & Cocoa Exch., Inc., N.Y.   T.661

United States Deliveries[1] of All Sugar by Primary Distributors   In Thousands of Short Tons, Raw Value

Year	Jan.	Feb.	Mar.	Apr.	May	June	July	Aug.	Sept.	Oct.	Nov.	Dec.	Total
1979	838	774	964	811	893	947	923	1,103	860	924	879	840	10,756
1980	794	848	866	772	943	882	910	904	909	825	717	818	10,189
1981		——2,208——			——2,532——			——2,725——			——2,305——		9,770
1982		——2,083——			——2,418——			——2,400——			——2,252——		9,153
1983		——2,078——			——2,195——			——2,349——			——2,190——		8,812
1984		——2,029——			——2,121——			——2,238——			——2,066——		8,454
1985		——1,909——			——1,972——			——2,150——			——2,004——		8,035
1986		——1,819——			——1,907——			——2,069——			——1,991——		7,786
1987[2]		——1,908——			——2,001——			——2,146——			——2,112——		8,167
1988[2]		——1,951——			——1,983——			——2,147——					

[1] Includes for domestic consumption and for export.   [2] Preliminary.   *Source: Department of Agriculture*   T.659

SUGAR

Centrifugal Sugar (Raw Value) Imported into Selected Countries In Thousands of Metric Tons

Crop Year	Algeria	Canada	China	France	Iran	Israel	Japan	Korea Rep.	Malaysia	Morocco	Nigeria	Peru	United Kingdom	United States	USSR	West Germany	World Total[2]
1978	437	1,030	1,438	117	875	195	2,284		398	294	595		1,689	3,616	3,993	152	23,843
1979	513	1,010	985	103	746	256	2,605		418	279	530		1,424	4,437	4,080	146	24,827
1980	569	859	946	69	785	119	2,265		510	332	709		1,404	3,802	4,981	150	26,480
1981–2	535	929	1,060	376	755	180	2,209		432	350	600		1,307	3,196	6,883	186	28,935
1982–3	636	912	2,563	357	472	302	2,239		433	205	941		1,050	2,393	7,363	183	29,085
1983–4	550	1,001	1,777	363	623	261	1,868		560	224	863	263	1,500	2,667	5,998	180	27,530
1984–5	595	1,054	1,348	360	607	319	1,903		580	319	439	130	1,300	3,021	5,704	175	27,937
1985–6	554	1,145	1,216	365	650	233	1,857	970	663	238	600	256	1,484	1,965	5,030	180	28,294
1986–7[1]	613	1,119	1,507	376	650		1,695	973	661	297	578	341	1,235	1,756	5,025	161	27,148
1987–8[3]	610	950	2,700	355	650		1,850	1,000	690	294	510	353	1,317	1,056	4,415	170	26,613

[1] Preliminary. [2] Excludes U.S. trade with Territories. [3] Estimate. *Source: Foreign Agricultural Service, U.S.D.A.* T.655

Centrifugal Sugar (Raw Value) Exported from Selected Countries In Thousands of Metric Tons

Crop Year	Australia	Brazil	Czecho-slovakia	Cuba	Dom. Re-public	France	Thai-land	Mau-ritius	Mex-ico	Peru	Philip-pines	South Africa	Taiwan	Un. King-dom	USSR	World Total[2]
1978	2,482	2,005	306	7,231	901	2,357	1,040	579		275	1,142	719	365	93	174	26,088
1979	2,002	1,860	242	7,269	986	2,347	1,190	641		181	1,150	884	387	76	244	26,373
1980	2,410	2,615	186	6,191	794	2,750	479	655		53	1,745	785	403	100	164	27,290
1981–2	2,620	2,984	160	7,734	816	3,226	2,419	560		63	1,314	851	380	122	268	33,044
1982–3	2,504	2,788	215	7,734	850	3,066	2,045	633		92	1,301	884	380	390	267	30,642
1983–4	2,425	2,801	115	6,792	956	3,300	1,411	644	833	120	999	569	186	240	148	28,842
1984–5	2,591	3,040	234	7,017	885	3,000	1,444	562	273	130	1,200	687	130	175	204	28,434
1985–6	2,858	2,690	200	7,000	480	2,580	2,060	622	192	55	296	1,207	177	275	176	29,365
1986–7[1]	2,658	1,720	200	6,630	587	1,917	1,960	691	505	33	197	850	25	366	200	28,055
1987–8[3]	2,797	1,900	100	6,350	575	2,455	2,050	697	1,000	26	125	750	20	340	500	27,593

[1] Preliminary. [2] Excludes U.S. trade with Territories. [3] Estimate. *Source: Agricultural Marketing Service, U.S.D.A.* T.656

Spot Raw Sugar (ISA) International Sugar Agreement World Price In Cents per Pound

Year	Jan.	Feb.	Mar.	Apr.	May	June	July	Aug.	Sept.	Oct.	Nov.	Dec.	Average
1979	7.57	8.23	8.46	7.82	7.85	8.14	8.52	8.85	9.90	11.94	13.68	14.93	9.65
1980	17.16	22.69	19.64	21.24	30.94	30.80	27.70	31.77	34.89	40.53	37.81	28.79	28.66
1981	27.78	24.09	21.81	17.83	15.06	16.38	16.34	14.76	11.65	12.04	11.97	12.98	16.89
1982	12.90	13.07	11.26	9.58	8.11	6.84	7.80	6.77	5.76	5.93	6.52	6.31	8.40
1983	6.03	6.43	6.20	6.71	9.24	10.74	10.53	10.56	9.43	9.69	8.33	7.67	8.46
1984	6.97	6.64	6.42	5.99	5.61	5.53	4.54	4.05	4.16	4.65	4.38	3.55	5.21
1985	3.62	3.70	3.83	3.42	2.82	2.78	3.18	4.39	5.14	5.01	5.48	5.34	4.06
1986	4.86	5.57	6.95	8.33	7.63	6.33	5.55	5.57	4.68	5.39	5.95	5.71	6.04
1987	6.44	7.36	7.56	6.68	6.73	6.44	6.10	5.62	5.82	6.65	7.33	8.30	6.75
1988[1]	9.66	8.53	8.53	8.54	8.90	10.56	14.02	11.15	10.15	10.28	10.84		

[1] Preliminary. *Source: Sugar Division, Commodity Stabilization Service* T.657

Average Refined Cane Sugar[1] (Wholesale)—Chicago-West In Cents per Pound

Year	Jan.	Feb.	Mar.	Apr.	May	June	July	Aug.	Sept.	Oct.	Nov.	Dec.	Average
1979	——	19.15	——	——	19.15	——	——	19.15	——	——	21.27	——	19.68
1980	——	28.71	——	——	36.30	——	——	41.17	——	——	47.00	——	38.30
1981	——	35.50	——	——	27.47	——	——	25.43	——	——	24.63	——	28.95
1982	——	27.50	——	——	26.77	——	——	28.20	——	——	28.00	——	27.62
1983	——	24.53	——	——	26.53	——	——	26.96	——	——	26.56	——	26.09
1984	——	26.62	——	——	26.42	——	——	25.35	——	——	24.24	——	25.66
1985	23.50	23.42	23.00	23.12	23.55	23.12	23.25	23.50	23.44	23.13	22.50	22.62	23.18
1986	23.45	23.31	23.25	23.50	23.30	23.00	23.38	24.20	24.19	23.50	23.00	23.00	23.42
1987	23.30	23.50	23.50	23.50	24.15	24.44	24.50	24.50	24.00	22.85	22.50	22.50	23.60
1988	23.25	22.75	22.75	23.45	24.19	25.25	27.10	27.75	27.50	27.25	26.75		

[1] These are f.o.b. basis prices in bulk, not delivered prices. To obtain delivered prices, add freight "prepays" & deduct discounts & allowances. Prior to 1982 prices are for 100-lb. paper bags. *Source: Economics & Statistics Service, U.S.D.A.* T.658

High, Low & Closing Prices of March World Sugar (#11) At New York   In Cents per Pound

Year of Delivery		Dec.	Jan.	Feb.	Mar.	Apr.	May	June	July	Aug.	Sept.	Oct.	Nov.	Dec.	Jan.	Feb.	Life of Delivery Range
							Year Prior to Delivery								Delivery Year		
1984	High	9.95	8.92	9.45	9.00	9.77	14.48	13.50	13.16	13.44	11.96	11.94	10.10	9.62	8.29	7.66	14.48
	Low	8.75	8.48	8.11	8.08	8.72	9.60	11.33	10.84	11.60	10.98	9.33	8.82	7.99	7.26	5.65	5.65
	Close	8.98	8.62	8.17	9.00	9.64	14.48	12.52	12.79	11.63	10.94	9.36	9.57	8.18	7.50	5.73	—
1985	High	11.50	10.25	9.60	9.44	9.12	8.39	7.70	6.74	6.08	6.17	6.27	6.05	5.35	4.84	4.45	13.60
	Low	10.06	9.38	8.63	8.74	8.28	7.19	6.61	5.62	4.94	5.05	5.33	5.08	4.02	4.01	3.74	3.74
	Close	10.16	9.56	8.75	9.04	8.40	7.45	6.73	5.72	5.80	5.44	5.83	5.28	4.16	4.32	4.10	—
1986	High	7.40	7.12	6.43	6.05	5.21	4.69	4.33	5.45	5.59	6.20	6.15	6.39	6.56	6.13	6.52	8.27
	Low	6.02	6.13	5.70	5.05	4.58	3.98	3.34	3.59	4.41	5.17	5.25	5.73	5.38	4.97	5.60	3.34
	Close	6.22	6.31	5.83	5.06	4.17	4.28	3.63	5.22	5.13	5.65	6.14	6.13	5.62	5.92	6.28	—
1987	High	7.68	7.60	7.50	9.48	9.67	9.50	8.30	7.54	7.62	6.53	7.10	7.30	7.07	8.32	8.30	9.67
	Low	6.70	6.45	6.95	7.33	8.31	7.65	6.70	6.17	6.15	5.83	5.75	6.45	5.99	5.77	7.09	5.75
	Close	6.96	7.36	7.37	9.43	9.43	8.00	7.51	7.20	6.16	6.28	6.90	6.60	6.16	7.74	8.24	—
1988	High	8.01	8.89	8.70	8.95	8.05	8.03	7.73	7.58	7.02	7.35	7.73	8.12	9.55	10.83	9.74	10.83
	Low	7.18	7.04	7.97	7.40	7.22	7.40	7.15	6.53	6.39	6.43	6.79	7.31	7.86	9.06	7.56	6.39
	Close	7.30	8.41	8.65	7.45	7.75	7.52	7.39	6.71	6.56	6.96	7.59	8.01	9.49	9.64	7.99	—
1989	High	9.65	10.32	9.42	9.02	9.07	9.70	12.10	13.64	10.90	10.37	10.27	10.98	11.52			
	Low	8.25	9.30	7.66	8.12	8.38	8.56	9.52	10.05	9.40	8.62	8.95	9.68	10.52			
	Close	9.61	9.56	8.05	8.83	8.84	9.35	11.87	10.37	10.00	9.46	10.26	10.73	10.95			
1990	High	10.62															
	Low	9.90															
	Close	10.16															

Source: Coffee, Sugar & Cocoa Exchange, Inc., N.Y.   T.662

SUGAR "11" NYCSC
Weekly high low & close of nearest futures

Sulfur

Nearly two-thirds of the elemental sulfur produced each year is a by-product of petroleum refining or natural gas processing. Since the sulfur must be removed for environmental reasons, sulfur output depends more upon the demand for fuels than on the demand for sulfur. As a result, production from U.S. deposits of elemental sulfur, the major source of discretionary sulfur, has fallen substantially. Prices have eroded to an estimated $89.67/tonne in 1988 from $105.22 in 1986, according to the Bureau of Mines. U.S. mines produce sulfur from sedimentary deposits, often associated with the cap rocks of salt domes, by the Frasch hot water process, in which the metal is melted underground and then brought to the surface.

While many products require sulfur at some point in their manufacture, usually in the form of sulfuric acid, fertilizer production dominates. Sulfuric acid is mixed with phospate rock to free the phosphates, leaving behind sulfur-containing wastes. In 1988, 74 percent of U.S. apparent sulfur consumption of 12,200 tonnes went into fertilizer production; chemical production (including rubber products) took 10 percent, petroleum refining - 8 percent, metals - 2 percent, and other uses - 6 percent.

Canada is the leading sulfur-exporting nation, but the U.S. is the major producer. Total U.S. sulfur output was estimated at 10.5 million tonnes for 1988, virtually unchanged from the previous year. World sulfur production in 1988 was estimated at 55.9 million tonnes.

World Production of Sulfur [All Forms]   In Thousands of Metric Tons

Year	Canada	Chile	China	France	West Germany	Israel	Italy	Japan	Mexico	Poland	Spain	Turkey	USSR	United States	Yugoslavia	World Total
1981	6,799	143	2,300	2,042	1,732	10	544	2,609	2,178	5,003	1,268	131	9,900	12,145	490	53,550
1982	6,280	137	2,300	2,035	1,821	10	489	2,595	1,916	5,130	1,172	109	9,650	9,787	557	50,559
1983	6,577	131	2,850	1,910	1,322	10	490	2,613	1,702	5,180	1,204	112	9,150	9,290	481	49,770
1984	6,596	86	2,650	1,862	1,481	10	400	2,592	1,985	5,210	1,231	119	9,200	10,652	464	51,859
1985	6,684	109	2,900	1,723	1,569	10	481	2,498	2,180	5,096	1,355	124	9,274	11,609	496	54,331
1986[1]	6,543	98	3,100	1,306	1,573	15	494	2,371	2,220	5,120	1,310	121	9,275	11,087	522	54,074
1987[2]	6,668	97	3,100	1,252	1,625	20	490	2,221	2,399	5,220	1,120	120	9,550	10,539	501	54,221

[1] Preliminary. [2] Estimate. [3] Content of ore. *Source: Bureau of Mines*   T.663

Salient Statistics of Sulfur in the United States   In Thousands of Metric Tons of Sulfur Content

Year	Frasch-Process Total (Native Sulfur[2])	Louisiana (Mines)	Texas (Mines)	Recovered Elemental Brimstone	Pyrites (Includ. Coal Brasses)	By-product Sulfuric Acid[3]	Other Sulf. Acid Compounds	Production (All Forms)	Imports Pyrites & Sulfur	Producers' Stocks Dec. 31[4]	Exports (Elemental)	Apparent Consumption (All Forms)	FAASCH ($ Per Tonne)	Recovered ($ Per Tonne)	Average ($ Per Tonne)
1980	6,390	2,309	4,081	4,073	322	1,003	78	11,866	2,523	3,094	1,673	13,659	97.36	74.13	89.06
1981	6,348	2,440	3,908	4,259	307	1,159	72	12,145	2,522	3,546	1,392	12,785	121.11	97.97	111.48
1982	4,210	1,312	2,898	4,404	265	828	80	9,787	1,905	4,218	961	10,059	120.79	97.89	108.27
1983	3,202	1,286	1,915	4,955	N.A.	831	302	9,290	1,695	3,223	992	10,988	100.76	76.22	87.24
1984	4,193	1,937	2,257	5,214	N.A.	962	283	10,652	2,557	2,419	1,334	12,679	109.20	80.02	94.31
1985	5,011	2,071	2,940	5,313	N.A.	957	328	11,609	2,104	2,799	1,365	11,968	122.62	92.11	106.46
1986	4,043	1,579	2,463	5,816	N.A.	919	309	11,087	1,347	2,748	1,895	10,586	123.79	92.06	105.22
1987[1]	3,202	1,369	1,833	6,161		1,003	173	10,539	1,599	2,316	1,242	11,323	107.15	79.63	89.78
1988[5]	3,100			6,300					1,700	1,700	1,150	12,000	105	78	85

[1] Preliminary. [2] Or sulfur ore. [3] Basis 100%, produced at Cu, Zn, & Pb plants. [4] Frasch & recovered. [5] Estimates. *Source: Bureau of Mines*
T.664

Sulfur Consumption & Foreign Trade of the United States   In Thousands of Metric Tons

Year	Net Import Reliance as a % of Apparent Consumption	Native Sulfur (Frasch)	Recovered Sulfur Shipm.	Total Pyrites Shipments	Smelter Acid Prod. Shipm.	Other Forms[2] Shipm.	Total	Imports of Recovered Sulfur	Shipments of Frasch Sulfur	Imports of Frasch Sulfur	Exports Quantity	Exports Value Ths. $	Imports Quantity	Imports Value Ths. $
1980	14	6,717	4,115	322	1,003	78	13,659	1,533	7,400	990	1,673	185,866	2,523	138,852
1981	5	5,550	4,207	307	1,159	72	12,785	1,666	5,910	856	1,392	187,407	2,522	209,766
1982	4	3,557	4,344	265	828	80	10,059	1,215	3,598	690	961	122,143	1,905	164,885
1983	15	4,114	5,041	N.A.	831	302	10,988	1,091	4,111	604	992	109,298	1,695	129,110
1984	16	4,812	5,210	N.A.	962	283	12,679	1,835	5,001	722	1,334	156,067	2,557	200,189
1985	3	4,416	5,266	N.A.	957	328	11,968	1,380	4,678	724	1,365	189,248	2,104	199,240
1986	—	3,584	5,798	N.A.	919	309	10,586	621	4,108	726	1,895	251,664	1,347	142,220
1987[1]	6	3,938	6,180		1,003	173	11,323	806	3,610	793	1,242	139,431	1,599	152,096

[1] Preliminary. [2] Includes hydrogen sulfide, liquid sulfur dioxide. [3] Crude sulfur equivalent. *Source: Bureau of Mines*   T.665

Sunflowerseed and Oil

World sunflower seed production in 1988/89 was projected by USDA at 21.3 million tonnes, 3 percent more than a year earlier. Sunseed comprises nearly 11 percent of world oilseed production.

The European Community was forecast to produce 4.1 million tonnes, 4 percent more than a year earlier. Argentina's crop was put at 3.2 million tonnes, up 14 percent. In the EC, acreage was lower, but yields improved. Argentina was expected to increase acreage, as dry planting conditions in many areas caused some switching out of corn and into oilseeds. The country's traditional sunflower areas received better moisture. The USSR's 1988/89 crop was put at 6.3 million tonnes, up 4 percent. The U.S. crop was pegged at 634,000 tonnes, down 47 percent due to drought. Sunflower yields in North and South Dakota, the two main producing states, fell by nearly 50 percent. The U.S. average yield was 823 pounds per acre, down 44 percent.

World sunseed exports were projected to decline by 3 percent to 2.1 million tonnes. With smaller crops, the U.S. continued to lose export market share. Mexico, the primary market for U.S. sunseed, was buying less.

The EC was producing more sunseed, led by France and Spain. Favorable price supports encourage production in the EC.

The world sunseed crush was projected at 18.8 million tonnes, 5 percent higher than in 1987/88. Argentina's crush was estimated at 3 milliion tonnes, up 15 percent. Under Argentina's system of differential export taxes, exports of sunoil and sunmeal are taxed less heavily than exports of sunseed. This acts as an economic incentive for processors to crush.

World sunseed meal production was put at 8.6 million tonnes, 5 percent more than a year earlier. The USSR was the largest producer with 2.1 million tonnes, while Argentina's output was 1.3 million tonnes. Virtually all of Argentina's production is exported. China and Spain are major exporters. Importers include the Netherlands, Great Britian, and West Germany. World sunmeal use was estimated at 8.3 million tonnes, 4 percent more than a year earlier. Meal ending stocks were put at 210,000 tonnes, down 2 percent.

World sunoil production in 1988/89 was estimated at 7.6 million tonnes, up 5 percent. Sunoil is the third largest oil produced, after soyoil and palmoil. Sunoil's high content of polyunsaturated fats has boosted its importance. Major producers have been the USSR, Argentina, and Turkey.

World sunoil exports were forecast at 2.1 million tonnes, 1 percent more than a year earlier. Argentine shipments were projected to be 830,000 tonnes, up 26 percent. Other exporters include Hungary, the U.S., and the Netherlands. The USDA has funds available to subsidize exports. Major importers of U.S. sunoil are Egypt, Algeria, the USSR and Venezuela.

Ending stocks of sunoil were put at 522,000 tonnes, 21 percent less than a year earlier. Spain and Argentina held 39 percent of world sunoil stocks.

World Production of Sunflowerseed In Thousands of Metric Tons

Crop Year	Argentina	Aus- tralia	Bul- garia	Burma	China	France	Hun- gary	India	Ro- mania	South Africa	Spain	Turkey	United States	USSR	Yugoslavia	World Total
1985–6	4,100	215	365	216	1,732	1,477	673	280	710	272	990	700	1,430	5,260	233	19,560
1986–7	2,500	145	489	253	1,544	1,902	857	436	1,004	404	920	940	1,210	5,258	449	19,250
1987–8[1]	2,800	139	400	274	1,241	2,508	784	500	650	540	1,000	1,000	1,183	6,075	493	20,620
1988–9[2]	3,300	135	400	250	1,450	2,348	755	600	750	550	1,200	1,100	634	6,300	343	21,310

[1] Preliminary. [2] Estimate. *Source: Foreign Agricultural Service, U.S.D.A.* T.668

Sunflowerseed Statistics in the United States

Crop Year Begin Sept.	Acres Harvested In Ths.	Yield per Harv. Acre Pounds	Farm Price $ Metric Ton	Value of Pro- duction Mil. $	Production	Imports	Stocks Sept. 1	Total	Crushings	Exports	Non-Oil Usage	Seed	Residual	Total
											In Thousands of Metric Tons			
1985–6	2,844	1,109	175	251.5	1,430	26	91	1,546	674	365		295		1,334
1986–7	1,955	1,369	152	184.5	1,214	8	212	1,434	635	324		222		1,181
1987–8[1]	1,775	1,469	196	231.9	1,183	10	253	1,446	855	275		119		1,249
1988–9[2]	1,699	823	276	175.0	634	19	197	850	550	125		125		800

[1] Preliminary. [2] Estimate. *Source: Economic Research Service, U.S.D.A.* T.666

Sunflowerseed Statistics in the United States In Metric Tons

Crop Year Begin. Oct.	Stocks Oct. 1	Production	Total	Ex- ports	Domestic	Total	Price $ per Metric Ton (Crude Mpls.)	Stocks Oct. 1	Production	Total	Ex- ports	Domestic	Total	Price $ per Metric Ton 28% Protein
	Sunflowerseed Oil Supply			Disappearance				Sunflowerseed Meal Supply			Disappearance			
1985–6	30	265	295	205	65	270	421	5	357	362	44	313	357	76
1986–7	25	266	291	156	84	240	353	5	305	310	45	260	305	84
1987–8[1]	51	369	420	335	50	385	520	5	428	433	45	383	428	109
1988–9[2]	35	220	255	190	45	235	585	5	275	280	50	225	275	175

[1] Preliminary. [2] Estimate. *Source: Economic Research Service, U.S.D.A.* T.667

Tall Oil

Tall Oil—Supply & Distribution in the U.S. In Millions of Pounds

Beginning Oct. 1	Supply (Crude)			Ex-ports	To U.S. Territ.	Disposition — Non Food Products								Total Nonfood Products
	Pro-duction	Stocks Oct. 1	Total Supply			Soap	Paint & Varnish	Lino-leum & Oilcloth	Resins & Plastics	Other Drying Oils	Lubri-cants & Similar Oils	Fatty Acids	Other	
1981–2	1,190	137	1,327			3	16		17		4	1,096	48	1,185
1982–3	1,557	151	1,708			4	30		25		4	1,042	64	1,151
1983–4	1,293	217	1,510				33		—			1,096		1,228
1984–5[2]	1,321	113	1,434				20		16			994		1,087
1985–6[2]	1,415	126	1,541			13	17		16		12	1,055		1,143
1986–7[2]	1,501	178	1,679			12	15		16		13	1,153		1,227

[1] Preliminary. [2] Estimated. *Source: Agricultural Marketing Service, U.S.D.A.* T.669

U.S. Tall Oil Consumption in Inedible Products In Millions of Pounds

Year	Jan.	Feb.	Mar.	Apr.	May	June	July	Aug.	Sept.	Oct.	Nov.	Dec.	Total
1982	95.4	107.4	121.8	105.2	96.8	95.6	84.7	95.8	88.3	94.4	84.3	66.9	1,136
1983	100.0	96.3	106.9	92.8	98.7	109.1	98.1	114.0	93.7	94.1	95.0	82.6	1,181
1984	100.8	100.7	105.6	97.8	104.2	113.6	117.2	105.2	111.2	100.6	95.7	85.2	1,238
1985	84.1	87.4	94.3	90.4	84.6	85.8	91.7	95.3	91.7	97.6	88.2	85.1	1,076
1986	86.3	93.1	106.0	106.1	95.3	99.5	93.7	101.4	91.1	103.4	80.3	93.7	1,150
1987[1]	109.2	101.8	107.9	104.5	100.1	112.1	109.9	99.3	104.8	111.4	94.8	87.6	1,243
1988[1]	109.2	103.2	111.0	108.0	112.3	104.0	105.9	110.6	111.4	104.6			

[1] Preliminary. *Source: Statistical Reporting Service, U.S.D.A.* T.670

Tall Oil Production in the United States In Millions of Pounds

Crop Year		Oct.	Nov.	Dec.	Jan.	Feb.	Mar.	Apr.	May	June	July	Aug.	Sept.	Total
1983–4	Crude	107.9	105.4	93.4	99.5	116.3	125.6	111.7	117.8	109.0	105.1	106.1	95.4	1,293.2
	Refined	12.1	14.8	9.9	13.0	11.6	13.4	12.0	13.4	10.7	13.0	12.9	12.6	149.4
1984–5	Crude	112.8	110.7	109.2	95.2	104.0	121.4	116.4	108.4	112.1	117.1	107.8	105.8	1,320.9
	Refined	12.9	11.7	10.9	10.2	9.9	11.8	9.9	10.3	9.7	7.3	10.0	10.5	125.1
1985–6	Crude	115.5	103.5	167.6	120.2	113.8	126.6	124.0	111.7	108.4	107.7	107.9	111.8	1,415.4
	Refined	9.8	9.2	8.7	8.3	8.0	7.9	8.7	8.7	8.2	8.2	9.4	9.7	104.8
1986–7	Crude	114.4	106.8	120.9	123.8	143.0	145.5	132.6	124.3	122.9	130.9	116.6	119.7	1,501.4
	Refined	9.1	7.8	8.2	9.0	8.9	8.6	9.2	10.4	8.4	10.5	9.7	9.6	109.4
1987–8[1]	Crude	123.0	116.2	127.9	121.7	126.3	141.3	124.3	119.3	117.1	124.2	116.4	125.6	1,483.3
	Refined	9.2	9.0	8.9	9.5	11.3	10.2	9.1	9.3	5.5	8.2	9.3	10.1	109.6
1988–9[1]	Crude	117.6												
	Refined	9.8												

[1] Preliminary. *Source: Bureau of the Census* T.0578

Tall Oil Stocks in the United States In Millions of Pounds

Crop Year		Oct. 1	Nov. 1	Dec. 1	Jan. 1	Feb. 1	Mar. 1	Apr. 1	May 1	June 1	July 1	Aug. 1	Sept. 1
1983–4	Crude	217.2	205.4	185.7	186.2	164.6	160.1	168.9	179.7	190.2	163.3	149.0	123.6
	Refined	19.9	18.8	18.1	17.4	16.3	15.9	15.5	12.9	11.7	9.2	11.1	11.1
1984–5	Crude	112.8	101.9	103.0	109.5	108.7	117.0	117.3	126.4	113.8	121.1	141.8	131.4
	Refined	9.9	10.9	12.6	13.0	13.6	17.7	18.3	21.9	22.9	23.8	25.9	29.4
1985–6	Crude	125.9	125.1	158.7	167.6	154.1	160.7	182.7	183.4	181.1	175.5	184.1	169.7
	Refined	19.7	19.7	19.9	19.0	21.2	19.3	25.3	29.2	27.6	26.5	25.3	30.1
1986–7	Crude	177.8	164.9	173.9	196.1	185.6	199.2	211.6	204.4	209.7	194.5	171.6	161.2
	Refined	29.1	27.7	23.4	28.3	26.5	27.3	35.8	29.3	30.9	31.8	33.4	33.7
1987–8[1]	Crude	160.1	144.0	147.7	161.8	148.3	159.1	165.4	155.9	138.7	145.3	148.8	115.0
	Refined	33.2	34.5	35.3	39.2	30.1	27.9	28.1	28.2	27.2	22.7	22.1	22.9
1988–9[1]	Crude	109.7	104.1										
	Refined	22.3	22.3										

[1] Preliminary. *Source: Bureau of the Census* T.0578A

Tallow and Greases

Tallow is primarily a by-product of the commercial beef industry. Edible tallow is used in processed foods and in frying fat in the fast food industry. Edible tallow competes with vegetable oils on a price basis. Together edible tallow, inedible tallow, and grease account for over 20 percent of U.S. consumption of fats and oils.

World production of edible and inedible tallow in 1988/89 was estimated by *Oil World* at 6.5 million tonnes, down 2 percent from the previous season. Declines in output were expected in both the U.S. and the European Community, the two largest producers. U.S. tallow output was forecast at 3.2 million tonnes, down 5 percent from the year before. U.S. commercial cattle slaughter was expected to be slightly below year-earlier levels. Tallow production in the EC was estimated at 919,000 tonnes, off 3 percent. Levels of output in the USSR, Australia, and China were expected to be above the previous season.

Global tallow exports in 1988/89 were forecast to drop about 4 percent from the previous year's strong pace. Shipments by the U.S., the leading exporter, were pegged at 1.22 million tonnes, down from 1.29 million the year before. Ample world vegetable oil supplies dampened prospects for U.S. edible tallow exports. Ex-

ports by the EC were placed at 578,000 tonnes, down 4 percent. Australia, New Zealand, and Canada were also slated to ship less in 1988/89 than the previous season.

The EC, the largest importer, was expected to purchase 881,000 tonnes in 1988/89, down 3 percent from the previous season. Egypt's imports were slated to fall 4 percent to 155,000 tonnes, while Mexico's were expected to rise 7 percent to 165,000 tonnes. China, Japan, and So. Korea were all forecast to import slightly more tallow than the year before.

Global tallow disappearance was expected to fall marginally to 6.56 million tonnes. In both the U.S. and EC, disappearance was expected to be slightly lower, while it was likely to rise in the USSR.

World ending stocks in 1988/89 were forecast at 455,000 tonnes, down 11 percent from the previous season and the lowest in some time. The U.S. held by far the largest stocks, and was followed by the EC and USSR.

In early 1988, prices of fancy, bleached U.S. tallow CIF Rotterdam were $439/tonne, the highest in nearly three years. In July 1988, the average price had risen to $473, but by October it had fallen to $368.

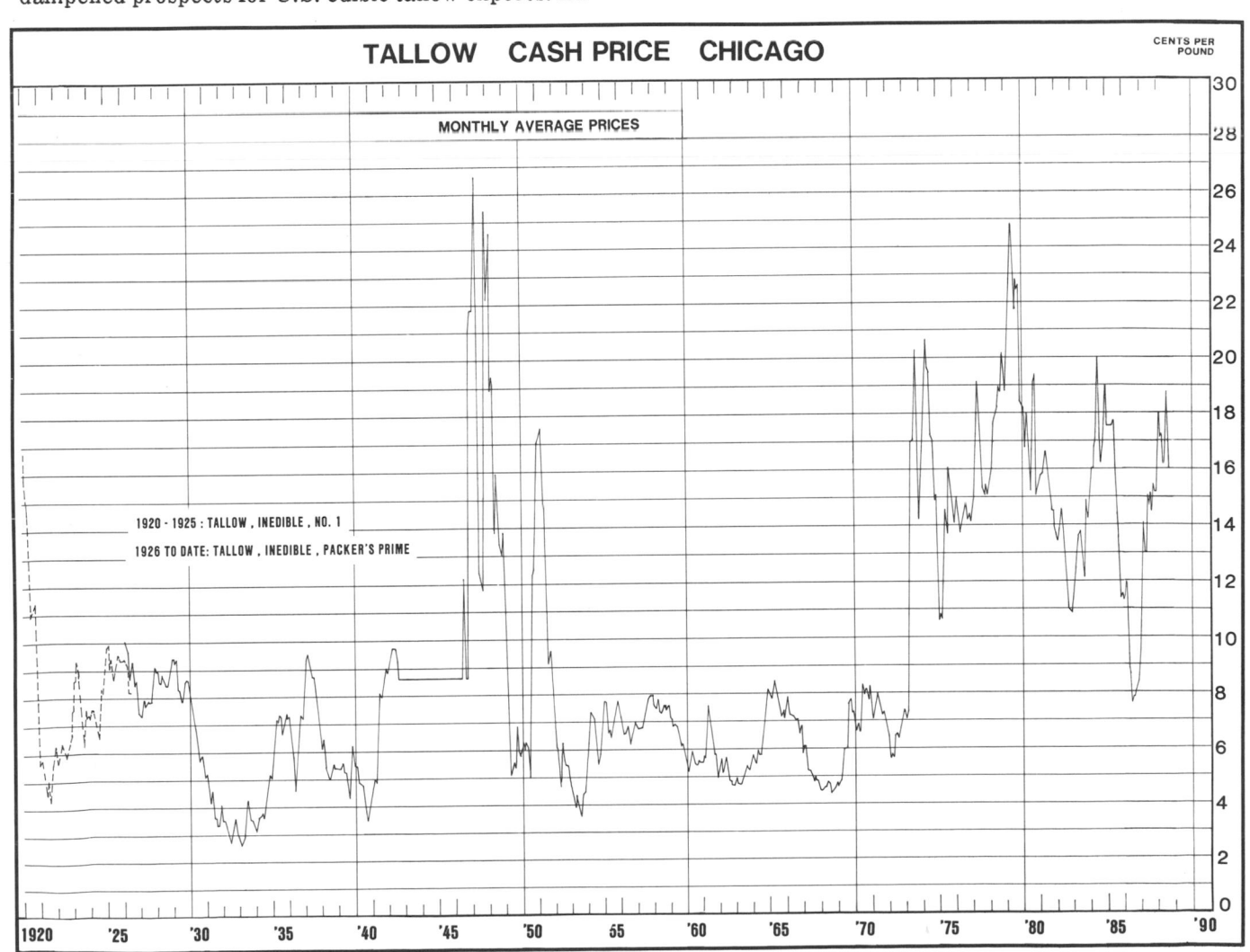

TALLOW   CASH PRICE   CHICAGO   CENTS PER POUND

MONTHLY AVERAGE PRICES

1920 - 1925 : TALLOW , INEDIBLE , NO. 1

1926 TO DATE: TALLOW , INEDIBLE , PACKER'S PRIME

TEA

Salient Statistics of Tea in the United States   In Thousands of Metric Tons

Year	Brazil	Argen-tina	Sri Lanka (Ceylon)	China (Main-land)	India	Indo-nesia	Japan	Kenya[2]	Mozam-bique	Nether-lands	Malawi	Tai-wan	Total	Tea Bags	Loose Tea	Inst-ant Tea	Inst-ant Mixes	Total Quan-tity
1975		1.8	18.3	2.0	6.8	12.9	1.7	8.4	2.7	2.4	2.2	4.0	72.3	31.6	4.1	19.8	8.0	63.5
1976		2.1	21.1	3.0	8.0	11.6	3.2	10.7	2.0	1.3	4.1	4.8	82.2	33.8	4.2	19.6	8.5	66.2
1977		4.9	16.6	4.2	12.3	14.7	3.4	9.5	2.3	3.0	5.6	5.7	92.1	36.2	5.2	20.0	10.7	72.1
1978	2.0	6.7	14.0	2.9	1.7	10.7	3.2	8.2	1.4	4.1	4.2	3.0	68.8	35.5	4.4	18.7	11.7	70.3
1979	3.5	7.0	14.7	6.5	5.9	11.2	2.9	9.4	2.4	4.7	2.5	2.3	79.2	36.1	4.1	18.0	11.7	69.9
1980	2.8	10.3	12.2	8.0	4.2	13.9	2.5	6.8	5.0	5.9	2.1	3.1	83.8	37.9	3.7	17.1	12.1	70.8
1981	3.5	10.0	13.0	7.1	4.7	14.7	2.5	5.5	4.2	7.7	2.4	4.2	86.3	39.7	3.3	15.9	12.0	70.8
1982	3.5	12.2	12.4	6.9	2.9	14.0	2.4	6.9	4.0	6.1	1.4	3.8	82.8	40.6	3.0	14.9	11.7	70.3
1983	3.9	15.1	8.1	6.4	2.9	14.4	1.8	4.5	3.5	4.7	1.3	3.5	77.3	41.9	2.7	14.9	13.1	72.6
1984	3.6	18.1	9.4	9.6	3.8	15.5	2.1	3.9	2.2	4.8	.9	6.3	88.3	40.7	2.3	13.3	12.2	68.5
1985	4.3	15.2	9.8	10.9	2.9	12.8	2.1	4.2	.7	4.2	.9	2.2	79.2	41.0	2.1	12.7	11.4	67.1
1986	5.6	16.4	7.8	16.9	3.9	16.3	1.2	4.3	.3	4.1	1.2	1.5	90.5	40.4	1.8	12.1	10.6	64.9
1987[1]	5.4	15.9	4.8	16.7	3.0	10.4	1.2	4.1	.2	3.3	2.0	.9	77.4	39.3	1.6	11.1	10.1	62.1
1988																		

[1] Preliminary.   Sources: Foreign Agricultural Service, U.S.D.A.; Bureau of Census   T.675

United States Imports of Tea   In Thousands of Pounds

Year	Jan.	Feb.	Mar.	Apr.	May	June	July	Aug.	Sept.	Oct.	Nov.	Dec.	Total
1972	12,914	16,907	10,276	10,165	12,885	16,563	10,835	11,581	12,830	14,348	11,460	10,731	151,495
1973	15,481	14,295	15,399	14,107	17,423	12,425	13,660	12,614	12,527	16,878	16,506	11,997	173,314
1974	11,675	14,974	16,583	17,177	18,122	17,489	21,788	16,432	13,954	10,460	7,735	11,844	178,326
1975	14,297	12,200	15,486	13,648	14,694	12,170	9,915	11,276	12,404	17,594	13,940	11,843	159,287
1976	11,842	12,309	15,779	15,805	13,053	13,893	14,259	15,051	19,224	15,683	16,133	18,273	181,304
1977	16,059	15,064	22,389	23,302	27,345	22,335	22,252	15,932	9,994	9,702	7,213	10,924	203,012
1978	9,023	12,791	18,648	15,450	17,523	8,286	13,141	13,788	9,390	12,502	8,877	12,332	151,751
1979	14,797	10,568	15,584	13,822	13,556	14,352	13,361	14,809	15,841	16,992	15,432	15,578	174,690
1980	18,749	17,562	17,456	18,501	15,871	16,460	14,099	11,883	11,870	14,271	12,126	15,936	184,786
1981	12,891	18,354	14,696	19,220	18,990	17,736	14,586	19,128	13,205	15,855	13,473	12,121	190,254
1982	15,055	15,464	13,787	13,176	16,518	14,309	14,286	15,598	17,425	16,207	18,222	12,567	182,613
1983	13,748	15,092	14,170	15,799	16,018	10,931	12,159	11,747	15,025	16,531	13,600	15,631	170,451
1984	15,599	15,956	20,235	18,031	17,546	12,803	22,287	12,023	14,169	20,946	12,386	12,585	194,565
1985	16,238	13,856	15,491	13,342	15,337	15,054	15,586	12,745	14,942	14,878	13,656	13,493	174,617
1986	16,923	13,219	21,719	19,002	15,747	14,970	19,732	14,626	18,110	14,864	14,965	14,086	197,963
1987[1]	15,206	14,495	19,830	14,634	16,835	12,421	12,838	13,538	11,207	15,569	12,562	11,480	170,616
1988[1]	14,377	15,800	17,770	19,962	18,596	19,386	17,609	17,356					

[1] Preliminary.   Source: Department of Commerce   T.679

London Auction Tea Prices   In U.S. Cents per Pound

Year	Jan.	Feb.	Mar.	Apr.	May	June	July	Aug.	Sept.	Oct.	Nov.	Dec.	Average
1979	102.4	97.4	98.3	96.7	96.5	96.6	95.9	97.3	92.8	99.4	102.0	101.0	98.0
1980	102.4	105.7	102.4	100.4	104.2	106.8	100.9	102.5	95.1	92.4	101.3	98.1	101.0
1981	98.6	101.2	100.5	97.9	94.7	90.4	84.6	80.0	81.7	87.4	91.3	91.6	91.7
1982	92.0	94.2	88.5	84.7	84.8	83.3	79.9	80.8	86.7	91.4	89.8	96.1	87.7
1983	98.5	93.1	89.8	92.1	91.0	85.2	86.6	90.6	99.0	117.4	158.8	163.8	105.5
1984	194.2	169.0	166.7	160.4	161.3	144.8	130.3	133.2	154.1	164.2	155.2	147.9	156.8
1985	143.1	127.3	110.4	98.6	75.2	74.6	71.5	72.2	73.3	78.7	80.2	75.3	90.0
1986	82.1	85.7	91.5	91.3	85.9	79.7	79.8	86.5	91.6	94.1	93.6	88.6	87.5
1987	89.7	83.6	83.2	67.9	65.4	60.8	69.5	72.3	72.7	84.1	87.4	94.0	77.6
1988	96.1	88.0	87.2										

Source: International Tea Committee   T.679a

Tin

Tin prices were stable in 1988, something remarkable considering the recently tumultuous history of the metal. Tin was the cause of ongoing financial problems for the International Tin Council (ITC), banks, international brokerage firms, and metals dealers, as well as a catalyst for changes in the venerable London Metal Exchange's (LME) clearing function.

The ITC was forced into default in 1985, when it was unable to meet its full financial commitments to take deliveries of tin on the LME. The council had given up warrants to various banks and clearing firms, and 1988 saw banks unloading some of that tin on the marketplace.

News reports indicated that the Bank of Tokyo alone had disposed of an estimated 3,000 tonnes of tin on the world market by October of 1988, and the sharp fall in LME stocks during the year indicated that creditors from around the globe were doing the same.

In January 1988, the LME stockpile of tin was just under 16,000 tonnes. By October, the inventory was down to 8,500 tonnes and dropping. As a result, world demand for direct producer business was off slightly as steelmakers were able, in part, to look to the LME as a source of supply. By late in the year, the market was seeing a small glut of LME "bank sale" tin. But analysts said that there would be renewed demand, as consumers began to realize that the current surplus was shrinking rapidly.

Tin prices ranged between $7,400 and $7,500 a tonne at year's end, with the relative firmness attributed to good European and Japanese offtake on the Kuala Lumpur tin market, where prices reached two and half year highs on brisk demand.

Tin, which leads a precarious price existence due to subsidized overproduction, notably in Malaysia, is the subject of another attempt to support prices through the mechanism of the Association of Tin Producing Countries, which has a "supply rationalization" scheme in place.

The ATPC, a successor to the ITC, groups Malaysia, Indonesia, Thailand, Australia, Nigeria, Zaire and Bolivia into a producers' cartel, and has asked two other major producers, Brazil and China, to be observers. The ATPC agreed to limit exports of tin to 101,900 tonnes between March 1988 and February 1989, after agreeing to 96,000 tonnes in the previous twelve-month period. According to the ATPC, the members were unable to export the full 96,000-tonne quota, with only 86,200 tonnes exported, which was a direct result of LME and stockpile sales. According to the ATPC, stocks in 1987 were drawn down by 25,500 tonnes to a total of 47,500 tonnes.

In important market decisions, Brazil and China, the two major exporters not in the ATPC, indicated that they would abide by quota allocations without formal membership. China pledged not to export more than 10,000 tonnes in the 1988/89 tin quota year, and Brazil pledged to restrict its sales to 26,500 tonnes.

In the U.S., consumption of tin for the first eight months of 1988 was 31,900 tons, a 17 percent gain over the comparable 1987 period's 27,100 tons. Total 1987 consumption included 35,597 tons for primary use and 8,599 tons for secondary consumption. Secondary consumption in the January through August 1988 period was 8,400 tons.

In 1987, solder was the largest consumer of tin, with about one third of the total 44,196 tonnes consumed. Solder's percentage in 1988 was running slightly behind 1987 at 6,230 tonnes, out of the total 22,756 tonnes consumed in the January-August period. Tin plate is the second largest use, accounting for 10,357 tonnes in all of 1987 and 7,195 tonnes for the first eight months of 1988. Other uses account for about 25 percent of yearly consumption.

Total imports for consumption in 1987 were 41,150 tons of metal and 2,953 tons of concentrates. Figures for the period of January through August 1988 were not yet released by the U.S. Bureau of Mines.

In keeping with the general drawdown of stocks worldwide, total stocks (not including those held in the U.S. strategic minerals stockpile), which were at 14,641 tons at the end of 1987, were down to 7,121 tons in August of 1988.

World Mine Production of Tin (Content of Ore) In Thousands of Metric Tons

Year	Australia	Bolivia[1]	Brazil	Burma	China[3]	Indonesia	Japan	Malaysia	Nigeria	Rwanda	South Africa	Thailand	United Kingdom	USSR	Zaire (Congo)	World Total
1984	7.9	19.9	20.0	2.0	15.0	23.2	.5	41.3	1.7	1.1	2.3	21.9	5.2	23.0	2.7	198.4
1985[2]	6.4	16.1	26.5	1.8	15.0	21.8	.5	36.9	1.0	.8	2.2	16.9	5.2	23.0	3.1	188.7
1986[3]	8.6	11.9	27.4	1.5	15.0	22.1	.5	28.1	1.1	—	2.1	16.8	4.6	23.5	2.8	180.2
1987[3]	6.0	9.0	29.0	1.5	15.0	18.0		26.0	1.0			16.0	3.0	23.0	2.5	163.0

[1] Exports. [2] Preliminary. [3] Estimate. *Source: Bureau of Mines*   T.682

World Smelter Production of Tin In Thousands of Metric Tons

Year	Australia	Thailand	Bolivia	Brazil	China	Zaire (Congo)	West Germany	Indonesia	Japan	Malaysia	Nigeria	Portugal	South Africa	United Kingdom	United States	USSR	Total
1983	2.9	18.5	14.2	13.0	15.0	.2	.4	28.4	1.3	53.3	1.2	.4	2.7	6.5	2.5	24.0	200.1
1984	2.9	19.7	15.8	18.9	15.0	.2	.4	22.5	1.4	46.9	1.4	.4	1.6	7.1	4.0	25.0	201.1
1985[2]	2.7	18.0	12.9	24.7	15.0	.1	.4	20.9	1.4	45.5	1.0	.4	1.4	7.5	3.0	25.0	196.6
1986[3]	1.3	18.5	8.5	25.5	15.0	.1	.4	22.0	1.3	44.0	1.0	.2	1.9	7.0	3.2	26.0	189.9

[1] Imports into the U.S. of tin concentrates (tin content). [2] Preliminary. [3] Estimate. *Source: Bureau of Mines*   T.683

Tin Foreign Trade of the United States   In Metric[5] Tons

Year	Exports (Metal[2])	Concentrates[3] (Ore) Total All Ore	Bolivia	Peru	Total All Metal	Imports (For Consumption) — Bars, Blocks, Pigs, etc.[4] (Metal) Australia	Belgium	Bolivia	Brazil	China	Indonesia	Malaysia	Nigeria	Singapore	Thailand	United Kingdom
1977	5,480	6,724	6,667	—	47,774	—	—	3,358	2,380	381	5,294	27,084	2	207	7,780	513
1978	4,692	3,873	3,541	—	46,776	—	155	5,768	1,810	1,571	5,664	23,448	—	230	6,865	468
1979	569	4,529	3,745	—	48,355	—	100	5,387	933	185	5,429	23,448	—	1,070	10,440	550
1980	595	840	528	—	45,982	145	190	5,597	2,031	858	6,477	15,548	770	864	12,414	416
1981	2,361	232	—	232	45,874	552	—	8,277	1,129	2,032	7,096	13,163	520	656	11,967	46
1982	5,769	1,961	192	1,416	27,939	334	10	4,340	2,409	2,632	5,744	2,364	124	600	9,116	55
1983	1,340	969	257	341	34,048	390	45	5,739	5,604	1,938	6,004	4,704	265	1,029	7,436	18
1984	1,429	3,272	271	2,502	41,224	288	137	5,438	10,220	1,640	4,985	6,622	60	781	9,531	583
1985	1,478	1,616	22	1,506	33,830	266	—	1,815	11,021	4,513	4,586	379	—	1,886	6,373	48
1986[1]	1,547	3,936	259	3,676	35,768	94	—	4,893	9,456	2,955	4,149	6,230	—	691	1,901	730
1987[1]	1,318	2,953	732	2,165	41,150	1,406	302	3,476	13,089	8,044	4,001	4,959	79	743	1,460	467
1988[5]	1,300	2,000	1,400	200	46,000	1,800		4,000	16,000	6,500	7,500	4,500	80	2,000	900	1,500

[1] Preliminary.   [2] Ingots, Pigs & Bars. Excludes re-exports from 1979.   [3] Tin content.   [4] Also grain, or granulated.   [5] Estimate.
Source: Department of Commerce

T.684

United States Tin (Pig) Consumption (Total)   In Metric Tons

Year	Jan.	Feb.	Mar.	Apr.	May	June	July	Aug.	Sept.	Oct.	Nov.	Dec.	Total
1977	5,600	5,500	6,800	5,800	5,800	6,000	5,200	5,800	5,900	5,400	5,000	5,100	60,732
1978	5,400	5,000	5,500	5,200	5,700	5,400	4,600	5,200	5,200	5,300	5,400	4,900	61,531
1979	5,400	5,500	6,400	5,400	5,400	5,300	4,900	4,900	5,000	5,500	5,000	4,600	62,465
1980	5,500	5,300	5,750	5,300	4,600	4,100	3,700	3,900	4,150	4,300	4,050	3,750	56,362
1981	4,300	4,400	4,100	4,600	4,400	4,350	3,900	4,200	3,950	3,900	3,400	2,950	54,373
1982	3,400	3,300	3,750	5,100	5,000	5,100	4,900	4,700	4,700	4,600	4,500	4,400	53,450
1983	4,400	4,700	4,900	4,700	4,700	4,800	4,300	4,600	4,700	4,800	4,400	4,800	55,800
1984	4,600	4,300	5,300	3,900	4,500	4,400	4,100	4,400	4,100	4,000	3,300	3,500	50,400
1985	4,000	3,900	4,600	4,500	4,600	4,400	4,200	4,400	4,300	4,500	4,200	4,000	51,600
1986	4,300	4,000	4,200	4,500	4,400	4,400	4,100	4,100	4,000	4,300	3,900	3,900	50,100
1987[1]	4,100	3,900	4,200	4,700	4,300	4,200	4,400	4,400	4,400	4,300	4,600	4,400	53,100
1988[1]	4,600	4,700	4,800	4,700	5,300	5,600	5,300	5,300	5,500				

[1] Preliminary.   *Source: Bureau of Mines.*

T.681

United States Tin Stocks (Pig—Industrial)   In Metric Tons

Year	Jan. 1	Feb. 1	Mar. 1	Apr. 1	May 1	June 1	July 1	Aug. 1	Sept. 1	Oct. 1	Nov. 1	Dec. 1
1977	7,282	8,032	7,883	5,874	6,157	5,644	4,720	6,305	5,557	5,378	9,124	7,272
1978	8,441	7,626	6,628	6,291	7,785	8,139	7,846	7,817	7,260	5,774	4,975	5,666
1979	5,040	4,594	4,254	5,891	6,097	5,938	6,317	6,270	6,096	5,058	4,901	4,244
1980	4,238	7,720	6,882	7,527	5,443	7,263	6,592	6,544	6,051	5,180	5,208	5,086
1981	5,504	5,968	5,745	5,229	5,725	5,978	6,227	6,465	5,663	5,710	5,325	5,563
1982	5,988	3,872	3,490	3,829	5,222	4,953	4,653	3,888	2,910	2,940	2,970	3,437
1983	3,152	4,609	3,513	3,815	4,026	3,527	3,634	3,931	4,091	3,604	3,074	3,180
1984	3,020	2,968	2,268	2,840	2,646	3,119	2,795	2,688	2,837	2,495	2,512	2,326
1985	2,592	2,766	2,283	2,407	2,228	2,853	3,042	2,762	2,663	2,985	4,121	4,913
1986	5,665	5,310	4,692	3,097	4,127	3,987	4,032	4,166	4,246	3,497	3,554	4,681
1987[1]	4,802	5,232	6,394	6,321	7,263	8,087	6,663	4,288	5,373	5,533	6,402	5,460
1988[1]	4,428	4,490	5,989	5,631	5,868	6,128	6,456	5,665	4,350	4,137		

[1] Preliminary.   *Source: Bureau of Mines*

T.680

TIN CASH PRICE NEW YORK

CENTS PER POUND

Monthly Average Prices
STRAITS TIN

NOT AVAILABLE SINCE 9/85

NO QUOTES

EX-DOCK TIN AT N.Y. FROM 1/84

Average Price of Ex–Dock Tin in New York[1]   In Cents per Pound

Year	Jan.	Feb.	Mar.	Apr.	May	June	July	Aug.	Sept.	Oct.	Nov.	Dec.	Average
1977	470.54	514.16	522.97	485.28	491.93	482.15	518.71	559.51	558.47	619.25	626.16	613.36	538.76
1978	591.19	595.93	557.48	537.85	570.58	600.95	606.21	641.80	679.66	739.69	758.84	695.86	631.34
1979	684.56	724.57	746.14	740.06	745.18	760.14	712.31	739.93	762.03	785.54	801.23	830.88	756.87
1980	836.46	866.39	900.23	872.21	861.84	845.19	836.95	834.61	861.92	832.92	788.67	751.36	840.73
1981	739.94	705.76	691.70	677.38	652.07	652.77	680.22	746.06	777.36	798.70	813.00	801.59	728.05
1982	787.41	749.93	669.51	649.58	662.35	643.00	638.00	636.33	644.33	627.94	627.93	630.18	663.88
1983	648.90	653.89	669.18	692.29	683.36	670.54	663.13	653.10	649.31	650.65	653.02	636.71	660.34
1984[1]	590.60	592.10	603.40	605.10	601.70	602.20	593.50	594.70	590.20	578.60	574.40	566.10	591.05
1985	542.10	532.00	533.80	559.10	557.70	576.30	594.90	593.80	578.60	580.50	N.Q.	N.Q.	564.88
1986	N.Q.	N.Q.	350.64	274.98	265.04	260.28	261.51	261.26	260.69	267.48	292.84	308.26	280.30
1987	321.56	320.39	317.66	320.98	323.60	316.96	307.59	314.63	321.86	324.81	332.21	327.65	320.83
1988	326.88	321.12	324.79	323.85	325.28	337.37	342.18	351.14	355.20	347.84	351.10	352.42	338.25

[1] Data prior to 1984 are for Straits (Alloyer Price).   *Source: American Metal Market*

T.685

Secondary Tin Recovered in the United States   In Metric Tons

Year	Tin-plate Scrap Treated (Ths. Tons)	Tin Recovered In the Form of Metal	Com-pounds²	Total	Weight of Tin Com-pounds Produced	Avg. Quantity of Tin Recov. Per Ton of Tin-Scrap (Kilog.)	Avg. Delivered cost of Tinplate Scrap. $ per Metric Ton	Tin Metal	Bronze & Brass	Solder	Type Metal	Babbitt	Anti-Monial Lead	Chemi-cal Com-pounds	Misc.³	Grand Total
1976	685.5	1,195	424	1,619	1,348	2.36		1,467	8,319	4,513	668	495	548	424	12	16,446
1977	667.4	1,376	365	1,741	1,516	2.61		1,668	10,397	4,094	708	694	565	365	12	18,503
1978	714.9	1,324	463	1,787	1,803	2.50	60.04	1,565	12,419	4,363	1,038	521	712	463	19	21,100
1979	841.4	1,536	433	1,969	1,256	2.34	90.73	1,767	12,090	5,282	584	441	867	433	29	21,493
1980	766.9	1,457	321	1,778	1,533	2.32	89.38	1,703	10,402	4,423	525	378	856	321	30	18,638
1981	668.0	1,328	265	1,593	1,220	2.38	102.42	1,587	8,894	3,035	576	261	791	265	29	15,438
1982	464.6	810	447	1,257	1,754	2.37	56.16	1,067	6,971	2,723	222	237	1,015	447	101	12,783
1983	486.5	928	182	1,110	1,284	1.98	60.60	1,180	8,517	3,072	172	185	803	182	94	14,205
1984	492.8	824	301	1,125	1,498	2.24	68.01	1,107	9,146	3,653	142	123	894	301	51	15,417
1985	460.1	1,302	186	1,488	338	3.23	53.69	1,302	8,045	3,565	122	88	791	186	10	14,109
1986¹	499.7	1,134	N.A.	1,134	N.A.	2.27	44.76	1,134	7,996	3,676	197	66	891	N.A.	17	13,977
1987¹		1,151						1,151	10,082	3,765	66	76	623		30	15,793

¹ Preliminary.   ² Tin content.   ³ Includes foil, cable lead & terne metal.   *Source: Bureau of Mines*   T.687

U.S. Consumption of Primary and Secondary Tin   In Metric Tons

Year	Net Import Reliance as a % of Apparent Consumption	Industry Stocks Jan. 1²	Net Receipts Primary	Secondary	Scrap	Total	Available Supply	Stocks Dec. 31 (Total Available Less Total Processed)	Total Processed	Consumed in Mfg. Pdt's.
1976	85	19,510	49,995	2,019	10,189	62,203	81,713		64,819	62,928
1977	82	16,894	48,215	4,025	10,604	62,844	79,738		62,880	60,732
1978	79	16,858	46,821	2,541	10,499	59,861	76,719		63,135	61,531
1979	80	13,584	50,126	2,636	10,659	63,421	77,005		64,067	62,465
1980	79	7,075	43,545	2,461	7,709	53,715	60,790	3,593	57,197	56,362
1981	77	8,835	41,162	5,692	8,050	54,904	63,739	8,640	55,099	54,373
1982	68	8,717	35,843	6,507	7,830	50,180	58,897	12,328	46,569	46,295
1983	73	7,549	36,494	5,412	7,435	49,341	56,890	11,098	45,792	45,547
1984	74	7,740	39,388	6,096	7,323	52,807	60,547	10,788	49,759	49,441
1985	72	8,130	38,939	8,904	7,909	55,752	63,882	13,901	49,981	49,767
1986¹	74	9,438	35,906	11,636	7,125	54,667	64,105	20,273	43,832	43,523
1987¹	73	6,914								

¹ Preliminary.   ² Includes tin in transit in the U.S.   *Source: Bureau of Mines*   T.686

Consumption of Tin in the United States by Finished Products   In Metric Tons of Contained Tin

Year	Alloys	Tin-plate²	Solder	Babbitt	Bronze & Brass	Collap. Tubes & Foil	Tinning	Chemi-cals³	Tin Powder	Type Metal	Bar Tin & Anodes	White Metal	Other	Total Primary	Total Secondary
1976		20,766	17,728	2,423	7,656	694	2,308	5,621	1,208	216	758	2,347		51,767	11,161
1977		18,539	17,315	2,093	8,606	787	2,323	5,727	1,287	202	578	1,655		47,596	13,136
1978		17,280	17,770	2,346	9,048	673	2,431	4,557	1,360	171	424	1,484		48,403	13,128
1979	2,428	17,929	18,022	2,243	8,690	686	2,584	4,797	1,435	140	567	1,258	1,686	49,496	12,969
1980	134	16,346	15,618	2,380	7,478	526	2,577	N.A.	1,109	N.A.	486	914	8,794	44,342	12,020
1981	2,435	13,306	15,799	3,844	7,041	561	2,491	4,417	983	52	455	1,201	1,788	40,229	14,144
1982	N.A.	11,134	13,142	1,915	4,400	N.A.	1,887	N.A.	906	N.A.	509	1,177	11,225	33,019	13,276
1983	N.A.	9,462	14,120	2,881	4,583	N.A.	1,759	N.A.	793	N.A.	654	937	10,358	34,301	11,246
1984	N.A.	8,825	17,249	2,684	4,998	N.A.	1,748	N.A.	1,057	N.A.	526	958	11,396	37,819	11,622
1985	N.A.	9,321	18,621	1,488	4,330	N.A.	1,511	N.A.	976	7	466	937	12,110	37,187	12,580
1986¹	N.A.	8,660	15,756	1,347	3,503	N.A.	1,422	N.A.	1,002	N.A.	480	1,134	10,219	32,548	10,975
1987⁴		10,357	15,240	1,060	3,559		1,398				703	1,175	10,704	35,597	8,599
1988⁴														60,000	11,000

¹ Preliminary.   ² Includes small quantity of secondary pig tin & tin acquired in chemicals.   ³ Including tin oxide.   ⁴ Estimate.
Source: Bureau of Mines   T.688

Titanium

Demand for titanium soared in 1988, because of heavy buying activity for military programs and commercial aircraft orders.

In 1988, demand for titanium mill products continued to show gains over previous quarters, and this produced price increases on the magnitude of 15 percent for the second quarter of 1988. Major U.S. dealers increased their prices for 0.5 inch-thick 6A1-4V plate to $11.73/lb. from $10.74. Aircraft grade titanium was increased to $8.98/lb. from $7.55 in the first quarter, and delivery lead times were being extended out to 30-38 weeks.

In the ten years from 1977 to 1987, titanium castings shipments more than doubled from 200 tons to 475 tons. Shipments were expected to expand further in 1988.

As the space age evolves, so have the technologies dedicated to the production of higher quality material. In 1988, Teledyne Allvac announced plans to install a new plasma arc cold-hearth melting system that was manufactured for Teledyne by Retech Inc. The system will be the first of its kind dedicated to titanium ingot production. The plasma arc process will produce alloys free from high and low density inclusions, as well as a wider variety of titanium scrap than any other system now in use.

As the demand for titanium metal has increased, so too has the demand for titanium pigment, or TiO2. In 1987, U.S. apparent consumption of titanium oxide totaled 1.04 million tons, and for the first five months of 1988, the total was already 470,971 tons. Stocks at the end of 1987 totaled 52,336 tons, and were whittled down to 43,711 tons after the first five months of 1988.

U.S. production is also running ahead of last year, and for the first five months totaled 429,800 tons, compared to full-year 1987 production of 951,685 tons.

For aircraft production, as well as high-tech space program uses, there is no substitute for titanium, which is as strong as steel, but lighter. There is also no cost effective substitute for titanium dioxide pigment.

After unprecedented levels of commercial aircraft bookings and production in 1988, steady demand for titanium was expected to continue in 1989.

Average Titanium Prices in the United States

Year	Ilmenite—F.O.B. Australian Ports[2] $ Tonne	Slag, 85% TiO$_2$ F.O.B. Richards Bay, South Africa $ Tonne	Ilmenite Large Lots Bulk, F.O.B. U.S. East Coast $ Tonne	Rutile Large Lots Bulk, F.O.B. U.S. East Coast[3] $ per Short Ton	Rutile Bagged F.O.B. Australian Ports $ per Short Ton	Synthetic F.O.B. Mobile, Ala. $ per Short Ton	Titanium Metal Sponge	Titanium Dioxide Pigments Anatase	Titanium Dioxide Rutile
1978	50			340			3.28	0.460	0.510
1979	50		—	390			3.98	0.530	0.590
1980	55		—	440		310	7.02	0.570	0.630
1981	70–75		39	450–475		340	7.65	0.690	0.750
1982	70–75	170–180	44–45	450–475		350	5.55	0.690	0.750
1983	70–75	187–198	44–45	400–430		350	5.55	0.690	0.750
1984	36–38	200	44–45	320–340	319–335	350	5.55	0.690	0.750
1985	38–42	212	50–56	350–360	315–328	350	3.50–4.00	.72–.73	0.780
1986[1]	47–53	225–230	50–56	355–375	374–386	350	3.90–4.30	.75–.77	0.820
1987[4]	50–56	235–245	50–56	355–375	397–417	350		.75–.77	.80–.82
1988[4]	55–66	250–275			469–491			.80–.85	.85–.90

Dec. 31 in $ per pound

[1] Preliminary. [2] Prior to 1984 prices are for TiO$_2$ F.O.B. Atlantic Seabord. [3] Prior to 1984 prices are for F.O.B. Eastern Ports. [4] Estimate
Source: U.S. Bureau of Mines
T.690

Salient Statistics of Titanium[4] in the United States   In Short Tons

Year	Ilmenite Production (Gross Wt.)	Ilmenite Shipments (TiO$_2$)	Ilmenite Imports[3]	Ilmenite Stocks Dec. 31 (TiO$_2$)	Titanium Slag Consumption (TiO$_2$)	Titanium Slag Imports[3]	Titanium Slag Stocks (TiO$_2$)	Rutile Imports[3, 4]	Rutile Stocks Dec. 31 (TiO$_2$)	Exports Ores & Concentrates	Exports Scrap	Exports Dioxide & Pigments	Exports Ingots, Billets, Etc.
1979	639,292	389,535	184,478	462,415	106,346	111,210	56,917	283,479	119,947	9,903	4,967	51,456	1,984
1980	556,646	358,181	357,488	584,280	133,933	194,994	127,981	281,605	147,670	17,830	3,300	45,795	3,278
1981	542,357	310,854	236,217	543,114	186,020	268,825	150,706	202,373	153,770	7,297	3,280	62,432	4,203
1982	263,391	145,725	348,366	470,776	168,433	247,845	103,667	163,325	165,762	21,682	4,287	72,823	2,196
1983	N.A.	N.A.	259,328	254,237	127,267	138,708	61,026	111,578	122,189	4,391	5,379	91,702	1,371
1984	N.A.	N.A.	409,605	128,507	152,534	209,839	52,397	180,508	96,186	8,651	4,109	106,124	2,071
1985	N.A.	N.A.	506,804	147,357	199,610	291,828	83,821	179,663	109,319	27,759	6,760	101,954	2,248
1986[1]	N.A.	N.A.	465,617	169,723	221,959	361,872	77,476	174,820	102,938	5,314	6,403	112,227	2,119
1987[2]			396,435			450,608		160,730			6,000	5,603	120,029	2,719

[1] Preliminary. [2] Estimate. [3] For consumption. [4] Natural & synthetic. *Source: Bureau of Mines*
T.693

TITANIUM

World Production of Titanium Ilmenite Concentrates[2] In Thousands of Short Tons

Year	Australia[7]	Brazil	Canada[2]	China	Finland	India	Sierra Leone	Malaysia (Exports)	Norway	South Africa[3]	Sri Lanka (Ceylon)	United States[4]	USSR	World Total[2 & 3]
1979	1,327	14.5	525.8	N.A.	131.9	161.9		220.3	903.7	316.0	61.0	639.3	450.0	4,752
1980	1,553	18.6	934.4	N.A.	175.3	185.1		208.3	912.5	379.0	37.4	556.6	460.0	5,420
1981	1,478	17.5	836.9	150.0	178.0	179.1		190.4	727.1	408.0	88.2	542.4	470.0	5,266
1982	1,289	12.5	737.4	150.0	185.0	168.6		111.6	608.2	420.0	75.3	263.4	475.0	4,496
1983	1,003	33.6	700.0	154.0	180.7	148.2		245.5	612.8	460.0	90.1	N.A.	480.0	4,108
1984	1,681	45.1	800.0	154.0	184.0	154.3		296.0	718.5	460.0	112.5	N.A.	485.0	5,091
1985	1,579	84.2	930.0	154.0	140.1	157.6		346.9	811.1	480.0	126.6	N.A.	490.0	5,301
1986[1]	1,380	83.2	937.0	154.0		154.0	6.2	457.4	885.8	480.0	110.0	N.A.	496.0	5,152
1987[6]	1,535	82.5	992.0	154.0		154.0		551.0	939.5	715.0	110.0	N.A.	500.0	5,768

[1] Preliminary. [2] Includes Ti slag containing approx. 70% TiO_2. [3] Contains 85% of TiO_2. [4] Includes a mixed product containing ilmenite, leucoxene, & rutile. [5] Includes slag & concentrate. [6] Estimate. [7] Includes leucoxene. *Source: Bureau of Mines*   T.692

World Production of Titanium Rutile Concentrates In Short Tons

Year	South Africa	Australia	USSR	Brazil	Sierra Leone	India	Sri Lanka (Ceylon)	United States	World Total
1979	46,000	302,620	11,000	484	8,267	5,445	16,176	N.A.	389,992
1980	53,000	343,639	11,000	472	52,356	5,908	14,097	N.A.	480,472
1981	55,000	254,432	11,000	190	55,992	7,397	14,662	N.A.	398,673
1982	52,000	243,277	11,000	258	52,590	6,374	7,950	N.A.	373,449
1983	62,000	180,089	11,000	510	79,146	6,100	8,921	N.A.	347,766
1984	62,000	187,860	11,000	454	100,641	6,600	7,129	N.A.	375,684
1985	61,000	233,265	11,000	786	88,858	7,496	9,434	N.A.	411,839
1986[1]	61,000	237,850	11,000	546	107,034	8,000	8,000	N.A.	433,430
1987[2]	61,000	283,000	11,000	550	124,892	8,000	8,000	N.A.	496,442

[1] Preliminary. [2] Estimate. *Source: Bureau of Mines*   T.691

World Production of Titanium Sponge Metal & U.S. Consumption of Titanium Concentrates

	Production of Titanium (in short tons) Sponge Metal[1]						U.S. Consumption of Titanium Concentrates, by Products (in short tons) Ilmenite (TiO_2 Content)			Rutile (TiO_2 Content)			
Year	China	USSR	United Kingdom	Japan	United States	Total	Pigments	Misc.	Total	Welding Rod Coatings	Pigments	Misc.	Total
1979		43,000	2,600	14,000	N.A.	—	475,342	11,886	478,228	9,947	230,776	52,189	292,912
1980		45,000	2,600	21,257	N.A.	—	502,108	11,207	513,315	6,876	211,599	59,407	277,882
1981	2,000	42,000	2,600	27,500	26,419	100,519	501,301	9,721	511,022	6,944	192,779	66,873	266,596
1982	1,500	44,000	2,600	18,600	15,600	82,300	345,618	6,775	352,393	5,275	184,403	35,435	225,113
1983	2,000	45,000	2,000	11,600	13,966	74,000	468,279	6,006	474,285	3,649	210,949	35,820	250,418
1984[3]	2,000	46,000	2,500	16,938	24,326	92,000	492,658	6,319	498,977	3,911	231,808	62,920	298,639
1985[2]	2,000	47,000	1,500	16,938	23,257	91,000	474,561	6,450	481,011	4,881	239,893	41,714	286,488
1986[2]	2,000	48,000	1,500	18,000	17,500	87,000	511,070	1,655	512,725	7,667	244,178	57,539	309,384
1987[2]					19,675								

[1] Unconsolidated metal in various forms. [2] Estimated. [3] Preliminary. *Source: Bureau of Mines*   T.689

Tobacco

U.S. tobacco production in 1988 was estimated by the USDA at 1.3 billion pounds, up 9 percent from 1987. Harvested acreage rose by 6 percent to 621,000. The average yield increased almost 4 percent to 2,101 lbs./acre. The major tobacco states were North Carolina, Kentucky and Tennessee.

U.S. supplies were expected to drop about 8 percent in 1988/89. Carry-in stocks were estimated at 2.8 billion pounds, 14 percent less than a year earlier. U.S. consumption was forecast to rise from 1.66 billion pounds in 1987/88, with more domestic tobacco used in cigarettes and higher cigarette production.

U.S. 1988 cigarette demand was forecast at 567 billion, down from 575 billion in 1987 and the fourth straight annual decline. Consumption had been trending lower since 1981, when it was 640 billion. Per capita 1988 consumption was estimated at 3,121 cigarettes, down from 3,196 in 1987 and 3,849 in 1980. The decline was linked to higher prices, rising health concerns, and new anti-smoking laws. But cigarette output was expected to rise, as exports increased by nearly 25 percent in the first 7 months of 1988. The major importers were Japan, Belgium-Luxembourg, and Hong Kong.

Retail tobacco prices in July 1988 were up 9 percent from July 1987. Manufacturers raised cigarette prices in December 1987 and June 1988. The increases were the largest in five years. Also, four states raised taxes an average of 4 cents a pack. The weighted average cigarette tax in mid-1988 was 17.8 cents, ranging from 2 cents in North Carolina to 38 cents in Minnesota. Cigarettes were taxed by many cities, and three-fourths of the states had a sales tax. The federal excise tax remained at 16 cents a pack.

Consumption of larger cigars in 1988 was expected to slip to 2.5 billion from 2.7 billion in 1987, following a long declining trend. Cigarillo or small cigar output had been trending lower since 1972. Consumption of smoking tobacco, used in pipes and self-rolled cigarettes, was forecast at 23 million pounds, down 3 percent. Chewing tobacco output was expected to drop in 1988; demand had been hurt by price hikes, bad publicity, and laws requiring warning labels on packages.

About 65 percent of U.S. tobacco was used domestically in 1988; the rest was exported. Flue-cured tobacco was the most commonly produced type, totaling about 780 million pounds.

Growing conditions were favorable in most areas in 1988, and quality was higher. Harvested flue-cured tobacco acreage was 354,000, nearly 30,000 acres more than in 1987. Yield was 2,201 lbs./acre, compared with 2,129 in 1986. With beginning stocks of 1.51 billion pounds, the total flue-cured supply was 2.27 billion. Flue-cured tobacco disappearance was 926 million pounds in 1987. Domestic use was 541 million pounds, up 13 percent from 1986. Exports of 385 million pounds were off 2 percent from 1986, reflecting lower demand in importing nations and lower-priced supplies from other countries. The major buyers of U.S. flue-cured tobacco were Japan, West Germany, Taiwan and Egypt.

The 1988 U.S. burley tobacco crop, used mostly in cigarettes, was 449 million pounds, up 7 percent from 1987. Harvested acreage increased almost 8,000 to 223,500, and yield rose 3 percent to 2,011 lbs./acre. With beginning stocks of 1.1 billion pounds, total supplies were 1.56 billion pounds, down 9 percent. Domestic 1987 use was about 460 million pounds, up 15 percent from 1986. Exports in 1987 were estimated at 150 million pounds, down 9 percent. Exports to Japan were significantly lower. West Germany was the other major importer. World burley output fell in 1988. Declines were reported in Mexico, Greece and Yugoslavia, but crops increased in Argentina, Brazil and Malawi.

Southern Maryland tobacco production, used in cigarettes, was put at 19.3 million pounds in 1988, down 7 percent. Harvested acreage fell 14 percent, but average yield increased 8 percent. Including stocks of 30 million pounds, total supply was 49.3 million pounds, 21 percent less than a year earlier.

Fire-cured tobacco is used in snuff, chewing tobacco, cigars and smoking tobacco. The 1988 crop of 26.2 million pounds was off 1.4 million from 1987. Yields of Kentucky-Tennessee fire-cured tobacco fell 8 percent, but the smaller Virginia fire-cured yield rose 30 percent. Domestic 1987 use was 20.2 million pounds, compared with 18.1 million in 1986. Exports fell in 1987.

U.S. Government Program

The 1988 national average flue-cured tobacco loan level was 144.2 cents/lb., 0.7 cent above 1987. The 1988 national acreage allotment was 379,588 acres. The national marketing quota of 744 million pounds was 7 percent larger than the 1987 quota.

The 1988 national average burley tobacco loan level was 150 cents/lb., 1.2 cents more than in 1987. The national marketing quota was 473 million pounds.

World Production of Leaf Tobacco In Thousands of Metric Tons (Farm Sales–Weight[3])

Year	United States	Brazil	Canada	China	USSR	France	Greece	India	Indonesia	Italy	Japan	Pakistan	Philippines	Turkey	World Total[1]
1981	936.3	325.0	112.4	1,497	273.0	42.8	127.4	440.8	109.7	131.0	137.7	67.6	80.9	168.0	5,939
1982	904.7	378.0	70.2	2,179	307.0	44.5	131.4	520.1	111.4	145.0	139.4	68.3	90.4	207.7	6,878
1983	648.2	378.0	111.7	1,381	385.0	44.5	111.7	590.6	126.0	156.0	136.7	64.6	91.7	234.0	6,044
1984	783.8	392.0	91.3	1,789	381.7	35.9	140.3	492.5	121.4	160.3	135.5	79.1	109.4	177.5	6,501
1985	685.5	411.0	85.9	2,320	376.0	34.9	148.5	472.8	172.5	166.5	116.2	87.4	75.9	171.0	6,883
1986[2]	527.4	385.0	70.1	1,670	381.0	38.6	148.8	439.4	154.1	145.5	118.2	78.3	72.8	161.5	6,021
1987[1]	540.1	410.0	60.7	2,095	381.0	36.3	134.5	447.7	178.4	149.4	105.8	73.3	83.2	175.0	6,468
1988[1]	604.1														6,500

[1] Estimated. [2] Preliminary. [3] Farm Sales–weight is about 10% above dry weight which is normally reported in trade statistics.
Source: Foreign Agricultural Service, U.S.D.A.

T.694

TOBACCO

Production and Consumption of Tobacco Products in the United States

Year	Production — Chewing Tobacco — Plug	Twist	Loose-leaf	Total	Cigar-ettes (Billion)	Cigars[2] (Billion)	Smoking Tobacco (Million Lbs.)	Snuff (Million Lbs.)	Consumption[3] — Cigars[2] (Number)	Cigar-ettes (Number)	Cigars[2] Per Capita[4]	Cigar-ettes Per Capita[4]	Smoking Tobacco (Pounds)	Chewing Tobacco (Pounds)	Total Pdt.'s
1980	17.2	1.9	72.1	105.7	714.1	3.45	32.2	25.5	51.1	3,849	.84	6.78	.48		7.98
1981	17.9	1.8	70.3	90.0	736.5	3.43	30.3	42.4[5]	48.9	3,836	.81	6.52	.46	1.13	7.59[5]
1982	15.7	1.7	73.0	90.4	694.2	3.17	28.3	43.8	45.2	3,739	.74	6.45	.42	1.09	7.46
1983	14.1	1.7	71.0	86.8	667.0	3.14	28.0	46.7	43.8	3,488	.72	6.19	.40	1.05	7.19
1984	12.7	1.7	74.4	88.8	668.8	3.13	24.5	49.4	41.9	3,446	.69	5.89	.35	1.05	6.85
1985	11.3	1.5	74.0	86.9	665.3	2.83	22.1	48.7	37.9	3,370	.62	5.91	.32	1.01	6.81
1986	10.4	1.4	69.6	81.4	658.0	2.93	19.4	47.5	35.8	3,274	.59	5.88	.29	.93	6.72
1987[1]	10.0	1.4	67.3	78.7	689.4	2.10	18.0	46.2	31.4	3,196	.52	5.59	.27	.89	6.37
1988[6]	9.1	1.4	65.5	76.0	705.0	2.00	17.5	49.0	28.9	3,121	.47	5.53	.26	.84	6.28

[1] Preliminary. [2] Large cigars & cigarillos. [3] Consumption of tax-paid tobacco products; Represents unstemmed equivalent of tobacco used in the manufacture of these products. [4] 18 years old & over. [5] New classifications. [6] Estimate.
Sources: Bureau of the Census; Internal Revenue Service

T.695

Production of Tobacco in the United States   In Millions of Pounds

Year	Conn.	Florida	Georgia	Indiana	Kentucky	Mary-land	Massa-chusetts	North Car.	Ohio	Pa.	South Car.	Tenn.	Virginia	Wis-consin	W. Virg.
1980	5.3	20.4	110.6	16.8	420.7	25.3	1.9	762.4	20.0	24.7	125.5	111.9	106.9	26.0	1.8
1981	5.6	22.8	121.0	18.8	509.6	33.0	2.0	795.9	22.9	27.3	149.6	161.5	157.8	26.4	2.4
1982	4.2	21.0	105.6	20.2	589.4	37.5	.9	700.7	31.9	25.9	124.2	178.2	125.4	20.1	3.6
1983	3.4	17.6	96.4	13.0	324.6	29.7	.8	546.9	17.7	22.0	112.9	118.2	99.1	16.7	3.8
1984	2.8	17.9	85.5	18.8	530.1	30.4	.8	590.0	26.5	22.4	105.5	154.6	115.9	16.4	4.5
1985	3.3	16.3	82.1	14.6	428.4	26.6	.8	556.5	16.9	21.9	98.9	127.4	91.1	18.0	3.4
1986	3.1	13.3	67.9	12.1	314.9	21.1	.6	444.8	13.6	21.8	75.5	82.8	73.5	11.9	2.6
1987	2.7	13.8	72.2	11.1	304.8	13.3	.7	466.6	12.0	20.7	94.1	87.3	76.9	8.4	2.6
1988[1]	2.8	16.9	83.3	11.2	337.2	13.5	.8	539.0	14.0	19.5	96.8	90.8	94.5	5.7	2.4

[1] Preliminary, December estimate. *Source: Crop Reporting Board, U.S.D.A.*

T.696

Salient Statistics of Tobacco in the United States

Year	Acres Harvested 1,000 Acres	Yield Per Acre Lbs.	Produc-tion Million Lbs.	Farm Price ¢ Lb.	Farm Value Mil. $	Tobacco (July–June) Ex-ports[2] (Mil. Lbs.)	Im-ports[3] (Mil. Lbs.)	Ciga-rettes (Millions)	U.S. Exports of — Cigars & Che-roots (Millions)	Chewing Tobacco & Snuff (Metric Tons)	Smoking Tobacco[5] (Metric Tons)	Stocks of Leaf Tobacco[4] — All Types — Jan. 1 (Billion Pounds)	April 1	July 1	Oct. 1
1980	920.5	1,939	1,786	152.3	2,720	553.4	439.8	81,998	200	191	6,103	4,974	4,608	4,284	4,548
1981	976.0	2,113	2,064	170.6	3,520	584.9	384.9	82,582	181	887	9,105	4,850	4,617	4,285	4,699
1982	912.7	2,185	1,994	176.4	3,519	553.4	434.0	73,585	181	1,073	10,345	5,080	4,909	4,675	5,034
1983	789.2	1,811	1,429	174.6	2,496	526.5	515.9	60,698	130	1,162	15,036	5,367	5,288	4,900	5,209
1984	791.7	2,183	1,728	180.6	3,121	519.8	425.1	56,517	104	525	19,156	5,357	5,210	4,987	5,186
1985	688.0	2,196	1,511	164.5	2,486	541.6	449.1	58,900	59	616	41,826	5,434	5,247	4,997	5,150
1986[1]	581.9	1,998	1,163	152.2	1,771	533.6	487.1	63,900	62	650	43,332	5,293	5,158	4,848	4,902
1987[1]	587.1	2,028	1,191	157.0	1,870	500.0	480.3	100,200	145			4,979	4,775	4,435	4,455
1988[1]	629.9	2,114	1,332	160.0	2,118	550.0	470.0	115,000	85			4,471	4,176	3,786	

[1] Preliminary. [2] Domestic. [3] For consumption. [4] Owned by dealer & mfgrs., converted to a farm-sales weight equivalent. [5] In packages & in bulk & other. *Source: Agricultural Marketing Service, U.S.D.A.*

T.700

Tobacco Production in the U.S., by Types   In Million Pounds (Farm–Sales Weight)

Types	11–14	31	32	21	22–23	35–36	37	41	42–44	72	51–52	54–55	61
1980	1,086	561	26.2	3.6	32.7	16.2	.4	24.7	2.4	.1	2.6	26.0	4.5
1981	1,170	730	46.4	5.2	32.4	15.7	.7	27.3	2.4	.1	3.5	26.4	4.1
1982	1,006	822	42.0	5.5	47.7	19.9	.7	21.4	3.5		3.5	20.1	1.6
1983	821.3	481.4	37.4	4.6	32.5	14.3	.4	14.2	1.9		2.5	16.7	1.7
1984	864.6	712.2	38.1	6.1	50.5	19.0	.6	14.6	2.2		1.9	16.4	1.7
1985	800.3	573.3	32.9	4.5	45.9	15.2	.2	15.6	1.7		2.1	18.0	2.0
1986	644.6	407.9	27.8	3.5	37.7	10.9	.2	15.2	.5		2.0	10.8	1.7
1987	690.9	419.4	20.7	2.6	25.0	6.8	.1	13.3	.1		1.8	8.4	1.6
1988[1]	795.9	458.9	20.0	3.0	23.9	7.6	.1	13.0	—		1.5	5.7	2.1

[1] Preliminary. *Source: Crop Reporting Board, U.S.D.A.*

T.701

U.S. Exports of Unmanufactured Tobacco In Millions of Pounds (Declared Weight)

Year	Aus-tralia	Belg.-Luxem.	Den-mark	Egypt	France	W. Ger-many	Thailand	Ireland	Japan	Nether-lands	Norway	Italy	Sweden	Switzer-land	United Kingdom	Total U.S. Exports
1980	13.4	7.9	17.5	17.4	4.5	100.7	22.6	3.6	82.1	44.9	6.8	30.7	15.4	20.1	32.5	598.7
1981	12.6	9.5	11.1	16.1	6.1	83.2	18.4	3.9	117.0	28.6	4.2	26.5	9.9	22.2	39.4	584.5
1982	10.1	15.2	16.8	22.0	5.3	68.2	27.7	4.7	110.3	25.1	3.6	28.1	8.7	26.7	30.7	572.0
1983	9.7	9.6	20.2	21.6	7.3	58.0	9.1	3.2	114.1	28.4	5.7	32.2	12.4	16.8	27.8	524.4
1984	8.2	9.4	19.8	37.4	5.1	66.0	14.6	8.0	92.1	22.3	4.7	31.3	11.5	25.3	31.8	542.7
1985	7.3	11.5	16.2	41.2	9.9	76.7	17.8	7.3	102.0	20.9	3.3	28.7	15.8	23.9	18.4	548.9
1986	11.7	10.1	14.5	46.5	8.4	82.7	13.0	3.4	83.2	31.2	4.3	22.5	10.2	11.5	21.8	477.5
1987[1]	8.5	8.2	15.6	11.0	6.7	69.3	7.5	1.2	105.4	32.1	3.3	22.4	8.0	12.6	16.7	430.0
1988[2]	9.5	10.0	17.0	20.0	6.5	82.0	15.0	2.4	58.0	45.0	4.4	35.0	9.9	14.0	19.0	480.0

[1] Preliminary. [2] Estimate. *Source: Bureau of the Census*   T.702

U.S. Salient Statistics for Flue-Cured Tobacco (Types 11–14)

Crop Year	Acres Har-vested 1,000	Yield Acre 100 Lbs.	Market-ings	Stocks, July 1	Total Supply	Exports	Dom. Disap-pearance	Total Disap-pearance	Farm Price ¢ Lb.	Crop Value Mil. $	Parity Price[2]	Price Support Level	Placed Under Gov't. Loan	Under Loan July 1
					Millions of Pounds						¢ Lb.		Mil. Lb.	
1979	502.8	18.8	946	2,075	3,021	520	563	1,083	140.0	1,324	203.0	129.3	72.0	564.0
1980	555.1	19.6	1,086	1,965	3,052	509	530	1,039	144.5	1,569	222.0	141.5	137.2	554.4
1981	540.6	21.6	1,144	2,013	3,157	523	489	1,012	166.4	1,947	243.0	158.7	105.9	595.8
1982	472.3	21.3	994	2,145	3,139	456	479	935	178.5	1,774	254.0	169.9	259.9	518.7
1983–4	409.8	20.0	855	2,205	3,060	453	442	894	177.9	1,521	267.0	169.9	194.8	688.4
1984–5	392.0	22.1	850	2,165	3,015	481	454	935	181.1	1,539	284.0	169.9	158.6	797.5
1985–6	357.1	22.4	789	2,080	2,870	435	477	912	171.9	1,376	289.0	169.9	131.6	833.1
1986–7	308.3	20.9	667	1,958	2,625	393	480	873	152.7	1,019	288.0	143.8	55.2	790.4
1987–8[1]	324.6	21.3	683	1,752	2,435	385	537	922	158.7	1,084		143.5	24.8	647.8
1988–9[3]	363.5	21.9	796	1,513	2,309	385	550	935	161.4	1,285		144.2		466.1

[1] Preliminary. [2] As of applicable date when support level was computed. [3] Estimate. *Source: Agricultural Marketing Service, U.S.D.A.*   T.697

U.S. Salient Statistics for Burley Tobacco (Type 31)

Crop Year	Placed Acres Har-vested 1,000	Yield Per Acre 100 Lbs.	Market-ings	Stocks, Oct. 1	Total Supply	Exports	Dom. Disap-pearance	Total Disap-pearance	Farm Price ¢ Lb.	Crop Value Mil. $	Parity Price[2]	Support Level	Under Gov't. Loan	Under Loan on Oct. 1
					Millions of Pounds						¢ Lb.		Mil. Lb.	
1979	238.1	18.7	446	1,212	1,658	133	499	632	145.2	700	210.0	133.3	7.3	155.4
1980	276.6	20.3	558	1,026	1,583	106	478	583	165.9	930	236.0	145.9	.0	66.3
1981	331.2	22.0	726	1,000	1,726	141	464	605	180.7	1,318	253.0	163.6	.8	0
1982	346.2	23.7	777	1,121	1,898	135	444	579	181.0	1,406	266.0	175.1	269.2	.7
1983–4	292.6	16.5	527	1,319	1,845	112	389	501	177.3	934	280.0	175.1	255.6	226.1
1984–5	315.7	22.6	674	1,344	2,018	154	403	556	187.6	1,264	294.0	175.1	201.0	377.2
1985–6	255.1	22.5	542	1,462	2,004	151	425	576	159.7	866	297.0	148.8	82.7	548.9
1986–7	210.7	19.4	420	1,428	1,848	165	402	567	156.5	657	297.0	148.8	38.8	525.7
1987–8[1]	215.8	19.4	428	1,281	1,709	157	478	635	156.3	669		148.8	90.0	329.7
1988–9[3]	223.5	20.5	475	1,074	1,549	160	480	640	162.0	770		150.0		240.0

[1] Preliminary. [2] As of applicable date when support level was computed. [3] Estimate. *Source: Agricultural Marketing Service, U.S.D.A.*   T.698

Exports[1] of Tobacco from the United States In Millions of Pounds

Year	Jan.	Feb.	Mar.	Apr.	May	June	July	Aug.	Sept.	Oct.	Nov.	Dec.	Total
1979	35.6	50.1	57.1	51.8	42.2	25.3	38.0	29.5	30.1	41.6	78.9	81.5	561.8
1980	28.0	52.5	80.1	54.6	53.2	43.0	40.9	28.3	32.3	47.6	64.4	66.6	591.5
1981	44.8	32.8	53.7	49.4	44.6	40.1	31.3	27.4	45.5	63.2	86.8	55.6	575.3
1982	31.7	39.4	62.1	41.8	54.0	37.2	23.9	30.2	24.8	74.5	92.2	50.5	562.3
1983	24.2	38.3	46.0	44.0	33.6	32.7	28.6	36.0	26.4	51.7	87.9	60.3	509.8
1984	42.0	40.2	43.3	32.4	26.5	28.9	14.8	18.4	39.1	68.0	97.9	77.1	528.5
1985	34.6	48.5	48.0	54.1	15.8	14.2	20.4	39.2	41.1	48.1	85.4	89.3	538.6
1986	21.6	31.9	48.8	45.9	28.4	22.4	16.4	23.7	22.1	32.9	66.3	106.1	466.6
1987[2]	59.6	25.4	43.1	41.4	32.3	20.7	19.4	15.7	21.6	28.1	53.7	64.8	425.9
1988[2]	72.0	37.7	48.4	56.7	34.9	22.8	26.0	24.7	31.5	32.6			

[1] Represents unmanufactured tobacco, including stems, trimmings and scrap. [2] Preliminary. *Source: Department of Commerce*   T.699

Tung Oil

The average price of tung oil, ex-tank, Rotterdam fell slightly in 1988 to $1,040 per tonne from the previous year's $1,060, and was well below the 5-year average of $1,443 in 1983-87, according to *Oil World*.

The U.S. imports all of its tung oil, and imports in 1988 were in line with the year-earlier level. According to the Census Bureau, U.S. imports in January to November 1988 were 6,030 tonnes, compared with 5,865 tonnes in the same period in 1987.

Total world tung oil production is around 100,000 tonnes a year. China, the leading producer and exporter, accounts for about 75 percent of global output. Produced from tung nuts, tung oil is used as an industrial lubricant and drying oil.

Supply and Distribution of Tung Oil in the United States   In Thousands of Pounds

Year	Stocks Jan. 1	Production	Imports	Exports[2]	Total Supply	Apparent Disappearance	Factory Consumption (Crop Yr. Beg. Oct.) Total	Paint & Varnish	Resins & Plastics	Other In-edible Prods	Oil Acquired By CCC
1977	2,300	—	18,821	1,200	19,900	16,900	20,100				
1978	3,000		17,912				13,500	7,200	3,700	2,600	
1979	1,200		20,038				15,700	10,400	3,000	2,300	
1980	3,500		16,239				16,600	8,300	3,700	4,600	
1981	2,800		15,033				14,600	5,800	3,200	5,600	
1982[1]	2,200		14,398				12,700	5,300	2,800	4,000	
1983[1]	2,217		13,635				19,700	5,600	3,400	10,800	
1984[3]	3,137		13,929				12,400	5,100	4,500	2,900	
1985[3]	2,546		15,298				11,600	5,200	4,300		
1986[3]	3,514		12,291				12,200	3,700	6,100		
1987[3]	4,516										

[1] Preliminary.   [2] Also including re-exports.   [3] Estimate.   *Source: Economic Research Service, U.S.D.A.*   T.703

U.S. Consumption of Tung Oil in Inedible Products   In Thousands of Pounds

Year	Jan.	Feb.	Mar.	Apr.	May	June	July	Aug.	Sept.	Oct.	Nov.	Dec.	Total
1985	1,110	1,079	887	1,039	818	1,197	1,303	1,096	1,105	1,068	911	891	12,504
1986[1]	884	964	959	989	923	1,093	976	895	949	1,091	854	734	11,311
1987[1]	875	940	861	1,054	1,265	1,134	978	1,055	1,146	1,232	1,260	1,847	13,647
1988[1]	2,169	1,143	988	1,117	1,072	878	713	1,148	1,276	2,213			

[1] Preliminary.   *Source: Bureau of the Census*

U.S. Stocks of Tung Oil at Factories & Warehouses   In Thousands of Pounds

Year	Jan. 1	Feb. 1	Mar. 1	Apr. 1	May 1	June 1	July 1	Aug. 1	Sept. 1	Oct. 1	Nov. 1	Dec. 1
1984	3,137	2,867	3,042	2,634	2,609	2,102	1,815	1,802	1,476	1,192	2,113	2,029
1985[1]	2,546	2,589	2,353	1,642	1,707	1,599	1,564	2,163	2,272	1,526	1,798	2,617
1986[1]	3,514	3,347	2,651	3,036	2,847	2,255	2,691	2,742	2,151	2,212	3,350	4,123
1987[1]	4,516	3,937	2,830	3,582	2,996	865	2,768	3,699	3,779	3,325	3,625	3,768
1988[1]	3,224	4,501	5,296	4,374	4,304	3,500	3,913	3,797	3,422	4,999	3,822	

[1] Preliminary.   *Source: Bureau of the Census*   T.703A

Average Price of Tung Oil[1] (Imported-Drums) F.O.B. New York   In Cents per Pound

Year	Jan.	Feb.	Mar.	Apr.	May	June	July	Aug.	Sept.	Oct.	Nov.	Dec.	Average
1981	69.6	68.0	64.0	60.3	62.9	64.5	64.0	64.0	62.1	60.3	58.5	58.5	63.1
1982	61.4	69.5	68.2	66.5	68.3	69.4	66.9	63.5	60.6	60.5	60.5	60.5	64.6
1983	60.5	57.0	57.0	61.9	86.4	102.5	102.5	107.3	133.4	136.0	138.0	138.0	98.4
1984	138.0	138.0	138.0	138.0	138.0	134.0	134.0	117.0	106.9	89.0	81.0	81.0	119.0
1985	81.0	81.0	81.0	81.0	81.0	N.A.	52.0	53.0	55.0	55.0	55.0	52.5	66.1
1986	52.0	46.5	46.1	44.5	43.5	40.1	36.5	34.8	33.0	32.0	32.0	32.0	31.2
1987	33.20	44.50	50.50	59.50	57.25	56.38	56.50	56.50	56.50	56.50	56.50	56.50	53.36
1988	57.63	58.00	58.00	56.88	53.50	52.00	51.00	49.80	49.00				

[1] Carlots, imported, f.o.b. New York.   *Source: Economic Research Service, U.S.D.A.*   T.704

Tungsten

Only one U.S. tungsten mine was open in 1988, producing an estimated 230 tonnes, used by the owner's ammonium paratungstate plant. Reopening of another mine was delayed, pending a common stock underwriting. Mining also was restrained in most market economies in 1988, although tungsten concentrate prices rose 15 percent from 1987 levels. U.S. apparent consumption grew 26 percent to 10,044 tonnes in 1988, reflecting strong demand from machine tool makers. U.S. net import reliance was 75 percent in 1988.

The U.S. Bureau of Mines estimated world 1988 mine production at 41,130 tonnes, up 2 percent from 1987.

China remained the largest producer and exporter, supplying 26 percent of U.S. needs under an orderly marketing agreement for ammonium paratungstate and tungstic acid. In 1988, the European Community investigated charges that China and So. Korea were dumping tungsten derivatives at artificially low prices, hurting European producers.

The International Tungsten Industry Association was established in February 1988. Its mandate included: compiling and publishing international tungsten statistics, promoting tungsten use, monitoring ecological issues, and organizing seminars.

World Concentrate Production of Tungsten   In Metric Tons of Contained Tungsten[3]

Year	Japan	Argentina	Australia	Bolivia	Brazil	Burma	China	Rep. of Korea	Canada	Portugal	Spain	Thailand	USSR	United States	World Total
1983	475	41	2,015	2,449	1,026	930	12,500	2,480	328	1,183	517	562	9,100	980	40,925
1984	477	37	1,709	1,893	1,037	1,096	13,500	2,702	3,715	1,509	565	741	9,100	1,203	46,148
1985	568	17	1,971	1,643	1,090	945	15,000	2,579	3,197	1,755	458	586	9,200	996	46,513
1986[1]	579	25	1,600	1,095	875	715	15,000	2,455	1,416	1,637	495	475	9,200	780	42,656
1987[2]	170	25	1,150	500	672	425	18,000	2,500	—	1,500	100	660	9,200	34	40,232

[1] Preliminary.   [2] Estimate.   [3] Conversion Factors: WO$_3$ to W, multiply by 0.7931; 60% WO$_3$ to W, multiply by 0.4758.
Source: Bureau of Mines

T.706

Salient Statistics of Tungsten in the U.S.   In Metric Tons of Contained Tungsten

Year	Net Import Reliance as a % of Apparent Consumption	Production[1]	Shipments from Mines[1]	Total Consumption	Tool	Steel Stainless & Heat Assisting	Alloy Steel[3]	Super-alloys	Cutting & Wear Resistant Materials	Pdt's. Made from Metal Powder	Miscellaneous	Chemicals & Ceramic	Exports	Consumers & Dealers	Producers[1]
1984	70	1,203	1,173	8,577	516	81	38	5	6,386	2,036	983	139	129	959	46
1985	68	996	983	6,838	326	76	19	13	5,033	1,858	674	85	124	1,077	60
1986	70	780	817	4,804	303	73	24	176	4,431	1,000	1,669	28	34	502	21
1987[2]	80	34	34	5,506	306	68	28	212	3,911	N.A.	2,662	41	2	329	21
1988[4]				7,000					4,200		2,500			500	

[1] Primary concentrates.   [2] Preliminary.   [3] Other than tool.   [4] Estimate.   *Source: Bureau of Mines*

T.707

U.S. Imports[1] of Tungsten Ores & Concentrates and Ferrotungsten   In Metric Tons[4] (Tungsten Content)

Year	Australia	Bolivia	Brazil	Canada	South Korea	Mexico	Portugal	Spain	Thailand	Peru	Total 1,000 Pounds	Value Mil. $	Austria	Portugal	China	Total 1,000 Lbs.
1983	28	662	78	649	117	215	339	—	142	199	2,861	25.7	25	19		48
1984	133	1,302	149	1,464	16	196	606	22	774	605	5,807	51.7	93	65		285
1985	414	627	69	1,371	4	183	555	11	472	282	4,746	36.7	27	41		93
1986	192	609	8	61	—	173	202	—	264	436	2,522	13.8	85	14	75	185
1987[2]	65	750	—	312	—	227	422	16	418	362	4,414	24.0	40	15	220	300
1988[4]											7,000					

[1] Imports for consumption.   [2] Preliminary.   [3] Estimate.   *Source: Bureau of Mines*

T.708

Tungsten Prices   In U.S. Dollars

Year	U.S.[1] Markets	European Markets	Total (Mil. $)	Avg. per Unit of WO$_3$	Avg. per Kilogram of Tungsten	Year	U.S.[1] Markets	European[1] Markets	Total (Mil. $)	Avg. per Unit of WO$_3$	Avg. per Kilogram of Tungsten
1982	106.00	107.00	22.1	111.06	14.00	1985	68.00	71.00	9.1	73.77	9.30
1983	85.00	81.00	10.5	82.17	10.36	1986	46.00	53.00	5.8	56.04	7.07
1984	85.00	87.00	13.4	90.63	11.43	1987[3]	50.00	52.00	.2	50.34	6.35

[1] Conc., Stu WO$_3$, Average (a short ton unit [stu] of tungsten trioxide [WO$_3$] contains 15,862 pounds of tungsten).   [2] Values apply to finished concentrate & are in some instances f.o.b. custom mill.   [3] Preliminary.   *Source: Bureau of Mines*

T.709

Turkeys

The 1988 U.S. turkey crop was almost 6 percent higher than in 1987, as first-quarter production was up 25 percent over a year earlier. Producers' net returns in 1988 were a negative 2.5 cents/lb. Negative returns were the result of heavy production increases during first-half 1988. Returns were positive in the second half of the year, as production decreased. North Carolina accounted for nearly 20 percent of domestic turkey production, while California and Minnesota were also major producers.

U.S. turkey exports were expected to be around 47-48 million pounds, up nearly 50 percent from 1987 levels. However, higher prices were likely to mean lower exports in 1989. Egypt, West Germany, and Mexico were all major importers of U.S. turkeys. Egypt dramatically increased its purchases of U.S. turkeys over the 1987 level. West Germany reclassified seasoned turkey into a higher EC duty category, raising the price of U.S. turkeys to non-competitive levels in that country.

U.S. per capita consumption of turkeys was expected to be 11 percent higher in 1988. This was in line with a steady uptrend in poultry consumption. Turkey consumption has become more evenly distributed over the course of the year than it once was. In 1988, less than 40 percent of turkey consumption occurred in the fourth quarter, the traditional holiday demand season.

In 1960, 57 percent of annual turkey consumption was in the fourth quarter. This change is due in part to the availability of turkey in other forms throughout the year.

Ending turkey stocks for 1988 were expected to be around 200 million pounds, about 30 percent below the 1987 level.

Wholesale hen turkey prices in the Eastern region averaged 61 cents/lb. in 1988, 5 percent higher than in 1987. Although prices were relatively low at the beginning of the year, they began to rise in the second quarter, when it appeared that production would be lower in the second half of the year. Prices in the second and third quarters averaged over 70 cents/lb. Prices came back down somewhat in December, as consumers purchased fewer frozen turkeys because of less Thanksgiving promotions than the previous year.

U.S. turkey production was expected to expand 2-4 percent in 1989. Net returns were likely to be negative in early-1989 because of high feed costs, but were expected to turn positive in the last two quarters. Although retail prices were expected to be higher for all of 1989, more Thanksgiving specials were anticipated, due to production increases in the second half. World production of turkeys was forecast to rise 2 percent in 1989. The U.S. was expected to continue as the leading producer.

Salient Statistics of Turkeys in the U.S.

Year	Turkey-Feed Price Ratio[3] Lbs.	(Breeds) Poults Placed — In Millions	Number Raised	(Liveweight) Produced Million - Lbs. -	Farm Price ¢ Lb.	Value of Production Million $	Production	Commercial Storage Jan. 1 — Million Pounds	Exports & Shipments	Military	Consumption Civilian Total	Per Capita Lb.	Production Costs Liveweight Feed	Production Costs Liveweight Total	Total Costs	Wholesale Ready-to-Cook 3-Regions Composite Price
1977	3.8	148.4	136.4	2,563	35.5	910	2,023	203	56	11	1,992	9.3	22.6	31.6	51.4	56.2
1978	4.6	157.5	138.9	2,655	43.6	1,157	2,098	168	57	15	2,019	9.2	22.1	31.7	51.7	68.8
1979	4.2	180.0	156.5	2,958	41.1	1,214	2,343	175	57	19	2,204	9.9	25.3	35.8	58.2	67.0
1980	3.6	188.7	164.9	3,077	41.3	1,272	2,425	240	81	16	2,370	10.5	26.1	37.1	61.0	66.0
1981	3.1	187.3	159.9	3,264	38.2	1,248	2,574	198	68	15	2,450	10.7	30.2	41.2	66.1	64.0
1982	3.3	184.2	164.5	3,175	39.5	1,255	2,522	238	56	12	2,489	10.8	24.5	36.3	60.1	63.6
1983	3.0	182.1	170.7	3,336	38.0	1,269	2,635	204	54	13	2,609	11.2	26.6	39.8	65.4	63.5
1984	3.9	184.2	171.2	3,386	48.9	1,655	2,685	162	33	13	2,676	11.4	29.0	42.0	69.0	72.0
1985	4.5	197.8	185.3	3,702	49.1	1,819	2,942	125	34	13	2,870	12.1	21.4	35.1	60.1	77.3
1986[1]	4.1	225.4	207.2	4,142	47.1	1,952	3,271	150	31	10	3,212	13.3	21.1	34.8	59.9	75.2
1987[2]	3.9	318.0	240.4	4,888	34.8	1,701	3,828	178	37	15	3,686	15.1	19.4	33.1	57.6	57.0
1988[2]	3.1		246.2				4,065	282	52		4,101	16.7				

[1] Preliminary. [2] Estimate. [3] Lbs. of feed = in value to 1 lb. of turkey live weight. *Source: Economic Research Service, U.S.D.A.* T.710

Turkey Per Capita Consumption in the U.S. by Quarters   In Pounds

Year	First	Second	Third	Fourth	Total	Year	First	Second	Third	Fourth	Total
1981	1.6	1.9	2.5	4.6	10.7	1985	2.1	2.3	2.9	4.9	12.1
1982	1.8	2.1	2.6	4.3	10.7	1986[1]	2.4	2.5	3.2	5.3	13.4
1983	2.1	2.2	2.5	4.4	11.2	1987[1]	2.6	3.0	3.5	6.0	15.1
1984	2.0	2.2	2.7	4.5	11.4	1988[1]	3.2	3.6			

[1] Preliminary. *Source: Economic Research Service, U.S.D.A.* T.711

U.S. Basis of Turkey-Feed Price Ratio   In Pounds[1]

Year	Jan.	Feb.	Mar.	Apr.	May	June	July	Aug.	Sept.	Oct.	Nov.	Dec.	Average
1985	4.7	3.8	3.7	3.7	3.7	3.9	4.2	4.5	5.0	5.5	5.5	5.5	4.5
1986	3.4	3.4	3.5	3.5	3.8	4.3	4.5	4.6	4.7	4.9	4.8	4.0	4.1
1987	3.3	3.4	3.6	3.5	3.3	3.4	3.1	3.0	2.9	2.8	3.1	3.6	3.9
1988[2]	2.8	2.6	2.5	2.7	2.8	3.0	2.9	3.1	3.4	3.6			

[1] Pounds of feed equal in value to one pound of turkey liveweight.   [2] Preliminary.   *Source: Agricultural Statistics Board, U.S.D.A.*

Wholesale Price of Turkeys[3] (Hens, 8–16 lbs.) N.Y.   In Cents per Pound

Year	Jan.	Feb.	Mar.	Apr.	May	June	July	Aug.	Sept.	Oct.	Nov.	Dec.	Avg.	Yearly Average Price — 4-Region Retail	Farm Price[2]
1977	72.5	70.2	68.8	68.8	69.0	70.1	72.1	73.2	73.6	74.6	75.5	78.2	72.2		35.5
1978	78.5	78.5	78.9	79.0	82.2	86.1	86.8	87.0	87.0	89.1	91.6	90.7	84.6		43.6
1979	91.0	90.8	90.0	89.5	90.9	91.0	91.0	91.5	91.4	93.1	94.5	92.9	91.5		41.9
1980[1]	62.3	57.8	56.8	54.1	53.3	55.5	63.3	67.2	74.5	77.0	75.0	67.0	63.6		40.0
1981	59.4	60.7	63.8	61.2	63.5	66.2	66.8	61.8	59.5	56.4	57.3	51.7	60.7	97.7	38.4
1982	53.6	55.8	56.0	55.8	58.8	61.8	64.1	64.1	68.0	69.6	67.2	54.2	60.8	92.6	39.5
1983	53.6	54.9	56.0	54.4	56.6	60.9	58.5	57.6	65.0	65.1	67.0	76.1	60.5	91.7	46.6
1984	72.2	64.7	66.1	67.0	66.8	67.0	68.6	72.4	76.2	82.6	91.5	97.3	74.4	98.7	48.0
1985	74.0	65.6	67.0	64.6	62.6	68.1	72.8	78.4	82.4	90.2	93.1	86.9	75.5	105.2	47.2
1986	60.3	61.7	63.9	64.6	67.1	73.8	77.9	80.5	81.2	83.2	80.7	71.1	72.2	106.6	44.4
1987	55.3	58.5	60.3	58.3	55.3	55.7	56.3	56.1	56.1	54.7	60.7	66.5	57.8	101.2	34.3
1988	52.8	47.1	47.0	46.9	49.2	57.1	70.8	70.5	76.5	80.0					

[1] Prior to 1980 prices are for frozen eviscerated tom turkeys (N.Y.C.); heaviest weights.   [2] Live weight.   [3] Ready-to-cook.
Source: Economic Research Service, U.S.D.A.   T.713

Certified Federally Inspected Turkey Slaughter in the U.S.   In Millions of Lbs.

Year	Jan.	Feb.	Mar.	Apr.	May	June	July	Aug.	Sept.	Oct.	Nov.	Dec.	Total
1974	97.3	59.8	58.9	80.1	113.2	159.7	213.1	237.2	220.2	261.1	215.2	119.9	1,836
1975	64.9	47.1	54.4	68.7	81.9	138.4	193.2	203.3	229.0	257.5	220.2	157.5	1,716
1976	76.3	61.7	68.6	79.9	106.5	182.2	213.9	243.8	252.8	256.6	261.5	146.4	1,950
1977	70.5	58.7	80.3	78.9	110.0	176.5	189.6	244.4	238.2	250.3	246.8	148.2	1,892
1978	81.8	59.7	86.3	80.8	129.3	189.5	199.9	248.8	230.9	271.2	248.9	156.3	1,983
1979	99.3	77.2	95.0	112.3	157.3	195.9	219.2	267.7	233.0	297.5	261.9	165.5	2,182
1980		378.6			528.3			711.6			713.9		2,232
1981		398.1			553.2			785.2			772.6		2,509
1982		410.4			527.9			761.5			759.1		2,459
1983		462.2			581.5			760.3			759.0		2,563
1984		432.3			589.3			777.2			775.3		2,574
1985		482.1			628.3			854.6			834.8		2,800
1986		174.6	193.6	205.2	236.4	275.8	307.6	299.4	331.4	365.8	307.1	248.2	3,133
1987	215.4	211.9	241.9	255.0	274.2	330.1	358.8	357.4	383.9	411.0	373.5	297.0	3,717
1988[1]	254.6	266.9	314.0	276.6	331.2	372.4	322.4	377.3	365.7	372.2			

[1] Preliminary.   *Source: Economic Research Service, U.S.D.A.*   T.714

Storage Stocks of Turkeys (Frozen) in the United States   In Millions of Pounds

Year	Jan. 1	Feb. 1	Mar. 1	Apr. 1	May 1	June 1	July 1	Aug. 1	Sept. 1	Oct. 1	Nov. 1	Dec. 1
1977	203.4	190.3	167.8	142.3	130.3	138.2	201.4	253.6	329.9	409.3	444.5	269.4
1978	167.9	168.2	136.6	113.0	101.1	103.9	152.8	213.6	301.2	373.3	425.4	236.2
1979	175.1	170.7	154.7	135.7	128.0	153.1	200.9	272.5	382.5	432.3	445.5	281.2
1980	240.0	246.8	225.0	208.9	206.6	233.8	286.6	325.8	384.0	398.8	420.2	257.6
1981	198.0	208.3	207.9	220.7	228.7	256.2	327.3	400.8	466.0	532.1	528.1	305.1
1982	238.4	236.9	236.4	232.8	—	—	281.7	—	—	435.8	—	—
1983	203.9	193.8	187.7	185.3	192.3	210.5	255.7	323.5	384.3	432.2	460.1	251.6
1984	161.8	161.5	145.8	144.4	142.2	180.9	226.3	278.2	331.3	390.6	415.4	195.7
1985	125.3	124.1	129.5	131.1	157.0	183.7	243.3	304.7	387.8	444.5	484.1	208.2
1986	150.2	159.2	163.6	150.5	188.9	229.5	297.8	388.1	449.3	511.6	543.2	249.0
1987	178.2	198.1	211.4	226.0	250.8	298.1	381.6	472.7	560.0	640.8	629.9	321.5
1988[1]	282.4	299.3	335.1	353.3	384.4	422.4	467.3	506.7	561.2	583.1	594.7	309.2

[1] Preliminary.   *Source: Crop Reporting Board, U.S.D.A.*   T.712

Uranium

U.S. spot prices for uranium have descended since 1979, the year of the nuclear accident at Three Mile Island. The average U.S. spot market price in 1988 was $14.55 per pound, down from $16.85 in 1987 and well under 1979's $42.57, according to NUEXCO, the nuclear fuel trading firm in Colorado.

U.S. uranium production in 1988 was estimated at 13.5 million pounds, up from 12.5 million the year before, but well below levels that prevailed in the early 1980s. Five years earlier, in 1983, U.S. uranium output was 21.2 million pounds. Sluggish demand, coupled with large inventories and the availability of cheap imports, has hurt the U.S. industry.

The U.S. is an importer of uranium, and net imports were estimated at 9.7 million pounds in 1987 and 12 million in 1986. Import data for 1988 were not available at this writing. Canada is the major U.S. supplier, while South Africa remains a supplier, despite U.S. trade restrictions. In 1986, Congress passed a South African sanctions bill which, among other provisions, prohibited U.S. imports of South African uranium ore and oxide.

The U.S. also exports small quantities of uranium, mainly to Asian countries under long-term contracts to provide uranium fuel, as well as nuclear reactors.

In 1988, two U.S. uranium/vanadium operations were closed, due to low uranium demand and prices. Atlas Corporation shut down its uranium/vanadium mill in Moab, Utah, and said that the mill's decommissioning and the reclamation of tailings were likely to take 6 to 7 years. The mill had been maintained at a cost of $1.5-$2 million annually in recent years. Many of the mill's 180 employees were to remain to decommission it.

Rio Algon Mining Corporation announced that it was shutting down its Lisbon vanadium mine in Utah, where 150 workers were employed.

In 1988, the re-election of Prime Minister Mulroney's Conservative party as Canada's majority government meant that Canada would implement the U.S.-Canada free trade agreement. There was some concern in the U.S. that the agreement would hurt the domestic uranium industry, since Canadian uranium, which is relatively inexpensive, would be brought in without restrictions. U.S. uranium producers were continuing their lawsuit against the Department of Energy to enforce enrichment restrictions on foreign uranium to help maintain a viable domestic industry.

Canada is the world's leading uranium producer, with annual output of about 30 million pounds, and is followed by the U.S., South Africa, Australia, and Central Africa.

In 1988, four Japanese electric power companies announced they would not extend their long-term uranium contracts with South African and Namibian suppliers. The utilities were expected to turn to Australia, Canada, and the U.S. for their supplies.

Free-World Production of Uranium Oxide (U$_3$O$_8$) Concentrate   In Thousands of Short Tons

Year	Argentina	Australia	Canada	Spain	Namibia	Central Africa	France	Portugal	Niger	Brazil	Sweden	South Africa	United States	World Total
1979	.2	.9	8.9		5.0		3.1		4.7	0		6.2	18.7	49.6
1980	.2	2.0	9.3		5.3		3.4		5.3	0		8.0	21.8	57.2
1981	.2	3.7	10.0		5.2		3.3		5.7	.1		8.0	19.2	57.1
1982	.2	5.7	10.5		4.9		3.7		5.5	.4		7.6	13.4	53.7
1983	.3	4.8	9.8		4.8		4.2		5.2	.4		7.5	10.6	49.3
1984		5.7	14.5		4.8	5.5	4.1					7.5	7.5	50.4
1985		4.3	14.2		4.5	5.3	4.2					6.3	5.7	45.2
1986[2]		5.4	15.3		4.6	5.2	4.3					6.0	7.0	48.4
1987[2]		4.9	16.7		4.6	5.0	4.3					5.2	6.3	47.4

[1] Less than 50 tons.   [2] Preliminary.   *Source: Bureau of Mines, Dept. of Energy; NUEXCO.*   T.720

Month–End Uranium (U$_3$O$_8$) Transaction Values[1]

Year	Jan.	Feb.	Mar.	Apr.	May	June	July	Aug.	Sept.	Oct.	Nov.	Dec.
1976	—	—	—	—	39.60	39.70	39.70	40.40	40.30	40.60	40.70	40.70
1977	41.30	41.30	41.40	41.50	42.80	42.90	43.00	42.60	42.50	42.80	42.90	42.90
1978	43.10	43.30	43.70	43.60	43.60	43.20	43.30	43.40	43.40	43.60	43.40	43.70
1979	43.60	43.80	43.70	43.40	43.60	43.70	43.70	43.60	43.60	43.60	43.50	42.30
1980	42.00	39.30	38.60	38.40	37.90	37.60	37.30	31.60	30.60	29.00	28.70	27.70
1981	27.20	27.20	27.00	25.70	25.70	24.50	24.40	24.30	23.90	24.10	24.10	24.00
1982	24.00	23.70	23.40	22.60	22.70	21.50	20.30	19.10	17.30	17.00	17.55	18.80
1983	19.35	20.00	21.35	21.40	22.35	22.45	23.50	23.60	23.65	23.65	23.85	23.85
1984	23.05	22.50	19.25	17.90	17.00	16.50	16.60	16.40	16.55	16.05	15.90	15.90
1985	16.20	15.70	15.05	14.90	14.45	14.60	14.75	15.10	15.10	15.75	15.80	16.55
1986	16.55	16.70	16.70	17.10	17.15	17.20	17.50	17.45	17.35	17.25	17.30	17.35
1987	17.35	16.90	16.95	17.00	17.20	17.10	17.30	17.55	18.20	18.05	17.80	17.20

[1] Transaction value is a weighted average price of recent natural uranium sales transactions, based on prices paid in transactions closed within the previous three-month period for which delivery is scheduled within one year of the transaction date; at least 10 transactions; and transactions involving a sum total of at least 2 million pounds of U$_3$O$_8$ equivalent.   *Source: NUEXCO.*

Vanadium

The domestic vanadium industry received a severe blow in 1988, when the Supreme Court overturned a Tenth Circuit Court of Appeals ruling stating that the uranium industry was entitled to protection from foreign enriched uranium. The decision was important because a significant number of U.S. uranium mills have vanadium recovery circuits.

The Supreme Court agreed with the U.S. government's opinion, as argued by the Environmental Protection Agency, that since the accident at Three Mile Island, the domestic uranium industry was not viable and therefore faced no threat to its livelihood.

The uranium-vanadium producers argued that the U.S. had become dependent on foreign supplies of vanadium and should look to protect the domestic industry for strategic purposes. It was expected that in 1989 Western senators would try to pass legislation to place duties against a certain proportion of U.S. vanadium and ferrovanadium imports.

Vanadium prices in Europe were up sharply in 1988, and ferrovanadium prices rallied up through the $20.00 a kilogram level. Vanadium pentoxide prices were also up to $3.60/kilogram. Most market observers said that the price strength was brought about by sharply in-creased buying by the Soviets, who have switched from their traditional role as net exporters of vanadium and ferrovanadium to net importers. Another factor in rising prices, according to industry sources, was the large-scale cancellation of export contracts by the Chinese.

While vanadium and ferrovanadium have been exempted from sanctions enacted against other U.S. imports from South Africa, the item is still a public relations problem for the five companies that are known to conduct mining operations in that country. South Africa is the world's largest producer of vanadium. Newmont Mining Corp Ltd. announced that it had sold its interests in several South African operations, including Highveld Steel and Vanadium Corp. Ltd. It said the divestiture was part of an ongoing effort to dispose of all its South African assets. Other firms with mining interests in South Africa are Phelps Dodge and Strategic Minerals Group.

Various metals that are interchangeable with vanadium are columbium, molybdenum, manganese, titanium, and tungsten. So far, there is no substitute for vanadium in aerospace titanium alloys.

World Production of Vanadium from Ores and Concentrates   In Short Tons (of Contained Vanadium)

Year	USSR	Chile	China	Finland	Aus-tralia	Norway	South West Africa[1]	South Africa	United States[1]	Other[4]	World Total
1978	10,000	760	2,200	3,092	—	510	485	12,400	4,272	1,697	35,416
1979	10,000	510	4,000	3,051	—	630	—	13,600	5,520	2,337	39,648
1980	10,500	300	5,000	3,135	—	540	—	16,428	4,806	2,230	42,939
1981	10,500	140	5,000	3,431	77	380	—	13,908	5,126	2,587	41,149
1982	10,500	—	5,000	3,470	25	120	—	12,911	4,098	2,267	38,391
1983	10,500	—	5,000	3,516	—	—	—	9,737	2,171	1,671	32,595
1984	10,500	—	5,000	3,376	—	—	—	13,798	1,617	2,471	36,762
1985[2]	10,500	—	5,000	2,350	—	—	—	15,449	N.A.	3,535	36,834
1986[3]	10,600	—	5,000	—	—	—	—	17,200	N.A.	4,292	37,092
1987[3]	10,500		5,000					17,000			32,500

[1] Recoverable vanadium.   [2] Preliminary.   [3] Estimate.   [4] Production from petroleum residues, ashes, & spent catalysts. Mainly in Japan & the United States.   *Source: Bureau of Mines*   T.722

Salient Statistics of Vanadium in the United States   In Short Tons of Contained Vanadium

Year	Vanadium in Ores & Concentrates — Mine Production	Recoverable Vanadium	Prod. of Vanad. Pentoxide (V_2O_5)	Consumer Stocks Dec. 31	Tool Steel	Cast Irons	High Strength Low Alloy	Non-ferrous Alloys	Chemicals	Carbon	Full Alloy	Total	$ Per Lb. Van. Pentoxide[3]	General Imports[5]	Ore & Concentrates[4]	Ferro-Vanadium (Gross Weight)
1978	4,446	1,309														
1979	5,841	880														
1980	5,832	4,806	9,829	879	653	54	1,986	728	59	1,114	1,420	6,139	3.54	1,786	960	803
1981	5,852	5,126	11,367	683	584	42	2,123	852	56	1,278	1,832	6,863	3.52	2,435	463	435
1982	4,093	4,098	8,689	326	273	20	1,148	461	29	698	811	3,496	3.50	1,112	2,000	326
1983	N.A.	2,171	4,344	374	426	10	966	505	19	577	716	3,277	3.50	58	2,802	775
1984	N.A.	1,617	4,678	449	610	18	1,636	905	22	683	816	4,761	3.50	633	4,029	469
1985	N.A.	N.A.	N.A.	360	522	22	1,383	788	14	1,135	944	4,883	3.50	303	1,852	454
1986[1]	N.A.	N.A.	N.A.	314	510	24	1,136	652	11	1,026	856	4,308	3.50	2,013	1,973	513
1987[1]												4,520	3.50	2,115	2,000	550

[1] Preliminary.   [2] Represent about 90% of the total consumption.   [3] Dealer export.   [4] Also includes fused vanadium oxide.   [5] Ores, slags, residues.   [6] Estimate.   *Source: Bureau of Mines*   T.723

Wheat

World wheat production in 1988/89 was projected by USDA at 503 million tonnes, near the previous season's 504 million. The U.S. spring wheat crop was severely reduced by drought in the upper Great Plains. The Canadian crop was cut by drought and fell 40 percent to 15.7 million tonnes. The USSR, the largest producer, harvested 88 million tonnes, 6 percent above 1987/88. China's crop of 87.5 million tonnes was close to the previous season's. The European Community produced 75.7 million tonnes, 6 percent more than in 1987/88. Eastern European countries produced a total of 45.1 million tonnes, up 13 percent. India's crop of 45 million tonnes was down slightly from 1987/88. Argentina's crop, cut by drought, was 7.4 million tonnes, down from 9 million.

Global use of wheat in 1988/89 was placed at 534 million tonnes, unchanged from a year earlier. Soviet consumption was put at 100 million tonnes, down slightly. Wheat use in China was placed at 106 million tonnes, the same as the previous year. While U.S. consumption slipped, foreign use was projected to rise slightly.

World wheat trade was projected to decline 6 percent to 108.4 million tonnes. The U.S. export market share was 38 percent, while the EC's was 29 percent. Canadian exports were projected at 11.7 million tonnes, 50 percent less than in 1987/88. Canada's export market share was expected to fall to only 11 percent from 20 percent. Argentine exports were 3.2 million tonnes, 14 percent less than a year earlier. Australia's exports were 12 million tonnes, up from 10 million.

The USSR, a major importer, was expected to purchase 13 million tonnes, 40 percent less than in 1987/88. China's imports were put at 15 million tonnes, the same as a year earlier.

Lower world production and a smaller carry-in meant that 1988/89 ending stocks would fall to 115.3 million tonnes, 2 percent below a year earlier. The trend in recent years has been to tighter world inventories.

U.S. wheat production in 1988/89 was estimated at 1.8 billion bushels, 14 percent less than the previous season. Harvested acreage was 53.2 million, compared to 55.9 million in 1987/88 and 60.7 million in 1986/87. The national average yield fell in 1988 to 34 bu./acre, down from 37.6 bushels in 1987. Production of hard red winter wheat, grown primarily in the Plains states, was 880 million bushels, 14 percent less than a year earlier. The soft red winter crop, produced mostly in the Corn Belt and the Southeast, was 474 million bushels, 36 percent more than a year earlier. In some important states like Missouri and Illinois, planted acreage expanded.

The hard red spring wheat crop, grown in the upper Great Plains, was cut by heat and drought. The hard red spring crop was only 181 million bushels, 48 percent less than in 1987. North Dakota's crop fell 62 percent, while Montana's was reduced by 73 percent. The durum crop, which is processed into pasta, fell to 45 million bushels, down 52 percent. The white wheat crop, grown in the Northwest, was 231 million bushels, 7 percent more than the previous year.

In 1988/89, U.S. carry-in stocks of 1.26 billion bushels were 31 percent below the previous season. Total wheat supplies were 3.09 billion bushels, down 22 percent from 1987/88. Food use of wheat was projected at 730 million bushels, 2 percent more than the previous season. With a reduced set-aside requirement in 1989, estimated seed use was raised to 100 million bushels, from 85 million in 1987/88. Feed use was put at 230 million bushels, 20 percent below a year earlier.

Having trended lower in the mid-1980s, U.S. wheat exports expanded in 1987/88. The USSR emerged as a major buyer, taking over 12 million tonnes, compared to none the previous season.

In 1988/89, U.S. exports were forecast at 1.5 billion bushels, 6 percent less than in 1987/88. In late 1988, the U.S. and USSR signed a new long-term grain agreement, under which the Soviets were obligated to purchase 4 million tonnes of wheat annually and could buy more without the permission of the U.S. government. The primary markets for U.S. wheat were China, the USSR, Japan, Egypt and India. The USDA aggressively used the Export Enhancement Program to promote wheat sales to the USSR, China, Egypt, and India, among others.

U.S. wheat ending stocks in 1988/89 were forecast at 534 million bushels, 48 percent less than the previous year. Stocks outside of government programs were expected to total only 109 million bushels, sharply below 511 million a year earlier. Commodity Credit Corporation stocks were also expected to decline sharply.

U.S. Government Program

The loan rate for 1989-crop wheat is $2.06/bu., down from $2.21 in 1988. The target price was lowered to $4.10/bu. from $4.23. Base acreage must be reduced by 10 percent in 1989, compared to 27.5 percent in 1988.

Futures Markets

Wheat futures and options are traded on the Chicago Board of Trade, Kansas City Board of Trade and the Minneapolis Grain Exchange. Feed wheat futures are traded on the Winnipeg Commodity Exchange.

World Production of Wheat In Thousands of Metric Tons

Crop Year	Argentina	Australia	Canada	China	France	West Germany	India	Italy	Pakistan	Spain	Turkey	United Kingdom	USSR	United States	World Total[1]
1984–5	13,200	18,700	21,200	87,800	33,241	10,223	45,500	10,005	10,882	5,800	13,300	14,957	68,600	70,600	512,000
1985–6	8,500	16,200	24,300	85,800	29,312	9,866	44,100	8,516	11,703	5,326	12,700	12,045	78,100	66,001	499,800
1986–7	8,900	16,100	31,400	90,000	26,555	10,406	47,100	9,000	13,900	4,292	14,000	14,000	92,300	56,925	530,200
1987–8[2]	9,000	12,400	26,000	87,800	(EC-12-71,500)		45,600	12,000			13,000		83,300	57,356	504,300
1988–9[1]	7,400	13,000	15,700	87,500	(EC-12-75,000)		45,000	12,600			15,000		88,000	49,317	502,500

[1] Estimated. [2] Preliminary. *Source: Foreign Agricultural Service, U.S.D.A.*

T.724

World Wheat Supply & Demand   In Millions of Metric Tons/Hectares

	Area Harvested	Yield	Production	World Trade	Utilization Total	Ending Stocks	Stocks as % of Util
1983/84	228.8	2.14	489.3	102.0	474.1	145.1	30.6
1984/85	231.0	2.22	512.0	107.0	493.2	163.9	33.2
1985/86	229.3	2.18	499.8	85.0	495.9	167.8	33.8
1986/87	227.8	2.33	530.2	90.7	523.0	175.1	33.5
1987/88[1]	219.6	2.30	504.3	104.6	533.9	145.5	27.3
1988/89[2]	219.1	2.29	502.5	93.1	535.2	112.8	21.1

[1] Preliminary.   [2] Estimate.   *Source: Foreign Agricultural Service, U.S.D.A.*   T.724a

Salient Statistics of Wheat in the United States

Crop Year	Planting Intentions 1,000 Acres	Acreage Harvested Winter 1,000 Acres	Acreage Harvested Spring 1,000 Acres	Acreage Harvested All	Avg.—All Yield Per Acre In Bushels	Farm Disposition Used for Seed (Million Bushels)	Farm Disposition Fed to Livestock (Million Bushels)	Sold	Value of Production Ths. $	Foreign Trade[5] Domestic Exports[2] Million Bushels	Foreign Trade[5] Imports[3] Million Bushels	Per Capita[1] Consumption Flour In Pounds	Per Capita[1] Consumption Cereal In Pounds
1983–4	76,419	47,584	13,806	61,390	39.4	No Longer Available			8,532,790	1,429	4.0	118	3.1
1984–5	79,213	51,513	15,415	66,928	38.8	No Longer Available			8,755,033	1,424	9.4	118	3.1
1985–6	75,575	47,953	16,781	64,734	37.5				7,652,444	915	16.0	123	3.1
1986–7	72,068	43,205	17,518	60,723	34.4				5,044,347	1,004	21.1	124	3.1
1987–8[4]	65,834	39,347	16,613	55,960	37.7				5,376,264	1,592	16.3	128	
1988–9[4]	65,725	39,785	13,485	53,270	34.0				6,705,000	1,450	15.0		

[1] Civilian only.   [2] Includes flour milled from imported wheat.   [3] Total wheat, flour & other products.   [4] Preliminary.   [5] Year beginning June.
Source: Economic Research Service, U.S.D.A.   T.728

Supply and Distribution of Wheat in the United States   In Millions of Bushels

Crop Yr. Beginning June	Stocks, June 1 On Farms	Stocks, June 1 Mills, Elevators[3]	Total Stocks	Production	Imports[1]	Total Supply	Food	Seed	Industry	Residual[5]	Feed (On Farms Where Grown)	Total Domestic Disap.	Exports[4]	Total Disappearance
1983–4	668.9	846.1	1,515.1	2,419.8	4.0	3,939	642.6	100.0	—		369.1	1,111.7	1,428.6	2,540
1984–5	591.7	806.7	1,398.6	2,594.8	9.4	4,003	651.0	98.0	—		404.5	1,153.5	1,424.1	2,578
1985–6	582.1	843.2	1,425.2	2,425.1	16.0	3,866	674.4	93.0	—		278.5	1,045.9	915.4	1,961
1986–7	681.1	1,223.9	1,905.0	2,091.6	21.1	4,018	696.0	84.0	—		413.3	1,193.3	1,003.5	2,197
1987–8[1]	560.0	1,260.9	1,820.9	2,107.5	16.3	3,942	719.0	85.0	—		280.1	1,084.2	1,592.1	2,676
1988–9[2]	520.0	735.7	1,255.7	1,812.1	15.0	3,083	735	100	—		270	1,105	1,450	2,555

[1] Preliminary.   [2] Estimated.   [3] Also warehouses and all off-farm storage not otherwise designated, including flour mills.   [4] Imports & exports are for wheat, including flour & other products in terms of wheat.   [5] Approximate feed use.   *Source: Economic Research Service, U.S.D.A.*   T.737

Stocks, Production, and Exports of Wheat, by Classes   In Millions of Bushels

Year Beginning June	Hard Spring June 1 Stocks	Hard Spring Production	Hard Spring Exports[2]	Durum[3] June 1 Stocks	Durum Production	Durum Exports[2]	Hard Winter June 1 Stocks	Hard Winter Production	Hard Winter Exports[2]	Soft Red Winter June 1 Stocks	Soft Red Winter Production	Soft Red Winter Exports[2]	White June 1 Stocks	White Production	White Exports[2]
1983–4	408	323	221	136	73	62	754	1,198	704	74	504	222	143	322	220
1984–5	314	409	183	99	103	61	745	1,251	717	74	531	253	167	301	210
1985–6	371	460	166	100	113	53	717	1,230	395	64	368	149	173	254	152
1986–7	498	451	200	121	98	82	1,009	1,018	432	79	292	115	198	232	175
1987–8[1]	490	431	255	95	93	62	973	1,021	905	77	348	160	185	216	210
1988–9[4]	391	182	220	83	46	30	572	888	710	75	473	270	135	222	220

[1] Preliminary.   [2] Includes flour made from U.S. wheat & shipments to territories.   [3] Includes "Red Durum."   [4] Estimate.
Source: Economic Research Service, U.S.D.A.   T.727

Seeded Acreage, Yield and Production of All Wheat in the United States

Year	Seeded Acreage—1,000,000 Acres Winter	Seeded Acreage Not Durum	Seeded Acreage Durum	Seeded Acreage All	Yield Per Harvested Acre—In Bushels Winter	Yield Not Durum	Yield Durum	Yield All	Production—1,000,000 Bushels Winter	Production Not Durum	Production Durum	Production All
1984	63.4	12.5	3.3	79.2	40.0	35.3	32.1	38.8	2,060.3	431.1	103.4	2,594.8
1985	57.8	14.6	3.2	75.6	38.1	35.4	36.4	37.5	1,827.6	485.0	112.5	2,425.1
1986	54.0	15.1	3.0	72.1	35.2	32.3	34.0	34.4	1,521.5	472.2	97.9	2,091.6
1987[1]	48.8	13.7	3.3	65.8	39.8	33.7	28.2	37.7	1,565.2	449.7	92.6	2,107.5
1988[2]	48.8	13.5	3.4	65.7	39.2	19.4	15.7	34.0	1,561.0	204.8	46.4	1,812.1

[1] Preliminary.   [2] Estimate.   *Source: Crop Reporting Board, U.S.D.A.*   T.726

WHEAT

Production of Winter Wheat in the United States   In Millions of Bushels

Year	Colo-rado	Idaho	Illinois	Indiana	Kansas	Michi-gan	Missouri	Mon-tana	Nebraska	Ohio	Okla-homa	Ore-gon	Pa.	Texas	Wash.	So. Dakota
1979	67.6	35.7	53.8	44.4	410.4	31.6	70.4	57.4	86.7	63.4	216.6	48.0	7.3	138.0	94.6	10.5
1980	107.2	51.9	75.4	53.9	420.0	35.2	89.0	54.8	108.3	67.1	195.0	72.0	9.3	130.0	143.0	20.9
1981	83.9	55.7	92.5	62.1	305.0	41.5	115.5	89.3	104.4	72.6	172.8	73.2	9.7	183.4	161.3	30.4
1982	81.5	53.0	67.5	43.3	458.5	23.0	74.8	80.6	101.5	51.6	227.7	59.4	8.2	144.0	125.4	36.3
1983	117.0	55.6	64.4	49.5	448.2	35.8	70.3	79.1	98.9	58.8	150.5	62.0	7.6	161.0	162.5	51.3
1984	110.4	56.7	70.4	48.3	431.2	45.6	84.1	67.0	81.0	48.4	190.8	66.2	8.4	150.0	148.8	61.2
1985	134.6	46.1	36.8	37.1	433.2	45.0	49.9	22.4	89.7	58.9	165.0	51.8	10.1	187.2	115.2	44.1
1986	92.8	51.9	36.1	30.1	336.6	30.6	18.8	64.0	76.0	48.3	150.8	53.9	9.7	120.0	102.9	57.6
1987	93.8	60.0	56.1	34.8	366.3	19.2	35.4	79.2	85.8	46.4	129.6	49.5	8.0	100.8	104.0	55.1
1988[1]	75.9	50.8	67.5	35.0	323.0	26.0	77.5	39.9	72.0	46.0	172.8	46.9	9.0	89.6	108.5	21.6

[1] Preliminary   *Source: Crop Reporting Board, U.S.D.A.*   T.734

United States Official Winter Wheat Crop Production Reports   In Thousands of Bushels

Crop Year	Previous December	May 1	June 1	July 1	August 1	Sept. 1	Current December	Final
1979–0	1,441,306	1,390,848	1,427,000	1,560,768	1,602,901	1,595,591	1,608,897	1,601,234
1980–1	1,567,817	1,711,010	1,757,170	1,848,000	1,870,000	1,878,000	1,891,251	1,895,383
1981–2	1,977,079	2,078,137	2,013,607	2,092,692	2,064,845	2,059,205	2,098,719	2,103,538
1982–3	2,128,133	2,063,336	2,131,214	2,124,854	2,095,554	2,106,149	2,108,246	2,073,560
1983–4	Discontinued	1,893,241	1,882,916	1,937,388	1,963,243	1,976,843	1,993,888	1,988,304
1984–5		1,979,366	1,972,776	2,021,918	2,045,088	2,036,028	2,060,646	2,060,266
1985–6		1,974,228	1,892,438	1,854,254	1,842,884	1,839,284	1,827,195	1,827,615
1986–7		1,603,127	1,578,277	1,553,026	1,532,526	1,532,526	1,519,143	1,521,498
1987–8		1,549,344	1,577,489	1,574,439	2,125,097	2,114,492	1,565,176	
1988–9		1,620,257	1,570,417	1,568,052	1,554,812	1,560,970		

Source: Crop Reporting Board, U.S.D.A.   T.736

Production of All Spring Wheat in the United States   In Millions of Bushels

	Durum Wheat							Other Spring Wheat									
Year	Ari-zona	Cali-fornia	Minne-sota	Mon-tana	North Dakota	South Dakota	Total Durum	Colo-rado	Idaho	Minne-sota	Mon-tana	North Dakota	Ore-gon	South Dakota	Utah	Wash-ington	Total
1979	5.3		2.8	6.8	84.5	3.6	106.7	2.6	38.4	85.8	52.3	165.1	9.3	46.0	1.6	23.4	426.2
1980	12.4	7.8	3.4	7.6	73.2	4.1	108.4	3.1	44.2	96.9	57.4	105.5	5.4	37.4	1.4	17.2	370.5
1981	18.3	14.7	5.4	11.0	130.8	5.8	185.9	4.0	34.1	134.0	72.5	197.4	4.2	52.8	1.4	7.0	509.3
1982	7.0	11.6	3.0	9.9	110.8	3.5	145.9	3.5	41.8	120.8	89.9	209.3	4.1	58.8	1.6	13.4	545.5
1983	5.0	6.3	1.2	4.1	54.3	2.1	73.0	5.1	36.1	75.1	53.7	135.0	3.6	36.4	1.4	10.1	358.5
1984	7.2	9.4	1.6	3.6	78.6	3.1	103.4	4.6	24.7	103.7	34.1	183.6	2.8	61.7	1.6	11.6	431.1
1985	3.9	7.4	1.7	1.4	95.5	2.6	112.5	4.8	25.9	130.4	26.4	212.0	4.2	64.5	1.6	13.1	485.0
1986	4.2	6.5	1.3	4.3	80.0	1.6	97.9	3.6	29.9	98.1	70.2	198.4	4.5	49.5	1.7	14.0	472.2
1987	3.8	5.1	1.2	5.3	74.1	3.0	92.6	3.6	25.5	98.4	66.7	189.1	3.4	48.6	1.7	10.3	449.7
1988[1]	4.3	5.6	.8	2.3	32.5	.8	46.4	3.3	24.7	48.3	18.0	71.3	4.9	15.6	1.2	16.1	204.8

[1] Preliminary.   *Source: Crop Reporting Board, U.S.D.A.*   T.735

Wheat Under Price Support Through the End of the Month
(Cumulative Total from Current Season's Crop)   In Millions of Bushels

Year	July	Aug.	Sept.	Oct.	Nov.	Dec.	Jan.	Feb.	Mar.	Apr.	May	June	Total
1979–0	6.5	30.1	55.6	82.8	103.3	115.5	138.2	145.4	161.0	176.4	179.4	180.5	180.5
1980–1	35.7	56.6	99.2	126.5	142.2	183.3	228.6	261.0	297.4	328.0	328.0	329.4	329.4
1981–2	84.6	164.4	254.8	296.1	314.1	344.7	392.3	411.7	427.4	443.3	444.5	445.8	
1982–3	106.7	206.5	335.2	414.0	467.2	501.1	579.1	606.1	629.4	638.6	640.9	643.4	
1983–4	196.3	335.2	357.5	462.8	494.7	520.4	571.5	595.4	619.2	627.5	629.1	630.3	
1984–5	48.8	104.9	195.5	213.4	225.6	237.7	263.5	270.2	275.7	279.7	280.1	280.8	
1985–6	269.5	414.2	567.7	679.0	714.3	740.7	786.2	803.8	813.5	825.0	827.3	828.1	
1986–7	81.7	155.7	274.6	400.5	441.6	456.0	487.9	500.7	505.6	512.6	513.5	513.4	513.4
1987–8	—	105.1	259.6	350.4	396.7	418.2	442.8	460.2	466.5	470.7	472.0	472.1	472.2
1988–9	—	60.0	85.9	91.3									

Source: Economic Research Service, U.S.D.A.   T.729

United States Grindings of Wheat by Mills   In Millions of Bushels (of 60 Pounds Each)

Year	July	Aug.	Sept.	Oct.	Nov.	Dec.	Jan.	Feb.	Mar.	Apr.	May	June	Total
1979–0	52.1	59.0	52.4	58.9	55.7	50.6	55.0	50.4	49.1	47.2	49.8	47.8	628.0
1980–1	51.8	53.0	54.8	58.4	54.6	56.9	53.9	51.1	55.3	53.4	52.2	52.6	648.0
1981–2	51.2	53.3	54.6	55.6	51.0	50.2	54.8	53.9	57.8	51.4	50.0	51.2	635.0
1982–3	53.4	57.0	55.4	57.5	54.9	55.9	55.7	53.6	60.1	54.8	59.1	57.7	675.1
1983–4	56.2	66.1	62.9	59.4	57.2	56.0	55.7	57.5	58.4	54.0	60.1	54.6	698.1
1984–5	51.8	59.2	55.2	58.7	56.6	53.4	56.7	57.4	58.8	55.3	58.1	53.9	675.1
1985–6	54.6	60.9	59.5	65.1	63.7	56.0	61.7	60.9	56.1	58.7	60.3	59.3	716.8
1986–7	61.7	67.3	67.8	71.1	67.7	65.9	61.7	61.6	63.8	63.5	67.6	66.9	786.6
1987–8[1]	63.0	65.7	65.2	68.9	66.2	61.9	58.8	57.6	60.4	57.6	64.9	63.0	753.2
1988–9[1]	63.0	69.2	65.2	69.2									

[1] Preliminary.   *Source: Bureau of the Census*   T.744

U.S. Wheat Foreign Trade and Domestic Disappearance   In Millions of Bushels

Year Begin. June	Imports (Grain Only)					Exports (Grain Only)					Domestic Disappearance				
	June–Aug.	Sep.–Nov.	Dec.–Feb.	Mar.–May	Total	June–Aug.	Sep.–Nov.	Dec.–Feb.	Mar.–May	Total	June–Aug.	Sep.–Nov.	Dec.–Feb.	Mar.–May	Total
1979–0	.7	.5	.5	.4	2.1	511	388	283	194	1,375	277	167	209	130	783
1980–1	.8	.6	.6	.5	2.5	375	379	399	360	1,514	194	243	171	174	783
1981–2	.7	.8	.7	.6	2.8	424	486	415	446	1,771	295	233	147	173	847
1982–3	1.2	3.0	2.6	.8	7.6	411	337	394	367	1,509	285	252	180	191	908
1983–4	1.1	.9	1.0	1.0	4.0	347	360	369	353	1,429	356	339	216	201	1,112
1984–5	4.6	1.8	1.2	1.8	9.4	399	486	335	204	1,424	439	337	204	174	1,154
1985–6	3.5	5.1	2.7	4.7	16.0	249	253	224	189	915	401	312	166	167	1,046
1986–7	4.3	3.6	5.9	7.3	21.1	321	263	203	217	1,004	524	223	226	220	1,193
1987–8[1]	5.1	5.1	2.7	3.5	16.3	410	309	413	461	1,592	533	180	172	200	1,084
1988–9[1]	8.6					363					473				

[1] Preliminary.   *Source: Crop Reporting Board, U.S.D.A.*   T.730

Wheat Government Loan Program Data in the United States   Loan Rates (Cents Per Bushel)

Crop Year Beginning June	Total Support Rate	National Avg.[1]	Target Rate	Corn Belt (Soft Red Winter)	Central & So. Plains (Hard Winter)	No. Plains (Spr. & Dur.)	Pacific North-West (White)	Placed Under Loan	% of Production	Acquired By CCC Under Program	Delivered To CCC	Total Stocks	Total CCC Stocks	CCC Loans	Farmer-Owned Reserve	"Free"
												Millions of Bushels				
1979–0	340	250	340	248	243	251	257	182.0	8.5	157	—	902.0	187.8	99.3	259.9	355.0
1980–1	363	300	363	300	294	302	308	331	14.0	—	—	989.1	199.7	54.6	359.6	375.2
1981–2	381	320	381	320	313	321	329	452	16.1	13	61.1	1,159	190.3	112.0	560.4	296.7
1982–3	405	355	405	356	347	357	365	646	23.0	148	9.3	1,515	192.0	65.2	1,060.6	197.3
1983–4	430	365	430	366	356	368	375	635	26.2	220	192.0	1,399	188.0	379.1	611.2	220.3
1984–5	438	330	438	332	323	334	343	284	10.9	244		1,425	377.6	175.0	657.1	215.5
1985–6	438	330	438	332	323	334	343	841	34.7	288		1,905	601.7	677.7	596.4	29.2
1986–7[2]	438	240	438	236	235	244	250	525	25.2	517		1,821	830.1	235.6	631.8	123.4
1987–8[3]	438	228	438									1,266	283.0	202.7	479.6	300.9
1988–9[3]	423	221	423									527.8				

[1] The national average loan rate at the farm as a percentage of the parity-priced wheat at the beginning of the marketing year.   [2] Preliminary.   [3] Estimate.   *Source: Agricultural Marketing Service, U.S.D.A.*   T.741

Exports of Wheat (Only) from the United States   In Millions of Bushels

Year	July	Aug.	Sept.	Oct.	Nov.	Dec.	Jan.	Feb.	Mar.	Apr.	May	June	Total
1979–0	133.3	117.8	129.6	149.0	108.9	114.9	82.7	89.5	94.7	98.3	88.6	96.2	1,305.5
1980–1	123.6	139.6	136.0	116.2	112.2	131.9	129.9	124.4	128.8	127.7	76.0	124.5	1,470.8
1981–2	138.1	145.4	194.1	156.9	127.5	137.4	124.2	138.7	159.1	147.4	114.8	155.7	1,739.3
1982–3	117.9	124.0	130.8	98.5	94.1	88.5	143.1	146.3	131.1	111.8	95.3	112.0	1,393.0
1983–4	115.8	87.5	119.2	114.8	102.3	128.4	118.3	111.0	118.7	94.3	111.7	104.8	1,326.8
1984–5	133.3	146.0	242.5	136.9	96.1	131.4	105.3	81.8	57.4	65.0	55.8	79.1	1,330.6
1985–6	63.6	85.6	72.0	85.6	81.3	60.5	68.6	67.7	60.1	54.0	46.3	79.5	824.8
1986–7	104.0	113.4	97.8	83.5	59.1	49.6	65.0	62.5	63.9	65.1	63.9	119.4	947.2
1987–8[1]	157.0	112.5	118.0	100.4	69.0	109.8	137.9	141.7	147.3	151.6	146.1	121.5	1,512.8
1988–9[1]	110.0	106.5	124.8	91.2									

[1] Preliminary.   *Source: Department of Commerce*   T.738

WHEAT

United States Wheat and Wheat Flour Imports and Exports   In Thousands of Bushels

Year Beginning June	Imports					Exports						
	Wheat		Flour (Wheat Equivalent)	Other Pdt's.[2]	Total	Public Law 480						Total Specified Gov't. Programs
	Suitable for Milling	Unfit for Human Consump-tion				Sales for Foreign Currency[3]	Long-Term $ & Conver. for Cur. Credit Sales	Gov't. to Gov't. Dona-tions[4]	Donations Thru Voluntary Relief Agencies	Foreign Donations Sec. 416	Mutual Security (A.I.D.)[5]	
1981–2	59	14	357	2,423	2,853	—	110,046	14,312	8,614	—	—	132,972
1982–3	3,901	35	624	3,036	7,596	—	113,322	22,081	8,724	—	6,805	150,932
1983–4	67	11	336	3,426	3,840	—	120,670	19,114	17,117	—	—	156,901
1984–5	4,825	3	329	4,283	9,440	—	151,605	23,188	8,930	—	2,726	186,449
1985–6[1]	9,758	71	475	4,400	14,704	—	128,438	18,322	6,172	1.84	17,124	171,905

[1] Preliminary.   [2] Includes macaroni, semolina & similar pdt's.   [3] Authorized by title, I, P.L. 480.   [4] Author, by title II, P.L. 480.   [5] Foreign Assist. Act of 1961.   *Source: Economic Research Service, U.S.D.A.*   T.732

Wheat Stocks in the United States   In Millions of Bushels

Year	On Farms				Off Farms				Total Stocks			
	Mar. 1	June 1	Sept. 1	Dec. 1	Mar. 1	June 1	Sept. 1	Dec. 1	Mar. 1	June 1	Sept. 1	Dec. 1
1985	N.A.	582.1	N.A.	N.A.	N.A.	843.2	N.A.	N.A.	1,800.8	1,425.2	3,203.5	2,643.4
1986	N.A.	681.1	1,293.0	1,063.0	N.A.	1,223.9	1,861.6	1,610.5	2,255.8	1,905.0	3,154.6	2,673.5
1987[1]	794.0	560.0	1,168.0	971.0	1,456.4	1,260.9	1,820.5	1,534.3	2,250.4	1,820.9	2,988.5	2,505.3
1988[1]	748.0	520.0	793.0		1,175.4	735.7	1,446.6		1,923.4	1,255.7	2,239.6	

[1] Preliminary.   *Source: Crop Reporting Board, U.S.D.A.*   T.731

Commercial Stocks of Domestic Wheat[1] in the United States, at First of Month   In Millions of Bushels

Year	July	Aug.	Sept.	Oct.	Nov.	Dec.	Jan.	Feb.	Mar.	Apr.	May	June
1983–4	285.0	403.1	462.1	477.0	442.0	385.4	334.9	294.9	273.0	255.1	236.6	212.4
1984–5	265.2	423.0	413.7	409.4	387.8	352.8	309.9	268.0	248.5	239.8	215.1	221.4
1985–6	312.5	434.8	474.8	510.9	504.2	473.9	446.3	435.7	413.0	400.3	399.0	407.2
1986–7	437.5	483.7	494.7	475.9	472.7	445.0	435.0	420.0	410.1	393.3	381.1	366.8
1987–8	417.8	436.5	443.7	451.9	439.9	421.4	387.1	361.1	302.6	261.2	235.6	203.7
1988–9	289.7	334.2	342.4	340.8	331.1	297.2						

[1] Domestic wheat in store in public and private elevators in 39 markets and wheat afloat in vessels or barges at lake and seaboard ports, the first Saturday of the month.   *Source: Department of Agriculture*   T.746

Comparative Average Cash Wheat Prices   In Dollars per Bushel

Crop Year— June to May	Re-ceived by U.S. Farm-ers	No. 2 Soft Red Winter Chicago	No. 1 Hd. Red Ordin. Protein Kansas City	No. 2 Soft Red Winter St. Louis	Minneapolis			No. 1 Soft Port-land Oregon	No. 2 Western White Pacific N.W.	No. 2 Soft White Toledo	Export Prices (U.S. $ per Metric Ton)				
					No. 1 Dark Northern Spring 14%	No. 1 Hard Amber Durum					Aust-ralia Std. White	Canada Vanc. No. 1 CWRS 13½%	Argen-tina F.O.B. B.A.	U.S. Gulf No. 2 H.W.	Rotter-dam C.I.F. U.S. No. 2 Hd. Winter
1982–3	3.45	3.32	3.94	3.32	4.09	4.25	4.39	3.93	3.33	160	165	166	161	187
1983–4	3.51	3.56	3.84	3.62	4.30	4.83	3.95	3.58	3.48	161	169	138	158	185
1984–5	3.39	3.51	3.74	3.57	4.06	4.44	3.82	3.44	3.42	153	166	135	153	180
1985–6	3.08	3.22	3.28	3.26	3.94	4.07	3.72	3.34	3.12	141	173	106	137	169
1986–7	2.42	2.76	2.72	2.87	3.07	3.57	2.90	2.58	2.66	120	161	88	117	148
1987–8[1]	2.64	2.89	2.96	2.95	3.15	4.13	3.06	2.74	2.94	115	134	89	114	141

[1] Preliminary.   *Source: Economic Research Service, U.S.D.A.*   T.733

Open Interest of All Wheat Futures Contracts at Chicago,[1] K.C. & Mpls.   In Millions of Bushels

Year	Jan.	Feb.	Mar.	April	May	End of Month[1]							Kansas City[3]		Minn.[2]
						June	July	Aug.	Sept.	Oct.	Nov.	Dec.	Jan. 1	July 1	Jan. 1
1984	291.5	281.3	288.9	248.4	256.7	215.3	246.6	233.0	217.9	222.5	209.9	213.3	89.0	92.8	23.7
1985	197.9	191.7	176.2	189.6	201.6	191.4	189.2	186.3	163.4	152.3	144.2	158.9	95.4	130.9	21.6
1986	167.4	162.8	164.1	183.5	167.0	190.9	178.0	165.7	191.6	165.4	143.5	115.8	63.0	101.0	23.4
1987	140.2	129.6	155.0	149.8	159.2	171.4	184.2	201.1	205.0	172.8	149.6	148.7	59.1	87.0	19.7
1988	195.1	194.4	224.2	192.0	231.0	297.1	264.1	287.7	358.2	352.9	313.1	321.9	96.3	141.9	34.3
1989													159.0		34.5

[1] Chicago Board of Trade.   [2] Minneapolis Grain Exchange.   [3] Kansas City Board of Trade.   *Source: Commodity Futures Trading Commission*   T.748

Wheat Supply and Distribution in Canada, Australia and Argentina   In Millions of Metric Tons

| | Canada (Yr. Beg. Aug. 1) | | | | | Australia (Yr. Beg. Oct. 1) | | | | | Argentina (Yr. Beg. Dec. 1) | | | | |
| | Supply | | | Disappearance | | Supply | | | Disappearance | | Supply | | | Disappearance | |
Crop Year	Stocks Aug. 1	New Crop	Total Supply	Domes-tic	Ex-ports[1]	Stocks Oct. 1	New Crop	Total Supply	Domes-tic	Ex-ports[1]	Stocks Dec. 1	New Crop	Total Supply	Domes-tic	Ex-ports[1]
1979–0	14.9	17.2	32.1	5.5	15.9	4.6	16.2	20.8	3.4	13.2	1.1	8.1	9.2	4.0	4.8
1980–1	10.7	19.3	30.0	5.2	16.3	4.3	10.9	15.2	3.5	9.6	.4	7.8	8.2	4.0	3.8
1981–2	8.6	24.8	33.4	5.2	18.4	2.0	16.4	18.4	2.6	11.0	.4	8.3	8.7	4.3	3.6
1982–3	9.7	26.7	36.4	5.1	21.4	4.8	8.9	13.7	4.1	7.3	.8	15.0	15.8	4.8	9.9
1983–4	10.0	26.5	36.5	5.5	21.8	2.3	22.0	24.3	3.4	13.3	1.1	12.8	13.9	4.7	7.8
1984–5	9.2	21.2	30.2	5.2	17.5	7.5	18.7	26.2	2.9	14.7	1.3	13.2	14.5	4.6	9.4
1985–6	7.6	24.3	31.9	5.6	17.7	8.6	16.2	24.8	2.9	16.0	.5	8.5	9.0	4.4	4.3
1986–7	8.6	31.4	40.0	6.4	20.8	5.9	16.1	22.0	2.6	15.7	.3	8.9	9.2	4.5	4.4
1987–8[2]	12.7	26.0	38.7	7.8	23.5	3.8	12.4	16.2	3.4	9.9	.2	9.0	9.2	4.7	3.7
1988–9[3]	7.3	15.7	23.0	5.1	11.7	2.9	13.0	15.9	2.7	10.8	.8	7.4	8.2	4.6	3.2
1989–0[3]	6.2					2.4					.4				

[1] Including flour.   [2] Preliminary.   [3] Forecast.   Source: *Foreign Agricultural Service, U.S.D.A.*   T.725

United States Wheat Quarterly Supply and Disappearance   In Millions of Bushels

| | Supply | | | | Disappearance — Domestic Use | | | | | Ex-ports[2] | Total Disap-pear-ance | Ending Stocks | | Total Stocks |
Year & Begin. June 1	Begin-ning Stocks	Pro-duction	Im-ports[2]	Total Supply	Food	Alc. Bever-ages	Seed	Feed & Residual	Total			Gov't. Owned[4]	Pri-vately Owned[5]	
1981–2	989.1	2,785	2.8	3,777	602.4	[6]	110.0	134.8	847.2	1,771	2,618	190.3	969.1	1,159
June–Sept.	989.1	2,785	.7	3,775	202.5	[6]	37.0	186.4	425.9	621.8	1,048	191.6	2,536	2,728
Oct.–Dec.	2,728	—	.8	2,728	159.0	[6]	45.0	–75.2	128.8	427.4	556.2	190.6	1,982	2,172
Jan.–Mar.	2,172	—	.8	2,173	151.7	[6]	1.0	27.6	180.3	441.0	621.3	189.1	1,362	1,551
Apr.–May	1,552	—	.5	1,552	89.2	[6]	27.0	–4.0	112.2	280.5	392.7	190.3	969.1	1,159
1982–3	1,159	2,765	7.6	3,932	616.4	[6]	97.0	194.8	908.2	1,509	2,417	192.0	1,323	1,515
June–Sept.	1,159	2,765	1.2	3,926	152.9	[6]	1.0	131.3	285.2	411.1	696.3	193.3	3,036	3,229
Oct.–Dec.	3,229	—	3.0	3,232	159.5	[6]	74.0	18.8	252.3	337.2	589.5	189.7	2,453	2,643
Jan.–Mar.	2,643	—	2.6	2,645	152.4	—	3.0	24.2	179.6	393.8	573.4	184.6	1,887	2,072
Apr.–May	2,072	—	.8	2,073	151.6	—	19.0	20.5	191.1	366.6	557.7	192.0	1,323	1,515
1983–4	1,515	2,420	4.0	3,939	642.6		100.0	369.1	1,112	1,429	2,540	188.0	1,211	1,399
June–Aug.	1,515	2,420	1.1	3,936	158.7	—	1.0	196.5	356.2	346.7	702.9	365.0	2,868	3,233
Sep.–Nov.	3,233	—	.9	3,234	163.1	—	75.0	100.5	338.6	359.7	698.3	375.8	2,160	2,536
Dec.–Feb.	2,536	—	1.0	2,537	166.8	—	3.0	46.4	216.2	369.0	585.2	313.8	1,638	1,952
Mar.–May	1,952	—	1.0	1,953	154.0	—	21.0	25.7	200.7	353.2	553.9	188.0	1,211	1,399
1984–5	1,399	2,595	9.4	4,003	651.0		98.0	404.5	1,154	1,424	2,578	377.6	1,048	1,425
June–Aug.	1,399	2,595	4.6	3,998	157.8	—	1.0	279.9	438.7	399.2	837.9	278.1	2,882	3,160
Sep.–Nov.	3,160	—	1.8	3,162	168.5	—	69.0	99.9	337.4	486.0	823.4	359.4	1,979	2,339
Dec.–Feb.	2,339	—	1.2	2,340	164.2	—	4.0	35.5	203.7	335.2	538.9	375.7	1,415	1,801
Mar.-May	1,801	—	1.8	1,803	160.5	—	24.0	–10.8	173.7	203.7	377.4	377.6	1,048	1,425
1985–6	1,425	2,425	16.0	3,866	674.4	—	93.0	278.5	1,046	915.4	1,961	601.7	1,303	1,905
June–Aug.	1,425	2,425	3.5	3,854	165.8	—	1.0	234.4	401.2	249.1	650.3	406.7	2,797	3,204
Sep.–Nov.	3,204	—	5.1	3,209	185.6	—	63.0	63.7	312.3	252.9	565.2	517.1	2,126	2,643
Dec.–Feb.	2,643	—	2.7	2,646	162.2	—	4.0	– .3	165.9	224.4	390.3	526.3	1,730	2,256
Mar.–May	2,256	—	4.7	2,261	160.8	—	25.0	–19.3	166.5	189.0	355.5	601.7	1,303	1,905
1986–7	1,905	2,092	21.1	4,018	696.0	—	84.0	413.3	1,193	1,004	2,197	830.1	990.8	1,821
June–Aug.	1,905	2,092	4.3	4,001	169.8	—	1.0	353.8	523.8	320.6	844.4	793.8	2,363	3,157
Sep.–Nov.	3,157	—	3.6	3,160	185.9	—	57.0	–19.7	223.2	263.4	486.6	863.9	1,810	2,674
Dec.–Feb.	2,674	—	5.9	2,679	166.8	—	3.0	56.5	226.3	202.7	429.0	905.3	1,345	2,250
Mar.–May	2,250	—	7.3	2,258	174.3	—	23.0	22.7	220.0	216.8	436.8	830.1	990.8	1,821
1987–8[1]	1,821	2,105	16.3	3,942	719.0	—	85.0	280.1	1,084	1,592	2,676	283.0	983.2	1,266
June–Aug.	1,821	2,105	5.1	3,931	179.3	—	1.0	352.5	532.8	409.9	940.3	798.8	2,190	2,989
Sep.–Nov.	2,989	—	5.1	2,994	191.1	—	58.0	–69.4	179.7	308.5	487.5	755.4	1,750	2,505
Dec.–Feb.	2,503	—	2.7	2,508	168.6	—	3.0	– .1	171.5	413.1	585.9	450.1	1,458	1,923
Mar.–May	1,923	—	3.5	1,927	180.0	—	23.0	– 2.9	200.2	460.6	662.3	283.0	983.2	1,266
1988–9[3]	1,256	1,812	15.0	3,083	735.0	—	100.0	290.0	1,105	1,450	2,555	150.0	377.8	527.8
June–Aug.	1,256	1,812	8.6	3,076	183.0	—	1.0	289.4	473.4	363.4	836.8	250.0	1,990	2,340

[1] Preliminary.   [2] Imports & exports include flour and other products expressed in wheat equivalent.   [3] Forecast.   [4] Uncommitted, Gov't. only.   [5] Includes total loans.   [6] Less than 50,000 bushels.   Source: *Economics Research Service, U.S.D.A.*   T.740

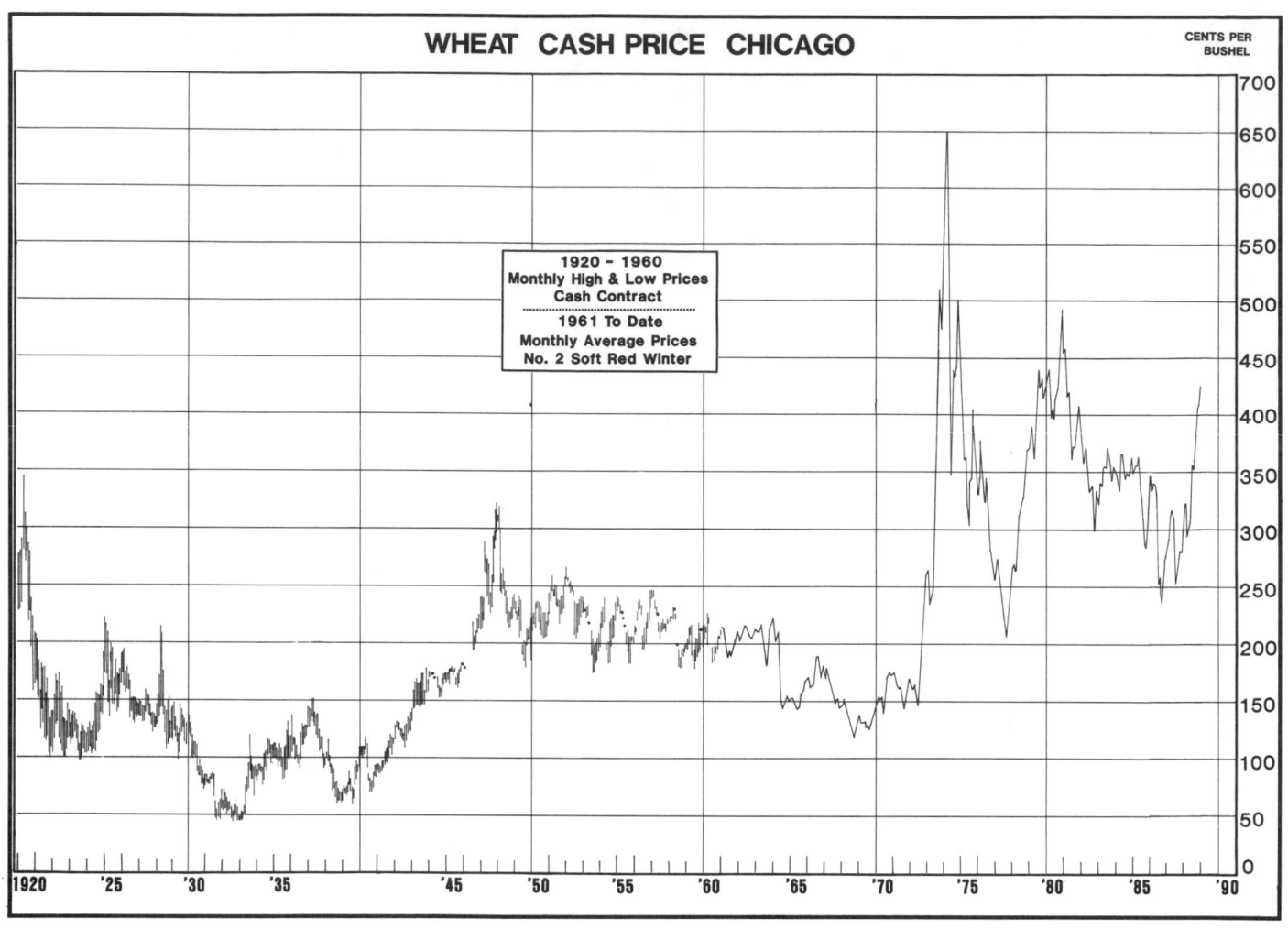

WHEAT CASH PRICE CHICAGO

CENTS PER BUSHEL

1920 – 1960
Monthly High & Low Prices
Cash Contract
1961 To Date
Monthly Average Prices
No. 2 Soft Red Winter

Average Price of No. 2 Soft Red Winter (30 Days) Wheat at Chicago   In Dollars per Bushel

Year	June	July	Aug.	Sept.	Oct.	Nov.	Dec.	Jan.	Feb.	Mar.	Apr.	May	Average
1978–9	3.18	3.22	3.32	3.42	3.51	3.68	3.68	3.73	3.88	3.79	3.60	3.86	3.57
1979–0	4.36	4.39	4.23	4.28	4.30	4.13	4.26	4.36	4.39	4.18	3.96	4.04	4.24
1980–1	3.96	4.17	4.21	4.38	4.70	4.92	4.54	4.57	4.34	4.15	4.18	3.80	4.33
1981–2	3.60	3.70	3.70	3.87	3.97	4.08	3.86	3.77	3.57	3.59	3.70	3.43	3.74
1982–3	3.31	3.36	3.35	3.18	2.98	3.33	3.23	3.32	3.40	3.36	3.51	3.55	3.32
1983–4	3.53	3.59	3.71	3.62	3.56	3.42	3.55	3.47	3.34	3.57	3.65	3.65	3.56
1984–5	3.51	3.44	3.49	3.47	3.51	3.62	3.49	3.51	3.55	3.58	3.63	3.34	3.51
1985–6	3.27	3.09	2.87	2.83	3.04	3.33	3.46	3.34	3.37	3.40	3.39	3.25	3.22
1986–7	2.52	2.58	2.44	2.36	2.57	2.73	2.76	2.87	2.91	3.11	3.16	3.08	2.76
1987–8	2.63	2.54	2.61	2.77	2.82	2.80	3.00	3.23	3.23	2.94	3.02	3.13	2.89
1988–9	3.56	3.52	3.61	3.84	4.07	4.09	4.25						

Source: Agricultural Marketing Service, Grain Division, U.S.D.A.   T.745

Stocks of Wheat Flour Held by Mills in the United States   In Thousands of Sacks (100 Pounds)

Year	Jan. 1	April 1	July 1	Oct. 1	Year	Jan. 1	April 1	July 1	Oct. 1
1981	3,842	3,897	3,895	4,222	1985	4,230	4,303	5,040	5,052
1982	3,460	3,384	3,744	3,563	1986	4,847	4,740	5,141	5,101
1983	4,276	3,760	3,490	3,599	1987[1]	5,228	5,738	5,581	5,258
1984	3,805	3,780	3,763	3,833	1988[1]	5,858	5,719	5,205	5,613

[1] Preliminary.   *Source: Department of Commerce*   T.755

High, Low & Closing Prices of May Wheat Futures on the Chicago Board of Trade   In Cents per Bushel

Year of Delivery		Apr.	May	June	July	Aug.	Sept.	Oct.	Nov.	Dec.	Jan.	Feb.	Mar.	April	May	Life of Delivery Range
					Year Prior to Delivery							**Delivery Year**				
1983	High	444¼	434½	411	403½	399	390½	354¼	368¼	355	356¾	363½	370½	366¼	360½	444¼
	Low	423	406¼	388½	381	374	343¼	327¼	338½	333¼	330½	318½	322¼	338¼	341¾	318½
	Close	431	406¼	395	392	383¼	349½	337¾	353¾	338½	351½	321½	360¼	351¼	346¾	—
1984	High	415	403	388	401¼	441	432	392½	376	365½	359	333¾	375	380	397	441
	Low	396	380¼	375¾	372½	397	386	364¾	347½	347	329¾	324½	330	349½	348½	324½
	Close	399	380¼	379½	398	431¼	390½	369½	355	360½	334	331¼	374	350¾	396½	—
1985	High	383½	405	392½	387	388	363	363½	362½	349¼	347¾	350	361¼	371½	349½	405
	Low	372	367¼	373½	369	355¼	350	351¼	347¼	334½	332½	333¾	335½	345	319¾	319¾
	Close	372	390½	385½	381½	357	353¾	361	349	341	343½	336¼	356½	349	320¾	—
1986	High	350	338¼	328¾	316	305	303	315	319½	326½	320½	294	312	328	360	360
	Low	335	316	314	286½	284	286½	294½	305¼	308½	281	274	285¼	275½	300	274
	Close	338¼	316	314	291¾	291½	300	311½	311¼	321	288¼	286¼	304¼	328	358	—
1987	High	283	300	255¼	250	253	250½	261½	267	269½	274	282	292½	290½	329	329
	Low	244	248	239	233¼	241½	237	244	252½	258	254½	263	278	273½	287¼	233¼
	Close	283	249	239	245¼	246½	244¼	255½	267	260¾	271¼	280	284½	289	295½	—
1988	High	270½	315	288½	282	296¾	302	318	317	319¼	334½	339	324¼	320½	341½	341½
	Low	264½	276	268	263	276½	280½	293	293	304¼	308	318	295½	298	294¾	263
	Close	275	281	268	278	282½	290	304	316¼	307½	327	323½	299¼	304½	336	—
1989	High	349	370	408	420	394	413½	416	417	430½						
	Low	335½	330	365	348	367	390½	396	397	398						
	Close	338½	370	398	363	391	394	403	412½	426						

Source: Chicago Board of Trade   T.750

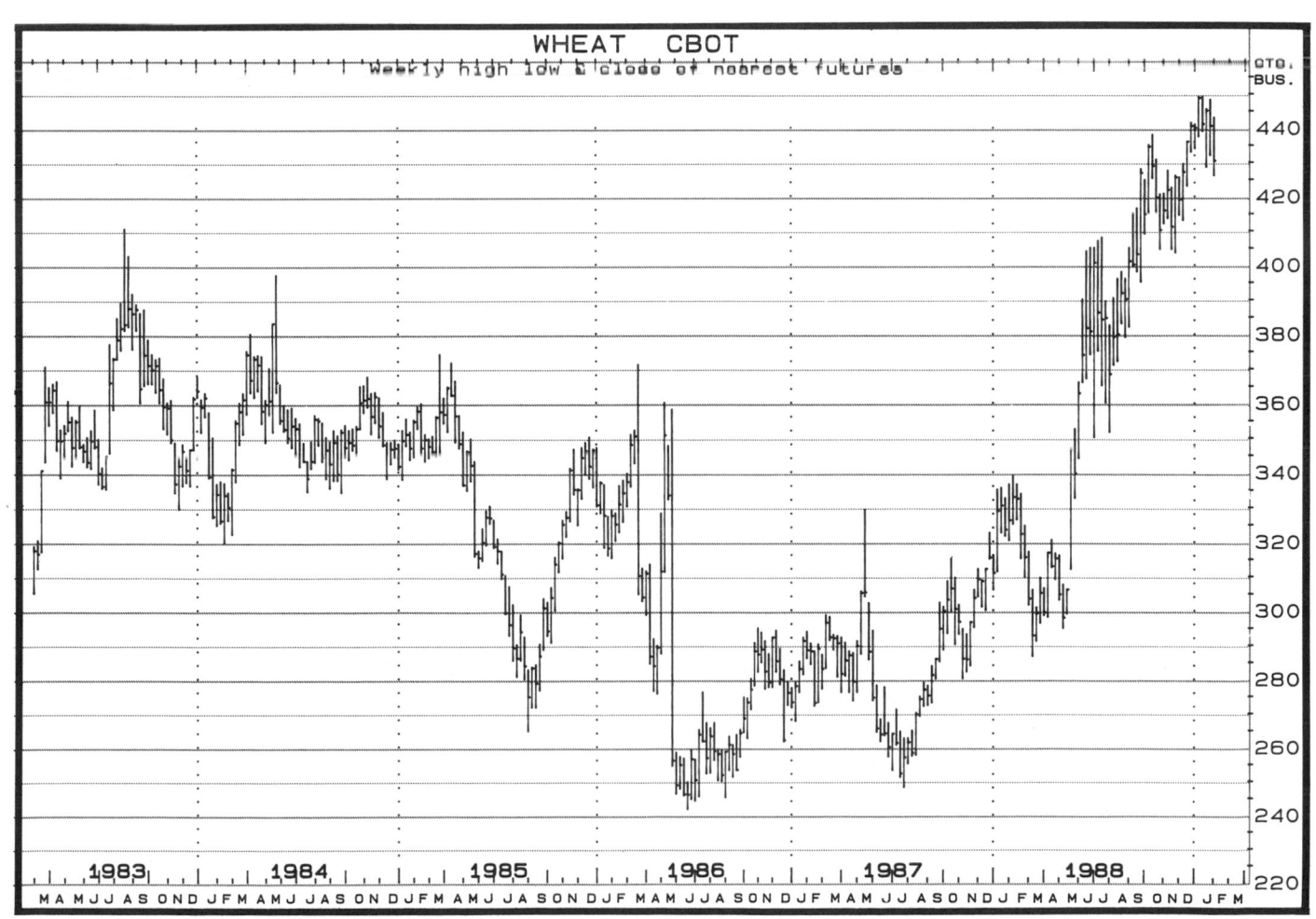

Average Price of No. 1 Hard Red Winter (Ordinary Protein) Wheat, at Kansas City   In Cents per Bushel

Year	July	Aug.	Sept.	Oct.	Nov.	Dec.	Jan.	Feb.	Mar.	Apr.	May	June	Average
1982–3	374	370	375	361	386	398	400	408	418	421	405	392	392
1983–4	371	388	390	384	382	385	381	371	385	393	389	380	384
1984–5	367	380	389	386	385	376	376	374	367	362	342	338	374
1985–6	317	303	307	315	335	342	332	330	336	345	340	280	328
1986–7	250	248	253	260	268	268	270	280	290	290	302	270	272
1987–8	259	265	278	290	290	310	320	328	310	314	320	379	296
1988–9	378	378	405	413	418	425							

Source: Agricultural Marketing Service, U.S.D.A.   T.739

Average Price of No. 1 Dark Northern Spring Wheat at Minneapolis (14% Protein)   In Cents per Bushel

Year	July	Aug.	Sept.	Oct.	Nov.	Dec.	Jan.	Feb.	Mar.	Apr.	May	June	Average
1982–3	416	396	402	400	408	396	393	392	408	440	440	439	409
1983–4	438	434	433	433	425	421	417	408	424	437	445	445	430
1984–5	434	407	397	403	402	392	390	392	394	436	402	399	406
1985–6	377	356	376	391	409	416	397	390	400	417	403	317	394
1986–7	300	286	285	298	309	304	308	313	319	317	324	307	307
1987–8	294	294	304	315	311	313	324	332	315	330	342	432	315
1988–9	423	424	432	433	422	426							

Source: Agricultural Marketing Service, U.S.D.A.   T.742

Average Price[1] Received by Farmers for Wheat in the U.S.   In Cents per Bushel

Year	July	Aug.	Sept.	Oct.	Nov.	Dec.	Jan.	Feb.	Mar.	Apr.	May	June	Average[2]
1982–3	326	334	338	343	348	351	357	357	366	375	373	350	355
1983–4	334	361	365	361	354	348	350	340	349	363	366	346	351
1984–5	328	343	343	343	345	338	338	338	338	334	329	309	339
1985–6	293	289	300	309	323	325	319	316	328	337	301	247	308
1986–7	225	226	228	230	243	249	253	258	257	263	266	244	242
1987–8	232	236	254	262	269	270	275	279	274	279	299	337	264
1988–9	350	361	374	384	388	389							

[1] Weighted average by sales.   [2] Includes an allowance for unredeemed loans at average loan values.
Source: Statistical Reporting Service, U.S.D.A.   T.743

Average Producer Price Index of Wheat Flour (Spring[1])   June 1983 = 100

Year	July	Aug.	Sept.	Oct.	Nov.	Dec.	Jan.	Feb.	Mar.	Apr.	May	June	Average
1984–5	99.5	96.9	96.9	97.3	97.7	96.8	98.2	98.7	98.3	100.3	97.0	96.3	97.8
1985–6	95.2	93.1	93.7	94.9	96.6	96.7	96.2	96.4	96.4	94.8	99.7	92.8	95.5
1986–7	87.9	87.0	85.4	86.9	86.8	86.9	87.0	89.1	89.2	89.8	93.5	90.1	88.3
1987–8	88.4	88.0	90.1	91.3	90.1	90.0	91.2	94.4	90.6	93.5	93.9	107.0	92.4
1988–9	106.0	107.4	110.1	111.1	109.0								

[1] Standard patent.   *Source: Bureau of Labor Statistics (0212–0301.99)*   T.758

World Wheat Flour Production   In Thousands of Metric Tons

Year	Argentina	Australia[2]	Rep. of Korea	France	India[3]	Mexico	Israel	Japan	W. Germany	Egypt	Poland	South Africa	Turkey	Un. Kingdom	United States	Yugoslavia
1981	2,456	1,069	1,439	3,481	2,327	2,422	464	4,184	2,601	3,512	2,815	718	2,400	3,596	12,884	2,330
1982	2,550	1,086	1,444	3,454	2,404	2,484	498	4,367	2,480	3,550	2,827	726	1,499	3,504	13,049	2,442
1983	2,678	1,055	1,476	4,386	3,092	2,435	506	4,356	2,280	3,686	2,539	694	1,582	3,420	13,883	2,414
1984	2,851	1,138	1,547	4,632	3,335	2,446	516	4,439	3,500	3,707	2,645	727	1,481	3,604	13,600	2,350
1985	2,899	1,159	1,612	4,284	3,430	2,366	508	4,402	3,523	3,598	2,645	564	1,490	3,648	14,234	2,411
1986[1]	2,856	1,178	1,596	4,922	3,720	2,126	529	4,534	3,415	3,731	2,498	520	1,518	3,700	15,475	2,323
1987[3]		1,217	1,613	5,021	3,526	2,256	529	4,496	3,449		2,723	577	1,596	3,829	15,100	2,282
1988[4]		1,230	1,700	4,800	3,800		525	4,350	3,500		2,800	650		3,800		2,100

[1] Preliminary.   [2] Twelve months ending June 30 of the year stated.   [3] Represents 60 percent of the total production.   [4] Estimate.
Source: United Nations   T.752

United States Wheat Flour Production   In Millions of Sacks (100 Pounds Each)

Year	July	Aug.	Sept.	Oct.	Nov.	Dec.	Jan.	Feb.	Mar.	Apr.	May	June	Total
1980–1	23.1	24.0	24.8	26.3	24.4	25.2	24.2	22.8	25.0	24.0	23.4	23.5	290.7
1981–2	23.3	23.7	24.2	24.7	22.8	22.3	24.5	24.0	25.8	22.9	22.3	22.9	283.4
1982–3	23.6	25.2	24.7	25.5	24.4	25.0	24.9	23.8	27.3	24.6	26.2	25.5	300.7
1983–4	25.1	29.4	27.9	26.6	25.4	24.9	24.8	25.5	25.9	24.1	26.6	24.3	310.5
1984–5	22.8	26.0	24.4	26.3	25.3	23.8	25.6	25.6	26.4	24.7	26.2	24.1	301.2
1985–6	24.3	27.3	26.8	29.1	28.4	25.2	27.8	27.5	25.6	26.5	27.2	26.7	322.4
1986–7[1]	27.6	30.2	30.4	31.8	30.3	29.5	28.1	28.0	29.0	27.5	30.0	28.5	352.2
1987–8[1]	27.4	29.5	29.1	31.1	29.5	27.7	26.2	25.6	26.5	25.6	28.9	28.2	335.3
1988–9[1]	28.3	31.2	29.1	31.0									

[1] Preliminary.   *Source: Bureau of the Census*   T.754

United States Wheat Flour Exports   In Thousands of 100 Pound Sacks

Year	July	Aug.	Sept.	Oct.	Nov.	Dec.	Jan.	Feb.	Mar.	Apr.	May	June	Total
1980–1	894	2,137	1,396	1,034	522	609	980	1,896	2,241	2,932	1,724	2,350	18,715
1981–2	987	1,420	724	284	117	184	605	2,165	2,336	2,858	1,760	944	14,384
1982–3	352	1,196	698	593	824	185	1,587	3,734	2,692	4,256	3,193	4,172	23,482
1983–4	3,293	3,095	3,621	3,469	1,122	395	830	883	2,842	2,802	3,213	2,457	28,022
1984–5	1,716	285	433	1,122	121	222	138	2,417	1,857	2,659	1,548	693	13,211
1985–6	850	381	132	131	1,079	2,569	1,374	2,312	2,171	2,526	888	2,089	16,502
1986–7[1]	2,044	2,791	1,824	2,544	941	2,240	2,800	1,508	2,417	2,852	2,856	2,233	27,047
1987–8[1]	2,633	1,902	1,528	1,081	2,777	1,779	3,057	883	273	782	831	2,941	20,467
1988–9[1]	2,490	2,385	689	2,411									

[1] Preliminary.   *Source: Department of Commerce*   T.756

Supply and Distribution of Wheat Flour in the United States   In Thousands of Cwt.

Year	Wheat Ground 1,000 Bu.	Milfeed Production 1,000 Tons	Flour Production[1]	Flour & Product Imports[2]	Total Supply	Exports Flour	Products[2]	Domestic Disappearance	Total Population July 1 Millions	Per Capita Disappearance Pounds
					— 1,000 Cwt. —					
1980	628,599	4,866	282,655	904	283,559	17,378	54	266,127	227.7	117
1981	634,381	5,045	283,966	1,166	285,132	18,655	84	266,393	229.8	116
1982	653,206	5,228	290,907	1,496	292,403	20,926	154	271,323	232.1	117
1983	689,951	5,655	311,587	1,590	313,177	37,315	150	275,712	234.3	118
1984	674,665	5,426	299,832	2,005	301,837	21,752	160	279,925	236.7	118
1985	700,151	5,556	313,815	2,064	315,879	20,766	141	294,972	239.3	123
1986	758,468	6,011	341,166	2,179	343,345	29,735	123	313,487	241.5	130
1987[3]	783,851	6,239	350,817	2,562	353,379	28,710	142	324,527	243.7	133

[1] Commercial production of wheat flour, whole wheat, industrial and durum flour and farina reported by Bureau of Census.   [2] Imports and exports of macaroni products (flour equivalent).   [3] Preliminary.   *Source: Economics & Statistics Service, U.S.D.A.*   T.753

Wheat and Flour—Price Relationships at Milling Centers   (In Dollars)

Crop Year (June-May)	At Kansas City Cost of Wheat to Produce 100 lb. Flour[1]	Bakery Flour Per 100 lb.[2]	By-Products Obtained 100 lb. Flour[3]	Total Products Actual	Over Cost of Wheat	At Minneapolis Cost of Wheat to Produce 100 lb. Flour[1]	Bakery Flour Per 100 lb.[2]	By-Products Obtained 100 lb. Flour[3]	Total Products Actual	Over Cost of Wheat
1980–1	10.30	10.38	1.99	12.37	2.07	10.95	11.00	1.78	12.78	1.83
1981–2	9.81	10.37	1.57	11.94	2.13	9.80	10.67	1.41	12.08	2.28
1982–3	9.46	10.22	1.52	11.74	2.28	9.45	10.54	1.26	11.80	2.35
1983–4	9.45	9.99	1.83	11.69	2.37	9.80	10.75	1.59	12.34	2.54
1984–5	8.96	9.78	1.32	11.09	2.13	9.27	10.84	1.01	11.85	2.58
1985–6	8.28	9.28	1.20	10.47	2.20	9.05	11.39	.91	12.30	3.25
1986–7	6.54	8.06	.84	8.90	2.36	6.99	9.22	.63	9.84	2.85
1987–8[4]	7.15	7.96	1.14	9.10	1.95	7.18	9.39	.89	10.28	3.10
Jun.–Aug.	8.83	9.57	1.57	11.14	2.31	9.72	11.00	1.48	12.48	2.76
Sept.	9.30	9.55	1.77	11.32	2.02	9.85	9.90	1.63	11.53	1.68
Oct.	9.48	10.05	1.80	11.85	2.37	9.87	9.95	1.66	11.61	1.74

[1] Cost of 2.28 bushels.   [2] Quoted as 95% patent at K.C. & standard patent at Minn., bulk basis.   [3] Assumes 50–50 millfeed distribution between bran & shorts or middlings, bulk basis.   [4] Preliminary.   *Source: Economic Research Service, U.S.D.A.*   T.751

Wool

World raw wool production in 1988/89 was estimated by USDA to be a record 4.06 billion pounds, up 2 percent from the previous season. Output in Australia, the world's largest producer, was expected to rise by about 4 percent to 1.15 billion. In both the Soviet Union and New Zealand, production was slated to fall. China, Argentina, Uruguay, and the United Kingdom were all expected to show increases.

In first quarter 1988, mill use of wool in nine major wool textile manufacturing countries accelerated, according to USDA. Consumption of raw wool at the carding stage in these countries was 383 million pounds, up 8 percent from fourth quarter 1987 and 6 percent above first quarter 1987. Yarn output in major producing countries was above the previous quarter and the year-earlier level.

Australian exports were strong in 1987/88 and by June, the end of the season, the Australian Wool Corporation's stocks were only 9,000 bales. This was well below ending stocks of 346,000 bales in 1986/87 and 895,000 in 1985/86. Australia's largest market was Japan, accounting for one-fifth of its exports, while China, the USSR, and Italy each took about 10 percent. At the beginning of the 1988/89 season, foreign demand for Australian wool continued to be firm.

New Zealand exported 736 million pounds of greasy wool in 1987/88, and China was the major destination, followed by the United Kingdom, USSR, and Japan. New Zealand's 1988/89 export season got off to a fairly strong start.

South Africa's 1987/88 wool season picked up as it progressed, and in the second half, the wool market indicator advanced on good Far Eastern buying and low fine wool stocks in other countries. In April 1988, the country's market indicator reached a record 2,231 cents/kg.

Calendar year estimates from USDA show that the U.S. began 1988 with wool stocks of 45 million pounds, clean content, the lowest in some time. Projected clean wool production of 48 million pounds was up 2 million from 1987 and the largest since 1984. Imports were expected to be 100 million pounds, down 5 percent from the previous year. Total U.S. supplies for the season were put at 193 million pounds, the highest in several years.

U.S. mill use in 1988 was expected to be strong at 145 million pounds, up from previous years. Exports were pegged at one million pounds, the same as the year before. Ending stocks were projected to rise slightly to 47 million pounds.

Under the National Wool Act of 1954, U.S. shorn wool prices are supported through payments to producers. The 1988 shorn wool support price was $1.78/lb. (greasy basis), and in 1989 it was $1.77.

Futures Markets

Greasy merino wool futures are traded on the Sydney Futures Exchange, and New Zealand crossbred futures are traded in London.

World Production of Wool[3]   In Thousands of Metric Tons (Greasy Basis)

Year	Brazil	Argentina	Australia	China	France	Morocco	India	New Zealand	Spain	Turkey	South Africa	United Kingdom	United States	Uruguay	USSR	World[1] Total
1980[2]	35	163	700	176	27	22	35	381	28	61	112	50	49	79	464	2,641
1981[2]	33	163	716	180	27	22	35	363	21	62	112	42	50	79	482	2,653
1982[1]			701					370							471	
1983[1]			672					370							474	

[1] Estimated.   [2] Preliminary.   [3] Includes shorn, pulled, & wool exported on skins.   *Source: Foreign Agricultural Service, U.S.D.A.*   T.760

Wool Goods[1] Production in the United States   In Millions of Square Yards

Year	First Quarter	Second Quarter	Third Quarter	Fourth Quarter	Total Year	Year	First Quarter	Second Quarter	Third Quarter	Fourth Quarter	Total Year
1981	50.6	52.9	39.0	35.5	178.1	1985	40.6	39.5	24.3	34.0	138.3
1982	41.0	36.3	20.2	23.6	121.1	1986	37.7	38.8	27.3	30.2	134.1
1983	36.0	41.8	28.8	37.0	143.5	1987[2]	48.0	45.9	36.0	40.9	168.9
1984	48.6	44.3	29.7	36.7	159.4	1988[2]					

[1] Woolen and worsted woven goods, except woven felts.   [2] Preliminary.   *Source: Bureau of Census*   T.763

Price Received by Farmers for Shorn[2] Wool in the U.S.   In Cents per Pound

Year	Jan.	Feb.	Mar.	Apr.	May	June	July	Aug.	Sept.	Oct.	Nov.	Dec.	Average[1]
1985	59.2	58.7	61.0	67.9	68.5	69.8	64.0	60.2	59.5	66.6	58.5	56.8	63.3
1986	52.2	54.4	61.9	70.0	73.7	75.5	67.5	65.9	57.6	69.7	64.0	59.4	66.8
1987	58.7	69.1	78.7	99.7	106.0	108.0	87.0	83.1	93.6	95.5	84.1	81.4	91.7
1988[3]	75.2	93.3	118.0	153.0	165.0	161.0	133.0	128.0	111.0	135.0	116.0	101.0	124.1

[1] Weighted average.   [2] Grease basis.   [3] Preliminary.   *Source: Crop Reporting Board, U.S.D.A.*   T.765

Salient Statistics of Wool in the United States

Year	Sheep & Lambs Shorn[2] Ths.	Weight per Fleece Lbs.	Shorn Wool Production Ths. Lbs.	Price per Lb.	Value of Production Mil. $	Shorn Wool Support —$ Per Lb.—	Shorn Wool Payment Rate —$ Per Lb.—	Total Wool Production[4]	Apparel Wool (Clean Content) Domestic Prod.	Exports Domestic Wool	Imports for Consumption[4]	Total New Supply[3]	Carpet Wool Imports for Cons.	Mill Consumption Apparel	Mill Consumption Carpet
											Thousand Pounds				
1979	13,069	8.02	104,867	86.3	90.5	115	28.7	105,767	56,022	313	20,283	98,039	22,047	106,533	10,513
1980	13,263	7.95	105,419	88.1	92.8	123	34.9	106,469	56,426	304	30,491	112,605	25,992	113,423	10,020
1981	13,493	8.14	109,787	94.4	103.7	135	40.5	110,937	58,806	307	48,106	132,750	26,145	127,752	10,896
1982	13,199	8.04	106,129	68.6	72.8	137	68.6	106,129	56,036	1,351	39,988	116,106	21,433	105,857	9,825
1983	12,865	8.00	102,886	61.2	63.0	153	91.7	102,886	54,324	1,014	49,371	131,369	28,688	126,729	13,851
1984	12,284	7.77	95,471	79.5	75.9	165	85.5	95,471	50,409	488	63,271	144,097	30,905	128,982	13,088
1985	11,158	7.88	87,941	63.3	55.7	165	101.7	87,941	46,433	1,415	50,164	124,490	29,308	106,051	10,562
1986[1]	10,852	7.82	84,829	66.8	56.7	178	111.2	84,829	44,790	788	66,090	150,131	30,901	126,768	9,960
1987[1]	11,027	7.78	85,757	91.7	78.6			85,757	45,280	1,037	74,054	158,774	31,066	129,677	13,092
1988[1]	11,300	8.00	90,400						48,000	1,000			25,000	128,100	16,500

[1] Preliminary. [2] Includes sheep shorn at commercial feeding yards. [3] Production minus exports plus imports; stocks not taken into consideration. [4] Apparel wool includes all dutiable wool; carpet wool includes all duty-free wool. *Sources: Economics Service, U.S.D.A.; Dept. of Commerce*

T.766

Consumption of Apparel Wool in the United States   In Millions of Pounds (Clean Basis)

Year	Jan.	Feb.	Mar.	Apr.	May	June	July	Aug.	Sept.	Oct.	Nov.	Dec.	Total
1980	11.3	10.2	9.8	11.4	9.2	8.3	7.5	8.4	7.7	10.8	8.8	10.0	113.4
1981	10.2	11.0	12.9	10.8	10.2	12.8	8.4	10.1	11.4	9.4	9.4	11.2	127.8
1982	9.4	9.6	12.9	9.2	8.3	9.4	5.9	8.0	8.4	7.2	7.8	9.6	105.9
1983	8.5	9.3	12.4	10.2	9.4	13.0	8.5	10.0	12.3	10.7	10.7	11.8	126.7
1984	10.6	12.0	14.0	11.3	11.9	13.0	8.2	9.9	11.2	8.5	8.9	9.4	129.0
1985	9.1	8.1	9.6	8.4	9.0	10.5	6.5	8.1	10.4	8.6	8.8	8.9	106.1
1986	11.9	10.6	10.0	12.7	10.2	10.8	11.3	9.4	9.4	11.1	9.3	10.1	126.8
1987[1]	12.4	11.7	10.0	10.9	10.6	12.7	9.0	9.4	11.7	10.9	9.6	11.2	129.7
1988[1]	10.1	10.1	13.5	10.1	9.6	13.6	9.8	9.7	10.6				

[1] Preliminary. *Source: Bureau of the Census*

T.767

Average Wool Prices[1]—Australian—64's, Type 62, Duty Paid—U.S. Mills   In Cents per Pound

Year	Jan.	Feb.	Mar.	Apr.	May	June	July	Aug.	Sept.	Oct.	Nov.	Dec.	Average
1980	292	310	306	299	310	321	311	306	311	306	320	321	309
1981	319	312	307	314	316	319	323	320	316	316	317	312	316
1982	301	303	313	323	336	321	304	294	287	276	269	267	299
1983	273	271	266	266	262	262	260	262	263	271	270	266	266
1984	268	276	279	276	271	269	255	259	247	249	255	251	263
1985	246	233	236	227	234	229	230	226	224	224	217	222	229
1986	231	229	231	238	252	242	N.A.	229	224	230	240	250	236
1987	252	259	288	325	327	335	332	373	341	348	347	356	324
1988	391	468	496	564	564	513	489	467	461	488	472		

[1] Raw, clean basis. *Source: U.S. Dept. of Agriculture*

T.768

Average Wool Prices—Domestic[1]—Graded Territory, 64's, Staple 2¾″ & Up—U.S. Mills   ¢/Lb.

Year	Jan.	Feb.	Mar.	Apr.	May	June	July	Aug.	Sept.	Oct.	Nov.	Dec.	Average
1980	238	253	256	231	225	233	245	251	253	253	253	253	245
1981	253	268	274	278	278	283	283	283	283	283	283	283	278
1982	275	263	244	240	240	240	240	240	240	—	—	—	247
1983	—	—	193	193	193	198	219	223	225	225	225	228	212
1984	230	230	230	245	234	230	230	230	230	221	218	214	228
1985	205	195	185	182	191	193	193	193	193	193	193	193	192
1986	193	189	180	188	198	198	193	190	190	190	190	190	191
1987	193	202	216	260	270	270	270	300	295	300	300	300	265
1988	315	397	435	453	463	460	450	450	450	463	475		

[1] Raw, shorn, clean basis. *Source: U.S. Dept. of Agriculture*

T.769

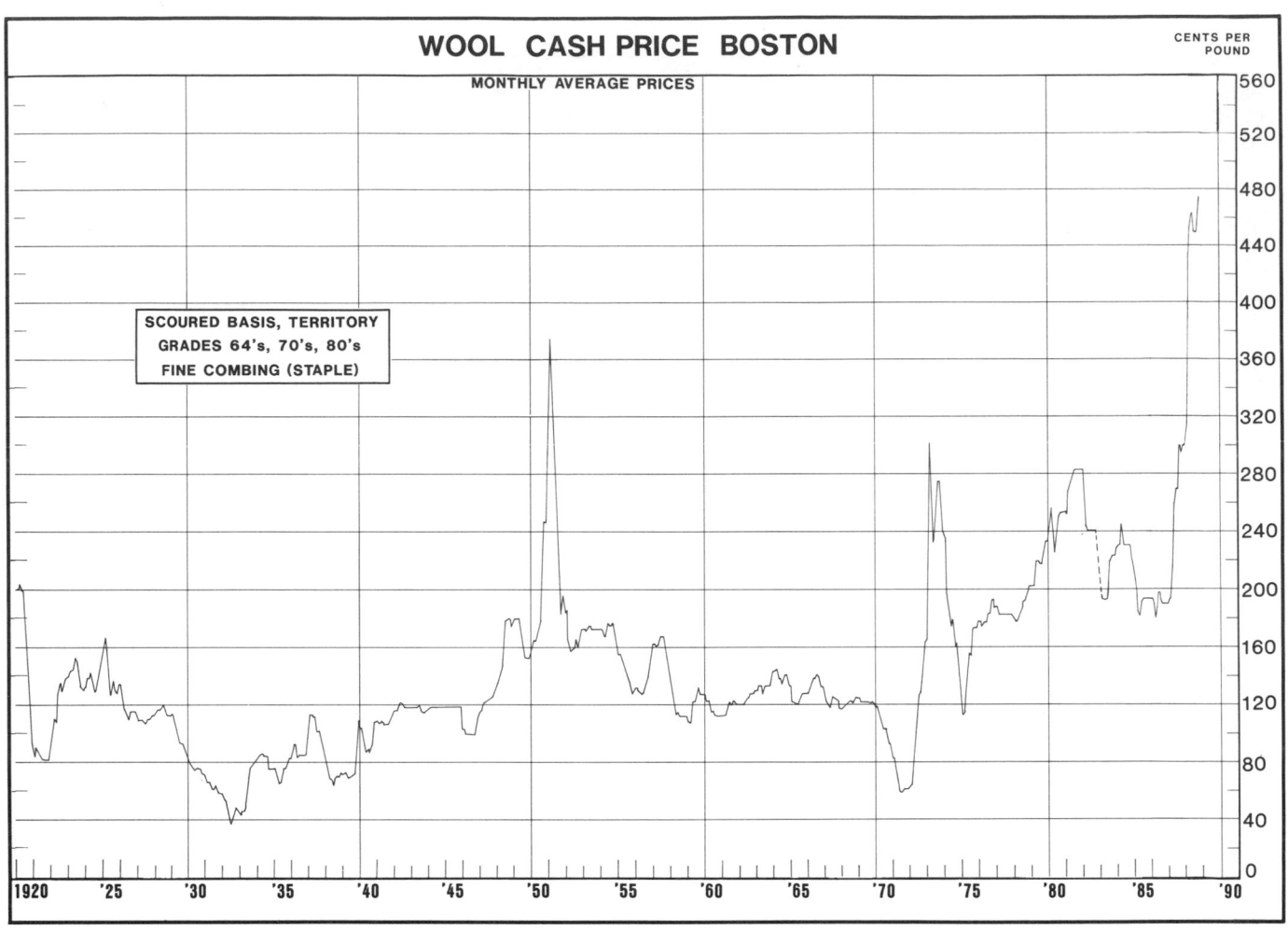

WOOL CASH PRICE BOSTON

MONTHLY AVERAGE PRICES

CENTS PER POUND

SCOURED BASIS, TERRITORY GRADES 64's, 70's, 80's FINE COMBING (STAPLE)

Wool: Mill Consumption, by Grades in the U.S., Scoured Basis   In Millions of Pounds

Year	Woolen System 60's & Finer	Woolen System 50's Up to 60's	Woolen System Total	Apparel Wool[1] Worsted System 60's & Finer	Apparel Wool[1] Worsted System Coarser Than 60's	Apparel Wool[1] Worsted System Total	All Total	Carpet Wool[2]
1982	23.8	24.6	48.4	36.2	21.3	57.5	105.9	9.8
1983	30.5	30.2	60.7	42.4	23.6	66.0	126.7	13.9
1984	32.9	32.2	65.2	39.7	24.1	63.8	129.0	13.1
1985	28.0	27.7	55.7	33.6	16.7	50.3	106.1	10.6
1986	34.1	32.2	66.3	41.7	18.8	60.5	126.8	10.0
1987[3]	32.4	28.6	61.0	53.8	14.8	68.7	129.7	13.1
1988[4]							128.1	16.5

[1] Domestic & duty-paid foreign.   [2] Duty-free foreign.   [3] Preliminary.   [4] Estimate.   *Source: Economic Research Service, U.S.D.A.*   T.762

United States Imports[1] of Unmanufactured Wool (Clean Yield)   In Millions of Pounds

Year	Jan.	Feb.	Mar.	Apr.	May	June	July	Aug.	Sept.	Oct.	Nov.	Dec.	Total
1982	8.0	6.3	6.6	4.9	6.0	6.6	4.0	4.2	4.7	2.9	3.6	3.7	61.4
1983	6.0	6.2	5.0	6.7	4.9	7.5	6.5	5.8	5.1	8.5	8.0	8.9	78.1
1984	11.2	9.0	7.8	7.8	10.4	6.7	9.6	6.4	6.0	6.9	5.6	6.8	94.2
1985	10.7	5.8	6.0	5.7	7.1	4.9	7.3	4.5	6.9	7.1	5.5	8.0	79.5
1986	10.2	8.8	7.6	7.5	8.0	8.6	7.8	6.3	7.0	5.0	9.2	10.8	97.0
1987[2]	8.6	8.2	9.5	8.7	13.4	8.9	8.6	8.4	6.7	7.0	8.2	9.0	105.1
1988[2]	12.0	12.7	8.8	9.1	8.6	7.4	7.7	5.0	3.3	6.7			

[1] Data are imports for consumption.   [2] Preliminary.   *Source: Department of Commerce*   T.764

Zinc

Zinc was among the industrial metals that rallied in 1988. In 1987, the average price for the full year was 41.92 cents/lb. for high grade, and for the first seven months of 1988, the price averaged 55.00 cents. In July 1988, it was 65.6 cents, the best level since 1983.

Total U.S. zinc consumption in 1987 was 1.094 million tonnes, for a monthly average of 91,166 tonnes. For the first eight months of 1988, consumption totaled 624,359 tonnes, for a monthly 78,044 tonnes. Of that 1988 total, 440,229 tonnes, or about 71 percent, was reported as slab zinc.

Construction materials accounted for about 45 percent of U.S. slab zinc consumption; transportation, for 25 percent; machinery, 10 percent; electrical uses, 10 percent, and other miscellaneous uses for the balance.

While total demand was off, apparent consumption (which is made up of smelter production (+) imports (-) exports (+) beginning stocks (-) ending stocks) totaled 722,900 tonnes for the first eight months of 1988, versus 1.052 million tonnes for all of 1987. Apparent consumption was running ahead of the year-earlier level.

Slab zinc smelter imports for 1988's first seven months totaled 437,548 tonnes, ahead of the 1987 pace, and implied stock building, possibly in anticipation of additional price increases.

Domestic slab zinc production for all of 1987 was 342,663 tonnes, for an average monthly output of 28,555 tonnes. Estimated January-August 1988 slab production was 235,131 tonnes, for an average 29,391 tonnes a month.

U.S. mine and smelter production was consistently steady in 1988, due to high metal prices and increased U.S. demand. New production facilities were opened, and others, closed for many years due to a dormant market, were reopened. For example, in 1988, Bunker Hill Mining Co. began initial lead-zinc-silver production at its mine in Kellog, Idaho. The mine had been closed since the end of 1981.

In response to the new buoyancy in the zinc market, brought on by years of hard-wrung capacity decreases, London Metal Exchange (LME) zinc futures took on added importance in 1988.

In October 1988, major European zinc producers linked their zinc prices to the recently introduced LME Special High Grade (SHG) zinc contract. It appeared that the industry was prepared to work with the LME in developing the contract.

Most U.S. imports come from Canada, which provided 399,755 tonnes out of total U.S. imports of 425,510 tonnes of ore and concentrates in 1987. Canada also supplied the U.S. with 360,729 tonnes of blocks, pigs, and slabs, out of total 1987 imports of 705,985 tonnes. Europe is another important supplier; imports of refined material coming from eleven European countries in 1987 accounted for 177,374 tons of 1987's total U.S. imports.

General imports of all types of zinc in 1987 totaled 1.138 million tonnes, compared with 1988's Jan.-July total of 685,755 tonnes. Imports for consumption in 1987 totaled 759,176 tonnes, and in the first eight months of 1988 were 491,207 tonnes.

Identified world zinc resources are estimated at 1.8 billion tonnes. Data on sphalerite-bearing coals in the mid-continent U.S. indicate a resource potential of millions of tonnes of zinc.

Aluminum, plastics, and magnesium are the major substitutes for zinc in numerous processes. Major co-products of zinc mining and smelting are lead, cadmium, silver and sulfur.

Futures Market

Zinc futures are traded on the London Metal Exchange (LME).

Salient Statistics of Zinc in the United States   In Thousands of Metric Tons

Year	Net Import Reliance as a % of Apparent Consumption	Production of Slab Zinc — Primary Domestic	For-eign	Total	Value Mil. $[6]	Redistilled Secondary	Total Production	Dec. 31 Stocks at Producer Plants	Consumer Plants	Gov't. Stockpile	Total All Stocks	Consumption Zinc Slab	Ores[2]	Zinc[3]	Copper	Aluminum[4]	Total
1976	59	346.4	106.1	452.6	359	62.2	514.7	88.0	109.9	349.4		1,028.9	91.8	138.4	139.2	.5	1,394
1977	57	322.2	86.2	408.4	309	45.9	454.3	83.8	86.5	347.8		999.5	86.5	139.6	139.6	.6	1,368
1978	66	267.4	139.3	406.7	207	34.8	441.5	37.9	99.3	345.9		1,050.6	90.0	73.2	141.5	.5	1,442
1979	63	255.3	217.1	472.5	220	53.2	525.7	59.1	92.6	345.7		1,000.6	79.7	146.7	166.4	.9	1,394
1980	60	231.9	108.6	340.5	262	29.4	369.9	22.6	69.6	342.4	125.8	811.1	59.0	133.0	138.2	1.1	1,142
1981	65	259.8	86.7	346.5	307	50.2	396.8	44.7	81.9	340.6	195.4	840.9	60.6	149.3	138.7	.7	1,189
1982	58	193.3	34.9	228.2	257	74.3	302.5	34.2	77.6	340.6	159.2	709.5	35.5	93.1	114.3	.7	953.1
1983	65	210.3	25.4	235.7	251	69.4	305.1	46.3	89.0	340.6	148.1	805.9	38.3	131.7	144.0	.7	1,121
1984	68	197.9	55.2	253.1	271	78.1	331.2	46.3	72.5	340.6	137.6	848.9	47.6	157.9	159.5	.7	1,215
1985	70	198.0	63.2	261.2	202	72.6	333.8	32.4	60.3	340.6	119.9	770.7	42.3	140.6	147.2	.6	1,095
1986[1]	73	191.1	62.3	253.4	170	62.9	316.3	19.9	54.2	340.6	100.7	706.0	21.9	141.8	131.4	.5	1,002
1987[5]	69						342.7	16.6	57.1		96.1	788.7	2.5	157.8	145.2	.5	1,095
1988[5]							340.0	12.0	50.0		81.0	675.0	3.0	130.0	160.0	.5	1,000

[1] Preliminary. [2] Recoverable zinc content. [3] Excludes redistilled slab & zinc produced by remelting. [4] Aluminum & magnesium-base scrap. [5] Estimate. [6] Domestic ores (recoverable content). *Source: Bureau of Mines*   T.770

ZINC

World Smelter Production of Zinc   In Thousands of Metric Tons

Year	Australia	Belgium	Canada	France	W. Germany	Italy	Japan	Mexico	Norway	Peru	Poland	Spain	USSR	United Kingdom[3]	United States	World Total
1979	310.4	252.6	580.4	248.6	355.5	202.3	789.4	161.7	77.8	68.2	209.0	182.7	880.0	76.7	525.7	6,260
1980	306.0	247.6	591.6	252.8	370.6	206.4	735.2	143.9	79.4	63.8	217.0	151.7	895.0	86.7	369.9	6,049
1981	300.4	234.7	618.6	257.1	366.6	180.9	670.2	126.5	80.3	126.2	167.1	179.5	905.0	81.6	396.8	6,081
1982	295.9	240.9	511.9	243.8	335.0	158.6	662.4	127.0	72.0	160.2	165.4	181.8	940.0	79.3	302.5	5,894
1983	303.0	275.8	617.0	249.5	356.5	155.9	701.3	175.7	90.7	154.0	170.3	189.9	965.0	87.7	305.1	6,249
1984	306.4	285.3	683.2	258.5	356.4	169.7	754.5	167.0	94.2	148.4	176.0	207.4	995.0	85.6	331.2	6,526
1985[1]	293.2	289.6	692.4	285.6	367.8	215.6	739.6	175.4	92.7	169.7	180.0	213.3	1,000	74.3	333.8	6,844
1986[2]	310.2	290.0	572.0	289.5	371.3	229.4	708.0	173.7	90.4	155.4	179.0	213.6	1,005	85.9	316.3	6,784

[1] Preliminary.   [2] Estimated.   [3] Some secondary metal included.   *Source: Bureau of Mines*   T.771

U.S. Mine Production of Recoverable Zinc   In Thousands of Metric Tons

Year	Arizona	Colorado	Idaho	Illinois	Missouri	Montana	Pennsylvania	New Mexico	New York	New Jersey	Tennessee	Utah	Virginia	Washington	Wisconsin	Total U.S.
1979	N.A.	9.9	29.7	N.A.	61.7	.1	21.4	N.A.	12.1	31.1	85.1	N.A.	11.4	—	N.A.	267.3
1980	N.A.	13.8	27.7	N.A.	62.9	.1	22.6	N.A.	33.6	28.9	111.8	N.A.	12.0	—	N.A.	317.1
1981	.1	N.A.	N.A.	N.A.	52.9	—	24.7	N.A.	36.9	16.2	117.7	1.6	9.7	—	—	312.4
1982	—	N.A.	N.A.	N.A.	63.7	N.A.	24.8	—	52.3	16.8	121.3	—	—	—	—	303.2
1983	—	N.A.	N.A.	N.A.	57.0	—	16.8	—	56.7	16.5	110.0	—	—	—	—	275.3
1984	—	N.A.	N.A.	N.A.	45.5	—	—	—	N.A.	N.A.	116.5	N.A.	—	—	—	252.8
1985	—	N.A.	N.A.	N.A.	49.3	—	—	—	N.A.	N.A.	104.5	—	—	—	—	226.5
1986[1]	—	N.A.	.4	N.A.	37.9	—	—	—	N.A.	N.A.	102.1	—	—	—	—	203.0
1987[1]					35.0						115.7					217.0
1988[2]					40.0						125.0					240.0

[1] Preliminary.   [2] Estimated.   *Source: Bureau of Mines*   T.772

Consumption of Slab Zinc in the United States, by Industries and Grades   In Thousands of Metric Tons

Year	Total	By Industries — Galvanizers	Brass Products	Zinc-Base Alloy[2]	Rolled Zinc	Zinc Oxide	Light-Metal Alloys	Other	By Grades — Special High Grade	High Grade	Contin.[5] Galvan. Grade	Contrd.[4] Lead Grade	Prime Western	Remelt
1979	1,000.6	452.8	141.4	314.1	22.0	35.5	12.9	21.9	443.1	108.6	22.5	86.8	336.8	2.8
1980	811.1	379.2	98.8	254.2	21.1	27.0	11.1	19.6	354.3	76.2	18.5	70.3	290.3	1.6
1981	840.9	411.0	113.0	243.4	23.2	25.7	8.2	16.5	361.5	97.6	18.2	80.3	275.3	1.2
1982	709.5	342.0	81.1	197.8	37.2	32.4	8.3	10.7	324.8	84.6	24.5	68.7	204.9	2.0
1983	805.9	373.2	107.9	212.9	56.3	36.2	12.5	6.9	406.7	91.0	62.6	60.8	179.1	5.6
1984	848.9	375.6	125.6	232.6	56.9	37.0	14.9	6.2	449.1	100.3	53.9	55.4	184.5	5.6
1985	770.7	362.4	77.9	218.4	48.0	44.4	15.2	4.3	420.6	87.4	37.1	39.3	174.8	5.5
1986	706.0	366.0	73.7	175.1	28.6	40.1	13.0	9.6	353.4	89.1	35.0	37.3	182.0	9.0
1987[3]	788.7	382.0	139.6	228.7	36.7	64.0	16.1	16.9						
1988[1]	675	420	150	240										

[1] Estimated.   [2] Die casters.   [3] Preliminary.   [4] Controlled.   [5] Continuous.   *Source: Bureau of Mines*   T.773

Zinc Foreign Trade of the United States   In Metric Tons

Year	Ores[1]	Imported for Consumption — Blocks, Pigs, Slabs	Zinc Fume	Waste & Scrap	Dross, & Skimmings	Dust, Powder & Flakes	Total Value Thous. $	Blocks, Pigs, Anodes, etc. — Unwrought	Unwrought Alloys	Zinc Ore & Manufactures Exported / Wrought & Alloys — Sheets, Plates & Strips	Angles Bars, Rods, etc.	Waste & Scrap	Dust (Blue Powder)	Zinc Ore & Concentrates
1979	87,499	524,130	28	3,259	4,454	3,586	434,677	279	366	1,824	1,451	28,149	966	20,095
1980	182,370	410,163	25	3,470	4,062	3,928	401,134	302	485	2,103	804	29,542	4,512	54,457
1981	245,710	612,007	184	5,782	7,629	7,993	676,299	323	378	1,500	1,160	30,046	5,003	54,232
1982	66,809	456,233	11	2,653	7,104	5,864	409,896	341	863	995	1,028	29,424	2,066	77,289
1983	63,156	617,679	631	3,900	6,508	6,533	533,398	427	662	957	1,046	28,255	1,914	60,168
1984	86,172	639,228	314	6,259	5,027	7,572	683,211	760	588	975	840	39,146	2,933	30,579
1985	90,186	610,900	—	3,247	4,942	8,681	559,434	1,011	1,243	776	1,434	43,947	2,037	23,264
1986[2]	75,786	665,126	11	4,521	6,087	7,446	522,473	1,938	1,610	721	1,050	68,660	1,551	3,269
1987[3]	46,464	705,985						1,082				88,277		16,921
1988[3]	65,000	775,000						800				100,000		35,000

[1] Zinc content.   [2] Preliminary.   [3] Estimate.   *Source: Bureau of Mines*   T.774